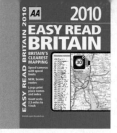

# Atlas contents

Scale 1:148,000 or 2.34 miles to 1 inch

| | |
|---|---|
| **Map pages south** | inside front cover |
| **Route planner** | II–VII |
| **Atlas symbols** | VIII–1 |
| **Road maps 1:148,000 scale** | 2–283 |
| Channel Islands 1:100,000 scale | 9 |
| Isle of Man 1:200,000 scale | 154 |
| Orkney Islands 1:450,000 scale | 275 |
| Shetland Islands 1:450,000 scale | 281 |
| Western Isles 1:480,000 scale | 282–283 |

| | |
|---|---|
| **Restricted junctions** | 284–285 |
| **Index to place names** | 286–368 |
| County, administrative area map | 286–287 |
| **Map pages north** | inside back cover |

**10th edition July 2009**

© AA Media Limited 2009
Original edition printed 2000.

**Cartography:**
All cartography in this atlas edited, designed and produced by the Mapping Services Department of AA Publishing (A04061).

 This product includes mapping data licensed from Ordnance Survey® with the permission of the Controller of Her Majesty's Stationery Office. © Crown copyright 2009. All rights reserved. Licence number 100021153.

**Publisher's notes:**
Published by AA Publishing (a trading name of AA Media Limited, whose registered office is Fanum House, Basing View, Basingstoke, Hampshire RG21 4EA, UK. Registered number 06112600).

ISBN: 978 0 7495 6257 1

A CIP catalogue record for this book is available from The British Library.

**Disclaimer:**
The contents of this atlas are believed to be correct at the time of the latest revision, it will not contain any subsequent amended, new or temporary information including diversions and traffic control or enforcement systems. The publishers cannot be held responsible or liable for any loss or damage occasioned to any person acting or refraining from action as a result of any use or reliance on material in this atlas, nor for any errors, omissions or changes in such material. This does not affect your statutory rights.

The publishers would welcome information to correct any errors or omissions and to keep this atlas up to date. Please write to the Atlas Editor, AA Publishing, The Automobile Association, Fanum House, Basing View, Basingstoke, Hampshire RG21 4EA, UK. E-mail: *roadatlasfeedback@theaa.com*

**Acknowledgements:**
AA Publishing would like to thank the following for their assistance in producing this atlas:

**RoadPilot**® Information on fixed speed camera locations provided by RoadPilot © 2009 RoadPilot® Driving Technology.
Information on truckstops and transport cafés kindly provided by John Eden (*www.transportcafe.co.uk*). Crematoria data provided by Cremation Society of Great Britain. Cadw, English Heritage, English Nature, Forestry Commission, Historic Scotland, Johnsons, National Trust and National Trust for Scotland, RSPB, Scottish Natural Heritage, The Countryside Agency, The Countryside Council for Wales.

**Printer:**
Printed in Spain by Graficas Estella, Estella, on paper sourced from sustainably managed forests.
Paper: 90gsm Oria Matt.

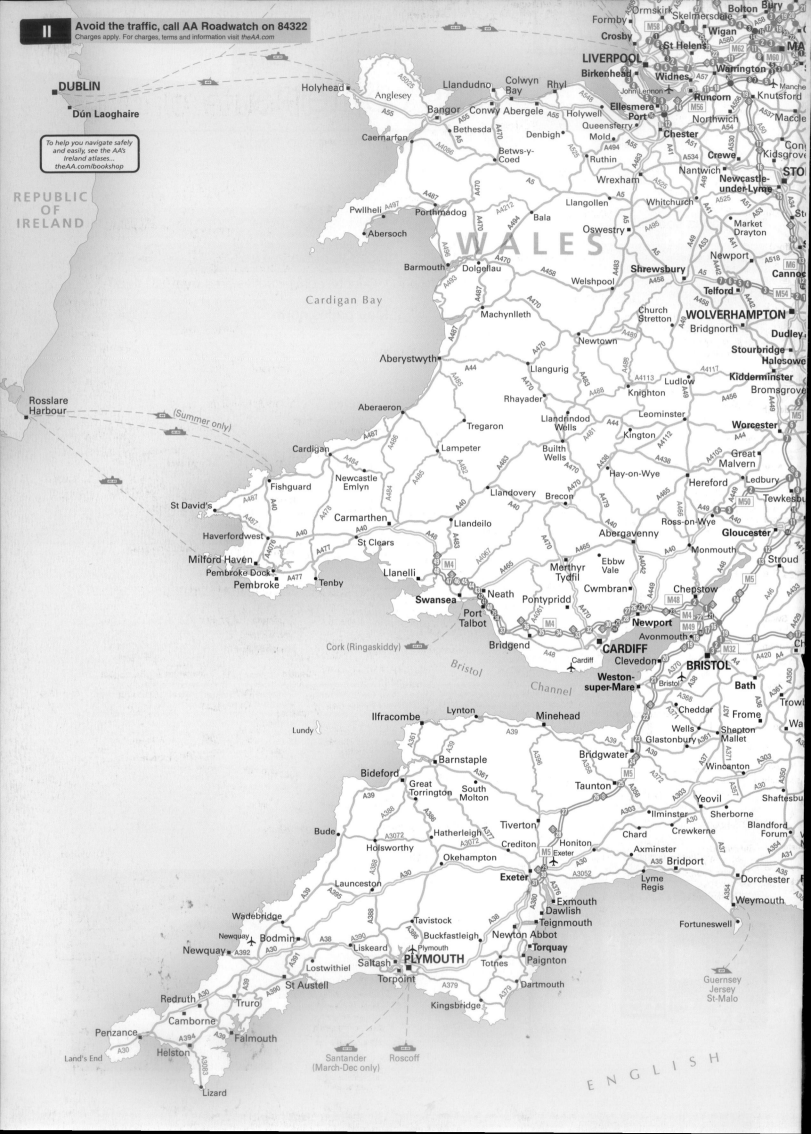

# Map pages south

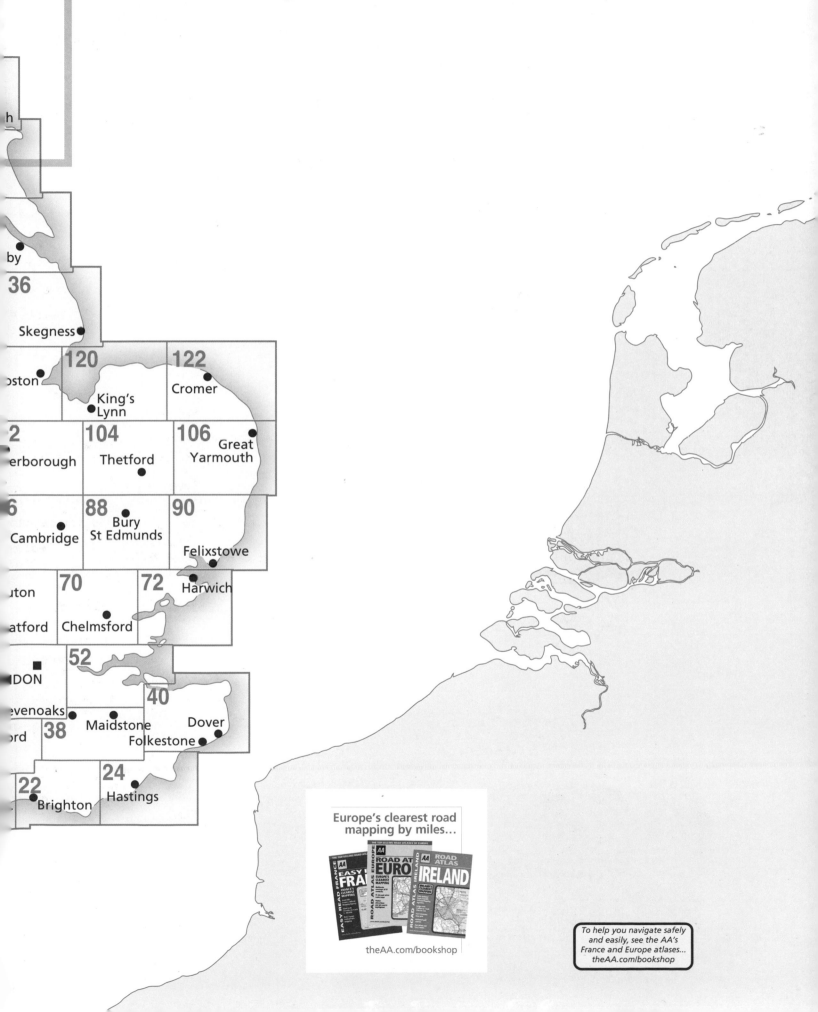

h

by

**36**

Skegness

**120**

oston

King's
Lynn

**122**

Cromer

**2**

erborough

**104**

Thetford

**106**

Great
Yarmouth

**6**

Cambridge

**88**

Bury
St Edmunds

**90**

Felixstowe

uton

**70**

atford

Chelmsford

**72**

Harwich

**52**

DON

evenoaks

**38**

rd

Maidstone

Folkestone

**40**

Dover

**22**

Brighton

**24**

Hastings

## Map Legend

| | | |
|---|---|---|
| | Motorway | |
| | Toll motorway | |
| | Primary route dual carriageway | |
| | Primary route single carriageway | |
| | Other A roads | |
| or V | Vehicle ferry | |
| | Fast vehicle ferry or catamaran | |

To help you navigate safely and easily, see the AA's France and Europe atlases...
theAA.com/bookshop

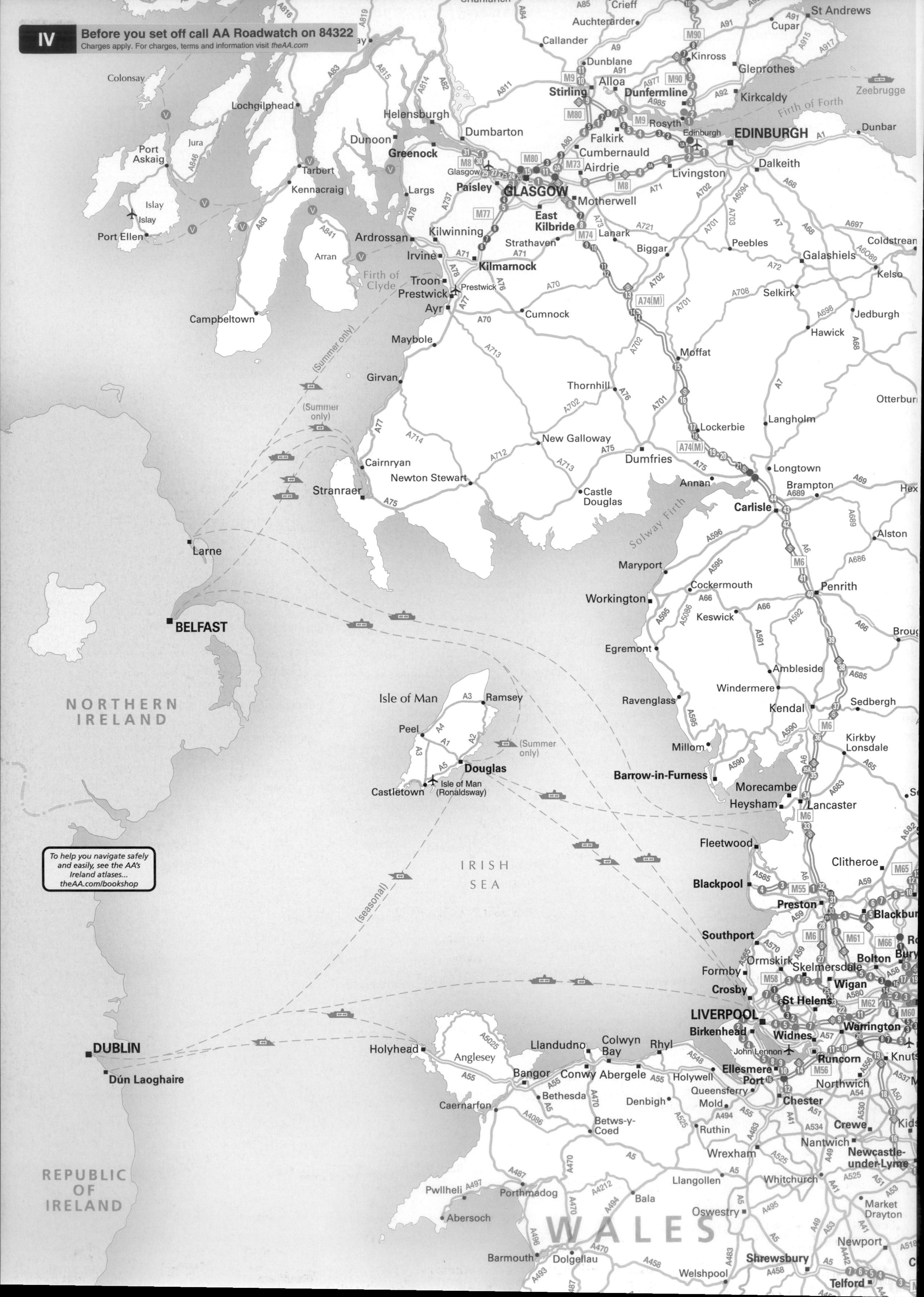

Colonsay

Crieff
St Andrews
Auchterarder
Cupar
Callander
Dunblane
Kinross
Glenrothes
Lochgilphead
Stirling
Alloa
Dunfermline
Kirkcaldy
Zeebrugge
Helensburgh
Rosyth
Port Askaig
Dunoon
Dumbarton
Edinburgh
EDINBURGH
Dunbar
Jura
Greenock
Falkirk
Cumbernauld
Kennacraig
Tarbert
Largs
Glasgow
Airdrie
Livingston
Dalkeith
Islay
Paisley
GLASGOW
Cumbernauld
Islay
GLASGOW
Motherwell
Peebles
Coldstream
Port Ellen
East Kilbride
Lanark
Biggar
Galashiels
Ardrossan
Kilwinning
Strathaven
Selkirk
Kelso
Campbeltown
Irvine
Kilmarnock
Hawick
Jedburgh
Arran
Troon
Prestwick
Cumnock
Otterburn
Firth of Clyde
Ayr
Maybole
Thornhill
Langholm
Girvan
New Galloway
Moffat
Lockerbie
Cairnryan
Newton Stewart
Dumfries
Longtown
Brampton
Hex
Stranraer
Castle Douglas
Annan
Carlisle
Alston
Larne
Solway Firth
Maryport
Penrith
BELFAST
Cockermouth
Workington
Keswick
Broug
NORTHERN IRELAND
Egremont
Ambleside
Ravenglass
Windermere
Sedbergh
Millom
Kendal
Isle of Man
Ramsey
Peel
Kirkby Lonsdale
Douglas
Barrow-in-Furness
Morecambe
Castletown
Isle of Man (Ronaldsway)
Heysham
Lancaster
Fleetwood
Clitheroe
IRISH SEA
Blackpool
Blackburn
Preston
Southport
Ormskirk
Skelmersdale
Bolton
Bury
Formby
Wigan
Crosby
St Helens
DUBLIN
LIVERPOOL
Warrington
Holyhead
Birkenhead
Widnes
Runcorn
Knuts
Dún Laoghaire
Llandudno
Colwyn Bay
Rhyl
John Lennon
Anglesey
Ellesmere Port
Northwich
Bangor
Conwy Abergele
Holywell
Queensferry
Chester
REPUBLIC OF IRELAND
Caernarfon
Bethesda
Denbigh
Mold
Ruthin
Crewe
Betws-y-Coed
Nantwich
Pwllheli
Wrexham
Newcastle-under-Lyme
Porthmadog
Llangollen
Whitchurch
Abersoch
Bala
Oswestry
Market Drayton
WALES
Barmouth
Dolgellau
Welshpool
Newport
Shrewsbury
Telford

*To help you navigate safely and easily, see the AA's Ireland atlases...*
*theAA.com/bookshop*

NORTH SEA

Motorway
Toll motorway
Primary route dual carriageway
Primary route single carriageway
Other A roads
Vehicle ferry
Fast vehicle ferry or catamaran

0        10        20        30 miles
0   10   20   30   40 kilometres

Eyemouth
Berwick-upon-Tweed
Wooler
Alnwick
Amble
Ashington
Morpeth
Newcastle
NorthShields  Tynemouth
Corbridge  South Shields
Gateshead  NEWCASTLE UPON TYNE  IJmuiden
Consett  SUNDERLAND
Chester-le-Street
Durham
Hartlepool
Bishop Auckland
Barnard Castle  Stockton-on-Tees  Middlesbrough
Darlington  Guisborough  Whitby
Durham Tees Valley
Richmond  Scotch Corner
Leyburn  Northallerton  Scarborough
Thirsk  Pickering  Filey
Helmsley
Ripon  Easingwold  Malton
Bridlington
Skipton  Harrogate  Driffield
Keighley  Otley  Wetherby  York
Leeds Bradford  Market Weighton  Beverley
BRADFORD  LEEDS  Selby
Burnley  Halifax  KINGSTON UPON HULL
Huddersfield  Goole  Immingham
Wakefield  Pontefract  Thorne  Scunthorpe  Grimsby
Oldham  Barnsley  Doncaster  Humberside  Cleethorpes  Rotterdam (Europoort) Zeebrugge
MANCHESTER  Brigg
Stockport  Rotherham  Robin Hood Doncaster Sheffield  Market Rasen
SHEFFIELD  Bawtry  Louth
Glossop  Worksop  Gainsborough  Mablethorpe
Buxton  CHESTERFIELD  Retford
Bakewell  ENGLAND  Lincoln
Congleton  Matlock  Alfreton  Horncastle  Skegness
Leek  Mansfield
STOKE-ON-TRENT  Ashbourne  Newark-on-Trent  The Wash
Ilkeston  Sleaford  Boston  Hunstanton  Sheringham  Cromer
Stafford  DERBY  Grantham
Rugeley  Burton upon Trent  East Midlands  King's Lynn  Aylsham  North Walsham
NOTTINGHAM  Long Eaton  Loughborough  Melton Mowbray  Bourne  Spalding  Fakenham  Dereham
Lichfield  LEICESTER  Oakham  Stamford  Wisbech  Swaffham  Norwich  Caister-on-Sea
Great

Western Isles

Outer Hebrides

Port Nis
(Port of Ness)

A857

The Minch

Scourie

A838

A894

A838

A836

Steornabhagh
(Stornoway)

Stornoway

Isle of
Lewis

A859

A835

A837

Taransay

Tairbeart
(Tarbert)

Ullapool

Bona
Bridg

A832

Harris

Sound of Harris

Gairloch

A832

Uibhist a Tuath
(North Uist)

A835

Kinlochewe

Dingwall

A832

Loch nam Madadh
(Lochmaddy)

Uig

Achnasheen

Inver

A87

Beinn na Faoghla
(Benbecula)

Benbecula

Dunvegan

A850

Portree

A890

Uibhist a Deas
(South Uist)

A865

Isle of
Skye

Kyle of
Lochalsh

Drumnadrochit

A87

A87

Invermoriston

Loch Baghasdail
(Lochboisdale)

A887

Sound of Barra

Rùm

Armadale

Invergarry

A87

Barra

Barraigh
(Barra)

Mallaig

Inner Hebrides

Eigg

New

A830

A82

A86

S

Coll

Fort William

Tiree

Tobermory

South
Ballachulish

A62

Killin

A861

A884

Lochaline

A828

Oban

Tyndrum

Craignure
Isle of Mull

A85

A85

Fionnphort

A849

Crianlarich

A816

Inveraray

A819

A83

A815

A814

A82

A811

Colonsay

Lochgilphead

Helensburgh

Dumbarto

Jura

A816

Dunoon

Greenock

Port
Askaig

A846

Tarbert

M8

Glasgow

Largs

Paisley

Kennacraig

A83

Islay

Islay

Ardrossan

A78

Kilwinning

A841

A737

Port Ellen

Arran

A71

Irvine

Kilmar

Firth of
Clyde

Troon

Campbeltown

Prestwick

A77

Ayr

A70

Maybole

Tongu

Alr

**Legend**

═══ Motorway

═══ Toll motorway

─── Primary route
dual carriageway

─── Primary route
single carriageway

─── Other A roads

🚢 or Ⓥ Vehicle ferry

⛴ Fast vehicle ferry
or catamaran

| 0 | | 10 | | 20 | | 30 miles |
|---|---|---|---|---|---|---|

| 0 | 10 | 20 | 30 | 40 kilometres |
|---|---|---|---|---|

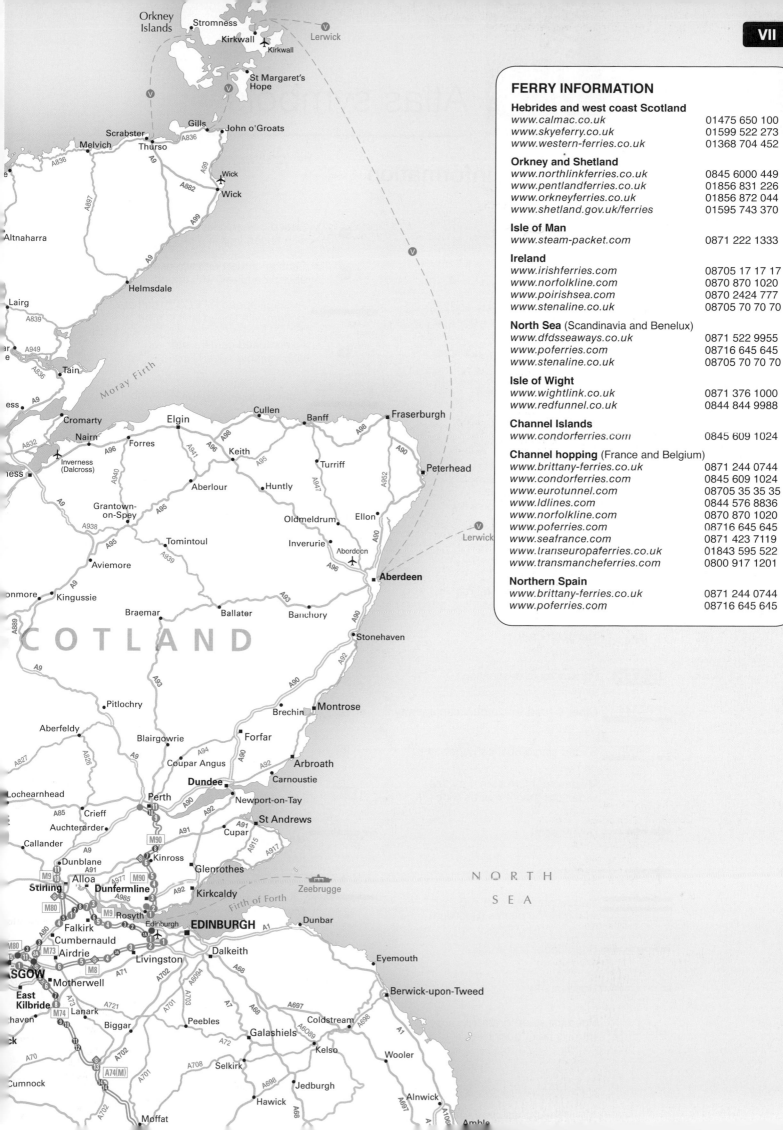

## FERRY INFORMATION

**Hebrides and west coast Scotland**
www.calmac.co.uk — 01475 650 100
www.skyeferry.co.uk — 01599 522 273
www.western-ferries.co.uk — 01368 704 452

**Orkney and Shetland**
www.northlinkferries.co.uk — 0845 6000 449
www.pentlandferries.co.uk — 01856 831 226
www.orkneyferries.co.uk — 01856 872 044
www.shetland.gov.uk/ferries — 01595 743 370

**Isle of Man**
www.steam-packet.com — 0871 222 1333

**Ireland**
www.irishferries.com — 08705 17 17 17
www.norfolkline.com — 0870 870 1020
www.poirishsea.com — 0870 2424 777
www.stenaline.co.uk — 08705 70 70 70

**North Sea** (Scandinavia and Benelux)
www.dfdsseaways.co.uk — 0871 522 9955
www.poferries.com — 08716 645 645
www.stenaline.co.uk — 08705 70 70 70

**Isle of Wight**
www.wightlink.co.uk — 0871 376 1000
www.redfunnel.co.uk — 0844 844 9988

**Channel Islands**
www.condorferries.com — 0845 609 1024

**Channel hopping** (France and Belgium)
www.brittany-ferries.co.uk — 0871 244 0744
www.condorferries.com — 0845 609 1024
www.eurotunnel.com — 08705 35 35 35
www.ldlines.com — 0844 576 8836
www.norfolkline.com — 0870 870 1020
www.poferries.com — 08716 645 645
www.seafrance.com — 0871 423 7119
www.transeuropaferries.co.uk — 01843 595 522
www.transmancheferries.com — 0800 917 1201

**Northern Spain**
www.brittany-ferries.co.uk — 0871 244 0744
www.poferries.com — 08716 645 645

# Atlas symbols

## Motoring information

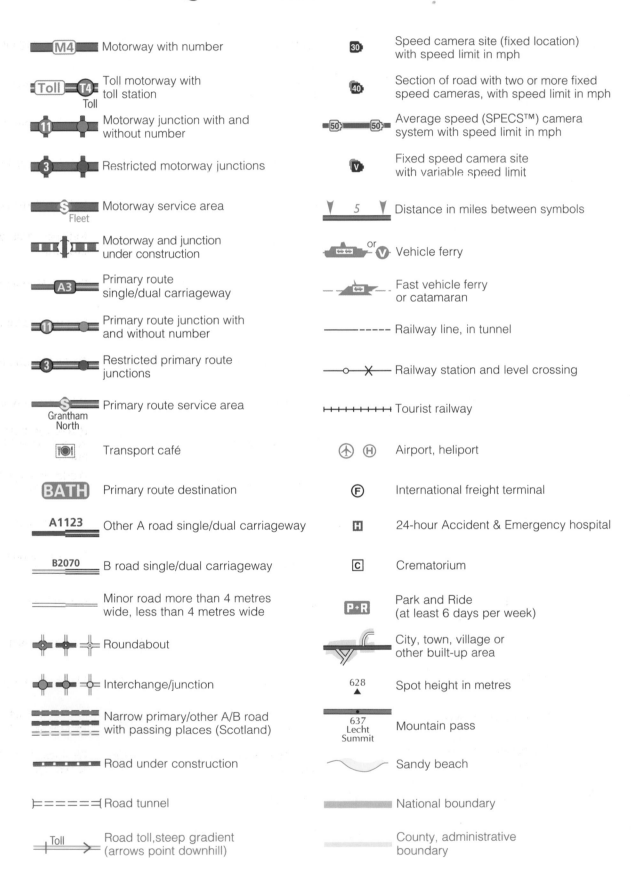

| | |
|---|---|
| Motorway with number | Speed camera site (fixed location) with speed limit in mph |
| Toll motorway with toll station | Section of road with two or more fixed speed cameras, with speed limit in mph |
| Motorway junction with and without number | Average speed (SPECS™) camera system with speed limit in mph |
| Restricted motorway junctions | Fixed speed camera site with variable speed limit |
| Motorway service area | Distance in miles between symbols |
| Motorway and junction under construction | Vehicle ferry |
| Primary route single/dual carriageway | Fast vehicle ferry or catamaran |
| Primary route junction with and without number | Railway line, in tunnel |
| Restricted primary route junctions | Railway station and level crossing |
| Primary route service area | Tourist railway |
| Transport café | Airport, heliport |
| Primary route destination | International freight terminal |
| Other A road single/dual carriageway | 24-hour Accident & Emergency hospital |
| B road single/dual carriageway | Crematorium |
| Minor road more than 4 metres wide, less than 4 metres wide | Park and Ride (at least 6 days per week) |
| Roundabout | City, town, village or other built-up area |
| Interchange/junction | Spot height in metres |
| Narrow primary/other A/B road with passing places (Scotland) | Mountain pass |
| Road under construction | Sandy beach |
| Road tunnel | National boundary |
| Road toll, steep gradient (arrows point downhill) | County, administrative boundary |

# Touring information
Before visiting check opening times, to avoid disappointment.

| Symbol | Description |
|---|---|
| | Scenic route |
| | Tourist Information Centre |
| | Tourist Information Centre (seasonal) |
| | Visitor or heritage centre |
| | Abbey, cathedral or priory |
| | Ruined abbey, cathedral or priory |
| | Castle |
| | Historic house or building |
| | Museum or art gallery |
| | Industrial interest |
| | Aqueduct or viaduct |
| | Garden |
| | Arboretum |
| | Vineyard |
| | Country park |
| | Agricultural showground |
| | Theme park |
| | Farm or animal centre |
| | Zoological or wildlife collection |
| | Bird collection |
| | Aquarium |

| Symbol | Description |
|---|---|
| RSPB | RSPB site |
| | National Nature Reserve (England, Scotland, Wales) |
| | Local nature reserve |
| | Forest drive |
| | National trail |
| | Viewpoint |
| | Picnic site |
| | Hill-fort |
| | Roman antiquity |
| | Prehistoric monument |
| 1066 | Battle site with year |
| | Steam railway centre |
| | Cave |
| | Windmill |
| | Monument |
| | Golf course |
| | County cricket ground |
| | Rugby Union national stadium |
| | International athletics stadium |
| | Horse racing |
| | Show jumping/equestrian circuit |

| Symbol | Description |
|---|---|
| | Motor-racing circuit |
| | Air show venue |
| | Ski slope (natural) |
| | Ski slope (artificial) |
| | National Trust property |
| | National Trust for Scotland property |
| | English Heritage site |
| | Historic Scotland site |
| | Cadw (Welsh heritage) site |
| ★ | Other place of interest |
| □ | Boxed symbols indicate attractions within urban areas |
| | World Heritage Site (UNESCO) |
| | National Park |
| | National Scenic Area (Scotland) |
| | Forest Park |
| | Heritage coast |
| | Major shopping centre |
| | Welcome Break or Moto Burger King |
| KFC | Kentucky Fried Chicken at Welcome Break |

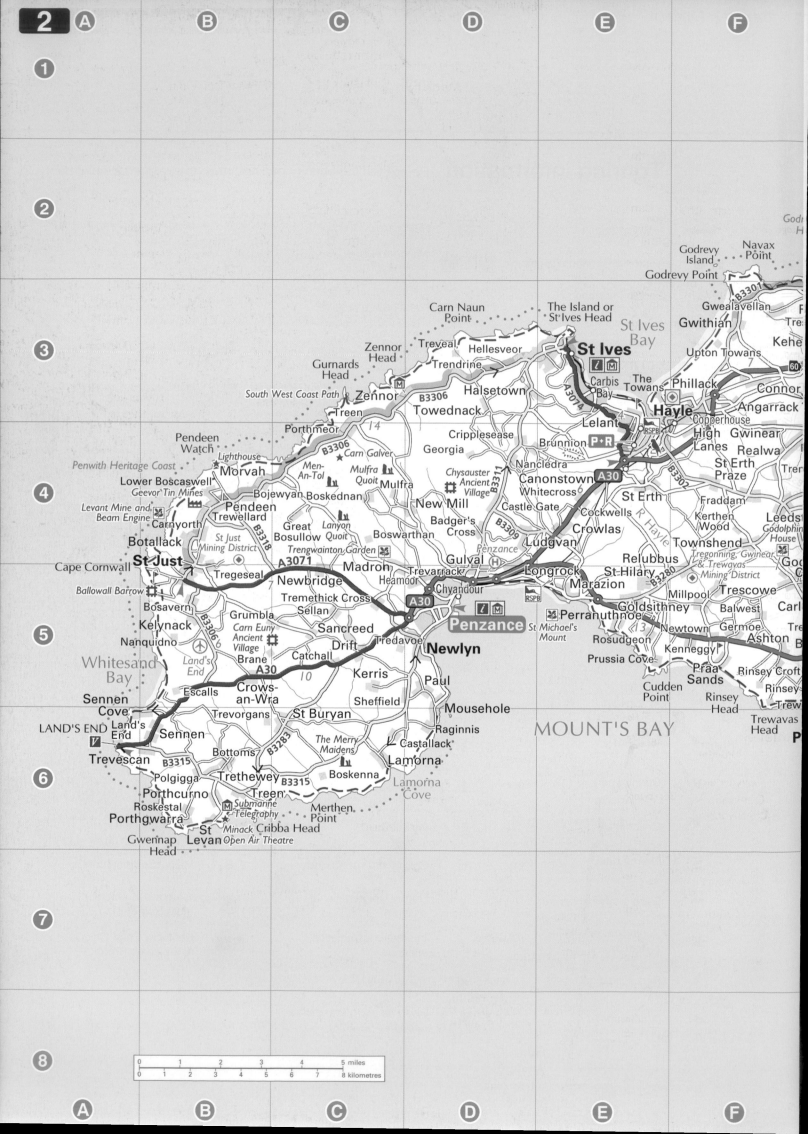

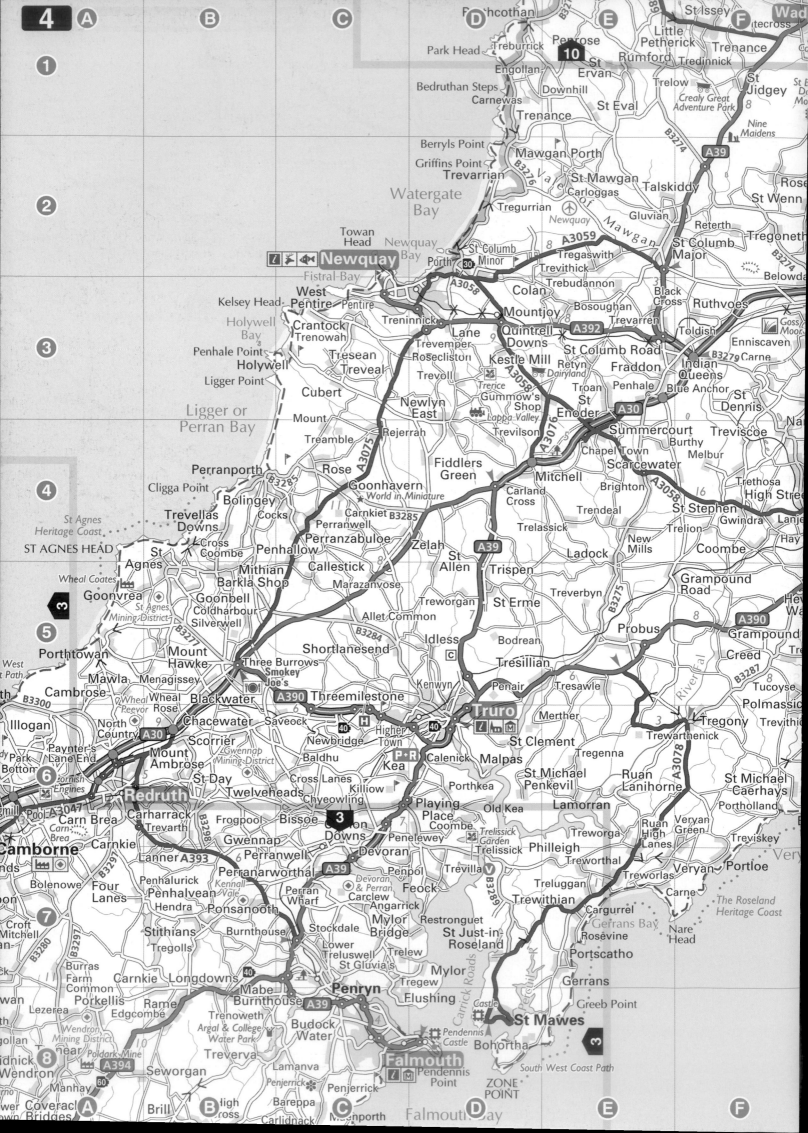

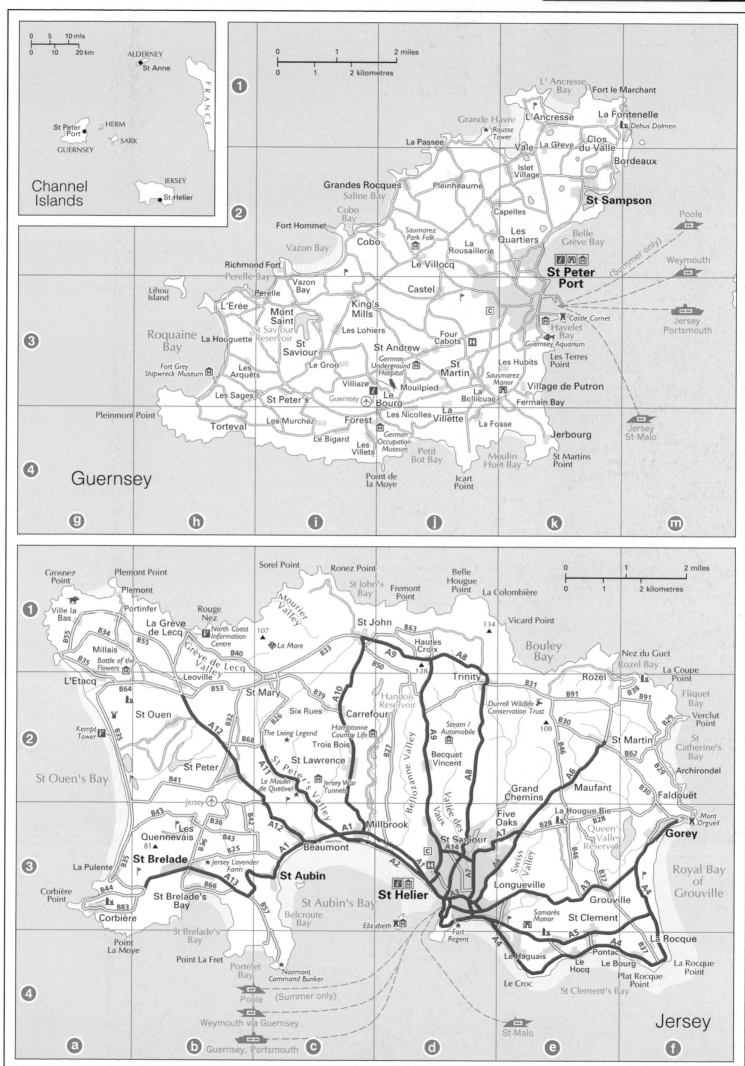

**Channel Islands**

Guernsey

Jersey

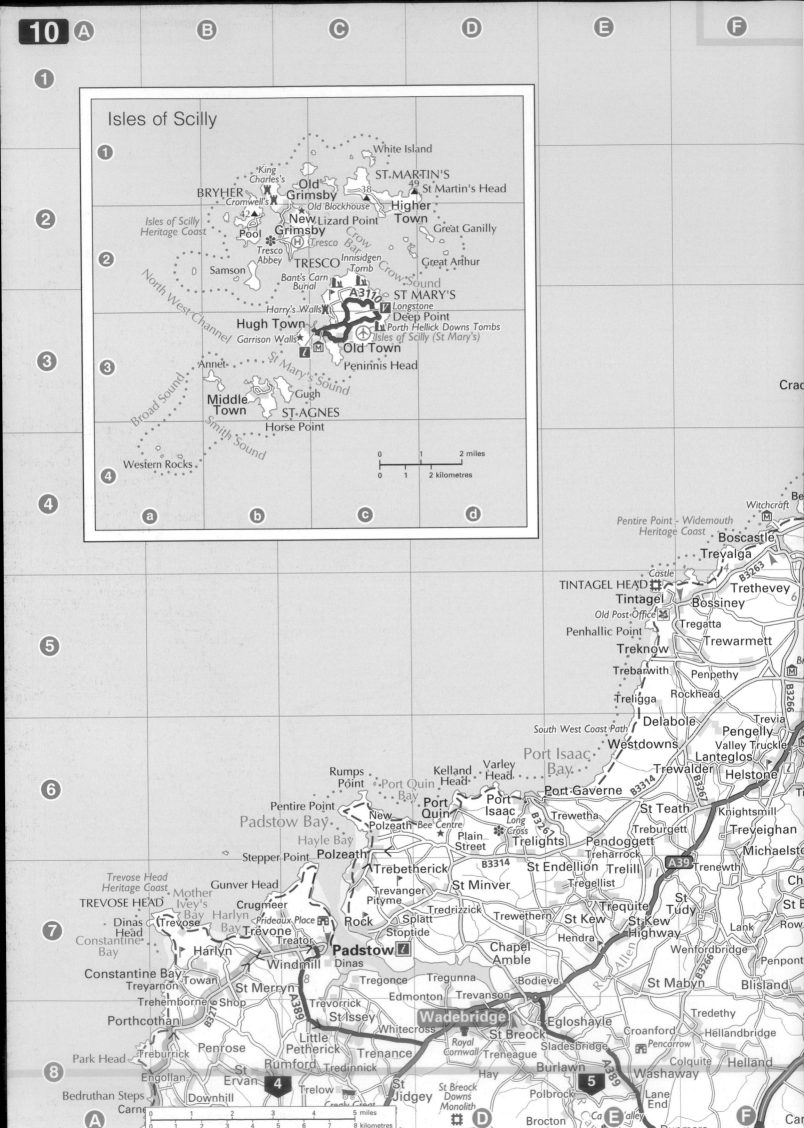

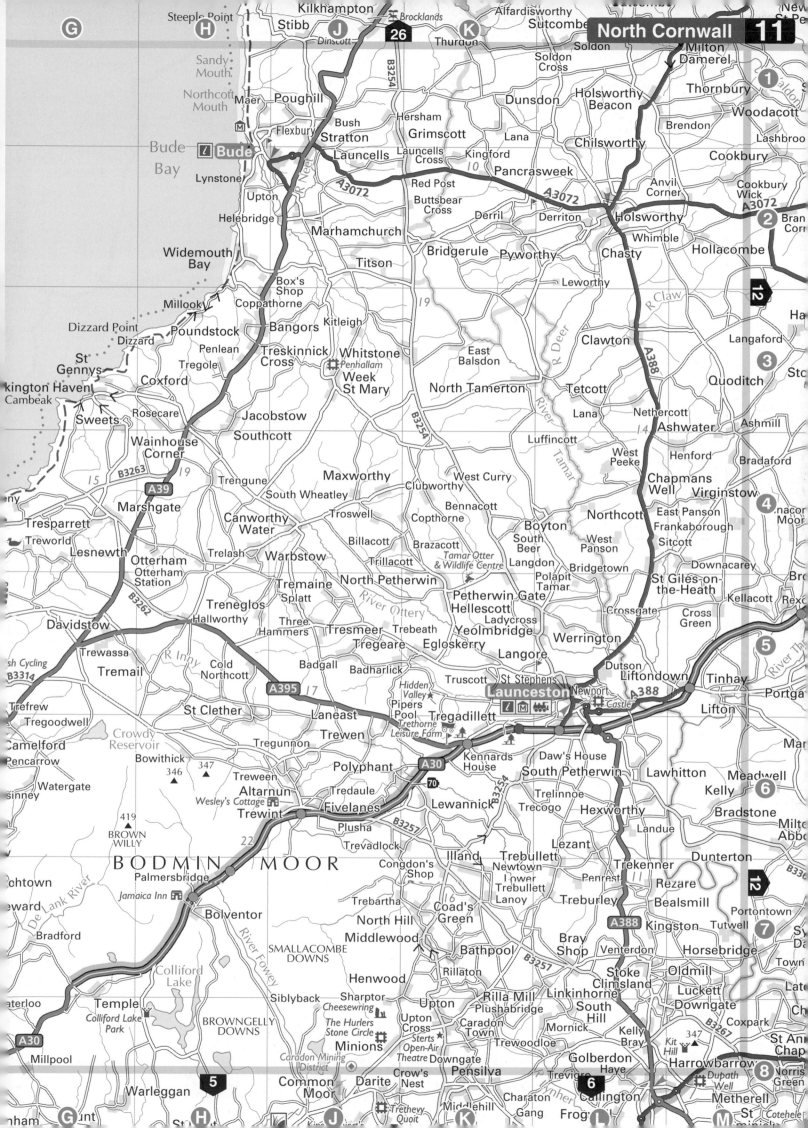

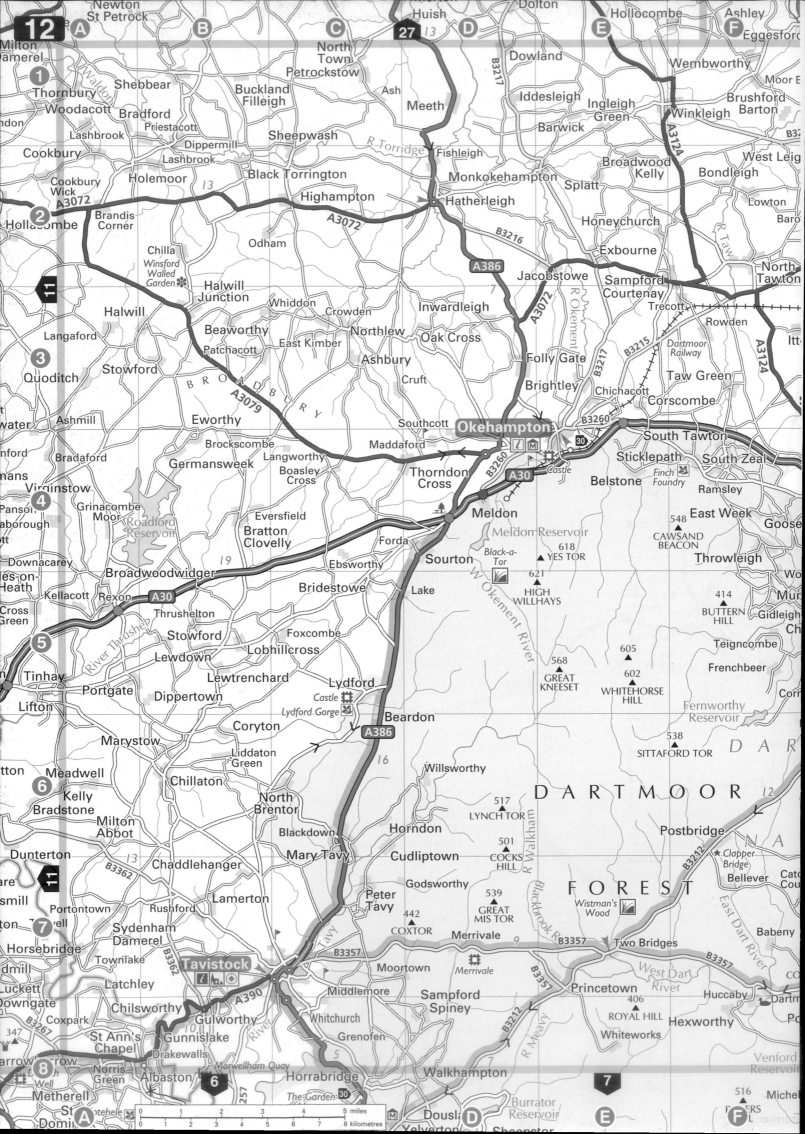

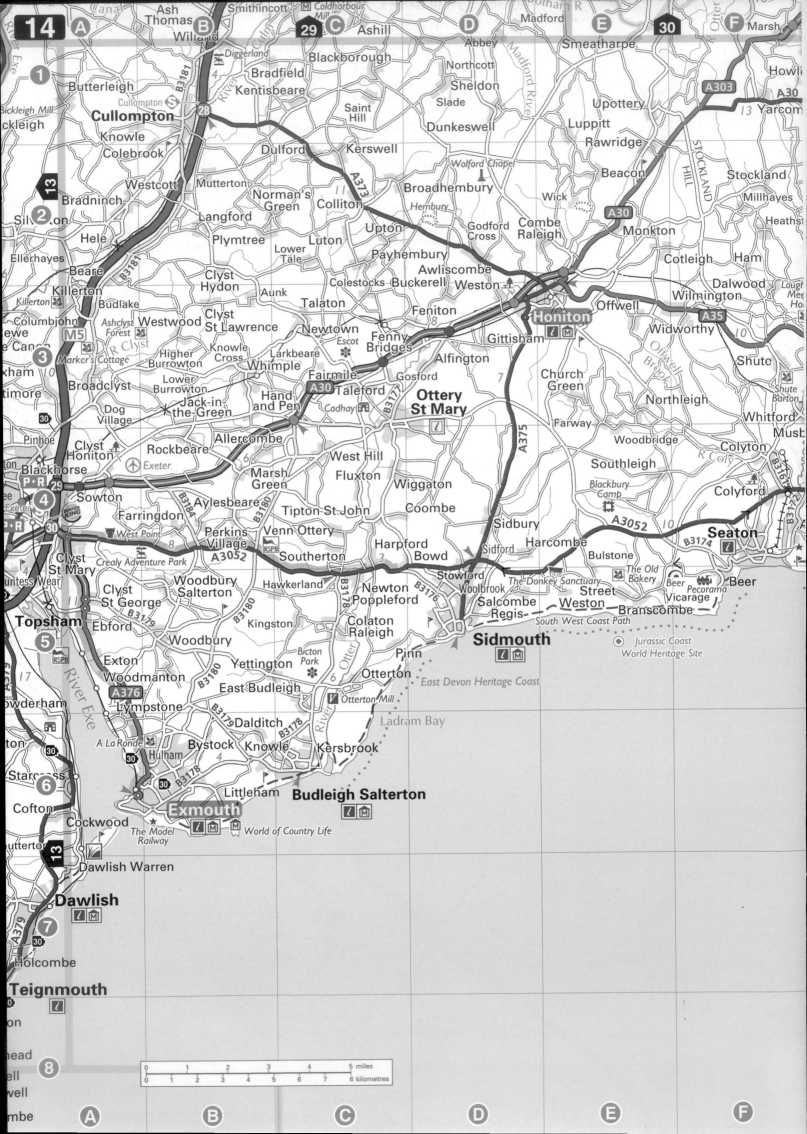

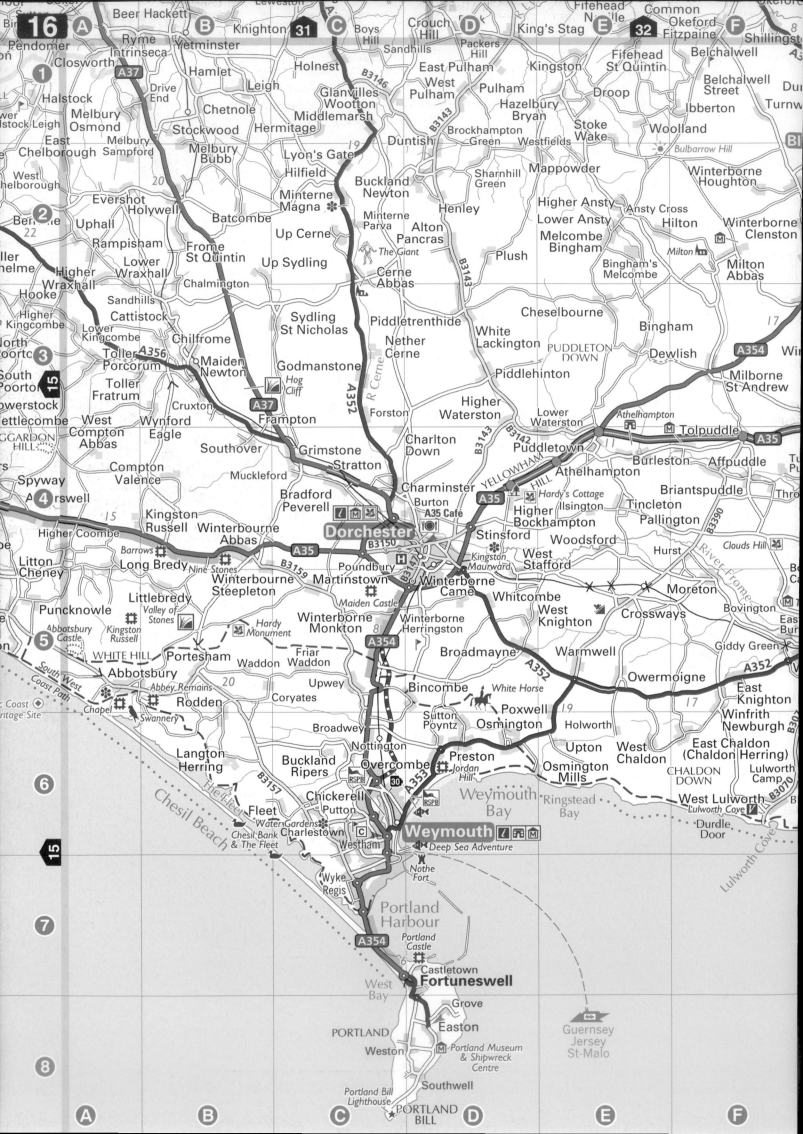

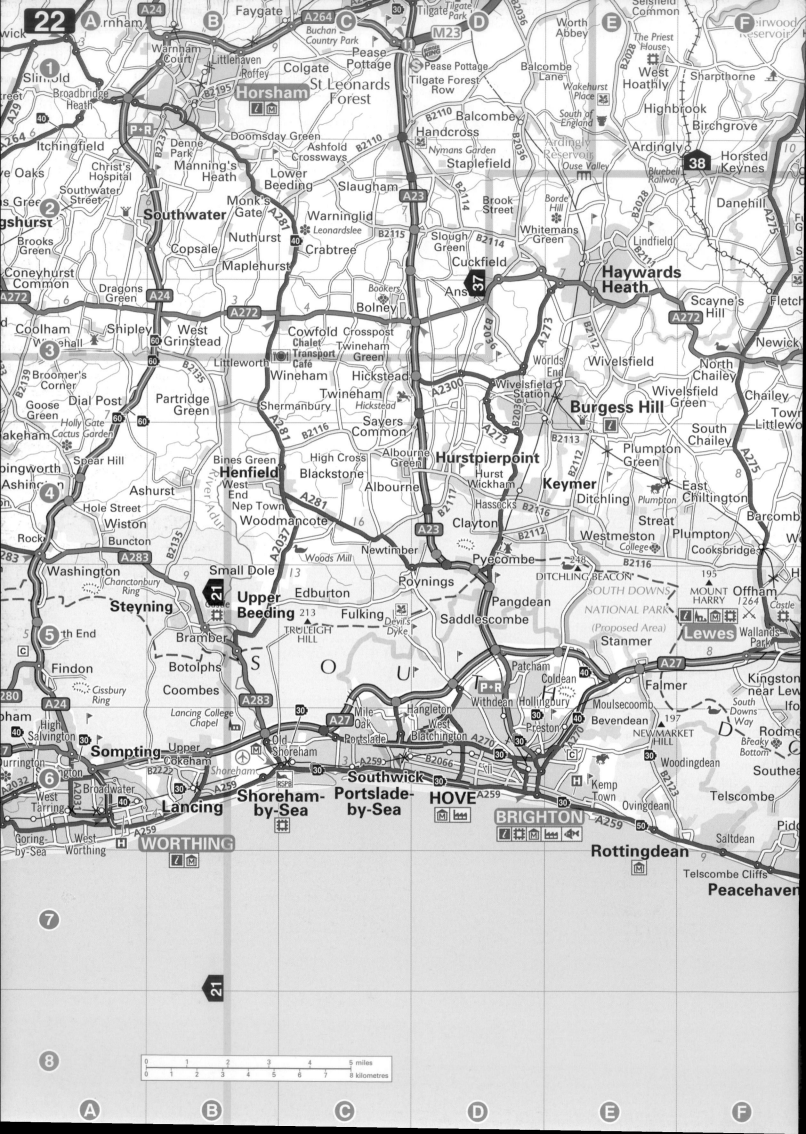

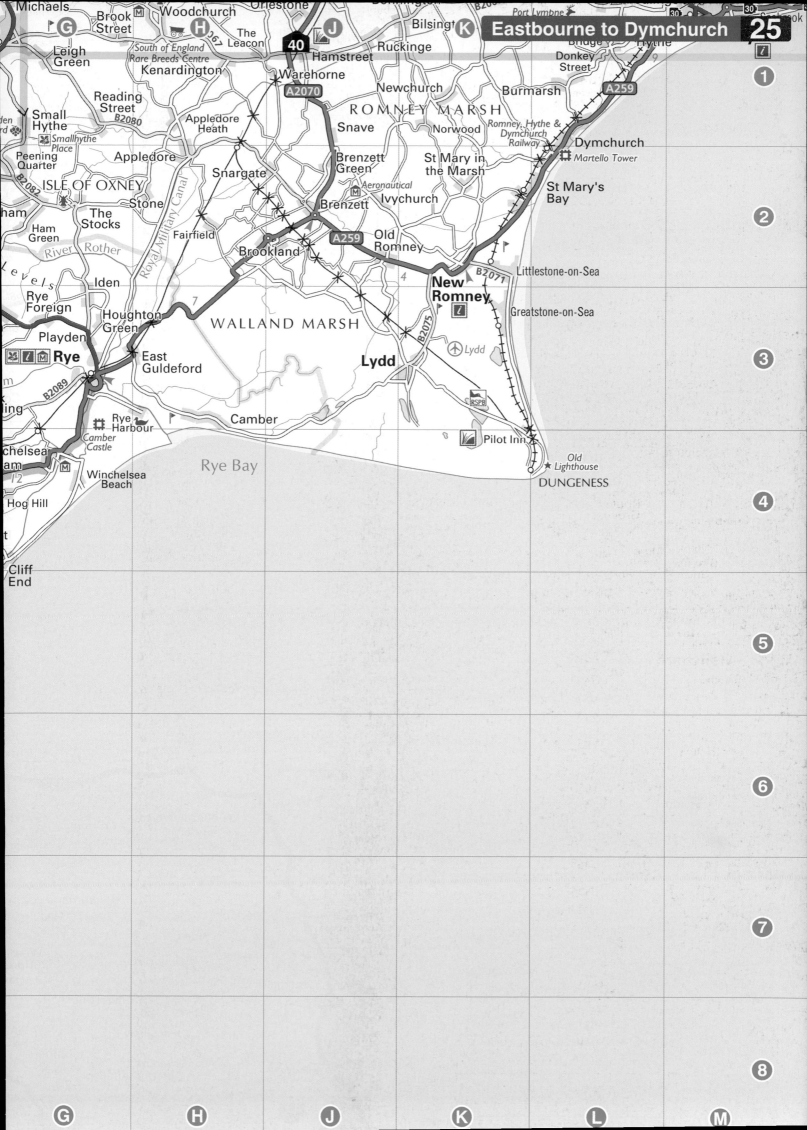

North West Point

*Lundy Heritage Coast*

LUNDY

142 ▲

*Marisco*

Surf Point

Shutter Point

BARNSTAPLE

OR

BIDEFORD BAY

*Shipload Bay*

HARTLAND POINT

Titchberry

Brownsham

Damehole Point

*Hartland Abbey & Garden*

Clovelly

*Hartland Heritage Coast*

Stoke

B3248

Velly

Buck's Mills

Fa...

Higher Clovelly

Hartland Quay

Hartland

*Spekes Mill Mouth*

Milford

*Docton Mill Gardens*

Buck's Cross

*Milky Way*

A39

Horn Cros...

Philham

Elmscott

Woolfardisworthy

Cranford

Parkh...

Hardisworthy

Parkham Ash

South Hole

Welcombe

Ashmansworthy

Mead

Darracott

Meddon

East Putford

Woolley

East Youlstone

Dinworthy

West Putford

*Gnome Reserve* ★

Gooseham

Eastcott

Colscott

Hay...

Morwenstow

West Youlstone

Bradworthy

Higher Sharpnose Point

Shop

*South West Coast Path*

Woodford

A39

Kimworthy

Lower Sharpnose Point

*Tamar Lakes*

Sutcombe

Ab... Bick...

Steeple Point

Kilkhampton

*Brocklands*

Alfardisworthy

Stibb

Sutcombemill

*Dinscott*

Thurdon

Soldon

Mil... Dam...

Soldon Cross

River...

0 1 2 3 4 5 miles

0 1 2 3 4 5 6 7 8 kilometres

**11**

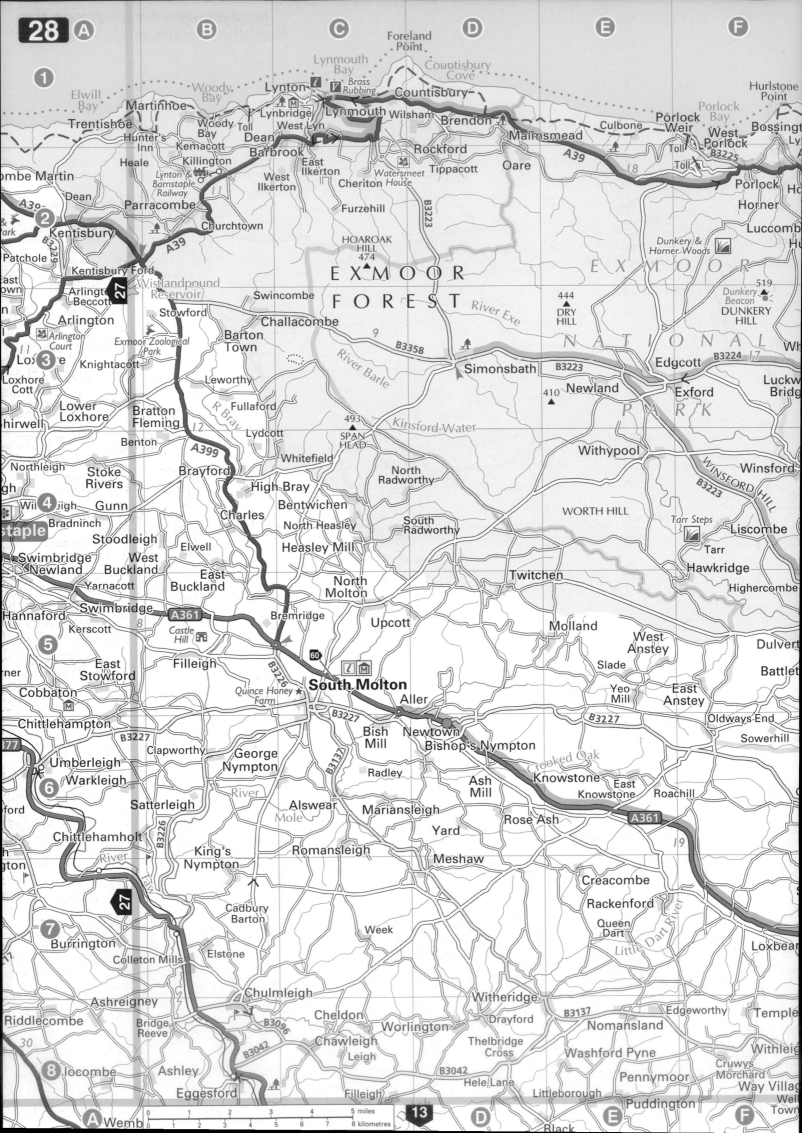

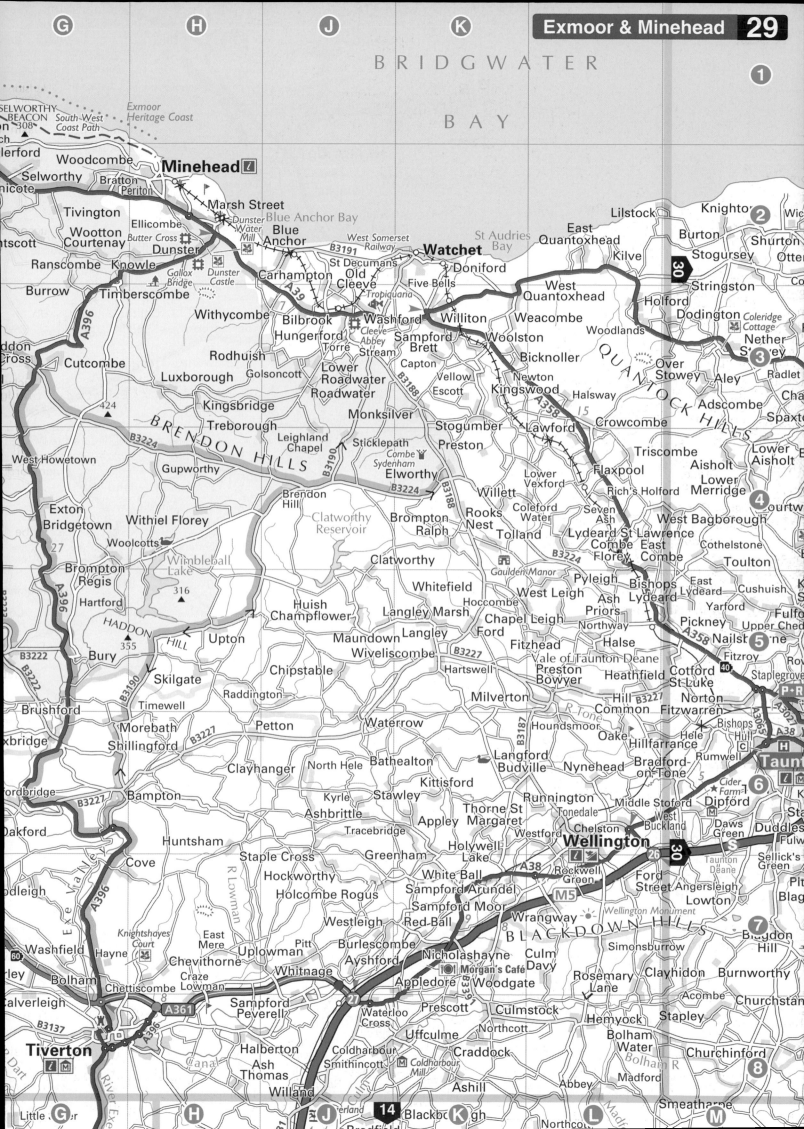

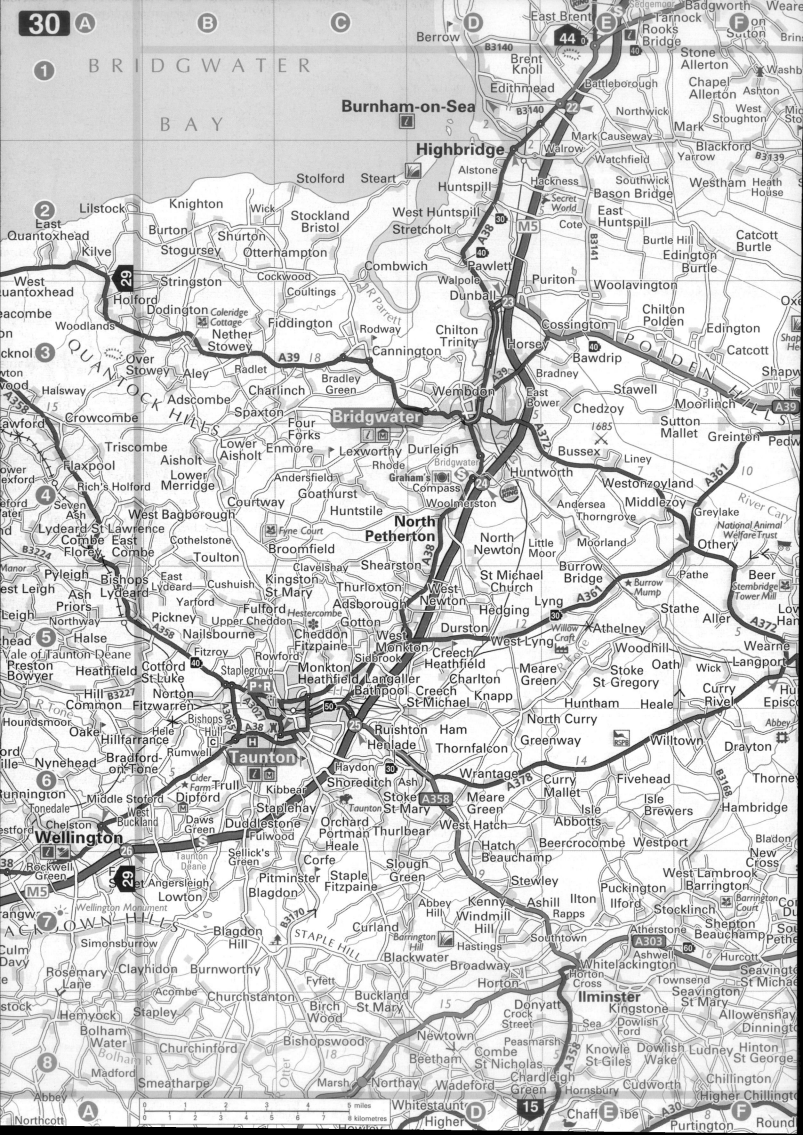

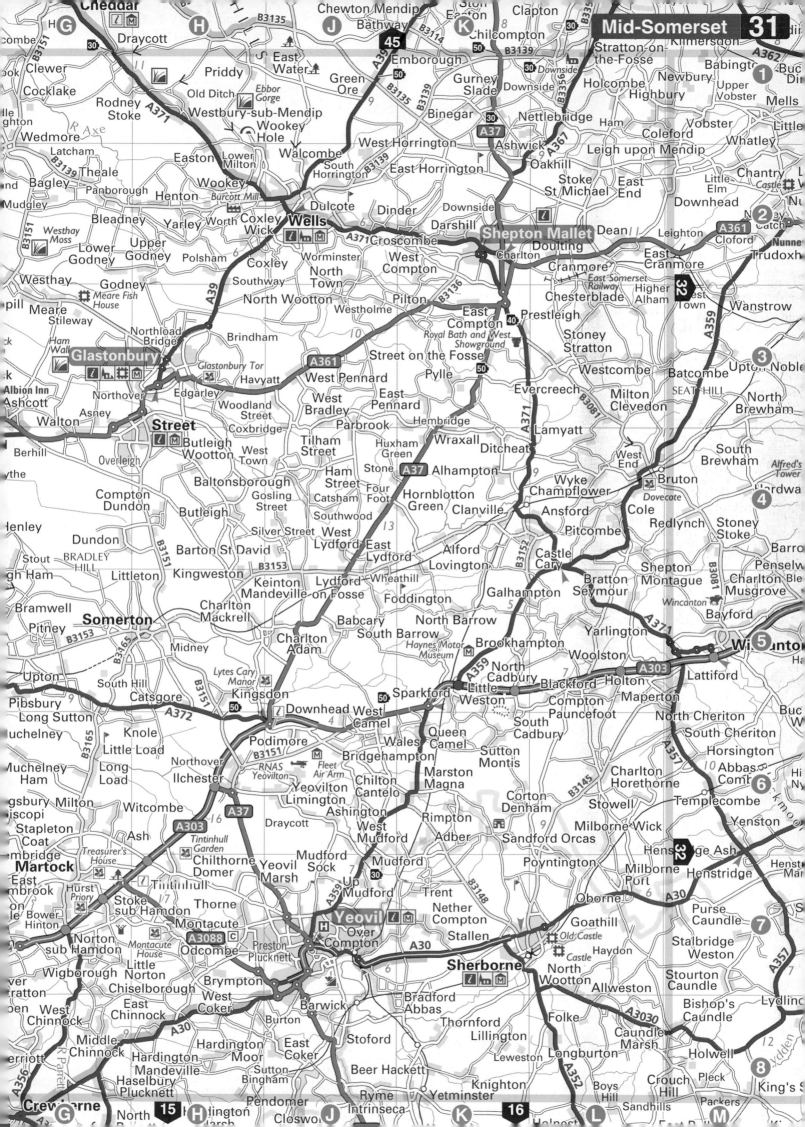

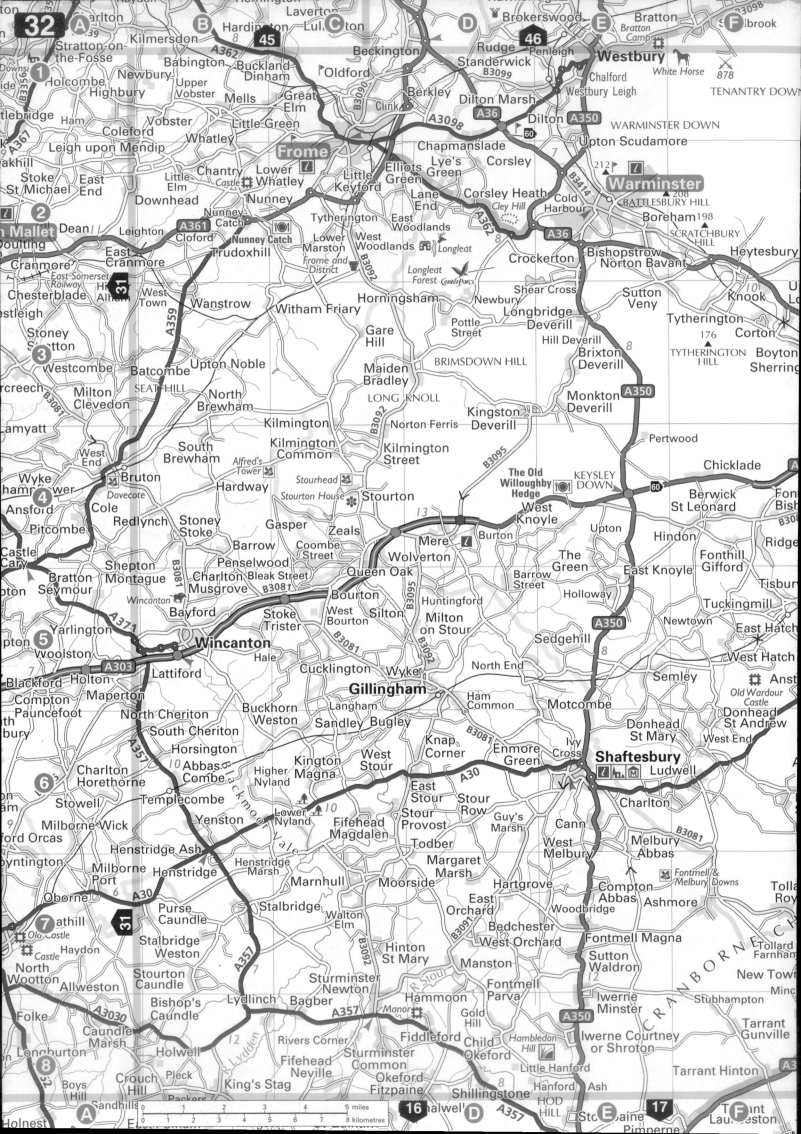

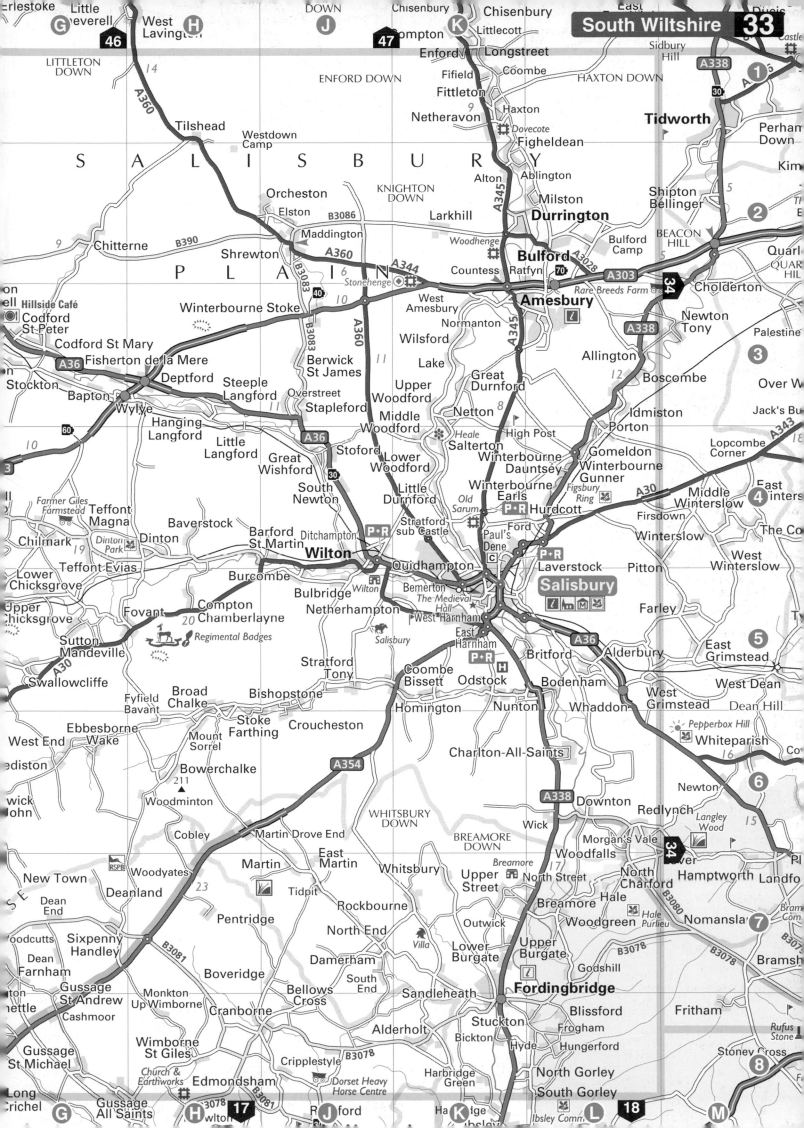

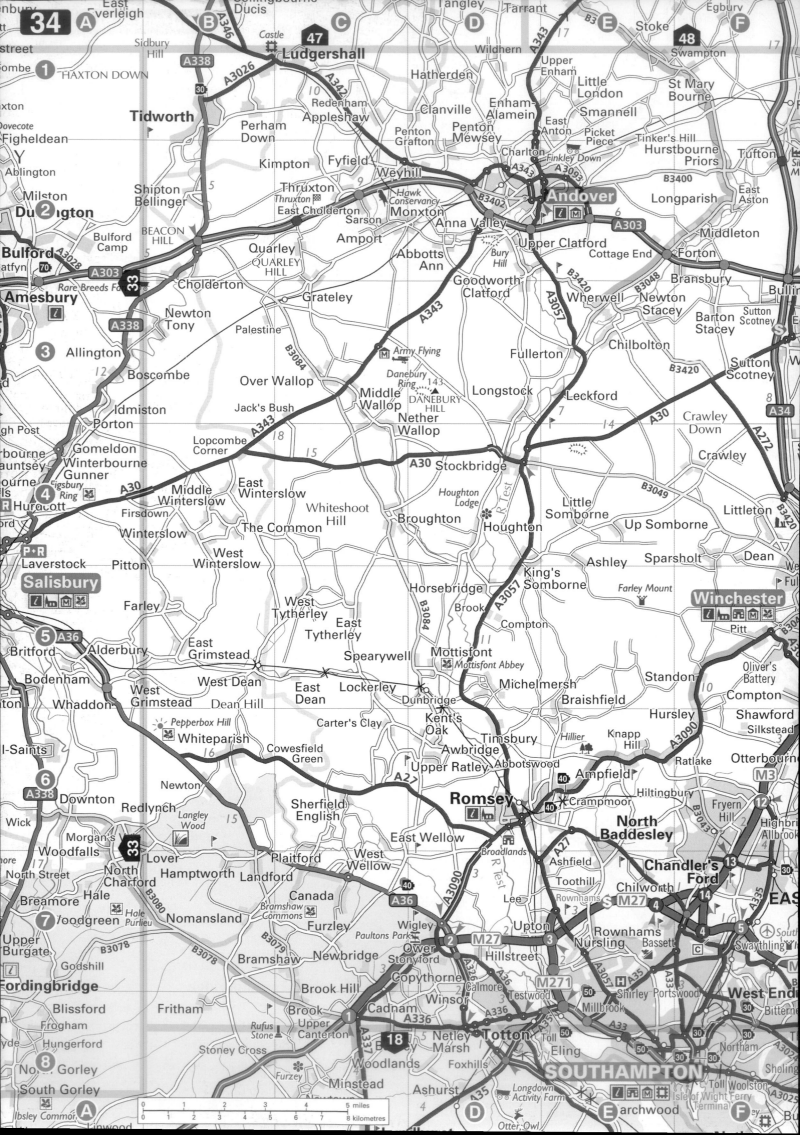

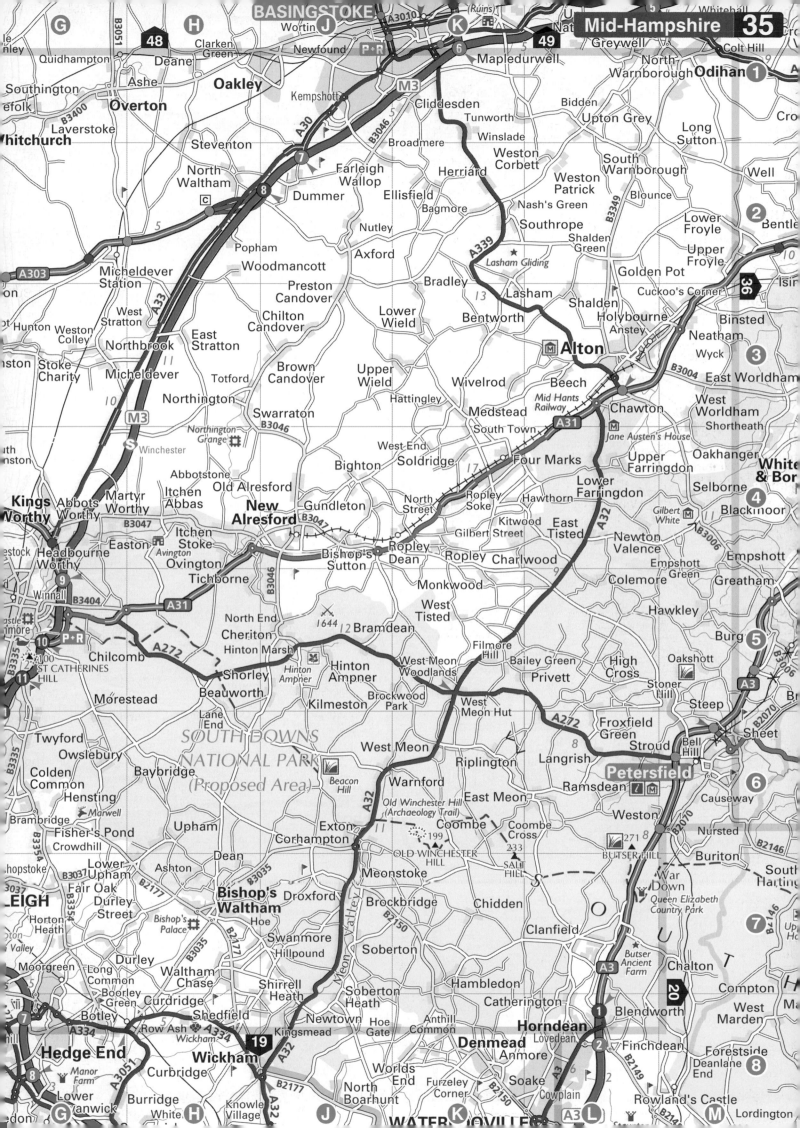

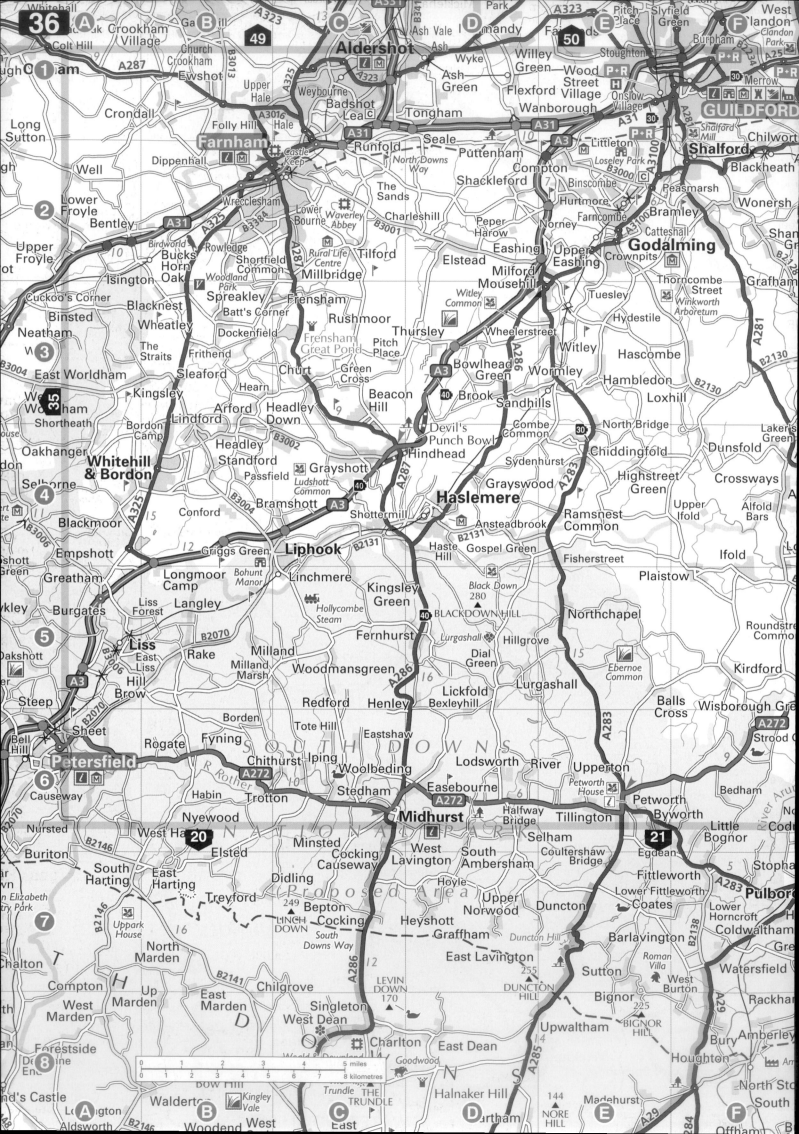

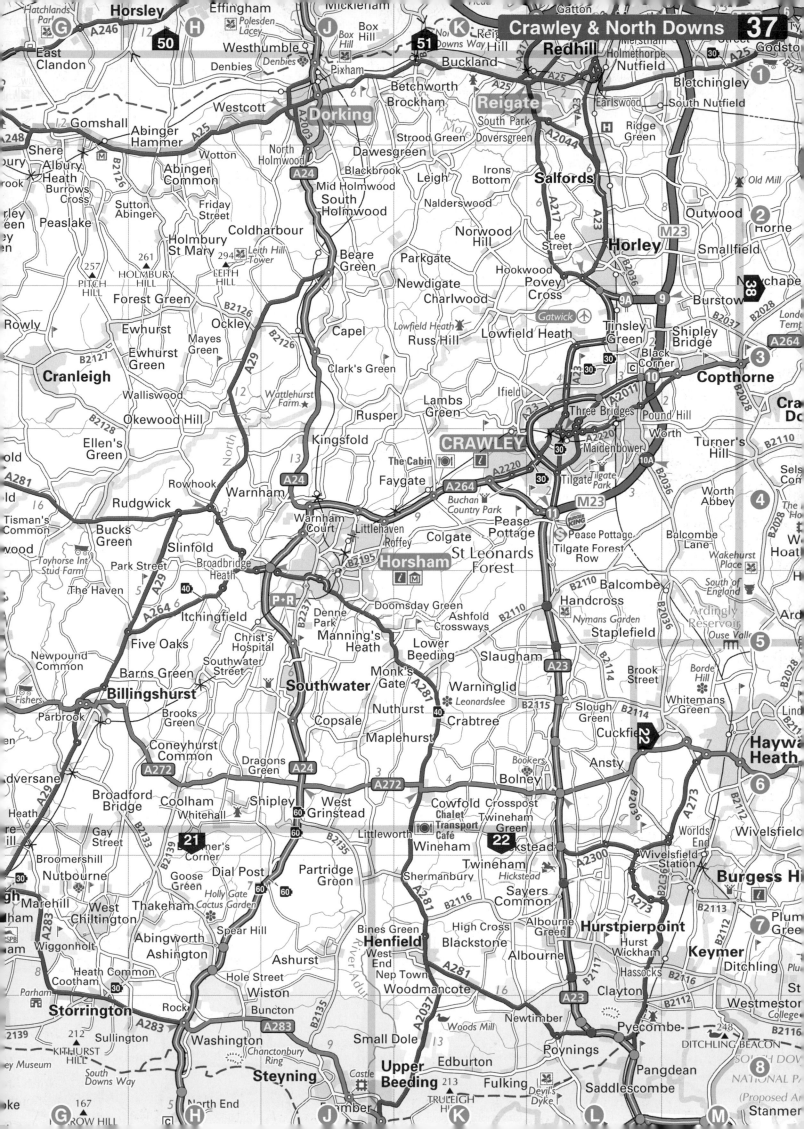

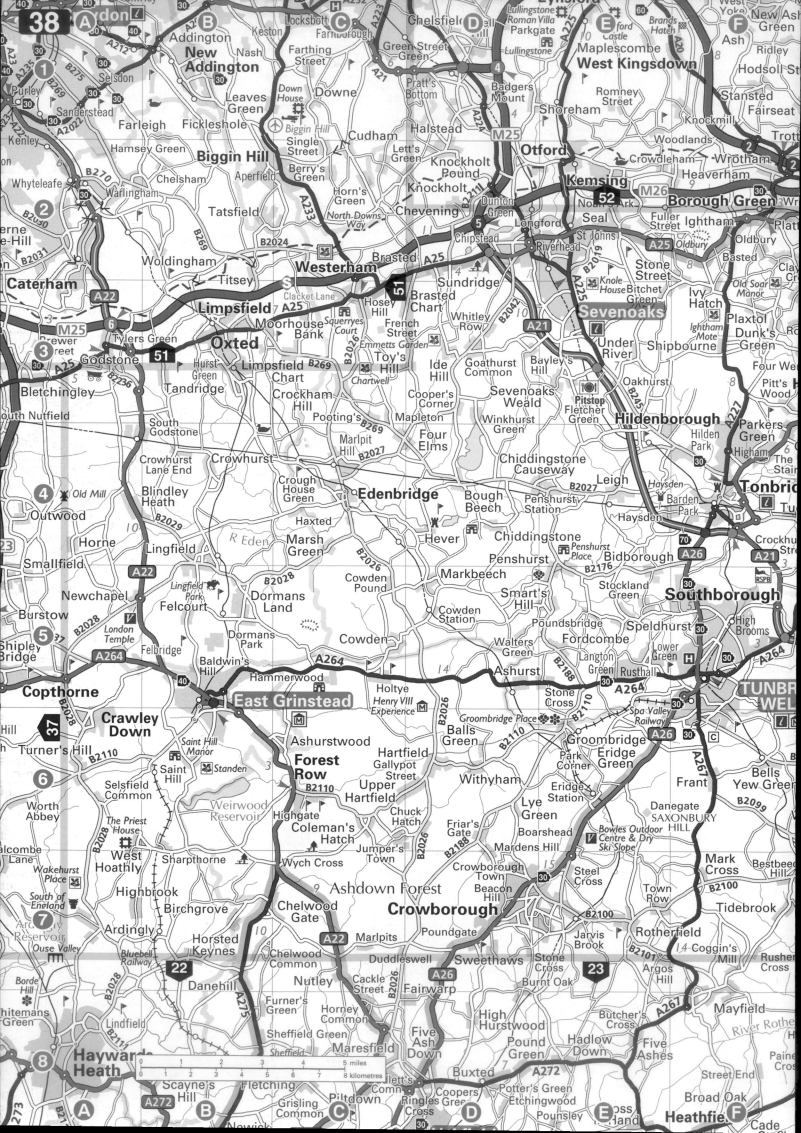

Sitting...

Snodland · Aylesford · Ditton · West Malling · Leybourne · Addington · Larkfield · Lunsford · New Hythe · Eccles · Boarley · Boxley · Sandling · Allington · British Legion Village · East Malling · East Malling Heath · Kings Hill · Offham · St Leonard's Street · Mereworth · Wateringbury · Teston · East Barming · Barming Heath · Tovil · Dean Street · Shepway · Otham · Loose · Coxheath · Linton · Boughton Green · Langley · Cock St · Chart Corner · Five Wents · Boughton Monchelsea · Chart Hill · Chart Sutton · Sutton Valence · East Sutton · Ulcombe · Chartway Street · Liverton Street · Platts Heath · Kingswood · Broomfield · Leeds · Otham Hole · Leadingcross Green · Sandway · Lenham Heath

**MAIDSTONE** · Bearsted · Grove Green · Ware Street · Detling · Thurnham · Broad Street · Hollingbourne · Eyhorne Street · Sutton Street · Willington · Ringlestone · Hucking · Wormshill · Frinsted · Milstead · Bicknor · Bredgar · Swanton Street · Stiff Street · Silver Street · South Green · Kemsley Street · Danaway · Borden · Tunstall · Hearts Delight · Highsted · Bexon · Rodmersham Green · Rawling Street · Dungate · Doddington · Frinsted · West Street · Woodside Green · Payden Street · Harrietsham · Lenham

Yalding · Hunton · Benover · Chainhurst · Stile Bridge · Underling Green · Little Pattenden · Milebush · Cross-at-Hand · Marden · Marden Thorn · Marden Beech · Staplehurst · Iden Croft Herbs · Sinkhurst Green · Frittenden · Lashenden · Rabbit's Cross · Farthing Green · Sweetlands Corner · Jubilee Corner · Plumtree Green · Southernden · Hawkenbury · Headcorn · Wheeler's Street · Smarden Bell · Smarden · Pembles Cross · Potter's Forstal · Bedlam Lane · The Forstal · Egerton · Mundy Bois · Swift's Green · The Quarter · Chambers Green · Biddenden Green · Pluckley · Maltman's Hill · Wissenden · Pluckley Station · Romden Castle · Haffenden Quarter

East Peckham · Hale Street · Snoll Hatch · Hop Farm · Beltring · Laddingford · Mockbeggar · Fowlhall · Whetsted · Five Oak Green · Rhoden Grn · Collier Street · Queen Street · Claygate · Paddock Wood · Matfield · Brenchley · Horsmonden · Corks Pond · Mile Oak · Castle Hill · The Corner · Pearson's Green · Grovenhurst · Hazel Street · Broad Ford · Colliers Green · Flishinghurst · Winchet Hill · Curtisden Green · Knox Bridge · Cranbrook Common · Wilsley Pound · Three Chimneys · Hareplain · Standen · Curteis Corner · Stede Quarter · Further Quarter · Biddenden · Woolpack · Goose Green · Sissinghurst Castle Garden · Middle Quarter · High Halden · Redbrook Street · St Michaels

Pembury · Tipping's Cross · Owl House · Hoathly · Bayham Abbey · Lamberhurst · Finchcocks · Spelmonden · Scotney Castle · Riseden · Kilndown · Glassenbury · Iden Green · Goudhurst · Bewlbridge · Bedgebury Cross · National Pinetum & Garden · Stonecrouch · Bewl Water · Pell Green · Hook Green · Cousley Wood · Lamberhurst Down · Wadhurst · Three Leg Cross · Flimwell · Union Street · Dale Hill · Hawkhurst · High Street · Gill's Green · Gun Green · Highgate · Four Throws · The Moor · Hartley · Goddard's Green · Benenden · Beacon Hill · Iden Green · Dingleden · Standen Street · Sandhurst · Wilsley Green · Sissinghurst · Union Mill · Golford · Golford Green · East End · Parkgate · Cranbrook · Arcadia · London Beach · Tenterden · Strood · Leigh Green · Historic Vehicles Collection · Rolvenden · Rolvenden Layne · Tenterden Vineyard Park · Peening Quarter · Small Hythe · Smallhythe Place · Reading Street

Ticehurst · Shover's Green · Bardown · Stonegate · Pashley Manor · Burgh Hill · Hurst Green · Merriments · Etchingham · Bodiam · Bodiam Castle · Great Dixter · Sandhurst Cross · Linkhill · Newenden · Kent & East Sussex Railway · Northiam · Beckley · Clayhill · Millcorner · Staple Cross · Cripp's Corner · Collier · Witherenden Hill · Burwash · Bateman's · Burwash Weald · Holton Hill · Willards Hill · Northbridge Street · Robertsbridge · Salehurst · Ewhurst Green · Four Oaks · Rye Foreign · Wittersham · Ham Green · The Stocks · Isle of Oxney · River Rother · Peasmarsh

Roads: M2 · M20 · A20 · A21 · A26 · A228 · A229 · A249 · A262 · A268 · A274 · B2010 · B2015 · B2016 · B2017 · B2079 · B2085 · B2086 · B2088 · B2099 · B2100 · B2160 · B2162 · B2163 · B2165 · B2244

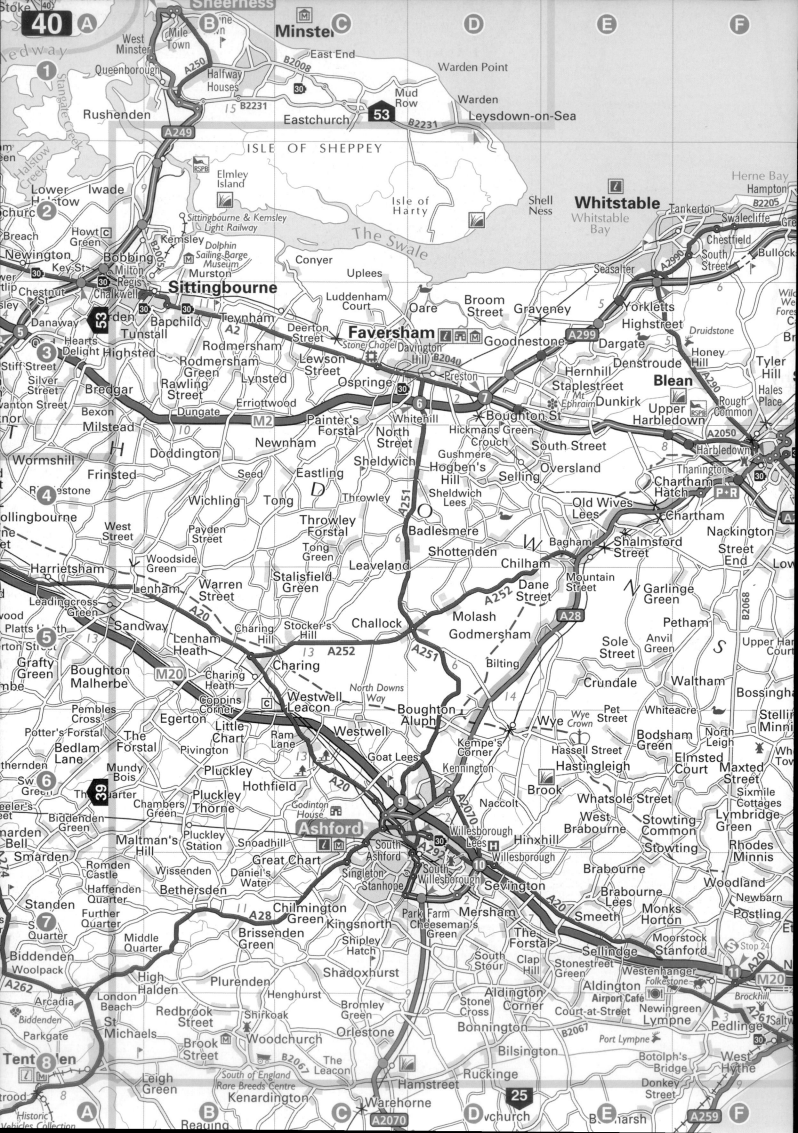

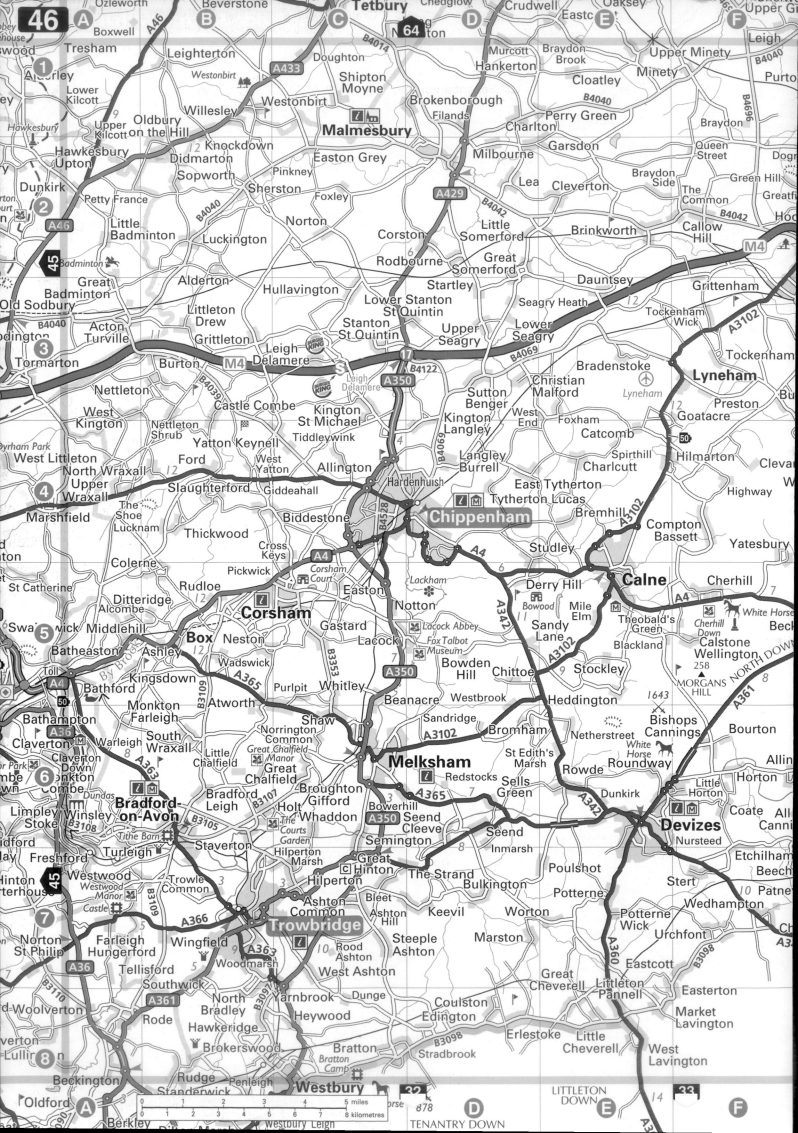

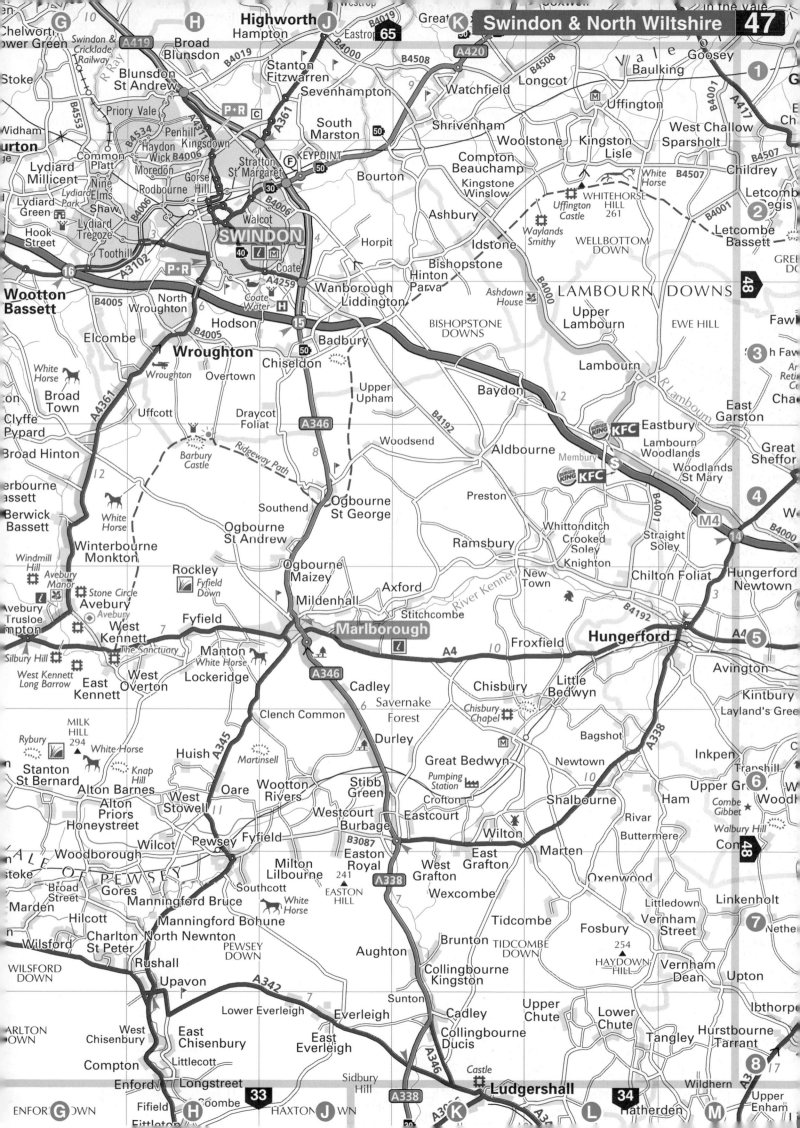

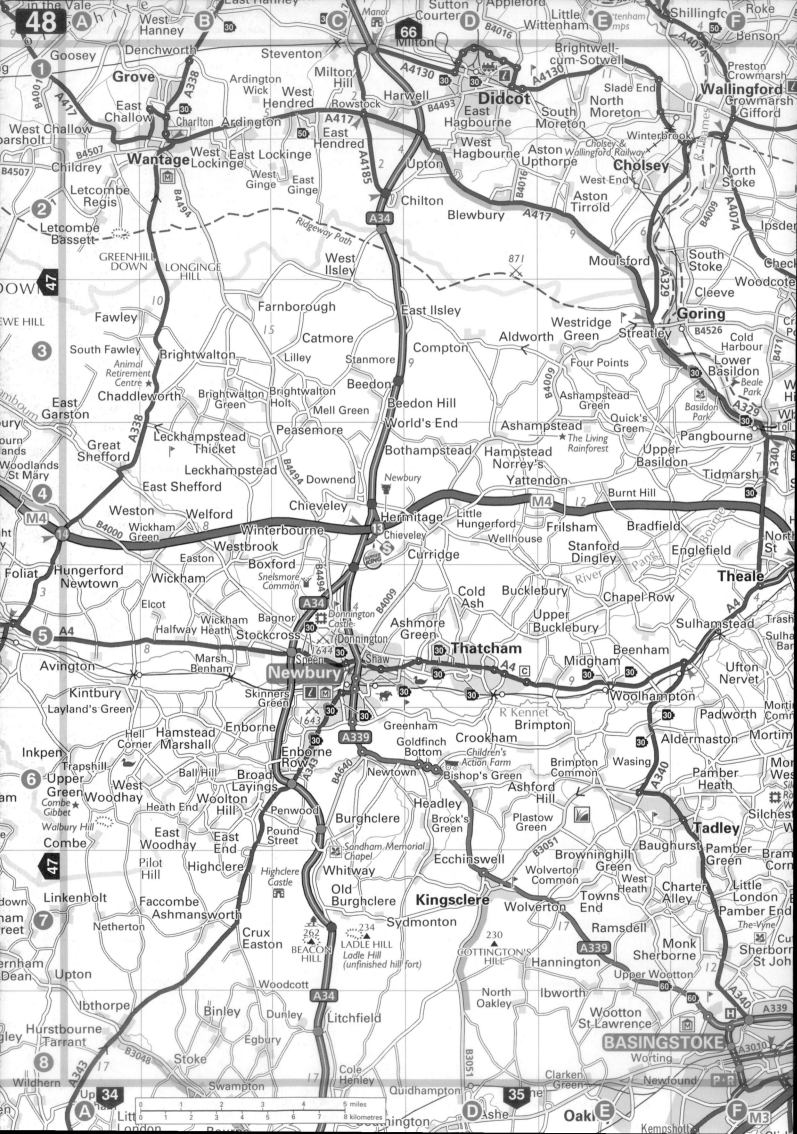

**G** **71** Shotgate  Rawreth  **H** ley  Paglesham  Island
A1245  **A129**  Hawkwell  Ashingdon  **J** **72**  Halesville  FOULNESS ISLAND
Nevendon  **Rayleigh**  B1013  Rochford  Great  Gore  Potton Is  ISLAND  **1**
A130  A127  Stroud  Great  Barling
New Thundersley  A1015  Green  Stambridge  R Roach
Thundersley  A129  Daws  **40**  Southend  Barling  Great Wakering
A13  Heath  **40**  Eastwood  Prittlewell  Little Wakering
Hadleigh  **40**  **C** A1159  Bournes Green  B1017  **2**
**South enfleet**  B1006  Hadleigh Castle  Leigh on-Sea  A13  **H**  North Shoebury
B1014  Westcliff -on-Sea  Southchurch  Shoeburyness
A130  Leigh Beck  Thorpe Bay  B1016  A3
**Canvey Island**  Canvey Point  **SOUTHEND-ON-SEA**  Shoebury Ness

THAMES  ESTUARY  **3**

Allhallows-on-Sea
St Mary's Hoo  Allhallows  Isle-of-Grain  Grain
Cooling  **40**  Lower Stoke  B2001  Wallend
High Halstow  Fenn Street  **40**  Middle Stoke  Sheerness  **Minster**  **4**
A228  Sharnal Street  North Street  Stoke  West Minster  Marine Town  East End
Hoo St Werburgh  Queenborough  A250  Warden Point
Broad Street  Halfway Houses  B2008  Mud Row  Warden
Lower Upnor  River Medway  Rushenden  15  B2231  Eastchurch  Leysdown-on-Sea  **5**
Upper Upnor  A249  **40**  ISLE OF SHEPPEY  B2231
The Historic Dockyard Chatham  Ham Green  Iwade  Elmley Island  Isle of Harty
Fort Amherst  **40**  Riverside  Lower Rainham  9
**GILLINGHAM**  Wetham Green  Lower Halstow  Dolphin Sailing Barge Museum  The Swale
Brompton  Grange  East Rainham  Sittingbourne & Kemsley Light Railway
HAM  A289  B2004  Upchurch  Howt Green  Kemsley  Conyer  Broom  **6**
Luton  A2  Otterham Quay  Breach  Murston  Luddenham Court  Oare  Gra
Darland  Rainham  Newington  Key St  Bobbing  Milton Regis  Uplees  **Faversham**  Goodnest
Capstone  Wigmore  Moor Street  **Sittingbourne**  Davington  Hill  B2040
Hempstead  Meresborough  Hartlip  Lower Hartlip  Chalkwell  Borden  Bapchild  Teynham  Deerton Street  Ospringe  Preston  **7**
Waldersade  Rainham  Chestnut St  Tunstall  A2  Rodmersham  Lewson Street  Whitehill  Boughton
Lords Wood  **M2**  Chesley  Danaway  Hearts Delight  Rodmersham Green  Lynsted  North Street  Hickmans Green
Lidsing  **4**  Guilstead  Hill Green  Oad St  **40**  Rawling Street  Painter's Forstal  Hogben's Hill  Selling
Bredhurst  Kemsley Street  **5**  Stiff Street  Bredgar  Erriottwood  Newnham  Sheldwich  **7**
Dunn Street  Stockbury  Silver Street  Bexon  Dungate  Eastling  Sheldwich Lees
Westfield Sole  A249  South Green  Milstead  Throwley  Badlesmere
Tyland Barn  Kent County  Bicknor  Wichling  Tong  Throwley Forstal  A251  Shottenden
Boarley  Boxley  Swanton Street  Doddington  Seed  Tong Green  Leaveland  Chilha
Sandling  Detling  Hucking  Wormshill  Frinsted  Eastling  Stalisfield Green  Molash
**Bearsted**  **39**  Thurnham  Broad Street  Ringlestone  Payden Street  Warren Street  Cadmersham
Maidstone  Woodside Green  **8**
Grove Green  Sutton Street  Hollingbourne  West Street  Lenham  Stocker's Hill  Charing Hill  Dan Stre
Willington  Bearsted  Eyhorne Street  Harrietsham  Leadingcross Green  Sandway  **L**  Molash
Shepway  Leeds  Otham  Leeds  Kingswood  Platts Heath  Charing  **M**
Otham Hole  Broomfield  Five Wents  A20  Challock
**G** Boughton  Langley  B2163  **H**  Liverton Street  **J** 13  Lenham  **K**  Len  **L**  Cadmersham

MYNYDD PRESELI
NATIONAL PARK

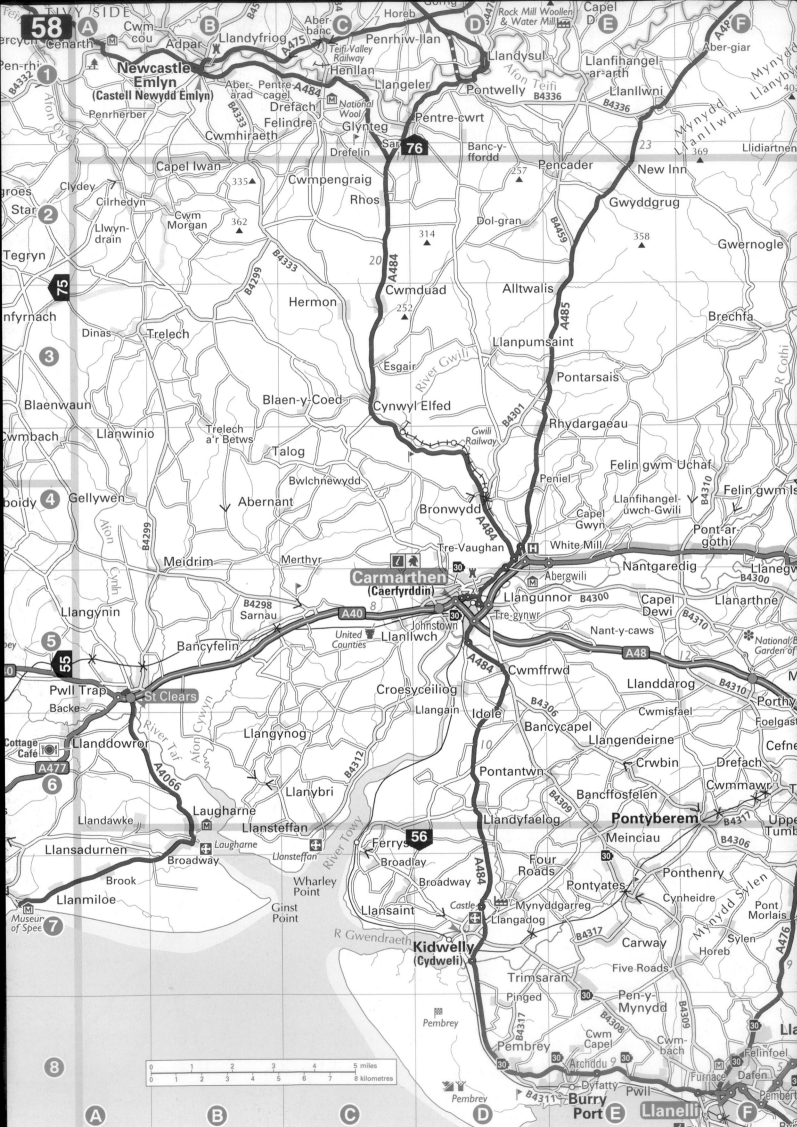

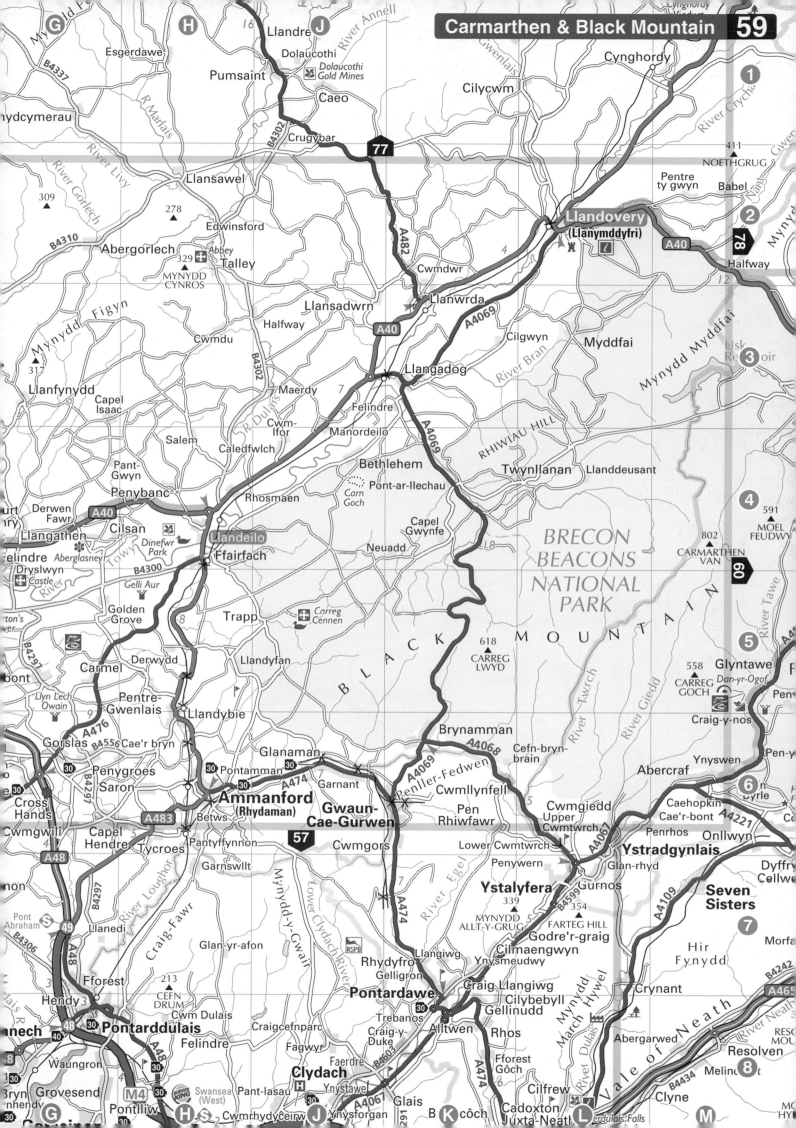

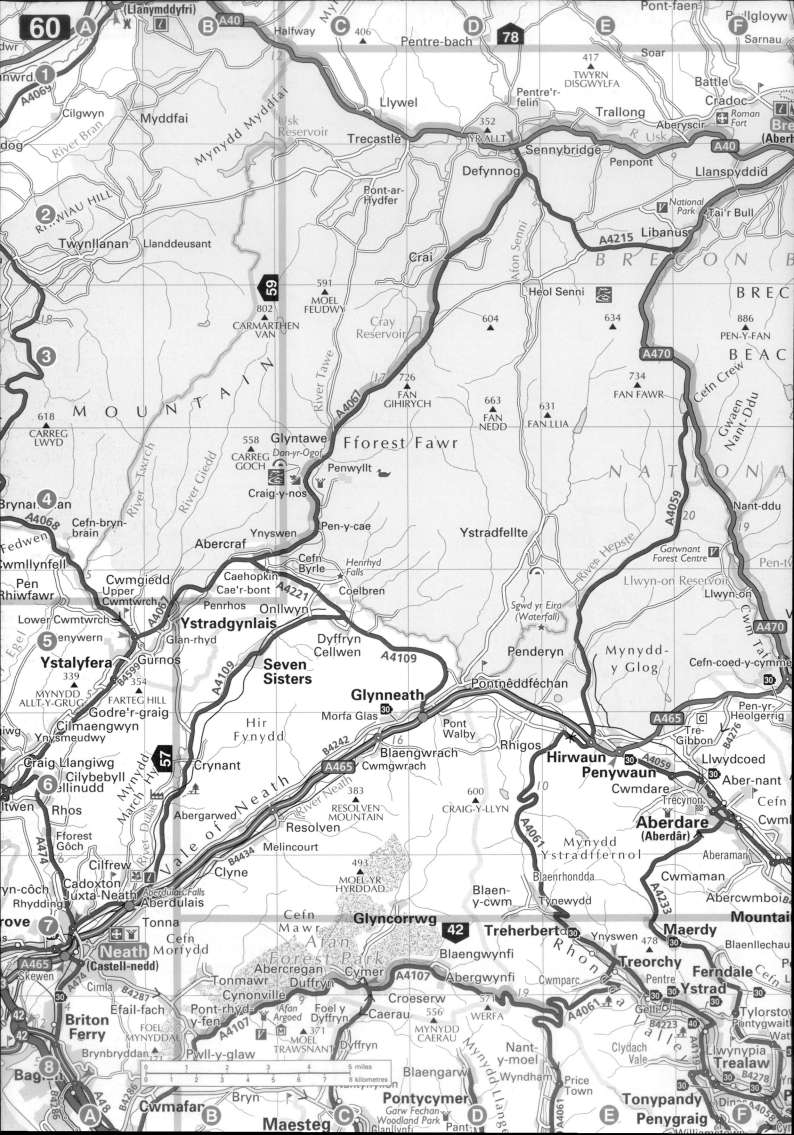

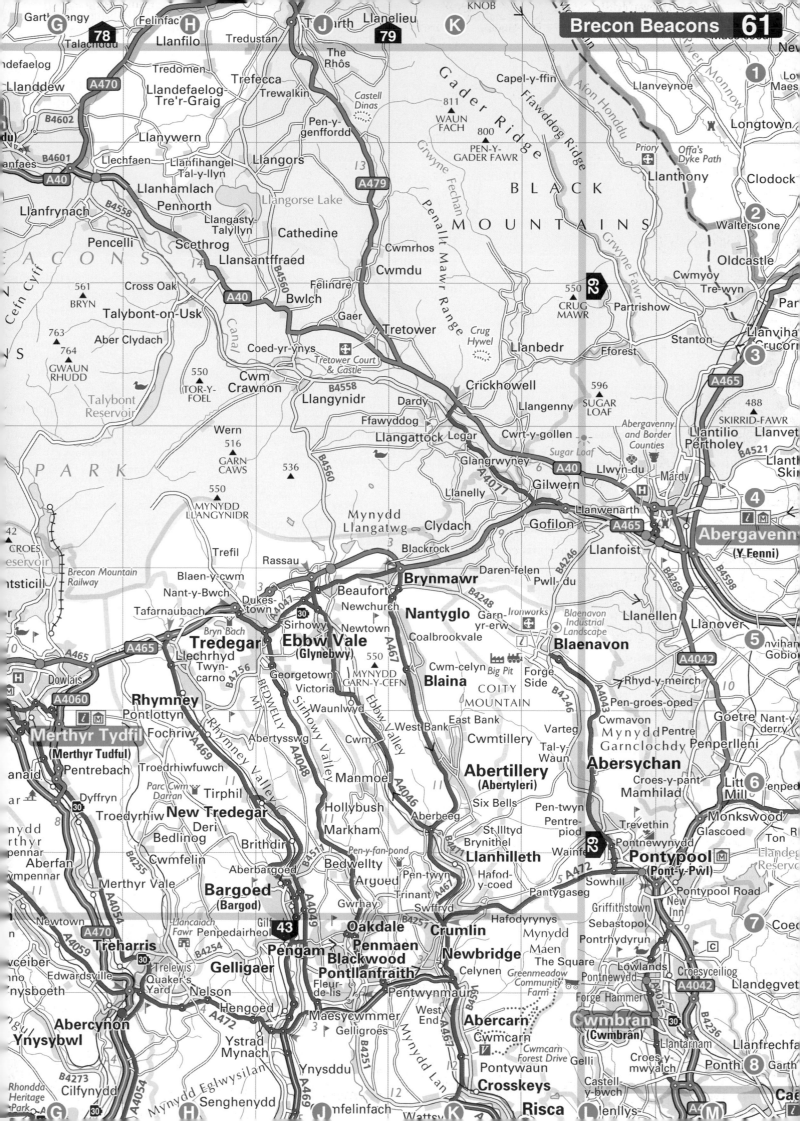

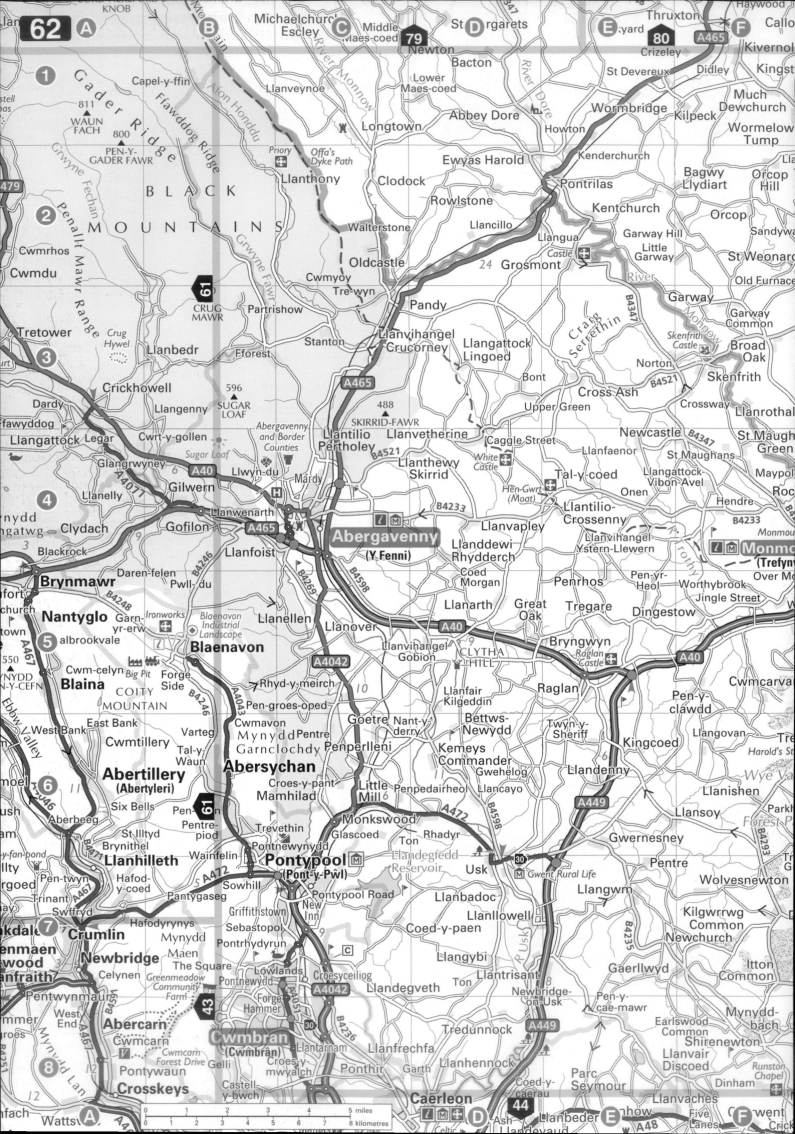

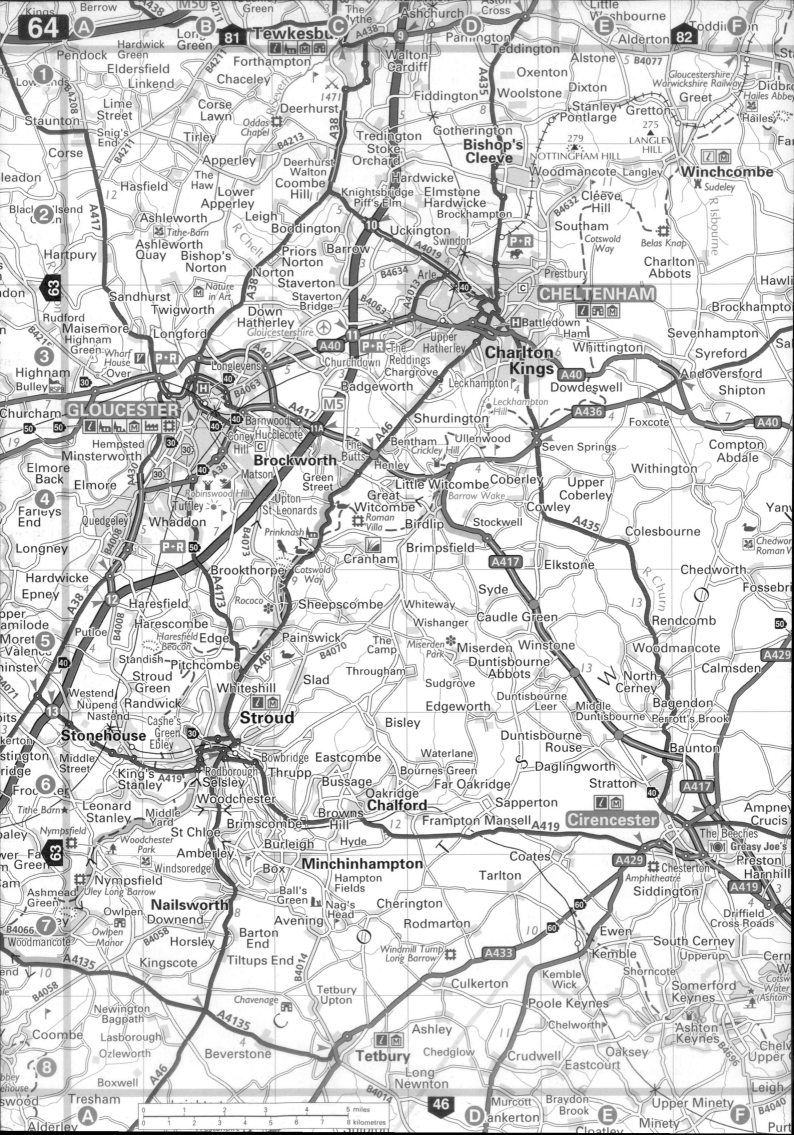

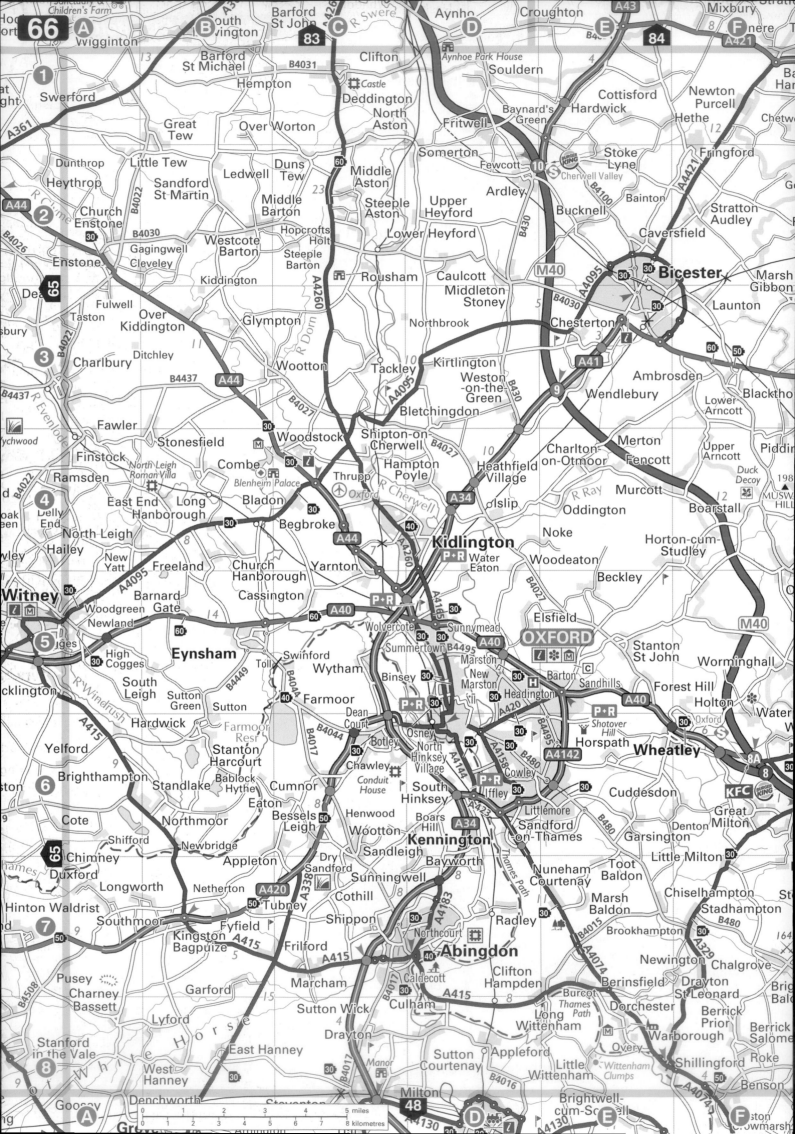

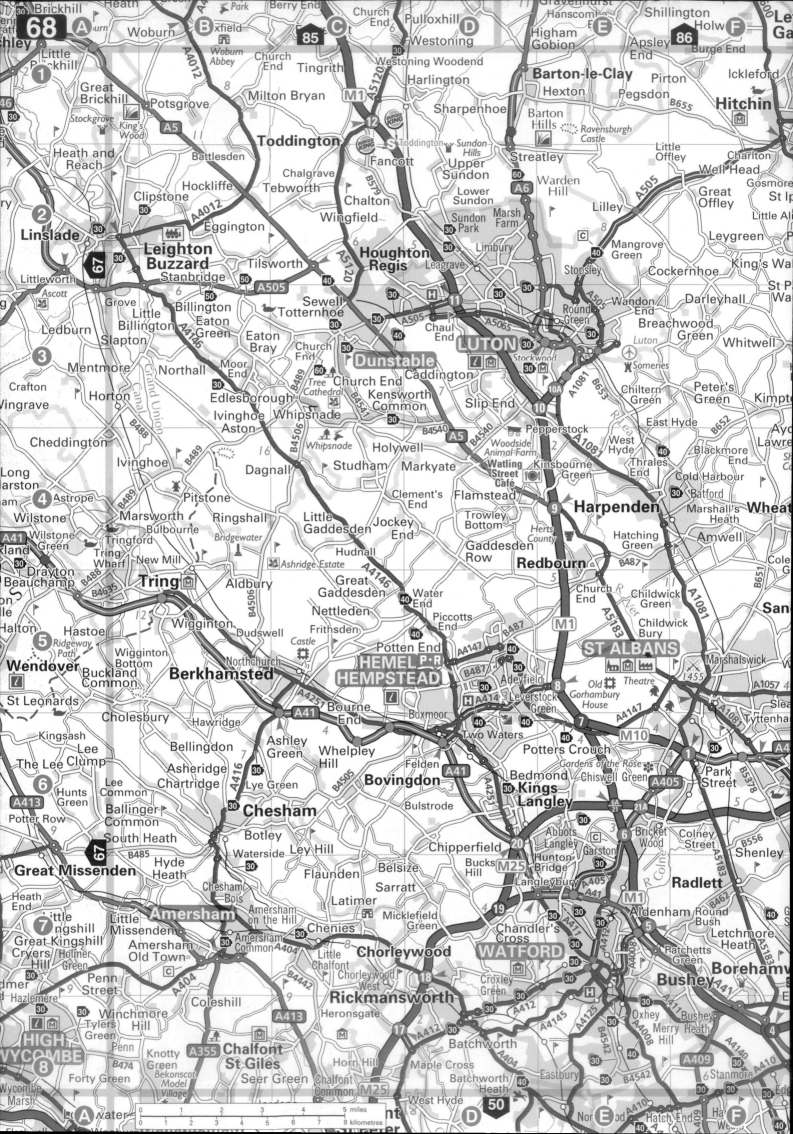

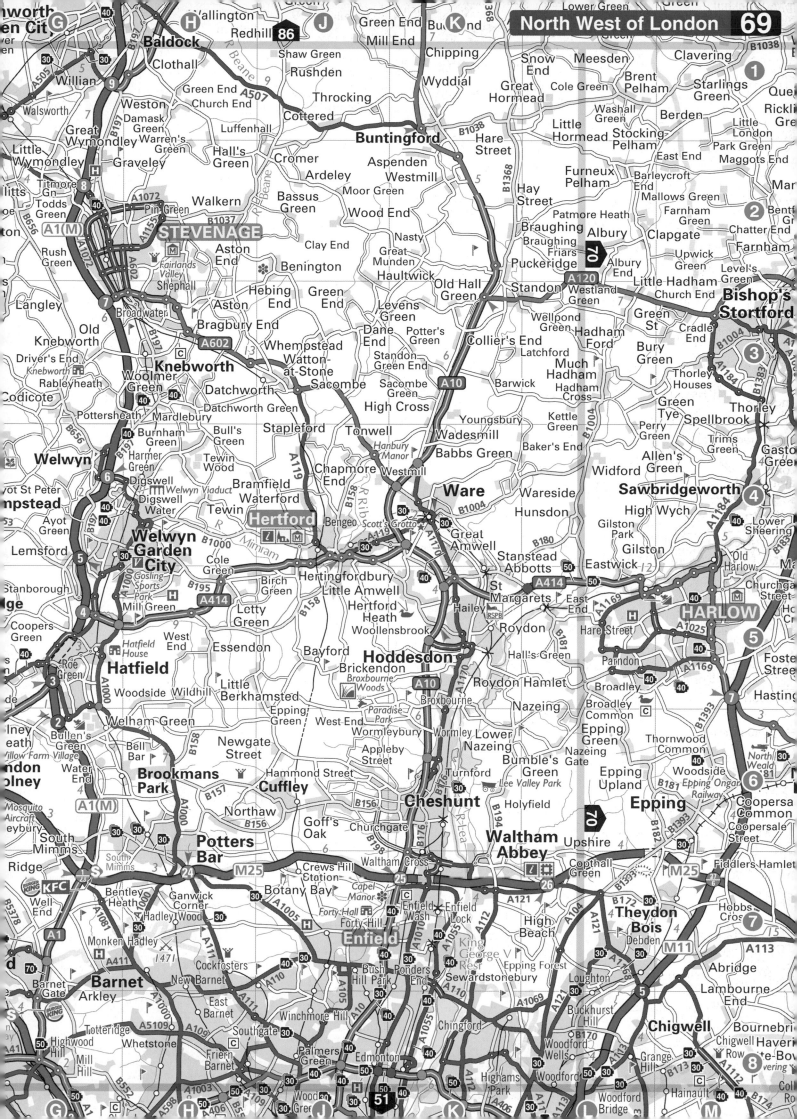

A | B | C | D | E | F

1

Mill End
Chipping
Wyddial
Anstey
Snow End
Meesden
Lower Green
Roast Green
Stickling Green
Clavering
Newport
Wicken Bonhunt
Rickling
Widdington
End
Thaxted

2

Huntingford
Aspenden
Westmill Green
od Er
Nasty
Great Munden
Haultwick
Great Hormead
Cole Green
Brent Pelham
Little Hormead
Starlings Green
Berden
Quendon
Rickling Green
Little London
Park Green
Maggots End
Ugley
Ugley Green
Henham
Woodend Green
Hamperden End
Cutler's Green
Bardfield End Greer
Hol Gr

Hare Street
Hay Street
Furneux Pelham
Stocking Pelham
Barleycroft End
Mallows Green
East End
Manuden
Bentfield Green
Elsenham
Pledgdon Green
Fuller's End
Gaunt's End
Tye Green
Molehill Green
Broxted
Monk Street
Sibley's Green
Duton Hill
Tilty
Great Easton
Lindse

3

Old Hall Green
Standon
Braughing
Braughing Friars
Puckeridge
Albury
Albury End
Clapgate
Upwick Green
Level's Green
Chatter End
Farnham
Bentfield Green
Birchanger
Stansted Mountfitchet
Burton End
Stansted
Brick End
Great Dunmow
Church
Li Du

Westland Green
Little Hadham
Church End
Bishop's Stortford
Takeley St
Brewers End
Smith's Green
Little Canfield
Takeley Green

Collier's End
Hadham Ford
Latchford
Much Hadham
Hadham Cross
Green St
Cradle End
Bury Green
Thorley Houses
Great Hallingbury
Hope End Green
Barnsto
Philpot End
Wellstye Green

Barwick
Kettle Green
Green Tye
Thorley
Spellbrook
Little Hallingbury
Wright's Green
Hatfield Broad Oak
Great Canfield
Taverners Green

4

Ware
Youngsbury
Wadesmill
Babbs Green
Westmill
Baker's End
Widford
Allen's Green
Perry Green
Trims Green
Gaston Green
Hatfield Heath
Broad Street
Aythorpe Roding
High Roding
THE RODINGS
Bishop's Green
High Eas

Wareside
Hunsdon
High Wych
Sawbridgeworth
Gilston Park
Gilston
Lower Sheering
Sheering
Ardley End
Roundbush Gn
White Roding
Leaden Roding
Clatterford End

5

Hoddesdon
Great Amwell
Stanstead Abbotts
St Margarets
Hailey
Roydon
Eastwick
East End
Hare Street
Old Harlow
Churchgate Street
HARLOW
Hobbs Cross
Matching Tye
Newman's End
Matching
Matching Green
Manwood Green
Abbess Roding
Nether Street
Margaret Roding
Beauchamp Roding
Good Easte
Boyto Cross

Hall's Green
Parndon
Carters Green
Threshers Bush
Little Laver
Birds Green
Miller's Green
Shellow Bowells

Roydon Hamlet
Broadley
Broadley Common
Foster Street
High Laver
Magdalen Laver
Norwood End
Fyfield
Willingale
Cooksmill Green
Radley Green

Nazeing
Nazeing Gate
Epping Green
Hastingwood
Tyler's Green
Moreton
Bobbingworth
Shelley
Norton Mandeville
Norton Heath

6

Cheshunt
Broxbourne
Wormley
Lower Nazeing
Bumble's Green
Holyfield
Thornwood Common
Woodside
North Weald
Bovinger
High Ongar
Chipping Ongar
Paslow Wood Common
Blackmore

Waltham Abbey
Upshire
Epping Upland
Epping
Coopersale Common
Coopersale Street
North Weald Bassett
Greensted
Toot Hill
Marden Ash
Stondon Massey
Mill Green

7

Enfield
Enfield Lock
High Beach
Debden
Copthall Green
Fiddlers Hamlet
Theydon Bois
Hobbs Cross
Stanford Rivers
Stapleford Tawney
Passingford Bridge
Kelvedon Hatch
Hook End
Fox Hatch
Fryerning
Wyatt's Green
Heybridge

Waltham Cross
Ponders End
Sewardstonebury
Loughton
Lambourne End
Abridge
Navestock
Navestock Side
Doddinghurst
Coxtie Green
Swallows Cross
Mountnessing

8

Chingford
Buckhurst Hill
Chigwell
Bournebridge
Chigwell Row
Havering-atte-Bower
Sabine's Green
Wattons Green
South Weald
Pilgrims Hatch
BRENTWOOD
Shenfield
Hutton
Ingrave

Woodford Wells
Grange Hill
Hainault
Collier Row
Noak Hill
Harold Hill
Brook Street
Ingrave

Scale: 0 1 2 3 4 5 miles / 8 kilometres

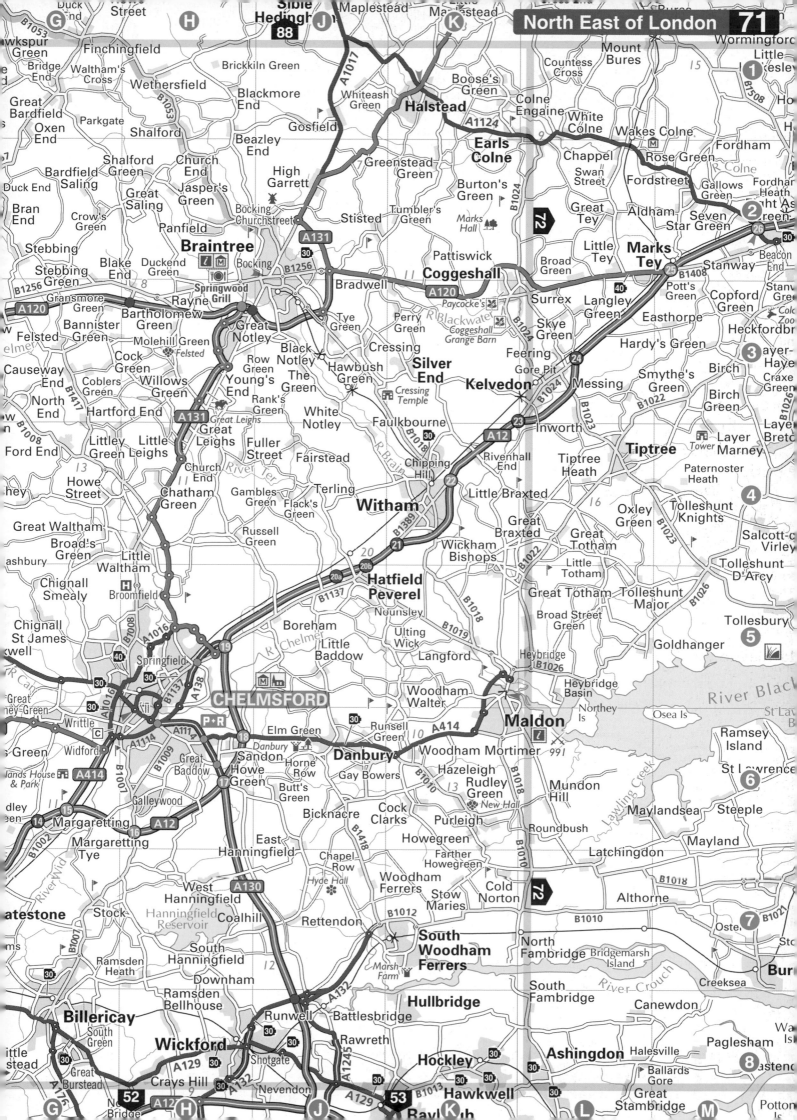

Brantham

**G** Cattawade
Flatford & Cottage
Mistley Towers
**Manningtree**
Mistley
New Mistley
rford
Mistley Heath
Little Bromley
Bradfield
**H**
Holbrook B
Holbrook
**90**
River Stour
Wrabness
Ramsey
**J**
International Ferry Terminal
Street
notley Gate
**K**
The Redoubt
Parkeston Quay
Parkeston
Upper Dovercourt
**30**
Bath Side
Dovercourt
Harwich Harbour
Landguard Fort
Landguard Point
**1**

Bradfield Heath
Horsleycross Street
Wix
**A120**
B1352
Little Oakley
**Harwich**
i

rnt
th
mley
ss
Great Bromley
19
Horsley Cross
Wix Green
Stones Green
Great Oakley
Pennyhole Bay
Hoek van Holland
Esbjerg
**2**

Great Bromley
Little Bentley
Tendring Heath
Tendring Green
Goose Green
B1414
17
Beaumont
Horsey Island
The Naze

stead
et
Frating
Green
Hare Green
**A133**
B1035
Tendring
Thorpe Green
Thorpe-le-Soken
Kirby le Soken
Walton on the Naze

Frating
stead Row
ford
Great Bentley
**C**
16
Weeley
B1033
B1441
Weeley Heath
Kirby Cross
B1033
B1034
**3**

Aingers Green
Thorrington
**A133**
B1414
Cook's Green
Frinton-on-Sea

Samson's Corner
Little Clacton
B1442
Great Holland
nny
eath
Hurst Green
B1027
**30**
**30**
Great Clacton
B1032
**30**
Holland-on-Sea

ea
Point Clear
**30**
Rush Green
St Osyth
B1032
**30**
**CLACTON-ON-SEA**
i
**4**

ore
ve
**Jaywick**

Colne Point

**5**

**6**

**7**

0   1   2   3   4   5 miles
0   1   2   3   4   5   6   7   8 kilometres
**8**

**G**          **H**          **J**          **K**          **L**          **M**

St Brides Bay

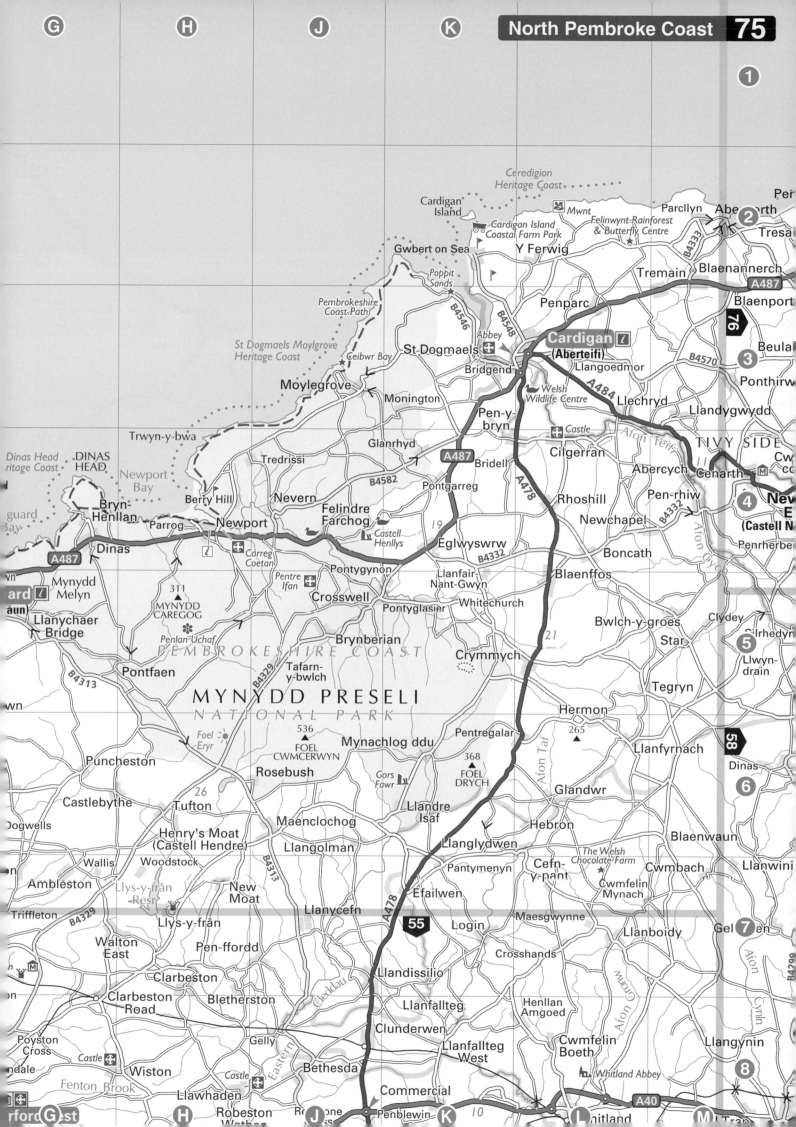

G    H    J    K

1

Ceredigion
Heritage Coast

Cardigan Island

Mwnt

Parcllyn    Abe    th    2
Felinwynt Rainforest
& Butterfly Centre

Cardigan Island
Coastal Farm Park

Tremain    Blaenannerch    A487

Gwbert on Sea    Y Ferwig    76    3

Poppit
Sands    Penparc    Beula

Pembrokeshire
Coast Path    Abbey    Cardigan    i    Ponthirw
Llangoedmor    (Aberteifi)

St Dogmaels Moylgrove
Heritage Coast    Ceibwr Bay    St-Dogmaels    A484    Llechryd    Llandygwydd

Bridgend    Welsh    TIVY SIDE
Moylegrove    Wildlife Centre    Cw
Monington    Pen-y-    Castle    co
bryn    Cilgerran    Afon Teifi
Trwyn-y-bwa    Glanrhyd    Abercych    Cenarth    4
A487    Bridell    Rhoshill    Pen-rhiw    New
Dinas Head    DINAS    Tredrissi    Pentre
ritage Coast    HEAD    B4582    Pontgarreg    Newchapel    (Castell N
Newport    Berry Hill    Nevern    Boncath    Penrherbe
Bay    Felindre    19    Eglwyswrw    B4332    Blaenffos
Bryn-    Farchog    Llanfair    Whitechurch    Bwlch-y-groes    Clydey
Henllan    Castell    Nant-Gwyn    Star    5
guard    Dinas    Henllys    Pontygynon    Pontyglasier    Cilrhedyn
Bay    Parrog    Newport    Crosswell    21    Llwyn-
Carreg    Pentre    drain
Mynydd    Coetan    Ifan    Crymmych    Tegryn
d    i    Melyn    311    Brynberian
Llanychaer    MYNYDD    P E M B R O K E S H I R E   C O A S T    Hermon
Bridge    CAREGOG    265
Penlan-Uchaf    Tafarn-    Pentregalar    Llanfyrnach    58
B4313    Pontfaen    y-bwlch    536    Mynachlog ddu    Dinas
wn    MYNYDD PRESELI    FOEL    Glandwr    6
Foel    N A T I O N A L   P A R K    CWMCERWYN    368
Eryr    Gors    FOEL    Hebron    Blaenwaun
Puncheston    Fawr    DRYCH    The Welsh
Castlebythe    Rosebush    Llandre    Chocolate Farm    Cwmbach    Llanwini
Dogwells    26    Tufton    Isaf    Llanglydwen    Cefn-
Maenclochog    Pantymenyn    y-pant    Cwmfelin
Ambleston    Henry's Moat    Mynach
Wallis    (Castell Hendre)    Woodstock    Efailwen
Triffleton    Llangolman    B4313    Maesgwynne    Gel    en    7
Walton    B4329    New    Llanycefn    55    Login    Llanboidy
East    Llys-y-frân    Moat    Crosshands    Llangynin
Pen-ffordd    Resr    Henllan
Clarbeston    Llys-y-frân    Llandissilio    Amgoed    Afon
Clarbeston    Bletherston    Llanfallteg    Cwmfelin
Poyston    Road    West    Boeth
Cross    Castle    Gelly    Clunderwen    Whitland Abbey    8
ndale    Wiston    Bethesda    Llanfallteg    A40
Castle    West
rford G est    Fenton Brook    Robeston    Commercial    Penblewin    10    itland    Tran
Llawhaden    Wether    H    J    K    L    M

55
A478
A478
A487
B4546
B4548
B4570
B4333
B4332
A484
B4582
B4329
B4313
B4329
A40
A487

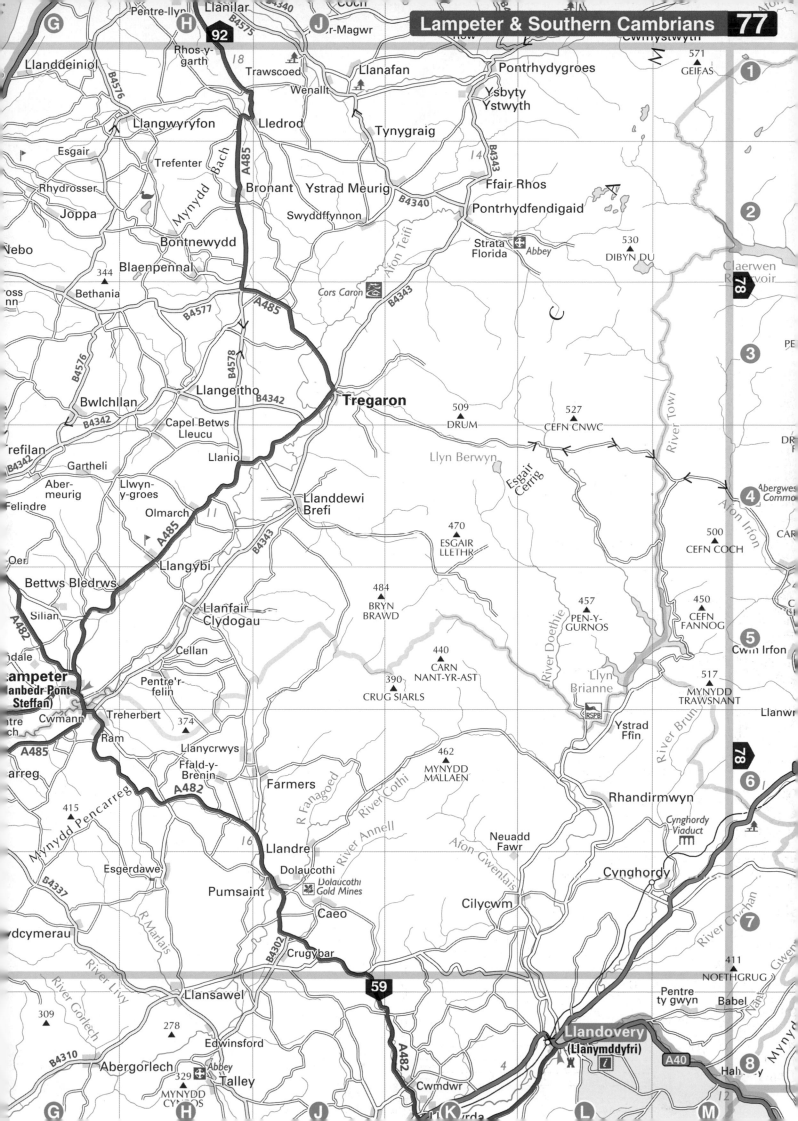

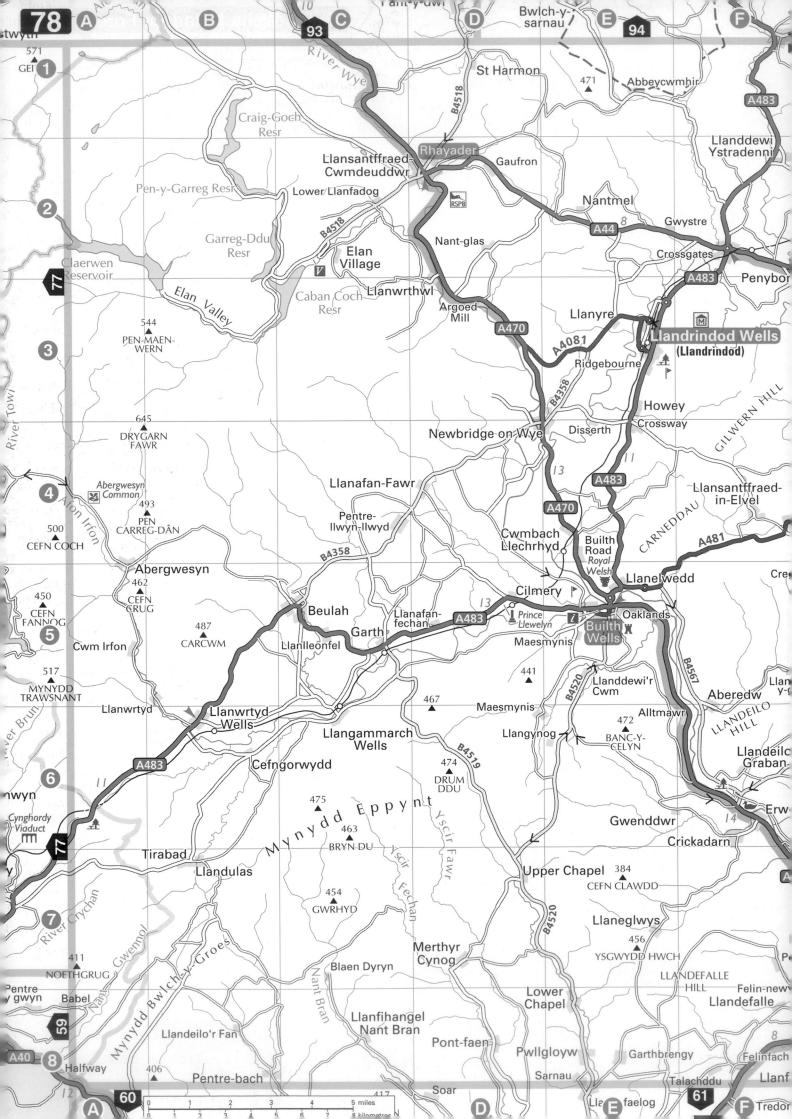

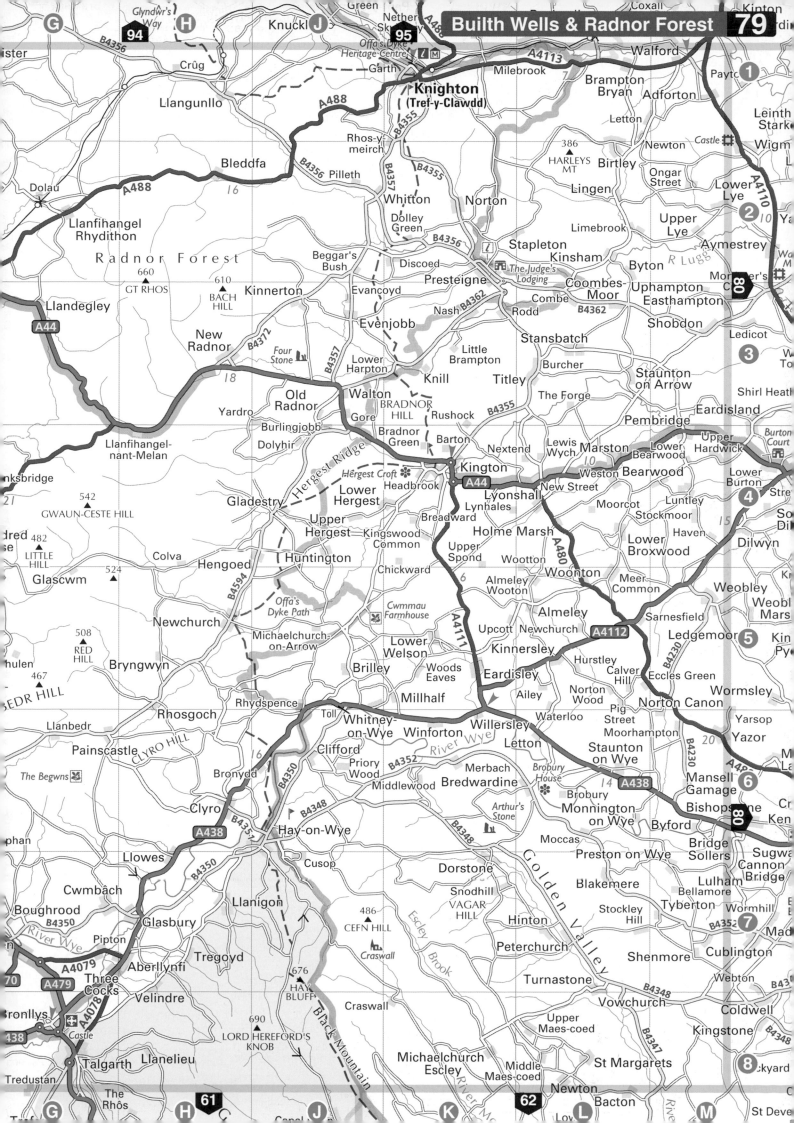

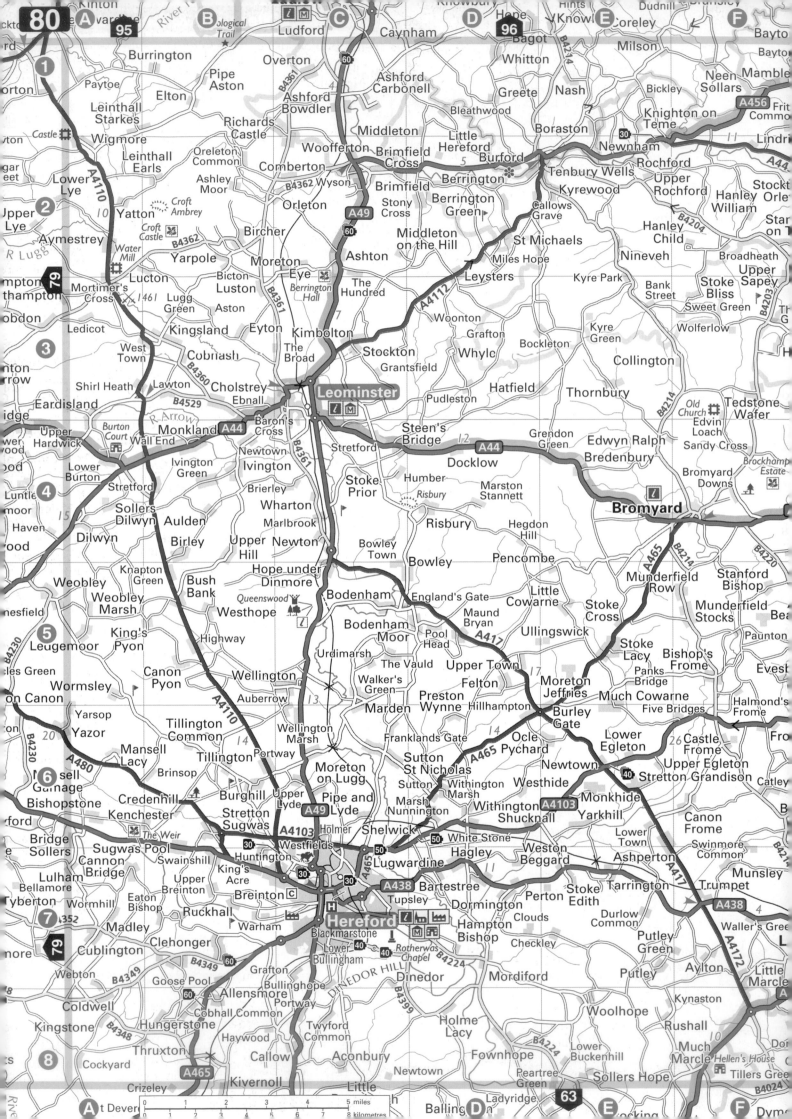

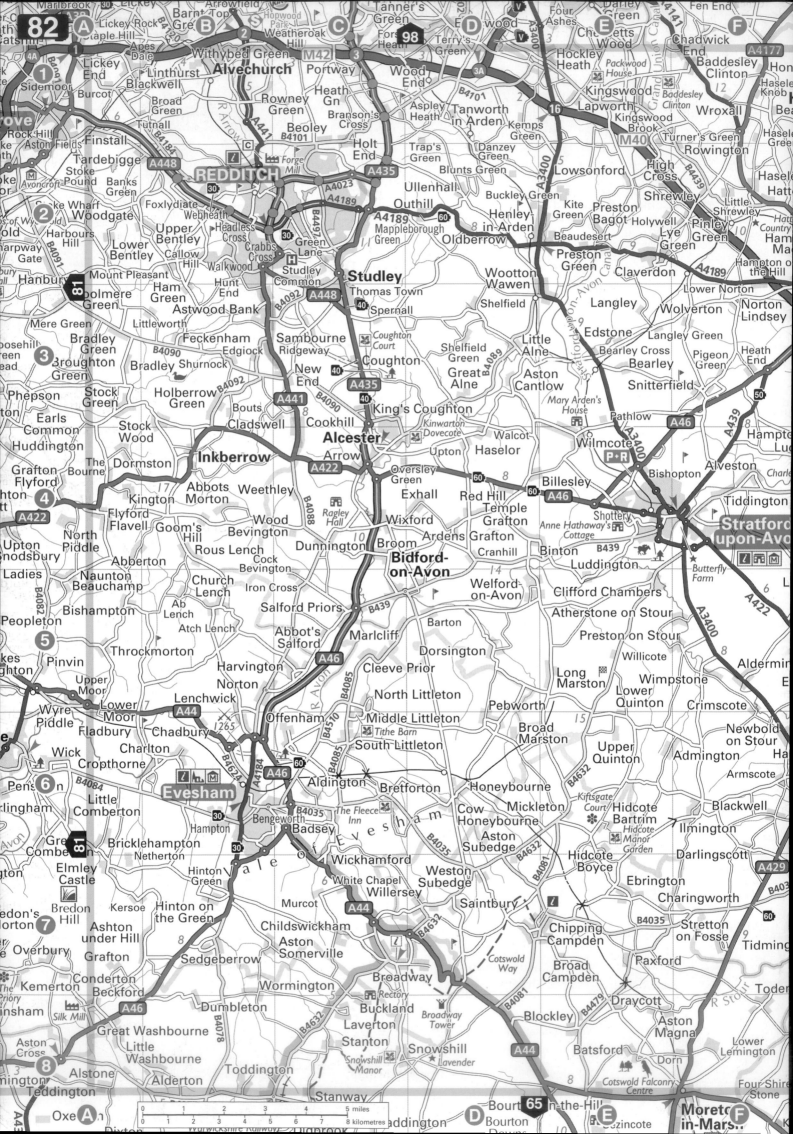

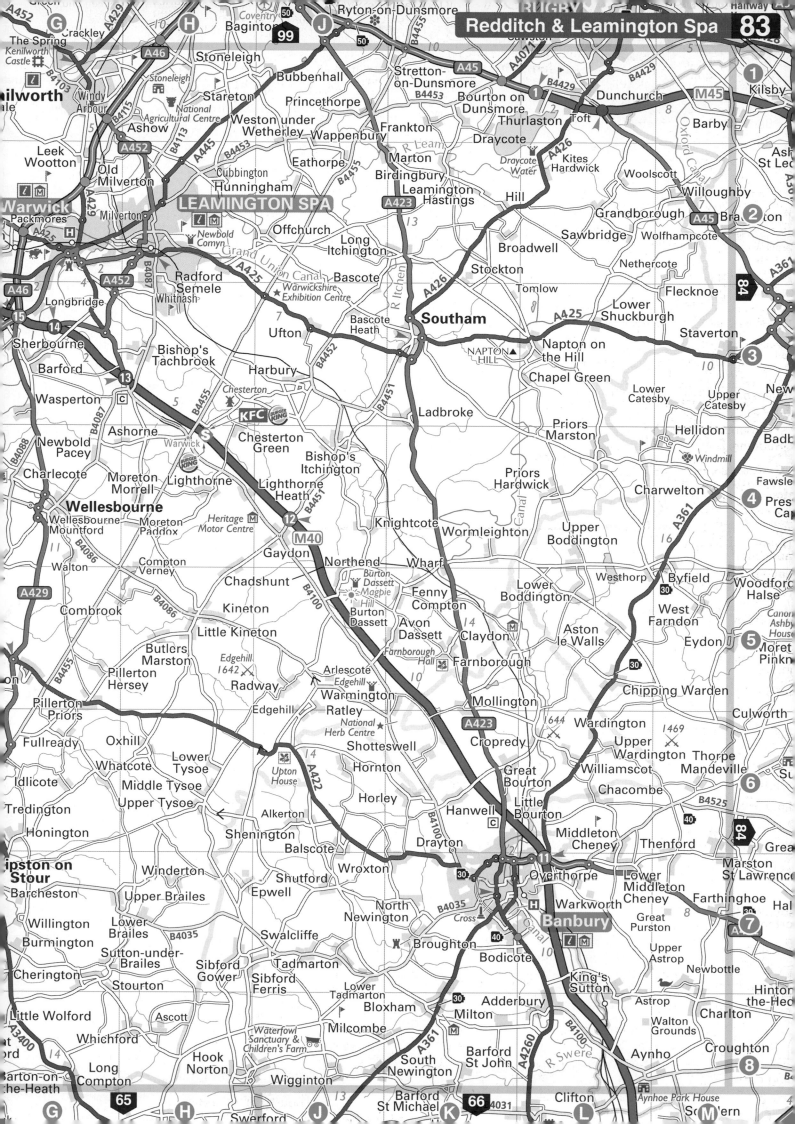

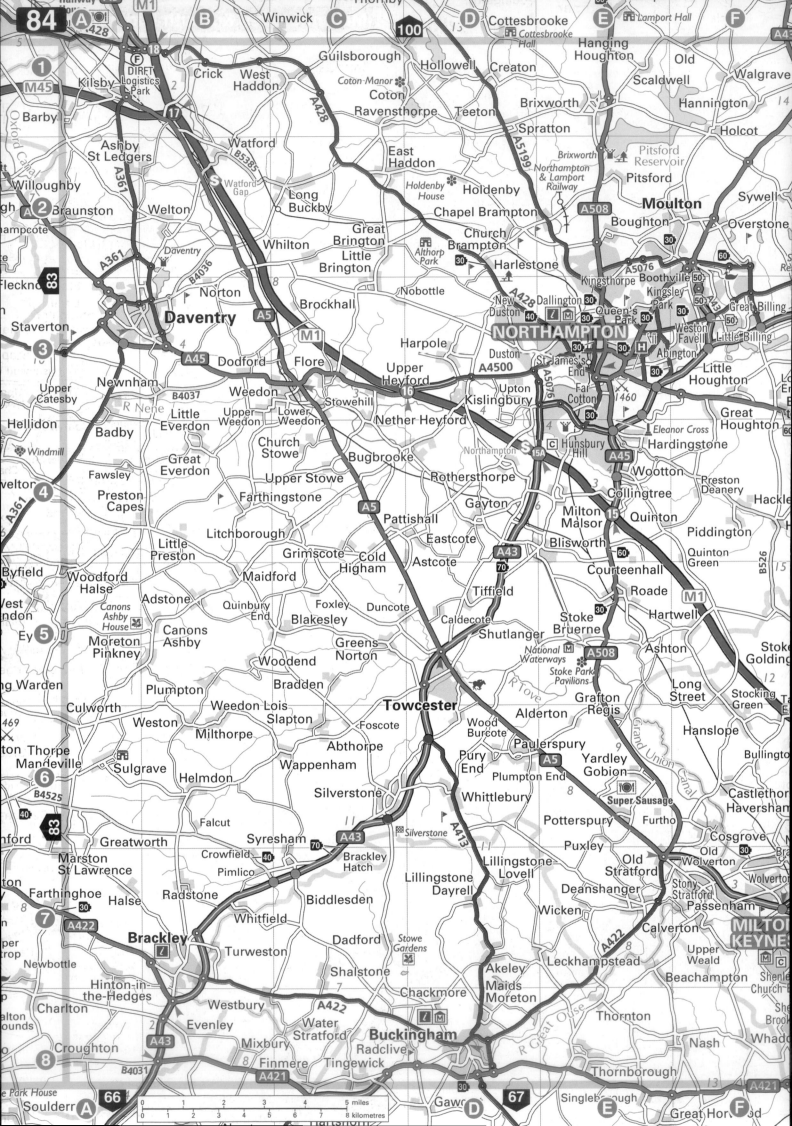

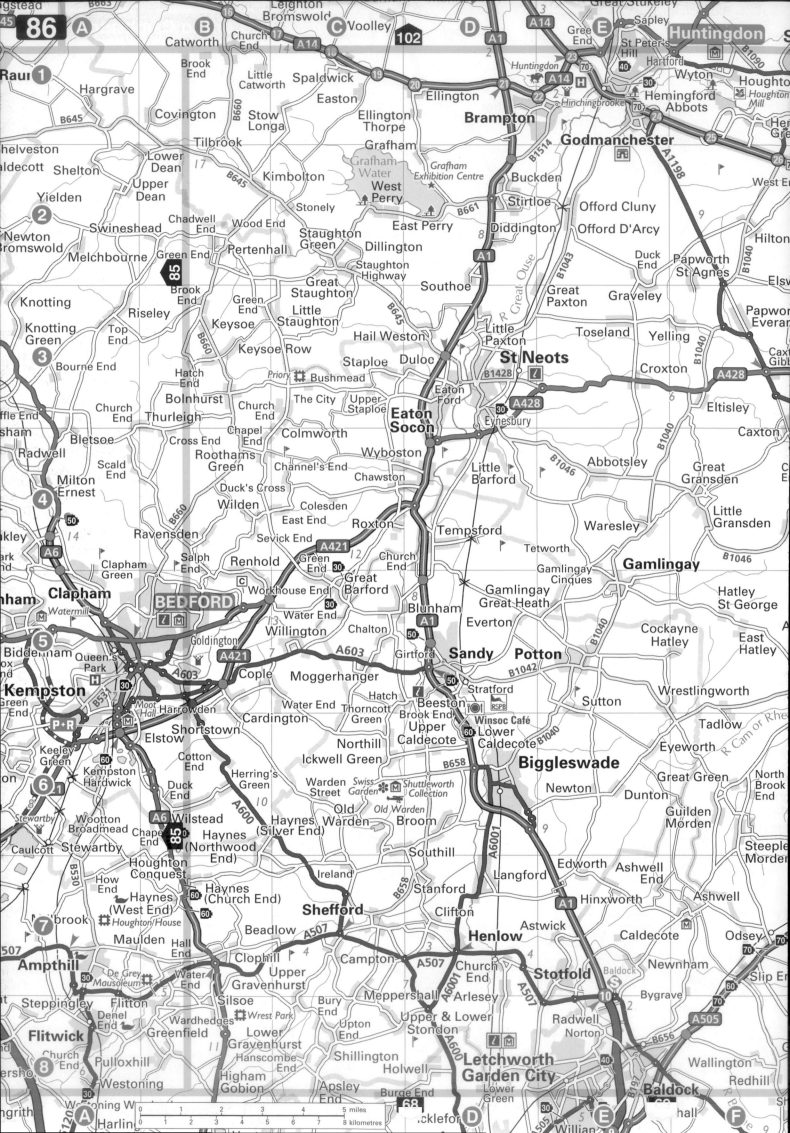

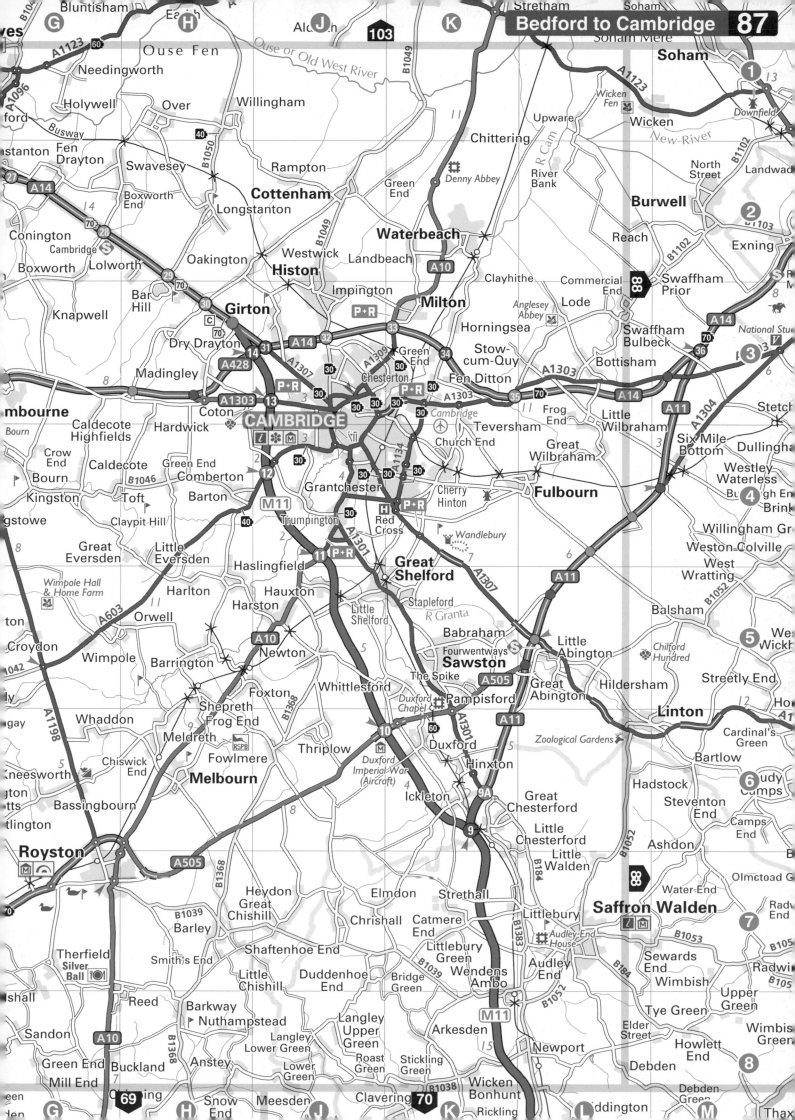

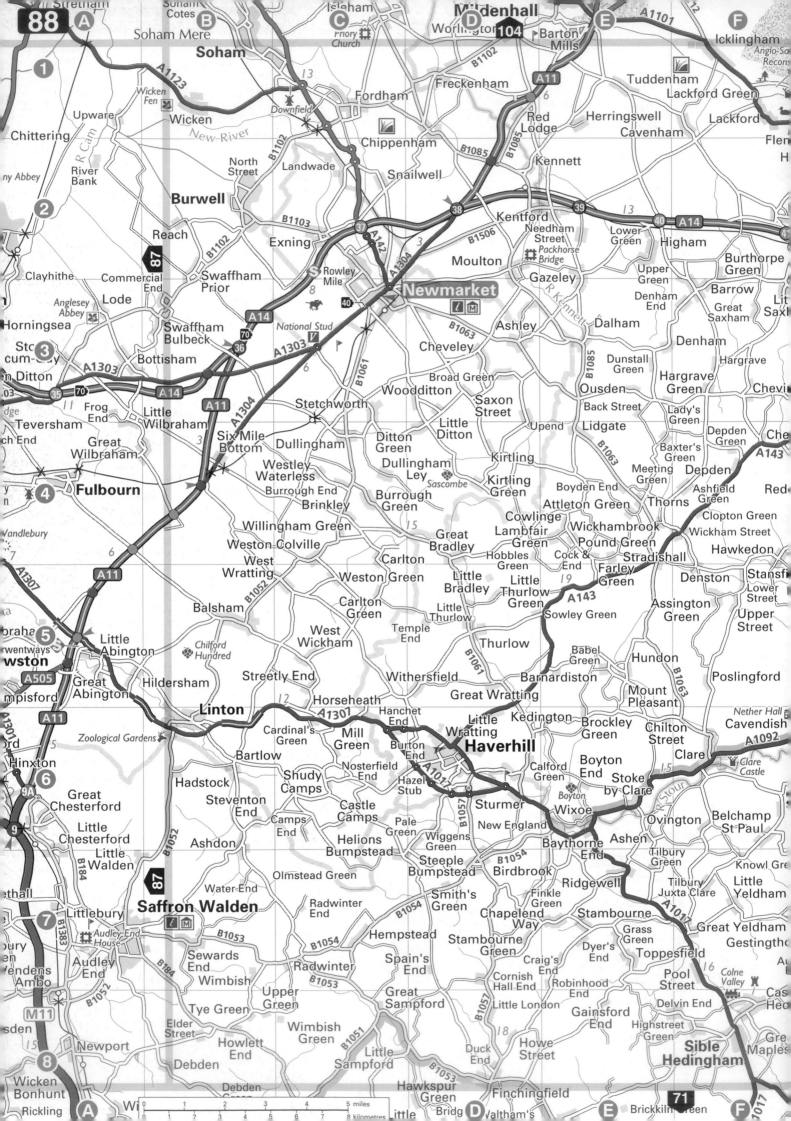

Bury St Edmunds
Sudbury
Stowmarket
Needham Market
Hadleigh
Long Melford
Lavenham
Woolpit
Ixworth
Thurston
Mendlesham

(Map 89 — Newmarket to Sudbury)

Place names shown include:
Thornham Parva, Thornham Magna, Wickham Street, Wickham Green, Wickham Skeith, Gislingham, Finningham, Westhorpe, Wyverstone, Wyverstone Street, Cotton, Bacton, Bacton Green, Brockford Street, Mendlesham, Mendlesham Green, Gipping, Old Newton, Saxham Street, Middlewood Green, Forward Green, Earl Stonham, Creeting St Mary, Stowupland, Haughley, Haughley Green, Wetherden, Harleston, Onehouse, Great Finborough, Combs, Combs Ford, Battisford, Battisford Tye, Ringshall, Ringshall Stocks, Barking, Barking Tye, Baylham, Lower Street, Upper Street, Great Blakenham, Little Blakenham, Somersham, Flowton, Elmsett, Bramford, Sproughton, Burstall, Hintlesham, Washbrook, Copdock, Coles Green, Chattisham, Little Wenham, Great Wenham, Capel St Mary, Bentley, East End, East Bergholt, Stratford St Mary, Higham, Holton St Mary, Raydon, Lower Raydon, Shelley, Polstead, Stoke-by-Nayland, Nayland, Wissington, Bures, Mount Bures, Wormingford, Boxted, Boxted Cross, Dedham, Flatford Mill & Cottages, Langham, Mistley, Manningtree.

Stanton, Upthorpe, Wattisfield, Allwood Green, Mill Street, Walsham le Willows, Cranmer Green, Crowland, Badwell Green, Four Ashes, Long Thurlow, Badwell Ash, Hunston, Hunston Green, Stowlangtoft, Langham, West Street, Norton, Norton Little Green, Great Ashfield, Earl's Green, Bacton Green, Cow Green, Ford's Green, Canhams Green, Brown Street, Elmswell, Tostock, Broadgrass Green, Base Green, Dagworth, Troston, Ampton, Ixworth Thorpe, Bardwell, Bangrove, Wyken, Ixworth, Great Livermere, Brockley, Ingham, Timworth, Culford, Timworth Green, Conyer's Green, Upper Town, Grimstone End, Pakenham, Great Barton, Cattishall, Thurston, Great Green, Hilltop Café, Battlies Green, Thurston Planch, Beyton, Beyton Gn, Broadgrass Gn, Hessett, Woolpit, Woolpit Green, Borley Green, Clopton Green, Drinkstone, Drinkstone Green, Rattlesden, Buxhall, Buxhall Fen Street, Poystreet Green, Gedding, Felsham, Mill Green, Great Finborough, Brettenham, Hitcham, Hitcham Causeway, Hitcham Street, Wattisham, Nedging, Nedging Tye, Great Bricett, Greenstreet Green, Naughton, Offton, Somersham.

Horringer, High Green, Nowton, Pinford End, Hawstead, Hawstead Green, Mickley Green, Bradfield Combust, Sicklesmere, Rougham Green, Kingshall Street, Blackthorpe, Rushbrooke, Little Welnetham, Great Welnetham, Bradfield St George, Maypole Green, Bradfield St Clare, Bush Green, Hoggards Green, Oldhall Green, Cross Green, Great Green, Cockfield, Thorpe Green, Thorpe Morieux, Preston, Kettlebaston, Brent Eleigh, Monks Eleigh, Chelsworth, Semer, Lindsey, Lindsey Tye, Milden, Rose Green, Kersey, Kersey Tye, Kersey Upland, Coram Street, Wicker Street Green, Groton, Horners Green, Calais Street, Hadleigh Heath, Bower House Tye, Polstead Heath, Whitestreet Green, Layham, Raydon.

Stanningfield, Harrow Green, Lawshall, Lawshall Green, Audley End, Cross Green, Windsor Green, Shimpling Street, Shimpling, Alpheton, Lavenham, Bridge Street, Stanstead, Stanstead Street, Glemsford, Acton, Long Melford, Newman's Green, Liston, Ballingdon, Borley, Borley Green, Bulmer, Bulmer Tye, Middleton, Little Cornard, Great Cornard, Cornard Tye, Newton, Chilton, Edwardstone, Great Waldingfield, Little Waldingfield, Mill Green, Boxford, Assington, Rose Green, Hagmore Green, Stone Street, Leavenheath, Honey Tye, Nayland, Wissington, Great Henny, Henny Street, Twinstead, Lamarsh, Alphamstone, Wickham St Paul, Pebmarsh, Cross End, Little Maplestead, Pentlow, Hartest, Boxted, Shimpling, Gifford's Hall, Kentwell Hall, Melford Hall, Guildhall.

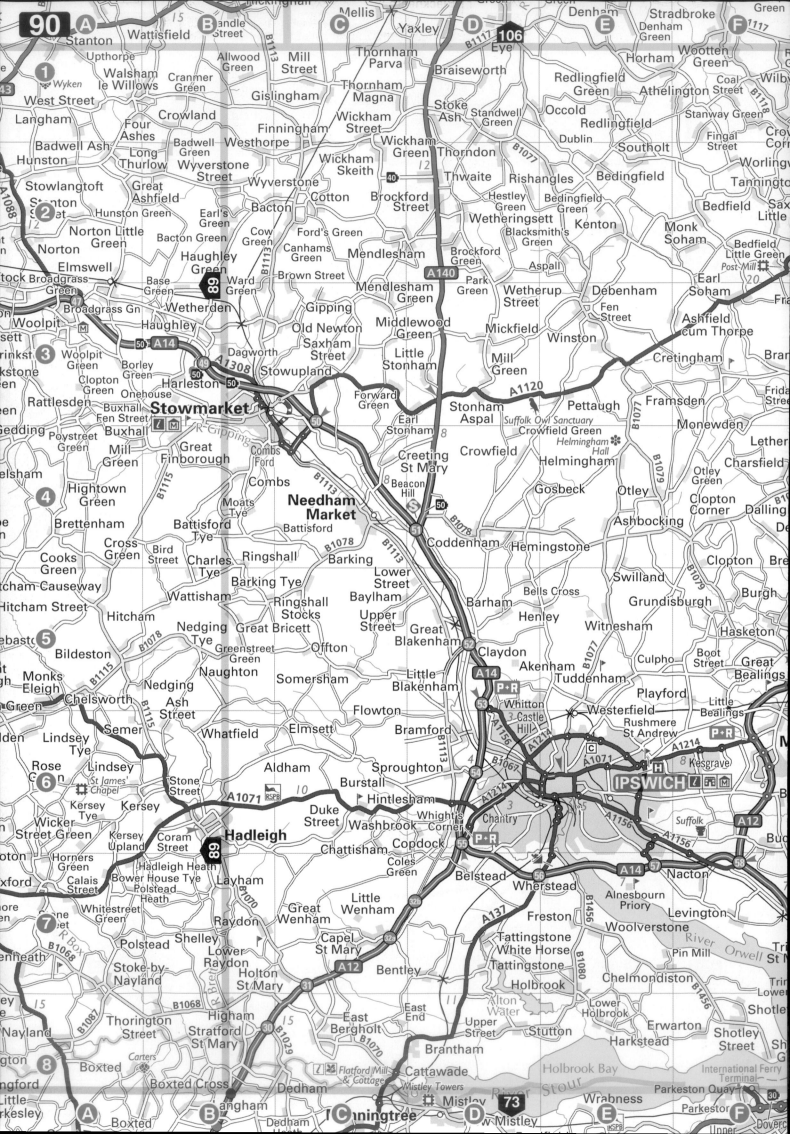

G
H B1117
J
K B1387

Huntingfield
Walpol
Tlington
Blackheath
Bramfield
107
B1125
Suffolk Coast

**1**

Laxfield
Heveningham
High Street
A144
A12
Darsham
Dunwich

undish Street
Ubbeston Green
Pouy Street
Grey Friars

undish
Owl's Green
Peasenhall
Sibton
Yoxford
Middleton
Westleton

Goddard's Corner
A1120
B1122
Minsmere
RSPB

ypole Green
Capon's Green
Badingham
Middleton Moor
North Green
Theberton
Eastbridge

**2**

Dennington
Bruisyard
A12
7
East Green
Poplar Street

axtead
Brabling Green
Bruisyard Street
Cransford
Rendham
Kelsale
Leiston Abbey

19
Castle
Shawsgate
B1119
Carlton
Saxmundham
Sizewell

ham
Swefling
B1119
Knodishall

North Green
Great Glemham
Benhall Street
Benhall Green
Sternfield
Coldfair Green
Leiston
M

**3**

Mill Green
50
Friday Street
B1121
Friston
Knodishall Common
Aldringham
Thorpe Ness

Parham
Stratford St Andrew
Farnham
Snape
B1353

Kettleburgh
Silverlace Green
Hacheston
Gromford
Snape Street
A1094
B1122
Thorpeness

Easton
Marlesford
Little Glemham
RSPB

Wickham Market
Lower Hacheston
Blaxhall
B1069
Iken
The Maltings
Aldeburgh
i

**4**

Pettistree
Campsea Ash
Tunstall
High Street
Aldeburgh Bay

Upper Ufford
10
Rendlesham
B1078
Sudbourne
River Alde

A12
B1438
Ufford
A1152
Chillesford
B1084

Lower Ufford
Friday Street
Butley
Castle
Orford

**5**

Melton
Eyke
Bromeswell
B1084
12
Butley High Corner
Orford Ness

**Woodbridge**
i
Capel Green
Capel St Andrew
RSPB

Sutton Hoo
B1083
Boyton
Orfordness-Havergate

sham
Sutton
River Ore
Suffolk Heritage Coast

ham
th
Waldringfield
Shottisham

**6**

Newbourne
Hemley
B1083
Hollesley
North Weir Point
Hollesley Bay

Ramsholt
Shingle Street

Kirton
Alderton

Bawdsey

**7**

59
Trimley St Mary
Felixstowe Ferry

Walton
Old Felixstowe

61
**Felixstowe**
i

dguard Fort

**8**

G
H
J
K
L
M

0 1 2 3 4 5 miles
0 1 2 3 4 5 6 7 8 kilometres

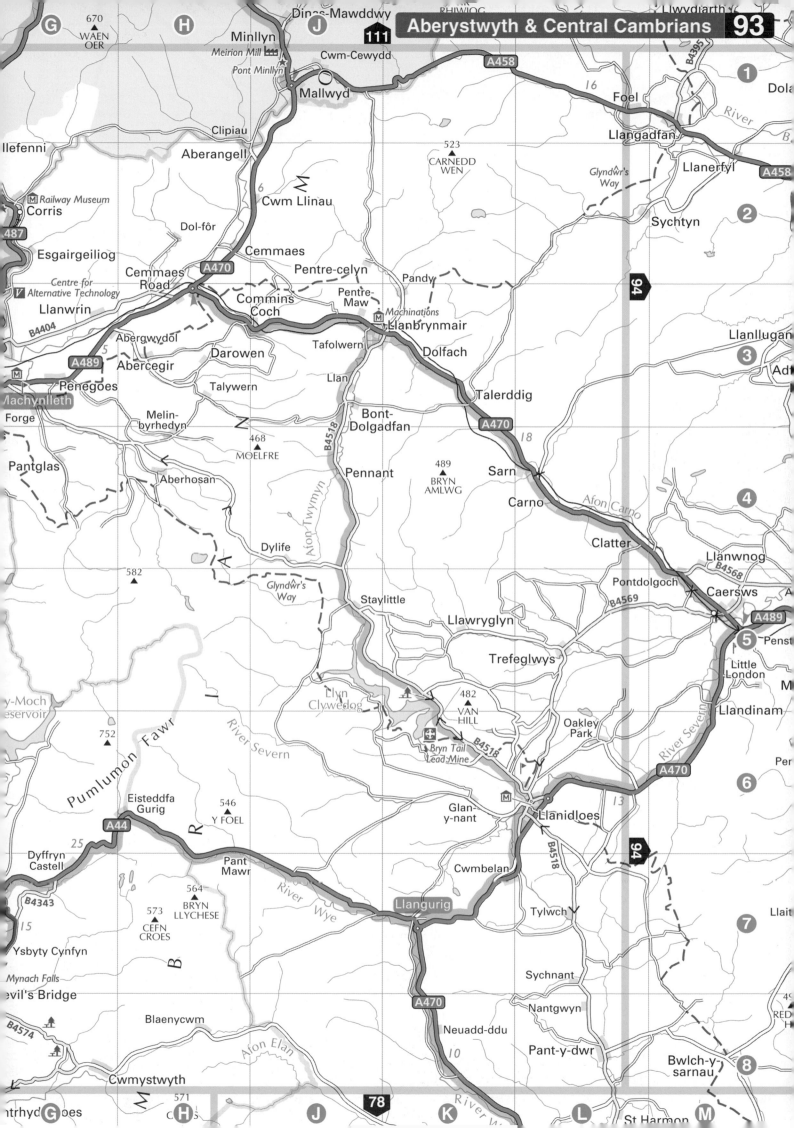

G
670
WAEN
OER
H
J
**111**

Dinas-Mawddwy
RHIWLOG
Llwydiarth
1

Minllyn
Meirion Mill
Pont Minllyn
Cwm-Cewydd
**A458**
16
Foel
River B

Mallwyd
Llangadfan

Clipiau
523
CARNEDD
WEN
Glyndŵr's
Way
Llanerfyl
**A458**

llefenni
Aberangell
Sychtyn
2

6
Cwm Llinau
Dol-fôr

Corris
Railway Museum
Cemmaes
Pentre-celyn
Pandy
**94**

487
Esgairgeiliog
**A470**
Pentre-
Maw
Machinations
Llanllugan

Cemmaes
Road
Centre for
Alternative Technology
Commins
Coch
Llanbrynmair
Llanwrin
Tafolwern
Dolfach
3
Adt

B4404
Abergwydol
Darowen
Llan
Talerddig

**A489**
Abercegir
Talywern
**A470**
18

Penegoes
Machynlleth
Bont-
Dolgadfan
Sarn
4

Forge
Melin-
byrhedyn
468
MOELFRE
B4518
489
BRYN
AMLWG
Afon Carno
Carno

Pantglas
Aberhosan
Pennant
Clatter
Llanwnog
B4568

582
Afon Twymyn
Dylife
Glyndŵr's
Way
Pontdolgoch
B4569
Caersws

y-Moch
eservoir
Staylittle
Llawryglyn
**A489**
5
Penst

Little
London
M

752
Pumlumon Fawr
Llyn
Clywedog
482
VAN
HILL
Trefeglwys
Oakley
Park
Llandinam

River Severn
Bryn Tail
Lead Mine
B4518
River Severn
**A470**
6

Eisteddfa
Gurig
546
Y FOEL
Glan-
y-nant
Llanidloes
13

**A44**
25
Dyffryn
Castell
Pant
Mawr
Cwmbelan
B4518
**94**

B4343
River Wye
564
BRYN
LLYCHESE
Llangurig
Tylwch
7

15
573
CEFN
CROES
**A470**
Sychnant

Ysbyty Cynfyn
Nantgwyn

Mynach Falls
evil's Bridge
B4574
Blaenycwm
Neuadd-ddu
Pant-y-dwr
Bwlch-y-
sarnau
8

Afon Elan
**A470**
10
REDA
H

ntrhyd-
oes
G
571
C S
H
J
**78**
K
River W
L
St Harmon
M

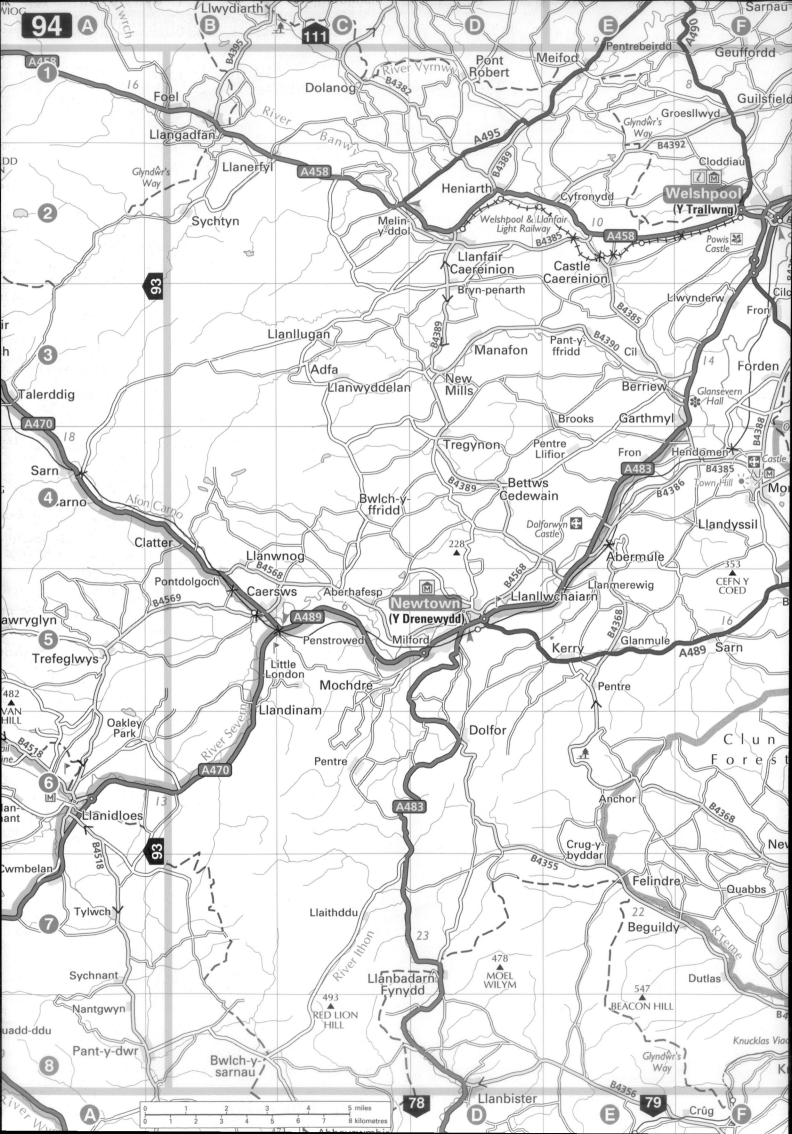

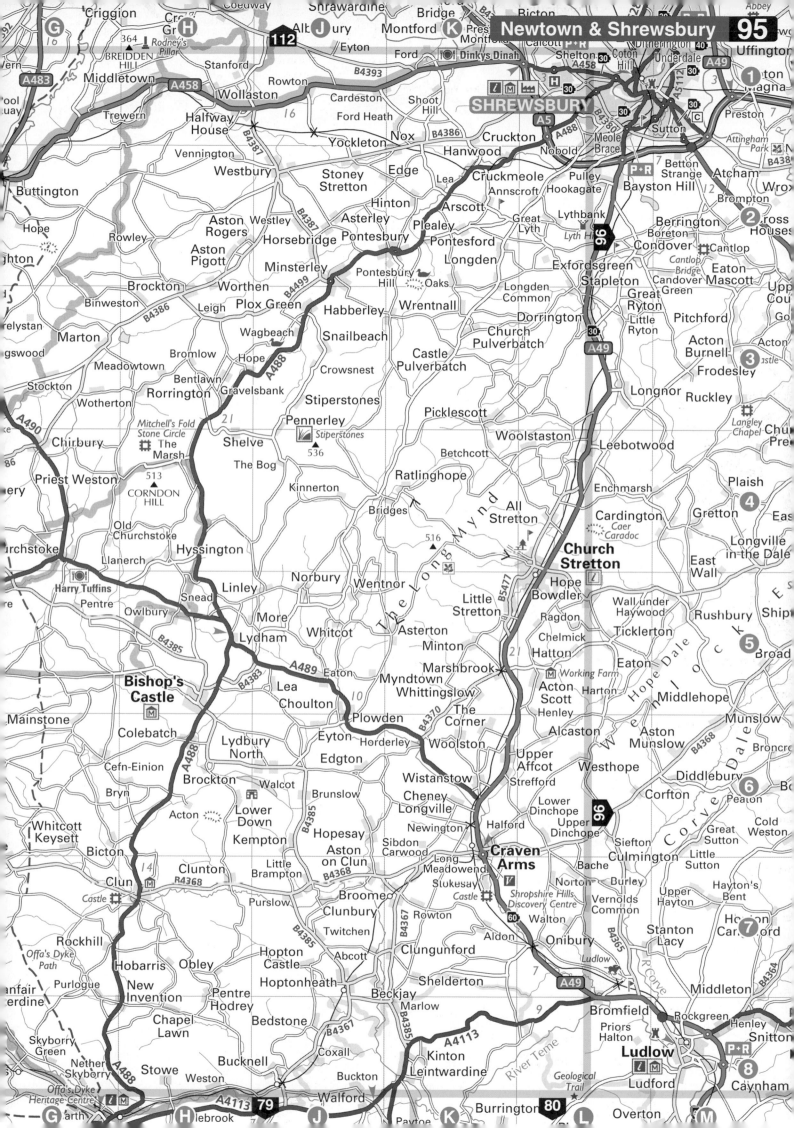

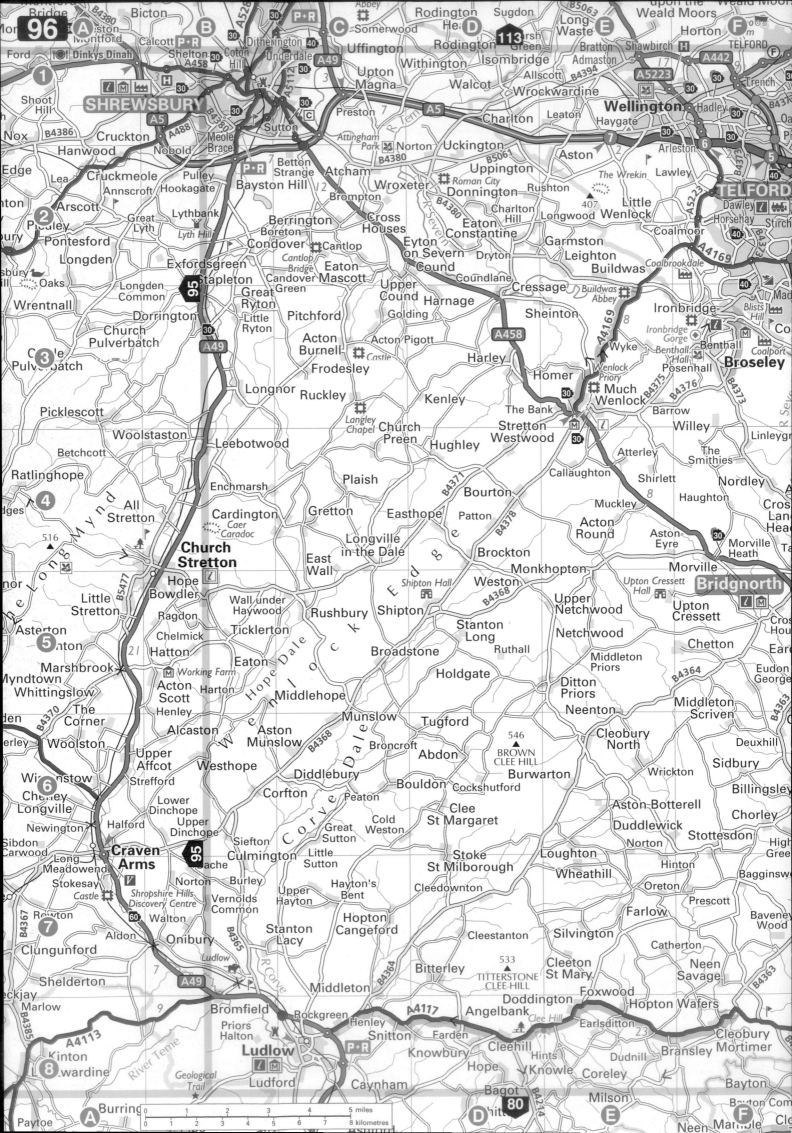

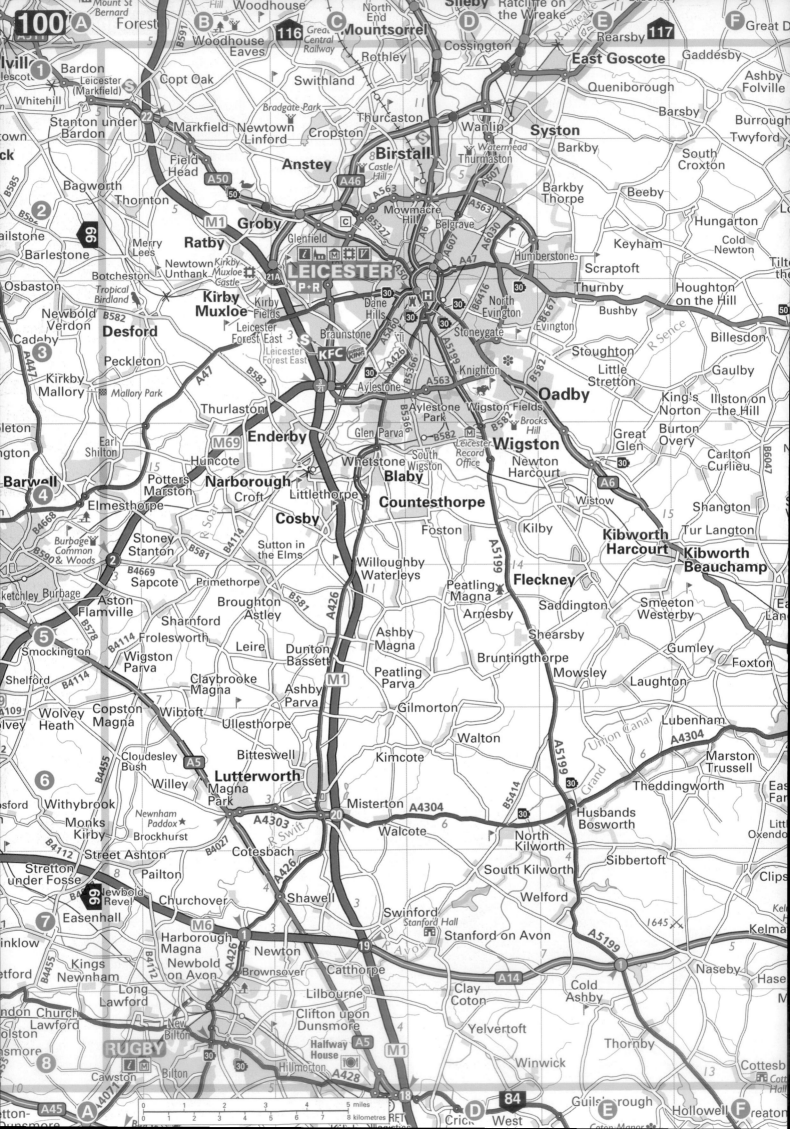

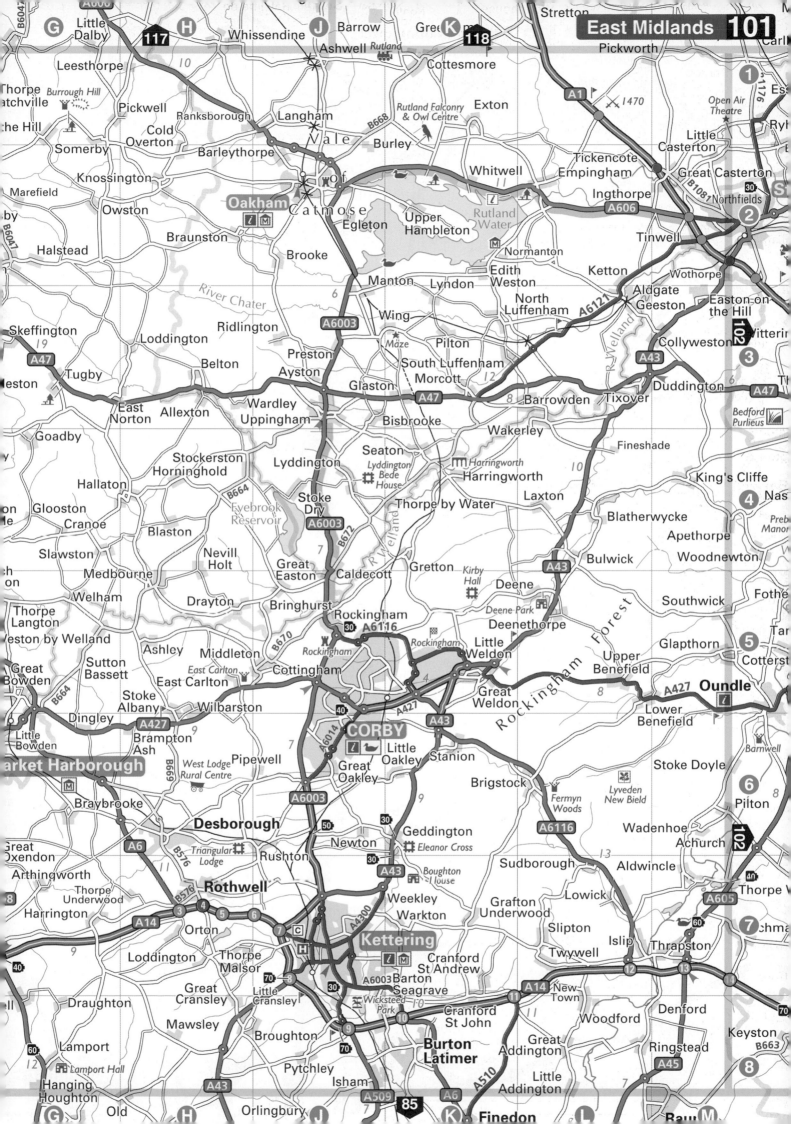

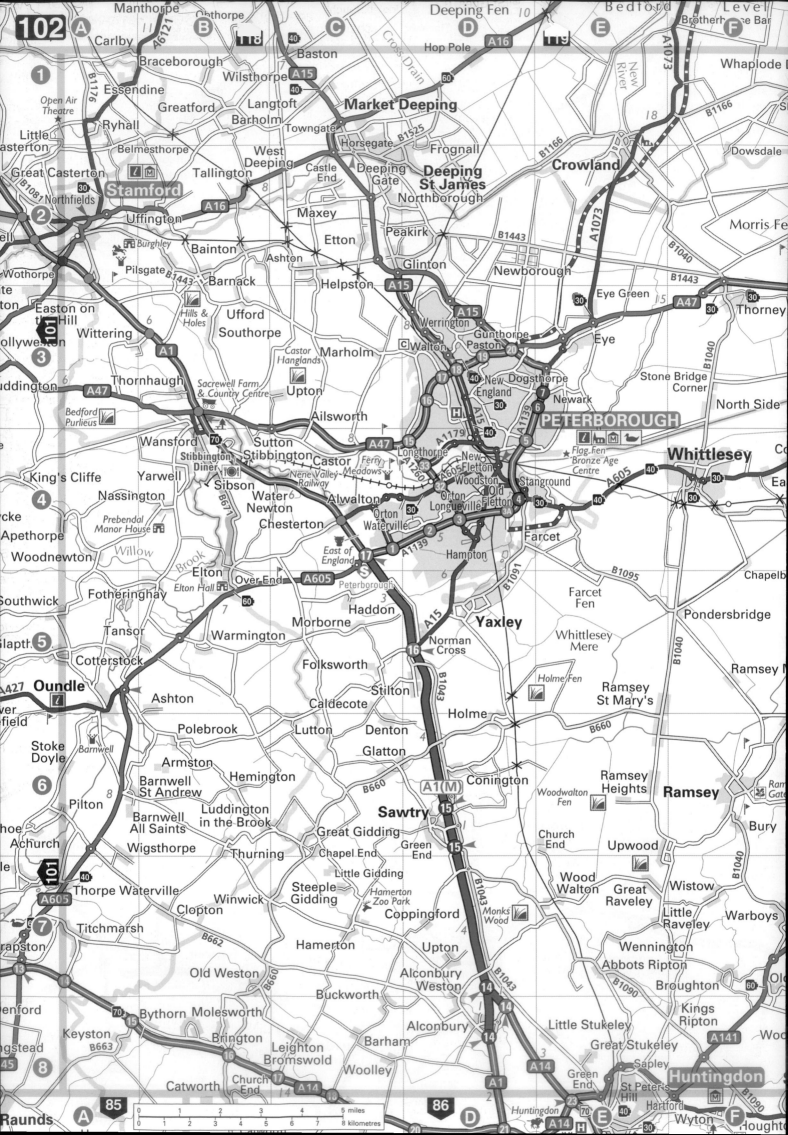

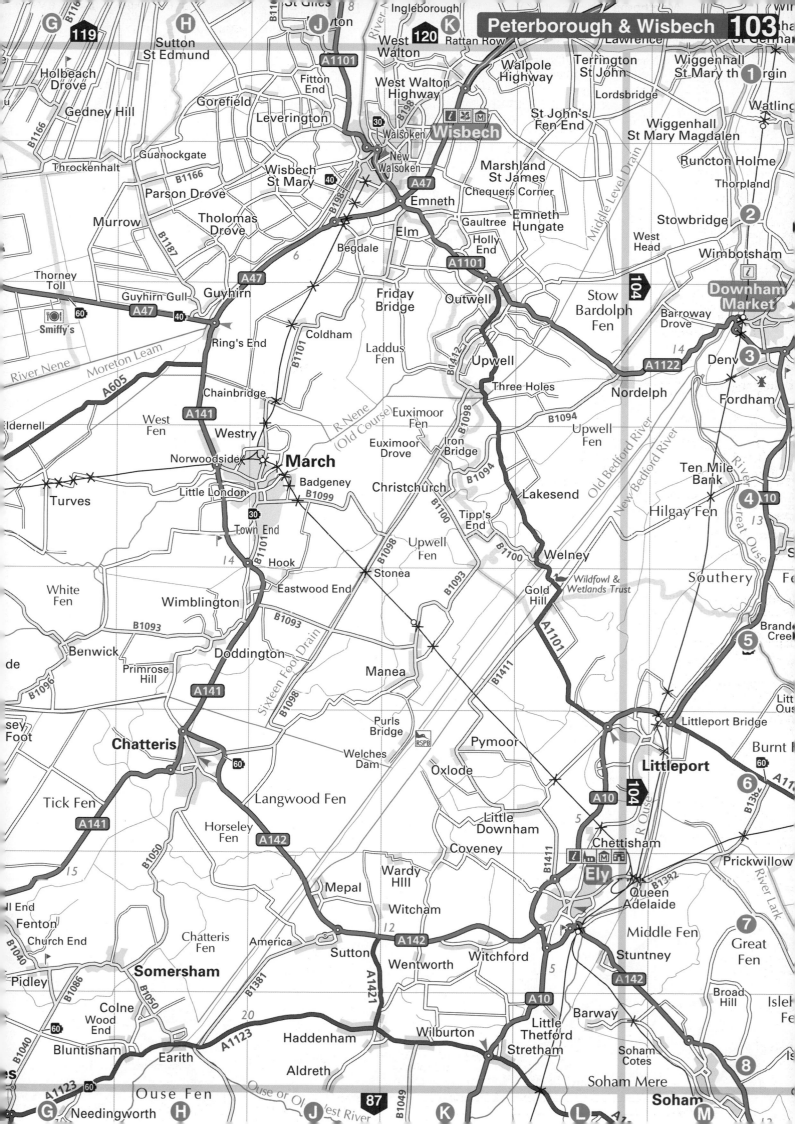

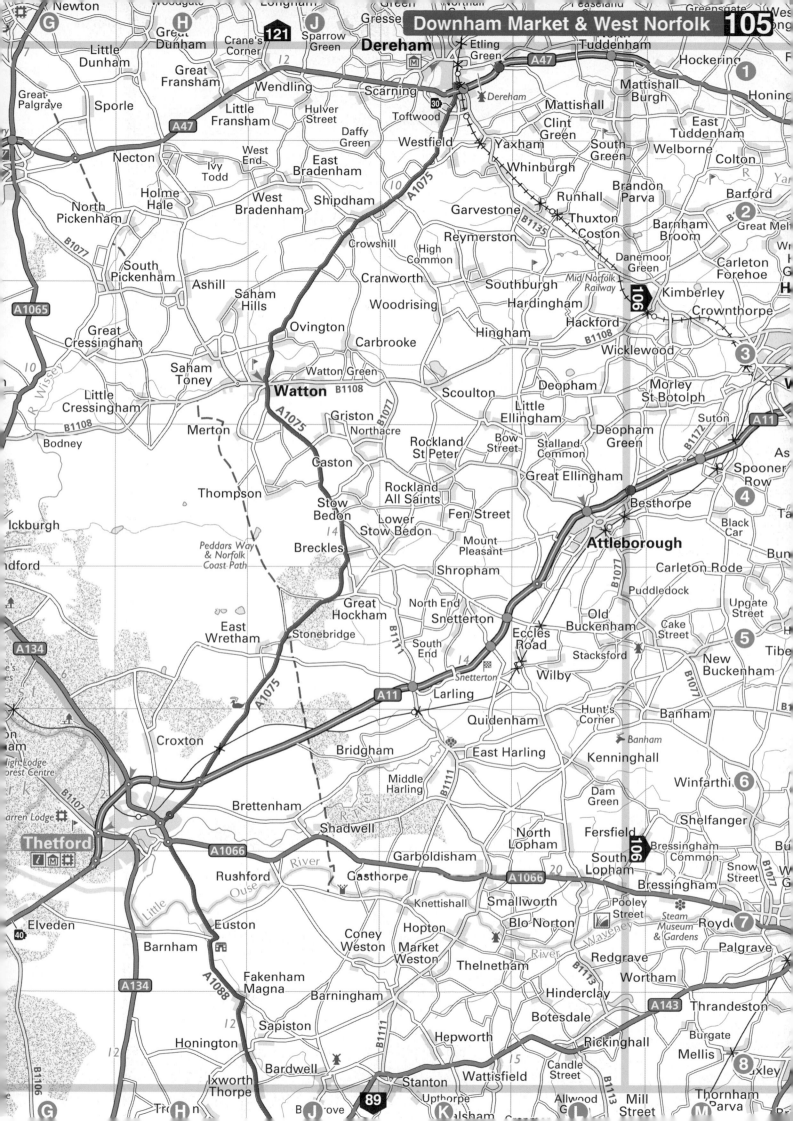

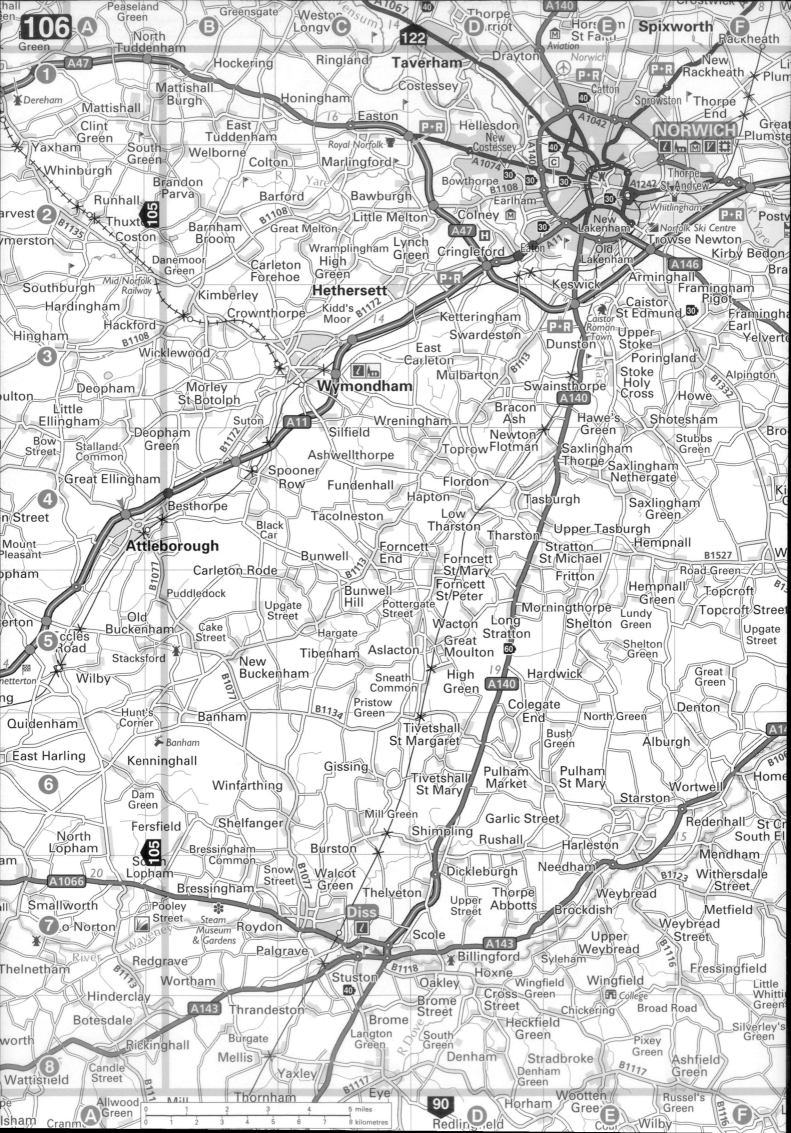

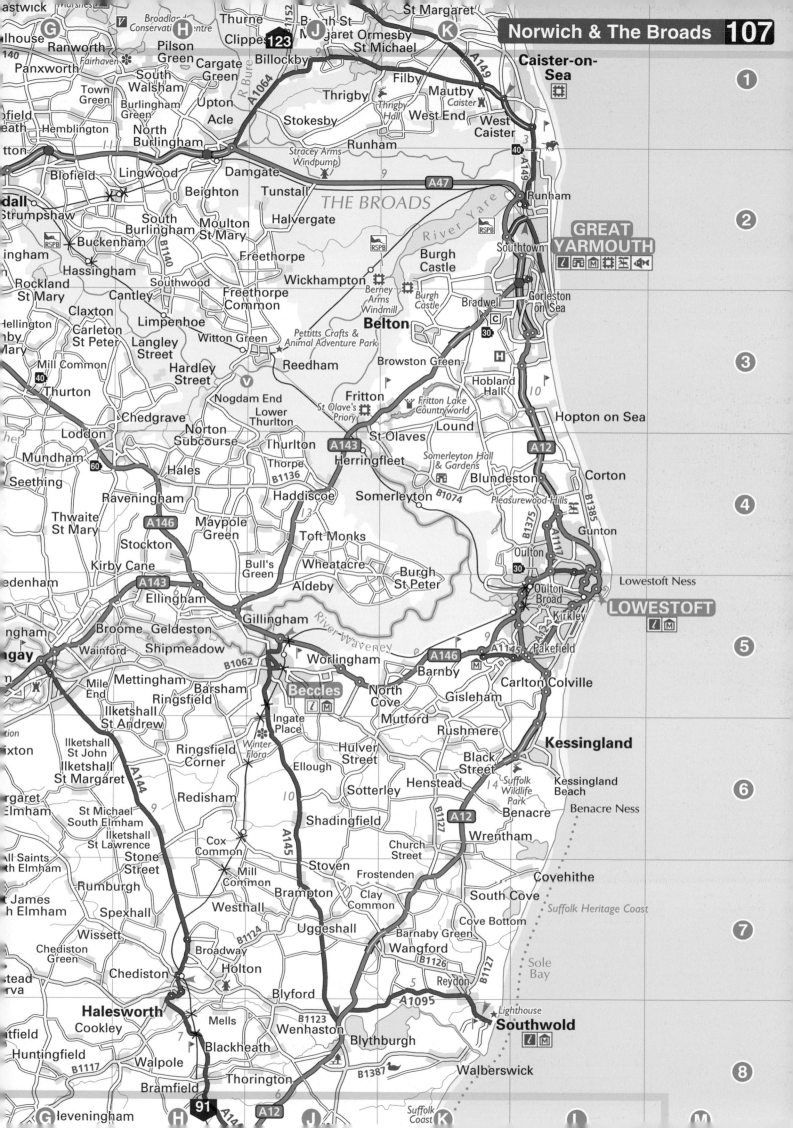

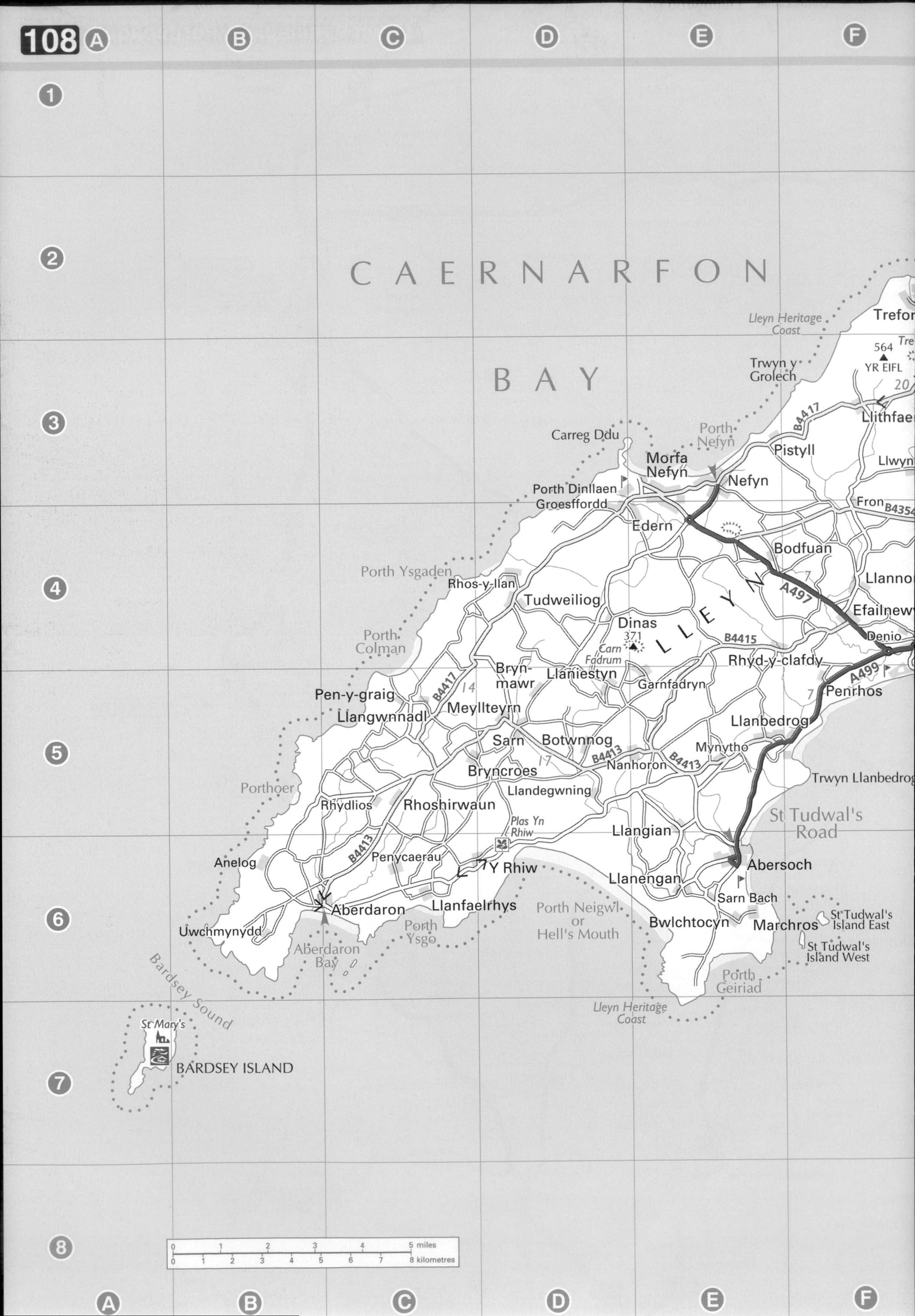

A　　B　　C　　D　　E　　F

1

2

C A E R N A R F O N

B A Y

*Lleyn Heritage Coast*

Trefor

564 ▲ YR EIFL

3

Carreg Ddu

*Porth Nefyn*

**Morfa Nefyn**

Trwyn y Grolech

Pistyll

Llithfae

Llwyn

Porth Dinllaen
Groesffordd

**Nefyn**

Edern

Fron B4354

Bodfuan

Llanno

4

*Porth Ysgaden*

Rhos-y-llan

Tudweiliog

**Dinas**

371 ▲ Carn Fadrum

A497

LLEYN

B4415

Efailnew

Denio

Rhyd-y-clafdy

*Porth Colman*

Bryn-mawr

Llaniestyn

Garnfadryn

A499

B4417 14

**Pen-y-graig**

Meyllteyrn

Rhydlios

**Llangwnnadl**

Sarn

Botwnnog

Nanhoron

B4413

B4413

Mynytho

Penrhos

Llanbedrog

Trwyn Llanbedrog

5

Bryncroes

17

*Porthoer*

Llandegwning

Rhoshirwaun

*Plas Yn Rhiw*

Llangian

St Tudwal's Road

Anelog

B4413

Penycaerau

Y Rhiw

Llanengan

**Abersoch**

6

Uwchmynydd

**Aberdaron**

Llanfaelrhys

*Porth Ysgo*

*Porth Neigwl or Hell's Mouth*

Sarn Bach

Bwlchtocyn

**Marchros**

St Tudwal's Island East

St Tudwal's Island West

*Aberdaron Bay*

*Porth Geiriad*

*Lleyn Heritage Coast*

*Bardsey Sound*

St Mary's

**BARDSEY ISLAND**

7

8

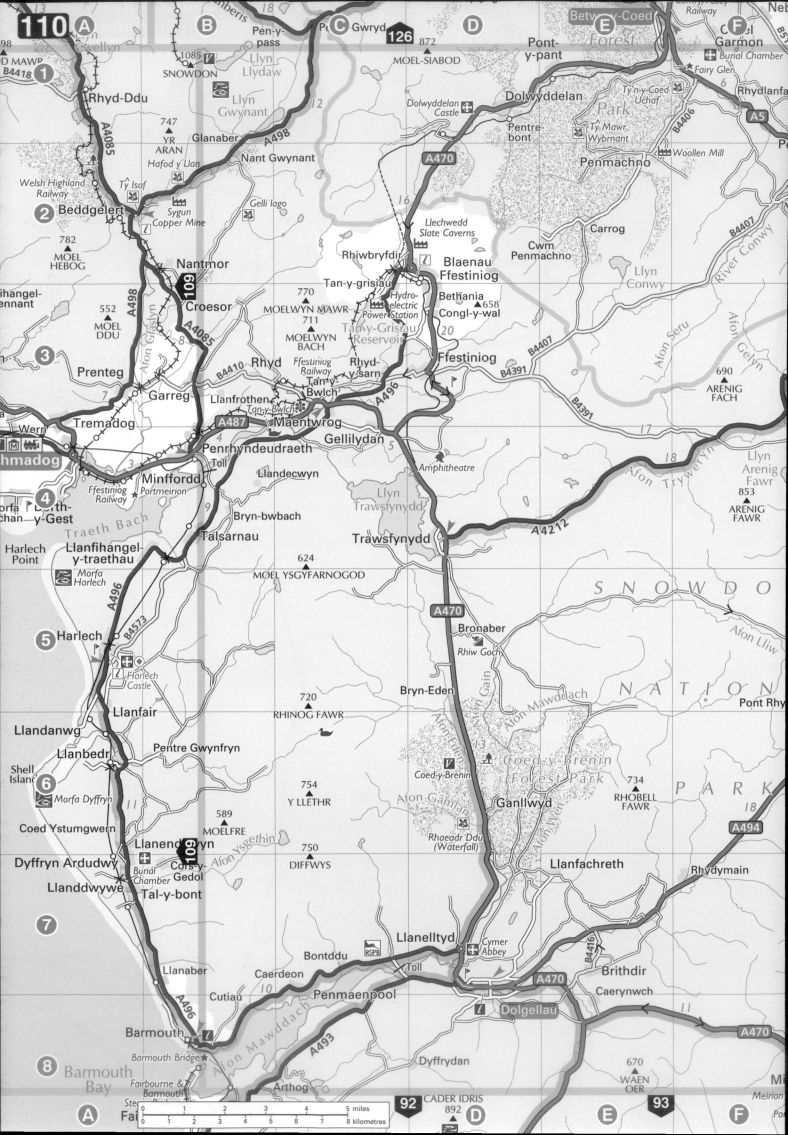

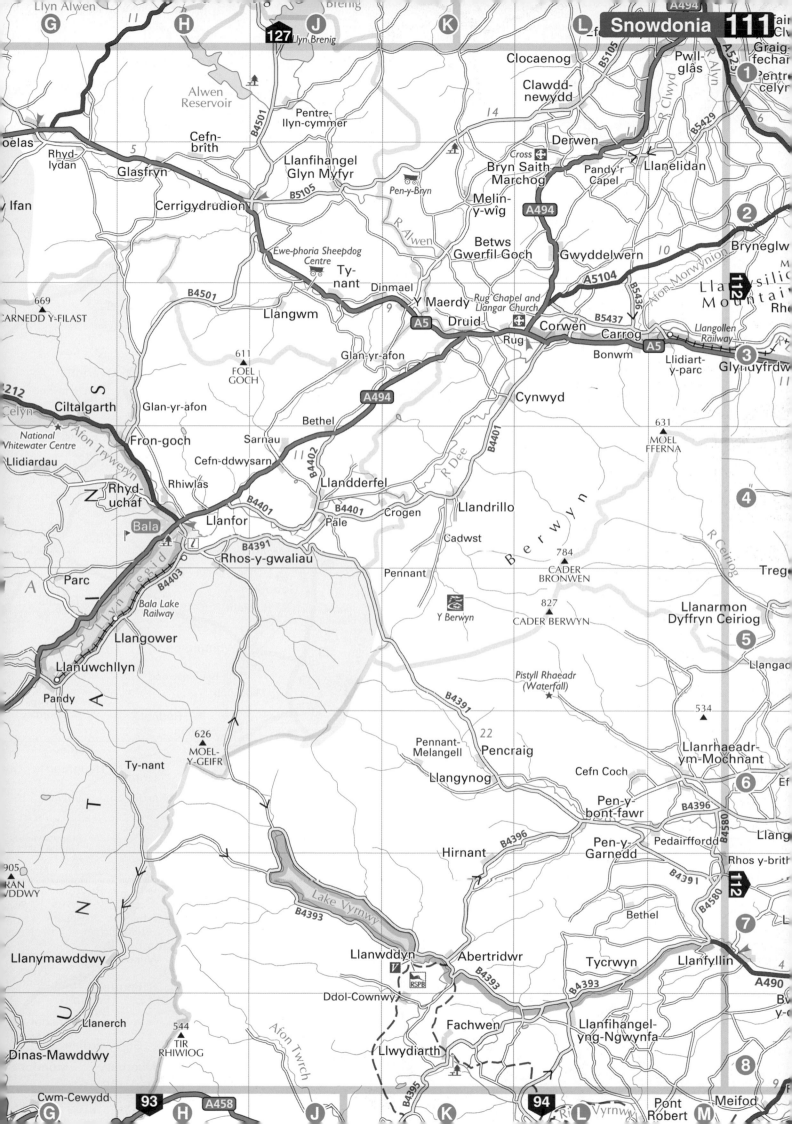

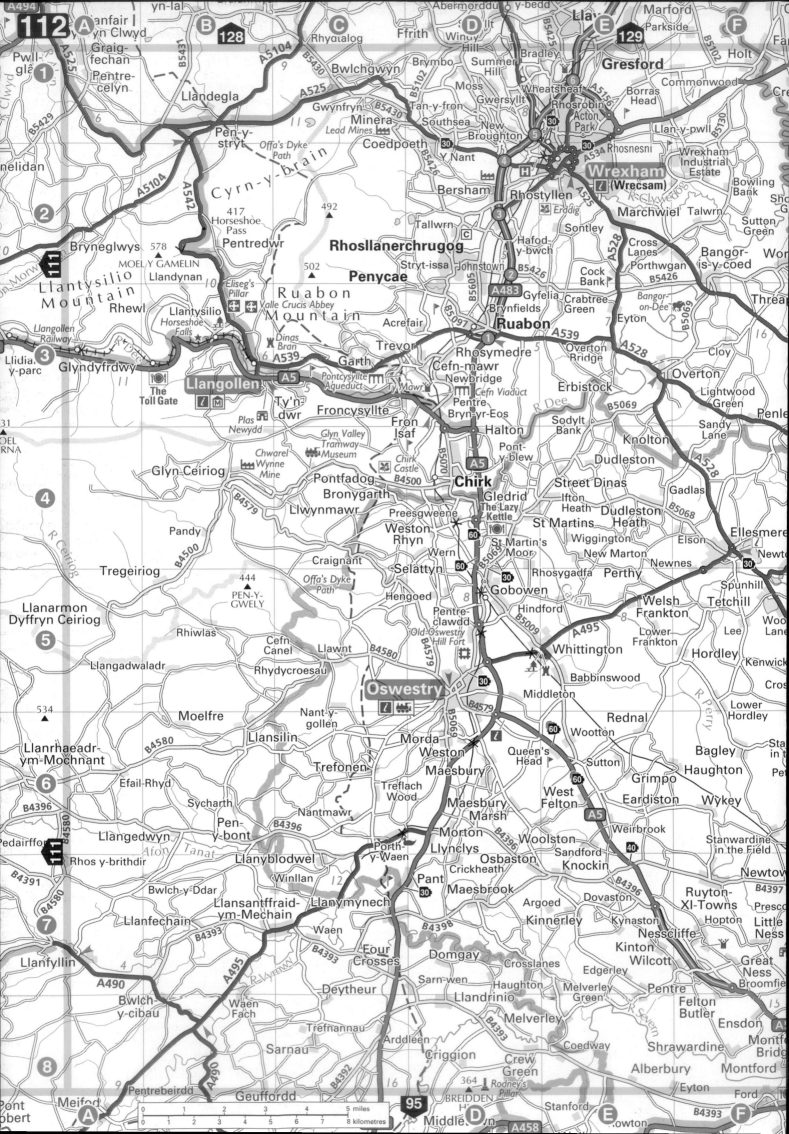

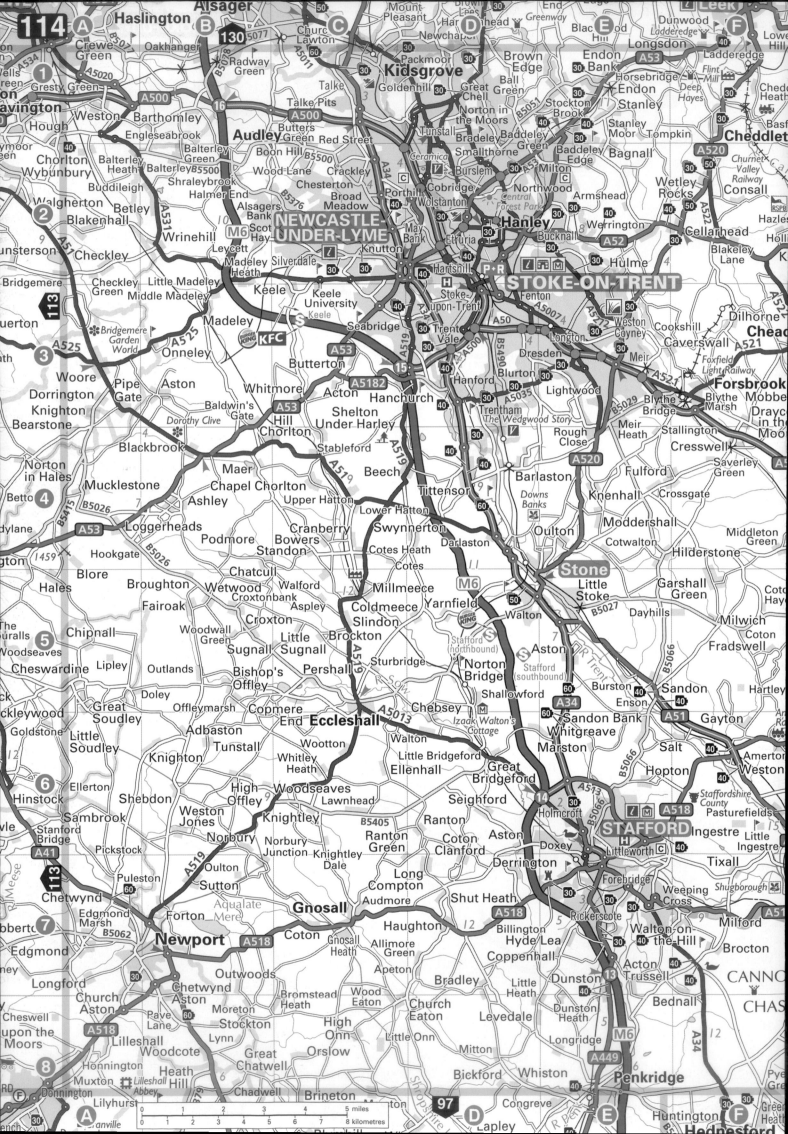

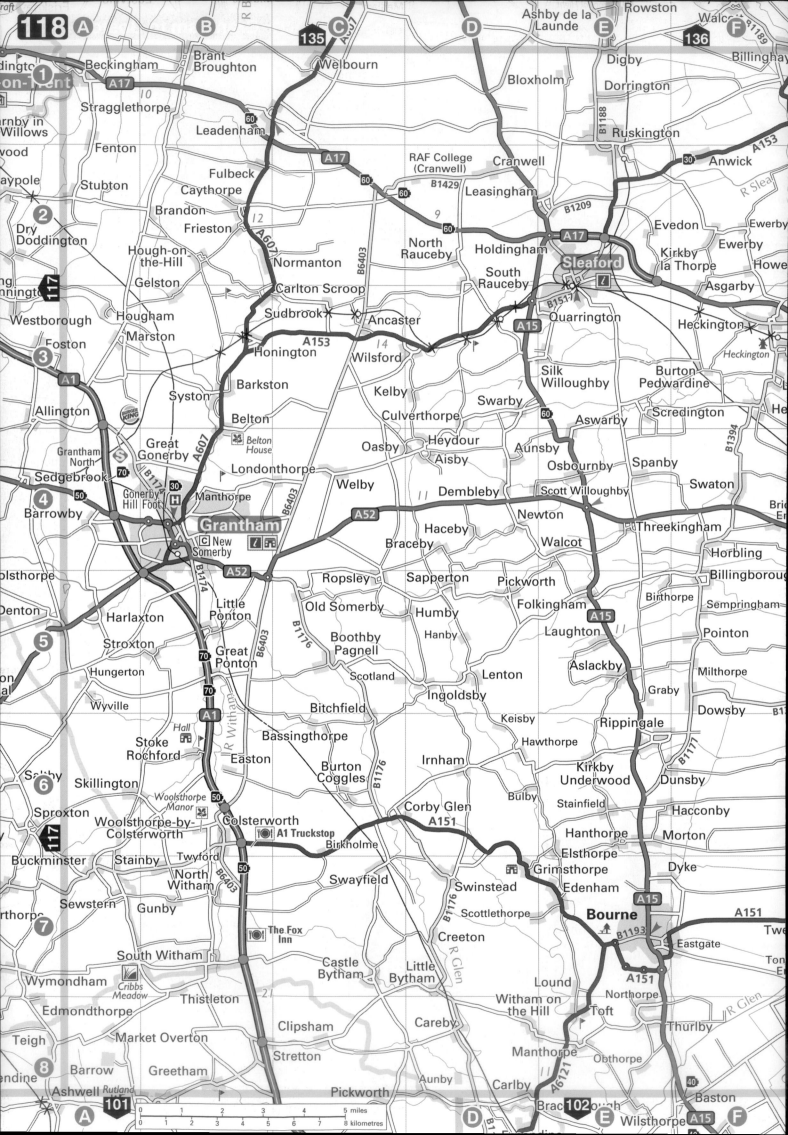

**137**

Friskney
Friskney Eaudike

Wrangle
Common **1**

**40**

Wrangle
Lowgate

Wrangle

Hurn's End **2**

casgate

ngton
End **119**

**3**

THE WASH

**4**

Holme
Dunes
Holme ne
the Sea

Old
Hunstanton

Hunstanton
Ringstead

A149

**40** Norfolk
Lavender

Heacham

Sedgeford

Snettisham

Park Farm

Southgate

RSPB
Ingoldisthorpe
Shernb

**5**

Dawsmere
Gedney
Drove End

B1359

12 B1440

**Dersingham**
Doddshill

Dersingham
Bog

Wolferton
Sandringha
West New

Babingley River
A149
B1439

**6** utton

Castle Rising

**119**

apelgate
Little London
★Butterfly & Falconry Park

The Wash

North
Wootton
Castle
A148
Congham

Roydon

**Long Sutton**
Sutton
Bridge

A1078
South Wootton

A148
A149

Pott
Row

**60**
**60**

Walpole
Cross Keys

Little
London

West
Lynn

Gaywood

**30** H
**4** C

Bawsey
B1145

Gayton

osses **7**

**Terrington
St Clement**
Clenchwarton
African Violet Centre
A17

11

Tilney
All Saints

Fairstead
**King's Lynn**

A148
Brow-of-
the-Hill

Ashwicke

Tydd
St Mary
Tydd
Gote

Walpole
St Andrew
Hay Green
Tilney High End
A47
Saddle
Bow
West
Winch
A10
A47
2
Middleton
East
Winch

Four
Gotes
Walpole
St Peter

Tydd
St Giles
B1165

Ingleborough

St John's
Highway
Tilney St
Lawrence
Wiggenhall
St Germans
North
Runcton
Blackborough
End
West
Bilney

**8** wton

River Nene
12
Rattan Row

West
Walton

Wiggenhall
St Mary t Virgin
Setchey
Pentney

0   1   2   3   4   5 miles
0     2     4     6     8 kilometres

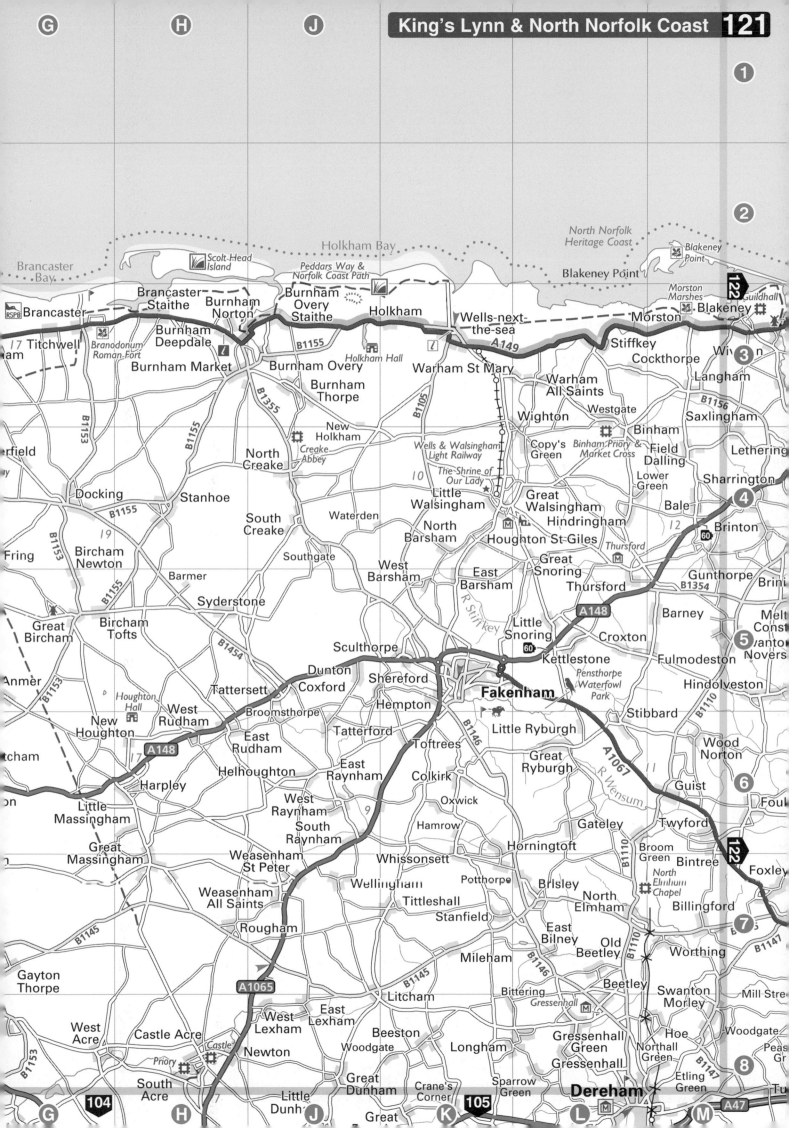

G   H   J

1

2

North Norfolk
Heritage Coast

Blakeney
Point

Brancaster
Bay

Scolt-Head
Island

Holkham Bay

Peddars Way &
Norfolk Coast Path

Blakeney Point

Morston
Marshes

122
Guildhall

Brancaster
RSPB

Brancaster
Staithe

Burnham
Norton

Burnham
Overy
Staithe

Holkham

Wells-next-
the-sea

Morston

Blakeney

3

17 Titchwell
ham

Branodunum
Roman Fort

Burnham
Deepdale

B1155

A149

Stiffkey
Cockthorpe

Wiv n

Burnham Market

Burnham Overy

Holkham Hall

Warham St Mary

Warham
All Saints

Langham

erfield

B1153

B1155

Burnham
Thorpe

B1355

B1105

Wighton

Westgate

Binham

B1156

Saxlingham

Lethering

New
Holkham

Creake
Abbey

Wells & Walsingham
Light Railway

Copy's
Green

Binham Priory &
Market Cross

Field
Dalling

Docking

North
Creake

The Shrine of
Our Lady

Lower
Green

Sharrington

Fring

B1153

B1155

Stanhoe

South
Creake

Waterden

Little
Walsingham

North
Barsham

Great
Walsingham

Hindringham

Bale

4

60
Brinton

Bircham
Newton

Barmer

Southgate

West
Barsham

Houghton St Giles

Thursford

12

B1354

Gunthorpe

Brini

Syderstone

East
Barsham

R Stiffkey

Great
Snoring

Barney

Melt
Const

Great
Bircham

Bircham
Tofts

B1454

Little
Snoring

A148

Thursford

Croxton

Fulmodeston

Novers

5

Anmer

B1153

Houghton
Hall

Sculthorpe

60

Kettlestone

Pensthorpe
Waterfowl
Park

Hindolveston

New
Houghton

West
Rudham

Dunton
Coxford

Shereford

Fakenham

Stibbard

B1110

Wood
Norton

6

A148

Broomsthorpe

Hempton

B1146

Little Ryburgh

Guist

cham

East
Rudham

Tatterford

Toftrees

Great
Ryburgh

A1067

Twyford

122

Little
Massingham

Harpley

Helhoughton

East
Raynham

Colkirk

R Wensum

Broom
Green

Bintree

Foxley

Great
Massingham

West
Raynham

Oxwick

Hamrow

Gateley

North
Elmham
Chapel

7

Weasenham
St Peter

South
Raynham

Whissonsett

Horningtoft

Brisley

North
Elmham

Billingford

Gayton
Thorpe

Weasenham
All Saints

Wellingham

Potthorpe

Tittleshall

East
Bilney

Old
Beetley

Worthing

B1147

Rougham

B1145

Stanfield

Mileham

B1146

Beetley

Swanton
Morley

Mill Stre

A1065

Litcham

Bittering
Gressenhall

Woodgate

West
Acre

West
Lexham

East
Lexham

Beeston
Woodgate

Longham

Gressenhall
Green

Hoe
Northall
Green

Peas
Gr

8

B1153

Castle Acre

Priory

Newton

Great
Dunham

Crane's
Corner

Sparrow
Green

Gressenhall

Etling
Green

B1147

South
Acre

Little
Dunh

Great

105

Dereham

M

A47

G   H   J   K   L   M

104

Mundesley
Stow Mill
Paston
B1159
Bacton
gthorpe
Walcott
Pollard
Street
rpe
Happisburgh
Witton    Ridlington
Ridlington
Street
Crostwight    Whimpwell Green
Happisburgh
Common    Eccles on Sea
ning    Hempstead
Lessingham
Ingham
riggate    East    Corner
Ruston    Sea Palling
stead    Ingham    Waxham
Stalham    Calthorpe
Dilham    Stalham    Street
Green
Low    Hickling
burgh    Street    A149
Barton    Horsey Corner
Pennygate    Turf    Sutton    Hickling Green    Horsey
Wood    Hickling    Hill Common
Street    Heath    Hickling    Horsey Windpump
gate    Barton    Broad
eet    Neatishead    Broad    Catfield
Irstead    Catfield    East
Common    Somerton
Threehammer    Sharp    West
Common    Green    Potter    Somerton    Winterton-on-Sea
Hoveton    Ludham    Heigham
A1062    Martham    Hemsby
pper    Johnson's    Bastwick    Hole
treet    Street    Cess    Newport
Horning    Repps    Hemsby    Scratby
stwick    Upper Street    Rollesby    Ormesby
Bure    Thurne    Burgh St    St Margaret
Marshes    Broadland    Margaret    Ormesby    California
house    Conservation Centre    Clippesby    St Michael
Ranworth    Pilson    Ormesby
40    Pan    Green    Cargate    Billockby    Caister-on-
Fairhaven    South    Green    B1152    107    Sea

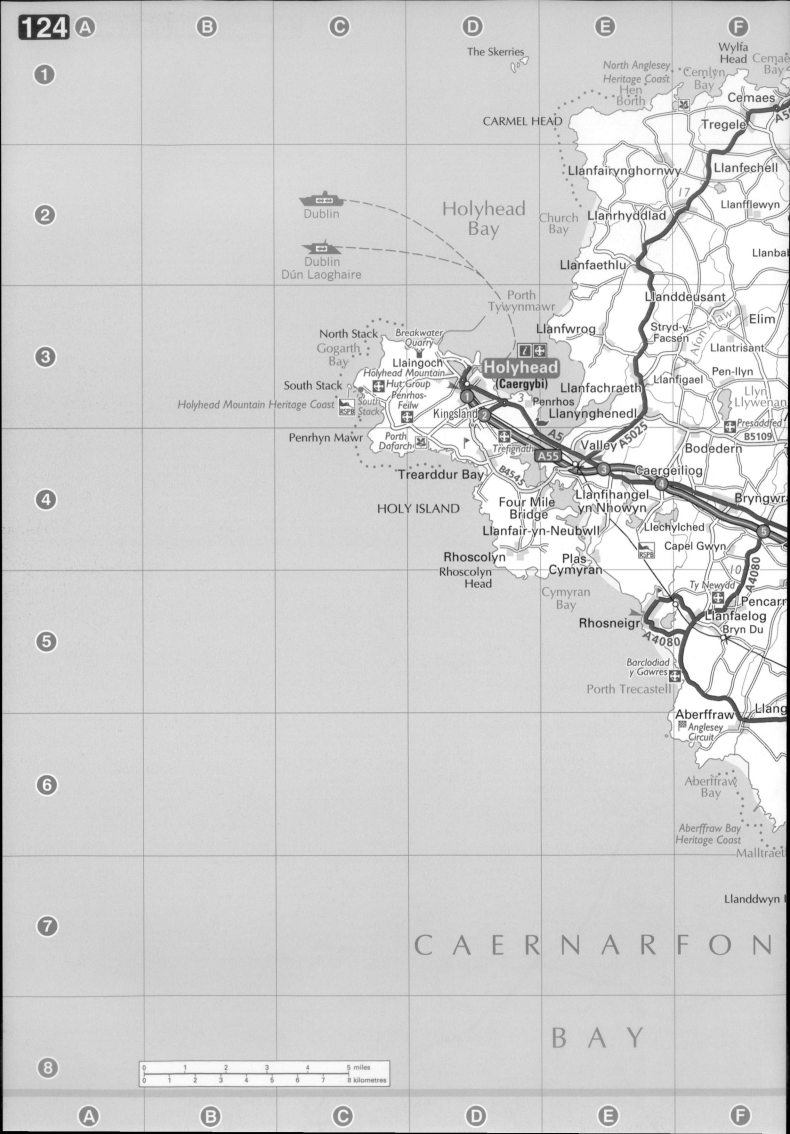

The Skerries

North Anglesey
Heritage Coast

Wylfa
Head

Cemaes
Bay

Cemlyn
Bay

CARMEL HEAD

Hen
Borth

Cemaes

Tregele

Llanfairynghornwy

Llanfechell

Holyhead
Bay

Church
Bay

Llanrhyddlad

Llanfflewyn

Llanbal

Llanfaethlu

Llanddeusant

Porth
Tywynmawr

Llanfwrog

Stryd-y-
Facsen

Elim

North Stack

Breakwater
Quarry

Llaingoch

Gogarth
Bay

Holyhead Mountain

South Stack

Hut Group

Penrhos-
Feilw

Holyhead Mountain Heritage Coast

RSPB

South
Stack

Holyhead
(Caergybi)

Penrhos

Llanfachraeth

Llanynghenedl

Penrhyn Mawr

Porth
Dafarch

Kingsland

Trefignath

Llantrisant

Pen-llyn

Llanfigael

Llyn
Llywenan

Presaddfed

B5109

Valley

Bodedern

Bryngwr

Caergeiliog

Four Mile
Bridge

Llanfihangel
yn Nhowyn

Llechylched

Trearddur Bay

HOLY ISLAND

Llanfair-yn-Neubwll

RSPB

Capel Gwyn

Rhoscolyn

Plas
Cymyran

Ty Newydd

Pencarn

Rhoscolyn
Head

Cymyran
Bay

Llanfaelog

Bryn Du

Rhosneigr

Barclodiad
y Gawres

Porth Trecastell

Llang

Aberffraw

Anglesey
Circuit

Aberffraw
Bay

Aberffraw Bay
Heritage Coast

Malltraeth

Llanddwyn

C A E R N A R F O N

B A Y

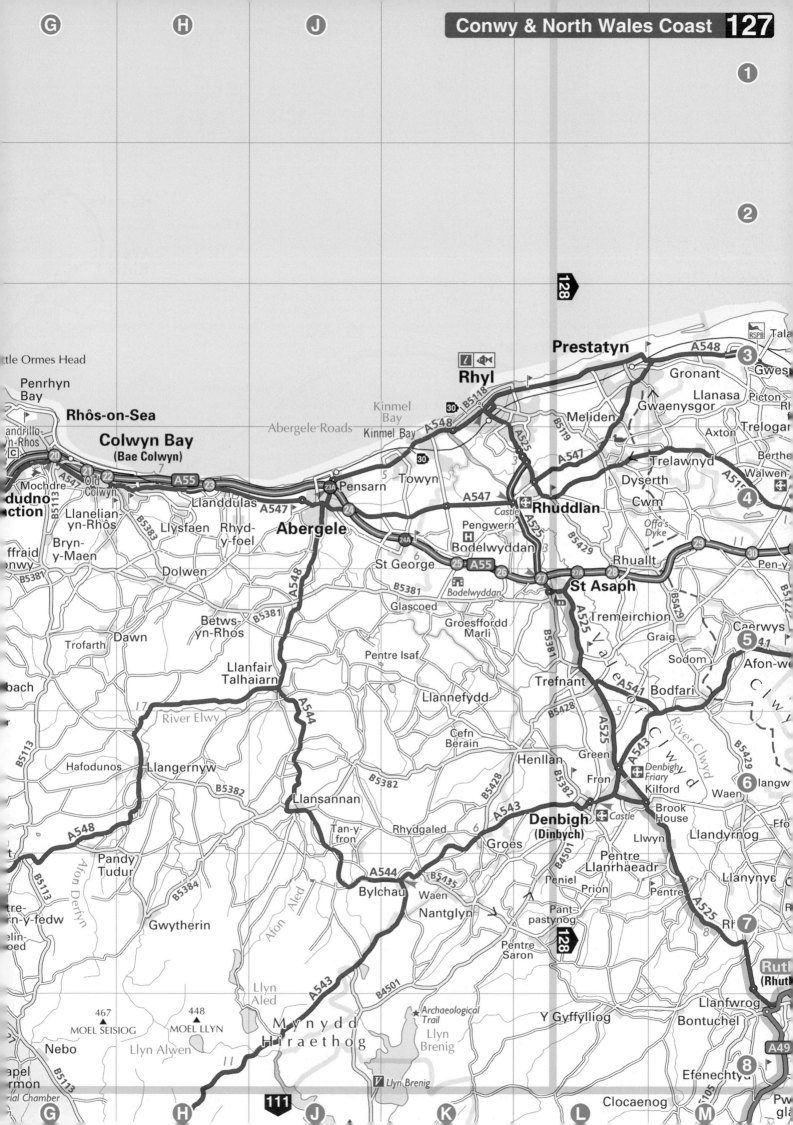

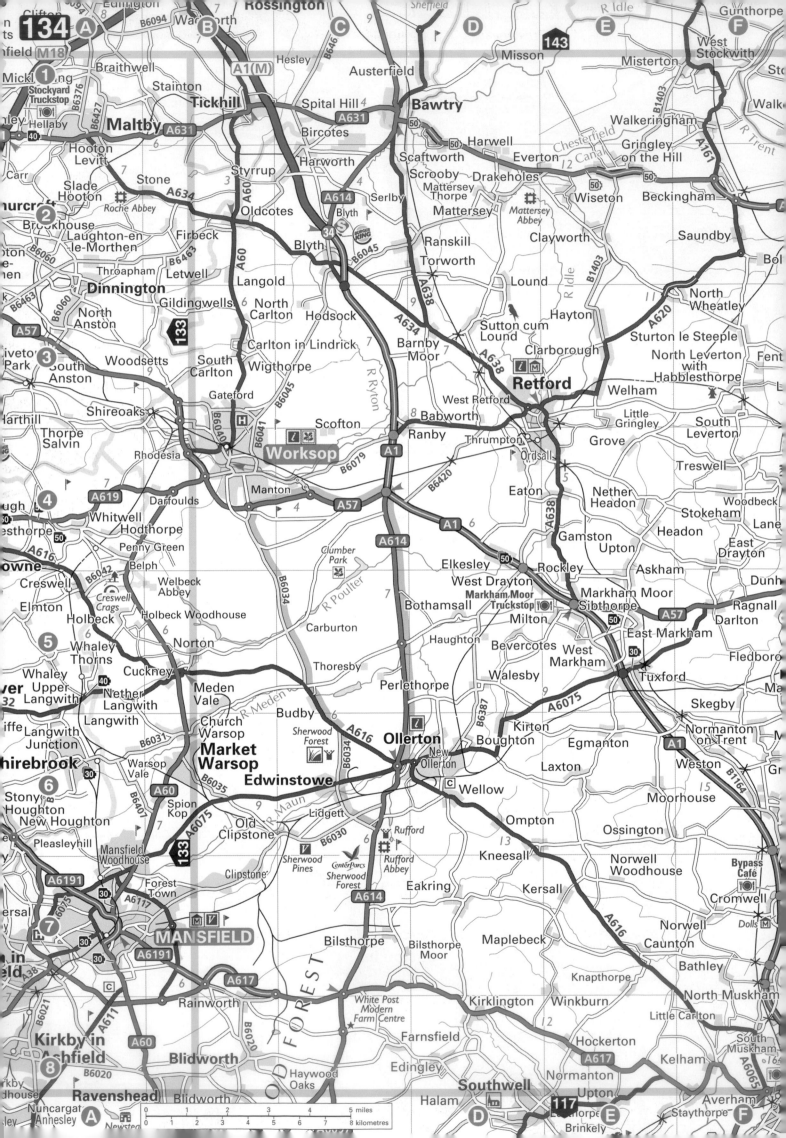

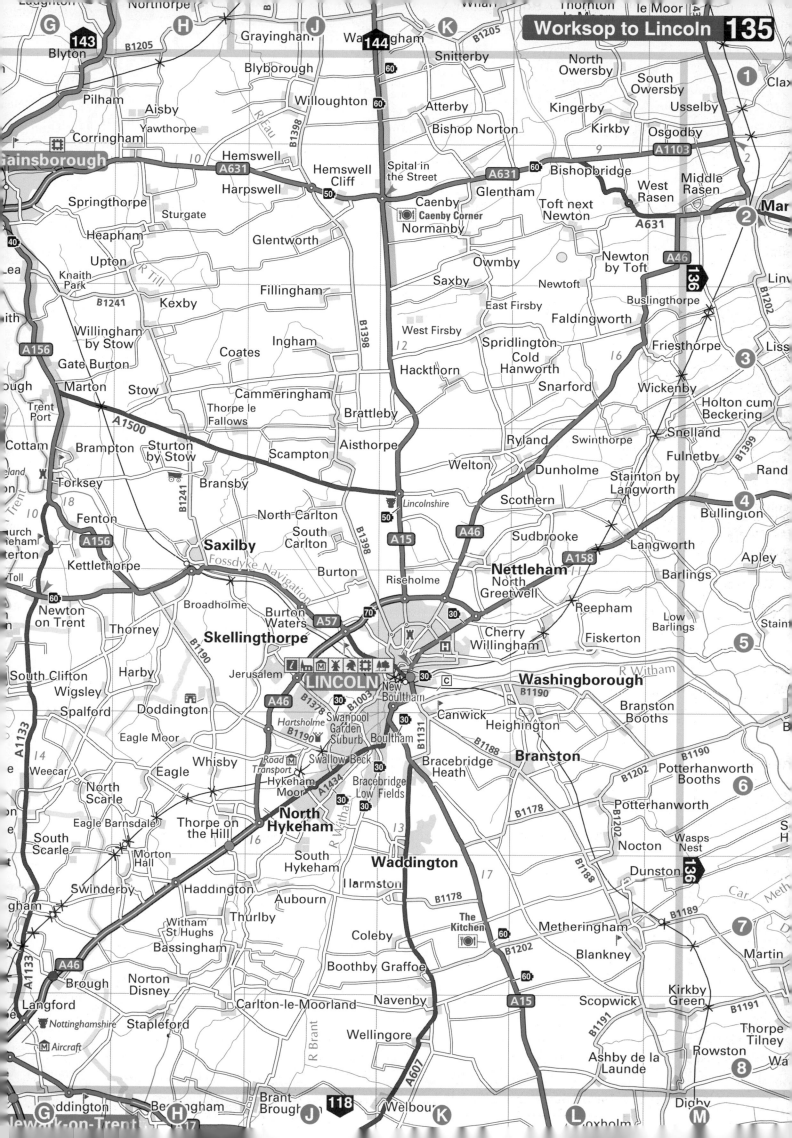

# 136

A | B | C | D | E | F

le Moor

144 | 145

Swinhope · Brookenby

Wold Newton · Ludborough

A16 · Lincoln Wolds Railway · Fulstow · Cov St B

1 South Owersby · Normanby le Wold · Claxby · Stainton le Vale · Binbrook · North Ormsby · Covenham St Mary

Usselby · Walesby · Kirmond le Mire · Great Tows · Utterby · Little Grimsby

Kirkby · Osgodby · A1103 · Tealby · Ludford · Kelstern · North Elkington · Fotherby

2 West Rasen · Middle Rasen · **Market Rasen** · North Willingham · A631 · South Elkington · A631

Newton by Toft · A46 · 135 · Linwood · Sixhills · Burgh on Bain · Welton le Wold · Little Welton · THE WOLDS

Buslingthorpe · Legsby · South Willingham · Biscathorpe · A157 · Hallington · Raithby · Lo

3 Friesthorpe · Bleasby · Hainton · East Torrington · Donington on Bain · Withcall · Maltby · A16

Wickenby · Lissington · West Torrington · Benniworth · A153 · Tathwell

Holton cum Beckering · East Barkwith · Market Stainton · Cawkwell · Cadwell Park · Haugham

Snelland · B1399 · West Barkwith · Goulceby · Asterby · Maidenwell · Burw

Fulnetby · Rand · B1202 · A157 · Panton · Sotby · Ranby · Scamblesby · Farforth · Ruck

4 Stainton by Langworth · Wragby · Hatton · B1225 · Oxcombe · Worlaby

Bullington · Langton by Wragby · Great Sturton · Belchford · Little London

Langworth · Apley · Low Langton · Hemingby · Far Thorpe · Tetford

A158 · Barlings · Kingthorpe · Baumber · Fulletby · Salmo

Reepham · Low Barlings · Bardney Limewoods · Minting · Furzehills · Mid Thorpe · West Ashby · Somersby

5 Fiskerton · Stainfield · Gautby · Wispington · **Horncastle** · Ashby Puerorum

ngborough · R Witham · Edlington · Low Toynton · Greetham

Branston Booths · Bucknall · Thimbleby · A158 · High Toynton · Scrafield · Hagwo

Bardney · B1190 · Langton · Thornton · Mareham on the Hill · Winceby

6 Potterhanworth Booths · Horsington · Hameringham · Asgarby

B1202 · Southrey · Woodhall · Martin · Scrivelsby · Hareby

Potterhanworth · Sots Hole · Stixwould · Dalderby · B1183 · Old Bolingbro

Reeds Beck · Roughton · Moorby · Miningsby

Noctorum · Wasps Nest · 135 · Woodhall Spa · Haltham · Wood Enderby

Dunston · Kirkstead · Toft Hill · Wilksby · East Kirkby · Lincoln Avia

7 Blankney · Martin Dales · **Woodhall Spa** · Kirkby on Bain · A153 · A155 · Revesby

Scopwick · Kirkby Green · Timberland · Tattershall Thorpe · Tumby · Mareham le Fen · Stic

Thorpe Tilney · Rowston · Tattershall · Tumby · Coningsby · Tumby Woodside · New Bolingbroke

8 Ashby de la Launde · Walcott · Billinghay · Dogdyke · Tattershall College · Tattershall Castle · Battle of Britain Memorial Flight · Moor Side · Sandy Bank · Medlam · Carrington

Bloxholm · Digby · Dorrington · Chapel Hill · Scrub Hill · Bunker's Hill · West Fen

Hawthorn Hill · New York · 119

A | B | C | D | E | F

0 1 2 3 4 5 miles
0 1 2 3 4 5 6 7 8 kilometres

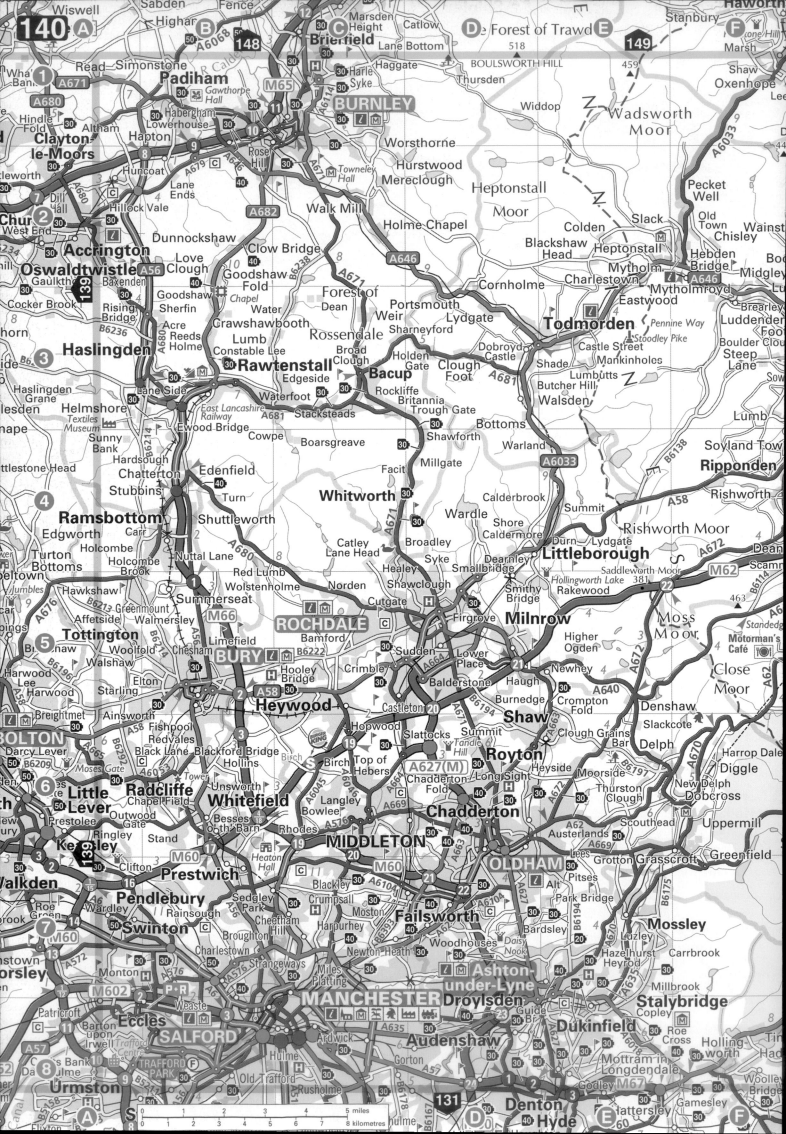

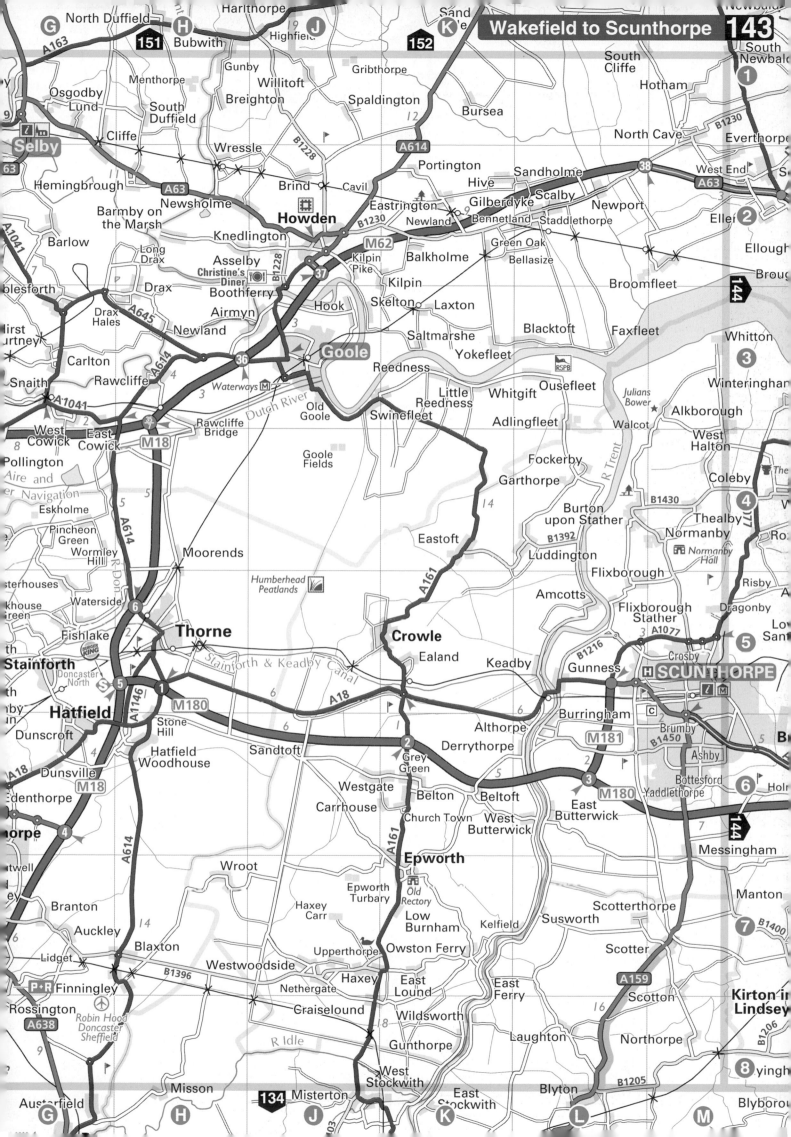

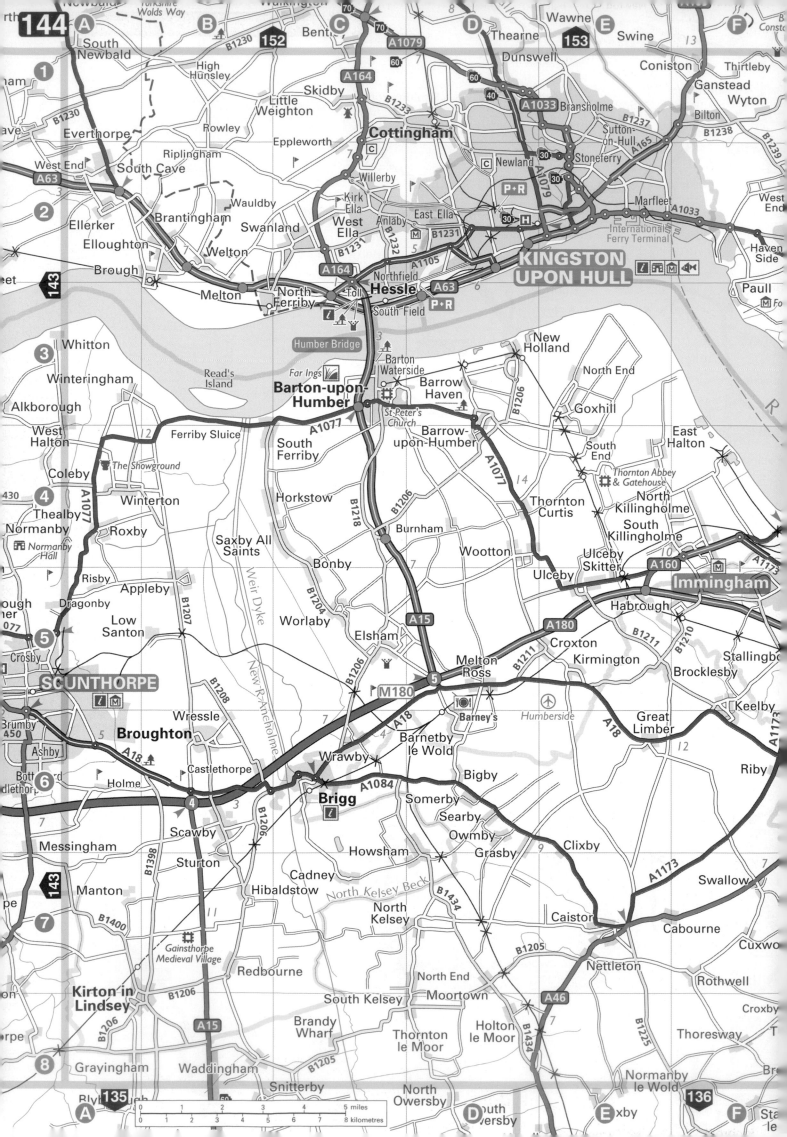

Flinto **G**
B1238 B1242 Newton **H** **J**

Broatley
Humbleton
Fitling
Grimston
153 Garton
Elley
R
Elstronwick
Danthorpe
North End
Hilston
Owstwick

St End
ston
Burton Pidsea
Roos
West End
Tunstall
Waxholme

Thorngumbald
E
S
Burstwick
Rimswell
Owthorne
**Withernsea**

A1033
Keyingham
West End
B1362
East End
B1242

Ryehill
16
Halsham
Winestead
Hollym
4
Holmpton

Ottringham
Patrington

Patrington Haven
Welwick
Out Newton

Sunk Island
Weeton
Skeffling
B1445
Easington

South End

Spurn Heritage Coast

Kilnsea

mingham
ck

HUMBER

Spurn Heritage Coast

SPURN HEAD

A180
**GRIMSBY**

B1210
West Marsh
Cleethorpes

ealing
Great Coates
A1136
Old Clee

ylesby
Little Coates
Thrunscoe
The Jungle

A46
Nunsthorpe
C
A46
Pleasure Island

70
H
A16
Scartho
A1098
**Humberston**

70
Laceby
B1203
B1219

by upon umber
**Waltham**
New Waltham
Holton le Clay
A1031

Barnoldby le Beck
Waltham Windmill
RSPB

Beelsby
A18
Brigsley
North End
Tetney Lock

Hatcliffe
Ashby cum Fenby
60
North Cotes

West Ravendale
Waithe
Tetney
Marshchapel

East Ravendale
Grainsby
Eskham

Wold Newton
North Thoresby
West End
29
Grainthorpe

B1201
Churchthorpe
North Somercotes

A16
Fulstow
Conisholme
A1031

15
Lincolnshire Wolds Railway
Canal
Church End
Skidbrooke North End

B1203
Ludborough
136
Covenham St Bartholomew
Saltf'
**M**

G H J K L

Rotterdam (Europoort) Zeebrugge

A  B  C  D  E  F

1

2

**155**

**156**

Haverigg
Point

Askam
in Furness

Marton

Swarthmoor

**A590**

Conishead Pri...

nal Foo...

Sandscale Haws

South Lakes
Animal Park

Lindal
in Furness

Great
Urswick

Bardsea

North Walney

Little
Urswick

Brow End

Dalton-
in-Furness

Scales

Baycliff

**BARROW-
IN-FURNESS**

Hawcoat

Newton

Stainton
with Adgarley

13

North Scale

Furness
Abbey

Bow
Bridge

Dendron

Watermill
Gleaston

Aldingham

Vickerstown

**A590**

Barrow
Island

**30**

Roose

Leece

Newbiggin

Roosebeck

Biggar

**A5087**

Rampside

ISLE OF
WALNEY

Roa
Island

Sheep
Island

Piel
Castle

Foulney Island

Piel Island

Hilpsford Point

Piel Bar

3

4

Douglas

5

Larne

**ℹ Ⓜ Fleetwood**

Rossall Point

6

**A587**

**ℹ Cleveleys**

**30**

**40**

Th...

7

Little Bispham

Norbreck

Bispha...

**A584**

**B5124**

Warbre...

North
Shore

**ℹ Ⓜ ⌖ 🐟 30**

**BLACKPOOL**

**138**

0  1  2  3  4  5 miles
0  1  2  3  4  5  6  7  8 kilometres

A  B  C  D  E  F

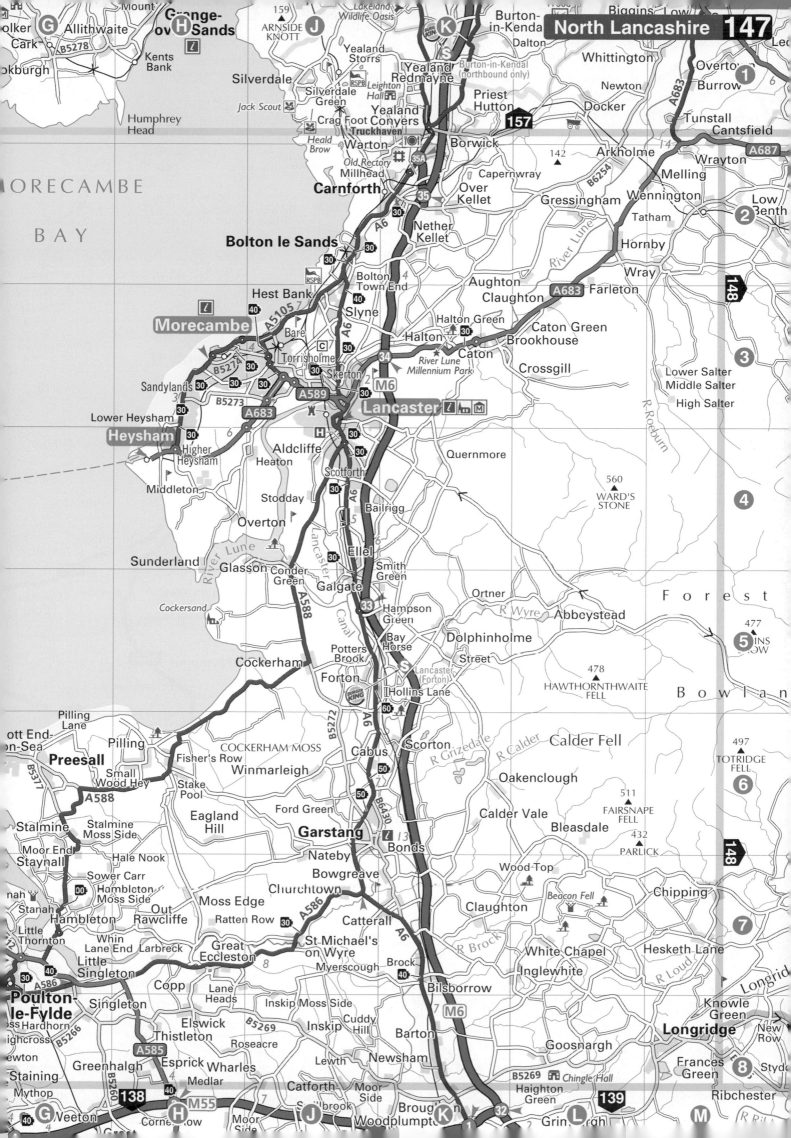

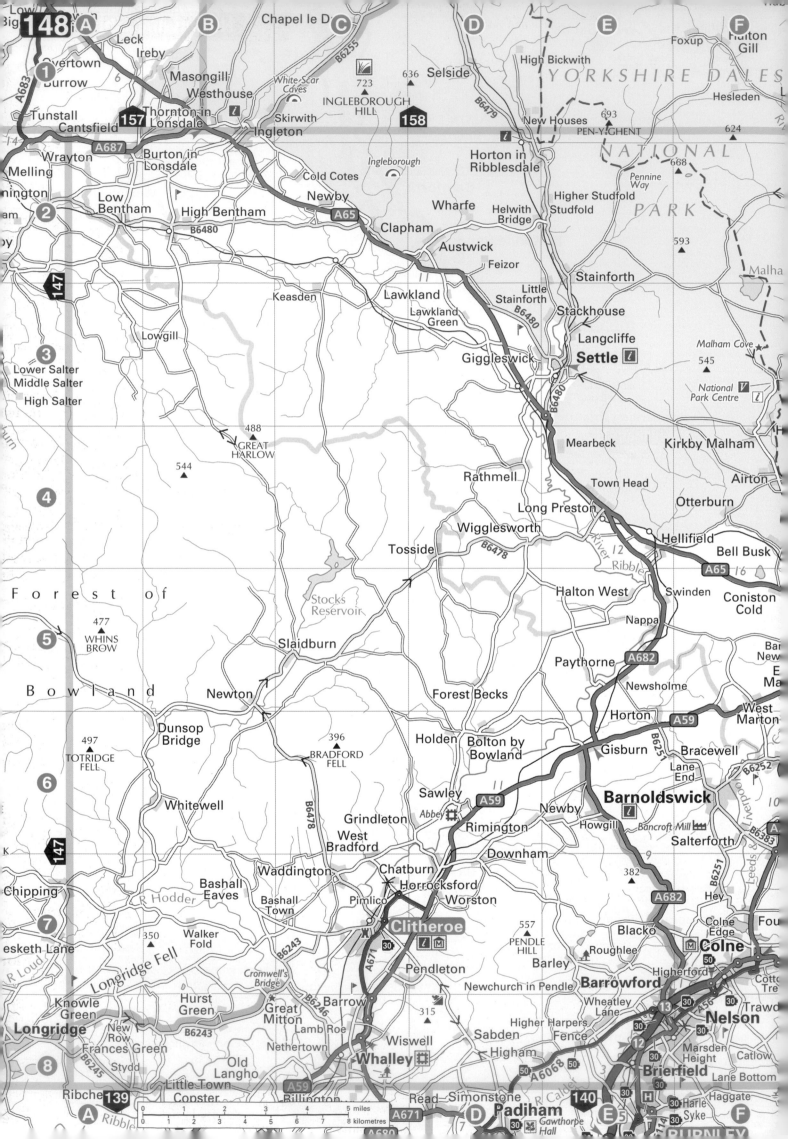

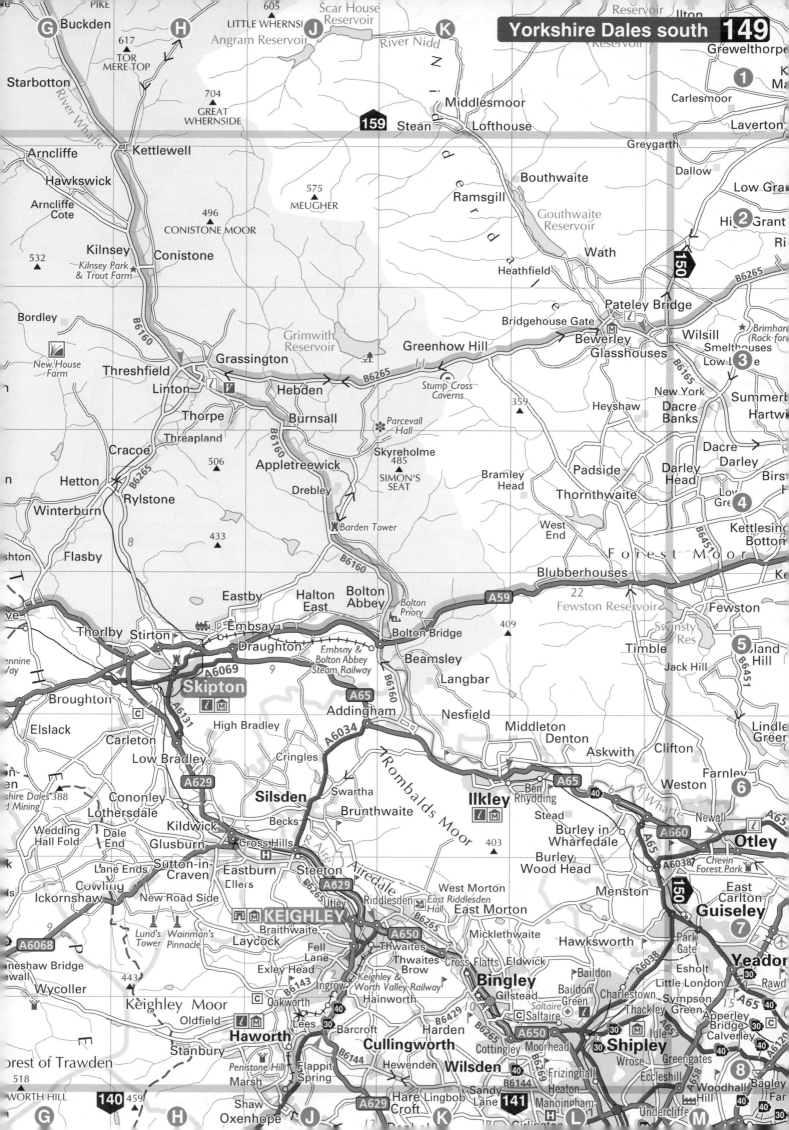

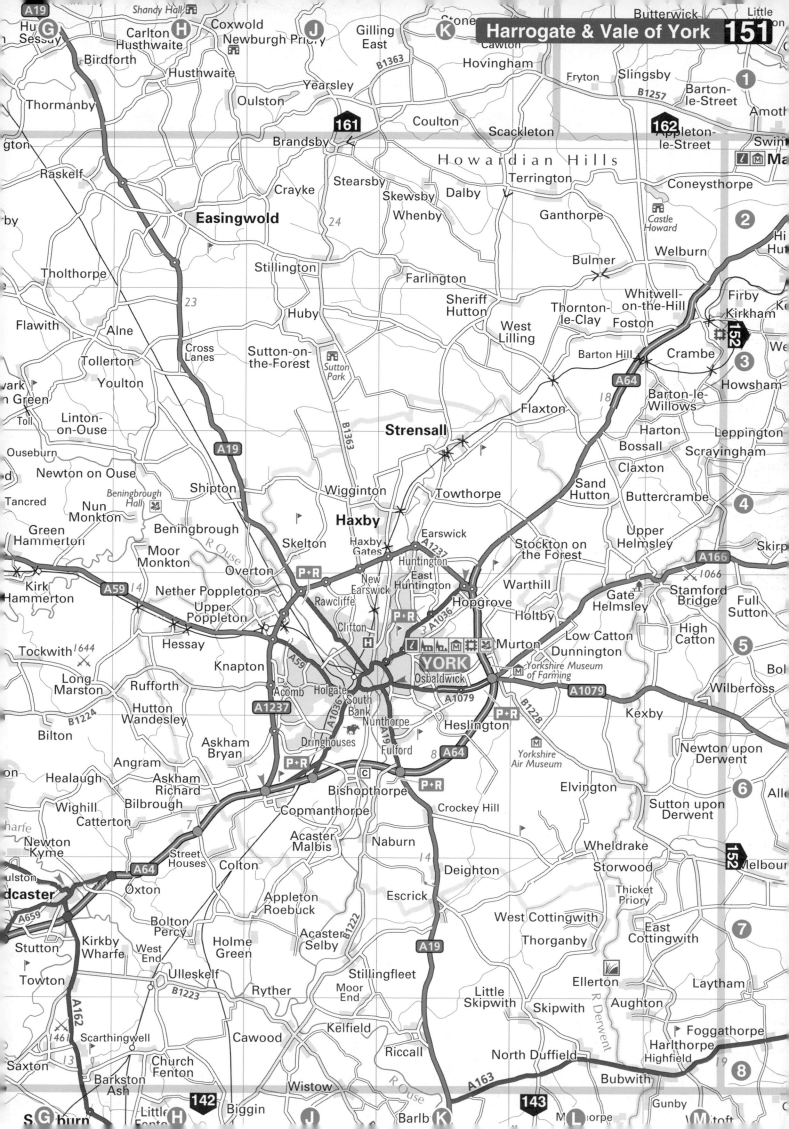

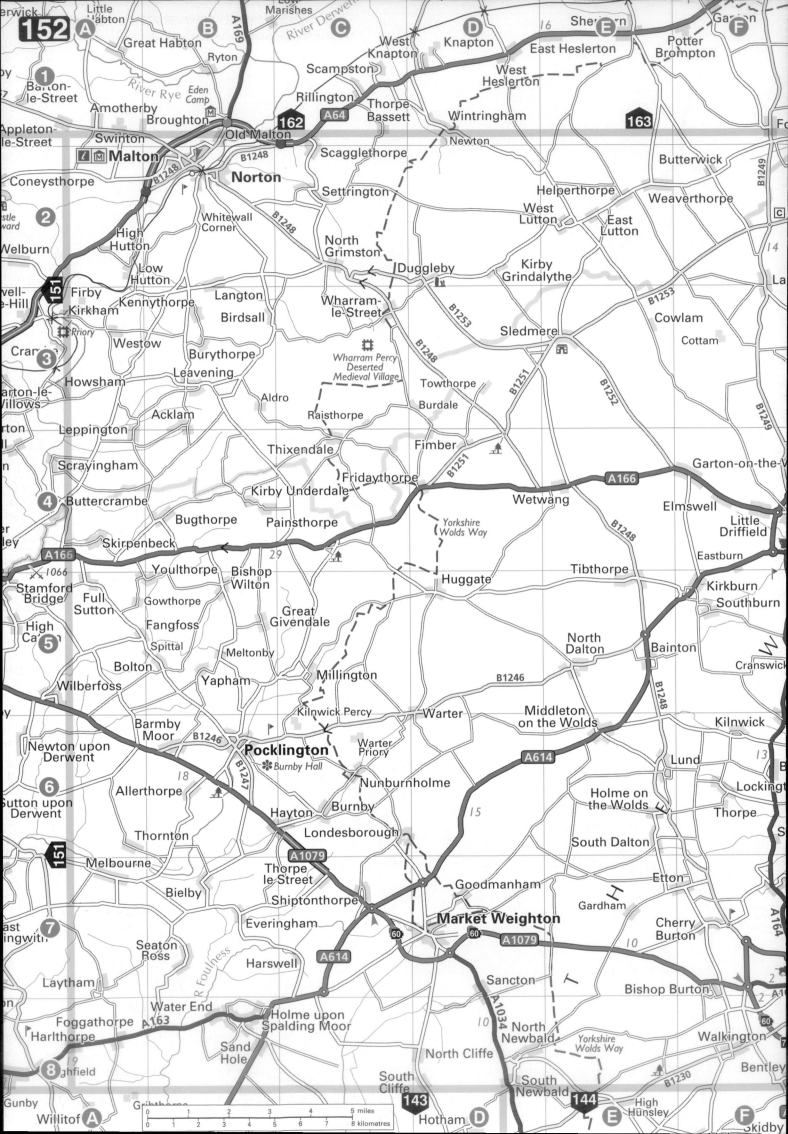

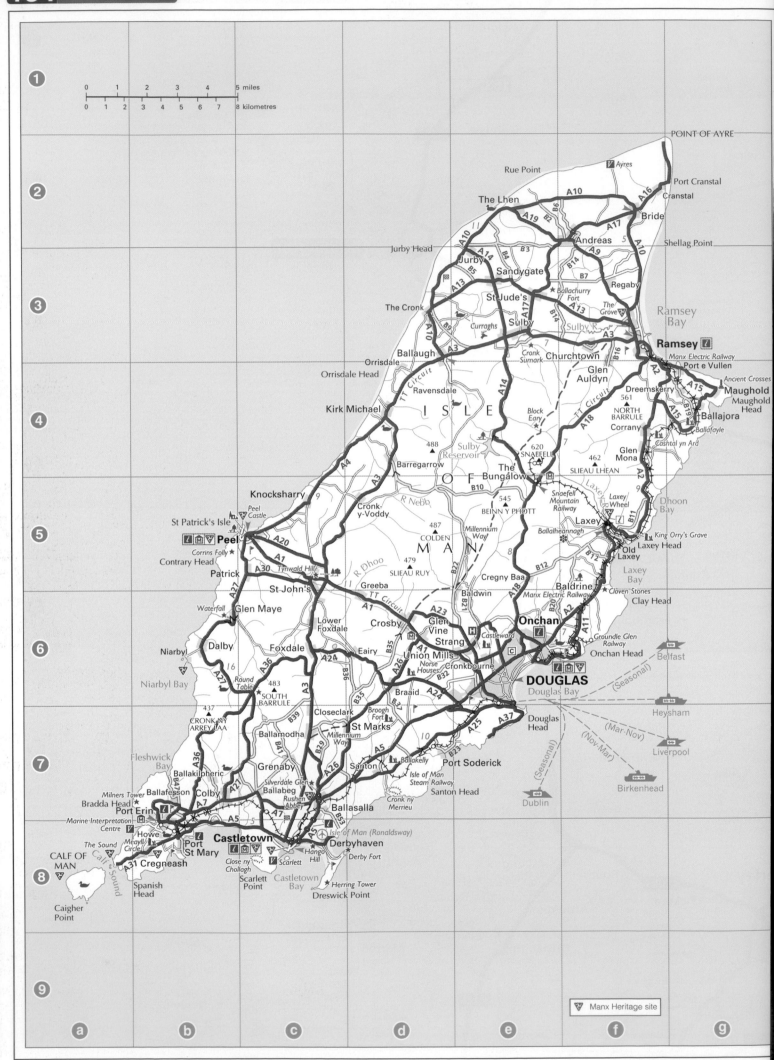

POINT OF AYRE

Rue Point
Ayres
Port Cranstal
The Lhen
A10
A16
Cranstal
A19
B6
B2
Bride
A17
Andreas
5
A10
Shellag Point
Jurby Head
A10
Jurby
A14
B4
B3
A9
B5
Sandygate
B14
Regaby
A13
St Jude's
Ballachurry
Fort
The
Grove
The Cronk
A17
B14
A13
Ramsey
Bay
Curraghs
Sulby
Sulby R.
A3
Ramsey
Churchtown
Manx Electric Railway
Port e Vullen
Ballaugh
A3
Cronk
Sumark
Glen
Auldyn
A2
A15
Ancient Crosses
Orrisdale
561
Dreemskerry
Maughold
Orrisdale Head
Ravensdale
NORTH
BARRULE
Corrany
A15
B19
Maughold
Head
Ballajora
Kirk Michael
ISLE
Block
Eary
620
Cashtal yn Ard
Ballafayle
488
Sulby
Reservoir
SNAEFELL
462
SLIEAU LHEAN
Glen
Mona
A2
Barregarrow
OF
The
Bungalow
B10
Snaefell
Mountain
Railway
Laxey
Wheel
Dhoon
Bay
Knocksharry
9
Cronk-
y-Voddy
R Nebb
545
BEINN Y PHOTT
Laxey
King Orry's Grave
St Patrick's Isle
Peel
Castle
487
MAN
Ballalheannagh
Laxey Head
Old
Laxey
Peel
Corrins Folly
COLDEN
479
Millennium
Way
B12
Laxey
Bay
Contrary Head
A20
SLIEAU RUY
8
B12
A1
Tynwald Hill
Patrick
A30
B22
Cregny Baa
Baldrine
St John's
Greeba
A18
Clay Head
A27
Glen Maye
Crosby
Glen
Vine
Baldwin
Manx Electric Railway
Cloven Stones
Waterfall
A1
B35
Strang
B21
B20
A2
Niarbyl
Dalby
Foxdale
Eairy
Union Mills
Onchan
A11
Groudle Glen
Railway
Belfast
Lower
Foxdale
A24
Norse
Houses
B32
Onchan Head
(Seasonal)
Niarbyl Bay
A27
16
A36
B36
B35
Cronkbourne
DOUGLAS
483
Braaid
A24
Douglas Bay
Heysham
Round
Table
SOUTH
BARRULE
Closeclark
Brough
Fort
A37
(Mar-Nov)
437
B39
St Marks
Douglas
Head
(Nov-Mar)
Liverpool
CRONK NY
ARREY LAA
Ballamodha
B41
Millennium
Way
A25
A5
B23
Fleshwick
Bay
B29
Santon
Ballakelly
Port Soderick
(Seasonal)
Birkenhead
Grenaby
A26
Isle of Man
Steam Railway
Santon Head
Ballakilpheric
A27
Silverdale Glen
Cronk ny
Merrieu
Dublin
Milners Tower
Colby
Ballabeg
Rushen
Abbey
Ballasalla
B53
Bradda Head
A7
Port Erin
Marine Interpretation
Centre
Howe
Meayll
Circle
Port
St Mary
Castletown
Isle of Man (Ronaldsway)
Derbyhaven
CALF OF
MAN
The Sound
A31
Cregneash
Close ny
Chollagh
Scarlett
Hango
Hill
Derby Fort
Spanish
Head
Scarlett
Point
Castletown
Bay
Herring Tower
Caigher
Point
Dreswick Point

Manx Heritage site

G   H   J   K   L

LAKE DISTRICT

Eskdale

St Bees   H
**Egremont**   J
Wilton
164
Florence Mine
Carleton
Coulderton
Middletown
Haile
Nethertown
Blackbeck
Beckermet
Calder Bridge
Braystones
Ponsonby
R Ehen
Sellafield
Visitor
Centre
Cross
Wellington
Calder
B5343
Gosforth
Santon
Santon Bridge
Seascale
Hallsenna Moor
Drigg   Holmrook
Muncaster
Mill
13
Saltcoats
Ravenglass
Roman
Bath
House
Muncaster
A595
Newbiggin
Broad Oak
Lane End
Waberthwaite
573
WHITFELL
Corney
Loganbeck
Beckfoot
Lower
Hawthwaite
Duddon
Bridge
Hycemoor
Selker Bay
Hyton
Bootle
Swinside Stone Circle
Annaside
600
BLACK
COMBE
Hallthwaites
Lady
Hall
Foxfiel
A595
Gutterby Spa
Whitbeck
The Green
Arnaby
Bridge End
Whicham
11
Silecroft
8
A5093
The Hill
Sand Side
Soutergate
Kirksanton
156
Millom
Steel Green
Borwick
Rails
RSPB
Haverigg
Haverigg
Point
Askam
in Furness
Sandscale Haws
North Walney
Dalto
in Fu
146
Hawcoat
BARROW-
IN-FURNESS
Furness
Abbey
North Scale
Vickerstown

PILLAR
HAYCOCK   L
Wasdale
Head
KIRK
FELL
GREAT
BLE   1
SEATALLAN   NAT
691
978
964   SCAFE
SCAFELL   SCAFELL PIKE
Nether
Wasdale
R Irt
Wast Water
Burnmoor
Tarn
156
Eskdale
Green
Boot   3
Beckfoot
Hardknott
Fort   Hard
Pa
652
HARTER
FELL
Ravenglass
and Eskdale
Railway
ESKDALE
River Esk
Devoke
Water
LAKE DISTRICT   Hall
Dunnerdale
NATIONAL   Ulpha   4
PARK
Broughton
Mills
5
Brou
2

Worm Gill
River Bleng

Wordsworth
0   1   2   3   4   5 miles
0   1   2   3   4   5   6   7   8 kilometres

G   H   J   K   1   M
7
8

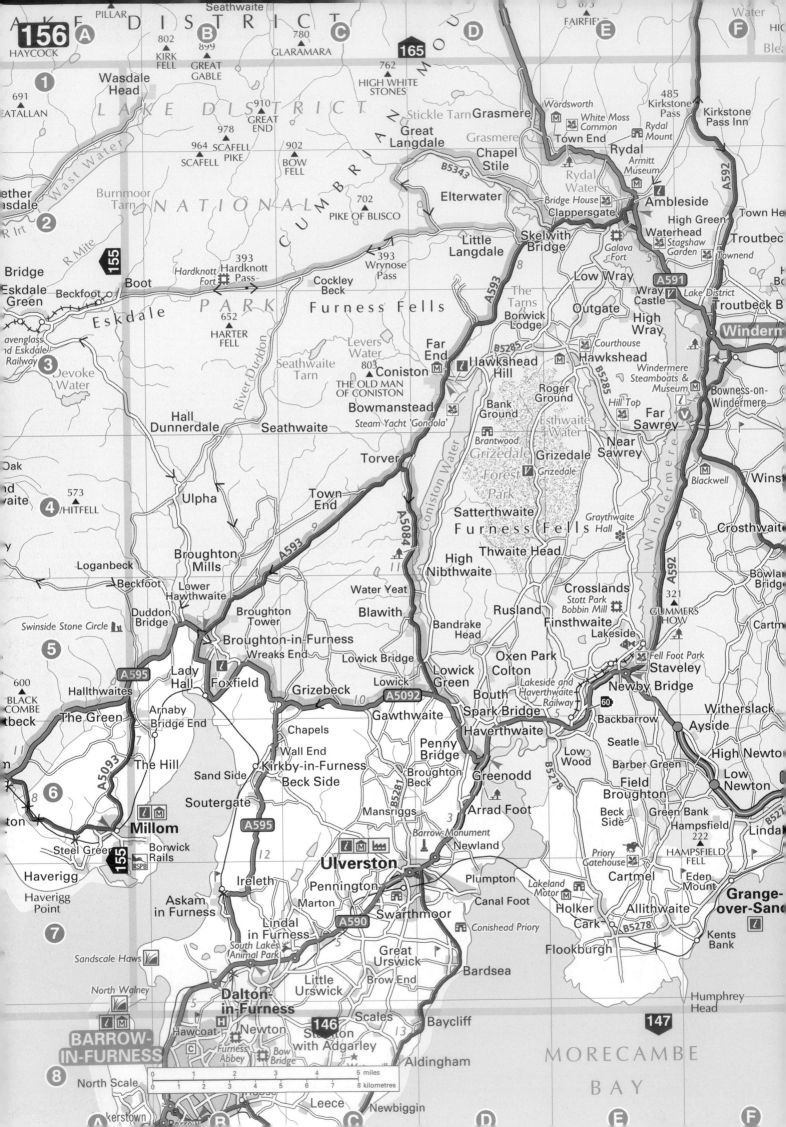

G
H
J
K

316
Shap Summit

166

Great Asby Scar

1
Crosby Garret
Wait

A6

15

6

B6261

Orton

412
387
GRANGE SCAR

Little Asby

Smardale

Smardale Gill

ntmere servoir

663
TARN CRAG

Sadgill

Green Quarter

Crookdale Beck

Borrow Beck

Greenholme
Bretherdale Head

Junction 38 Truckstop

Tebay

38

Old Tebay

R Lune
Kelleth

Brownber

Coldbeck

A685

Sunbiggin
Raisbeck

Gaisgill

Newbiggin-on-Lune

2

Raven oned

Weasdale

Long Sleddale

60

A6

A685

Low Borrowbridge

Langdale

Bowderdale Beck

158

River Kent

Staveley

Garnett Bridge

Selside
Watchgate

Lowgill

Beck Foot

9

Cautley Spout (Waterfall)

677
THE CALF

Cross Keys Temperance Inn

14

River Rawthey

70

3

WILD BO

Bowston

Garth Row

Grayrigg

12

Burneside

Meal Bank

A591

A685

M6

37

Firbank

B6257

WINDER
473

National Park Centre

V

Sedbergh

676

4

Crook
Plumgarths

A5284

2

Kendal

Castle Green

A684

New Hutton

Killington Lake (southbound only)

5

Millthrop

A684

Garsdale

Garso

Underbarrow

30

A6

217

4
40

Oxenholme

Garths

B6254

Middleshaw

8

Killington

Hallbeck

60

Gawthrop

556

Garso

Brigsteer

Natland

Old Hutton
Halfpenny

Beckside

11

Dent

A5074

A591

Sizergh Castle

Cotes

Homescales

Summerlands

Middleton

609
CALF TOP

Deepdale

5

owgill

Causeway End

Levens

Sedgwick
Stainton

Gatebeck

B6254

A683

686
CRAGHILL

Leasgill

60

Hincaster

A590

Westmorland

Crooklands

Endmoor
Preston Patrick

Rigmadon Park

Old Town

Barbon

6

WHERNSIDE

Heversham

Levens Hall

Milnthorpe

36

Milness

284

Nook
Lupton

Mansergh

Ribblehead Viaduct

B5282

Whasset

Farleton

Underley Hall

Kearstwick

40

Casterton

Chapel le Dale

Ulpha
hop

River Kent

Sandside

Beetham

A6070

Holme Park Fell

Hutton Roof

High Biggins

Kirkby Lonsdale

High Casterton

158

Storth
Slack Head

Holme

Clawthorpe

Park Wood

Low Biggins

Cowan Bridge

Leck

White Scar Caves

723

Hale

Lakeland Wildlife Oasis

Burton-in-Kendal

Dalton

Whittington

Ireby

Masongill

Skirwith

INGLEBOROUGH HILL

Yealand Storrs

Yealand Redmayne

Leighton Hall

Burton-in-Kendal (northbound only)

Priest Hutton

Newton

Overtown
Burrow

Westhouse

Thornton in Lonsdale

Ingleton

SIDE OTT

Silverdale Green

Yealand Conyers

Crag Foot

Truckhaven

Docker

A683

Tunstall

Cantsfield

Burton in Lonsdale

Ingleboro

Heald Brow

Warton

Old Rectory

Borwick

147

142

Arkholme

14

Wrayton

A687

148

Cold Cotes

8

Newby

Millhead

Carnforth

35A

35

30

A6

Over Kellet

Capernwray

B6254

Gressingham

Melling

Wennington

Tatham

Low Bentham

High Bentham

A65

Nether Kell

e Sa

G
H
J
K
L
M

Clap

B5254

Hornby

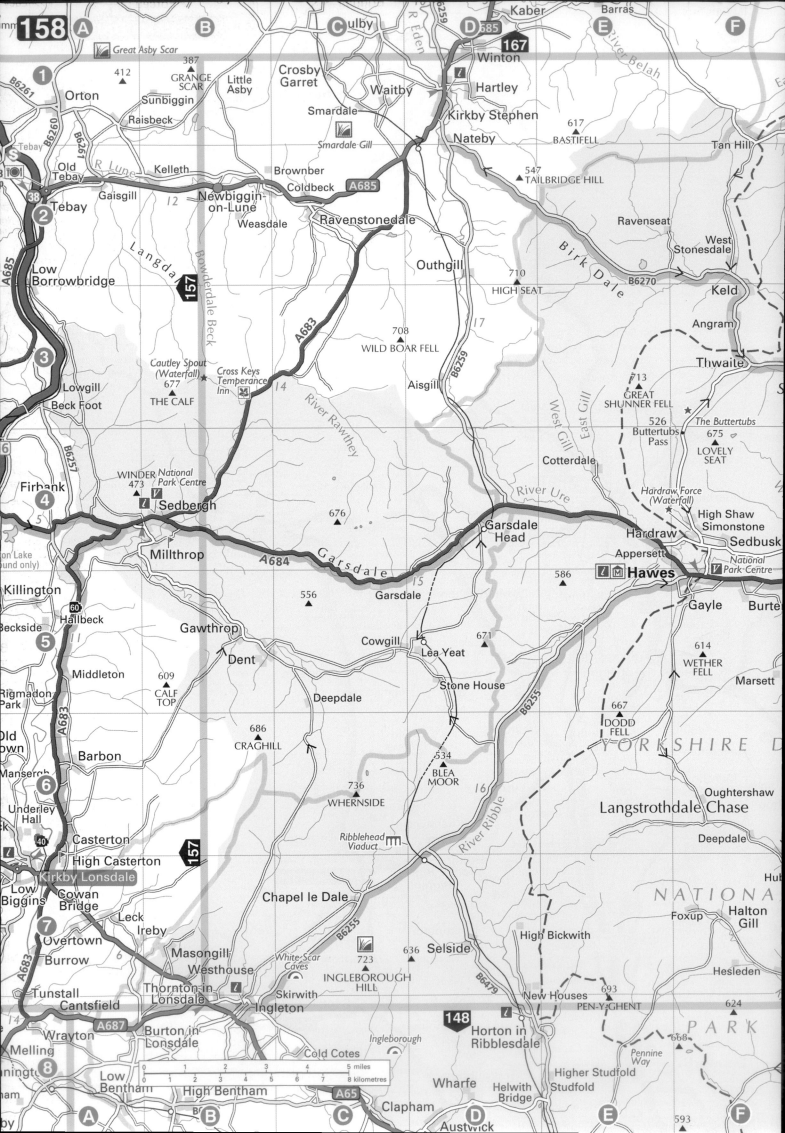

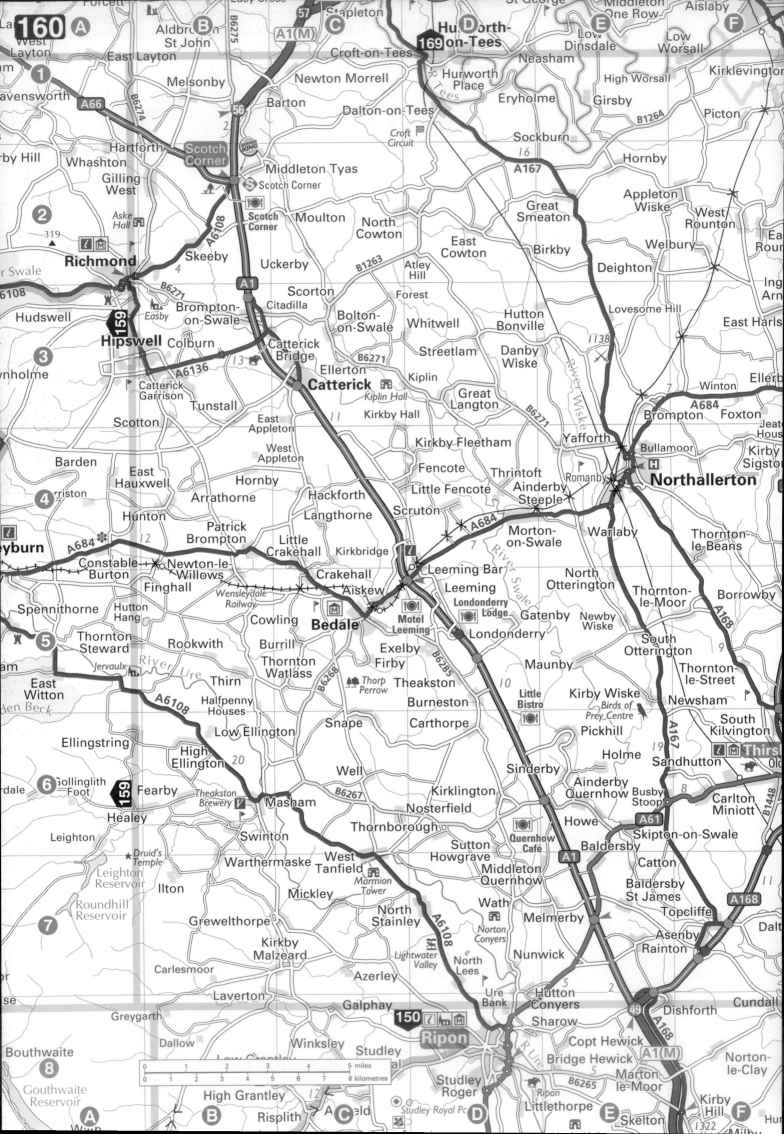

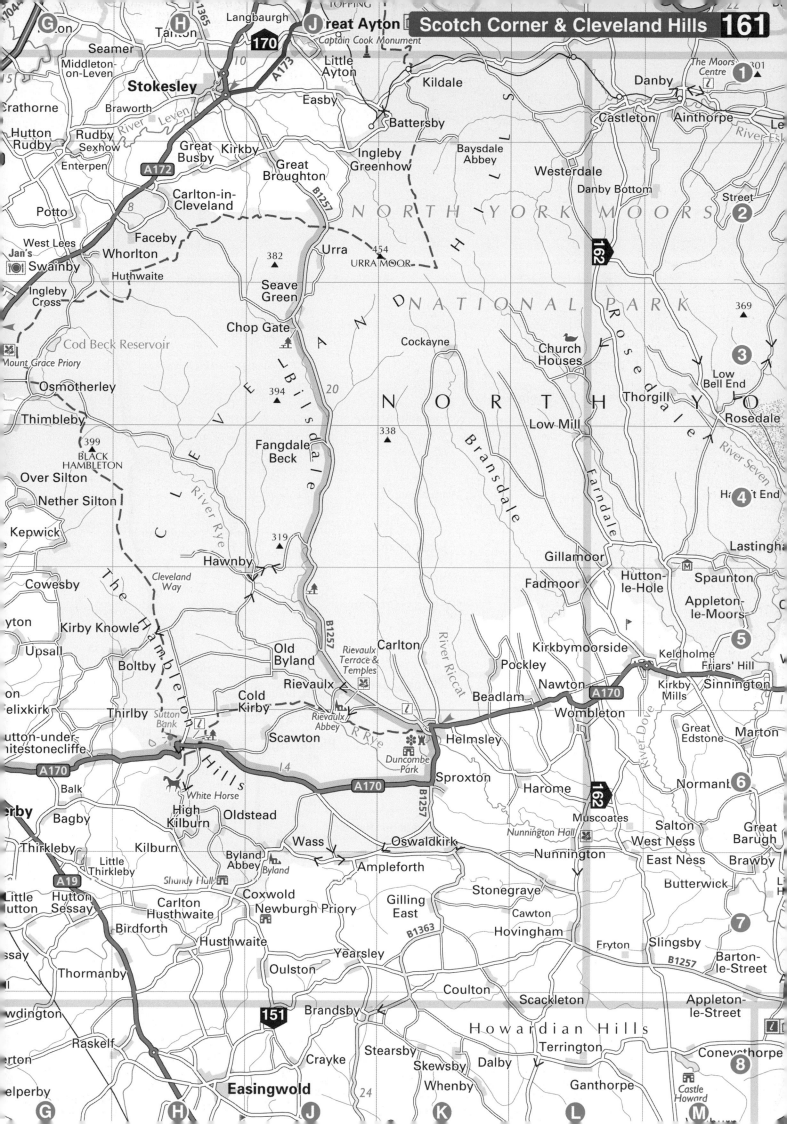

G    H    J **reat Ayton**

Langbaurgh

TOPPING

*Captain Cook Monument*

170    10

Tanton

Seamer

Middleton-on-Leven

15    **Stokesley**

Crathorne    Braworth

Hutton    Rudby    Sexhow
Rudby

Enterpen

Potto

West Lees

Jan's    Swainby

A172

Great
Busby    Kirkby

Carlton-in-
Cleveland

Faceby

Whorlton

Huthwaite

Ingleby
Cross

Little
Ayton

Easby

Battersby

Ingleby
Greenhow

Great
Broughton

B1257

Urra    454
382    URRA MOOR

Seave
Green

Kildale

Baysdale
Abbey

**NORTH YORK MOORS**

Westerdale

Danby Bottom

The Moors
Centre    1

Danby

Castleton    Ainthorpe    Le

River Esk

Street    2

162

Cod Beck Reservoir

Mount Grace Priory

Osmotherley

Thimbleby

399
BLACK
HAMBLETON

Over Silton

Nether Silton

Kepwick

Cowesby

...yton

Upsall

Kirby Knowle

Boltby

Thirlby    *Sutton
Bank*

...on
...elixkirk

Chop Gate

394

Fangdale
Beck

River Rye

319

Hawnby

*Cleveland
Way*

Old
Byland

Cold
Kirby

Cockayne

Church
Houses

338

N O R T H

Bransdale

Low Mill

B1257

Rievaulx
Terrace &
Temples

Rievaulx

Carlton

River Riccal

A I O N A L    P A R K

Rosedale

369    3

Low
Bell End

Thorgill

Low Mill

Gillamoor

Fadmoor

Kirkbymoorside

Pockley

Friars' Hill

Hutton-
le-Hole

Spaunton

Appleton-
le-Moors

Keldholme    Kirkby
Mills    Sinnington

...utton-under-
...itestonecliffe

A170

Scawton

Rievaulx
Abbey

R Rye

Duncombe
Park

Helmsley

Sproxton

A170

Nawton

Beadlam

Wombleton

A170

Marton

Great
Edstone

Normanb...    6

Hills

White Horse

14

A170

Balk

...by

Bagby

Thirkleby

High
Kilburn    Oldstead

Wass

Harome

162

Muscoates

Nunnington Hall

Salton

West Ness

Great
Barugh

A19

Little
Thirkleby

Hutton
Sessay

...ay

Kilburn

Byland
Abbey    Byland

*Shandy Hall*

Oswaldkirk

Ampleforth

Nunnington

East Ness

Butterwick

Brawby

Li...

Coxwold

Carlton
Husthwaite

Birdforth

Husthwaite

Newburgh Priory

Gilling
East

Stonegrave

Cawton

Hovingham

Fryton

Slingsby

B1257

Barton-
le-Street

Thormanby

...ssy

Yearsley

Oulston

B1363

Coulton

Scackleton

Appleton-
le-Street

Brandsby

151

Stearsby

Crayke

Skewsby    Dalby

Whenby    Ganthorpe

**H o w a r d i a n    H i l l s**

Terrington

*Castle
Howard*

Conev...horpe

8

**Easingwold**

...wdington

Raskelf

...rton

...elperby

G    H    J    K    L    M

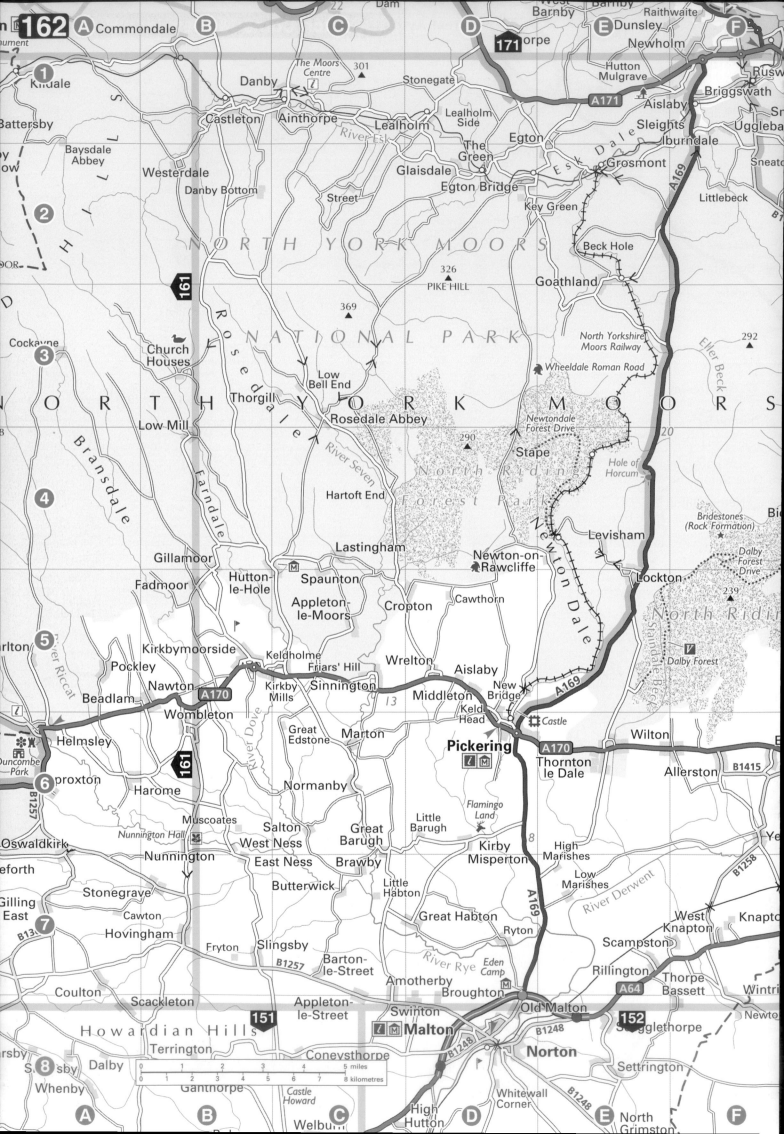

G H J

1
2
3
4
5
6
7
8

bby
G rick Bay
ainsacre
High Hawsker
B1447
w sker
Raw
Fylingthorpe
Ness Point or North Cheek
Robin Hood's Bay
Robin Hood's Bay
Old Peak or South Cheek
171
Ravenscar
20
Harwood Dale
Staintondale
Shire Horse Centre
Hayburn Wyke
Cloughton Newlands
Cloughton Wyke
Broxa
Silpho
Suffield
Cloughton
A165
Cromer Point
Burniston
Cleveland Way
Langdale End
Hackness
Newby
Scalby
Scarborough
Wrench Green
Everley
Castle
Falsgrave
Hatherleigh Deep Sea Trawler
est Park
River Derwent
Sea Cut
A171
H
C
P+R
A170
Oliver's Mount
Bee Dale
West Ayton
East Ayton
A165
Sawdon
Irton
Eastfield
P+R
Osgodby
Cayton Bay
Hutton Buscel
Seamer
Crossgates
High Killerby
The Wyke
Ruston
Wykeham
B1261
7
Cayton
7
Snainton
Brompton
B1261
Lebberston
Filey Brigg
A1039
6
Gristhorpe
A64
R-Hertford
Filey
Folkton
A1039
Muston
Willerby
West Flotmanby
Flixton
7
Filey Bay
Staxton
Yorkshire Wolds Way
Hunmanby
16
Sherburn
Ganton
Flamborough Head Heritage Coast
East Heslerton
Potter Brompton
Fordon
Reighton
Speeton
Bempton Cliffs
RSPB
Foxholes
Wold Newton
153
Burton Fleming
Buckton
Bempton
B1229
Butterwick
B1249
Grindale
A165
Helperthorpe
est tton
Weaverthorpe
Octon
Thwing
B1255
East Lutton
H
J
K
L
erby
M
14

G H J K

Abbey Town
Raby
Drumleaning
Thornby
Whinnow
Baldwinholme
Brisco
Holm Cultram
Kelsick
Oulton
Lessonhall
Dockray
Micklethwaite
Crofton
Thursby
Cardew
Dalston
Cotehill
177
596
Dundraw
Moor Row
Aikhead
East Curthwaite
Green Head
Buckabank
Ratten Row
Burthwaite
1
Wheyrigg
Blencogo
Waverbridge
Waverton
Wigton
Highmoor
West Curthwaite
Cumdivock
Hawksdale
Bridge End
Unthank
Raughton
Sceugh
Wreay
Foulbridge
Low Hesket
field
B5302
Howrigg
Gaitsgill
Mellguards
Southwa
High Scales
Low Row
Bolton Low Houses
Red Dial
Brackenthwaite
Rosley
Welton
Raughton Head
Nether Welton
Skiprigg
Stockdalewath
Burger King
S
Southwaite
i
A595
18
B5305
Grassgarth
Thethwaite
Low Braithwaite
2
Watchill
Crookdake
Westward
Sebergham
Ivegill
Middlesceugh
13
M6
Baggrow
Blennerhasset
Mealsgate
Bolton New Houses
343
FAULDS BROW
Ratten Row
Caldbeck
Newlands
Southernby
Sowerby Row
B5305
Ivegill
Thomas Close
Morton
166
Kirkland Guards
Torpenhow
Boltongate
Sandale
Whelpo
Upton
Hesket Newmarket
Hutton End
3
reapland
Bothel
Whitrigg
Ireby
B5299
Fell Side
Nether Row
Millhouse
Haltcliff Bridge
Lamonby
Unthank
land
A591
High Ireby
Uldale
Aughertree
Branthwaite
Longlands
Low Row
High Row
Ellonby
Skelton
New
Sunderland
Bewaldeth
447
BINSEY
663
CARROCK FELL
Hutton Roof
Little Blencow
Ca
13
Trotters World of Animals
High Bewaldeth
Kilnhill
Orthwaite
710
KNOTT
Johnby
Great Blencow
4
R Derwent
B5291
North Row
Bassenthwaite
Chapel
690
GREAT CALVA
Mosedale
Bowscale
357
BERRIER HILL
Greystoke
Laith
Embleton
High Side
703
BOWSCALE FELL
Mungrisdale
Gill
Wythop Mill
Scarness
931
SKIDDAW
Berrier
Motherby
Newbigg
92
Mirehouse
Little Crosthwaite
868
SADDLEBACK
Scales
17
Tarn Moss
Penruddock
A66
S
13
552
LORDS SEAT
A66
Millbeck
Applethwaite
Threlkeld
Wallthwaite
Troutbeck
Hutton Sparket
Dac
aside
Thornthwaite
Whinlatter
V
Great Crosthwaite
Ormathwaite
367
LATRIGG R Greta
Quarry and Mining
A5091
Thackthwaite
536
GREAT MELL FELL
506
Bennet Head
Soulby
High orton
318
Whinlatter Pass
Braithwaite
Portinscale
Briery
Matterdale End
Thornythwaite
LITTLE MELL FELL
Longthwaite
Wreay
Grisedale Pike
Swinside
Keswick
Brigham
Castlerigg Stone Circle
B5322
Matterdale End
High Row
Ulcat Row
Dockray
Watermi
790
770
HOBCARTON PIKE
Stair
Dale Bottom
Fornside
856
GREAT DODD
Aira Force
6
851
GRASMOOR
Little Town
Derwent Water
Borrowdale
A591
840
STYBARROW DODD
Sandwick
Howtown
Martindale
STRICT
Grange
Lodore Falls
608
HIGH SEAT
Legburthwaite
Glenridding
657
PLACE FELL
671
LOADPOT HILL
mere
Hassness
Gatesgarth
DALE HEAD
754
356
Bowder Stone
Watendlath
27
Thirlmere
Patterdale
7
806
HIGH STILE
B5289
Honister Pass
Rosthwaite
Borrowdale
Stonethwaite
Seatoller
17
950
HELVELLYN
Wythburn
Brothers Water
Bridgend
Hartsop
803
HIGH RAISE
L
892
PILLAR
Seathwaite
Grisdale Tarn
873
FAIRFIELD
Hayes Water
817
HIGH STREET
8
802
KIRK FELL
899
GREAT GABLE
780
GLARAMARA
762
HIGH WHITE STC
Blea Wate
Wasdale He
DISTRICT
156

G H J K L M Kentmere

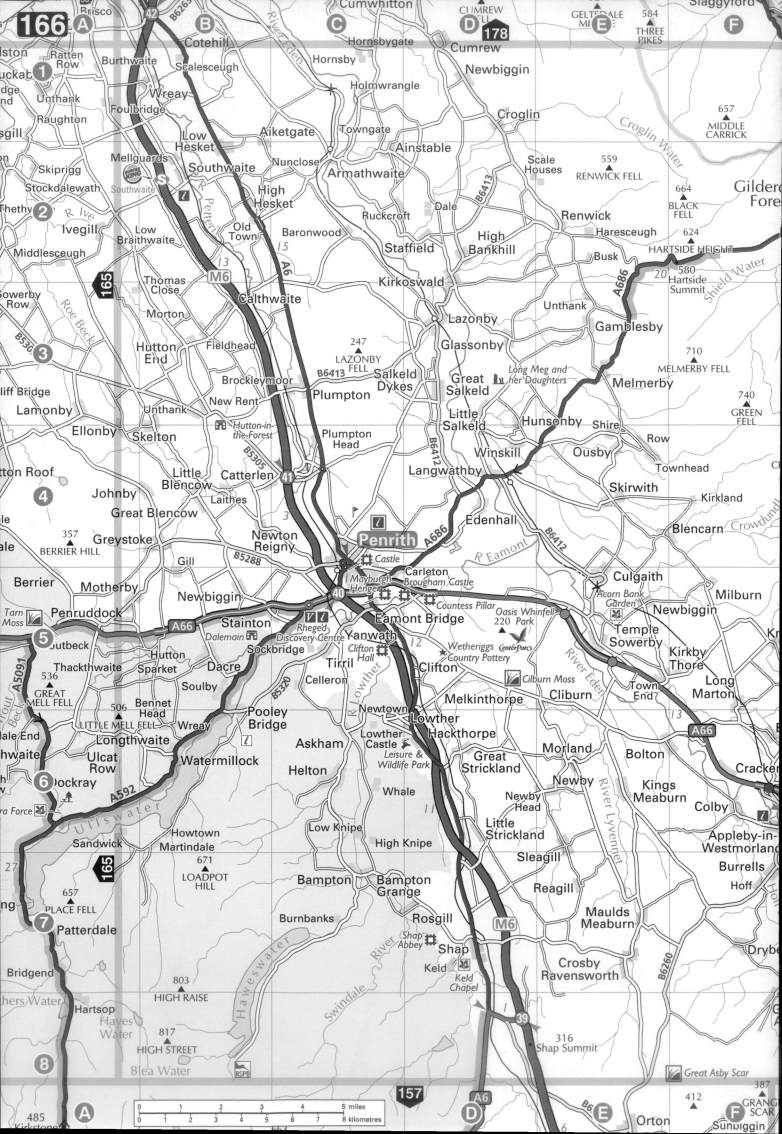

G  H  179  J  Sinderhope  K  HANGMAN HILL

Dianemund

khaugh
Ayle
Keirsley Row
Limestone Brae
R West Allen
R East Allen
B6295
River Derwent
Baybridge
Edmund
1

South Tynedale Railway
Blagill
B6294
Alston
Nenthall
Carr Shield
572 HARTLEY MOOR
Spartylea
Dirt Pot
Allenheads
478 NOOKTON FELL
Hunstanworth
Ramshaw
540 BOLT'S LAW
2

aise
Nenthead
20 A689
627 Killhope Summit
Killhope Lead Mining Centre
Lanehead
Cornriggs
Cowshill
Wearhead
Rookhope Burn
Rookhope
B6278
C
Crawleyside
Sta
3

Garrigill
B6277
R South Tyne
747 BURNHOPE SEAT
Ireshopeburn
St John's Chapel
Daddry Shield
Weardale
Westgate
Eastgate A689
Brotherlee
Bri

22
Moor House
Milburn Forest
847
EAT DUN FELL
Trout Beck
Harwood
Cow Green Reservoir
Langdon Beck
Forest-in-Teesdale
Ettersgill
559 BLACK HILL
653 OUTBERRY PLAIN
Bollihope Burn
4

601 CARRS HILL

Dufton Fell
Cauldron Snout (Waterfall)
River Tees
B6271
High Force (Waterfall)
Newbiggin
B6278
5

481
TON PIKE
ton
Pennine Way
Maize Beck
672 MURTON FELL
Upper Teesdale
Holwick
Middleton-in-Teesdale
Tees

Keisley
n
790 MICKLE FELL
618
Bowbank
Thringarth
Mickleton
B6282
Hill
B6281
6

746 HILTON FELL
Fish Loch
Grassholme Reservoir
Romaldkirk

Murton
Hilton
Lune Forest
B6276
Selset Reservoir
Hunderthwaite
Hury
West Briscoe
East Briscoe
Larting

on
Great Ormside
Eden Valley Railway
Sandford
8
562 IRON BAND
Balderhead Reservoir
168
Deepdale Beck
7

ttle side
Warcop
A66
Hillbeck
North Stainmore
478 BELDOO HILL
13 A66
Bow
Gilm

Bleatarn
Great Musgrave
Little Musgrave
Castle
Church Brough
Brough
Brough Sowerby
Kaber
Barras
Argill Beck
The Otter Trust
Stainmore Forest
8

Soulby
B6259
R Eden
5
A685
Winton
158
Hartley
River Belah
Ease Gill
Sleightholme
Eller B

Crosby et
Waitby
G  H  J  K  L  M

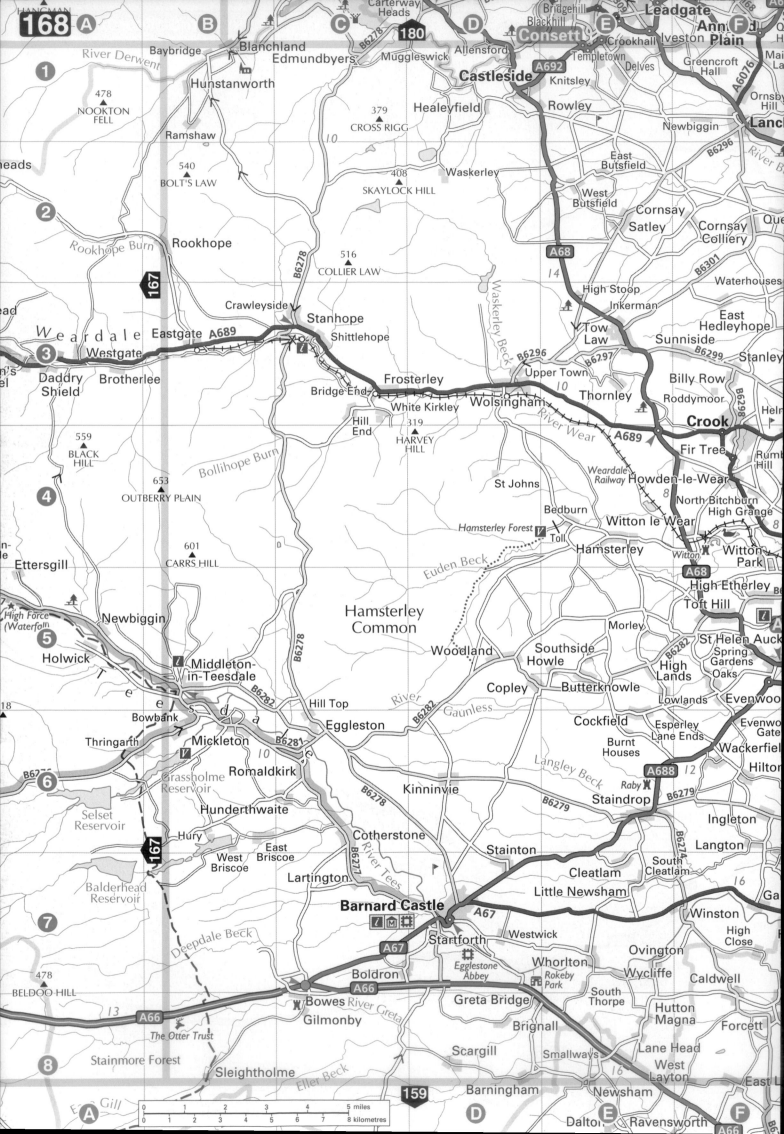

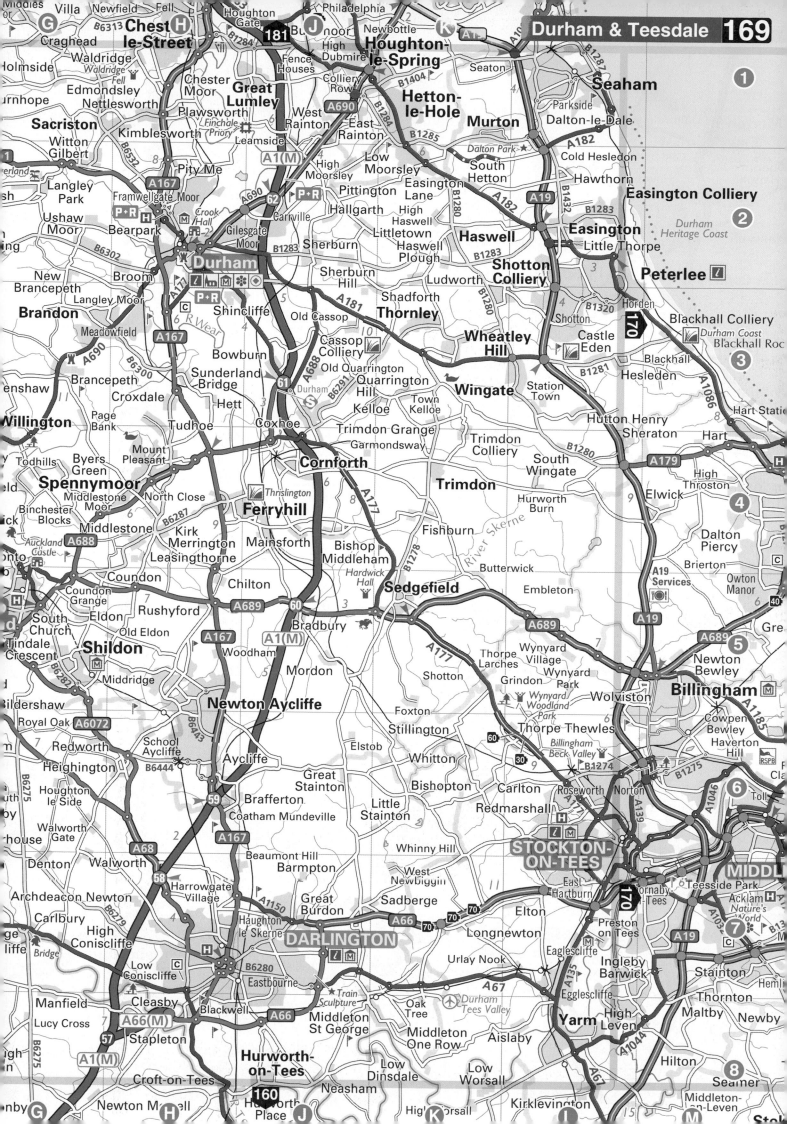

G          H          J

1

2

3

4

5

6

agglers,
Brotton
Hummersea Scar
Carlin
How          Skinningrove
Upton          Boulby
Loftus          Staithes
Daléhouse          Heritage Centre
n          Liverton          Easington          16          Port Mulgrave
rpe          Mines          Hinderwell          Runswick          North Yorkshire and
e          Roxby          Newton          Bay          Cleveland Heritage Coast
n          Handale          Mulgrave          Runswick
Borrowby          Kettleness          Goldsborough          7
holm          Scaling          Ellerby          Overdale
          B1266          Wyke
Gerrick          Scaling          Mickleby          A174          Lythe
          Dam          West          East          Sandsend          Sandsend
          Barnby          Barnby          Raithwaite          Wyke
          Dunsley          Whitby
          Ugthorpe          Newholm          Abbey          Saltwick
The Moors          301          Bay
Centre          Hutton          Rusward
Stone          Mulgrave          8
G          H          162          J          K          St          L          acre          M

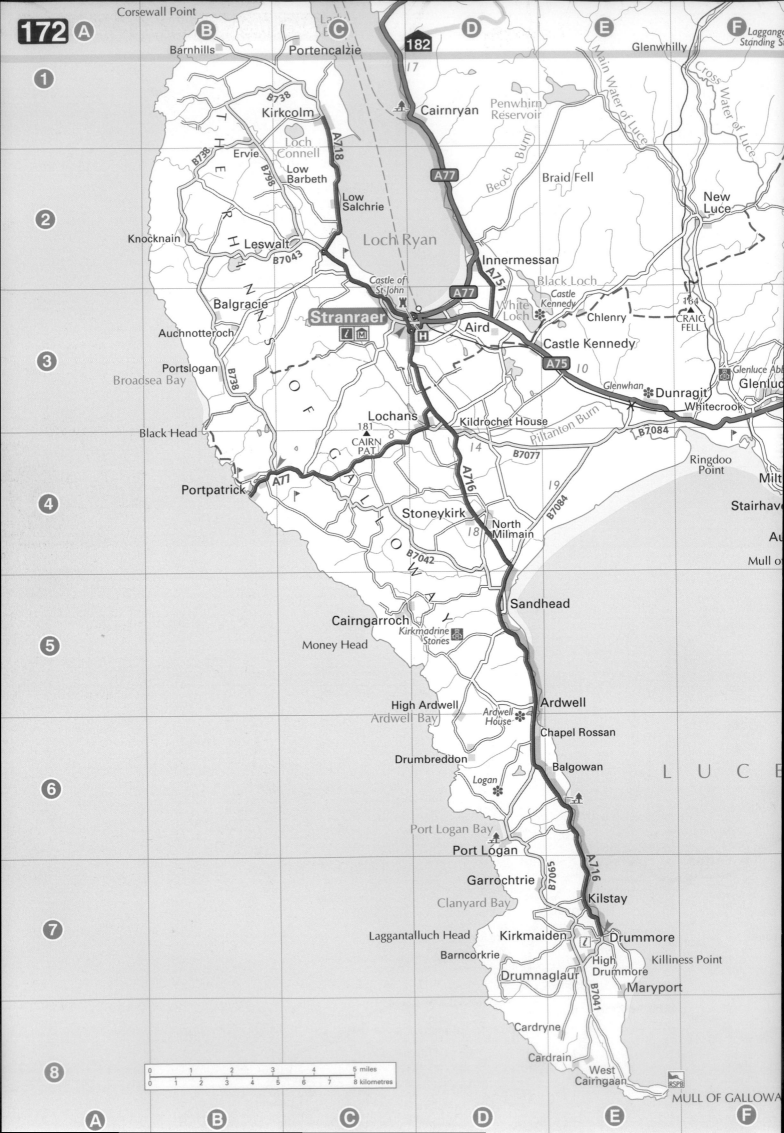

Corsewall Point

Barnhills

Portencalzie

**182**

Glenwhilly

Laggang
Standing S

Kirkcolm

B738

Ervie

B798

Low
Barbeth

Cairnryan

Penwhirm
Reservoir

Braid Fell

New
Luce

A77

Knocknain

Leswalt

B7043

Low
Salchrie

Loch Ryan

Innermessan

Black Loch

Castle
Kennedy

White
Loch

Chlenry

CRAIG
FELL

164

Loch
Connell

Balgracie

Castle of
St John

**Stranraer**

Aird

Castle Kennedy

A77

A751

Auchnotteroch

Portslogan

B738

Broadsea Bay

A75

10

Glenwhan

Dunragit

Glenluce Abb

Glenluc

Whitecrook

Black Head

Lochans

181

CAIRN
PAT

8

Kildrochet House

Piltanton Burn

B7084

Ringdoo
Point

Milt

Portpatrick

A71

Stoneykirk

14

B7077

A716

19

B7084

Stairhav

Au

18

North
Milmain

Mull o

B7042

Sandhead

Cairngarroch

Kirkmadrine
Stones

Money Head

Ardwell
Bay

High Ardwell

Ardwell
House

Ardwell

Chapel Rossan

Balgowan

L U C E

Drumbreddon

Logan

Port Logan Bay

Port Logan

B7065

Garrochtrie

Clanyard Bay

A716

Kilstay

Laggantalluch Head

Barncorkrie

Kirkmaiden

Drummore

Killiness Point

High
Drummore

Maryport

Drumnaglaur

B7041

Cardryne

Cardrain

West
Cairngaan

RSPB

MULL OF GALLOWA

| 0 | 1 | 2 | 3 | 4 | 5 miles |
| 0 | 1 | 2 | 3 | 4 | 5 | 6 | 7 | 8 kilometres |

G H J K L M

1
2
3
4
5
6
7
8

GALLOWAY

Knowe 183

River Bladnoch

Black Burn

184 ▲ URRALL FELL

271 ▲ ARTFIELD FELL

Carseriggan

Challoch

Penkill Burn

R. Cree

RSPB

Minnigaff

710 ▲ CAIRNSMORE OF FLEET

Barfad

214 ▲ CULVENNAN FELL

Loch Ronald

Newton Stewart

Creebridge

Kirroughtree

Grani

Big

Shennanton

A714

Tarf Water

15

B733 B735

Palnure

A75

A747

Craighlaw

Kirkcowan

Baltersan

174

Dernaglar Loch

A75

B733

R Bladnoch

Causeway End

Gem Rock

Creetown

Fell Loch

Clugston

B7052

Torhouse Stone Circle

18

Kirkmabreck

Castle Loch

THE

B7005

Wigtown

Bladnoch

Carsluith

CAIRN

Cairnholy Chambered Cairn

Carsluith Castle

Mochrum Loch

MACHARS

Kirwaugh

Braehead

Orchardton Bay

Ravenshall Point

Ig

Water of Malzie

B7005

Kirkinner

B7052

B7085

Whauphill

11

B7004

Culscadden

Auchenmalg Bay

Chapel Finian (ruin)

Culshabbin

Barrachan

Little Airies

A746

5

Wig

A747

13

Elrig

Druchtag Motte

B7085

Sorbie

B7052

Pouton

Garlieston

Cruggleton Bay

Mochrum

Drumtrodden Cup & Ring

Drumtrodden Standing Stones

Drummoddie

Broughton Mains

B7004

B7063

Port William

Big Balcraig

174

Priory

'Wren's Egg' Standing Stones

B7021

BAY

Barsalloch Fort

Monreith

Whithorn Story

Barsalloch Point

Point of Leg

A747

10

Rispain Camp

A746

Whithorn

Portyerrock

St Ninian's Cave

Kidsdale

B7004

Isle of Whithorn

St Ninian's Chapel (ruin)

Cutcloy

BURROW HEAD

G H J K L M

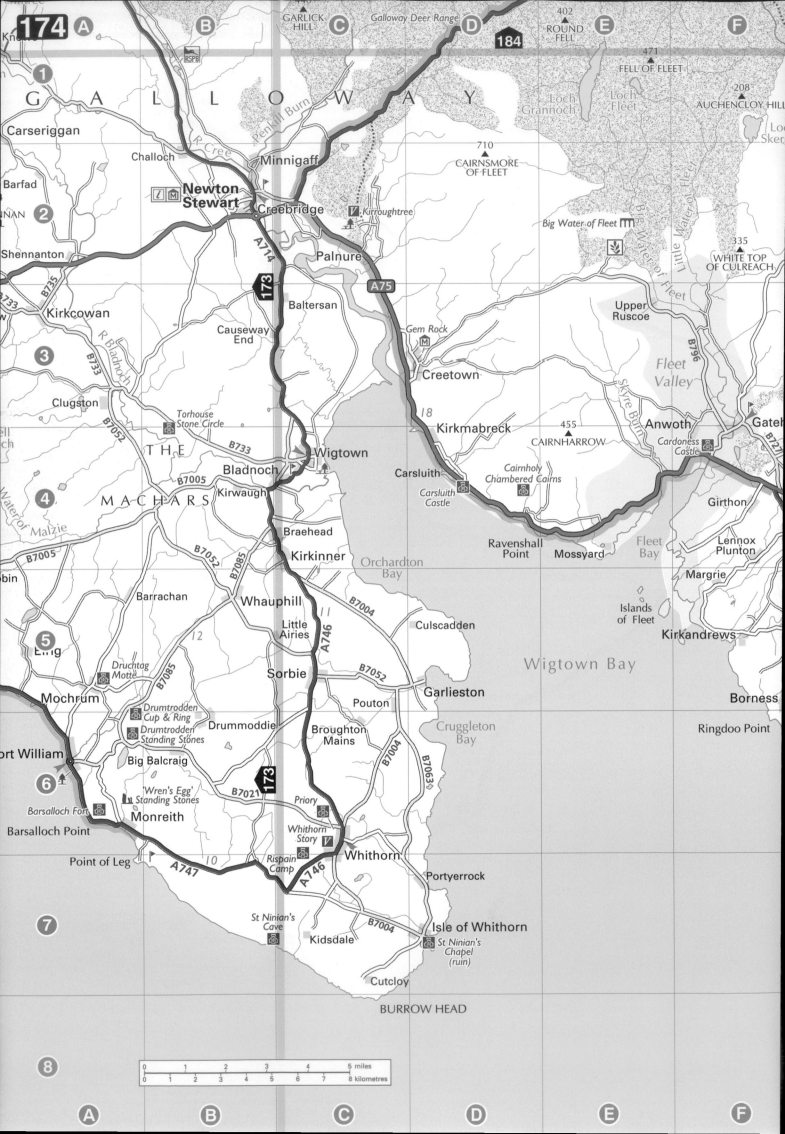

**A** **B** **C** **D** **E** **F**

**1**
GALLOWAY

Knowe
Carseriggan
Challoch
RSPB
Barfad
Minnigaff
GARLICK HILL
Galloway Deer Range
184
ROUND FELL 402
FELL OF FLEET 471

**2**
Newton Stewart
Creebridge
NAN
Penkill Burn
R Cree
Kirroughtree
Cairnsmore of Fleet 710
Loch Grannoch
Loch Fleet
AUCHENCLOY HILL 208
Loch Sker

Shennanton
B735
B733
A714
173
Palnure
A75
Baltersan
Big Water of Fleet
WHITE TOP OF CULREACH 335

**3**
Kirkcowan
B733
R Bladnoch
Clugston
B7052
Causeway End
Gem Rock
Creetown
Upper Ruscoe
B796
Fleet Valley

**4**
THE
Torhouse Stone Circle
B733
Wigtown
Bladnoch
B7005
Kirwaugh
18
Kirkmabreck
Carsluith
Carsluith Castle
Cairnholy Chambered Cairns
CAIRNHARROW 455
Skyre Burn
Anwoth
Cardoness Castle
Gate
B7217
Girthon

**5**
Waterof Malzie
B7005
MACHARS
B7052
B7085
Braehead
Kirkinner
Orchardton Bay
B7004
Barrachan
Whauphill
11
Little Airies
A746
Culscadden
Ravenshall Point
Mossyard
Fleet Bay
Lennox Plunton
Margrie
Islands of Fleet
Kirkandrews

Elrig
12
Druchtag Motte
B7085
Sorbie
B7052
Garlieston
Wigtown Bay
Borness

**6**
Mochrum
Drumtrodden Cup & Ring
Drumtrodden Standing Stones
Drummoddie
Pouton
Broughton Mains
B7004
B7063
Cruggleton Bay
Ringdoo Point

ort William
Big Balcraig
'Wren's Egg' Standing Stones
B7021
173
Priory
Barsalloch Fort
Monreith
Whithorn Story
Rispain Camp
A746
Whithorn

**7**
Barsalloch Point
Point of Leg
A747
10
A746
Portyerrock
St Ninian's Cave
Kidsdale
B7004
Isle of Whithorn
St Ninian's Chapel (ruin)
Cutcloy
BURROW HEAD

**8**

0    1    2    3    4    5 miles
0  1  2  3  4  5  6  7  8 kilometres

**A** **B** **C** **D** **E** **F**

G  H  J  185  B794  K  Auchel Loch  Crocketfc  1

Mossdale  A713  Airds of Kells  Knockvennie Smithy  Kirkpatrick Durham  Springholm  Milton  Drumcoltran Tower  Beeswing

Slogarie  A762  Loch Ken  16  Loch Roan  Walbutt  Old Bridge of Urr  Hardgate  Kirkgunzeon  14  Kinhar  LOTUS HILL  334  Glensone Burn

Laurieston  B795  Glenlochar  Crossmichael  Clarebrand  B795  Haugh of Urr  Redcastle  A711  Kirkgunzeon  2

Woodhall Loch  19  Townhead of Greenlaw  Hillowton  A745  B794  Edingham  430  CUIL HILL

Kirkconnell  Longwood  Threave Castle  A75  Castle Douglas  6  Little Knox  Dalbeattie  176  3

Bridge of Dee  Threave Garden  Carlingwark Loch  A711  A710  B793  8

Rhonehouse  Gelston  B736  Barlochan  Palnackie  10  Caulkerbush

Ringford  River Dee  10  Craigley  Airieland  343 SCREEL HILL  Orchardton Tower  Kippford or Scaur  Barnbarroch  Fairgirth  Drumburn  Sandyhills  RSPB  L

Twynholm  A762  A711  15  390 BENGAIRN  Mote of Mark  East Stewartry Coast  Rockcliffe  Colvend  Portling  4

A75  Tongland  B727  Little Sypland  Castlehill Point

Compstonend  Hydros Visitor Centre  Whinnie Liggate  Auchencairn  Auchencairn Bay

A755  Wildlife Park  Kirkchrist  MacLellan's Castle  Kirkcudbright  Culnaightrie  18  Balcary  Heston Island

edpark  Mutehill  Balcary Point

orgue  B727  Dundrennan  Rascarrel  5

Imangan  Kirkcudbright Bay  A711  Dundrennan Abbey  Orroland

Ross  Balmae  Netherlaw

Little Ross  Abbey Head  6

7

G  H  J  K  L  M  8

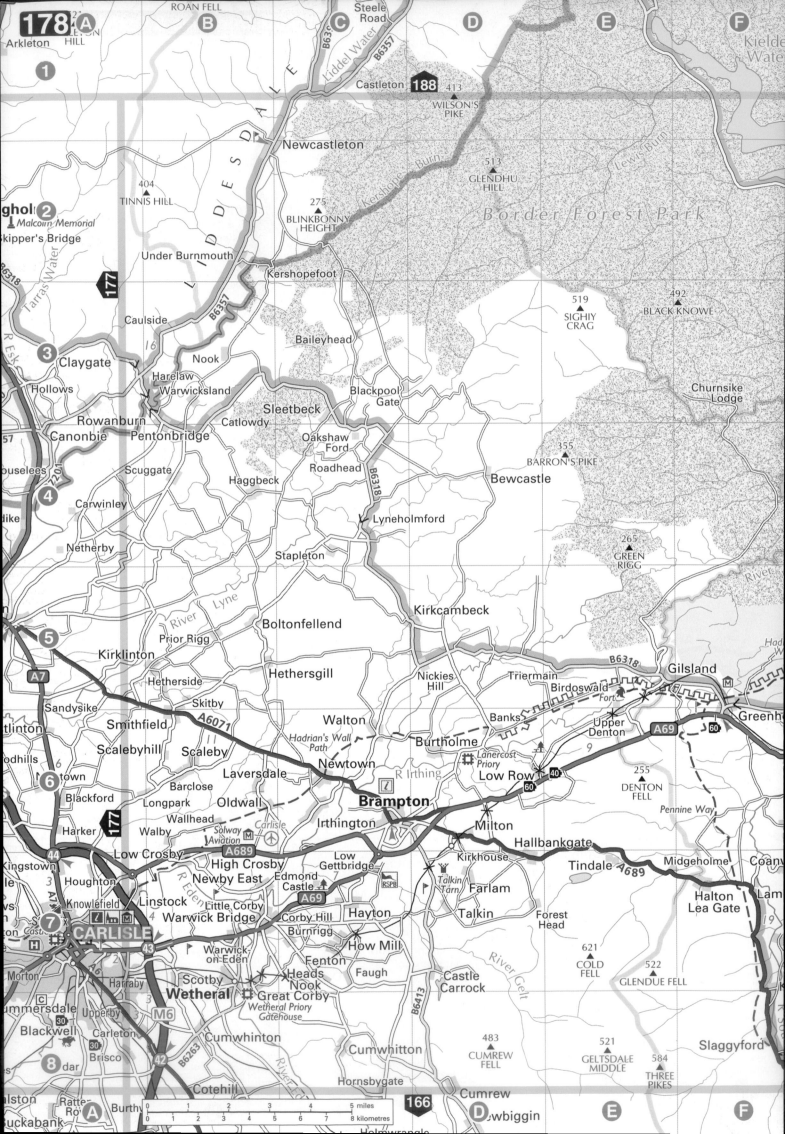

G   H   J   Troughend   K   Old Town   1

EARL SEA

Highgreen Manor

A68

190

A696

Black Middens Bastle House

189

Harwo

Gatehouse

307 ▲ WHITE HILL

West Woodburn

East Woodburn

Ray Fell

14

Falstone

Greenhaugh

Fort

Ridsdale

Kirkwhelping

2

Tower Knowe

Stannersburn

Hott

Lanehead

Charlton

180

Kirkha

15

Hesleyside

Bellingham

B6320

9

NORTHUMBERLAND

Redesmouth

Sweethope Loughs

Great Bavington

3

Chirdon Burn

NATIONAL    PARK

Birtley

Colt Craig Reservoir

Thockrington

Little Swinburne

8

Little Bavingto

325 ▲ ROUND TOP

Stonehaugh

Wark

Chipchase Castle

Gunnerton

Great Swinburne

B6342

Hallington Reservoir

Hallingt

Warks Burn

Park End

R North Tyne

A6079

Colwell

4

Black Fell

Simonburn

Nunwick

B6320

Great Swinburne

Barrasford

A68

Chollerton

4

Bingfield

Pennine Way

Carrawburgh: Temple of Mithras

Humshaugh

Chollerford

7

Wh

Greenlee Lough

Broomlee Lough

Hadrian's Wall Path

Walwick

Hadrian's Wall

Little Whitting

17

Chesters Fort

B6318

5

B6318

Grindon Hill

Wall

Fallowfield

Halton

Housesteads Fort

Newbrough

Fourstones

High Warden

Acomb

Sandhoe

Aydon Castle

Chesterholm (Vindolanda)

B6319

R South Tyne

Warden

5

Anick

Once Brewed

Birkshaw

Westend Town

Chesterwood

Haydon Bridge

Wharmley

A69

30

Oakwood

70

3

Haltwhistle

Henshaw

Westwood

Thorngrafton

Low Gate

B6531

Tyne Green

Corbridge

B6

60

Redburn

Bardon Mill

Ridley

30

Hexham

A695

Di

6

Melkridge

13

Beltingham

Elrington

Langley Castle

Warden

A695

B6306

180

Plenmeller

Deanraw

A686

Langley

B6305

West Dipton Burn

Diptonmill

Allen Banks and Staward Gorge

B6304

Juniper

Ordley

Steel

Slaley

nehouse

Wolf Hills

Whitfield

Catton

Whitley Chapel

7

Whitfield Hall

Thornley Gate

Allendale

357 ▲ DUKESFIELD FELL

B6306

Fellhouse Fell

ot

17

Ninebanks

Derwent Reservoir

A686

443 ▲ HANGMAN HILL

8

Keirsleywell Row

Sinderhope

Blanchland L

South Tynedale Railway

haugh

G   le   H   Limesto J rae   K   Spartyles   River Derwent   L   Baybridge   M   Edmund

B6295

R East

A1068
G Ellington
Linton
Lynemouth

1

A189
191 Beacon Point
Woodhorn
A197 Woodhorn Demesne
Wansbeck
Riverside
Hirst H
eepwash North M 30 **Newbiggin-by-the-Sea**
Seaton
Stakeford B1334
Guide Post North Seaton Colliery

2

Scotland
Gate
on 30 Bomarsund
dlington 30 East Cambois
Sleekburn North Blyth
B1331 A193 C **Blyth**
East Cowpen
Hartford Bebside
A189 Newsham 30

3

A192 New
Shankhouse Delaval
5 A1061
New A193 Seaton
ington East Hartley 30 Sluice
Cramlington A190 Seaton Hartley
B1326 Seaton **Seaton** C St Mary's Lighthouse
Seghill **Delaval** A192 ★
19 2 A192 Holywell B1325 9 ☐
eaton Annitsford B1322 B1325
**Dudley** 30 7 A1148
Burradon Earsdon
de Camperdown Monkseaton **Whitley** ℹ
pen Backworth **Bay**
1056 Killingworth B1317 Shiremoor Cullercoats
Forest Hall Murton H A193
A189 Rising A191 New H **Tynemouth**
A19 York ⌂ ◀◼
Sun C ℹ 4 ⌂ Tynemouth Priory
**Longbenton** ℹ 4 & Castle IJmuiden
A1058 North
osforth 30 **Shields** A187 **SOUTH**
Jesmond 50 Willington **SHIELDS** ℹ M ♣
**Wallsend** Quay Int. Ferry- A183
40 Heaton Terminal Westoe
A187 M ⌂ Toll Harton Marsden
Walker **Jarrow** Tyne Tunnel A185 Bay
Byker B1313 Monkton Marsden C Souter Lighthouse
**Hebburn** A1300 H
Monkton Souter Point
**Felling** 2 C 30 Cleadon **Whitburn**
A184 A19 West B1298 40 A183
**GATESHEAD** Wardley Boldon Boldon
50 A184 Colliery B1299 A1018
C ℹ B1288 East 30 Whitburn
H Boldon A184 Bay
Wrekenton Seaburn
Bowes Railway A194(M) Fulwell Roker
& Museum Hylton Southwick
Springwell A1290 A19 Castletown Monkwearmouth
Usworth Wildfowl & ℹ M
**Birtley** 65 A1231 Wetlands Trust **SUNDERLAND**
Portobello South Grindon
30 **WASHINGTON** Hylton A183 H B1522 Hendon
S 64 Offerton 30 Grangetown
Ouston A195 Penshaw A183 High Newport B1405
Perkinsville Monument A690 New Tunstall Durham
**Penshaw** Silksworth Heritage Coast
Fatfield **Herrington** Silksworth B1286 Ryhope
A693 River Wear Shiney Row New Herrington A19 Newbottle
Pelton A183 Philadelphia A1018
Fell Houghton Burnmoor High Newbottle
**Chester-** Gate B1284 Dubmire **Houghton-** Seaton
e-Street 169 Ferry le-Spri B1287
Chester H Colliery B1404 K
G H J

Ⓐ 1   Ⓑ 1   Ⓒ 1   Ⓓ 1   Ⓔ 1   Ⓕ 1

Maiden Bay

**Maide**

2

*Turnberry*

**Turnberry**

*Turnberry Bay*

60

**A77**

340 ▲ Ailsa Craig

3

RSPB

60

O

60   **Girvan**

Douneparl

Woodland

60

Pinmin 8

4

60

297 ▲ GREY HILL

Pinmore

13

▲

Lendalfoot   A714

5

**A77**

Bennane Head

**Colmonell** 9   B734

River Stinchar

B734

B7044

Heronsford

Water of Tig

6

**Ballantrae**

437 ▲ BENERAIRD

🚢 Larne

🚢 Larne   *(Summer only)*   Currarie Port

7   🚢 Belfast

321 ▲ CARLOCK HILL

387 ▲ ALTIMEG HILL

🚢 Belfast

Glen App

Milleur Point

Corsewall Point   Lady Bay

8   Glenwhilly

Barnhills   **Portencalzie**   Laggan Standing

Ⓐ   0   1   2   3   4   5 miles

0   1   2   3   4   5   6   7   8 kilometres

17   **172**

Ⓓ   Ⓔ   Ⓕ

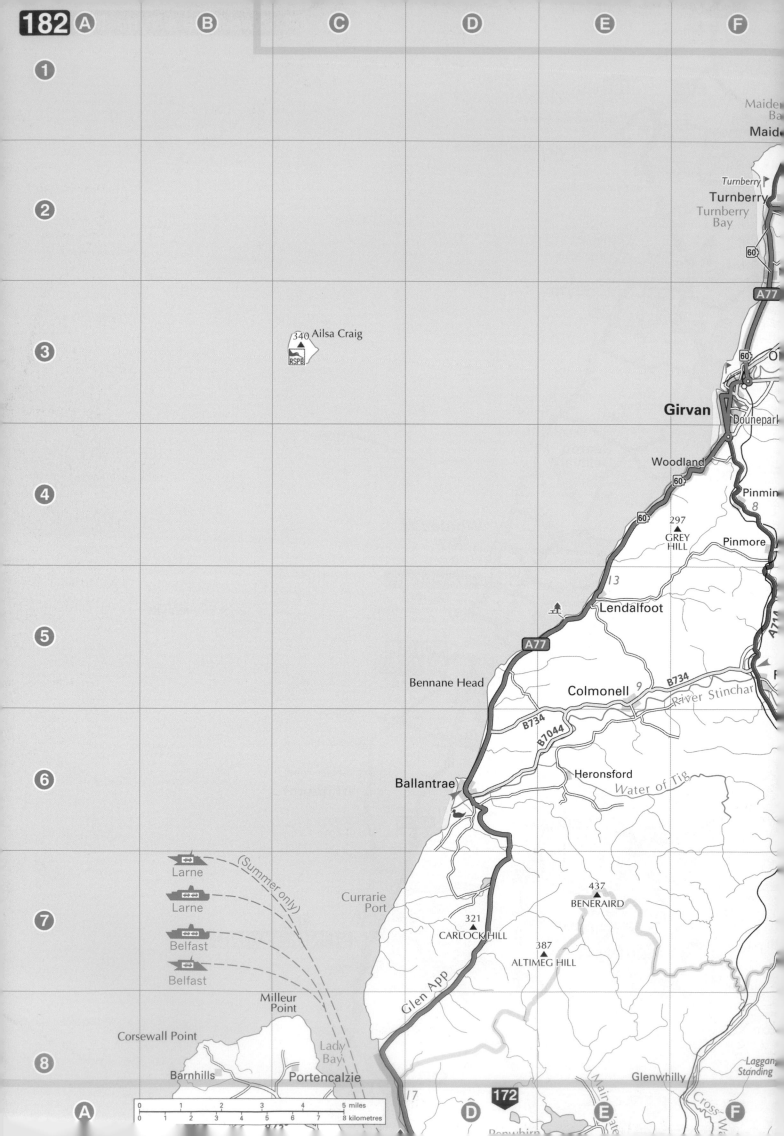

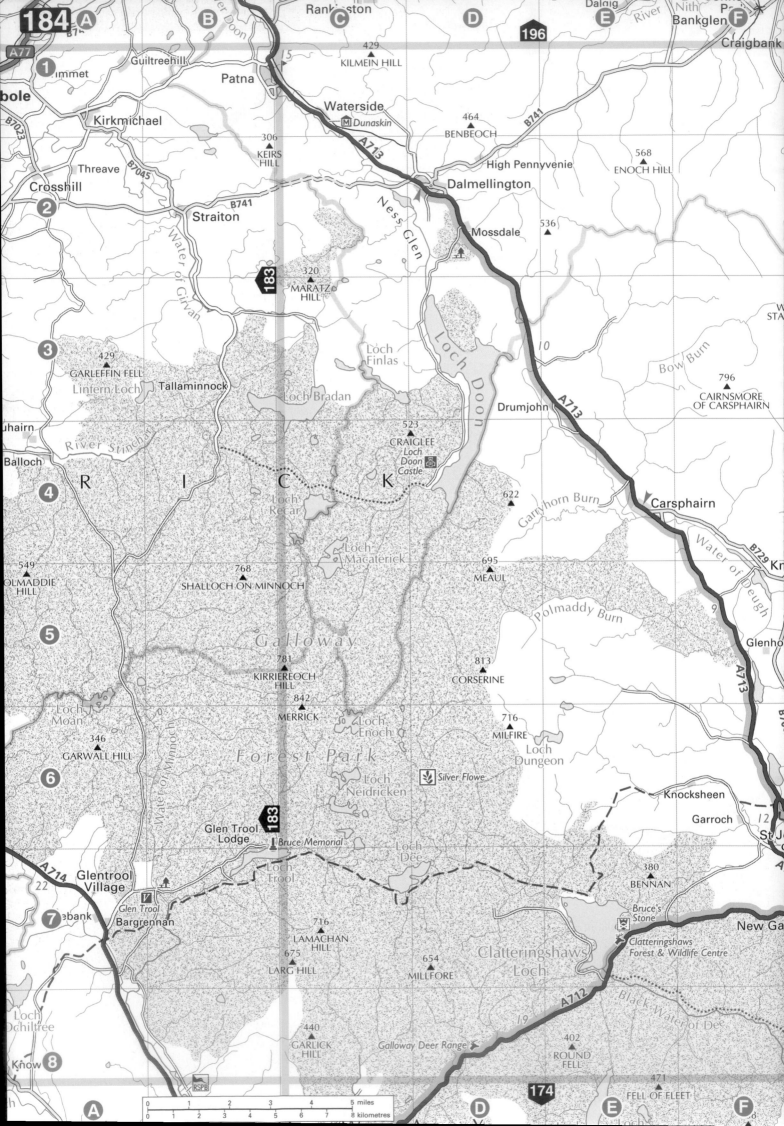

A   B   C   D   196   E   F

A77
Rankston
Dalaig
River Nith
Bankglen
Craigbank

1
immet
Guiltreehill
Patna
429
KILMEIN HILL

Kirkmichael
Waterside
Dunaskin
464
BENBEOCH
B741

Threave
B7045
306
KEIRS HILL
High Pennyvenie
568
ENOCH HILL

B7023
Crosshill

2
Straiton
B741
Dalmellington

Mossdale
536

183
320
MARATZ HILL
Ness Glen

3
429
GARLEFFIN FELL
Linfern Loch
Tallaminnock
Loch Finlas
Loch Bradan
Loch Doon
Drumjohn
A713
Cairnsmore of Carsphairn
796
STA

uhairn
Balloch
River Stinchar
523
CRAIGLEE
Loch Doon Castle

R   I   C   K

4
549
OLMADDIE HILL
Loch Recar
Loch Macaterick
622
695
MEAUL
Garryhorn Burn
Carsphairn
B729
Kr
Water of Deugh

5
Galloway
768
SHALLOCH ON MINNOCH
781
KIRRIEREOCH HILL
813
CORSERINE
Polmaddy Burn
9
Glenho

6
Loch Moan
346
GARWALL HILL
Water of Minnoch
842
MERRICK
Loch Enoch
Forest Park
716
MILFIRE
Loch Dungeon
Silver Flowe
Knocksheen
Garroch
12

7
A714
22
Glentrool Village
Bargrennan
Glen Trool
183
Glen Trool Lodge
Bruce Memorial
Loch Trool
Loch Neidricken
Loch Dee
Loch
380
BENNAN
Bruce's Stone
New Ga
Clatteringshaws Loch
Clatteringshaws Forest & Wildlife Centre

8
Loch Ochiltree
Know
ebank
716
LAMACHAN HILL
675
LARG HILL
654
MILLFORE
A712
19
402
ROUND FELL
Black Water of Dee
471
FELL OF FLEET
174
RSPB
440
GARLICK HILL
Galloway Deer Range

0  1  2  3  4  5 miles
0  1  2  3  4  5  6  7  8 kilometres

A   B   C   D   E   F

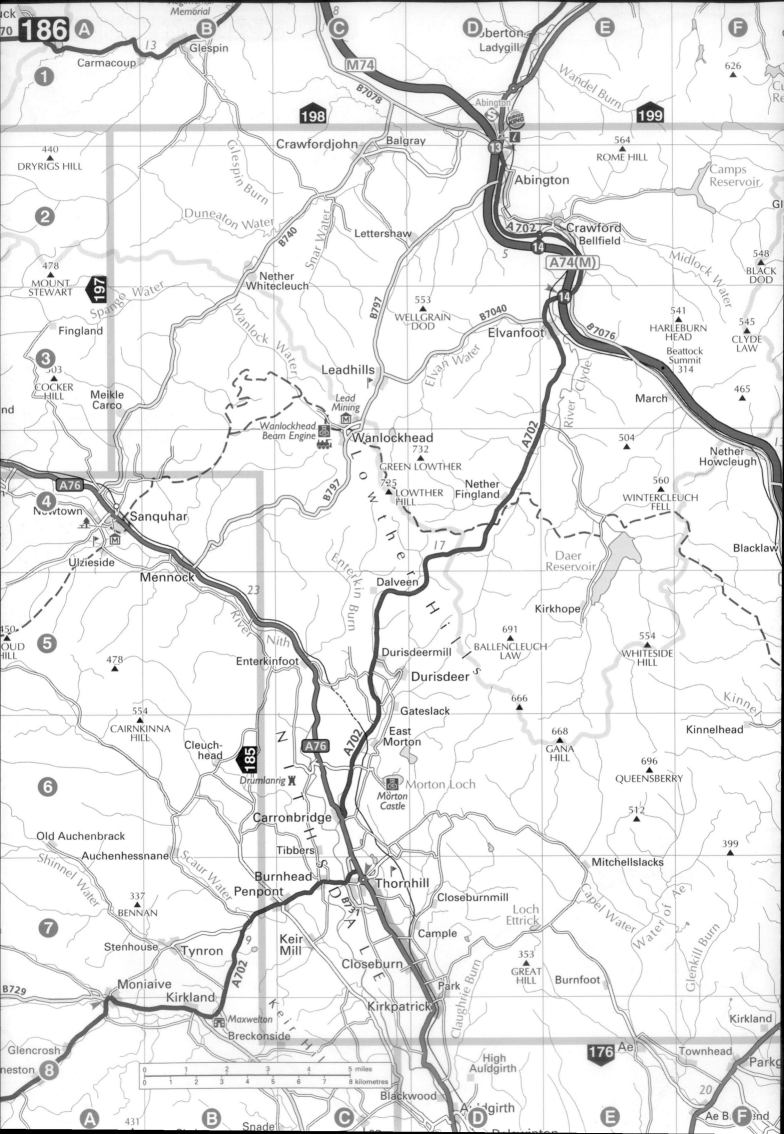

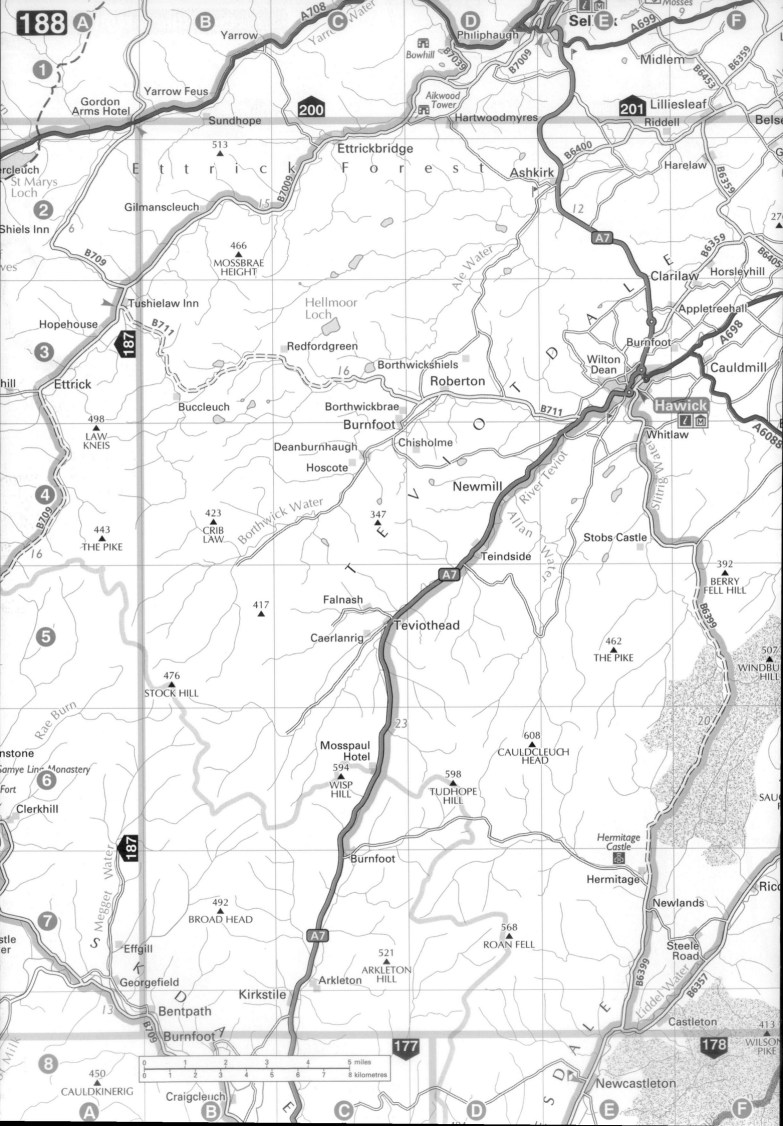

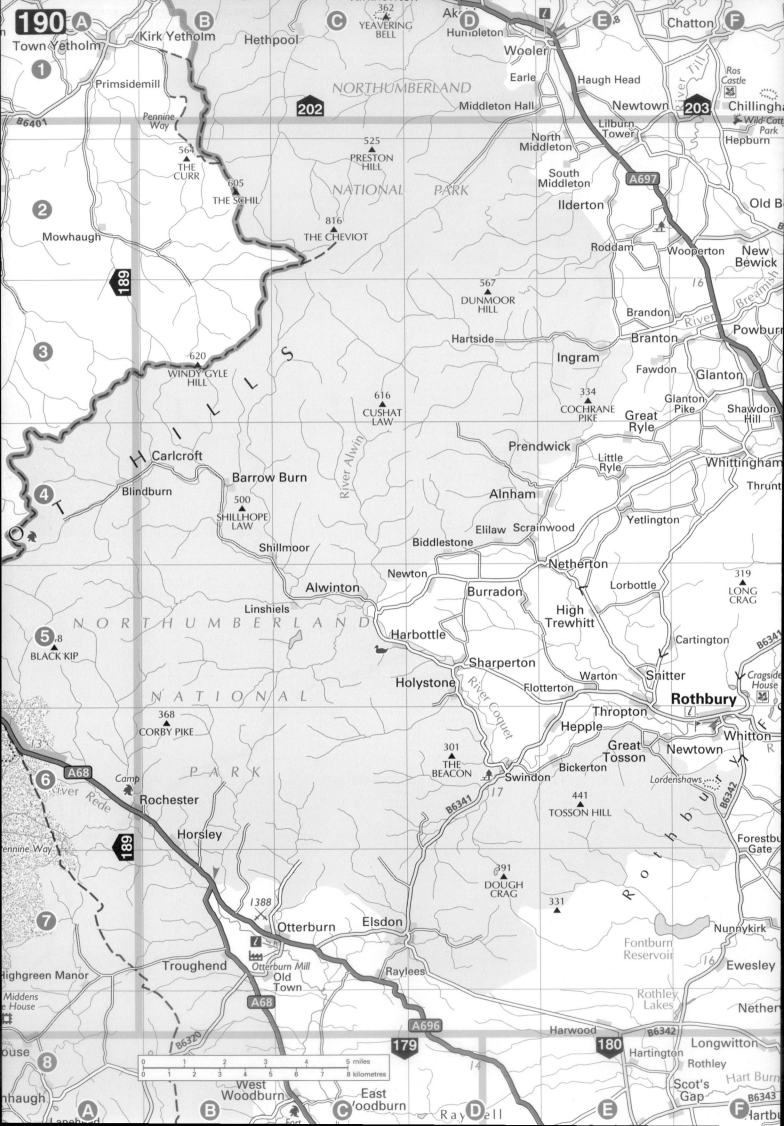

G  H  J  K

Warenford  Newham  Beadnell

Newstead  Chathill  Swinhoe  Beadnell Bay

A1  Ellingham  Tughall

Preston  Brunton  203  Newton-by-the-Sea

Preston Pele Tower  Embleton & Newton Links

267 TERAN HILL  Brownieside  Doxford  Christon Bank  Embleton

North Charlton  Falloden  Dunstan Steads  Dunstanburgh Castle  Embleton Bay

Ditchburn  South Charlton  Dunstan  Craster

Eglingham  Rock  Stamford  Howick Hall  Howick

Rennington  Cullernose Point

Broxfield  Littlehoughton

East Bolton  Longhoughton

River Aln  Denwick  Boulmer

Abberwick  Hawkhill  Seaton Point

Alnwick  Lesbury

Broome Park  Bilton  Hipsburn

B6341  Alnmouth

Castle  Bilton Banks  High Buston  Alnmouth Bay

Edlingham  A1  Low Buston  A1068

Shilbottle  Birling

260 GLANTLEES HILL  Newton-on-the-Moor  Warkworth Castle & Hermitage  Warkworth

A697  Amble  Coquet Island

Swarland Estate  Guyzance  Gloster Hill  High Hauxley

Swarland  Togston  Radcliffe

North End  Acklington

amlington  70 Felton  Broomhill

Pauperhaugh  East Thirston  B6345  South Broomhill  East Chevington  60

Weldon Bridge  West Thirston  Red Row  Druridge Bay

Brinkburn Priory  Eshott  Chevington Drift

Todburn  Helm  West Chevington  Druridge  Druridge Bay

Wingates  Causey Park  Stobswood  Widdrington  North Northumberland Heritage Coast

Longhorsley  Causey Park Bridge  Earsdon  B1337  Widdrington Station  Cresswell

Stanton  Fenrother  Tritlington  Ulgham  A1068  Ellington

A697  A1  Linton  Lynemouth

Hebron  Beacon Point

Pigdon  60  Longhirst  180  Woodhorn

River Font  Ashington  A189  Woodhorn Demesne

Newton Underwood  Pegswood  A197  Hirst North Seaton  Newbiggin-by-the-Sea

Bothal Sheepwash  Wansbeck River  B1334

G  H  J  K  L  M

1  2  3  4  5  6  7  8

Muasdale

Glenacardoch
Point

Belloch

Barr Water

Brie
D

Glenbarr

MacAlister Clan

454
BEINN AN TUIRC

Torr

Cleongart

319

408
BORD
MOR

Sadde

Bellochantuy Bay

Bellochantuy

N

194

396
SGREADAN
HILL

Ugadale

Tangy Loch

Glen Lussa

Peninver

Ardnacr
Bay

Kilkenzie

A83

Kilmichael

B842

Machrihanish
Bay

Campbeltown

Campbeltown

Machrihanish

B842

Campbeltown
Loch

Island Da

Drumlemble

6

B843

Kilkerran

Kildalloig

Earadale Point

385
THE
STATE

352
BEINN GHUILEAN

Achinhoan

446
CNOC
MOY

10

Conie Glen

Glen Kerran

Ru

Dalsmeran

Glen Breakevie

Strone Glen

B842

Cattadale

Polliwilline Bay

MULL
OF
KINTYRE

BEINN NA LICE

428

Carskey

Southend

Macharioch

Dunaverty

Carskey Bay

Sanda Sound

Borgadalemore Point

Sheep Island

Sanda Island

G Carradale
B879
Carradale House
Carradale Point
Carradale Bay

H Balliekine
Imachar

J

792 BEINN NUIS

K

Glen Rosa

6 Merkland Point
Brodick Castle, Garden & Country Club
Brodick Bay
1

A R R A N

Iorsa Water

Auchagallon Stone Circle
Machrie
Machrie Bay
Tormore
B880
Machrie Moor Stone Circles
Moss Farm Road Stone Circle
Balmichael
V
503
BEINN BHREAC
512 A'CHRUACH
Balmichael

M
Brodick
i
Strathwhillan
Corriegills
4
A841
Lamlash
Clauchlands Point
2
Margnaheglish
Lamlash Bay
Holy Island

Torbeg
Shiskine
Cordon

K I L B R A N
Drumadoon Bay
Blackwaterfoot
Kilpatrick
Kilpatrick Dun
194 Brown Head

Glen Scorrodale
Carn Ban
Kilmory Water

4
Auchencairn
Kingscross
Knockenkelly
3
Whiting Bay
Whiting Bay
Glen Ashdale
Largymore

Corriecravie
Torr a' Chaisteal Fort
Sliddery
16
Lagg
Torrylin Cairn
Kilmory
Bennan

Largybeg
Dippen
Dippen Head
Bennan Head
Pladda
Kildonan
4

195

5

6

7

340 Ailsa Craig
RSPB

8

G H J K L M

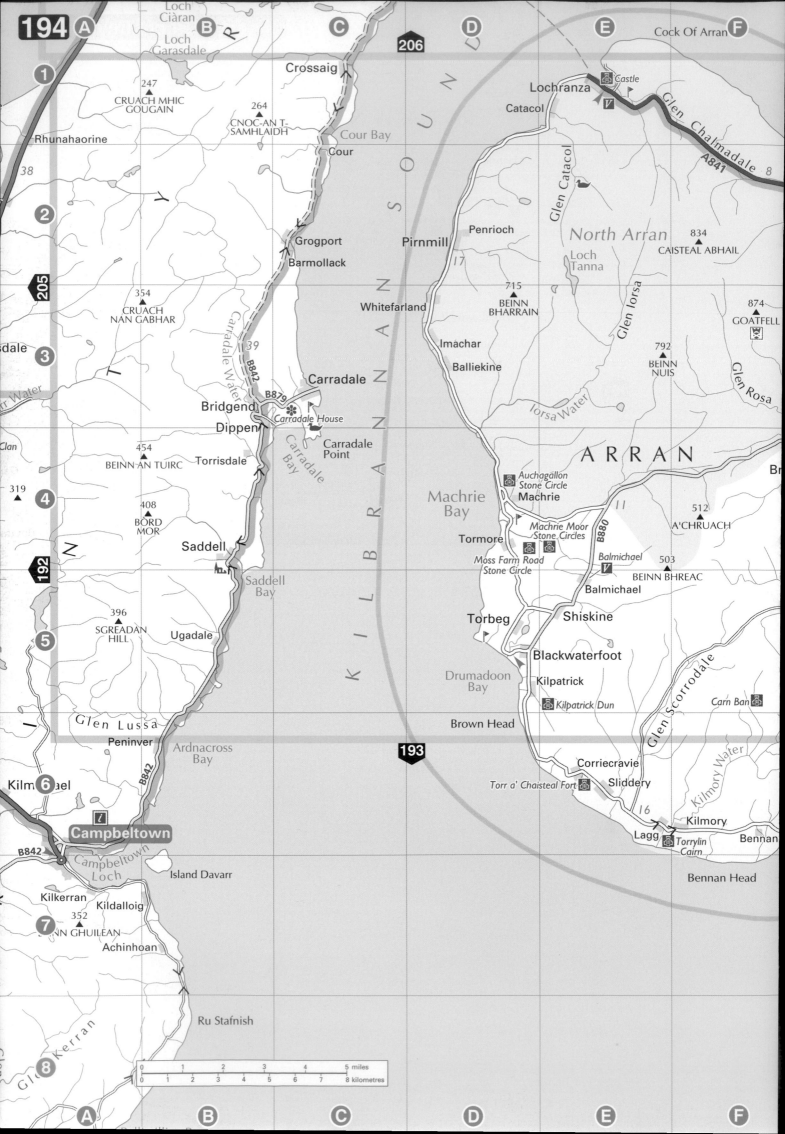

G    **H** nty    J    **207**

Ga    **H** nty    Garroch Head

Little
Cumbrae
Island

Fairlie R    **K**

Hunterston
Power Station

12

Crosbie

Blackshaw

Munnoch

Drakemyre

Hig

**1**

**Dalry**

Portencross
Farland Head

B7048

B7047

B781    B780

B780

**West
Kilbride**

C    U    N

A737

Dalgarven
Mill

7

**Seamill**

A78

B780

B714

Dalgarven

**2**

B778

nnox

**Kilwinning**

A78

B779

B785

**Corrie**

**Ardrossan**
Horse Isle

A738

A738

**196**

**Stevenston**

30    30

Ardeer

B780

6    Merkland Point

odick Castle, Garden
Country Club

Brodick
Bay

V

**Saltcoats**

**3**

B779

30

**Irvine**

Maritime

**Strathwhillan**

Corriegills

Fullar

The Big Idea

Irvine

Bay

Ga

F I R T H

Clauchlands Point

**4**

O F

Barass

B746

h

**Margnaheglish**

Lamlash
Bay

Holy Island

C L Y D E

(Summer only)

**Troon**

Cordon

hencairn    Kingscross

Knockenkelly

Whiting
Bay

Larne

**5**

Royal

iting Bay

4

Largymore

A y r
Bay

**6**

Ashdale

Largybeg

Dippen    Dippen Head

Kildonan

**196**

i    m    Ay

Heads
of Ay

Doonfoot

Burns Cottag

Heads of Ayr

Allo

a

Fisherton

A719

**7**

Do

Dunure

Culroy

Drumshang

Croy Brae
(Electric Brae)
Knoweside

Culzean
Bay

Culzean Castle
& Country Park

**8**

A77

Pennyglen    E    **M**

G    **H**    J    **182**    **K**    L

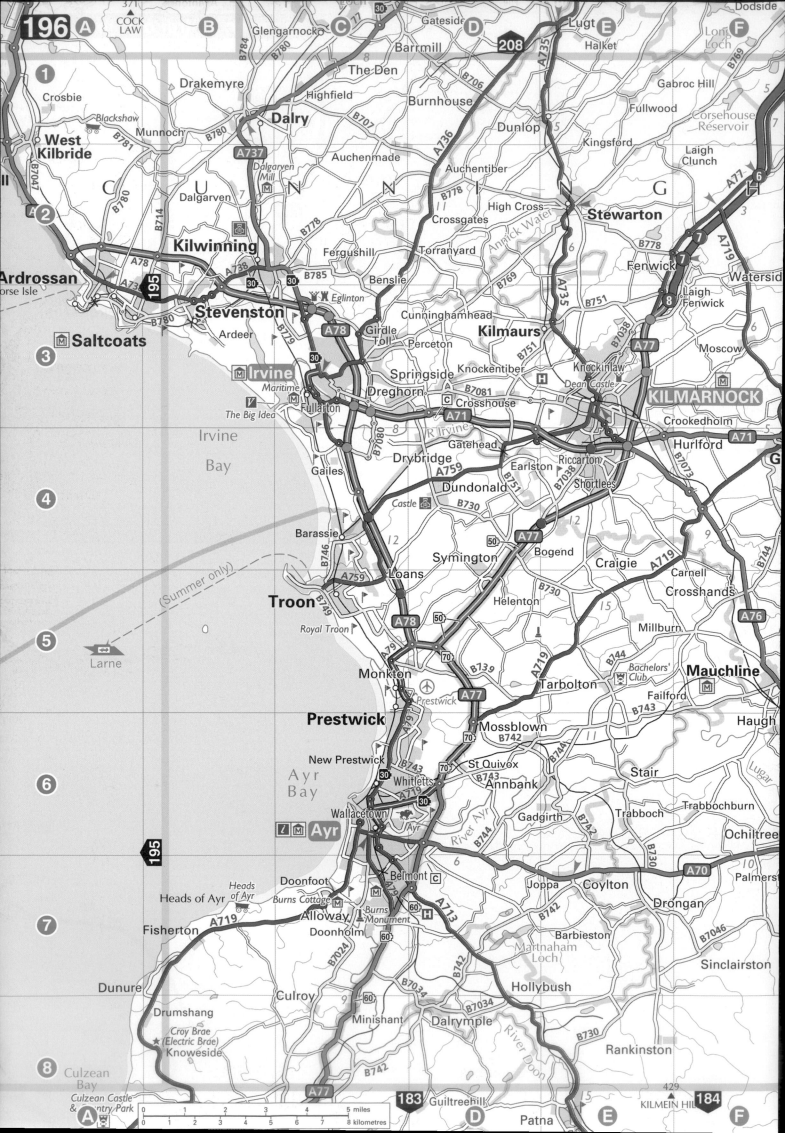

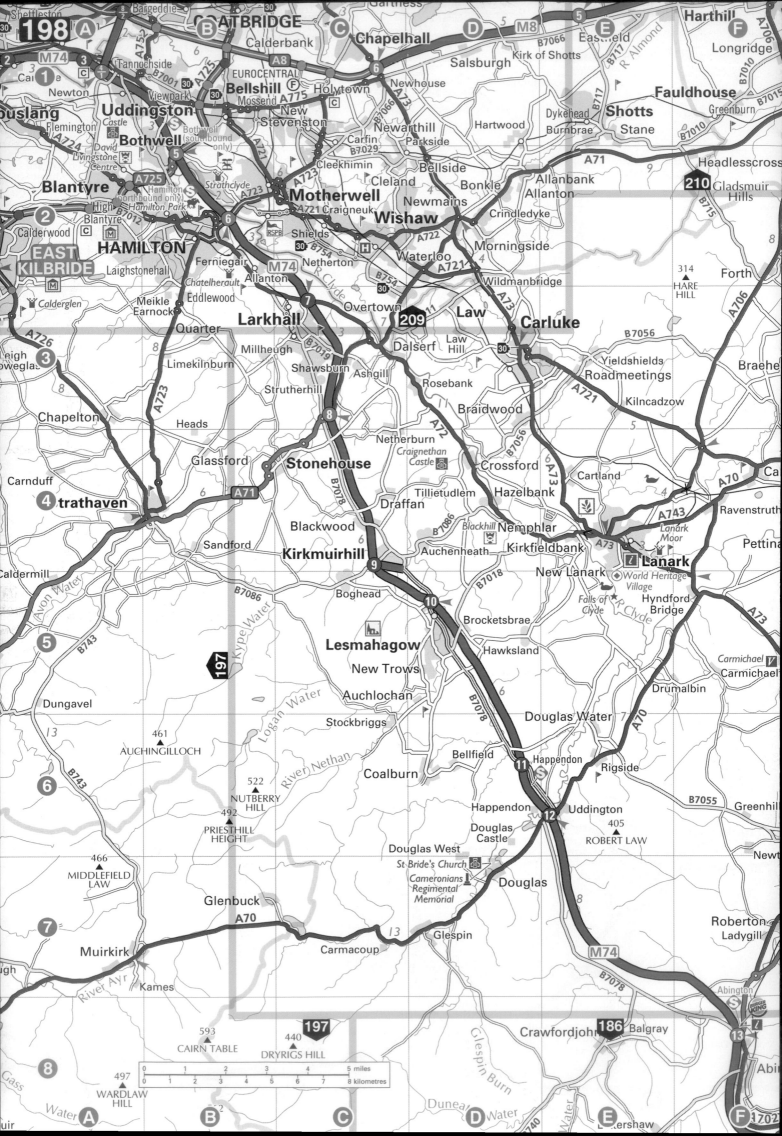

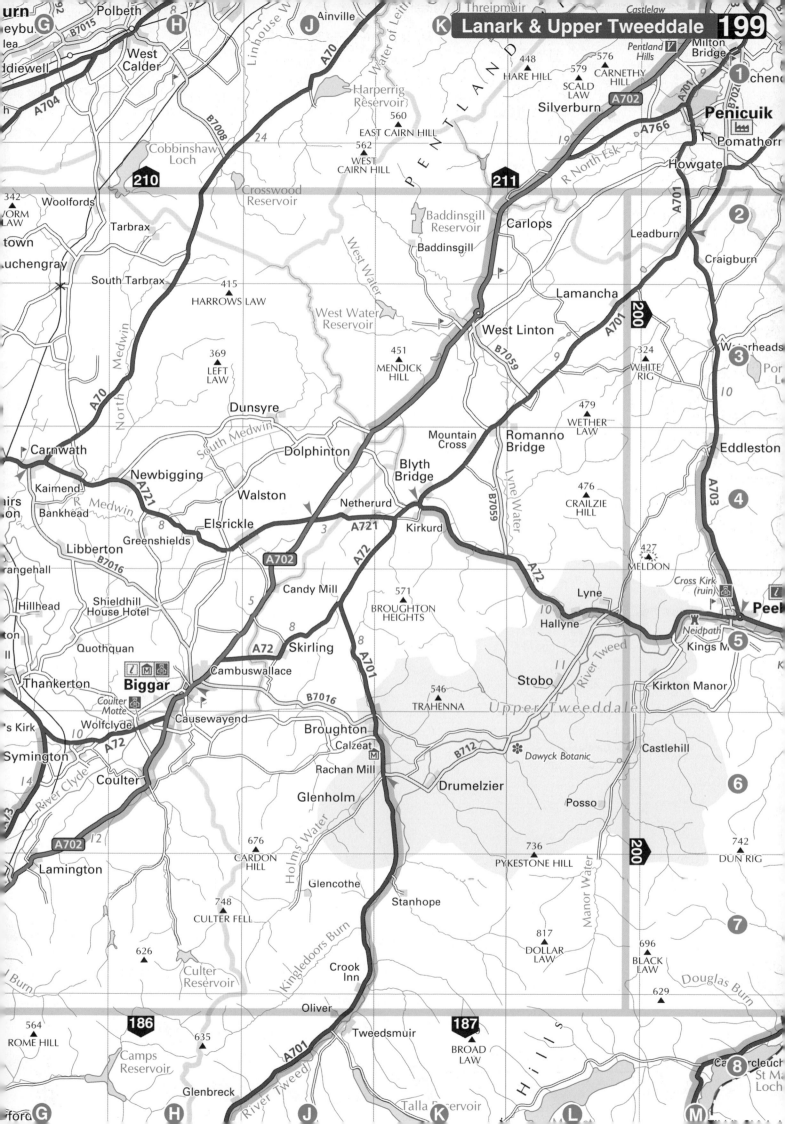

G  H  J  K

Polbeth
Ainville
Threipmuir
Castlelaw
Milton Bridge
eybu
B7015
Pentland Hills
chen
West Calder
Pentland Hills
448 HARE HILL
576
579
CARNETHY HILL
diewell
A704
SCALD LAW
Silverburn
A702
Penicuik
1
Harperrig Reservoir
A701
A701
A766
A702
Pomathorn
B7008
24
East Cairn Hill
560
Cobbinshaw Loch
210
562 WEST CAIRN HILL
211
R North Esk
Howgate
Crosswood Reservoir
Baddinsgill Reservoir
Carlops
A701
Leadburn
2
342
Woolfords
Baddinsgill
Craigburn
WORM LAW
Tarbrax
Lamancha
200
town
West Water
White Rig 324
Water heads
uchengray
South Tarbrax
415 HARROWS LAW
West Linton
B7059
9
Por
3
10
Medwin
West Water Reservoir
451 MENDICK HILL
479 WETHER LAW
369 LEFT LAW
Dunsyre
Mountain Cross
Romanno Bridge
Crailzie Hill 476
Eddleston
A70
South Medwin
Dolphinton
A703
Carnwath
Newbigging
Blyth Bridge
Netherurd
Lyne Water
427 MELDON
Kaimend
A721
Walston
B7059
Cross Kirk (ruin)
airs
Bankhead
R Medwin
8
Kirkurd
A721
A72
Peeb
on
Libberton
Elsrickle
Greenshields
3
A702
A72
rangehall
B7016
Candy Mill
571 BROUGHTON HEIGHTS
Lyne
Hillhead
5
8
Hallyne
427
Shieldhill House Hotel
A72
Skirling
8
10
Neidpath
5
Quothquan
A701
Stobo
Kings M
Thankerton
Cambuswallace
546 TRAHENNA
Upper Tweeddale
Kirkton Manor
Biggar
River Tweed
11
Coulter Motte
B7016
Broughton
Calzeat
Castlehill
s Kirk
Wolfclyde
Causewayend
Rachan Mill
Drumelzier
6
Symington
A72
10
B712
Dawyck Botanic
Posso
14
River Clyde
Coulter
Glenholm
742 DUN RIG
A702
12
676 CARDON HILL
736 PYKESTONE HILL
200
Lamington
Glencothe
817 DOLLAR LAW
696 BLACK LAW
748 CULTER FELL
Stanhope
Manor Water
629
626
Douglas Burn
Burn
Culter Reservoir
Crook Inn
564 ROME HILL
186
635
Oliver
187
M
Camps Reservoir
Tweedsmuir
BROAD LAW
8
cleuch St Ma Loch
ford
G
Glenbreck
H
River Tweed
A701
J
Talla Reservoir
K
L
Hills
M

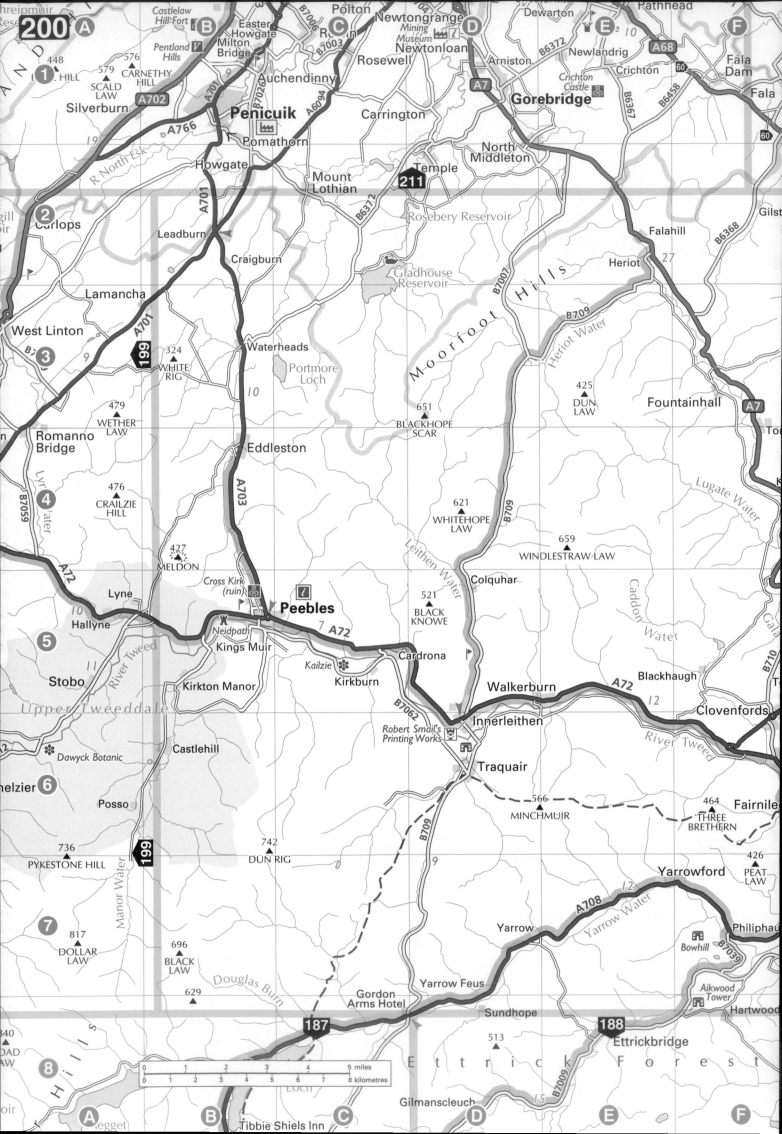

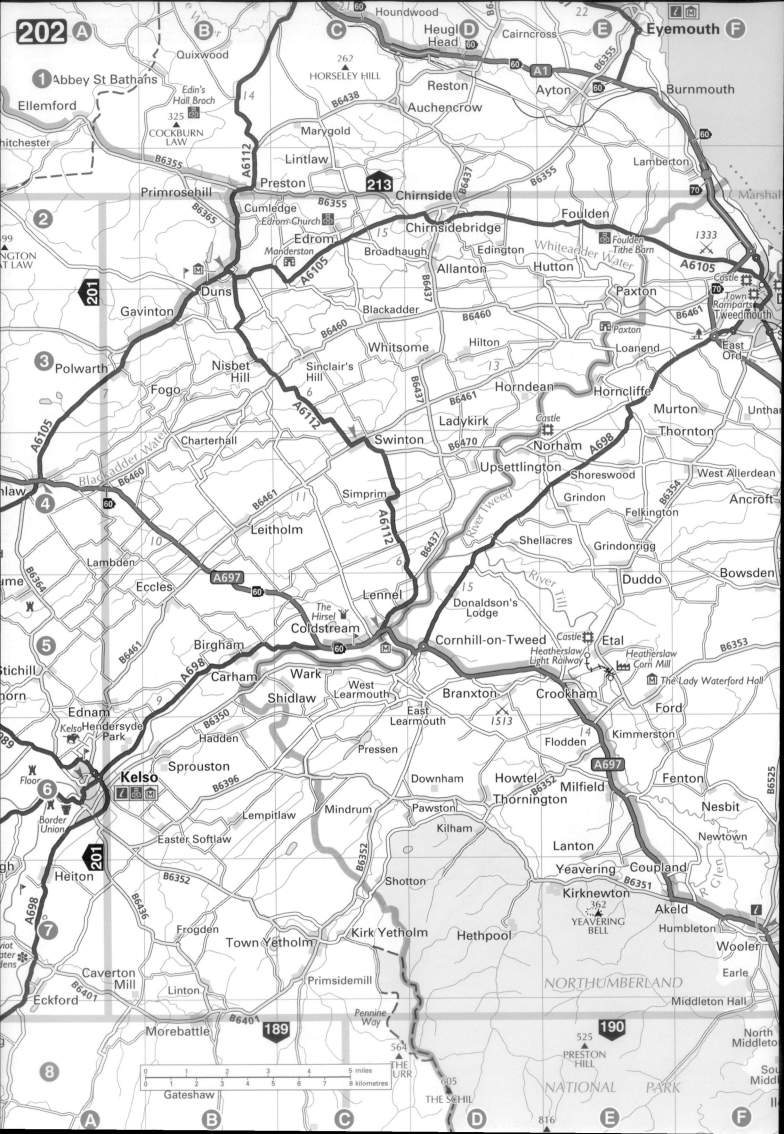

G    H    J

1

2

...ws Bay

*Northumberland Heritage Coast*

...ck-upon-Tweed
ℹ️ Ⓜ️

3

...uds
...ead
...erston

Cheswick

Goswick

Haggerston

*15*

Beal

60

Fenham

West Kyloe

...wick

Fenwick

Buckton

Detchant

Smeafield

Elwick

Ross

CAUSEWAY
FLOODED
AT HIGH TIDE

HOLY ISLAND

Holy
Island

*Lindisfarne
Priory*

*Lindisfarne
Castle*
Castle Point

Guile Point

4

*Longstone
Lighthouse*

FARNE
ISLANDS

*Staple
Sound*

*North Northumberland
Heritage Coast*

5

Holburn

*St Cuthbert's
Cave*

Middleton

Hetton
Steads

North
Hazelrigg

Belford

B6349

South
Hazelrigg

Low
Middleton

Easington

Outchester

Spindlestone

Bradford

Budle
Bay

Waren
Mill

Budle

*Bamburgh*

B1342

Bamburgh

Ⓜ️

B1340

New
Shoreston

Burton

*Inner
Sound*

Seahouses

ℹ️

6

East
Horton

...on

...t

Chatton

*River Till*

*Ros
Castle*

...ead

...wtown

Chillingham

*Wild Cattle
Park*

Hepburn

190

A697

Warenton

B6348

Bellshill

60

Adderstone

Warenford

*9*

B1341

Lucker

Newham

Elford

North Sunderland

Beadnell

Swinhoe

*Beadnell
Bay*

B1340

7

Chathill

Newstead

Ellingham

Tughall

Preston

Newton-by-the-Sea

*Preston
Pele Tower*

191

Brunton

Christon
Bank

*Embleton &
Newton Links*

Embleton

*14*

Brownieside

▲ *267*
CATERAN
HILL

North
Charlton

Falloden

Doxford

B347

*Embleton
Bay*

Dunstan
Steads

*Dunstanburgh Castle*

8

Old Bewick

Ditchbur...

South
Ch...

A1

G    H    J    K    L    M

A  B  C  D  E  F

1

Rudha
Bholsa

363
SGARB
BREA

2

Nave Island
Ardnave
Point
Gortantaoid
Point

316
GUIR-
BHEINN

Bunnahabhair

Ton Mhòr

Kilnave

**Sanaigmore**

Eilean Mòr

Finlaggan

Kiells

Rudha Lamanais

Loch
Gòrr

Lecht Gruinart

Loch
Finlaggan

Loch
Bal

A

3

Saligo Bay

Loch
Gorm

B8018

RSPB

B8017

Gruinart

Gleann Mòr

**Ballygrant**

A846
8

Coul Point

Sunderland

B8018

L
L

**Kilchoman**

A847

Machir
Bay

4

**Bruichladdich**

Loch
Indaal

**Bridgend**

Gartachossan

Kilennan Burn

Kilchiaran Bay

O
F

**Bowmore**

15
M

i

3

5

Lossit Bay

R
H
I
N
N
S

Nereabolls

231
BEINN TART A'MHILL

**Port
Charlotte**

River Laggan

Duich R.

A846

B8016

**I S L A Y**

454
BEINN URAR
Loch

Rudha na
Faing

A847

**Portnahaven**

**Port Wemyss**

Orsay

RHINNS
POINT

6

L a g g a n

B a y

Glenegedale

Islay

346
BEINN SHOLUM

7

Rudha Mòr

Kintra

165
MAOL BUIDHE

**T H E   O A**

Lower
Killeyan

Risabus

Port
Ellen

A846

Ar
Laga

**Laphroaig**

Texa

Kilnaughton
Bay

RSPB

Kinnabus

American
Monument

Loch
Kinnabus

MULL
OF OA

Rudha nan Leacan

8

A  B  C  D  E  F

G    H    J    K

214    215

dha' a' Ghil

Sween

Danna Island

Ellary

506
▲
SCRINADLE

398
▲
BEINN
TARSUINN

Jura Forest

St Cormac's Chapel

Kilmory Knap Chapel

Kilmory

784
▲
BEINN
AN OIR

Paps of Jura

Kilmory Bay

Loch a' Chnuic Bhric

734
▲

Point of Knap

Jura

24

Knockrome

Ardfernal

J U R A

560
▲
GLASS BHEINN

v
Feolin Ferry

A846

529
▲
DUBHA BHEINN

Keils

Craighouse

Small Isles

Kilberry Sculptured Stones

C henga

Coulaghailt

Kilberry

342
▲
BRAT BHEINN

Rudha na Gaillich

Kilberry Head

Keppoch Point

Tiretigan

213
▲
CRUACH AI

206

Cabrach

Am Fraoch Eilean

Rudha na Tràille

Brosdale Island

Loch Stornoway

NAM ANN

McArthur's Head

v

Port Askaig - Kennacraig

We

Rona n Poin

GEIR

Rudha Liath

Ardtalla

Claggain Bay

v

Kinerarach

Tarbert

Kintour

Kildalton Cross

Ardmore Point

GIGHA

Rhunahaorine Point

Sound of Gigha

Eilean a' Chuirn

v

Ardminish

Achamore

Rhunahaorine

Rudha na Gainmhich

Port Ellen - Kennacraig

v

Cara

Tayinloan

38

194

A83

Muasdale

Glenacardoch Point

Belloch

G    H    J    K    L    M

192

1   2   3   4   5   6   7   8

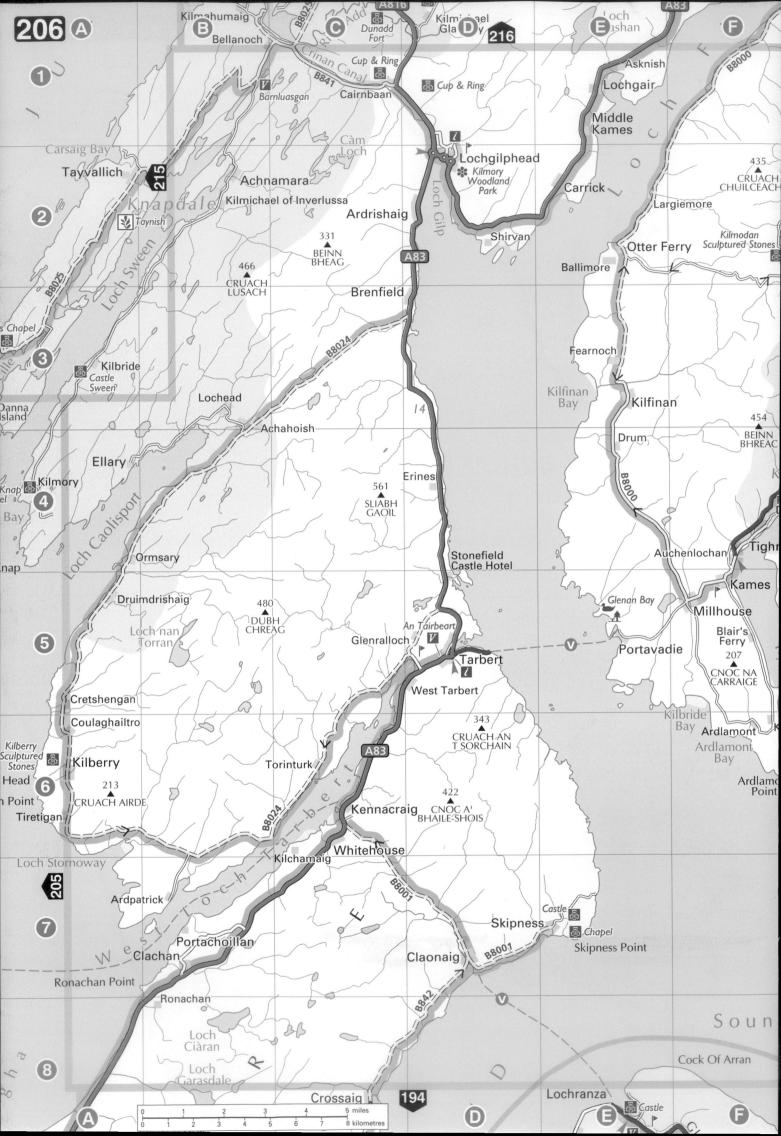

CRUACH AN LOCHAIN

**G** A886 **H** J **217** BE BHL **J** Whistlefield Inn **K** **K** A814 BEINN CHAORACH **207**

655
BEI THARSUINN

**1**

Dunans Castle
643

742
BEINN MHOR

Argyll Forest Park

657
CREACHAN MOR

Sligrachan

Garelochhead

Rockville

Greenfield

B872

Glen Fruin

Glenmassen

Glen Massen

643
CLACH BHEINN

664
BEINN RUADH

Ardentinny

Coulport

B833

Shandon

7

**2**

Benmore

Benmore

548
STRONCHULLIN HILL

Clynder

Rhu

Hill House

**208**

432
CRUACH NAN CUILEAN

Loch Tarsan

601
SGORACH MOR

B836

Glen Lean

Rashfield

Ardbeg

Blairmore

Loch Long

Cove

Rosneath

daruel

Stronafian

7

606

Clachaig

Kilmun

A880

Strone

Kilcreggan

Firth of

**3**

A886

505
BEINN BHREAC

Glenkin

Glenstriven

611
CRUACH NAN CAPULL

Sandbank

Ardnadam

A885

A815

Holy Loch

Hunter's Quay

Kirn

Cloch Point

Gourock

3

GREENOCK

Ardmo

Ardentraive

Colintraive

Altgaltraig

Loch Striven

503
BISHOP'S SEAT

**Dunoon**

Ardhallow

Ashton

Lyle Hill

**C**

A770

Larkfield

30

A78

 ubodach

Kyles of Bute

391
KILMARNOCK HILL

Knockdow

Ardgowan

Lunderston Bay

Braeside

Chrisswell

8

Loch Thom

**4**

**BUTE**

A886

322
BEINN RUADH

Dunan

Innellan

Inverkip

Cornalees Bridge

Gryffe Reservoir

267
KAMES HILL

Ardmaleish

8

A815

Wemyss Bay

Shielhill

Garvock

Cairncurra

Kilbride

St Colmac

Ardyre Point

Ardbeg

Port Bannatyne

Toward

Toward Quay

Skelmorlie

Upper Skelmorlie

441
CREUCH HILL

**5**

B875

Kildavanan

Castle

Bogany Point

A78

6

Ettrick Bay

B878

Rothesay

A844

St Mary's Chapel (ruin)

Ardencraig

Ascog

Knock Castle

522
HILL OF STAKE

**6**

**208**

Ballanlay

A844

B881

Loch Ascog

Kerrycroy

Quarter

Routenburn

Midpark

Meikle Kilmory

Loch Fada

8

Mount Stuart

Skelmorlie Aisle

Vikingar!

483
IRISH LAW

River Garnoc

**7**

Ardscalpsie Bay

Bruchag

GREAT CUMBRAE ISLAND

B896

Largs

Kelburn

A760

Kelburn Country Centre

14

Kingarth

B881

Kilchattan Bay

B899

B896

Millport

M

Fairlie

Camphill Reservoir

**Kilbirnie**

Stravanan Bay

Kilchattan

St Blane's Church

371
COCK LAW

B784

B780

**8**

Garrochty

f Bute

Garroch Head

Little Cu

**195**

Hunterston Power Station

Fairlie Roads

Drak re

**G** **H** **J** **K** **L** **M**

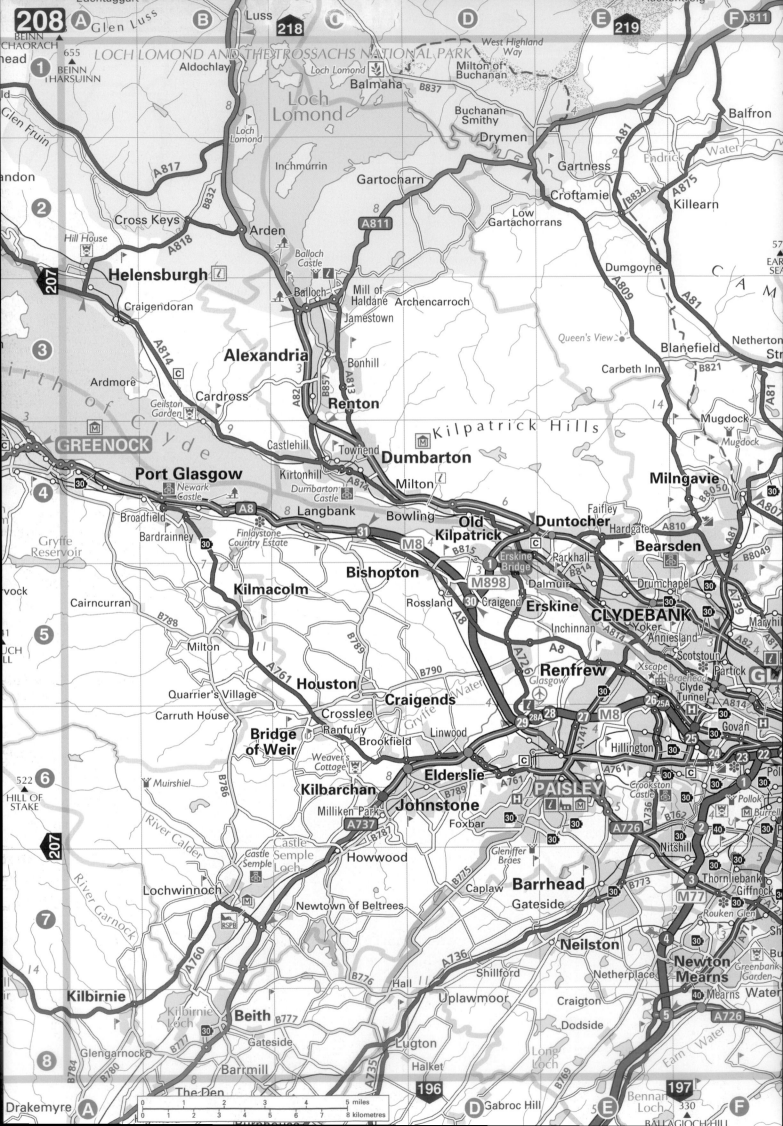

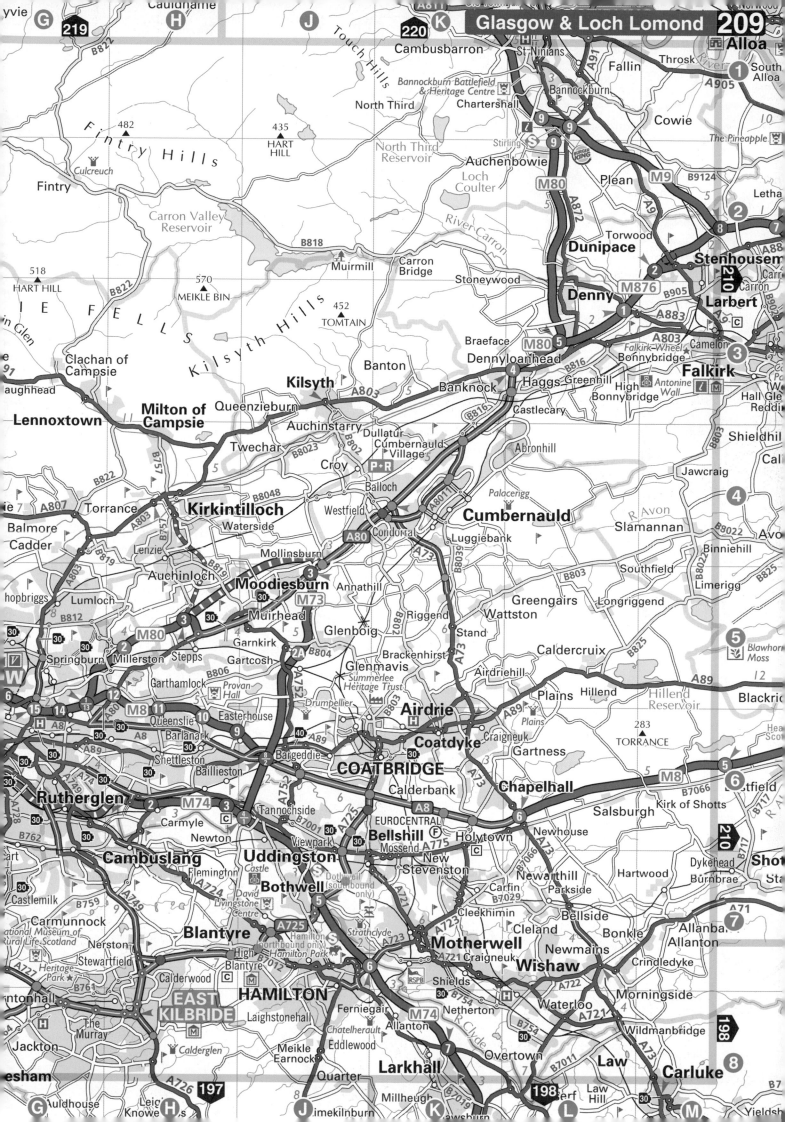

**G** Lumphinnans  Loch Gelly  **222**  **H**  **J** Dysart

**Cowdenbeath**
B925
Auchtertool
Pathhead
Ravenscraig Castle
**Kirkcaldy**
Linktown
B9157
B925
B923
Donibristle
Balmule
A909  B923
A921  A921
Aberdour  Castle  Kinghorn
St Bridget's Kirk  Pettycur Bay  Pettycur
Silversands Bay  **Burntisland**
Dalgety Bay  Inchcolm Abbey
Cramond Island
Inchkeith
Zeebrugge

**1**
**2**
Gullane B
Gullane Point  **212**
Aberlady Bay
Craigelaw Point  **3**
Aberlady

F I R T H  O F  F O R T H

sferry
Eagle Rock  Dalmeny
Gosford Bay
A90  Cramond  Granton  Britannia  **EDINBURGH**
Lauriston Castle  Newhaven  A902  A900  30
Barnton  Davidson's Mains  B9085  Leith  C  St Triduana's Chapel
Blackhall  Warriston  A199
Dovecot  A90  A8  Portobello  **Musselburgh**  **Cockenzie and Port Seton**
A902  B701  Corstorphine  Castle  A1  Joppa  40  Seton Collegiate Church
Cockenzie and Port Seton
Preston Market Cross
South Gyle  ARTHUR'S SEAT 251  Newcraighall  Fisherrow  **Prestonpans**  Longnidd
Duddingston  Craigmillar  Inveresk  Heritage Museum
Craiglockhart  Royal Observatory  Lodge Garden  Inveresk  **4**
Morningside  A772  Craigmillar Castle  H  P+R  A1  70  **Tranent**  Macmerry
M8  A71  Blackford Hill  A7  Newton  Whitecraig  Wallyford  Elphinstone  New Winton
Juniper Green  Water of Leith  Liberton  30  Gilmerton  Danderhall  A720  Millerhill  Crossgatehall  Ormiston Market Cross  Boggs Holding
Colinton  Gilmerton  A7  Dalkeith Park  Ormiston
Currie  Bonaly  B701  C  Straiton  Butterfly Farm  Eskbank  **Dalkeith**  Cousland  A6093  Pencaitland  **5**
Kinleith  Hillend  Newbattle  60  B6367
Malleny Garden  ALLERMUIR HILL  **Loanhead**  Bilston  **Bonnyrigg**  Lasswade  Mayfield  Chesterhill  Pathhead
Malleny Mills  Boghall  A703  Polton  Newtongrange  Dewarton  Vogrie  A68  **6**
Woodhouselee  Castlelaw Hill Fort  Roslin  Mining Museum  Newtonloan  Arniston  Newlandrig  Crichton  Fala Dam
Easter Howgate  Milton Bridge  Rosewell  Crichton Castle  Crichton  Fala
Pentland Hills  Auchendinny  **212**
SCALD LAW  CARNETHY HILL  A701  A6094  **Gorebridge**
Silverburn  A702  **Penicuik**  A7
Pomathorn  Carrington  North Middleton  **7**  DUN LAW
Howgate  Mount Lothian  Temple
**199**  **200**
Carlops  Leadburn  A701  Rosebery Reservoir  Gilston
Craigburn  Falahill
Lamancha  Gladhouse Reservoir  B7007  Heriot
Linton  Waterheads  B709  Heriot Water

**G**  **H**  **J**  **K**  **L**  **M**

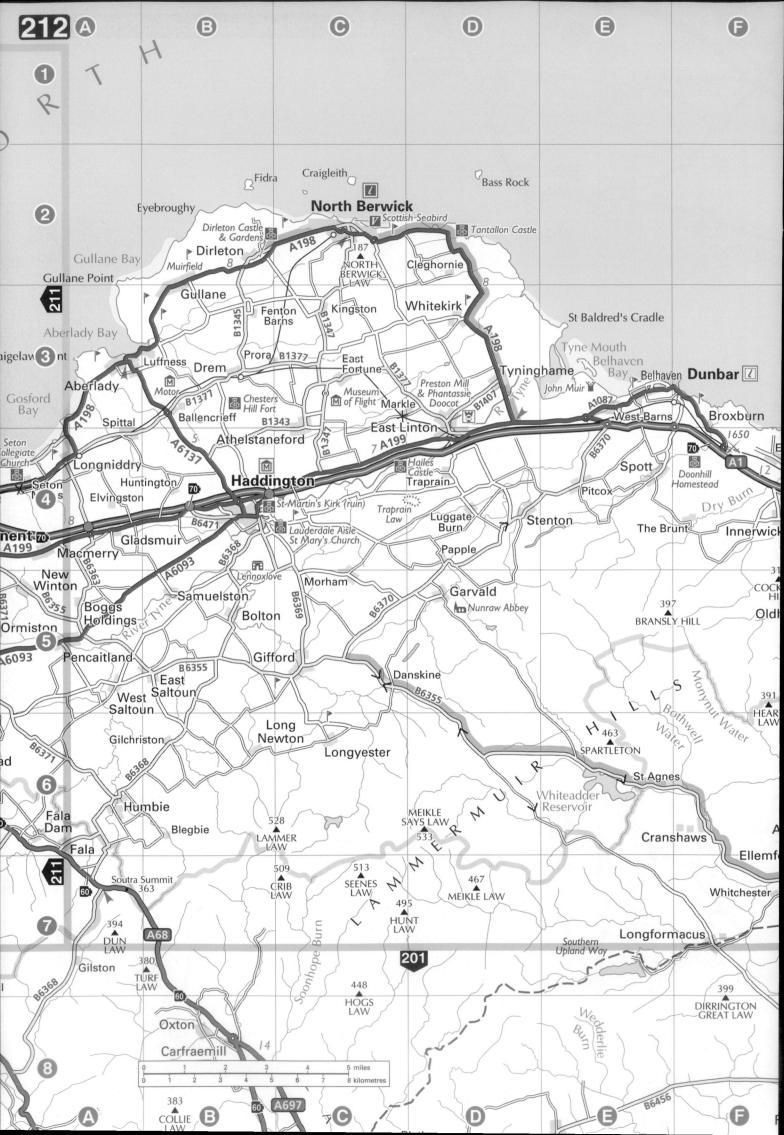

G  H  J

1

2

3

Chapel Point

Thorntonloch

60

owhill

Dunglass
Collegiate
Church

Reed
Point
Cove  Pease
Bay

Siccar
Point

Fast Castle Head

ST ABB'S HEAD

4

70

Cockburnspath

A1107

196
BROWN
RIG

Coldingham
Loch

St Abbs

5

Ecclaw

Southern
Upland Way

60

Grantshouse

Coldingham

A1107

22

Coldingham
Bay

Butterdean

Eye Water

21  60

Houndwood

B6438

Eyemouth

6

Quixwood

Heugh
Head  60

Cairncross

Bathans

Edin's
Hall Broch

262
HORSELEY HILL

14

B6438

Reston

60

A1  B6355

Ayton  60

Burnmouth

325

COCKBURN
LAW

Marygold

Auchencrow

60

B6355

A6112

Lintlaw

B6437

B6355

Lamberton

7

Primrosehill

B6365

Preston

B6355

Chirnside

202

Foulden

70

Marshall Meadows Bay

Cumledge

Edrom Church

15

Chirnsidebridge

Whiteadder Water

Foulden
Tithe Barn

1333

North Northumberlan

Edrom

Broadhaugh

Edington

Manderston

Allanton

Hutton

A6105

Berwick-upon

Duns

B6437

Paxton

Castle

70
Town
Ramparts

Barracks

H

Gavinton

Blackadder

B6460

B6461

Tweedmouth

8

Paxton

Whitsome

Hilton

Loanend

East
Ord

Spittal

Huds
Head

G  Nisbet  H  Sinclair's  J  13  K  L  M

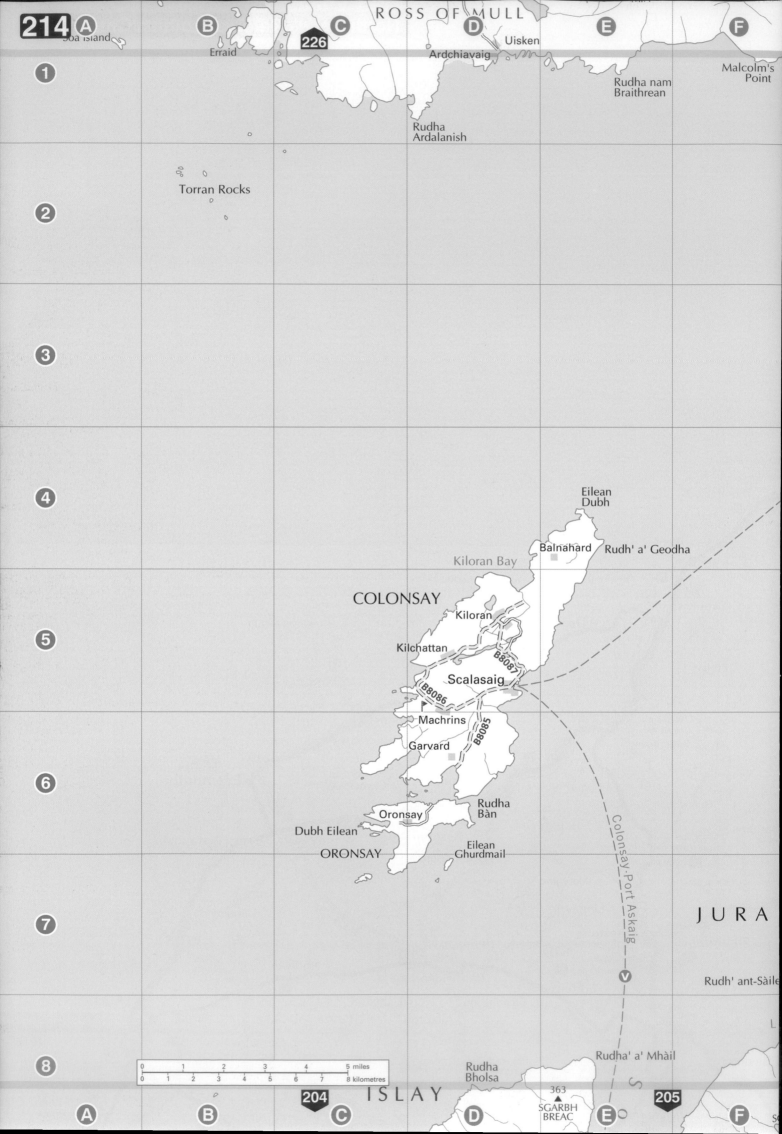

ROSS OF MULL

Soa Island

Erraid

**226**

Ardchiavaig

Uisken

**1**

Malcolm's
Point

Rudha nam
Braithrean

Rudha
Ardalanish

Torran Rocks

**2**

**3**

Eilean
Dubh

**4**

Balnahard

Rudh' a' Geodha

Kiloran Bay

COLONSAY

Kiloran

**5**

Kilchattan

B8087

Scalasaig

B8086

Machrins

B8085

Garvard

**6**

Rudha
Bàn

Oronsay

Dubh Eilean

ORONSAY

Eilean
Ghurdmail

JURA

**7**

Colonsay-Port Askaig

Rudh' ant-Sàile

Ⓥ

Rudha' a' Mhàil

Rudha
Bholsa

**8**

| 0 | 1 | 2 | 3 | 4 | 5 miles |
| 0 | 1 | 2 | 3 | 4 | 5 | 6 | 7 | 8 kilometres |

**204**

ISLAY

363
▲
SGARBH
BREAC

**205**

Dubh

G  H  J  **227**  K

Insh Island

Clachan

Clachan-Seil

Ellanbeich

**SEIL**  Easdale

Balvicar

Easdale

B844

B8003

V  Cuan Ferry Village

Cullipool House

Torsay Island

Degnish

**Loch Melfort**

Garbh Eileach

LUING

Seil Sound

Arduaine Garden

Arduaine

Eilean Dubh Mòr

**GARVELLACHS**
*Monastery & Beehive Cells*

Eileach an Naoimh

**LUNGA**

Toberonochy

Shuna Sound

**216**

**SHUNA**

Cra Haven

A8

*Scarba, Lunga*

*and the*

*Garvellachs*

Shuna Point

Craigdhu

Ardfern

Kintr

**SCARBA**

448 ▲
CRUACH SCARBA

B8002

En Mhic

En Righ

Carn

Gulf of Corryvreckan

Aird

Loch Craignish

Craignish Point

Island Macaskin

Slockavullin
*Temple Wood*
*Stone Circles*

Glengarrisdale Bay

295 ▲
CRUACH NA
SEILCHEIG

*Ri Cruin Cair*
Poltalloch

Glendebadel Bay

Loch Crinan

**Crinan**

364 ▲
BEN
GARRISDALE

Lealt Burn

Kilmahumaig

B8025

Bellanoch

Crinan River

Corpach Bay

466 ▲
BEINN
BHREAC

Lussa River

Glen Grundale

J  U  R  A

Carsaig Bay

Barnluc  V

B841

Bay

453 ▲
RAINBERG MÒR

Tayvallich

Achnamara

Kilmichael of Inverluss

Loch Mòr

A846

Ardlussa

Lussa Point
Lussagiven

*Knapdale*

**206**

7

331 ▲
BEINN
BHEAG

arbert

N  O  R  T  H

O  F

Taynish

Loch Sween

466 ▲
CRUACH
LUSACH

Keills Chapel

B8025

B802

G  H  **205**  J  K

Loch na Cille

Danna Island

Kilbride
*Castle*
*Sween*

Lochead

L  M  hahoish

1

2

3

4

5

6

7

8

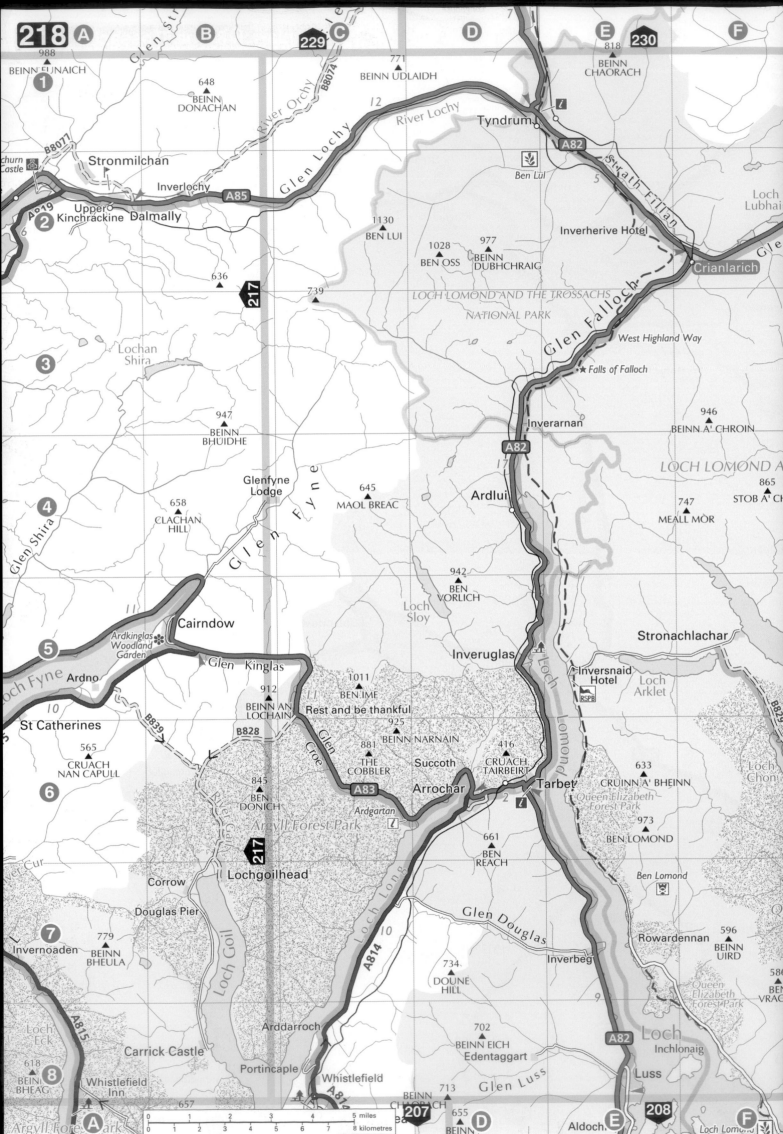

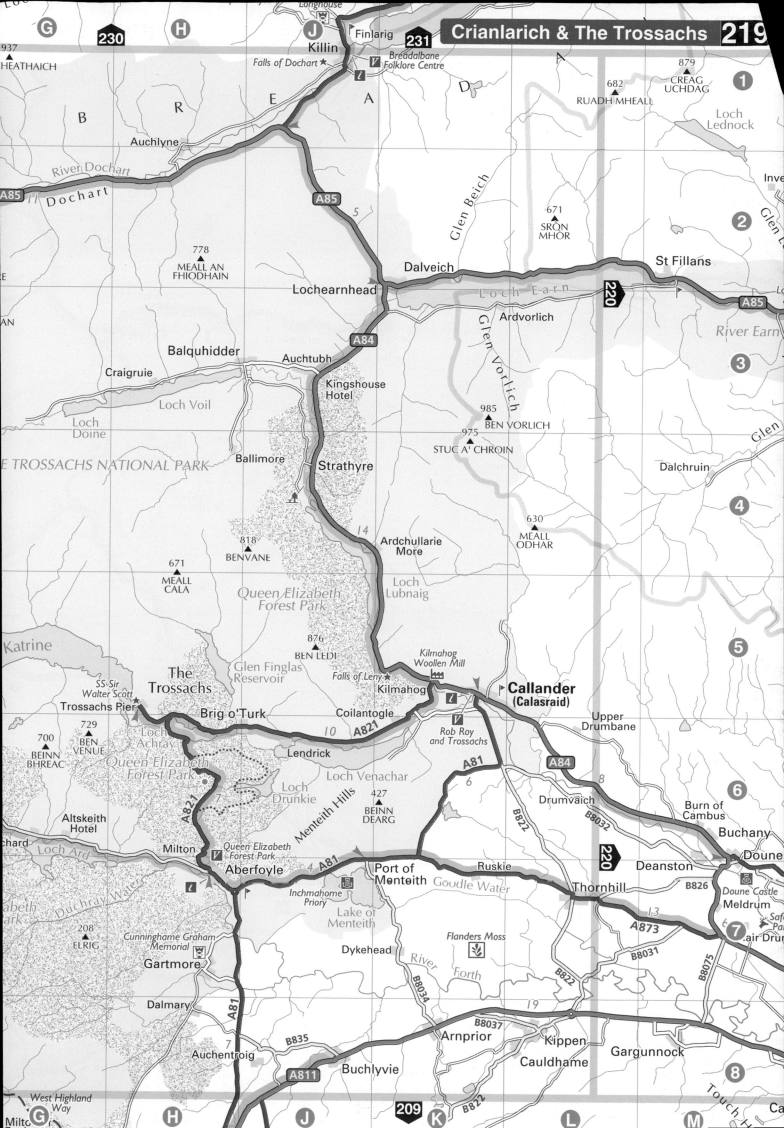

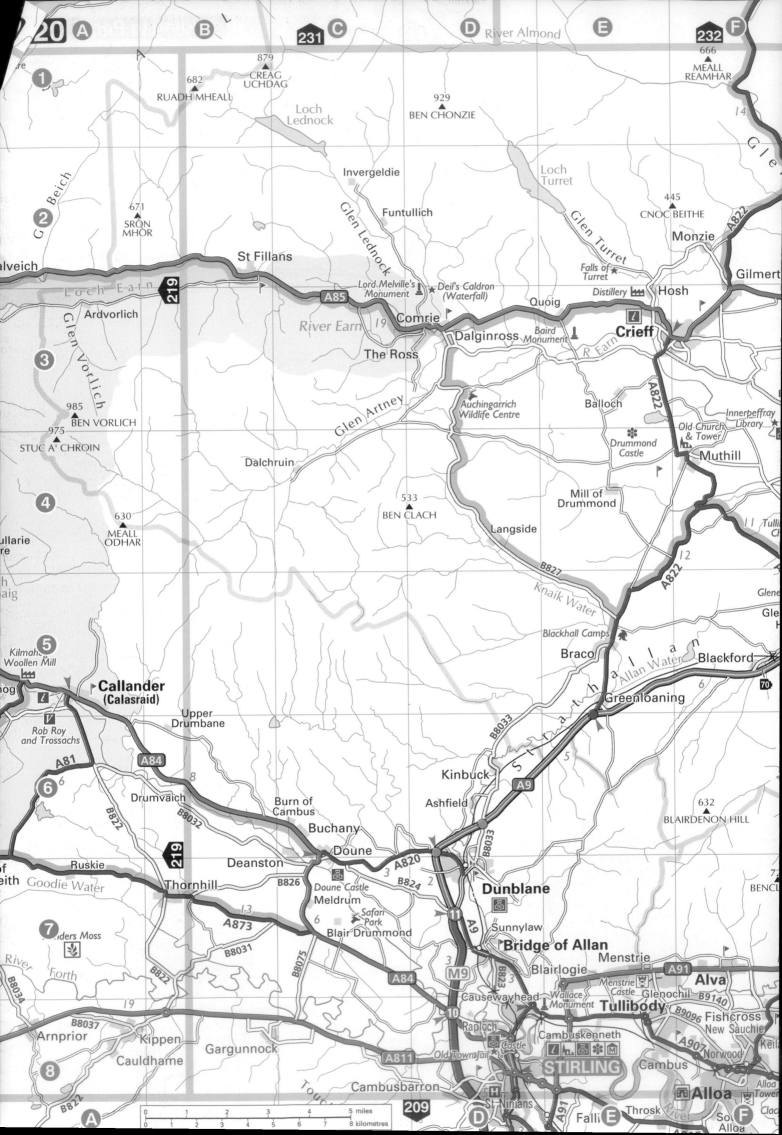

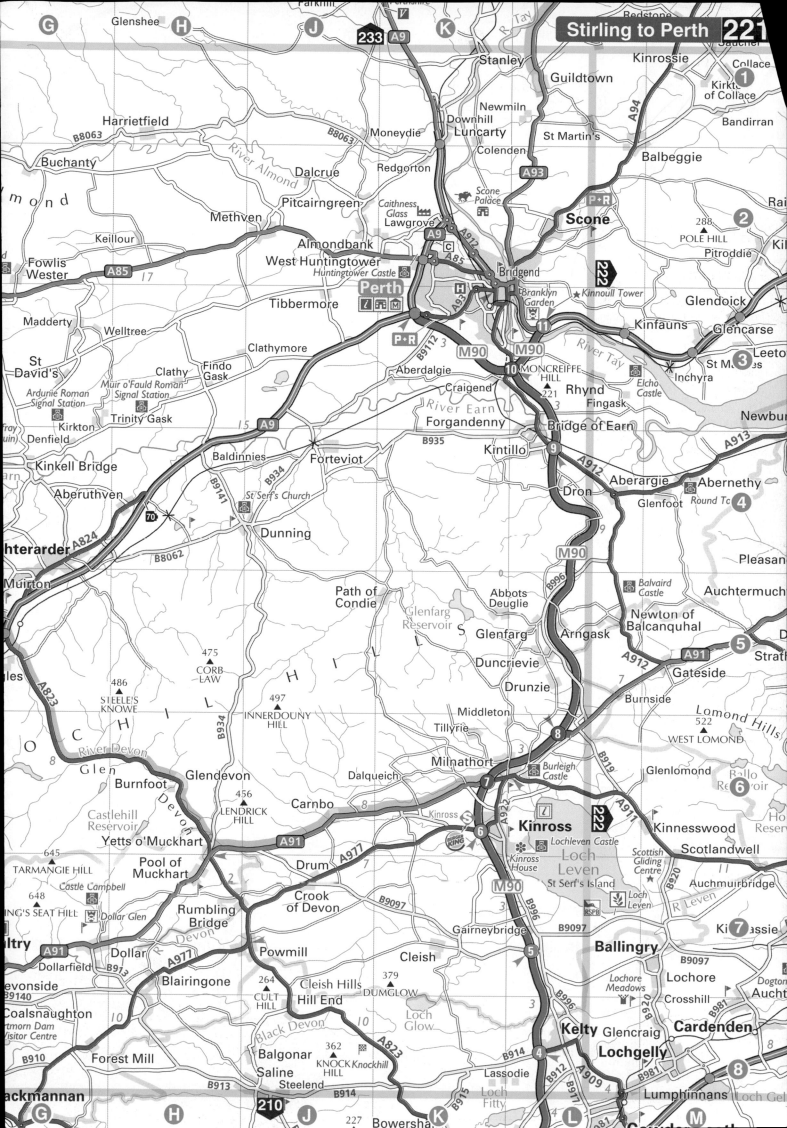

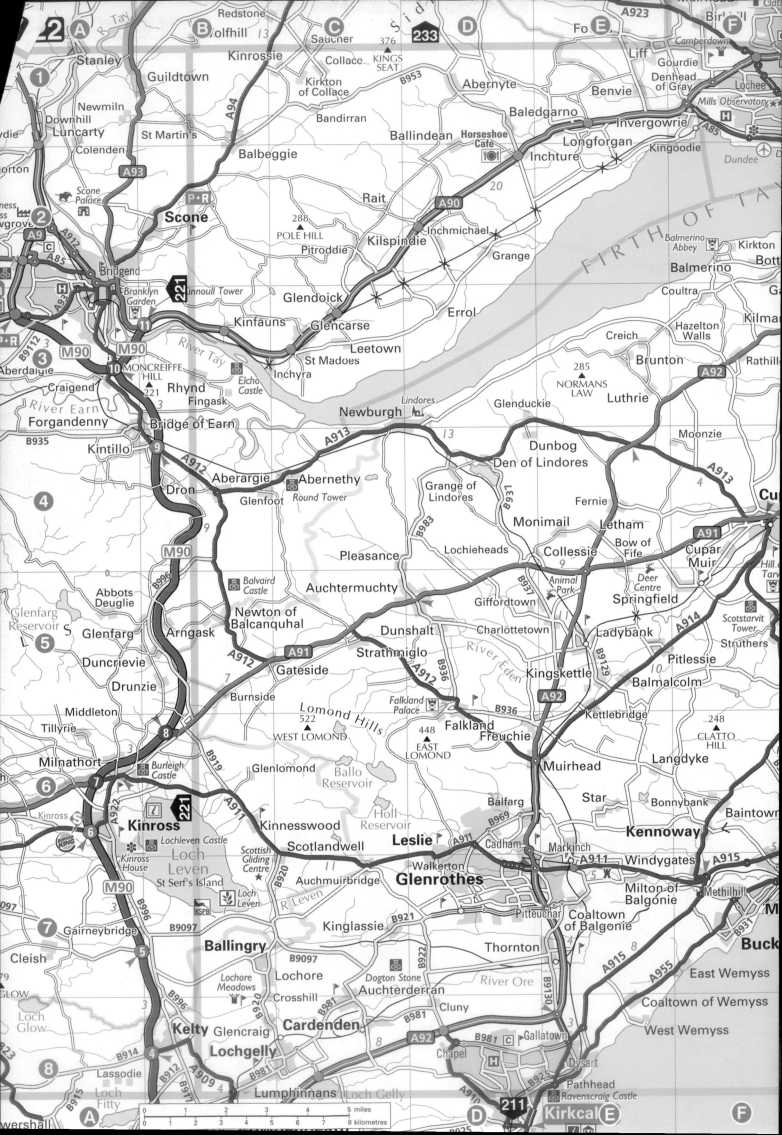

A   B   C   D   E   F

1

2

3

Grish
Clabhach

Hogh Bay   Ballyh

Totrona

4   °Feall   Arileod   Ach
Bay

Uig

RSPB

Calgary Point   Crossapol   Rudh
Bay   Fàsach

Gunna   Loch Breachacha

5   Caoles   Rudha Dubh

Rudha Port   Clachan   B8069
Bhiosd   Mor   Balephetrish   Ruaig
Loch   Bay   B8068
Bhàsapoll

Haugh   Gott
Bay   Ballevullin   Cornoigmore   Kenovay   Bay

6   Kilkenneth   Tiree   Scarinish
B8068   B8065
Moss   Heylipoll
Middleton   Crossapoll   TIREE
B8065
Barrapoll   Hynish Bay
B8067
Loch a'   Balemartine
Phuill
Mannel

Rinn   Balephuil   Hynish
7   Thorbhais   Bay

8   0   1   2   3   4   5 miles
0   1   2   3   4   5   6   7   8 kilometres

A   B   C   D   E   F

**1**

Sanna Point

Sanna Bay

Sanna
Bay

Portuairk    Achnaha

Ardnamurchan
Point

MEALL

**2**

B8007

Achosnich

342
BEINN
NA SEILG

*i* Kilc

Ormsaigmore

**236** Eilean Mòr

Bagh a Chaisteil
(Castlebay)
Loch Baghasdail
(Lochboisdale)

Rudha
Mòr

Rudha
Sgor-innis

**236**

**3**

Cliad
Bay

Bousd

Sorisdale

B8072

Ardmore Point

ost

B8071

Sorne
Point

Glengorm Castle

Quinish Point

ch
ad

Arinagour

**COLL**

Coll - Oban

To more **4**

B8070

*i*

Eilean
Ornsay

d

292
'S AIRDE
BEINN

Caliach Point

Dervaig

Achnadrish House

5

B8073

6

**5**

44
SPEINNE

Calgary

Loch Frisa

**Calgary Bay**

Treshnish Point

Ensay

342
CÀRN MÒR

Fladda

Rudh' a' Chaoil

Burg

390
Fanmore
CNOC AN DÀ CHINN

**6**

Lunga

Ballygown

Eas Fors (Waterfall)

3

BE
NAN

**226**

**TRESHNISH
ISLES**

Loch Tuath

19

Oskamull

Gometra

**ULVA**

**7**

Bac Mòr or Dutchmans Cap

Eorsa

Bac Beag

Loch

Little Colonsay

Inch Kenneth
Inchkenneth Chapel
(ruin)

B8035 17

Staffa

Fingal's Cave

*Loch na Keal,
Isle of Mull*

Balnahard

**8**

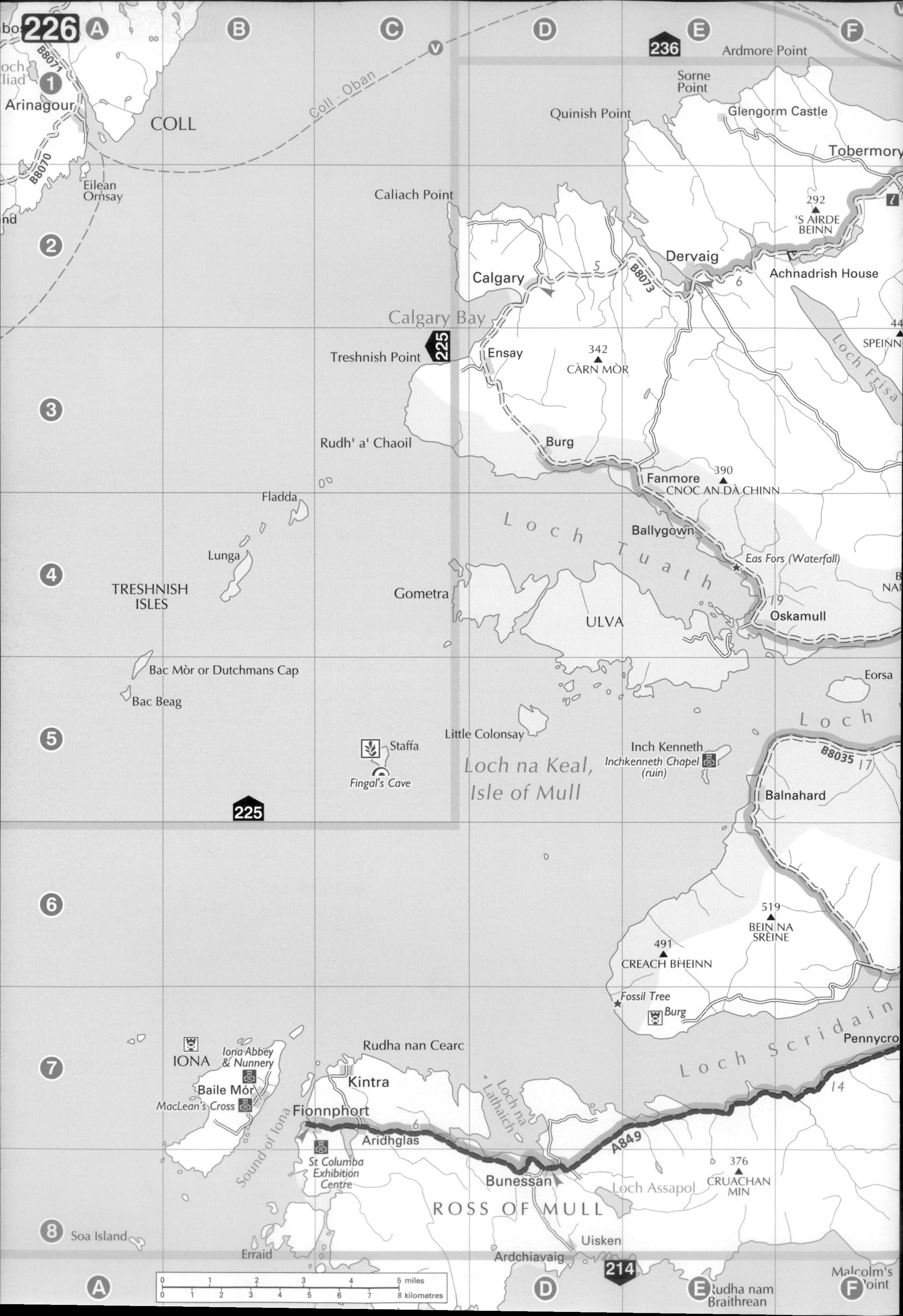

A
B
C
D
**236**
E
F

1

Arinagour
COLL
Coll · Oban
Ardmore Point
Sorne
Point
Quinish Point
Glengorm Castle
Tobermory

2

Eilean
Ornsay
Caliach Point
292 ▲
'S AIRDE
BEINN
Achnadrish House
Dervaig

B8070
B8071
B8073

Calgary
5
6
44 ▲
SPEINN
Loch Frisa

Calgary Bay

3

Treshnish Point **225**
Ensay
342 ▲
CÀRN MÒR
Burg
Rudh' a' Chaoil

Fanmore
390 ▲
CNOC AN DÀ CHINN

4

Fladda
Ballygown
Eas Fors (Waterfall) ★
Loch Tuath

Lunga
TRESHNISH
ISLES
Gometra
ULVA
Oskamull
19

Bac Mòr or Dutchmans Cap
Eorsa
Loch
B8035 17

Bac Beag

5

Staffa
Little Colonsay
Inch Kenneth
Inchkenneth Chapel
(ruin)
Balnahard

Fingal's Cave
Loch na Keal,
Isle of Mull

**225**

6

519 ▲
BEIN NA
SRÈINE
491 ▲
CREACH BHEINN

Fossil Tree ★
Burg

7

Iona Abbey
& Nunnery
Rudha nan Cearc
Pennycross
Loch Scridain

IONA
Kintra
Loch na Lathaich
14

Baile Mór
MacLean's Cross
Fionnphort
Aridhglas
6
A849

St Columba
Exhibition
Centre
Bunessan
376 ▲
CRUACHAN
MIN
Loch Assapol

8

Soa Island
ROSS OF MULL
Uisken

Erraid
Ardchiavaig
**214**
Malcolm's
Point

A
0   1   2   3   4   5 miles
0 1 2 3 4 5 6 7 8 kilometres
D
E
Rudha nam
Braithrean
F

Arùslignish

GEÀRR CHREAG

Camasine

Ardnastang

Liddesdale

Carna

Oronsay

Auliston
Point

Calve
Island

Drimnin

571
▲
BEINN
LADAIN

522
▲
MEALL A' CHOISE

Lochuisge

Loch
Teacuis

738
▲
BEINN MHEADHOIN

Glen Dubh

20

437
▲
BEINN
BHUIDHE

550
▲
SÌTHEAN NA RAPLAICH

Loch
Arienas

Acharn

Gleann Geal

Claggan

339
▲
MEALL DAMH

Larachbeg

Fuinary

Rannoch River

Achranich

Loch
Àline

Loch
Téarnait

n Aros

Aros

Lochaline

Glenaros House

464
▲
GLAIS
BHEINN

514
▲
AN
SLEAGHOCH

Salen

Fishnish
Point

A849

Fishnish Pier

Killiechronan

B8035
2

Gruline

Macquarie
Mausoleum

408
▲
BEINN
NAN LUS

Glen Forsa

Scallastle Bay

Rudha an
Ridire

Bernera
Island

Kilchera

591
▲
BEINN A' GHRÀIG

Loch Bà

636
▲
BEINN
MHEADHON

Altcreich

ISLE

Craignure

Mull & West Highland
Narrow Gauge Railway

766
▲
DÙN DA
GHAOITHE

OF

Torosay Castle

Duart
Bay

Duart
Point

Duart

966
▲
BEN
MORE

704
▲
CRUACHAN
DEARG

MULL

Lochdonhead

Lochdon

Gorten

247
▲
CÀRN
BÀN

Loch Don

Grass Point

KERRERA

Glen More

A849

Strathcoil

Loch Fuaran

717
▲
BEN
BUIE

698
▲
BEN CREACH

Loch Spelve

Croggan

216

Leidle Water

503
▲
BEINN NA
CROISE

Lochbuie

Loch
Uisg

337
▲
MAOL
BÀN

Rudha Seanach

Ard

A849

nnyghael

Carsaig

Loch Buie

377
▲
DRUIM
FADA

Barrnacarry Bay

B844

ACH

Rudha
Dubh

Colonsay - Oban

Clachan

Insh
Island

SEIL
asdale

Ellanbeic

Clachan-Seil

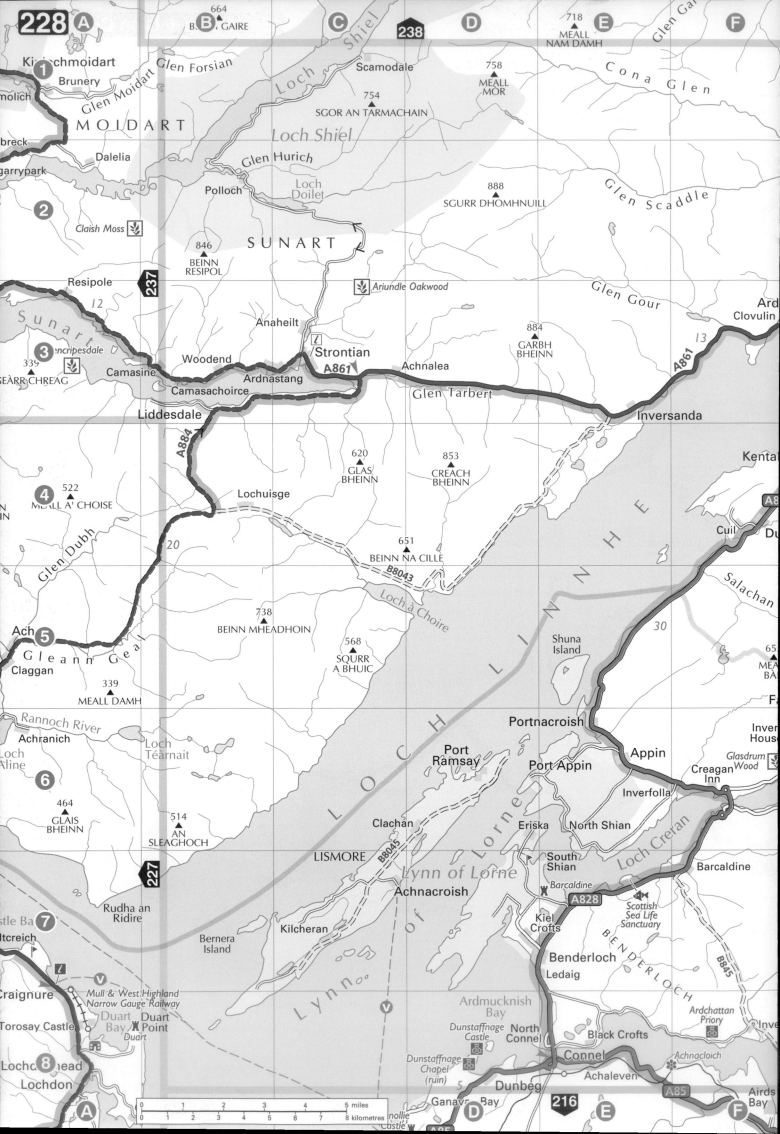

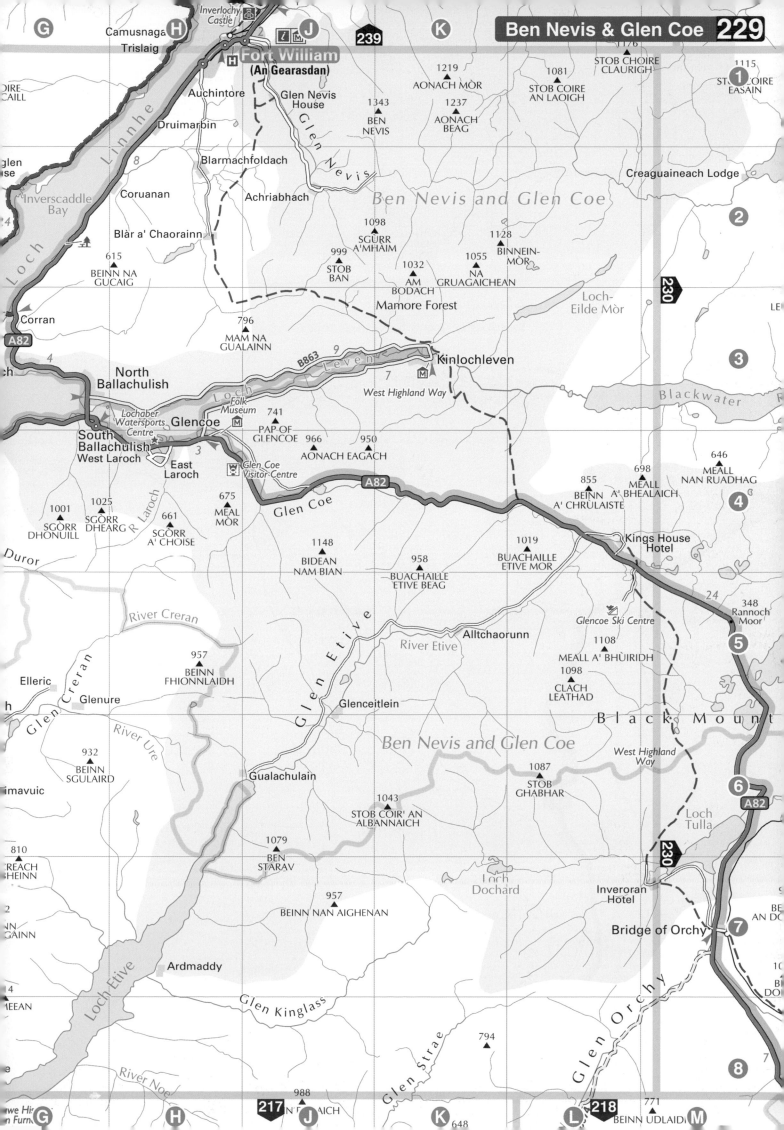

G **H** J K

Camusnaga
Trislaig

Inverlochy Castle

**Fort William**
**(An Gearasdan)**

239

**Ben Nevis & Glen Coe** 229

1176
STOB CHOIRE
CLAURIGH

1115
STOB COIRE
EASAIN 1

Auchintore

Glen Nevis House

1219
AONACH MÒR

1081
STOB COIRE
AN LAOIGH

Druimarbin

1343
BEN
NEVIS

1237
AONACH
BEAG

Blarmachfoldach

Creaguaineach Lodge

*Ben Nevis and Glen Coe* 2

OIRE
CAILL

Inverscaddle
Bay

Coruanan

Achriabhach

Blàr a' Chaorainn

1098
SGURR
A'MHAIM

1128
BINNEIN-
MÒR

glen
use

615
BEINN NA
GUCAIG

999
STOB
BAN

1032
AM
BODACH

1055
NA
GRUAGAICHEAN

230

Corran

796
MAM NA
GUALAINN

Mamore Forest

Loch-
Eilde Mòr

3

A82

B863 9

Leven

Kinlochleven

North
Ballachulish

7

Loch

West Highland Way

*Blackwater*

Folk
Museum

741

Lochaber
Watersports
Centre

Glencoe

PAP OF
GLENCOE

966

950

855
BEINN
A' CHRULAISTE

698
MEALL
A' BHEALAICH

646
MEALL
NAN RUADHAG 4

South
Ballachulish

AONACH EAGACH

West Laroch

East
Laroch

Glen Coe
Visitor Centre

675
MEAL
MÒR

Glen Coe

A82

Kings House
Hotel

Duror

1001
SGORR
DHONUILL

1025
SGORR
DHEARG

R Laroch

661
SGORR
A' CHOISE

1148
BIDEAN
NAM BIAN

958
BUACHAILLE
ETIVE BEAG

1019
BUACHAILLE
ETIVE MOR

*River Creran*

Glencoe Ski Centre

24

348
Rannoch
Moor 5

Elleric

Glenure

Glen Creran

957
BEINN
FHIONNLAIDH

Glen Etive

River Etive

Alltchaorunn

1108
MEALL A' BHÙIRIDH

1098
CLACH
LEATHAD

River Ure

Glenceitlein

B l a c k   M o u n t

932
BEINN
SGULAIRD

*Ben Nevis and Glen Coe*

West Highland
Way

imavuic

Gualachulain

1087
STOB
GHABHAR

6

A82

Loch
Tulla

810
REACH
HEINN

1043
STOB COIR' AN
ALBANNAICH

Loch
Dochard

230

2

1079
BEN
STARAV

Inveroran
Hotel

NN
GAINN

957
BEINN NAN AIGHENAN

**Bridge of Orchy**

7

AN DO

Ardmaddy

Loch Etive

Glen Kinglass

Glen Strae

794

Glen Orchy

8

River Noe

River

G H J 217 K 218 L M

988
N     AICH

648

771
BEINN UDLAID

awe Hi
Furn

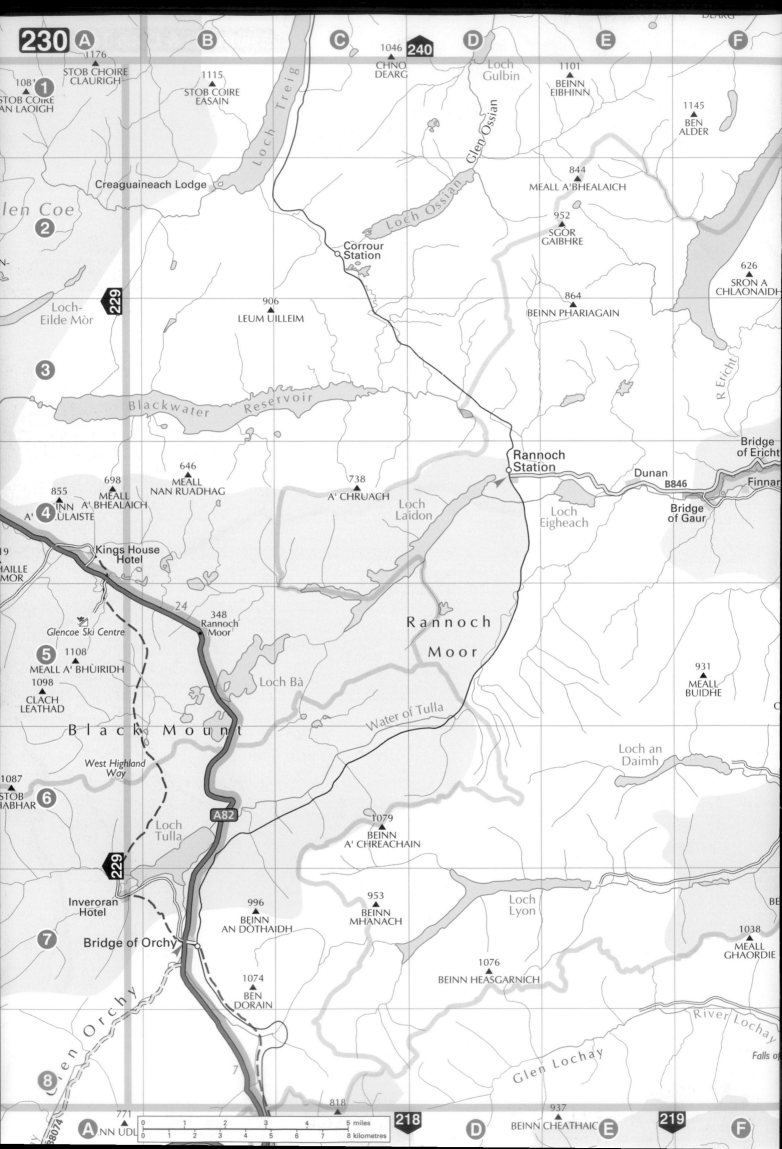

G H J 241 K

1

Loch Fri...
BEINN UDLAMAIN 1008
SGAIRNEACH MHOR 991
Dalnaspidal

A' MHARCONAICH

Glen Garry

Loch Garry
20
Dalnacardoch

A9

Glen

CRAIG BHAGAILTEACH 491

2
Calvine
M Donnachaidh
Cl... Bruar
Struan
Pitagowan
Old Struan
232
Blair

Loch Con

Loch Errochty

BEINN MHOLACH 841

Trinafour
B847

Glen Errochty

14
TORR DUBH 511

Tay Forest Park

Tressait B8019

3
Queen's View

BEINN A' CHUALLAICH 892

7 B846
R Tummel
Dunalastair
Loch Tummel

...chonan 16

Loch Rannoch

Kinloch Rannoch
Drumchastle
Tummel Bridge
Foss
Daloist
Frenich
Tay Forest Park
13
Loch Tumm...

Inverhadden
Tempar

Dunalastair Water

4

Carie

Camghouran

Tay Forest Park

SCHIEHALLION 1081

Tay Forest Park

MEALL TAIRNEACHAN 780

FARRAGON HILL 780

Loch Glassie

Glengoulandie Deer Park

B846
14

5
Menzies We...
Camserney
Dull
Dewars

Loch Rannoch and Glen Lyon

MEALL A' MHUIC 745

BEINN DEARG 824

CÀRN GORM 1027

CÀRN MAIRG 1042

Coshieville
Keltneyburn

River Tay

en Lyon

Bridge of Balgie

River Lyon

Fortingall

Tay Forest Park

Croftmoraig Stone Circle
A827
6

MEALL LUAIDHE 780

MEALL A' CHOIRE LEITH 924

MEALL GARBH 1116

MEALL GREIGH 1000

Fearnan

Kenmore
Acharn

232

...GHREAG

BEN LAWERS 1214

Lochan na Làirige

Leckbuie
BEINN BHREAC 713

The Crannog Centre

Glen Quaic...
MEAL...

7

Ben Lawers Information Centre

Lawers

A827
25

Loch Tay

SRÒN A' CHAOINEIDH 864

River Quaich

MEALL NAM FUARAN 802

Ben Lawers

Milton Morenish
Morenish

Ardeonaig

River Almond

8

Moirlanich Longhouse

Finlarig

Killin
Loch...
Breadalbane Folklore Centre

G H 219 J K 220 L M

CREAG 879

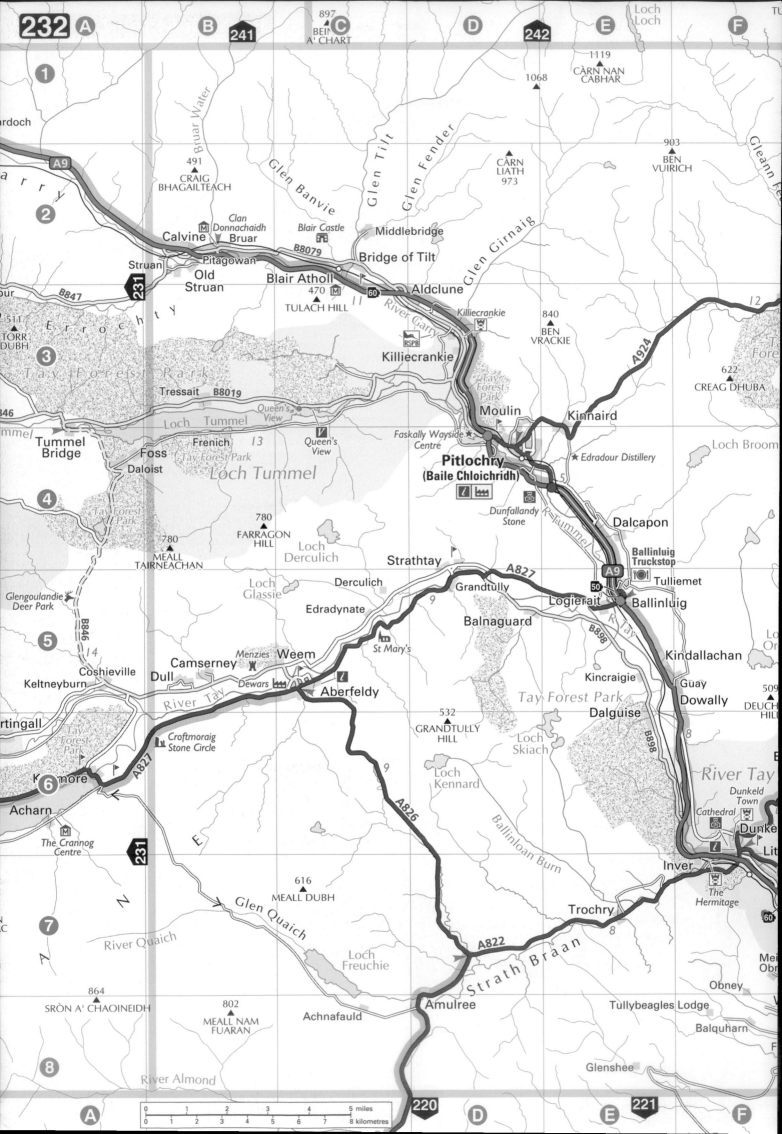

A | B | C | D | E | F

897
BEIN
A' CHART

1119
CÀRN NAN
CABHAR

1068

**1**

903
BEN
VUIRICH

Gleann

491
CRAIG
BHAGAILTEACH

Glen Banvie

Glen Tilt

Glen Fender

CÀRN
LIATH
973

ardoch

A9

Glen Girnaig

Clan
Donnachaidh
Bruar

Blair Castle

Middlebridge

**2**

Calvine

Bruar

Bridge of Tilt

B8079

Struan

Pitagowan

Old
Struan

Blair Atholl

Aldclune

511

231

B847

60

River Garry

Killiecrankie

840
BEN
VRACKIE

Kinnaird

12

**3**

TORR
DUBH

Tay Forest Park

470
TULACH HILL

RSPB

Killiecrankie

Tay
Forest
Park

622
CREAG DHUBA

T
Fore

Tressait

B8019

Loch Tummel

Queen's
View

Moulin

A924

846

Tummel

Tummel
Bridge

Foss

Frenich

Queen's
View

Faskally Wayside
Centre

**Pitlochry**
**(Baile Chloichridh)**

Edradour Distillery

Loch Broom

13

Tay Forest Park

Daloist

Loch Tummel

i

Dunfallandy
Stone

R. Tummel

Dalcapon

**4**

Tay
Forest
Park

780
FARRAGON
HILL

Loch
Derculich

Ballinluig
Truckstop

780
MEALL
TAIRNEACHAN

Strathtay

A827

A9

5

Tulliemet

Glengoulandie
Deer Park

B846

Derculich

Grantully

50

Lo
On

**5**

14

Loch
Glassie

Edradynate

9

Balnaguard

Logierait

Ballinluig

Kindallachan

Coshieville

Menzies

Weem

St Mary's

Kincraigie

Guay

Keltneyburn

Camserney

Dull

Dewars

Aberfeldy

Tay Forest Park

Dowally

509
DEUCH
HILL

tingall

River Tay

532
GRANDTULLY
HILL

Dalguise

River Tay

Tay Forest
Park

Croftmoraig
Stone Circle

A827

Loch
Skiach

Dunkeld
Town

**6**

K more

Acharn

231

The Crannog
Centre

A826

Loch
Kennard

Cathedral

i

Dunke

Inver

Lit

616
MEALL DUBH

9

Ballinloan Burn

The
Hermitage

60

**7**

Glen Quaich

Trochry

8

Me
Obr

River Quaich

Loch
Freuchie

A822

Strath Braan

Obney

864
SRÒN A' CHAOINEIDH

802
MEALL NAM
FUARAN

Achnafauld

Amulree

Tullybeagles Lodge

Balquharn

**8**

River Almond

Glenshee

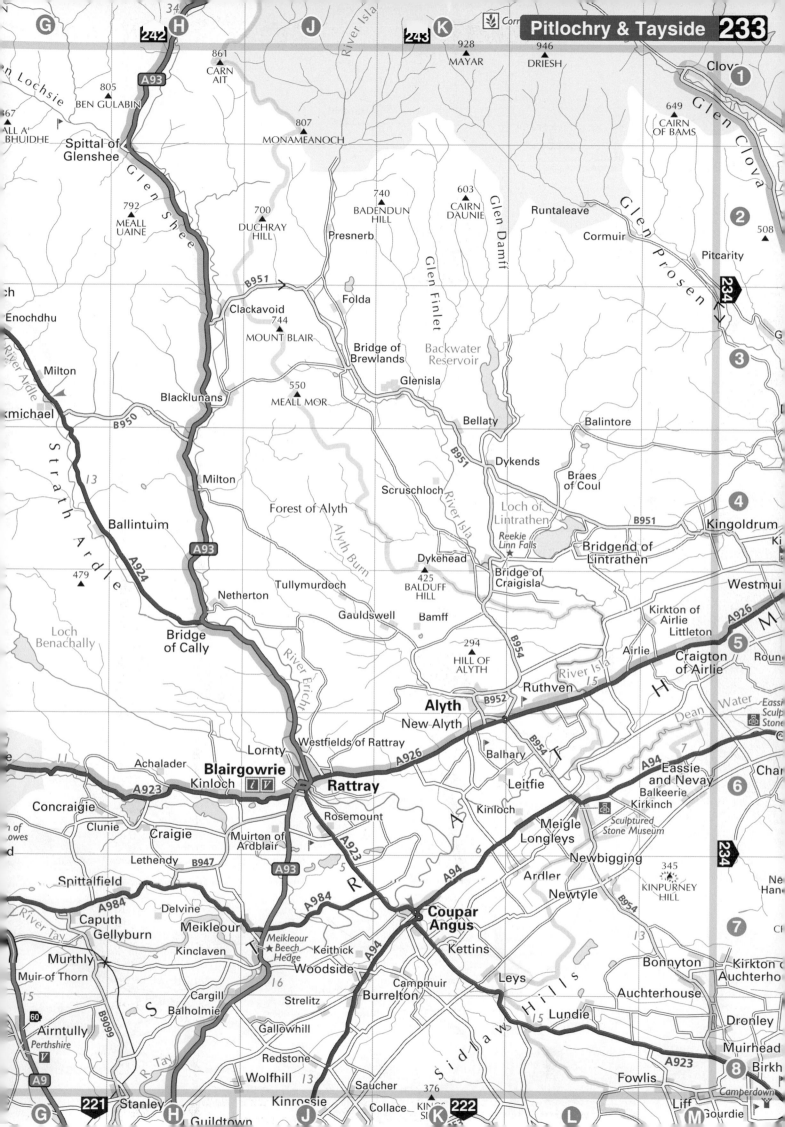

G  242  H  J  243  K

Glen Lochsie

34

River Isla

Corr

928 ▲
MAYAR

946 ▲
DRIESH

Clova
1

805 ▲
BEN GULABIN

A93

861 ▲
CARN
AIT

649 ▲
CAIRN
OF BAMS

Glen Clova

67 ▲
ALL A'
BHUIDHE

807 ▲
MONAMEANOCH

2

508 ▲

Spittal of
Glenshee

Glen Shee

792 ▲
MEALL
UAINE

700 ▲
DUCHRAY
HILL

740 ▲
BADENDUN
HILL

603 ▲
CAIRN
DAUNIE

Runtaleave

Cormuir

Pitcarity

Glen Damff

Glen Prosen

234

ch
Enochdhu

B951

Clackavoid

Presnerb

Folda

Glen Finlet

3

River Ardle

Milton

744 ▲
MOUNT BLAIR

Bridge of
Brewlands

Backwater
Reservoir

kmichael

Blacklunans

B950

550 ▲
MEALL MOR

Glenisla

Bellaty

Balintore

Braes
of Coul

Strath Ardle

13

Milton

Forest of Alyth

Scruschloch

River Isla

B951

Dykends

Loch of
Lintrathen

Reekie
Linn Falls ★

B951

Bridgend of
Lintrathen

Kingoldrum

4

Ki

Ballintuim

A93

479 ▲

Alyth Burn

Dykehead

425 ▲
BALDUFF
HILL

Bridge of
Craigisla

Westmui

Kirkton of
Airlie
Littleton

A926

M

A924

Netherton

Tullymurdoch

Gauldswell

Bamff

B954

Airlie

Craigton
of Airlie

5

Roun

Loch
Benachally

Bridge
of Cally

294 ▲
HILL OF
ALYTH

River Isla

15

H

Dean Water

Eassi
Sculp
Stone

River Ericht

Ruthven

B952

**Alyth**

New Alyth

A926

Balhary

B954

T

A94

Eassie
and Nevay

6

Char

Achalader

Westfields of Rattray

Lornty

**Blairgowrie**

Kinloch  i V

**Rattray**

Balharry

Leitfie

Kinloch

A

Balkeerie
Kirkinch

Meigle
Longleys

Sculptured
Stone Museum

234

Concraigie

Clunie

Craigie

Muirton of
Ardblair

Rosemount

A923

A923

5

6

Ardler

Newbigging

Newtyle

B954

345 ▲
KINPURNEY
HILL

Ne
Han

of
owes
d

Lethendy

B947

Spittalfield

A984

Delvine

Meikleour

A93

A984

R

Coupar
Angus

A94

Kettins

Campmuir

Leys

Bonnyton

Auchterho

Kirkton of
Auchterhouse

7

River Tay

Caputh
Gellyburn

Kinclaven

Meikleour
Beech ★
Hedge

Keithick

Woodside

Burrelton

Sidlaw Hills

Lundie

Auchterhouse

Dronley

Murthly

Muir of Thorn

15

B9099

Cargill
Balholmie

16

S

Strelitz

15

Muirhead

A923

60

Airntully

Perthshire V

B9009

Gallowhill

Redstone

376 ▲

Camperdown

Birkh

8

A9

221  Stanley

Guildtown

H

Wolfhill

13

Kinrossie

J

Saucher

Collace

KING
SI

222  K

L

Fowlis

M  Liff  Gourdie

G

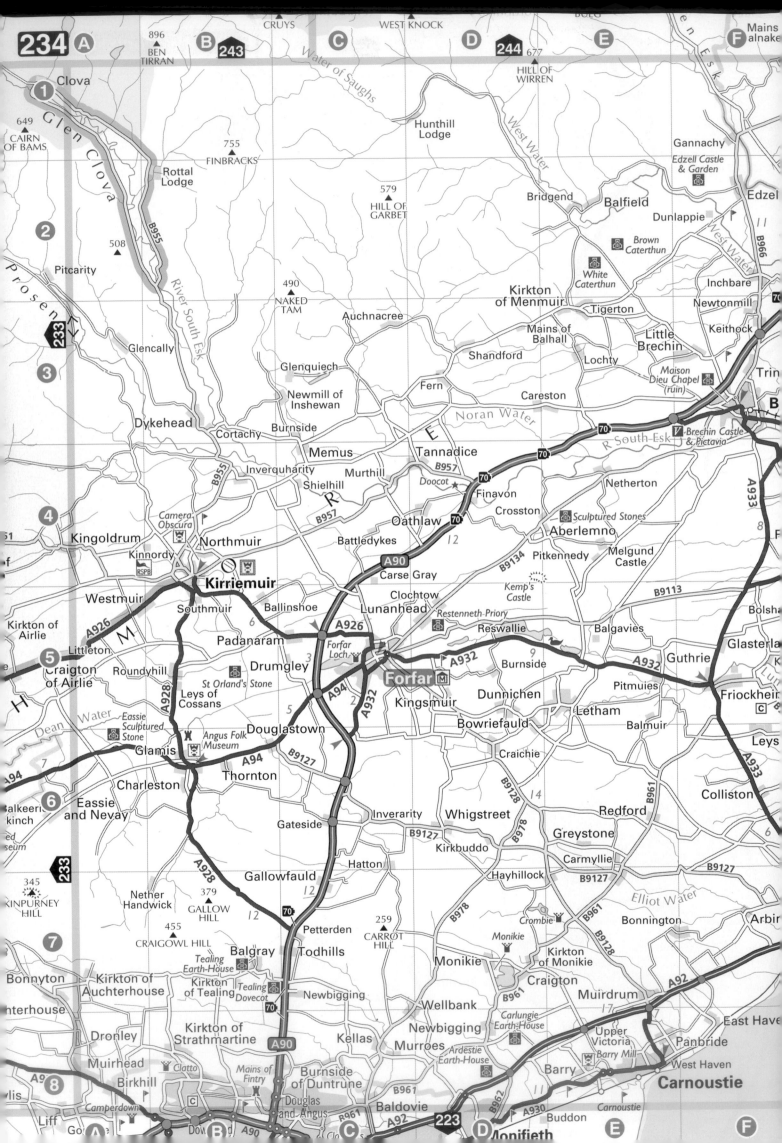

G H J K

1

Pittarrow

244

Fordoun
edmyre

245

Airbuthnott

A

Inverbervie

Bervie
Bay

Gourdon

airn

Mains of
Haulkerton

B9120

50

70

25

Laurencekirk

B9120

Redford

Benholm

2

Sauchieburn
l
s
hermuir

B974

70

70

A90

B974

North

Esk

o Hospital

Dykelands

Marykirk

Craigo

Logie Pert

Logie

Lochside

Morphie

A937

Bush

St Cyrus

Johnshaven

Milton Ness

Gogmuir

North

3

Hillside

A92

House of
Dun

Dun

Montrose Air Station

Montrose

A935

9

Montrose
Basin

4

Barnhead

Maryton

Craig

A934

Scurdie Ness

Ferryden

Usan

Westerton

5

Braehead

Boddin Point

Lunan

Lunan Bay

Inverkeilor

13

Red Head

pelton

Cauldcots

6

A92

Marywell

Auchmithie

eans

Carlingheugh
Bay

The Deil's
Head

7

Arbroath

i

8

G H J K L M

A Bhrideanach

MULLACH MÒR

Rubha na Roinne

Kinloch

Loch Scresort

570
▲
ORVAL

RÙM

810
▲
ASKIVAL

763
▲
SGÙRR NAN GILLEAN

*The Small Isles*

Rudha nam Meirleach

*S o u n d   o f   R u m*

Bay of Laig

Cleadale

299
▲
AN CRUACHAN

Rudha an Fhasaidh

Laig

EIGG

Kildon

393
▲
AN SGÙRR

Sandavor

Eilean Chathastail

*S o u n d   o f   E i g g*

Eilean nan Each

MUCK

Port Mor

Sanna Point

Sanna Bay

Sanna Bay

Portuairk

Achnaha

MEAL

Ardnamurchan Point

Achosnich

B8007

342
▲
BEINN NA SEILG

Ki

Ormsaigmo

V Bagh a Chaisteil (Castlebay)
Loch Baghasdail (Lochboisdale)

Eilean Mòr

225

Rudha Mòr

Rudha Sgor-innis

Bousd

Sorisdale

COLL

Cliad Bay

B8072

abost

B8071

Loch Cliad

Coll - Oban V

0  1  2  3  4  5 miles
0  1  2  3  4  5  6  7  8 kilometres

Ardmore Point

Sorne P

226

Glengorm Castle

G   H   J   247   V   K   Cand.   KNOYD

Sleat
Ard Thurinish
Point of Sleat

Inverie Bay

Rudha Raonuill

Courteachan
Mallaigvaig
Mallaig (Malaig)   V   547   CÀRN A'GHOBHAIR
Glasnacardoch Bay
Loch an Nostaire   437   SGÙRR BHUIDHE

Loch Nevis

Beoraidbeg
Morar   Bracora   Bracorina

Glenancross   238   Swordland

Loch Morar

Lettermorar   jesm

BEINN B

B8008   A830

Meoble   7   MEITH

Eilean Ighe
Bunacaimb   503   CÀRN A' MHÀDAIDH-RUAIDH

Back of Keppoch
Luinga Mhòr   Arisaig   600   SIDHEAN MÒR

Loch nan Ceall   10

Rudh' Arisaig   Druimindarroch   Prince Charlie's Cairn
103   CRUACH DOIRE   Arisaig House   Kinlochnanuagh

Loch nan Uamh   Polnish   Loch

Sound of Arisaig   Ardnish   Lochailort   4   Loch Eilt
Rudha Choalais   Inverailort

Loch Ailort   A861   877   ROIS-BHEINN

Smearisary   Glenuig   712   5

Eilean Shona   664   BEINN GAIRE

Rudha Aird Druimnich   Loch Moidart   Kinlochmoidart   Glen Forsian

Morar, Moidart and Ardnamurchan   Tioram   Brunery   Glen Moidart

Ockle Point   239   Ardmolich   MOIDART   6   Loch S
Ardtoe   BEINN BHREAC
mory   Ockle   Shielfoot   Dalnabreck   Dalelia
Branault   356   BEINN BHREAC   Kentra   Blain   Mingarrypark   228   Glen Hurich
B8044   Polloch   Loch Doile

ARDNAMURCHAN   Arevegaig   Acharacle   A861   Claish Moss   SUNAR

Loch Mudle   437   846   BEINN RESIPOL   7

527   BEN HIANT   Salen   Resipole   12   Anaheilt
19   Glenbeg   512   BEN LAGA   B8007   Loch Sunart   Glencripesdale
Ardslignish   Glenborrodale   Laga   RSPB   339   GEÀRR CHREAG   Camasine   Woodend   Ardnastang
Oronsay   Carna   Camasachoirce   A884   S

Auliston Point   227   Liddesdale   8

G   H   J   227   K   L   M

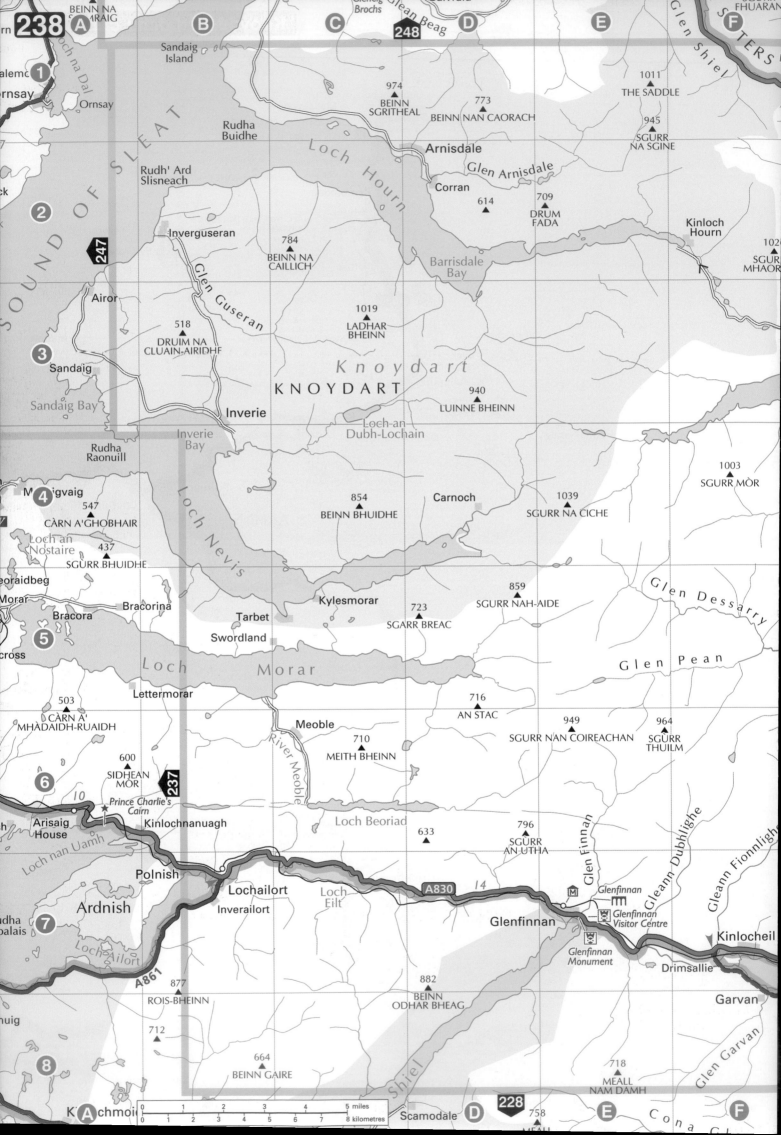

A     B     C     **248**     D     E     F

BEINN NA
...MRAIG

Glen Beag
Brochs

Glenelg Glen Beag

Glen Shiel

Glen
FHUARAN

STERS

1

alemc
Loch na Dal
rn
Ornsay
Ornsay

Sandaig
Island

974
▲
BEINN
SGRITHEAL

773
▲
BEINN NAN CAORACH

Arnisdale

Glen Arnisdale

1011
▲
THE SADDLE

2

**247**

Rudha
Buidhe

Rudh' Ard
Slisneach

Corran

614
▲

945
▲
SGURR
NA SGINE

709
▲
DRUM
FADA

Kinloch
Hourn

102
SGUR
MHAOR

Inverguseran

Glen Guseran

784
▲
BEINN NA
CAILLICH

Loch Hourn

Barrisdale
Bay

3

Airor

518
▲
DRUIM NA
CLUAIN-AIRIDHF

1019
▲
LADHAR
BHEINN

Sandaig

Sandaig Bay

*Knoydart*

**KNOYDART**

940
▲
LUINNE BHEINN

Loch-an
Dubh-Lochain

1003
▲
SGURR MÒR

Inverie

Inverie
Bay

Rudha
Raonuill

4

M...igvaig

547
▲
CÀRN A'GHOBHAIR

Loch an
Nostaire

437
▲
SGURR BHUIDHE

854
▲
BEINN BHUIDHE

Carnoch

1039
▲
SGURR NA CICHE

Glen Dessarry

...eoraidbeg

...Morar

Bracora

Bracorina

Kylesmorar

859
▲
SGURR NAH-AIDE

5

Tarbet

Swordland

723
▲
SGARR BREAC

Glen Pean

cross

Loch    Morar

Lettermorar

503
▲
CÀRN A'
MHÀDAIDH-RUAIDH

Meoble

716
▲
AN STAC

949
▲
SGURR NAN COIREACHAN

964
▲
SGURR
THUILM

6

600
▲
SIDHEAN
MÒR

**237**

10

Prince Charlie's
Cairn

Kinlochnanuagh

River Meoble

710
▲
MEITH BHEINN

Loch Beoriad

633
▲

796
▲
SGURR
AN UTHA

Glen Finnan

Gleann Dubhlighe

Gleann Fionnligh

Arisaig
House

Polnish

Loch nan Uamh

Lochailort

Inverailort

Loch
Eilt

**A830**

14

Glenfinnan

Glenfinnan
Visitor Centre

7

...dha
...alais

Ardnish

Loch Ailort

A861

877
▲
ROIS-BHEINN

Glenfinnan
Monument

Drimsallie

Kinlocheil

Garvan

Glen Garvan

...nuig

712
▲

882
▲
BEINN
ODHAR BHEAG

8

664
▲
BEINN GAIRE

Shiel

**228**

758
MEA...

Meall
Nam Damh

718
▲
MEALL
NAM DAMH

Glen Cl

K...chmoi

A   0   1   2   3   4   5 miles
  0   1   2   3   4   5   6   7   8 kilometres

Scamodale   D    E    Cona   F

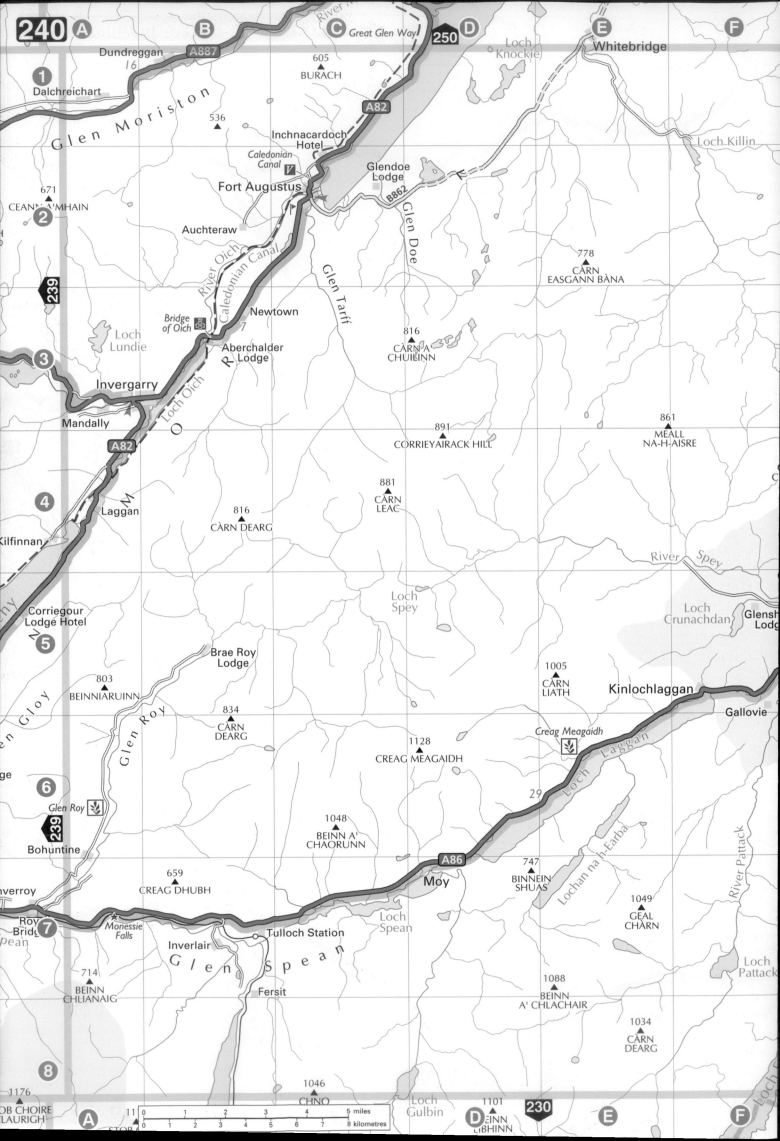

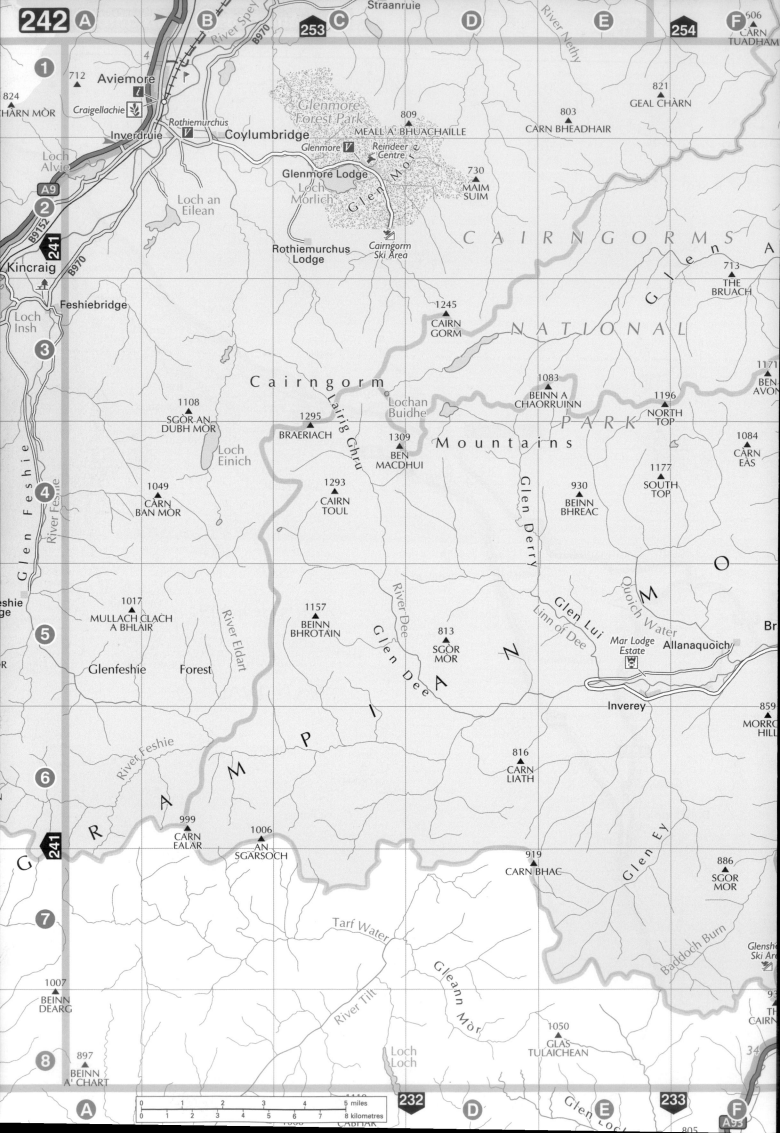

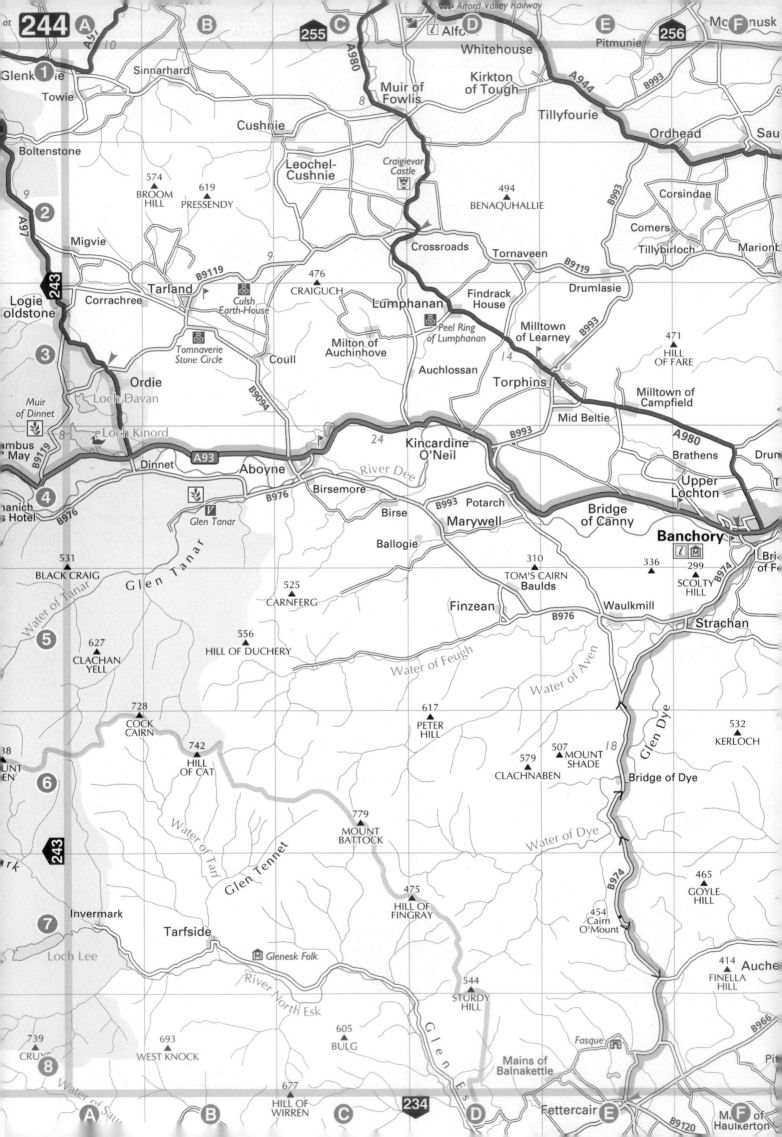

Ke**G**ay
Kintore
Cottown
gearn
Leylodge
le Fraser
B994
B977
B979
256
J
Dyce-Symbol Stones
Overton
Aberdeen
Dyce
Parkhill House
Blackdog
B999
B997
1

Lyne of Skene
Blackburn
A96
Stoneywood
40
Denmore
P+R
Bridge of Don
V
Kirkwall
Lerwick
2

Clinterty
Bucksburn
Bankhead
A90
30
40
30
40
Northfield
Old Aberdeen

necht
Skene House
B9126
Millbuie
B9979
265
BRIMMOND HILL
Kittybrewster
H

in
Loch of Skene
B977
Kirkton of Skene
Westhill
Kingswells
P+R

Garlogie
Carnie
Elrick
Kingsford
A944
B9119
C
Ruthrieston
Torry
Nigg Bay

Echt
Redhill
B9119
B9979
ABERDEEN
Mannofield
A956
2

erberry
Cullerlie
B9125
Cullerlie Stone Circle
Easter Ord
Blacktop
Cults
Kincorth
40
Nigg
Altens Haven

Hardgate
Benthoul
Milltimber
Bieldside
Banchory-Devenick
Cove Bay
3

Hirn
Drum Castle
18
Craigton
B9077
Kingcausie
Charlestown
A90

Myrebird
West Park
River Dee
Peterculter
Marywell

Crathes Castle
A93
Maryculter
Hillside

rathes
Deeside lway
B9077
B979
Auchlee
70
Findon
4

Durris
Denside
Portlethen
Cammachmore Bay

Woodlands
Downies

Crossroads
Cammachmore

Cookney
Newtonhill
5

A957
Netherley
Skateraw

376
MONGOUR
B979
Muchalls

15
Doonie Point
A90
70

320
HILL OF TRUSTA
Garron Point
Stonehaven Bay
6

390
HIE HILL
Elfhill
Kirktown of Fetteresso
70
Stonehaven
i M

Tannachie
A90
70
Dunnottar

osecruives
New Mill

Water
Drumlithie
70
Temple of Fiddes
10
Crawton
7

Glenbervie
Mondynes
70
RSPB
Fowlsheugh
Trelong Bay

B967
Kinneff
Catterline

doun
Redmyre
70
Arbuthnott
A92
Todhead Point
8

| 0 | 1 | 2 | 3 | 4 | 5 miles |
| 0 | 1 2 3 | 4 5 | 6 7 | 8 kilometres |

G
235
H
J
K
L
M

Harlosh

HEALAVAL
BHEAG
B

C **258** Colbost
Point

Loch

Os D

E

F

Glen

Loch Duagrich

Mug

**1**

368
▲
BEINN NA
BOINEID

Harlosh
Island

Tarner
Island

Dun
Beag

Bracadale

Loch Bracadale

Ullinish
Lodge Hotel

Struan

Coillore

Wiay

23

**2**

Idrigill
Point

Oronsay

Portnalong

Fiskavaig

Loch Harport

439
▲
ROINEVAL

Rudha nan Clach

B8009

Fernilea

Drynoch

A863

369
▲
ARNAVAL

Carbost

Merkadale

Glen Dryno

**3**

Talisker
Bay

Talisker

Glen Eynort

369
▲
BEINN BHR

447
▲
BEINN
BHREAC

Grula

**4**

Loch Eynort

434
▲
AN CRUACHIN

Glenbrittle House

9
SGU
A' GHE

C u

Bualintur

S
ALA

**5**

Loch Brittle

225
▲
CEANN NA BEINNE

Rudh' an Dùnain

Soay Soun

**6**

Ru
Aong

C
U
I
L
L
I

**7**

CANNA

Garrisdale Point

210
▲
CÀRN A' GHAILL

A'Chill

Canna
Harbour

Rudha
Shamhnan Insir

Sanday

RÙM

**8**

Sound of Canna

302
▲
MULLACH
MÒR

Rudha na
Roinne

Kinloch   Loch
Screscort

0   1   2   3   4   5 miles
0   1   2   3   4   5   6   7   8 kilometres

A Bhrideanach

**236**

570
▲
ORVAL

A         B         C         D         E         F

259

Penifiler

412
BEN TIANAVAIG

G

H

J

444
DÙN CAAN

Camusterrach

Culduie

A87

Camastianavaig
Tianavaig Bay

Ollach

Oskaig

Rudha na' Leac

Toscaig

River Toscaig

1

Clachan

B883

Inverarish

310
BEINN NA LEAC

Caolas Mòr

2

The Braes

Eilean Meadhonach

Eilean Mòr

Port-an-Eo

Glen Varragill

444
BEN LEE

Peinchorran

Suisnish Point

Eyre Point

SCALPAY

CROWLIN ISLANDS

Drumbu

V

Sconser

67
Longay

248

Clachan

773
GLAMAIG

A87

Loch Ainort

Dunan

Luib

17

Caolas Scalpay

396
MULLACH NA CARN

Pabay

27

Badicaul

Kyle of Loch
(Caol Loch Ailse)

3

ISLE OF SKYE

564
GLAS BHEIN MHÒRN

M

Luib Folk

Broadford Bay

Lower Breakish

Skye Bridge

Kyleakin

965

N GILLEAN

The Cuillin Hills

Hills

732
BEINN NA CAILLICH

Corry

Broadford

Waterloo

Upper Breakish

A87

708
BEINN DEORG MHÒR

B8083

Harrapool

Skulamus

4

732
SGURR NA COINNICH

927
BLAVEN

Torrin

14

605
BEN ASLAK

Ky

Loch na Crèitheach

A851

Loch ruisk

4

RS NN

Kirkibost

B8083

Loch Slapin

300
BEINN NAN CARN

Heast

561
BEINN NA SEAMRAIG

5

344
BEN MEABOST

Suisnish

Drumfearn

Loch na Dal

Sandaig Island

Loch Scavaig

Elgol

Rudha Suisnish

Loch Eishort

Duisdalemore

6

hlach

Glasnakille

298
SGORACH BREAC

Isleornsay

Ornsay

AY

Strathaird Point

Tokavaig

Ord River

SOUND OF SLEAT

Rudh' Ard Slisneach

Tarskavaig

Teangue

17

238

Tarskavaig Bay

Achnacloich

Loch nam Uamph

Knock

Invergusera

7

Ferrindonald

Knock Bay

Airor

Glen G

Kilmore

Kilbeg

518
DRUM NA CLUAIN-AIRIDHE

Aird of Sleat

Clan Donald

V

Ardvasar

A851

Armadale

Calligarry

Sandaig

G

H

J

K

L

M

Point of Sleat

Ard Thurinish

237

Sandaig Bay

Rudha Raonuill

Inverie Bay

8

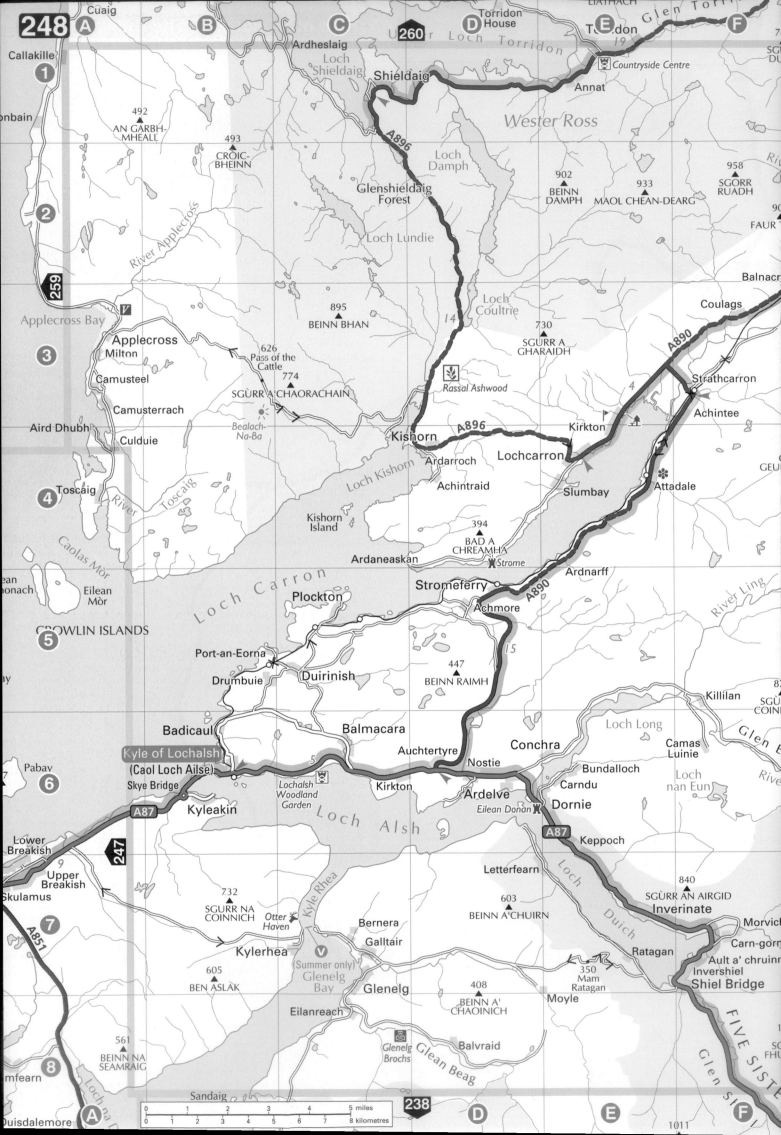

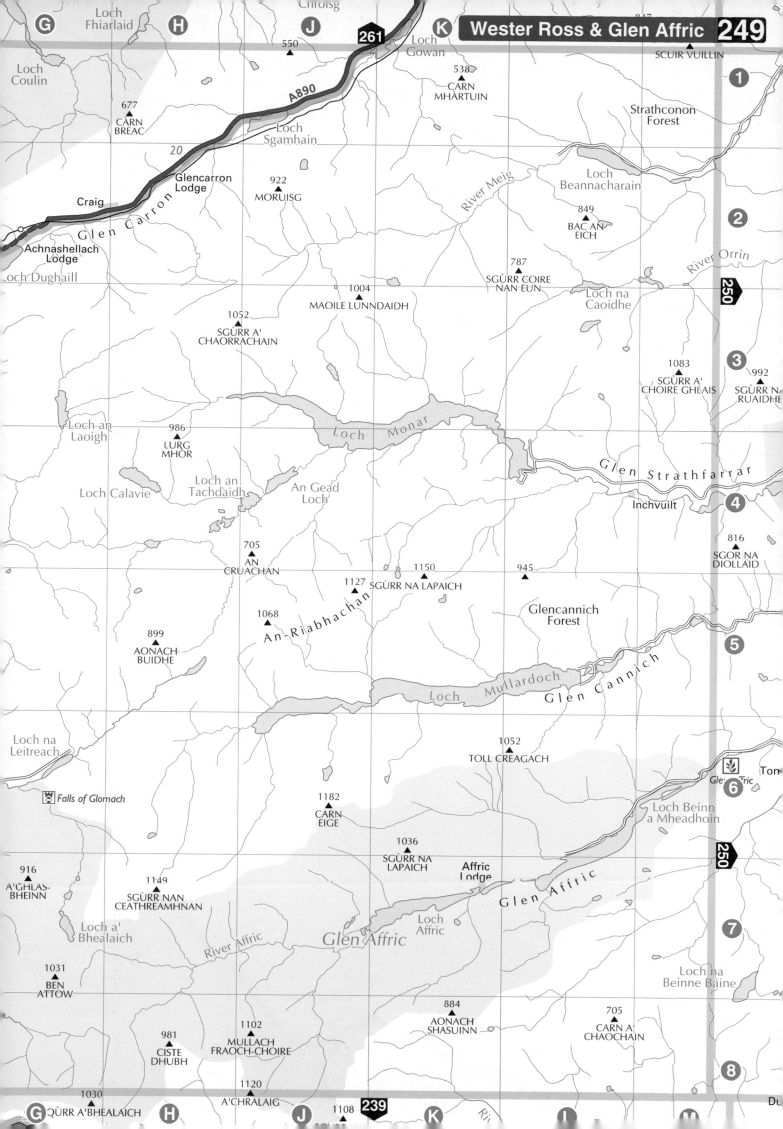

G
H
J
K

Loch Fhiarlaid
Chroisg
Loch Gowan
SCUIR VUILLIN

**1**

Loch Coulin
550 ▲
538 ▲ CARN MHÀRTUIN
Strathconon Forest

A890
677 ▲ CARN BREAC
Loch Sgamhain
River Meig
Loch Beannacharain

**2**

20
Glencarron Lodge
922 ▲ MORUISG
849 ▲ BAC AN EICH
River Orrin

Craig
Glen Carron
787 ▲ SGÙRR COIRE NAN EUN
**250**

Achnashellach Lodge
1004 ▲ MAOILE LUNNDAIDH
Loch na Caoidhe

och Dughaill

1052 ▲ SGÙRR A' CHAORRACHAIN
1083 ▲ SGÙRR A' CHOIRE GHLAIS
992 ▲ SGÙRR N. RUAIDHE

**3**

Loch-an Laoigh
986 ▲ LURG MHOR
Loch Monar
Glen Strathfarrar

Loch Calavie
Loch an Tachdaidh
An Gead Loch
Inchvuilt

**4**

816 ▲ SGOR NA DIOLLAID

705 ▲ AN CRUACHAN
1150 ▲
945 ▲

1127 ▲ SGÙRR NA LAPAICH

1068 ▲
An-Riabhachan
Glencannich Forest

899 ▲ AONACH BUIDHE

**5**

Loch Mullardoch
Glen Cannich

Loch na Leitreach

1052 ▲ TOLL CREAGACH

Glen Affric
Ton

**6**

Falls of Glomach

1182 ▲ CARN EIGE
Loch Beinn a Mheadhoin

1036 ▲ SGÙRR NA LAPAICH
**250**

916 ▲ A'GHLAS-BHEINN
1149 ▲ SGÙRR NAN CEATHREAMHNAN
Affric Lodge

Glen Affric

**7**

Loch a' Bhealaich
River Affric
Glen Affric
Loch Affric
Loch na Beinne Bàine

1031 ▲ BEN ATTOW

884 ▲ AONACH SHASUINN
705 ▲ CARN A' CHAOCHAIN

1102 ▲ MULLACH FRAOCH-CHOIRE
981 ▲ CISTE DHUBH

1030 ▲ SGÙRR A'BHEALAICH
1120 ▲ A'CHRALAIG
1108 ▲
**239**

**8**

G
H
J
K
I
M

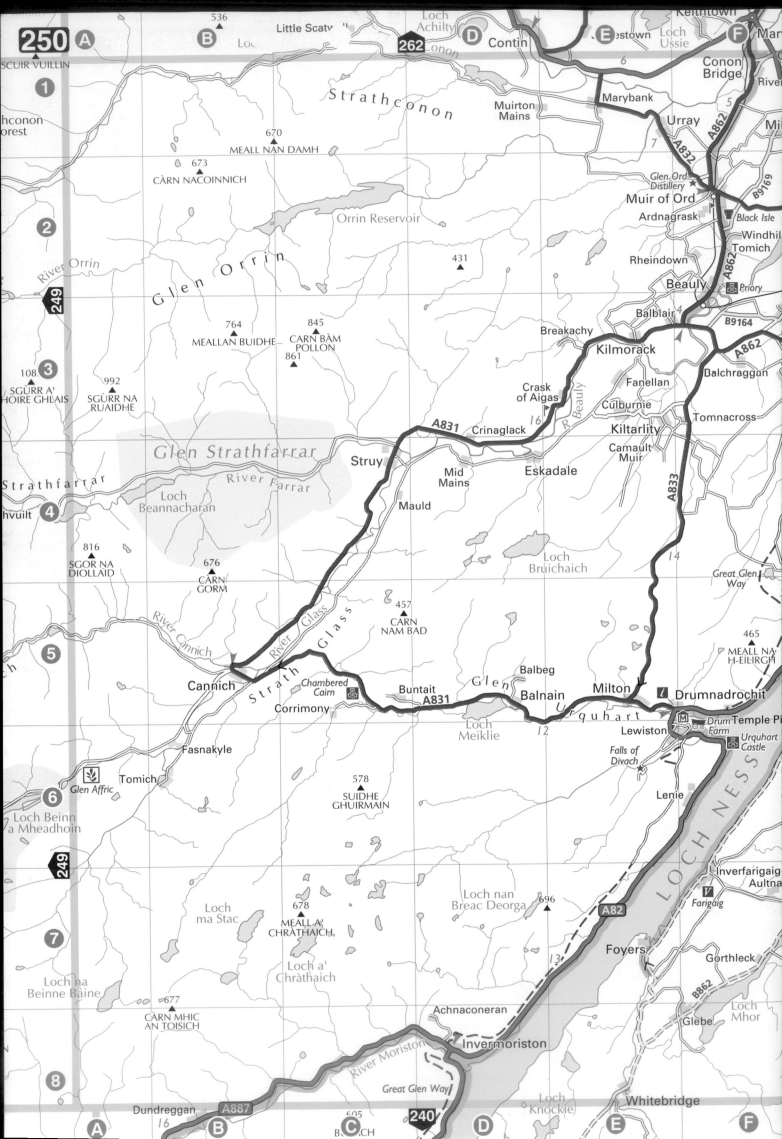

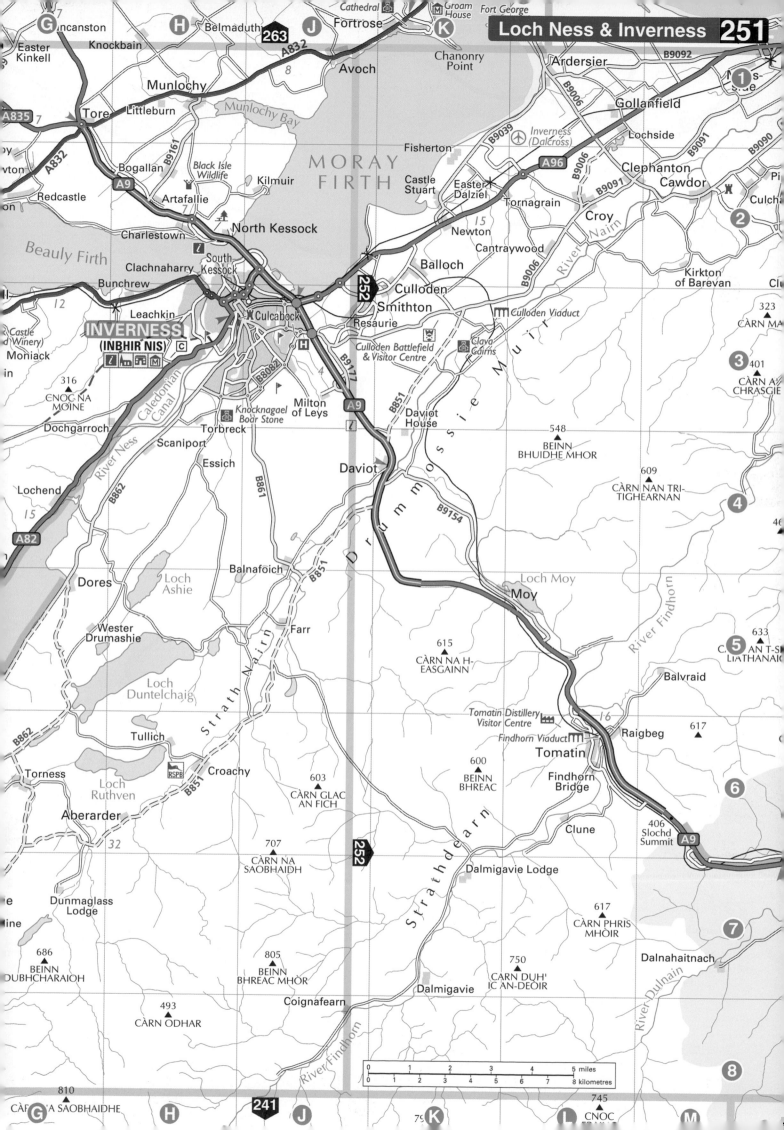

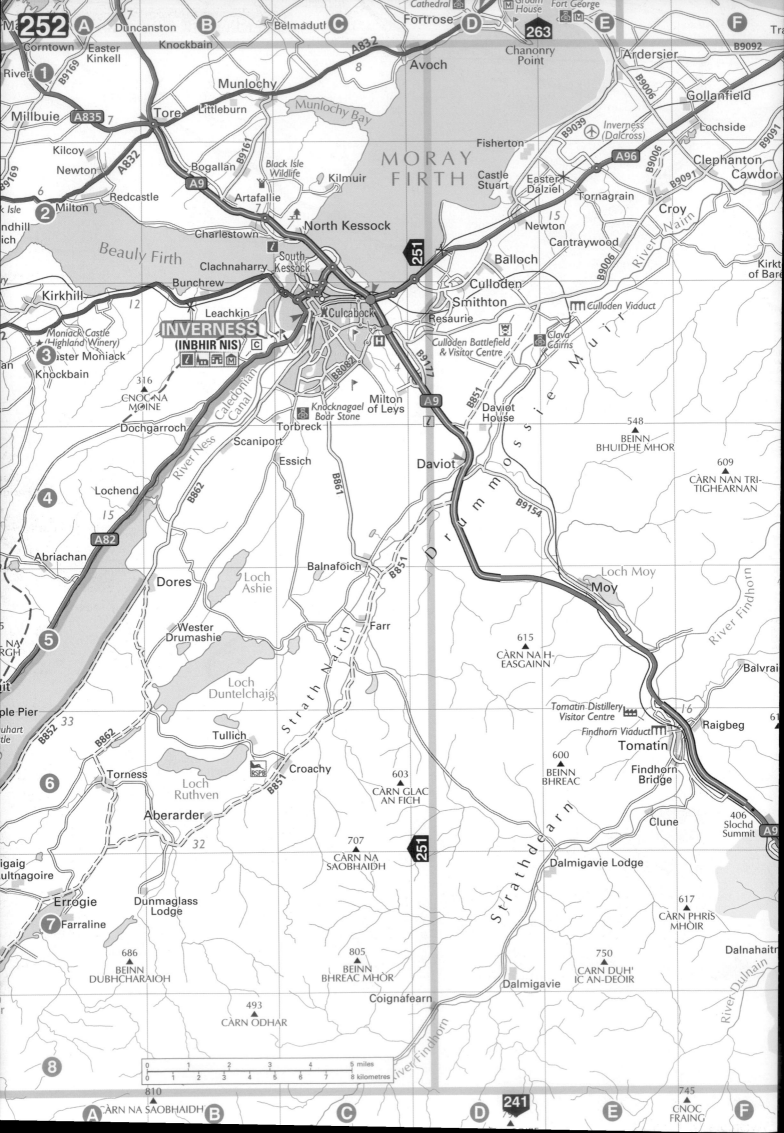

G   H   A96   10   Brc   J   River Findhorn   K   Dava Dhu Distillery   Barnhill

1   Kellas

Boath Doocot   Househill   Auldearn   Whitemire   Conicavel   B9010   Branchill   River   Dallas

Foynesfield   Righoul   Fornighty   Logie Steading   Logie

B9101   Littlemill   A940   Relugas   Dunphail   371 MILL BUIE   266

Piperhill   ulcharry   Clunas   Redburn   B9007   Glenerney   543 LARIG HILL   522 CÀRN KITTY   Glen Lossie   2

A939   22   River Divie   3

323 N MAOL   Ardclach Bell Tower   Ferness   23   Dava Way   515   STRAT H

Bridge of Dulsie   A939   A940   Dava   464   Lochindorb   Dava Moor   548 CÀRN NA LOINE   B9102   Bla Pitchr   4   Ballindalloch

33 N T-SEAN-ANAICH   Lochindorb Lodge   483   A939   Advie   Lettoch   14   A95   Mains of Dalvey   5

485 CÀRN SGRIOB   Camerory   Delliefure   Hills of Cromdale   River Avon

659 CÀRN GLAS-CHOIRE   471   Grantown-on-Spey   Cromdale   254   B9136 Strath Avon   6

Glenbeg   River Spey   Speybridge   Glen Lochy

Dulnain Bridge   10   Craggan   A939   Bridge of Brown   7

A938   Duthil   Skye of Curr   Speyside Way   459 CÀRN NA LOINNE   14   Bridge of Avon   Tor

Bogroy   2   Carrbridge   A95   13   Nethy Bridge   Lettoch   Glen Brown   Bridge of Avon

Kinveachy   B9153   Auchterblair   Landmark Forest Heritage Park   Drumuillie   Dell Wood (Abernethy)   RSPB   Glen Brown   M

Boat of Garten   Loch Garten   C A I R N G O R M S

Strathspey Railway   River Spey   B970   Straanruie   Dorback Lodge   N A T I O N A L   P A R K   River Nethy   Delnabo

242   606 CÀRN TUADHAM   8

G   H   J   K   I   M

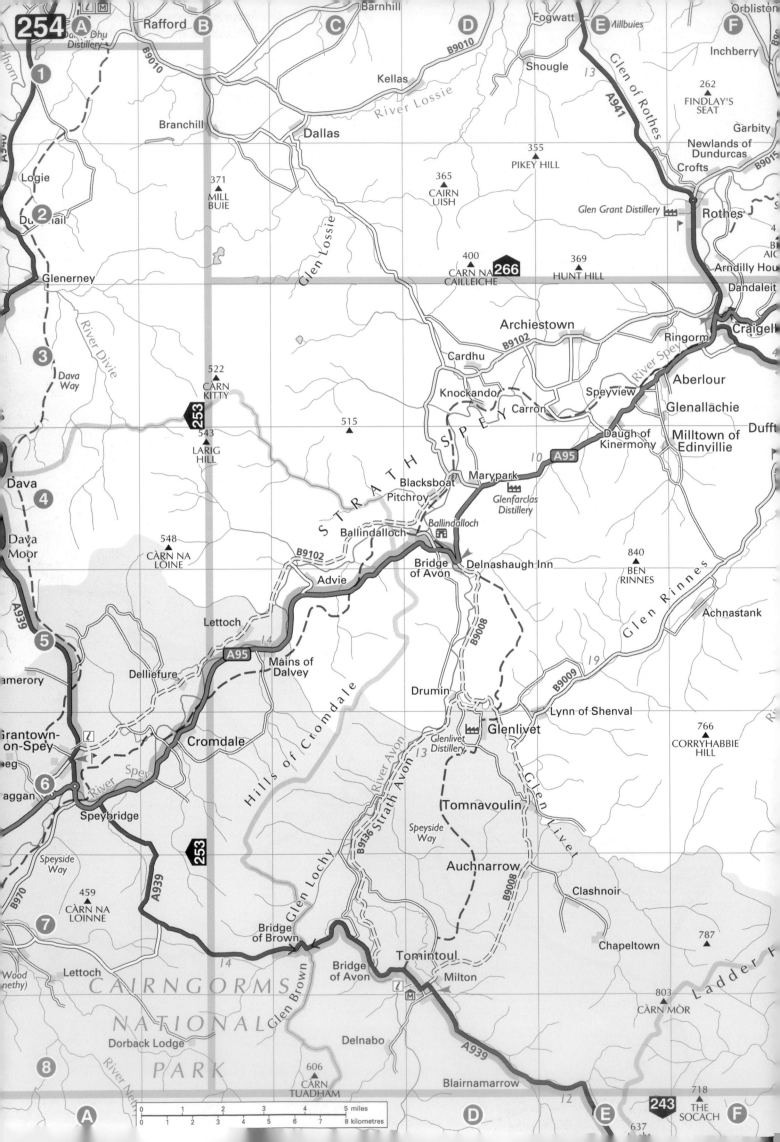

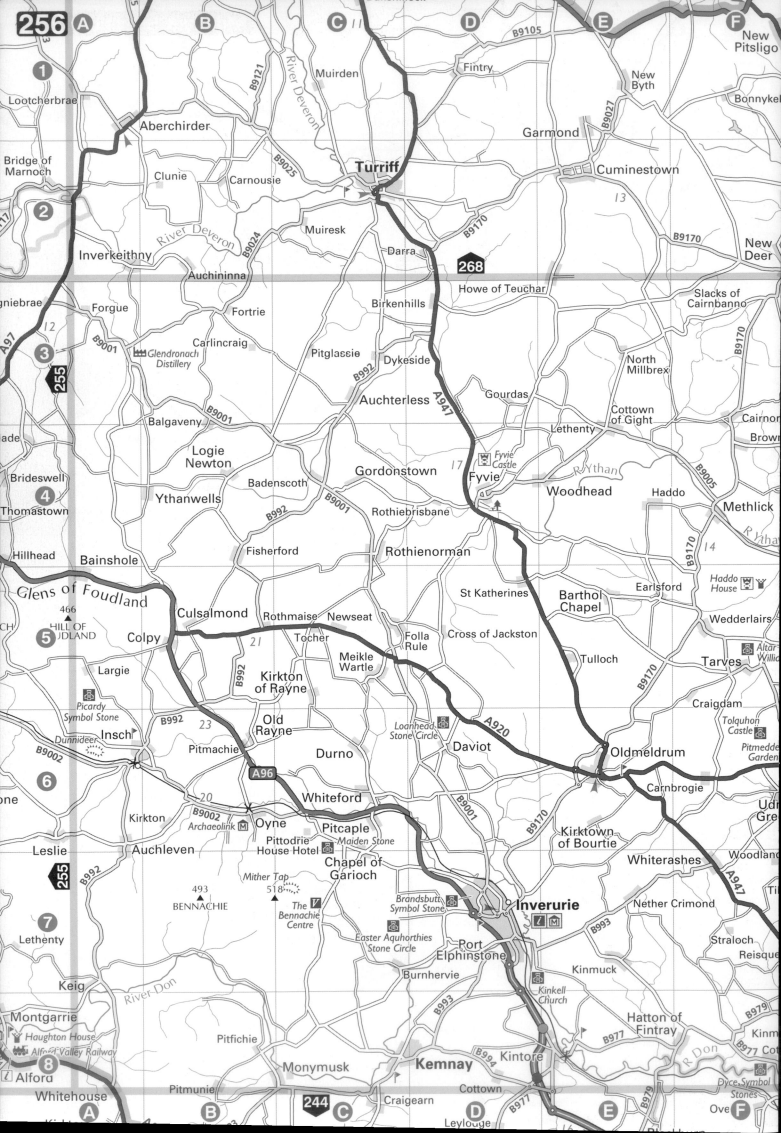

G   H   J   K

1

B9093
G
Strichen
New Leeds
B9093
Leys
Denhead
Backfolds
Crimond
K
60
Blackhill
18
Kirktown
St Fergus
A90
60
1

Fetterangus
A981  A950
Maud
6
B9106
Deer Abbey
Dunshillock
Aden
Mintlaw
Rora
River Ugie
Inverugie
Peterhead
Buchanhaven
**Peterhead**
2

B9029
Blackhill of Clackriach
B9029
Old Deer
Longside
269
A950
Inverquhomery
9
H
Peterhead
Burnhaven
Peterhead Bay
2

Drymuir
Bulwark
Stuartfield
Millbreck
Nether Kinmundy
Hillhead of Cocklaw
B9028
Nethermuir
Clola
Blackhill
Stirling
Buchan Ness
Boddam
3

B9030
Kinnadie
12
Inkhorn
A948
Kinknockie
Ardallie
Lendrum Terrace
Longhaven
3

Coldwells
Muirtack
14
Hatton
17
A952
A90
Auchiries
Bullers of Buchan
North Haven
Slains
4

Arthrath
Bogbrae
Chapel Hill
A975
Cruden Bay
Bay of Cruden
4

Ythanbank
Birness
Whinnyfold
The Skares
5

uchedly
Artrochie
Kinharrachie
Ellon
P+R
B9005
Kirkton of Logie Buchan
Kirktown of Slains
5

Esslemont
A920
medden
Logierieve
10
B9000
Collieston
32
Forvie
6

ousieside
Udny Station
B9000
A90
Newburgh
6

Culterullen
Foveran
A975
7

Delfrigs
17
7

machar
B979
Causeyend
8

hitecairns
B999
B977
Belhelvie
Balmedie
Balmedie
8

Potterton
G
245
H
B999
Blackog
J
K
I
M

0  1  2  3  4  5 miles
0  1  2  3  4  5  6  7  8 kilometres

A  B  C  D  E  F

1
2
3
4
5
6
7
8

Fladda-chùain

Rudha Hun

Lùb Score

Tairbeart
(Tarbert)

Borneskitaig

Kilmuir

Kilva

Balgown

Lin

Loch nam Madadh
(Lochmaddy)

Waternish Point

Totscore

Idrigill

Ascrib
Islands

Uig Bay

Ear

283
BEN
GEARY

Geary

Loch Snizort

A87

16

Trumpan

Ardmore
Point

Gillen

Hallin

DUNVEGAN
HEAD

Isay  Mingay

Stein  Lusta

Loch
Bay

214
BEN
DIUBAIG

Greshornish
House
Hotel

Loch Greshornish

Loch Snizort

Claigan

Boreraig

Uig

Loch Dunvegan

327
BEINN
BHREAC

Bay

B886

Treaslane

Flashader

22

A850

Loch
Pooltiel

Feriniquarrie

Totaig

Upperglen

Edinbane

Bernisdale

Oisgill Bay

Milovaig

Glendale

Lephin

B884

Colbost

Colbost Croft

Toy

Skinidin

Dunvegan

Dunvegan

Giant Angus MacAskill

ISLE OF

Waterstein

Neist
Point

Kilmuir

Lonmore

Roskhill

Caroy River

265
BEN
AKETIL

271
CRUACHAN BEINN
A' CHEARCAILL

SKYE

Moonen Bay

469
HEALAVAL
MORE

Roag

Orbost

Vatten

A863

Loch Caroy

Glen Ose

Ramasaig

Hoe Rape

488
HEALAVAL
BHEAG

Harlosh

Ose

Hoe Point

368
BEINN NA

**246**

Harlosh
Island

Colbost
Point

Dun
Beag

Bracadale

Tarner Island

A  B  C  D  E  F

0  1  2  3  4  5 miles
0            8 kilometres

G　H　J　K　L

1
2
3
4
5
6
7
8

260
248
247

n Trodday

North
Duntulm
Kilmaluag

useum
d Life
Flodigarry
Eilean Flodigarry

Poldorais

542
MEAL NA　Digg
SUIREAMACH
Brogaig

Staffin
Bay
Staffin Island

Stenscholl
Staffin

464
BIODA
BUIDHE
Trotternish

Kilt Rock Waterfall
Ellishader

Maligar

Marishader
Valtos

611
BEINN
EDRA
Garros

Rudha nam Brathairean
Culnaknock

Lealt

River Conon

Tote

608
CREAG A' LAIN
A855

inlich

nisdal

451
BEINN
A' SGA

Loch a' Bhràige

RONA

Rudha
na Fearn

Òb
Chuaig

uaig

Callakille

Old Man
of Storr
719
THE
STORR

River Romesdal

esdal

Lonbain

AN
M

Kensaleyre
River Haulton

Loch
Leathan

Eilean
Tigh

16

Loch
Fada

Eilean
Fladday

SOUND OF RAASAY

INNER SO

248

Carbost
Borve

Manish
Point
Loch
Arnish
Torran

Drumuie

Arnish

Glengrasco

A855

312

Brochel

RAASAY

Torvaig

Applecross Bay

App

Portree
Seafield

Milton

417
BEINN NA
GRÉINE

Penifiler
412
BEN
TIANAVAIG

Camust

Cam

Glenmore

444
DÙN CAAN

Aird Dhu'

Glenvarragill

A87
247

Mugeary
Camastianav
Tianavaig
Bay
Oskaig
Rudha na' Leac

G　H　J　K　L　M

G · H · **270** · J · **K** · **271**

Scoraig

Ardmair

Annat Bay

Morefield

Ullapool (Ulapul)

Rhireavach

635 ▲ BEINN GHOBHLACH

Loch Achall

Glen Achall

Loch an Daimh

**1**

Badrallach

558 ▲ BEINN EILIDEACH

**A835**

Leckmelm

Ardcharnich

642 ▲ MEALL DUBH

677 ▲ MEALL NAM BRADHAN

**2**

Badcaul

Ardessie

Camusnagaul

764 ▲ SAIL MHOR

32

Dundonnell

Lochan Gaineamhaich

Ardindrean

Letters

Loch a' Choire Mhò

647 ▲ CÀRN MÒR

**262**

Little Loch Broom

Loch na Sealga

Strathnasheallag Forest

1062 ▲ AN TEALLACH

507 ▲ CÀRN BHIORAIN

Croftown

Inverlael

12

River Lael

R Broom

**3**

906 ▲ BEINN DEARG MHOR

387 ▲ CARN BREAC BEAG

Braemore

Corrieshalloch Gorge

1081 ▲ BEINN DEARG

**4**

974 ▲ SGÙRRBÀN

1019 ▲ MULLACH COIRE MHIC FHEARCHAIR

601 ▲ MEALL AN T-SITHE

★ Falls of Measach

618 ▲ MEALL LEACACHAIN

Loch Coire Làir

**A832**

Lochan Fada

Loch a' Bhraoin

662 ▲ BEINN LIATH BHEAG

Loch Droma

**5**

981 ▲ SLIOCH

999 ▲ A' CHAILLEACH

1109 ▲ SGÙRR MÒR

680 ▲ BEINN DEARG

**6**

680 ▲ BEINN A' MHÙINIDH

Kinlochewe Forest

711 ▲ BEINN NAN RAMH

Fannich Lodge

Loch Fannich

**262**

558 ▲ AN CABAR

Beinn Eighe

Incheril

Kinlochewe

933 ▲ FIONN BHEINN

Strath Bran

Achanalt

**7** **A832**

Loch Achanalt

Glen Docherty

**A832**

10

Achnasheen

847 ▲

Loch a' Chroisg

Loch Fhiarlaid

550 ▲

**249**

Loch Gowan

538 ▲

867 ▲ SCUIR VUILLIN

**8**

Loch Coulin

G · H · J · K · L · M

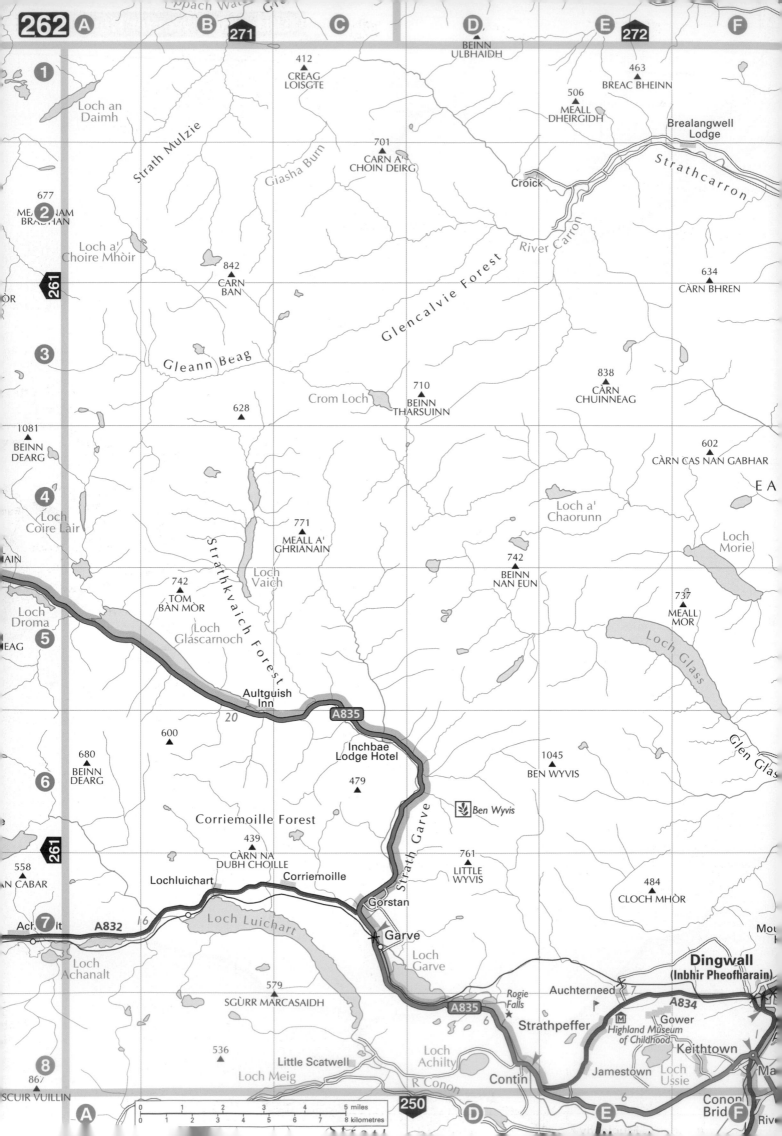

**A**    **B** 271    **C**    **D**    **E** 272    **F**

BEINN
ULBHAIDH

412
▲
CREAG
LOISGTE

463
▲
BREAC BHEINN

Brealangwell
Lodge

506
▲
MEALL
DHEIRGIDH

Strath Mulzie

Giasha Burn

701
▲
CARN A'
CHOIN DEIRG

Croick

Strathcarron

River Carron

677
▲
MEA    NAM
BRA  HAN

Loch an
Daimh

Loch a'
Choire Mhòir

261

842
▲
CARN
BAN

Glencalvie Forest

634
▲
CÀRN BHREN

Gleann Beag

628
▲

Crom Loch

710
▲
BEINN
THARSUINN

838
▲
CÀRN
CHUINNEAG

1081
▲
BEINN
DEARG

602
▲
CÀRN CAS NAN GABHAR

E A

Loch
Coire Làir

771
▲
MEALL A'
GHRIANAIN

Loch a'
Chaorunn

Loch
Moriel

AIN

Strathvaich Forest

Loch
Vaich

742
▲
BEINN
NAN EUN

737
▲
MEALL
MOR

742
▲
TOM
BÀN MÒR

Loch
Droma

Loch
Glascarnoch

Loch Glass

EAG

Glen Glas

Aultguish
Inn

20

A835

600
▲

Inchbae
Lodge Hotel

1045
▲
BEN WYVIS

680
▲
BEINN
DEARG

479
▲

Strath Garve

🌿 Ben Wyvis

Corriemoille Forest

439
▲
CÀRN NA
DUBH CHOILLE

761
▲
LITTLE
WYVIS

484
▲
CLOCH MHÒR

261

Lochluichart

Corriemoille

558
▲
N CABAR

Gorstan

Loch
Garve

Dingwall
(Inbhir Pheofharain)

Ach    lt    A832   16

Loch Luichart

Garve

Auchterneed

7

Loch
Achanalt

579
▲
SGÙRR MARCASAIDH

Rogie
Falls
★

A835   6

Strathpeffer

A834

Gower
M
Highland Museum
of Childhood

Keithtown

536
▲

Little Scatwell

Loch
Achilty

Contin

Jamestown

Loch
Ussie

867
▲
SCUIR VUILLIN

Loch Meig

R Conon

Conon
Brid

Riv

**A**    0 1 2 3 4 5 miles    0 1 2 3 4 5 6 7 8 kilometres    250    **D**    **E** 6    **F**

G  H  J  K  L

1
2
3
4
5
6
7
8

Branderburgh
Stotfield
**Lossiemouth**
B9040
Burnside
Burghead
Well
Hopeman
Burghead
Kinneddar
Duffus
St Peter's Kirk
& Parish Cross
B9012
Cummingston
B9135
Loch
Spynie
Roseisle
B9013
B9012
Duffus
Castle
Burghead Bay
A941
Spynie
Palace
College of
Roseisle
Stonewells
King
on S
Lochill
B9103
Findhorn
Hempriggs
B9089
Quarrywood
Viewfield
Calcots
Innesmill
Newton
Bishopmill
Elgin
Urquhart
Coltfield
A96
H
7
Kinloss
Findhorn
Bay
B9011
Glen Moray
Distillery
Lhanbryde
The
Lochs
9
Alves
New Elgin
266
Grange Hall
Kilbuiack
12
Linkwood
Mosstodloch
Muir of
Miltonduff
Clackmarras
Crofts
of Dipple
B9103
eno's Stone
Forres
Pluscarden
Longmorn
Califer
Barnhill
Orb ton
8
Rafford
Fogwatt
Millbuies
Dallas Dhu
Distillery
253
B9010
Inchberry
B9015
G  H  J  K  L  M
Shougle

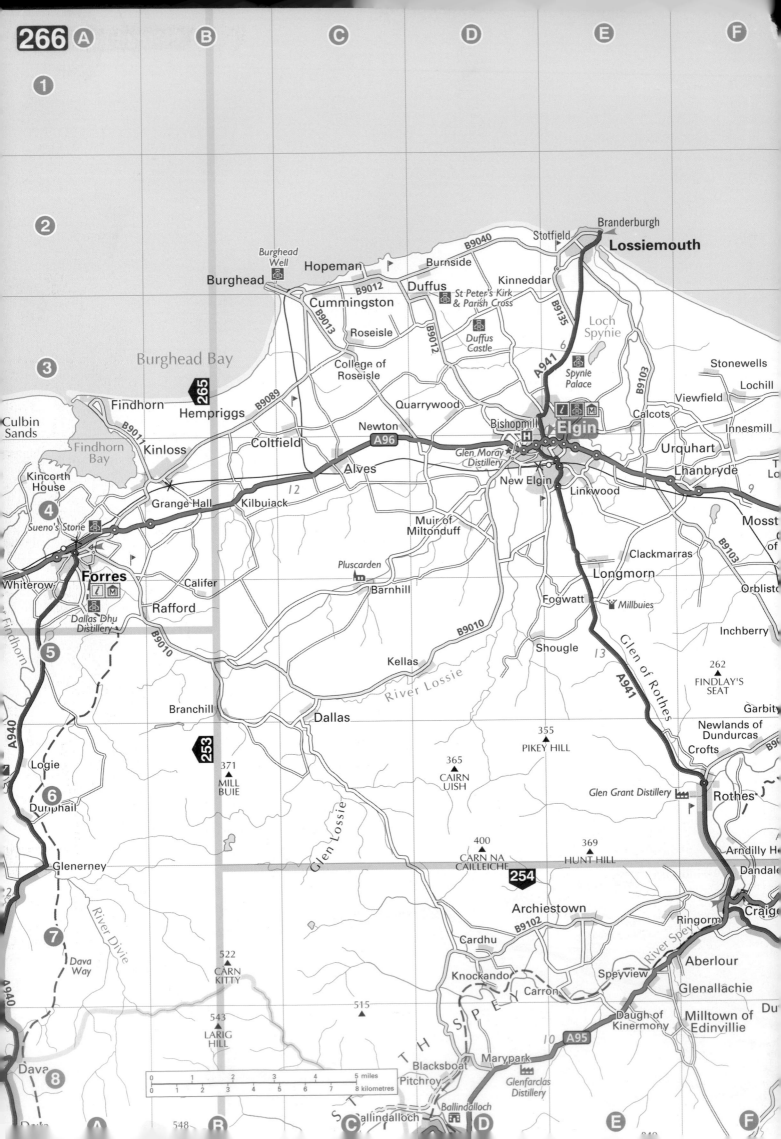

A  B  C  D  E  F

1

2

Branderburgh
Stotfield
B9040
**Lossiemouth**

Burnside
Burghead Well
Hopeman
Burghead
Kinneddar
B9012
Duffus
St Peter's Kirk & Parish Cross
B9135
Loch Spynie
Cummingston
B9013
Roseisle
B9012
Duffus Castle
Stonewells
Lochill
College of Roseisle
A941
Spynie Palace
B9103
Viewfield
Calcots
Innesmill

3

Burghead Bay
Findhorn
**265**
Hempriggs
B9089
Quarrywood
Bishopmill
Elgin
Urquhart
Lhanbryde
Culbin Sands
Findhorn Bay
B9011
Kinloss
Coltfield
Newton
A96
Alves
Glen Moray Distillery
H
New Elgin
Linkwood
Mosst

4

Kincorth House
Grange Hall
Kilbuiack
12
Muir of Miltonduff
Clackmarras
B9103
Sueno's Stone
Whiterow
**Forres**
Califer
Pluscarden
Barnhill
Longmorn
Fogwatt
Millbuies
Orblisto

5

Rafford
Dallas Dhu Distillery
B9010
Kellas
River Lossie
Shougle
13
Glen of Rothes
A941
Inchberry
262
FINDLAY'S SEAT
Garbity

Branchill
Dallas
**253**
355
PIKEY HILL
Newlands of Dundurcas
Crofts

6

Logie
371
MILL BUIE
365
CAIRN UISH
Glen Grant Distillery
Rothes
Dunphail
A940

7

Glenerney
River Divie
Glen Lossie
400
CARN NA CAILLEICHE
369
HUNT HILL
Arndilly H
Dandale
Dava Way
**254**
Craig
Archiestown
B9102
Ringorm
River Spey
Cardhu
Speyview
Aberlour
Carn Kitty
522
CARN KITTY
Knockando
Carron
Glenallachie
515
Daugh of Kinermony
Milltown of Edinvillie
Du

8

543
LARIG HILL
10  A95
Dava
Blacksboat
Marypark
Pitchroy
Glenfarclas Distillery
Ballindalloch

0  1  2  3  4  5 miles
0  1  2  3  4  5  6  7  8 kilometres

548

A  B  C  D  E  F

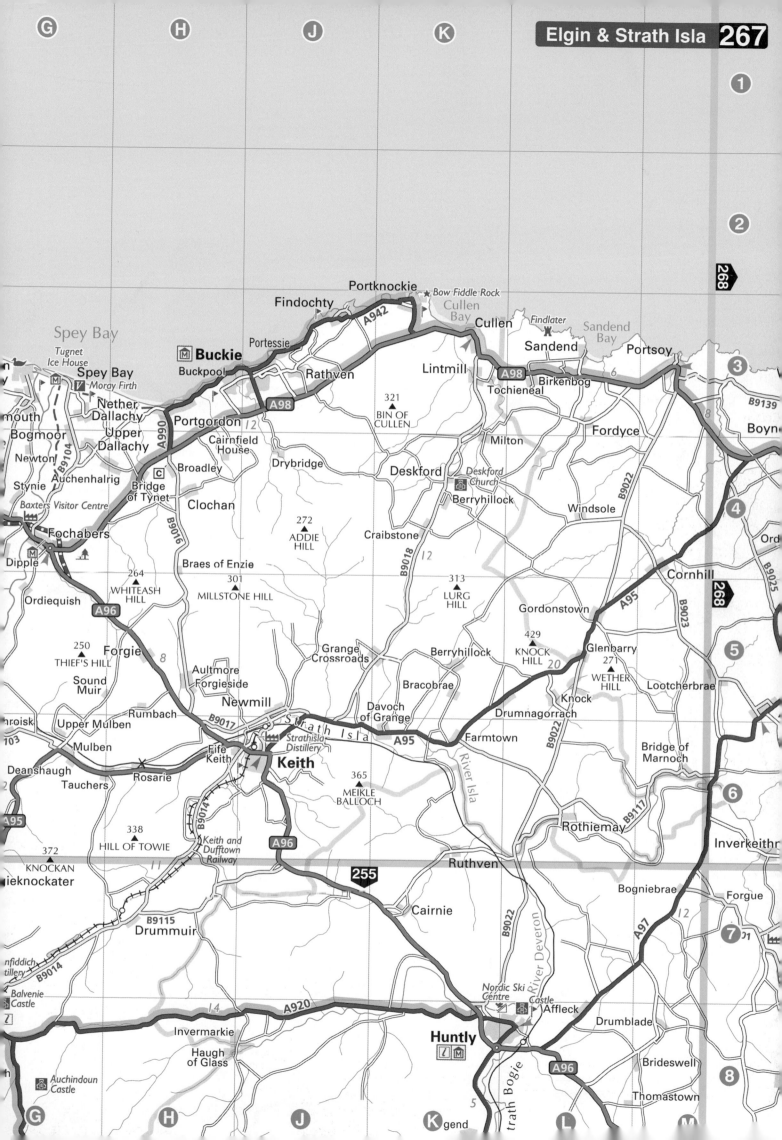

G   H   J   K

1

2

268

3

4

5

6

7

8

Spey Bay

Tugnet
Ice House

Moray Firth

Spey Bay

Nether
Dallachy

mouth

Bogmoor

Newton

Stynie

Auchenhalrig

Upper
Dallachy

Baxters Visitor Centre

Fochabers

Dipple

Ordiequish

Forgie

250
THIEF'S HILL

Sound
Muir

Upper Mulben

hroisk

Deanshaugh

Tauchers

Mulben

Rosarie

A95

372
KNOCKAN
ieknockater

nfiddich
tilley

Balvenie
Castle

Auchindoun
Castle

B9016

B9104

A990

C

Bridge
of Tynet

Broadley

Clochan

264
WHITEASH
HILL

301
MILLSTONE HILL

Braes of Enzie

Aultmore
Forgieside

Newmill

B9017

Fife
Keith

Keith

Strathisla
Distillery

Strath Isla

338
HILL OF TOWIE

Keith and
Dufftown
Railway

B9115

Drummuir

B9014

A920

Invermarkie

Haugh
of Glass

Buckie

Buckpool

Portgordon

Cairnfield
House

Drybridge

Findochty

Portessie

Rathven

A942

A98

12

272
ADDIE
HILL

Grange
Crossroads

Davoch
of Grange

B9014

365
MEIKLE
BALLOCH

A96

255

Cairnie

Portknockie

Bow Fiddle Rock

Cullen
Bay

Findlater

Cullen

Sandend

Lintmill

321
BIN OF
CULLEN

Tochieneal

Milton

Deskford

Deskford
Church

Berryhillock

Craibstone

B9018

12

313
LURG
HILL

Berryhillock

Bracobrae

A95

Farmtown

River Isla

Ruthven

Nordic Ski
Centre

Castle
Affleck

Huntly

strath Bogie

5

A96

Sandend
Bay

Portsoy

A98

Birkenbog

Fordyce

Windsole

Gordonstown

429
KNOCK
HILL

20

Knock

Drumnagorrach

B9022

Rothiemay

B9117

B9022

River Deveron

A97

12

Bogniebrae

Drumblade

Brideswell

Thomastown

Boyn

B9139

8

6

4

Cornhill

268

A95

B9023

Glenbarry

271
WETHER
HILL

Lootcherbrae

Bridge of
Marnoch

Inverkeithr

Forgue

01

Ord

B9025

103

A95

2

G   H   J   K   gend   L   M

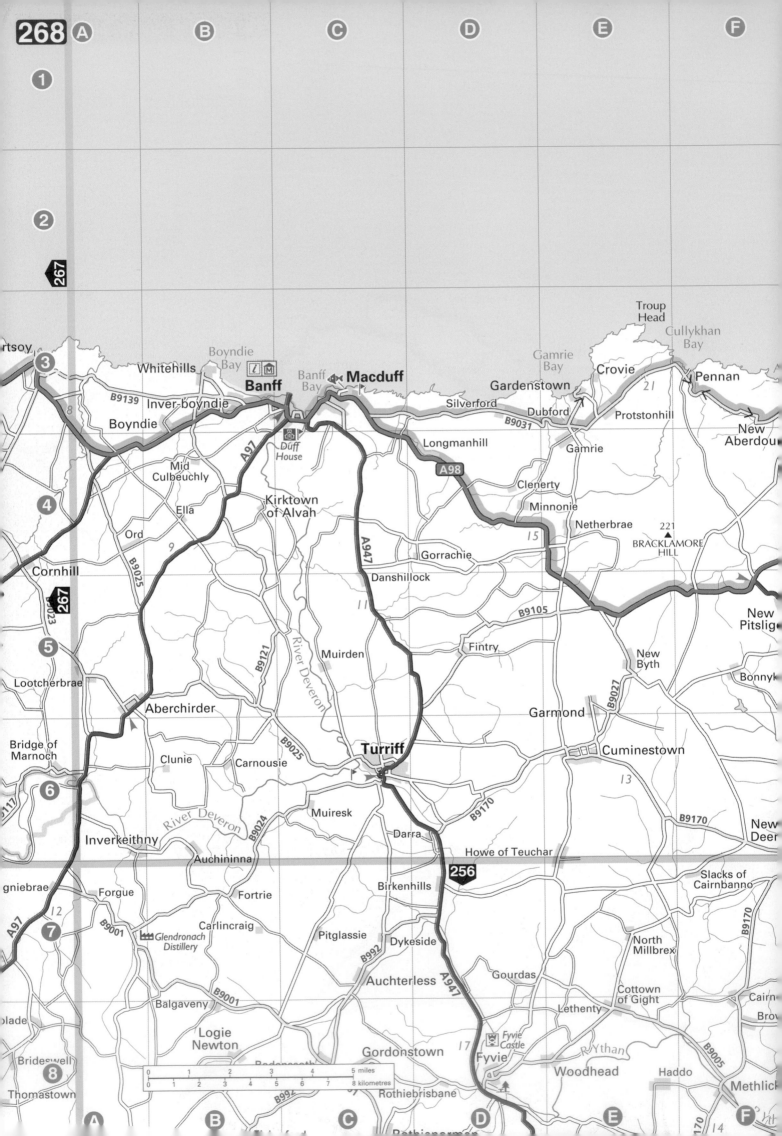

G H J K

1

2

Rosehearty

Castle Lighthouse & Museum

Sandhaven Kinnaird Head

Pittulie

**Fraserburgh** ℹ️

Peathill Kirktown Fraserburgh Bay

raigiefold Cairnbulg

Percyhorner Pitblae Maggie's Hoosie **Inverallochy**

B9031 Coburby Whitelinks Bay

Mid Ardlaw A90 B9033

ndlie 10 St Combs

A98 B9032 Memsie 60

Crofts of Savoch

A981 Memsie Cairn 60 Rathen

12 Newburgh Lonmay Rattray Head

234 60 RSPB Loch of Strathbeg

WAUGHTON HILL 12 A952

B9093 Crimond 60 Blackhill

Strichen 18

New Leeds 60

B9093

Leys St Fergus

Denhead Backfolds Kirktown

Fetterangus Rora A90

A981 A950 60

6 River Ugie

Deer Abbey Dunshillock Inverugie

Maud B9106 Longside Buchanhaven **Peterhead**

B9029 Aden Mintlaw A950 Peterhead

Blackhill of Clackriach Old Deer Peterhead H Peterhead Bay

Stuartfield 257 Inverquhomery 9 Burnhaven

Drymuir Bulwark Millbreck Nether Kinmundy Hillhead of Cocklaw Buchan Ness

Nethermuir Clola Blackhill Stirling Boddam

B9030 Kinnadie Lendrum Terrace

uchnagatt Kinknockie

12 Ardallie Longhaven

Inkhorn A948 A90 Bullers of Buchan

Coldwells A952 Auchiries

Hatton North Haven

uchnagatt A948 Arthrat Muirtack 14 J 17 K Slains L Cruden Bay M

1
2
3
4
5
6
7
8

A    B    C    D    E    F

1

Point of Stoer

Old Man
of Stoer

OLDANY
ISLAND

Eddrachi
Bay

Culkein

Culkein
Drumbeg

Clashnessie
Bay

Achnacarnin

Oldany

Drumbeg

2

Clashmore

Clashnessie

Nedd

Loch
Poll

Stoer

Clachtoll

B869

Loch
Beannac

Bay of Clachtoll

3

Rhicarn

A837

Achmelvich
Bay

Achmelvich

Baddidarrach

Lochinver

Soyea Island

Loch Inver

Strathan

Assyr

Inverkirkaig

4

River Kirkaig

Fionn
Loch

Rhu
Coigach

Eilean Mòr

Enard Bay

5

Rubha Mòr

Reiff

Achnahaird

Altandhu

Eilean Mullagrach

Loch
Osgaig

Loch
Sionasc

Isle Ristol

Polbain

612 ▲
STAC POLLAIDH

Glas-leac Mòr

SUMMER ISLES

Achiltibuie

769 ▲
CUL BE

6

Badentarbat
Bay

Polglass

Loch
Lurgainn

Tanera
Beg

V

Steornabhagh
(Stornoway)

Tanera
Mòr

Horse
Island

Horse
Sound

COIGACH

Glas-leac Beag

652 ▲
BEN MORE
COIGACH

Achduart

Culnacraig

7

Eilean Dubh

Strathcana

Priest
Island

Leac Dhonn

Isle
Martin

Strath

A835

Greenstone
Point

Cailleach Head

8

Rudha Beag

Ardmair

A    D    E    F

ellon

Scoraig

Rhireavach

Mo ld

Annat
Bay

Ullap

0  1  2  3  4  5 miles
0  1  2  3  4  5  6  7  8 kilometres

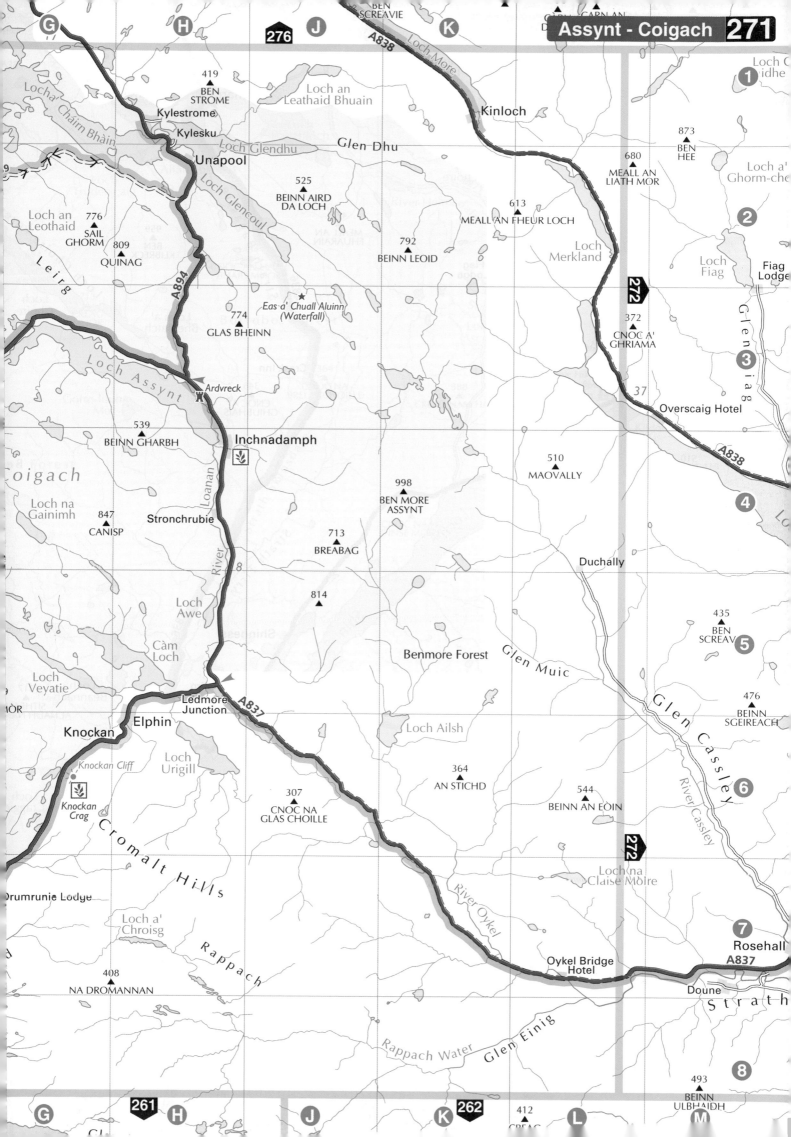

G  H  276  J  A838  Loch More  K  BEN SCREAVIE  1

Loch a' Chàirn Bhàin

419 ▲ BEN STROME

Kylestrome

Kylesku

Loch an Leathaid Bhuain

Kinloch

873 ▲ BEN HEE

680 ▲ MEALL AN LIATH MOR

Loch a' Ghorm-che

Unapool

Loch Glendhu

Glen Dhu

Loch Glencoul

2

525 ▲ BEINN AIRD DA LOCH

613 ▲ MEALL AN FHEUR LOCH

Loch Merkland

Loch Fiag

Fiag Lodge

Loch an Leothaid

776 ▲ SAIL GHORM

809 ▲ QUINAG

792 ▲ BEINN LEOID

Leirg

Eas a' Chuall Aluinn (Waterfall) ★

A894

272

3

774 ▲ GLAS BHEINN

372 ▲ CNOC A' GHRIAMA

Loch Assynt

Ardvreck ⚔

37

Overscaig Hotel

539 ▲ BEINN GHARBH

Inchnadamph

Coigach

Loch na Gainimh

510 ▲ MAOVALLY

A838

4

847 ▲ CANISP

Stronchrubie

Loanan

998 ▲ BEN MORE ASSYNT

Duchally

435 ▲ BEN SCREAV

5

Loch Awe

River

8

713 ▲ BREABAG

814 ▲

Càm Loch

Loch Veyatie

Benmore Forest

Glen Muic

476 ▲ BEINN SGEIREACH

Glen Cassley

Loch Ailsh

MÒR

Ledmore Junction

A837

River Cassley

6

Knockan

Elphin

Loch Urigill

364 ▲ AN STICHD

544 ▲ BEINN AN EOIN

Knockan Cliff

Knockan Crag

307 ▲ CNOC NA GLAS CHOILLE

272

Cromalt Hills

Loch na Claise Mòre

7

Drumrunie Lodge

Rappach

River Oykel

Loch a' Chroisg

Oykel Bridge Hotel

Rosehall

A837

408 ▲ NA DROMANNAN

Doune

Strath

Rappach Water

Glen Einig

8

493 ▲ BEINN ULBHAIDH

G  261  H  J  K  262  412 ▲ CREAG  L  M

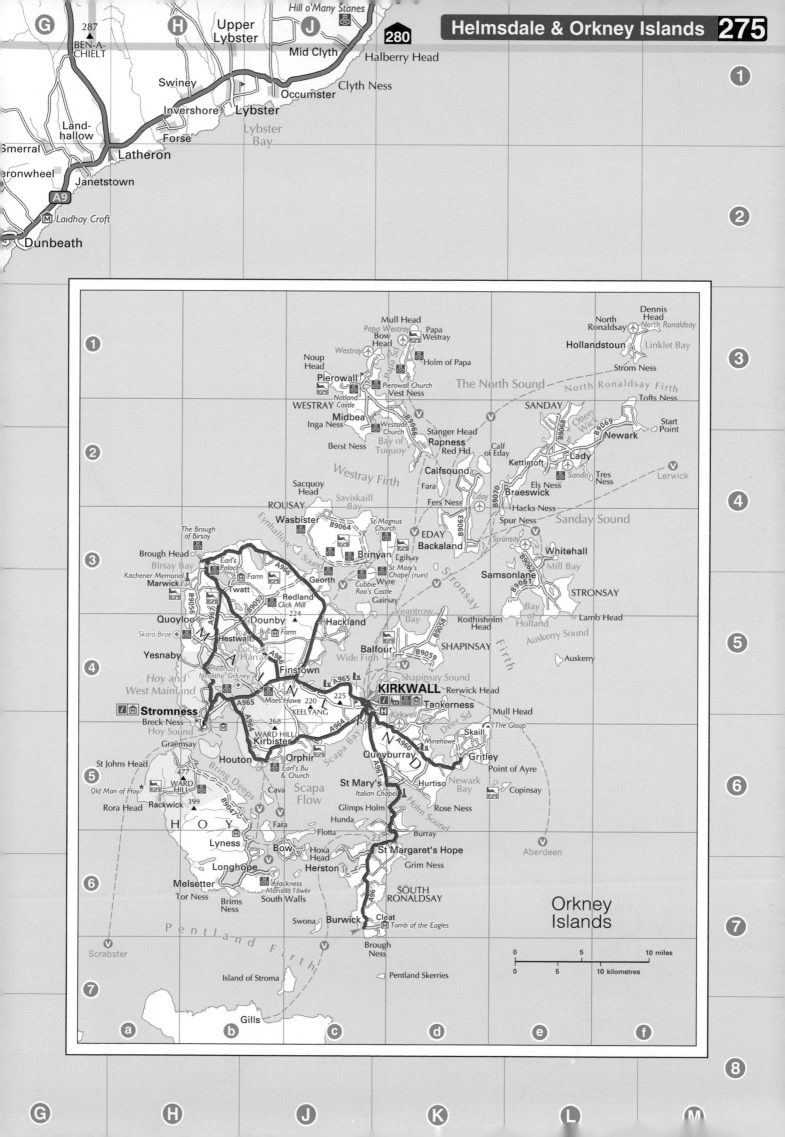

Orkney
Islands

| 0 | | 5 | | 10 miles |
| 0 | 5 | | 10 kilometres |

**Map labels (partial):**

G · BEN-A-CHIELT · 287
H · Upper Lybster
J · Hill o'Many Stanes
280

Mid Clyth
Halberry Head
Swiney
Clyth Ness
Invershore · Occumster
Lybster
Forse · Lybster Bay
Land-hallow
Latheron
Smerral
eronwheel · Janetstown
A9
Laidhay Croft
Dunbeath

Mull Head
Papa Westray · Bow Head · Papa Westray
Noup Head · Westray · Holm of Papa
Pierowall · Pierowall Church · Vest Ness
Notland Castle
WESTRAY · The North Sound
North Ronaldsay · Dennis Head · North Ronaldsay
Hollandstoun · Linklet Bay
Strom Ness
Midbea · Westside Church
Inga Ness · Bay of Tuquoy
Berst Ness · Rapness · Stanger Head
Red Hd · Calf of Eday
Tofts Ness
Start Point
Newark
SANDAY · Otters Wick
Lady
Kettletoft · Sanday · Tres Ness
Els Ness
Braeswick · Hacks Ness
Westray Firth
Sacquoy Head
Fara · Fers Ness · Eday
Calfsound
Lerwick
ROUSAY · Saviskaill Bay
Wasbister · St Magnus Church
Spur Ness · Sanday Sound
Stronsay · Whitehall
Samsonlane · Mill Bay
The Brough of Birsay
Brough Head · Earl's Palace
Kitchener Memorial · Birsay Bay
Marwick · Twatt · Farm
Quoyloo · Redland · Click Mill · Dounby · Hackland
EDAY · Backaland · Egilsay
Brinyan · St Mary's Chapel (ruin)
Cubbie Roo's Castle · Wyre · Gairsay
Veantrow Bay · Koithisholm Head
Bay of Holland · STRONSAY · Lamb Head
Auskerry
STRONSAY Firth
Skara Brae · Hestwall · Loch of Harray · Heart of Neolithic Orkney
Yesnaby · Finstown
Hoy and West Mainland
Stromness · Breck Ness · Hoy Sound
Maes Howe · KEELYANG
Balfour · SHAPINSAY
Wide Firth · Shapinsay Sound
KIRKWALL · Tankerness · Rerwick Head
Mull Head · The Gloup · Skaill · Deer Sd
Ward Hill · Kirbister
Graemsay · Houton · Orphir · Quoyburray · Gritley
Earl's Bu & Church · Point of Ayre
St Johns Head · Minehowe
Old Man of Hoy · WARD HILL · 477 · Rackwick · 399
Bring Deeps · Scapa Bay · Newark Bay
Copinsay
Rora Head · Cava · Scapa Flow
St Mary's · Italian Chapel · Hurtiso · Rose Ness
HOY · Fara · Glimps Holm · Hunda
Lyness · Flotta · Burray
Bow · Hoxa Head · St Margaret's Hope · Grim Ness
Longhope · Herston
Melsetter · Hackness · Martello Tower
Tor Ness · Brims Ness · South Walls · SOUTH RONALDSAY
Swona · Burwick · Cleat · Tomb of the Eagles
Scrabster · Brough Ness
Pentland Firth
Island of Stroma · Pentland Skerries · Gills
Aberdeen

A    B    C    D    E    F

1
2
3
4
5
6
7
8

CAPE WRATH

Cléit
Dhubh

Faraid
Head

371
SGRIBHIS-
BHEINN

297
CNOC A
GHIUBHAIS

300
MAOVALLY

THE PARPH

Balnakeil
Bay

Balnakeil

Durness

Sangomo

457
FASHVEN

Keold

Loch Airigh
na Beinne

Sandwood
Bay

Kyle of Durness

Sandwood
Loch

485
CREAG
RIABACH

Rudh' an Fhir Leithe

Strath Shinary

468
BEINN
DEARG MHÒR

464
MEALL
NA MÒINE

331
GHLAS-
BHEINN

A838

Sheigra

489
MEALL
NA CRÀ

Balchreick

Blairmore

521
FARVEALL

19

Oldshoremore

355
AN
SOCACH

773
BEINN
SPIONNAIDH

801
CRANSTACKIE

Kinlochbervie

Loch Clash

Badcall

Strath Beag

B801

Achriesgill

Loch Inchard

Strath Dionard

Rhiconich

Loch-na
Claise Càrnaich

River Dionard

Rudha Ruadh

908
FOINAVEN

Fanagmore

Skerricha

Loch Laxford

A838

Tarbet

North-west Sutherland

Loch na Tuadh

HANDA
ISLAND

Foindle

786
ARKLE

River Laxford

Scourie Bay

7

Laxford
Bridge

A894

Loch
Stack

729
SÀBHAL BEAG

Scourie

721
BEN STACK

Scourie More

Badcall

386
BEN
AUSKAIRD

Strath Stack

800

796
CARN
DEARG

757
CARN
TION

Badcall Bay

Loch a'
Mhuilinn

Achfary

333
BEN
SCREAVIE

Rudh' a'
Mhucard

17

A838

Loch More

A    D    E    F

Loch an

0  1  2  3  4  5 miles
0  1  2  3  4  5  6  7  8 kilometres

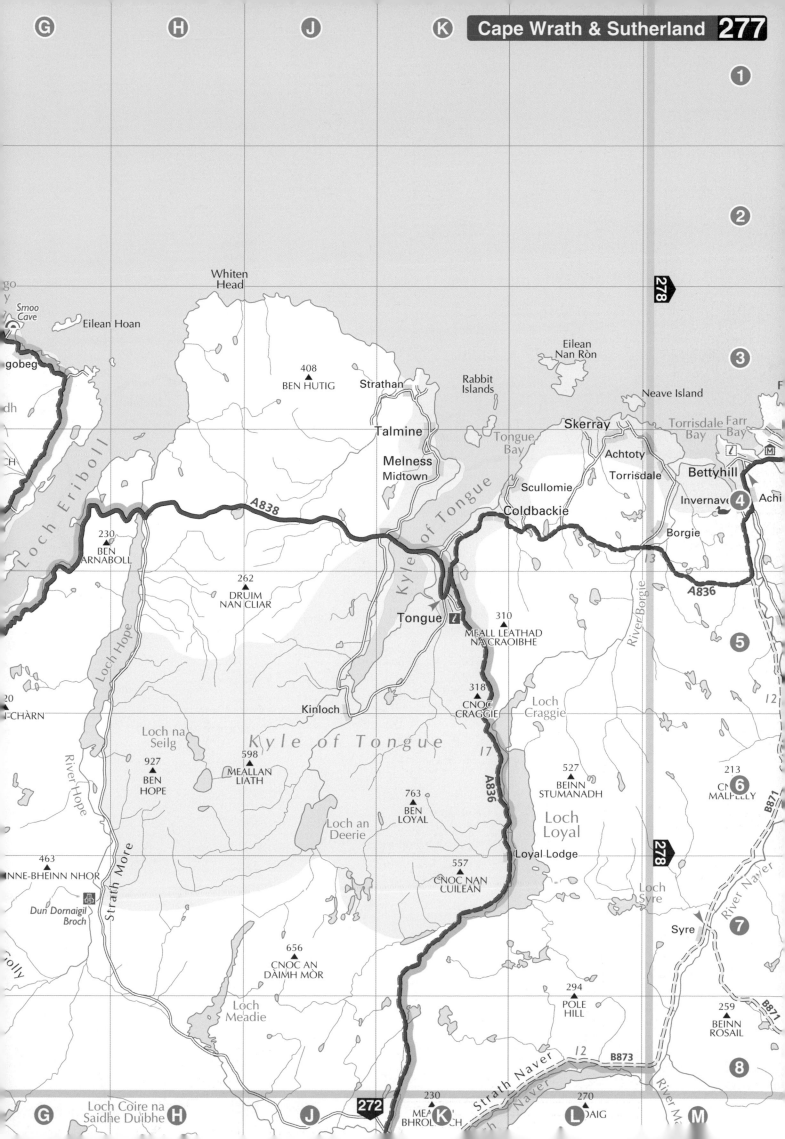

G    H    J    K

1
2
3
4
5
6
7
8

Whiten Head

Smoo Cave

Eilean Hoan

gobeg

dh

H

Loch Eriboll

408
BEN HUTIG

Strathan

Talmine

Melness
Midtown

A838

230
BEN ARNABOLL

262
DRUIM NAN CLIAR

Kinloch

Loch Hope

Loch na Seilg

927
BEN HOPE

598
MEALLAN LIATH

Loch an Deerie

Strath More

463
INNE-BHEINN NHOR

Dun Dornaigil Broch

656
CNOC AN DÀIMH MÒR

Loch Meadie

River Hope

20

I-CHÀRN

Loch Coire na Saidhe Duibhe

G

Rabbit Islands

Tongue Bay

Kyle of Tongue

Tongue

763
BEN LOYAL

Kyle of Tongue

Eilean Nan Ròn

Skerray

Achtoty
Torrisdale

Scullomie

Coldbackie

310
MEALL LEATHAD NA CRAOIBHE

318
CNOC CRAGGIE

Loch Craggie

527
BEINN STUMANADH

Loch Loyal

Loyal Lodge

557
CNOC NAN CUILEAN

294
POLE HILL

230
MEAL BHROL CH

12

Strath Naver

Naver

B873

270
AIG

Neave Island

Torrisdale Bay    Farr Bay

Bettyhill

Invernave

Borgie

13

A836

River Borgie

17

A836

213
CN MALFELLY

6

259
BEINN ROSAIL

River Naver

Syre

Loch Syre

278

278

B871

B871

Achi

M

River M

272

H    J    K    L    M

12

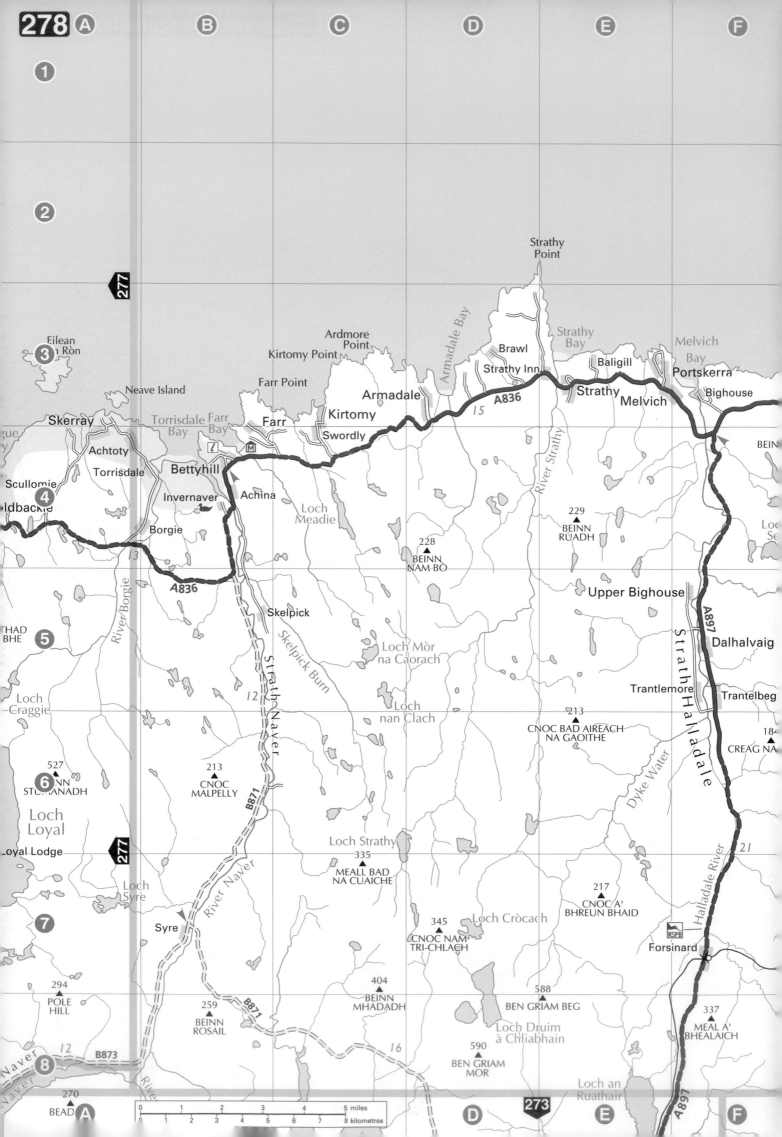

G   H   J   K   1

DUNNET HEAD   127

Stromness V

Briga Head

121
DUNNET
HILL   Brough   i M
St John's
Loch

Holborn
Head   West Dunnet   2
Dunnet

Brims Ness

St Mary's
Chapel (ruin)   Scrabster   Dunnet
Bay   stlehill   B855

Crosskirk   A9   Thurso Bay   i M
Thurso   Murkle   280   Castletown

A836   Bridge of Forss   16   A836   5

Skiall   B874   Olrig
House   Tai   3

Upper
Dounreay   Achreamie   Lythmore   Weydale   B876

Sandside
Bay   Isauld   Cnoc Freiceadain
Long Cairns   Glengolly   Hilliclay   Bower

Reay   Achvarasdal   Shebster   Forss Water   Westfield   A9   Sordale

242
BEINN
RATHA   Loch
Calder   Knockdee   Loch
Scarmclate   4   Halcr

Broubster   B874   Roadside   Clayock   Gillock   B874

Shurrery   Halkirk   Georgemas
Junction
Station   21   Loch Watten

Shurrery
Lodge   B870   Scotscalder
Station   Harpsdale   176
SPITTAL
HILL   5   Watten

290
BEIN NAM
BAD MHÒR   Loch
Scye   Dorrery   Spittal   B870

243
CNOC AN
DARAIN BHÀIN   Loch
Shurrery   Olgrinmore   Mybster   Loch of
Toftingall

160
BRAIGH FÉITH HEMIGAL   132
DRUIM A'
CHRACAIRNIE   River Thurso   Westerdale   23

Loch Tuim
Ghlais   Loch
Caluim

203
CNOC PREAS
A'MHADAIDH   200
CNOC BEUL
NA FAIRE   Strath Beg   280   6

136
BEINN CHÀITEAG   A9

Altnabreac Station   7   BALLH
HIL

75
OC
GALL   Loch
More   Loch
Ruard   Achavanich   Loch
Stemster

Rumsdale Water   Strathmore Water   Loch an
Thulachan   Loch
Sand   Loch
Rangag   248
STEMSTER HILL

Dalnawillan Lodge   Clutt Water   226
COIRE
NA BEINN   287
BEN-A-
CHIELT   8   U
Ly

348
BEN
ALISKY

G   Lodge   H   J   274   K   L   M

PENTLAND FIRTH

DUNNET HEAD
127
Briga Head

Langaton Point
Nethertown
ISLAND OF STROMA
Mell Head
Uppertown

St John's Point
St Margaret's Hope
Inner Sound

121
DUNNET HILL

Brough
Scarfskerry
Castle of Mey
Gills Bay
Huna
DUNCANSBY HEAD

St John's Loch
Loch Mey
A836
15
Kirkstyle

Rattar
Mey
Gills
Muckle Stack

West Dunnet
Barrock
Canisbay
John o' Groats

Dunnet
Dunnet Bay
Stacks of Duncansby

Murkle
279
Castlehill
Inkstack
Brabstermire
Skirza

5
A836
Castletown
Greenland
Loch Heilen
Gill Burn
Freswick
Freswick Bay

Olrig House
Tain
Slickly
Ness Head

Hilliclay
B876
Bowermadden
Kirk Burn
Auckengill

Sordale
Bower
Lyth
Sortat
Nybster

Knockdee
Halcro
Howe
17
Brough Head

Loch Scarmclate
16
Kirk
Mireland
A99
Keiss

Clayock
Gillock
B874
B870
Loch of Wester

Georgemas Junction Station
21
Killimster
Sinclair Bay

Loch Watten
B876
Noss Head

176
SPITTAL HILL
Watten
B874
Reiss
Castle Girnigoe & Sinclair

Spittal
B870
Bilbster
Wick River
Winless
Ackergill
Staxigoe

Mybster
Loch of Toftingall
Haster
Milton
Janetstown
A99
Wick
Wick Bay
Papigoe

23
Achairn Burn
Newton
Old Wick
South Head

Strath Beg
279
Badlipster
Loch Hempriggs
Whiterow
Castle of Old Wick

A9
Tannach
Thrumster

145
BALLHARN HILL
Grey Cairns of Camster
212
Loch of Yarrows
17
Sarclet

Achavanich
Loch Stemster
HILL OF YARROWS
A99
Ulbster

Loch Rangag
248
STEMSTER HILL
Cairn o' Get
Whaligoe
Whaligoe Steps

226
COIRE NA BEINN
287
BEN-A-CHIELT
Roster
Hill o'Many Stanes
Bruan

Upper Lybster
275
Mid Clyth
Halberry Head

Clyth Ness

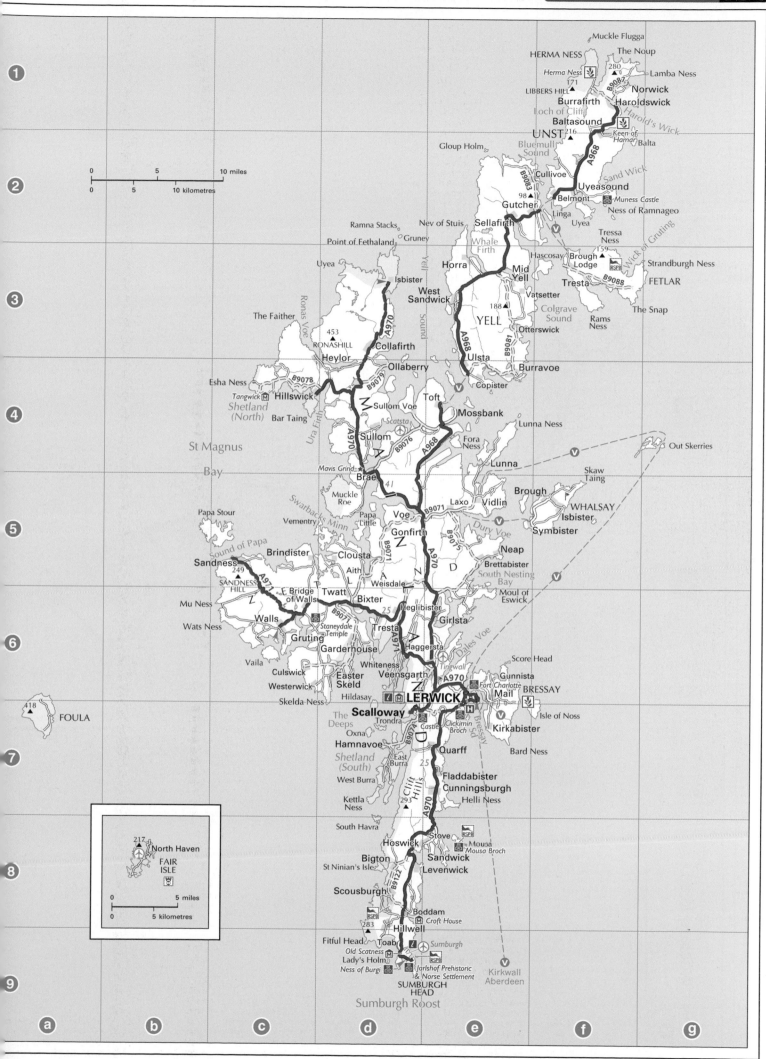

Muckle Flugga
HERMA NESS
The Noup
*Herma Ness* 280
LIBBERS HILL 171 ▲ B9087 Lamba Ness
Burrafirth Norwick
Loch of Cliff Haroldswick
Baltasound
UNST Keen of 216 ▲ Balta
Bluemull Hamar
Gloup Holm Sound Sand Wick
B9083 Cullivoe
Uyeasound Harold's Wick
98 ▲ Belmont
Gutcher Linga Muness Castle
Ness of Ramnageo
Sellafirth Uyea
Ramna Stacks Nev of Stuis Tressa
Point of Fethaland Gruney Whale Ness
Firth Hascosay Brough 159 Wick of Gruting
Uyea Horra Lodge RSPB
Mid Strandburgh Ness
Isbister West Yell Tresta B9088 FETLAR
Sandwick Vatsetter
The Faither A970 188 ▲ YELL The Snap
Ronas Voe Colgrave
453 ▲ Yell Otterswick Sound Rams
RONASHILL Collafirth A968 Ness
Heylor Sound Ulsta B9081
Ollaberry Burravoe
Esha Ness B9078 B9079 Copister
Tangwick Hillswick Sullom Voe Toft V
*Shetland* Sullom Voe Mossbank
*(North)* Bar Taing Scatsta Fora Lunna Ness
Ura Firth A970 B9076 Ness Out Skerries
St Magnus Sullom Lunna
Mavis Grind ★ A968 Skaw
Bay Brae Laxo Taing
41 B9071 Vidlin WHALSAY
Muckle Brough
Roe Isbister
Papa Stour Voe Symbister
Vementry Papa Gonfirth B9075 Neap
Little Dury Voe
Sandness Brindister Clousta Brettabister V
249 ▲ A971 Aith South Nesting
SANDNESS Weisdale Bay Moul of
HILL Twatt Eswick
Mu Ness Bridge Bixter
of Walls Heglibister
Walls B9071 Score Head
Wats Ness Tresta 25 Girlsta
Staneydale Gunnista
Temple A971 Haggersta Tingwall
Gruting Whiteness Fort BRESSAY
Gardenhouse Veensgarth Charlotte Mail
Vaila A970
Culswick LERWICK Isle of Noss
Easter Clickimin
Westerwick Skeld Hildasay Scalloway Broch Kirkabister
Skelda Ness The Castle Bard Ness
Deeps Trondra B9074
FOULA Oxna Quarff
418 ▲ Hamnavoe
*Shetland* East Fladdabister
*(South)* Burra Cunningsburgh
West Burra 25 Helli Ness
Kettla A970
Ness Stove
South Havra RSPB
Hoswick Mousa
Bigton Sandwick Mousa Broch
St Ninian's Isle Levenwick
Scousburgh
B9122 Boddam
283 ▲ Croft House
Hillwell
Fitful Head Toab Sumburgh
Old Scatness RSPB
Lady's Holm Jarlshof Prehistoric Kirkwall
Ness of Burgi & Norse Settlement Aberdeen
SUMBURGH
HEAD
Sumburgh Roost

0 5 10 miles
0 5 10 kilometres

217 ▲
North Haven
FAIR
ISLE
0 5 miles
0 5 kilometres

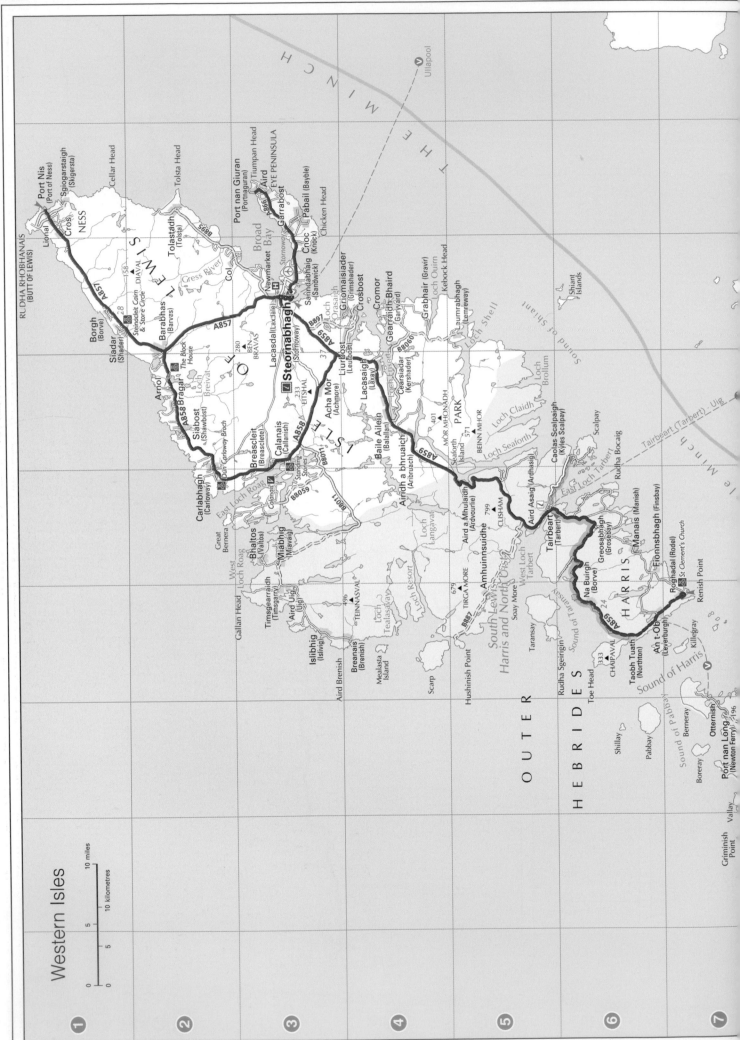

## Western Isles

10 miles

10 kilometres

THE MINCH

Ullapool

RUDHA RHOBHANAIS
(BUTT OF LEWIS)
Port Nis
(Port of Ness)
Sgiogarstaigh
(Skigersta)
Lional
Cros
NESS
Cellar Head
Tolsta Head

A857
Borgh
(Borve)
Siadar
(Shader)
Steinacleit Cairn
& Store Circle
DIAVAL
158
Barabhas
(Barvas)
A857
Tolastadh
(Tolsta)
B895
Gress River
Col

Port nan Giuran
(Portnaguran)
Tiumpan Head
Aird
A866
EYE PENINSULA
Garrabost
Pabail (Bayble)
Chicken Head

Arnol
Bragar
A858
The Block
House
Loch
Breivat
280
BEN
BRAVAS
L E W I S
Newmarket Bay
Broad
Bay
Stornoway
Sandabhaig
(Sandwick)
Cnoc
(Knock)

Siabost
(Shawbost)
Breascleit
(Breasclete)
A858
Dun Carloway Broch
233
EITSHAL
Acha Mor
(Achmore)
A857
Steornabhagh
Lacasdall (Laxdale)
(Stornoway)
A859
Liurbost
(Leurbost)
A859
B897
Loch
Orasaigh
Griomaisiader
(Grimshader)
Crosbost
Cromor
Gearraidh-Bhaird
(Garyvard)
Grabhair (Gravir)
Loch Ouirn
Kebock Head

Carlabhagh
(Carloway)
Calanais
(Callanish)
Standing
Stones
B8011
B8059
Cearsiadar
(Kershader)
Lacasaigh
(Laxay)
Baile Ailein
(Balallan)
Airidh a bhruaich
(Aribruach)
A859
Seaforth
Island
MOR MHONADH
401
PARK
BEINN MHOR
571
Loch Shell
Loch
Brollum
Sound of Shiant
Shiant
Islands
Seumrabhagh
(Lemreway)
Loch Claidh
Loch Seaforth

Great
Bernera
East Loch Roag
Colbost
Bhaltos
(Valtos)
Miabhig
(Miavaig)
West Loch Roag
Gallan Head
Aird Uig
(Uig)
Timsgearraidh
(Timsgarry)
TEINNASVAL
396
Loch
Tealasavay
Loch
Langavat
West Loch
Tairbeart
679
TIRGA MORE
B887
Amhuinnsuidhe
Aird a Mhulaidh
(Ardvourlie)
CLISHAM
799
Aird Asaig
(Ardhasig)
Tairbeart
(Tarbert)
East Loch Tarbert
Caolas Scalpaigh
(Kyles Scalpay)
Scalpa
Scalpay
Rudha Bocaig

Islibhig
(Islivig)
Breanais
(Brenish)
Mealasta
Island
Scarp
Hushinish Point
Aird Brenish
Taransay
South Lewis,
Harris and North Uist
Soay Mor
Rudha Sgeirigin
Na Buirgh
(Borve)
24
A859
Greosabhagh
(Grosebay)
Manais (Manish)
Fionnsbhagh (Finsbay)
HARRIS

Shillay
Pabbay
Boreray
Bernera
Toe Head
CHAIPAVAL
333
Taobh Tuath
(Northton)
An t-Ob
(Leverburgh)
Killegray
Sound of Harris
Otternish
Port nan Long
(Newton Ferry)
Valtay
Griminish
Point
OUTER
HEBRIDES
Sound of Pabbay
Sound of Taransay
St Clement's Church
Roghadal (Rodel)
Renish Point

Tairbeart (Tarbert) · Uig
le Minch
THE MINCH

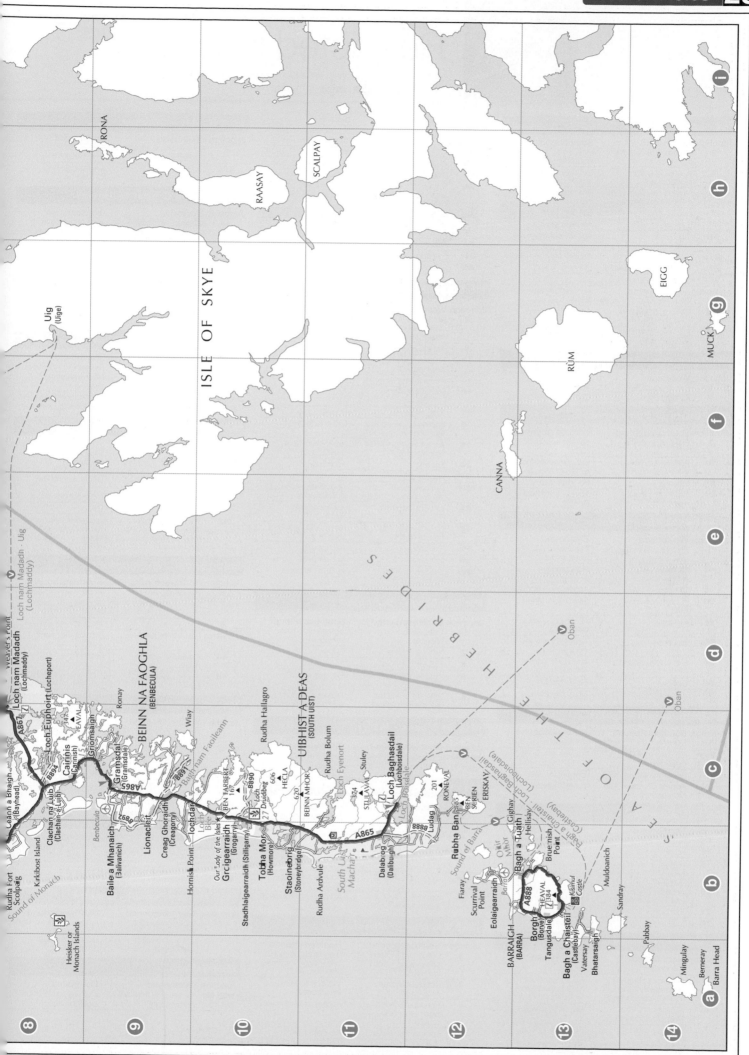

ISLE OF SKYE

RONA

RAASAY

SCALPAY

EIGG

MUCK

RÙM

CANNA

Uig
(Uige)

Oban

Oban

SEA OF THE HEBRIDES

Weaver's Point

Loch nam Madadh · Uig
(Lochmaddy)

Loch nam Madadh
(Lochmaddy)

Loch Euphoirt (Locheport)

Leann a bhaigh
(Bayhead)

A867

A865

B894

Cairinis
(Carinish)

Gramsdal
(Gramsdale)

BEINN NA FAOGHLA
(BENBECULA)

Ronay

EAVAL
347

Grìomsaigh

Clachan na Luib
(Clachan-a-Luib)

Rudha Fort
Scolpaig

Sound of Kirkibost Island

Heisker or
Monach Islands

Baile a Mhanaich
(Balivanich)

Benbecula

B892

Lìonacleit

Creag Ghoraidh
(Creagorry)

Iochdar
(Stilligarry)

Loch
Bee

Wiay

Bagh nam Faoileann

Hornish Point

Our Lady of the Isles

Grcigearraidh
(Grogarry)

Stadhlaigearraidh
(Stilligarry)

BEN TARBERT
167

Loch
Druidibeg

B890

Tobha Mòr
(Howmore)

Staoinebrig
(Stoneybridge)

27 Druidibeg

Rudha Hallagro

UIBHIST A DEAS
(SOUTH UIST)

HECLA
606

BEINN MHOR
620

South Uist

Machair

Rudha Ardvule

Dalabrog
(Daliburgh)

Loch
Eynort

Rudha Bolum

374

STULAVAL

Stuley

A865

Loch Baghasdail
(Lochboisdale)

Loch Boisdale

Ludag

B888

201

RONEVAL

Loch Baghasdail · Lochboisdale
(Lochboisdale)

ERISKAY

Rubha a' Chaisteil
(Castlebay)

Bàgh a' Tuath

BEN
SCRIEN
185

Rubha Bàn

Gighay

Hellisay

Brue-nish
Point

Scurrival
Point

Fiaray

Sound of Barra

Oitir
Mhòr

Muldoanich

Eolaigearraidh

BARRAIGH
(BARRA)

Borgh
(Borve)

Tangusdale

Bàgh a' Chaisteil
(Castlebay)

A888

HEAVAL
384

Kisimul
Castle

Vatersay

Bhatarsaigh

Sandray

Pabbay

Mingulay

Berneray

Barra Head

# Restricted junctions

Motorway and Primary Route junctions which have access or exit restrictions are shown thus 3, 56 on the map pages.

## M1 London - Leeds

| Junction | Northbound | Southbound |
|---|---|---|
| 2 | Access only from A1 (northbound) | Exit only to A1 (southbound) |
| 4 | Access only from A41 (northbound) | Exit only to A41 (southbound) |
| 6A | Access only from M25 (no link from A405) | Exit only to M25 (no link from A405) |
| 7 | Access only from M10 | Exit only to M10 |
| 17 | Exit only to M45 | Access only from M45 |
| 19 | Exit only to northbound M6 | Access only from M6 |
| 21A | Exit only to A46 | Access only from A46 |
| 23A | Access only from A42 | Exit only to A42 |
| 24A | Access only from A50 | Exit only to A50 |
| 35A | Exit only to A616 | Access only from A616 |
| 43 | Exit only to M621 | Access only from M621 |
| 48 | Exit only to A1(M) (northbound) | Access only from A1(M) (southbound) |

## M2 Rochester - Faversham

| Junction | Westbound | Eastbound |
|---|---|---|
| 1 | Exit only to A289 (eastbound) | Access only from A289 (westbound) |

## M3 Sunbury - Southampton

| Junction | Southwestbound | Northeastbound |
|---|---|---|
| 8 | Exit only to A303 | Access only from A303 |
| 10 | Access only from Winchester & A31 | Exit only to Winchester & A31 |
| 13 | Exit only | No restriction |
| 14 | No access to M27 westbound | Access from M27 only No exit |

## M4 London - South Wales

| Junction | Westbound | Eastbound |
|---|---|---|
| 1 | Access only from A4 (westbound) | Exit only to A4 (eastbound) |
| 4A | No exit to A4 (westbound) | No restriction |
| 21 | Exit only to M48 | Access only from M48 |
| 23 | Access only from M48 | Exit only to M48 |
| 25 | Exit only | Access only from B4596 |
| 25A | Exit only | Access only from A4042 |
| 29 | Exit only to A48(M) | Access only from A48(M) |
| 38 | Exit only | No restriction |
| 39 | Access only | No access/exit |

## M5 Birmingham - Exeter

| Junction | Southwestbound | Northeastbound |
|---|---|---|
| 10 | Exit only | Access only |
| 11A | Exit only to A417 (eastbound) | Access only from A417 (westbound) |
| 18A | Access only from M49 | Exit only to M49 |
| 29 | Access only from A30 (westbound) | No restriction |

## M6 Toll Motorway

| Junction | Northbound | Southbound |
|---|---|---|
| T1 | Access only | No access or exit |
| T2 | No access or exit | Exit only |
| T3 | Staggered junction; follow signs - access only from A38 | Staggered junction; follow signs - no restriction |
| T5 | Access only from A5127 (southbound) | Exit only to A5148 (northbound) |
| T7 | Exit only | Access only |
| T8 | Exit only | Access only |

## M6 Rugby - Carlisle

| Junction | Northbound | Southbound |
|---|---|---|
| 3A | Exit only | Access only |
| 4 | No access from M42 (southbound). No exit to M42 (northbound) | No access from M42 (southbound). No exit to M42 |
| 4A | Access only from M42 (southbound) | Exit only to M42 |
| 5 | Exit only to A452 | Access only from A452 |
| 10A | Exit only to M54 | Access only from M54 |
| 11A | Access only | Exit only |
| 20A (with M56) | No restriction | No access from M56 (westbound) |
| 20 | Access only from A50 | No restriction |
| 24 | Access only from A58 | Exit only to A58 |
| 25 | Exit only | Access only |
| 29 | No direct access, use adjacent slip road to jct 29A | No direct exit, use adjacent slip road from jct 29A |
| 29A | No direct exit, use adjacent slip road from jct 29 | No direct access, use adjacent slip road to jct 29 |
| 30 | Access only from M61 | Exit only to M61 |
| 31A | Exit only | Access only |
| 45 | Exit only | Access only |

## M8 Edinburgh - Bishopton

| Junction | Westbound | Eastbound |
|---|---|---|
| 8 | No access from M73 (southbound) or from A8 (eastbound) & A89 | No exit to M73 (northbound) or to A8 (westbound) & A89 |
| 9 | Access only | Exit only |
| 13 | Access only from M80 (southbound) | Exit only to M80 (northbound) |
| 14 | Access only | Exit only |
| 16 | Exit only to A804 | Access only from A879 |
| 17 | Exit only to A82 | No restriction |
| 18 | Access only from A82 (eastbound) | Exit only to A814 |
| 19 | No access from A814 (westbound) | Exit only to A814 (westbound) |
| 20 | Exit only | Access only |
| 21 | Access only | Exit only to A8 |
| 22 | Exit only to M77 (southbound) | Access only from M77 (northbound) |
| 23 | Exit only to B768 | Access only from B768 |
| 25 | No access or exit from or to A8 | No access or exit from or to A8 |
| 25A | Exit only | Access only |
| 28 | Exit only | Access only |
| 28A | Exit only to A737 | Access only from A737 |

## M9 Edinburgh - Dunblane

| Junction | Northwestbound | Southeastbound |
|---|---|---|
| 1A | Exit only to M9 spur | Access only from M9 spur |
| 2 | Access only | Exit only |
| 3 | Exit only | Access only |
| 6 | Access only from A904 | Exit only to A905 |
| 8 | Exit only to M876 (southwestbound) | Access only from M876 (northeastbound) |

## M10 St Albans - M1

| Junction | Northwestbound | Southeastbound |
|---|---|---|
| with M1 (jct 7) | Exit only to M1 (northbound) | Access only from M1 (southbound) |

## M11 London - Cambridge

| Junction | Northbound | Southbound |
|---|---|---|
| 4 | Access only from A406 | Exit only to A406 |
| 5 | Exit only to A1168 | Access only from A1168 |
| 9 | Exit only to A11 | Access only from A11 |
| 13 | Exit only to A1303 | Access only from A1303 |
| 14 | Exit only to A14 (eastbound) | Access only from A14 |

## M20 Swanley - Folkestone

| Junction | Southeastbound | Northwestbound |
|---|---|---|
| 2 | Staggered junction; follow signs - exit only to A227 | Staggered junction; follow signs - access only from A227 |
| 3 | Access only from M26 (eastbound) | Exit only to M26 (westbound) |
| 5 | For access follow signs - exit only to A20 | Access only from A20 |
| 6 | For exit follow signs | No restriction |
| 11A | Exit only | Access only |

## M23 Hooley - Crawley

| Junction | Southbound | Northbound |
|---|---|---|
| 7 | Access only from A23 (southbound) | Exit only to A23 (northbound) |
| 10A | Exit only to B2036 | Access only from B2036 |

## M25 London Orbital Motorway

| Junction | Clockwise | Anticlockwise |
|---|---|---|
| 1B | No direct access, use slip road to Jct 2. Exit only to A296 | Access only from A296. No exit - use jct 2 |
| 5 | No exit to M26 | No access from M26 |
| 19 | Exit only to A41 | Access only from A41 |
| 21 | Access only from M1 (southbound). Exit only to M1 (northbound) | Access only from M1 (southbound). Exit only to M1 (northbound) |
| 31 | No exit (use slip road via jct 30) | For access follow signs |

## M26 Sevenoaks - Wrotham

| Junction | Eastbound | Westbound |
|---|---|---|
| with M25 (jct 5) | Access only from anticlockwise M25 (eastbound) | Exit only to clockwise M25 (westbound) |
| with M20 (jct 3) | Exit only to M20 (southeastbound) | Access only from M20 (northwestbound) |

## M27 Cadnam - Portsmouth

| Junction | Eastbound | Westbound |
|---|---|---|
| 4 | Staggered junction; follow signs - access only from M3 (southbound). Exit only to M3 (northbound) | Staggered junction; follow signs - access only from M3 (southbound). Exit only to M3 (northbound) |
| 10 | Access only | Exit only |
| 12 | Staggered junction; follow signs - access only from M275 (northbound) | Staggered junction; follow signs - exit only to M275 (southbound) |

## M40 London - Birmingham

| Junction | Northwestbound | Southeastbound |
|---|---|---|
| 3 | Exit only to A40 | Access only from A40 |
| 7 | Exit only to A329 | Access only from A329 |
| 8 | Exit only to A40 | Access only from A40 |
| 13 | Exit only to A452 | Access only from A452 |
| 14 | Access only from A452 | Exit only to A452 |
| 16 | Access only from A3400 | Exit only to A3400 |

## M42 Bromsgrove - Measham

| Junction | Northeastbound | Southwestbound |
|---|---|---|
| 1 | Access only from A38 | Exit only to A38 |
| 7 | Exit only to M6 (northwestbound) | Access only from M6 (northwestbound) |
| 7A | Exit only to M6 (southeastbound) | No access or exit |
| 8 | Access only from M6 (southeastbound) | Exit only to M6 (northwestbound) |

## M45 Coventry - M1

| Junction | Eastbound | Westbound |
|---|---|---|
| unnumbered (Dunchurch) | Exit only to A45 & B4429 | Access only from A45 & B4429 |
| with M1 (jct 17) | Exit only to M1 (southbound) | Access only from M1 (northbound) |

## M53 Mersey Tunnel - Chester

| Junction | Southeastbound | Northwestbound |
|---|---|---|
| 11 | Access only from M56 (westbound). Exit only to M56 (eastbound) | Access only from M56 (westbound). Exit only to M56 (eastbound) |

## M54 Telford

| Junction | Westbound | Eastbound |
|---|---|---|
| with M6 (jct 10A) | Access only from M6 (northbound) | Exit only to M6 (southbound) |

## M56 North Cheshire

| Junction | Westbound | Eastbound |
|---|---|---|
| 1 | Access only from M60 (*westbound*) | Exit only to M60 (*eastbound*) & A34 (*northbound*) |
| 2 | Exit only to A560 | Access only from A560 |
| 3 | Access only from A5103 | Exit only to A5103 & A560 |
| 4 | Exit only | Access only |
| 9 | Exit to M6 (*southbound*) via A50 interchange | Access from M6 (*northbound*) via A50 interchange |
| 15 | Exit only to M53 | Access only from M53 |

## M57 Liverpool Outer Ring Road

| Junction | Northwestbound | Southeastbound |
|---|---|---|
| 3 | Access only from A526 | Exit only to A526 |
| 5 | Access only from A580 (*westbound*) | Exit only to A580 |

## M58 Liverpool - Wigan

| Junction | Eastbound | Westbound |
|---|---|---|
| 1 | Access only | Exit Only |

## M60 Manchester Orbital

| Junction | Clockwise | Anticlockwise |
|---|---|---|
| 2 | Access only from A560 | Exit only to A560 |
| 3 | No access from M56 | Access only from A34 (*northbound*) |
| 4 | Access only from A34 (*northbound*). Exit only to M56 | Access only from M56 (*eastbound*). Exit only to A34 (*southbound*) |
| 5 | Access and exit only from and to A5103 (*northbound*) | Access and exit only from and to A5103 (*southbound*) |
| 7 | No direct access, use slip road to jct 8. Exit only to A56 | Access only from A56. No exit - use jct 8 |
| 14 | Access from A580 (*eastbound*) | Exit only to A580 (*westbound*) |
| 16 | Access only from A666 | Exit only to A666 |
| 20 | Exit only to A664 | Access only from A664 |
| 22 | No restriction | Exit only to A62 |
| 25 | Exit only to A6017 | No restriction |
| 26 | No restriction | No access or exit |
| 27 | Access only from A626 | Exit only to A626 |

## M61 Manchester - Preston

| Junction | Northwestbound | Southeastbound |
|---|---|---|
| 3 | No access or exit | Exit only to A666 |
| with M6 (jct 30) | Exit only to M6 (*northbound*) | Access only from M6 (*southbound*) |

## M62 Liverpool - Kingston upon Hull

| Junction | Eastbound | Westbound |
|---|---|---|
| 23 | Exit only to A640 | Access only from A640 |

## M65 Preston - Colne

| Junction | Northeastbound | Southwestbound |
|---|---|---|
| 1 | Access and exit to M6 only | Access and exit to M6 only |
| 9 | Exit only to A679 | Access only from A679 |
| 11 | Access only | Exit only |

## M66 Bury

| Junction | Southbound | Northbound |
|---|---|---|
| with A56 | Access only from A56 (*southbound*) | Exit only to A56 (*northbound*) |
| 1 | Access only from A56 | Exit only to A56 |

## M67 Hyde Bypass

| Junction | Eastbound | Westbound |
|---|---|---|
| 1 | Exit only to A6017 | Access only from A6017 |
| 2 | Access only | Exit only to A57 |
| 3 | No restriction | Exit only to A627 |

## M69 Coventry - Leicester

| Junction | Northbound | Southbound |
|---|---|---|
| 2 | Access only from B4669 | Exit only to B4669 |

## M73 East of Glasgow

| Junction | Northbound | Southbound |
|---|---|---|
| 2 | No access from or exit to A89. No access from M8 (*eastbound*). | No access from or exit to A89. No exit to M8 (*westbound*) |
| 3 | Exit only to A80 (*northeastbound*) | Access only from A80 (*southwestbound*) |

## M74 and A74(M) Glasgow - Gretna

| Junction | Southbound | Northbound |
|---|---|---|
| 2 | Access only from A763 | Exit only to A763 |
| 3 | Exit only | Access only |
| 7 | Exit only to A72 | Access only from A72 |
| 9 | Exit only to B7078 | No access or exit |
| 10 | Access only from B7078 | No restrictions |
| 11 | Exit only to B7078 | Access only from B7078 |
| 12 | Access only from A70 | Exit only to A70 |
| 18 | Access only from B723 | Exit only to B723 |
| 21 | Exit only to B6357 | Access only from B6357 |
| 22 | Exit only | Access only |
| 23 | Access only from A75 | Exit only to A75 |

## M77 South of Glasgow

| Junction | Southbound | Northbound |
|---|---|---|
| with M8 (jct 22) | No access from M8 (*eastbound*) | No exit to M8 (*westbound*) |
| 4 | Exit only | Access only |
| 6 | Exit only | Access only |
| 7 | No restriction | Access only |
| 8 | No restriction | Access only from A77 |

## M80 Stepps Bypass

| Junction | Northeastbound | Southwestbound |
|---|---|---|
| 1 | Access only | No restriction |
| 3 | Exit only | Access only |

## M80 Bonnybridge - Stirling

| Junction | Northbound | Southbound |
|---|---|---|
| 5 | Exit only to M876 (*northeastbound*) | Access only from M876 (*southwestbound*) |

## M90 Forth Road Bridge - Perth

| Junction | Northbound | Southbound |
|---|---|---|
| 2A | Exit only to A92 (*eastbound*) | Access only from A92 (*westbound*) |
| 7 | Access only from A91 | Exit only to A91 |
| 8 | Exit only to A91 | Access only from A91 |
| 10 | No access from A912. No exit to A912 (*southbound*) | No access from A912 (*northbound*). No exit to A912 |

## M180 Doncaster - Grimsby

| Junction | Eastbound | Westbound |
|---|---|---|
| 1 | Exit only A18 | Access only from A18 |

## M606 Bradford Spur

| Junction | Northbound | Southbound |
|---|---|---|
| 2 | Exit only | No restriction |

## M621 Leeds - M1

| Junction | Clockwise | Anticlockwise |
|---|---|---|
| 2A | Access only | Exit only |
| 4 | Exit only | No restriction |
| 5 | Access only | Exit only |
| 6 | Access only | Exit only |
| with M1 (jct 43) | Exit only to M1 (*southbound*) | Access only from M1 (*northbound*) |

## M876 Bonnybridge - Kincardine Bridge

| Junction | Northeastbound | Southwestbound |
|---|---|---|
| with M80 (jct 5) | Access only from M80 (*northbound*) | Exit only to M80 (*southbound*) |
| 2 | Exit only to A9 | Access only from A9 |
| with M9 (jct 8) | Exit only to M9 (*eastbound*) | Access only from M9 (*westbound*) |

## A1(M) South Mimms - Baldock

| Junction | Northbound | Southbound |
|---|---|---|
| 2 | Exit only to A1001 | Access only from A1001 |
| 3 | No restriction | Exit only |
| 5 | Access only | No access or exit |

## A1(M) East of Leeds

| Junction | Northbound | Southbound |
|---|---|---|
| 44 | Access only from M1 (*northbound*) | Exit only to M1 (*southbound*) |

## A1(M) Scotch Corner - Newcastle upon Tyne

| Junction | Northbound | Southbound |
|---|---|---|
| 57 | Exit only to A66(M) (*eastbound*) | Access only from A66(M) (*westbound*) |
| 65 | No access. Exit only to A194(M) & A1 (*northbound*) | No exit. Access only from A194(M) and A1 (*southbound*) |

## A3(M) Horndean - Havant

| Junction | Southbound | Northbound |
|---|---|---|
| 1 | Exit only to A3 | Access only from A3 |
| 4 | Access only | Exit only |

## A48(M) Cardiff Spur

| Junction | Westbound | Eastbound |
|---|---|---|
| 29 | Access only from M4 | Exit only to M4 (*eastbound*) |
| 29A | Exit only to A48 (*westbound*) | Access only from A48 (*eastbound*) |

## A66(M) Darlington Spur

| Junction | Eastbound | Westbound |
|---|---|---|
| with A1(M) (jct 57) | Access only from A1(M) (*northbound*) | Exit only to A1(M) (*southbound*) |

## A194(M) Newcastle upon Tyne

| Junction | Northbound | Southbound |
|---|---|---|
| with A1(M) (jct 65) | Access only from A1(M) (*northbound*) | Exit only to A1(M) (*southbound*) |

## A12 M25 - Ipswich

| Junction | Northeastbound | Southwestbound |
|---|---|---|
| 13 | Access only from B1002 | No restriction |
| 14 | Exit only | Access only |
| 20A | Exit only to B1137 | Access only from B1137 |
| 20B | Access only B1137 | Exit only to B1137 |
| 21 | No restriction | Access only from B1389 |
| 23 | Exit only to B1024 | Access only from B1024 |
| 24 | Access only from B1024 | Exit only from B1024 |
| 27 | Exit only to A113 | Access only from A113 |
| unnumbered (with A120) | Exit only A120 | Access only from A120 |
| 29 | Access only from A120 and A1232 | Exit only to A120 and A1232 |
| unnumbered | Exit only | Access only |

## A14 M1 - Felixstowe

| Junction | Eastbound | Westbound |
|---|---|---|
| With M1/M6 (jct 19) | Access only from M6 and M1 (*southbound*) | Exit only to M6 and M1 (*northbound*) |
| 4 | Access only from B669 | Exit only to B669 |
| 31 | Access only from A428 & M11. Exit only to A1307 | Exit only to A428 & M11. Access only from A1307 |
| 34 | Exit only to B1047 | Access only from B1047 |
| 36 | Access only from A11 | Exit only to A11 |
| 38 | Exit only to A11 | Access only from A11 |
| 39 | Access only from B1506 | Exit only to B1506 |
| 49 | Exit only to A1308 | Access only from A1308 |
| 61 | Exit only to A154 | Access only from A154 |

## A55 Holyhead - Chester

| Junction | Eastbound | Westbound |
|---|---|---|
| 8A | Access only from A5 | Exit only to A5 |
| 23A | Exit only | Access only |
| 24A | No access or exit | Exit only |
| 33A | No access from or exit to B5126 | Exit only to B5126 |
| 33B | Access only from A494 | Exit only to A494 |
| 35A (west) | Exit only A5104 | Access only from A5104 |
| 35B (east) | Access only from A5104 | Exit only to A5104 |

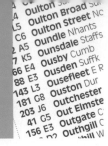

# Index to place names

This index lists places appearing in the main-map section of the atlas in alphabetical order. The reference before each name gives the atlas page number and grid reference of the square in which the place appears. The map shows counties, unitary authorities and administrative areas, together with a list of the abbreviated name forms used in the index.

## England

| | |
|---|---|
| BaNES | **Bath & N E Somerset (18)** |
| Barns | **Barnsley (19)** |
| Bed | **Bedford** |
| Birm | **Birmingham** |
| Bl w D | **Blackburn with Darwen (20)** |
| Bmouth | **Bournemouth** |
| Bolton | **Bolton (21)** |
| Bpool | **Blackpool** |
| Br & H | **Brighton & Hove (22)** |
| Br For | **Bracknell Forest (23)** |
| Bristl | **City of Bristol** |
| Bucks | **Buckinghamshire** |
| Bury | **Bury (24)** |
| C Beds | **Central Bedfordshire** |
| C Brad | **City of Bradford** |
| C Derb | **City of Derby** |
| C KuH | **City of Kingston upon Hull** |
| C Leic | **City of Leicester** |
| C Nott | **City of Nottingham** |
| C Pete | **City of Peterborough** |
| C Plym | **City of Plymouth** |
| C Port | **City of Portsmouth** |
| C Sotn | **City of Southampton** |
| C Stke | **City of Stoke-on-Trent** |
| C York | **City of York** |
| Calder | **Calderdale (25)** |
| Cambs | **Cambridgeshire** |
| Ches E | **Cheshire East** |
| Ches W | **Cheshire West and Chester** |
| Cnwll | **Cornwall** |
| Covtry | **Coventry** |
| Cumb | **Cumbria** |
| Darltn | **Darlington (26)** |
| Derbys | **Derbyshire** |
| Devon | **Devon** |
| Donc | **Doncaster (27)** |
| Dorset | **Dorset** |
| Dudley | **Dudley (28)** |
| Dur | **Durham** |
| E R Yk | **East Riding of Yorkshire** |
| E Susx | **East Sussex** |
| Essex | **Essex** |
| Gatesd | **Gateshead (29)** |
| Gloucs | **Gloucestershire** |
| Gt Lon | **Greater London** |
| Halton | **Halton (30)** |
| Hants | **Hampshire** |
| Hartpl | **Hartlepool (31)** |
| Herefs | **Herefordshire** |
| Herts | **Hertfordshire** |
| IoS | **Isles of Scilly** |
| IoW | **Isle of Wight** |
| Kent | **Kent** |
| Kirk | **Kirklees (32)** |
| Knows | **Knowsley (33)** |
| Lancs | **Lancashire** |
| Leeds | **Leeds** |
| Leics | **Leicestershire** |
| Lincs | **Lincolnshire** |
| Lpool | **Liverpool** |

| | |
|---|---|
| Luton | **Luton** |
| M Keyn | **Milton Keynes** |
| Manch | **Manchester** |
| Medway | **Medway** |
| Middsb | **Middlesbrough** |
| NE Lin | **North East Lincolnshire** |
| N Linc | **North Lincolnshire** |
| N Som | **North Somerset (34)** |
| N Tyne | **North Tyneside (35)** |
| N u Ty | **Newcastle upon Tyne** |
| N York | **North Yorkshire** |
| Nhants | **Northamptonshire** |
| Norfk | **Norfolk** |
| Notts | **Nottinghamshire** |
| Nthumb | **Northumberland** |
| Oldham | **Oldham (36)** |
| Oxon | **Oxfordshire** |
| Poole | **Poole** |
| R & Cl | **Redcar & Cleveland** |
| Readg | **Reading** |
| Rochdl | **Rochdale (37)** |
| Rothm | **Rotherham (38)** |
| Rutlnd | **Rutland** |
| S Glos | **South Gloucestershire (39)** |
| S on T | **Stockton-on-Tees (40)** |
| S Tyne | **South Tyneside (41)** |
| Salfd | **Salford (42)** |
| Sandw | **Sandwell (43)** |
| Sefton | **Sefton (44)** |
| Sheff | **Sheffield** |
| Shrops | **Shropshire** |
| Slough | **Slough (45)** |
| Solhll | **Solihull (46)** |
| Somset | **Somerset** |
| St Hel | **St Helens (47)** |
| Staffs | **Staffordshire** |
| Sthend | **Southend-on-Sea** |
| Stockp | **Stockport (48)** |
| Suffk | **Suffolk** |
| Sundld | **Sunderland** |
| Surrey | **Surrey** |
| Swindn | **Swindon** |
| Tamesd | **Tameside (49)** |
| Thurr | **Thurrock (50)** |
| Torbay | **Torbay** |
| Traffd | **Trafford (51)** |
| W & M | **Windsor and Maidenhead (52)** |
| W Berk | **West Berkshire** |
| W Susx | **West Sussex** |
| Wakefd | **Wakefield (53)** |
| Warrtn | **Warrington (54)** |
| Warwks | **Warwickshire** |
| Wigan | **Wigan (55)** |
| Wilts | **Wiltshire** |
| Wirral | **Wirral (56)** |
| Wokham | **Wokingham (57)** |
| Wolves | **Wolverhampton (58)** |
| Worcs | **Worcestershire** |
| Wrekin | **Telford & Wrekin (59)** |
| Wsall | **Walsall (60)** |

## Scotland

| | |
|---|---|
| Abers | **Aberdeenshire** |
| Ag & B | **Argyll and Bute** |
| Angus | **Angus** |
| Border | **Scottish Borders** |
| C Aber | **City of Aberdeen** |
| C Dund | **City of Dundee** |
| C Edin | **City of Edinburgh** |
| C Glas | **City of Glasgow** |
| Clacks | **Clackmannanshire (1)** |
| D & G | **Dumfries & Galloway** |
| E Ayrs | **East Ayrshire** |
| E Duns | **East Dunbartonshire (2)** |
| E Loth | **East Lothian** |
| E Rens | **East Renfrewshire (3)** |
| Falk | **Falkirk** |
| Fife | **Fife** |
| Highld | **Highland** |
| Inver | **Inverclyde (4)** |
| Mdloth | **Midlothian (5)** |
| Moray | **Moray** |
| N Ayrs | **North Ayrshire** |
| N Lans | **North Lanarkshire (6)** |
| Ork | **Orkney Islands** |
| P & K | **Perth & Kinross** |
| Rens | **Renfrewshire (7)** |
| S Ayrs | **South Ayrshire** |
| Shet | **Shetland Islands** |
| S Lans | **South Lanarkshire** |
| Stirlg | **Stirling** |
| W Duns | **West Dunbartonshire (8)** |
| W Isls | **Western Isles (Na h-Eileanan an Iar)** |
| W Loth | **West Lothian** |

## Wales

| | |
|---|---|
| Blae G | **Blaenau Gwent (9)** |
| Brdgnd | **Bridgend (10)** |
| Caerph | **Caerphilly (11)** |
| Cardif | **Cardiff** |
| Carmth | **Carmarthenshire** |
| Cerdgn | **Ceredigion** |
| Conwy | **Conwy** |
| Denbgs | **Denbighshire** |
| Flints | **Flintshire** |
| Gwynd | **Gwynedd** |
| IoA | **Isle of Anglesey** |
| Mons | **Monmouthshire** |
| Myr Td | **Merthyr Tydfil (12)** |
| Neath | **Neath Port Talbot (13)** |
| Newpt | **Newport (14)** |
| Pembks | **Pembrokeshire** |
| Powys | **Powys** |
| Rhondd | **Rhondda Cynon Taff (15)** |
| Swans | **Swansea** |
| Torfn | **Torfaen (16)** |
| V Glam | **Vale of Glamorgan (17)** |
| Wrexhm | **Wrexham** |

## Channel Islands & Isle of Man

| | |
|---|---|
| Guern | **Guernsey** |
| Jersey | **Jersey** |
| IoM | **Isle of Man** |

ORKNEY ISLANDS

SHETLAND ISLANDS

WESTERN ISLES (Na h-Eileanan an Iar)

HIGHLAND

MORAY

S C O T L A N D

ABERDEENSHIRE

Aberdeen

ANGUS

PERTH & KINROSS

Dundee

ARGYLL & BUTE

STIRLING

FIFE

1

FALK

8
2
4
Glasgow
7
W LOTH
6
3

Edinburgh

E LOTH

5

NORTH AYRSHIRE

S LANS

E AYRS

SCOTTISH BORDERS

S AYRS

DUMFRIES & GALLOWAY

NORTHUMBERLAND

Newcastle upon Tyne
35
29
41
Sunderland

CUMBRIA

DURHAM

31
26
40
R & Cl
Middlesbrough

IoM

NORTH YORKSHIRE

Bradford

York

EAST RIDING OF YORKSHIRE

Blackpool

LANCASHIRE

Leeds

Kingston upon Hull

20
25
32
53

N LINCS

N E LINCS

21 24 37
55
44
47 42
33
51
54
56 30

36
49
Manchester
48

19
38
Sheffield

27

IoA

CHES W

CHES E

DERBYS

NOTTS

LINCOLNSHIRE

CONWY
FLINTS

Stoke-on-Trent

Derby

Nottingham

DENBGS

WREXHAM

GWYNEDD

STAFFS

LEICS

RUTLAND

Peterborough

NORFOLK

59

SHROPSHIRE

58 60
28 43
Birmingham
46
Coventry

NHANTS

CAMBS

SUFFOLK

POWYS

WORCS

WARWKS

Milton Keynes

BED

CERDGN

HEREFS

W A L E S

E N G L A N D

BEDS
Luton

HFRTS

ESSEX

PEMBKS

CARMTH

MONS
9
12
10
15 11
10
13
14
Cardiff
17

GLOUCS

OXON

BUCKS

GREATER LONDON

Southend-on-Sea

Swansea

Bristol
39
34
18

Swindon

Reading
52 45
57 23
W BERKS

MEDWAY
50

WILTSHIRE

SURREY

KENT

HAMPSHIRE

W SUSX

E SUSX

SOMERSET

DORSET

Southampton

22

DEVON

Bournemouth
Poole

Portsmouth

IoW

CORNWALL

Plymouth

Torbay

Guernsey

CHANNEL ISLANDS

Jersey

IoS

288 Abbas Combe - Aldoth

## A


32 B6 Abbas Combe Somset
81 H2 Abberley Worcs
81 G2 Abberley Common Worcs
72 E3 Abberton Essex
82 A4 Abberton Worcs
191 G3 Abberwick Nthumb
70 E5 Abbess Roding Essex
29 L8 Abbey Devon
78 E1 Abbeycwmhir Powys
132 F3 Abbeydale Sheff
62 D1 Abbey Dore Herefs
131 J8 Abbey Green Staffs
30 D7 Abbey Hill Somset
213 G6 Abbey St Bathans Border
147 L5 Abbeystead Lancs
177 G8 Abbey Town Cumb
139 J3 Abbey Village Lancs
52 A3 Abbey Wood Gt Lon
189 G4 Abbotrule Border
27 G8 Abbots Bickington Devon
115 H6 Abbots Bromley Staffs
16 A5 Abbotsbury Dorset
131 K2 Abbot's Chair Derbys
221 K5 Abbots Deuglie P & K
27 G5 Abbotsham Devon
8 C1 Abbotskerswell Devon
68 E6 Abbots Langley Herts
8 B5 Abbotsleigh Devon
45 G4 Abbots Leigh N Som
86 E4 Abbotsley Cambs
82 B4 Abbots Morton Worcs
102 E7 Abbots Ripton Cambs
82 C5 Abbot's Salford Warwks
35 H4 Abbotstone Hants
34 D6 Abbotswood Hants
35 G4 Abbots Worthy Hants
34 D2 Abbotts Ann Hants
17 J2 Abbott Street Dorset
95 J7 Abcott Shrops
96 D6 Abdon Shrops
63 K4 Abenhall Gloucs
76 E3 Aberaeron Cerdgn
60 F7 Aberaman Rhondd
93 J2 Aberangell Gwynd
76 B7 Aber-arad Carmth
251 H6 Aberarder Highld
222 B4 Aberargie P & K
76 E3 Aberarth Cerdgn
57 K7 Aberavon Neath
76 C7 Aber-banc Cerdgn
61 J7 Aberbargoed Caerph
61 K6 Aberbeeg Blae G
61 G6 Abercanaid Myr Td
43 K3 Abercarn Caerph
74 D5 Abercastle Pembks
93 H3 Abercegir Powys
240 B3 Aberchalder Lodge Highld
268 A5 Aberchirder Abers
61 H3 Aber Clydach Powys
59 M6 Abercraf Powys
42 C2 Abercregan Neath
60 F7 Abercwmboi Rhondd
75 M4 Abercych Pembks
43 G3 Abercynon Rhondd
221 K3 Aberdalgie P & K
60 F6 Aberdare Rhondd
108 C6 Aberdaron Gwynd
245 L2 Aberdeen C Aber
109 G1 Aberdesach Gwynd
211 G2 Aberdour Fife
57 L5 Aberdulais Neath
92 D4 Aberdyfi Gwynd
78 F6 Aberedw Powys
74 C6 Abereiddy Pembks
109 G4 Abererch Gwynd
61 G7 Aberfan Myr Td
232 C5 Aberfeldy P & K
124 F6 Aberffraw IoA
92 E7 Aberffrwd Cerdgn
150 F8 Aberford Leeds
219 H7 Aberfoyle Stirlg
42 D5 Abergarw Brdgnd
60 B6 Abergarwed Neath
62 C4 Abergavenny Mons
127 J4 Abergele Conwy
76 F7 Aber-giar Carmth
59 G2 Abergorlech Carmth
78 A4 Abergwesyn Powys
58 D5 Abergwili Carmth
93 G3 Abergwydol Powys
42 D3 Abergwynfi Neath
126 C5 Abergwyngregyn Gwynd
92 E2 Abergynolwyn Gwynd
94 C5 Aberhafesp Powys
93 H4 Aberhosan Powys
42 D5 Aberkenfig Brdgnd
212 A3 Aberlady E Loth
234 E4 Aberlemno Angus
93 G2 Aberllefenni Gwynd
79 H7 Aberllynfi Powys
254 E3 Aberlour Moray
92 E8 Aber-Magwr Cerdgn
77 G4 Aber-meurig Cerdgn
129 G8 Abermorddu Flints
94 E4 Abermule Powys
58 C4 Abernant Carmth
60 F6 Aber-nant Rhondd
222 C4 Abernethy P & K
222 D1 Abernyte P & K
76 A5 Aberporth Cerdgn
108 E6 Abersoch Gwynd
62 B6 Abersychan Torfn
42 F6 Aberthin V Glam
61 K6 Abertillery Blae G
43 H4 Abertridwr Caerph
111 K7 Abertridwr Powys
61 H6 Abertysswg Caerph
221 H4 Aberuthven P & K
60 F1 Aberyscir Powys
92 C7 Aberystwyth Cerdgn
92 D6 Aberystwyth Crematorium Cerdgn
66 C7 Abingdon Oxon
37 H2 Abinger Common Surrey
37 G2 Abinger Hammer Surrey
84 F3 Abington Nhants
186 D2 Abington S Lans
86 F6 Abington Pigotts Cambs
21 J3 Abingworth W Susx
117 J7 Ab Kettleby Leics
82 B5 Ab Lench Worcs
65 G5 Ablington Gloucs
33 K2 Ablington Wilts
132 D4 Abney Derbys
115 G2 Above Church Staffs
244 C4 Aboyne Abers
139 J7 Abram Wigan
250 F4 Abriachan Highld
70 C7 Abridge Essex
209 L4 Abronhill N Lans
45 L4 Abson S Glos
84 C6 Abthorpe Nhants
137 H4 Aby Lincs
151 J6 Acaster Malbis C York
151 J7 Acaster Selby N York
139 M2 Accrington Lancs
140 A2 Accrington Crematorium Lancs
224 F4 Acha Ag & B
206 B3 Achahoish Ag & B
233 H6 Achalader P & K
228 E8 Achaleven Ag & B
282 f3 Acha Mor W Isls
261 M7 Achanalt Highld
263 H5 Achandunie Highld
272 E7 Achany Highld
237 K7 Acharacle Highld
227 K2 Acharn Highld
231 L6 Acharn P & K
279 L7 Achavanich Highld
270 D7 Achduart Highld
276 D8 Achfary Highld
246 C7 A'Chill Highld
270 D6 Achiltibuie Highld
278 B4 Achina Highld
192 F5 Achinhoan Ag & B
248 F3 Achintee Highld
248 D4 Achintraid Highld
270 E3 Achmelvich Highld
248 D5 Achmore Highld
282 f3 Achmore W Isls
270 D2 Achnacarnin Highld
239 K6 Achnacarry Highld
247 J6 Achnacloich Highld
250 D8 Achnaconeran Highld
228 C7 Achnacroish Ag & B
226 F2 Achnadrish House Ag & B
232 C8 Achnafauld P & K
263 J6 Achnagarron Highld
236 F6 Achnaha Highld
270 D5 Achnahaird Highld
272 E5 Achnairn Highld
228 C3 Achnalea Highld
206 B2 Achnamara Ag & B
261 K8 Achnasheen Highld
249 G2 Achnashellach Lodge Highld
254 F5 Achnastank Moray
236 E7 Achosnich Highld
227 K3 Achranich Highld
279 H3 Achreamie Highld
229 J2 Achriabhach Highld
276 D5 Achriesgill Highld
277 M4 Achtoty Highld
102 A6 Achurch Nhants
263 J1 Achvaich Highld
279 H3 Achvarasdal Highld
280 E5 Ackergill Highld
170 C7 Acklam Middsb
152 B3 Acklam N York
97 H4 Ackleton Shrops
191 J6 Acklington Nthumb
142 C3 Ackton Wakefd
142 C4 Ackworth Moor Top Wakefd
107 H1 Acle Norfk
98 E6 Acock's Green Birm
41 J2 Acol Kent
151 J5 Acomb C York
179 L5 Acomb Nthumb
30 B8 Acombe Somset
80 C8 Aconbury Herefs
140 B3 Acre Lancs
112 D3 Acrefair Wrexhm
113 K1 Acton Ches E
17 J6 Acton Dorset
51 G3 Acton Gt Lon
95 H6 Acton Shrops
114 C3 Acton Staffs
89 H6 Acton Suffk
81 J2 Acton Worcs
80 F5 Acton Beauchamp Herefs
130 B4 Acton Bridge Ches W
96 C3 Acton Burnell Shrops
81 G5 Acton Green Herefs
112 E1 Acton Park Wrexhm
96 C3 Acton Pigott Shrops
96 E4 Acton Round Shrops
95 L5 Acton Scott Shrops
114 E7 Acton Trussell Staffs
46 A3 Acton Turville S Glos
114 B6 Adbaston Staffs
31 K6 Adber Dorset
117 G4 Adbolton Notts
83 L8 Adderbury Oxon
113 L3 Adderley Shrops
203 J7 Adderstone Nthumb
210 C6 Addiewell W Loth
149 K6 Addingham C Brad
67 H2 Addington Bucks
51 K6 Addington Gt Lon
52 E7 Addington Kent
51 J5 Addiscombe Gt Lon
50 D6 Addlestone Surrey
50 D6 Addlestonemoor Surrey
137 K6 Addlethorpe Lincs
113 M7 Adeney Wrekin
68 D5 Adeyfield Herts
94 C3 Adfa Powys
79 M1 Adforton Herefs
41 H4 Adisham Kent
65 K2 Adlestrop Gloucs
143 L3 Adlingfleet E R Yk
131 H4 Adlington Ches E
139 J5 Adlington Lancs
115 G7 Admaston Staffs
96 E1 Admaston Wrekin
82 E6 Admington Warwks
76 B7 Adpar Cerdgn
30 D5 Adsborough Somset
30 B3 Adscombe Somset
67 H1 Adstock Bucks
84 B5 Adstone Nhants
131 H2 Adswood Stockp
37 G6 Adversane W Susx
254 C5 Advie Highld
141 K2 Adwalton Leeds
67 G7 Adwell Oxon
142 E6 Adwick Le Street Donc
142 D7 Adwick upon Dearne Donc
176 C1 Ae D & G
176 D2 Ae Bridgend D & G
139 M5 Affetside Bury
255 L4 Affleck Abers
16 F4 Affpuddle Dorset
249 K7 Affric Lodge Highld
128 D5 Afon-wen Flints
8 C2 Afton Devon
18 E6 Afton IoW
140 B7 Agecroft Crematorium Salfd
159 K5 Agglethorpe N York
129 J2 Aigburth Lpool
153 G6 Aike E R Yk
166 B1 Aiketgate Cumb
165 H1 Aikhead Cumb
177 J8 Aikton Cumb
137 H4 Ailby Lincs
79 L5 Ailey Herefs
102 C4 Ailsworth C Pete
160 E6 Ainderby Quernhow N York
160 E4 Ainderby Steeple N York
73 G3 Aingers Green Essex
138 C5 Ainsdale Sefton
138 C5 Ainsdale-on-Sea Sefton
166 C2 Ainstable Cumb
139 M5 Ainsworth Bury
162 C1 Ainthorpe N York
138 D8 Aintree Sefton
210 F6 Ainville W Loth
216 B7 Aird Ag & B
172 D3 Aird D & G
282 h3 Aird W Isls
282 e5 Aird a Mhulaidh W Isls
282 e5 Aird Asaig W Isls
248 A4 Aird Dhubh Highld
216 F1 Airdeny Ag & B
227 G6 Aird of Kinloch Ag & B
247 J8 Aird of Sleat Highld
209 K6 Airdrie N Lans
209 K5 Airdriehill N Lans
216 F1 Airds Bay Ag & B
175 G1 Airds of Kells D & G
282 d3 Aird Uig W Isls
282 f4 Airidh a bhruaich W Isls
175 J3 Airieland D & G
233 M5 Airlie Angus
143 J3 Airmyn E R Yk
233 G8 Airntully P & K
247 M7 Airor Highld
210 B2 Airth Falk
148 F4 Airton N York
118 D4 Aisby Lincs
135 H1 Aisby Lincs
158 D3 Aisgill Cumb
7 K3 Aish Devon
8 C3 Aish Devon
30 B4 Aisholt Somset
160 C5 Aiskew N York
162 D5 Aislaby N York
162 F1 Aislaby N York
169 L8 Aislaby S on T
135 J4 Aisthorpe Lincs
281 d5 Aith Shet
202 E7 Akeld Nthumb
84 D7 Akeley Bucks
90 D5 Akenham Suffk
12 A8 Albaston Cnwll
112 E8 Alberbury Shrops
22 C4 Albourne W Susx
22 C4 Albourne Green W Susx
97 H3 Albrighton Shrops
113 H7 Albrighton Shrops
106 F6 Alburgh Norfk
70 B2 Albury Herts
67 G6 Albury Oxon
37 G2 Albury Surrey
70 B2 Albury End Herts
37 G2 Albury Heath Surrey
122 D5 Alby Hill Norfk
263 G8 Alcaig Highld
95 L6 Alcaston Shrops
82 C4 Alcester Warwks
98 D7 Alcester Lane End Birm
23 H6 Alciston E Susx
46 A5 Alcombe Wilts
102 D8 Alconbury Cambs
102 D7 Alconbury Weston Cambs
150 F3 Aldborough N York
122 D5 Aldborough Norfk
47 K4 Aldbourne Wilts
153 L8 Aldbrough E R Yk
169 G8 Aldbrough St John N York
68 B4 Aldbury Herts
147 J4 Aldcliffe Lancs
232 D3 Aldclune P & K
91 K4 Aldeburgh Suffk
107 J5 Aldeby Norfk
68 F7 Aldenham Herts
33 L5 Alderbury Wilts
116 D2 Aldercar Derbys
122 C7 Alderford Norfk
33 K8 Alderholt Dorset
45 M1 Alderley Gloucs
131 G4 Alderley Edge Ches E
99 K6 Aldermans Green Covtry
48 E6 Aldermaston W Berk
82 F5 Alderminster Warwks
115 L6 Alder Moor Staffs
129 K8 Aldersey Green Ches W
36 C1 Aldershot Hants
82 B8 Alderton Gloucs
84 E6 Alderton Nhants
113 H6 Alderton Shrops
91 H7 Alderton Suffk
46 B2 Alderton Wilts
116 A1 Alderwasley Derbys
150 C2 Aldfield N York
129 K7 Aldford Ches W
101 L3 Aldgate Rutlnd
72 D2 Aldham Essex
90 B6 Aldham Suffk
20 F5 Aldingbourne W Susx
146 E2 Aldingham Cumb
40 E8 Aldington Kent
82 C6 Aldington Worcs
40 E7 Aldington Corner Kent
255 G6 Aldivalloch Moray
208 B1 Aldochlay Ag & B
95 K7 Aldon Shrops
164 F1 Aldoth Cumb

103 J8 **Aldreth** Cambs
98 D3 **Aldridge** Wsall
91 K3 **Aldringham** Suffk
152 B3 **Aldro** N York
65 H5 **Aldsworth** Gloucs
20 C5 **Aldsworth** W Susx
255 G6 **Aldunie** Moray
132 E8 **Aldwark** Derbys
151 G3 **Aldwark** N York
20 E7 **Aldwick** W Susx
101 M7 **Aldwincle** Nhants
48 E3 **Aldworth** W Berk
208 C3 **Alexandria** W Duns
30 B3 **Aley** Somset
26 E8 **Alfardisworthy** Devon
14 D3 **Alfington** Devon
36 F4 **Alfold** Surrey
36 F4 **Alfold Bars** W Susx
36 F4 **Alfold Crossways** Surrey
255 M8 **Alford** Abers
137 H4 **Alford** Lincs
31 K4 **Alford** Somset
137 H4 **Alford Crematorium** Lincs
133 H8 **Alfreton** Derbys
81 H4 **Alfrick** Worcs
81 G5 **Alfrick Pound** Worcs
23 H6 **Alfriston** E Susx
119 J4 **Algarkirk** Lincs
31 K4 **Alhampton** Somset
143 M3 **Alkborough** N Linc
63 M6 **Alkerton** Gloucs
83 J6 **Alkerton** Oxon
41 H6 **Alkham** Kent
113 H4 **Alkington** Shrops
115 K4 **Alkmonton** Derbys
8 B4 **Allaleigh** Devon
242 F5 **Allanaquoich** Abers
209 M7 **Allanbank** N Lans
202 D2 **Allanton** Border
209 M7 **Allanton** N Lans
209 K8 **Allanton** S Lans
63 J6 **Allaston** Gloucs
34 F6 **Allbrook** Hants
46 F6 **All Cannings** Wilts
179 J7 **Allendale** Nthumb
98 F4 **Allen End** Warwks
167 K2 **Allenheads** Nthumb
168 D1 **Allensford** Dur
70 C4 **Allen's Green** Herts
80 B8 **Allensmore** Herefs
116 B5 **Allenton** C Derb
28 D5 **Aller** Devon
30 F5 **Aller** Somset
164 E3 **Allerby** Cumb
14 B3 **Allercombe** Devon
28 F2 **Allerford** Somset
162 F6 **Allerston** N York
152 B6 **Allerthorpe** E R Yk
141 H1 **Allerton** C Brad
263 K6 **Allerton** Highld
129 J2 **Allerton** Lpool
142 C2 **Allerton Bywater** Leeds
150 F4 **Allerton Mauleverer** N York
99 J7 **Allesley** Covtry
116 B4 **Allestree** C Derb
4 C5 **Allet Common** Cnwll
101 H3 **Allexton** Leics
131 J6 **Allgreave** Ches E
53 H3 **Allhallows** Medway
53 H3 **Allhallows-on-Sea** Medway
260 D8 **Alligin Shuas** Highld
114 D7 **Allimore Green** Staffs
15 K4 **Allington** Dorset
53 G7 **Allington** Kent
117 M3 **Allington** Lincs
33 L3 **Allington** Wilts
46 C4 **Allington** Wilts
46 F6 **Allington** Wilts
156 E7 **Allithwaite** Cumb
220 F8 **Alloa** Clacks
164 E2 **Allonby** Cumb
130 E5 **Allostock** Ches W
196 C7 **Alloway** S Ayrs
30 F8 **Allowenshay** Somset
107 G7 **All Saints South Elmham** Suffk
97 G4 **Allscott** Shrops
96 E1 **Allscott** Wrekin
95 L4 **All Stretton** Shrops
129 G6 **Alltami** Flints
229 K5 **Alltchaorunn** Highld
78 F6 **Alltmawr** Powys
58 E3 **Alltwalis** Carmth
57 K4 **Alltwen** Neath
76 F6 **Alltyblaca** Cerdgn
31 L8 **Allweston** Dorset
90 B1 **Allwood Green** Suffk
79 L5 **Almeley** Herefs
79 L5 **Almeley Wooton** Herefs
17 H3 **Almer** Dorset
142 F6 **Almholme** Donc

113 M4 **Almington** Staffs
20 D7 **Almodington** W Susx
221 J2 **Almondbank** P & K
141 J5 **Almondbury** Kirk
45 J2 **Almondsbury** S Glos
151 G3 **Alne** N York
90 E7 **Alnesbourn Priory** Suffk
263 H6 **Alness** Highld
190 E4 **Alnham** Nthumb
191 J4 **Alnmouth** Nthumb
191 H3 **Alnwick** Nthumb
50 F2 **Alperton** Gt Lon
89 H8 **Alphamstone** Essex
89 H5 **Alpheton** Suffk
13 L4 **Alphington** Devon
106 F3 **Alpington** Norfk
132 D6 **Alport** Derbys
130 B7 **Alpraham** Ches E
72 F3 **Alresford** Essex
115 K8 **Alrewas** Staffs
130 F8 **Alsager** Ches E
114 C2 **Alsagers Bank** Staffs
132 C8 **Alsop en le Dale** Derbys
167 G2 **Alston** Cumb
15 G2 **Alston** Devon
82 A8 **Alstone** Gloucs
30 D2 **Alstone** Somset
132 C8 **Alstonefield** Staffs
44 E8 **Alston Sutton** Somset
28 C6 **Alswear** Devon
140 E7 **Alt** Oldham
270 C5 **Altandhu** Highld
11 J6 **Altarnun** Cnwll
272 D8 **Altass** Highld
227 K5 **Altcreich** Ag & B
207 G4 **Altgaltraig** Ag & B
140 A1 **Altham** Lancs
72 D7 **Althorne** Essex
143 L6 **Althorpe** N Linc
279 H7 **Altnabreac Station** Highld
216 C2 **Altnacraig** Ag & B
272 E1 **Altnaharra** Highld
142 B3 **Altofts** Wakefd
133 G6 **Alton** Derbys
35 L3 **Alton** Hants
115 H3 **Alton** Staffs
33 K2 **Alton** Wilts
47 G6 **Alton Barnes** Wilts
16 D2 **Alton Pancras** Dorset
47 G6 **Alton Priors** Wilts
130 E2 **Altrincham** Traffd
130 E2 **Altrincham Crematorium** Traffd
219 G6 **Altskeith Hotel** Stirlg
220 F7 **Alva** Clacks
129 L5 **Alvanley** Ches W
116 C5 **Alvaston** C Derb
82 B1 **Alvechurch** Worcs
99 H3 **Alvecote** Warwks
33 G6 **Alvediston** Wilts
97 G6 **Alveley** Shrops
27 J6 **Alverdiscott** Devon
19 K4 **Alverstoke** Hants
19 K6 **Alverstone** IoW
141 M3 **Alverthorpe** Wakefd
117 L3 **Alverton** Notts
266 C4 **Alves** Moray
65 K6 **Alvescot** Oxon
45 J1 **Alveston** S Glos
82 F4 **Alveston** Warwks
137 G2 **Alvingham** Lincs
63 J7 **Alvington** Gloucs
102 C4 **Alwalton** C Pete
190 C5 **Alwinton** Nthumb
150 C7 **Alwoodley** Leeds
150 D7 **Alwoodley Gates** Leeds
233 K5 **Alyth** P & K
116 B1 **Ambergate** Derbys
119 H2 **Amber Hill** Lincs
64 B6 **Amberley** Gloucs
21 H4 **Amberley** W Susx
133 G8 **Amber Row** Derbys
23 K5 **Amberstone** E Susx
191 K5 **Amble** Nthumb
97 K6 **Amblecote** Dudley
141 H2 **Ambler Thorn** C Brad
156 E2 **Ambleside** Cumb
75 G7 **Ambleston** Pembks
66 F3 **Ambrosden** Oxon
143 L5 **Amcotts** N Linc
103 J7 **America** Cambs
68 B7 **Amersham** Bucks
68 B7 **Amersham Common** Bucks
68 B7 **Amersham Old Town** Bucks
68 B7 **Amersham on the Hill** Bucks
114 F6 **Amerton** Staffs
33 K3 **Amesbury** Wilts
282 d5 **Amhuinnsuidhe** W Isls
99 G3 **Amington** Staffs
176 D2 **Amisfield Town** D & G
125 H1 **Amlwch** IoA

59 H6 **Ammanford** Carmth
162 C7 **Amotherby** N York
34 E6 **Ampfield** Hants
161 J7 **Ampleforth** N York
64 F6 **Ampney Crucis** Gloucs
65 G6 **Ampney St Mary** Gloucs
65 G6 **Ampney St Peter** Gloucs
34 C2 **Amport** Hants
85 K7 **Ampthill** C Beds
89 H1 **Ampton** Suffk
55 K5 **Amroth** Pembks
232 D8 **Amulree** P & K
68 F4 **Amwell** Herts
228 C3 **Anaheilt** Highld
118 C3 **Ancaster** Lincs
94 E6 **Anchor** Shrops
202 F4 **Ancroft** Nthumb
189 H1 **Ancrum** Border
21 G6 **Ancton** W Susx
137 K4 **Anderby** Lincs
30 E4 **Andersea** Somset
30 C4 **Andersfield** Somset
17 G3 **Anderson** Dorset
130 C4 **Anderton** Ches W
6 E4 **Anderton** Cnwll
34 D2 **Andover** Hants
64 F3 **Andoversford** Gloucs
154 f2 **Andreas** IoM
108 B6 **Anelog** Gwynd
51 J5 **Anerley** Gt Lon
129 J1 **Anfield** Lpool
129 J1 **Anfield Crematorium** Lpool
2 F3 **Angarrack** Cnwll
3 K4 **Angarrick** Cnwll
96 D8 **Angelbank** Shrops
30 B7 **Angersleigh** Somset
177 H7 **Angerton** Cumb
54 D6 **Angle** Pembks
21 H6 **Angmering** W Susx
151 H6 **Angram** N York
158 F3 **Angram** N York
3 H7 **Angrouse** Cnwll
179 L5 **Anick** Nthumb
264 C5 **Ankerville** Highld
117 K7 **Ankle Hill** Leics
144 C2 **Anlaby** E R Yk
121 G5 **Anmer** Norfk
19 L1 **Anmore** Hants
177 G5 **Annan** D & G
155 K5 **Annaside** Cumb
248 E1 **Annat** Highld
209 J5 **Annathill** N Lans
34 D2 **Anna Valley** Hants
196 E6 **Annbank** S Ayrs
116 E1 **Annesley** Notts
116 E1 **Annesley Woodhouse** Notts
180 E8 **Annfield Plain** Dur
208 F5 **Anniesland** C Glas
181 G4 **Annitsford** N Tyne
95 L2 **Annscroft** Shrops
138 D2 **Ansdell** Lancs
31 L4 **Ansford** Somset
99 J5 **Ansley** Warwks
115 L6 **Anslow** Staffs
115 K6 **Anslow Gate** Staffs
115 K6 **Anslow Lees** Staffs
36 D4 **Ansteadbrook** Surrey
35 L3 **Anstey** Hants
87 H8 **Anstey** Herts
100 C2 **Anstey** Leics
223 K6 **Anstruther** Fife
37 L6 **Ansty** W Susx
99 L6 **Ansty** Warwks
33 G5 **Ansty** Wilts
16 E2 **Ansty Cross** Dorset
19 L1 **Anthill Common** Hants
50 C6 **Anthonys** Surrey
177 G7 **Anthorn** Cumb
122 F5 **Antingham** Norfk
282 d6 **An t-Ob** W Isls
119 J2 **Anton's Gowt** Lincs
6 D4 **Antony** Cnwll
130 C4 **Antrobus** Ches W
11 M2 **Anvil Corner** Devon
40 E5 **Anvil Green** Kent
118 F2 **Anwick** Lincs
174 F4 **Anwoth** D & G
51 L7 **Aperfield** Gt Lon
82 A1 **Apes Dale** Worcs
102 A4 **Apethorpe** Nhants
114 D7 **Apeton** Staffs
136 B5 **Apley** Lincs
133 H4 **Apperknowle** Derbys
64 B2 **Apperley** Gloucs
150 B8 **Apperley Bridge** C Brad
180 C7 **Apperley Dene** Nthumb
158 E4 **Appersett** N York
228 E6 **Appin** Ag & B
144 B5 **Appleby** N Linc
166 F6 **Appleby-in-Westmorland** Cumb

99 J2 **Appleby Magna** Leics
99 J2 **Appleby Parva** Leics
69 J6 **Appleby Street** Herts
248 A3 **Applecross** Highld
27 H5 **Appledore** Devon
29 K7 **Appledore** Devon
25 H2 **Appledore** Kent
25 H1 **Appledore Heath** Kent
66 D8 **Appleford** Oxon
176 F2 **Applegarth Town** D & G
142 A5 **Applehaigh** Wakefd
34 C1 **Appleshaw** Hants
165 J5 **Applethwaite** Cumb
129 M2 **Appleton** Halton
66 C6 **Appleton** Oxon
130 B3 **Appleton** Warrtn
162 C5 **Appleton-le-Moors** N York
162 C7 **Appleton-le-Street** N York
151 J7 **Appleton Roebuck** N York
130 C3 **Appleton Thorn** Warrtn
160 F2 **Appleton Wiske** N York
188 F3 **Appletreehall** Border
149 J4 **Appletreewick** N York
29 K6 **Appley** Somset
139 G6 **Appley Bridge** Lancs
19 J7 **Apse Heath** IoW
86 C8 **Apsley End** C Beds
20 D6 **Apuldram** W Susx
264 C5 **Arabella** Highld
234 F7 **Arbirlot** Angus
264 D3 **Arboll** Highld
49 H5 **Arborfield** Wokham
49 J5 **Arborfield Cross** Wokham
133 G3 **Arbourthorne** Sheff
235 G7 **Arbroath** Angus
245 H8 **Arbuthnott** Abers
39 L6 **Arcadia** Kent
56 E4 **Archddu** Carmth
169 H7 **Archdeacon Newton** Darltn
208 C3 **Archencarroch** W Duns
254 E3 **Archiestown** Moray
9 f2 **Archirondel** Jersey
130 F7 **Arclid Green** Ches E
257 J4 **Ardallie** Abers
217 H2 **Ardanaiseig Hotel** Ag & B
248 D4 **Ardaneaskan** Highld
248 D4 **Ardarroch** Highld
204 F7 **Ardbeg** Ag & B
207 H5 **Ardbeg** Ag & B
207 K2 **Ardbeg** Ag & B
261 K2 **Ardcharnich** Highld
214 D1 **Ardchiavaig** Ag & B
216 F5 **Ardchonnel** Ag & B
219 K4 **Ardchullarie More** Stirlg
218 C8 **Arddarroch** Ag & B
112 C8 **Arddleen** Powys
239 J5 **Ardechive** Highld
196 B3 **Ardeer** N Ayrs
69 J6 **Ardeley** Herts
248 D6 **Ardelve** Highld
208 B2 **Arden** Ag & B
82 D4 **Ardens Grafton** Warwks
216 C2 **Ardentallen** Ag & B
207 K2 **Ardentinny** Ag & B
207 G4 **Ardentraive** Ag & B
231 J8 **Ardeonaig** Stirlg
252 E1 **Ardersier** Highld
261 H2 **Ardessie** Highld
216 C6 **Ardfern** Ag & B
205 J2 **Ardfernal** Ag & B
263 G2 **Ardgay** Highld
229 G3 **Ardgour** Highld
207 L4 **Ardgowan** Inver
207 K4 **Ardhallow** Ag & B
282 e5 **Ardhasig** W Isls
260 C8 **Ardheslaig** Highld
261 K2 **Ardindrean** Highld
38 A7 **Ardingly** W Susx
48 B1 **Ardington** Oxon
48 B1 **Ardington Wick** Oxon
206 F6 **Ardlamont** Ag & B
72 F1 **Ardleigh** Essex
72 F1 **Ardleigh Heath** Essex
233 L7 **Ardler** P & K
66 D2 **Ardley** Oxon
70 D4 **Ardley End** Essex
218 D4 **Ardlui** Ag & B
215 J6 **Ardlussa** Ag & B
229 H7 **Ardmaddy** Ag & B
270 F8 **Ardmair** Highld
207 H5 **Ardmaleish** Ag & B
205 L6 **Ardminish** Ag & B
237 K6 **Ardmolich** Highld
208 A3 **Ardmore** Ag & B
263 J3 **Ardmore** Highld
207 K3 **Ardnadam** Ag & B
250 F2 **Ardnagrask** Highld
248 E4 **Ardnarff** Highld
228 B3 **Ardnastang** Highld
217 J5 **Ardno** Ag & B

206 B7 **Ardpatrick** Ag & B
206 D2 **Ardrishaig** Ag & B
263 H5 **Ardross** Highld
195 L3 **Ardrossan** N Ayrs
142 B6 **Ardsley** Barns
141 M3 **Ardsley East** Leeds
237 H8 **Ardslignish** Highld
205 G5 **Ardtalla** Ag & B
237 J6 **Ardtoe** Highld
216 B5 **Arduaine** Ag & B
263 G7 **Ardullie** Highld
247 K7 **Ardvasar** Highld
219 K3 **Ardvorlich** P & K
282 e5 **Ardvourlie** W Isls
172 D5 **Ardwell** D & G
140 C8 **Ardwick** Manch
81 H1 **Areley Kings** Worcs
237 J7 **Arevegaig** Highld
36 B3 **Arford** Hants
61 J7 **Argoed** Caerph
112 E7 **Argoed** Shrops
78 D3 **Argoed Mill** Powys
23 J2 **Argos Hill** E Susx
282 f4 **Aribruach** W Isls
226 C7 **Aridhglas** Ag & B
224 F4 **Arileod** Ag & B
225 G4 **Arinagour** Ag & B
216 D2 **Ariogan** Ag & B
237 J3 **Arisaig** Highld
237 K4 **Arisaig House** Highld
150 E4 **Arkendale** N York
87 K8 **Arkesden** Essex
147 L2 **Arkholme** Lancs
164 F3 **Arkleby** Cumb
188 C7 **Arkleton** D & G
159 H2 **Arkle Town** N York
69 G7 **Arkley** Gt Lon
142 F6 **Arksey** Donc
133 H5 **Arkwright Town** Derbys
64 D2 **Arle** Gloucs
164 D7 **Arlecdon** Cumb
83 J5 **Arlescote** Warwks
86 D7 **Arlesey** C Beds
96 F1 **Arleston** Wrekin
130 C3 **Arley** Ches E
99 H5 **Arley** Warwks
63 L5 **Arlingham** Gloucs
27 L3 **Arlington** Devon
23 J5 **Arlington** E Susx
65 G5 **Arlington** Gloucs
27 L3 **Arlington Beccott** Devon
247 K7 **Armadale** Highld
278 D3 **Armadale** Highld
210 B5 **Armadale** W Loth
164 F5 **Armaside** Cumb
166 C2 **Armathwaite** Cumb
106 E3 **Arminghall** Norfk
115 H8 **Armitage** Staffs
141 H5 **Armitage Bridge** Kirk
141 L1 **Armley** Leeds
82 F6 **Armscote** Warwks
114 E2 **Armshead** Staffs
102 B6 **Armston** Nhants
143 G6 **Armthorpe** Donc
225 G3 **Arnabost** Ag & B
156 A5 **Arnaby** Cumb
149 G2 **Arncliffe** N York
149 G2 **Arncliffe Cote** N York
223 J6 **Arncroach** Fife
266 F6 **Arndilly House** Moray
17 J5 **Arne** Dorset
100 D5 **Arnesby** Leics
221 L5 **Arngask** P & K
238 D2 **Arnisdale** Highld
259 K7 **Arnish** Highld
211 K6 **Arniston** Mdloth
282 f2 **Arnol** W Isls
153 H7 **Arnold** E R Yk
117 G2 **Arnold** Notts
219 K8 **Arnprior** Stirlg
157 G7 **Arnside** Cumb
227 G3 **Aros** Ag & B
113 G4 **Arowry** Wrexhm
156 D6 **Arrad Foot** Cumb
153 G7 **Arram** E R Yk
160 B4 **Arrathorne** N York
19 J6 **Arreton** IoW
260 B8 **Arrina** Highld
87 G5 **Arrington** Cambs
218 D6 **Arrochar** Ag & B
82 C4 **Arrow** Warwks
98 C8 **Arrowfield Top** Worcs
95 K2 **Arscott** Shrops
251 H2 **Artafallie** Highld
150 C6 **Arthington** Leeds
101 G7 **Arthingworth** Nhants
110 C8 **Arthog** Gwynd
257 H4 **Arthrath** Abers
150 E8 **Arthursdale** Leeds
257 J5 **Artrochie** Abers

21 G5 **Arundel** W Susx
164 E6 **Asby** Cumb
207 J6 **Ascog** Ag & B
50 A5 **Ascot** W & M
83 H8 **Ascott** Warwks
65 L3 **Ascott Earl** Oxon
65 L3 **Ascott-under-Wychwood** Oxon
160 F7 **Asenby** N York
117 J7 **Asfordby** Leics
117 J7 **Asfordby Hill** Leics
118 F3 **Asgarby** Lincs
136 F6 **Asgarby** Lincs
8 C5 **Ash** Devon
12 C1 **Ash** Devon
32 E8 **Ash** Dorset
41 J4 **Ash** Kent
52 D6 **Ash** Kent
30 D6 **Ash** Somset
31 G6 **Ash** Somset
36 D1 **Ash** Surrey
48 E4 **Ashampstead** W Berk
48 E3 **Ashampstead Green** W Berk
90 E4 **Ashbocking** Suffk
115 K2 **Ashbourne** Derbys
29 J6 **Ashbrittle** Somset
24 C4 **Ashburnham Place** E Susx
13 H8 **Ashburton** Devon
12 C3 **Ashbury** Devon
47 K2 **Ashbury** Oxon
143 M6 **Ashby** N Linc
137 H6 **Ashby by Partney** Lincs
145 H7 **Ashby cum Fenby** NE Lin
135 L8 **Ashby de la Launde** Lincs
116 B8 **Ashby-de-la-Zouch** Leics
100 F1 **Ashby Folville** Leics
100 C5 **Ashby Magna** Leics
100 C5 **Ashby Parva** Leics
136 F5 **Ashby Puerorum** Lincs
84 B2 **Ashby St Ledgers** Nhants
107 G3 **Ashby St Mary** Norfk
81 L8 **Ashchurch** Gloucs
13 L6 **Ashcombe** Devon
44 C6 **Ashcombe** N Som
31 G3 **Ashcott** Somset
88 B6 **Ashdon** Essex
35 H1 **Ashe** Hants
72 E6 **Asheldham** Essex
88 E6 **Ashen** Essex
67 H4 **Ashendon** Bucks
68 B6 **Asheridge** Bucks
34 E7 **Ashfield** Hants
63 H2 **Ashfield** Herefs
220 D6 **Ashfield** Stirlg
90 F3 **Ashfield cum Thorpe** Suffk
88 F4 **Ashfield Green** Suffk
106 F8 **Ashfield Green** Suffk
37 K5 **Ashfold Crossways** W Susx
7 K5 **Ashford** Devon
27 J4 **Ashford** Devon
40 D6 **Ashford** Kent
50 D4 **Ashford** Surrey
80 C1 **Ashford Bowdler** Shrops
80 C1 **Ashford Carbonell** Shrops
48 E6 **Ashford Hill** Hants
132 D5 **Ashford in the Water** Derbys
198 C3 **Ashgill** S Lans
36 D1 **Ash Green** Surrey
99 J6 **Ash Green** Warwks
29 K8 **Ashill** Devon
105 H3 **Ashill** Norfk
30 D7 **Ashill** Somset
72 C8 **Ashingdon** Essex
181 G1 **Ashington** Nthumb
17 K3 **Ashington** Poole
31 J6 **Ashington** Somset
21 K4 **Ashington** W Susx
188 E2 **Ashkirk** Border
19 G3 **Ashlett** Hants
64 A2 **Ashleworth** Gloucs
64 B2 **Ashleworth Quay** Gloucs
88 D3 **Ashley** Cambs
130 F3 **Ashley** Ches E
28 B8 **Ashley** Devon
18 A3 **Ashley** Dorset
64 D8 **Ashley** Gloucs
18 C4 **Ashley** Hants
34 E4 **Ashley** Hants
41 J5 **Ashley** Kent
101 H5 **Ashley** Nhants
114 B4 **Ashley** Staffs
46 B5 **Ashley** Wilts
68 B6 **Ashley Green** Bucks
17 M2 **Ashley Heath** Dorset
80 B2 **Ashley Moor** Herefs
113 J4 **Ash Magna** Shrops
48 B7 **Ashmansworth** Hants
26 F7 **Ashmansworthy** Devon
63 M7 **Ashmead Green** Gloucs
11 M3 **Ashmill** Devon
28 D6 **Ash Mill** Devon

32 F7 **Ashmore** Dorset
48 D5 **Ashmore Green** W Berk
83 G4 **Ashorne** Warwks
133 G7 **Ashover** Derbys
133 G7 **Ashover Hay** Derbys
83 H1 **Ashow** Warwks
113 J4 **Ash Parva** Shrops
80 E7 **Ashperton** Herefs
8 B3 **Ashprington** Devon
29 L5 **Ash Priors** Somset
27 L8 **Ashreigney** Devon
89 K6 **Ash Street** Suffk
50 F7 **Ashtead** Surrey
29 H8 **Ash Thomas** Devon
102 B2 **Ashton** C Pete
129 L6 **Ashton** Ches W
2 F5 **Ashton** Cnwll
13 K5 **Ashton** Devon
35 H7 **Ashton** Hants
80 C2 **Ashton** Herefs
207 L4 **Ashton** Inver
84 E5 **Ashton** Nhants
102 B5 **Ashton** Nhants
30 F1 **Ashton** Somset
46 C7 **Ashton Common** Wilts
46 C7 **Ashton Hill** Wilts
139 H7 **Ashton-in-Makerfield** Wigan
64 F8 **Ashton Keynes** Wilts
82 A7 **Ashton under Hill** Worcs
140 E7 **Ashton-under-Lyne** Tamesd
130 F1 **Ashton upon Mersey** Traffd
18 E2 **Ashurst** Hants
38 D5 **Ashurst** Kent
21 L4 **Ashurst** W Susx
38 B6 **Ashurstwood** W Susx
49 L8 **Ash Vale** Surrey
11 M3 **Ashwater** Devon
86 F7 **Ashwell** Herts
101 J1 **Ashwell** Rutlnd
30 E7 **Ashwell** Somset
86 E7 **Ashwell End** Herts
106 C4 **Ashwellthorpe** Norfk
31 K1 **Ashwick** Somset
120 F7 **Ashwicken** Norfk
97 K5 **Ashwood** Staffs
156 B7 **Askam in Furness** Cumb
142 F3 **Askern** Donc
15 M4 **Askerswell** Dorset
67 K6 **Askett** Bucks
166 C6 **Askham** Cumb
134 E5 **Askham** Notts
151 H6 **Askham Bryan** C York
151 H6 **Askham Richard** C York
206 E1 **Asknish** Ag & B
159 L6 **Askrigg** N York
149 L6 **Askwith** N York
118 E5 **Aslackby** Lincs
106 D5 **Aslacton** Norfk
117 K3 **Aslockton** Notts
31 G3 **Asney** Somset
90 E2 **Aspall** Suffk
164 F2 **Aspatria** Cumb
69 K2 **Aspenden** Herts
131 K2 **Aspenshaw** Derbys
119 J4 **Asperton** Lincs
114 C5 **Asperton** Staffs
85 J8 **Aspley Guise** C Beds
85 H8 **Aspley Heath** C Beds
82 C1 **Aspley Heath** Warwks
139 J6 **Aspull** Wigan
139 J8 **Aspull Common** Wigan
143 H2 **Asselby** E R Yk
137 J4 **Asserby** Lincs
137 J4 **Asserby Turn** Lincs
89 J7 **Assington** Suffk
88 F5 **Assington Green** Suffk
131 G7 **Astbury** Ches E
84 D4 **Astcote** Nhants
136 E4 **Asterby** Lincs
95 J2 **Asterley** Shrops
95 K5 **Asterton** Shrops
65 L5 **Asthall** Oxon
65 L5 **Asthall Leigh** Oxon
263 K2 **Astle** Highld
142 B2 **Astley** Leeds
113 H7 **Astley** Shrops
99 J5 **Astley** Warwks
139 L7 **Astley** Wigan
81 H2 **Astley** Worcs
96 F4 **Astley Abbots** Shrops
139 L5 **Astley Bridge** Bolton
81 J1 **Astley Cross** Worcs
139 L7 **Astley Green** Wigan
98 D5 **Aston** Birm
113 K2 **Aston** Ches E
130 A4 **Aston** Ches W
132 D3 **Aston** Derbys
129 G6 **Aston** Flints
80 B3 **Aston** Herefs
69 H3 **Aston** Herts

65 M6 **Aston** Oxon
133 J3 **Aston** Rothm
97 H5 **Aston** Shrops
113 H6 **Aston** Shrops
114 B3 **Aston** Staffs
114 D6 **Aston** Staffs
114 E5 **Aston** Staffs
49 J2 **Aston** Wokham
96 E2 **Aston** Wrekin
67 K3 **Aston Abbotts** Bucks
96 E6 **Aston Botterell** Shrops
82 D3 **Aston Cantlow** Warwks
67 L4 **Aston Clinton** Bucks
63 K3 **Aston Crews** Herefs
81 L8 **Aston Cross** Gloucs
69 H2 **Aston End** Herts
96 E4 **Aston-Eyre** Shrops
81 M2 **Aston Fields** Worcs
100 A5 **Aston Flamville** Leics
130 A4 **Aston Heath** Ches W
63 K3 **Aston Ingham** Herefs
130 C8 **Aston juxta Mondrum** Ches E
83 L5 **Aston le Walls** Nhants
82 E8 **Aston Magna** Gloucs
96 C6 **Aston Munslow** Shrops
95 J7 **Aston on Clun** Shrops
95 H2 **Aston Pigott** Shrops
95 H2 **Aston Rogers** Shrops
67 H7 **Aston Rowant** Oxon
67 J5 **Aston Sandford** Bucks
82 B7 **Aston Somerville** Worcs
82 D7 **Aston Subedge** Gloucs
48 E2 **Aston Tirrold** Oxon
116 C5 **Aston-upon-Trent** Derbys
48 E2 **Aston Upthorpe** Oxon
83 L7 **Astrop** Nhants
67 L4 **Astrope** Herts
86 E7 **Astwick** C Beds
133 J6 **Astwith** Derbys
85 J5 **Astwood** M Keyn
81 L2 **Astwood** Worcs
82 B3 **Astwood Bank** Worcs
81 K4 **Astwood Crematorium** Worcs
118 E4 **Aswarby** Lincs
137 G5 **Aswardby** Lincs
96 C2 **Atcham** Shrops
82 B5 **Atch Lench** Worcs
16 E4 **Athelhampton** Dorset
90 F1 **Athelington** Suffk
30 E5 **Athelney** Somset
212 C4 **Athelstaneford** E Loth
19 G7 **Atherfield Green** IoW
27 L6 **Atherington** Devon
21 G6 **Atherington** W Susx
30 F7 **Atherstone** Somset
99 J4 **Atherstone** Warwks
82 F5 **Atherstone on Stour** Warwks
139 K7 **Atherton** Wigan
160 D2 **Atley Hill** N York
115 L2 **Atlow** Derbys
248 E4 **Attadale** Highld
116 E5 **Attenborough** Notts
135 K1 **Atterby** Lincs
133 G2 **Attercliffe** Sheff
96 E4 **Atterley** Shrops
99 K4 **Atterton** Leics
105 L4 **Attleborough** Norfk
99 K5 **Attleborough** Warwks
122 C8 **Attlebridge** Norfk
88 E4 **Attleton Green** Suffk
153 K5 **Atwick** E R Yk
46 B6 **Atworth** Wilts
80 C6 **Auberrow** Herefs
135 J7 **Aubourn** Lincs
257 G5 **Auchedly** Abers
244 F7 **Auchenblae** Abers
209 L2 **Auchenbowie** Stirlg
175 K4 **Auchencairn** D & G
176 C2 **Auchencairn** D & G
195 G5 **Auchencairn** N Ayrs
213 J7 **Auchencrow** Border
211 H6 **Auchendinny** Mdloth
199 G2 **Auchengray** S Lans
267 H4 **Auchenhalrig** Moray
198 D4 **Auchenheath** S Lans
185 K4 **Auchenhessnane** D & G
206 F4 **Auchenlochan** Ag & B
196 C2 **Auchenmade** N Ayrs
173 G4 **Auchenmalg** D & G
196 D2 **Auchentiber** N Ayrs
219 J8 **Auchentroig** Stirlg
261 K4 **Auchindrean** Highld
268 B6 **Auchininna** Abers
197 G6 **Auchinleck** E Ayrs
209 H5 **Auchinloch** N Lans
209 J4 **Auchinstarry** N Lans
229 H1 **Auchintore** Highld
257 K4 **Auchiries** Abers
245 K4 **Auchlee** Abers
256 A6 **Auchleven** Abers

| | | | |
|---|---|---|---|
| 98 D5 **Auchlochan** S Lans | 100 C3 **Aylestone** C Leic | 283 b13 **Bagh a Chaisteil** W Isls | 154 C7 **Ballamodha** IoM |
| 44 D3 **Auchlossan** Abers | 100 D3 **Aylestone Park** C Leic | 40 E4 **Bagham** Kent | 207 G6 **Ballanlay** Ag & B |
| 19 H1 **Auchlyne** Stirlg | 122 D4 **Aylmerton** Norfk | 283 b13 **Bagh a Tuath** W Isls | 182 D6 **Ballantrae** S Ayrs |
| 97 G5 **Auchmillan** E Ayrs | 122 D6 **Aylsham** Norfk | 128 F4 **Bagillt** Flints | 72 C8 **Ballards Gore** Essex |
| 35 G6 **Auchmithie** Angus | 80 F7 **Aylton** Herefs | 99 K8 **Baginton** Warwks | 99 H5 **Ballards Green** Warwks |
| 22 C7 **Auchmuirbridge** Fife | 65 G3 **Aylworth** Gloucs | 57 K6 **Baglan** Neath | 154 C7 **Ballasalla** IoM |
| 34 C3 **Auchnacree** Angus | 80 A2 **Aymestrey** Herefs | 141 K1 **Bagley** Leeds | 243 L4 **Ballater** Abers |
| 57 G3 **Auchnagatt** Abers | 83 L8 **Aynho** Nhants | 112 F6 **Bagley** Shrops | 154 d3 **Ballaugh** IoM |
| 54 D7 **Auchnarrow** Moray | 69 G4 **Ayot Green** Herts | 31 G2 **Bagley** Somset | 263 K5 **Ballchraggan** Highld |
| 72 B3 **Auchnotteroch** D & G | 69 G4 **Ayot St Lawrence** Herts | 35 K2 **Bagmore** Hants | 212 B3 **Ballencrieff** E Loth |
| 67 G6 **Auchroisk** Moray | 69 G4 **Ayot St Peter** Herts | 114 E1 **Bagnall** Staffs | 224 B6 **Ballevullin** Ag & B |
| 21 G4 **Auchterarder** P & K | 196 C6 **Ayr** S Ayrs | 48 C5 **Bagnor** W Berk | 114 D1 **Ball Green** C Stke |
| 40 B2 **Auchteraw** Highld | 159 H5 **Aysgarth** N York | 96 D8 **Bagot** Shrops | 131 K8 **Ball Haye Green** Staffs |
| 53 H7 **Auchterblair** Highld | 29 J7 **Ayshford** Devon | 49 M6 **Bagshot** Surrey | 48 B6 **Ball Hill** Hants |
| 60 C4 **Auchtercairn** Highld | 156 F6 **Ayside** Cumb | 47 L6 **Bagshot** Wilts | 115 K1 **Ballidon** Derbys |
| 22 C8 **Auchterderran** Fife | 101 J3 **Ayston** Rutlnd | 45 K2 **Bagstone** S Glos | 194 D3 **Balliekine** N Ayrs |
| 33 M7 **Auchterhouse** Angus | 70 E4 **Aythorpe Roding** Essex | 116 D1 **Bagthorpe** Notts | 217 H7 **Balliemore** Ag & B |
| 56 C3 **Auchterless** Abers | 213 K6 **Ayton** Border | 99 M2 **Bagworth** Leics | 183 G5 **Balligmorrie** S Ayrs |
| 22 D5 **Auchtermuchty** Fife | 160 C7 **Azerley** N York | 62 F2 **Bagwy Llydiart** Herefs | 206 E2 **Ballimore** Ag & B |
| 62 E7 **Auchterneed** Highld | | 149 L7 **Baildon** C Brad | 219 H4 **Ballimore** Stirlg |
| 11 H1 **Auchtertool** Fife | | 149 L7 **Baildon Green** C Brad | 254 D4 **Ballindalloch** Moray |
| 48 D6 **Auchtertyre** Highld | **B** | 282 f4 **Baile Ailein** W Isls | 222 D2 **Ballindean** P & K |
| 19 J3 **Auchtubh** Stirlg | | 283 c9 **Baile a Mhanaich** W Isls | 89 H7 **Ballingdon** Suffk |
| 80 E3 **Auckengill** Highld | 8 D2 **Babbacombe** Torbay | 226 B7 **Baile Mor** Ag & B | 67 M6 **Ballinger Common** Bucks |
| 43 G7 **Auckley** Donc | 116 E3 **Babbington** Notts | 35 K5 **Bailey Green** Hants | 63 H1 **Ballingham** Herefs |
| 40 D8 **Audenshaw** Tamesd | 112 E5 **Babbinswood** Shrops | 178 C3 **Baileyhead** Cumb | 222 B7 **Ballingry** Fife |
| 13 L3 **Audlem** Ches E | 69 K4 **Babbs Green** Herts | 141 J3 **Bailiff Bridge** Calder | 232 E5 **Ballinluig** P & K |
| 14 C2 **Audley** Staffs | 31 J5 **Babcary** Somset | 209 H6 **Baillieston** C Glas | 234 B5 **Ballinshoe** Angus |
| 87 L7 **Audley End** Essex | 59 M2 **Babel** Carmth | 147 J4 **Bailrigg** Lancs | 233 G4 **Ballintuim** P & K |
| 89 G7 **Audley End** Essex | 88 E5 **Babel Green** Suffk | 159 G4 **Bainbridge** N York | 252 D2 **Balloch** Highld |
| 89 G4 **Audley End** Suffk | 128 E5 **Babell** Flints | 256 A5 **Bainshole** Abers | 209 K4 **Balloch** N Lans |
| 14 C7 **Audmore** Staffs | 12 F7 **Babeny** Devon | 102 B2 **Bainton** C Pete | 220 E3 **Balloch** P & K |
| 97 K6 **Audnam** Dudley | 32 B1 **Babington** Somset | 152 E5 **Bainton** E R Yk | 183 J4 **Balloch** S Ayrs |
| 65 H3 **Aughertree** Cumb | 66 B6 **Bablock Hythe** Oxon | 66 E2 **Bainton** Oxon | 208 C3 **Balloch** W Duns |
| 51 L8 **Aughton** E R Yk | 87 K5 **Babraham** Cambs | 222 F6 **Baintown** Fife | 244 D4 **Ballogie** Abers |
| 38 E6 **Aughton** Lancs | 134 D3 **Babworth** Notts | 189 H3 **Bairnkine** Border | 36 E5 **Balls Cross** W Susx |
| 47 L2 **Aughton** Lancs | 125 H3 **Bachau** IoA | 69 L4 **Baker's End** Herts | 38 D6 **Balls Green** E Susx |
| 33 J2 **Aughton** Rothm | 95 L7 **Bache** Shrops | 52 D3 **Baker Street** Thurr | 64 B7 **Ball's Green** Gloucs |
| 47 K7 **Aughton** Wilts | 94 F5 **Bacheldre** Powys | 132 D6 **Bakewell** Derbys | 226 E4 **Ballygown** Ag & B |
| 38 E6 **Aughton Park** Lancs | 24 F5 **Bachelor's Bump** E Susx | 111 H4 **Bala** Gwynd | 204 F3 **Ballygrant** Ag & B |
| 53 H1 **Auldearn** Highld | 275 d3 **Backaland** Ork | 282 f4 **Balallan** W Isls | 224 F4 **Ballyhaugh** Ag & B |
| 80 B4 **Aulden** Herefs | 156 E5 **Backbarrow** Cumb | 250 D5 **Balbeg** Highld | 248 C6 **Balmacara** Highld |
| 76 B2 **Auldgirth** D & G | 58 A5 **Backe** Carmth | 222 B1 **Balbeggie** P & K | 185 G7 **Balmaclellan** D & G |
| 97 J1 **Auldhouse** S Lans | 269 J5 **Backfolds** Abers | 250 E3 **Balblair** Highld | 175 H6 **Balmae** D & G |
| 48 F7 **Ault a' chruinn** Highld | 129 J5 **Backford** Ches W | 263 J6 **Balblair** Highld | 208 C1 **Balmaha** Stirlg |
| 60 D2 **Aultbea** Highld | 129 J5 **Backford Cross** Ches W | 142 E7 **Balby** Donc | 222 E5 **Balmalcolm** Fife |
| 60 B3 **Aultgrishin** Highld | 273 K7 **Backies** Highld | 175 K5 **Balcary** D & G | 175 G5 **Balmangan** D & G |
| 52 B6 **Aultguish Inn** Highld | 257 J3 **Back of Keppoch** Highld | 250 F3 **Balchraggan** Highld | 257 H8 **Balmedie** Abers |
| 33 J6 **Ault Hucknall** Derbys | 115 H1 **Back o' th' Brook** Staffs | 276 B4 **Balchreick** Highld | 113 G4 **Balmer Heath** Shrops |
| 67 H5 **Aultmore** Moray | 88 E3 **Back Street** Suffk | 37 M5 **Balcombe** W Susx | 222 F2 **Balmerino** Fife |
| 50 F7 **Aultnagoire** Highld | 44 F5 **Backwell** N Som | 37 M4 **Balcombe Lane** W Susx | 18 D3 **Balmerlawn** Hants |
| 63 J4 **Aultnamain Inn** Highld | 181 H4 **Backworth** N Tyne | 223 L5 **Balcomie Links** Fife | 194 E5 **Balmichael** N Ayrs |
| 18 D8 **Aunby** Lincs | 98 F6 **Bacon's End** Solhll | 160 E7 **Baldersby** N York | 209 G4 **Balmore** E Duns |
| 14 B2 **Aunk** Devon | 122 C4 **Baconsthorpe** Norfk | 160 E7 **Baldersby St James** N York | 264 D4 **Balmuchy** Highld |
| 18 D4 **Aunsby** Lincs | 62 D1 **Bacton** Herefs | 139 J1 **Balderstone** Lancs | 234 E5 **Balmuir** Angus |
| 45 H1 **Aust** S Glos | 123 G5 **Bacton** Norfk | 140 D5 **Balderstone** Rochdl | 211 H2 **Balmule** Fife |
| 49 J7 **Austendike** Lincs | 90 C2 **Bacton** Suffk | 117 L1 **Balderton** Notts | 223 G3 **Balmullo** Fife |
| 54 D1 **Austerfield** Donc | 90 B2 **Bacton Green** Suffk | 4 C6 **Baldhu** Cnwll | 273 K5 **Balnacoil Lodge** Highld |
| 40 E6 **Austerlands** Oldham | 140 D3 **Bacup** Lancs | 223 G5 **Baldinnie** Fife | 248 F3 **Balnacra** Highld |
| 42 B1 **Austhorpe** Leeds | 260 C5 **Badachro** Highld | 221 J4 **Baldinnies** P & K | 243 J5 **Balnacroft** Abers |
| 41 H6 **Austonley** Kirk | 47 J3 **Badbury** Swindn | 86 E8 **Baldock** Herts | 251 J4 **Balnafoich** Highld |
| 99 J2 **Austrey** Warwks | 84 A3 **Badby** Nhants | 234 C8 **Baldovie** C Dund | 232 D5 **Balnaguard** P & K |
| 48 D2 **Austwick** N York | 276 B7 **Badcall** Highld | 154 f5 **Baldrine** IoM | 214 E4 **Balnahard** Ag & B |
| 37 G3 **Authorpe** Lincs | 276 C5 **Badcall** Highld | 24 E4 **Baldslow** E Susx | 226 E5 **Balnahard** Ag & B |
| 37 K5 **Authorpe Row** Lincs | 261 G2 **Badcaul** Highld | 154 e6 **Baldwin** IoM | 250 D5 **Balnain** Highld |
| 47 G5 **Avebury** Wilts | 114 E1 **Baddeley Edge** C Stke | 177 K8 **Baldwinholme** Cumb | 276 F3 **Balnakeil** Highld |
| 47 G5 **Avebury Trusloe** Wilts | 114 E1 **Baddeley Green** C Stke | 114 B3 **Baldwin's Gate** Staffs | 264 B6 **Balnapaling** Highld |
| 52 C3 **Aveley** Thurr | 82 F1 **Baddesley Clinton** Warwks | 38 B5 **Baldwin's Hill** W Susx | 142 F4 **Balne** N York |
| 64 C7 **Avening** Gloucs | 99 H4 **Baddesley Ensor** Warwks | 121 M4 **Bale** Norfk | 232 F8 **Balquharn** P & K |
| 47 K1 **Averham** Notts | 270 E3 **Baddidarrach** Highld | 222 D1 **Baledgarno** P & K | 219 H3 **Balquhidder** Stirlg |
| 7 K5 **Aveton Gifford** Devon | 199 K2 **Baddinsgill** Border | 224 C7 **Balemartine** Ag & B | 99 G8 **Balsall Common** Solhll |
| 42 B1 **Aviemore** Highld | 256 C4 **Badenscoth** Abers | 211 G5 **Balerno** C Edin | 98 D6 **Balsall Heath** Birm |
| 48 A5 **Avington** W Berk | 255 G7 **Badenyon** Abers | 222 D6 **Balfarg** Fife | 99 G8 **Balsall Street** Solhll |
| 61 J1 **Avoch** Highld | 11 J5 **Badgall** Cnwll | 234 E2 **Balfield** Angus | 83 J3 **Balscote** Oxon |
| 18 A4 **Avon** Hants | 103 J4 **Badgeney** Cambs | 275 d4 **Balfour** Ork | 88 B5 **Balsham** Cambs |
| 10 B4 **Avonbridge** Falk | 97 H3 **Badger** Shrops | 208 F1 **Balfron** Stirlg | 281 f1 **Baltasound** Shet |
| 83 K5 **Avon Dassett** Warwks | 2 D4 **Badger's Cross** Cnwll | 256 B4 **Balgaveny** Abers | 114 B2 **Balterley** Staffs |
| 45 G3 **Avonmouth** Bristl | 52 B6 **Badgers Mount** Kent | 234 E5 **Balgavies** Angus | 114 B2 **Balterley Green** Staffs |
| 7 K3 **Avonwick** Devon | 64 C7 **Badgeworth** Gloucs | 221 J8 **Balgonar** Fife | 114 B2 **Balterley Heath** Staffs |
| 14 D6 **Awbridge** Hants | 44 E8 **Badgworth** Somset | 172 E6 **Balgowan** D & G | 174 C3 **Baltersan** D & G |
| 45 H2 **Awkley** S Glos | 11 J5 **Badharlick** Cnwll | 241 H4 **Balgowan** Highld | 31 J4 **Baltonsborough** Somset |
| 14 D2 **Awliscombe** Devon | 248 B6 **Badicaul** Highld | 258 F3 **Balgown** Highld | 216 B4 **Balvicar** Ag & B |
| 63 L5 **Awre** Gloucs | 91 G2 **Badingham** Suffk | 172 B3 **Balgracie** D & G | 248 D8 **Balvraid** Highld |
| 16 E3 **Awsworth** Notts | 40 D4 **Badlesmere** Kent | 234 B7 **Balgray** Angus | 252 F5 **Balvraid** Highld |
| 7 J7 **Axborough** Worcs | 187 G2 **Badlieu** Border | 186 C2 **Balgray** S Lans | 2 F5 **Balwest** Cnwll |
| 14 E8 **Axbridge** Somset | 280 B6 **Badlipster** Highld | 51 H4 **Balham** Gt Lon | 139 H3 **Bamber Bridge** Lancs |
| 45 J2 **Axford** Hants | 261 G1 **Badluachrach** Highld | 233 L6 **Balhary** P & K | 70 E3 **Bamber's Green** Essex |
| 47 K5 **Axford** Wilts | 263 K1 **Badninish** Highld | 233 H8 **Balholmie** P & K | 203 K6 **Bamburgh** Nthumb |
| 5 G3 **Axminster** Devon | 261 H2 **Badrallach** Highld | 278 E3 **Baligill** Highld | 233 K5 **Bamff** P & K |
| 74 F4 **Axmouth** Devon | 82 C6 **Badsey** Worcs | 233 L4 **Balintore** Angus | 132 D3 **Bamford** Derbys |
| 78 D4 **Axton** Flints | 36 C1 **Badshot Lea** Surrey | 264 D5 **Balintore** Highld | 140 C5 **Bamford** Rochdl |
| 79 H6 **Aycliffe** Dur | 142 D5 **Badsworth** Wakefd | 263 K5 **Balintraid** Highld | 166 C7 **Bampton** Cumb |
| 80 B5 **Aydon** Nthumb | 89 K2 **Badwell Ash** Suffk | 283 c9 **Balivanich** W Isls | 29 G6 **Bampton** Devon |
| 63 J6 **Aylburton** Gloucs | 89 K2 **Badwell Green** Suffk | 161 G6 **Balk** N York | 65 L6 **Bampton** Oxon |
| 27 G1 **Ayle** Nthumb | 32 C8 **Bagber** Dorset | 233 M6 **Balkeerie** Angus | 166 C7 **Bampton Grange** Cumb |
| 74 B4 **Aylesbeare** Devon | 161 G6 **Bagby** N York | 143 K2 **Balkholme** E R Yk | 239 J8 **Banavie** Highld |
| 67 K4 **Aylesbury** Bucks | 136 F5 **Bag Enderby** Lincs | 154 c7 **Ballabeg** IoM | 83 K7 **Banbury** Oxon |
| 37 G6 **Aylesby** NE Lin | 64 E5 **Bagendon** Gloucs | 154 b7 **Ballafesson** IoM | 83 K6 **Banbury Crematorium** Oxon |
| 82 F7 **Aylesford** Kent | 96 F7 **Bagginswood** Shrops | 154 g4 **Ballajora** IoM | 58 E6 **Bancffosfelen** Carmth |
| 81 H5 **Aylesham** Kent | 165 G2 **Baggrow** Cumb | 154 b7 **Ballakilpheric** IoM | 244 F4 **Banchory** Abers |

245 K3 Banchory-Devenick Abers
58 D6 Bancycapel Carmth
58 B5 Bancyfelin Carmth
76 D7 Banc-y-ffordd Carmth
222 C1 Bandirran P & K
156 B5 Bandrake Head Cumb
268 C3 Banff Abers
125 K5 Bangor Gwynd
125 L5 Bangor Crematorium Gwynd
112 F2 Bangor-is-y-coed Wrexhm
11 H3 Bangors Cnwll
138 D6 Bangor's Green Lancs
89 J1 Bangrove Suffk
106 B6 Banham Norfk
18 D2 Bank Hants
176 D5 Bankend D & G
233 G8 Bankfoot P & K
197 H8 Bankglen E Ayrs
156 D3 Bank Ground Cumb
245 K2 Bankhead C Aber
199 G4 Bankhead S Lans
148 F5 Bank Newton N York
209 K3 Banknock Falk
178 D6 Banks Cumb
138 E4 Banks Lancs
82 A2 Banks Green Worcs
177 G3 Bankshill D & G
80 E3 Bank Street Worcs
141 H3 Bank Top Calder
139 G6 Bank Top Lancs
122 E5 Banningham Norfk
71 G3 Bannister Green Essex
209 L1 Bannockburn Stirlg
51 H7 Banstead Surrey
7 K6 Bantham Devon
209 K3 Banton N Lans
44 E7 Banwell N Som
40 B3 Bapchild Kent
33 G3 Bapton Wilts
282 g2 Barabhas W Isls
196 C4 Barassie S Ayrs
263 K5 Barbaraville Highld
132 B3 Barber Booth Derbys
156 F6 Barber Green Cumb
196 E7 Barbieston S Ayrs
157 K6 Barbon Cumb
130 B8 Barbridge Ches E
28 C2 Barbrook Devon
84 A1 Barby Nhants
228 F7 Barcaldine Ag & B
83 G7 Barcheston Warwks
178 B6 Barclose Cumb
22 F4 Barcombe E Susx
23 G4 Barcombe Cross E Susx
149 J8 Barcroft C Brad
159 L4 Barden N York
38 F4 Barden Park Kent
70 F1 Bardfield End Green Essex
71 G2 Bardfield Saling Essex
136 B6 Bardney Lincs
99 M1 Bardon Leics
179 H6 Bardon Mill Nthumb
209 L4 Bardowie E Duns
39 G7 Bardown E Susx
208 B4 Bardrainney Inver
156 D7 Bardsea Cumb
150 E7 Bardsey Leeds
140 D7 Bardsley Oldham
105 J8 Bardwell Suffk
147 J3 Bare Lancs
3 K5 Bareppa Cnwll
173 J2 Barfad D & G
106 C2 Barford Norfk
83 G3 Barford Warwks
83 K8 Barford St John Oxon
33 J4 Barford St Martin Wilts
83 K8 Barford St Michael Oxon
41 H5 Barfrestone Kent
116 B2 Bargate Derbys
209 J6 Bargeddie N Lans
61 J7 Bargoed Caerph
183 J7 Bargrennan D & G
102 C8 Barham Cambs
41 G5 Barham Kent
90 D5 Barham Suffk
41 H5 Barham Crematorium Kent
87 H3 Bar Hill Cambs
102 B1 Barholm Lincs
100 E2 Barkby Leics
100 E2 Barkby Thorpe Leics
113 H6 Barkers Green Shrops
117 K4 Barkestone-le-Vale Leics
49 J5 Barkham Wokham
51 L2 Barking Gt Lon
90 C4 Barking Suffk
51 L1 Barkingside Gt Lon
90 C5 Barking Tye Suffk
141 G4 Barkisland Calder
4 B5 Barkla Shop Cnwll
118 B3 Barkston Lincs

151 G8 Barkston Ash N York
87 H8 Barkway Herts
209 H6 Barlanark C Glas
114 D4 Barlaston Staffs
21 G4 Barlavington W Susx
133 J4 Barlborough Derbys
143 G1 Barlby N York
99 L2 Barlestone Leics
87 H7 Barley Herts
148 E7 Barley Lancs
70 B2 Barleycroft End Herts
142 B8 Barley Hole Rothm
101 J2 Barleythorpe Rutlnd
53 K1 Barling Essex
135 M5 Barlings Lincs
175 K3 Barlochan D & G
133 G5 Barlow Derbys
180 E6 Barlow Gatesd
143 G2 Barlow N York
152 B6 Barmby Moor E R Yk
143 H2 Barmby on the Marsh E R Yk
121 H5 Barmer Norfk
39 J2 Barming Heath Kent
194 C2 Barmollack Ag & B
109 L8 Barmouth Gwynd
169 J7 Barmpton Darltn
153 J4 Barmston E R Yk
107 K7 Barnaby Green Suffk
216 F8 Barnacarry Ag & B
102 B2 Barnack C Pete
99 K6 Barnacle Warwks
168 D7 Barnard Castle Dur
66 B5 Barnard Gate Oxon
88 E5 Barnardiston Suffk
175 L3 Barnbarroch D & G
142 D7 Barnburgh Donc
107 K5 Barnby Suffk
142 F6 Barnby Dun Donc
117 M1 Barnby in the Willows Notts
134 D3 Barnby Moor Notts
172 D7 Barncorkrie D & G
52 B4 Barnehurst Gt Lon
51 G4 Barnes Gt Lon
39 G4 Barnes Street Kent
69 H7 Barnet Gt Lon
144 D6 Barnetby le Wold N Linc
69 G8 Barnet Gate Gt Lon
121 M5 Barney Norfk
105 H7 Barnham Suffk
20 F6 Barnham W Susx
106 B2 Barnham Broom Norfk
235 G4 Barnhead Angus
223 H1 Barnhill C Dund
113 H1 Barnhill Ches W
266 C5 Barnhill Moray
182 B8 Barnhills D & G
168 D8 Barningham Dur
105 K8 Barningham Suffk
145 G7 Barnoldby le Beck NE Lin
148 F6 Barnoldswick Lancs
142 D5 Barnsdale Bar Donc
37 H5 Barns Green W Susx
142 A6 Barnsley Barns
65 G6 Barnsley Gloucs
97 G5 Barnsley Shrops
142 B6 Barnsley Crematorium Barns
41 J4 Barnsole Kent
27 K4 Barnstaple Devon
70 F3 Barnston Essex
129 G3 Barnston Wirral
117 J4 Barnstone Notts
98 C8 Barnt Green Worcs
211 G4 Barnton C Edin
130 C5 Barnton Ches W
102 A6 Barnwell All Saints Nhants
102 A6 Barnwell St Andrew Nhants
64 B3 Barnwood Gloucs
80 B4 Baron's Cross Herefs
13 G2 Barons Wood Devon
166 C2 Baronwood Cumb
183 H4 Barr S Ayrs
173 J5 Barrachan D & G
224 B6 Barrapoll Ag & B
167 J8 Barras Cumb
179 L4 Barrasford Nthumb
154 d4 Barregarrow IoM
130 B7 Barrets Green Ches E
208 E7 Barrhead E Rens
183 G6 Barrhill S Ayrs
87 H5 Barrington Cambs
30 F7 Barrington Somset
3 G3 Barripper Cnwll
196 D1 Barrmill N Ayrs
216 C3 Barrnacarry Bay Ag & B
280 C2 Barrock Highld
64 C2 Barrow Gloucs
148 C8 Barrow Lancs
118 A8 Barrow Rutlnd
96 E3 Barrow Shrops
32 B4 Barrow Somset

88 F3 Barrow Suffk
104 B3 Barroway Drove Norfk
139 K5 Barrow Bridge Bolton
190 B4 Barrow Burn Nthumb
118 A4 Barrowby Lincs
101 L3 Barrowden Rutlnd
148 E7 Barrowford Lancs
45 G5 Barrow Gurney N Som
144 D3 Barrow Haven N Linc
133 H4 Barrow Hill Derbys
146 D2 Barrow-in-Furness Cumb
146 D2 Barrow Island Cumb
138 F7 Barrow Nook Lancs
130 D8 Barrow's Green Ches E
129 M2 Barrow's Green Halton
32 D5 Barrow Street Wilts
144 D4 Barrow-upon-Humber N Linc
116 F8 Barrow upon Soar Leics
116 B6 Barrow upon Trent Derbys
45 J7 Barrow Vale BaNES
234 E8 Barry Angus
43 H7 Barry V Glam
43 H8 Barry Island V Glam
100 F1 Barsby Leics
107 H5 Barsham Suffk
99 G7 Barston Solhll
80 D7 Bartestree Herefs
256 E5 Barthol Chapel Abers
71 H3 Bartholomew Green Essex
114 B1 Barthomley Ches E
18 D1 Bartley Hants
98 C7 Bartley Green Birm
88 B6 Bartlow Cambs
87 H4 Barton Cambs
113 G1 Barton Ches W
65 G2 Barton Gloucs
79 K4 Barton Herefs
138 D6 Barton Lancs
147 K8 Barton Lancs
160 C1 Barton N York
66 E5 Barton Oxon
8 D2 Barton Torbay
82 D5 Barton Warwks
104 E2 Barton Bendish Norfk
64 B7 Barton End Gloucs
115 K7 Barton Green Staffs
66 F1 Barton Hartshorn Bucks
151 L3 Barton Hill N York
116 E5 Barton in Fabis Notts
99 L2 Barton in the Beans Leics
68 D1 Barton-le-Clay C Beds
162 C7 Barton-le-Street N York
151 M3 Barton-le-Willows N York
104 E8 Barton Mills Suffk
18 C5 Barton-on-Sea Hants
83 G8 Barton-on-the-Heath Warwks
31 J4 Barton St David Somset
101 J7 Barton Seagrave Nhants
34 F3 Barton Stacey Hants
28 B3 Barton Town Devon
123 G7 Barton Turf Norfk
115 K7 Barton-under-Needwood Staffs
144 C3 Barton-upon-Humber N Linc
140 A8 Barton upon Irwell Salfd
144 C3 Barton Waterside N Linc
141 M6 Barugh Barns
141 M6 Barugh Green Barns
282 g2 Barvas W Isls
103 L8 Barway Cambs
99 L4 Barwell Leics
12 E1 Barwick Devon
69 K3 Barwick Herts
31 J8 Barwick Somset
150 F8 Barwick in Elmet Leeds
112 F7 Baschurch Shrops
83 J3 Bascote Warwks
83 J3 Bascote Heath Warwks
89 L3 Base Green Suffk
114 F1 Basford Green Staffs
148 B7 Bashall Eaves Lancs
148 C7 Bashall Town Lancs
18 C4 Bashley Hants
52 F1 Basildon Essex
53 G2 Basildon & District Crematorium Essex
48 F8 Basingstoke Hants
35 H2 Basingstoke Crematorium Hants
132 E5 Baslow Derbys
30 E2 Bason Bridge Somset
44 B2 Bassaleg Newpt
201 K4 Bassendean Border
165 H4 Bassenthwaite Cumb
34 F7 Bassett C Sotn
87 G6 Bassingbourn Cambs
117 G4 Bassingfield Notts
135 H7 Bassingham Lincs
118 C6 Bassingthorpe Lincs
69 J2 Bassus Green Herts
38 F2 Basted Kent

102 C1 Baston Lincs
123 J8 Bastwick Norfk
44 C7 Batch Somset
68 D8 Batchworth Herts
68 D8 Batchworth Heath Herts
16 B2 Batcombe Dorset
31 M3 Batcombe Somset
130 D4 Bate Heath Ches E
68 F4 Batford Herts
45 L6 Bath BaNES
45 M5 Bathampton BaNES
29 K6 Bathealton Somset
45 M5 Batheaston BaNES
46 A5 Bathford BaNES
210 C5 Bathgate W Loth
134 F7 Bathley Notts
11 K7 Bathpool Cnwll
30 C5 Bathpool Somset
73 K1 Bath Side Essex
210 B5 Bathville W Loth
45 H8 Bathway Somset
141 K3 Batley Kirk
82 E8 Batsford Gloucs
7 L7 Batson Devon
161 K1 Battersby N York
51 H4 Battersea Gt Lon
7 H5 Battisborough Cross Devon
90 C4 Battisford Suffk
89 L4 Battisford Tye Suffk
24 D4 Battle E Susx
60 F1 Battle Powys
30 E1 Battleborough Somset
64 D3 Battledown Gloucs
234 C4 Battledykes Angus
113 H8 Battlefield Shrops
71 J8 Battlesbridge Essex
68 B2 Battlesden C Beds
29 G5 Battleton Somset
89 H2 Battlies Green Suffk
18 E4 Battramsley Cross Hants
36 B3 Batt's Corner Hants
141 J4 Battyeford Kirk
81 K6 Baughton Worcs
48 E7 Baughurst Hants
244 D5 Baulds Abers
47 L1 Baulking Oxon
136 D5 Baumber Lincs
64 E6 Baunton Gloucs
96 F7 Baveney Wood Shrops
33 H4 Baverstock Wilts
106 D2 Bawburgh Norfk
122 A7 Bawdeswell Norfk
30 E3 Bawdrip Somset
91 H7 Bawdsey Suffk
120 E7 Bawsey Norfk
134 C1 Bawtry Donc
140 A2 Baxenden Lancs
99 H4 Baxterley Warwks
88 E4 Baxter's Green Suffk
258 D6 Bay Highld
282 h3 Bayble W Isls
35 H6 Baybridge Hants
168 B1 Baybridge Nthumb
146 F2 Baycliff Cumb
47 L3 Baydon Wilts
69 J5 Bayford Herts
32 B5 Bayford Somset
283 b8 Bayhead W Isls
147 K5 Bay Horse Lancs
38 D3 Bayley's Hill Kent
90 C5 Baylham Suffk
66 E1 Baynard's Green Oxon
161 K1 Baysdale Abbey N York
63 H2 Baysham Herefs
96 B2 Bayston Hill Shrops
88 E6 Baythorne End Essex
96 F8 Bayton Worcs
81 G1 Bayton Common Worcs
66 D6 Bayworth Oxon
45 L5 Beach S Glos
84 E7 Beachampton Bucks
104 E2 Beachamwell Norfk
45 H1 Beachley Gloucs
14 E2 Beacon Devon
72 D2 Beacon End Essex
38 D7 Beacon Hill E Susx
39 K6 Beacon Hill Kent
117 L1 Beacon Hill Notts
36 C3 Beacon Hill Surrey
67 J8 Beacon's Bottom Bucks
50 B1 Beaconsfield Bucks
161 L5 Beadlam N York
86 C7 Beadlow C Beds
203 L7 Beadnell Nthumb
27 K7 Beaford Devon
142 E3 Beal N York
203 H4 Beal Nthumb
6 D2 Bealbury Cnwll
11 L7 Bealsmill Cnwll
115 L6 Beam Hill Staffs

Beamhurst - Bickerton 293


115 H4 Beamhurst Staffs
15 L2 Beaminster Dorset
180 F8 Beamish Dur
149 K5 Beamsley N York
52 C4 Bean Kent
46 C5 Beanacre Wilts
190 F3 Beanley Nthumb
12 C5 Beardon Devon
139 K2 Beardwood Bl w D
14 A2 Beare Devon
37 J2 Beare Green Surrey
82 E3 Bearley Warwks
82 E3 Bearley Cross Warwks
169 G2 Bearpark Dur
208 F4 Bearsden E Duns
39 K2 Bearsted Kent
114 A4 Bearstone Shrops
98 C6 Bearwood Birm
79 M4 Bearwood Herefs
17 L3 Bearwood Poole
187 G6 Beattock D & G
70 E5 Beauchamp Roding Essex
132 F3 Beauchief Sheff
82 E2 Beaudesert Warwks
61 J5 Beaufort Blae G
18 F3 Beaulieu Hants
18 E2 Beaulieu Road Station Hants
250 F2 Beauly Highld
126 B4 Beaumaris IoA
177 K7 Beaumont Cumb
73 H2 Beaumont Essex
9 c3 Beaumont Jersey
169 J7 Beaumont Hill Darltn
82 F1 Beausale Warwks
35 J5 Beauworth Hants
12 B3 Beaworthy Devon
71 H1 Beazley End Essex
129 H3 Bebington Wirral
181 G3 Bebside Nthumb
107 J5 Beccles Suffk
138 F3 Becconsall Lancs
97 H3 Beckbury Shrops
51 K5 Beckenham Gt Lon
51 K5 Beckenham Crematorium Gt Lon
155 J1 Beckermet Cumb
104 F4 Beckett End Norfk
155 L3 Beckfoot Cumb
156 B5 Beckfoot Cumb
157 K3 Beck Foot Cumb
164 E1 Beckfoot Cumb
82 A8 Beckford Worcs
47 G5 Beckhampton Wilts
162 E2 Beck Hole N York
118 A1 Beckingham Lincs
134 F2 Beckingham Notts
46 A8 Beckington Somset
95 J7 Beckjay Shrops
24 F3 Beckley E Susx
18 C4 Beckley Hants
66 E5 Beckley Oxon
104 D7 Beck Row Suffk
149 J6 Becks C Brad
156 B6 Beck Side Cumb
156 E6 Beck Side Cumb
157 K5 Beckside Cumb
51 L3 Beckton Gt Lon
150 C5 Beckwithshaw N York
52 A2 Becontree Gt Lon
9 d2 Becquet Vincent Jersey
160 C5 Bedale N York
168 E4 Bedburn Dur
32 E7 Bedchester Dorset
43 G4 Beddau Rhondd
109 L2 Beddgelert Gwynd
23 G5 Beddingham E Susx
51 J6 Beddington Gt Lon
51 H5 Beddington Corner Gt Lon
90 F2 Bedfield Suffk
90 F2 Bedfield Little Green Suffk
85 L5 Bedford Bed
86 B5 Bedford Crematorium Bed
39 H6 Bedgebury Cross Kent
36 F6 Bedham W Susx
20 A5 Bedhampton Hants
90 E2 Bedingfield Suffk
90 E2 Bedingfield Green Suffk
150 C3 Bedlam N York
39 M4 Bedlam Lane Kent
181 G3 Bedlington Nthumb
61 H6 Bedlinog Myr Td
45 H5 Bedminster Bristl
45 H5 Bedminster Down Bristl
68 E6 Bedmond Herts
114 F7 Bednall Staffs
189 G3 Bedrule Border
95 J8 Bedstone Shrops
43 J4 Bedwas Caerph
61 J7 Bedwellty Caerph
99 K6 Bedworth Warwks
99 K6 Bedworth Woodlands Warwks
100 E2 Beeby Leics
35 L3 Beech Hants
114 D4 Beech Staffs
49 G6 Beech Hill W Berk
47 G7 Beechingstoke Wilts
48 C3 Beedon W Berk
48 C3 Beedon Hill W Berk
153 H5 Beeford E R Yk
132 E6 Beeley Derbys
145 G7 Beelsby NE Lin
48 E5 Beenham W Berk
49 K4 Beenham's Heath W & M
11 G4 Beeny Cnwll
14 F4 Beer Devon
30 F4 Beer Somset
30 D6 Beercrocombe Somset
31 K8 Beer Hackett Dorset
8 B6 Beesands Devon
137 J4 Beesby Lincs
8 B6 Beeson Devon
86 D5 Beeston C Beds
129 M7 Beeston Ches W
141 L2 Beeston Leeds
121 K8 Beeston Norfk
116 E4 Beeston Notts
122 D3 Beeston Regis Norfk
176 A5 Beeswing D & G
157 H6 Beetham Cumb
30 D8 Beetham Somset
121 L8 Beetley Norfk
43 K5 Began Cardif
66 C4 Begbroke Oxon
103 J2 Begdale Cambs
55 J5 Begelly Pembks
141 L3 Beggarington Hill Leeds
79 J2 Beggar's Bush Powys
94 F7 Beguildy Powys
107 H2 Beighton Norfk
133 J3 Beighton Sheff
115 M1 Beighton Hill Derbys
208 B8 Beith N Ayrs
41 G4 Bekesbourne Kent
41 G4 Bekesbourne Hill Kent
122 F7 Belaugh Norfk
97 L7 Belbroughton Worcs
16 F1 Belchalwell Dorset
16 F1 Belchalwell Street Dorset
88 F6 Belchamp Otten Essex
88 F6 Belchamp St Paul Essex
89 G7 Belchamp Walter Essex
136 E4 Belchford Lincs
203 H6 Belford Nthumb
100 D2 Belgrave C Leic
212 E3 Belhaven E Loth
257 H8 Belhelvie Abers
255 J6 Belhinnie Abers
243 K1 Bellabeg Abers
79 M7 Bellamore Herefs
216 B8 Bellanoch Ag & B
143 K2 Bellasize E R Yk
233 K3 Bellaty Angus
69 H6 Bell Bar Herts
148 F4 Bell Busk N York
137 G4 Belleau Lincs
97 L7 Bell End Worcs
159 K4 Bellerby N York
12 F7 Bellever Devon
177 L7 Belle Vue Cumb
142 A4 Belle Vue Wakefd
186 E2 Bellfield S Lans
198 D6 Bellfield S Lans
97 L7 Bell Heath Worcs
35 M6 Bell Hill Hants
68 B6 Bellingdon Bucks
179 J2 Bellingham Nthumb
192 D1 Belloch Ag & B
192 D2 Bellochantuy Ag & B
113 H2 Bell o' th' Hill Ches W
33 J0 Bellows Cross Dorset
90 D5 Bells Cross Suffk
209 J7 Bellshill N Lans
203 J7 Bellshill Nthumb
209 L7 Bellside N Lans
210 D6 Bellsquarry W Loth
38 F6 Bells Yew Green E Susx
45 J6 Belluton BaNES
263 H8 Belmaduthy Highld
102 A2 Belmesthorpe Rutlnd
139 K4 Belmont Bl w D
51 H6 Belmont Gt Lon
196 C7 Belmont S Ayrs
281 f2 Belmont Shet
255 H8 Belnacraig Abers
4 F3 Belowda Cnwll
116 B2 Belper Derbys
116 B2 Belper Lane End Derbys
133 L4 Belph Derbys
180 D3 Belsay Nthumb
201 J8 Belses Border
7 L3 Belsford Devon
68 D7 Belsize Herts
90 D7 Belstead Suffk
12 E4 Belstone Devon
139 L3 Belthorn Lancs
41 G2 Beltinge Kent
179 H6 Beltingham Nthumb
143 K6 Beltoft N Linc
116 D7 Belton Leics
118 B3 Belton Lincs
143 K6 Belton N Linc
107 K3 Belton Norfk
101 H3 Belton Rutlnd
39 H4 Beltring Kent
52 B3 Belvedere Gt Lon
117 L5 Belvoir Leics
19 L6 Bembridge IoW
33 K5 Bemerton Wilts
153 K2 Bempton E R Yk
107 K6 Benacre Suffk
185 H4 Benbuie D & G
228 D7 Benderloch Ag & B
39 K6 Benenden Kent
180 D8 Benfieldside Dur
122 F6 Bengates Norfk
69 J4 Bengeo Herts
82 B6 Bengeworth Worcs
91 J3 Benhall Green Suffk
91 H3 Benhall Street Suffk
235 K2 Benholm Abers
151 H4 Beningbrough N York
69 J2 Benington Herts
119 L2 Benington Lincs
119 L2 Benington Sea End Lincs
125 J3 Benllech IoA
207 J2 Benmore Ag & B
11 K4 Bennacott Cnwll
193 K4 Bennan N Ayrs
166 B6 Bennet Head Cumb
143 L2 Bennetland E R Yk
67 J7 Bennett End Bucks
136 D3 Benniworth Lincs
39 H4 Benover Kent
149 L6 Ben Rhydding C Brad
196 C2 Benslie N Ayrs
66 F8 Benson Oxon
70 D2 Bentfield Green Essex
96 F3 Benthall Shrops
64 C4 Bentham Gloucs
245 H3 Benthoul C Aber
95 H3 Bentlawn Shrops
142 E6 Bentley Donc
152 F8 Bentley E R Yk
36 A2 Bentley Hants
90 D7 Bentley Suffk
99 H4 Bentley Warwks
69 H7 Bentley Heath Herts
98 F8 Bentley Heath Solhll
28 B4 Benton Devon
188 B8 Bentpath D & G
28 C4 Bentwichen Devon
35 K3 Bentworth Hants
222 E1 Benvie Angus
15 M2 Benville Dorset
103 G5 Benwick Cambs
82 C1 Beoley Worcs
237 K2 Beoraidbeg Highld
20 D3 Bepton W Susx
70 C1 Berden Essex
74 C6 Berea Pembks
6 E2 Bere Alston Devon
6 E2 Bere Ferrers Devon
3 G6 Berepper Cnwll
17 G3 Bere Regis Dorset
106 F3 Bergh Apton Norfk
31 G4 Berhill Somset
66 E7 Berinsfield Oxon
63 K7 Berkeley Gloucs
63 K7 Berkeley Heath Gloucs
63 L7 Berkeley Road Gloucs
68 C5 Berkhamsted Herts
32 D1 Berkley Somset
99 H7 Berkswell Solhll
51 J3 Bermondsey Gt Lon
99 K5 Bermuda Warwks
248 C7 Bernera Highld
258 F6 Bernisdale Highld
66 F8 Berrick Prior Oxon
66 F8 Berrick Salome Oxon
274 F3 Berriedale Highld
165 L5 Berrier Cumb
94 E3 Berriew Powys
202 F4 Berrington Nthumb
96 C2 Berrington Shrops
80 D2 Berrington Worcs
80 D2 Berrington Green Worcs
44 C8 Berrow Somset
81 H8 Berrow Worcs
81 H3 Berrow Green Worcs
141 H5 Berry Brow Kirk
27 H7 Berry Cross Devon
27 K2 Berry Down Cross Devon
63 H4 Berry Hill Gloucs
75 H4 Berry Hill Pembks
267 K4 Berryhillock Moray
267 K5 Berryhillock Moray
27 K2 Berrynarbor Devon
8 B3 Berry Pomeroy Devon
51 L7 Berry's Green Gt Lon
112 D2 Bersham Wrexhm
128 D4 Berthengam Flints
23 H6 Berwick E Susx
47 G4 Berwick Bassett Wilts
180 E4 Berwick Hill Nthumb
33 J3 Berwick St James Wilts
32 F6 Berwick St John Wilts
32 F4 Berwick St Leonard Wilts
202 F3 Berwick-upon-Tweed Nthumb
117 L6 Bescaby Leics
138 E5 Bescar Lancs
113 J6 Besford Shrops
81 L6 Besford Worcs
142 F7 Bessacarr Donc
66 C6 Bessels Leigh Oxon
140 B6 Besses o' th' Barn Bury
153 J3 Bessingby E R Yk
122 D4 Bessingham Norfk
38 F7 Bestbeech Hill E Susx
106 B4 Besthorpe Norfk
135 G6 Besthorpe Notts
116 F2 Bestwood Village Notts
152 F6 Beswick E R Yk
95 K4 Betchcott Shrops
37 K1 Betchworth Surrey
77 G3 Bethania Cerdgn
110 D3 Bethania Gwynd
111 J4 Bethel Gwynd
125 J6 Bethel Gwynd
125 G5 Bethel IoA
111 L7 Bethel Powys
40 B7 Bethersden Kent
126 C6 Bethesda Gwynd
55 J3 Bethesda Pembks
59 J4 Bethlehem Carmth
51 K2 Bethnal Green Gt Lon
114 B2 Betley Staffs
52 D4 Betsham Kent
41 J5 Betteshanger Kent
15 J2 Bettiscombe Dorset
113 G4 Bettisfield Wrexhm
113 M4 Betton Shrops
96 C2 Betton Strange Shrops
44 C1 Bettws Newpt
77 H5 Bettws Bledrws Cerdgn
94 D4 Bettws Cedewain Powys
76 B5 Bettws Evan Cerdgn
62 D6 Bettws-Newydd Mons
278 B4 Bettyhill Highld
42 D4 Betws Brdgnd
59 H6 Betws Carmth
125 K8 Betws Garmon Gwynd
111 K2 Betws Gwerfil Goch Denbgs
126 F8 Betws-y-Coed Conwy
127 H5 Betws-yn-Rhos Conwy
76 B6 Beulah Cerdgn
78 C5 Beulah Powys
22 E6 Bevendean Br & H
134 D5 Bevercotes Notts
153 G7 Beverley E R Yk
64 B8 Beverstone Gloucs
63 K7 Bevington Gloucs
165 H4 Bewaldeth Cumb
178 D4 Bewcastle Cumb
97 H8 Bewdley Worcs
149 L3 Bewerley N York
153 J6 Bewholme E R Yk
39 H6 Bewlbridge Kent
24 D5 Bexhill E Susx
52 B4 Bexley Gt Lon
52 A4 Bexleyheath Gt Lon
36 D6 Bexleyhill W Susx
53 J7 Bexon Kent
104 C3 Bexwell Norfk
89 J3 Beyton Suffk
89 J3 Beyton Green Suffk
282 e3 Bhaltos W Isls
283 b13 Bhatarsaigh W Isls
45 K1 Bibstone S Glos
65 G5 Bibury Gloucs
66 E3 Bicester Oxon
99 G7 Bickenhill Solhll
119 H4 Bicker Lincs
119 H4 Bicker Bar Lincs
119 H4 Bicker Gauntlet Lincs
139 J7 Bickershaw Wigan
138 F7 Bickerstaffe Lancs
113 H1 Bickerton Ches E
8 B7 Bickerton Devon
151 G5 Bickerton N York
190 E6 Bickerton Nthumb

114 D8 **Bickford** Staffs
13 J7 **Bickington** Devon
27 J4 **Bickington** Devon
7 G2 **Bickleigh** Devon
13 M1 **Bickleigh** Devon
27 J5 **Bickleton** Devon
113 J2 **Bickley** Ches W
51 L5 **Bickley** Gt Lon
163 G4 **Bickley** N York
80 E1 **Bickley** Worcs
113 J2 **Bickley Moss** Ches W
71 J6 **Bicknacre** Essex
29 K3 **Bicknoller** Somset
53 J7 **Bicknor** Kent
33 K8 **Bickton** Hants
80 B2 **Bicton** Herefs
95 G6 **Bicton** Shrops
113 G8 **Bicton** Shrops
38 E5 **Bidborough** Kent
35 L1 **Bidden** Hants
39 L5 **Biddenden** Kent
39 M5 **Biddenden Green** Kent
85 K5 **Biddenham** Bed
46 B4 **Biddestone** Wilts
44 D8 **Biddisham** Somset
84 C7 **Biddlesden** Bucks
190 D4 **Biddlestone** Nthumb
131 H7 **Biddulph** Staffs
131 H8 **Biddulph Moor** Staffs
27 H5 **Bideford** Devon
82 D5 **Bidford-on-Avon** Warwks
129 G2 **Bidston** Wirral
152 B7 **Bielby** E R Yk
245 K3 **Bieldside** C Aber
19 H8 **Bierley** IoW
67 K4 **Bierton** Bucks
173 K6 **Big Balcraig** D & G
7 K5 **Bigbury** Devon
7 J6 **Bigbury-on-Sea** Devon
144 D6 **Bigby** Lincs
185 G3 **Big Carlae** D & G
146 D3 **Biggar** Cumb
199 H5 **Biggar** S Lans
115 L2 **Biggin** Derbys
132 C7 **Biggin** Derbys
142 E1 **Biggin** N York
51 L7 **Biggin Hill** Gt Lon
86 D6 **Biggleswade** C Beds
177 K3 **Bigholms** D & G
278 F3 **Bighouse** Highld
35 J4 **Bighton** Hants
177 H8 **Biglands** Cumb
21 G4 **Bignor** W Susx
164 D8 **Bigrigg** Cumb
260 B4 **Big Sand** Highld
281 d8 **Bigton** Shet
116 E3 **Bilborough** C Nott
29 J3 **Bilbrook** Somset
97 K3 **Bilbrook** Staffs
151 H6 **Bilbrough** N York
280 C5 **Bilbster** Highld
169 G6 **Bildershaw** Dur
89 K5 **Bildeston** Suffk
11 J4 **Billacott** Cnwll
71 G8 **Billericay** Essex
100 F3 **Billesdon** Leics
82 D4 **Billesley** Warwks
118 F5 **Billingborough** Lincs
139 G7 **Billinge** St Hel
106 D7 **Billingford** Norfk
121 M7 **Billingford** Norfk
170 B6 **Billingham** S on T
136 C8 **Billinghay** Lincs
142 C6 **Billingley** Barns
37 G5 **Billingshurst** W Susx
96 F6 **Billingsley** Shrops
68 B3 **Billington** C Beds
148 C8 **Billington** Lancs
114 D7 **Billington** Staffs
107 J1 **Billockby** Norfk
168 F3 **Billy Row** Dur
147 K7 **Bilsborrow** Lancs
137 J4 **Bilsby** Lincs
21 G6 **Bilsham** W Susx
40 D8 **Bilsington** Kent
134 C7 **Bilsthorpe** Notts
134 C7 **Bilsthorpe Moor** Notts
211 J6 **Bilston** Mdloth
98 B4 **Bilston** Wolves
99 K2 **Bilstone** Leics
40 D5 **Bilting** Kent
144 F1 **Bilton** E R Yk
150 D4 **Bilton** N York
151 G6 **Bilton** N York
191 J4 **Bilton** Nthumb
100 B8 **Bilton** Warwks
191 J4 **Bilton Banks** Nthumb
136 D1 **Binbrook** Lincs
169 G4 **Binchester Blocks** Dur
16 D5 **Bincombe** Dorset

31 K1 **Binegar** Somset
21 L3 **Bines Green** W Susx
49 K4 **Binfield** Br For
49 H3 **Binfield Heath** Oxon
180 A4 **Bingfield** Nthumb
117 J3 **Bingham** Notts
16 E2 **Bingham's Melcombe** Dorset
149 K7 **Bingley** C Brad
113 J7 **Bings** Shrops
121 L4 **Binham** Norfk
99 K7 **Binley** Covtry
48 B8 **Binley** Hants
99 L7 **Binley Woods** Warwks
17 G5 **Binnegar** Dorset
209 M4 **Binniehill** Falk
36 E2 **Binscombe** Surrey
66 C5 **Binsey** Oxon
19 K5 **Binstead** IoW
36 A3 **Binsted** Hants
21 G5 **Binsted** W Susx
82 D4 **Binton** Warwks
121 M7 **Bintree** Norfk
95 H3 **Binweston** Shrops
72 D3 **Birch** Essex
140 C6 **Birch** Rochdl
121 G5 **Bircham Newton** Norfk
121 G5 **Bircham Tofts** Norfk
70 D3 **Birchanger** Essex
115 J5 **Birch Cross** Staffs
141 H4 **Birchencliffe** Kirk
80 B2 **Bircher** Herefs
98 D5 **Birchfield** Birm
72 D3 **Birch Green** Essex
69 J5 **Birch Green** Herts
81 K6 **Birch Green** Worcs
43 J5 **Birchgrove** Cardif
57 K5 **Birchgrove** Swans
38 B7 **Birchgrove** W Susx
130 A7 **Birch Heath** Ches W
129 M5 **Birch Hill** Ches W
41 J2 **Birchington** Kent
99 H4 **Birchley Heath** Warwks
99 H3 **Birchmoor** Warwks
85 J8 **Birchmoor Green** C Beds
132 E7 **Birchover** Derbys
131 K2 **Birch Vale** Derbys
30 C8 **Birch Wood** Somset
130 C2 **Birchwood** Warrtn
134 C2 **Bircotes** Notts
88 E7 **Birdbrook** Essex
161 G7 **Birdforth** N York
20 D6 **Birdham** W Susx
83 K2 **Birdingbury** Warwks
64 D4 **Birdlip** Gloucs
178 E5 **Birdoswald** Cumb
152 B3 **Birdsall** N York
141 K6 **Birds Edge** Kirk
70 E5 **Birds Green** Essex
97 H6 **Birdsgreen** Shrops
15 J2 **Birdsmoorgate** Dorset
89 K5 **Bird Street** Suffk
142 A7 **Birdwell** Barns
63 L3 **Birdwood** Gloucs
202 B5 **Birgham** Border
263 K2 **Birichin** Highld
139 H5 **Birkacre** Lancs
160 D2 **Birkby** N York
138 C5 **Birkdale** Sefton
267 L3 **Birkenbog** Abers
129 H2 **Birkenhead** Wirral
256 D3 **Birkenhills** Abers
141 K2 **Birkenshaw** Kirk
243 K5 **Birkhall** Abers
234 A8 **Birkhill** Angus
187 J3 **Birkhill** D & G
118 C6 **Birkholme** Lincs
142 E2 **Birkin** N York
141 L2 **Birks** Leeds
179 H5 **Birkshaw** Nthumb
80 B4 **Birley** Herefs
133 G1 **Birley Carr** Sheff
52 E6 **Birling** Kent
191 K5 **Birling** Nthumb
23 J8 **Birling Gap** E Susx
81 L6 **Birlingham** Worcs
98 D6 **Birmingham** Birm
232 F7 **Birnam** P & K
257 H5 **Birness** Abers
244 C4 **Birse** Abers
244 C4 **Birsemore** Abers
141 K3 **Birstall** Kirk
100 D2 **Birstall** Leics
150 B4 **Birstwith** N York
118 E5 **Birthorpe** Lincs
181 G7 **Birtley** Gatesd
79 L2 **Birtley** Herefs
179 K3 **Birtley** Nthumb
181 G7 **Birtley Crematorium** Gatesd
81 H7 **Birts Street** Worcs
101 J3 **Bisbrooke** Rutlnd

136 D3 **Biscathorpe** Lincs
5 H4 **Biscovey** Cnwll
49 K2 **Bisham** W & M
82 A5 **Bishampton** Worcs
28 C6 **Bish Mill** Devon
169 G5 **Bishop Auckland** Dur
135 L2 **Bishopbridge** Lincs
209 G5 **Bishopbriggs** E Duns
152 F7 **Bishop Burton** E R Yk
169 J4 **Bishop Middleham** Dur
266 E3 **Bishopmill** Moray
150 D3 **Bishop Monkton** N York
135 K1 **Bishop Norton** Lincs
41 G5 **Bishopsbourne** Kent
46 F6 **Bishops Cannings** Wilts
95 H5 **Bishop's Castle** Shrops
32 B8 **Bishop's Caundle** Dorset
64 D2 **Bishop's Cleeve** Gloucs
80 F5 **Bishop's Frome** Herefs
50 B5 **Bishops Gate** Surrey
70 F3 **Bishop's Green** Essex
48 D6 **Bishop's Green** Hants
30 B6 **Bishops Hull** Somset
83 J4 **Bishop's Itchington** Warwks
29 M5 **Bishops Lydeard** Somset
64 B2 **Bishop's Norton** Gloucs
28 D6 **Bishop's Nympton** Devon
114 B5 **Bishop's Offley** Staffs
70 C3 **Bishop's Stortford** Herts
35 J4 **Bishop's Sutton** Hants
83 H3 **Bishop's Tachbrook** Warwks
27 K5 **Bishop's Tawton** Devon
13 L7 **Bishopsteignton** Devon
34 F7 **Bishopstoke** Hants
57 G7 **Bishopston** Swans
67 J5 **Bishopstone** Bucks
23 G7 **Bishopstone** E Susx
80 A6 **Bishopstone** Herefs
41 G2 **Bishopstone** Kent
47 K2 **Bishopstone** Swindn
33 J5 **Bishopstone** Wilts
32 E2 **Bishopstrow** Wilts
45 H7 **Bishop Sutton** BaNES
35 H7 **Bishop's Waltham** Hants
97 J2 **Bishop's Wood** Staffs
45 H5 **Bishopsworth** Bristl
150 C3 **Bishop Thornton** N York
151 J6 **Bishopthorpe** C York
169 K6 **Bishopton** Darltn
208 D5 **Bishopton** Rens
82 E4 **Bishopton** Warwks
152 B5 **Bishop Wilton** E R Yk
44 D2 **Bishton** Newpt
115 G7 **Bishton** Staffs
64 C6 **Bisley** Gloucs
50 B7 **Bisley** Surrey
50 B7 **Bisley Camp** Surrey
146 F7 **Bispham** Bpool
138 F5 **Bispham Green** Lancs
3 K3 **Bissoe** Cnwll
18 A3 **Bisterne** Hants
38 E7 **Bitchet Green** Kent
118 C6 **Bitchfield** Lincs
27 K3 **Bittadon** Devon
7 K3 **Bittaford** Devon
121 K8 **Bittering** Norfk
96 D7 **Bitterley** Shrops
34 F8 **Bitterne** C Sotn
100 C6 **Bitteswell** Leics
45 K5 **Bitton** S Glos
49 H2 **Bix** Oxon
281 d6 **Bixter** Shet
100 C4 **Blaby** Leics
202 C3 **Blackadder** Border
8 B4 **Blackawton** Devon
155 J1 **Blackbeck** Cumb
14 C1 **Blackborough** Devon
120 E8 **Blackborough End** Norfk
65 L6 **Black Bourton** Oxon
23 J3 **Blackboys** E Susx
116 B2 **Blackbrook** Derbys
139 G8 **Blackbrook** St Hel
114 B4 **Blackbrook** Staffs
37 J2 **Blackbrook** Surrey
245 J1 **Blackburn** Abers
139 K2 **Blackburn** Bl w D
133 H1 **Blackburn** Rothm
210 C6 **Blackburn** W Loth
180 E5 **Black Callerton** N u Ty
106 B4 **Black Car** Norfk
37 L3 **Black Corner** W Susx
185 G1 **Blackcraig** E Ayrs
228 E8 **Black Crofts** Ag & B
4 E3 **Black Cross** Cnwll
130 F5 **Blackden Heath** Ches E
245 L1 **Blackdog** Abers
13 J1 **Black Dog** Devon
12 C6 **Blackdown** Devon
15 J2 **Blackdown** Dorset

176 F8 **Blackdyke** Cumb
142 A5 **Blacker** Barns
142 B7 **Blacker Hill** Barns
51 M4 **Blackfen** Gt Lon
19 G3 **Blackfield** Hants
177 L6 **Blackford** Cumb
220 F5 **Blackford** P & K
30 F2 **Blackford** Somset
31 L5 **Blackford** Somset
140 B6 **Blackford Bridge** Bury
116 B7 **Blackfordby** Leics
19 H8 **Blackgang** IoW
211 G4 **Blackhall** C Edin
170 B3 **Blackhall** Dur
170 B3 **Blackhall Colliery** Dur
200 F5 **Blackhaugh** Border
72 E3 **Blackheath** Essex
51 K4 **Blackheath** Gt Lon
98 B6 **Blackheath** Sandw
107 J8 **Blackheath** Suffk
36 F2 **Blackheath** Surrey
180 C4 **Black Heddon** Nthumb
257 K3 **Blackhill** Abers
269 K5 **Blackhill** Abers
180 D8 **Blackhill** Dur
269 G7 **Blackhill of Clackriach** Abers
14 A4 **Blackhorse** Devon
119 H4 **Blackjack** Lincs
46 E5 **Blackland** Wilts
140 A6 **Black Lane** Bury
149 G3 **Black Lane Ends** Lancs
186 F4 **Blacklaw** D & G
140 C7 **Blackley** Manch
140 C7 **Blackley Crematorium** Manch
233 H3 **Blacklunans** P & K
80 C7 **Blackmarstone** Herefs
42 E4 **Blackmill** Brdgnd
36 A4 **Blackmoor** Hants
150 D7 **Black Moor** Leeds
44 F6 **Blackmoor** N Som
141 H5 **Blackmoorfoot** Kirk
70 F6 **Blackmore** Essex
71 H1 **Blackmore End** Essex
68 F4 **Blackmore End** Herts
210 E3 **Blackness** Falk
36 B3 **Blacknest** Hants
50 B5 **Blacknest** W & M
71 J3 **Black Notley** Essex
148 E7 **Blacko** Lancs
57 H6 **Black Pill** Swans
146 F8 **Blackpool** Bpool
8 C5 **Blackpool** Devon
13 J7 **Blackpool** Devon
178 C3 **Blackpool Gate** Cumb
210 A5 **Blackridge** W Loth
3 G4 **Blackrock** Cnwll
61 K4 **Blackrock** Mons
139 J5 **Blackrod** Bolton
254 D4 **Blacksboat** Moray
176 D5 **Blackshaw** D & G
140 E2 **Blackshaw Head** Calder
90 D2 **Blacksmith's Green** Suffk
139 L3 **Blacksnape** Bl w D
22 C4 **Blackstone** W Susx
107 K6 **Black Street** Suffk
55 G5 **Black Tar** Pembks
66 F3 **Blackthorn** Oxon
89 H3 **Blackthorpe** Suffk
143 L3 **Blacktoft** E R Yk
245 J3 **Blacktop** C Aber
12 B2 **Black Torrington** Devon
115 L2 **Blackwall** Derbys
4 B5 **Blackwater** Cnwll
49 K7 **Blackwater** Hants
19 H6 **Blackwater** IoW
30 C7 **Blackwater** Somset
194 D5 **Blackwaterfoot** N Ayrs
177 L8 **Blackwell** Cumb
169 H8 **Blackwell** Darltn
132 C5 **Blackwell** Derbys
133 J7 **Blackwell** Derbys
82 F6 **Blackwell** Warwks
82 A1 **Blackwell** Worcs
63 M2 **Blackwellsend Green** Gloucs
43 J2 **Blackwood** Caerph
176 B2 **Blackwood** D & G
198 C4 **Blackwood** S Lans
131 H8 **Blackwood Hill** Staffs
129 J6 **Blacon** Ches W
41 G6 **Bladbean** Kent
174 C4 **Bladnoch** D & G
66 C4 **Bladon** Oxon
30 F6 **Bladon** Somset
75 M2 **Blaenannerch** Cerdgn
110 D2 **Blaenau Ffestiniog** Gwynd
61 L5 **Blaenavon** Torfn
78 C7 **Blaen Dyryn** Powys
75 L5 **Blaenffos** Pembks
42 D3 **Blaengarw** Brdgnd
92 E7 **Blaengeuffordd** Cerdgn

60 C6 **Blaengwrach** Neath
42 D2 **Blaengwynfi** Neath
42 F2 **Blaenllechau** Rhondd
77 H2 **Blaenpennal** Cerdgn
92 C8 **Blaenplwyf** Cerdgn
76 A5 **Blaenporth** Cerdgn
60 D7 **Blaenrhondda** Rhondd
75 M6 **Blaenwaun** Carmth
58 C3 **Blaen-y-Coed** Carmth
61 H5 **Blaen-y-cwm** Blae G
93 H8 **Blaenycwm** Cerdgn
60 D7 **Blaen-y-cwm** Rhondd
45 G7 **Blagdon** N Som
30 B7 **Blagdon** Somset
8 C3 **Blagdon** Torbay
30 B7 **Blagdon Hill** Somset
167 G1 **Blagill** Cumb
138 F6 **Blaguegate** Lancs
239 G8 **Blaich** Highld
237 K6 **Blain** Highld
61 K5 **Blaina** Blae G
232 C2 **Blair Atholl** P & K
220 C7 **Blair Drummond** Stirlg
233 J6 **Blairgowrie** P & K
210 C2 **Blairhall** Fife
221 H7 **Blairingone** P & K
220 E7 **Blairlogie** Stirlg
207 K2 **Blairmore** Ag & B
276 B4 **Blairmore** Highld
254 D8 **Blairnamarrow** Moray
206 F5 **Blair's Ferry** Ag & B
63 K4 **Blaisdon** Gloucs
97 J8 **Blakebrook** Worcs
97 K7 **Blakedown** Worcs
71 H3 **Blake End** Essex
114 F2 **Blakeley Lane** Staffs
130 A5 **Blakemere** Ches W
79 L7 **Blakemere** Herefs
7 M3 **Blakemore** Devon
98 C3 **Blakenall Heath** Wsall
63 K5 **Blakeney** Gloucs
122 A3 **Blakeney** Norfk
114 A2 **Blakenhall** Ches E
97 K4 **Blakenhall** Wolves
97 J7 **Blakeshall** Worcs
84 C5 **Blakesley** Nhants
168 B1 **Blanchland** Nthumb
17 H1 **Blandford Camp** Dorset
17 G1 **Blandford Forum** Dorset
17 G1 **Blandford St Mary** Dorset
150 B5 **Bland Hill** N York
208 F3 **Blanefield** Stirlg
135 L7 **Blankney** Lincs
209 J7 **Blantyre** S Lans
229 H2 **Blar a' Chaorainn** Highld
241 G4 **Blargie** Highld
229 H2 **Blarmachfoldach** Highld
18 A2 **Blashford** Hants
101 H4 **Blaston** Leics
101 L4 **Blatherwycke** Nhants
156 C5 **Blawith** Cumb
184 F6 **Blawquhairn** D & G
91 J4 **Blaxhall** Suffk
143 H7 **Blaxton** Donc
180 F6 **Blaydon** Gatesd
31 H2 **Bleadney** Somset
44 C7 **Bleadon** N Som
32 C4 **Bleak Street** Somset
40 F3 **Blean** Kent
136 B3 **Bleasby** Lincs
117 J2 **Bleasby** Notts
147 L6 **Bleasdale** Lancs
167 G7 **Bleatarn** Cumb
80 D1 **Bleathwood** Herefs
223 G4 **Blebocraigs** Fife
79 H2 **Bleddfa** Powys
65 K3 **Bledington** Gloucs
67 J6 **Bledlow** Bucks
67 J7 **Bledlow Ridge** Bucks
46 C7 **Bleet** Wilts
212 B6 **Blegbie** E Loth
166 E4 **Blencarn** Cumb
165 G1 **Blencogo** Cumb
35 L8 **Blendworth** Hants
165 G2 **Blennerhasset** Cumb
66 D3 **Bletchingdon** Oxon
37 M1 **Bletchingley** Surrey
85 G8 **Bletchley** M Keyn
113 K6 **Bletchley** Shrops
55 H3 **Bletherston** Pembks
85 K4 **Bletsoe** Bed
48 D2 **Blewbury** Oxon
122 D6 **Blickling** Norfk
134 B8 **Blidworth** Notts
117 G1 **Blidworth Bottoms** Notts
189 L4 **Blindburn** Nthumb
164 F4 **Blindcrake** Cumb
38 A4 **Blindley Heath** Surrey
10 F7 **Blisland** Cnwll
33 L8 **Blissford** Hants

81 G1 **Bliss Gate** Worcs
84 D4 **Blisworth** Nhants
115 H7 **Blithbury** Staffs
176 F8 **Blitterlees** Cumb
82 E8 **Blockley** Gloucs
107 G2 **Blofield** Norfk
107 G1 **Blofield Heath** Norfk
105 K7 **Blo Norton** Norfk
189 G2 **Bloomfield** Border
114 A4 **Blore** Staffs
115 J2 **Blore** Staffs
35 L2 **Blounce** Hants
115 H5 **Blounts Green** Staffs
138 D4 **Blowick** Sefton
83 K8 **Bloxham** Oxon
118 E1 **Bloxholm** Lincs
98 C3 **Bloxwich** Wsall
17 G3 **Bloxworth** Dorset
149 L5 **Blubberhouses** N York
4 E3 **Blue Anchor** Cnwll
29 J2 **Blue Anchor** Somset
52 F6 **Blue Bell Hill** Kent
138 C7 **Blundellsands** Sefton
107 L4 **Blundeston** Suffk
86 C5 **Blunham** C Beds
47 H1 **Blunsdon St Andrew** Swindn
97 K8 **Bluntington** Worcs
103 H8 **Bluntisham** Cambs
6 C2 **Blunts** Cnwll
82 D2 **Blunts Green** Warwks
114 D3 **Blurton** C Stke
135 J1 **Blyborough** Lincs
107 J8 **Blyford** Suffk
97 H1 **Blymhill** Staffs
97 J1 **Blymhill Lawn** Staffs
134 C2 **Blyth** Notts
181 H3 **Blyth** Nthumb
199 K4 **Blyth Bridge** Border
107 J8 **Blythburgh** Suffk
181 H3 **Blyth Crematorium** Nthumb
201 J3 **Blythe** Border
114 F3 **Blythe Bridge** Staffs
99 G5 **Blythe End** Warwks
114 F3 **Blythe Marsh** Staffs
135 G1 **Blyton** Lincs
223 K4 **Boarhills** Fife
19 K2 **Boarhunt** Hants
53 G7 **Boarley** Kent
140 C4 **Boarsgreave** Lancs
38 E6 **Boarshead** E Susx
139 H6 **Boar's Head** Wigan
66 D6 **Boars Hill** Oxon
66 F4 **Boarstall** Bucks
12 C4 **Boasley Cross** Devon
263 G5 **Boath** Highld
253 H7 **Boat of Garten** Highld
53 J6 **Bobbing** Kent
97 H5 **Bobbington** Staffs
70 D6 **Bobbingworth** Essex
5 L3 **Bocaddon** Cnwll
71 J2 **Bocking** Essex
71 J2 **Bocking Churchstreet** Essex
80 D3 **Bockleton** Worcs
5 K3 **Boconnoc** Cnwll
257 L3 **Boddam** Abers
281 d8 **Boddam** Shet
64 C2 **Boddington** Gloucs
124 F4 **Bodedern** IoA
127 K4 **Bodelwyddan** Denbgs
80 C5 **Bodenham** Herefs
33 L5 **Bodenham** Wilts
80 D5 **Bodenham Moor** Herefs
125 G2 **Bodewryd** IoA
128 C5 **Bodfari** Denbgs
125 G2 **Bodffordd** IoA
108 E4 **Bodfuan** Gwynd
122 C3 **Bodham** Norfk
24 E2 **Bodiam** E Susx
83 K7 **Bodicote** Oxon
10 D7 **Bodieve** Cnwll
5 K4 **Bodinnick** Cnwll
23 L4 **Bodle Street Green** E Susx
5 H2 **Bodmin** Cnwll
105 G4 **Bodney** Norfk
125 G6 **Bodorgan** IoA
4 D5 **Bodrean** Cnwll
40 E6 **Bodsham Green** Kent
5 H3 **Bodwen** Cnwll
99 G4 **Bodymoor Heath** Warwks
251 H2 **Bogallan** Highld
257 J4 **Bogbrae** Abers
196 D4 **Bogend** S Ayrs
212 A5 **Boggs Holdings** E Loth
211 H6 **Boghall** Mdloth
210 C5 **Boghall** W Loth
198 C5 **Boghead** S Lans
267 G4 **Bogmoor** Moray
235 G1 **Bogmuir** Abers
255 M3 **Bogniebrae** Abers
20 F7 **Bognor Regis** W Susx

253 G7 **Bogroy** Highld
185 G6 **Bogue** D & G
6 E1 **Bohetherick** Cnwll
3 L4 **Bohortha** Cnwll
240 A6 **Bohuntine** Highld
2 B4 **Bojewyan** Cnwll
5 H2 **Bokiddick** Cnwll
169 G6 **Bolam** Dur
180 D2 **Bolam** Nthumb
7 K7 **Bolberry** Devon
129 M2 **Bold Heath** St Hel
98 E4 **Boldmere** Birm
181 J6 **Boldon Colliery** S Tyne
18 E4 **Boldre** Hants
168 C7 **Boldron** Dur
134 F2 **Bole** Notts
132 F8 **Bolehill** Derbys
133 G5 **Bole Hill** Derbys
3 H3 **Bolenowe** Cnwll
29 G7 **Bolham** Devon
29 L8 **Bolham Water** Devon
4 C4 **Bolingey** Cnwll
131 J4 **Bollington** Ches E
131 H4 **Bollington Cross** Ches E
63 L4 **Bollow** Gloucs
37 L6 **Bolney** W Susx
86 B3 **Bolnhurst** Bed
234 F5 **Bolshan** Angus
133 J5 **Bolsover** Derbys
141 G5 **Bolster Moor** Kirk
141 L8 **Bolsterstone** Sheff
161 H5 **Boltby** N York
243 M2 **Boltenstone** Abers
67 J8 **Bolter End** Bucks
139 L6 **Bolton** Bolton
166 E6 **Bolton** Cumb
212 B5 **Bolton** E Loth
152 B5 **Bolton** E R Yk
191 G3 **Bolton** Nthumb
149 K5 **Bolton Abbey** N York
149 K5 **Bolton Bridge** N York
148 D6 **Bolton by Bowland** Lancs
178 B5 **Boltonfellend** Cumb
165 H3 **Boltongate** Cumb
147 J2 **Bolton le Sands** Lancs
165 H2 **Bolton Low Houses** Cumb
165 H2 **Bolton New Houses** Cumb
160 C3 **Bolton-on-Swale** N York
151 H7 **Bolton Percy** N York
147 J2 **Bolton Town End** Lancs
142 C7 **Bolton Upon Dearne** Barns
11 H7 **Bolventor** Cnwll
181 G2 **Bomarsund** Nthumb
113 G7 **Bomere Heath** Shrops
263 G2 **Bonar Bridge** Highld
228 F8 **Bonawe** Ag & B
144 C5 **Bonby** N Linc
75 L4 **Boncath** Pembks
189 G4 **Bonchester Bridge** Border
19 K8 **Bonchurch** IoW
12 F2 **Bondleigh** Devon
147 J6 **Bonds** Lancs
13 G7 **Bonehill** Devon
99 G3 **Bonehill** Staffs
210 D3 **Bo'ness** Falk
98 D2 **Boney Hay** Staffs
208 C3 **Bonhill** W Duns
97 J3 **Boningale** Shrops
189 H2 **Bonjedward** Border
209 M7 **Bonkle** N Lans
234 F7 **Bonnington** Angus
40 D8 **Bonnington** Kent
222 F6 **Bonnybank** Fife
209 L3 **Bonnybridge** Falk
268 F5 **Bonnykelly** Abers
211 J6 **Bonnyrigg** Mdloth
233 M7 **Bonnyton** Angus
93 J3 **Bont-Dolgadfan** Powys
92 E6 **Bont-goch or Elerch** Cerdgn
137 J5 **Bonthorpe** Lincs
77 H2 **Bontnewydd** Cerdgn
125 J7 **Bontnewydd** Gwynd
128 C8 **Bontuchel** Denbgs
43 G7 **Bonvilston** V Glam
111 L3 **Bonwm** Denbgs
57 J6 **Bon-y-maen** Swans
27 J3 **Boode** Devon
49 K1 **Booker** Bucks
113 J6 **Booley** Shrops
201 J4 **Boon** Border
114 C2 **Boon Hill** Staffs
35 G8 **Boorley Green** Hants
170 F7 **Boosbeck** R & Cl
71 K1 **Boose's Green** Essex
155 M3 **Boot** Cumb
141 G2 **Booth** Calder

135 K7 **Boothby Graffoe** Lincs
118 C5 **Boothby Pagnell** Lincs
143 J3 **Boothferry** E R Yk
131 H3 **Booth Green** Ches E
139 L7 **Boothstown** Salfd
141 G2 **Booth Town** Calder
84 F2 **Boothville** Nhants
155 K5 **Bootle** Cumb
138 D8 **Bootle** Sefton
130 E5 **Boots Green** Ches W
90 C3 **Boot Street** Suffk
159 H2 **Booze** N York
80 E1 **Boraston** Shrops
9 k2 **Bordeaux** Guern
53 J6 **Borden** Kent
36 B6 **Borden** W Susx
177 G8 **Border** Cumb
149 G3 **Bordley** N York
36 B4 **Bordon Camp** Hants
71 J5 **Boreham** Essex
32 E2 **Boreham** Wilts
24 B5 **Boreham Street** E Susx
69 G7 **Borehamwood** Herts
187 J8 **Boreland** D & G
258 B6 **Boreraig** Highld
96 C2 **Boreton** Shrops
282 g1 **Borgh** W Isls
283 b13 **Borgh** W Isls
278 B4 **Borgie** Highld
175 G5 **Borgue** D & G
274 F7 **Borgue** Highld
89 G6 **Borley** Essex
89 G6 **Borley Green** Essex
89 K3 **Borley Green** Suffk
258 B6 **Borneskitaig** Highld
174 F5 **Borness** D & G
150 E3 **Boroughbridge** N York
38 F2 **Borough Green** Kent
112 E1 **Borras Head** Wrexhm
116 C4 **Borrowash** Derbys
160 F5 **Borrowby** N York
171 H7 **Borrowby** N York
165 H7 **Borrowdale** Cumb
210 D3 **Borrowstoun** Falk
52 F5 **Borstal** Medway
92 D5 **Borth** Cerdgn
188 C3 **Borthwickbrae** Border
188 D3 **Borthwickshiels** Border
109 K4 **Borth-y-Gest** Gwynd
259 G7 **Borve** Highld
282 d6 **Borve** W Isls
282 g1 **Borve** W Isls
283 b13 **Borve** W Isls
147 K1 **Borwick** Lancs
156 E3 **Borwick Lodge** Cumb
156 A6 **Borwick Rails** Cumb
2 B5 **Bosavern** Cnwll
80 F6 **Bosbury** Herefs
5 H1 **Boscarne** Cnwll
10 F4 **Boscastle** Cnwll
17 M4 **Boscombe** Bmouth
33 L3 **Boscombe** Wilts
5 H4 **Boscoppa** Cnwll
20 C6 **Bosham** W Susx
20 D6 **Bosham Hoe** W Susx
54 F7 **Bosherston** Pembks
2 C4 **Boskednan** Cnwll
2 C6 **Boskenna** Cnwll
131 H6 **Bosley** Ches E
4 E3 **Bosoughan** Cnwll
151 M4 **Bossall** N York
10 F4 **Bossiney** Cnwll
40 F5 **Bossingham** Kent
28 F1 **Bossington** Somset
130 C6 **Bostock Green** Ches W
119 K3 **Boston** Lincs
119 K3 **Boston Crematorium** Lincs
150 F6 **Boston Spa** Leeds
2 C4 **Boswarthan** Cnwll
5 G6 **Boswinger** Cnwll
2 B4 **Botallack** Cnwll
69 J7 **Botany Bay** Gt Lon
100 B2 **Botcheston** Leics
105 L8 **Botesdale** Suffk
180 F2 **Bothal** Nthumb
48 D4 **Bothampstead** W Berk
134 D5 **Bothamsall** Notts
165 G3 **Bothel** Cumb
15 L4 **Bothenhampton** Dorset
209 J7 **Bothwell** S Lans
68 B6 **Botley** Bucks
35 G8 **Botley** Hants
66 C6 **Botley** Oxon
67 H2 **Botolph Claydon** Bucks
21 L5 **Botolphs** W Susx
40 F8 **Botolph's Bridge** Kent
117 L4 **Bottesford** Leics
143 M6 **Bottesford** N Linc
87 L3 **Bottisham** Cambs
222 F2 **Bottomcraig** Fife

138 F2 **Bottom of Hutton** Lancs
139 K5 **Bottom o' th' Moor** Bolton
140 D3 **Bottoms** Calder
2 B6 **Bottoms** Cnwll
99 H5 **Botts Green** Warwks
6 E3 **Botusfleming** Cnwll
108 D5 **Botwnnog** Gwynd
38 D4 **Bough Beech** Kent
79 G7 **Boughrood** Powys
63 H7 **Boughspring** Gloucs
84 E2 **Boughton** Nhants
104 D3 **Boughton** Norfk
134 D6 **Boughton** Notts
40 D6 **Boughton Aluph** Kent
85 J7 **Boughton End** C Beds
39 J3 **Boughton Green** Kent
39 M3 **Boughton Malherbe** Kent
39 J3 **Boughton Monchelsea** Kent
40 D3 **Boughton Street** Kent
171 H7 **Boulby** R & Cl
140 F3 **Boulder Clough** Calder
18 F5 **Bouldnor** IoW
96 C6 **Bouldon** Shrops
191 K3 **Boulmer** Nthumb
55 G4 **Boulston** Pembks
135 J6 **Boultham** Lincs
87 G4 **Bourn** Cambs
118 E7 **Bourne** Lincs
70 D8 **Bournebridge** Essex
98 D6 **Bournebrook** Birm
85 K3 **Bourne End** Bed
49 L2 **Bourne End** Bucks
85 J6 **Bourne End** C Beds
68 C6 **Bourne End** Herts
17 L4 **Bournemouth** Bmouth
17 M4 **Bournemouth Crematorium** Bmouth
64 C6 **Bournes Green** Gloucs
53 K2 **Bournes Green** Sthend
98 B8 **Bournheath** Worcs
63 L8 **Bournstream** Gloucs
98 D7 **Bournville** Birm
32 C5 **Bourton** Dorset
44 D6 **Bourton** N Som
47 K2 **Bourton** Oxon
96 D4 **Bourton** Shrops
46 F6 **Bourton** Wilts
83 K1 **Bourton on Dunsmore** Warwks
65 J1 **Bourton-on-the-Hill** Gloucs
65 H3 **Bourton-on-the-Water** Gloucs
225 H3 **Bousd** Ag & B
177 J7 **Boustead Hill** Cumb
156 D5 **Bouth** Cumb
149 L2 **Bouthwaite** N York
82 B3 **Bouts** Worcs
50 B3 **Boveney** Bucks
33 J7 **Boveridge** Dorset
13 J6 **Bovey Tracey** Devon
68 C6 **Bovingdon** Herts
49 K2 **Bovingdon Green** Bucks
70 D6 **Bovinger** Essex
16 F5 **Bovington** Dorset
16 F4 **Bovington Camp** Dorset
177 K7 **Bow** Cumb
8 B3 **Bow** Devon
13 G2 **Bow** Devon
51 K2 **Bow** Gt Lon
275 c6 **Bow** Ork
168 B6 **Bowbank** Dur
85 H8 **Bow Brickhill** M Keyn
64 B6 **Bowbridge** Gloucs
169 J3 **Bowburn** Dur
19 H6 **Bowcombe** IoW
14 D4 **Bowd** Devon
201 H7 **Bowden** Border
8 C5 **Bowden** Devon
46 D5 **Bowden Hill** Wilts
130 E2 **Bowdon** Traffd
280 B4 **Bower** Highld
45 H4 **Bower Ashton** Bristl
33 H6 **Bowerchalke** Wilts
46 C6 **Bowerhill** Wilts
31 G7 **Bower Hinton** Somset
89 K7 **Bower House Tye** Suffk
280 B3 **Bowermadden** Highld
114 C4 **Bowers** Staffs
53 G1 **Bowers Gifford** Essex
210 E1 **Bowershall** Fife
142 B2 **Bower's Row** Leeds
168 C7 **Bowes** Dur
147 K7 **Bowgreave** Lancs
176 D5 **Bowhouse** D & G
11 H6 **Bowithick** Cnwll
138 E6 **Bowker's Green** Lancs
200 F5 **Bowland** Border
156 F5 **Bowland Bridge** Cumb
140 C6 **Bowlee** Rochdl
80 C5 **Bowley** Herefs
80 C5 **Bowley Town** Herefs
36 D3 **Bowlhead Green** Surrey

141 J2 **Bowling** C Brad
208 D4 **Bowling** W Duns
112 F2 **Bowling Bank** Wrexhm
81 J5 **Bowling Green** Worcs
156 D3 **Bowmanstead** Cumb
204 D4 **Bowmore** Ag & B
177 H6 **Bowness-on-Solway** Cumb
156 F3 **Bowness-on-Windermere** Cumb
222 E4 **Bow of Fife** Fife
234 D6 **Bowriefauld** Angus
165 K4 **Bowscale** Cumb
202 F5 **Bowsden** Nthumb
157 H3 **Bowston** Cumb
92 D6 **Bow Street** Cerdgn
105 L4 **Bow Street** Norfk
106 D2 **Bowthorpe** Norfk
64 B7 **Box** Gloucs
46 B5 **Box** Wilts
63 K3 **Boxbush** Gloucs
63 L4 **Boxbush** Gloucs
85 K5 **Box End** Bed
89 K7 **Boxford** Suffk
48 B4 **Boxford** W Berk
20 E5 **Boxgrove** W Susx
51 G8 **Box Hill** Surrey
53 G7 **Boxley** Kent
68 D6 **Boxmoor** Herts
11 H2 **Box's Shop** Cnwll
72 E1 **Boxted** Essex
89 K8 **Boxted** Essex
89 G5 **Boxted** Suffk
72 E1 **Boxted Cross** Essex
64 A8 **Boxwell** Gloucs
87 G2 **Boxworth** Cambs
87 G2 **Boxworth End** Cambs
88 E4 **Boyden End** Suffk
41 H2 **Boyden Gate** Kent
115 K4 **Boylestone** Derbys
268 B3 **Boyndie** Abers
269 G4 **Boyndlie** Abers
153 J2 **Boynton** E R Yk
234 F5 **Boysack** Angus
16 C1 **Boys Hill** Dorset
133 G5 **Boythorpe** Derbys
11 L4 **Boyton** Cnwll
91 J6 **Boyton** Suffk
32 F3 **Boyton** Wilts
70 F5 **Boyton Cross** Essex
88 E6 **Boyton End** Suffk
85 H3 **Bozeat** Nhants
154 d6 **Braaid** IoM
91 G2 **Brabling Green** Suffk
40 E7 **Brabourne** Kent
40 E7 **Brabourne Lees** Kent
280 D2 **Brabstermire** Highld
246 E1 **Bracadale** Highld
102 B3 **Braceborough** Lincs
135 K6 **Bracebridge Heath** Lincs
135 J6 **Bracebridge Low Fields** Lincs
118 D4 **Braceby** Lincs
148 F6 **Bracewell** Lancs
133 G7 **Brackenfield** Derbys
209 K5 **Brackenhirst** N Lans
165 J1 **Brackenthwaite** Cumb
150 C5 **Brackenthwaite** N York
20 C7 **Bracklesham** W Susx
239 K7 **Brackletter** Highld
84 B7 **Brackley** Nhants
84 C7 **Brackley Hatch** Nhants
49 L5 **Bracknell** Br For
220 E5 **Braco** P & K
267 K5 **Bracobrae** Moray
106 D3 **Bracon Ash** Norfk
237 L2 **Bracora** Highld
237 L2 **Bracorina** Highld
11 M4 **Bradaford** Devon
115 K1 **Bradbourne** Derbys
169 J5 **Bradbury** Dur
84 C5 **Bradden** Nhants
5 K2 **Braddock** Cnwll
114 D1 **Bradeley** C Stke
67 K7 **Bradenham** Bucks
46 E3 **Bradenstoke** Wilts
14 B1 **Bradfield** Devon
73 H1 **Bradfield** Essex
122 F5 **Bradfield** Norfk
132 E1 **Bradfield** Sheff
48 F4 **Bradfield** W Berk
89 H4 **Bradfield Combust** Suffk
130 D7 **Bradfield Green** Ches E
73 H1 **Bradfield Heath** Essex
89 H4 **Bradfield St Clare** Suffk
89 H3 **Bradfield St George** Suffk
141 J1 **Bradford** C Brad
11 G7 **Bradford** Cnwll
12 A1 **Bradford** Devon
180 C2 **Bradford** Nthumb
203 J6 **Bradford** Nthumb
31 K8 **Bradford Abbas** Dorset

46 B6 **Bradford Leigh** Wilts
46 B6 **Bradford-on-Avon** Wilts
30 B6 **Bradford-on-Tone** Somset
16 C4 **Bradford Peverell** Dorset
27 K4 **Bradiford** Devon
19 K6 **Brading** IoW
115 L2 **Bradley** Derbys
35 K3 **Bradley** Hants
141 J4 **Bradley** Kirk
159 J6 **Bradley** N York
145 G6 **Bradley** NE Lin
114 D7 **Bradley** Staffs
98 B4 **Bradley** Wolves
82 A3 **Bradley** Worcs
112 E1 **Bradley** Wrexhm
113 H2 **Bradley Common** Ches W
30 C3 **Bradley Green** Somset
99 H3 **Bradley Green** Warwks
82 A3 **Bradley Green** Worcs
115 H3 **Bradley in the Moors** Staffs
45 J3 **Bradley Stoke** S Glos
117 G5 **Bradmore** Notts
30 E3 **Bradney** Somset
14 A2 **Bradninch** Devon
27 L4 **Bradninch** Devon
131 K8 **Bradnop** Staffs
79 K4 **Bradnor Green** Herefs
15 L4 **Bradpole** Dorset
139 L5 **Bradshaw** Bolton
141 G2 **Bradshaw** Calder
141 G5 **Bradshaw** Kirk
11 M6 **Bradstone** Devon
130 E7 **Bradwall Green** Ches E
132 C3 **Bradwell** Derbys
27 J2 **Bradwell** Devon
71 K3 **Bradwell** Essex
85 G7 **Bradwell** M Keyn
107 K3 **Bradwell** Norfk
114 D2 **Bradwell Crematorium** Staffs
72 E5 **Bradwell-on-Sea** Essex
72 E5 **Bradwell Waterside** Essex
26 E8 **Bradworthy** Devon
263 H7 **Brae** Highld
281 d4 **Brae** Shet
209 K3 **Braeface** Falk
235 H5 **Braehead** Angus
173 K4 **Braehead** D & G
198 F3 **Braehead** S Lans
243 G5 **Braemar** Abers
261 L4 **Braemore** Highld
274 E2 **Braemore** Highld
240 B5 **Brae Roy Lodge** Highld
207 L4 **Braeside** Inver
233 L4 **Braes of Coul** Angus
267 H4 **Braes of Enzie** Moray
275 e2 **Braeswick** Ork
216 E5 **Braevallich** Ag & B
169 H6 **Brafferton** Darltn
150 F2 **Brafferton** N York
84 F3 **Brafield-on-the-Green** Nhants
282 f2 **Bragar** W Isls
69 H3 **Bragbury End** Herts
198 D3 **Braidwood** S Lans
115 L3 **Brailsford** Derbys
115 L3 **Brailsford Green** Derbys
63 K5 **Brain's Green** Gloucs
71 J2 **Braintree** Essex
90 D1 **Braiseworth** Suffk
34 E6 **Braishfield** Hants
149 J7 **Braithwaite** C Brad
165 H6 **Braithwaite** Cumb
133 K1 **Braithwell** Donc
142 C4 **Braken Hill** Wakefd
21 L5 **Bramber** W Susx
35 G6 **Brambridge** Hants
116 E4 **Bramcote** Notts
99 L5 **Bramcote** Warwks
116 E4 **Bramcote Crematorium** Notts
35 J5 **Bramdean** Hants
106 F2 **Bramerton** Norfk
69 H4 **Bramfield** Herts
107 H8 **Bramfield** Suffk
90 D6 **Bramford** Suffk
131 H3 **Bramhall** Stockp
150 F7 **Bramham** Leeds
150 C7 **Bramhope** Leeds
49 G7 **Bramley** Hants
141 K1 **Bramley** Leeds
133 K1 **Bramley** Rothm
36 F2 **Bramley** Surrey
48 F7 **Bramley Corner** Hants
49 G7 **Bramley Green** Hants
149 L4 **Bramley Head** N York
41 H4 **Bramling** Kent
13 L3 **Brampford Speke** Devon
86 E1 **Brampton** Cambs
166 F6 **Brampton** Cumb
178 C6 **Brampton** Cumb
135 G4 **Brampton** Lincs
122 E6 **Brampton** Norfk

142 C7 **Brampton** Rothm
107 J7 **Brampton** Suffk
63 J2 **Brampton Abbotts** Herefs
101 H6 **Brampton Ash** Nhants
79 L1 **Brampton Bryan** Herefs
133 J2 **Brampton-en-le-Morthen** Rothm
115 H5 **Bramshall** Staffs
34 C7 **Bramshaw** Hants
49 H6 **Bramshill** Hants
36 C4 **Bramshott** Hants
31 G5 **Bramwell** Somset
237 G6 **Branault** Highld
121 G3 **Brancaster** Norfk
121 H3 **Brancaster Staithe** Norfk
169 G3 **Brancepeth** Dur
266 B5 **Branchill** Moray
119 L3 **Brand End** Lincs
266 E2 **Branderburgh** Moray
153 H6 **Brandesburton** E R Yk
90 F3 **Brandeston** Suffk
63 L2 **Brand Green** Gloucs
12 A2 **Brandis Corner** Devon
122 C7 **Brandiston** Norfk
169 G3 **Brandon** Dur
118 B2 **Brandon** Lincs
190 F3 **Brandon** Nthumb
104 F6 **Brandon** Suffk
99 L8 **Brandon** Warwks
104 C5 **Brandon Bank** Norfk
104 C5 **Brandon Creek** Norfk
106 B2 **Brandon Parva** Norfk
151 J1 **Brandsby** N York
144 C8 **Brandy Wharf** Lincs
2 B5 **Brane** Cnwll
71 G2 **Bran End** Essex
17 L4 **Branksome** Poole
17 L4 **Branksome Park** Poole
34 F2 **Bransbury** Hants
135 H4 **Bransby** Lincs
14 E5 **Branscombe** Devon
81 H5 **Bransford** Worcs
18 B4 **Bransgore** Hants
144 E1 **Bransholme** C KuH
96 E3 **Bransley** Shrops
82 C1 **Branson's Cross** Worcs
117 L5 **Branston** Leics
135 K6 **Branston** Lincs
115 L7 **Branston** Staffs
135 L6 **Branston Booths** Lincs
19 J7 **Branstone** IoW
118 B1 **Brant Broughton** Lincs
90 D8 **Brantham** Suffk
164 E5 **Branthwaite** Cumb
165 J3 **Branthwaite** Cumb
144 B2 **Brantingham** E R Yk
143 G7 **Branton** Donc
190 F3 **Branton** Nthumb
150 F3 **Branton Green** N York
202 D5 **Branxton** Nthumb
129 M7 **Brassey Green** Ches W
115 L1 **Brassington** Derbys
38 D2 **Brasted** Kent
51 M8 **Brasted Chart** Kent
244 F4 **Brathens** Abers
137 J6 **Bratoft** Lincs
135 J3 **Brattleby** Lincs
29 G2 **Bratton** Somset
46 C8 **Bratton** Wilts
96 E1 **Bratton** Wrekin
12 B4 **Bratton Clovelly** Devon
27 M3 **Bratton Fleming** Devon
31 L5 **Bratton Seymour** Somset
69 K2 **Braughing** Herts
70 B2 **Braughing Friars** Herts
83 M2 **Braunston** Nhants
101 H2 **Braunston** Rutlnd
100 C5 **Braunstone** Leics
27 J4 **Braunton** Devon
162 C7 **Brawby** N York
54 D2 **Brawdy** Pembks
278 D3 **Brawl** Highld
161 H1 **Braworth** N York
49 L3 **Bray** W & M
101 G6 **Braybrooke** Nhants
46 F1 **Braydon** Wilts
64 E8 **Braydon Brook** Wilts
46 E2 **Braydon Side** Wilts
28 B4 **Brayford** Devon
24 B4 **Bray's Hill** E Susx
11 L7 **Bray Shop** Cnwll
155 H2 **Braystones** Cumb
150 C6 **Braythorn** N York
142 F2 **Brayton** N York
49 L3 **Braywick** W & M
49 L4 **Braywoodside** W & M
11 K4 **Brazacott** Cnwll
41 G6 **Breach** Kent
53 H6 **Breach** Kent
68 F3 **Breachwood Green** Herts

113 G4 **Breaden Heath** Shrops
116 B4 **Breadsall** Derbys
63 L7 **Breadstone** Gloucs
79 K4 **Breadward** Herefs
3 G5 **Breage** Cnwll
250 E3 **Breakachy** Highld
50 D1 **Breakspear Crematorium** Gt Lon
262 F1 **Brealangwell Lodge** Highld
63 J6 **Bream** Gloucs
33 L7 **Breamore** Hants
44 C7 **Brean** Somset
282 d4 **Breanais** W Isls
140 F3 **Brearley** Calder
150 D4 **Brearton** N York
282 f3 **Breascleit** W Isls
282 f3 **Breasclete** W Isls
116 D5 **Breaston** Derbys
58 F3 **Brechfa** Carmth
234 F3 **Brechin** Angus
105 J4 **Breckles** Norfk
185 L5 **Breckonside** D & G
61 G2 **Brecon** Powys
131 H2 **Bredbury** Stockp
24 E4 **Brede** E Susx
80 E4 **Bredenbury** Herefs
91 G4 **Bredfield** Suffk
53 J7 **Bredgar** Kent
53 G6 **Bredhurst** Kent
81 L7 **Bredon** Worcs
81 L8 **Bredon's Hardwick** Worcs
81 L7 **Bredon's Norton** Worcs
79 L6 **Bredwardine** Herefs
116 C7 **Breedon on the Hill** Leics
210 C7 **Breich** W Loth
139 L6 **Breightmet** Bolton
143 H1 **Breighton** E R Yk
80 B7 **Breinton** Herefs
46 E4 **Bremhill** Wilts
28 B5 **Bremridge** Devon
39 H5 **Brenchley** Kent
11 L1 **Brendon** Devon
28 D1 **Brendon** Devon
29 J4 **Brendon Hill** Somset
206 D3 **Brenfield** Ag & B
282 d4 **Brenish** W Isls
80 F4 **Brenkley** N u Ty
89 J5 **Brent Eleigh** Suffk
50 F3 **Brentford** Gt Lon
117 K7 **Brentingby** Leics
30 E1 **Brent Knoll** Somset
7 K3 **Brent Mill** Devon
70 B1 **Brent Pelham** Herts
70 D2 **Brentwood** Essex
25 J2 **Brenzett** Kent
25 J2 **Brenzett Green** Kent
115 G8 **Brereton** Staffs
130 F6 **Brereton Green** Ches E
130 F6 **Brereton Heath** Ches E
115 G8 **Brereton Hill** Staffs
106 B7 **Bressingham** Norfk
106 B7 **Bressingham Common** Norfk
116 A7 **Bretby** Derbys
115 M7 **Bretby Crematorium** Derbys
99 L7 **Bretford** Warwks
82 C6 **Bretforton** Worcs
157 J2 **Bretherdale Head** Cumb
138 F4 **Bretherton** Lancs
281 e5 **Brettabister** Shet
105 J6 **Brettenham** Norfk
89 K4 **Brettenham** Suffk
132 D4 **Bretton** Derbys
129 H7 **Bretton** Flints
70 E3 **Brewers End** Essex
51 J8 **Brewer Street** Surrey
97 K2 **Brewood** Staffs
16 F4 **Briantspuddle** Dorset
70 E2 **Brick End** Essex
69 J5 **Brickendon** Herts
68 E6 **Bricket Wood** Herts
132 F3 **Brick Houses** Sheff
71 H1 **Brickkiln Green** Essex
82 A6 **Bricklehampton** Worcs
154 f2 **Bride** IoM
154 F4 **Bridekirk** Cumb
75 L4 **Bridell** Pembks
12 C4 **Bridestowe** Devon
255 M4 **Brideswell** Abers
3 J5 **Bridford** Devon
41 G4 **Bridge** Kent
156 A6 **Bridge End** Cumb
155 L1 **Bridge End** Cumb
7 K5 **Bridge End** Devon
148 C3 **Bridge End** Dur
71 G1 **Bridge End** Essex
103 F4 **Bridge End** Lincs
154 E5 **Bridgefoot** Cumb
57 K7 **Bridge Green** Essex
31 J6 **Bridgehampton** Somset
150 D2 **Bridge Hewick** N York

180 D8 **Bridgehill** Dur
149 L3 **Bridgehouse Gate** N York
19 K3 **Bridgemary** Hants
113 M2 **Bridgemere** Ches E
255 K4 **Bridgend** Abers
204 E4 **Bridgend** Ag & B
234 E2 **Bridgend** Angus
42 D5 **Bridgend** Brdgnd
75 L3 **Bridgend** Cerdgn
165 L7 **Bridgend** Cumb
187 G4 **Bridgend** D & G
7 G5 **Bridgend** Devon
223 G5 **Bridgend** Fife
255 H5 **Bridgend** Moray
221 L2 **Bridgend** P & K
210 D4 **Bridgend** W Loth
233 L4 **Bridgend of Lintrathen** Angus
255 L8 **Bridge of Alford** Abers
220 D7 **Bridge of Allan** Stirlg
254 C7 **Bridge of Avon** Moray
254 D4 **Bridge of Avon** Moray
231 G6 **Bridge of Balgie** P & K
233 J3 **Bridge of Brewlands** Angus
254 C7 **Bridge of Brown** Highld
233 H5 **Bridge of Cally** P & K
244 E4 **Bridge of Canny** Abers
233 K4 **Bridge of Craigisla** Angus
175 J3 **Bridge of Dee** D & G
245 L2 **Bridge of Don** C Aber
253 H3 **Bridge of Dulsie** Highld
244 E6 **Bridge of Dye** Abers
221 L3 **Bridge of Earn** P & K
230 F4 **Bridge of Ericht** P & K
244 F4 **Bridge of Feugh** Abers
279 J3 **Bridge of Forss** Highld
243 K4 **Bridge of Gairn** Abers
230 F4 **Bridge of Gaur** P & K
267 M6 **Bridge of Marnoch** Abers
230 B7 **Bridge of Orchy** Ag & B
232 C2 **Bridge of Tilt** P & K
267 H4 **Bridge of Tynet** Moray
281 c6 **Bridge of Walls** Shet
208 C6 **Bridge of Weir** Rens
28 B8 **Bridge Reeve** Devon
11 K2 **Bridgerule** Devon
95 J4 **Bridges** Shrops
80 A6 **Bridge Sollers** Herefs
89 H5 **Bridge Street** Suffk
11 L4 **Bridgetown** Cnwll
29 G4 **Bridgetown** Somset
129 K5 **Bridge Trafford** Ches W
45 K4 **Bridge Yate** S Glos
105 J6 **Bridgham** Norfk
97 G5 **Bridgnorth** Shrops
30 D3 **Bridgwater** Somset
153 K3 **Bridlington** E R Yk
15 K4 **Bridport** Dorset
68 H2 **Bridstow** Herefs
148 E8 **Brierfield** Lancs
142 B5 **Brierley** Barns
63 J4 **Brierley** Gloucs
80 C4 **Brierley** Herefs
97 L6 **Brierley Hill** Dudley
170 B5 **Brierton** Hartpl
165 J6 **Briery** Cumb
144 C6 **Brigg** N Linc
123 G6 **Briggate** Norfk
162 F1 **Briggswath** N York
164 E4 **Brigham** Cumb
165 J6 **Brigham** Cumb
153 H5 **Brigham** E R Yk
141 J3 **Brighouse** Calder
19 G7 **Brighstone** IoW
132 E7 **Brightgate** Derbys
66 A6 **Brighthampton** Oxon
132 F1 **Brightholmlee** Sheff
12 E3 **Brightley** Devon
24 C3 **Brightling** E Susx
73 G4 **Brightlingsea** Essex
22 D6 **Brighton** Br & H
4 E4 **Brighton** Cnwll
138 C7 **Brighton le Sands** Sefton
210 B3 **Brightons** Falk
48 B3 **Brightwalton** W Berk
48 B3 **Brightwalton Green** W Berk
48 B3 **Brightwalton Holt** W Berk
90 F6 **Brightwell** Suffk
67 G8 **Brightwell Baldwin** Oxon
48 E1 **Brightwell-cum-Sotwell** Oxon
67 G8 **Brightwell Upperton** Oxon
168 D8 **Brignall** Dur
219 J6 **Brig o'Turk** Stirlg
145 H7 **Brigsley** NE Lin
157 G5 **Brigsteer** Cumb
101 L6 **Brigstock** Nhants
67 G4 **Brill** Bucks
3 J5 **Brill** Cnwll
79 J5 **Brilley** Herefs
80 C2 **Brimfield** Herefs
80 C2 **Brimfield Cross** Herefs

133 H5 **Brimington** Derbys
13 J7 **Brimley** Devon
64 D4 **Brimpsfield** Gloucs
48 E6 **Brimpton** W Berk
48 E6 **Brimpton Common** W Berk
64 C6 **Brimscombe** Gloucs
129 G3 **Brimstage** Wirral
132 F3 **Brincliffe** Sheff
143 J2 **Brind** E R Yk
31 H3 **Brindham** Somset
281 c5 **Brindister** Shet
139 J3 **Brindle** Lancs
97 H1 **Brineton** Staffs
101 J5 **Bringhurst** Leics
81 G4 **Bringsty** Herefs
102 B8 **Brington** Cambs
122 A5 **Briningham** Norfk
117 J1 **Brinkely** Notts
137 G5 **Brinkhill** Lincs
88 C4 **Brinkley** Cambs
99 L7 **Brinklow** Warwks
46 E2 **Brinkworth** Wilts
139 J3 **Brinscall** Lancs
44 E8 **Brinscombe** Somset
44 F6 **Brinsea** N Som
116 D2 **Brinsley** Notts
80 B6 **Brinsop** Herefs
133 H2 **Brinsworth** Rothm
122 A4 **Brinton** Norfk
275 C3 **Brinyan** Ork
178 A8 **Brisco** Cumb
121 L7 **Brisley** Norfk
45 J5 **Brislington** Bristl
40 B7 **Brissenden Green** Kent
45 H4 **Bristol** Bristl
122 B5 **Briston** Norfk
7 G2 **Brisworthy** Devon
140 C3 **Britannia** Lancs
33 L5 **Britford** Wilts
61 J6 **Brithdir** Caerph
110 E7 **Brithdir** Gwynd
52 F7 **British Legion Village** Kent
57 K6 **Briton Ferry** Neath
67 G8 **Britwell Salome** Oxon
8 D4 **Brixham** Torbay
7 G4 **Brixton** Devon
51 J4 **Brixton** Gt Lon
32 E3 **Brixton Deverill** Wilts
84 E1 **Brixworth** Nhants
65 L5 **Brize Norton** Oxon
81 K2 **Broad Alley** Worcs
47 H1 **Broad Blunsdon** Swindn
131 K1 **Broadbottom** Tamesd
20 D6 **Broadbridge** W Susx
37 H4 **Broadbridge Heath** W Susx
82 E7 **Broad Campden** Gloucs
141 H4 **Broad Carr** Calder
33 H5 **Broad Chalke** Wilts
140 C3 **Broad Clough** Lancs
14 A3 **Broadclyst** Devon
208 B4 **Broadfield** Inver
55 K6 **Broadfield** Pembks
247 K4 **Bradford** Highld
39 H5 **Broad Ford** Kent
37 G6 **Broadford Bridge** W Susx
187 K4 **Broadgairhill** Border
89 K3 **Broadgrass Green** Suffk
88 D3 **Broad Green** Cambs
72 C2 **Broad Green** Essex
81 H4 **Broad Green** Worcs
82 A1 **Broad Green** Worcs
202 D2 **Broadhaugh** Border
54 D4 **Broad Haven** Pembks
130 E2 **Broadheath** Traffd
80 F2 **Broadheath** Worcs
14 C2 **Broadhembury** Devon
8 B2 **Broadhempston** Devon
104 B8 **Broad Hill** Cambs
47 G4 **Broad Hinton** Wilts
135 H5 **Broadholme** Lincs
24 F3 **Broadland Row** E Susx
56 C3 **Broadlay** Carmth
48 B6 **Broad Layings** Hants
70 B5 **Broadley** Essex
140 C4 **Broadley** Lancs
267 H4 **Broadley** Moray
70 B5 **Broadley Common** Essex
82 D6 **Broad Marston** Worcs
16 D5 **Broadmayne** Dorset
114 C2 **Broad Meadow** Staffs
35 J2 **Broadmere** Hants
63 J4 **Broadmoor** Gloucs
55 J5 **Broadmoor** Pembks
13 G2 **Broadnymett** Devon
155 K4 **Broad Oak** Cumb
15 K3 **Broadoak** Dorset
23 K3 **Broad Oak** E Susx
24 E3 **Broad Oak** E Susx
63 K4 **Broadoak** Gloucs
49 H8 **Broad Oak** Hants

62 F3 **Broad Oak** Herefs
41 G3 **Broad Oak** Kent
139 G8 **Broad Oak** St Hel
129 J7 **Broadoak** Wrexhm
106 F8 **Broad Road** Suffk
71 G4 **Broad's Green** Essex
41 L2 **Broadstairs** Kent
63 G6 **Broadstone** Mons
17 K3 **Broadstone** Poole
96 C5 **Broadstone** Shrops
24 F4 **Broad Street** E Susx
70 E4 **Broad Street** Essex
39 L2 **Broad Street** Kent
53 G4 **Broad Street** Medway
47 G7 **Broad Street** Wilts
72 B5 **Broad Street Green** Essex
47 G3 **Broad Town** Wilts
81 H4 **Broadwas** Worcs
69 H3 **Broadwater** Herts
21 K6 **Broadwater** W Susx
97 J7 **Broadwaters** Worcs
56 B3 **Broadway** Carmth
56 C3 **Broadway** Carmth
54 E4 **Broadway** Pembks
30 D7 **Broadway** Somset
107 H7 **Broadway** Suffk
82 C7 **Broadway** Worcs
63 H5 **Broadwell** Gloucs
65 J2 **Broadwell** Gloucs
65 K6 **Broadwell** Oxon
83 K2 **Broadwell** Warwks
16 C5 **Broadwey** Dorset
15 K2 **Broadwindsor** Dorset
12 E1 **Broadwood Kelly** Devon
12 A4 **Broadwoodwidger** Devon
79 L6 **Brobury** Herefs
259 K7 **Brochel** Highld
147 K7 **Brock** Lancs
81 H4 **Brockamin** Worcs
35 J7 **Brockbridge** Hants
106 E7 **Brockdish** Norfk
97 K8 **Brockencote** Worcs
18 D3 **Brockenhurst** Hants
198 D5 **Brocketsbrae** S Lans
90 D2 **Brockford Green** Suffk
90 D2 **Brockford Street** Suffk
84 C3 **Brockhall** Nhants
37 J1 **Brockham** Surrey
64 D2 **Brockhampton** Gloucs
64 F3 **Brockhampton** Gloucs
20 B5 **Brockhampton** Hants
63 H1 **Brockhampton** Herefs
16 D1 **Brockhampton Green** Dorset
141 J5 **Brockholes** Kirk
133 G6 **Brockhurst** Derbys
100 A6 **Brockhurst** Warwks
165 J2 **Brocklebank** Cumb
144 E5 **Brocklesby** Lincs
44 F5 **Brockley** N Som
89 G1 **Brockley** Suffk
88 E6 **Brockley Green** Suffk
89 G4 **Brockley Green** Suffk
166 C3 **Brockleymoor** Cumb
97 K5 **Brockmoor** Dudley
12 B3 **Brockscombe** Devon
48 D6 **Brock's Green** Hants
95 H3 **Brockton** Shrops
95 H6 **Brockton** Shrops
96 D4 **Brockton** Shrops
97 G3 **Brockton** Shrops
114 C5 **Brockton** Staffs
63 G6 **Brockweir** Gloucs
35 K5 **Brockwood Park** Hants
64 C4 **Brockworth** Gloucs
5 G1 **Brocton** Cnwll
114 F7 **Brocton** Staffs
195 G4 **Brodick** N Ayrs
264 F8 **Brodie** Moray
142 D6 **Brodsworth** Donc
259 H3 **Brogaig** Highld
85 J7 **Brogborough** C Beds
46 D1 **Brokenborough** Wilts
131 H5 **Broken Cross** Ches E
130 D5 **Broken Cross** Ches W
46 B8 **Brokerswood** Wilts
129 H3 **Bromborough** Wirral
106 C8 **Brome** Suffk
106 C8 **Brome Street** Suffk
91 G5 **Bromeswell** Suffk
165 L5 **Bromfield** Cumb
96 B8 **Bromfield** Shrops
85 K5 **Bromham** Bed
46 D6 **Bromham** Wilts
141 M7 **Bromley** Barns
97 K5 **Bromley** Dudley
51 L5 **Bromley** Gt Lon
97 G4 **Bromley** Shrops
51 L5 **Bromley Common** Gt Lon
72 F2 **Bromley Cross** Essex
40 C8 **Bromley Green** Kent

95 H3 **Bromlow** Shrops
53 G5 **Brompton** Medway
160 E3 **Brompton** N York
163 G6 **Brompton** N York
96 C2 **Brompton** Shrops
160 B3 **Brompton-on-Swale** N York
29 K4 **Brompton Ralph** Somset
29 G4 **Brompton Regis** Somset
63 J2 **Bromsash** Herefs
81 G8 **Bromsberrow** Gloucs
81 G8 **Bromsberrow Heath** Gloucs
81 M1 **Bromsgrove** Worcs
114 B8 **Bromstead Heath** Staffs
80 F4 **Bromyard** Herefs
80 F4 **Bromyard Downs** Herefs
110 D5 **Bronaber** Gwynd
77 H2 **Bronant** Cerdgn
96 C6 **Broncroft** Shrops
76 B6 **Brongest** Cerdgn
113 H3 **Bronington** Wrexhm
79 G8 **Bronllys** Powys
58 D4 **Bronwydd** Carmth
79 J6 **Bronydd** Powys
112 C4 **Brongarth** Shrops
127 G4 **Bron-y-Nant Crematorium**
Conwy
56 A3 **Brook** Carmth
34 C8 **Brook** Hants
34 D5 **Brook** Hants
18 F6 **Brook** IoW
40 E6 **Brook** Kent
36 D3 **Brook** Surrey
37 G2 **Brook** Surrey
106 F3 **Brooke** Norfk
101 J2 **Brooke** Rutlnd
145 G8 **Brookenby** Lincs
86 B3 **Brook End** Bed
86 D5 **Brook End** C Beds
86 B1 **Brook End** Cambs
85 H6 **Brook End** M Keyn
208 C6 **Brookfield** Rens
66 F7 **Brookhampton** Oxon
31 K5 **Brookhampton** Somset
34 C7 **Brook Hill** Hants
128 C6 **Brook House** Denbgs
147 K3 **Brookhouse** Lancs
133 K2 **Brookhouse** Rothm
130 F7 **Brookhouse Green** Ches E
131 K2 **Brookhouses** Derbys
25 J2 **Brookland** Kent
130 F2 **Brooklands** Traffd
69 H6 **Brookmans Park** Herts
94 E3 **Brooks** Powys
117 H8 **Brooksby** Leics
41 J2 **Brooks End** Kent
37 H6 **Brooks Green** W Susx
70 E8 **Brook Street** Essex
40 B8 **Brook Street** Kent
89 G5 **Brook Street** Suffk
22 D2 **Brook Street** W Susx
64 B4 **Brookthorpe** Gloucs
104 E4 **Brookville** Norfk
50 B7 **Brookwood** Surrey
86 D6 **Broom** C Beds
169 H2 **Broom** Dur
133 J1 **Broom** Rothm
82 C4 **Broom** Warwks
107 G5 **Broome** Norfk
95 K7 **Broome** Shrops
97 K7 **Broome** Worcs
130 D3 **Broomedge** Warrtn
191 G4 **Broome Park** Nthumb
21 K3 **Broomer's Corner** W Susx
21 H3 **Broomershill** W Susx
71 H5 **Broomfield** Essex
39 L3 **Broomfield** Kent
41 G2 **Broomfield** Kent
30 B4 **Broomfield** Somset
112 F7 **Broomfields** Shrops
143 M2 **Broomfleet** E R Yk
121 L6 **Broom Green** Norfk
50 B5 **Broomhall** W & M
180 B6 **Broomhaugh** Nthumb
142 C7 **Broom Hill** Barns
17 K2 **Broom Hill** Dorset
116 F2 **Broom Hill** Notts
191 J6 **Broomhill** Nthumb
97 L8 **Broom Hill** Worcs
113 K2 **Broomhill Green** Ches E
180 C6 **Broomley** Nthumb
81 G8 **Broom's Green** Gloucs
121 J6 **Broomsthorpe** Norfk
40 D3 **Broom Street** Kent
274 B7 **Brora** Highld
96 F3 **Broseley** Shrops
119 J8 **Brotherhouse Bar** Lincs
167 L3 **Brotherlee** Dur
119 J2 **Brothertoft** Lincs
142 D3 **Brotherton** N York
170 F6 **Brotton** R & Cl

279 J4 **Broubster** Highld
167 J7 **Brough** Cumb
132 D3 **Brough** Derbys
144 B2 **Brough** E R Yk
280 B2 **Brough** Highld
135 G7 **Brough** Notts
281 f5 **Brough** Shet
113 J3 **Broughall** Shrops
281 f3 **Brough Lodge** Shet
167 J8 **Brough Sowerby** Cumb
199 K6 **Broughton** Border
67 K4 **Broughton** Bucks
102 F7 **Broughton** Cambs
129 H7 **Broughton** Flints
34 C4 **Broughton** Hants
139 G1 **Broughton** Lancs
85 H7 **Broughton** M Keyn
144 B6 **Broughton** N Linc
149 G5 **Broughton** N York
162 D8 **Broughton** N York
101 H8 **Broughton** Nhants
83 K7 **Broughton** Oxon
140 B7 **Broughton** Salfd
114 B5 **Broughton** Staffs
42 D7 **Broughton** V Glam
100 C5 **Broughton Astley** Leics
156 C6 **Broughton Beck** Cumb
46 C6 **Broughton Gifford** Wilts
81 M3 **Broughton Green** Worcs
81 L4 **Broughton Hackett** Worcs
156 B5 **Broughton-in-Furness** Cumb
174 C6 **Broughton Mains** D & G
156 B4 **Broughton Mills** Cumb
164 E4 **Broughton Moor** Cumb
65 K6 **Broughton Poggs** Oxon
156 B5 **Broughton Tower** Cumb
223 H1 **Broughty Ferry** C Dund
156 C7 **Brow End** Cumb
158 B2 **Brownber** Cumb
35 J3 **Brown Candover** Hants
138 D5 **Brown Edge** Lancs
114 E1 **Brown Edge** Staffs
129 K6 **Brown Heath** Ches W
113 G5 **Brownheath** Shrops
256 F4 **Brownhill** Abers
223 J4 **Brownhills** Fife
98 D2 **Brownhills** Wsall
191 H2 **Brownieside** Nthumb
48 E7 **Browninghill Green** Hants
131 G8 **Brown Lees** Staffs
131 G7 **Brownlow Heath** Ches E
164 D6 **Brownrigg** Cumb
177 G8 **Brownrigg** Cumb
98 D5 **Brown's Green** Birm
26 E5 **Brownsham** Devon
64 C6 **Browns Hill** Gloucs
100 B7 **Brownsover** Warwks
7 K4 **Brownston** Devon
90 C3 **Brown Street** Suffk
120 E7 **Brow-of-the-Hill** Norfk
107 K3 **Browston Green** Norfk
163 G4 **Broxa** N York
69 K5 **Broxbourne** Herts
212 F3 **Broxburn** E Loth
210 E4 **Broxburn** W Loth
191 J3 **Broxfield** Nthumb
70 E2 **Broxted** Essex
113 H1 **Broxton** Ches W
23 G4 **Broyle Side** E Susx
280 D8 **Bruan** Highld
232 B2 **Bruar** P & K
264 E3 **Brucefield** Highld
207 J7 **Bruchag** Ag & B
129 K7 **Bruera** Ches W
65 K3 **Bruern Abbey** Oxon
204 C4 **Bruichladdich** Ag & B
91 H2 **Bruisyard** Suffk
91 H2 **Bruisyard Street** Suffk
143 M6 **Brumby** N Linc
132 B7 **Brund** Staffs
107 G2 **Brundall** Norfk
91 G1 **Brundish** Suffk
91 G1 **Brundish Street** Suffk
237 L6 **Brunery** Highld
2 D4 **Brunnion** Cnwll
95 J6 **Brunslow** Shrops
180 F4 **Brunswick Village** N u Ty
141 L2 **Bruntcliffe** Leeds
149 J6 **Brunthwaite** C Brad
100 D5 **Bruntingthorpe** Leics
222 E3 **Brunton** Fife
191 J1 **Brunton** Nthumb
47 K7 **Brunton** Wilts
29 G5 **Brushford** Somset
12 F1 **Brushford Barton** Devon
31 L4 **Bruton** Somset
81 K2 **Bryan's Green** Worcs
17 G1 **Bryanston** Dorset
67 L7 **Bryant's Bottom** Bucks
177 G5 **Brydekirk** D & G

112 D1 **Brymbo** Wrexhm
31 H7 **Brympton** Somset
57 G5 **Bryn** Carmth
130 B5 **Bryn** Ches W
42 B3 **Bryn** Neath
95 H6 **Bryn** Shrops
139 H7 **Bryn** Wigan
59 K6 **Brynamman** Carmth
75 J5 **Brynberian** Pembks
57 L6 **Brynbryddan** Neath
110 B4 **Bryn-bwbach** Gwynd
42 F5 **Bryncae** Rhondd
42 D5 **Bryncethin** Brdgnd
109 H3 **Bryncir** Gwynd
57 K5 **Bryn-coch** Neath
108 C5 **Bryncroes** Gwynd
92 D3 **Bryncrug** Gwynd
124 F5 **Bryn Du** IoA
110 D5 **Bryn-Eden** Gwynd
112 A2 **Bryneglwys** Denbgs
112 D3 **Brynfields** Wrexhm
128 E5 **Brynford** Flints
139 J7 **Bryn Gates** Wigan
42 F4 **Bryn Golau** Rhondd
124 F4 **Bryngwran** IoA
62 D5 **Bryngwyn** Mons
79 H5 **Bryngwyn** Powys
75 G4 **Bryn-Henllan** Pembks
76 B5 **Brynhoffnant** Cerdgn
138 E2 **Bryning** Lancs
61 K6 **Brynithel** Blae G
61 J5 **Brynmawr** Blae G
108 D5 **Bryn-mawr** Gwynd
42 D5 **Brynmenyn** Brdgnd
57 H6 **Brynmill** Swans
42 F5 **Brynna** Rhondd
94 D3 **Bryn-penarth** Powys
125 K7 **Brynrefail** Gwynd
125 H2 **Brynrefail** IoA
42 F5 **Brynsadler** Rhondd
111 L2 **Bryn Saith Marchog** Denbgs
125 H6 **Brynsiencyn** IoA
125 J3 **Brynteg** IoA
128 F6 **Bryn-y-bal** Flints
127 G4 **Bryn-y-Maen** Conwy
112 D3 **Bryn-yr-Eos** Wrexhm
246 F4 **Bualintur** Highld
128 E4 **Buarth-draw** Flints
83 J1 **Bubbenhall** Warwks
151 M8 **Bubwith** E R Yk
188 B3 **Buccleuch** Border
208 D1 **Buchanan Smithy** Stirlg
269 L6 **Buchanhaven** Abers
221 G2 **Buchanty** P & K
220 C6 **Buchany** Stirlg
219 J8 **Buchlyvie** Stirlg
165 L1 **Buckabank** Cumb
86 D2 **Buckden** Cambs
159 G7 **Buckden** N York
107 G2 **Buckenham** Norfk
14 D2 **Buckerell** Devon
7 L2 **Buckfast** Devon
7 L2 **Buckfastleigh** Devon
222 F7 **Buckhaven** Fife
63 G4 **Buckholt** Mons
32 C6 **Buckhorn Weston** Dorset
69 L8 **Buckhurst Hill** Essex
267 J3 **Buckie** Moray
84 D8 **Buckingham** Bucks
67 L4 **Buckland** Bucks
7 K6 **Buckland** Devon
82 C8 **Buckland** Gloucs
18 E4 **Buckland** Hants
87 G8 **Buckland** Herts
41 J6 **Buckland** Kent
65 M7 **Buckland** Oxon
37 K1 **Buckland** Surrey
27 G6 **Buckland Brewer** Devon
68 A5 **Buckland Common** Bucks
32 C1 **Buckland Dinham** Somset
12 B1 **Buckland Filleigh** Devon
13 G7 **Buckland in the Moor** Devon
6 F1 **Buckland Monachorum** Devon
16 D2 **Buckland Newton** Dorset
16 C6 **Buckland Ripers** Dorset
30 C8 **Buckland St Mary** Somset
7 L5 **Buckland-Tout-Saints** Devon
48 E5 **Bucklebury** W Berk
18 F4 **Bucklers Hard** Hants
90 F6 **Bucklesham** Suffk
129 G7 **Buckley** Flints
82 E2 **Buckley Green** Warwks
130 E3 **Bucklow Hill** Ches E
118 A7 **Buckminster** Leics
114 E2 **Bucknall** C Stke
136 C6 **Bucknall** Lincs
66 E2 **Bucknell** Oxon
95 J8 **Bucknell** Shrops
267 H3 **Buckpool** Moray
245 K2 **Bucksburn** C Aber

26 F6 **Buck's Cross** Devon
37 G4 **Bucks Green** W Susx
139 H4 **Buckshaw Village** Lancs
68 D7 **Bucks Hill** Herts
36 B3 **Bucks Horn Oak** Hants
26 F6 **Buck's Mills** Devon
153 K1 **Buckton** E R Yk
95 J8 **Buckton** Herefs
203 H5 **Buckton** Nthumb
102 C8 **Buckworth** Cambs
134 C5 **Budby** Notts
114 B2 **Buddileigh** Staffs
223 J1 **Buddon** Angus
11 H1 **Bude** Cnwll
6 C3 **Budge's Shop** Cnwll
14 A2 **Budlake** Devon
203 J6 **Budle** Nthumb
14 C6 **Budleigh Salterton** Devon
23 H3 **Budlett's Common** E Susx
3 K5 **Budock Water** Cnwll
113 L3 **Buerton** Ches E
84 D4 **Bugbrooke** Nhants
8 B5 **Bugford** Devon
131 G7 **Buglawton** Ches E
5 G3 **Bugle** Cnwll
32 C6 **Bugley** Dorset
152 B4 **Bugthorpe** E R Yk
96 E2 **Buildwas** Shrops
78 E4 **Builth Road** Powys
78 E5 **Builth Wells** Powys
68 B4 **Bulbourne** Herts
33 J5 **Bulbridge** Wilts
118 D6 **Bulby** Lincs
33 L2 **Bulford** Wilts
33 L2 **Bulford Camp** Wilts
113 J1 **Bulkeley** Ches E
99 K6 **Bulkington** Warwks
46 D7 **Bulkington** Wilts
27 G8 **Bulkworthy** Devon
160 F4 **Bullamoor** N York
125 G1 **Bull Bay** IoA
116 B1 **Bullbridge** Derbys
49 L5 **Bullbrook** Br For
69 G6 **Bullen's Green** Herts
63 M3 **Bulley** Gloucs
164 E3 **Bullgill** Cumb
80 C7 **Bullinghope** Herefs
34 F3 **Bullington** Hants
136 A4 **Bullington** Lincs
84 F6 **Bullington End** M Keyn
41 G2 **Bullockstone** Kent
69 H4 **Bull's Green** Herts
107 J4 **Bull's Green** Norfk
89 G7 **Bulmer** Essex
151 L2 **Bulmer** N York
89 G7 **Bulmer Tye** Essex
52 D2 **Bulphan** Thurr
14 E4 **Bulstone** Devon
68 C6 **Bulstrode** Herts
24 D5 **Bulverhythe** E Susx
257 G3 **Bulwark** Abers
116 F3 **Bulwell** C Nott
101 L4 **Bulwick** Nhants
69 L6 **Bumble's Green** Essex
237 J3 **Bunacaimb** Highld
239 K6 **Bunarkaig** Highld
130 A8 **Bunbury** Ches E
130 A8 **Bunbury Heath** Ches E
251 H3 **Bunchrew** Highld
21 K4 **Buncton** W Susx
248 E6 **Bundalloch** Highld
226 D8 **Bunessan** Ag & B
107 G5 **Bungay** Suffk
119 J1 **Bunker's Hill** Lincs
204 F2 **Bunnahabhain** Ag & B
117 G5 **Bunny** Notts
250 C5 **Buntait** Highld
69 K1 **Buntingford** Herts
106 C4 **Bunwell** Norfk
106 C5 **Bunwell Hill** Norfk
115 L4 **Bupton** Derbys
131 L6 **Burbage** Derbys
99 L5 **Burbage** Leics
47 K6 **Burbage** Wilts
79 L3 **Burcher** Herefs
39 G7 **Burchett's Green** E Susx
49 K3 **Burchett's Green** W & M
33 J5 **Burcombe** Wilts
66 E7 **Burcot** Oxon
82 A1 **Burcot** Worcs
97 G4 **Burcote** Shrops
67 K4 **Burcott** Bucks
67 L2 **Burcott** Bucks
152 D3 **Burdale** N York
89 H8 **Bures** Essex
65 K5 **Burford** Oxon
80 D2 **Burford** Shrops
226 D3 **Burg** Ag & B
106 B8 **Burgate** Suffk
36 A5 **Burgates** Hants

| | |
|---|---|
| 68 F1 | **Burge End** Herts |
| 22 E3 | **Burgess Hill** W Susx |
| 90 F5 | **Burgh** Suffk |
| 177 K7 | **Burgh by Sands** Cumb |
| 107 K2 | **Burgh Castle** Norfk |
| 48 C6 | **Burghclere** Hants |
| 266 C2 | **Burghead** Moray |
| 49 G5 | **Burghfield** W Berk |
| 49 G5 | **Burghfield Common** W Berk |
| 51 H7 | **Burgh Heath** Surrey |
| 24 C2 | **Burgh Hill** E Susx |
| 80 B6 | **Burghill** Herefs |
| 137 J6 | **Burgh le Marsh** Lincs |
| 122 E6 | **Burgh next Aylsham** Norfk |
| 136 D2 | **Burgh on Bain** Lincs |
| 123 J8 | **Burgh St Margaret** Norfk |
| 107 K5 | **Burgh St Peter** Norfk |
| 142 E5 | **Burghwallis** Donc |
| 52 F6 | **Burham** Kent |
| 20 B3 | **Buriton** Hants |
| 113 K1 | **Burland** Ches E |
| 10 D8 | **Burlawn** Cnwll |
| 64 C6 | **Burleigh** Gloucs |
| 29 K7 | **Burlescombe** Devon |
| 16 E3 | **Burleston** Dorset |
| 8 B5 | **Burlestone** Devon |
| 18 C3 | **Burley** Hants |
| 101 J1 | **Burley** Rutlnd |
| 96 B7 | **Burley** Shrops |
| 113 K3 | **Burleydam** Ches E |
| 80 E6 | **Burley Gate** Herefs |
| 149 L6 | **Burley in Wharfedale** C Brad |
| 18 C3 | **Burley Lawn** Hants |
| 18 B3 | **Burley Street** Hants |
| 149 L7 | **Burley Wood Head** C Brad |
| 107 H1 | **Burlingham Green** Norfk |
| 79 J4 | **Burlingjobb** Powys |
| 97 H1 | **Burlington** Shrops |
| 113 G6 | **Burlton** Shrops |
| 25 L1 | **Burmarsh** Kent |
| 83 G7 | **Burmington** Warwks |
| 142 F2 | **Burn** N York |
| 131 G1 | **Burnage** Manch |
| 115 M5 | **Burnaston** Derbys |
| 166 C7 | **Burnbanks** Cumb |
| 210 A7 | **Burnbrae** N Lans |
| 152 C6 | **Burnby** E R Yk |
| 142 A8 | **Burn Cross** Sheff |
| 21 G6 | **Burndell** W Susx |
| 139 L6 | **Burnden** Bolton |
| 140 D5 | **Burnedge** Rochdl |
| 157 H3 | **Burneside** Cumb |
| 160 D5 | **Burneston** N York |
| 45 K6 | **Burnett** BaNES |
| 188 C4 | **Burnfoot** Border |
| 188 F3 | **Burnfoot** Border |
| 177 K1 | **Burnfoot** D & G |
| 186 E7 | **Burnfoot** D & G |
| 188 C6 | **Burnfoot** D & G |
| 221 H6 | **Burnfoot** P & K |
| 50 A3 | **Burnham** Bucks |
| 144 D4 | **Burnham** N Linc |
| 121 H3 | **Burnham Deepdale** Norfk |
| 69 H4 | **Burnham Green** Herts |
| 121 H3 | **Burnham Market** Norfk |
| 121 H3 | **Burnham Norton** Norfk |
| 72 D7 | **Burnham-on-Crouch** Essex |
| 30 D1 | **Burnham-on-Sea** Somset |
| 121 J3 | **Burnham Overy** Norfk |
| 121 J3 | **Burnham Overy Staithe** Norfk |
| 121 J3 | **Burnham Thorpe** Norfk |
| 257 L3 | **Burnhaven** Abers |
| 186 C7 | **Burnhead** D & G |
| 256 C7 | **Burnhervie** Abers |
| 97 H3 | **Burnhill Green** Staffs |
| 169 G1 | **Burnhope** Dur |
| 96 D1 | **Burnhouse** N Ayrs |
| 163 H4 | **Burniston** N York |
| 140 C1 | **Burnley** Lancs |
| 140 B2 | **Burnley Crematorium** Lancs |
| 181 H8 | **Burnmoor** Dur |
| 213 L6 | **Burnmouth** Border |
| 147 G7 | **Burn Naze** Lancs |
| 220 C6 | **Burn of Cambus** Stirlg |
| 180 E7 | **Burnopfield** Dur |
| 78 C7 | **Burnrigg** Cumb |
| 149 J3 | **Burnsall** N York |
| 234 C3 | **Burnside** Angus |
| 234 D5 | **Burnside** Angus |
| 222 B5 | **Burnside** Fife |
| 266 D2 | **Burnside** Moray |
| 210 E4 | **Burnside** W Loth |
| 234 C8 | **Burnside of Duntrune** Angus |
| 50 D8 | **Burntcommon** Surrey |
| 115 L5 | **Burntheath** Derbys |
| 72 F2 | **Burnt Heath** Essex |
| 48 E4 | **Burnt Hill** W Berk |
| 3 K4 | **Burnthouse** Cnwll |
| 168 E6 | **Burnt Houses** Dur |

| | |
|---|---|
| 211 H2 | **Burntisland** Fife |
| 23 H2 | **Burnt Oak** E Susx |
| 98 D2 | **Burntwood** Staffs |
| 98 D2 | **Burntwood Green** Staffs |
| 150 C4 | **Burnt Yates** N York |
| 30 B7 | **Burnworthy** Somset |
| 50 C8 | **Burpham** Surrey |
| 21 H5 | **Burpham** W Susx |
| 181 G4 | **Burradon** N Tyne |
| 190 D5 | **Burradon** Nthumb |
| 281 f1 | **Burrafirth** Shet |
| 3 H4 | **Burras** Cnwll |
| 6 E2 | **Burraton** Cnwll |
| 281 e4 | **Burravoe** Shet |
| 166 F7 | **Burrells** Cumb |
| 233 J7 | **Burrelton** P & K |
| 15 H1 | **Burridge** Devon |
| 27 K4 | **Burridge** Devon |
| 19 J2 | **Burridge** Hants |
| 160 C5 | **Burrill** N York |
| 143 L6 | **Burringham** N Linc |
| 27 L7 | **Burrington** Devon |
| 80 B1 | **Burrington** Herefs |
| 44 F7 | **Burrington** N Som |
| 88 C4 | **Burrough End** Cambs |
| 88 C4 | **Burrough Green** Cambs |
| 101 G1 | **Burrough on the Hill** Leics |
| 157 K7 | **Burrow** Lancs |
| 29 G2 | **Burrow** Somset |
| 30 E5 | **Burrow Bridge** Somset |
| 50 B6 | **Burrowhill** Surrey |
| 37 G2 | **Burrows Cross** Surrey |
| 56 E6 | **Burry** Swans |
| 56 E6 | **Burry Green** Swans |
| 56 E5 | **Burry Port** Carmth |
| 138 E5 | **Burscough** Lancs |
| 138 F5 | **Burscough Bridge** Lancs |
| 143 K1 | **Bursea** E R Yk |
| 153 H6 | **Burshill** E R Yk |
| 19 H2 | **Bursledon** Hants |
| 114 D2 | **Burslem** C Stke |
| 90 C6 | **Burstall** Suffk |
| 15 K2 | **Burstock** Dorset |
| 106 C6 | **Burston** Norfk |
| 114 E5 | **Burston** Staffs |
| 37 M3 | **Burstow** Surrey |
| 145 G2 | **Burstwick** E R Yk |
| 158 F5 | **Burtersett** N York |
| 178 D6 | **Burtholme** Cumb |
| 88 F2 | **Burthorpe Green** Suffk |
| 165 M1 | **Burthwaite** Cumb |
| 4 E4 | **Burthy** Cnwll |
| 30 F2 | **Burtle Hill** Somset |
| 119 J4 | **Burtoft** Lincs |
| 129 H5 | **Burton** Ches W |
| 129 L7 | **Burton** Ches W |
| 16 D4 | **Burton** Dorset |
| 18 B5 | **Burton** Dorset |
| 135 J5 | **Burton** Lincs |
| 203 K6 | **Burton** Nthumb |
| 55 G5 | **Burton** Pembks |
| 30 B2 | **Burton** Somset |
| 31 H8 | **Burton** Somset |
| 32 D4 | **Burton** Wilts |
| 46 B3 | **Burton** Wilts |
| 153 H3 | **Burton Agnes** E R Yk |
| 15 L4 | **Burton Bradstock** Dorset |
| 118 C6 | **Burton Coggles** Lincs |
| 83 J5 | **Burton Dassett** Warwks |
| 70 D2 | **Burton End** Essex |
| 88 D6 | **Burton End** Suffk |
| 153 H2 | **Burton Fleming** E R Yk |
| 99 H8 | **Burton Green** Warwks |
| 129 H7 | **Burton Green** Wrexhm |
| 99 L5 | **Burton Hastings** Warwks |
| 157 H7 | **Burton-in-Kendal** Cumb |
| 148 A2 | **Burton in Lonsdale** N York |
| 117 H3 | **Burton Joyce** Notts |
| 101 K8 | **Burton Latimer** Nhants |
| 117 K8 | **Burton Lazars** Leics |
| 150 D3 | **Burton Leonard** N York |
| 117 G7 | **Burton on the Wolds** Leics |
| 100 E4 | **Burton Overy** Leics |
| 118 F3 | **Burton Pedwardine** Lincs |
| 145 H2 | **Burton Pidsea** E R Yk |
| 142 D2 | **Burton Salmon** N York |
| 71 K2 | **Burton's Green** Essex |
| 143 L4 | **Burton upon Stather** N Linc |
| 115 L6 | **Burton upon Trent** Staffs |
| 135 J5 | **Burton Waters** Lincs |
| 130 A1 | **Burtonwood** Warrtn |
| 129 L8 | **Burwardsley** Ches W |
| 96 E6 | **Burwarton** Shrops |
| 24 B2 | **Burwash** E Susx |
| 23 L3 | **Burwash Common** E Susx |
| 23 L3 | **Burwash Weald** E Susx |
| 88 B2 | **Burwell** Cambs |
| 137 G4 | **Burwell** Lincs |
| 125 G1 | **Burwen** IoA |

| | |
|---|---|
| 275 C6 | **Burwick** Ork |
| 140 B5 | **Bury** Bury |
| 102 F6 | **Bury** Cambs |
| 29 G4 | **Bury** Somset |
| 21 G4 | **Bury** W Susx |
| 86 C8 | **Bury End** C Beds |
| 70 C3 | **Bury Green** Herts |
| 89 G2 | **Bury St Edmunds** Suffk |
| 152 B3 | **Burythorpe** N York |
| 208 F7 | **Busby** E Rens |
| 160 E6 | **Busby Stoop** N York |
| 65 J7 | **Buscot** Oxon |
| 235 J2 | **Bush** Abers |
| 11 J1 | **Bush** Cnwll |
| 80 B5 | **Bush Bank** Herefs |
| 97 L3 | **Bushbury** Wolves |
| 97 L3 | **Bushbury Crematorium** Wolves |
| 100 E3 | **Bushby** Leics |
| 68 E8 | **Bushey** Herts |
| 68 F8 | **Bushey Heath** Herts |
| 106 E6 | **Bush Green** Norfk |
| 89 H4 | **Bush Green** Suffk |
| 69 J7 | **Bush Hill Park** Gt Lon |
| 81 K8 | **Bushley** Worcs |
| 81 K8 | **Bushley Green** Worcs |
| 86 C3 | **Bushmead** Bed |
| 46 F3 | **Bushton** Wilts |
| 166 E2 | **Busk** Cumb |
| 135 M3 | **Buslingthorpe** Lincs |
| 64 C6 | **Bussage** Gloucs |
| 30 E4 | **Bussex** Somset |
| 140 D3 | **Butcher Hill** Calder |
| 23 J2 | **Butcher's Cross** E Susx |
| 45 G6 | **Butcombe** N Som |
| 31 H4 | **Butleigh** Somset |
| 31 H4 | **Butleigh Wootton** Somset |
| 67 K5 | **Butler's Cross** Bucks |
| 116 F2 | **Butler's Hill** Notts |
| 83 H5 | **Butlers Marston** Warwks |
| 91 J5 | **Butley** Suffk |
| 91 J5 | **Butley High Corner** Suffk |
| 151 M4 | **Buttercrambe** N York |
| 213 H6 | **Butterdean** Border |
| 168 E5 | **Butterknowle** Dur |
| 14 A1 | **Butterleigh** Devon |
| 116 C1 | **Butterley** Derbys |
| 165 G7 | **Buttermere** Cumb |
| 47 M6 | **Buttermere** Wilts |
| 114 C2 | **Butters Green** Staffs |
| 141 H2 | **Buttershaw** C Brad |
| 233 G6 | **Butterstone** P & K |
| 114 C3 | **Butterton** Staffs |
| 131 L8 | **Butterton** Staffs |
| 169 K5 | **Butterwick** Dur |
| 119 L3 | **Butterwick** Lincs |
| 152 F2 | **Butterwick** N York |
| 162 C7 | **Butterwick** N York |
| 113 L1 | **Butt Green** Ches E |
| 95 G2 | **Buttington** Powys |
| 97 G7 | **Buttonbridge** Shrops |
| 97 G7 | **Buttonoak** Shrops |
| 19 G2 | **Buttsash** Hants |
| 11 K2 | **Buttsbear Cross** Cnwll |
| 71 J6 | **Butt's Green** Essex |
| 89 K4 | **Buxhall** Suffk |
| 89 K3 | **Buxhall Fen Street** Suffk |
| 23 H3 | **Buxted** E Susx |
| 131 L5 | **Buxton** Derbys |
| 122 E7 | **Buxton** Norfk |
| 122 D7 | **Buxton Heath** Norfk |
| 61 J3 | **Bwlch** Powys |
| 112 C1 | **Bwlchgwyn** Wrexhm |
| 77 G3 | **Bwlchllan** Cerdgn |
| 58 C4 | **Bwlchnewydd** Carmth |
| 108 E6 | **Bwlchtocyn** Gwynd |
| 112 B8 | **Bwlch-y-cibau** Powys |
| 112 B7 | **Bwlch-y-Ddar** Powys |
| 76 D5 | **Bwlchyfadfa** Cerdgn |
| 94 C4 | **Bwlch-y-ffridd** Powys |
| 75 M5 | **Bwlch-y-groes** Pembks |
| 57 G5 | **Bwlchymyrdd** Swans |
| 94 B8 | **Bwlch-y-sarnau** Powys |
| 180 F7 | **Byermoor** Gatesd |
| 169 G4 | **Byers Green** Dur |
| 83 M4 | **Byfield** Nhants |
| 50 D6 | **Byfleet** Surrey |
| 79 M6 | **Byford** Herefs |
| 86 F7 | **Bygrave** Herts |
| 181 G6 | **Byker** N u Ty |
| 161 J6 | **Byland Abbey** N York |
| 127 K7 | **Bylchau** Conwy |
| 130 E6 | **Byley** Ches W |
| 57 G5 | **Bynea** Carmth |
| 189 K5 | **Byrness** Nthumb |
| 14 B5 | **Bystock** Devon |
| 102 B8 | **Bythorn** Cambs |
| 79 L2 | **Byton** Herefs |
| 180 C6 | **Bywell** Nthumb |
| 36 E6 | **Byworth** W Susx |

**C**

| | |
|---|---|
| 27 G6 | **Cabbacott** Devon |
| 144 E7 | **Cabourne** Lincs |
| 205 H3 | **Cabrach** Ag & B |
| 255 H6 | **Cabrach** Moray |
| 147 J6 | **Cabus** Lancs |
| 23 G2 | **Cackle Street** E Susx |
| 24 C3 | **Cackle Street** E Susx |
| 24 E3 | **Cackle Street** E Susx |
| 13 L2 | **Cadbury** Devon |
| 28 B7 | **Cadbury Barton** Devon |
| 209 G4 | **Cadder** E Duns |
| 68 D3 | **Caddington** C Beds |
| 200 F6 | **Caddonfoot** Border |
| 142 E7 | **Cadeby** Donc |
| 99 L3 | **Cadeby** Leics |
| 13 L1 | **Cadeleigh** Devon |
| 23 K3 | **Cade Street** E Susx |
| 3 J8 | **Cadgwith** Cnwll |
| 222 D6 | **Cadham** Fife |
| 130 D1 | **Cadishead** Salfd |
| 57 H5 | **Cadle** Swans |
| 139 G2 | **Cadley** Lancs |
| 47 J5 | **Cadley** Wilts |
| 47 K8 | **Cadley** Wilts |
| 67 J8 | **Cadmore End** Bucks |
| 34 C8 | **Cadnam** Hants |
| 144 C7 | **Cadney** N Linc |
| 128 E7 | **Cadole** Flints |
| 43 H7 | **Cadoxton** V Glam |
| 57 L5 | **Cadoxton Juxta-Neath** Neath |
| 111 K4 | **Cadwst** Denbgs |
| 125 J7 | **Caeathro** Gwynd |
| 59 M6 | **Caehopkin** Powys |
| 135 K2 | **Caenby** Lincs |
| 77 J7 | **Caeo** Carmth |
| 42 C3 | **Caerau** Brdgnd |
| 43 H6 | **Caerau** Cardif |
| 59 M6 | **Cae'r-bont** Powys |
| 59 H6 | **Cae'r bryn** Carmth |
| 110 C7 | **Caerdeon** Gwynd |
| 74 C6 | **Caer Farchell** Pembks |
| 124 E4 | **Caergeiliog** IoA |
| 129 G8 | **Caergwrle** Flints |
| 126 F5 | **Caerhun** Conwy |
| 188 C5 | **Caerlanrig** Border |
| 44 D1 | **Caerleon** Newpt |
| 125 H7 | **Caernarfon** Gwynd |
| 43 J4 | **Caerphilly** Caerph |
| 94 B5 | **Caersws** Powys |
| 76 C4 | **Caerwedros** Cerdgn |
| 44 F1 | **Caerwent** Mons |
| 128 D5 | **Caerwys** Flints |
| 110 E8 | **Caerynwch** Gwynd |
| 62 D4 | **Caggle Street** Mons |
| 126 C3 | **Caim** IoA |
| 283 C8 | **Cairinis** W Isls |
| 206 C1 | **Cairnbaan** Ag & B |
| 269 J3 | **Cairnbulg** Abers |
| 213 K6 | **Cairncross** Border |
| 208 A5 | **Cairncurran** Inver |
| 217 K5 | **Cairndow** Ag & B |
| 210 D2 | **Cairneyhill** Fife |
| 267 H4 | **Cairnfield House** Moray |
| 172 C5 | **Cairngarroch** D & G |
| 255 K3 | **Cairnie** Abers |
| 256 F3 | **Cairnorrie** Abers |
| 172 D1 | **Cairnryan** D & G |
| 267 G5 | **Cairnty** Moray |
| 107 L1 | **Caister-on-Sea** Norfk |
| 144 E7 | **Caistor** Lincs |
| 106 E3 | **Caistor St Edmund** Norfk |
| 81 K1 | **Cakebole** Worcs |
| 106 B5 | **Cake Street** Norfk |
| 89 K7 | **Calais Street** Suffk |
| 282 f3 | **Calanais** W Isls |
| 19 G6 | **Calbourne** IoW |
| 137 G4 | **Calceby** Lincs |
| 128 E5 | **Calcot** Flints |
| 65 G5 | **Calcot** Gloucs |
| 49 G4 | **Calcot** W Berk |
| 49 G4 | **Calcot Row** W Berk |
| 266 E3 | **Calcots** Moray |
| 41 G3 | **Calcott** Kent |
| 113 G8 | **Calcott** Shrops |
| 150 E4 | **Calcutt** N York |
| 65 G8 | **Calcutt** Wilts |
| 165 K3 | **Caldbeck** Cumb |
| 159 K5 | **Caldbergh** N York |
| 87 G4 | **Caldecote** Cambs |
| 102 C5 | **Caldecote** Cambs |
| 86 E7 | **Caldecote** Herts |
| 84 D5 | **Caldecote** Nhants |
| 87 G3 | **Caldecote Highfields** Cambs |
| 85 K2 | **Caldecott** Nhants |
| 66 D7 | **Caldecott** Oxon |
| 101 J4 | **Caldecott** Rutlnd |
| 85 H8 | **Caldecotte** M Keyn |

155 J2 **Calder** Cumb
209 K6 **Calderbank** N Lans
155 J2 **Calder Bridge** Cumb
140 E4 **Calderbrook** Rochdl
209 L5 **Caldercruix** N Lans
141 M4 **Calder Grove** Wakefd
197 J3 **Caldermill** S Lans
140 D4 **Caldermore** Rochdl
147 K6 **Calder Vale** Lancs
209 H7 **Calderwood** S Lans
44 F1 **Caldicot** Mons
98 C4 **Caldmore** Wsall
168 F8 **Caldwell** N York
128 F3 **Caldy** Wirral
59 J4 **Caledfwlch** Carmth
4 D6 **Calenick** Cnwll
88 D6 **Calford Green** Suffk
275 d2 **Calfsound** Ork
226 D2 **Calgary** Ag & B
265 H8 **Califer** Moray
210 B4 **California** Falk
123 K8 **California** Norfk
7 K4 **California Cross** Devon
116 B7 **Calke** Derbys
259 M5 **Callakille** Highld
219 K5 **Callander** Stirlg
282 f3 **Callanish** W Isls
96 E4 **Callaughton** Shrops
4 C5 **Callestick** Cnwll
247 K7 **Calligarry** Highld
6 D1 **Callington** Cnwll
115 K6 **Callingwood** Staffs
80 C8 **Callow** Herefs
81 J5 **Callow End** Worcs
46 F2 **Callow Hill** Wilts
82 B2 **Callow Hill** Worcs
97 G8 **Callow Hill** Worcs
80 D2 **Callows Grave** Worcs
34 D7 **Calmore** Hants
64 F5 **Calmsden** Gloucs
46 E5 **Calne** Wilts
133 H5 **Calow** Derbys
19 H3 **Calshot** Hants
6 E1 **Calstock** Cnwll
46 F5 **Calstone Wellington** Wilts
122 D5 **Calthorpe** Norfk
123 H6 **Calthorpe Street** Norfk
166 B3 **Calthwaite** Cumb
148 F4 **Calton** N York
115 H2 **Calton** Staffs
130 B7 **Calveley** Ches E
132 E5 **Calver** Derbys
113 K4 **Calverhall** Shrops
79 L5 **Calver Hill** Herefs
29 G8 **Calverleigh** Devon
150 B8 **Calverley** Leeds
132 E5 **Calver Sough** Derbys
67 G2 **Calvert** Bucks
84 F7 **Calverton** M Keyn
117 G2 **Calverton** Notts
232 B2 **Calvine** P & K
176 F8 **Calvo** Cumb
199 K6 **Calzeat** Border
63 M7 **Cam** Gloucs
228 B3 **Camasachoirce** Highld
237 L8 **Camasine** Highld
248 F6 **Camas Luinie** Highld
247 L2 **Camastianavaig** Highld
250 E4 **Camault Muir** Highld
25 H3 **Camber** E Susx
49 L6 **Camberley** Surrey
51 J4 **Camberwell** Gt Lon
143 G3 **Camblesforth** N York
180 B2 **Cambo** Nthumb
181 H2 **Cambois** Nthumb
3 G3 **Camborne** Cnwll
87 G3 **Cambourne** Cambs
87 J3 **Cambridge** Cambs
63 L6 **Cambridge** Gloucs
87 H3 **Cambridge City Crematorium** Cambs
4 A5 **Cambrose** Cnwll
220 E8 **Cambus** Clacks
263 L1 **Cambusavie Platform** Highld
220 D8 **Cambusbarron** Stirlg
220 D8 **Cambuskenneth** Stirlg
209 H7 **Cambuslang** S Lans
243 M4 **Cambus o' May** Abers
199 H5 **Cambuswallace** S Lans
51 H2 **Camden Town** Gt Lon
45 J7 **Cameley** BaNES
10 F5 **Camelford** Cnwll
209 M3 **Camelon** Falk
253 K5 **Camerory** Highld
81 H8 **Camer's Green** Worcs
45 K7 **Camerton** BaNES
164 D4 **Camerton** Cumb
231 G4 **Camghouran** P & K
201 J7 **Camieston** Border
245 K4 **Cammachmore** Abers

135 J3 **Cammeringham** Lincs
263 L2 **Camore** Highld
192 E4 **Campbeltown** Ag & B
181 G4 **Camperdown** N Tyne
186 D7 **Cample** D & G
233 K7 **Campmuir** P & K
210 E5 **Camps** W Loth
142 E5 **Campsall** Donc
91 H4 **Campsea Ash** Suffk
88 C6 **Camps End** Cambs
86 C7 **Campton** C Beds
189 J4 **Camptown** Border
54 F3 **Camrose** Pembks
232 B5 **Camserney** P & K
239 H8 **Camusnagaul** Highld
261 H2 **Camusnagaul** Highld
248 A3 **Camusteel** Highld
248 A3 **Camusterrach** Highld
34 C7 **Canada** Hants
156 D7 **Canal Foot** Cumb
55 H4 **Canaston Bridge** Pembks
243 K4 **Candacraig** Abers
137 H6 **Candlesby** Lincs
105 L8 **Candle Street** Suffk
96 C2 **Candover Green** Shrops
199 J5 **Candy Mill** Border
49 G3 **Cane End** Oxon
72 C8 **Canewdon** Essex
17 K2 **Canford Bottom** Dorset
17 L4 **Canford Cliffs** Poole
45 H3 **Canford Crematorium** Bristl
17 K4 **Canford Heath** Poole
17 K3 **Canford Magna** Poole
90 C2 **Canhams Green** Suffk
280 D2 **Canisbay** Highld
133 H2 **Canklow** Rothm
99 J7 **Canley** Covtry
99 J8 **Canley Crematorium** Covtry
32 E6 **Cann** Dorset
250 B5 **Cannich** Highld
30 C3 **Cannington** Somset
51 L3 **Canning Town** Gt Lon
98 B2 **Cannock** Staffs
98 D1 **Cannock Wood** Staffs
80 A7 **Cannon Bridge** Herefs
177 L4 **Canonbie** D & G
80 F6 **Canon Frome** Herefs
80 B5 **Canon Pyon** Herefs
84 B5 **Canons Ashby** Nhants
2 E4 **Canonstown** Cnwll
40 F4 **Canterbury** Kent
107 H3 **Cantley** Norfk
96 C2 **Cantlop** Shrops
43 J6 **Canton** Cardif
252 E2 **Cantraywood** Highld
147 M1 **Cantsfield** Lancs
53 G2 **Canvey Island** Essex
135 K6 **Canwick** Lincs
11 J4 **Canworthy Water** Cnwll
239 J8 **Caol** Highld
282 f6 **Caolas Scalpaigh** W Isls
224 D5 **Caoles** Ag & B
239 H5 **Caonich** Highld
39 G4 **Capel** Kent
37 J3 **Capel** Surrey
92 E7 **Capel Bangor** Cerdgn
77 H4 **Capel Betws Lleucu** Cerdgn
125 H3 **Capel Coch** IoA
126 E8 **Capel Curig** Conwy
76 C5 **Capel Cynon** Cerdgn
58 E5 **Capel Dewi** Carmth
76 E6 **Capel Dewi** Cerdgn
92 D7 **Capel-Dewi** Cerdgn
127 G8 **Capel Garmon** Conwy
91 J5 **Capel Green** Suffk
58 E4 **Capel Gwyn** Carmth
124 F4 **Capel Gwyn** IoA
59 K4 **Capel Gwynfe** Carmth
59 G6 **Capel Hendre** Carmth
59 G3 **Capel Isaac** Carmth
58 B2 **Capel Iwan** Carmth
41 H7 **Capel le Ferne** Kent
9 j2 **Capelles** Guern
43 H5 **Capel Llanilltern** Cardif
125 G5 **Capel Mawr** IoA
125 H2 **Capel Parc** IoA
91 J5 **Capel St Andrew** Suffk
90 C7 **Capel St Mary** Suffk
92 D7 **Capel Seion** Cerdgn
92 F8 **Capel Trisant** Cerdgn
109 H2 **Capeluchaf** Gwynd
126 E4 **Capelulo** Conwy
61 L1 **Capel-y-ffin** Powys
125 K6 **Capel-y-graig** Gwynd
129 J5 **Capenhurst** Ches W
147 K2 **Capernwray** Lancs
180 C3 **Capheaton** Nthumb
208 D7 **Caplaw** E Rens
91 G2 **Capon's Green** Suffk
187 K2 **Cappercleuch** Border

53 G6 **Capstone** Medway
8 C4 **Capton** Devon
29 K3 **Capton** Somset
233 G7 **Caputh** P & K
11 K8 **Caradon Town** Cnwll
208 E3 **Carbeth Inn** Stirlg
5 G3 **Carbis** Cnwll
2 E3 **Carbis Bay** Cnwll
246 E2 **Carbost** Highld
259 G7 **Carbost** Highld
133 G2 **Carbrook** Sheff
105 J3 **Carbrooke** Norfk
134 C5 **Carburton** Notts
5 H4 **Carclaze** Cnwll
3 K3 **Carclew** Cnwll
117 J3 **Car Colston** Notts
142 E6 **Carcroft** Donc
222 C8 **Cardenden** Fife
95 J1 **Cardeston** Shrops
177 K8 **Cardewlees** Cumb
254 D3 **Cardhu** Moray
43 J6 **Cardiff** Cardif
75 L3 **Cardigan** Cerdgn
88 C6 **Cardinal's Green** Cambs
86 B5 **Cardington** Bed
96 C4 **Cardington** Shrops
5 J1 **Cardinham** Cnwll
172 E8 **Cardrain** D & G
200 C5 **Cardrona** Border
208 B3 **Cardross** Ag & B
172 E8 **Cardryne** D & G
177 G7 **Cardurnock** Cumb
118 D8 **Careby** Lincs
234 E3 **Careston** Angus
55 H6 **Carew** Pembks
55 H6 **Carew Cheriton** Pembks
55 H6 **Carew Newton** Pembks
63 H1 **Carey** Herefs
209 K7 **Carfin** N Lans
201 G2 **Carfraemill** Border
107 H1 **Cargate Green** Norfk
176 C4 **Cargenbridge** D & G
233 H8 **Cargill** P & K
177 L7 **Cargo** Cumb
6 E2 **Cargreen** Cnwll
3 M4 **Cargurrel** Cnwll
202 B5 **Carham** Nthumb
29 H2 **Carhampton** Somset
3 J3 **Carharrack** Cnwll
231 H4 **Carie** P & K
283 c8 **Carinish** W Isls
19 H6 **Carisbrooke** IoW
156 E7 **Cark** Cumb
6 E3 **Carkeel** Cnwll
282 e2 **Carlabhagh** W Isls
4 D4 **Carland Cross** Cnwll
169 G7 **Carlbury** Darltn
102 A1 **Carlby** Lincs
190 B4 **Carlcroft** Nthumb
141 J7 **Carlecotes** Barns
3 G5 **Carleen** Cnwll
160 B7 **Carlesmoor** N York
155 J1 **Carleton** Cumb
166 C5 **Carleton** Cumb
178 A8 **Carleton** Cumb
146 F7 **Carleton** Lancs
149 H6 **Carleton** N York
142 D4 **Carleton** Wakefd
146 F7 **Carleton Crematorium** Bpool
106 B2 **Carleton Forehoe** Norfk
106 C5 **Carleton Rode** Norfk
107 G3 **Carleton St Peter** Norfk
3 K5 **Carlidnack** Cnwll
256 B3 **Carlincraig** Abers
45 K7 **Carlingcott** BaNES
171 G6 **Carlin How** R & Cl
177 L7 **Carlisle** Cumb
177 L8 **Carlisle Crematorium** Cumb
4 E2 **Carloggas** Cnwll
199 K2 **Carlops** Border
282 e2 **Carloway** W Isls
142 B5 **Carlton** Barns
85 J4 **Carlton** Bed
88 C4 **Carlton** Cambs
142 A2 **Carlton** Leeds
99 L2 **Carlton** Leics
143 G3 **Carlton** N York
159 J5 **Carlton** N York
161 K5 **Carlton** N York
117 G3 **Carlton** Notts
169 K6 **Carlton** S on T
91 J2 **Carlton** Suffk
107 K5 **Carlton Colville** Suffk
100 F4 **Carlton Curlieu** Leics
88 C5 **Carlton Green** Cambs
161 H7 **Carlton Husthwaite** N York
161 H2 **Carlton-in-Cleveland** N York
134 B3 **Carlton in Lindrick** Notts
135 H8 **Carlton-le-Moorland** Lincs
160 F6 **Carlton Miniott** N York

134 F7 **Carlton-on-Trent** Notts
118 B3 **Carlton Scroop** Lincs
198 D3 **Carluke** S Lans
5 H4 **Carlyon Bay** Cnwll
198 C7 **Carmacoup** S Lans
58 D5 **Carmarthen** Carmth
59 G5 **Carmel** Carmth
128 E4 **Carmel** Flints
125 J8 **Carmel** Gwynd
198 F5 **Carmichael** S Lans
114 E2 **Carmountside Crematorium** C Stke
209 G7 **Carmunnock** C Glas
209 H6 **Carmyle** C Glas
234 E6 **Carmyllie** Angus
153 J3 **Carnaby** E R Yk
223 J6 **Carnbee** Fife
221 J6 **Carnbo** P & K
3 H3 **Carn Brea** Cnwll
256 F6 **Carnbrogie** Abers
248 E6 **Carndu** Highld
197 J2 **Carnduff** S Lans
3 K6 **Carne** Cnwll
4 E7 **Carne** Cnwll
4 F3 **Carne** Cnwll
196 F4 **Carnell** E Ayrs
4 D1 **Carnewas** Cnwll
147 K2 **Carnforth** Lancs
248 F7 **Carn-gorm** Highld
74 C6 **Carnhedryn** Pembks
3 G4 **Carnhell Green** Cnwll
245 H2 **Carnie** Abers
3 H3 **Carnkie** Cnwll
3 H4 **Carnkie** Cnwll
4 C4 **Carnkiet** Cnwll
93 L4 **Carno** Powys
238 D4 **Carnoch** Highld
210 D1 **Carnock** Fife
3 K3 **Carnon Downs** Cnwll
268 B6 **Carnousie** Abers
234 E8 **Carnoustie** Angus
5 G3 **Carnsmerry** Cnwll
199 G4 **Carnwath** S Lans
2 B4 **Carnyorth** Cnwll
99 H7 **Carol Green** Solhll
4 F4 **Carpalla** Cnwll
159 H5 **Carperby** N York
140 B4 **Carr** Bury
133 K2 **Carr** Rothm
194 C3 **Carradale** Ag & B
253 G7 **Carrbridge** Highld
140 E7 **Carrbrook** Tamesd
9 c2 **Carrefour** Jersey
125 G2 **Carreglefn** IoA
141 M3 **Carr Gate** Wakefd
143 K6 **Carrhouse** N Linc
206 E2 **Carrick** Ag & B
217 K8 **Carrick Castle** Ag & B
210 D3 **Carriden** Falk
136 F8 **Carrington** Lincs
211 K7 **Carrington** Mdloth
130 C1 **Carrington** Traffd
110 E2 **Carrog** Conwy
111 L3 **Carrog** Denbgs
210 A3 **Carron** Falk
254 E3 **Carron** Moray
186 C6 **Carronbridge** D & G
209 K2 **Carron Bridge** Stirlg
210 A2 **Carronshore** Falk
44 E1 **Carrow Hill** Mons
167 J1 **Carr Shield** Nthumb
176 E4 **Carrutherstown** D & G
208 B6 **Carruth House** Inver
133 J5 **Carr Vale** Derbys
169 J2 **Carrville** Dur
227 G8 **Carsaig** Ag & B
234 C4 **Carse Gray** Angus
173 H1 **Carseriggan** D & G
176 C7 **Carsethorn** D & G
51 H6 **Carshalton** Gt Lon
115 L1 **Carsington** Derbys
192 D6 **Carskey** Ag & B
174 D4 **Carsluith** D & G
184 E4 **Carsphairn** D & G
198 F4 **Carstairs** S Lans
198 F4 **Carstairs Junction** S Lans
65 L7 **Carswell Marsh** Oxon
34 C6 **Carter's Clay** Hants
70 D5 **Carters Green** Essex
65 L5 **Carterton** Oxon
180 C8 **Carterway Heads** Nthumb
5 G4 **Carthew** Cnwll
160 D6 **Carthorpe** N York
190 E5 **Cartington** Nthumb
198 E4 **Cartland** S Lans
132 F4 **Cartledge** Derbys
156 E7 **Cartmel** Cumb
156 F5 **Cartmel Fell** Cumb
56 E3 **Carway** Carmth
177 L4 **Carwinley** Cumb

Cashe's Green - Charmouth 301


64 B6 **Cashe's Green** Gloucs
33 G8 **Cashmoor** Dorset
66 C5 **Cassington** Oxon
169 K3 **Cassop Colliery** Dur
2 C6 **Castallack** Cnwll
9 j3 **Castel** Guern
126 F6 **Castell** Conwy
62 B8 **Castell-y-bwch** Torfn
157 K6 **Casterton** Cumb
5 J3 **Castle** Cnwll
121 H8 **Castle Acre** Norfk
85 G3 **Castle Ashby** Nhants
283 b13 **Castlebay** W Isls
159 J4 **Castle Bolton** N York
98 F5 **Castle Bromwich** Solhll
118 C7 **Castle Bytham** Lincs
75 H6 **Castlebythe** Pembks
94 E2 **Castle Caereinion** Powys
88 C6 **Castle Camps** Cambs
178 D7 **Castle Carrock** Cumb
209 L3 **Castlecary** Falk
31 L4 **Castle Cary** Somset
46 B3 **Castle Combe** Wilts
116 D6 **Castle Donington** Leics
175 J2 **Castle Douglas** D & G
65 H7 **Castle Eaton** Swindn
169 L3 **Castle Eden** Dur
102 C2 **Castle End** C Pete
142 C3 **Castleford** Wakefd
80 F6 **Castle Frome** Herefs
2 D4 **Castle Gate** Cnwll
157 H4 **Castle Green** Cumb
50 B6 **Castle Green** Surrey
115 M7 **Castle Gresley** Derbys
88 F8 **Castle Hedingham** Essex
200 B6 **Castlehill** Border
280 B3 **Castlehill** Highld
39 H5 **Castle Hill** Kent
90 D6 **Castle Hill** Suffk
208 C4 **Castlehill** W Duns
172 D3 **Castle Kennedy** D & G
217 G8 **Castle Lachlan** Ag & B
54 E7 **Castlemartin** Pembks
209 G7 **Castlemilk** C Glas
74 E6 **Castle Morris** Pembks
81 H7 **Castlemorton** Worcs
187 K7 **Castle O'er** D & G
95 K3 **Castle Pulverbatch** Shrops
120 E6 **Castle Rising** Norfk
168 D1 **Castleside** Dur
140 E3 **Castle Street** Calder
252 D2 **Castle Stuart** Highld
84 F6 **Castlethorpe** M Keyn
144 B6 **Castlethorpe** N Linc
188 E8 **Castleton** Border
132 C3 **Castleton** Derbys
162 B1 **Castleton** N York
43 L5 **Castleton** Newpt
140 C5 **Castleton** Rochdl
16 D7 **Castletown** Dorset
280 A3 **Castletown** Highld
154 c8 **Castletown** IoM
181 J7 **Castletown** Sundld
150 C6 **Castley** N York
105 J4 **Caston** Norfk
102 C4 **Castor** C Pete
57 G7 **Caswell Bay** Swans
194 E1 **Catacol** N Ayrs
131 K5 **Cat and Fiddle** Derbys
45 H3 **Catbrain** S Glos
63 G6 **Catbrook** Mons
128 F5 **Catch** Flints
2 C5 **Catchall** Cnwll
99 H8 **Catchem's Corner** Solhll
180 E8 **Catchgate** Dur
133 H2 **Catcliffe** Rothm
46 E4 **Catcomb** Wilts
30 F3 **Catcott** Somset
30 F2 **Catcott Burtle** Somset
51 J7 **Caterham** Surrey
123 H7 **Catfield** Norfk
123 H7 **Catfield Common** Norfk
51 K4 **Catford** Gt Lon
138 F1 **Catforth** Lancs
209 G7 **Cathcart** C Glas
61 J2 **Cathedine** Powys
98 F7 **Catherine-de-Barnes** Solhll
141 G2 **Catherine Slack** C Brad
35 L8 **Catherington** Hants
15 J3 **Catherston Leweston** Dorset
96 E7 **Catherton** Shrops
19 J2 **Catisfield** Hants
80 F6 **Catley** Herefs
140 C4 **Catley Lane Head** Rochdl
241 H5 **Catlodge** Highld
148 F8 **Catlow** Lancs
178 B3 **Catlowdy** Cumb
87 K7 **Catmere End** Essex
48 C3 **Catmore** W Berk
13 H8 **Caton** Devon
147 K3 **Caton** Lancs
147 L3 **Caton Green** Lancs
13 G7 **Cator Court** Devon
197 G6 **Catrine** E Ayrs
44 D1 **Cat's Ash** Newpt
24 C4 **Catsfield** E Susx
24 C4 **Catsfield Stream** E Susx
31 H5 **Catsgore** Somset
31 J4 **Catsham** Somset
98 B8 **Catshill** Worcs
97 G4 **Catstree** Shrops
192 D6 **Cattadale** Ag & B
150 F5 **Cattal** N York
90 C8 **Cattawade** Suffk
147 K7 **Catterall** Lancs
113 J3 **Catteralslane** Shrops
160 C3 **Catterick** N York
160 B3 **Catterick Bridge** N York
160 B3 **Catterick Garrison** N York
166 B4 **Catterlen** Cumb
245 J7 **Catterline** Abers
151 H6 **Catterton** N York
36 E2 **Catteshall** Surrey
100 C7 **Catthorpe** Leics
89 H2 **Cattishall** Suffk
16 B3 **Cattistock** Dorset
160 E7 **Catton** N York
106 E1 **Catton** Norfk
179 J7 **Catton** Nthumb
153 J6 **Catwick** E R Yk
86 B1 **Catworth** Cambs
64 D5 **Caudle Green** Gloucs
85 K6 **Caulcott** C Beds
66 D2 **Caulcott** Oxon
235 G6 **Cauldcots** Angus
219 L8 **Cauldhame** Stirlg
188 F3 **Cauldmill** Border
115 H2 **Cauldon** Staffs
115 H2 **Cauldon Lowe** Staffs
115 L8 **Cauldwell** Derbys
176 B7 **Caulkerbush** D & G
178 B3 **Caulside** D & G
31 L8 **Caundle Marsh** Dorset
97 J7 **Caunsall** Worcs
134 E7 **Caunton** Notts
35 M6 **Causeway** Hants
157 G5 **Causeway End** Cumb
173 K3 **Causeway End** D & G
71 G3 **Causeway End** Essex
199 H6 **Causewayend** S Lans
176 F8 **Causewayhead** Cumb
220 D8 **Causewayhead** Stirlg
257 H7 **Causeyend** Abers
191 H7 **Causey Park** Nthumb
191 H7 **Causey Park Bridge** Nthumb
88 F6 **Cavendish** Suffk
88 F1 **Cavenham** Suffk
66 E2 **Caversfield** Oxon
49 H4 **Caversham** Readg
114 F3 **Caverswall** Staffs
202 A7 **Caverton Mill** Border
143 J2 **Cavil** E R Yk
252 F2 **Cawdor** Highld
136 E4 **Cawkwell** Lincs
151 J8 **Cawood** N York
6 E5 **Cawsand** Cnwll
122 C6 **Cawston** Norfk
100 A8 **Cawston** Warwks
162 D5 **Cawthorn** N York
141 L6 **Cawthorne** Barns
161 K7 **Cawton** N York
86 F3 **Caxton** Cambs
87 G4 **Caxton End** Cambs
86 F3 **Caxton Gibbet** Cambs
80 D1 **Caynham** Shrops
118 B2 **Caythorpe** Lincs
117 J2 **Caythorpe** Notts
163 J6 **Cayton** N York
283 b8 **Ceann a Bhaigh** W Isls
239 L1 **Ceannacroc Lodge** Highld
282 f4 **Cearsiadar** W Isls
63 G6 **Ceciliford** Mons
44 B1 **Cefn** Newpt
127 K6 **Cefn Berain** Conwy
111 H2 **Cefn-brith** Conwy
59 K6 **Cefn-bryn-brain** Carmth
60 C5 **Cefn Byrle** Powys
112 C5 **Cefn Canel** Powys
111 L6 **Cefn Coch** Powys
60 F5 **Cefn-coed-y-cymmer** Myr Td
42 C5 **Cefn Cribwr** Brdgnd
42 C5 **Cefn Cross** Brdgnd
111 J4 **Cefn-ddwysarn** Gwynd
95 G6 **Cefn-Einion** Shrops
59 G6 **Cefneithin** Carmth
78 B6 **Cefngorwydd** Powys
43 K5 **Cefn Mably** Caerph
112 D3 **Cefn-mawr** Wrexhm
61 G7 **Cefnpennar** Rhondd
129 H8 **Cefn-y-bedd** Flints
75 L7 **Cefn-y-pant** Carmth
125 J4 **Ceint** IoA
77 H5 **Cellan** Cerdgn
223 K6 **Cellardyke** Fife
114 F2 **Cellarhead** Staffs
166 C5 **Celleron** Cumb
43 K3 **Celynen** Caerph
124 F1 **Cemaes** IoA
93 H2 **Cemmaes** Powys
93 H3 **Cemmaes Road** Powys
76 A7 **Cenarth** Cerdgn
74 D6 **Cerbyd** Pembks
223 G5 **Ceres** Fife
16 C2 **Cerne Abbas** Dorset
65 G7 **Cerney Wick** Gloucs
125 G5 **Cerrigceinwen** IoA
111 J2 **Cerrigydrudion** Conwy
123 J7 **Cess** Norfk
125 J7 **Ceunant** Gwynd
64 B1 **Chaceley** Gloucs
4 B6 **Chacewater** Cnwll
84 D8 **Chackmore** Bucks
83 L6 **Chacombe** Nhants
82 B6 **Chadbury** Worcs
140 D6 **Chadderton** Oldham
140 D6 **Chadderton Fold** Oldham
116 C4 **Chaddesden** C Derb
97 K8 **Chaddesley Corbett** Worcs
12 B6 **Chaddlehanger** Devon
48 B3 **Chaddleworth** W Berk
65 M3 **Chadlington** Oxon
83 H4 **Chadshunt** Warwks
117 K6 **Chadwell** Leics
114 B8 **Chadwell** Shrops
86 B2 **Chadwell End** Bed
52 A1 **Chadwell Heath** Gt Lon
52 E3 **Chadwell St Mary** Thurr
81 J2 **Chadwick** Worcs
82 F1 **Chadwick End** Solhll
139 G7 **Chadwick Green** St Hel
15 H1 **Chaffcombe** Somset
52 D3 **Chafford Hundred** Thurr
13 G5 **Chagford** Devon
22 F3 **Chailey** E Susx
103 J3 **Chainbridge** Cambs
39 J4 **Chainhurst** Kent
17 K1 **Chalbury** Dorset
17 K1 **Chalbury Common** Dorset
51 J7 **Chaldon** Surrey
19 H8 **Chale** IoW
19 H7 **Chale Green** IoW
68 C8 **Chalfont Common** Bucks
68 C8 **Chalfont St Giles** Bucks
50 C1 **Chalfont St Peter** Bucks
64 C6 **Chalford** Gloucs
67 H7 **Chalford** Oxon
32 E1 **Chalford** Wilts
68 C2 **Chalgrave** C Beds
66 F7 **Chalgrove** Oxon
52 E4 **Chalk** Kent
70 F5 **Chalk End** Essex
49 H3 **Chalkhouse Green** Oxon
15 J1 **Chalkway** Somset
53 J6 **Chalkwell** Kent
7 J6 **Challaborough** Devon
28 B3 **Challacombe** Devon
173 K2 **Challoch** D & G
40 C5 **Challock** Kent
16 B2 **Chalmington** Dorset
68 C2 **Chalton** C Beds
86 C5 **Chalton** C Beds
20 B4 **Chalton** Hants
50 B3 **Chalvey** Slough
23 H5 **Chalvington** E Susx
40 B6 **Chambers Green** Kent
68 D7 **Chandler's Cross** Herts
81 H7 **Chandlers Cross** Worcs
34 F7 **Chandler's Ford** Hants
86 C4 **Channel's End** Bed
144 D2 **Chanterlands Crematorium** C KuH
32 B2 **Chantry** Somset
90 D6 **Chantry** Suffk
165 H4 **Chapel** Cumb
222 D8 **Chapel** Fife
150 D8 **Chapel Allerton** Leeds
30 F1 **Chapel Allerton** Somset
10 D7 **Chapel Amble** Cnwll
84 E2 **Chapel Brampton** Nhants
102 F4 **Chapelbridge** Cambs
114 C4 **Chapel Chorlton** Staffs
23 K3 **Chapel Cross** E Susx
86 B4 **Chapel End** Bed
85 L6 **Chapel End** C Beds
102 C6 **Chapel End** Cambs
99 J5 **Chapel End** Warwks
88 E7 **Chapelend Way** Essex
131 L3 **Chapel-en-le-Frith** Derbys
140 B6 **Chapel Field** Bury
119 L6 **Chapelgate** Lincs
83 L3 **Chapel Green** Warwks
99 H6 **Chapel Green** Warwks
142 F3 **Chapel Haddlesey** N York
209 K6 **Chapelhall** N Lans
257 K4 **Chapel Hill** Abers
119 G1 **Chapel Hill** Lincs
63 G7 **Chapel Hill** Mons
150 D6 **Chapel Hill** N York
187 K2 **Chapelhope** Border
177 K4 **Chapelknowe** D & G
95 H8 **Chapel Lawn** Shrops
158 C7 **Chapel le Dale** N York
29 L5 **Chapel Leigh** Somset
131 L3 **Chapel Milton** Derbys
256 C7 **Chapel of Garioch** Abers
172 D6 **Chapel Rossan** D & G
23 L5 **Chapel Row** E Susx
71 J7 **Chapel Row** Essex
48 E5 **Chapel Row** W Berk
156 B6 **Chapels** Cumb
137 K5 **Chapel St Leonards** Lincs
156 D2 **Chapel Stile** Cumb
234 F6 **Chapelton** Angus
27 K5 **Chapelton** Devon
197 K1 **Chapelton** S Lans
139 L4 **Chapeltown** Bl w D
4 E4 **Chapel Town** Cnwll
254 E7 **Chapeltown** Moray
142 A8 **Chapeltown** Sheff
32 D1 **Chapmanslade** Wilts
11 L4 **Chapmans Well** Devon
69 J4 **Chapmore End** Herts
72 C2 **Chappel** Essex
6 B1 **Charaton** Cnwll
15 H1 **Chard** Somset
15 H2 **Chard Junction** Somset
30 D8 **Chardleigh Green** Somset
15 G2 **Chardstock** Devon
63 L8 **Charfield** S Glos
64 D3 **Chargrove** Gloucs
40 B5 **Charing** Kent
40 B5 **Charing Crematorium** Kent
40 B5 **Charing Heath** Kent
40 B5 **Charing Hill** Kent
82 E7 **Charingworth** Gloucs
66 A3 **Charlbury** Oxon
45 L5 **Charlcombe** BaNES
46 E4 **Charlcutt** Wilts
83 G4 **Charlecote** Warwks
98 C4 **Charlemont** Sandw
28 B4 **Charles** Devon
36 D2 **Charleshill** Surrey
234 B6 **Charleston** Angus
245 L3 **Charlestown** C Aber
149 L8 **Charlestown** C Brad
140 E2 **Charlestown** Calder
5 H4 **Charlestown** Cnwll
131 L1 **Charlestown** Derbys
16 C6 **Charlestown** Dorset
210 E2 **Charlestown** Fife
251 H2 **Charlestown** Highld
260 C5 **Charlestown** Highld
140 B7 **Charlestown** Salfd
89 L5 **Charles Tye** Suffk
131 K1 **Charlesworth** Derbys
30 C3 **Charlinch** Somset
222 E5 **Charlottetown** Fife
51 L3 **Charlton** Gt Lon
34 D2 **Charlton** Hants
68 F2 **Charlton** Herts
83 M8 **Charlton** Nhants
179 J2 **Charlton** Nthumb
48 B1 **Charlton** Oxon
30 D5 **Charlton** Somset
31 K2 **Charlton** Somset
45 K8 **Charlton** Somset
50 D5 **Charlton** Surrey
20 E4 **Charlton** W Susx
32 F6 **Charlton** Wilts
46 D1 **Charlton** Wilts
81 J1 **Charlton** Worcs
82 B6 **Charlton** Worcs
96 D1 **Charlton** Wrekin
64 F2 **Charlton Abbots** Gloucs
31 J5 **Charlton Adam** Somset
33 L6 **Charlton-All-Saints** Wilts
16 C3 **Charlton Down** Dorset
96 D2 **Charlton Hill** Shrops
31 L6 **Charlton Horethorne** Somset
64 D3 **Charlton Kings** Gloucs
31 H5 **Charlton Mackrell** Somset
17 H2 **Charlton Marshall** Dorset
32 B5 **Charlton Musgrove** Somset
66 E4 **Charlton-on-Otmoor** Oxon
17 H2 **Charlton on the Hill** Dorset
47 G7 **Charlton St Peter** Wilts
35 K4 **Charlwood** Hants
37 K3 **Charlwood** Surrey
16 C4 **Charminster** Dorset
15 H4 **Charmouth** Dorset

| | |
|---|---|
| 67 G2 | **Charndon** Bucks |
| 66 A8 | **Charney Bassett** Oxon |
| 139 H4 | **Charnock Green** Lancs |
| 139 H4 | **Charnock Richard** Lancs |
| 139 H4 | **Charnock Richard Crematorium** Lancs |
| 90 F4 | **Charsfield** Suffk |
| 39 K3 | **Chart Corner** Kent |
| 48 E7 | **Charter Alley** Hants |
| 202 B4 | **Charterhall** Border |
| 45 G7 | **Charterhouse** Somset |
| 209 L1 | **Chartershall** Stirlg |
| 65 L5 | **Charterville Allotments** Oxon |
| 40 E4 | **Chartham** Kent |
| 40 E4 | **Chartham Hatch** Kent |
| 39 K3 | **Chart Hill** Kent |
| 68 B6 | **Chartridge** Bucks |
| 39 K3 | **Chart Sutton** Kent |
| 39 L3 | **Chartway Street** Kent |
| 49 J4 | **Charvil** Wokham |
| 83 M4 | **Charwelton** Nhants |
| 98 D2 | **Chase Terrace** Staffs |
| 98 D2 | **Chasetown** Staffs |
| 65 K1 | **Chastleton** Oxon |
| 11 L2 | **Chasty** Devon |
| 148 D7 | **Chatburn** Lancs |
| 114 B4 | **Chatcull** Staffs |
| 43 K4 | **Chatham** Caerph |
| 53 G5 | **Chatham** Medway |
| 71 H4 | **Chatham Green** Essex |
| 203 K7 | **Chathill** Nthumb |
| 81 J3 | **Chatley** Worcs |
| 53 G4 | **Chattenden** Medway |
| 70 C2 | **Chatter End** Essex |
| 103 H6 | **Chatteris** Cambs |
| 140 B4 | **Chatterton** Lancs |
| 90 C6 | **Chattisham** Suffk |
| 189 K3 | **Chatto** Border |
| 203 G7 | **Chatton** Nthumb |
| 68 D3 | **Chaul End** C Beds |
| 28 C8 | **Chawleigh** Devon |
| 66 C6 | **Chawley** Oxon |
| 86 C4 | **Chawston** Bed |
| 35 L3 | **Chawton** Hants |
| 63 L4 | **Chaxhill** Gloucs |
| 49 G3 | **Chazey Heath** Oxon |
| 115 G3 | **Cheadle** Staffs |
| 131 G2 | **Cheadle** Stockp |
| 131 G2 | **Cheadle Heath** Stockp |
| 131 G2 | **Cheadle Hulme** Stockp |
| 51 H6 | **Cheam** Gt Lon |
| 50 B5 | **Cheapside** W & M |
| 67 H5 | **Chearsley** Bucks |
| 114 D6 | **Chebsey** Staffs |
| 49 G2 | **Checkendon** Oxon |
| 114 A2 | **Checkley** Ches E |
| 80 E7 | **Checkley** Herefs |
| 115 G4 | **Checkley** Staffs |
| 114 A2 | **Checkley Green** Ches E |
| 88 F4 | **Chedburgh** Suffk |
| 44 F8 | **Cheddar** Somset |
| 68 A4 | **Cheddington** Bucks |
| 114 F1 | **Cheddleton** Staffs |
| 114 F1 | **Cheddleton Heath** Staffs |
| 30 C5 | **Cheddon Fitzpaine** Somset |
| 64 D8 | **Chedglow** Wilts |
| 107 H3 | **Chedgrave** Norfk |
| 15 L2 | **Chedington** Dorset |
| 107 G7 | **Chediston** Suffk |
| 107 G7 | **Chediston Green** Suffk |
| 64 F5 | **Chedworth** Gloucs |
| 30 E3 | **Chedzoy** Somset |
| 40 D7 | **Cheeseman's Green** Kent |
| 140 C7 | **Cheetham Hill** Manch |
| 28 C8 | **Cheldon** Devon |
| 130 F5 | **Chelford** Ches E |
| 116 C5 | **Chellaston** C Derb |
| 85 J4 | **Chellington** Bed |
| 97 G5 | **Chelmarsh** Shrops |
| 95 L5 | **Chelmick** Shrops |
| 90 E7 | **Chelmondiston** Suffk |
| 132 B5 | **Chelmorton** Derbys |
| 71 H5 | **Chelmsford** Essex |
| 71 G6 | **Chelmsford Crematorium** Essex |
| 98 F6 | **Chelmsley Wood** Solhll |
| 51 H3 | **Chelsea** Gt Lon |
| 52 A6 | **Chelsfield** Gt Lon |
| 51 K7 | **Chelsham** Surrey |
| 29 L6 | **Chelston** Somset |
| 89 K5 | **Chelsworth** Suffk |
| 64 D3 | **Cheltenham** Gloucs |
| 64 E3 | **Cheltenham Crematorium** Gloucs |
| 85 K1 | **Chelveston** Nhants |
| 44 F5 | **Chelvey** N Som |
| 45 J6 | **Chelwood** BaNES |
| 38 B7 | **Chelwood Common** E Susx |
| 38 B7 | **Chelwood Gate** E Susx |
| 64 E8 | **Chelworth** Wilts |
| 65 G8 | **Chelworth Lower Green** Wilts |

| | |
|---|---|
| 65 G8 | **Chelworth Upper Green** Wilts |
| 95 K6 | **Cheney Longville** Shrops |
| 68 C7 | **Chenies** Bucks |
| 63 G8 | **Chepstow** Mons |
| 139 K6 | **Chequerbent** Bolton |
| 103 K2 | **Chequers Corner** Norfk |
| 46 F5 | **Cherhill** Wilts |
| 64 C7 | **Cherington** Gloucs |
| 83 G7 | **Cherington** Warwks |
| 28 C2 | **Cheriton** Devon |
| 35 J5 | **Cheriton** Hants |
| 41 G7 | **Cheriton** Kent |
| 56 E6 | **Cheriton** Swans |
| 13 H4 | **Cheriton Bishop** Devon |
| 13 K1 | **Cheriton Fitzpaine** Devon |
| 55 G7 | **Cheriton or Stackpole Elidor** Pembks |
| 113 L7 | **Cherrington** Wrekin |
| 152 F7 | **Cherry Burton** E R Yk |
| 87 K4 | **Cherry Hinton** Cambs |
| 81 K4 | **Cherry Orchard** Worcs |
| 135 L5 | **Cherry Willingham** Lincs |
| 50 D5 | **Chertsey** Surrey |
| 16 E3 | **Cheselbourne** Dorset |
| 68 B6 | **Chesham** Bucks |
| 140 B5 | **Chesham** Bury |
| 68 B7 | **Chesham Bois** Bucks |
| 69 K6 | **Cheshunt** Herts |
| 53 J6 | **Chesley** Kent |
| 98 B2 | **Cheslyn Hay** Staffs |
| 99 G8 | **Chessetts Wood** Warwks |
| 50 F6 | **Chessington** Gt Lon |
| 129 J6 | **Chester** Ches W |
| 31 L3 | **Chesterblade** Somset |
| 129 J6 | **Chester Crematorium** Ches W |
| 133 G5 | **Chesterfield** Derbys |
| 98 E2 | **Chesterfield** Staffs |
| 133 H5 | **Chesterfield Crematorium** Derbys |
| 211 L6 | **Chesterhill** Mdloth |
| 181 G8 | **Chester-le-Street** Dur |
| 169 H1 | **Chester Moor** Dur |
| 189 G2 | **Chesters** Border |
| 189 H4 | **Chesters** Border |
| 87 K3 | **Chesterton** Cambs |
| 102 C4 | **Chesterton** Cambs |
| 64 E7 | **Chesterton** Gloucs |
| 66 E3 | **Chesterton** Oxon |
| 97 H4 | **Chesterton** Shrops |
| 114 C2 | **Chesterton** Staffs |
| 83 H4 | **Chesterton Green** Warwks |
| 179 J6 | **Chesterwood** Nthumb |
| 40 F2 | **Chestfield** Kent |
| 53 J6 | **Chestnut Street** Kent |
| 7 K3 | **Cheston** Devon |
| 114 A5 | **Cheswardine** Shrops |
| 113 M8 | **Cheswell** Wrekin |
| 203 G4 | **Cheswick** Nthumb |
| 98 E8 | **Cheswick Green** Solhll |
| 16 B1 | **Chetnole** Dorset |
| 29 H7 | **Chettiscombe** Devon |
| 103 L6 | **Chettisham** Cambs |
| 32 F8 | **Chettle** Dorset |
| 96 F5 | **Chetton** Shrops |
| 66 F1 | **Chetwode** Bucks |
| 114 A7 | **Chetwynd** Wrekin |
| 114 B8 | **Chetwynd Aston** Wrekin |
| 88 D3 | **Cheveley** Cambs |
| 52 A7 | **Chevening** Kent |
| 19 G6 | **Cheverton** IoW |
| 88 F3 | **Chevington** Suffk |
| 191 K6 | **Chevington Drift** Nthumb |
| 29 H7 | **Chevithorne** Devon |
| 45 H6 | **Chew Magna** BaNES |
| 139 K6 | **Chew Moor** Bolton |
| 45 H6 | **Chew Stoke** BaNES |
| 45 K5 | **Chewton Keynsham** BaNES |
| 45 H8 | **Chewton Mendip** Somset |
| 12 E3 | **Chichacott** Devon |
| 85 H6 | **Chicheley** M Keyn |
| 20 E6 | **Chichester** W Susx |
| 20 E5 | **Chichester Crematorium** W Susx |
| 16 C6 | **Chickerell** Dorset |
| 106 E8 | **Chickering** Suffk |
| 32 F4 | **Chicklade** Wilts |
| 79 K4 | **Chickward** Herefs |
| 35 K7 | **Chidden** Hants |
| 36 E4 | **Chiddingfold** Surrey |
| 23 J4 | **Chiddingly** E Susx |
| 38 D2 | **Chiddingstone** Kent |
| 38 E4 | **Chiddingstone Causeway** Kent |
| 15 K4 | **Chideock** Dorset |
| 20 C6 | **Chidham** W Susx |
| 141 L3 | **Chidswell** Kirk |
| 48 C4 | **Chieveley** W Berk |
| 71 G5 | **Chignall St James** Essex |
| 71 G5 | **Chignall Smealy** Essex |
| 70 B8 | **Chigwell** Essex |
| 70 C8 | **Chigwell Row** Essex |

| | |
|---|---|
| 34 E3 | **Chilbolton** Hants |
| 35 G5 | **Chilcomb** Hants |
| 15 M4 | **Chilcombe** Dorset |
| 45 J8 | **Chilcompton** Somset |
| 99 H1 | **Chilcote** Leics |
| 129 J4 | **Childer Thornton** Ches W |
| 32 D8 | **Child Okeford** Dorset |
| 48 A2 | **Childrey** Oxon |
| 113 L6 | **Child's Ercall** Shrops |
| 82 C7 | **Childswickham** Worcs |
| 129 K2 | **Childwall** Lpool |
| 68 F5 | **Childwick Bury** Herts |
| 68 F5 | **Childwick Green** Herts |
| 16 B3 | **Chilfrome** Dorset |
| 20 D4 | **Chilgrove** W Susx |
| 40 E4 | **Chilham** Kent |
| 12 B2 | **Chilla** Devon |
| 12 B6 | **Chillaton** Devon |
| 41 J4 | **Chillenden** Kent |
| 19 H6 | **Chillerton** IoW |
| 91 J5 | **Chillesford** Suffk |
| 203 G8 | **Chillingham** Nthumb |
| 8 B6 | **Chillington** Devon |
| 30 F8 | **Chillington** Somset |
| 33 G4 | **Chilmark** Wilts |
| 40 C7 | **Chilmington Green** Kent |
| 65 L3 | **Chilson** Oxon |
| 12 A7 | **Chilsworthy** Cnwll |
| 11 L1 | **Chilsworthy** Devon |
| 68 E3 | **Chiltern Green** C Beds |
| 68 B7 | **Chilterns Crematorium** Bucks |
| 31 H7 | **Chilthorne Domer** Somset |
| 67 G5 | **Chilton** Bucks |
| 13 K2 | **Chilton** Devon |
| 169 H5 | **Chilton** Dur |
| 41 J6 | **Chilton** Kent |
| 48 C2 | **Chilton** Oxon |
| 89 H6 | **Chilton** Suffk |
| 35 J3 | **Chilton Candover** Hants |
| 31 J6 | **Chilton Cantelo** Somset |
| 47 L5 | **Chilton Foliat** Wilts |
| 30 E3 | **Chilton Polden** Somset |
| 88 E6 | **Chilton Street** Suffk |
| 30 D3 | **Chilton Trinity** Somset |
| 116 E4 | **Chilwell** Notts |
| 34 F7 | **Chilworth** Hants |
| 36 F2 | **Chilworth** Surrey |
| 65 M7 | **Chimney** Oxon |
| 49 G7 | **Chineham** Hants |
| 69 K8 | **Chingford** Gt Lon |
| 131 L3 | **Chinley** Derbys |
| 67 J6 | **Chinnor** Oxon |
| 179 K4 | **Chipchase Castle** Nthumb |
| 114 A5 | **Chipnall** Shrops |
| 88 D1 | **Chippenham** Cambs |
| 46 D4 | **Chippenham** Wilts |
| 68 D6 | **Chipperfield** Herts |
| 69 K1 | **Chipping** Herts |
| 147 M7 | **Chipping** Lancs |
| 82 E7 | **Chipping Campden** Gloucs |
| 71 K4 | **Chipping Hill** Essex |
| 65 L2 | **Chipping Norton** Oxon |
| 70 E6 | **Chipping Ongar** Essex |
| 45 L3 | **Chipping Sodbury** S Glos |
| 83 L5 | **Chipping Warden** Nhants |
| 29 J5 | **Chipstable** Somset |
| 38 D2 | **Chipstead** Kent |
| 51 H7 | **Chipstead** Surrey |
| 95 G4 | **Chirbury** Shrops |
| 112 D4 | **Chirk** Wrexhm |
| 202 D2 | **Chirnside** Border |
| 202 C2 | **Chirnsidebridge** Border |
| 47 G7 | **Chirton** Wilts |
| 47 K5 | **Chisbury** Wilts |
| 31 G7 | **Chiselborough** Somset |
| 47 J3 | **Chiseldon** Swindn |
| 66 E7 | **Chiselhampton** Oxon |
| 188 D4 | **Chisholme** Border |
| 51 L5 | **Chislehurst** Gt Lon |
| 41 H2 | **Chislet** Kent |
| 140 F2 | **Chisley** Calder |
| 68 E6 | **Chiswell Green** Herts |
| 51 G3 | **Chiswick** Gt Lon |
| 87 H6 | **Chiswick End** Cambs |
| 131 K2 | **Chisworth** Derbys |
| 24 E3 | **Chitcombe** E Susx |
| 36 C6 | **Chithurst** W Susx |
| 87 K1 | **Chittering** Cambs |
| 33 G2 | **Chitterne** Wilts |
| 28 B6 | **Chittlehamholt** Devon |
| 27 L5 | **Chittlehampton** Devon |
| 46 D5 | **Chittoe** Wilts |
| 8 A7 | **Chivelstone** Devon |
| 27 J4 | **Chivenor** Devon |
| 172 E3 | **Chlenry** D & G |
| 50 B6 | **Chobham** Surrey |
| 34 B2 | **Cholderton** Wilts |
| 68 B5 | **Cholesbury** Bucks |
| 179 L5 | **Chollerford** Nthumb |
| 179 L4 | **Chollerton** Nthumb |

| | |
|---|---|
| 130 C7 | **Cholmondeston** Ches E |
| 48 E2 | **Cholsey** Oxon |
| 80 B3 | **Cholstrey** Herefs |
| 161 J3 | **Chop Gate** N York |
| 181 G2 | **Choppington** Nthumb |
| 180 D7 | **Chopwell** Gatesd |
| 113 J1 | **Chorley** Ches E |
| 139 H4 | **Chorley** Lancs |
| 96 F6 | **Chorley** Shrops |
| 98 D1 | **Chorley** Staffs |
| 68 D7 | **Chorleywood** Herts |
| 68 C7 | **Chorleywood West** Herts |
| 114 A2 | **Chorlton** Ches E |
| 130 F1 | **Chorlton-cum-Hardy** Manch |
| 113 G2 | **Chorlton Lane** Ches W |
| 95 J5 | **Choulton** Shrops |
| 129 L8 | **Chowley** Ches W |
| 87 J7 | **Chrishall** Essex |
| 207 L4 | **Chrisswell** Inver |
| 103 K4 | **Christchurch** Cambs |
| 18 B5 | **Christchurch** Dorset |
| 63 H4 | **Christchurch** Gloucs |
| 44 D1 | **Christchurch** Newpt |
| 46 D3 | **Christian Malford** Wilts |
| 129 K6 | **Christleton** Ches W |
| 67 H8 | **Christmas Common** Oxon |
| 44 D7 | **Christon** N Som |
| 191 J2 | **Christon Bank** Nthumb |
| 13 J5 | **Christow** Devon |
| 37 H5 | **Christ's Hospital** W Susx |
| 38 D6 | **Chuck Hatch** E Susx |
| 13 K6 | **Chudleigh** Devon |
| 13 K7 | **Chudleigh Knighton** Devon |
| 28 B8 | **Chulmleigh** Devon |
| 131 L2 | **Chunal** Derbys |
| 139 L2 | **Church** Lancs |
| 63 M3 | **Churcham** Gloucs |
| 114 A8 | **Church Aston** Wrekin |
| 84 D2 | **Church Brampton** Nhants |
| 167 J7 | **Church Brough** Cumb |
| 115 K5 | **Church Broughton** Derbys |
| 3 H8 | **Church Cove** Cnwll |
| 49 K8 | **Church Crookham** Hants |
| 64 C3 | **Churchdown** Gloucs |
| 114 C8 | **Church Eaton** Staffs |
| 85 L3 | **Church End** Bed |
| 86 C3 | **Church End** Bed |
| 67 H5 | **Church End** Bucks |
| 68 C3 | **Church End** C Beds |
| 68 C3 | **Church End** C Beds |
| 85 J8 | **Church End** C Beds |
| 85 K8 | **Church End** C Beds |
| 86 D4 | **Church End** C Beds |
| 86 D7 | **Church End** C Beds |
| 87 K4 | **Church End** Cambs |
| 102 B8 | **Church End** Cambs |
| 102 E6 | **Church End** Cambs |
| 103 G7 | **Church End** Cambs |
| 70 F3 | **Church End** Essex |
| 71 H2 | **Church End** Essex |
| 71 H4 | **Church End** Essex |
| 72 E8 | **Churchend** Essex |
| 51 H1 | **Church End** Gt Lon |
| 49 G7 | **Church End** Hants |
| 68 E5 | **Church End** Herts |
| 69 H1 | **Church End** Herts |
| 70 C3 | **Church End** Herts |
| 119 H5 | **Church End** Lincs |
| 145 L8 | **Church End** Lincs |
| 99 H5 | **Church End** Warwks |
| 99 H5 | **Church End** Warwks |
| 66 A2 | **Church Enstone** Oxon |
| 151 H8 | **Church Fenton** N York |
| 98 C5 | **Churchfield** Sandw |
| 69 K6 | **Churchgate** Herts |
| 70 C5 | **Churchgate Street** Essex |
| 14 E3 | **Church Green** Devon |
| 115 M7 | **Church Gresley** Derbys |
| 66 B4 | **Church Hanborough** Oxon |
| 98 C1 | **Church Hill** Staffs |
| 161 L3 | **Church Houses** N York |
| 15 G2 | **Churchill** Devon |
| 27 L3 | **Churchill** Devon |
| 44 E7 | **Churchill** N Som |
| 65 L2 | **Churchill** Oxon |
| 81 L4 | **Churchill** Worcs |
| 97 K7 | **Churchill** Worcs |
| 30 B8 | **Churchinford** Somset |
| 17 H6 | **Church Knowle** Dorset |
| 135 G4 | **Church Laneham** Notts |
| 100 F5 | **Church Langton** Leics |
| 99 M8 | **Church Lawford** Warwks |
| 130 F8 | **Church Lawton** Ches E |
| 115 G4 | **Church Leigh** Staffs |
| 82 B5 | **Church Lench** Worcs |
| 115 J3 | **Church Mayfield** Staffs |
| 130 C7 | **Church Minshull** Ches E |
| 20 E7 | **Church Norton** W Susx |
| 100 B7 | **Churchover** Warwks |
| 96 C4 | **Church Preen** Shrops |

95 K3 **Church Pulverbatch** Shrops
30 B7 **Churchstanton** Somset
95 G4 **Churchstoke** Powys
7 K5 **Churchstow** Devon
84 C4 **Church Stowe** Nhants
88 F6 **Church Street** Essex
52 F4 **Church Street** Kent
107 K6 **Church Street** Suffk
95 L4 **Church Stretton** Shrops
145 J8 **Churchthorpe** Lincs
146 F7 **Churchtown** Bpool
10 F7 **Churchtown** Cnwll
132 E7 **Churchtown** Derbys
28 B2 **Churchtown** Devon
154 f3 **Churchtown** IoM
147 J7 **Churchtown** Lancs
143 K6 **Church Town** N Linc
138 D4 **Churchtown** Sefton
43 G4 **Church Village** Rhondd
133 L6 **Church Warsop** Notts
116 D5 **Church Wilne** Derbys
178 F3 **Churnsike Lodge** Nthumb
8 D4 **Churston Ferrers** Torbay
36 C3 **Churt** Surrey
129 K8 **Churton** Ches W
141 L2 **Churwell** Leeds
109 H4 **Chwilog** Gwynd
2 D5 **Chyandour** Cnwll
3 G6 **Chyanvounder** Cnwll
3 K3 **Chyeowling** Cnwll
3 G6 **Chyvarloe** Cnwll
94 E3 **Cil** Powys
128 E6 **Cilcain** Flints
76 F3 **Cilcennin** Cerdgn
94 F3 **Cilcewydd** Powys
57 L5 **Cilfrew** Neath
43 H3 **Cilfynydd** Rhondd
75 L4 **Cilgerran** Pembks
59 K3 **Cilgwyn** Carmth
109 J1 **Cilgwyn** Gwynd
76 F4 **Ciliau-Aeron** Cerdgn
57 K4 **Cilmaengwyn** Neath
78 D5 **Cilmery** Powys
58 A2 **Cilrhedyn** Pembks
59 H4 **Cilsan** Carmth
111 G3 **Ciltalgarth** Gwynd
77 L7 **Cilycwm** Carmth
57 L5 **Cimla** Neath
63 K4 **Cinderford** Gloucs
97 L4 **Cinder Hill** Wolves
50 B3 **Cippenham** Slough
64 F6 **Cirencester** Gloucs
160 B3 **Citadilla** N York
51 J3 **City** Gt Lon
42 F6 **City** V Glam
125 H2 **City Dulas** IoA
51 L2 **City of London Crematorium** Gt Lon
224 F3 **Clabhach** Ag & B
207 J3 **Clachaig** Ag & B
206 B7 **Clachan** Ag & B
216 B3 **Clachan** Ag & B
228 D6 **Clachan** Ag & B
247 H1 **Clachan** Highld
283 c8 **Clachan-a-Luib** W Isls
224 C5 **Clachan Mor** Ag & B
283 c8 **Clachan na Luib** W Isls
209 G3 **Clachan of Campsie** E Duns
216 B3 **Clachan-Seil** Ag & B
251 H2 **Clachnaharry** Highld
270 D3 **Clachtoll** Highld
233 H3 **Clackavoid** P & K
210 B1 **Clackmannan** Clacks
266 B2 **Clackmarras** Moray
73 J4 **Clacton-on-Sea** Essex
17 H3 **Cladich** Ag & B
82 C3 **Cladswell** Worcs
27 K3 **Claggan** Highld
58 C6 **Claigan** Highld
45 K7 **Clandown** BaNES
35 L7 **Clanfield** Hants
65 L6 **Clanfield** Oxon
13 H2 **Clannaborough** Devon
34 D1 **Clanville** Hants
31 K4 **Clanville** Somset
206 D7 **Claonaig** Ag & B
17 K2 **Clapgate** Dorset
70 C2 **Clapgate** Herts
85 K5 **Clapham** Bed
13 L5 **Clapham** Devon
51 H4 **Clapham** Gt Lon
148 C2 **Clapham** N York
21 J5 **Clapham** W Susx
85 K4 **Clapham Green** Bed
40 D7 **Clap Hill** Kent
56 E2 **Clappersgate** Cumb
31 J1 **Clapton** Somset
15 J1 **Clapton** Somset
44 F4 **Clapton-in-Gordano** N Som
65 H3 **Clapton-on-the-Hill** Gloucs

28 B6 **Clapworthy** Devon
92 D6 **Clarach** Cerdgn
180 E6 **Claravale** Gatesd
55 H3 **Clarbeston** Pembks
55 G3 **Clarbeston Road** Pembks
134 E3 **Clarborough** Notts
88 F6 **Clare** Suffk
175 J2 **Clarebrand** D & G
176 E5 **Clarencefield** D & G
180 B5 **Clarewood** Nthumb
188 F3 **Clarilaw** Border
35 H1 **Clarken Green** Hants
37 J3 **Clark's Green** Surrey
208 F7 **Clarkston** E Rens
263 K2 **Clashmore** Highld
270 D2 **Clashmore** Highld
270 E2 **Clashnessie** Highld
254 E7 **Clashnoir** Moray
221 H3 **Clathy** P & K
221 H3 **Clathymore** P & K
255 L6 **Clatt** Abers
94 B4 **Clatter** Powys
70 F4 **Clatterford End** Essex
29 J4 **Clatworthy** Somset
147 K7 **Claughton** Lancs
147 L3 **Claughton** Lancs
129 G2 **Claughton** Wirral
30 C4 **Clavelshay** Somset
82 E2 **Claverdon** Warwks
44 F5 **Claverham** N Som
70 C1 **Clavering** Essex
97 H5 **Claverley** Shrops
46 A6 **Claverton** BaNES
45 M6 **Claverton Down** BaNES
43 G6 **Clawdd-coch** V Glam
111 L1 **Clawdd-newydd** Denbgs
157 H7 **Clawthorpe** Cumb
11 L3 **Clawton** Devon
136 B1 **Claxby** Lincs
137 H5 **Claxby** Lincs
151 L4 **Claxton** N York
107 G3 **Claxton** Norfk
100 B5 **Claybrooke Magna** Leics
107 K7 **Clay Common** Suffk
100 D8 **Clay Coton** Nhants
133 H7 **Clay Cross** Derbys
83 K5 **Claydon** Oxon
90 D5 **Claydon** Suffk
69 J2 **Clay End** Herts
177 L3 **Claygate** D & G
39 H4 **Claygate** Kent
50 F6 **Claygate** Surrey
38 F2 **Claygate Cross** Kent
51 L1 **Clayhall** Gt Lon
29 J6 **Clayhanger** Devon
98 D3 **Clayhanger** Wsall
29 L7 **Clayhidon** Devon
24 F3 **Clayhill** E Susx
18 D2 **Clayhill** Hants
87 K2 **Clayhithe** Cambs
279 L4 **Clayock** Highld
87 G4 **Claypit Hill** Cambs
63 M6 **Claypits** Gloucs
117 M2 **Claypole** Lincs
137 H4 **Claythorpe** Lincs
141 H2 **Clayton** C Brad
142 C6 **Clayton** Donc
22 D4 **Clayton** W Susx
139 H3 **Clayton Green** Lancs
139 M2 **Clayton-le-Moors** Lancs
139 H3 **Clayton-le-Woods** Lancs
141 L5 **Clayton West** Kirk
134 E2 **Clayworth** Notts
236 F3 **Cleadale** Highld
181 J6 **Cleadon** S Tyne
7 G2 **Clearbrook** Devon
63 H5 **Clearwell** Gloucs
63 H5 **Clearwell Meend** Gloucs
169 H8 **Cleasby** N York
275 c6 **Cleat** Ork
168 E7 **Cleatlam** Dur
164 D7 **Cleator** Cumb
164 D7 **Cleator Moor** Cumb
141 J3 **Cleckheaton** Kirk
96 D7 **Cleedownton** Shrops
96 D8 **Cleehill** Shrops
209 K7 **Cleekhimin** N Lans
96 D6 **Clee St Margaret** Shrops
96 D7 **Cleestanton** Shrops
145 J6 **Cleethorpes** NE Lin
96 E7 **Cleeton St Mary** Shrops
44 F5 **Cleeve** N Som
48 F3 **Cleeve** Oxon
64 E2 **Cleeve Hill** Gloucs
82 C5 **Cleeve Prior** Worcs
212 D2 **Cleghornie** E Loth
80 B7 **Clehonger** Herefs
221 K7 **Cleish** P & K
209 L7 **Cleland** N Lans
68 C4 **Clement's End** C Beds

52 B5 **Clement Street** Kent
216 E2 **Clenamacrie** Ag & B
47 H6 **Clench Common** Wilts
120 D7 **Clenchwarton** Norfk
268 D4 **Clenerty** Abers
97 L7 **Clent** Worcs
96 F8 **Cleobury Mortimer** Shrops
96 E6 **Cleobury North** Shrops
192 D2 **Cleongart** Ag & B
252 F2 **Clephanton** Highld
187 L6 **Clerkhill** D & G
185 K3 **Cleuch-head** D & G
46 F4 **Clevancy** Wilts
44 E5 **Clevedon** N Som
66 B2 **Cleveley** Oxon
146 F7 **Cleveleys** Lancs
46 E2 **Cleverton** Wilts
31 G1 **Clewer** Somset
122 A3 **Cley next the Sea** Norfk
166 E5 **Cliburn** Cumb
35 K1 **Cliddesden** Hants
99 G4 **Cliff** Warks
139 L1 **Cliffe** Lancs
52 F4 **Cliffe** Medway
143 G2 **Cliffe** N York
169 G2 **Cliffe** N York
25 G4 **Cliff End** E Susx
52 F4 **Cliffe Woods** Medway
79 J6 **Clifford** Herefs
150 F7 **Clifford** Leeds
82 E5 **Clifford Chambers** Warwks
63 K2 **Clifford's Mesne** Gloucs
41 K2 **Cliffsend** Kent
45 H4 **Clifton** Bristl
86 D7 **Clifton** C Beds
116 F4 **Clifton** C Nott
151 J5 **Clifton** C York
141 J3 **Clifton** Calder
166 C5 **Clifton** Cumb
115 K3 **Clifton** Derbys
27 L3 **Clifton** Devon
142 E8 **Clifton** Donc
138 F2 **Clifton** Lancs
150 B6 **Clifton** N York
180 F2 **Clifton** Nthumb
66 C1 **Clifton** Oxon
140 A7 **Clifton** Salfd
81 J6 **Clifton** Worcs
99 H1 **Clifton Campville** Staffs
66 D7 **Clifton Hampden** Oxon
85 H5 **Clifton Reynes** M Keyn
100 C8 **Clifton upon Dunsmore** Warwks
81 G3 **Clifton upon Teme** Worcs
41 L1 **Cliftonville** Kent
21 G6 **Climping** W Susx
32 C1 **Clink** Somset
150 C4 **Clint** N York
245 J1 **Clinterty** C Aber
105 L1 **Clint Green** Norfk
201 J6 **Clintmains** Border
93 H1 **Clipiau** Gwynd
123 J8 **Clippesby** Norfk
118 C8 **Clipsham** Rutlnd
100 F7 **Clipston** Nhants
117 H5 **Clipston** Notts
68 B2 **Clipstone** C Beds
134 B7 **Clipstone** Notts
148 C7 **Clitheroe** Lancs
113 H6 **Clive** Shrops
144 E7 **Clixby** Lincs
46 E1 **Cloatley** Wilts
111 L1 **Clocaenog** Denbgs
267 H4 **Clochan** Moray
234 D5 **Clochtow** Angus
129 M2 **Clock Face** St Hel
94 F2 **Cloddiau** Powys
62 C2 **Clodock** Herefs
32 B2 **Cloford** Somset
257 I3 **Clola** Abers
86 B7 **Clophill** C Beds
102 B7 **Clopton** Nhants
90 F4 **Clopton** Suffk
90 F4 **Clopton Corner** Suffk
88 F4 **Clopton Green** Suffk
89 K3 **Clopton Green** Suffk
9 k1 **Clos du Valle** Guern
186 D7 **Closeburn** D & G
186 D7 **Closeburnmill** D & G
154 c7 **Closeclark** IoM
16 A1 **Closworth** Somset
69 H1 **Clothall** Herts
129 M6 **Clotton** Ches W
100 A6 **Cloudesley Bush** Warwks
80 D7 **Clouds** Herefs
140 E6 **Clough** Oldham
140 D3 **Clough Foot** Calder
141 H4 **Clough Head** Calder
163 H4 **Cloughton** N York
163 H3 **Cloughton Newlands** N York
281 d5 **Clousta** Shet

233 M1 **Clova** Angus
26 E6 **Clovelly** Devon
200 F6 **Clovenfords** Border
228 F3 **Clovulin** Highld
140 B2 **Clow Bridge** Lancs
133 K4 **Clowne** Derbys
81 G1 **Clows Top** Worcs
112 F3 **Cloy** Wrexhm
239 H1 **Cluanie Inn** Highld
239 H2 **Cluanie Lodge** Highld
11 K4 **Clubworthy** Cnwll
173 J3 **Clugston** D & G
95 H7 **Clun** Shrops
253 G2 **Clunas** Highld
95 J7 **Clunbury** Shrops
55 J3 **Clunderwen** Carmth
252 E6 **Clune** Highld
239 K6 **Clunes** Highld
95 K7 **Clungunford** Shrops
268 B6 **Clunie** Abers
233 H6 **Clunie** P & K
95 H7 **Clunton** Shrops
222 D8 **Cluny** Fife
45 J7 **Clutton** BaNES
113 G1 **Clutton** Ches W
45 J7 **Clutton Hill** BaNES
125 K7 **Clwt-y-bont** Gwynd
61 K4 **Clydach** Mons
57 J4 **Clydach** Swans
42 E3 **Clydach Vale** Rhondd
208 E5 **Clydebank** W Duns
75 M5 **Clydey** Pembks
47 G3 **Clyffe Pypard** Wilts
207 L2 **Clynder** Ag & B
60 B7 **Clyne** Neath
109 G2 **Clynnog-fawr** Gwynd
79 H6 **Clyro** Powys
14 A4 **Clyst Honiton** Devon
14 B2 **Clyst Hydon** Devon
14 A5 **Clyst St George** Devon
14 B2 **Clyst St Lawrence** Devon
14 A4 **Clyst St Mary** Devon
282 g3 **Cnoc** W Isls
92 E8 **Cnwch Coch** Cerdgn
11 K7 **Coad's Green** Cnwll
133 G4 **Coal Aston** Derbys
61 K5 **Coalbrookvale** Blae G
198 D6 **Coalburn** S Lans
180 D6 **Coalburns** Gatesd
63 M6 **Coaley** Gloucs
71 J7 **Coalhill** Essex
96 F2 **Coalmoor** Wrekin
45 K3 **Coalpit Heath** S Glos
98 C3 **Coal Pool** Wsall
96 F3 **Coalport** Wrekin
221 G8 **Coalsnaughton** Clacks
90 F1 **Coal Street** Suffk
222 E7 **Coaltown of Balgonie** Fife
222 E8 **Coaltown of Wemyss** Fife
116 D8 **Coalville** Leics
178 F7 **Coanwood** Nthumb
31 G6 **Coat** Somset
209 J6 **Coatbridge** N Lans
209 K6 **Coatdyke** N Lans
47 J2 **Coate** Swindn
46 F6 **Coate** Wilts
102 F4 **Coates** Cambs
64 E7 **Coates** Gloucs
135 H3 **Coates** Lincs
135 G3 **Coates** Notts
21 G3 **Coates** W Susx
170 E5 **Coatham** R & Cl
169 H6 **Coatham Mundeville** Darltn
27 L5 **Cobbaton** Devon
64 D4 **Coberley** Gloucs
80 B8 **Cobhall Common** Herefs
52 E5 **Cobham** Kent
50 E7 **Cobham** Surrey
71 G3 **Coblers Green** Essex
33 H6 **Cobley** Dorset
80 B3 **Cobnash** Herefs
9 j2 **Cobo** Guern
114 D2 **Cobridge** C Stke
269 G3 **Coburby** Abers
133 H5 **Cock Alley** Derbys
161 K3 **Cockayne** N York
86 F5 **Cockayne Hatley** C Beds
112 E2 **Cock Bank** Wrexhm
82 C5 **Cock Bevington** Warwks
243 J2 **Cock Bridge** Abers
213 G5 **Cockburnspath** Border
71 K6 **Cock Clarks** Essex
88 E4 **Cock & End** Suffk
211 L4 **Cockenzie and Port Seton** E Loth
139 G3 **Cocker Bar** Lancs
139 L3 **Cocker Brook** Lancs
147 J5 **Cockerham** Lancs
164 F4 **Cockermouth** Cumb
68 E2 **Cockernhoe** Herts

| Ref | Place | Area |
|---|---|---|
| 141 K2 | Cockersdale | Leeds |
| 57 H6 | Cockett | Swans |
| 168 E6 | Cockfield | Dur |
| 89 H4 | Cockfield | Suffk |
| 69 H7 | Cockfosters | Gt Lon |
| 71 G3 | Cock Green | Essex |
| 20 E3 | Cocking | W Susx |
| 20 E3 | Cocking Causeway | W Susx |
| 8 D2 | Cockington | Torbay |
| 31 G1 | Cocklake | Somset |
| 156 C2 | Cockley Beck | Cumb |
| 104 F3 | Cockley Cley | Norfk |
| 24 F3 | Cock Marling | E Susx |
| 49 J3 | Cockpole Green | Wokham |
| 4 C4 | Cocks | Cnwll |
| 96 D6 | Cockshutford | Shrops |
| 113 G5 | Cockshutt | Shrops |
| 39 K3 | Cock Street | Kent |
| 121 L3 | Cockthorpe | Norfk |
| 2 E4 | Cockwells | Cnwll |
| 14 A6 | Cockwood | Devon |
| 30 B2 | Cockwood | Somset |
| 131 L4 | Cockyard | Derbys |
| 80 A8 | Cockyard | Herefs |
| 90 D4 | Coddenham | Suffk |
| 129 K8 | Coddington | Ches W |
| 81 G6 | Coddington | Herefs |
| 117 L1 | Coddington | Notts |
| 33 G3 | Codford St Mary | Wilts |
| 33 G3 | Codford St Peter | Wilts |
| 69 G3 | Codicote | Herts |
| 21 H3 | Codmore Hill | W Susx |
| 116 C2 | Codnor | Derbys |
| 45 L3 | Codrington | S Glos |
| 97 K3 | Codsall | Staffs |
| 97 J2 | Codsall Wood | Staffs |
| 125 H3 | Coedana | IoA |
| 42 F4 | Coedely | Rhondd |
| 44 B2 | Coedkernew | Newpt |
| 62 D5 | Coed Morgan | Mons |
| 112 D1 | Coedpoeth | Wrexhm |
| 129 G7 | Coed Talon | Flints |
| 112 E8 | Coedway | Powys |
| 76 C6 | Coed-y-Bryn | Cerdgn |
| 44 D1 | Coed-y-caerau | Newpt |
| 62 C7 | Coed-y-paen | Mons |
| 61 J3 | Coed-yr-ynys | Powys |
| 109 K6 | Coed Ystumgwern | Gwynd |
| 60 C5 | Coelbren | Powys |
| 8 D1 | Coffinswell | Devon |
| 85 K3 | Coffle End | Bed |
| 13 M6 | Cofton | Devon |
| 98 C8 | Cofton Hackett | Worcs |
| 43 J7 | Cogan | V Glam |
| 84 F3 | Cogenhoe | Nhants |
| 65 M5 | Cogges | Oxon |
| 71 K3 | Coggeshall | Essex |
| 23 K2 | Coggin's Mill | E Susx |
| 251 J8 | Coignafearn | Highld |
| 243 K4 | Coilacriech | Abers |
| 219 K5 | Coilantogle | Stirlg |
| 246 E1 | Coillore | Highld |
| 42 D5 | Coity | Brdgnd |
| 282 g3 | Col | W Isls |
| 272 E6 | Colaboll | Highld |
| 4 E3 | Colan | Cnwll |
| 14 C5 | Colaton Raleigh | Devon |
| 258 C7 | Colbost | Highld |
| 160 B3 | Colburn | N York |
| 166 F6 | Colby | Cumb |
| 154 b7 | Colby | IoM |
| 122 E5 | Colby | Norfk |
| 72 E2 | Colchester | Essex |
| 72 E2 | Colchester Crematorium | Essex |
| 48 D5 | Cold Ash | W Berk |
| 100 E8 | Cold Ashby | Nhants |
| 45 L4 | Cold Ashton | S Glos |
| 65 H3 | Cold Aston | Gloucs |
| 277 K4 | Coldbackie | Highld |
| 158 C2 | Coldbeck | Cumb |
| 55 J4 | Cold Blow | Pembks |
| 85 H5 | Cold Brayfield | M Keyn |
| 148 C2 | Cold Cotes | N York |
| 22 E5 | Coldean | Br & H |
| 13 J7 | Coldeast | Devon |
| 140 E2 | Colden | Calder |
| 35 G6 | Colden Common | Hants |
| 91 K3 | Coldfair Green | Suffk |
| 103 J3 | Coldham | Cambs |
| 135 L3 | Cold Hanworth | Lincs |
| 4 B5 | Coldharbour | Cnwll |
| 29 J8 | Coldharbour | Devon |
| 63 H6 | Coldharbour | Gloucs |
| 68 F4 | Cold Harbour | Herts |
| 48 F3 | Cold Harbour | Oxon |
| 37 H2 | Coldharbour | Surrey |
| 32 E2 | Cold Harbour | Wilts |
| 113 K7 | Cold Hatton | Wrekin |
| 113 K7 | Cold Hatton Heath | Wrekin |
| 169 L2 | Cold Hesleden | Dur |
| 142 B5 | Cold Hiendley | Wakefd |
| 84 C4 | Cold Higham | Nhants |
| 213 K6 | Coldingham | Border |
| 161 H6 | Cold Kirby | N York |
| 114 D5 | Coldmeece | Staffs |
| 100 F2 | Cold Newton | Leics |
| 11 H5 | Cold Northcott | Cnwll |
| 71 K7 | Cold Norton | Essex |
| 101 H2 | Cold Overton | Leics |
| 41 J6 | Coldred | Kent |
| 13 G1 | Coldridge | Devon |
| 202 C5 | Coldstream | Border |
| 21 H3 | Coldwaltham | W Susx |
| 80 A8 | Coldwell | Herefs |
| 257 H4 | Coldwells | Abers |
| 96 C6 | Cold Weston | Shrops |
| 31 L4 | Cole | Somset |
| 95 H6 | Colebatch | Shrops |
| 7 G3 | Colebrook | C Plym |
| 14 B1 | Colebrook | Devon |
| 13 H3 | Colebrooke | Devon |
| 135 K7 | Coleby | Lincs |
| 143 M4 | Coleby | N Linc |
| 99 G5 | Cole End | Warwks |
| 13 H2 | Coleford | Devon |
| 63 H5 | Coleford | Gloucs |
| 31 L1 | Coleford | Somset |
| 29 L4 | Coleford Water | Somset |
| 106 D6 | Colegate End | Norfk |
| 69 H5 | Cole Green | Herts |
| 70 B1 | Cole Green | Herts |
| 34 F1 | Cole Henley | Hants |
| 17 K2 | Colehill | Dorset |
| 69 G4 | Coleman Green | Herts |
| 38 C2 | Coleman's Hatch | E Susx |
| 113 G5 | Colemere | Shrops |
| 35 L5 | Colemore | Hants |
| 97 G4 | Colemore Green | Shrops |
| 221 K1 | Colenden | P & K |
| 116 C8 | Coleorton | Leics |
| 46 B5 | Colerne | Wilts |
| 64 E4 | Colesbourne | Gloucs |
| 8 A5 | Cole's Cross | Devon |
| 15 J2 | Coles Cross | Dorset |
| 86 C4 | Colesden | Bed |
| 90 C7 | Coles Green | Suffk |
| 68 B8 | Coleshill | Bucks |
| 65 K8 | Coleshill | Oxon |
| 99 G5 | Coleshill | Warwks |
| 14 C2 | Colestocks | Devon |
| 45 H7 | Coley | BaNES |
| 37 K4 | Colgate | W Susx |
| 223 H6 | Colinsburgh | Fife |
| 211 H5 | Colinton | C Edin |
| 207 G4 | Colintraive | Ag & B |
| 121 K6 | Colkirk | Norfk |
| 222 C1 | Collace | P & K |
| 281 d3 | Collafirth | Shet |
| 7 L7 | Collaton | Devon |
| 8 C3 | Collaton St Mary | Torbay |
| 266 C3 | College of Roseisle | Moray |
| 49 K6 | College Town | Br For |
| 222 D4 | Collessie | Fife |
| 28 B7 | Colleton Mills | Devon |
| 52 B1 | Collier Row | Gt Lon |
| 69 K3 | Collier's End | Herts |
| 24 C3 | Collier's Green | E Susx |
| 39 J5 | Colliers Green | Kent |
| 39 H4 | Collier Street | Kent |
| 169 J1 | Colliery Row | Sundld |
| 257 J6 | Collieston | Abers |
| 176 D4 | Collin | D & G |
| 47 K8 | Collingbourne Ducis | Wilts |
| 47 K7 | Collingbourne Kingston | Wilts |
| 150 E6 | Collingham | Leeds |
| 135 G7 | Collingham | Notts |
| 80 F3 | Collington | Herefs |
| 84 E4 | Collingtree | Nhants |
| 130 A1 | Collins Green | Warrtn |
| 81 G4 | Collins Green | Worcs |
| 234 F6 | Colliston | Angus |
| 14 C2 | Colliton | Devon |
| 101 M3 | Collyweston | Nhants |
| 182 E5 | Colmonell | S Ayrs |
| 86 C4 | Colmworth | Bed |
| 50 C3 | Colnbrook | Slough |
| 103 H8 | Colne | Cambs |
| 148 F7 | Colne | Lancs |
| 141 J4 | Colne Bridge | Kirk |
| 148 F7 | Colne Edge | Lancs |
| 71 K1 | Colne Engaine | Essex |
| 106 D2 | Colney | Norfk |
| 69 G6 | Colney Heath | Herts |
| 68 F6 | Colney Street | Herts |
| 65 G5 | Coln Rogers | Gloucs |
| 65 H6 | Coln St Aldwyns | Gloucs |
| 65 G5 | Coln St Dennis | Gloucs |
| 256 B5 | Colpy | Abers |
| 200 D1 | Colquhar | Border |
| 10 E8 | Colquite | Cnwll |
| 26 F7 | Colscott | Devon |
| 159 L6 | Colsterdale | N York |
| 118 B6 | Colsterworth | Lincs |
| 117 J5 | Colston Bassett | Notts |
| 266 C3 | Coltfield | Moray |
| 49 H8 | Colt Hill | Hants |
| 122 F7 | Coltishall | Norfk |
| 156 D5 | Colton | Cumb |
| 142 B1 | Colton | Leeds |
| 151 H6 | Colton | N York |
| 106 C2 | Colton | Norfk |
| 115 G7 | Colton | Staffs |
| 39 G4 | Colt's Hill | Kent |
| 81 H6 | Colwall | Herefs |
| 179 M4 | Colwell | Nthumb |
| 115 G7 | Colwich | Staffs |
| 117 G3 | Colwick | Notts |
| 42 E6 | Colwinston | V Glam |
| 20 F6 | Colworth | W Susx |
| 127 G4 | Colwyn Bay | Conwy |
| 14 F4 | Colyford | Devon |
| 14 F4 | Colyton | Devon |
| 7 L7 | Combe | Devon |
| 79 L3 | Combe | Herefs |
| 66 B4 | Combe | Oxon |
| 48 A6 | Combe | W Berk |
| 17 J3 | Combe Almer | Dorset |
| 36 E4 | Combe Common | Surrey |
| 45 M6 | Combe Down | BaNES |
| 8 C2 | Combe Fishacre | Devon |
| 29 L4 | Combe Florey | Somset |
| 45 L7 | Combe Hay | BaNES |
| 13 L8 | Combeinteignhead | Devon |
| 27 K2 | Combe Martin | Devon |
| 14 E2 | Combe Raleigh | Devon |
| 130 C4 | Comberbach | Ches W |
| 99 G2 | Comberford | Staffs |
| 87 H4 | Comberton | Cambs |
| 80 C2 | Comberton | Herefs |
| 30 D8 | Combe St Nicholas | Somset |
| 15 G4 | Combpyne | Devon |
| 115 H4 | Combridge | Staffs |
| 83 H5 | Combrook | Warwks |
| 131 L4 | Combs | Derbys |
| 90 B4 | Combs | Suffk |
| 90 B4 | Combs Ford | Suffk |
| 30 C2 | Combwich | Somset |
| 244 F2 | Comers | Abers |
| 81 J2 | Comhampton | Worcs |
| 55 K3 | Commercial | Pembks |
| 87 L3 | Commercial End | Cambs |
| 93 H3 | Commins Coch | Powys |
| 170 F8 | Commondale | N York |
| 138 C1 | Common Edge | Bpool |
| 164 D6 | Common End | Cumb |
| 6 A1 | Common Moor | Cnwll |
| 47 G2 | Common Platt | Wilts |
| 130 A5 | Commonside | Ches W |
| 115 L3 | Commonside | Derbys |
| 133 G4 | Common Side | Derbys |
| 113 H6 | Commonwood | Shrops |
| 112 F1 | Commonwood | Wrexhm |
| 30 D4 | Compass | Somset |
| 131 J2 | Compstall | Stockp |
| 175 G4 | Compstonend | D & G |
| 8 C2 | Compton | Devon |
| 34 D5 | Compton | Hants |
| 34 F5 | Compton | Hants |
| 97 J6 | Compton | Staffs |
| 36 E2 | Compton | Surrey |
| 48 D3 | Compton | W Berk |
| 20 C4 | Compton | W Susx |
| 47 H8 | Compton | Wilts |
| 32 E7 | Compton Abbas | Dorset |
| 64 F4 | Compton Abdale | Gloucs |
| 46 F4 | Compton Bassett | Wilts |
| 47 K2 | Compton Beauchamp | Oxon |
| 44 E7 | Compton Bishop | Somset |
| 33 H5 | Compton Chamberlayne | Wilts |
| 45 J6 | Compton Dando | BaNES |
| 31 H4 | Compton Dundon | Somset |
| 30 F7 | Compton Durville | Somset |
| 45 H3 | Compton Greenfield | S Glos |
| 45 G7 | Compton Martin | BaNES |
| 31 L5 | Compton Pauncefoot | Somset |
| 16 B4 | Compton Valence | Dorset |
| 83 H5 | Compton Verney | Warwks |
| 210 D1 | Comrie | Fife |
| 220 D3 | Comrie | P & K |
| 229 G2 | Conaglen House | Highld |
| 248 E6 | Conchra | Highld |
| 233 G6 | Concraigie | P & K |
| 147 J4 | Conder Green | Lancs |
| 81 M7 | Conderton | Worcs |
| 65 H2 | Condicote | Gloucs |
| 209 K4 | Condorrat | N Lans |
| 96 B2 | Condover | Shrops |
| 64 B3 | Coney Hill | Gloucs |
| 37 H6 | Coneyhurst Common | W Susx |
| 151 M2 | Coneysthorpe | N York |
| 150 E4 | Coneythorpe | N York |
| 105 J7 | Coney Weston | Suffk |
| 36 B4 | Conford | Hants |
| 11 K6 | Congdon's Shop | Cnwll |
| 99 K2 | Congerstone | Leics |
| 120 F6 | Congham | Norfk |
| 131 G7 | Congleton | Ches E |
| 110 D3 | Congl-y-wal | Gwynd |
| 44 E6 | Congresbury | N Som |
| 97 K1 | Congreve | Staffs |
| 176 C5 | Conheath | D & G |
| 253 J1 | Conicavel | Moray |
| 136 D8 | Coningsby | Lincs |
| 87 G2 | Conington | Cambs |
| 102 D6 | Conington | Cambs |
| 142 D8 | Conisbrough | Donc |
| 145 K8 | Conisholme | Lincs |
| 156 D3 | Coniston | Cumb |
| 144 F1 | Coniston | E R Yk |
| 148 F5 | Coniston Cold | N York |
| 149 H2 | Conistone | N York |
| 129 G6 | Connah's Quay | Flints |
| 228 E8 | Connel | Ag & B |
| 197 H8 | Connel Park | E Ayrs |
| 2 F3 | Connor Downs | Cnwll |
| 250 F1 | Conon Bridge | Highld |
| 149 H6 | Cononley | N York |
| 114 F2 | Consall | Staffs |
| 180 D8 | Consett | Dur |
| 159 L4 | Constable Burton | N York |
| 140 B3 | Constable Lee | Lancs |
| 3 J5 | Constantine | Cnwll |
| 10 B7 | Constantine Bay | Cnwll |
| 262 D8 | Contin | Highld |
| 126 F4 | Conwy | Conwy |
| 40 C2 | Conyer | Kent |
| 89 H2 | Conyer's Green | Suffk |
| 24 C6 | Cooden | E Susx |
| 12 A1 | Cookbury | Devon |
| 11 M2 | Cookbury Wick | Devon |
| 49 L2 | Cookham | W & M |
| 49 L2 | Cookham Dean | W & M |
| 49 L2 | Cookham Rise | W & M |
| 82 C3 | Cookhill | Worcs |
| 107 G8 | Cookley | Suffk |
| 97 J7 | Cookley | Worcs |
| 49 G1 | Cookley Green | Oxon |
| 245 J5 | Cookney | Abers |
| 22 F4 | Cooksbridge | E Susx |
| 81 L1 | Cooksey Green | Worcs |
| 73 J3 | Cook's Green | Essex |
| 89 K4 | Cooks Green | Suffk |
| 114 E3 | Cookshill | Staffs |
| 5 J1 | Cooksland | Cnwll |
| 70 F6 | Cooksmill Green | Essex |
| 130 B5 | Cookson Green | Ches W |
| 37 H6 | Coolham | W Susx |
| 53 G4 | Cooling | Medway |
| 52 F4 | Cooling Street | Medway |
| 3 G3 | Coombe | Cnwll |
| 3 L3 | Coombe | Cnwll |
| 4 F4 | Coombe | Cnwll |
| 13 J5 | Coombe | Devon |
| 13 L7 | Coombe | Devon |
| 14 C4 | Coombe | Devon |
| 63 M8 | Coombe | Gloucs |
| 35 K6 | Coombe | Hants |
| 33 K1 | Coombe | Wilts |
| 33 K5 | Coombe Bissett | Wilts |
| 13 L8 | Coombe Cellars | Devon |
| 35 K6 | Coombe Cross | Hants |
| 64 C2 | Coombe Hill | Gloucs |
| 17 G5 | Coombe Keynes | Dorset |
| 8 D2 | Coombe Pafford | Torbay |
| 21 L5 | Coombes | W Susx |
| 79 L3 | Coombes-Moor | Herefs |
| 32 C4 | Coombe Street | Somset |
| 98 B6 | Coombeswood | Dudley |
| 70 C6 | Coopersale Common | Essex |
| 70 C6 | Coopersale Street | Essex |
| 38 D3 | Cooper's Corner | Kent |
| 23 H3 | Coopers Green | E Susx |
| 69 G5 | Coopers Green | Herts |
| 41 J3 | Cooper Street | Kent |
| 139 J6 | Cooper Turning | Bolton |
| 21 J4 | Cootham | W Susx |
| 90 D6 | Copdock | Suffk |
| 72 D3 | Copford Green | Essex |
| 150 D3 | Copgrove | N York |
| 281 e4 | Copister | Shet |
| 86 C5 | Cople | Bed |
| 141 G3 | Copley | Calder |
| 168 D5 | Copley | Dur |
| 140 E8 | Copley | Tamesd |
| 132 C4 | Coplow Dale | Derbys |
| 151 J6 | Copmanthorpe | C York |
| 114 C5 | Copmere End | Staffs |

Copp - Cranworth 305


147 H7 **Copp** Lancs
11 H2 **Coppathorne** Cnwll
114 E7 **Coppenhall** Staffs
130 D8 **Coppenhall Moss** Ches E
2 F3 **Copperhouse** Cnwll
97 G7 **Coppicegate** Shrops
102 D7 **Coppingford** Cambs
40 B5 **Coppins Corner** Kent
13 H2 **Copplestone** Devon
139 H5 **Coppull** Lancs
139 H5 **Coppull Moor** Lancs
37 J6 **Copsale** W Susx
139 K1 **Copster Green** Lancs
99 M5 **Copston Magna** Warwks
41 J3 **Cop Street** Kent
70 B7 **Copthall Green** Essex
98 F7 **Copt Heath** Solhll
150 D2 **Copt Hewick** N York
11 K4 **Copthorne** Cnwll
37 M3 **Copthorne** W Susx
100 B1 **Copt Oak** Leics
121 L4 **Copy's Green** Norfk
34 C8 **Copythorne** Hants
89 K6 **Coram Street** Suffk
52 C2 **Corbets Tey** Gt Lon
9 a3 **Corbiere** Jersey
180 B6 **Corbridge** Nthumb
101 K5 **Corby** Nhants
118 C6 **Corby Glen** Lincs
178 B7 **Corby Hill** Cumb
195 G5 **Cordon** N Ayrs
132 F4 **Cordwell** Derbys
96 E8 **Coreley** Shrops
49 L2 **Cores End** Bucks
30 C7 **Corfe** Somset
17 J6 **Corfe Castle** Dorset
17 J3 **Corfe Mullen** Dorset
96 B6 **Corfton** Shrops
243 J2 **Corgarff** Abers
35 J6 **Corhampton** Hants
39 G5 **Corks Pond** Kent
99 J6 **Corley** Warwks
99 J6 **Corley Ash** Warwks
99 H6 **Corley Moor** Warwks
233 L2 **Cormuir** Angus
89 H7 **Cornard Tye** Suffk
13 G5 **Corndon** Devon
138 E1 **Corner Row** Lancs
155 K4 **Corney** Cumb
169 J4 **Cornforth** Dur
267 M4 **Cornhill** Abers
202 D5 **Cornhill-on-Tweed** Nthumb
140 D3 **Cornholme** Calder
88 D7 **Cornish Hall End** Essex
224 C6 **Cornoigmore** Ag & B
167 K2 **Cornriggs** Dur
168 F2 **Cornsay** Dur
168 F2 **Cornsay Colliery** Dur
262 F8 **Corntown** Highld
42 D6 **Corntown** V Glam
65 K2 **Cornwell** Oxon
7 H3 **Cornwood** Devon
8 B4 **Cornworthy** Devon
239 H8 **Corpach** Highld
122 C5 **Corpusty** Norfk
244 B3 **Corrachree** Abers
5 G5 **Corran** Cnwll
229 G3 **Corran** Highld
238 D2 **Corran** Highld
154 f4 **Corrany** IoM
177 G2 **Corrie** D & G
195 G2 **Corrie** N Ayrs
193 J4 **Corriecravie** N Ayrs
195 G4 **Corriegills** N Ayrs
239 M5 **Corriegour Lodge Hotel** Highld
262 C7 **Corriemoille** Highld
250 C5 **Corrimony** Highld
135 H2 **Corringham** Lincs
52 F2 **Corringham** Thurr
93 G2 **Corris** Gwynd
92 F2 **Corris Uchaf** Gwynd
217 K7 **Corrow** Ag & B
247 K4 **Corry** Highld
12 E3 **Corscombe** Devon
15 L1 **Corscombe** Dorset
64 A2 **Corse** Gloucs
64 B1 **Corse Lawn** Gloucs
46 C5 **Corsham** Wilts
244 F2 **Corsindae** Abers
32 D2 **Corsley** Wilts
32 D2 **Corsley Heath** Wilts
185 J7 **Corsock** D & G
45 K6 **Corston** BaNES
46 D2 **Corston** Wilts
211 G4 **Corstorphine** C Edin
109 L7 **Cors-y-Gedol** Gwynd
234 B3 **Cortachy** Angus
107 L4 **Corton** Suffk
32 F3 **Corton** Wilts
31 K6 **Corton Denham** Somset
229 H2 **Coruanan** Highld
111 L3 **Corwen** Denbgs
16 B5 **Coryates** Dorset
12 B5 **Coryton** Devon
52 F2 **Coryton** Thurr
100 C4 **Cosby** Leics
97 L4 **Coseley** Dudley
97 H2 **Cosford** Shrops
84 F6 **Cosgrove** Nhants
19 L3 **Cosham** C Port
55 G6 **Cosheston** Pembks
231 L5 **Coshieville** P & K
116 E3 **Cossall** Notts
116 E3 **Cossall Marsh** Notts
100 D1 **Cossington** Leics
30 E3 **Cossington** Somset
106 D1 **Costessey** Norfk
116 F6 **Costock** Notts
117 M7 **Coston** Leics
106 B2 **Coston** Norfk
65 M6 **Cote** Oxon
30 E2 **Cote** Somset
130 B6 **Cotebrook** Ches W
166 B1 **Cotehill** Cumb
157 G5 **Cotes** Cumb
116 F7 **Cotes** Leics
114 C4 **Cotes** Staffs
100 C7 **Cotesbach** Leics
114 C4 **Cotes Heath** Staffs
30 A5 **Cotford St Luke** Somset
117 H4 **Cotgrave** Notts
256 F8 **Cothal** Abers
117 L2 **Cotham** Notts
30 B4 **Cothelstone** Somset
168 C6 **Cotherstone** Dur
66 C7 **Cothill** Oxon
14 E2 **Cotleigh** Devon
116 D3 **Cotmanhay** Derbys
87 H3 **Coton** Cambs
84 D1 **Coton** Nhants
113 J4 **Coton** Shrops
98 F2 **Coton** Staffs
114 C7 **Coton** Staffs
114 F5 **Coton** Staffs
114 D7 **Coton Clanford** Staffs
114 F5 **Coton Hayes** Staffs
96 B1 **Coton Hill** Shrops
115 K5 **Coton in the Clay** Staffs
115 L8 **Coton in the Elms** Derbys
115 M7 **Coton Park** Derbys
8 B3 **Cott** Devon
34 E2 **Cottage End** Hants
152 F3 **Cottam** E R Yk
139 G1 **Cottam** Lancs
135 G4 **Cottam** Notts
87 J2 **Cottenham** Cambs
158 E4 **Cotterdale** N York
69 J1 **Cottered** Herts
98 D7 **Cotteridge** Birm
102 A5 **Cotterstock** Nhants
100 F8 **Cottesbrooke** Nhants
101 K1 **Cottesmore** Rutlnd
144 D1 **Cottingham** E R Yk
101 J5 **Cottingham** Nhants
149 K8 **Cottingley** C Brad
141 L2 **Cottingley Hall Crematorium** Leeds
66 E1 **Cottisford** Oxon
90 C2 **Cotton** Suffk
86 B6 **Cotton End** Bed
148 F7 **Cotton Tree** Lancs
255 K6 **Cottown** Abers
256 D8 **Cottown** Abers
256 E4 **Cottown of Gight** Abers
43 G6 **Cottrell** V Glam
6 E2 **Cotts** Devon
113 K8 **Cotwall** Wrekin
114 E4 **Cotwalton** Staffs
5 K3 **Couch's Mill** Cnwll
63 H3 **Coughton** Herefs
82 C3 **Coughton** Warwks
206 A6 **Coulaghailtro** Ag & B
248 F3 **Coulags** Highld
155 H1 **Coulderton** Cumb
244 B3 **Coull** Abers
207 L2 **Coulport** Ag & B
51 J7 **Coulsdon** Gt Lon
46 D8 **Coulston** Wilts
199 H6 **Coulter** S Lans
21 G3 **Coultershaw Bridge** W Susx
30 C3 **Coultings** Somset
161 K7 **Coulton** N York
222 F3 **Coultra** Fife
96 D2 **Cound** Shrops
96 D2 **Coundlane** Shrops
169 G5 **Coundon** Dur
169 G5 **Coundon Grange** Dur
159 G5 **Countersett** N York
33 K2 **Countess** Wilts
72 C1 **Countess Cross** Essex
13 M4 **Countess Wear** Devon
100 D4 **Countesthorpe** Leics
28 C1 **Countisbury** Devon
233 K7 **Coupar Angus** P & K
139 H2 **Coup Green** Lancs
167 G7 **Coupland** Cumb
202 E7 **Coupland** Nthumb
194 C2 **Cour** Ag & B
40 E8 **Court-at-Street** Kent
237 K1 **Courteachan** Highld
84 E4 **Courteenhall** Nhants
59 G4 **Court Henry** Carmth
72 F8 **Courtsend** Essex
30 B4 **Courtway** Somset
211 L5 **Cousland** Mdloth
39 G6 **Cousley Wood** E Susx
207 L3 **Cove** Ag & B
213 G4 **Cove** Border
29 G7 **Cove** Devon
49 L7 **Cove** Hants
260 C2 **Cove** Highld
245 L3 **Cove Bay** C Aber
107 K7 **Cove Bottom** Suffk
107 L7 **Covehithe** Suffk
97 K2 **Coven** Staffs
103 K7 **Coveney** Cambs
136 F1 **Covenham St Bartholomew** Lincs
136 F1 **Covenham St Mary** Lincs
97 K2 **Coven Heath** Staffs
99 J7 **Coventry** Covtry
3 K7 **Coverack** Cnwll
3 H5 **Coverack Bridges** Cnwll
159 K5 **Coverham** N York
85 L1 **Covington** Cambs
199 G5 **Covington** S Lans
157 K7 **Cowan Bridge** Lancs
23 K4 **Cowbeech** E Susx
119 H7 **Cowbit** Lincs
42 F6 **Cowbridge** V Glam
132 B5 **Cowdale** Derbys
38 C5 **Cowden** Kent
211 G1 **Cowdenbeath** Fife
38 C5 **Cowden Pound** Kent
38 D5 **Cowden Station** Kent
116 A2 **Cowers Lane** Derbys
19 H4 **Cowes** IoW
161 G5 **Cowesby** N York
34 B6 **Cowesfield Green** Wilts
37 K6 **Cowfold** W Susx
158 C5 **Cowgill** Cumb
90 C2 **Cow Green** Suffk
45 J1 **Cowhill** S Glos
82 D6 **Cow Honeybourne** Worcs
209 M1 **Cowie** Stirlg
152 E3 **Cowlam** E R Yk
13 L3 **Cowley** Devon
64 D4 **Cowley** Gloucs
50 D3 **Cowley** Gt Lon
66 D6 **Cowley** Oxon
139 J4 **Cowling** Lancs
149 H7 **Cowling** N York
160 C5 **Cowling** N York
88 E4 **Cowlinge** Suffk
141 J4 **Cowmes** Kirk
140 C4 **Cowpe** Lancs
181 H3 **Cowpen** Nthumb
170 B5 **Cowpen Bewley** S on T
19 M2 **Cowplain** Hants
167 K3 **Cowshill** Dur
44 F6 **Cowslip Green** N Som
150 F5 **Cowthorpe** N York
95 J8 **Coxall** Herefs
113 L3 **Coxbank** Ches E
116 C3 **Coxbench** Derbys
31 J3 **Coxbridge** Somset
107 H7 **Cox Common** Suffk
11 H3 **Coxford** Cnwll
121 J5 **Coxford** Norfk
97 H6 **Coxgreen** Staffs
39 J3 **Coxheath** Kent
169 J3 **Coxhoe** Dur
31 H2 **Coxley** Somset
141 L4 **Coxley** Wakefd
31 H2 **Coxley Wick** Somset
12 A8 **Coxpark** Cnwll
70 E7 **Coxtie Green** Essex
161 H7 **Coxwold** N York
42 E6 **Coychurch** Brdgnd
42 D5 **Coychurch Crematorium** Brdgnd
196 E7 **Coylton** S Ayrs
242 B1 **Coylumbridge** Highld
42 D4 **Coytrahen** Brdgnd
82 B2 **Crabbs Cross** Worcs
17 L1 **Crab Orchard** Dorset
37 K6 **Crabtree** W Susx
112 E3 **Crabtree Green** Wrexhm
166 F6 **Crackenthorpe** Cumb
11 G3 **Crackington Haven** Cnwll
114 C2 **Crackley** Staffs
99 J8 **Crackley** Warwks
97 G1 **Crackleybank** Shrops
159 H3 **Crackpot** N York
149 H4 **Cracoe** N York
29 K8 **Craddock** Devon
70 C3 **Cradle End** Herts
97 L6 **Cradley** Dudley
81 G6 **Cradley** Herefs
97 L6 **Cradley Heath** Sandw
60 F1 **Cradoc** Powys
6 D4 **Crafthole** Cnwll
67 L3 **Crafton** Bucks
157 G7 **Crag Foot** Lancs
253 K6 **Craggan** Highld
150 B8 **Cragg Hill** Leeds
180 F8 **Craghead** Dur
60 D2 **Crai** Powys
267 K4 **Craibstone** Moray
234 D6 **Craichie** Angus
235 H4 **Craig** Angus
249 H2 **Craig** Highld
197 H8 **Craigbank** E Ayrs
200 B2 **Craigburn** Border
57 J4 **Craigcefnparc** Swans
177 K2 **Craigcleuch** D & G
256 F5 **Craigdam** Abers
216 C6 **Craigdhu** Ag & B
245 G1 **Craigearn** Abers
254 F3 **Craigellachie** Moray
221 K3 **Craigend** P & K
208 D5 **Craigend** Rens
208 A3 **Craigendoran** Ag & B
208 C6 **Craigends** Rens
173 H3 **Craighlaw** D & G
205 H3 **Craighouse** Ag & B
233 H6 **Craigie** P & K
196 E4 **Craigie** S Ayrs
269 G3 **Craigiefold** Abers
175 J3 **Craigley** D & G
57 K4 **Craig Llangiwg** Neath
211 H5 **Craiglockhart** C Edin
211 J4 **Craigmillar** C Edin
112 C4 **Craignant** Shrops
185 J5 **Craigneston** D & G
209 K6 **Craigneuk** N Lans
209 K7 **Craigneuk** N Lans
227 L5 **Craignure** Ag & B
235 H3 **Craigo** Angus
42 E6 **Craig Penllyn** V Glam
222 F5 **Craigrothie** Fife
219 H3 **Craigruie** Stirlg
88 E7 **Craig's End** Essex
234 D7 **Craigton** Angus
245 J3 **Craigton** C Aber
208 E8 **Craigton** E Rens
233 M5 **Craigton of Airlie** Angus
57 K4 **Craig-y-Duke** Neath
60 C4 **Craig-y-nos** Powys
223 L5 **Crail** Fife
189 J1 **Crailing** Border
143 J8 **Craiselound** N Linc
160 C5 **Crakehall** N York
160 F7 **Crakehill** N York
115 H4 **Crakemarsh** Staffs
151 M3 **Crambe** N York
181 G3 **Cramlington** Nthumb
211 G4 **Cramond** C Edin
211 G4 **Cramond Bridge** C Edin
34 E6 **Crampmoor** Hants
130 E6 **Cranage** Ches E
114 C4 **Cranberry** Staffs
33 H8 **Cranborne** Dorset
50 A4 **Cranbourne** Br For
39 J6 **Cranbrook** Kent
39 K5 **Cranbrook Common** Kent
141 M7 **Crane Moor** Barns
105 J1 **Crane's Corner** Norfk
85 J6 **Cranfield** C Beds
26 F6 **Cranford** Devon
50 E4 **Cranford** Gt Lon
101 K7 **Cranford St Andrew** Nhants
101 K8 **Cranford St John** Nhants
64 C4 **Cranham** Gloucs
52 C2 **Cranham** Gt Lon
82 D4 **Cranhill** Warwks
139 G7 **Crank** St Hel
37 G3 **Cranleigh** Surrey
89 L1 **Cranmer Green** Suffk
18 F5 **Cranmore** IoW
31 L2 **Cranmore** Somset
101 G4 **Cranoe** Leics
91 H2 **Cransford** Suffk
212 F6 **Cranshaws** Border
154 f2 **Cranstal** IoM
152 F5 **Cranswick** E R Yk
4 C3 **Crantock** Cnwll
118 D2 **Cranwell** Lincs
104 F4 **Cranwich** Norfk
105 K3 **Cranworth** Norfk

216 B5 **Craobh Haven** Ag & B
6 F1 **Crapstone** Devon
216 F7 **Crarae** Ag & B
272 D3 **Crask Inn** Highld
250 E3 **Crask of Aigas** Highld
191 K2 **Craster** Nthumb
79 K8 **Craswall** Herefs
97 K2 **Crateford** Staffs
107 G8 **Cratfield** Suffk
245 G4 **Crathes** Abers
243 J4 **Crathie** Abers
241 G5 **Crathie** Highld
161 G1 **Crathorne** N York
95 K6 **Craven Arms** Shrops
180 D6 **Crawcrook** Gatesd
139 G7 **Crawford** Lancs
186 E2 **Crawford** S Lans
186 C2 **Crawfordjohn** S Lans
34 F4 **Crawley** Hants
65 M4 **Crawley** Oxon
37 L4 **Crawley** W Susx
38 A6 **Crawley Down** W Susx
168 C3 **Crawleyside** Dur
140 B3 **Crawshawbooth** Lancs
245 J7 **Crawton** Abers
72 D3 **Craxe's Green** Essex
159 G6 **Cray** N York
52 B4 **Crayford** Gt Lon
151 J2 **Crayke** N York
122 B5 **Craymere Beck** Norfk
71 H8 **Crays Hill** Essex
48 F3 **Cray's Pond** Oxon
115 L6 **Craythorne** Staffs
29 H8 **Craze Lowman** Devon
49 J3 **Crazies Hill** Wokham
28 E7 **Creacombe** Devon
228 F6 **Creagan Inn** Ag & B
283 C9 **Creag Ghoraidh** W Isls
283 C9 **Creagorry** W Isls
230 B2 **Creaguaineach Lodge** Highld
113 H5 **Creamore Bank** Shrops
84 D1 **Creaton** Nhants
177 H5 **Creca** D & G
80 B6 **Credenhill** Herefs
13 J2 **Crediton** Devon
183 J7 **Creebank** D & G
173 K2 **Creebridge** D & G
17 H5 **Creech** Dorset
30 D5 **Creech Heathfield** Somset
30 C6 **Creech St Michael** Somset
4 F5 **Creed** Cnwll
51 M3 **Creekmouth** Gt Lon
72 D7 **Creeksea** Essex
90 C4 **Creeting St Mary** Suffk
118 D7 **Creeton** Lincs
174 D3 **Creetown** D & G
154 b8 **Cregneash** IoM
154 e5 **Cregny Baa** IoM
79 G5 **Cregrina** Powys
222 E3 **Creich** Fife
43 G5 **Creigiau** Cardif
6 E4 **Cremyll** Cnwll
96 D3 **Cressage** Shrops
132 C5 **Cressbrook** Derbys
55 H5 **Cresselly** Pembks
67 K8 **Cressex** Bucks
71 J3 **Cressing** Essex
191 K7 **Cresswell** Nthumb
55 H5 **Cresswell** Pembks
114 F4 **Cresswell** Staffs
133 K5 **Creswell** Derbys
98 D1 **Creswell Green** Staffs
90 F3 **Cretingham** Suffk
206 A5 **Cretshengan** Ag & B
130 D8 **Crewe** Ches E
112 F1 **Crewe** Ches W
130 D8 **Crewe Crematorium** Ches E
130 E8 **Crewe Green** Ches E
112 D8 **Crew Green** Powys
15 K1 **Crewkerne** Somset
69 J7 **Crews Hill Station** Gt Lon
116 C5 **Crewton** C Derb
218 F2 **Crianlarich** Stirlg
76 F5 **Cribyn** Cerdgn
109 J4 **Criccieth** Gwynd
116 B1 **Crich** Derbys
116 B1 **Crich Carr** Derbys
211 L6 **Crichton** Mdloth
44 F1 **Crick** Mons
84 B1 **Crick** Nhants
78 F6 **Crickadarn** Powys
15 J1 **Cricket St Thomas** Somset
112 D7 **Crickheath** Shrops
61 K3 **Crickhowell** Powys
65 G8 **Cricklade** Wilts
51 G2 **Cricklewood** Gt Lon
142 E3 **Cridling Stubbs** N York
220 F3 **Crieff** P & K
5 G3 **Criggan** Cnwll
112 D8 **Criggion** Powys

141 M4 **Crigglestone** Wakefd
140 C5 **Crimble** Rochdl
269 K5 **Crimond** Abers
104 C3 **Crimplesham** Norfk
82 F5 **Crimscote** Warwks
250 D4 **Crinaglack** Highld
216 B8 **Crinan** Ag & B
209 L7 **Crindledyke** N Lans
106 D2 **Cringleford** Norfk
149 J6 **Cringles** C Brad
55 K4 **Crinow** Pembks
2 D4 **Crippleease** Cnwll
33 J8 **Cripplestyle** Dorset
24 D3 **Cripp's Corner** E Susx
62 F1 **Crizeley** Herefs
251 H6 **Croachy** Highld
10 E8 **Croanford** Cnwll
52 B5 **Crockenhill** Kent
49 H2 **Crocker End** Oxon
20 F5 **Crockerhill** W Susx
13 H4 **Crockernwell** Devon
63 G4 **Crocker's Ash** Herefs
32 E2 **Crockerton** Wilts
185 K8 **Crocketford** D & G
151 K6 **Crockey Hill** C York
38 C3 **Crockham Hill** Kent
39 G4 **Crockhurst Street** Kent
72 F2 **Crockleford Heath** Essex
30 D8 **Crock Street** Somset
42 C3 **Croeserw** Neath
74 D6 **Croes-goch** Pembks
76 C6 **Croes-lan** Cerdgn
110 B3 **Croesor** Gwynd
58 D5 **Croesyceiliog** Carmth
62 C7 **Croesyceiliog** Torfn
62 C8 **Croes-y-mwyalch** Torfn
62 C6 **Croes-y-pant** Mons
100 B4 **Croft** Leics
137 J7 **Croft** Lincs
130 C1 **Croft** Warrtn
208 E2 **Croftamie** Stirlg
3 H4 **Croft Mitchell** Cnwll
165 J1 **Crofton** Cumb
142 B4 **Crofton** Wakefd
47 K6 **Crofton** Wilts
160 D1 **Croft-on-Tees** N York
261 K3 **Croftown** Highld
266 F6 **Crofts** Moray
139 M8 **Crofts Bank** Traffd
267 G4 **Crofts of Dipple** Moray
269 J4 **Crofts of Savoch** Abers
56 F6 **Crofty** Swans
111 K4 **Crogen** Gwynd
227 K7 **Croggan** Ag & B
166 D1 **Croglin** Cumb
262 D2 **Croick** Highld
264 B6 **Cromarty** Highld
210 E2 **Crombie** Fife
253 L6 **Cromdale** Highld
69 J2 **Cromer** Herts
122 E3 **Cromer** Norfk
132 F8 **Cromford** Derbys
45 K1 **Cromhall** S Glos
45 K1 **Cromhall Common** S Glos
282 g4 **Cromor** W Isls
140 E6 **Crompton Fold** Oldham
134 F7 **Cromwell** Notts
197 H6 **Cronberry** E Ayrs
36 B1 **Crondall** Hants
154 e6 **Cronkbourne** IoM
154 d5 **Cronk-y-Voddy** IoM
129 L2 **Cronton** Knows
157 G4 **Crook** Cumb
168 F4 **Crook** Dur
165 G2 **Crookdake** Cumb
139 H6 **Crooke** Wigan
63 J3 **Crooked End** Gloucs
196 E3 **Crookedholm** E Ayrs
47 L4 **Crooked Soley** Wilts
132 F2 **Crookes** Sheff
180 D8 **Crookhall** Dur
202 E5 **Crookham** Nthumb
48 D6 **Crookham** W Berk
49 J8 **Crookham Village** Hants
199 J7 **Crook Inn** Border
157 H6 **Crooklands** Cumb
221 J7 **Crook of Devon** P & K
115 L4 **Cropper** Derbys
83 L6 **Cropredy** Oxon
100 C1 **Cropston** Leics
82 B6 **Cropthorne** Worcs
162 D5 **Cropton** N York
117 H4 **Cropwell Bishop** Notts
117 J4 **Cropwell Butler** Notts
282 h1 **Cros** W Isls
195 K1 **Crosbie** N Ayrs
282 g4 **Crosbost** W Isls
164 E3 **Crosby** Cumb
154 d6 **Crosby** IoM
143 M5 **Crosby** N Linc

138 C8 **Crosby** Sefton
158 C1 **Crosby Garret** Cumb
166 E7 **Crosby Ravensworth** Cumb
164 E3 **Crosby Villa** Cumb
31 K2 **Croscombe** Somset
113 G5 **Crosemere** Shrops
141 H5 **Crosland Edge** Kirk
141 H5 **Crosland Hill** Kirk
44 E8 **Cross** Somset
194 C1 **Crossaig** Ag & B
224 C6 **Crossapoll** Ag & B
62 E3 **Cross Ash** Mons
39 K4 **Cross-at-Hand** Kent
21 H5 **Crossbush** W Susx
164 E3 **Crosscanonby** Cumb
4 B4 **Cross Coombe** Cnwll
122 E4 **Crossdale Street** Norfk
85 L4 **Cross End** Bed
89 G8 **Cross End** Essex
138 D4 **Crossens** Sefton
149 K7 **Cross Flatts** C Brad
210 E2 **Crossford** Fife
198 D4 **Crossford** S Lans
11 L5 **Crossgate** Cnwll
119 H6 **Crossgate** Lincs
114 E4 **Crossgate** Staffs
211 L5 **Crossgatehall** E Loth
196 D2 **Crossgates** E Ayrs
210 F1 **Crossgates** Fife
142 B1 **Cross Gates** Leeds
163 J6 **Crossgates** N York
78 F2 **Crossgates** Powys
147 L3 **Crossgill** Lancs
11 M5 **Cross Green** Devon
141 M2 **Cross Green** Leeds
97 K2 **Cross Green** Staffs
89 G4 **Cross Green** Suffk
89 H4 **Cross Green** Suffk
89 K4 **Cross Green** Suffk
55 L2 **Crosshands** Carmth
59 G6 **Cross Hands** Carmth
196 F5 **Crosshands** E Ayrs
55 H4 **Cross Hands** Pembks
116 C2 **Cross Hill** Derbys
222 B7 **Crosshill** Fife
183 J2 **Crosshill** S Ayrs
149 H6 **Cross Hills** N York
196 D3 **Crosshouse** E Ayrs
96 C2 **Cross Houses** Shrops
96 F5 **Cross Houses** Shrops
23 J3 **Cross in Hand** E Susx
76 D4 **Cross Inn** Cerdgn
77 G2 **Cross Inn** Cerdgn
55 J5 **Cross Inn** Pembks
43 G5 **Cross Inn** Rhondd
208 B2 **Cross Keys** Ag & B
43 K3 **Crosskeys** Caerph
46 C5 **Cross Keys** Wilts
279 H2 **Crosskirk** Highld
156 E5 **Crosslands** Cumb
19 H5 **Cross Lane** IoW
97 G4 **Cross Lane Head** Shrops
3 H6 **Cross Lanes** Cnwll
4 C6 **Cross Lanes** Cnwll
151 H3 **Cross Lanes** N York
112 E7 **Crosslanes** Shrops
112 E2 **Cross Lanes** Wrexhm
208 C6 **Crosslee** Rens
141 K3 **Crossley** Kirk
175 J2 **Crossmichael** D & G
61 H2 **Cross Oak** Powys
256 D5 **Cross of Jackston** Abers
115 M2 **Cross o' th' hands** Derbys
37 L6 **Crosspost** W Susx
244 D2 **Crossroads** Abers
245 G5 **Crossroads** Abers
106 D8 **Cross Street** Suffk
234 E4 **Crosston** Angus
130 E4 **Cross Town** Ches E
62 F3 **Crossway** Mons
78 E4 **Crossway** Powys
63 G8 **Crossway Green** Mons
81 J2 **Crossway Green** Worcs
16 E5 **Crossways** Dorset
75 J5 **Crosswell** Pembks
157 H6 **Crosthwaite** Cumb
138 F4 **Croston** Lancs
122 E8 **Crostwick** Norfk
123 G5 **Crostwight** Norfk
38 F2 **Crouch** Kent
40 D4 **Crouch** Kent
51 J1 **Crouch End** Gt Lon
33 J6 **Croucheston** Wilts
32 B8 **Crouch Hill** Dorset
38 C4 **Crough House Green** Kent
84 A8 **Croughton** Nhants
268 E3 **Crovie** Abers
18 B3 **Crow** Hants
3 G4 **Crowan** Cnwll
38 D7 **Crowborough** E Susx

38 D7 **Crowborough Town** E Susx
29 L3 **Crowcombe** Somset
132 B6 **Crowdecote** Derbys
141 G7 **Crowden** Derbys
12 C3 **Crowden** Devon
35 G6 **Crowdhill** Hants
52 C7 **Crowdleham** Kent
141 J6 **Crow Edge** Barns
67 H7 **Crowell** Oxon
87 G4 **Crow End** Cambs
84 B7 **Crowfield** Nhants
90 D4 **Crowfield** Suffk
90 D4 **Crowfield Green** Suffk
123 G7 **Crowgate Street** Norfk
70 E7 **Crow Green** Essex
213 G4 **Crowhill** E Loth
63 J2 **Crow Hill** Herefs
133 G4 **Crowhole** Derbys
24 D5 **Crowhurst** E Susx
38 B4 **Crowhurst** Surrey
38 B4 **Crowhurst Lane End** Surrey
102 E2 **Crowland** Lincs
89 K1 **Crowland** Suffk
2 E4 **Crowlas** Cnwll
143 K5 **Crowle** N Linc
81 L4 **Crowle** Worcs
81 L4 **Crowle Green** Worcs
48 F1 **Crowmarsh Gifford** Oxon
90 F1 **Crown Corner** Suffk
6 F3 **Crownhill** C Plym
84 F7 **Crownhill Crematorium** M Keyn
36 E2 **Crownpits** Surrey
106 B3 **Crownthorpe** Norfk
3 G5 **Crowntown** Cnwll
2 B5 **Crows-an-Wra** Cnwll
71 G2 **Crow's Green** Essex
105 J2 **Crowshill** Norfk
6 B1 **Crow's Nest** Cnwll
95 J3 **Crowsnest** Shrops
49 K6 **Crowthorne** Wokham
130 B5 **Crowton** Ches W
99 G1 **Croxall** Staffs
144 F8 **Croxby** Lincs
169 H3 **Croxdale** Dur
115 H4 **Croxden** Staffs
68 D7 **Croxley Green** Herts
86 E3 **Croxton** Cambs
144 E5 **Croxton** N Linc
105 H6 **Croxton** Norfk
121 L5 **Croxton** Norfk
114 B5 **Croxton** Staffs
114 B5 **Croxtonbank** Staffs
113 J1 **Croxton Green** Ches E
117 L5 **Croxton Kerrial** Leics
252 E2 **Croy** Highld
209 J4 **Croy** N Lans
27 H3 **Croyde** Devon
27 G3 **Croyde Bay** Devon
87 G5 **Croydon** Cambs
51 J6 **Croydon** Gt Lon
51 J5 **Croydon Crematorium** Gt Lon
241 J5 **Crubenmore** Highld
95 K2 **Cruckmeole** Shrops
95 K1 **Cruckton** Shrops
257 K4 **Cruden Bay** Abers
113 K7 **Crudgington** Wrekin
64 D8 **Crudwell** Wilts
12 C3 **Cruft** Devon
79 H1 **Crug** Powys
10 C7 **Crugmeer** Cnwll
77 J7 **Crugybar** Carmth
94 E7 **Crug-y-byddar** Powys
43 K2 **Crumlin** Caerph
5 L4 **Crumplehorn** Cnwll
140 C7 **Crumpsall** Manch
40 E5 **Crundale** Kent
54 F3 **Crundale** Pembks
55 L5 **Crunwear** Pembks
28 F8 **Cruwys Morchard** Devon
48 B7 **Crux Easton** Hants
16 B3 **Cruxton** Dorset
58 E6 **Crwbin** Carmth
67 L7 **Cryers Hill** Bucks
75 L5 **Crymmych** Pembks
60 B6 **Crynant** Neath
51 J5 **Crystal Palace** Gt Lon
260 A8 **Cuaig** Highld
215 L2 **Cuan Ferry Village** Ag & B
83 H2 **Cubbington** Warwks
4 C3 **Cubert** Cnwll
141 K7 **Cubley** Barns
67 K3 **Cublington** Bucks
79 M7 **Cublington** Herefs
32 D2 **Cuckfield** W Susx
32 C5 **Cucklington** Somset
133 L5 **Cuckney** Notts
119 G7 **Cuckoo Bridge** Lincs
35 M3 **Cuckoo's Corner** Hants
129 J7 **Cuckoo's Nest** Ches W
66 F6 **Cuddesdon** Oxon

| Page | Grid | Place | County |
|---|---|---|---|
| 67 | H5 | **Cuddington** | Bucks |
| 130 | B5 | **Cuddington** | Ches W |
| 113 | G2 | **Cuddington Heath** | Ches W |
| 147 | J8 | **Cuddy Hill** | Lancs |
| 51 | L7 | **Cudham** | Gt Lon |
| 12 | C6 | **Cudliptown** | Devon |
| 17 | L3 | **Cudnell** | Bmouth |
| 142 | B6 | **Cudworth** | Barns |
| 30 | F8 | **Cudworth** | Somset |
| 139 | H3 | **Cuerden Green** | Lancs |
| 130 | A2 | **Cuerdley Cross** | Warrtn |
| 49 | G7 | **Cufaude** | Hants |
| 69 | J6 | **Cuffley** | Herts |
| 228 | F4 | **Cuil** | Highld |
| 263 | G7 | **Culbokie** | Highld |
| 28 | E1 | **Culbone** | Somset |
| 250 | E3 | **Culburnie** | Highld |
| 251 | J3 | **Culcabock** | Highld |
| 253 | G2 | **Culcharry** | Highld |
| 130 | C1 | **Culcheth** | Warrtn |
| 255 | K5 | **Culdrain** | Abers |
| 248 | A4 | **Culduie** | Highld |
| 89 | G1 | **Culford** | Suffk |
| 166 | E5 | **Culgaith** | Cumb |
| 66 | D8 | **Culham** | Oxon |
| 270 | D2 | **Culkein** | Highld |
| 270 | F1 | **Culkein Drumbeg** | Highld |
| 64 | D7 | **Culkerton** | Gloucs |
| 267 | K3 | **Cullen** | Moray |
| 181 | J4 | **Cullercoats** | N Tyne |
| 245 | G3 | **Cullerlie** | Abers |
| 263 | H7 | **Cullicudden** | Highld |
| 149 | J8 | **Cullingworth** | C Brad |
| 215 | L2 | **Cullipool House** | Ag & B |
| 281 | e2 | **Cullivoe** | Shet |
| 252 | D3 | **Culloden** | Highld |
| 14 | B1 | **Cullompton** | Devon |
| 29 | L7 | **Culm Davy** | Devon |
| 96 | B7 | **Culmington** | Shrops |
| 29 | K8 | **Culmstock** | Devon |
| 270 | E7 | **Culnacraig** | Highld |
| 175 | J5 | **Culnaightrie** | D & G |
| 259 | J4 | **Culnaknock** | Highld |
| 90 | F5 | **Culpho** | Suffk |
| 263 | G1 | **Culrain** | Highld |
| 210 | C2 | **Culross** | Fife |
| 196 | C8 | **Culroy** | S Ayrs |
| 256 | B5 | **Culsalmond** | Abers |
| 74 | D5 | **Culscadden** | D & G |
| 173 | H4 | **Culshabbin** | D & G |
| 281 | c6 | **Culswick** | Shet |
| 257 | G7 | **Cultercullen** | Abers |
| 245 | K3 | **Cults** | C Aber |
| 52 | D6 | **Culverstone Green** | Kent |
| 118 | D3 | **Culverthorpe** | Lincs |
| 84 | A6 | **Culworth** | Nhants |
| 209 | K4 | **Cumbernauld** | N Lans |
| 209 | K4 | **Cumbernauld Village** | N Lans |
| 37 | J5 | **Cumberworth** | Lincs |
| 165 | K1 | **Cumdivock** | Cumb |
| 268 | E6 | **Cuminestown** | Abers |
| 202 | B2 | **Cumledge** | Border |
| 77 | L8 | **Cummersdale** | Cumb |
| 176 | F5 | **Cummertrees** | D & G |
| 266 | C2 | **Cummingston** | Moray |
| 197 | H7 | **Cumnock** | E Ayrs |
| 66 | C6 | **Cumnor** | Oxon |
| 78 | D8 | **Cumrew** | Cumb |
| 76 | E2 | **Cumrue** | D & G |
| 78 | B8 | **Cumwhinton** | Cumb |
| 78 | C8 | **Cumwhitton** | Cumb |
| 150 | F1 | **Cundall** | N York |
| 196 | D3 | **Cunninghamhead** | N Ayrs |
| 281 | e7 | **Cunningsburgh** | Shet |
| 22 | F4 | **Cupar** | Fife |
| 22 | F4 | **Cupar Muir** | Fife |
| 32 | E5 | **Curbar** | Derbys |
| 19 | J1 | **Curbridge** | Hants |
| 65 | M5 | **Curbridge** | Oxon |
| 35 | H8 | **Curdridge** | Hants |
| 98 | F5 | **Curdworth** | Warwks |
| 30 | C7 | **Curland** | Somset |
| 48 | C4 | **Curridge** | W Berk |
| 211 | G5 | **Currie** | C Edin |
| 30 | E6 | **Curry Mallet** | Somset |
| 30 | F6 | **Curry Rivel** | Somset |
| 39 | L5 | **Curteis Corner** | Kent |
| 39 | J5 | **Curtisden Green** | Kent |
| 7 | L4 | **Curtisknowle** | Devon |
| 3 | H6 | **Cury** | Cnwll |
| 244 | C1 | **Cushnie** | Abers |
| 30 | B5 | **Cushuish** | Somset |
| 79 | J7 | **Cusop** | Herefs |
| 74 | C7 | **Cutcloy** | D & G |
| 29 | G3 | **Cutcombe** | Somset |
| 40 | C5 | **Cutgate** | Rochdl |
| 263 | K2 | **Cuthill** | Highld |
| 10 | B8 | **Cutiau** | Gwynd |
| 70 | E1 | **Cutler's Green** | Essex |
| 5 | J2 | **Cutmadoc** | Cnwll |
| 6 | C3 | **Cutmere** | Cnwll |
| 81 | K2 | **Cutnall Green** | Worcs |
| 65 | G1 | **Cutsdean** | Gloucs |
| 142 | C3 | **Cutsyke** | Wakefd |
| 133 | G5 | **Cutthorpe** | Derbys |
| 6 | D2 | **Cuttivett** | Cnwll |
| 67 | G8 | **Cuxham** | Oxon |
| 52 | F5 | **Cuxton** | Medway |
| 144 | F7 | **Cuxwold** | Lincs |
| 61 | J6 | **Cwm** | Blae G |
| 128 | C4 | **Cwm** | Denbgs |
| 57 | L6 | **Cwmafan** | Neath |
| 60 | F7 | **Cwmaman** | Rhondd |
| 77 | G6 | **Cwmann** | Carmth |
| 62 | B6 | **Cwmavon** | Torfn |
| 56 | E4 | **Cwm-bach** | Carmth |
| 75 | M7 | **Cwmbach** | Carmth |
| 79 | G7 | **Cwmbach** | Powys |
| 60 | F6 | **Cwmbach** | Rhondd |
| 78 | E4 | **Cwmbach Llechrhyd** | Powys |
| 93 | K7 | **Cwmbelan** | Powys |
| 62 | C8 | **Cwmbran** | Torfn |
| 92 | F7 | **Cwmbrwyno** | Cerdgn |
| 56 | E4 | **Cwm Capel** | Carmth |
| 43 | K3 | **Cwmcarn** | Caerph |
| 62 | F5 | **Cwmcarvan** | Mons |
| 61 | K5 | **Cwm-celyn** | Blae G |
| 93 | J1 | **Cwm-Cewydd** | Gwynd |
| 76 | B6 | **Cwm-cou** | Cerdgn |
| 61 | J3 | **Cwm Crawnon** | Powys |
| 60 | F6 | **Cwmdare** | Rhondd |
| 59 | H3 | **Cwmdu** | Carmth |
| 61 | J2 | **Cwmdu** | Powys |
| 57 | H6 | **Cwmdu** | Swans |
| 58 | C3 | **Cwmduad** | Carmth |
| 57 | H4 | **Cwm Dulais** | Swans |
| 59 | K2 | **Cwmdwr** | Carmth |
| 42 | C4 | **Cwmfelin** | Brdgnd |
| 61 | H6 | **Cwmfelin** | Myr Td |
| 55 | L3 | **Cwmfelin Boeth** | Carmth |
| 43 | J3 | **Cwmfelinfach** | Caerph |
| 75 | L7 | **Cwmfelin Mynach** | Carmth |
| 58 | D5 | **Cwmffrwd** | Carmth |
| 59 | L6 | **Cwmgiedd** | Powys |
| 57 | K3 | **Cwmgorse** | Carmth |
| 57 | G3 | **Cwmgwili** | Carmth |
| 60 | C6 | **Cwmgwrach** | Neath |
| 76 | C7 | **Cwmhiraeth** | Carmth |
| 59 | J4 | **Cwm-Ifor** | Carmth |
| 78 | A5 | **Cwm Irfon** | Powys |
| 58 | F5 | **Cwmisfael** | Carmth |
| 93 | J2 | **Cwm Llinau** | Powys |
| 59 | K6 | **Cwmllynfell** | Neath |
| 58 | F6 | **Cwmmawr** | Carmth |
| 58 | B2 | **Cwm Morgan** | Carmth |
| 42 | E3 | **Cwmparc** | Rhondd |
| 58 | C2 | **Cwmpengraig** | Carmth |
| 110 | E2 | **Cwm Penmachno** | Conwy |
| 61 | G7 | **Cwmpennar** | Rhondd |
| 61 | J2 | **Cwmrhos** | Powys |
| 57 | J5 | **Cwmrhydyceirw** | Swans |
| 76 | E6 | **Cwmsychbant** | Cerdgn |
| 61 | K6 | **Cwmtillery** | Blae G |
| 59 | G6 | **Cwm-y-glo** | Carmth |
| 125 | K7 | **Cwm-y-glo** | Gwynd |
| 62 | C3 | **Cwmyoy** | Mons |
| 93 | G8 | **Cwmystwyth** | Cerdgn |
| 92 | E3 | **Cwrt** | Gwynd |
| 76 | E5 | **Cwrt-newydd** | Cerdgn |
| 61 | K4 | **Cwrt-y-gollen** | Powys |
| 94 | E2 | **Cyfronydd** | Powys |
| 57 | K4 | **Cylibebyll** | Neath |
| 42 | C3 | **Cymer** | Neath |
| 42 | F3 | **Cymmer** | Rhondd |
| 77 | M7 | **Cynghordy** | Carmth |
| 56 | E3 | **Cynheidre** | Carmth |
| 42 | C3 | **Cynonville** | Neath |
| 111 | K3 | **Cynwyd** | Denbgs |
| 58 | C3 | **Cynwyl Elfed** | Carmth |

**D**

| Page | Grid | Place | County |
|---|---|---|---|
| 8 | D1 | **Daccombe** | Devon |
| 166 | B5 | **Dacre** | Cumb |
| 150 | B4 | **Dacre** | N York |
| 150 | B3 | **Dacre Banks** | N York |
| 167 | K3 | **Daddry Shield** | Dur |
| 84 | C7 | **Dadford** | Bucks |
| 99 | L4 | **Dadlington** | Leics |
| 56 | F4 | **Dafen** | Carmth |
| 105 | J2 | **Daffy Green** | Norfk |
| 52 | B2 | **Dagenham** | Gt Lon |
| 64 | E6 | **Daglingworth** | Gloucs |
| 68 | C4 | **Dagnall** | Bucks |
| 89 | L3 | **Dagworth** | Suffk |
| 183 | H3 | **Dailly** | S Ayrs |
| 8 | C2 | **Dainton** | Devon |
| 223 | G4 | **Dairsie** | Fife |
| 139 | K6 | **Daisy Hill** | Bolton |
| 141 | L2 | **Daisy Hill** | Leeds |
| 283 | b11 | **Dalabrog** | W Isls |
| 216 | F5 | **Dalavich** | Ag & B |
| 175 | L3 | **Dalbeattie** | D & G |
| 115 | M5 | **Dalbury** | Derbys |
| 154 | b6 | **Dalby** | IoM |
| 137 | H5 | **Dalby** | Lincs |
| 151 | K2 | **Dalby** | N York |
| 232 | E4 | **Dalcapon** | P & K |
| 274 | B6 | **Dalchalm** | Highld |
| 240 | A1 | **Dalchreichart** | Highld |
| 220 | C4 | **Dalchruin** | P & K |
| 221 | J2 | **Dalcrue** | P & K |
| 136 | E6 | **Dalderby** | Lincs |
| 14 | B5 | **Dalditch** | Devon |
| 166 | D2 | **Dale** | Cumb |
| 116 | D4 | **Dale** | Derbys |
| 54 | C5 | **Dale** | Pembks |
| 165 | J6 | **Dale Bottom** | Cumb |
| 132 | D7 | **Dale End** | Derbys |
| 149 | G6 | **Dale End** | N York |
| 39 | H7 | **Dale Hill** | E Susx |
| 171 | H7 | **Dalehouse** | N York |
| 237 | L6 | **Dalelia** | Highld |
| 196 | B2 | **Dalgarven** | N Ayrs |
| 211 | G2 | **Dalgety Bay** | Fife |
| 197 | G8 | **Dalgig** | E Ayrs |
| 220 | D3 | **Dalginross** | P & K |
| 232 | E6 | **Dalguise** | P & K |
| 252 | D7 | **Dalhalvaig** | Highld |
| 88 | E3 | **Dalham** | Suffk |
| 283 | b11 | **Daliburgh** | W Isls |
| 211 | K5 | **Dalkeith** | Mdloth |
| 266 | C5 | **Dallas** | Moray |
| 91 | G4 | **Dallinghoo** | Suffk |
| 24 | B3 | **Dallington** | E Susx |
| 84 | E3 | **Dallington** | Nhants |
| 150 | B2 | **Dallow** | N York |
| 217 | K2 | **Dalmally** | Ag & B |
| 219 | H8 | **Dalmary** | Stirlg |
| 184 | D2 | **Dalmellington** | E Ayrs |
| 210 | F3 | **Dalmeny** | C Edin |
| 252 | D7 | **Dalmigavie** | Highld |
| 252 | E7 | **Dalmigavie Lodge** | Highld |
| 263 | H6 | **Dalmore** | Highld |
| 208 | E5 | **Dalmuir** | W Duns |
| 237 | K6 | **Dalnabreck** | Highld |
| 231 | K1 | **Dalnacardoch** | P & K |
| 252 | F7 | **Dalnahaitnach** | Highld |
| 231 | J1 | **Dalnaspidal** | P & K |
| 279 | H8 | **Dalnawillan Lodge** | Highld |
| 231 | L4 | **Daloist** | P & K |
| 221 | K6 | **Dalqueich** | P & K |
| 183 | J4 | **Dalquhairn** | S Ayrs |
| 273 | H6 | **Dalreavoch Lodge** | Highld |
| 196 | B1 | **Dalry** | N Ayrs |
| 196 | D8 | **Dalrymple** | E Ayrs |
| 198 | C3 | **Dalserf** | S Lans |
| 192 | D5 | **Dalsmeran** | Ag & B |
| 165 | L1 | **Dalston** | Cumb |
| 51 | J2 | **Dalston** | Gt Lon |
| 176 | B2 | **Dalswinton** | D & G |
| 157 | H7 | **Dalton** | Cumb |
| 176 | F4 | **Dalton** | D & G |
| 139 | G6 | **Dalton** | Lancs |
| 159 | K1 | **Dalton** | N York |
| 160 | F7 | **Dalton** | N York |
| 180 | D4 | **Dalton** | Nthumb |
| 133 | J1 | **Dalton** | Rothm |
| 156 | B7 | **Dalton-in-Furness** | Cumb |
| 169 | L1 | **Dalton-le-Dale** | Dur |
| 133 | J1 | **Dalton Magna** | Rothm |
| 160 | D1 | **Dalton-on-Tees** | N York |
| 133 | J1 | **Dalton Parva** | Rothm |
| 170 | B4 | **Dalton Piercy** | Hartpl |
| 186 | C5 | **Dalveen** | D & G |
| 219 | K2 | **Dalveich** | Stirlg |
| 241 | H6 | **Dalwhinnie** | Highld |
| 14 | F2 | **Dalwood** | Devon |
| 69 | H1 | **Damask Green** | Herts |
| 33 | J7 | **Damerham** | Hants |
| 107 | H2 | **Damgate** | Norfk |
| 105 | L6 | **Dam Green** | Norfk |
| 53 | J6 | **Danaway** | Kent |
| 71 | J6 | **Danbury** | Essex |
| 162 | C1 | **Danby** | N York |
| 162 | B2 | **Danby Bottom** | N York |
| 160 | E3 | **Danby Wiske** | N York |
| 254 | F3 | **Dandaleith** | Moray |
| 211 | J5 | **Danderhall** | Mdloth |
| 131 | J6 | **Danebridge** | Ches E |
| 69 | J3 | **Dane End** | Herts |
| 38 | E6 | **Danegate** | E Susx |
| 22 | F2 | **Danehill** | E Susx |
| 100 | C3 | **Dane Hills** | C Leic |
| 105 | L2 | **Danemoor Green** | Norfk |
| 97 | G5 | **Danesford** | Shrops |
| 133 | H7 | **Danesmoor** | Derbys |
| 40 | D5 | **Dane Street** | Kent |
| 40 | C7 | **Daniel's Water** | Kent |
| 268 | C5 | **Danshillock** | Abers |
| 212 | C5 | **Danskine** | E Loth |
| 145 | H1 | **Danthorpe** | E R Yk |
| 82 | D2 | **Danzey Green** | Warwks |
| 115 | G6 | **Dapple Heath** | Staffs |
| 49 | K7 | **Darby Green** | Hants |
| 139 | L6 | **Darcy Lever** | Bolton |
| 61 | K3 | **Dardy** | Powys |
| 61 | K4 | **Daren-felen** | Mons |
| 52 | C5 | **Darenth** | Kent |
| 130 | B3 | **Daresbury** | Halton |
| 142 | C6 | **Darfield** | Barns |
| 133 | L4 | **Darfoulds** | Notts |
| 40 | E3 | **Dargate** | Kent |
| 6 | B1 | **Darite** | Cnwll |
| 53 | G6 | **Darland** | Medway |
| 129 | J8 | **Darland** | Wrexhm |
| 114 | D4 | **Darlaston** | Staffs |
| 98 | B4 | **Darlaston** | Wsall |
| 98 | B4 | **Darlaston Green** | Wsall |
| 150 | B4 | **Darley** | N York |
| 116 | B4 | **Darley Abbey** | C Derb |
| 132 | E7 | **Darley Bridge** | Derbys |
| 132 | E7 | **Darley Dale** | Derbys |
| 98 | F8 | **Darley Green** | Solhll |
| 68 | F3 | **Darleyhall** | Herts |
| 150 | B4 | **Darley Head** | N York |
| 82 | F6 | **Darlingscott** | Warwks |
| 169 | H7 | **Darlington** | Darltn |
| 169 | H7 | **Darlington Crematorium** | Darltn |
| 113 | J5 | **Darliston** | Shrops |
| 134 | F5 | **Darlton** | Notts |
| 98 | E2 | **Darnford** | Staffs |
| 201 | H6 | **Darnick** | Border |
| 93 | H3 | **Darowen** | Powys |
| 268 | D6 | **Darra** | Abers |
| 26 | D7 | **Darracott** | Devon |
| 27 | H3 | **Darracott** | Devon |
| 180 | E5 | **Darras Hall** | Nthumb |
| 142 | D4 | **Darrington** | Wakefd |
| 91 | K1 | **Darsham** | Suffk |
| 31 | K2 | **Darshill** | Somset |
| 52 | B4 | **Dartford** | Kent |
| 8 | B2 | **Dartington** | Devon |
| 12 | F7 | **Dartmeet** | Devon |
| 8 | C4 | **Dartmouth** | Devon |
| 141 | M5 | **Darton** | Barns |
| 197 | H3 | **Darvel** | E Ayrs |
| 24 | C3 | **Darwell Hole** | E Susx |
| 139 | K3 | **Darwen** | Bl w D |
| 50 | C3 | **Datchet** | W & M |
| 69 | H3 | **Datchworth** | Herts |
| 69 | H3 | **Datchworth Green** | Herts |
| 139 | L6 | **Daubhill** | Bolton |
| 254 | E3 | **Daugh of Kinermony** | Moray |
| 46 | E3 | **Dauntsey** | Wilts |
| 253 | J4 | **Dava** | Highld |
| 130 | C5 | **Davenham** | Ches W |
| 131 | H2 | **Davenport** | Stockp |
| 131 | G4 | **Davenport Green** | Ches E |
| 130 | F2 | **Davenport Green** | Traffd |
| 84 | B3 | **Daventry** | Nhants |
| 211 | H4 | **Davidson's Mains** | C Edin |
| 11 | G5 | **Davidstow** | Cnwll |
| 52 | E6 | **David Street** | Kent |
| 187 | K5 | **Davington** | D & G |
| 40 | D3 | **Davington Hill** | Kent |
| 256 | D6 | **Daviot** | Abers |
| 252 | D4 | **Daviot** | Highld |
| 252 | D4 | **Daviot House** | Highld |
| 23 | J4 | **Davis's Town** | E Susx |
| 267 | K6 | **Davoch of Grange** | Moray |
| 139 | M8 | **Davyhulme** | Traffd |
| 98 | C3 | **Daw End** | Wsall |
| 37 | K2 | **Dawesgreen** | Surrey |
| 96 | F2 | **Dawley** | Wrekin |
| 13 | M7 | **Dawlish** | Devon |
| 14 | A6 | **Dawlish Warren** | Devon |
| 127 | G5 | **Dawn** | Conwy |
| 30 | B6 | **Daws Green** | Somset |
| 53 | H1 | **Daws Heath** | Essex |
| 11 | K6 | **Daw's House** | Cnwll |
| 120 | A5 | **Dawsmere** | Lincs |
| 116 | F3 | **Daybrook** | Notts |
| 130 | F8 | **Day Green** | Ches E |
| 114 | F5 | **Dayhills** | Staffs |
| 98 | B7 | **Dayhouse Bank** | Worcs |
| 65 | K2 | **Daylesford** | Gloucs |
| 128 | D5 | **Ddol** | Flints |
| 111 | K8 | **Ddol-Cownwy** | Powys |
| 41 | L5 | **Deal** | Kent |
| 164 | E5 | **Dean** | Cumb |
| 7 | L2 | **Dean** | Devon |
| 27 | L2 | **Dean** | Devon |
| 28 | C1 | **Dean** | Devon |
| 33 | G7 | **Dean** | Dorset |
| 34 | F4 | **Dean** | Hants |
| 35 | H7 | **Dean** | Hants |
| 140 | C3 | **Dean** | Lancs |
| 65 | M3 | **Dean** | Oxon |

308 Dean - Doulting


31 L2 **Dean** Somset
52 C5 **Dean Bottom** Kent
188 C4 **Deanburnhaugh** Border
7 L2 **Deancombe** Devon
66 C6 **Dean Court** Oxon
139 K6 **Deane** Bolton
35 H1 **Deane** Hants
33 G7 **Dean End** Dorset
141 L7 **Dean Head** Barns
141 G4 **Deanhead** Kirk
33 G7 **Deanland** Dorset
20 B4 **Deanlane End** W Susx
7 L2 **Dean Prior** Devon
179 J6 **Deanraw** Nthumb
131 G3 **Dean Row** Ches E
210 D5 **Deans** W Loth
164 E5 **Deanscales** Cumb
84 E7 **Deanshanger** Nhants
267 G6 **Deanshaugh** Moray
220 C6 **Deanston** Stirlg
39 J3 **Dean Street** Kent
164 E3 **Dearham** Cumb
140 D4 **Dearnley** Rochdl
90 F4 **Debach** Suffk
70 C7 **Debden** Essex
87 L8 **Debden** Essex
70 E1 **Debden Green** Essex
90 E3 **Debenham** Suffk
81 J5 **Deblin's Green** Worcs
210 D5 **Dechmont** W Loth
210 D5 **Dechmont Road** W Loth
66 C1 **Deddington** Oxon
90 C8 **Dedham** Essex
72 F1 **Dedham Heath** Essex
50 B4 **Dedworth** W & M
101 L5 **Deene** Nhants
101 L5 **Deenethorpe** Nhants
141 L8 **Deepcar** Sheff
49 L7 **Deepcut** Surrey
158 C5 **Deepdale** Cumb
158 F6 **Deepdale** N York
102 C2 **Deeping Gate** C Pete
102 D2 **Deeping St James** Lincs
119 H8 **Deeping St Nicholas** Lincs
64 C1 **Deerhurst** Gloucs
64 C2 **Deerhurst Walton** Gloucs
40 C3 **Deerton Street** Kent
81 L6 **Defford** Worcs
60 D2 **Defynnog** Powys
126 F4 **Deganwy** Conwy
216 B5 **Degnish** Ag & B
151 K7 **Deighton** C York
160 E2 **Deighton** N York
125 K7 **Deiniolen** Gwynd
10 F5 **Delabole** Cnwll
130 A6 **Delamere** Ches W
257 H7 **Delfrigs** Abers
27 K6 **Delley** Devon
253 L5 **Delliefure** Highld
20 D6 **Dell Quay** W Susx
65 M4 **Delly End** Oxon
254 C8 **Delnabo** Moray
254 D4 **Delnashaugh Inn** Moray
263 K5 **Delny** Highld
140 E6 **Delph** Oldham
168 E1 **Delves** Dur
233 H7 **Delvine** P & K
88 F8 **Delvin End** Essex
118 D4 **Dembleby** Lincs
5 G2 **Demelza** Cnwll
142 D7 **Denaby** Donc
142 D7 **Denaby Main** Donc
37 H1 **Denbies** Surrey
128 C6 **Denbigh** Denbgs
222 F3 **Denbrae** Fife
8 B1 **Denbury** Devon
116 C2 **Denby** Derbys
116 C2 **Denby Bottles** Derbys
141 K6 **Denby Dale** Kirk
48 A1 **Denchworth** Oxon
146 E2 **Dendron** Cumb
85 K8 **Denel End** C Beds
221 G4 **Denfield** P & K
101 L8 **Denford** Nhants
72 E6 **Dengie** Essex
50 D2 **Denham** Bucks
88 E3 **Denham** Suffk
106 D8 **Denham** Suffk
88 F3 **Denham End** Suffk
50 D1 **Denham Green** Bucks
106 D8 **Denham Green** Suffk
269 J5 **Denhead** Abers
223 H4 **Denhead** Fife
222 F1 **Denhead of Gray** C Dund
189 G3 **Denholm** Border
141 G1 **Denholme** C Brad
141 G1 **Denholme Clough** C Brad
108 F4 **Denio** Gwynd
19 L1 **Denmead** Hants
245 L1 **Denmore** C Aber
37 J5 **Denne Park** W Susx
91 G2 **Dennington** Suffk
209 L3 **Denny** Falk
209 L3 **Dennyloanhead** Falk
222 D4 **Den of Lindores** Fife
140 E5 **Denshaw** Oldham
245 H4 **Denside** Abers
41 G7 **Densole** Kent
88 F5 **Denston** Suffk
115 H3 **Denstone** Staffs
40 E3 **Denstroude** Kent
158 B5 **Dent** Cumb
102 C6 **Denton** Cambs
169 G7 **Denton** Darltn
23 G6 **Denton** E Susx
41 G6 **Denton** Kent
52 E4 **Denton** Kent
117 M5 **Denton** Lincs
149 L6 **Denton** N York
85 G4 **Denton** Nhants
106 F5 **Denton** Norfk
66 E6 **Denton** Oxon
131 H1 **Denton** Tamesd
104 C3 **Denver** Norfk
191 J3 **Denwick** Nthumb
105 L3 **Deopham** Norfk
105 L4 **Deopham Green** Norfk
88 F4 **Depden** Suffk
88 F4 **Depden Green** Suffk
51 K3 **Deptford** Gt Lon
33 H3 **Deptford** Wilts
116 B4 **Derby** C Derb
27 K4 **Derby** Devon
154 c8 **Derbyhaven** IoM
232 C5 **Derculich** P & K
105 K1 **Dereham** Norfk
61 H6 **Deri** Caerph
11 K2 **Derril** Devon
41 G5 **Derringstone** Kent
114 D7 **Derrington** Staffs
11 L2 **Derriton** Devon
46 D5 **Derry Hill** Wilts
143 L6 **Derrythorpe** N Linc
120 F5 **Dersingham** Norfk
226 E2 **Dervaig** Ag & B
111 L2 **Derwen** Denbgs
59 G4 **Derwen Fawr** Carmth
92 F4 **Derwenlas** Powys
59 H5 **Derwydd** Carmth
101 H6 **Desborough** Nhants
100 B3 **Desford** Leics
267 K4 **Deskford** Moray
203 H6 **Detchant** Nthumb
53 G7 **Detling** Kent
96 F6 **Deuxhill** Shrops
62 F7 **Devauden** Mons
92 F8 **Devil's Bridge** Cerdgn
99 H5 **Devitts Green** Warwks
46 E6 **Devizes** Wilts
6 E4 **Devonport** C Plym
221 G7 **Devonside** Clacks
3 K3 **Devoran** Cnwll
211 L6 **Dewarton** Mdloth
16 E3 **Dewlish** Dorset
141 K3 **Dewsbury** Kirk
141 K3 **Dewsbury Moor** Kirk
141 K3 **Dewsbury Moor Crematorium** Kirk
112 C8 **Deytheur** Powys
45 G5 **Dial** N Som
36 D5 **Dial Green** W Susx
21 K3 **Dial Post** W Susx
15 K2 **Dibberford** Dorset
18 F2 **Dibden** Hants
18 F2 **Dibden Purlieu** Hants
98 E8 **Dickens Heath** Solhll
106 D7 **Dickleburgh** Norfk
64 F1 **Didbrook** Gloucs
48 D1 **Didcot** Oxon
86 D2 **Diddington** Cambs
96 C6 **Diddlebury** Shrops
62 F1 **Didley** Herefs
20 D3 **Didling** W Susx
46 B2 **Didmarton** Gloucs
131 G1 **Didsbury** Manch
7 K2 **Didworthy** Devon
135 M8 **Digby** Lincs
259 H3 **Digg** Highld
140 F6 **Diggle** Oldham
139 G6 **Digmoor** Lancs
69 H4 **Digswell** Herts
69 H4 **Digswell Water** Herts
76 E4 **Dihewyd** Cerdgn
123 G6 **Dilham** Norfk
114 F3 **Dilhorne** Staffs
139 M2 **Dill Hall** Lancs
86 C2 **Dillington** Cambs
180 A6 **Dilston** Nthumb
32 E1 **Dilton** Wilts
32 D1 **Dilton Marsh** Wilts
80 A4 **Dilwyn** Herefs
139 L4 **Dimple** Bolton
132 F7 **Dimple** Derbys
58 A3 **Dinas** Carmth
10 C7 **Dinas** Cnwll
108 D4 **Dinas** Gwynd
75 G4 **Dinas** Pembks
42 F3 **Dinas** Rhondd
125 H8 **Dinas Dinlle** Gwynd
111 G8 **Dinas-Mawddwy** Gwynd
43 J7 **Dinas Powys** V Glam
31 J2 **Dinder** Somset
80 C7 **Dinedor** Herefs
62 F5 **Dingestow** Mons
129 J2 **Dingle** Lpool
39 K7 **Dingleden** Kent
101 G6 **Dingley** Nhants
262 F8 **Dingwall** Highld
62 F8 **Dinham** Mons
111 J3 **Dinmael** Conwy
244 A4 **Dinnet** Abers
180 F4 **Dinnington** N u Ty
133 K3 **Dinnington** Rothm
30 F8 **Dinnington** Somset
125 L7 **Dinorwic** Gwynd
67 J5 **Dinton** Bucks
33 H4 **Dinton** Wilts
187 H8 **Dinwoodie** D & G
26 E7 **Dinworthy** Devon
30 B6 **Dipford** Somset
49 H7 **Dipley** Hants
194 B3 **Dippen** Ag & B
195 G6 **Dippen** N Ayrs
36 B2 **Dippenhall** Surrey
12 B1 **Dippermill** Devon
12 B5 **Dippertown** Devon
267 G4 **Dipple** Moray
182 F2 **Dipple** S Ayrs
7 L3 **Diptford** Devon
180 E8 **Dipton** Dur
179 L6 **Diptonmill** Nthumb
212 B2 **Dirleton** E Loth
167 K2 **Dirt Pot** Nthumb
79 K2 **Discoed** Powys
116 D6 **Diseworth** Leics
160 E8 **Dishforth** N York
131 J3 **Disley** Ches E
106 C7 **Diss** Norfk
78 E4 **Disserth** Powys
164 D6 **Distington** Cumb
164 D6 **Distington Hall Crematorium** Cumb
33 J4 **Ditchampton** Wilts
191 G2 **Ditchburn** Nthumb
31 K4 **Ditcheat** Somset
107 G5 **Ditchingham** Norfk
66 A3 **Ditchley** Oxon
22 E4 **Ditchling** E Susx
113 H8 **Ditherington** Shrops
46 B5 **Ditteridge** Wilts
8 C4 **Dittisham** Devon
129 L2 **Ditton** Halton
52 F7 **Ditton** Kent
88 D4 **Ditton Green** Cambs
96 E5 **Ditton Priors** Shrops
64 E1 **Dixton** Gloucs
63 G4 **Dixton** Mons
11 H3 **Dizzard** Cnwll
140 F6 **Dobcross** Oldham
140 D3 **Dobroyd Castle** Calder
5 L2 **Dobwalls** Cnwll
13 H5 **Doccombe** Devon
251 H3 **Dochgarroch** Highld
36 B3 **Dockenfield** Surrey
157 J7 **Docker** Lancs
121 G4 **Docking** Norfk
80 D4 **Docklow** Herefs
165 J1 **Dockray** Cumb
165 L6 **Dockray** Cumb
7 L6 **Dodbrooke** Devon
70 E7 **Doddinghurst** Essex
103 H5 **Doddington** Cambs
40 B4 **Doddington** Kent
135 H5 **Doddington** Lincs
202 F6 **Doddington** Nthumb
96 E8 **Doddington** Shrops
13 K5 **Doddiscombsleigh** Devon
113 K3 **Dodd's Green** Ches E
120 F5 **Doddshill** Norfk
6 C2 **Doddy Cross** Cnwll
84 B3 **Dodford** Nhants
97 L8 **Dodford** Worcs
45 L3 **Dodington** S Glos
30 A3 **Dodington** Somset
129 J7 **Dodleston** Ches W
27 K7 **Dodscott** Devon
208 E8 **Dodside** E Rens
115 G4 **Dod's Leigh** Staffs
141 M6 **Dodworth** Barns
141 M7 **Dodworth Bottom** Barns
141 M6 **Dodworth Green** Barns
98 E4 **Doe Bank** Birm
133 J6 **Doe Lea** Derbys
136 D8 **Dogdyke** Lincs
141 J5 **Dogley Lane** Kirk
49 J8 **Dogmersfield** Hants
47 G2 **Dogridge** Wilts
102 D3 **Dogsthorpe** C Pete
14 A3 **Dog Village** Devon
94 C1 **Dolanog** Powys
79 G2 **Dolau** Powys
77 J7 **Dolaucothi** Carmth
109 J3 **Dolbenmaen** Gwynd
114 A5 **Doley** Staffs
93 K3 **Dolfach** Powys
93 H2 **Dol-for** Powys
94 D6 **Dolfor** Powys
126 F6 **Dolgarrog** Conwy
110 D7 **Dolgellau** Gwynd
92 E3 **Dolgoch** Gwynd
58 D2 **Dol-gran** Carmth
273 L7 **Doll** Highld
221 G7 **Dollar** Clacks
221 G7 **Dollarfield** Clacks
79 K2 **Dolley Green** Powys
92 E7 **Dollwen** Cerdgn
128 E5 **Dolphin** Flints
147 K5 **Dolphinholme** Lancs
199 J4 **Dolphinton** S Lans
27 K8 **Dolton** Devon
127 H5 **Dolwen** Conwy
110 D1 **Dolwyddelan** Conwy
92 D5 **Dolybont** Cerdgn
79 J4 **Dolyhir** Powys
112 D7 **Domgay** Powys
202 D5 **Donaldson's Lodge** Nthumb
142 F7 **Doncaster** Donc
142 F7 **Doncaster Carr** Donc
32 F6 **Donhead St Andrew** Wilts
32 F6 **Donhead St Mary** Wilts
211 G1 **Donibristle** Fife
29 K2 **Doniford** Somset
119 H4 **Donington** Lincs
136 D3 **Donington on Bain** Lincs
119 G5 **Donington Southing** Lincs
99 J1 **Donisthorpe** Leics
25 L1 **Donkey Street** Kent
50 B6 **Donkey Town** Surrey
65 J2 **Donnington** Gloucs
81 G8 **Donnington** Herefs
96 D2 **Donnington** Shrops
48 C5 **Donnington** W Berk
20 D6 **Donnington** W Susx
113 M8 **Donnington** Wrekin
97 G1 **Donnington Wood** Wrekin
30 E8 **Donyatt** Somset
37 J5 **Doomsday Green** W Susx
196 C7 **Doonfoot** S Ayrs
196 C7 **Doonholm** S Ayrs
253 L8 **Dorback Lodge** Highld
16 D4 **Dorchester** Dorset
66 E8 **Dorchester** Oxon
99 H3 **Dordon** Warwks
132 F3 **Dore** Sheff
251 G5 **Dores** Highld
37 J1 **Dorking** Surrey
89 J7 **Dorking Tye** Suffk
38 B5 **Dormans Land** Surrey
38 B5 **Dormans Park** Surrey
80 D7 **Dormington** Herefs
82 A4 **Dormston** Worcs
82 F8 **Dorn** Gloucs
50 B3 **Dorney** Bucks
248 D6 **Dornie** Highld
264 B2 **Dornoch** Highld
177 H5 **Dornock** D & G
279 J5 **Dorrery** Highld
98 F8 **Dorridge** Solhll
118 E1 **Dorrington** Lincs
96 B3 **Dorrington** Shrops
114 A3 **Dorrington** Shrops
82 D5 **Dorsington** Warwks
79 K7 **Dorstone** Herefs
67 G4 **Dorton** Bucks
99 G3 **Dosthill** Staffs
124 F5 **Dothan** IoA
15 K3 **Dottery** Dorset
5 L2 **Doublebois** Cnwll
46 C1 **Doughton** Gloucs
154 e6 **Douglas** IoM
198 D7 **Douglas** S Lans
234 C8 **Douglas and Angus** C Dund
154 e6 **Douglas Borough Crematorium** IoM
198 D6 **Douglas Castle** S Lans
217 K7 **Douglas Pier** Ag & B
234 B6 **Douglastown** Angus
198 E6 **Douglas Water** S Lans
198 D6 **Douglas West** S Lans
31 L2 **Doulting** Somset

Dounby - Durley Street 309


275 b4 **Dounby** Ork
272 B7 **Doune** Highld
220 C6 **Doune** Stirlg
182 F3 **Dounepark** S Ayrs
263 G2 **Dounie** Highld
7 G1 **Dousland** Devon
112 E7 **Dovaston** Shrops
116 D1 **Dove Green** Notts
131 L4 **Dove Holes** Derbys
164 E4 **Dovenby** Cumb
41 K7 **Dover** Kent
139 J7 **Dover** Wigan
73 K1 **Dovercourt** Essex
81 K2 **Doverdale** Worcs
115 J5 **Doveridge** Derbys
37 L1 **Doversgreen** Surrey
232 F5 **Dowally** P & K
138 E2 **Dowbridge** Lancs
64 E3 **Dowdeswell** Gloucs
61 G5 **Dowlais** Myr Td
12 D1 **Dowland** Devon
30 E8 **Dowlish Ford** Somset
30 E8 **Dowlish Wake** Somset
11 M4 **Downacarey** Devon
65 G7 **Down Ampney** Gloucs
6 C4 **Downderry** Cnwll
51 L6 **Downe** Gt Lon
64 B7 **Downend** Gloucs
19 J6 **Downend** IoW
45 K3 **Downend** S Glos
48 C4 **Downend** W Berk
223 G1 **Downfield** C Dund
11 K8 **Downgate** Cnwll
11 L7 **Downgate** Cnwll
71 H7 **Downham** Essex
51 K4 **Downham** Gt Lon
148 D7 **Downham** Lancs
202 D6 **Downham** Nthumb
104 C3 **Downham Market** Norfk
64 C3 **Down Hatherley** Gloucs
31 J6 **Downhead** Somset
32 A2 **Downhead** Somset
4 D1 **Downhill** Cnwll
221 K1 **Downhill** P & K
138 D6 **Downholland Cross** Lancs
159 K3 **Downholme** N York
245 K4 **Downies** Abers
128 D4 **Downing** Flints
67 K8 **Downley** Bucks
13 H2 **Down St Mary** Devon
22 E6 **Downs Crematorium** Br & H
31 K2 **Downside** Somset
31 L1 **Downside** Somset
50 E7 **Downside** Surrey
6 F5 **Down Thomas** Devon
18 D5 **Downton** Hants
33 L6 **Downton** Wilts
118 F5 **Dowsby** Lincs
102 F2 **Dowsdale** Lincs
114 D6 **Doxey** Staffs
191 H2 **Doxford** Nthumb
45 L4 **Doynton** S Glos
43 K4 **Draethen** Caerph
198 C4 **Draffan** S Lans
143 M5 **Dragonby** N Linc
37 H6 **Dragons Green** W Susx
134 E2 **Drakeholes** Notts
97 J7 **Drakelow** Worcs
196 B1 **Drakemyre** N Ayrs
81 L5 **Drakes Broughton** Worcs
12 B8 **Drakewalls** Cnwll
149 J5 **Draughton** N York
101 G8 **Draughton** Nhants
143 H3 **Drax** N York
143 H3 **Drax Hales** N York
83 K1 **Draycote** Warwks
47 J3 **Draycot Foliat** Swindn
116 D5 **Draycott** Derbys
82 E8 **Draycott** Gloucs
97 H5 **Draycott** Shrops
31 G1 **Draycott** Somset
31 J6 **Draycott** Somset
81 K5 **Draycott** Worcs
115 J6 **Draycott in the Clay** Staffs
114 F3 **Draycott in the Moors** Staffs
28 D8 **Drayford** Devon
19 L3 **Drayton** C Port
101 H5 **Drayton** Leics
119 H4 **Drayton** Lincs
106 D1 **Drayton** Norfk
66 C8 **Drayton** Oxon
83 K7 **Drayton** Oxon
30 F6 **Drayton** Somset
97 K8 **Drayton** Worcs
99 G3 **Drayton Bassett** Staffs
67 L5 **Drayton Beauchamp** Bucks
67 K2 **Drayton Parslow** Bucks
66 E7 **Drayton St Leonard** Oxon
149 J4 **Drebley** N York
154 g4 **Dreemskerry** IoM
54 F4 **Dreen Hill** Pembks
58 F6 **Drefach** Carmth
76 C7 **Drefach** Carmth
76 F6 **Drefach** Cerdgn
76 C7 **Drefelin** Carmth
196 C3 **Dreghorn** N Ayrs
41 H7 **Drellingore** Kent
212 B3 **Drem** E Loth
114 E3 **Dresden** C Stke
13 H4 **Drewsteignton** Devon
137 G5 **Driby** Lincs
152 F4 **Driffield** E R Yk
65 G7 **Driffield** Gloucs
64 F7 **Driffield Cross Roads** Gloucs
2 C5 **Drift** Cnwll
155 K3 **Drigg** Cumb
141 K2 **Drighlington** Leeds
227 G2 **Drimnin** Highld
15 K2 **Drimpton** Dorset
238 F7 **Drimsallie** Highld
153 J5 **Dringhoe** E R Yk
151 J6 **Dringhouses** C York
89 J3 **Drinkstone** Suffk
89 J3 **Drinkstone Green** Suffk
16 B1 **Drive End** Dorset
69 G3 **Driver's End** Herts
115 G6 **Drointon** Staffs
81 K3 **Droitwich** Worcs
221 L4 **Dron** P & K
133 G4 **Dronfield** Derbys
133 G4 **Dronfield Woodhouse** Derbys
196 E7 **Drongan** E Ayrs
234 A8 **Dronley** Angus
16 E1 **Droop** Dorset
133 H1 **Dropping Well** Rothm
35 J7 **Droxford** Hants
140 D8 **Droylsden** Tamesd
111 K3 **Druid** Denbgs
54 E3 **Druidston** Pembks
229 H1 **Druimarbin** Highld
229 G6 **Druimavuic** Ag & B
206 A5 **Druimdrishaig** Ag & B
237 K4 **Druimindarroch** Highld
206 E4 **Drum** Ag & B
221 J7 **Drum** P & K
198 F5 **Drumalbin** S Lans
270 F2 **Drumbeg** Highld
255 M4 **Drumblade** Abers
172 D6 **Drumbreddon** D & G
248 B5 **Drumbuie** Highld
177 J7 **Drumburgh** Cumb
175 L4 **Drumburn** D & G
208 E5 **Drumchapel** C Glas
231 J4 **Drumchastle** P & K
197 J3 **Drumclog** S Lans
223 G6 **Drumeldrie** Fife
199 K6 **Drumelzier** Border
247 L5 **Drumfearn** Highld
244 F4 **Drumfrennie** Abers
234 C5 **Drumgley** Angus
241 L3 **Drumguish** Highld
254 D5 **Drumin** Moray
184 E3 **Drumjohn** D & G
183 H7 **Drumlamford** S Ayrs
244 E2 **Drumlasie** Abers
177 J8 **Drumleaning** Cumb
192 D4 **Drumlemble** Ag & B
245 H7 **Drumlithie** Abers
173 K6 **Drummoddie** D & G
172 E7 **Drummore** D & G
255 H3 **Drummuir** Moray
250 E5 **Drumnadrochit** Highld
172 E7 **Drumnaglaur** D & G
267 L5 **Drumnagorrach** Moray
185 L7 **Drumpark** D & G
271 G7 **Drumrunie Lodge** Highld
195 L8 **Drumshang** S Ayrs
259 G7 **Drumuie** Highld
253 H7 **Drumuillie** Highld
220 B6 **Drumvaich** Stirlg
221 L5 **Drunzie** P & K
191 K7 **Druridge** Nthumb
129 G6 **Drury** Flints
166 F7 **Drybeck** Cumb
267 J4 **Drybridge** Moray
196 D4 **Drybridge** N Ayrs
63 J4 **Drybrook** Gloucs
201 J6 **Dryburgh** Border
117 M2 **Dry Doddington** Lincs
87 H3 **Dry Drayton** Cambs
208 E1 **Drymen** Stirlg
257 G3 **Drymuir** Abers
246 F2 **Drynoch** Highld
66 C7 **Dry Sandford** Oxon
59 G5 **Dryslwyn** Carmth
52 E2 **Dry Street** Essex
96 D2 **Dryton** Shrops
268 E3 **Dubford** Abers
90 E1 **Dublin** Suffk
271 L4 **Duchally** Highld
85 L6 **Duck End** Bed
86 E2 **Duck End** Cambs
71 G2 **Duck End** Essex
88 D8 **Duck End** Essex
71 H3 **Duckend Green** Essex
113 H1 **Duckington** Ches W
65 M5 **Ducklington** Oxon
86 C4 **Duck's Cross** Bed
87 J7 **Duddenhoe End** Essex
211 J4 **Duddingston** C Edin
101 L3 **Duddington** Nhants
30 C6 **Duddlestone** Somset
38 C7 **Duddleswell** E Susx
96 F6 **Duddlewick** Shrops
202 E4 **Duddo** Nthumb
129 L6 **Duddon** Ches W
156 B5 **Duddon Bridge** Cumb
129 M6 **Duddon Common** Ches W
112 E4 **Dudleston** Shrops
112 E4 **Dudleston Heath** Shrops
97 L5 **Dudley** Dudley
181 G4 **Dudley** N Tyne
141 J2 **Dudley Hill** C Brad
98 B5 **Dudley Port** Sandw
96 E8 **Dudnill** Shrops
17 L3 **Dudsbury** Dorset
68 B5 **Dudswell** Herts
116 B3 **Duffield** Derbys
42 C3 **Duffryn** Neath
255 G4 **Dufftown** Moray
266 D3 **Duffus** Moray
166 F5 **Dufton** Cumb
152 D2 **Duggleby** N York
248 C5 **Duirinish** Highld
247 L6 **Duisdalemore** Highld
239 G8 **Duisky** Highld
61 J5 **Dukestown** Blae G
90 C6 **Duke Street** Suffk
140 E8 **Dukinfield** Tamesd
140 E8 **Dukinfield Crematorium** Tamesd
125 H2 **Dulas** IoA
31 J2 **Dulcote** Somset
14 C1 **Dulford** Devon
232 B5 **Dull** P & K
209 K4 **Dullatur** N Lans
88 C4 **Dullingham** Cambs
88 C4 **Dullingham Ley** Cambs
253 J6 **Dulnain Bridge** Highld
86 D3 **Duloe** Bed
5 M3 **Duloe** Cnwll
29 G5 **Dulverton** Somset
51 J4 **Dulwich** Gt Lon
208 C4 **Dumbarton** W Duns
82 B8 **Dumbleton** Gloucs
176 C4 **Dumfries** D & G
208 E2 **Dumgoyne** Stirlg
35 J2 **Dummer** Hants
41 L2 **Dumpton** Kent
235 G3 **Dun** Angus
231 K4 **Dunalastair** P & K
207 J5 **Dunan** Ag & B
247 J3 **Dunan** Highld
230 E4 **Dunan** P & K
192 E6 **Dunaverty** Ag & B
30 D3 **Dunball** Somset
212 E3 **Dunbar** E Loth
275 G2 **Dunbeath** Highld
228 D8 **Dunbeg** Ag & B
220 D7 **Dunblane** Stirlg
222 D4 **Dunbog** Fife
34 D5 **Dunbridge** Hants
263 G8 **Duncanston** Highld
255 L6 **Duncanstone** Abers
13 K5 **Dunchideock** Devon
83 L1 **Dunchurch** Warwks
84 C5 **Duncote** Nhants
176 C2 **Duncow** D & G
221 L5 **Duncrievie** P & K
20 F3 **Duncton** W Susx
223 G1 **Dundee** C Dund
222 F1 **Dundee Crematorium** C Dund
31 G4 **Dundon** Somset
196 D4 **Dundonald** S Ayrs
261 J2 **Dundonnell** Highld
165 H1 **Dundraw** Cumb
240 B1 **Dundreggan** Highld
175 J5 **Dundrennan** D & G
45 H5 **Dundry** N Som
245 G2 **Dunecht** Abers
210 E1 **Dunfermline** Fife
210 F2 **Dunfermline Crematorium** Fife
65 H7 **Dunfield** Gloucs
141 J7 **Dunford Bridge** Barns
40 B3 **Dungate** Kent
197 J3 **Dungavel** S Lans
46 C8 **Dunge** Wilts
132 E2 **Dungworth** Sheff
135 G5 **Dunham** Notts
129 L5 **Dunham-on-the-Hill** Ches W
81 L3 **Dunhampstead** Worcs
81 J2 **Dunhampton** Worcs
130 E2 **Dunham Town** Traffd
130 E2 **Dunham Woodhouses** Traffd
135 L4 **Dunholme** Lincs
223 J5 **Dunino** Fife
209 L2 **Dunipace** Falk
232 F6 **Dunkeld** P & K
45 L7 **Dunkerton** BaNES
14 D1 **Dunkeswell** Devon
150 D6 **Dunkeswick** N York
129 J5 **Dunkirk** Ches W
40 E3 **Dunkirk** Kent
46 A2 **Dunkirk** S Glos
46 E6 **Dunkirk** Wilts
38 F3 **Dunk's Green** Kent
234 F2 **Dunlappie** Angus
48 C8 **Dunley** Hants
81 H2 **Dunley** Worcs
196 E1 **Dunlop** E Ayrs
251 G7 **Dunmaglass** Highld
5 H1 **Dunmere** Cnwll
210 A1 **Dunmore** Falk
280 B2 **Dunnet** Highld
234 D5 **Dunnichen** Angus
221 J4 **Dunning** P & K
151 L5 **Dunnington** C York
153 J5 **Dunnington** E R Yk
82 C4 **Dunnington** Warwks
140 B2 **Dunnockshaw** Lancs
53 G6 **Dunn Street** Kent
207 K4 **Dunoon** Ag & B
253 J2 **Dunphail** Moray
172 E3 **Dunragit** D & G
202 B2 **Duns** Border
132 E5 **Dunsa** Derbys
118 E6 **Dunsby** Lincs
139 L5 **Dunscar** Bolton
185 L6 **Dunscore** D & G
143 G6 **Dunscroft** Donc
170 E6 **Dunsdale** R & Cl
49 H3 **Dunsden Green** Oxon
11 K1 **Dunsdon** Devon
36 F4 **Dunsfold** Surrey
13 J4 **Dunsford** Devon
222 D5 **Dunshalt** Fife
269 H6 **Dunshillock** Abers
133 J7 **Dunsill** Notts
171 K8 **Dunsley** N York
97 J6 **Dunsley** Staffs
67 L6 **Dunsmore** Bucks
148 B6 **Dunsop Bridge** Lancs
68 C3 **Dunstable** C Beds
115 K7 **Dunstall** Staffs
81 K6 **Dunstall Common** Worcs
88 E3 **Dunstall Green** Suffk
191 K2 **Dunstan** Nthumb
191 J2 **Dunstan Steads** Nthumb
29 H2 **Dunster** Somset
66 C2 **Duns Tew** Oxon
180 F6 **Dunston** Gatesd
135 L7 **Dunston** Lincs
106 E3 **Dunston** Norfk
114 E8 **Dunston** Staffs
7 H4 **Dunstone** Devon
13 G7 **Dunstone** Devon
114 E8 **Dunston Heath** Staffs
143 G6 **Dunsville** Donc
144 D1 **Dunswell** E R Yk
199 J3 **Dunsyre** S Lans
11 M6 **Dunterton** Devon
65 M2 **Dunthrop** Oxon
64 E5 **Duntisbourne Abbots** Gloucs
64 E5 **Duntisbourne Leer** Gloucs
64 E6 **Duntisbourne Rouse** Gloucs
16 D1 **Duntish** Dorset
208 E4 **Duntocher** W Duns
67 K2 **Dunton** Bucks
86 F6 **Dunton** C Beds
121 J5 **Dunton** Norfk
100 C5 **Dunton Bassett** Leics
38 D2 **Dunton Green** Kent
52 E1 **Dunton Wayletts** Essex
259 G2 **Duntulm** Highld
195 L7 **Dunure** S Ayrs
57 G6 **Dunvant** Swans
258 C7 **Dunvegan** Highld
91 L1 **Dunwich** Suffk
131 J8 **Dunwood** Staffs
177 L8 **Durdar** Cumb
3 K5 **Durgan** Cnwll
169 H2 **Durham** Dur
169 H3 **Durham Crematorium** Dur
186 C5 **Durisdeer** D & G
186 C5 **Durisdeermill** D & G
141 M4 **Durkar** Wakefd
30 C4 **Durleigh** Somset
35 G7 **Durley** Hants
47 K6 **Durley** Wilts
35 H7 **Durley Street** Hants

41 J2 **Durlock** Kent
41 J4 **Durlock** Kent
80 E7 **Durlow Common** Herefs
140 E4 **Durn** Rochdl
276 F3 **Durness** Highld
256 C6 **Durno** Abers
228 F4 **Duror** Highld
216 F5 **Durran** Ag & B
21 J6 **Durrington** W Susx
33 K2 **Durrington** Wilts
245 G4 **Durris** Abers
63 M7 **Dursley** Gloucs
63 K3 **Dursley Cross** Gloucs
30 D5 **Durston** Somset
17 G1 **Durweston** Dorset
84 D3 **Duston** Nhants
253 H6 **Duthil** Highld
94 F7 **Dutlas** Powys
70 F2 **Duton Hill** Essex
11 L5 **Dutson** Cnwll
130 B4 **Dutton** Ches W
87 K6 **Duxford** Cambs
66 A7 **Duxford** Oxon
126 E4 **Dwygyfylchi** Conwy
125 H6 **Dwyran** IoA
245 K1 **Dyce** C Aber
88 E7 **Dyer's End** Essex
56 E5 **Dyfatty** Carmth
110 D8 **Dyffrydan** Gwynd
42 C3 **Dyffryn** Brdgnd
61 G6 **Dyffryn** Myr Td
43 H7 **Dyffryn** V Glam
109 K7 **Dyffryn Ardudwy** Gwynd
93 G7 **Dyffryn Castell** Cerdgn
60 C5 **Dyffryn Cellwen** Neath
118 E7 **Dyke** Lincs
264 F8 **Dyke** Moray
233 K4 **Dykehead** Angus
234 B3 **Dykehead** Angus
210 A7 **Dykehead** N Lans
219 K7 **Dykehead** Stirlg
235 H2 **Dykelands** Abers
233 K4 **Dykends** Angus
256 C3 **Dykeside** Abers
93 J4 **Dylife** Powys
25 L1 **Dymchurch** Kent
63 K1 **Dymock** Gloucs
45 L4 **Dyrham** S Glos
222 E8 **Dysart** Fife
128 C4 **Dyserth** Denbgs

**E**

98 C8 **Eachway** Worcs
180 D4 **Eachwick** Nthumb
147 H6 **Eagland Hill** Lancs
135 H6 **Eagle** Lincs
135 H6 **Eagle Barnsdale** Lincs
135 H6 **Eagle Moor** Lincs
169 L7 **Eaglescliffe** S on T
164 E5 **Eaglesfield** Cumb
177 H4 **Eaglesfield** D & G
208 F8 **Eaglesham** E Rens
139 L5 **Eagley** Bolton
154 d6 **Eairy** IoM
134 D7 **Eakring** Notts
143 K5 **Ealand** N Linc
50 F3 **Ealing** Gt Lon
178 F7 **Eals** Nthumb
166 C5 **Eamont Bridge** Cumb
148 F6 **Earby** Lancs
139 K3 **Earcroft** Bl w D
97 G5 **Eardington** Shrops
80 A4 **Eardisland** Herefs
79 K5 **Eardisley** Herefs
112 E6 **Eardiston** Shrops
80 F2 **Eardiston** Worcs
103 H8 **Earith** Cambs
202 F7 **Earle** Nthumb
130 B1 **Earlestown** St Hel
49 H4 **Earley** Wokham
106 D2 **Earlham** Norfk
106 E2 **Earlham Crematorium** Norfk
258 F4 **Earlish** Highld
85 G3 **Earls Barton** Nhants
71 L1 **Earls Colne** Essex
81 M3 **Earls Common** Worcs
81 K6 **Earl's Croome** Worcs
96 E8 **Earlsditton** Shrops
99 J7 **Earlsdon** Covtry
23 L3 **Earl's Down** E Susx
223 H7 **Earlsferry** Fife
51 H4 **Earlsfield** Gt Lon
256 E5 **Earlsford** Abers
90 B2 **Earl's Green** Suffk
141 L3 **Earlsheaton** Kirk
100 A4 **Earl Shilton** Leics
90 F3 **Earl Soham** Suffk
132 B6 **Earl Sterndale** Derbys

201 J5 **Earlston** Border
196 D4 **Earlston** E Ayrs
90 D3 **Earl Stonham** Suffk
37 L1 **Earlswood** Surrey
98 E8 **Earlswood** Warwks
62 F8 **Earlswood Common** Mons
20 D7 **Earnley** W Susx
139 G3 **Earnshaw Bridge** Lancs
181 H4 **Earsdon** N Tyne
191 J7 **Earsdon** Nthumb
107 G5 **Earsham** Norfk
151 K4 **Earswick** C York
20 F5 **Eartham** W Susx
45 K2 **Earthcott** S Glos
161 J1 **Easby** N York
215 L1 **Easdale** Ag & B
36 D6 **Easebourne** W Susx
100 A7 **Easenhall** Warwks
36 E2 **Eashing** Surrey
67 G5 **Easington** Bucks
169 L2 **Easington** Dur
145 K4 **Easington** E R Yk
203 J6 **Easington** Nthumb
67 G7 **Easington** Oxon
171 H7 **Easington** R & Cl
169 L2 **Easington Colliery** Dur
169 K2 **Easington Lane** Sundld
151 H2 **Easingwold** N York
41 H5 **Easole Street** Kent
233 M6 **Eassie and Nevay** Angus
42 F8 **East Aberthaw** V Glam
7 M5 **East Allington** Devon
28 F5 **East Anstey** Devon
34 E1 **East Anton** Hants
160 C3 **East Appleton** N York
19 K6 **East Ashey** IoW
20 D5 **East Ashling** W Susx
34 F2 **East Aston** Hants
163 H5 **East Ayton** N York
11 K3 **East Balsdon** Cnwll
61 K6 **East Bank** Blae G
136 C3 **East Barkwith** Lincs
39 H3 **East Barming** Kent
171 J8 **East Barnby** N York
69 H8 **East Barnet** Gt Lon
212 F4 **East Barns** E Loth
121 K5 **East Barsham** Norfk
122 D4 **East Beckham** Norfk
50 D4 **East Bedfont** Gt Lon
90 C8 **East Bergholt** Suffk
141 J2 **East Bierley** Kirk
121 L7 **East Bilney** Norfk
23 H7 **East Blatchington** E Susx
17 H4 **East Bloxworth** Dorset
181 J6 **East Boldon** S Tyne
18 F4 **East Boldre** Hants
191 G3 **East Bolton** Nthumb
169 J7 **Eastbourne** Darltn
23 K7 **Eastbourne** E Susx
23 L6 **Eastbourne Crematorium** E Susx
30 D3 **East Bower** Somset
105 J2 **East Bradenham** Norfk
44 D8 **East Brent** Somset
91 K2 **Eastbridge** Suffk
117 J3 **East Bridgford** Notts
168 B6 **East Briscoe** Dur
43 J7 **Eastbrook** V Glam
28 B4 **East Buckland** Devon
14 C5 **East Budleigh** Devon
149 J7 **Eastburn** C Brad
152 F4 **Eastburn** E R Yk
50 B2 **East Burnham** Bucks
16 F5 **East Burton** Dorset
68 E8 **Eastbury** Herts
47 M3 **Eastbury** W Berk
168 E2 **East Butsfield** Dur
143 L6 **East Butterwick** N Linc
149 J5 **Eastby** N York
210 E5 **East Calder** W Loth
106 D3 **East Carleton** Norfk
150 B7 **East Carlton** Leeds
101 H5 **East Carlton** Nhants
16 F6 **East Chaldon (Chaldon Herring)** Dorset
48 A1 **East Challow** Oxon
7 L6 **East Charleton** Devon
16 A1 **East Chelborough** Dorset
191 K6 **East Chevington** Nthumb
22 F4 **East Chiltington** E Susx
31 H8 **East Chinnock** Somset
47 H8 **East Chisenbury** Wilts
34 C2 **East Cholderton** Hants
53 L5 **Eastchurch** Kent
50 D8 **East Clandon** Surrey
67 H2 **East Claydon** Bucks
44 E5 **East Clevedon** N Som
31 J8 **East Coker** Somset
64 C6 **Eastcombe** Gloucs
29 L4 **East Combe** Somset

31 K3 **East Compton** Somset
8 C4 **East Cornworthy** Devon
176 F7 **East Cote** Cumb
50 E1 **Eastcote** Gt Lon
84 D4 **Eastcote** Nhants
99 G7 **Eastcote** Solhll
26 D7 **Eastcott** Cnwll
46 F7 **Eastcott** Wilts
151 L7 **East Cottingwith** E R Yk
47 K6 **Eastcourt** Wilts
64 E8 **Eastcourt** Wilts
19 H4 **East Cowes** IoW
143 G4 **East Cowick** E R Yk
160 D2 **East Cowton** N York
181 G4 **East Cramlington** Nthumb
31 L2 **East Cranmore** Somset
17 H6 **East Creech** Dorset
165 K1 **East Curthwaite** Cumb
23 J7 **East Dean** E Susx
63 K3 **East Dean** Gloucs
34 C5 **East Dean** Hants
20 E4 **East Dean** W Susx
8 B5 **Eastdown** Devon
27 L3 **East Down** Devon
134 F4 **East Drayton** Notts
51 J4 **East Dulwich** Gt Lon
45 H5 **East Dundry** N Som
144 D2 **East Ella** C KuH
86 C4 **East End** Bed
85 J6 **East End** C Beds
145 G2 **East End** E R Yk
145 H2 **East End** E R Yk
70 B5 **East End** Essex
72 D8 **Eastend** Essex
18 E4 **East End** Hants
48 B6 **East End** Hants
70 C2 **East End** Herts
39 L6 **East End** Kent
53 L4 **East End** Kent
85 J6 **East End** M Keyn
44 F5 **East End** N Som
66 B4 **East End** Oxon
31 L2 **East End** Somset
90 C8 **East End** Suffk
243 J5 **Easter Balmoral** Abers
45 H2 **Easter Compton** S Glos
252 E2 **Easter Dalziel** Highld
20 F6 **Eastergate** W Susx
209 J6 **Easterhouse** C Glas
211 H6 **Easter Howgate** Mdloth
263 G8 **Easter Kinkell** Highld
250 F3 **Easter Moniack** Highld
99 H7 **Eastern Green** Covtry
245 J3 **Easter Ord** Abers
223 K6 **Easter Pitkierie** Fife
281 d6 **Easter Skeld** Shet
202 B6 **Easter Softlaw** Border
46 F8 **Easterton** Wilts
44 D8 **Eastertown** Somset
47 J8 **East Everleigh** Wilts
39 J3 **East Farleigh** Kent
100 F6 **East Farndon** Nhants
143 K7 **East Ferry** Lincs
210 A6 **Eastfield** N Lans
163 J6 **Eastfield** N York
135 K3 **East Firsby** Lincs
212 C3 **East Fortune** E Loth
142 C1 **East Garforth** Leeds
47 M4 **East Garston** W Berk
168 B3 **Eastgate** Dur
118 F7 **Eastgate** Lincs
122 C7 **Eastgate** Norfk
48 C2 **East Ginge** Oxon
100 E1 **East Goscote** Leics
47 K6 **East Grafton** Wilts
91 J2 **East Green** Suffk
34 B5 **East Grimstead** Wilts
38 B5 **East Grinstead** W Susx
25 H3 **East Guldeford** E Susx
84 C2 **East Haddon** Nhants
48 D1 **East Hagbourne** Oxon
144 E4 **East Halton** N Linc
51 L2 **East Ham** Gt Lon
129 H4 **Eastham** Wirral
129 J3 **Eastham Ferry** Wirral
80 A3 **Easthampton** Herefs
66 B8 **East Hanney** Oxon
71 J6 **East Hanningfield** Essex
142 D4 **East Hardwick** Wakefd
105 K6 **East Harling** Norfk
160 F3 **East Harlsey** N York
33 K5 **East Harnham** Wilts
45 H7 **East Harptree** BaNES
169 L7 **East Hartburn** S on T
181 G3 **East Hartford** Nthumb
20 C3 **East Harting** W Susx
32 F5 **East Hatch** Wilts
86 F5 **East Hatley** Cambs

159 L4 **East Hauxwell** N York
234 F8 **East Haven** Angus
49 J5 **Eastheath** Wokham
119 G3 **East Heckington** Lincs
168 F3 **East Hedleyhope** Dur
274 D5 **East Helmsdale** Highld
48 C1 **East Hendred** Oxon
163 G7 **East Heslerton** N York
44 E6 **East Hewish** N Som
23 H4 **East Hoathly** E Susx
17 H5 **East Holme** Dorset
96 D4 **Easthope** Shrops
72 C3 **Easthorpe** Essex
117 J1 **Easthorpe** Notts
31 J2 **East Horrington** Somset
50 E8 **East Horsley** Surrey
203 G7 **East Horton** Nthumb
17 L3 **East Howe** Bmouth
151 K5 **East Huntington** C York
30 E2 **East Huntspill** Somset
68 E4 **East Hyde** C Beds
28 C2 **East Ilkerton** Devon
48 C3 **East Ilsley** W Berk
13 H1 **Eastington** Devon
63 M6 **Eastington** Gloucs
65 H4 **Eastington** Gloucs
137 G7 **East Keal** Lincs
47 G5 **East Kennett** Wilts
150 B7 **East Keswick** Leeds
209 H8 **East Kilbride** S Lans
12 C3 **East Kimber** Devon
136 F7 **East Kirkby** Lincs
16 F5 **East Knighton** Dorset
28 E6 **East Knowstone** Devon
32 E5 **East Knoyle** Wilts
31 G7 **East Lambrook** Somset
140 A6 **East Lancashire Crematorium** Bury
185 K8 **Eastlands** D & G
41 K6 **East Langdon** Kent
100 F5 **East Langton** Leics
229 H4 **East Laroch** Highld
20 D5 **East Lavant** W Susx
20 F4 **East Lavington** W Susx
159 L1 **East Layton** N York
65 J6 **Eastleach Martin** Gloucs
65 J6 **Eastleach Turville** Gloucs
116 F6 **East Leake** Notts
202 D5 **East Learmouth** Nthumb
7 K4 **East Leigh** Devon
7 L3 **East Leigh** Devon
13 G2 **East Leigh** Devon
27 J5 **Eastleigh** Devon
34 F7 **Eastleigh** Hants
121 J8 **East Lexham** Norfk
40 C4 **Eastling** Kent
212 D3 **East Linton** E Loth
36 A5 **East Liss** Hants
48 B2 **East Lockinge** Oxon
143 K7 **East Lound** N Linc
17 G6 **East Lulworth** Dorset
152 E2 **East Lutton** N York
30 B5 **East Lydeard** Somset
31 J4 **East Lydford** Somset
39 H2 **East Malling** Kent
39 H2 **East Malling Heath** Kent
20 C4 **East Marden** W Susx
134 E5 **East Markham** Notts
33 J7 **East Martin** Hants
148 F5 **East Marton** N York
35 L6 **East Meon** Hants
29 H7 **East Mere** Devon
72 F4 **East Mersea** Essex
50 F5 **East Molesey** Surrey
104 E3 **Eastmoor** Norfk
17 H3 **East Morden** Dorset
149 K7 **East Morton** C Brad
186 C6 **East Morton** D & G
162 B7 **East Ness** N York
153 L8 **East Newton** E R Yk
19 L4 **Eastney** C Port
81 G7 **Eastnor** Herefs
101 G3 **East Norton** Leics
143 K4 **Eastoft** N Linc
13 J8 **East Ogwell** Devon
86 C1 **Easton** Cambs
177 J7 **Easton** Cumb
13 G4 **Easton** Devon
16 D8 **Easton** Dorset
35 G4 **Easton** Hants
118 B6 **Easton** Lincs
106 C1 **Easton** Norfk
31 H2 **Easton** Somset
91 G3 **Easton** Suffk
48 B4 **Easton** W Berk
46 C5 **Easton** Wilts
46 C2 **Easton Grey** Wilts
45 G4 **Easton-in-Gordano** N Som
85 H3 **Easton Maudit** Nhants
101 M3 **Easton on the Hill** Nhants

Easton Royal - Elton 311


47 J7 **Easton Royal** Wilts
32 D7 **East Orchard** Dorset
202 F3 **East Ord** Nthumb
11 L4 **East Panson** Devon
17 M3 **East Parley** Dorset
39 G4 **East Peckham** Kent
54 F6 **East Pennar** Pembks
31 K3 **East Pennard** Somset
86 C2 **East Perry** Cambs
7 L7 **East Portlemouth** Devon
8 A7 **East Prawle** Devon
21 J6 **East Preston** W Susx
16 D1 **East Pulham** Dorset
26 F7 **East Putford** Devon
29 L2 **East Quantoxhead** Somset
53 H5 **East Rainham** Medway
169 J1 **East Rainton** Sundld
145 G7 **East Ravendale** NE Lin
121 J6 **East Raynham** Norfk
102 F4 **Eastrea** Cambs
152 F2 **East Riding Crematorium** E R Yk
177 H5 **Eastriggs** D & G
150 E7 **East Rigton** Leeds
143 K2 **Eastrington** E R Yk
44 E6 **East Rolstone** N Som
65 J8 **Eastrop** Swindn
160 F2 **East Rounton** N York
121 H6 **East Rudham** Norfk
122 D3 **East Runton** Norfk
123 G6 **East Ruston** Norfk
41 J4 **Eastry** Kent
212 B5 **East Saltoun** E Loth
36 C6 **Eastshaw** W Susx
51 G4 **East Sheen** Gt Lon
48 A4 **East Shefford** W Berk
181 G2 **East Sleekburn** Nthumb
123 K7 **East Somerton** Norfk
134 F1 **East Stockwith** Lincs
17 G5 **East Stoke** Dorset
117 K2 **East Stoke** Notts
32 D6 **East Stour** Dorset
41 H3 **East Stourmouth** Kent
27 L5 **East Stowford** Devon
35 H3 **East Stratton** Hants
41 J5 **East Studdal** Kent
39 L3 **East Sutton** Kent
5 L2 **East Taphouse** Cnwll
27 H5 **East-the-Water** Devon
191 J6 **East Thirston** Nthumb
52 E3 **East Tilbury** Thurr
35 L4 **East Tisted** Hants
136 B3 **East Torrington** Lincs
106 B1 **East Tuddenham** Norfk
34 C5 **East Tytherley** Hants
46 D4 **East Tytherton** Wilts
13 K2 **East Village** Devon
45 J4 **Eastville** Bristl
137 H8 **Eastville** Lincs
96 C4 **East Wall** Shrops
121 G8 **East Walton** Norfk
31 J1 **East Water** Somset
12 F4 **East Week** Devon
117 K6 **Eastwell** Leics
34 C6 **East Wellow** Hants
222 F7 **East Wemyss** Fife
210 C6 **East Whitburn** W Loth
70 B5 **Eastwick** Herts
51 M3 **East Wickham** Gt Lon
55 J6 **East Williamston** Pembks
120 F8 **East Winch** Norfk
34 B4 **East Winterslow** Wilts
20 C7 **East Wittering** W Susx
159 L5 **East Witton** N York
140 E3 **Eastwood** Calder
116 D2 **Eastwood** Notts
53 H2 **Eastwood** Sthend
179 L2 **East Woodburn** Nthumb
103 J5 **Eastwood End** Cambs
48 B6 **East Woodhay** Hants
32 C2 **East Woodlands** Somset
35 M3 **East Worldham** Hants
105 J5 **East Wretham** Norfk
26 D7 **East Youlstone** Devon
83 J2 **Eathorpe** Warwks
131 G6 **Eaton** Ches E
130 B7 **Eaton** Ches W
117 L5 **Eaton** Leics
106 D2 **Eaton** Norfk
134 E4 **Eaton** Notts
66 C6 **Eaton** Oxon
95 J5 **Eaton** Shrops
96 B5 **Eaton** Shrops
80 B7 **Eaton Bishop** Herefs
68 B3 **Eaton Bray** C Beds
96 D2 **Eaton Constantine** Shrops
86 D3 **Eaton Ford** Cambs
68 B3 **Eaton Green** C Beds
65 K7 **Eaton Hastings** Oxon
96 C2 **Eaton Mascott** Shrops
86 D3 **Eaton Socon** Cambs
113 L7 **Eaton upon Tern** Shrops
130 C1 **Eaves Brow** Warrtn
99 H6 **Eaves Green** Solhll
162 F6 **Ebberston** N York
33 G6 **Ebbesborne Wake** Wilts
61 J5 **Ebbw Vale** Blae G
180 D7 **Ebchester** Dur
44 D6 **Ebdon** N Som
14 A5 **Ebford** Devon
64 B6 **Ebley** Gloucs
113 H2 **Ebnal** Ches W
80 B3 **Ebnall** Herefs
82 E7 **Ebrington** Gloucs
12 C4 **Ebsworthy** Devon
48 D7 **Ecchinswell** Hants
213 G5 **Ecclaw** Border
177 G4 **Ecclefechan** D & G
202 B5 **Eccles** Border
52 F6 **Eccles** Kent
140 A8 **Eccles** Salfd
132 F3 **Ecclesall** Sheff
139 M8 **Eccles Crematorium** Salfd
133 G1 **Ecclesfield** Sheff
79 L5 **Eccles Green** Herefs
114 C5 **Eccleshall** Staffs
149 M8 **Eccleshill** C Brad
210 E4 **Ecclesmachan** W Loth
123 H5 **Eccles on Sea** Norfk
105 L5 **Eccles Road** Norfk
129 J7 **Eccleston** Ches W
139 G4 **Eccleston** Lancs
138 F8 **Eccleston** St Hel
139 G4 **Eccleston Green** Lancs
245 G2 **Echt** Abers
201 L7 **Eckford** Border
133 H4 **Eckington** Derbys
81 L7 **Eckington** Worcs
84 F3 **Ecton** Nhants
132 B8 **Ecton** Staffs
132 B3 **Edale** Derbys
22 C5 **Edburton** W Susx
164 E2 **Edderside** Cumb
263 J3 **Edderton** Highld
41 G2 **Eddington** Kent
200 B4 **Eddleston** Border
209 J8 **Eddlewood** S Lans
38 C4 **Edenbridge** Kent
140 B4 **Edenfield** Lancs
166 D4 **Edenhall** Cumb
118 E7 **Edenham** Lincs
156 F7 **Eden Mount** Cumb
51 K5 **Eden Park** Gt Lon
132 E5 **Edensor** Derbys
218 D8 **Edentaggart** Ag & B
143 G6 **Edenthorpe** Donc
108 E4 **Edern** Gwynd
31 H3 **Edgarley** Somset
98 D6 **Edgbaston** Birm
3 J4 **Edgcombe** Cnwll
67 G3 **Edgcott** Bucks
28 E3 **Edgcott** Somset
64 B5 **Edge** Gloucs
95 K2 **Edge** Shrops
113 J7 **Edgebolton** Shrops
63 H4 **Edge End** Gloucs
122 B5 **Edgefield** Norfk
122 B4 **Edgefield Green** Norfk
139 L6 **Edgefold** Bolton
113 H1 **Edge Green** Ches W
83 J5 **Edgehill** Warwks
112 E7 **Edgerley** Shrops
141 H4 **Edgerton** Kirk
140 C3 **Edgeside** Lancs
64 D6 **Edgeworth** Gloucs
28 E8 **Edgeworthy** Devon
8 C2 **Edginswell** Torbay
82 B3 **Edgiock** Worcs
114 A7 **Edgmond** Wrekin
114 A7 **Edgmond Marsh** Wrekin
95 J6 **Edgton** Shrops
51 G1 **Edgware** Gt Lon
139 L4 **Edgworth** Bl w D
258 E6 **Edinbane** Highld
211 J4 **Edinburgh** C Edin
99 G1 **Edingale** Staffs
175 L2 **Edingham** D & G
134 D8 **Edingley** Notts
123 G5 **Edingthorpe** Norfk
122 F5 **Edingthorpe Green** Norfk
202 D2 **Edington** Border
180 E2 **Edington** Nthumb
30 F3 **Edington** Somset
46 D8 **Edington** Wilts
30 F2 **Edington Burtle** Somset
44 D8 **Edingworth** Somset
30 E1 **Edithmead** Somset
101 K2 **Edith Weston** Rutlnd
68 B3 **Edlesborough** Bucks
191 G4 **Edlingham** Nthumb
136 D5 **Edlington** Lincs
178 C7 **Edmond Castle** Cumb
33 J8 **Edmondsham** Dorset
169 G1 **Edmondsley** Dur
117 M8 **Edmondthorpe** Leics
10 D7 **Edmonton** Cnwll
69 J8 **Edmonton** Gt Lon
168 C1 **Edmundbyers** Dur
202 A5 **Ednam** Border
115 L3 **Ednaston** Derbys
232 C5 **Edradynate** P & K
202 C2 **Edrom** Border
113 H5 **Edstaston** Shrops
82 E3 **Edstone** Warwks
80 F3 **Edvin Loach** Herefs
117 G4 **Edwalton** Notts
89 J6 **Edwardstone** Suffk
43 G2 **Edwardsville** Myr Td
59 H2 **Edwinsford** Carmth
134 C6 **Edwinstowe** Notts
86 E7 **Edworth** C Beds
80 F4 **Edwyn Ralph** Herefs
234 F2 **Edzell** Angus
234 F2 **Edzell Woods** Abers
57 L6 **Efail-fach** Neath
43 H5 **Efail Isaf** Rhondd
108 F4 **Efailnewydd** Gwynd
112 A6 **Efail-Rhyd** Powys
75 K7 **Efailwen** Carmth
128 D8 **Efenechtyd** Denbgs
187 L7 **Effgill** D & G
50 E8 **Effingham** Surrey
115 K8 **Efflinch** Staffs
13 K2 **Efford** Devon
6 F3 **Efford Crematorium** C Plym
48 B8 **Egbury** Hants
21 G3 **Egdean** W Susx
139 L5 **Egerton** Bolton
40 B6 **Egerton** Kent
6 F3 **Eggbuckland** C Plym
28 B8 **Eggesford** Devon
68 B2 **Eggington** C Beds
115 M6 **Egginton** Derbys
169 L7 **Egglescliffe** S on T
168 C6 **Eggleston** Dur
50 C5 **Egham** Surrey
50 B5 **Egham Wick** Surrey
101 J2 **Egleton** Rutlnd
191 G2 **Eglingham** Nthumb
10 D8 **Egloshayle** Cnwll
11 K5 **Egloskerry** Cnwll
126 F5 **Eglwysbach** Conwy
42 F7 **Eglwys-Brewis** V Glam
113 G3 **Eglwys Cross** Wrexhm
92 F4 **Eglwys Fach** Cerdgn
75 K4 **Eglwyswrw** Pembks
134 E6 **Egmanton** Notts
164 D8 **Egremont** Cumb
129 H1 **Egremont** Wirral
162 E2 **Egton** N York
162 D2 **Egton Bridge** N York
50 B2 **Egypt** Bucks
34 F3 **Egypt** Hants
72 D2 **Eight Ash Green** Essex
248 C8 **Eilanreach** Highld
93 H6 **Eisteddfa Gurig** Cerdgn
78 C2 **Elan Village** Powys
45 J1 **Elberton** S Glos
20 F6 **Elbridge** W Susx
7 G4 **Elburton** C Plym
47 H3 **Elcombe** Swindn
48 B5 **Elcot** W Berk
103 G4 **Eldernell** Cambs
64 A1 **Eldersfield** Worcs
208 D6 **Elderslie** Rens
88 B8 **Elder Street** Essex
169 G5 **Eldon** Dur
149 L7 **Eldwick** C Brad
245 H6 **Elfhill** Abers
203 K7 **Elford** Nthumb
98 F1 **Elford** Staffs
266 E4 **Elgin** Moray
247 H6 **Elgol** Highld
41 G6 **Elham** Kent
223 J7 **Elie** Fife
190 D4 **Elilaw** Nthumb
124 F3 **Elim** IoA
18 F1 **Eling** Hants
134 D4 **Elkesley** Notts
64 D4 **Elkstone** Gloucs
268 B4 **Ella** Abers
8 D2 **Ellacombe** Torbay
215 L1 **Ellanbeich** Ag & B
141 H4 **Elland** Calder
141 H3 **Elland Lower Edge** Calder
206 A4 **Ellary** Ag & B
115 J3 **Ellastone** Staffs
147 J4 **Ellel** Lancs
212 F7 **Ellemford** Border
164 D3 **Ellenborough** Cumb
139 L7 **Ellenbrook** Salfd
114 C6 **Ellenhall** Staffs
37 G4 **Ellen's Green** Surrey
160 F3 **Ellerbeck** N York
171 J7 **Ellerby** N York
113 K7 **Ellerdine Heath** Wrekin
14 A2 **Ellerhayes** Devon
229 G5 **Elleric** Ag & B
144 A2 **Ellerker** E R Yk
149 H7 **Ellers** N York
151 L7 **Ellerton** E R Yk
160 C3 **Ellerton** N York
113 M6 **Ellerton** Shrops
67 K6 **Ellesborough** Bucks
112 F4 **Ellesmere** Shrops
129 J4 **Ellesmere Port** Ches W
29 H2 **Ellicombe** Somset
18 A2 **Ellingham** Hants
107 H5 **Ellingham** Norfk
203 K8 **Ellingham** Nthumb
159 M6 **Ellingstring** N York
86 D1 **Ellington** Cambs
191 K7 **Ellington** Nthumb
86 D1 **Ellington Thorpe** Cambs
32 D2 **Elliots Green** Somset
35 K2 **Ellisfield** Hants
259 H3 **Ellishader** Highld
99 L1 **Ellistown** Leics
257 H5 **Ellon** Abers
166 A4 **Ellonby** Cumb
107 J6 **Ellough** Suffk
144 B2 **Elloughton** E R Yk
63 H5 **Ellwood** Gloucs
103 K2 **Elm** Cambs
81 K2 **Elmbridge** Worcs
87 J7 **Elmdon** Essex
98 F6 **Elmdon** Solhll
98 F7 **Elmdon Heath** Solhll
21 G6 **Elmer** W Susx
51 K5 **Elmers End** Gt Lon
139 G6 **Elmer's Green** Lancs
100 A4 **Elmesthorpe** Leics
71 J6 **Elm Green** Essex
98 E1 **Elmhurst** Staffs
82 A7 **Elmley Castle** Worcs
81 K1 **Elmley Lovett** Worcs
64 A4 **Elmore** Gloucs
63 M4 **Elmore Back** Gloucs
52 B2 **Elm Park** Gt Lon
26 D6 **Elmscott** Devon
90 C6 **Elmsett** Suffk
81 G2 **Elms Green** Worcs
72 F3 **Elmstead Heath** Essex
72 F2 **Elmstead Market** Essex
72 F3 **Elmstead Row** Essex
40 F6 **Elmsted Court** Kent
41 H3 **Elmstone** Kent
64 D2 **Elmstone Hardwicke** Gloucs
152 F4 **Elmswell** E R Yk
89 K2 **Elmswell** Suffk
133 K5 **Elmton** Derbys
271 H6 **Elphin** Highld
211 L5 **Elphinstone** E Loth
245 H2 **Elrick** Abers
173 J5 **Elrig** D & G
179 K6 **Elrington** Nthumb
190 C7 **Elsdon** Nthumb
142 B7 **Elsecar** Barns
70 D2 **Elsenham** Essex
66 D5 **Elsfield** Oxon
144 C5 **Elsham** N Linc
122 B8 **Elsing** Norfk
149 G6 **Elslack** N York
19 K3 **Elson** Hants
112 F4 **Elson** Shrops
199 J4 **Elsrickle** S Lans
36 D2 **Elstead** Surrey
20 D3 **Elsted** W Susx
118 E6 **Elsthorpe** Lincs
169 J6 **Elstob** Dur
139 J1 **Elston** Lancs
117 K2 **Elston** Notts
33 J2 **Elston** Wilts
28 B7 **Elstone** Devon
85 L6 **Elstow** Bed
68 F8 **Elstree** Herts
145 G1 **Elstronwick** E R Yk
147 H8 **Elswick** Lancs
180 F6 **Elswick** N u Ty
87 G3 **Elsworth** Cambs
156 D2 **Elterwater** Cumb
51 L4 **Eltham** Gt Lon
51 L4 **Eltham Crematorium** Gt Lon
86 F3 **Eltisley** Cambs
140 B5 **Elton** Bury
102 B4 **Elton** Cambs
129 K4 **Elton** Ches W
132 D7 **Elton** Derbys
63 K4 **Elton** Gloucs
80 B1 **Elton** Herefs
117 K4 **Elton** Notts

169 L7 **Elton** S on T
129 K5 **Elton Green** Ches W
180 C6 **Eltringham** Nthumb
186 E3 **Elvanfoot** S Lans
116 C5 **Elvaston** Derbys
105 G7 **Elveden** Suffk
49 K7 **Elvetham Heath** Hants
212 A4 **Elvingston** E Loth
151 L6 **Elvington** C York
41 J5 **Elvington** Kent
28 B4 **Elwell** Devon
170 B4 **Elwick** Hartpl
203 J5 **Elwick** Nthumb
130 E7 **Elworth** Ches E
29 K4 **Elworthy** Somset
103 L7 **Ely** Cambs
43 J6 **Ely** Cardif
85 H5 **Emberton** M Keyn
165 G4 **Embleton** Cumb
169 L5 **Embleton** Dur
191 J2 **Embleton** Nthumb
264 C1 **Embo** Highld
31 K1 **Emborough** Somset
264 C2 **Embo Street** Highld
149 H5 **Embsay** N York
18 D2 **Emery Down** Hants
141 K5 **Emley** Kirk
141 K5 **Emley Moor** Kirk
49 J5 **Emmbrook** Wokham
49 H4 **Emmer Green** Readg
133 J4 **Emmett Carr** Derbys
67 H6 **Emmington** Oxon
103 K2 **Emneth** Norfk
103 K2 **Emneth Hungate** Norfk
101 L2 **Empingham** Rutlnd
35 M4 **Empshott** Hants
35 M5 **Empshott Green** Hants
96 C1 **Emstrey Crematorium** Shrops
20 B5 **Emsworth** Hants
48 B6 **Enborne** W Berk
48 C6 **Enborne Row** W Berk
96 B4 **Enchmarsh** Shrops
100 C3 **Enderby** Leics
157 H5 **Endmoor** Cumb
114 E1 **Endon** Staffs
114 E1 **Endon Bank** Staffs
69 K7 **Enfield** Gt Lon
69 K7 **Enfield Crematorium** Gt Lon
69 K7 **Enfield Lock** Gt Lon
69 K7 **Enfield Wash** Gt Lon
47 H8 **Enford** Wilts
45 K2 **Engine Common** S Glos
80 D5 **England's Gate** Herefs
48 F4 **Englefield** W Berk
50 C4 **Englefield Green** Surrey
114 B1 **Engleseabrook** Ches E
63 H4 **English Bicknor** Gloucs
45 L6 **Englishcombe** BaNES
113 G5 **English Frankton** Shrops
10 B8 **Engollan** Cnwll
34 D1 **Enham-Alamein** Hants
30 C4 **Enmore** Somset
32 E6 **Enmore Green** Dorset
164 E7 **Ennerdale Bridge** Cumb
4 F3 **Enniscaven** Cnwll
233 G3 **Enochdhu** P & K
226 D3 **Ensay** Ag & B
17 L3 **Ensbury** Bmouth
112 F8 **Ensdon** Shrops
27 K5 **Ensis** Devon
114 E6 **Enson** Staffs
66 A2 **Enstone** Oxon
186 C5 **Enterkinfoot** D & G
161 G2 **Enterpen** N York
97 J6 **Enville** Staffs
283 b12 **Eolaigearraidh** W Isls
63 M5 **Epney** Gloucs
117 H2 **Epperstone** Notts
70 C6 **Epping** Essex
70 B6 **Epping Green** Essex
69 J5 **Epping Green** Herts
70 C6 **Epping Upland** Essex
168 F8 **Eppleby** N York
144 C2 **Eppleworth** E R Yk
51 G6 **Epsom** Surrey
83 H7 **Epwell** Oxon
143 K7 **Epworth** N Linc
143 J7 **Epworth Turbary** N Linc
112 E3 **Erbistock** Wrexhm
98 E5 **Erdington** Birm
38 E6 **Eridge Green** E Susx
38 E6 **Eridge Station** E Susx
206 D4 **Erines** Ag & B
228 D6 **Eriska** Ag & B
104 E7 **Eriswell** Suffk
52 B3 **Erith** Gt Lon
46 D8 **Erlestoke** Wilts
7 J4 **Ermington** Devon
122 D5 **Erpingham** Norfk
40 B3 **Erriottwood** Kent

250 F7 **Errogie** Highld
222 D3 **Errol** P & K
208 D5 **Erskine** Rens
172 B1 **Ervie** D & G
90 F8 **Erwarton** Suffk
78 F6 **Erwood** Powys
160 D1 **Eryholme** N York
128 E8 **Eryrys** Denbgs
2 B5 **Escalls** Cnwll
168 F4 **Escomb** Dur
29 K3 **Escott** Somset
151 K7 **Escrick** N York
58 C3 **Esgair** Carmth
77 G2 **Esgair** Cerdgn
93 G2 **Esgairgeiliog** Powys
77 H7 **Esgerdawe** Carmth
126 F4 **Esgyryn** Conwy
169 G2 **Esh** Dur
50 E6 **Esher** Surrey
150 A7 **Esholt** C Brad
191 J6 **Eshott** Nthumb
149 G4 **Eshton** N York
169 G2 **Esh Winning** Dur
250 D4 **Eskadale** Highld
211 K5 **Eskbank** Mdloth
155 L3 **Eskdale Green** Cumb
187 K6 **Eskdalemuir** D & G
164 E7 **Eskett** Cumb
145 K8 **Eskham** Lincs
143 G4 **Eskholme** Donc
168 E6 **Esperley Lane Ends** Dur
147 H8 **Esprick** Lancs
102 A1 **Essendine** Rutlnd
69 H5 **Essendon** Herts
251 H4 **Essich** Highld
98 B3 **Essington** Staffs
257 G6 **Esslemont** Abers
170 D7 **Eston** R & Cl
202 E5 **Etal** Nthumb
46 F7 **Etchilhampton** Wilts
24 C2 **Etchingham** E Susx
41 G7 **Etchinghill** Kent
115 G7 **Etchinghill** Staffs
23 H3 **Etchingwood** E Susx
153 L8 **Etherdwick** E R Yk
105 K1 **Etling Green** Norfk
63 K6 **Etloe** Gloucs
50 B3 **Eton** W & M
50 B3 **Eton Wick** W & M
114 D2 **Etruria** C Stke
241 J5 **Etteridge** Highld
167 K5 **Ettersgill** Dur
130 E7 **Ettiley Heath** Ches E
97 L4 **Ettingshall** Wolves
83 G5 **Ettington** Warwks
102 C2 **Etton** C Pete
152 F7 **Etton** E R Yk
187 L3 **Ettrick** Border
188 C1 **Ettrickbridge** Border
187 L3 **Ettrickhill** Border
115 M5 **Etwall** Derbys
96 F5 **Eudon George** Shrops
105 H7 **Euston** Suffk
103 K4 **Euximoor Drove** Cambs
139 H4 **Euxton** Lancs
79 J3 **Evancoyd** Powys
263 G6 **Evanton** Highld
118 E2 **Evedon** Lincs
97 G2 **Evelith** Shrops
263 L2 **Evelix** Highld
79 J3 **Evenjobb** Powys
84 B8 **Evenley** Nhants
65 J1 **Evenlode** Gloucs
168 F5 **Evenwood** Dur
168 F6 **Evenwood Gate** Dur
31 L3 **Evercreech** Somset
152 B7 **Everingham** E R Yk
47 J8 **Everleigh** Wilts
163 H5 **Everley** N York
12 B4 **Eversfield** Devon
85 K8 **Eversholt** C Beds
16 A2 **Evershot** Dorset
49 J6 **Eversley** Hants
49 J6 **Eversley Cross** Hants
144 A2 **Everthorpe** E R Yk
86 D5 **Everton** C Beds
18 D5 **Everton** Hants
129 H1 **Everton** Lpool
134 D2 **Everton** Notts
177 K4 **Evertown** D & G
80 F5 **Evesbatch** Herefs
82 B6 **Evesham** Worcs
100 D3 **Evington** C Leic
141 M3 **Ewden Village** Sheff
97 G4 **Ewdness** Shrops
51 G6 **Ewell** Surrey
41 H6 **Ewell Minnis** Kent
48 F1 **Ewelme** Oxon
64 E7 **Ewen** Gloucs
42 D6 **Ewenny** V Glam

118 F2 **Ewerby** Lincs
118 F2 **Ewerby Thorpe** Lincs
190 F7 **Ewesley** Nthumb
37 G3 **Ewhurst** Surrey
24 E2 **Ewhurst Green** E Susx
37 G3 **Ewhurst Green** Surrey
129 G6 **Ewloe** Flints
129 G6 **Ewloe Green** Flints
139 K3 **Ewood** Bl w D
140 B4 **Ewood Bridge** Lancs
12 B3 **Eworthy** Devon
36 B1 **Ewshot** Hants
62 D2 **Ewyas Harold** Herefs
12 E2 **Exbourne** Devon
29 G6 **Exbridge** Somset
19 G4 **Exbury** Hants
23 H7 **Exceat** E Susx
160 D5 **Exelby** N York
13 L4 **Exeter** Devon
13 L4 **Exeter & Devon Crematorium** Devon
28 E3 **Exford** Somset
95 L2 **Exfordsgreen** Shrops
82 D4 **Exhall** Warwks
99 K6 **Exhall** Warwks
49 G3 **Exlade Street** Oxon
149 J7 **Exley Head** C Brad
13 M5 **Exminster** Devon
14 A6 **Exmouth** Devon
88 C2 **Exning** Suffk
41 G6 **Exted** Kent
14 A5 **Exton** Devon
35 J6 **Exton** Hants
101 K1 **Exton** Rutlnd
29 G4 **Exton** Somset
13 L4 **Exwick** Devon
132 D4 **Eyam** Derbys
83 M5 **Eydon** Nhants
102 E3 **Eye** C Pete
80 C2 **Eye** Herefs
106 C8 **Eye** Suffk
102 E3 **Eye Green** C Pete
117 K8 **Eye Kettleby** Leics
213 L6 **Eyemouth** Border
86 E6 **Eyeworth** C Beds
39 L2 **Eyhorne Street** Kent
91 H5 **Eyke** Suffk
86 D3 **Eynesbury** Cambs
52 C6 **Eynsford** Kent
66 B5 **Eynsham** Oxon
15 K4 **Eype** Dorset
259 G6 **Eyre** Highld
41 J5 **Eythorne** Kent
80 B3 **Eyton** Herefs
95 J6 **Eyton** Shrops
112 F8 **Eyton** Shrops
113 G7 **Eyton** Shrops
112 E3 **Eyton** Wrexhm
96 D2 **Eyton on Severn** Shrops
113 L8 **Eyton upon the Weald Moors** Wrekin

## F

48 A7 **Faccombe** Hants
161 H2 **Faceby** N York
111 K8 **Fachwen** Powys
140 D4 **Facit** Lancs
133 J7 **Fackley** Notts
113 K1 **Faddiley** Ches E
161 L5 **Fadmoor** N York
57 J4 **Faerdre** Swans
57 J4 **Fagwyr** Swans
208 E4 **Faifley** W Duns
45 G4 **Failand** N Som
196 F5 **Failford** S Ayrs
140 D7 **Failsworth** Oldham
92 D1 **Fairbourne** Gwynd
142 D2 **Fairburn** N York
131 L5 **Fairfield** Derbys
25 H2 **Fairfield** Kent
97 L8 **Fairfield** Worcs
65 H6 **Fairford** Gloucs
65 H6 **Fairford Park** Gloucs
175 L3 **Fairgirth** D & G
138 C2 **Fairhaven** Lancs
50 B8 **Fairlands** Surrey
207 L8 **Fairlie** N Ayrs
24 F5 **Fairlight** E Susx
14 C3 **Fairmile** Devon
50 E6 **Fairmile** Surrey
200 F6 **Fairnilee** Border
35 G7 **Fair Oak** Hants
114 B5 **Fairoak** Staffs
49 G6 **Fair Oak Green** Hants
52 D6 **Fairseat** Kent
71 J4 **Fairstead** Essex
120 E7 **Fairstead** Norfk
122 F6 **Fairstead** Norfk

23 G2 **Fairwarp** E Susx
43 J6 **Fairwater** Cardif
27 G6 **Fairy Cross** Devon
121 K5 **Fakenham** Norfk
105 H8 **Fakenham Magna** Suffk
211 M6 **Fala** Mdloth
211 M6 **Fala Dam** Mdloth
200 E2 **Falahill** Border
77 G5 **Falcondale** Cerdgn
84 B6 **Falcut** Nhants
135 L3 **Faldingworth** Lincs
9 f2 **Faldouet** Jersey
63 K8 **Falfield** S Glos
91 G7 **Falkenham** Suffk
210 A3 **Falkirk** Falk
222 D5 **Falkland** Fife
191 H2 **Falloden** Nthumb
131 G1 **Fallowfield** Manch
179 L5 **Fallowfield** Nthumb
216 F4 **Falls of Blarghour** Ag & B
22 E5 **Falmer** E Susx
3 K4 **Falmouth** Cnwll
188 C5 **Falnash** Border
163 J5 **Falsgrave** N York
179 G2 **Falstone** Nthumb
276 B6 **Fanagmore** Highld
68 C2 **Fancott** C Beds
250 E3 **Fanellan** Highld
161 J4 **Fangdale Beck** N York
152 A5 **Fangfoss** E R Yk
226 E3 **Fanmore** Ag & B
261 L6 **Fannich Lodge** Highld
201 J5 **Fans** Border
85 G8 **Far Bletchley** M Keyn
102 D4 **Farcet** Cambs
84 E3 **Far Cotton** Nhants
96 D8 **Farden** Shrops
19 K2 **Fareham** Hants
156 D3 **Far End** Cumb
98 D1 **Farewell** Staffs
97 G8 **Far Forest** Worcs
136 F4 **Farforth** Lincs
63 M7 **Far Green** Gloucs
65 L8 **Faringdon** Oxon
139 G3 **Farington** Lancs
232 F8 **Farkhill** P & K
178 D7 **Farlam** Cumb
45 G5 **Farleigh** N Som
51 K7 **Farleigh** Surrey
46 A7 **Farleigh Hungerford** Somset
35 J2 **Farleigh Wallop** Hants
137 J5 **Farlesthorpe** Lincs
157 H6 **Farleton** Cumb
147 L2 **Farleton** Lancs
132 F7 **Farley** Derbys
115 H3 **Farley** Staffs
34 B5 **Farley** Wilts
88 E4 **Farley Green** Suffk
37 G2 **Farley Green** Surrey
49 H6 **Farley Hill** Wokham
63 M4 **Farleys End** Gloucs
19 M3 **Farlington** C Port
151 K2 **Farlington** N York
96 E7 **Farlow** Shrops
45 K7 **Farmborough** BaNES
70 F5 **Farmbridge End** Essex
64 F1 **Farmcote** Gloucs
97 H5 **Farmcote** Shrops
77 J6 **Farmers** Carmth
65 H4 **Farmington** Gloucs
66 C5 **Farmoor** Oxon
139 G7 **Far Moor** Wigan
3 H4 **Farms Common** Cnwll
116 C8 **Farm Town** Leics
267 K6 **Farmtown** Moray
116 B2 **Farnah Green** Derbys
51 L6 **Farnborough** Gt Lon
49 L8 **Farnborough** Hants
48 B3 **Farnborough** W Berk
83 K5 **Farnborough** Warwks
49 L7 **Farnborough Park** Hants
49 L7 **Farnborough Street** Hants
36 E2 **Farncombe** Surrey
85 H3 **Farndish** Bed
112 F1 **Farndon** Ches W
117 K1 **Farndon** Notts
235 G4 **Farnell** Angus
33 G7 **Farnham** Dorset
70 C2 **Farnham** Essex
150 E4 **Farnham** N York
91 H3 **Farnham** Suffk
36 B2 **Farnham** Surrey
50 B2 **Farnham Common** Bucks
70 C2 **Farnham Green** Essex
50 B2 **Farnham Royal** Bucks
52 C5 **Farningham** Kent
141 L1 **Farnley** Leeds

Farnley - Fochabers 313

150 B6 **Farnley** N York
141 J5 **Farnley Tyas** Kirk
134 C8 **Farnsfield** Notts
139 L6 **Farnworth** Bolton
129 L2 **Farnworth** Halton
64 D6 **Far Oakridge** Gloucs
241 L3 **Farr** Highld
251 J5 **Farr** Highld
278 B4 **Farr** Highld
251 G7 **Farraline** Highld
14 B4 **Farringdon** Devon
45 J7 **Farrington Gurney** BaNES
156 E4 **Far Sawrey** Cumb
141 K1 **Farsley** Leeds
71 K6 **Farther Howegreen** Essex
39 K4 **Farthing Green** Kent
83 M7 **Farthinghoe** Nhants
41 J7 **Farthingloe** Kent
84 B4 **Farthingstone** Nhants
51 L6 **Farthing Street** Gt Lon
136 E5 **Far Thorpe** Lincs
141 J4 **Fartown** Kirk
141 K1 **Fartown** Leeds
14 E3 **Farway** Devon
229 G6 **Fasnacloich** Ag & B
250 B6 **Fasnakyle** Highld
239 G7 **Fassfern** Highld
181 H8 **Fatfield** Sundld
178 C7 **Faugh** Cumb
115 K6 **Fauld** Staffs
210 B6 **Fauldhouse** W Loth
71 J4 **Faulkbourne** Essex
45 L8 **Faulkland** Somset
113 K5 **Fauls** Shrops
40 D3 **Faversham** Kent
150 F1 **Fawdington** N York
180 F5 **Fawdon** N u Ty
190 E3 **Fawdon** Nthumb
131 L7 **Fawfieldhead** Staffs
52 C6 **Fawkham Green** Kent
66 A4 **Fawler** Oxon
49 J2 **Fawley** Bucks
19 G3 **Fawley** Hants
48 B3 **Fawley** W Berk
63 H1 **Fawley Chapel** Herefs
128 F6 **Fawnog** Flints
84 A4 **Fawsley** Nhants
143 L3 **Faxfleet** E R Yk
37 K4 **Faygate** W Susx
138 D8 **Fazakerley** Lpool
99 G3 **Fazeley** Staffs
160 B6 **Fearby** N York
264 C4 **Fearn** Highld
231 K6 **Fearnan** P & K
260 B7 **Fearnbeg** Highld
130 C2 **Fearnhead** Warrtn
260 A7 **Fearnmore** Highld
06 E3 **Fearnoch** Ag & B
97 L2 **Featherstone** Staffs
42 C3 **Featherstone** Wakefd
82 B3 **Feckenham** Worcs
72 C3 **Feering** Essex
59 H3 **Feetham** N York
48 D2 **Feizor** N York
38 B5 **Felbridge** Surrey
22 E4 **Felbrigg** Norfk
38 B5 **Felcourt** Surrey
68 D6 **Felden** Herts
59 G4 **Felindre** Carmth
59 K3 **Felindre** Carmth
76 C7 **Felindre** Carmth
77 G4 **Felindre** Cerdgn
61 J2 **Felindre** Powys
94 E7 **Felindre** Powys
57 H4 **Felindre** Swans
75 J4 **Felindre Farchog** Pembks
76 F4 **Felin Fach** Cerdgn
78 F8 **Felinfach** Powys
56 F4 **Felinfoel** Carmth
58 F4 **Felin gwm Isaf** Carmth
58 F4 **Felin gwm Uchaf** Carmth
78 F8 **Felin-newydd** Powys
61 G5 **Felixkirk** N York
91 G8 **Felixstowe** Suffk
91 H7 **Felixstowe Ferry** Suffk
02 E4 **Felkington** Nthumb
42 B5 **Felkirk** Wakefd
81 G6 **Felling** Gatesd
49 J7 **Fell Lane** C Brad
65 J3 **Fell Side** Cumb
35 K4 **Felmersham** Bed
22 E5 **Felmingham** Norfk
20 F7 **Felpham** W Susx
39 J4 **Felsham** Suffk
71 G3 **Felsted** Essex
50 E4 **Feltham** Gt Lon
50 E5 **Felthamhill** Surrey
22 D7 **Felthorpe** Norfk
30 D5 **Felton** Herefs
35 G6 **Felton** N Som
191 H6 **Felton** Nthumb
112 F8 **Felton Butler** Shrops
104 E5 **Feltwell** Norfk
141 J4 **Fenay Bridge** Kirk
148 E8 **Fence** Lancs
133 J3 **Fence** Rothm
169 J1 **Fence Houses** Sundld
160 D4 **Fencote** N York
66 E4 **Fencott** Oxon
137 H7 **Fendike Corner** Lincs
87 K3 **Fen Ditton** Cambs
87 G2 **Fen Drayton** Cambs
119 H7 **Fen End** Lincs
99 G8 **Fen End** Solhll
203 H5 **Fenham** Nthumb
139 K2 **Feniscliffe** Bl w D
139 K3 **Feniscowles** Bl w D
14 D3 **Feniton** Devon
97 H6 **Fenn Green** Shrops
53 G4 **Fenn Street** Medway
115 K2 **Fenny Bentley** Derbys
14 D3 **Fenny Bridges** Devon
83 K5 **Fenny Compton** Warwks
99 K4 **Fenny Drayton** Leics
85 G8 **Fenny Stratford** M Keyn
191 H7 **Fenrother** Nthumb
87 G2 **Fenstanton** Cambs
88 F5 **Fenstead End** Suffk
105 K4 **Fen Street** Norfk
90 E3 **Fen Street** Suffk
114 D3 **Fenton** C Stke
103 G7 **Fenton** Cambs
178 C7 **Fenton** Cumb
118 A1 **Fenton** Lincs
135 G4 **Fenton** Lincs
134 F3 **Fenton** Notts
202 F6 **Fenton** Nthumb
212 B3 **Fenton Barns** E Loth
142 F4 **Fenwick** Donc
196 F2 **Fenwick** E Ayrs
180 C4 **Fenwick** Nthumb
203 H5 **Fenwick** Nthumb
3 L3 **Feock** Cnwll
205 G3 **Feolin Ferry** Ag & B
196 C2 **Fergushill** N Ayrs
258 B6 **Feriniquarrie** Highld
9 k3 **Fermain Bay** Guern
234 D3 **Fern** Angus
42 F2 **Ferndale** Rhondd
17 L2 **Ferndown** Dorset
253 J3 **Ferness** Highld
65 L8 **Fernham** Oxon
81 K3 **Fernhill Heath** Worcs
36 D5 **Fernhurst** W Susx
222 E4 **Fernie** Fife
209 K8 **Ferniegair** S Lans
246 E2 **Fernilea** Highld
131 K4 **Fernilee** Derbys
117 L2 **Fernwood** Notts
150 E4 **Ferrensby** N York
144 B4 **Ferriby Sluice** N Linc
247 L7 **Ferrindonald** Highld
21 J6 **Ferring** W Susx
142 D3 **Ferrybridge** Wakefd
235 H4 **Ferryden** Angus
169 H4 **Ferryhill** Dur
263 K3 **Ferry Point** Highld
56 C3 **Ferryside** Carmth
263 K2 **Ferrytown** Highld
106 B6 **Fersfield** Norfk
240 B7 **Fersit** Highld
241 M3 **Feshiebridge** Highld
50 F7 **Fetcham** Surrey
269 H6 **Fetterangus** Abers
235 G1 **Fettercairn** Abers
66 D2 **Fewcott** Oxon
150 B5 **Fewston** N York
59 H4 **Ffairfach** Carmth
77 K2 **Ffair Rhos** Cerdgn
77 H6 **Ffald-y-Brenin** Carmth
61 K3 **Ffawyddog** Powys
110 D3 **Ffestiniog** Gwynd
128 D6 **Ffordd-las** Denbgs
57 G4 **Fforest** Carmth
62 B3 **Fforest** Mons
57 H5 **Fforest Fach** Swans
57 K4 **Fforest Goch** Neath
76 C5 **Ffostrasol** Cerdgn
129 G8 **Ffrith** Flints
76 C4 **Ffynnonddewi** Cerdgn
128 D3 **Ffynnongroyw** Flints
76 F4 **Ffynnon-Oer** Cerdgn
272 C2 **Fiag Lodge** Highld
51 K6 **Fickleshole** Surrey
64 D1 **Fiddington** Gloucs
30 B3 **Fiddington** Somset
32 D8 **Fiddleford** Dorset
4 D4 **Fiddlers Green** Cnwll
70 C6 **Fiddlers Hamlet** Essex
115 G5 **Field** Staffs
156 E6 **Field Broughton** Cumb
121 M4 **Field Dalling** Norfk
166 B3 **Fieldhead** Cumb
100 B2 **Field Head** Leics
32 C6 **Fifehead Magdalen** Dorset
32 C8 **Fifehead Neville** Dorset
16 E1 **Fifehead St Quintin** Dorset
267 H6 **Fife Keith** Moray
65 K3 **Fifield** Oxon
49 L4 **Fifield** W & M
33 K1 **Fifield** Wilts
33 K2 **Figheldean** Wilts
46 D1 **Filands** Wilts
107 K1 **Filby** Norfk
163 L6 **Filey** N York
85 G5 **Filgrave** M Keyn
65 K6 **Filkins** Oxon
28 B5 **Filleigh** Devon
28 C8 **Filleigh** Devon
135 J3 **Fillingham** Lincs
99 H6 **Fillongley** Warwks
35 K5 **Filmore Hill** Hants
45 J3 **Filton** S Glos
152 D4 **Fimber** E R Yk
234 D4 **Finavon** Angus
104 D2 **Fincham** Norfk
49 J6 **Finchampstead** Wokham
216 D6 **Fincharn** Ag & B
20 B4 **Finchdean** Hants
88 D8 **Finchingfield** Essex
51 H1 **Finchley** Gt Lon
116 A5 **Findern** Derbys
265 G7 **Findhorn** Moray
252 E6 **Findhorn Bridge** Highld
267 J3 **Findochty** Moray
221 H3 **Findo Gask** P & K
245 L4 **Findon** Abers
21 J5 **Findon** W Susx
263 G7 **Findon Mains** Highld
244 D3 **Findrack House** Abers
85 H1 **Finedon** Nhants
101 L4 **Fineshade** Nhants
90 F1 **Fingal Street** Suffk
222 B3 **Fingask** P & K
49 J1 **Fingest** Bucks
160 B5 **Finghall** N York
177 H7 **Fingland** Cumb
197 L7 **Fingland** D & G
41 K4 **Finglesham** Kent
72 F3 **Fingringhoe** Essex
88 D7 **Finkle Green** Essex
141 M7 **Finkle Street** Barns
231 G8 **Finlarig** Stirlg
84 C8 **Finmere** Oxon
230 F4 **Finnart** P & K
90 C2 **Finningham** Suffk
143 H7 **Finningley** Donc
282 e6 **Finsbay** W Isls
82 A1 **Finstall** Worcs
156 E5 **Finsthwaite** Cumb
66 A4 **Finstock** Oxon
275 c4 **Finstown** Ork
268 D5 **Fintry** Abers
209 G2 **Fintry** Stirlg
244 D5 **Finzean** Abers
226 B7 **Fionnphort** Ag & B
282 e6 **Fionnsbhagh** W Isls
157 K4 **Firbank** Cumb
133 L2 **Firbeck** Rothm
152 A3 **Firby** N York
160 C5 **Firby** N York
140 D5 **Firgrove** Rochdl
23 G6 **Firle** E Susx
137 H7 **Firsby** Lincs
34 B4 **Firsdown** Wilts
168 F4 **Fir Tree** Dur
19 J5 **Fishbourne** IoW
20 D6 **Fishbourne** W Susx
169 K4 **Fishburn** Dur
220 F8 **Fishcross** Clacks
20 E6 **Fisher** W Susx
256 B4 **Fisherford** Abers
211 K4 **Fisherrow** E Loth
35 G6 **Fisher's Pond** Hants
147 H6 **Fisher's Row** Lancs
36 E4 **Fisherstreet** W Susx
252 D2 **Fisherton** Highld
196 B7 **Fisherton** S Ayrs
33 G3 **Fisherton de la Mere** Wilts
98 F2 **Fisherwick** Staffs
49 L3 **Fishery Estate** W & M
74 F5 **Fishguard** Pembks
143 G5 **Fishlake** Donc
12 D1 **Fishleigh** Devon
119 J4 **Fishmere End** Lincs
227 J4 **Fishnish Pier** Ag & B
15 J3 **Fishpond Bottom** Dorset
45 J4 **Fishponds** Bristl
140 B6 **Fishpool** Bury
119 K3 **Fishtoft** Lincs
119 K2 **Fishtoft Drove** Lincs
139 H2 **Fishwick** Lancs
246 D2 **Fiskavaig** Highld
135 L5 **Fiskerton** Lincs
117 K1 **Fiskerton** Notts
145 H1 **Fitling** E R Yk
33 K1 **Fittleton** Wilts
21 G3 **Fittleworth** W Susx
103 J1 **Fitton End** Cambs
113 G7 **Fitz** Shrops
29 L5 **Fitzhead** Somset
30 B5 **Fitzroy** Somset
142 C5 **Fitzwilliam** Wakefd
23 H3 **Five Ash Down** E Susx
23 J2 **Five Ashes** E Susx
29 K2 **Five Bells** Somset
80 F6 **Five Bridges** Herefs
129 M4 **Fivecrosses** Ches W
30 E6 **Fivehead** Somset
11 J6 **Fivelanes** Cnwll
44 F1 **Five Lanes** Mons
39 G4 **Five Oak Green** Kent
9 e3 **Five Oaks** Jersey
37 G5 **Five Oaks** W Susx
56 E4 **Five Roads** Carmth
39 K3 **Five Wents** Kent
71 J4 **Flack's Green** Essex
49 L1 **Flackwell Heath** Bucks
82 A6 **Fladbury** Worcs
281 e7 **Fladdabister** Shet
132 C6 **Flagg** Derbys
153 K2 **Flamborough** E R Yk
68 D4 **Flamstead** Herts
20 F6 **Flansham** W Susx
141 M4 **Flanshaw** Wakefd
149 J8 **Flappit Spring** C Brad
149 G4 **Flasby** N York
131 K6 **Flash** Staffs
258 E6 **Flashader** Highld
68 C7 **Flaunden** Herts
117 K3 **Flawborough** Notts
151 G3 **Flawith** N York
45 G5 **Flax Bourton** N Som
150 E4 **Flaxby** N York
63 K4 **Flaxley** Gloucs
130 A5 **Flaxmere** Ches W
29 L4 **Flaxpool** Somset
151 L3 **Flaxton** N York
100 E5 **Fleckney** Leics
83 M3 **Flecknoe** Warwks
134 F5 **Fledborough** Notts
16 C6 **Fleet** Dorset
20 B6 **Fleet** Hants
49 K8 **Fleet** Hants
119 L6 **Fleet** Lincs
19 H3 **Fleetend** Hants
119 L6 **Fleet Hargate** Lincs
146 F6 **Fleetwood** Lancs
42 F7 **Flemingston** V Glam
209 H7 **Flemington** S Lans
89 G1 **Flempton** Suffk
38 E3 **Fletcher Green** Kent
5 J2 **Fletchersbridge** Cnwll
165 G2 **Fletchertown** Cumb
23 G3 **Fletching** E Susx
43 J3 **Fleur-de-lis** Caerph
11 J1 **Flexbury** Cnwll
36 D1 **Flexford** Surrey
164 D4 **Flimby** Cumb
39 H7 **Flimwell** E Susx
128 F5 **Flint** Flints
117 K2 **Flintham** Notts
128 F5 **Flint Mountain** Flints
153 K8 **Flinton** E R Yk
99 H7 **Flint's Green** Solhll
39 J6 **Flishinghurst** Kent
120 F6 **Flitcham** Norfk
85 L8 **Flitton** C Beds
85 K8 **Flitwick** C Beds
143 L5 **Flixborough** N Linc
143 L5 **Flixborough Stather** N Linc
163 J6 **Flixton** N York
107 G6 **Flixton** Suffk
130 E1 **Flixton** Traffd
141 K5 **Flockton** Kirk
141 L5 **Flockton Green** Kirk
202 E6 **Flodden** Nthumb
259 H2 **Flodigarry** Highld
156 E7 **Flookburgh** Cumb
106 D4 **Flordon** Norfk
84 C3 **Flore** Nhants
190 E5 **Flotterton** Nthumb
23 L5 **Flowers Green** E Susx
90 C6 **Flowton** Suffk
141 L3 **Flushdyke** Wakefd
3 K4 **Flushing** Cnwll
14 C4 **Fluxton** Devon
82 A4 **Flyford Flavell** Worcs
52 F2 **Fobbing** Thurr
267 G4 **Fochabers** Moray

314 Fochriw - Full Sutton

61 H6 Fochriw Caerph
143 L4 Fockerby N Linc
31 J5 Foddington Somset
94 B1 Foel Powys
59 G6 Foelgastell Carmth
42 C3 Foel y Dyffryn Brdgnd
152 A8 Foggathorpe E R Yk
202 B3 Fogo Border
266 E5 Fogwatt Moray
276 B6 Foindle Highld
233 J3 Folda Angus
115 G4 Fole Staffs
99 K7 Foleshill Covtry
31 L8 Folke Dorset
41 H8 Folkestone Kent
118 E5 Folkingham Lincs
23 J6 Folkington E Susx
102 C5 Folksworth Cambs
163 J6 Folkton N York
256 C5 Folla Rule Abers
150 D5 Follifoot N York
12 D3 Folly Gate Devon
36 B1 Folly Hill Surrey
43 G8 Fonmon V Glam
32 F4 Fonthill Bishop Wilts
32 F4 Fonthill Gifford Wilts
32 E7 Fontmell Magna Dorset
32 D7 Fontmell Parva Dorset
20 F5 Fontwell W Susx
43 G8 Font-y-gary V Glam
132 D4 Foolow Derbys
52 A5 Foots Cray Gt Lon
243 L1 Forbestown Abers
168 F8 Forcett N York
216 D6 Ford Ag & B
67 J5 Ford Bucks
133 H4 Ford Derbys
7 J5 Ford Devon
8 B6 Ford Devon
27 G6 Ford Devon
65 G1 Ford Gloucs
202 E5 Ford Nthumb
95 K1 Ford Shrops
29 K5 Ford Somset
45 H8 Ford Somset
115 H1 Ford Staffs
21 G6 Ford W Susx
33 L4 Ford Wilts
46 B4 Ford Wilts
12 D4 Forda Devon
38 E5 Fordcombe Kent
211 G1 Fordell Fife
94 F3 Forden Powys
71 G4 Ford End Essex
8 B2 Forder Green Devon
147 J6 Ford Green Lancs
88 C1 Fordham Cambs
72 D2 Fordham Essex
104 C3 Fordham Norfk
72 D2 Fordham Heath Essex
95 K1 Ford Heath Shrops
33 K8 Fordingbridge Hants
163 J7 Fordon E R Yk
245 G8 Fordoun Abers
90 C2 Ford's Green Suffk
72 D2 Fordstreet Essex
29 L7 Ford Street Somset
13 J3 Fordton Devon
65 L4 Fordwells Oxon
41 G3 Fordwich Kent
267 L3 Fordyce Abers
114 E7 Forebridge Staffs
116 B6 Foremark Derbys
9 j4 Forest Guern
160 C3 Forest N York
148 D5 Forest Becks Lancs
190 F7 Forestburn Gate Nthumb
131 J5 Forest Chapel Ches E
51 L2 Forest Gate Gt Lon
37 H3 Forest Green Surrey
181 G5 Forest Hall N Tyne
178 D7 Forest Head Cumb
51 K4 Forest Hill Gt Lon
66 E5 Forest Hill Oxon
167 K4 Forest-in-Teesdale Dur
150 D4 Forest Lane Head N York
221 G8 Forest Mill Clacks
70 C8 Forest Park Crematorium Gt Lon
38 C6 Forest Row E Susx
19 H5 Forest Side IoW
20 C4 Forestside W Susx
133 L7 Forest Town Notts
234 C5 Forfar Angus
221 K3 Forgandenny P & K
93 G3 Forge Powys
62 B7 Forge Hammer Torfn
61 L5 Forge Side Torfn
267 H5 Forgie Moray
267 H5 Forgieside Moray
256 A3 Forgue Abers
98 D8 Forhill Worcs
138 C6 Formby Sefton
106 C4 Forncett End Norfk
106 D4 Forncett St Mary Norfk
106 D5 Forncett St Peter Norfk
89 G2 Fornham All Saints Suffk
89 G2 Fornham St Martin Suffk
253 H2 Fornighty Highld
165 K6 Fornside Cumb
265 G8 Forres Moray
114 F3 Forsbrook Staffs
275 H1 Forse Highld
98 E8 Forshaw Heath Warwks
278 F7 Forsinard Highld
16 C3 Forston Dorset
240 C2 Fort Augustus Highld
221 J4 Forteviot P & K
198 F2 Forth S Lans
64 B1 Forthampton Gloucs
9 i2 Fort Hommet Guern
231 K6 Fortingall P & K
9 k1 Fort le Marchant Guern
34 F2 Forton Hants
147 J5 Forton Lancs
113 G8 Forton Shrops
15 H1 Forton Somset
114 B7 Forton Staffs
256 B3 Fortrie Abers
263 K8 Fortrose Highld
16 D7 Fortuneswell Dorset
239 J8 Fort William Highld
50 A1 Forty Green Bucks
69 J7 Forty Hill Gt Lon
90 C3 Forward Green Suffk
47 L7 Fosbury Wilts
65 K3 Foscot Oxon
84 C6 Foscote Nhants
119 K5 Fosdyke Lincs
119 K5 Fosdyke Bridge Lincs
231 L4 Foss P & K
65 G5 Fossebridge Gloucs
76 E3 Foss-y-ffin Cerdgn
143 G5 Fosterhouses Donc
70 C5 Foster Street Essex
115 K5 Foston Derbys
100 D4 Foston Leics
117 M3 Foston Lincs
151 L3 Foston N York
153 H4 Foston on the Wolds E R Yk
136 F2 Fotherby Lincs
164 D4 Fothergill Cumb
102 B5 Fotheringhay Nhants
165 M1 Foulbridge Cumb
142 B4 Foulby Wakefd
202 E2 Foulden Border
104 F4 Foulden Norfk
99 H4 Foul End Warwks
23 K4 Foul Mile E Susx
9 j3 Foulon Vale Crematorium Guern
148 F7 Foulridge Lancs
122 A6 Foulsham Norfk
200 F3 Fountainhall Border
98 F8 Four Ashes Solhll
97 H6 Four Ashes Staffs
97 L2 Four Ashes Staffs
89 K1 Four Ashes Suffk
9 j3 Four Cabots Guern
112 C7 Four Crosses Powys
98 B2 Four Crosses Staffs
38 C4 Four Elms Kent
31 J4 Four Foot Somset
30 C3 Four Forks Somset
139 J6 Four Gates Bolton
120 A8 Four Gotes Cambs
141 L7 Four Lane End Barns
130 A7 Four Lane Ends Ches W
3 H3 Four Lanes Cnwll
130 F7 Fourlanes End Ches E
35 K4 Four Marks Hants
124 E4 Four Mile Bridge IoA
98 E4 Four Oaks Birm
24 F2 Four Oaks E Susx
63 K2 Four Oaks Gloucs
99 H7 Four Oaks Solhll
264 C1 Fourpenny Highld
48 E3 Four Points W Berk
56 E3 Four Roads Carmth
65 K1 Four Shire Stone Warwks
179 K5 Fourstones Nthumb
39 J7 Four Throws Kent
38 F3 Four Wents Kent
33 H5 Fovant Wilts
257 H7 Foveran Abers
5 K4 Fowey Cnwll
139 K8 Fowley Common Warrtn
39 H4 Fowlhall Kent
233 M8 Fowlis Angus
221 G2 Fowlis Wester P & K
87 J6 Fowlmere Cambs
80 D8 Fownhope Herefs
208 D6 Foxbar Rens
12 C5 Foxcombe Devon
50 B7 Fox Corner Surrey
64 E3 Foxcote Gloucs
45 L7 Foxcote Somset
154 c6 Foxdale IoM
89 G6 Foxearth Essex
52 E5 Foxendown Kent
156 B5 Foxfield Cumb
46 E3 Foxham Wilts
70 E7 Fox Hatch Essex
18 E1 Foxhills Hants
4 F4 Foxhole Cnwll
163 H8 Foxholes N York
23 J4 Foxhunt Green E Susx
84 C5 Foxley Nhants
122 A7 Foxley Norfk
46 C2 Foxley Wilts
82 B2 Foxlydiate Worcs
72 F2 Fox Street Essex
115 G2 Foxt Staffs
87 H5 Foxton Cambs
169 K5 Foxton Dur
100 F5 Foxton Leics
160 F3 Foxton N York
158 F7 Foxup N York
130 C6 Foxwist Green Ches W
96 E8 Foxwood Shrops
63 H2 Foy Herefs
250 E7 Foyers Highld
253 G1 Foynesfield Highld
2 F4 Fraddam Cnwll
4 E3 Fraddon Cnwll
98 F1 Fradley Staffs
114 F5 Fradswell Staffs
153 J3 Fraisthorpe E R Yk
23 H3 Framfield E Susx
106 F3 Framingham Earl Norfk
106 F3 Framingham Pigot Norfk
91 G3 Framlingham Suffk
16 B3 Frampton Dorset
119 K4 Frampton Lincs
45 K3 Frampton Cotterell S Glos
64 D6 Frampton Mansell Gloucs
63 L5 Frampton on Severn Gloucs
119 J3 Frampton West End Lincs
90 E3 Framsden Suffk
169 H2 Framwellgate Moor Dur
148 A8 Frances Green Lancs
97 J7 Franche Worcs
130 C4 Frandley Ches W
11 M4 Frankaborough Devon
128 F2 Frankby Wirral
122 F6 Frankfort Norfk
80 C6 Franklands Gate Herefs
98 C7 Frankley Worcs
78 F4 Franksbridge Powys
83 K1 Frankton Warwks
38 F6 Frant E Susx
269 J3 Fraserburgh Abers
73 G3 Frating Essex
73 G2 Frating Green Essex
19 L4 Fratton C Port
6 D4 Freathy Cnwll
88 D1 Freckenham Suffk
138 E2 Freckleton Lancs
132 F5 Freebirch Derbys
117 L7 Freeby Leics
35 G1 Freefolk Hants
115 G3 Freehay Staffs
66 B4 Freeland Oxon
107 H2 Freethorpe Norfk
107 H2 Freethorpe Common Norfk
119 L3 Freiston Lincs
27 J4 Fremington Devon
159 J3 Fremington N York
45 J3 Frenchay S Glos
12 F5 Frenchbeer Devon
51 M8 French Street Kent
232 B4 Frenich P & K
36 C3 Frensham Surrey
138 C6 Freshfield Sefton
46 A7 Freshford Wilts
18 E6 Freshwater IoW
18 E6 Freshwater Bay IoW
55 G7 Freshwater East Pembks
106 F7 Fressingfield Suffk
90 E7 Freston Suffk
280 E3 Freswick Highld
63 L5 Fretherne Gloucs
122 E8 Frettenham Norfk
222 D6 Freuchie Fife
54 F4 Freystrop Pembks
98 C4 Friar Park Sandw
38 D6 Friar's Gate E Susx
162 C5 Friars' Hill N York
16 C5 Friar Waddon Dorset
103 K2 Friday Bridge Cambs
90 F3 Friday Street Suffk
91 H5 Friday Street Suffk
91 J3 Friday Street Suffk
37 H2 Friday Street Surrey
152 D4 Fridaythorpe E R Yk
132 C7 Friden Derbys
141 G3 Friendly Calder
69 H8 Friern Barnet Gt Lon
225 G4 Friesland Bay Ag & B
135 M3 Friesthorpe Lincs
118 B2 Frieston Lincs
49 J1 Frieth Bucks
116 D2 Friezeland Notts
66 B7 Frilford Oxon
48 E4 Frilsham W Berk
49 L7 Frimley Surrey
49 L7 Frimley Green Surrey
52 F5 Frindsbury Medway
121 G4 Fring Norfk
66 F1 Fringford Oxon
40 A4 Frinsted Kent
73 K3 Frinton-on-Sea Essex
234 F5 Friockheim Angus
92 D1 Friog Gwynd
117 J8 Frisby on the Wreake Leics
137 J8 Friskney Lincs
137 J8 Friskney Eaudike Lincs
23 J7 Friston E Susx
91 J3 Friston Suffk
116 B1 Fritchley Derbys
34 B8 Fritham Hants
119 K2 Frith Bank Lincs
80 F1 Frith Common Worcs
27 H7 Frithelstock Devon
27 H7 Frithelstock Stone Devon
36 B3 Frithend Hants
68 C5 Frithsden Herts
119 K2 Frithville Lincs
39 K5 Frittenden Kent
8 B6 Frittiscombe Devon
106 E5 Fritton Norfk
107 K3 Fritton Norfk
66 D1 Fritwell Oxon
149 L8 Frizinghall C Brad
164 D7 Frizington Cumb
63 M6 Frocester Gloucs
96 C3 Frodesley Shrops
129 M4 Frodsham Ches W
202 B7 Frogden Border
87 H6 Frog End Cambs
87 L3 Frog End Cambs
132 E4 Froggatt Derbys
115 G2 Froghall Staffs
33 L8 Frogham Hants
41 H5 Frogham Kent
7 M6 Frogmore Devon
102 D2 Frognall Lincs
3 J3 Frogpool Cnwll
81 J2 Frog Pool Worcs
6 C1 Frogwell Cnwll
100 B5 Frolesworth Leics
32 C1 Frome Somset
16 B2 Frome St Quintin Dorset
80 F6 Fromes Hill Herefs
128 C6 Fron Denbgs
108 F4 Fron Gwynd
109 J1 Fron Gwynd
94 E4 Fron Powys
94 F3 Fron Powys
112 C3 Froncysyllte Denbgs
111 H4 Fron-goch Gwynd
112 C3 Fron Isaf Wrexhm
107 K7 Frostenden Suffk
168 C3 Frosterley Dur
85 J8 Froxfield C Beds
47 L5 Froxfield Wilts
35 L5 Froxfield Green Hants
34 F6 Fryern Hill Hants
70 F7 Fryerning Essex
162 B7 Fryton N York
227 J3 Fuinary Highld
118 B2 Fulbeck Lincs
87 L4 Fulbourn Cambs
65 K4 Fulbrook Oxon
35 G5 Fulflood Hants
151 K6 Fulford C York
30 B5 Fulford Somset
114 F4 Fulford Staffs
51 H4 Fulham Gt Lon
22 C5 Fulking W Susx
28 B3 Fullaford Devon
196 C3 Fullarton N Ayrs
70 D2 Fuller's End Essex
113 H1 Fuller's Moor Ches W
71 H4 Fuller Street Essex
38 E2 Fuller Street Kent
34 E3 Fullerton Hants
136 E5 Fulletby Lincs
83 G6 Fullready Warwks
152 A5 Full Sutton E R Yk

196 E1 **Fullwood** E Ayrs
50 C2 **Fulmer** Bucks
121 M5 **Fulmodeston** Norfk
136 B4 **Fulnetby** Lincs
119 J6 **Fulney** Lincs
141 J6 **Fulstone** Kirk
145 J8 **Fulstow** Lincs
66 A3 **Fulwell** Oxon
181 J7 **Fulwell** Sundld
139 H2 **Fulwood** Lancs
133 J8 **Fulwood** Notts
132 F3 **Fulwood** Sheff
30 B6 **Fulwood** Somset
66 C4 **Fundenhall** Norfk
20 C5 **Funtington** W Susx
19 J2 **Funtley** Hants
220 C2 **Funtullich** P & K
15 G2 **Furley** Devon
217 G7 **Furnace** Ag & B
56 F4 **Furnace** Carmth
92 E4 **Furnace** Cerdgn
99 H5 **Furnace End** Warwks
22 F2 **Furner's Green** E Susx
131 K3 **Furness Vale** Derbys
70 B2 **Furneux Pelham** Herts
39 M5 **Further Quarter** Kent
84 E6 **Furtho** Nhants
28 C2 **Furzehill** Devon
17 K2 **Furzehill** Dorset
136 E5 **Furzehills** Lincs
19 L2 **Furzeley Corner** Hants
49 L3 **Furze Platt** W & M
34 C7 **Furzley** Hants
30 C7 **Fyfett** Somset
70 E5 **Fyfield** Essex
34 C2 **Fyfield** Hants
66 B7 **Fyfield** Oxon
47 H5 **Fyfield** Wilts
47 H6 **Fyfield** Wilts
33 H6 **Fyfield Bavant** Wilts
163 G2 **Fylingthorpe** N York
36 B6 **Fyning** W Susx
255 D4 **Fyvie** Abers

**G**

196 E1 **Gabroc Hill** E Ayrs
100 F1 **Gaddesby** Leics
68 D4 **Gaddesden Row** Herts
125 H2 **Gadfa** IoA
196 E6 **Gadgirth** S Ayrs
112 E4 **Gadlas** Shrops
61 J3 **Gaer** Powys
62 F7 **Gaer-llwyd** Mons
125 H5 **Gaerwen** IoA
66 B2 **Gagingwell** Oxon
196 C4 **Gailes** N Ayrs
97 K1 **Galley** Staffs
168 F7 **Gainford** Dur
135 G2 **Gainsborough** Lincs
88 E8 **Gainsford End** Essex
260 C4 **Gairloch** Highld
239 K6 **Gairlochy** Highld
221 L7 **Gairneybridge** P & K
157 K2 **Gaisgill** Cumb
165 L1 **Gaitsgill** Cumb
201 G6 **Galashiels** Border
47 J5 **Galgate** Lancs
31 K5 **Galhampton** Somset
216 C2 **Gallanach** Ag & B
13 H1 **Gallantry Bank** Ches E
222 E8 **Gallatown** Fife
99 J5 **Galley Common** Warwks
71 H6 **Galleywood** Essex
240 F5 **Gallovie** Highld
234 C7 **Gallowfauld** Angus
233 J8 **Gallowhill** P & K
72 D2 **Gallows Green** Essex
81 L3 **Gallows Green** Worcs
49 G5 **Gallowstree Common** Oxon
248 C7 **Galltair** Highld
125 K7 **Gallt-y-foel** Gwynd
49 K8 **Gally Hill** Hants
38 D6 **Gallypot Street** E Susx
7 K6 **Galmpton** Devon
8 D4 **Galmpton** Torbay
150 C1 **Galphay** N York
196 F4 **Galston** E Ayrs
88 E2 **Gamballs Green** Staffs
31 L6 **Gamblesby** Cumb
71 J4 **Gambles Green** Essex
77 H8 **Gamelsby** Cumb
131 K1 **Gamesley** Derbys
86 E5 **Gamlingay** Cambs
86 E4 **Gamlingay Cinques** Cambs
86 E5 **Gamlingay Great Heath** Cambs
59 J6 **Gammersgill** N York
268 E4 **Gamrie** Abers
117 G4 **Gamston** Notts

134 E4 **Gamston** Notts
63 G4 **Ganarew** Herefs
216 D1 **Ganavan Bay** Ag & B
6 C1 **Gang** Cnwll
110 D6 **Ganllwyd** Gwynd
234 F1 **Gannachy** Angus
144 F1 **Ganstead** E R Yk
151 L2 **Ganthorpe** N York
163 H7 **Ganton** N York
69 H7 **Ganwick Corner** Herts
13 K7 **Gappah** Devon
266 F5 **Garbity** Moray
105 K7 **Garboldisham** Norfk
243 J2 **Garchory** Abers
129 H6 **Garden City** Flints
49 K5 **Gardeners Green** Wokham
268 E3 **Gardenstown** Abers
141 L8 **Garden Village** Sheff
281 d6 **Garderhouse** Shet
152 E7 **Gardham** E R Yk
32 C3 **Gare Hill** Somset
207 L1 **Garelochhead** Ag & B
66 B7 **Garford** Oxon
142 B1 **Garforth** Leeds
142 B1 **Garforth Bridge** Leeds
149 G5 **Gargrave** N York
220 B8 **Gargunnock** Stirlg
126 D4 **Garizim** Conwy
106 E6 **Garlic Street** Norfk
174 D5 **Garlieston** D & G
41 K2 **Garlinge** Kent
40 F5 **Garlinge Green** Kent
245 H2 **Garlogie** Abers
268 E5 **Garmond** Abers
169 J4 **Garmondsway** Dur
267 G3 **Garmouth** Moray
96 E2 **Garmston** Shrops
59 J6 **Garnant** Carmth
109 J3 **Garn-Dolbenmaen** Gwynd
157 H3 **Garnett Bridge** Cumb
108 E5 **Garnfadryn** Gwynd
209 H5 **Garnkirk** N Lans
57 H3 **Garnswllt** Swans
61 K5 **Garn-yr-erw** Torfn
282 h3 **Garrabost** W Isls
197 G7 **Garrallan** E Ayrs
3 H6 **Garras** Cnwll
109 L3 **Garreg** Gwynd
167 H2 **Garrigill** Cumb
159 L4 **Garriston** N York
184 F6 **Garroch** D & G
172 D7 **Garrochtrie** D & G
207 H8 **Garrochty** Ag & B
259 H4 **Garros** Highld
158 C5 **Garsdale** Cumb
158 D4 **Garsdale Head** Cumb
46 D2 **Garsdon** Wilts
114 F5 **Garshall Green** Staffs
66 E6 **Garsington** Oxon
147 J6 **Garstang** Lancs
68 E7 **Garston** Herts
129 J3 **Garston** Lpool
204 E4 **Gartachossan** Ag & B
209 J5 **Gartcosh** N Lans
42 C4 **Garth** Brdgnd
62 D8 **Garth** Mons
78 C5 **Garth** Powys
79 J1 **Garth** Powys
112 C3 **Garth** Wrexhm
209 H5 **Garthamlock** C Glas
78 E8 **Garthbrengy** Powys
77 G4 **Gartheli** Cerdgn
94 F3 **Garthmyl** Powys
117 L7 **Garthorpe** Leics
143 L4 **Garthorpe** N Linc
92 E6 **Garth Penrhyncoch** Cerdgn
157 H3 **Garth Row** Cumb
157 H5 **Garths** Cumb
255 K5 **Gartly** Abers
210 H7 **Gartmore** Stirlg
209 K6 **Gartness** N Lans
208 E2 **Gartness** Stirlg
208 D2 **Gartocharn** W Duns
145 H1 **Garton** E R Yk
152 F4 **Garton-on-the-Wolds** E R Yk
274 D5 **Gartymore** Highld
212 D5 **Garvald** E Loth
238 F8 **Garvan** Highld
214 D6 **Garvard** Ag & B
262 C7 **Garve** Highld
105 L2 **Garvestone** Norfk
207 L5 **Garvock** Inver
62 F3 **Garway** Herefs
62 F3 **Garway Common** Herefs
62 F2 **Garway Hill** Herefs
282 g4 **Garyvard** W Isls
32 C4 **Gasper** Wilts
46 C5 **Gastard** Wilts
105 K7 **Gasthorpe** Norfk
70 D4 **Gaston Green** Essex

19 H6 **Gatcombe** IoW
157 J5 **Gatebeck** Cumb
135 G3 **Gate Burton** Lincs
134 B3 **Gateford** Notts
142 E2 **Gateforth** N York
196 D4 **Gatehead** E Ayrs
151 L5 **Gate Helmsley** N York
179 H1 **Gatehouse** Nthumb
174 F4 **Gatehouse of Fleet** D & G
121 L6 **Gateley** Norfk
160 D5 **Gatenby** N York
165 G7 **Gatesgarth** Cumb
189 L2 **Gateshaw** Border
181 G6 **Gateshead** Gatesd
129 L7 **Gates Heath** Ches W
234 C6 **Gateside** Angus
208 E7 **Gateside** E Rens
222 B5 **Gateside** Fife
208 B8 **Gateside** N Ayrs
186 C5 **Gateslack** D & G
139 G6 **Gathurst** Wigan
131 G2 **Gatley** Stockp
51 H8 **Gatton** Surrey
201 H6 **Gattonside** Border
78 D2 **Gaufron** Powys
100 F3 **Gaulby** Leics
222 F2 **Gauldry** Fife
233 K5 **Gauldswell** P & K
139 M3 **Gaulkthorn** Lancs
103 K2 **Gaultree** Norfk
113 J2 **Gaunton's Bank** Ches E
17 K2 **Gaunt's Common** Dorset
70 E2 **Gaunt's End** Essex
136 C5 **Gautby** Lincs
202 B3 **Gavinton** Border
141 M6 **Gawber** Barns
67 G1 **Gawcott** Bucks
131 H5 **Gawsworth** Ches E
141 L3 **Gawthorpe** Wakefd
158 B5 **Gawthrop** Cumb
156 C5 **Gawthwaite** Cumb
71 J6 **Gay Bowers** Essex
83 J4 **Gaydon** Warwks
85 G6 **Gayhurst** M Keyn
158 F5 **Gayle** N York
159 L1 **Gayles** N York
21 J3 **Gay Street** W Susx
84 D4 **Gayton** Nhants
120 F7 **Gayton** Norfk
114 F6 **Gayton** Staffs
129 G4 **Gayton** Wirral
137 H3 **Gayton le Marsh** Lincs
121 G7 **Gayton Thorpe** Norfk
120 E7 **Gaywood** Norfk
88 E2 **Gazeley** Suffk
3 J6 **Gear** Cnwll
282 g4 **Gearraidh Bhaird** W Isls
258 D4 **Geary** Highld
89 J4 **Gedding** Suffk
101 K6 **Geddington** Nhants
117 G3 **Gedling** Notts
119 L6 **Gedney** Lincs
119 L7 **Gedney Broadgate** Lincs
120 A5 **Gedney Drove End** Lincs
119 L6 **Gedney Dyke** Lincs
103 G1 **Gedney Hill** Lincs
131 J1 **Gee Cross** Tamesd
101 L3 **Geeston** Rutlnd
107 H5 **Geldeston** Norfk
42 E3 **Gelli** Rhondd
62 B8 **Gelli** Torfn
128 D7 **Gellifor** Denbgs
43 H2 **Gelligaer** Caerph
43 J3 **Gelligroes** Caerph
57 K4 **Gelligron** Neath
110 C4 **Gellilydan** Gwynd
57 K4 **Gellinudd** Neath
55 J3 **Gelly** Pembks
233 C7 **Gellyburn** P & K
58 A4 **Gellywen** Carmth
175 J3 **Gelston** D & G
118 B3 **Gelston** Lincs
153 H4 **Gembling** E R Yk
98 D1 **Gentleshaw** Staffs
187 L7 **Georgefield** D & G
50 C3 **George Green** Bucks
27 H3 **Georgeham** Devon
279 L4 **Georgemas Junction Station** Highld
28 B6 **George Nympton** Devon
61 J5 **Georgetown** Blae G
2 D4 **Georgia** Cnwll
275 C3 **Georth** Ork
126 C6 **Gerlan** Gwynd
12 B4 **Germansweek** Devon
2 F5 **Germoe** Cnwll
3 M4 **Gerrans** Cnwll
50 C1 **Gerrards Cross** Bucks
171 G8 **Gerrick** R & Cl
89 G7 **Gestingthorpe** Essex

112 B8 **Geuffordd** Powys
130 C4 **Gib Hill** Ches W
137 K7 **Gibraltar** Lincs
117 J2 **Gibsmere** Notts
46 B4 **Giddeahall** Wilts
16 F5 **Giddy Green** Dorset
52 B1 **Gidea Park** Gt Lon
12 F5 **Gidleigh** Devon
208 F7 **Giffnock** E Rens
212 C5 **Gifford** E Loth
222 E5 **Giffordtown** Fife
148 D3 **Giggleswick** N York
143 L2 **Gilberdyke** E R Yk
81 J6 **Gilbert's End** Worcs
35 K4 **Gilbert Street** Hants
212 B6 **Gilchriston** E Loth
164 F3 **Gilcrux** Cumb
141 K2 **Gildersome** Leeds
133 L3 **Gildingwells** Rothm
169 J2 **Gilesgate Moor** Dur
42 F8 **Gileston** V Glam
43 J2 **Gilfach** Caerph
42 E4 **Gilfach Goch** Brdgnd
76 D3 **Gilfachrheda** Cerdgn
164 D6 **Gilgarran** Cumb
166 B5 **Gill** Cumb
162 B4 **Gillamoor** N York
3 K6 **Gillan** Cnwll
258 D5 **Gillen** Highld
187 J7 **Gillesbie** D & G
161 K7 **Gilling East** N York
32 D5 **Gillingham** Dorset
53 G5 **Gillingham** Medway
107 H5 **Gillingham** Norfk
160 B2 **Gilling West** N York
280 B4 **Gillock** Highld
131 H7 **Gillow Heath** Staffs
280 D2 **Gills** Highld
39 J7 **Gill's Green** Kent
188 B2 **Gilmanscleuch** Border
211 J5 **Gilmerton** C Edin
220 F2 **Gilmerton** P & K
168 C8 **Gilmonby** Dur
100 C6 **Gilmorton** Leics
100 C2 **Gilroes Crematorium** C Leic
178 E5 **Gilsland** Nthumb
99 G5 **Gilson** Warwks
149 L7 **Gilstead** C Brad
200 F2 **Gilston** Border
70 C4 **Gilston** Herts
70 B4 **Gilston Park** Herts
116 E2 **Giltbrook** Notts
61 L4 **Gilwern** Mons
122 F4 **Gimingham** Norfk
131 J4 **Ginclough** Ches E
23 K5 **Gingers Green** E Susx
90 C3 **Gipping** Suffk
119 J2 **Gipsey Bridge** Lincs
196 C3 **Girdle Toll** N Ayrs
141 H1 **Girlington** C Brad
281 e6 **Girlsta** Shet
160 E1 **Girsby** N York
86 D5 **Girtford** C Beds
174 F4 **Girthon** D & G
87 J3 **Girton** Cambs
135 G6 **Girton** Notts
182 F3 **Girvan** S Ayrs
148 E6 **Gisburn** Lancs
107 K5 **Gisleham** Suffk
90 C1 **Gislingham** Suffk
106 C6 **Gissing** Norfk
14 D3 **Gittisham** Devon
79 J4 **Gladestry** Powys
212 A4 **Gladsmuir** E Loth
57 K5 **Glais** Swans
162 D2 **Glaisdale** N York
234 B6 **Glamis** Angus
110 B1 **Glanaber** Gwynd
54 F3 **Glanafon** Pembks
59 J6 **Glanaman** Carmth
122 A3 **Glandford** Norfk
76 F6 **Glan-Duar** Carmth
75 L6 **Glandwr** Pembks
109 J3 **Glan-Dwyfach** Gwynd
92 F4 **Glandyfi** Cerdgn
61 K4 **Glangrwyney** Powys
42 C3 **Glanllynfi** Brdgnd
94 E5 **Glanmule** Powys
75 K4 **Glanrhyd** Pembks
57 L3 **Glan-rhyd** Powys
190 F3 **Glanton** Nthumb
190 F3 **Glanton Pike** Nthumb
16 C1 **Glanvilles Wootton** Dorset
128 E4 **Glan-y-don** Flints
43 H5 **Glan-y-llyn** Rhondd
93 K6 **Glan-y-nant** Powys
111 H3 **Glan-yr-afon** Gwynd
111 K3 **Glan-yr-afon** Gwynd
126 B4 **Glan-yr-afon** IoA
57 H4 **Glan-yr-afon** Swans

101 M5 **Glapthorn** Nhants
133 J6 **Glapwell** Derbys
79 H7 **Glasbury** Powys
127 K5 **Glascoed** Denbgs
62 C6 **Glascoed** Mons
99 G3 **Glascote** Staffs
79 G5 **Glascwm** Powys
111 H2 **Glasfryn** Conwy
209 G6 **Glasgow** C Glas
125 K6 **Glasinfryn** Gwynd
237 K2 **Glasnacardoch Bay** Highld
247 H6 **Glasnakille** Highld
92 F4 **Glaspwll** Powys
39 J6 **Glassenbury** Kent
197 L2 **Glassford** S Lans
142 C3 **Glass Houghton** Wakefd
63 L3 **Glasshouse** Gloucs
63 L3 **Glasshouse Hill** Gloucs
149 L3 **Glasshouses** N York
177 H6 **Glasson** Cumb
147 J4 **Glasson** Lancs
166 D3 **Glassonby** Cumb
234 F5 **Glasterlaw** Angus
101 K3 **Glaston** Rutlnd
31 H3 **Glastonbury** Somset
102 C6 **Glatton** Cambs
130 D1 **Glazebrook** Warrtn
139 K8 **Glazebury** Warrtn
96 F5 **Glazeley** Shrops
133 G3 **Gleadless** Sheff
130 F6 **Gleadsmoss** Ches E
146 E2 **Gleaston** Cumb
250 F8 **Glebe** Highld
150 D8 **Gledhow** Leeds
175 G5 **Gledpark** D & G
112 D4 **Gledrid** Shrops
89 G5 **Glemsford** Suffk
254 E3 **Glenallachie** Moray
237 K2 **Glenancross** Highld
227 G4 **Glenaros House** Ag & B
154 f4 **Glen Auldyn** IoM
192 D1 **Glenbarr** Ag & B
267 L5 **Glenbarry** Abers
237 H8 **Glenbeg** Highld
253 J6 **Glenbeg** Highld
245 G7 **Glenbervie** Abers
209 J5 **Glenboig** N Lans
237 H8 **Glenborrodale** Highld
217 J7 **Glenbranter** Ag & B
187 G2 **Glenbreck** Border
246 F4 **Glenbrittle House** Highld
198 B7 **Glenbuck** E Ayrs
234 A3 **Glencally** Angus
176 C5 **Glencaple** D & G
249 H2 **Glencarron Lodge** Highld
222 C3 **Glencarse** P & K
229 J5 **Glenceitlein** Highld
242 F7 **Glen Clunie Lodge** Abers
229 H4 **Glencoe** Highld
199 J7 **Glencothe** Border
222 B8 **Glencraig** Fife
185 J5 **Glencrosh** D & G
258 B6 **Glendale** Highld
206 F2 **Glendaruel** Ag & B
221 H6 **Glendevon** P & K
240 C2 **Glendoe Lodge** Highld
222 C3 **Glendoick** P & K
222 D3 **Glenduckie** Fife
221 G5 **Gleneagles** P & K
221 G5 **Gleneagles Hotel** P & K
204 E6 **Glenegedale** Ag & B
248 C7 **Glenelg** Highld
253 K2 **Glenerney** Moray
221 L5 **Glenfarg** P & K
241 M5 **Glenfeshie Lodge** Highld
100 C2 **Glenfield** Leics
238 E7 **Glenfinnan** Highld
239 L6 **Glenfintaig Lodge** Highld
222 B4 **Glenfoot** P & K
218 B4 **Glenfyne Lodge** Ag & B
208 B8 **Glengarnock** N Ayrs
279 K3 **Glengolly** Highld
226 E1 **Glengorm Castle** Ag & B
259 G2 **Glengrasco** Highld
199 J6 **Glenholm** Border
184 F5 **Glenhoul** D & G
233 K3 **Glenisla** Angus
207 J3 **Glenkin** Ag & B
243 M1 **Glenkindie** Abers
254 D6 **Glenlivet** Moray
175 J2 **Glenlochar** D & G
222 B6 **Glenlomond** P & K
172 F3 **Glenluce** D & G
207 H2 **Glenmassen** Ag & B
209 K5 **Glenmavis** N Lans
154 b6 **Glen Maye** IoM
154 f4 **Glen Mona** IoM
259 G8 **Glenmore** Highld
242 C2 **Glenmore Lodge** Highld
229 J1 **Glen Nevis House** Highld

220 F8 **Glenochil** Clacks
100 C4 **Glen Parva** Leics
234 C3 **Glenquiech** Angus
206 D5 **Glenralloch** Ag & B
165 L7 **Glenridding** Cumb
222 D7 **Glenrothes** Fife
232 E8 **Glenshee** P & K
240 F5 **Glenshero Lodge** Highld
207 H3 **Glenstriven** Ag & B
135 K2 **Glentham** Lincs
241 L4 **Glentromie Lodge** Highld
183 K7 **Glen Trool Lodge** D & G
183 J7 **Glentrool Village** D & G
241 J4 **Glentruim House** Highld
135 J2 **Glentworth** Lincs
237 K5 **Glenuig** Highld
229 G5 **Glenure** Ag & B
259 H8 **Glenvarragill** Highld
154 d6 **Glen Vine** IoM
182 F8 **Glenwhilly** D & G
198 D7 **Glespin** S Lans
63 H3 **Glewstone** Herefs
64 B3 **Gloucester** Gloucs
64 B4 **Gloucester Crematorium** Gloucs
149 H6 **Glusburn** N York
274 D1 **Glutt Lodge** Highld
4 F2 **Gluvian** Cnwll
66 B3 **Glympton** Oxon
76 B5 **Glynarthen** Cerdgn
112 B4 **Glyn Ceiriog** Wrexhm
60 C7 **Glyncorrwg** Neath
23 G5 **Glynde** E Susx
23 G5 **Glyndebourne** E Susx
112 A3 **Glyndyfrdwy** Denbgs
60 D5 **Glynneath** Neath
5 J2 **Glynn Valley Crematorium** Cnwll
43 H4 **Glyntaff** Rhondd
43 H4 **Glyntaff Crematorium** Rhondd
60 C4 **Glyntawe** Powys
76 C7 **Glynteg** Carmth
114 C7 **Gnosall** Staffs
114 C7 **Gnosall Heath** Staffs
101 G4 **Goadby** Leics
117 K6 **Goadby Marwood** Leics
46 F4 **Goatacre** Wilts
217 G7 **Goatfield** Ag & B
24 E3 **Goatham Green** E Susx
31 L7 **Goathill** Dorset
162 E2 **Goathland** N York
30 C4 **Goathurst** Somset
38 D3 **Goathurst Common** Kent
40 D6 **Goat Lees** Kent
112 D5 **Gobowen** Shrops
36 E2 **Godalming** Surrey
91 G2 **Goddard's Corner** Suffk
39 K6 **Goddard's Green** Kent
14 D2 **Godford Cross** Devon
66 F2 **Godington** Oxon
140 E8 **Godley** Tamesd
86 E1 **Godmanchester** Cambs
16 C3 **Godmanstone** Dorset
40 D5 **Godmersham** Kent
31 H2 **Godney** Somset
2 F5 **Godolphin Cross** Cnwll
57 L3 **Godre'r-graig** Neath
33 L7 **Godshill** Hants
19 J7 **Godshill** IoW
115 G5 **Godstone** Staffs
51 K8 **Godstone** Surrey
12 C7 **Godsworthy** Devon
18 B4 **Godwinscroft** Hants
62 C6 **Goetre** Mons
69 J6 **Goff's Oak** Herts
61 L4 **Gofilon** Mons
211 G4 **Gogar** C Edin
92 E7 **Goginan** Cerdgn
109 J3 **Golan** Gwynd
5 K4 **Golant** Cnwll
11 L8 **Golberdon** Cnwll
139 J8 **Golborne** Wigan
141 H4 **Golcar** Kirk
44 D2 **Goldcliff** Newpt
23 J5 **Golden Cross** E Susx
39 G4 **Golden Green** Kent
59 G5 **Golden Grove** Carmth
114 D1 **Goldenhill** C Stke
55 G6 **Golden Hill** Pembks
35 L2 **Golden Pot** Hants
116 C1 **Golden Valley** Derbys
51 H2 **Golders Green** Gt Lon
51 H1 **Golders Green Crematorium** Gt Lon
48 D6 **Goldfinch Bottom** W Berk
72 C5 **Goldhanger** Essex
103 L5 **Gold Hill** Cambs

32 D8 **Gold Hill** Dorset
96 C3 **Golding** Shrops
86 B5 **Goldington** Bed
150 E4 **Goldsborough** N York
171 J7 **Goldsborough** N York
98 C5 **Golds Green** Sandw
2 E5 **Goldsithney** Cnwll
41 J3 **Goldstone** Kent
113 M6 **Goldstone** Shrops
50 C7 **Goldsworth Park** Surrey
142 C7 **Goldthorpe** Barns
27 G6 **Goldworthy** Devon
39 K6 **Golford** Kent
39 K6 **Golford Green** Kent
252 F1 **Gollanfield** Highld
159 L6 **Gollinglith Foot** N York
129 H7 **Golly** Wrexhm
29 J3 **Golsoncott** Somset
273 K8 **Golspie** Highld
33 L4 **Gomeldon** Wilts
141 K3 **Gomersal** Kirk
37 G1 **Gomshall** Surrey
117 H2 **Gonalston** Notts
118 B4 **Gonerby Hill Foot** Lincs
281 d5 **Gonfirth** Shet
7 G2 **Goodameavy** Devon
70 F5 **Good Easter** Essex
104 F3 **Gooderstone** Norfk
27 L4 **Goodleigh** Devon
152 D7 **Goodmanham** E R Yk
51 M2 **Goodmayes** Gt Lon
40 D3 **Goodnestone** Kent
41 H4 **Goodnestone** Kent
63 H3 **Goodrich** Herefs
8 D3 **Goodrington** Torbay
140 B3 **Goodshaw** Lancs
140 B2 **Goodshaw Fold** Lancs
13 H8 **Goodstone** Devon
74 F4 **Goodwick** Pembks
34 D2 **Goodworth Clatford** Hants
99 J6 **Goodyers End** Warwks
143 J3 **Goole** E R Yk
143 J4 **Goole Fields** E R Yk
82 B4 **Goom's Hill** Worcs
4 B5 **Goonbell** Cnwll
4 C4 **Goonhavern** Cnwll
4 B5 **Goonvrea** Cnwll
245 G7 **Goosecruives** Abers
12 F4 **Gooseford** Devon
73 H2 **Goose Green** Essex
39 G3 **Goose Green** Kent
39 L6 **Goose Green** Kent
45 K4 **Goose Green** S Glos
21 J3 **Goose Green** W Susx
139 H7 **Goose Green** Wigan
26 D7 **Gooseham** Cnwll
81 L3 **Goosehill Green** Worcs
80 B7 **Goose Pool** Herefs
47 M1 **Goosey** Oxon
147 L8 **Goosnargh** Lancs
130 F5 **Goostrey** Ches E
126 D5 **Gorddinog** Conwy
201 K4 **Gordon** Border
200 C8 **Gordon Arms Hotel** Border
256 C4 **Gordonstown** Abers
267 L5 **Gordonstown** Abers
79 J3 **Gore** Powys
211 K6 **Gorebridge** Mdloth
103 J1 **Gorefield** Cambs
72 C3 **Gore Pit** Essex
47 G7 **Gores** Wilts
41 J2 **Gore Street** Kent
9 f3 **Gorey** Jersey
48 F3 **Goring** Oxon
21 J6 **Goring-by-Sea** W Susx
49 G3 **Goring Heath** Oxon
107 L3 **Gorleston on Sea** Norfk
97 K5 **Gornal Wood Crematorium** Dudley
268 D4 **Gorrachie** Abers
5 G6 **Gorran** Cnwll
5 G6 **Gorran Haven** Cnwll
5 G6 **Gorran High Lanes** Cnwll
76 D6 **Gorrig** Cerdgn
92 D7 **Gors** Cerdgn
128 E4 **Gorsedd** Flints
47 H2 **Gorse Hill** Swindn
57 G5 **Gorseinon** Swans
115 M1 **Gorseybank** Derbys
76 E5 **Gorsgoch** Cerdgn
59 G6 **Gorslas** Carmth
63 K2 **Gorsley** Gloucs
63 K2 **Gorsley Common** Herefs
130 B5 **Gorstage** Ches W
262 C7 **Gorstan** Highld
129 H7 **Gorstella** Ches W
97 G8 **Gorst Hill** Worcs
115 H6 **Gorsty Hill** Staffs
227 L6 **Gorten** Ag & B
250 F7 **Gorthleck** Highld

140 C8 **Gorton** Manch
90 D4 **Gosbeck** Suffk
119 H5 **Gosberton** Lincs
119 G5 **Gosberton Clough** Lincs
71 J1 **Gosfield** Essex
14 C3 **Gosford** Devon
155 J2 **Gosforth** Cumb
180 F5 **Gosforth** N u Ty
31 J4 **Gosling Street** Somset
68 F2 **Gosmore** Herts
97 K4 **Gospel End** Staffs
36 D4 **Gospel Green** W Susx
19 K4 **Gosport** Hants
85 J6 **Gossard's Green** C Beds
63 L6 **Gossington** Gloucs
203 G4 **Goswick** Nthumb
116 F5 **Gotham** Notts
64 D1 **Gotherington** Gloucs
30 C5 **Gotton** Somset
39 H6 **Goudhurst** Kent
136 E4 **Goulceby** Lincs
256 D3 **Gourdas** Abers
222 F1 **Gourdie** C Dund
235 K1 **Gourdon** Abers
207 L3 **Gourock** Inver
208 F6 **Govan** C Glas
7 L5 **Goveton** Devon
143 G3 **Gowdall** E R Yk
262 E8 **Gower** Highld
57 G5 **Gowerton** Swans
210 E1 **Gowkhall** Fife
152 A5 **Gowthorpe** E R Yk
153 K6 **Goxhill** E R Yk
144 E3 **Goxhill** N Linc
282 g4 **Grabhair** W Isls
118 E5 **Graby** Lincs
3 H8 **Grade** Cnwll
113 K1 **Gradeley Green** Ches E
20 F3 **Graffham** W Susx
86 D2 **Grafham** Cambs
36 F3 **Grafham** Surrey
80 C7 **Grafton** Herefs
150 F3 **Grafton** N York
65 K7 **Grafton** Oxon
113 G7 **Grafton** Shrops
80 D3 **Grafton** Worcs
82 A7 **Grafton** Worcs
81 M4 **Grafton Flyford** Worcs
84 E6 **Grafton Regis** Nhants
101 K7 **Grafton Underwood** Nhants
39 L4 **Grafty Green** Kent
128 F8 **Graianrhyd** Denbgs
126 F5 **Graig** Conwy
128 C5 **Graig** Denbgs
112 A1 **Graig-fechan** Denbgs
53 J4 **Grain** Medway
140 E6 **Grains Bar** Oldham
145 H7 **Grainsby** Lincs
145 K8 **Grainthorpe** Lincs
4 F5 **Grampound** Cnwll
4 E5 **Grampound Road** Cnwll
283 c9 **Gramsdal** W Isls
283 c9 **Gramsdale** W Isls
67 J2 **Granborough** Bucks
117 K4 **Granby** Notts
83 L2 **Grandborough** Warwks
9 e3 **Grand Chemins** Jersey
9 J2 **Grandes Rocques** Guern
232 D5 **Grandtully** P & K
165 H7 **Grange** Cumb
53 G5 **Grange** Medway
222 D2 **Grange** P & K
128 F2 **Grange** Wirral
267 K5 **Grange Crossroads** Moray
265 H7 **Grange Hall** Moray
199 G4 **Grangehall** S Lans
70 C8 **Grange Hill** Essex
132 E8 **Grangemill** Derbys
141 K4 **Grange Moor** Kirk
210 B3 **Grangemouth** Falk
222 D4 **Grange of Lindores** Fife
156 F7 **Grange-over-Sands** Cumb
210 D3 **Grangepans** Falk
170 D6 **Grangetown** R & Cl
181 K8 **Grangetown** Sundld
180 F8 **Grange Villa** Dur
153 H4 **Gransmoor** E R Yk
71 G3 **Gransmore Green** Essex
74 E5 **Granston** Pembks
87 J4 **Grantchester** Cambs
118 B4 **Grantham** Lincs
118 B4 **Grantham Crematorium** Lincs
211 H4 **Granton** C Edin
253 K6 **Grantown-on-Spey** Highld
80 C3 **Grantsfield** Herefs
213 H6 **Grantshouse** Border
130 C2 **Grappenhall** Warrtn
144 D6 **Grasby** Lincs
156 D1 **Grasmere** Cumb
140 E6 **Grasscroft** Oldham

129 J3 **Grassendale** Lpool
165 K2 **Grassgarth** Cumb
88 E7 **Grass Green** Essex
149 H3 **Grassington** N York
133 H6 **Grassmoor** Derbys
134 F6 **Grassthorpe** Notts
34 C3 **Grateley** Hants
115 G5 **Gratwich** Staffs
86 E3 **Graveley** Cambs
69 G2 **Graveley** Herts
98 E5 **Gravelly Hill** Birm
95 H3 **Gravelsbank** Shrops
40 D3 **Graveney** Kent
52 E4 **Gravesend** Kent
282 g4 **Gravir** W Isls
144 A8 **Grayingham** Lincs
157 J3 **Grayrigg** Cumb
52 D3 **Grays** Thurr
36 C4 **Grayshott** Hants
164 C5 **Grayson Green** Cumb
36 D4 **Grayswood** Surrey
170 C5 **Graythorpe** Hartpl
49 G5 **Grazeley** Wokham
142 C8 **Greasbrough** Rothm
128 F2 **Greasby** Wirral
116 E2 **Greasley** Notts
87 L5 **Great Abington** Cambs
101 L8 **Great Addington** Nhants
82 D3 **Great Alne** Warwks
138 C6 **Great Altcar** Lancs
69 K4 **Great Amwell** Herts
166 F8 **Great Asby** Cumb
89 K2 **Great Ashfield** Suffk
170 D8 **Great Ayton** N York
71 H6 **Great Baddow** Essex
46 A2 **Great Badminton** S Glos
71 G1 **Great Bardfield** Essex
86 C5 **Great Barford** Bed
98 D4 **Great Barr** Sandw
65 J4 **Great Barrington** Gloucs
129 L6 **Great Barrow** Ches W
89 H2 **Great Barton** Suffk
162 C6 **Great Barugh** N York
180 B3 **Great Bavington** Nthumb
90 F5 **Great Bealings** Suffk
47 K6 **Great Bedwyn** Wilts
73 G3 **Great Bentley** Essex
84 F3 **Great Billing** Nhants
121 G5 **Great Bircham** Norfk
90 D5 **Great Blakenham** Suffk
166 B4 **Great Blencow** Cumb
113 L7 **Great Bolas** Wrekin
50 E8 **Great Bookham** Surrey
2 C4 **Great Bosullow** Cnwll
83 K6 **Great Bourton** Oxon
101 G5 **Great Bowden** Leics
88 D4 **Great Bradley** Suffk
72 B4 **Great Braxted** Essex
90 B5 **Great Bricett** Suffk
67 L1 **Great Brickhill** Bucks
114 D6 **Great Bridgeford** Staffs
84 C2 **Great Brington** Nhants
73 G2 **Great Bromley** Essex
164 E4 **Great Broughton** Cumb
161 J2 **Great Broughton** N York
130 C4 **Great Budworth** Ches W
169 J7 **Great Burdon** Darltn
71 G8 **Great Burstead** Essex
161 H2 **Great Busby** N York
70 E3 **Great Canfield** Essex
137 H3 **Great Carlton** Lincs
101 M2 **Great Casterton** Rutlnd
46 B6 **Great Chalfield** Wilts
40 C7 **Great Chart** Kent
114 B8 **Great Chatwell** Staffs
114 D1 **Great Chell** C Stke
87 K6 **Great Chesterford** Essex
46 E8 **Great Cheverell** Wilts
87 J7 **Great Chishill** Cambs
73 J4 **Great Clacton** Essex
141 M4 **Great Cliffe** Wakefd
104 D5 **Great Clifton** Cumb
145 G6 **Great Coates** NE Lin
81 L6 **Great Comberton** Worcs
39 G2 **Great Comp** Kent
78 B7 **Great Corby** Cumb
89 H7 **Great Cornard** Suffk
153 L7 **Great Cowden** E R Yk
65 K8 **Great Coxwell** Oxon
101 H8 **Great Cransley** Nhants
105 G3 **Great Cressingham** Norfk
165 J6 **Great Crosthwaite** Cumb
115 K4 **Great Cubley** Derbys
117 K8 **Great Dalby** Leics
85 H2 **Great Doddington** Nhants
63 G4 **Great Doward** Herefs
21 J8 **Great Dunham** Norfk
70 F3 **Great Dunmow** Essex
33 K3 **Great Durnford** Wilts
70 F2 **Great Easton** Essex

101 J5 **Great Easton** Leics
147 H7 **Great Eccleston** Lancs
162 C6 **Great Edstone** N York
105 L4 **Great Ellingham** Norfk
32 C1 **Great Elm** Somset
84 B4 **Great Everdon** Nhants
87 H4 **Great Eversden** Cambs
47 G2 **Greatfield** Wilts
89 K4 **Great Finborough** Suffk
102 B1 **Greatford** Lincs
105 H1 **Great Fransham** Norfk
68 C5 **Great Gaddesden** Herts
115 G3 **Greatgate** Staffs
102 C6 **Great Gidding** Cambs
152 B5 **Great Givendale** E R Yk
91 H3 **Great Glemham** Suffk
100 E4 **Great Glen** Leics
118 B4 **Great Gonerby** Lincs
86 F4 **Great Gransden** Cambs
106 F5 **Great Green** Norfk
89 J2 **Great Green** Suffk
89 J4 **Great Green** Suffk
162 D7 **Great Habton** N York
118 F3 **Great Hale** Lincs
70 D3 **Great Hallingbury** Essex
36 A5 **Greatham** Hants
170 C5 **Greatham** Hartpl
21 H4 **Greatham** W Susx
67 K6 **Great Hampden** Bucks
85 G1 **Great Harrowden** Nhants
139 L1 **Great Harwood** Lancs
66 F6 **Great Haseley** Oxon
153 K7 **Great Hatfield** E R Yk
114 F7 **Great Haywood** Staffs
142 F3 **Great Heck** N York
89 H7 **Great Henny** Essex
46 C7 **Great Hinton** Wilts
105 J5 **Great Hockham** Norfk
73 J3 **Great Holland** Essex
49 L5 **Great Hollands** Br For
72 E1 **Great Horkesley** Essex
69 L1 **Great Hormead** Herts
141 J2 **Great Horton** C Brad
67 J1 **Great Horwood** Bucks
142 C6 **Great Houghton** Barns
84 F3 **Great Houghton** Nhants
132 D4 **Great Hucklow** Derbys
153 H4 **Great Kelk** E R Yk
67 K6 **Great Kimble** Bucks
67 L7 **Great Kingshill** Bucks
156 D2 **Great Langdale** Cumb
160 D3 **Great Langton** N York
71 H4 **Great Leighs** Essex
144 E6 **Great Limber** Lincs
85 G6 **Great Linford** M Keyn
89 H1 **Great Livermere** Suffk
132 D5 **Great Longstone** Derbys
169 J1 **Great Lumley** Dur
95 L2 **Great Lyth** Shrops
81 H6 **Great Malvern** Worcs
89 G8 **Great Maplestead** Essex
138 C1 **Great Marton** Bpool
121 H7 **Great Massingham** Norfk
106 C2 **Great Melton** Norfk
128 F2 **Great Meols** Wirral
66 F6 **Great Milton** Oxon
67 L6 **Great Missenden** Bucks
148 C8 **Great Mitton** Lancs
41 K5 **Great Mongeham** Kent
106 D5 **Great Moulton** Norfk
69 K2 **Great Munden** Herts
167 H7 **Great Musgrave** Cumb
112 F7 **Great Ness** Shrops
71 H3 **Great Notley** Essex
62 D5 **Great Oak** Mons
73 J2 **Great Oakley** Essex
101 J6 **Great Oakley** Nhants
68 F2 **Great Offley** Herts
167 G7 **Great Ormside** Cumb
177 K7 **Great Orton** Cumb
150 F3 **Great Ouseburn** N York
100 F6 **Great Oxendon** Nhants
71 G6 **Great Oxney Green** Essex
105 G1 **Great Palgrave** Norfk
39 J4 **Great Pattenden** Kent
86 E2 **Great Paxton** Cambs
138 D1 **Great Plumpton** Lancs
106 F2 **Great Plumstead** Norfk
118 B5 **Great Ponton** Lincs
27 J7 **Great Potheridge** Devon
142 B2 **Great Preston** Leeds
83 M7 **Great Purston** Nhants
102 E7 **Great Raveley** Cambs
65 J4 **Great Rissington** Gloucs
65 L1 **Great Rollright** Oxon
54 F3 **Great Rudbaxton** Pembks
121 L6 **Great Ryburgh** Norfk
190 E4 **Great Ryle** Nthumb
96 B3 **Great Ryton** Shrops

71 G2 **Great Saling** Essex
166 D3 **Great Salkeld** Cumb
88 C8 **Great Sampford** Essex
130 B2 **Great Sankey** Warrtn
98 B2 **Great Saredon** Staffs
129 H5 **Great Saughall** Ches W
88 F3 **Great Saxham** Suffk
48 A4 **Great Shefford** W Berk
87 J5 **Great Shelford** Cambs
160 E2 **Great Smeaton** N York
121 L4 **Great Snoring** Norfk
46 D2 **Great Somerford** Wilts
114 A5 **Great Soudley** Shrops
169 J6 **Great Stainton** Darltn
53 J1 **Great Stambridge** Essex
86 C2 **Great Staughton** Cambs
137 H6 **Great Steeping** Lincs
45 J3 **Great Stoke** S Glos
41 K3 **Great Stonar** Kent
25 K3 **Greatstone-on-Sea** Kent
166 D6 **Great Strickland** Cumb
102 E8 **Great Stukeley** Cambs
136 D4 **Great Sturton** Lincs
129 J4 **Great Sutton** Ches W
96 C6 **Great Sutton** Shrops
179 L4 **Great Swinburne** Nthumb
66 B1 **Great Tew** Oxon
72 C2 **Great Tey** Essex
27 J7 **Great Torrington** Devon
190 E6 **Great Tosson** Nthumb
72 B5 **Great Totham** Essex
72 C4 **Great Totham** Essex
136 D2 **Great Tows** Lincs
156 C7 **Great Urswick** Cumb
53 K2 **Great Wakering** Essex
89 J6 **Great Waldingfield** Suffk
121 L4 **Great Walsingham** Norfk
71 G4 **Great Waltham** Essex
130 F4 **Great Warford** Ches E
52 C1 **Great Warley** Essex
82 A8 **Great Washbourne** Gloucs
13 G5 **Great Weeke** Devon
101 K5 **Great Weldon** Nhants
89 H3 **Great Welnetham** Suffk
90 C7 **Great Wenham** Suffk
180 B5 **Great Whittington** Nthumb
72 D4 **Great Wigborough** Essex
87 L4 **Great Wilbraham** Cambs
33 J4 **Great Wishford** Wilts
122 C7 **Great Witchingham** Norfk
64 D4 **Great Witcombe** Gloucs
81 H2 **Great Witley** Worcs
82 F8 **Great Wolford** Warwks
84 A6 **Greatworth** Nhants
88 D5 **Great Wratting** Suffk
69 G2 **Great Wymondley** Herts
98 C2 **Great Wyrley** Staffs
113 J7 **Great Wytheford** Shrops
107 L2 **Great Yarmouth** Norfk
107 K3 **Great Yarmouth Crematorium** Norfk
88 F7 **Great Yeldham** Essex
137 H6 **Grebby** Lincs
154 d6 **Greeba** IoM
128 C6 **Green** Denbgs
156 E6 **Green Bank** Cumb
210 B7 **Greenburn** W Loth
168 F1 **Greencroft Hall** Dur
36 C3 **Green Cross** Surrey
45 H8 **Green Down** Somset
85 K5 **Green End** Bed
86 B2 **Green End** Bed
86 B3 **Green End** Bed
86 C5 **Green End** Bed
87 H4 **Green End** Cambs
87 K2 **Green End** Cambs
87 K3 **Green End** Cambs
102 D6 **Green End** Cambs
102 E8 **Green End** Cambs
69 H1 **Green End** Herts
69 J3 **Green End** Herts
87 G8 **Green End** Herts
65 L3 **Greenend** Oxon
99 H6 **Green End** Warwks
207 L1 **Greenfield** Ag & B
85 L8 **Greenfield** C Beds
128 E4 **Greenfield** Flints
239 L3 **Greenfield** Highld
140 F7 **Greenfield** Oldham
49 H1 **Greenfield** Oxon
50 F3 **Greenford** Gt Lon
209 L5 **Greengairs** N Lans
150 B8 **Greengates** C Brad
164 F3 **Greengill** Cumb
147 H8 **Greenhalgh** Lancs
29 K6 **Greenham** Somset
48 C6 **Greenham** W Berk
151 G4 **Green Hammerton** N York
179 J2 **Greenhaugh** Nthumb
165 L1 **Green Head** Cumb

178 F6 **Greenhead** Nthumb
98 C1 **Green Heath** Staffs
139 L7 **Greenheys** Salfd
176 F3 **Greenhill** D & G
209 L3 **Greenhill** Falk
81 G5 **Greenhill** Herefs
40 F2 **Greenhill** Kent
198 F6 **Greenhill** S Lans
46 F2 **Green Hill** Wilts
116 C2 **Greenhillocks** Derbys
52 C4 **Greenhithe** Kent
197 G3 **Greenholm** E Ayrs
157 J2 **Greenholme** Cumb
188 F2 **Greenhouse** Border
149 K3 **Greenhow Hill** N York
280 B3 **Greenland** Highld
133 H2 **Greenland** Sheff
49 J2 **Greenlands** Bucks
13 H7 **Green Lane** Devon
82 C2 **Green Lane** Worcs
201 L4 **Greenlaw** Border
176 D4 **Greenlea** D & G
220 E5 **Greenloaning** P & K
141 L7 **Green Moor** Barns
140 A5 **Greenmount** Bury
143 K2 **Green Oak** E R Yk
207 M4 **Greenock** Inver
156 D6 **Greenodd** Cumb
31 J1 **Green Ore** Somset
157 G2 **Green Quarter** Cumb
122 B8 **Greensgate** Norfk
199 H4 **Greenshields** S Lans
180 E6 **Greenside** Gatesd
141 J4 **Greenside** Kirk
84 C5 **Greens Norton** Nhants
72 E2 **Greenstead** Essex
71 K2 **Greenstead Green** Essex
70 D6 **Greensted** Essex
24 D5 **Green Street** E Susx
64 C4 **Green Street** Gloucs
69 G7 **Green Street** Herts
70 C3 **Green Street** Herts
81 K5 **Green Street** Worcs
51 M6 **Green Street Green** Gt Lon
52 C5 **Green Street Green** Kent
90 B5 **Greenstreet Green** Suffk
70 C3 **Green Tye** Herts
81 G8 **Greenway** Gloucs
30 D6 **Greenway** Somset
43 G7 **Greenway** V Glam
81 G1 **Greenway** Worcs
51 K3 **Greenwich** Gt Lon
64 F1 **Greet** Gloucs
80 D1 **Greete** Shrops
136 F5 **Greetham** Lincs
118 B8 **Greetham** Rutlnd
141 G3 **Greetland** Calder
139 J2 **Gregson Lane** Lancs
30 F4 **Greinton** Somset
154 c7 **Grenaby** IoM
85 G3 **Grendon** Nhants
99 H3 **Grendon** Warwks
80 E4 **Grendon Green** Herefs
67 G3 **Grendon Underwood** Bucks
12 C8 **Grenofen** Devon
133 G1 **Grenoside** Sheff
132 F1 **Grenoside Crematorium** Sheff
282 e6 **Greosabhagh** W Isls
112 E1 **Gresford** Wrexhm
122 D4 **Gresham** Norfk
258 E6 **Greshornish House Hotel** Highld
121 L8 **Gressenhall** Norfk
121 L8 **Gressenhall Green** Norfk
147 L2 **Gressingham** Lancs
113 M1 **Gresty Green** Ches E
168 D8 **Greta Bridge** Dur
177 K5 **Gretna** D & G
177 K5 **Gretna Green** D & G
64 E1 **Gretton** Gloucs
101 K4 **Gretton** Nhants
96 C4 **Gretton** Shrops
160 C7 **Grewelthorpe** N York
91 L1 **Grey Friars** Suffk
150 A1 **Greygarth** N York
143 K6 **Grey Green** N Linc
30 F4 **Greylake** Somset
176 E1 **Greyrigg** D & G
49 H2 **Greys Green** Oxon
164 E5 **Greysouthen** Cumb
166 B4 **Greystoke** Cumb
234 E6 **Greystone** Angus
35 L1 **Greywell** Hants
15 J2 **Gribb** Dorset
143 J1 **Gribthorpe** E R Yk
99 K5 **Griff** Warwks
62 C7 **Griffithstown** Torfn
116 C7 **Griffydam** Leics
36 B4 **Griggs Green** Hants
139 J5 **Grimeford Village** Lancs
133 G2 **Grimesthorpe** Sheff

142 C6 **Grimethorpe** Barns
81 J3 **Grimley** Worcs
183 J1 **Grimmet** S Ayrs
137 G2 **Grimoldby** Lincs
112 E6 **Grimpo** Shrops
139 H1 **Grimsargh** Lancs
145 H5 **Grimsby** NE Lin
145 H6 **Grimsby Crematorium** NE Lin
84 C4 **Grimscote** Nhants
11 J1 **Grimscott** Cnwll
282 g4 **Grimshader** W Isls
139 L3 **Grimshaw** Bl w D
139 G5 **Grimshaw Green** Lancs
118 D7 **Grimsthorpe** Lincs
145 H1 **Grimston** E R Yk
117 J7 **Grimston** Leics
120 F7 **Grimston** Norfk
16 C4 **Grimstone** Dorset
89 J2 **Grimstone End** Suffk
12 A4 **Grinacombe Moor** Devon
153 J2 **Grindale** E R Yk
97 G3 **Grindle** Shrops
132 E4 **Grindleford** Derbys
148 D6 **Grindleton** Lancs
113 H3 **Grindley Brook** Shrops
132 D4 **Grindlow** Derbys
202 E4 **Grindon** Nthumb
169 K5 **Grindon** S on T
115 H1 **Grindon** Staffs
181 J7 **Grindon** Sundld
179 J5 **Grindon Hill** Nthumb
202 E4 **Grindonrigg** Nthumb
134 E2 **Gringley on the Hill** Notts
177 L7 **Grinsdale** Cumb
113 H6 **Grinshill** Shrops
159 J3 **Grinton** N York
282 g4 **Griomaisiader** W Isls
283 c9 **Griomsaigh** W Isls
224 F3 **Grishipoll** Ag & B
23 G3 **Grisling Common** E Susx
163 K6 **Gristhorpe** N York
105 J4 **Griston** Norfk
275 d5 **Gritley** Ork
46 F2 **Grittenham** Wilts
46 B3 **Grittleton** Wilts
156 C5 **Grizebeck** Cumb
156 D4 **Grizedale** Cumb
100 B2 **Groby** Leics
127 K6 **Groes** Conwy
43 G5 **Groes-faen** Rhondd
108 D4 **Groesffordd** Gwynd
127 K5 **Groesffordd Marli** Denbgs
94 F1 **Groesllwyd** Powys
125 H8 **Groeslon** Gwynd
125 J7 **Groeslon** Gwynd
43 H4 **Groes-Wen** Caerph
283 c10 **Grogarry** W Isls
194 C2 **Grogport** Ag & B
283 c10 **Groigearraidh** W Isls
91 J3 **Gromford** Suffk
128 C3 **Gronant** Flints
38 E6 **Groombridge** E Susx
282 e6 **Grosebay** W Isls
62 E2 **Grosmont** Mons
162 E2 **Grosmont** N York
89 J7 **Groton** Suffk
140 E6 **Grotton** Oldham
9 e3 **Grouville** Jersey
67 M3 **Grove** Bucks
16 D7 **Grove** Dorset
41 H3 **Grove** Kent
134 E4 **Grove** Notts
48 B1 **Grove** Oxon
55 G6 **Grove** Pembks
39 K2 **Grove Green** Kent
39 H5 **Grovenhurst** Kent
51 L4 **Grove Park** Gt Lon
45 K1 **Grovesend** S Glos
57 G5 **Grovesend** Swans
52 C5 **Grubb Street** Kent
260 F2 **Gruinard** Highld
204 D3 **Gruinart** Ag & B
246 E3 **Grula** Highld
227 G4 **Gruline** Ag & B
2 C5 **Grumbla** Cnwll
90 F5 **Grundisburgh** Suffk
281 c6 **Gruting** Shet
229 J6 **Gualachulain** Highld
103 H2 **Guanockgate** Lincs
223 H3 **Guardbridge** Fife
81 J6 **Guarlford** Worcs
232 F5 **Guay** P & K
24 F4 **Guestling Green** E Susx
24 F4 **Guestling Thorn** E Susx
122 B6 **Guestwick** Norfk
139 L3 **Guide** Bl w D
140 D8 **Guide Bridge** Tamesd
181 G2 **Guide Post** Nthumb
86 F6 **Guilden Morden** Cambs
129 K6 **Guilden Sutton** Ches W

36 F1 **Guildford** Surrey
36 E2 **Guildford Crematorium** Surrey
53 H6 **Guildstead** Kent
221 L1 **Guildtown** P & K
84 D1 **Guilsborough** Nhants
94 F1 **Guilsfield** Powys
41 J4 **Guilton** Kent
183 J1 **Guiltreehill** S Ayrs
27 K3 **Guineaford** Devon
170 E7 **Guisborough** R & Cl
150 B7 **Guiseley** Leeds
121 M6 **Guist** Norfk
65 G2 **Guiting Power** Gloucs
212 B2 **Gullane** E Loth
89 G4 **Gulling Green** Suffk
2 D5 **Gulval** Cnwll
12 B7 **Gulworthy** Devon
55 J6 **Gumfreston** Pembks
100 F5 **Gumley** Leics
4 E3 **Gummow's Shop** Cnwll
143 H1 **Gunby** E R Yk
118 B7 **Gunby** Lincs
137 J6 **Gunby** Lincs
35 J4 **Gundleton** Hants
39 J7 **Gun Green** Kent
23 J4 **Gun Hill** E Susx
99 H5 **Gun Hill** Warwks
27 L4 **Gunn** Devon
159 G3 **Gunnerside** N York
179 L4 **Gunnerton** Nthumb
143 L5 **Gunness** N Linc
12 B8 **Gunnislake** Cnwll
281 e6 **Gunnista** Shet
102 D3 **Gunthorpe** C Pete
143 K8 **Gunthorpe** N Linc
121 M4 **Gunthorpe** Norfk
117 H3 **Gunthorpe** Notts
107 L4 **Gunton** Suffk
3 G6 **Gunwalloe** Cnwll
29 H4 **Gupworthy** Somset
19 H4 **Gurnard** IoW
131 H5 **Gurnett** Ches E
31 K1 **Gurney Slade** Somset
57 L3 **Gurnos** Powys
40 D4 **Gushmere** Kent
33 G8 **Gussage All Saints** Dorset
33 G8 **Gussage St Andrew** Dorset
33 G8 **Gussage St Michael** Dorset
41 K6 **Guston** Kent
281 f2 **Gutcher** Shet
234 E5 **Guthrie** Angus
103 H3 **Guyhirn** Cambs
103 H3 **Guyhirn Gull** Cambs
32 D6 **Guy's Marsh** Dorset
191 J5 **Guyzance** Nthumb
128 C3 **Gwaenysgor** Flints
125 G4 **Gwalchmai** IoA
126 C8 **Gwastadnant** Gwynd
59 J6 **Gwaun-Cae-Gurwen** Carmth
75 K2 **Gwbert on Sea** Cerdgn
2 F3 **Gwealavellan** Cnwll
3 H5 **Gweek** Cnwll
62 D6 **Gwehelog** Mons
78 E6 **Gwenddwr** Powys
3 J3 **Gwennap** Cnwll
62 C7 **Gwent Crematorium** Mons
3 J7 **Gwenter** Cnwll
128 F6 **Gwernaffield** Flints
62 E6 **Gwernesney** Mons
58 F2 **Gwernogle** Carmth
128 F7 **Gwernymynydd** Flints
112 D1 **Gwersyllt** Wrexhm
128 D3 **Gwespyr** Flints
4 F4 **Gwindra** Cnwll
2 F4 **Gwinear** Cnwll
2 F3 **Gwithian** Cnwll
125 G3 **Gwredog** IoA
61 J7 **Gwrhay** Caerph
111 L2 **Gwyddelwern** Denbgs
58 E2 **Gwyddgrug** Carmth
112 C1 **Gwynfryn** Wrexhm
78 E2 **Gwystre** Powys
127 H7 **Gwytherin** Conwy
112 E3 **Gyfelia** Wrexhm
109 E3 **Gyrn-goch** Gwynd

### H

95 K3 **Habberley** Shrops
97 H7 **Habberley** Worcs
140 B1 **Habergham** Lancs
137 J6 **Habertoft** Lincs
36 B6 **Habin** W Susx
144 F5 **Habrough** NE Lin
118 E6 **Hacconby** Lincs
118 D4 **Haceby** Lincs
91 G3 **Hacheston** Suffk
51 H5 **Hackbridge** Gt Lon
133 H3 **Hackenthorpe** Sheff

106 B3 **Hackford** Norfk
160 C4 **Hackforth** N York
113 L2 **Hack Green** Ches E
275 C4 **Hackland** Ork
84 D1 **Hackleton** Nhants
41 K4 **Hacklinge** Kent
97 K7 **Hackman's Gate** Worcs
163 H4 **Hackness** N York
30 E2 **Hackness** Somset
51 K2 **Hackney** Gt Lon
135 K3 **Hackthorn** Lincs
166 D6 **Hackthorpe** Cumb
52 C2 **Hacton** Gt Lon
202 B6 **Hadden** Border
67 H5 **Haddenham** Bucks
103 J8 **Haddenham** Cambs
212 B4 **Haddington** E Loth
135 H7 **Haddington** Lincs
107 J4 **Haddiscoe** Norfk
256 E4 **Haddo** Abers
102 C5 **Haddon** Cambs
141 J6 **Hade Edge** Kirk
140 F8 **Hadfield** Derbys
70 B3 **Hadham Cross** Herts
70 B3 **Hadham Ford** Herts
53 H2 **Hadleigh** Essex
89 L6 **Hadleigh** Suffk
89 K7 **Hadleigh Heath** Suffk
81 K2 **Hadley** Worcs
96 F1 **Hadley** Wrekin
115 J7 **Hadley End** Staffs
69 H7 **Hadley Wood** Gt Lon
39 G3 **Hadlow** Kent
23 J2 **Hadlow Down** E Susx
113 H7 **Hadnall** Shrops
88 B6 **Hadstock** Essex
81 L3 **Hadzor** Worcs
39 M5 **Haffenden Quarter** Kent
127 H6 **Hafodunos** Conwy
112 D2 **Hafod-y-bwch** Wrexhm
61 K7 **Hafod-y-coed** Blae G
61 K7 **Hafodyrynys** Caerph
140 C1 **Haggate** Lancs
178 B4 **Haggbeck** Cumb
281 d6 **Haggersta** Shet
203 G4 **Haggerston** Nthumb
27 K2 **Haggington Hill** Devon
209 L3 **Haggs** Falk
80 D7 **Hagley** Herefs
97 K7 **Hagley** Worcs
89 J7 **Hagmore Green** Suffk
136 F3 **Hagnaby** Lincs
137 J4 **Hagnaby** Lincs
136 F6 **Hagworthingham** Lincs
139 J6 **Haigh** Wigan
139 H1 **Haighton Green** Lancs
155 J1 **Haile** Cumb
64 F1 **Hailes** Gloucs
69 K5 **Hailey** Herts
48 F2 **Hailey** Oxon
65 M4 **Hailey** Oxon
23 K5 **Hailsham** E Susx
86 D3 **Hail Weston** Cambs
70 C8 **Hainault** Gt Lon
41 K2 **Haine** Kent
122 E7 **Hainford** Norfk
136 C3 **Hainton** Lincs
149 J8 **Hainworth** C Brad
153 H3 **Haisthorpe** E R Yk
54 E5 **Hakin** Pembks
117 H1 **Halam** Notts
210 F1 **Halbeath** Fife
29 H8 **Halberton** Devon
280 B4 **Halcro** Highld
157 H7 **Hale** Cumb
129 L3 **Hale** Halton
33 L7 **Hale** Hants
32 C5 **Hale** Somset
36 C1 **Hale** Surrey
130 F2 **Hale** Traffd
129 L3 **Hale Bank** Halton
130 F3 **Halebarns** Traffd
23 J4 **Hale Green** E Susx
147 G7 **Hale Nook** Lancs
107 H4 **Hales** Norfk
113 M5 **Hales** Staffs
119 K6 **Halesgate** Lincs
115 K3 **Hales Green** Derbys
98 B6 **Halesowen** Dudley
40 F3 **Hales Place** Kent
39 G3 **Hale Street** Kent
72 C8 **Halesville** Essex
107 H7 **Halesworth** Suffk
129 K3 **Halewood** Knows
13 J7 **Halford** Devon
95 K6 **Halford** Shrops
83 G6 **Halford** Warwks
157 H5 **Halfpenny** Cumb
97 J5 **Halfpenny Green** Staffs
160 B5 **Halfpenny Houses** N York

59 J3 **Halfway** Carmth
59 M2 **Halfway** Carmth
133 J3 **Halfway** Sheff
48 B5 **Halfway** W Berk
36 D6 **Halfway Bridge** W Susx
95 H1 **Halfway House** Shrops
53 K4 **Halfway Houses** Kent
141 H3 **Halifax** Calder
208 D8 **Halket** E Ayrs
279 K4 **Halkirk** Highld
128 F5 **Halkyn** Flints
208 C8 **Hall** E Rens
116 D4 **Hallam Fields** Derbys
23 H4 **Halland** E Susx
101 H4 **Hallaton** Leics
45 J7 **Hallatrow** BaNES
178 D7 **Hallbankgate** Cumb
157 K5 **Hallbeck** Cumb
141 L4 **Hall Cliffe** Wakefd
138 E2 **Hall Cross** Lancs
156 B3 **Hall Dunnerdale** Cumb
45 H3 **Hallen** S Glos
85 K6 **Hall End** Bed
86 B7 **Hall End** C Beds
133 H8 **Hallfield Gate** Derbys
169 J2 **Hallgarth** Dur
210 A3 **Hall Glen** Falk
98 E7 **Hall Green** Birm
258 C5 **Hallin** Highld
52 F6 **Halling** Medway
136 F3 **Hallington** Lincs
180 B4 **Hallington** Nthumb
139 L5 **Halliwell** Bolton
117 J1 **Halloughton** Notts
81 J3 **Hallow** Worcs
81 J3 **Hallow Heath** Worcs
8 B7 **Hallsands** Devon
69 L5 **Hall's Green** Essex
69 H2 **Hall's Green** Herts
156 A5 **Hallthwaites** Cumb
11 H5 **Hallworthy** Cnwll
199 L5 **Hallyne** Border
114 B2 **Halmer End** Staffs
80 F5 **Halmond's Frome** Herefs
63 K6 **Halmore** Gloucs
20 E5 **Halnaker** W Susx
138 D5 **Halsall** Lancs
84 A7 **Halse** Nhants
29 L5 **Halse** Somset
2 D3 **Halsetown** Cnwll
145 H2 **Halsham** E R Yk
27 J3 **Halsinger** Devon
71 K1 **Halstead** Essex
52 A6 **Halstead** Kent
101 G2 **Halstead** Leics
15 M1 **Halstock** Dorset
29 L3 **Halsway** Somset
165 L3 **Haltcliff Bridge** Cumb
144 C2 **Haltemprice Crematorium** E R Yk
136 D7 **Haltham** Lincs
119 L3 **Haltoft End** Lincs
67 L5 **Halton** Bucks
129 M3 **Halton** Halton
147 K3 **Halton** Lancs
142 A1 **Halton** Leeds
180 B5 **Halton** Nthumb
112 D3 **Halton** Wrexhm
149 J5 **Halton East** N York
137 H7 **Halton Fenside** Lincs
158 F7 **Halton Gill** N York
147 K3 **Halton Green** Lancs
137 H6 **Halton Holegate** Lincs
178 F7 **Halton Lea Gate** Nthumb
6 E2 **Halton Quay** Cnwll
180 B5 **Halton Shields** Nthumb
148 E5 **Halton West** N York
179 G6 **Haltwhistle** Nthumb
107 J2 **Halvergate** Norfk
8 A4 **Halwell** Devon
12 B3 **Halwill** Devon
12 B2 **Halwill Junction** Devon
14 F2 **Ham** Devon
63 K7 **Ham** Gloucs
64 E3 **Ham** Gloucs
50 F4 **Ham** Gt Lon
41 K4 **Ham** Kent
30 D6 **Ham** Somset
31 L1 **Ham** Somset
47 L6 **Ham** Wilts
49 J2 **Hambleden** Bucks
35 K7 **Hambledon** Hants
36 E3 **Hambledon** Surrey
19 H2 **Hamble-le-Rice** Hants
147 G7 **Hambleton** Lancs
142 E2 **Hambleton** N York
147 G7 **Hambleton Moss Side** Lancs
30 F6 **Hambridge** Somset
45 J3 **Hambrook** S Glos
20 C5 **Hambrook** W Susx

32 D5 **Ham Common** Dorset
136 F6 **Hameringham** Lincs
102 C7 **Hamerton** Cambs
81 H6 **Ham Green** Herefs
25 G2 **Ham Green** Kent
53 H5 **Ham Green** Kent
45 G4 **Ham Green** N Som
82 B3 **Ham Green** Worcs
52 F6 **Ham Hill** Kent
209 J7 **Hamilton** S Lans
16 B1 **Hamlet** Dorset
23 K5 **Hamlins** E Susx
21 H5 **Hammerpot** W Susx
51 G3 **Hammersmith** Gt Lon
98 D2 **Hammerwich** Staffs
38 C5 **Hammerwood** E Susx
69 J6 **Hammond Street** Herts
32 D7 **Hammoon** Dorset
281 d7 **Hamnavoe** Shet
23 K6 **Hampden Park** E Susx
70 E1 **Hamperden End** Essex
65 G4 **Hampnett** Gloucs
142 D5 **Hampole** Donc
17 L3 **Hampreston** Dorset
156 F6 **Hampsfield** Cumb
147 J5 **Hampson Green** Lancs
51 H2 **Hampstead** Gt Lon
48 D4 **Hampstead Norrey's** W Berk
150 C4 **Hampsthwaite** N York
102 D4 **Hampton** C Pete
15 G3 **Hampton** Devon
50 F5 **Hampton** Gt Lon
40 F2 **Hampton** Kent
97 G6 **Hampton** Shrops
65 J8 **Hampton** Swindn
82 B6 **Hampton** Worcs
80 D7 **Hampton Bishop** Herefs
64 C7 **Hampton Fields** Gloucs
113 H2 **Hampton Green** Ches W
113 H2 **Hampton Heath** Ches W
99 G7 **Hampton in Arden** Solhll
97 G6 **Hampton Loade** Shrops
81 K2 **Hampton Lovett** Worcs
83 G4 **Hampton Lucy** Warwks
83 G2 **Hampton Magna** Warwks
82 F2 **Hampton on the Hill** Warwks
66 D4 **Hampton Poyle** Oxon
50 F5 **Hampton Wick** Gt Lon
34 B7 **Hamptworth** Wilts
121 K6 **Hamrow** Norfk
22 F5 **Hamsey** E Susx
51 K7 **Hamsey Green** Surrey
115 H7 **Hamstall Ridware** Staffs
98 D5 **Hamstead** Birm
18 F5 **Hamstead** IoW
48 B6 **Hamstead Marshall** W Berk
168 E4 **Hamsterley** Dur
180 D7 **Hamsterley** Dur
40 C8 **Hamstreet** Kent
31 J4 **Ham Street** Somset
44 D7 **Hamwood** N Som
17 K4 **Hamworthy** Poole
115 K6 **Hanbury** Staffs
81 M2 **Hanbury** Worcs
118 D5 **Hanby** Lincs
88 C6 **Hanchet End** Suffk
114 C3 **Hanchurch** Staffs
171 G7 **Handale** R & Cl
14 B3 **Hand and Pen** Devon
129 J6 **Handbridge** Ches W
37 L5 **Handcross** W Susx
131 G3 **Handforth** Ches E
130 A7 **Hand Green** Ches W
129 L8 **Handley** Ches W
133 G7 **Handley** Derbys
71 G6 **Handley Green** Essex
115 H8 **Handsacre** Staffs
98 D5 **Handsworth** Birm
133 H2 **Handsworth** Sheff
49 K1 **Handy Cross** Bucks
114 D3 **Hanford** C Stke
32 D8 **Hanford** Dorset
141 L3 **Hanging Heaton** Kirk
101 G8 **Hanging Houghton** Nhants
33 H3 **Hanging Langford** Wilts
22 D6 **Hangleton** Br & H
21 J6 **Hangleton** W Susx
45 J4 **Hanham** S Glos
113 L2 **Hankelow** Ches E
46 E1 **Hankerton** Wilts
23 K6 **Hankham** E Susx
114 D2 **Hanley** C Stke
114 D2 **Hanley** C Stke
81 J6 **Hanley Castle** Worcs
80 F2 **Hanley Child** Worcs
81 J6 **Hanley Swan** Worcs
80 F2 **Hanley William** Worcs
148 H7 **Hanlith** N York
113 G3 **Hanmer** Wrexhm
27 L5 **Hannaford** Devon

137 J4 **Hannah** Lincs
48 D7 **Hannington** Hants
84 F1 **Hannington** Nhants
65 H8 **Hannington** Swindn
65 H8 **Hannington Wick** Swindn
86 C8 **Hanscombe End** C Beds
84 F6 **Hanslope** M Keyn
118 E6 **Hanthorpe** Lincs
50 F3 **Hanwell** Gt Lon
83 K6 **Hanwell** Oxon
95 K2 **Hanwood** Shrops
50 E5 **Hanworth** Gt Lon
122 D4 **Hanworth** Norfk
198 E6 **Happendon** S Lans
123 H5 **Happisburgh** Norfk
123 H5 **Happisburgh Common** Norfk
129 L5 **Hapsford** Ches W
140 B2 **Hapton** Lancs
106 D4 **Hapton** Norfk
8 A3 **Harberton** Devon
8 A4 **Harbertonford** Devon
40 F4 **Harbledown** Kent
98 C6 **Harborne** Birm
100 B7 **Harborough Magna** Warwks
190 C5 **Harbottle** Nthumb
7 K2 **Harbourneford** Devon
81 M2 **Harbours Hill** Worcs
18 A2 **Harbridge** Hants
33 K8 **Harbridge Green** Hants
83 J3 **Harbury** Warwks
117 K5 **Harby** Leics
135 H5 **Harby** Notts
13 K6 **Harcombe** Devon
14 D4 **Harcombe** Devon
15 H3 **Harcombe Bottom** Devon
149 K8 **Harden** C Brad
98 C3 **Harden** Wsall
46 C4 **Hardenhuish** Wilts
245 H3 **Hardgate** Abers
175 K2 **Hardgate** D & G
150 C3 **Hardgate** N York
208 E4 **Hardgate** W Duns
21 H3 **Hardham** W Susx
147 G8 **Hardhorn** Lancs
105 L3 **Hardingham** Norfk
84 E4 **Hardingstone** Nhants
45 L8 **Hardington** Somset
31 H8 **Hardington Mandeville** Somset
15 L1 **Hardington Marsh** Somset
31 H8 **Hardington Moor** Somset
26 D6 **Hardisworthy** Devon
19 G3 **Hardley** Hants
107 H3 **Hardley Street** Norfk
85 H5 **Hardmead** M Keyn
158 F4 **Hardraw** N York
140 B4 **Hardsough** Lancs
133 J7 **Hardstoft** Derbys
19 K3 **Hardway** Hants
32 B4 **Hardway** Somset
67 K3 **Hardwick** Bucks
87 H3 **Hardwick** Cambs
85 G1 **Hardwick** Nhants
106 E5 **Hardwick** Norfk
66 A6 **Hardwick** Oxon
66 E1 **Hardwick** Oxon
133 K3 **Hardwick** Rothm
98 D4 **Hardwick** Wsall
64 A4 **Hardwicke** Gloucs
64 C2 **Hardwicke** Gloucs
81 J8 **Hardwick Green** Worcs
72 D3 **Hardy's Green** Essex
23 K5 **Harebeating** E Susx
136 F6 **Hareby** Lincs
149 K8 **Hare Croft** C Brad
50 D1 **Harefield** Gt Lon
73 G2 **Hare Green** Essex
49 J3 **Hare Hatch** Wokham
115 K4 **Harehill** Derbys
141 M1 **Harehills** Leeds
191 G2 **Harehope** Nthumb
188 F2 **Harelaw** Border
178 B3 **Harelaw** D & G
180 E8 **Harelaw** Dur
39 L5 **Hareplain** Kent
166 E2 **Haresceugh** Cumb
64 B5 **Harescombe** Gloucs
64 A5 **Haresfield** Gloucs
34 F4 **Harestock** Hants
70 B5 **Hare Street** Essex
70 D7 **Hare Street** Essex
69 K1 **Hare Street** Herts
150 D6 **Harewood** Leeds
63 G2 **Harewood End** Herefs
7 J3 **Harford** Devon
106 C5 **Hargate** Norfk
132 B4 **Hargatewall** Derbys
129 L7 **Hargrave** Ches W
85 K1 **Hargrave** Nhants
88 F3 **Hargrave** Suffk
88 F3 **Hargrave Green** Suffk

177 L6 **Harker** Cumb
90 E8 **Harkstead** Suffk
99 G1 **Harlaston** Staffs
118 A5 **Harlaxton** Lincs
109 K5 **Harlech** Gwynd
113 H8 **Harlescott** Shrops
51 G2 **Harlesden** Gt Lon
133 K4 **Harlesthorpe** Derbys
8 B6 **Harleston** Devon
106 E6 **Harleston** Norfk
89 L3 **Harleston** Suffk
84 D2 **Harlestone** Nhants
140 C1 **Harle Syke** Lancs
142 B8 **Harley** Rothm
96 D3 **Harley** Shrops
68 D1 **Harlington** C Beds
142 D7 **Harlington** Donc
50 E3 **Harlington** Gt Lon
258 D8 **Harlosh** Highld
70 C5 **Harlow** Essex
180 C5 **Harlow Hill** Nthumb
152 A8 **Harlthorpe** E R Yk
87 H5 **Harlton** Cambs
10 B7 **Harlyn** Cnwll
17 J6 **Harman's Cross** Dorset
159 L5 **Harmby** N York
69 H4 **Harmer Green** Herts
113 H7 **Harmer Hill** Shrops
50 D3 **Harmondsworth** Gt Lon
135 K7 **Harmston** Lincs
96 D3 **Harnage** Shrops
180 C3 **Harnham** Nthumb
64 F7 **Harnhill** Gloucs
70 D8 **Harold Hill** Gt Lon
54 D4 **Haroldston West** Pembks
281 f1 **Haroldswick** Shet
52 C1 **Harold Wood** Gt Lon
161 L6 **Harome** N York
68 E4 **Harpenden** Herts
14 C4 **Harpford** Devon
153 H3 **Harpham** E R Yk
121 H6 **Harpley** Norfk
80 F3 **Harpley** Worcs
84 D3 **Harpole** Nhants
279 K5 **Harpsdale** Highld
49 J3 **Harpsden** Oxon
135 J2 **Harpswell** Lincs
140 C7 **Harpurhey** Manch
131 L5 **Harpur Hill** Derbys
177 M7 **Harraby** Cumb
27 K5 **Harracott** Devon
247 K4 **Harrapool** Highld
221 H1 **Harrietfield** P & K
39 L3 **Harrietsham** Kent
51 J1 **Harringay** Gt Lon
164 C5 **Harrington** Cumb
137 G5 **Harrington** Lincs
101 G7 **Harrington** Nhants
101 K4 **Harringworth** Nhants
131 G8 **Harriseahead** Staffs
165 G2 **Harriston** Cumb
150 D5 **Harrogate** N York
150 D5 **Harrogate Crematorium** N York
85 J4 **Harrold** Bed
140 F6 **Harrop Dale** Oldham
50 F1 **Harrow** Gt Lon
12 A8 **Harrowbarrow** Cnwll
85 L6 **Harrowden** Bed
169 H7 **Harrowgate Village** Darltn
89 H4 **Harrow Green** Suffk
50 F2 **Harrow on the Hill** Gt Lon
50 F1 **Harrow Weald** Gt Lon
87 J5 **Harston** Cambs
117 L5 **Harston** Leics
152 C7 **Harswell** E R Yk
170 B4 **Hart** Hartpl
180 D2 **Hartburn** Nthumb
89 G5 **Hartest** Suffk
38 D6 **Hartfield** E Susx
88 E1 **Hartford** Cambs
130 C5 **Hartford** Ches W
29 G5 **Hartford** Somset
49 J7 **Hartfordbridge** Hants
71 G3 **Hartford End** Essex
159 L2 **Hartforth** N York
32 D7 **Hartgrove** Dorset
129 L8 **Harthill** Ches W
210 B6 **Harthill** N Lans
133 K3 **Harthill** Rothm
132 C7 **Hartington** Derbys
180 B1 **Hartington** Nthumb
26 D6 **Hartland** Devon
26 C6 **Hartland Quay** Devon
81 J1 **Hartlebury** Worcs
170 C4 **Hartlepool** Hartpl
170 C4 **Hartlepool Crematorium** Hartpl
158 D1 **Hartley** Cumb
39 J6 **Hartley** Kent
52 D5 **Hartley** Kent
181 H4 **Hartley** Nthumb

52 D5 **Hartley Green** Kent
114 F5 **Hartley Green** Staffs
49 G7 **Hartley Wespall** Hants
49 J7 **Hartley Wintney** Hants
53 H6 **Hartlip** Kent
162 C4 **Hartoft End** N York
151 L3 **Harton** N York
181 J6 **Harton** S Tyne
96 B5 **Harton** Shrops
64 A2 **Hartpury** Gloucs
141 J3 **Hartshead** Kirk
114 D2 **Hartshill** C Stke
99 J4 **Hartshill** Warwks
116 B7 **Hartshorne** Derbys
190 D3 **Hartside** Nthumb
165 L8 **Hartsop** Cumb
170 B3 **Hart Station** Hartpl
29 K5 **Hartswell** Somset
84 F5 **Hartwell** Nhants
150 B3 **Hartwith** N York
209 M7 **Hartwood** N Lans
188 D1 **Hartwoodmyres** Border
52 E6 **Harvel** Kent
82 C5 **Harvington** Worcs
97 K8 **Harvington** Worcs
134 D2 **Harwell** Notts
48 C1 **Harwell** Oxon
73 K1 **Harwich** Essex
139 L5 **Harwood** Bolton
167 J4 **Harwood** Dur
190 E8 **Harwood** Nthumb
163 H3 **Harwood Dale** N York
139 L5 **Harwood Lee** Bolton
69 H3 **Harwood Park Crematorium** Herts
134 C2 **Harworth** Notts
98 B6 **Hasbury** Dudley
36 F3 **Hascombe** Surrey
100 F7 **Haselbech** Nhants
31 G8 **Haselbury Plucknett** Somset
82 F2 **Haseley** Warwks
82 F1 **Haseley Green** Warwks
82 F1 **Haseley Knob** Warwks
82 D4 **Haselor** Warwks
64 B2 **Hasfield** Gloucs
54 D5 **Hasguard** Pembks
138 D2 **Haskayne** Lancs
90 F5 **Hasketon** Suffk
133 H5 **Hasland** Derbys
36 D4 **Haslemere** Surrey
140 B3 **Haslingden** Lancs
139 M3 **Haslingden Grane** Lancs
87 H5 **Haslingfield** Cambs
130 E8 **Haslington** Ches E
130 E8 **Hassall** Ches E
130 F7 **Hassall Green** Ches E
40 E6 **Hassell Street** Kent
107 H2 **Hassingham** Norfk
165 G7 **Hassness** Cumb
22 D4 **Hassocks** W Susx
132 D5 **Hassop** Derbys
36 D4 **Haste Hill** Surrey
280 D6 **Haster** Highld
137 J5 **Hasthorpe** Lincs
40 E6 **Hastingleigh** Kent
24 E5 **Hastings** E Susx
30 D7 **Hastings** Somset
24 E5 **Hastings Borough Crematorium** E Susx
70 C5 **Hastingwood** Essex
68 A5 **Hastoe** Herts
169 K2 **Haswell** Dur
169 K2 **Haswell Plough** Dur
86 D5 **Hatch** C Beds
30 D6 **Hatch Beauchamp** Somset
86 B3 **Hatch End** Bed
50 E1 **Hatch End** Gt Lon
18 F3 **Hatchet Gate** Hants
68 E4 **Hatching Green** Herts
130 A5 **Hatchmere** Ches W
145 G7 **Hatcliffe** NE Lin
143 G6 **Hatfield** Donc
80 E3 **Hatfield** Herefs
69 G5 **Hatfield** Herts
81 K5 **Hatfield** Worcs
70 E4 **Hatfield Broad Oak** Essex
70 D4 **Hatfield Heath** Essex
71 J5 **Hatfield Peverel** Essex
143 H6 **Hatfield Woodhouse** Donc
65 M8 **Hatford** Oxon
34 D1 **Hatherden** Hants
12 D2 **Hatherleigh** Devon
116 E7 **Hathern** Leics
65 H6 **Hatherop** Gloucs
132 E3 **Hathersage** Derbys
132 E3 **Hathersage Booths** Derbys
113 L2 **Hatherton** Ches E
98 B1 **Hatherton** Staffs
86 F5 **Hatley St George** Cambs
6 D2 **Hatt** Cnwll

209 L5 **Hillend** N Lans
56 D6 **Hillend** Swans
63 H4 **Hillersland** Gloucs
13 G3 **Hillerton** Devon
67 G1 **Hillesden** Bucks
45 M1 **Hillesley** Gloucs
29 L6 **Hillfarrance** Somset
53 H6 **Hill Green** Kent
36 D5 **Hillgrove** W Susx
80 D6 **Hillhampton** Herefs
255 M4 **Hillhead** Abers
8 D4 **Hillhead** Devon
19 J3 **Hill Head** Hants
199 G5 **Hillhead** S Lans
257 K3 **Hillhead of Cocklaw** Abers
98 F1 **Hilliard's Cross** Staffs
279 L3 **Hilliclay** Highld
50 D2 **Hillingdon** Gt Lon
208 E6 **Hillington** C Glas
120 F6 **Hillington** Norfk
19 H5 **Hillis Corner** IoW
100 C8 **Hillmorton** Warwks
140 A2 **Hillock Vale** Lancs
210 F1 **Hill of Beath** Fife
264 C4 **Hill of Fearn** Highld
175 J2 **Hillowton** D & G
97 K8 **Hillpool** Worcs
35 J7 **Hillpound** Hants
115 H8 **Hill Ridware** Staffs
245 K4 **Hillside** Abers
235 H3 **Hillside** Angus
7 K3 **Hillside** Devon
141 J4 **Hill Side** Kirk
81 H3 **Hill Side** Worcs
133 J5 **Hills Town** Derbys
34 D7 **Hillstreet** Hants
281 c4 **Hillswick** Shet
168 C6 **Hill Top** Dur
18 F3 **Hill Top** Hants
141 G5 **Hill Top** Kirk
133 H1 **Hill Top** Rothm
98 C5 **Hill Top** Sandw
142 A4 **Hill Top** Wakefd
281 d8 **Hillwell** Shet
46 E4 **Hilmarton** Wilts
46 C7 **Hilperton** Wilts
46 C7 **Hilperton Marsh** Wilts
19 L3 **Hilsea** C Port
145 H1 **Hilston** E R Yk
34 F6 **Hiltingbury** Hants
202 D3 **Hilton** Border
86 F2 **Hilton** Cambs
167 G6 **Hilton** Cumb
115 L5 **Hilton** Derbys
16 E2 **Hilton** Dorset
168 F6 **Hilton** Dur
264 D4 **Hilton** Highld
170 B8 **Hilton** S on T
97 H4 **Hilton** Shrops
81 L3 **Himbleton** Worcs
97 K5 **Himley** Staffs
157 H5 **Hincaster** Cumb
50 F6 **Hinchley Wood** Surrey
99 L4 **Hinckley** Leics
105 L8 **Hinderclay** Suffk
171 J7 **Hinderwell** N York
112 E5 **Hindford** Shrops
36 C4 **Hindhead** Surrey
139 L1 **Hindle Fold** Lancs
180 C7 **Hindley** Nthumb
139 J6 **Hindley** Wigan
139 J7 **Hindley Green** Wigan
81 K3 **Hindlip** Worcs
122 A5 **Hindolveston** Norfk
32 F4 **Hindon** Wilts
121 L4 **Hindringham** Norfk
105 L3 **Hingham** Norfk
97 J5 **Hinksford** Staffs
113 M6 **Hinstock** Shrops
90 C6 **Hintlesham** Suffk
63 K6 **Hinton** Gloucs
18 C4 **Hinton** Hants
79 L7 **Hinton** Herefs
45 L4 **Hinton** S Glos
95 K2 **Hinton** Shrops
96 E7 **Hinton** Shrops
18 C4 **Hinton Admiral** Hants
35 J5 **Hinton Ampner** Hants
45 H7 **Hinton Blewett** BaNES
45 M7 **Hinton Charterhouse** BaNES
82 B7 **Hinton Green** Worcs
84 A7 **Hinton-in-the-Hedges** Nhants
35 J5 **Hinton Marsh** Hants
17 K1 **Hinton Martell** Dorset
82 B7 **Hinton on the Green** Worcs
47 K2 **Hinton Parva** Swindn
30 F8 **Hinton St George** Somset
32 C7 **Hinton St Mary** Dorset
66 A7 **Hinton Waldrist** Oxon
96 E8 **Hints** Shrops

98 F3 **Hints** Staffs
85 J3 **Hinwick** Bed
40 D6 **Hinxhill** Kent
87 K6 **Hinxton** Cambs
86 E7 **Hinxworth** Herts
141 H3 **Hipperholme** Calder
191 J4 **Hipsburn** Nthumb
160 B3 **Hipswell** N York
245 G3 **Hirn** Abers
111 K7 **Hirnant** Powys
181 G2 **Hirst** Nthumb
142 F3 **Hirst Courtney** N York
128 D7 **Hirwaen** Denbgs
60 E6 **Hirwaun** Rhondd
27 K5 **Hiscott** Devon
87 J3 **Histon** Cambs
89 K5 **Hitcham** Suffk
89 K5 **Hitcham Causeway** Suffk
89 K5 **Hitcham Street** Suffk
68 F1 **Hitchin** Herts
51 K4 **Hither Green** Gt Lon
13 G3 **Hittisleigh** Devon
13 G3 **Hittisleigh Cross** Devon
143 K2 **Hive** E R Yk
114 F6 **Hixon** Staffs
41 J3 **Hoaden** Kent
115 J7 **Hoar Cross** Staffs
63 G1 **Hoarwithy** Herefs
41 G2 **Hoath** Kent
39 G6 **Hoathly** Kent
95 H7 **Hobarris** Shrops
88 D4 **Hobbles Green** Suffk
70 C7 **Hobbs Cross** Essex
70 D5 **Hobbs Cross** Essex
189 G4 **Hobkirk** Border
107 K3 **Hobland Hall** Norfk
116 D2 **Hobsick** Notts
180 E7 **Hobson** Dur
117 H8 **Hoby** Leics
29 K5 **Hoccombe** Somset
106 B1 **Hockering** Norfk
134 E8 **Hockerton** Notts
131 J3 **Hockley** Ches E
99 H7 **Hockley** Covtry
71 K8 **Hockley** Essex
99 G3 **Hockley** Staffs
82 E1 **Hockley Heath** Solhll
68 B2 **Hockliffe** C Beds
104 E6 **Hockwold cum Wilton** Norfk
29 J7 **Hockworthy** Devon
69 K5 **Hoddesdon** Herts
139 L3 **Hoddlesden** Bl w D
177 G4 **Hoddom Cross** D & G
177 G4 **Hoddom Mains** D & G
131 G5 **Hodgehill** Ches E
55 H7 **Hodgeston** Pembks
113 K6 **Hodnet** Shrops
134 C3 **Hodsock** Notts
52 D6 **Hodsoll Street** Kent
47 H3 **Hodson** Swindn
133 L4 **Hodthorpe** Derbys
35 H7 **Hoe** Hants
121 M8 **Hoe** Norfk
35 K8 **Hoe Gate** Hants
166 F7 **Hoff** Cumb
40 D4 **Hogben's Hill** Kent
89 H4 **Hoggards Green** Suffk
67 K2 **Hoggeston** Bucks
99 G5 **Hoggrill's End** Warwks
25 G4 **Hog Hill** E Susx
139 J2 **Hoghton** Lancs
139 J2 **Hoghton Bottoms** Lancs
115 L2 **Hognaston** Derbys
137 K5 **Hogsthorpe** Lincs
119 K6 **Holbeach** Lincs
119 K6 **Holbeach Bank** Lincs
119 K6 **Holbeach Clough** Lincs
103 G1 **Holbeach Drove** Lincs
119 L6 **Holbeach Hurn** Lincs
119 K7 **Holbeach St Johns** Lincs
119 L5 **Holbeach St Mark's** Lincs
119 L5 **Holbeach St Matthew** Lincs
133 L5 **Holbeck** Notts
133 L5 **Holbeck Woodhouse** Notts
82 B3 **Holberrow Green** Worcs
7 J5 **Holbeton** Devon
51 J3 **Holborn** Gt Lon
52 F6 **Holborough** Kent
116 B3 **Holbrook** Derbys
133 J3 **Holbrook** Sheff
90 E7 **Holbrook** Suffk
116 B3 **Holbrook Moor** Derbys
99 J6 **Holbrooks** Covtry
203 G6 **Holburn** Nthumb
19 G3 **Holbury** Hants
140 A4 **Holcombe** Bury
13 M7 **Holcombe** Devon
31 L1 **Holcombe** Somset
140 A5 **Holcombe Brook** Bury
29 J7 **Holcombe Rogus** Devon

84 F1 **Holcot** Nhants
148 D6 **Holden** Lancs
84 D2 **Holdenby** Nhants
140 D3 **Holden Gate** Calder
70 F1 **Holder's Green** Essex
96 D5 **Holdgate** Shrops
118 E2 **Holdingham** Lincs
15 H2 **Holditch** Dorset
141 G2 **Holdsworth** Calder
131 K1 **Holehouse** Derbys
63 J2 **Hole-in-the-Wall** Herefs
12 A1 **Holemoor** Devon
21 K4 **Hole Street** W Susx
29 L3 **Holford** Somset
151 J5 **Holgate** C York
156 E7 **Holker** Cumb
121 K3 **Holkham** Norfk
11 M2 **Hollacombe** Devon
119 H2 **Holland Fen** Lincs
139 G6 **Holland Lees** Lancs
73 J4 **Holland-on-Sea** Essex
275 f1 **Hollandstoun** Ork
177 J5 **Hollee** D & G
91 H6 **Hollesley** Suffk
8 D2 **Hollicombe** Torbay
39 L2 **Hollingbourne** Kent
22 D5 **Hollingbury** Br & H
67 L2 **Hollingdon** Bucks
142 B2 **Hollingthorpe** Leeds
115 L4 **Hollington** Derbys
115 G4 **Hollington** Staffs
140 F8 **Hollingworth** Tamesd
131 G3 **Hollinlane** Ches E
140 B6 **Hollins** Bury
132 F5 **Hollins** Derbys
114 F2 **Hollins** Staffs
131 L6 **Hollinsclough** Staffs
133 H3 **Hollins End** Sheff
130 D2 **Hollins Green** Warrtn
147 K5 **Hollins Lane** Lancs
96 F2 **Hollinswood** Wrekin
113 H4 **Hollinwood** Shrops
140 D7 **Hollinwood Crematorium**
       Oldham
24 C3 **Holllingrove** E Susx
27 L8 **Hollocombe** Devon
132 F8 **Holloway** Derbys
51 J2 **Holloway** Gt Lon
32 E5 **Holloway** Wilts
84 D1 **Hollowell** Nhants
129 L6 **Hollowmoor Heath** Ches W
177 L3 **Hollows** D & G
61 J6 **Hollybush** Caerph
196 D7 **Hollybush** E Ayrs
81 H7 **Hollybush** Herefs
103 K2 **Holly End** Norfk
81 K7 **Holly Green** Worcs
113 J3 **Hollyhurst** Ches E
145 J3 **Hollym** E R Yk
98 D7 **Hollywood** Worcs
141 H6 **Holmbridge** Kirk
37 H2 **Holmbury St Mary** Surrey
5 H4 **Holmbush** Cnwll
114 E6 **Holmcroft** Staffs
102 D6 **Holme** Cambs
157 H7 **Holme** Cumb
141 H6 **Holme** Kirk
144 A6 **Holme** N Linc
160 E6 **Holme** N York
134 F7 **Holme** Notts
140 C2 **Holme Chapel** Lancs
151 J7 **Holme Green** N York
105 H2 **Holme Hale** Norfk
80 D8 **Holme Lacy** Herefs
79 L4 **Holme Marsh** Herefs
120 F3 **Holme next the Sea** Norfk
152 E6 **Holme on the Wolds** E R Yk
117 G4 **Holme Pierrepont** Notts
80 C6 **Holmer** Herefs
67 L7 **Holmer Green** Bucks
164 F1 **Holme St Cuthbert** Cumb
130 E6 **Holmes Chapel** Ches E
132 F4 **Holmesfield** Derbys
23 J4 **Holmes Hill** E Susx
138 E4 **Holmeswood** Lancs
51 H8 **Holmethorpe** Surrey
152 B8 **Holme upon Spalding Moor**
       E R Yk
133 H6 **Holmewood** Derbys
141 G2 **Holmfield** Calder
141 H6 **Holmfirth** Kirk
197 H7 **Holmhead** E Ayrs
145 K3 **Holmpton** E R Yk
155 K3 **Holmrook** Cumb
196 D3 **Holmsford Bridge**
       **Crematorium** N Ayrs
23 L2 **Holmshurst** E Susx
169 G1 **Holmside** Dur
166 C1 **Holmwrangle** Cumb
7 K1 **Holne** Devon

16 C1 **Holnest** Dorset
29 G2 **Holnicote** Somset
11 L2 **Holsworthy** Devon
11 L1 **Holsworthy Beacon** Devon
17 K2 **Holt** Dorset
122 B4 **Holt** Norfk
46 B6 **Holt** Wilts
81 J3 **Holt** Worcs
112 F1 **Holt** Wrexhm
151 L5 **Holtby** C York
82 C1 **Holt End** Worcs
81 J3 **Holt Fleet** Worcs
138 E6 **Holt Green** Lancs
17 L2 **Holt Heath** Dorset
81 J3 **Holt Heath** Worcs
66 F5 **Holton** Oxon
31 L5 **Holton** Somset
107 H7 **Holton** Suffk
136 B3 **Holton cum Beckering** Lincs
17 J4 **Holton Heath** Dorset
24 B2 **Holton Hill** E Susx
145 H7 **Holton le Clay** Lincs
144 D8 **Holton le Moor** Lincs
90 C7 **Holton St Mary** Suffk
41 H5 **Holt Street** Kent
38 C5 **Holtye** E Susx
128 E4 **Holway** Flints
32 B8 **Holwell** Dorset
86 D8 **Holwell** Herts
117 J6 **Holwell** Leics
65 K5 **Holwell** Oxon
167 L5 **Holwick** Dur
16 E5 **Holworth** Dorset
35 M3 **Holybourne** Hants
97 L7 **Holy Cross** Worcs
69 K6 **Holyfield** Essex
124 D3 **Holyhead** IoA
203 J5 **Holy Island** Nthumb
133 G6 **Holymoorside** Derbys
49 L3 **Holyport** W & M
190 D5 **Holystone** Nthumb
209 K6 **Holytown** N Lans
68 C4 **Holywell** C Beds
87 G1 **Holywell** Cambs
4 C3 **Holywell** Cnwll
16 B2 **Holywell** Dorset
128 E4 **Holywell** Flints
181 H4 **Holywell** Nthumb
82 E2 **Holywell** Warwks
141 G4 **Holywell Green** Calder
29 K6 **Holywell Lake** Somset
104 E7 **Holywell Row** Suffk
176 B3 **Holywood** D & G
176 C3 **Holywood Village** D & G
96 E3 **Homer** Shrops
138 D7 **Homer Green** Sefton
106 F6 **Homersfield** Suffk
157 J5 **Homescales** Cumb
63 H3 **Hom Green** Herefs
33 K5 **Homington** Wilts
54 F5 **Honeyborough** Pembks
82 D6 **Honeybourne** Worcs
12 E2 **Honeychurch** Devon
40 F3 **Honey Hill** Kent
47 G6 **Honeystreet** Wilts
89 J8 **Honey Tye** Suffk
82 F1 **Honiley** Warwks
123 G4 **Honing** Norfk
106 C1 **Honingham** Norfk
118 B3 **Honington** Lincs
105 H8 **Honington** Suffk
83 G6 **Honington** Warwks
14 E2 **Honiton** Devon
141 H5 **Honley** Kirk
114 A8 **Honnington** Wrekin
51 K4 **Honor Oak Crematorium** Gt Lon
41 J2 **Hoo** Kent
97 J8 **Hoobrook** Worcs
141 M7 **Hood Green** Barns
142 B8 **Hood Hill** Rothm
6 F4 **Hooe** C Plym
24 C5 **Hooe** E Susx
68 F3 **Hoo End** Herts
130 D3 **Hoo Green** Ches E
146 F8 **Hoohill** Bpool
103 J5 **Hook** Cambs
15 G2 **Hook** Devon
143 J3 **Hook** E R Yk
50 F6 **Hook** Gt Lon
19 H3 **Hook** Hants
49 H8 **Hook** Hants
55 G4 **Hook** Pembks
47 G2 **Hook** Wilts
95 L2 **Hookagate** Shrops
81 J7 **Hook Bank** Worcs
15 M2 **Hooke** Dorset
70 E7 **Hook End** Essex
114 A4 **Hookgate** Staffs
39 G6 **Hook Green** Kent
52 D5 **Hook Green** Kent

Hook Norton - Hurstbourne Tarrant 323


83 H8 **Hook Norton** Oxon
63 K7 **Hook Street** Gloucs
47 G2 **Hook Street** Wilts
13 K3 **Hookway** Devon
37 L2 **Hookwood** Surrey
51 H7 **Hooley** Surrey
140 C5 **Hooley Bridge** Rochdl
7 G2 **Hoo Meavy** Devon
53 G4 **Hoo St Werburgh** Medway
129 J4 **Hooton** Ches W
133 K2 **Hooton Levitt** Rothm
142 D6 **Hooton Pagnell** Donc
142 D8 **Hooton Roberts** Rothm
66 C2 **Hopcrofts Holt** Oxon
132 C3 **Hope** Derbys
7 K6 **Hope** Devon
129 G7 **Hope** Flints
95 G2 **Hope** Powys
95 H3 **Hope** Shrops
96 D8 **Hope** Shrops
132 B8 **Hope** Staffs
95 L5 **Hope Bowdler** Shrops
70 E3 **Hope End Green** Essex
187 L3 **Hopehouse** Border
266 C2 **Hopeman** Moray
63 J3 **Hope Mansell** Herefs
95 J6 **Hopesay** Shrops
142 B3 **Hopetown** Wakefd
80 C5 **Hope under Dinmore** Herefs
151 K5 **Hopgrove** C York
150 F4 **Hopperton** N York
102 D1 **Hop Pole** Lincs
99 L6 **Hopsford** Warwks
97 H4 **Hopstone** Shrops
115 L1 **Hopton** Derbys
112 F7 **Hopton** Shrops
114 E6 **Hopton** Staffs
105 K7 **Hopton** Suffk
96 C7 **Hopton Cangeford** Shrops
95 J7 **Hopton Castle** Shrops
95 J7 **Hoptonheath** Shrops
107 L3 **Hopton on Sea** Norfk
96 E8 **Hopton Wafers** Shrops
98 F3 **Hopwas** Staffs
140 C6 **Hopwood** Rochdl
98 C8 **Hopwood** Worcs
23 K4 **Horam** E Susx
118 F4 **Horbling** Lincs
141 L4 **Horbury** Wakefd
65 H7 **Horcott** Gloucs
170 B3 **Horden** Dur
95 K6 **Horderley** Shrops
18 D4 **Hordle** Hants
112 F5 **Hordley** Shrops
56 F4 **Horeb** Carmth
76 D6 **Horeb** Cerdgn
45 H4 **Horfield** Bristl
90 F1 **Horham** Suffk
72 E1 **Horkesley Heath** Essex
144 B4 **Horkstow** N Linc
83 K6 **Horley** Oxon
37 L2 **Horley** Surrey
31 K4 **Hornblotton Green** Somset
147 L2 **Hornby** Lancs
160 B4 **Hornby** N York
160 E2 **Hornby** N York
136 E6 **Horncastle** Lincs
52 B2 **Hornchurch** Gt Lon
202 E3 **Horncliffe** Nthumb
202 D3 **Horndean** Border
35 L8 **Horndean** Hants
12 C6 **Horndon** Devon
52 E2 **Horndon on the Hill** Thurr
38 A4 **Horne** Surrey
28 F2 **Horner** Somset
71 J6 **Horne Row** Essex
89 K7 **Horners Green** Suffk
23 G2 **Horney Common** E Susx
68 C8 **Horn Hill** Bucks
123 G8 **Horning** Norfk
101 H4 **Horninghold** Leics
115 L6 **Horninglow** Staffs
87 K3 **Horningsea** Cambs
32 D3 **Horningsham** Wilts
121 K6 **Horningtoft** Norfk
6 B3 **Horningtops** Cnwll
30 E8 **Hornsbury** Somset
166 C1 **Hornsby** Cumb
166 C1 **Hornsbygate** Cumb
27 G6 **Horns Cross** Devon
24 E3 **Horns Cross** E Susx
153 K6 **Hornsea** E R Yk
51 J1 **Hornsey** Gt Lon
51 M7 **Horn's Green** Gt Lon
41 G8 **Horn Street** Kent
83 J6 **Hornton** Oxon
47 J2 **Horpit** Swindn
281 e3 **Horra** Shet
7 G1 **Horrabridge** Devon
13 H7 **Horridge** Devon
89 G3 **Horringer** Suffk
19 J6 **Horringford** IoW
139 L5 **Horrocks Fold** Bolton
148 C7 **Horrocksford** Lancs
27 J4 **Horsacott** Devon
12 A7 **Horsebridge** Devon
23 K5 **Horsebridge** E Susx
34 D5 **Horsebridge** Hants
95 J2 **Horsebridge** Shrops
114 F1 **Horsebridge** Staffs
97 K1 **Horsebrook** Staffs
44 E5 **Horsecastle** N Som
3 G4 **Horsedown** Cnwll
102 C2 **Horsegate** Lincs
96 F2 **Horsehay** Wrekin
88 C5 **Horseheath** Cambs
159 J6 **Horsehouse** N York
50 C7 **Horsell** Surrey
113 G3 **Horseman's Green** Wrexhm
67 J6 **Horsenden** Bucks
123 J7 **Horsey** Norfk
30 D3 **Horsey** Somset
123 J6 **Horsey Corner** Norfk
122 D8 **Horsford** Norfk
150 B8 **Horsforth** Leeds
37 J5 **Horsham** W Susx
81 G4 **Horsham** Worcs
122 E8 **Horsham St Faith** Norfk
136 C6 **Horsington** Lincs
32 B6 **Horsington** Somset
116 C3 **Horsley** Derbys
64 B7 **Horsley** Gloucs
180 D5 **Horsley** Nthumb
190 B6 **Horsley** Nthumb
73 H2 **Horsley Cross** Essex
73 G1 **Horsleycross Street** Essex
132 F4 **Horsley-Gate** Derbys
188 F2 **Horsleyhill** Border
67 J8 **Horsley's Green** Bucks
116 C3 **Horsley Woodhouse** Derbys
39 H5 **Horsmonden** Kent
66 E6 **Horspath** Oxon
122 F7 **Horstead** Norfk
22 F2 **Horsted Keynes** W Susx
68 A3 **Horton** Bucks
17 K1 **Horton** Dorset
148 E6 **Horton** Lancs
84 F4 **Horton** Nhants
45 M2 **Horton** S Glos
113 H5 **Horton** Shrops
30 D7 **Horton** Somset
131 J8 **Horton** Staffs
51 G6 **Horton** Surrey
56 E7 **Horton** Swans
50 C4 **Horton** W & M
46 F6 **Horton** Wilts
113 L8 **Horton** Wrekin
30 E7 **Horton Cross** Somset
66 F4 **Horton-cum-Studley** Oxon
113 G2 **Horton Green** Ches W
35 G7 **Horton Heath** Hants
148 D2 **Horton in Ribblesdale** N York
52 C5 **Horton Kirby** Kent
139 J5 **Horwich** Bolton
131 K3 **Horwich End** Derbys
27 J5 **Horwood** Devon
138 F5 **Hoscar** Lancs
188 C4 **Hoscote** Border
117 J5 **Hose** Leics
51 M8 **Hosey Hill** Kent
220 E3 **Hosh** P & K
281 e8 **Hoswick** Shet
143 M1 **Hotham** E R Yk
40 C6 **Hothfield** Kent
116 F7 **Hoton** Leics
179 H2 **Hott** Nthumb
113 M1 **Hough** Ches E
131 G4 **Hough** Ches E
118 A3 **Hougham** Lincs
141 K1 **Hough End** Leeds
129 L2 **Hough Green** Halton
118 B2 **Hough-on-the-Hill** Lincs
86 F1 **Houghton** Cambs
177 L7 **Houghton** Cumb
34 D4 **Houghton** Hants
180 D5 **Houghton** Nthumb
55 G5 **Houghton** Pembks
21 H4 **Houghton** W Susx
85 L7 **Houghton Conquest** C Beds
181 H8 **Houghton Gate** Dur
25 G3 **Houghton Green** E Susx
130 C1 **Houghton Green** Warrtn
169 G6 **Houghton le Side** Darltn
169 J1 **Houghton-le-Spring** Sundld
100 E3 **Houghton on the Hill** Leics
68 C2 **Houghton Regis** C Beds
121 K4 **Houghton St Giles** Norfk
49 H7 **Hound Green** Hants
201 K4 **Houndslow** Border
29 L5 **Houndsmoor** Somset
213 J6 **Houndwood** Border
50 F4 **Hounslow** Gt Lon
253 G1 **Househill** Highld
141 K4 **Houses Hill** Kirk
257 G6 **Housieside** Abers
208 C5 **Houston** Rens
275 G1 **Houstry** Highld
275 b5 **Houton** Ork
22 D6 **Hove** Br & H
141 H3 **Hove Edge** Calder
117 J2 **Hoveringham** Notts
122 F7 **Hoveton** Norfk
161 L7 **Hovingham** N York
141 M8 **Howbrook** Barns
63 J1 **How Caple** Herefs
143 J2 **Howden** E R Yk
168 F4 **Howden-le-Wear** Dur
280 D4 **Howe** Highld
154 b8 **Howe** IoM
160 E6 **Howe** N York
106 F3 **Howe** Norfk
139 K7 **Howe Bridge** Wigan
139 K7 **Howe Bridge Crematorium** Wigan
71 H6 **Howe Green** Essex
71 K6 **Howegreen** Essex
118 F2 **Howell** Lincs
85 K7 **How End** C Beds
268 E6 **Howe of Teuchar** Abers
177 G5 **Howes** D & G
71 G4 **Howe Street** Essex
88 D8 **Howe Street** Essex
78 E3 **Howey** Powys
164 C6 **Howgate** Cumb
211 H7 **Howgate** Mdloth
148 E6 **Howgill** Lancs
191 K3 **Howick** Nthumb
168 E5 **Howle** Dur
113 M6 **Howle** Wrekin
63 J3 **Howle Hill** Herefs
88 B8 **Howlett End** Essex
15 G1 **Howley** Somset
178 C7 **How Mill** Cumb
283 b10 **Howmore** W Isls
189 L2 **Hownam** Border
165 K1 **Howrigg** Cumb
144 D6 **Howsham** N Linc
151 M3 **Howsham** N York
202 D6 **Howtel** Nthumb
53 J6 **Howt Green** Kent
62 E1 **Howton** Herefs
166 B6 **Howtown** Cumb
208 C7 **Howwood** Rens
106 D7 **Hoxne** Suffk
128 F2 **Hoylake** Wirral
142 B7 **Hoyland Common** Barns
142 B7 **Hoyland Nether** Barns
141 L6 **Hoyland Swaine** Barns
20 E3 **Hoyle** W Susx
142 A6 **Hoyle Mill** Barns
159 G7 **Hubberholme** N York
54 E5 **Hubberston** Pembks
119 J3 **Hubbert's Bridge** Lincs
150 C6 **Huby** N York
151 J3 **Huby** N York
12 F7 **Huccaby** Devon
64 C4 **Hucclecote** Gloucs
53 H7 **Hucking** Kent
116 F2 **Hucknall** Notts
141 H4 **Huddersfield** Kirk
141 J4 **Huddersfield Crematorium** Kirk
81 L4 **Huddington** Worcs
68 C4 **Hudnall** Herts
159 L3 **Hudswell** N York
152 D5 **Huggate** E R Yk
99 L1 **Hugglescote** Leics
67 L7 **Hughenden Valley** Bucks
96 D4 **Hughley** Shrops
10 c3 **Hugh Town** IoS
27 J8 **Huish** Devon
47 H6 **Huish** Wilts
29 J5 **Huish Champflower** Somset
31 G5 **Huish Episcopi** Somset
85 J7 **Hulcote** C Beds
67 K4 **Hulcott** Bucks
14 B6 **Hulham** Devon
115 L2 **Hulland** Derbys
115 L2 **Hulland Ward** Derbys
46 C3 **Hullavington** Wilts
71 K8 **Hullbridge** Essex
140 C8 **Hulme** Manch
114 E2 **Hulme** Staffs
130 B2 **Hulme** Warrtn
132 B7 **Hulme End** Staffs
131 G6 **Hulme Walfield** Ches E
130 E3 **Hulse Heath** Ches E
139 K6 **Hulton Lane Ends** Bolton
18 F6 **Hulverstone** IoW
105 J1 **Hulver Street** Norfk
107 K6 **Hulver Street** Suffk
13 L7 **Humber** Devon
80 C4 **Humber** Herefs
145 J6 **Humberston** NE Lin
100 E2 **Humberstone** C Leic
150 F2 **Humberton** N York
212 A6 **Humbie** E Loth
145 G1 **Humbleton** E R Yk
202 F7 **Humbleton** Nthumb
118 D5 **Humby** Lincs
201 L5 **Hume** Border
179 L4 **Humshaugh** Nthumb
280 E2 **Huna** Highld
140 A2 **Huncoat** Lancs
100 B4 **Huncote** Leics
189 H3 **Hundalee** Border
133 H4 **Hundall** Derbys
168 C6 **Hunderthwaite** Dur
137 G6 **Hundleby** Lincs
119 H1 **Hundle Houses** Lincs
54 F6 **Hundleton** Pembks
88 E5 **Hundon** Suffk
138 E3 **Hundred End** Lancs
78 F4 **Hundred House** Powys
100 F2 **Hungarton** Leics
33 L8 **Hungerford** Hants
29 J3 **Hungerford** Somset
47 M5 **Hungerford** W Berk
47 M4 **Hungerford Newtown** W Berk
139 K6 **Hunger Hill** Bolton
139 G5 **Hunger Hill** Lancs
80 B8 **Hungerstone** Herefs
118 A5 **Hungerton** Lincs
113 L6 **Hungryhatton** Shrops
163 K7 **Hunmanby** N York
83 J2 **Hunningham** Warwks
98 B7 **Hunnington** Worcs
84 E4 **Hunsbury Hill** Nhants
69 L4 **Hunsdon** Herts
150 F5 **Hunsingore** N York
141 M2 **Hunslet** Leeds
166 D4 **Hunsonby** Cumb
120 E3 **Hunstanton** Norfk
168 B1 **Hunstanworth** Dur
113 M2 **Hunsterson** Ches E
89 K2 **Hunston** Suffk
20 D6 **Hunston** W Susx
89 K2 **Hunston Green** Suffk
45 J6 **Hunstrete** BaNES
141 J2 **Hunsworth** Kirk
82 B2 **Hunt End** Worcs
28 B1 **Hunter's Inn** Devon
207 K3 **Hunter's Quay** Ag & B
30 E5 **Huntham** Somset
234 D1 **Hunthill Lodge** Angus
86 E1 **Huntingdon** Cambs
107 G8 **Huntingfield** Suffk
32 D5 **Huntingford** Dorset
151 K4 **Huntington** C York
129 K6 **Huntington** Ches W
212 B4 **Huntington** E Loth
79 J4 **Huntington** Herefs
80 B6 **Huntington** Herefs
98 B1 **Huntington** Staffs
63 L3 **Huntley** Gloucs
255 L4 **Huntly** Abers
35 G3 **Hunton** Hants
39 H3 **Hunton** Kent
160 B4 **Hunton** N York
68 D7 **Hunton Bridge** Herts
105 L5 **Hunt's Corner** Norfk
29 G2 **Huntscott** Somset
129 K3 **Hunt's Cross** Lpool
67 L6 **Hunts Green** Bucks
98 F4 **Hunts Green** Warwks
29 H6 **Huntsham** Devon
27 J6 **Huntshaw** Devon
27 J6 **Huntshaw Cross** Devon
30 D2 **Huntspill** Somset
30 C4 **Huntstile** Somset
30 D4 **Huntworth** Somset
168 F4 **Hunwick** Dur
122 B4 **Hunworth** Norfk
30 F7 **Hurcott** Somset
33 L4 **Hurdcott** Wilts
131 H5 **Hurdsfield** Ches E
49 K2 **Hurley** W & M
99 H4 **Hurley** Warwks
49 K2 **Hurley Bottom** W & M
99 H4 **Hurley Common** Warwks
196 E4 **Hurlford** E Ayrs
138 E5 **Hurlston Green** Lancs
18 A4 **Hurn** Dorset
119 M2 **Hurn's End** Lincs
34 F6 **Hursley** Hants
16 F4 **Hurst** Dorset
159 J2 **Hurst** N York
31 G7 **Hurst** Somset
49 J4 **Hurst** Wokham
34 F2 **Hurstbourne Priors** Hants
48 A8 **Hurstbourne Tarrant** Hants

24 D2 **Hurst Green** E Susx
73 G4 **Hurst Green** Essex
148 B8 **Hurst Green** Lancs
51 K8 **Hurst Green** Surrey
97 L4 **Hurst Hill** Dudley
79 L5 **Hurstley** Herefs
22 D4 **Hurstpierpoint** W Susx
22 D4 **Hurst Wickham** W Susx
140 C2 **Hurstwood** Lancs
275 d5 **Hurtiso** Ork
36 E2 **Hurtmore** Surrey
169 L4 **Hurworth Burn** Dur
169 J8 **Hurworth-on-Tees** Darltn
160 D1 **Hurworth Place** Darltn
168 B6 **Hury** Dur
100 E6 **Husbands Bosworth** Leics
85 J8 **Husborne Crawley** C Beds
161 H7 **Husthwaite** N York
8 A5 **Hutcherleigh** Devon
133 G3 **Hutcliffe Wood Crematorium** Sheff
142 F3 **Hut Green** N York
161 G2 **Huthwaite** N York
133 J7 **Huthwaite** Notts
137 K4 **Huttoft** Lincs
202 E2 **Hutton** Border
166 B5 **Hutton** Cumb
152 F5 **Hutton** E R Yk
70 F8 **Hutton** Essex
139 G2 **Hutton** Lancs
44 D7 **Hutton** N Som
160 E3 **Hutton Bonville** N York
163 H6 **Hutton Buscel** N York
160 D7 **Hutton Conyers** N York
153 G5 **Hutton Cranswick** E R Yk
166 B3 **Hutton End** Cumb
159 L5 **Hutton Hang** N York
169 L3 **Hutton Henry** Dur
162 B4 **Hutton-le-Hole** N York
170 E7 **Hutton Lowcross** R & Cl
168 E8 **Hutton Magna** Dur
162 E1 **Hutton Mulgrave** N York
157 J7 **Hutton Roof** Cumb
165 L4 **Hutton Roof** Cumb
161 G2 **Hutton Rudby** N York
161 G7 **Hutton Sessay** N York
151 H5 **Hutton Wandesley** N York
13 M3 **Huxham** Devon
31 K4 **Huxham Green** Somset
129 L7 **Huxley** Ches W
129 K2 **Huyton** Knows
155 K5 **Hycemoor** Cumb
64 C6 **Hyde** Gloucs
33 L8 **Hyde** Hants
131 J1 **Hyde** Tamesd
49 H5 **Hyde End** Wokham
68 B7 **Hyde Heath** Bucks
114 E7 **Hyde Lea** Staffs
36 E3 **Hydestile** Surrey
135 J6 **Hykeham Moor** Lincs
198 F5 **Hyndford Bridge** S Lans
224 C7 **Hynish** Ag & B
95 H4 **Hyssington** Powys
63 K7 **Hystfield** Gloucs
19 G2 **Hythe** Hants
41 G8 **Hythe** Kent
44 F8 **Hythe** Somset
50 C4 **Hythe End** W & M
155 K5 **Hyton** Cumb

## I

16 F1 **Ibberton** Dorset
132 E8 **Ible** Derbys
18 A2 **Ibsley** Hants
99 L2 **Ibstock** Leics
67 J8 **Ibstone** Bucks
48 A8 **Ibthorpe** Hants
162 F1 **Iburndale** N York
48 E7 **Ibworth** Hants
44 D6 **Icelton** N Som
105 G4 **Ickburgh** Norfk
50 D2 **Ickenham** Gt Lon
66 F5 **Ickford** Bucks
41 H4 **Ickham** Kent
68 F1 **Ickleford** Herts
24 F4 **Icklesham** E Susx
87 K6 **Ickleton** Cambs
88 F1 **Icklingham** Suffk
149 G7 **Ickornshaw** N York
86 C6 **Ickwell Green** C Beds
65 J3 **Icomb** Gloucs
65 K3 **Idbury** Oxon
12 D1 **Iddesleigh** Devon
13 L4 **Ide** Devon
13 K7 **Ideford** Devon
38 D3 **Ide Hill** Kent
25 G3 **Iden** E Susx
39 J6 **Iden Green** Kent

39 K7 **Iden Green** Kent
149 M8 **Idle** C Brad
4 D5 **Idless** Cnwll
83 G6 **Idlicote** Warwks
33 L3 **Idmiston** Wilts
58 D5 **Idole** Carmth
115 M2 **Idridgehay** Derbys
258 F4 **Idrigill** Highld
47 K2 **Idstone** Oxon
66 D6 **Iffley** Oxon
37 K3 **Ifield** W Susx
36 F4 **Ifold** W Susx
18 A5 **Iford** Bmouth
22 F5 **Iford** E Susx
44 F1 **Ifton** Mons
112 E4 **Ifton Heath** Shrops
113 K4 **Ightfield** Shrops
38 F2 **Ightham** Kent
91 J4 **Iken** Suffk
115 J2 **Ilam** Staffs
31 H6 **Ilchester** Somset
190 E2 **Ilderton** Nthumb
51 L2 **Ilford** Gt Lon
30 E7 **Ilford** Somset
27 J2 **Ilfracombe** Devon
116 D3 **Ilkeston** Derbys
107 H6 **Ilketshall St Andrew** Suffk
107 H6 **Ilketshall St John** Suffk
107 H6 **Ilketshall St Lawrence** Suffk
107 G6 **Ilketshall St Margaret** Suffk
149 K6 **Ilkley** C Brad
11 K6 **Illand** Cnwll
98 B7 **Illey** Dudley
130 F7 **Illidge Green** Ches E
141 G2 **Illingworth** Calder
3 H2 **Illogan** Cnwll
100 F3 **Illston on the Hill** Leics
67 J6 **Ilmer** Bucks
82 F6 **Ilmington** Warwks
30 E7 **Ilminster** Somset
13 H7 **Ilsington** Devon
16 E4 **Ilsington** Dorset
57 G6 **Ilston** Swans
160 B7 **Ilton** N York
30 E7 **Ilton** Somset
194 D3 **Imachar** N Ayrs
144 F5 **Immingham** NE Lin
145 G4 **Immingham Dock** NE Lin
87 J3 **Impington** Cambs
129 K4 **Ince** Ches W
138 C7 **Ince Blundell** Sefton
139 J6 **Ince-in-Makerfield** Wigan
262 C6 **Inchbae Lodge Hotel** Highld
234 F2 **Inchbare** Angus
266 F5 **Inchberry** Moray
261 G7 **Incheril** Highld
208 E5 **Inchinnan** Rens
239 K3 **Inchlaggan** Highld
222 D2 **Inchmichael** P & K
240 C2 **Inchnacardoch Hotel** Highld
271 H4 **Inchnadamph** Highld
222 D2 **Inchture** P & K
249 L4 **Inchvuilt** Highld
222 C3 **Inchyra** P & K
4 E3 **Indian Queens** Cnwll
107 J5 **Ingate Place** Suffk
70 F7 **Ingatestone** Essex
141 K6 **Ingbirchworth** Barns
150 C3 **Ingerthorpe** N York
114 F6 **Ingestre** Staffs
135 J3 **Ingham** Lincs
123 H6 **Ingham** Norfk
89 G1 **Ingham** Suffk
123 H6 **Ingham Corner** Norfk
120 B8 **Ingleborough** Norfk
116 B6 **Ingleby** Derbys
161 G3 **Ingleby Arncliffe** N York
170 B7 **Ingleby Barwick** S on T
161 G3 **Ingleby Cross** N York
161 J2 **Ingleby Greenhow** N York
12 E1 **Ingleigh Green** Devon
45 L6 **Inglesbatch** BaNES
65 J7 **Inglesham** Swindn
176 C6 **Ingleston** D & G
168 F6 **Ingleton** Dur
158 B8 **Ingleton** N York
147 L2 **Inglewhite** Lancs
180 C4 **Ingoe** Nthumb
139 G1 **Ingol** Lancs
120 F5 **Ingoldisthorpe** Norfk
137 K6 **Ingoldmells** Lincs
118 D5 **Ingoldsby** Lincs
190 E3 **Ingram** Nthumb
52 D1 **Ingrave** Essex
149 J7 **Ingrow** C Brad
157 G3 **Ings** Cumb
45 H2 **Ingst** S Glos
101 M2 **Ingthorpe** Rutlnd
122 D5 **Ingworth** Norfk
82 B4 **Inkberrow** Worcs

168 E3 **Inkerman** Dur
257 G4 **Inkhorn** Abers
48 A6 **Inkpen** W Berk
280 C2 **Inkstack** Highld
46 D6 **Inmarsh** Wilts
207 J5 **Innellan** Ag & B
200 D6 **Innerleithen** Border
222 F7 **Innerleven** Fife
172 D2 **Innermessan** D & G
212 F4 **Innerwick** E Loth
266 F5 **Innesmill** Moray
256 A6 **Insch** Abers
241 L3 **Insh** Highld
147 J8 **Inskip** Lancs
147 J8 **Inskip Moss Side** Lancs
27 H5 **Instow** Devon
6 E4 **Insworke** Cnwll
133 H3 **Intake** Sheff
243 H3 **Inver** Abers
264 D3 **Inver** Highld
232 F7 **Inver** P & K
238 B7 **Inverailort** Highld
260 D8 **Inveralligin** Highld
269 J3 **Inverallochy** Abers
272 E8 **Inveran** Highld
217 H5 **Inveraray** Ag & B
247 H2 **Inverarish** Highld
234 C6 **Inverarity** Angus
218 D3 **Inverarnan** Stirlg
260 C3 **Inverasdale** Highld
217 G1 **Inverawe** Ag & B
218 E7 **Inverbeg** Ag & B
235 K1 **Inverbervie** Abers
268 B3 **Inver-boyndie** Abers
229 G6 **Invercreran House Hotel** Ag & B
242 B1 **Inverdruie** Highld
211 K5 **Inveresk** E Loth
228 F8 **Inveresragan** Ag & B
242 E5 **Inverey** Abers
250 F7 **Inverfarigaig** Highld
228 E6 **Inverfolla** Ag & B
240 A3 **Invergarry** Highld
220 C2 **Invergeldie** P & K
239 L6 **Invergloy** Highld
263 J6 **Invergordon** Highld
222 F1 **Invergowrie** P & K
238 B2 **Inverguseran** Highld
231 J4 **Inverhadden** P & K
218 E2 **Inverherive Hotel** Stirlg
238 B3 **Inverie** Highld
216 F4 **Inverinan** Ag & B
248 E7 **Inverinate** Highld
235 G5 **Inverkeilor** Angus
210 F2 **Inverkeithing** Fife
268 A6 **Inverkeithny** Abers
207 K4 **Inverkip** Inver
270 E4 **Inverkirkaig** Highld
261 K3 **Inverlael** Highld
240 B7 **Inverlair** Highld
216 D6 **Inverliever Lodge** Ag & B
217 K2 **Inverlochy** Ag & B
244 A7 **Invermark** Angus
255 J4 **Invermarkie** Abers
250 D8 **Invermoriston** Highld
278 B4 **Invernaver** Highld
251 H3 **Inverness** Highld
251 H3 **Inverness Crematorium** Highld
217 J7 **Invernoaden** Ag & B
229 M7 **Inveroran Hotel** Ag & B
234 B4 **Inverquharity** Angus
257 J2 **Inverquhomery** Abers
239 M7 **Inverroy** Highld
228 E3 **Inversanda** Highld
248 F7 **Invershiel** Highld
272 E8 **Invershin** Highld
275 H1 **Invershore** Highld
218 E5 **Inversnaid Hotel** Stirlg
269 L6 **Inverugie** Abers
218 D5 **Inveruglas** Ag & B
241 L3 **Inveruglass** Highld
256 D7 **Inverurie** Abers
12 D3 **Inwardleigh** Devon
72 C3 **Inworth** Essex
283 b9 **Iochdar** W Isls
36 C6 **Iping** W Susx
8 B2 **Ipplepen** Devon
48 F2 **Ipsden** Oxon
115 G2 **Ipstones** Staffs
90 E6 **Ipswich** Suffk
90 E6 **Ipswich Crematorium** Suffk
128 F3 **Irby** Wirral
137 J7 **Irby in the Marsh** Lincs
145 G6 **Irby upon Humber** NE Lin
85 H2 **Irchester** Nhants
165 H3 **Ireby** Cumb
157 L7 **Ireby** Lancs
86 C7 **Ireland** C Beds
156 B7 **Ireleth** Cumb
167 K3 **Ireshopeburn** Dur

115 M2 **Ireton Wood** Derbys
130 E1 **Irlam** Salfd
118 D6 **Irnham** Lincs
45 K2 **Iron Acton** S Glos
103 K4 **Iron Bridge** Cambs
96 F3 **Ironbridge** Wrekin
82 C5 **Iron Cross** Warwks
185 G7 **Ironmacannie** D & G
37 K2 **Irons Bottom** Surrey
116 D1 **Ironville** Derbys
123 H7 **Irstead** Norfk
178 C6 **Irthington** Cumb
85 J1 **Irthlingborough** Nhants
163 H6 **Irton** N York
196 C3 **Irvine** N Ayrs
279 G3 **Isauld** Highld
281 d3 **Isbister** Shet
281 f5 **Isbister** Shet
23 G4 **Isfield** E Susx
101 J8 **Isham** Nhants
36 A2 **Isington** Hants
97 K7 **Islandpool** Worcs
30 E6 **Isle Abbotts** Somset
30 E6 **Isle Brewers** Somset
104 C8 **Isleham** Cambs
51 K3 **Isle of Dogs** Gt Lon
174 D7 **Isle of Whithorn** D & G
19 J5 **Isle of Wight Crematorium** IoW
247 L6 **Isleornsay** Highld
176 C4 **Islesteps** D & G
9 k2 **Islet Village** Guern
50 F4 **Isleworth** Gt Lon
116 C6 **Isley Walton** Leics
282 d3 **Islibhig** W Isls
51 J2 **Islington** Gt Lon
51 H1 **Islington Crematorium** Gt Lon
101 L7 **Islip** Nhants
66 D4 **Islip** Oxon
282 d3 **Islivig** W Isls
96 E1 **Isombridge** Wrekin
52 D5 **Istead Rise** Kent
35 H4 **Itchen Abbas** Hants
35 H4 **Itchen Stoke** Hants
37 H5 **Itchingfield** W Susx
45 K2 **Itchington** S Glos
122 C5 **Itteringham** Norfk
12 F3 **Itton** Devon
62 F8 **Itton** Mons
62 F7 **Itton Common** Mons
165 M2 **Ivegill** Cumb
159 G3 **Ivelet** N York
50 D3 **Iver** Bucks
50 C2 **Iver Heath** Bucks
168 E1 **Iveston** Dur
68 B4 **Ivinghoe** Bucks
68 B3 **Ivinghoe Aston** Bucks
80 B4 **Ivington** Herefs
80 B4 **Ivington Green** Herefs
7 J4 **Ivybridge** Devon
25 J2 **Ivychurch** Kent
32 E6 **Ivy Cross** Dorset
38 F3 **Ivy Hatch** Kent
105 H2 **Ivy Todd** Norfk
40 A2 **Iwade** Kent
32 E8 **Iwerne Courtney or Shroton** Dorset
32 E8 **Iwerne Minster** Dorset
89 J1 **Ixworth** Suffk
89 J1 **Ixworth Thorpe** Suffk

## J

139 J3 **Jack Green** Lancs
150 B5 **Jack Hill** N York
14 B3 **Jack-in-the-Green** Devon
34 C3 **Jack's Bush** Hants
116 D1 **Jacksdale** Notts
141 J6 **Jackson Bridge** Kirk
209 G8 **Jackton** S Lans
11 H3 **Jacobstow** Cnwll
12 E2 **Jacobstowe** Devon
50 C8 **Jacobs Well** Surrey
55 H7 **Jameston** Pembks
262 E8 **Jamestown** Highld
208 C3 **Jamestown** W Duns
275 G2 **Janetstown** Highld
280 D6 **Janets-town** Highld
176 E1 **Jardine Hall** D & G
181 H6 **Jarrow** S Tyne
38 E7 **Jarvis Brook** E Susx
71 H2 **Jasper's Green** Essex
209 M4 **Jawcraig** Falk
73 H4 **Jaywick** Essex
49 L4 **Jealott's Hill** Br For
160 F4 **Jeater Houses** N York
189 H2 **Jedburgh** Border
55 J5 **Jeffreyston** Pembks
263 K7 **Jemimaville** Highld

9 k4 **Jerbourg** Guern
9 d3 **Jersey Crematorium** Jersey
57 K6 **Jersey Marine** Neath
135 J5 **Jerusalem** Lincs
181 G5 **Jesmond** N u Ty
23 J7 **Jevington** E Susx
62 F5 **Jingle Street** Mons
68 D4 **Jockey End** Herts
130 F5 **Jodrell Bank** Ches E
166 B4 **Johnby** Cumb
280 E2 **John o' Groats** Highld
24 D3 **John's Cross** E Susx
235 K2 **Johnshaven** Abers
123 H8 **Johnson's Street** Norfk
54 F5 **Johnston** Pembks
187 K6 **Johnstone** D & G
208 D6 **Johnstone** Rens
187 G7 **Johnstonebridge** D & G
58 D5 **Johnstown** Carmth
112 D2 **Johnstown** Wrexhm
211 K4 **Joppa** C Edin
77 G2 **Joppa** Cerdgn
196 E7 **Joppa** S Ayrs
50 B1 **Jordans** Bucks
74 F5 **Jordanston** Pembks
133 G3 **Jordanthorpe** Sheff
52 B4 **Joyden's Wood** Kent
39 L4 **Jubilee Corner** Kent
142 B7 **Jump** Barns
38 C6 **Jumper's Town** E Susx
179 L7 **Juniper** Nthumb
211 G5 **Juniper Green** C Edin
154 e3 **Jurby** IoM
13 G5 **Jurston** Devon

**K**

167 J8 **Kaber** Cumb
199 G4 **Kaimend** S Lans
206 F5 **Kames** Ag & B
197 K5 **Kames** E Ayrs
4 C6 **Kea** Cnwll
143 L5 **Keadby** N Linc
137 G7 **Keal Cotes** Lincs
150 E6 **Kearby Town End** N York
139 M6 **Kearsley** Bolton
180 B4 **Kearsley** Nthumb
41 I6 **Kearsney** Kent
157 K6 **Kearstwick** Cumb
159 H3 **Kearton** N York
148 C3 **Keasden** N York
7 J4 **Keaton** Devon
130 B3 **Keckwick** Halton
136 F2 **Keddington** Lincs
137 G2 **Keddington Corner** Lincs
88 E6 **Kedington** Suffk
116 A3 **Kedleston** Derbys
144 F5 **Keelby** Lincs
114 C3 **Keele** Staffs
114 C3 **Keele University** Staffs
85 K6 **Keeley Green** Bed
141 G1 **Keelham** C Brad
54 E3 **Keeston** Pembks
46 D7 **Keevil** Wilts
116 E6 **Kegworth** Leics
3 G3 **Kehelland** Cnwll
256 A7 **Keig** Abers
149 J7 **Keighley** C Brad
149 J8 **Keighley Crematorium** C Brad
220 F8 **Keilarsbrae** Clacks
221 H2 **Keillour** P & K
243 G5 **Keiloch** Abers
205 H3 **Keils** Ag & B
31 J5 **Keinton Mandeville** Somset
186 C7 **Keir Mill** D & G
179 H8 **Keirsleywell Row** Nthumb
118 D6 **Keisby** Lincs
167 G6 **Keisley** Cumb
280 D4 **Keiss** Highld
267 J6 **Keith** Moray
233 I7 **Keithick** P & K
234 F3 **Keithock** Angus
262 F8 **Keithtown** Highld
148 F7 **Kelbrook** Lancs
207 L7 **Kelburn** N Ayrs
118 D3 **Kelby** Lincs
166 D7 **Keld** Cumb
158 F3 **Keld** N York
162 D5 **Keld Head** N York
162 C5 **Keldholme** N York
143 L7 **Kelfield** N Linc
151 J8 **Kelfield** N York
134 F8 **Kelham** Notts
12 A5 **Kellacott** Devon
138 E2 **Kellamergh** Lancs
234 C8 **Kellas** Angus
266 D5 **Kellas** Moray
8 B7 **Kellaton** Devon

157 L2 **Kelleth** Cumb
122 B3 **Kelling** Norfk
142 E3 **Kellington** N York
169 K3 **Kelloe** Dur
185 J1 **Kelloholm** D & G
164 C7 **Kells** Cumb
11 M6 **Kelly** Dcvon
11 L8 **Kelly Bray** Cnwll
101 G7 **Kelmarsh** Nhants
65 K7 **Kelmscott** Oxon
91 J2 **Kelsale** Suffk
129 M6 **Kelsall** Ches W
87 G7 **Kelshall** Herts
165 G1 **Kelsick** Cumb
201 M6 **Kelso** Border
133 G7 **Kelstedge** Derbys
136 D2 **Kelstern** Lincs
129 G5 **Kelsterton** Flints
45 K5 **Kelston** BaNES
231 L5 **Keltneyburn** P & K
176 C5 **Kelton** D & G
221 L8 **Kelty** Fife
72 C3 **Kelvedon** Essex
70 E7 **Kelvedon Hatch** Essex
2 B5 **Kelynack** Cnwll
28 B2 **Kemacott** Devon
223 G4 **Kemback** Fife
97 G3 **Kemberton** Shrops
64 E7 **Kemble** Gloucs
64 E7 **Kemble Wick** Gloucs
81 L7 **Kemerton** Worcs
62 D6 **Kemeys Commander** Mons
256 D8 **Kemnay** Abers
40 D6 **Kempe's Corner** Kent
63 K1 **Kempley** Gloucs
63 K1 **Kempley Green** Gloucs
81 J5 **Kempsey** Worcs
65 H7 **Kempsford** Gloucs
82 D1 **Kemps Green** Warwks
35 J1 **Kempshott** Hants
85 K5 **Kempston** Bed
85 K6 **Kempston Hardwick** Bed
95 J6 **Kempton** Shrops
22 E6 **Kemp Town** Br & H
52 C7 **Kemsing** Kent
40 B2 **Kemsley** Kent
53 H6 **Kemsley Street** Kent
25 H1 **Kenardington** Kent
80 B6 **Kenchester** Herefs
65 K6 **Kencot** Oxon
157 H4 **Kendal** Cumb
62 E2 **Kenderchurch** Herefs
45 K3 **Kendleshire** S Glos
42 B5 **Kenfig** Brdgnd
42 C5 **Kenfig Hill** Brdgnd
83 G1 **Kenilworth** Warwks
51 J7 **Kenley** Gt Lon
96 D3 **Kenley** Shrops
260 B8 **Kenmore** Highld
231 L6 **Kenmore** P & K
13 L5 **Kenn** Devon
44 E5 **Kenn** N Som
206 C6 **Kennacraig** Ag & B
11 K6 **Kennards House** Cnwll
2 F5 **Kenneggy** Cnwll
13 J1 **Kennerleigh** Devon
138 D7 **Kennessee Green** Sefton
210 B1 **Kennet** Clacks
255 L6 **Kennethmont** Abers
88 D2 **Kennett** Cambs
13 L5 **Kennford** Devon
105 L6 **Kenninghall** Norfk
40 D6 **Kennington** Kent
66 D6 **Kennington** Oxon
222 F6 **Kennoway** Fife
30 D7 **Kenny** Somset
104 D7 **Kennyhill** Suffk
152 B3 **Kennythorpe** N York
224 C6 **Kenovay** Ag & B
259 G6 **Kensaleyre** Highld
51 H3 **Kensington** Gt Lon
68 C3 **Kensworth Common** C Beds
38 F6 **Kent and Sussex Crematorium** Kent
62 E2 **Kentchurch** Herefs
88 E2 **Kentford** Suffk
131 G8 **Kent Green** Ches E
14 C1 **Kentisbeare** Devon
27 L2 **Kentisbury** Devon
27 L2 **Kentisbury Ford** Devon
51 H2 **Kentish Town** Gt Lon
157 G2 **Kentmere** Cumb
13 M6 **Kenton** Devon
50 F1 **Kenton** Gt Lon
180 F5 **Kenton** N u Ty
90 E2 **Kenton** Suffk
180 F5 **Kenton Bankfoot** N u Ty
237 J6 **Kentra** Highld
156 F7 **Kents Bank** Cumb

63 L2 **Kent's Green** Gloucs
34 D6 **Kent's Oak** Hants
24 E4 **Kent Street** E Susx
39 G2 **Kent Street** Kent
112 F5 **Kenwick** Shrops
4 D5 **Kenwyn** Cnwll
139 J8 **Kenyon** Warrtn
276 F3 **Keoldale** Highld
248 E6 **Keppoch** Highld
161 G4 **Kepwick** N York
99 J6 **Keresley** Covtry
130 F6 **Kermincham** Ches E
8 B6 **Kernborough** Devon
63 H3 **Kerne Bridge** Herefs
131 J4 **Kerridge** Ches E
131 J4 **Kerridge-end** Ches E
2 C5 **Kerris** Cnwll
94 E5 **Kerry** Powys
207 J6 **Kerrycroy** Ag & B
134 E7 **Kersall** Notts
14 C6 **Kersbrook** Devon
27 L5 **Kerscott** Devon
89 K6 **Kersey** Suffk
89 K6 **Kersey Tye** Suffk
89 K6 **Kersey Upland** Suffk
282 f4 **Kershader** W Isls
178 B2 **Kershopefoot** Cumb
82 A7 **Kersoe** Worcs
14 C1 **Kerswell** Devon
81 K6 **Kerswell Green** Worcs
2 F4 **Kerthen Wood** Cnwll
90 F6 **Kesgrave** Suffk
107 L6 **Kessingland** Suffk
107 L6 **Kessingland Beach** Suffk
5 G5 **Kestle** Cnwll
4 D3 **Kestle Mill** Cnwll
51 L6 **Keston** Gt Lon
165 J6 **Keswick** Cumb
106 E2 **Keswick** Norfk
137 G4 **Ketsby** Lincs
101 J7 **Kettering** Nhants
101 J7 **Kettering Crematorium** Nhants
106 D3 **Ketteringham** Norfk
233 K7 **Kettins** P & K
89 K5 **Kettlebaston** Suffk
222 E5 **Kettlebridge** Fife
99 G3 **Kettlebrook** Staffs
91 G3 **Kettleburgh** Suffk
69 L3 **Kettle Green** Herts
176 F3 **Kettleholm** D & G
171 J7 **Kettleness** N York
131 K4 **Kettleshulme** Ches E
150 B4 **Kettlesing** N York
150 B4 **Kettlesing Bottom** N York
121 L5 **Kettlestone** Norfk
135 G4 **Kettlethorpe** Lincs
275 e2 **Kettletoft** Ork
149 H2 **Kettlewell** N York
101 L3 **Ketton** Rutlnd
50 F4 **Kew** Gt Lon
44 C6 **Kewstoke** N Som
141 M6 **Kexbrough** Barns
151 L5 **Kexby** C York
135 H3 **Kexby** Lincs
131 H7 **Key Green** Ches E
162 D2 **Key Green** N York
100 E2 **Keyham** Leics
18 D5 **Keyhaven** Hants
145 H3 **Keyingham** E R Yk
22 D4 **Keymer** W Susx
45 K5 **Keynsham** BaNES
86 B3 **Keysoe** Bed
86 B3 **Keysoe Row** Bed
102 A8 **Keyston** Cambs
53 J6 **Key Street** Kent
117 G5 **Keyworth** Notts
30 B6 **Kibbear** Somset
181 G7 **Kibblesworth** Gatesd
100 F4 **Kibworth Beauchamp** Leics
100 F4 **Kibworth Harcourt** Leics
51 L4 **Kidbrooke** Gt Lon
164 E6 **Kidburngill** Cumb
97 J2 **Kiddemore Green** Staffs
97 J8 **Kidderminster** Worcs
66 B3 **Kiddington** Oxon
106 D4 **Kidd's Moor** Norfk
66 D4 **Kidlington** Oxon
49 G3 **Kidmore End** Oxon
174 C7 **Kidsdale** D & G
131 G8 **Kidsgrove** Staffs
159 G6 **Kidstones** N York
56 D3 **Kidwelly** Carmth
228 D7 **Kiel Crofts** Ag & B
189 H7 **Kielder** Nthumb
204 F3 **Kiells** Ag & B
208 C6 **Kilbarchan** Rens
247 K7 **Kilbeg** Highld
206 A6 **Kilberry** Ag & B
208 A8 **Kilbirnie** N Ayrs
207 G5 **Kilbride** Ag & B

215 L8 **Kilbride** Ag & B
216 C2 **Kilbride** Ag & B
266 B4 **Kilbuiack** Moray
116 C2 **Kilburn** Derbys
51 H2 **Kilburn** Gt Lon
161 H6 **Kilburn** N York
100 D4 **Kilby** Leics
206 D6 **Kilchamaig** Ag & B
207 H8 **Kilchattan** Ag & B
214 D5 **Kilchattan** Ag & B
228 C7 **Kilcheran** Ag & B
236 F7 **Kilchoan** Highld
204 B4 **Kilchoman** Ag & B
217 G3 **Kilchrenan** Ag & B
223 H6 **Kilconquhar** Fife
63 K2 **Kilcot** Gloucs
251 G2 **Kilcoy** Highld
207 L3 **Kilcreggan** Ag & B
161 K1 **Kildale** N York
192 F4 **Kildalloig** Ag & B
263 K5 **Kildary** Highld
206 F6 **Kildavaig** Ag & B
207 G5 **Kildavanan** Ag & B
274 B4 **Kildonan** Highld
195 G6 **Kildonan** N Ayrs
274 B4 **Kildonan Lodge** Highld
236 F3 **Kildonnan** Highld
172 D4 **Kildrochet House** D & G
255 J8 **Kildrummy** Abers
149 H6 **Kildwick** N York
206 E3 **Kilfinan** Ag & B
239 M4 **Kilfinnan** Highld
128 C6 **Kilford** Denbgs
55 K5 **Kilgetty** Pembks
183 G3 **Kilgrammie** S Ayrs
62 F7 **Kilgwrrwg Common** Mons
153 G3 **Kilham** E R Yk
202 D6 **Kilham** Nthumb
224 B6 **Kilkenneth** Ag & B
192 D3 **Kilkenzie** Ag & B
192 E4 **Kilkerran** Ag & B
26 D8 **Kilkhampton** Cnwll
133 J3 **Killamarsh** Derbys
57 H6 **Killay** Swans
208 E2 **Killearn** Stirlg
263 J8 **Killen** Highld
169 G6 **Killerby** Darltn
14 A2 **Killerton** Devon
231 G4 **Killichonan** P & K
239 L7 **Killiechonate** Highld
227 G4 **Killiechronan** Ag & B
232 D3 **Killiecrankie** P & K
248 F5 **Killilan** Highld
280 D5 **Killimster** Highld
231 G8 **Killin** Stirlg
150 C4 **Killinghall** N York
157 K5 **Killington** Cumb
28 B2 **Killington** Devon
181 G5 **Killingworth** N Tyne
4 C6 **Killiow** Cnwll
200 F4 **Killochyett** Border
208 B5 **Kilmacolm** Inver
219 K5 **Kilmahog** Stirlg
216 B8 **Kilmahumaig** Ag & B
259 G2 **Kilmaluag** Highld
222 F3 **Kilmany** Fife
196 E3 **Kilmarnock** E Ayrs
216 C7 **Kilmartin** Ag & B
196 E3 **Kilmaurs** E Ayrs
216 C4 **Kilmelford** Ag & B
45 K8 **Kilmersdon** Somset
35 J5 **Kilmeston** Hants
192 E4 **Kilmichael** Ag & B
216 D8 **Kilmichael Glassary** Ag & B
206 B2 **Kilmichael of Inverlussa** Ag & B
15 G3 **Kilmington** Devon
32 C3 **Kilmington** Wilts
32 C4 **Kilmington Common** Wilts
32 C4 **Kilmington Street** Wilts
250 E3 **Kilmorack** Highld
216 D2 **Kilmore** Ag & B
247 K7 **Kilmore** Highld
205 M2 **Kilmory** Ag & B
237 G6 **Kilmory** Highld
193 K4 **Kilmory** N Ayrs
251 J2 **Kilmuir** Highld
258 D7 **Kilmuir** Highld
258 F3 **Kilmuir** Highld
263 K5 **Kilmuir** Highld
207 K3 **Kilmun** Ag & B
204 D2 **Kilnave** Ag & B
198 E3 **Kilncadzow** S Lans
39 H6 **Kilndown** Kent
49 K3 **Kiln Green** Wokham
165 H4 **Kilnhill** Cumb
130 C6 **Kilnhouses** Ches W
142 C8 **Kilnhurst** Rothm
216 C3 **Kilninver** Ag & B
180 C7 **Kiln Pit Hill** Nthumb
145 L4 **Kilnsea** E R Yk

| | | |
|---|---|---|
| 149 H2 | **Kilnsey** N York |
| 152 F6 | **Kilnwick** E R Yk |
| 152 C6 | **Kilnwick Percy** E R Yk |
| 214 D5 | **Kiloran** Ag & B |
| 194 D5 | **Kilpatrick** N Ayrs |
| 62 F1 | **Kilpeck** Herefs |
| 143 K2 | **Kilpin** E R Yk |
| 143 J2 | **Kilpin Pike** E R Yk |
| 223 K6 | **Kilrenny** Fife |
| 84 A1 | **Kilsby** Nhants |
| 222 C2 | **Kilspindie** P & K |
| 172 E7 | **Kilstay** D & G |
| 209 J3 | **Kilsyth** N Lans |
| 250 E3 | **Kiltarlity** Highld |
| 171 G7 | **Kilton** R & Cl |
| 171 G7 | **Kilton Thorpe** R & Cl |
| 258 F3 | **Kilvaxter** Highld |
| 29 L2 | **Kilve** Somset |
| 117 L3 | **Kilvington** Notts |
| 196 B2 | **Kilwinning** N Ayrs |
| 106 B3 | **Kimberley** Norfk |
| 116 E3 | **Kimberley** Notts |
| 133 H1 | **Kimberworth** Rothm |
| 169 H1 | **Kimblesworth** Dur |
| 67 J5 | **Kimble Wick** Bucks |
| 86 B2 | **Kimbolton** Cambs |
| 80 C3 | **Kimbolton** Herefs |
| 100 D6 | **Kimcote** Leics |
| 17 H6 | **Kimmeridge** Dorset |
| 202 E6 | **Kimmerston** Nthumb |
| 34 C2 | **Kimpton** Hants |
| 68 F3 | **Kimpton** Herts |
| 26 E8 | **Kimworthy** Devon |
| 273 L2 | **Kinbrace** Highld |
| 220 D6 | **Kinbuck** Stirlg |
| 223 H3 | **Kincaple** Fife |
| 210 B2 | **Kincardine** Fife |
| 263 G2 | **Kincardine** Highld |
| 244 D4 | **Kincardine O'Neil** Abers |
| 233 H7 | **Kinclaven** P & K |
| 245 L3 | **Kincorth** C Aber |
| 265 G7 | **Kincorth House** Moray |
| 241 M2 | **Kincraig** Highld |
| 232 E5 | **Kincraigie** P & K |
| 232 E5 | **Kindallachan** P & K |
| 205 L5 | **Kinerarach** Ag & B |
| 65 G2 | **Kineton** Gloucs |
| 83 H5 | **Kineton** Warwks |
| 222 B3 | **Kinfauns** P & K |
| 207 H7 | **Kingarth** Ag & B |
| 245 J3 | **Kingcausie** Abers |
| 62 E6 | **Kingcoed** Mons |
| 135 L1 | **Kingerby** Lincs |
| 11 K1 | **Kingford** Devon |
| 65 K2 | **Kingham** Oxon |
| 176 C4 | **Kingholm Quay** D & G |
| 211 J2 | **Kinghorn** Fife |
| 222 C7 | **Kinglassie** Fife |
| 233 M4 | **Kingoldrum** Angus |
| 222 F1 | **Kingoodie** P & K |
| 80 B7 | **King's Acre** Herefs |
| 6 E5 | **Kingsand** Cnwll |
| 67 L6 | **Kingsash** Bucks |
| 223 K5 | **Kingsbarns** Fife |
| 7 L6 | **Kingsbridge** Devon |
| 29 H3 | **Kingsbridge** Somset |
| 57 G5 | **Kings Bridge** Swans |
| 115 J8 | **King's Bromley** Staffs |
| 258 F5 | **Kingsburgh** Highld |
| 51 G1 | **Kingsbury** Gt Lon |
| 99 G4 | **Kingsbury** Warwks |
| 31 G6 | **Kingsbury Episcopi** Somset |
| 63 H2 | **King's Caple** Herefs |
| 48 D7 | **Kingsclere** Hants |
| 101 M4 | **King's Cliffe** Nhants |
| 64 B7 | **Kingscote** Gloucs |
| 27 K7 | **Kingscott** Devon |
| 82 C3 | **King's Coughton** Warwks |
| 195 G5 | **Kingscross** N Ayrs |
| 31 H5 | **Kingsdon** Somset |
| 41 L5 | **Kingsdown** Kent |
| 47 H1 | **Kingsdown** Swindn |
| 46 A5 | **Kingsdown** Wilts |
| 47 H1 | **Kingsdown Crematorium** Swindn |
| 210 F1 | **Kingseat** Fife |
| 67 H6 | **Kingsey** Bucks |
| 37 J4 | **Kingsfold** W Susx |
| 245 J2 | **Kingsford** C Aber |
| 196 E2 | **Kingsford** E Ayrs |
| 97 J7 | **Kingsford** Worcs |
| 41 L1 | **Kingsgate** Kent |
| 81 H8 | **Kings Green** Gloucs |
| 89 J3 | **Kingshall Street** Suffk |
| 27 K3 | **Kingsheanton** Devon |
| 98 D7 | **King's Heath** Birm |
| 39 H2 | **Kings Hill** Kent |
| 98 C4 | **King's Hill** Wsall |
| 229 L4 | **Kings House Hotel** Highld |
| 219 J3 | **Kingshouse Hotel** Stirlg |

| | | |
|---|---|---|
| 98 F5 | **Kingshurst** Solhll |
| 177 G8 | **Kingside Hill** Cumb |
| 8 C1 | **Kingskerswell** Devon |
| 222 E5 | **Kingskettle** Fife |
| 15 K3 | **Kingsland** Dorset |
| 80 B3 | **Kingsland** Herefs |
| 124 D3 | **Kingsland** IoA |
| 68 D6 | **Kings Langley** Herts |
| 130 A5 | **Kingsley** Ches W |
| 36 B3 | **Kingsley** Hants |
| 115 G2 | **Kingsley** Staffs |
| 36 D5 | **Kingsley Green** W Susx |
| 84 E3 | **Kingsley Park** Nhants |
| 97 H4 | **Kingslow** Shrops |
| 120 D7 | **King's Lynn** Norfk |
| 166 E6 | **Kings Meaburn** Cumb |
| 35 J8 | **Kingsmead** Hants |
| 9 i3 | **King's Mills** Guern |
| 139 G7 | **King's Moss** St Hel |
| 234 D5 | **Kingsmuir** Angus |
| 200 B5 | **Kings Muir** Border |
| 223 J5 | **Kingsmuir** Fife |
| 99 M7 | **Kings Newnham** Warwks |
| 116 C6 | **King's Newton** Derbys |
| 40 C7 | **Kingsnorth** Kent |
| 98 D7 | **King's Norton** Birm |
| 100 F3 | **King's Norton** Leics |
| 28 B7 | **King's Nympton** Devon |
| 80 B5 | **King's Pyon** Herefs |
| 102 F8 | **Kings Ripton** Cambs |
| 34 D4 | **King's Somborne** Hants |
| 32 B8 | **King's Stag** Dorset |
| 64 A6 | **King's Stanley** Gloucs |
| 83 L8 | **King's Sutton** Nhants |
| 98 D4 | **Kingstanding** Birm |
| 13 K7 | **Kingsteignton** Devon |
| 132 B5 | **King Sterndale** Derbys |
| 63 G1 | **Kingsthorne** Herefs |
| 84 E3 | **Kingsthorpe** Nhants |
| 87 G4 | **Kingston** Cambs |
| 11 L7 | **Kingston** Cnwll |
| 7 J5 | **Kingston** Devon |
| 14 C5 | **Kingston** Devon |
| 16 E1 | **Kingston** Dorset |
| 17 J6 | **Kingston** Dorset |
| 212 C3 | **Kingston** E Loth |
| 18 A3 | **Kingston** Hants |
| 19 H7 | **Kingston** IoW |
| 41 G5 | **Kingston** Kent |
| 21 J6 | **Kingston** W Susx |
| 66 B7 | **Kingston Bagpuize** Oxon |
| 67 H7 | **Kingston Blount** Oxon |
| 32 D3 | **Kingston Deverill** Wilts |
| 80 A8 | **Kingstone** Herefs |
| 30 E8 | **Kingstone** Somset |
| 115 H5 | **Kingstone** Staffs |
| 47 K2 | **Kingstone Winslow** Oxon |
| 47 L2 | **Kingston Lisle** Oxon |
| 22 F5 | **Kingston near Lewes** E Susx |
| 116 E6 | **Kingston on Soar** Notts |
| 267 G3 | **Kingston on Spey** Moray |
| 16 A4 | **Kingston Russell** Dorset |
| 30 B5 | **Kingston St Mary** Somset |
| 44 E5 | **Kingston Seymour** N Som |
| 67 H7 | **Kingston Stert** Oxon |
| 144 D2 | **Kingston upon Hull** C KuH |
| 50 F5 | **Kingston upon Thames** Gt Lon |
| 51 G5 | **Kingston upon Thames Crematorium** Gt Lon |
| 177 L7 | **Kingstown** Cumb |
| 68 F2 | **King's Walden** Herts |
| 8 C4 | **Kingswear** Devon |
| 245 J2 | **Kingswells** C Aber |
| 45 G3 | **Kings Weston** Bristl |
| 97 K5 | **Kingswinford** Dudley |
| 67 G3 | **Kingswood** Bucks |
| 63 L8 | **Kingswood** Gloucs |
| 39 L3 | **Kingswood** Kent |
| 94 F3 | **Kingswood** Powys |
| 45 J4 | **Kingswood** S Glos |
| 29 K3 | **Kingswood** Somset |
| 51 H7 | **Kingswood** Surrey |
| 82 E1 | **Kingswood** Warwks |
| 82 E1 | **Kingswood Brook** Warwks |
| 79 K4 | **Kingswood Common** Herefs |
| 97 J3 | **Kingswood Common** Staffs |
| 35 G4 | **Kings Worthy** Hants |
| 136 B4 | **Kingthorpe** Lincs |
| 79 K4 | **Kington** Herefs |
| 45 J1 | **Kington** S Glos |
| 82 A4 | **Kington** Worcs |
| 46 D3 | **Kington Langley** Wilts |
| 32 C6 | **Kington Magna** Dorset |
| 46 C3 | **Kington St Michael** Wilts |
| 241 K3 | **Kingussie** Highld |
| 31 H5 | **Kingweston** Somset |
| 257 G5 | **Kinharrachie** Abers |
| 176 B5 | **Kinharvie** D & G |
| 221 G4 | **Kinkell Bridge** P & K |
| 257 J3 | **Kinknockie** Abers |

| | | |
|---|---|---|
| 211 G5 | **Kinleith** C Edin |
| 97 G7 | **Kinlet** Shrops |
| 246 E8 | **Kinloch** Highld |
| 271 K1 | **Kinloch** Highld |
| 277 J5 | **Kinloch** Highld |
| 233 H6 | **Kinloch** P & K |
| 233 L6 | **Kinloch** P & K |
| 219 G6 | **Kinlochard** Stirlg |
| 276 C5 | **Kinlochbervie** Highld |
| 238 F7 | **Kinlocheil** Highld |
| 261 G7 | **Kinlochewe** Highld |
| 238 F2 | **Kinloch Hourn** Highld |
| 240 F5 | **Kinlochlaggan** Highld |
| 229 K3 | **Kinlochleven** Highld |
| 237 K6 | **Kinlochmoidart** Highld |
| 237 L4 | **Kinlochnanuagh** Highld |
| 231 J4 | **Kinloch Rannoch** P & K |
| 265 H7 | **Kinloss** Moray |
| 127 K4 | **Kinmel Bay** Conwy |
| 256 E7 | **Kinmuck** Abers |
| 256 F8 | **Kinmundy** Abers |
| 204 D7 | **Kinnabus** Ag & B |
| 257 H3 | **Kinnadie** Abers |
| 232 E4 | **Kinnaird** P & K |
| 235 G4 | **Kinnaird Castle** Angus |
| 266 E2 | **Kinneddar** Moray |
| 245 J8 | **Kinneff** Abers |
| 186 F6 | **Kinnelhead** D & G |
| 234 F5 | **Kinnell** Angus |
| 112 E7 | **Kinnerley** Shrops |
| 79 L5 | **Kinnersley** Herefs |
| 81 K6 | **Kinnersley** Worcs |
| 79 J3 | **Kinnerton** Powys |
| 95 J4 | **Kinnerton** Shrops |
| 129 H7 | **Kinnerton Green** Flints |
| 222 B6 | **Kinnesswood** P & K |
| 168 D6 | **Kinninvie** Dur |
| 234 B4 | **Kinnordy** Angus |
| 117 H5 | **Kinoulton** Notts |
| 221 K6 | **Kinross** P & K |
| 222 C1 | **Kinrossie** P & K |
| 68 E4 | **Kinsbourne Green** Herts |
| 113 L3 | **Kinsey Heath** Ches E |
| 79 L2 | **Kinsham** Herefs |
| 81 L8 | **Kinsham** Worcs |
| 142 C5 | **Kinsley** Wakefd |
| 17 L3 | **Kinson** Bmouth |
| 48 A5 | **Kintbury** W Berk |
| 264 F7 | **Kintessack** Moray |
| 221 L4 | **Kintillo** P & K |
| 95 K8 | **Kinton** Herefs |
| 112 E7 | **Kinton** Shrops |
| 256 E8 | **Kintore** Abers |
| 205 G6 | **Kintour** Ag & B |
| 204 D6 | **Kintra** Ag & B |
| 226 C7 | **Kintra** Ag & B |
| 216 C6 | **Kintraw** Ag & B |
| 253 G7 | **Kinveachy** Highld |
| 97 J6 | **Kinver** Staffs |
| 160 C3 | **Kiplin** N York |
| 142 C2 | **Kippax** Leeds |
| 219 L8 | **Kippen** Stirlg |
| 175 L4 | **Kippford or Scaur** D & G |
| 39 G5 | **Kipping's Cross** Kent |
| 275 c5 | **Kirbister** Ork |
| 106 F2 | **Kirby Bedon** Norfk |
| 117 J7 | **Kirby Bellars** Leics |
| 107 H5 | **Kirby Cane** Norfk |
| 99 J8 | **Kirby Corner** Covtry |
| 73 J3 | **Kirby Cross** Essex |
| 100 B3 | **Kirby Fields** Leics |
| 152 D2 | **Kirby Grindalythe** N York |
| 150 E2 | **Kirby Hill** N York |
| 159 L2 | **Kirby Hill** N York |
| 161 G5 | **Kirby Knowle** N York |
| 73 J3 | **Kirby le Soken** Essex |
| 162 D6 | **Kirby Misperton** N York |
| 100 B3 | **Kirby Muxloe** Leics |
| 160 F4 | **Kirby Sigston** N York |
| 152 B4 | **Kirby Underdale** E R Yk |
| 160 E5 | **Kirby Wiske** N York |
| 36 F5 | **Kirdford** W Susx |
| 280 C4 | **Kirk** Highld |
| 281 e7 | **Kirkabister** Shet |
| 174 F5 | **Kirkandrews** D & G |
| 177 K7 | **Kirkandrews upon Eden** Cumb |
| 177 J7 | **Kirkbampton** Cumb |
| 176 C7 | **Kirkbean** D & G |
| 143 G5 | **Kirk Bramwith** Donc |
| 177 H7 | **Kirkbride** Cumb |
| 160 C4 | **Kirkbridge** N York |
| 234 D6 | **Kirkbuddo** Angus |
| 200 C5 | **Kirkburn** Border |
| 152 F5 | **Kirkburn** E R Yk |
| 141 K5 | **Kirkburton** Kirk |
| 138 E7 | **Kirkby** Knows |
| 135 L1 | **Kirkby** Lincs |
| 161 H2 | **Kirkby** N York |
| 160 D4 | **Kirkby Fleetham** N York |
| 136 A8 | **Kirkby Green** Lincs |

| | | |
|---|---|---|
| 160 C3 | **Kirkby Hall** N York |
| 133 K8 | **Kirkby in Ashfield** Notts |
| 156 B6 | **Kirkby-in-Furness** Cumb |
| 118 E2 | **Kirkby la Thorpe** Lincs |
| 157 K7 | **Kirkby Lonsdale** Cumb |
| 148 F4 | **Kirkby Malham** N York |
| 99 M3 | **Kirkby Mallory** Leics |
| 160 C7 | **Kirkby Malzeard** N York |
| 162 C5 | **Kirkby Mills** N York |
| 162 B5 | **Kirkbymoorside** N York |
| 136 D7 | **Kirkby on Bain** Lincs |
| 150 D6 | **Kirkby Overblow** N York |
| 158 D1 | **Kirkby Stephen** Cumb |
| 166 E5 | **Kirkby Thore** Cumb |
| 118 E6 | **Kirkby Underwood** Lincs |
| 151 H7 | **Kirkby Wharf** N York |
| 116 E1 | **Kirkby Woodhouse** Notts |
| 211 J1 | **Kirkcaldy** Fife |
| 222 D8 | **Kirkcaldy Crematorium** Fife |
| 178 C5 | **Kirkcambeck** Cumb |
| 175 G4 | **Kirkchrist** D & G |
| 172 C1 | **Kirkcolm** D & G |
| 197 L8 | **Kirkconnel** D & G |
| 175 G3 | **Kirkconnell** D & G |
| 176 C5 | **Kirkconnell** D & G |
| 173 J3 | **Kirkcowan** D & G |
| 175 H5 | **Kirkcudbright** D & G |
| 129 H1 | **Kirkdale** Lpool |
| 150 F5 | **Kirk Deighton** N York |
| 144 C2 | **Kirk Ella** E R Yk |
| 198 E4 | **Kirkfieldbank** S Lans |
| 175 L2 | **Kirkgunzeon** D & G |
| 116 D3 | **Kirk Hallam** Derbys |
| 138 E1 | **Kirkham** Lancs |
| 151 M3 | **Kirkham** N York |
| 141 L3 | **Kirkhamgate** Wakefd |
| 151 G5 | **Kirk Hammerton** N York |
| 180 B2 | **Kirkharle** Nthumb |
| 167 G1 | **Kirkhaugh** Nthumb |
| 141 J4 | **Kirkheaton** Kirk |
| 180 B3 | **Kirkheaton** Nthumb |
| 250 F3 | **Kirkhill** Highld |
| 186 E5 | **Kirkhope** S Lans |
| 178 D7 | **Kirkhouse** Cumb |
| 143 G5 | **Kirkhouse Green** Donc |
| 247 H5 | **Kirkibost** Highld |
| 233 L6 | **Kirkinch** P & K |
| 174 C4 | **Kirkinner** D & G |
| 209 H4 | **Kirkintilloch** E Duns |
| 115 M2 | **Kirk Ireton** Derbys |
| 164 E7 | **Kirkland** Cumb |
| 166 F4 | **Kirkland** Cumb |
| 185 K5 | **Kirkland** D & G |
| 186 F8 | **Kirkland** D & G |
| 197 L8 | **Kirkland** D & G |
| 165 G3 | **Kirkland Guards** Cumb |
| 115 M4 | **Kirk Langley** Derbys |
| 170 E6 | **Kirkleatham** R & Cl |
| 160 F1 | **Kirklevington** S on T |
| 107 L5 | **Kirkley** Suffk |
| 160 D6 | **Kirklington** N York |
| 134 D8 | **Kirklington** Notts |
| 178 B5 | **Kirklinton** Cumb |
| 210 F4 | **Kirkliston** C Edin |
| 174 D4 | **Kirkmabreck** D & G |
| 172 E7 | **Kirkmaiden** D & G |
| 169 H4 | **Kirk Merrington** Dur |
| 154 d4 | **Kirk Michael** IoM |
| 233 G3 | **Kirkmichael** P & K |
| 183 J1 | **Kirkmichael** S Ayrs |
| 198 C4 | **Kirkmuirhill** S Lans |
| 202 E7 | **Kirknewton** Nthumb |
| 210 F5 | **Kirknewton** W Loth |
| 255 K5 | **Kirkney** Abers |
| 209 M6 | **Kirk of Shotts** N Lans |
| 166 D3 | **Kirkoswald** Cumb |
| 183 G2 | **Kirkoswald** S Ayrs |
| 186 D8 | **Kirkpatrick** D & G |
| 175 K1 | **Kirkpatrick Durham** D & G |
| 177 J5 | **Kirkpatrick-Fleming** D & G |
| 142 F6 | **Kirk Sandall** Donc |
| 155 L6 | **Kirksanton** Cumb |
| 142 E4 | **Kirk Smeaton** N York |
| 150 C8 | **Kirkstall** Leeds |
| 136 C7 | **Kirkstead** Lincs |
| 255 L5 | **Kirkstile** Abers |
| 188 C8 | **Kirkstile** D & G |
| 156 F1 | **Kirkstone Pass Inn** Cumb |
| 280 D2 | **Kirkstyle** Highld |
| 142 B3 | **Kirkthorpe** Wakefd |
| 256 B6 | **Kirkton** Abers |
| 176 C3 | **Kirkton** D & G |
| 222 F2 | **Kirkton** Fife |
| 248 C6 | **Kirkton** Highld |
| 248 E3 | **Kirkton** Highld |
| 221 G3 | **Kirkton** P & K |
| 200 B5 | **Kirkton Manor** Border |
| 233 M5 | **Kirkton of Airlie** Angus |
| 234 A7 | **Kirkton of Auchterhouse** Angus |
| 252 F2 | **Kirkton of Barevan** Highld |

222 C1 **Kirkton of Collace** P & K
255 H8 **Kirkton of Glenbuchat** Abers
257 H6 **Kirkton of Logie Buchan** Abers
234 E3 **Kirkton of Menmuir** Angus
234 D7 **Kirkton of Monikie** Angus
256 C5 **Kirkton of Rayne** Abers
245 H2 **Kirkton of Skene** Abers
234 B8 **Kirkton of Strathmartine** Angus
234 B7 **Kirkton of Tealing** Angus
244 D1 **Kirkton of Tough** Abers
269 J3 **Kirktown** Abers
269 K6 **Kirktown** Abers
268 B4 **Kirktown of Alvah** Abers
256 E6 **Kirktown of Bourtie** Abers
245 J6 **Kirktown of Fetteresso** Abers
254 F4 **Kirktown of Mortlach** Moray
257 J6 **Kirktown of Slains** Abers
199 K4 **Kirkurd** Border
275 c4 **Kirkwall** Ork
180 B2 **Kirkwhelpington** Nthumb
202 C7 **Kirk Yetholm** Border
144 E5 **Kirmington** N Linc
136 C1 **Kirmond le Mire** Lincs
207 K3 **Kirn** Ag & B
234 B4 **Kirriemuir** Angus
106 F4 **Kirstead Green** Norfk
177 H4 **Kirtlebridge** D & G
88 D4 **Kirtling** Cambs
88 D4 **Kirtling Green** Cambs
66 D3 **Kirtlington** Oxon
278 C3 **Kirtomy** Highld
119 J4 **Kirton** Lincs
134 D6 **Kirton** Notts
91 G7 **Kirton** Suffk
119 J3 **Kirton End** Lincs
208 C4 **Kirtonhill** W Duns
119 J3 **Kirton Holme** Lincs
144 A8 **Kirton in Lindsey** N Linc
173 K4 **Kirwaugh** D & G
248 D4 **Kishorn** Highld
84 D3 **Kislingbury** Nhants
65 K1 **Kitebrook** Warwks
82 E2 **Kite Green** Warwks
83 L2 **Kites Hardwick** Warwks
11 J3 **Kitleigh** Cnwll
139 H6 **Kitt Green** Wigan
29 K6 **Kittisford** Somset
57 G7 **Kittle** Swans
98 F6 **Kitt's Green** Birm
245 K2 **Kittybrewster** C Aber
35 K4 **Kitwood** Hants
62 F1 **Kivernoll** Herefs
133 K3 **Kiveton Park** Rothm
135 G3 **Knaith** Lincs
135 G3 **Knaith Park** Lincs
32 D6 **Knap Corner** Dorset
50 B7 **Knaphill** Surrey
30 D5 **Knapp** Somset
34 E6 **Knapp Hill** Hants
134 E7 **Knapthorpe** Notts
151 J5 **Knapton** C York
162 F7 **Knapton** N York
122 F5 **Knapton** Norfk
80 B5 **Knapton Green** Herefs
87 G3 **Knapwell** Cambs
150 E4 **Knaresborough** N York
178 F8 **Knarsdale** Nthumb
257 G3 **Knaven** Abers
160 F5 **Knayton** N York
69 H3 **Knebworth** Herts
143 J2 **Knedlington** E R Yk
134 D6 **Kneesall** Notts
87 G6 **Kneesworth** Cambs
117 J2 **Kneeton** Notts
56 E7 **Knelston** Swans
114 E4 **Knenhall** Staffs
105 K7 **Knettishall** Suffk
28 B3 **Knightacott** Devon
83 J4 **Knightcote** Warwks
114 C6 **Knightley** Staffs
114 C6 **Knightley Dale** Staffs
100 D3 **Knighton** C Leic
7 G5 **Knighton** Devon
31 K8 **Knighton** Dorset
17 L3 **Knighton** Poole
79 K1 **Knighton** Powys
30 B2 **Knighton** Somset
114 A3 **Knighton** Staffs
114 B6 **Knighton** Staffs
47 L4 **Knighton** Wilts
80 E1 **Knighton on Teme** Worcs
64 C2 **Knightsbridge** Gloucs
10 F6 **Knightsmill** Cnwll
81 G4 **Knightwick** Worcs
79 K3 **Knill** Herefs
117 L5 **Knipton** Leics
168 E1 **Knitsley** Dur
115 K2 **Kniveton** Derbys
166 F5 **Knock** Cumb
247 L6 **Knock** Highld

267 L5 **Knock** Moray
282 g3 **Knock** W Isls
274 F2 **Knockally** Highld
271 H6 **Knockan** Highld
254 D3 **Knockando** Moray
250 F3 **Knockbain** Highld
263 H8 **Knockbain** Highld
207 K6 **Knock Castle** N Ayrs
279 L4 **Knockdee** Highld
207 J5 **Knockdow** Ag & B
46 B1 **Knockdown** Wilts
183 H4 **Knockeen** S Ayrs
195 G5 **Knockenkelly** N Ayrs
196 D3 **Knockentiber** E Ayrs
52 C4 **Knockhall** Kent
51 M7 **Knockholt** Kent
52 A7 **Knockholt Pound** Kent
112 E7 **Knockin** Shrops
196 E3 **Knockinlaw** E Ayrs
52 C6 **Knockmill** Kent
172 B2 **Knocknain** D & G
205 J2 **Knockrome** Ag & B
154 c5 **Knocksharry** IoM
184 F6 **Knocksheen** D & G
175 J1 **Knockvennie Smithy** D & G
91 K3 **Knodishall** Suffk
91 K3 **Knodishall Common** Suffk
31 G6 **Knole** Somset
45 H2 **Knole Park** S Glos
130 F4 **Knolls Green** Ches E
112 F4 **Knolton** Wrexhm
32 F3 **Knook** Wilts
101 H2 **Knossington** Leics
147 G6 **Knott End-on-Sea** Lancs
85 K3 **Knotting** Bed
85 K3 **Knotting Green** Bed
142 D3 **Knottingley** Wakefd
129 J1 **Knotty Ash** Lpool
68 B8 **Knotty Green** Bucks
96 D8 **Knowbury** Shrops
183 H8 **Knowe** D & G
184 F5 **Knowehead** D & G
195 L8 **Knoweside** S Ayrs
45 J5 **Knowle** Bristl
13 H2 **Knowle** Devon
14 B1 **Knowle** Devon
14 B6 **Knowle** Devon
27 J3 **Knowle** Devon
96 D8 **Knowle** Shrops
98 F8 **Knowle** Solhll
29 H2 **Knowle** Somset
14 B3 **Knowle Cross** Devon
177 L7 **Knowlefield** Cumb
148 A8 **Knowle Green** Lancs
50 C5 **Knowle Hill** Surrey
30 E8 **Knowle St Giles** Somset
19 J2 **Knowle Village** Hants
88 F7 **Knowl Green** Essex
49 K3 **Knowl Hill** W & M
17 K1 **Knowlton** Dorset
41 J4 **Knowlton** Kent
138 E8 **Knowsley** Knows
28 E6 **Knowstone** Devon
150 C4 **Knox** N York
39 K5 **Knox Bridge** Kent
95 G8 **Knucklas** Powys
85 H2 **Knuston** Nhants
130 E4 **Knutsford** Ches E
114 C2 **Knutton** Staffs
141 G4 **Krumlin** Calder
3 J7 **Kuggar** Cnwll
248 B6 **Kyleakin** Highld
248 B6 **Kyle of Lochalsh** Highld
248 C7 **Kylerhea** Highld
271 H1 **Kylesku** Highld
238 C5 **Kylesmorar** Highld
282 f6 **Kyles Scalpay** W Isls
271 H1 **Kylestrome** Highld
80 E8 **Kynaston** Herefs
112 E7 **Kynaston** Shrops
113 L8 **Kynnersley** Wrekin
80 E3 **Kyre Green** Worcs
80 E3 **Kyre Park** Worcs
80 E2 **Kyrewood** Worcs
29 J6 **Kyrle** Somset

**L**

9 j3 **La Bellieuse** Guern
282 f4 **Lacasaigh** W Isls
282 g3 **Lacasdal** W Isls
145 G6 **Laceby** NE Lin
67 K7 **Lacey Green** Bucks
130 D5 **Lach Dennis** Ches W
170 D6 **Lackenby** R & Cl
88 F1 **Lackford** Suffk
88 F1 **Lackford Green** Suffk
46 C5 **Lacock** Wilts
83 K3 **Ladbroke** Warwks

114 F1 **Ladderedge** Staffs
39 H4 **Laddingford** Kent
119 L1 **Lade Bank** Lincs
4 E5 **Ladock** Cnwll
275 e2 **Lady** Ork
222 E5 **Ladybank** Fife
11 L5 **Ladycross** Cnwll
198 F7 **Ladygill** S Lans
156 B5 **Lady Hall** Cumb
202 D3 **Ladykirk** Border
63 H1 **Ladyridge** Herefs
88 E3 **Lady's Green** Suffk
98 D6 **Ladywood** Birm
81 K3 **Ladywood** Worcs
9 k1 **La Fontenelle** Guern
9 j4 **La Fosse** Guern
185 L5 **Lag** D & G
237 J8 **Laga** Highld
204 F7 **Lagavulin** Ag & B
193 K4 **Lagg** N Ayrs
240 A4 **Laggan** Highld
241 G5 **Laggan** Highld
9 k2 **La Greve** Guern
9 b1 **La Greve de Lecq** Jersey
9 e3 **La Hougue Bie** Jersey
9 h3 **La Houguette** Guern
277 G4 **Laid** Highld
260 E2 **Laide** Highld
236 F3 **Laig** Highld
196 F2 **Laigh Clunch** E Ayrs
196 F3 **Laigh Fenwick** E Ayrs
197 J7 **Laigh Glenmuir** E Ayrs
209 J8 **Laighstonehall** S Lans
52 E1 **Laindon** Essex
272 E6 **Lairg** Highld
141 J1 **Laisterdyke** C Brad
166 B4 **Laithes** Cumb
12 C4 **Lake** Devon
27 K4 **Lake** Devon
19 K7 **Lake** IoW
17 J4 **Lake** Poole
33 K3 **Lake** Wilts
104 E6 **Lakenheath** Suffk
103 L4 **Lakesend** Norfk
156 F5 **Lakeside** Cumb
50 D5 **Laleham** Surrey
42 C5 **Laleston** Brdgnd
199 L3 **Lamancha** Border
3 J5 **Lamanva** Cnwll
89 H8 **Lamarsh** Essex
122 E7 **Lamas** Norfk
202 A4 **Lambden** Border
39 H6 **Lamberhurst** Kent
39 G6 **Lamberhurst Down** Kent
213 L7 **Lamberton** Border
51 J3 **Lambeth** Gt Lon
51 H4 **Lambeth Crematorium** Gt Lon
88 E4 **Lambfair Green** Suffk
117 H2 **Lambley** Notts
178 F7 **Lambley** Nthumb
47 L3 **Lambourn** W Berk
70 C8 **Lambourne End** Essex
47 L4 **Lambourn Woodlands** W Berk
148 C8 **Lamb Roe** Lancs
37 K3 **Lambs Green** W Susx
54 E3 **Lambston** Pembks
6 A2 **Lamellion** Cnwll
12 B7 **Lamerton** Devon
181 G2 **Lamesley** Gatesd
199 G7 **Lamington** S Lans
195 G5 **Lamlash** N Ayrs
165 L3 **Lamonby** Cumb
5 H2 **Lamorick** Cnwll
2 C6 **Lamorna** Cnwll
4 E6 **Lamorran** Cnwll
5 L2 **Lampen** Cnwll
77 G5 **Lampeter** Cerdgn
55 K4 **Lampeter Velfrey** Pembks
55 G6 **Lamphey** Pembks
164 E6 **Lamplugh** Cumb
101 G8 **Lamport** Nhants
31 L4 **Lamyatt** Somset
11 K1 **Lana** Devon
11 L3 **Lana** Devon
198 E4 **Lanark** S Lans
147 J3 **Lancaster** Lancs
147 J3 **Lancaster & Morecambe Crematorium** Lancs
63 G7 **Lancaut** Gloucs
168 F1 **Lanchester** Dur
21 L6 **Lancing** W Susx
9 k1 **L'Ancresse** Guern
87 K2 **Landbeach** Cambs
27 H6 **Landcross** Devon
245 G3 **Landerberry** Abers
34 B7 **Landford** Wilts
275 G2 **Land-hallow** Highld
129 G3 **Landican Crematorium** Wirral
56 E6 **Landimore** Swans

27 L4 **Landkey** Devon
57 J5 **Landore** Swans
6 D3 **Landrake** Cnwll
7 M2 **Landscove** Devon
2 A6 **Land's End** Cnwll
55 G4 **Landshipping** Pembks
11 L6 **Landue** Cnwll
6 E3 **Landulph** Cnwll
88 C2 **Landwade** Suffk
4 D3 **Lane** Cnwll
11 J5 **Laneast** Cnwll
140 C1 **Lane Bottom** Lancs
49 K1 **Lane End** Bucks
5 H1 **Lane End** Cnwll
35 H5 **Lane End** Hants
52 C4 **Lane End** Kent
148 F6 **Lane End** Lancs
130 D2 **Lane End** Warrtn
32 D2 **Lane End** Wilts
115 L4 **Lane Ends** Derbys
140 B2 **Lane Ends** Lancs
149 H7 **Lane Ends** N York
155 K4 **Lane End Waberthwaite** Cumb
97 K3 **Lane Green** Staffs
134 F4 **Laneham** Notts
167 J2 **Lanehead** Dur
168 E8 **Lane Head** Dur
179 H2 **Lanehead** Nthumb
139 J8 **Lane Head** Wigan
98 B3 **Lane Head** Wsall
147 H7 **Lane Heads** Lancs
149 G7 **Laneshaw Bridge** Lancs
140 B3 **Lane Side** Lancs
12 A3 **Langaford** Devon
30 C5 **Langaller** Somset
117 J4 **Langar** Notts
208 C4 **Langbank** Rens
149 K5 **Langbar** N York
170 D8 **Langbaurgh** N York
148 E3 **Langcliffe** N York
163 G4 **Langdale End** N York
11 K4 **Langdon** Cnwll
167 K4 **Langdon Beck** Dur
19 G2 **Langdown** Hants
222 E6 **Langdyke** Fife
72 E3 **Langenhoe** Essex
86 D7 **Langford** C Beds
14 B2 **Langford** Devon
71 K5 **Langford** Essex
44 F6 **Langford** N Som
135 G7 **Langford** Notts
65 K6 **Langford** Oxon
29 K6 **Langford Budville** Somset
32 C5 **Langham** Dorset
72 F1 **Langham** Essex
121 M3 **Langham** Norfk
101 J1 **Langham** Rutlnd
89 K1 **Langham** Suffk
139 L1 **Langho** Lancs
177 L2 **Langholm** D & G
57 H7 **Langland** Swans
201 G6 **Langlee** Border
131 J5 **Langley** Ches E
116 D2 **Langley** Derbys
64 E2 **Langley** Gloucs
19 G3 **Langley** Hants
69 G3 **Langley** Herts
39 K3 **Langley** Kent
179 J6 **Langley** Nthumb
65 L4 **Langley** Oxon
140 C6 **Langley** Rochdl
50 C3 **Langley** Slough
29 K5 **Langley** Somset
36 B5 **Langley** W Susx
82 E3 **Langley** Warwks
46 D4 **Langley Burrell** Wilts
68 D7 **Langleybury** Herts
179 J6 **Langley Castle** Nthumb
115 M4 **Langley Common** Derbys
115 M4 **Langley Green** Derbys
72 C3 **Langley Green** Essex
82 E3 **Langley Green** Warwks
87 J8 **Langley Lower Green** Essex
29 K5 **Langley Marsh** Somset
116 D2 **Langley Mill** Derbys
169 H3 **Langley Moor** Dur
169 G2 **Langley Park** Dur
107 H3 **Langley Street** Norfk
87 J8 **Langley Upper Green** Essex
23 L6 **Langney** E Susx
134 B2 **Langold** Notts
11 K5 **Langore** Cnwll
30 F5 **Langport** Somset
119 J2 **Langrick** Lincs
45 L5 **Langridge** BaNES
27 K6 **Langridgeford** Devon
165 G2 **Langrigg** Cumb
35 L6 **Langrish** Hants
141 K7 **Langsett** Barns
220 D4 **Langside** P & K

| | | |
|---|---|---|
| 20 B6 | **Langstone** | Hants |
| 44 D1 | **Langstone** | Newpt |
| 160 C4 | **Langthorne** | N York |
| 150 E2 | **Langthorpe** | N York |
| 159 H2 | **Langthwaite** | N York |
| 152 F3 | **Langtoft** | E R Yk |
| 102 C1 | **Langtoft** | Lincs |
| 168 F6 | **Langton** | Dur |
| 136 D6 | **Langton** | Lincs |
| 137 G5 | **Langton** | Lincs |
| 152 B2 | **Langton** | N York |
| 136 C4 | **Langton by Wragby** | Lincs |
| 38 E5 | **Langton Green** | Kent |
| 106 C8 | **Langton Green** | Suffk |
| 16 B6 | **Langton Herring** | Dorset |
| 17 H1 | **Langton Long Blandford** | Dorset |
| 17 K6 | **Langton Matravers** | Dorset |
| 27 H7 | **Langtree** | Devon |
| 27 H7 | **Langtree Week** | Devon |
| 166 D4 | **Langwathby** | Cumb |
| 274 F3 | **Langwell House** | Highld |
| 133 K5 | **Langwith** | Derbys |
| 133 K6 | **Langwith Junction** | Derbys |
| 135 L4 | **Langworth** | Lincs |
| 12 C3 | **Langworthy** | Devon |
| 5 H2 | **Lanivet** | Cnwll |
| 5 G4 | **Lanjeth** | Cnwll |
| 10 F7 | **Lank** | Cnwll |
| 5 J3 | **Lanlivery** | Cnwll |
| 3 J3 | **Lanner** | Cnwll |
| 11 K7 | **Lanoy** | Cnwll |
| 5 L3 | **Lanreath** | Cnwll |
| 5 K4 | **Lansallos** | Cnwll |
| 10 F6 | **Lanteglos** | Cnwll |
| 5 K4 | **Lanteglos Highway** | Cnwll |
| 189 G2 | **Lanton** | Border |
| 202 E6 | **Lanton** | Nthumb |
| 9 j2 | **La Passee** | Guern |
| 13 G1 | **Lapford** | Devon |
| 204 F7 | **Laphroaig** | Ag & B |
| 97 K1 | **Lapley** | Staffs |
| 9 a3 | **La Pulente** | Jersey |
| 82 E1 | **Lapworth** | Warwks |
| 227 K3 | **Larachbeg** | Highld |
| 209 M3 | **Larbert** | Falk |
| 147 H7 | **Larbreck** | Lancs |
| 256 A5 | **Largie** | Abers |
| 206 E2 | **Largiemore** | Ag & B |
| 223 H5 | **Largoward** | Fife |
| 207 K7 | **Largs** | N Ayrs |
| 195 G6 | **Largybeg** | N Ayrs |
| 195 G6 | **Largymore** | N Ayrs |
| 14 C3 | **Larkbeare** | Devon |
| 207 L4 | **Larkfield** | Inver |
| 52 F7 | **Larkfield** | Kent |
| 198 C3 | **Larkhall** | S Lans |
| 33 K2 | **Larkhill** | Wilts |
| 105 K5 | **Larling** | Norfk |
| 9 f4 | **La Rocque** | Jersey |
| 9 j2 | **La Rousaillerie** | Guern |
| 168 C7 | **Lartington** | Dur |
| 64 B8 | **Lasborough** | Gloucs |
| 35 K2 | **Lasham** | Hants |
| 12 A1 | **Lashbrook** | Devon |
| 12 B1 | **Lashbrook** | Devon |
| 39 L5 | **Lashenden** | Kent |
| 131 H8 | **Lask Edge** | Staffs |
| 221 K8 | **Lassodie** | Fife |
| 211 J6 | **Lasswade** | Mdloth |
| 162 C4 | **Lastingham** | N York |
| 31 G2 | **Latcham** | Somset |
| 69 K3 | **Latchford** | Herts |
| 67 G6 | **Latchford** | Oxon |
| 72 C7 | **Latchingdon** | Essex |
| 12 A7 | **Latchley** | Cnwll |
| 139 K8 | **Lately Common** | Warrtn |
| 85 G6 | **Lathbury** | M Keyn |
| 275 G2 | **Latheron** | Highld |
| 275 G2 | **Latheronwheel** | Highld |
| 223 H5 | **Lathones** | Fife |
| 68 C7 | **Latimer** | Bucks |
| 45 K2 | **Latteridge** | S Glos |
| 32 B5 | **Lattiford** | Somset |
| 65 G7 | **Latton** | Wilts |
| 201 H4 | **Lauder** | Border |
| 56 B3 | **Laugharne** | Carmth |
| 135 G4 | **Laughterton** | Lincs |
| 23 H4 | **Laughton** | E Susx |
| 100 E5 | **Laughton** | Leics |
| 118 E5 | **Laughton** | Lincs |
| 143 L8 | **Laughton** | Lincs |
| 133 K2 | **Laughton-en-le-Morthen** | Rothm |
| 11 J1 | **Launcells** | Cnwll |
| 11 K1 | **Launcells Cross** | Cnwll |
| 11 L5 | **Launceston** | Cnwll |
| 66 F3 | **Launton** | Oxon |
| 235 H1 | **Laurencekirk** | Abers |
| 175 H2 | **Laurieston** | D & G |
| 210 B3 | **Laurieston** | Falk |
| 85 H4 | **Lavendon** | M Keyn |
| 89 J5 | **Lavenham** | Suffk |
| 43 J8 | **Lavernock** | V Glam |
| 178 B6 | **Laversdale** | Cumb |
| 33 L5 | **Laverstock** | Wilts |
| 35 G1 | **Laverstoke** | Hants |
| 82 C8 | **Laverton** | Gloucs |
| 160 B7 | **Laverton** | N York |
| 45 M8 | **Laverton** | Somset |
| 9 j3 | **La Villette** | Guern |
| 129 J8 | **Lavister** | Wrexhm |
| 209 L8 | **Law** | S Lans |
| 231 J7 | **Lawers** | P & K |
| 73 G1 | **Lawford** | Essex |
| 29 L4 | **Lawford** | Somset |
| 221 K2 | **Lawgrove** | P & K |
| 209 L8 | **Law Hill** | S Lans |
| 11 L6 | **Lawhitton** | Cnwll |
| 148 D3 | **Lawkland** | N York |
| 148 D3 | **Lawkland Green** | N York |
| 96 F2 | **Lawley** | Wrekin |
| 114 C6 | **Lawnhead** | Staffs |
| 150 C8 | **Lawns Wood Crematorium** | Leeds |
| 55 G5 | **Lawrenny** | Pembks |
| 89 H4 | **Lawshall** | Suffk |
| 89 H4 | **Lawshall Green** | Suffk |
| 80 B3 | **Lawton** | Herefs |
| 282 f4 | **Laxay** | W Isls |
| 282 g3 | **Laxdale** | W Isls |
| 154 f5 | **Laxey** | IoM |
| 91 G1 | **Laxfield** | Suffk |
| 276 C7 | **Laxford Bridge** | Highld |
| 281 e5 | **Laxo** | Shet |
| 143 K3 | **Laxton** | E R Yk |
| 101 L4 | **Laxton** | Nhants |
| 134 E6 | **Laxton** | Notts |
| 149 J7 | **Laycock** | C Brad |
| 72 D3 | **Layer Breton** | Essex |
| 72 D3 | **Layer-de-la-Haye** | Essex |
| 72 D4 | **Layer Marney** | Essex |
| 89 L7 | **Layham** | Suffk |
| 48 A5 | **Layland's Green** | W Berk |
| 15 J2 | **Laymore** | Dorset |
| 50 C1 | **Layter's Green** | Bucks |
| 152 A7 | **Laytham** | E R Yk |
| 177 H7 | **Laythes** | Cumb |
| 170 D6 | **Lazenby** | R & Cl |
| 166 D3 | **Lazonby** | Cumb |
| 132 F8 | **Lea** | Derbys |
| 63 K3 | **Lea** | Herefs |
| 135 G2 | **Lea** | Lincs |
| 95 J5 | **Lea** | Shrops |
| 95 K2 | **Lea** | Shrops |
| 46 D2 | **Lea** | Wilts |
| 251 H3 | **Leachkin** | Highld |
| 200 B2 | **Leadburn** | Border |
| 118 B1 | **Leadenham** | Lincs |
| 70 E4 | **Leaden Roding** | Essex |
| 180 D8 | **Leadgate** | Dur |
| 180 D7 | **Leadgate** | Nthumb |
| 186 C3 | **Leadhills** | S Lans |
| 39 M3 | **Leadingcross Green** | Kent |
| 132 E4 | **Leadmill** | Derbys |
| 65 L4 | **Leafield** | Oxon |
| 68 D2 | **Leagrave** | Luton |
| 130 D6 | **Leahead** | Ches W |
| 115 G6 | **Lea Heath** | Staffs |
| 160 F4 | **Leake** | N York |
| 119 L1 | **Leake Common Side** | Lincs |
| 162 D1 | **Lealholm** | N York |
| 162 D1 | **Lealholm Side** | N York |
| 259 H4 | **Lealt** | Highld |
| 132 E4 | **Leam** | Derbys |
| 99 G5 | **Lea Marston** | Warwks |
| 83 K2 | **Leamington Hastings** | Warwks |
| 83 H2 | **Leamington Spa** | Warwks |
| 169 J1 | **Leamside** | Dur |
| 23 K5 | **Leap Cross** | E Susx |
| 157 H6 | **Leasgill** | Cumb |
| 118 E2 | **Leasingham** | Lincs |
| 169 H4 | **Leasingthorne** | Dur |
| 50 F7 | **Leatherhead** | Surrey |
| 150 B6 | **Leathley** | N York |
| 113 G7 | **Leaton** | Shrops |
| 96 E1 | **Leaton** | Wrekin |
| 138 F7 | **Lea Town** | Lancs |
| 40 C4 | **Leaveland** | Kent |
| 89 J7 | **Leavenheath** | Suffk |
| 152 B3 | **Leavening** | N York |
| 51 L6 | **Leaves Green** | Gt Lon |
| 158 D5 | **Lea Yeat** | Cumb |
| 163 K6 | **Lebberston** | N York |
| 9 j4 | **Le Bigard** | Guern |
| 9 j4 | **Le Bourg** | Guern |
| 9 f4 | **Le Bourg** | Jersey |
| 65 J7 | **Lechlade on Thames** | Gloucs |
| 204 D3 | **Lecht Gruinart** | Ag & B |
| 157 K7 | **Leck** | Lancs |
| 231 K7 | **Leckbuie** | P & K |
| 34 E3 | **Leckford** | Hants |
| 84 D7 | **Leckhampstead** | Bucks |
| 48 B4 | **Leckhampstead** | W Berk |
| 48 B4 | **Leckhampstead Thicket** | W Berk |
| 64 D3 | **Leckhampton** | Gloucs |
| 261 K2 | **Leckmelm** | Highld |
| 43 J6 | **Leckwith** | V Glam |
| 152 F7 | **Leconfield** | E R Yk |
| 228 E7 | **Ledaig** | Ag & B |
| 67 L3 | **Ledburn** | Bucks |
| 81 G7 | **Ledbury** | Herefs |
| 80 F8 | **Leddington** | Gloucs |
| 80 A5 | **Ledgemoor** | Herefs |
| 80 A3 | **Ledicot** | Herefs |
| 271 K4 | **Ledmore Junction** | Highld |
| 129 H5 | **Ledsham** | Ches W |
| 142 C2 | **Ledsham** | Leeds |
| 142 C2 | **Ledston** | Leeds |
| 7 L5 | **Ledstone** | Devon |
| 142 C2 | **Ledston Luck** | Leeds |
| 66 B2 | **Ledwell** | Oxon |
| 27 H2 | **Lee** | Devon |
| 51 K4 | **Lee** | Gt Lon |
| 34 D7 | **Lee** | Hants |
| 112 F5 | **Lee** | Shrops |
| 96 B4 | **Leebotwood** | Shrops |
| 113 J6 | **Lee Brockhurst** | Shrops |
| 146 E2 | **Leece** | Cumb |
| 52 E2 | **Lee Chapel** | Essex |
| 67 M6 | **Lee Clump** | Bucks |
| 67 M6 | **Lee Common** | Bucks |
| 39 K3 | **Leeds** | Kent |
| 141 L1 | **Leeds** | Leeds |
| 2 F4 | **Leedstown** | Cnwll |
| 130 C7 | **Lee Green** | Ches E |
| 131 K8 | **Leek** | Staffs |
| 83 G2 | **Leek Wootton** | Warwks |
| 7 H4 | **Lee Mill** | Devon |
| 141 G1 | **Leeming** | C Brad |
| 160 D5 | **Leeming** | N York |
| 160 D4 | **Leeming Bar** | N York |
| 7 H3 | **Lee Moor** | Devon |
| 19 J3 | **Lee-on-the-Solent** | Hants |
| 149 J8 | **Lees** | C Brad |
| 115 L4 | **Lees** | Derbys |
| 140 E6 | **Lees** | Oldham |
| 115 L4 | **Lees Green** | Derbys |
| 101 H1 | **Leesthorpe** | Leics |
| 37 L2 | **Lee Street** | Surrey |
| 129 G7 | **Leeswood** | Flints |
| 222 C3 | **Leetown** | P & K |
| 130 C5 | **Leftwich** | Ches W |
| 61 K4 | **Legar** | Powys |
| 137 G3 | **Legbourne** | Lincs |
| 165 K6 | **Legburthwaite** | Cumb |
| 201 J4 | **Legerwood** | Border |
| 9 i3 | **Le Gron** | Guern |
| 136 B3 | **Legsby** | Lincs |
| 9 e4 | **Le Haguais** | Jersey |
| 9 e4 | **Le Hocq** | Jersey |
| 100 D3 | **Leicester** | C Leic |
| 100 B3 | **Leicester Forest East** | Leics |
| 28 C8 | **Leigh** | Devon |
| 16 B1 | **Leigh** | Dorset |
| 64 C2 | **Leigh** | Gloucs |
| 38 E4 | **Leigh** | Kent |
| 95 H3 | **Leigh** | Shrops |
| 37 K2 | **Leigh** | Surrey |
| 139 K7 | **Leigh** | Wigan |
| 64 F8 | **Leigh** | Wilts |
| 81 H4 | **Leigh** | Worcs |
| 53 H2 | **Leigh Beck** | Essex |
| 46 C3 | **Leigh Delamere** | Wilts |
| 40 A8 | **Leigh Green** | Kent |
| 197 J1 | **Leigh Knoweglass** | S Lans |
| 29 J4 | **Leighland Chapel** | Somset |
| 53 H2 | **Leigh-on-Sea** | Sthend |
| 17 K3 | **Leigh Park** | Dorset |
| 81 H5 | **Leigh Sinton** | Worcs |
| 98 D3 | **Leighswood** | Wsall |
| 46 B1 | **Leighterton** | Gloucs |
| 159 L6 | **Leighton** | N York |
| 94 F2 | **Leighton** | Powys |
| 96 E2 | **Leighton** | Shrops |
| 32 B2 | **Leighton** | Somset |
| 102 C8 | **Leighton Bromswold** | Cambs |
| 68 A2 | **Leighton Buzzard** | C Beds |
| 31 M2 | **Leigh upon Mendip** | Somset |
| 45 H4 | **Leigh Woods** | N Som |
| 80 B2 | **Leinthall Earls** | Herefs |
| 80 A1 | **Leinthall Starkes** | Herefs |
| 95 K8 | **Leintwardine** | Herefs |
| 100 B5 | **Leire** | Leics |
| 91 K3 | **Leiston** | Suffk |
| 233 L6 | **Leitfie** | P & K |
| 211 J4 | **Leith** | C Edin |
| 202 B4 | **Leitholm** | Border |
| 2 E4 | **Lelant** | Cnwll |
| 145 G1 | **Lelley** | E R Yk |
| 97 G8 | **Lem Hill** | Worcs |
| 202 B6 | **Lempitlaw** | Border |
| 282 g5 | **Lemreway** | W Isls |
| 69 G4 | **Lemsford** | Herts |
| 82 B6 | **Lenchwick** | Worcs |
| 182 E5 | **Lendalfoot** | S Ayrs |
| 219 J6 | **Lendrick** | Stirlg |
| 257 L3 | **Lendrum Terrace** | Abers |
| 40 A5 | **Lenham** | Kent |
| 40 B5 | **Lenham Heath** | Kent |
| 250 F6 | **Lenie** | Highld |
| 202 C5 | **Lennel** | Border |
| 174 F4 | **Lennox Plunton** | D & G |
| 209 G3 | **Lennoxtown** | E Duns |
| 50 A3 | **Lent** | Bucks |
| 116 F4 | **Lenton** | C Nott |
| 118 D5 | **Lenton** | Lincs |
| 122 B7 | **Lenwade** | Norfk |
| 209 H4 | **Lenzie** | E Duns |
| 244 C2 | **Leochel-Cushnie** | Abers |
| 98 E2 | **Leomansley** | Staffs |
| 80 C3 | **Leominster** | Herefs |
| 64 A6 | **Leonard Stanley** | Gloucs |
| 9 b2 | **Leoville** | Jersey |
| 19 G4 | **Lepe** | Hants |
| 258 B6 | **Lephin** | Highld |
| 152 A4 | **Leppington** | N York |
| 141 K5 | **Lepton** | Kirk |
| 9 h3 | **L'Eree** | Guern |
| 5 K3 | **Lerryn** | Cnwll |
| 281 e6 | **Lerwick** | Shet |
| 9 h3 | **Les Arquets** | Guern |
| 191 J4 | **Lesbury** | Nthumb |
| 9 k3 | **Les Hubits** | Guern |
| 255 M6 | **Leslie** | Abers |
| 222 D6 | **Leslie** | Fife |
| 9 i3 | **Les Lohiers** | Guern |
| 198 D5 | **Lesmahagow** | S Lans |
| 9 i4 | **Les Murchez** | Guern |
| 11 G4 | **Lesnewth** | Cnwll |
| 9 j4 | **Les Nicolles** | Guern |
| 9 j2 | **Les Quartiers** | Guern |
| 9 b3 | **Les Quennevais** | Jersey |
| 9 i3 | **Les Sages** | Guern |
| 123 H6 | **Lessingham** | Norfk |
| 165 H1 | **Lessonhall** | Cumb |
| 3 K6 | **Lestowder** | Cnwll |
| 9 i4 | **Les Villets** | Guern |
| 172 C2 | **Leswalt** | D & G |
| 9 a2 | **L'Etacq** | Jersey |
| 68 F7 | **Letchmore Heath** | Herts |
| 86 E8 | **Letchworth Garden City** | Herts |
| 48 A2 | **Letcombe Bassett** | Oxon |
| 48 A2 | **Letcombe Regis** | Oxon |
| 234 E5 | **Letham** | Angus |
| 189 J4 | **Letham** | Border |
| 210 B2 | **Letham** | Falk |
| 222 E4 | **Letham** | Fife |
| 235 G6 | **Letham Grange** | Angus |
| 233 H7 | **Lethendy** | P & K |
| 255 M7 | **Lethenty** | Abers |
| 256 E4 | **Lethenty** | Abers |
| 91 G4 | **Letheringham** | Suffk |
| 122 B4 | **Letheringsett** | Norfk |
| 13 G5 | **Lettaford** | Devon |
| 260 F5 | **Letterewe** | Highld |
| 248 D7 | **Letterfearn** | Highld |
| 239 L5 | **Letterfinlay Lodge Hotel** | Highld |
| 237 L3 | **Lettermorar** | Highld |
| 261 K2 | **Letters** | Highld |
| 186 D2 | **Lettershaw** | S Lans |
| 74 F6 | **Letterston** | Pembks |
| 253 K7 | **Lettoch** | Highld |
| 254 B5 | **Lettoch** | Highld |
| 79 L1 | **Letton** | Herefs |
| 79 L6 | **Letton** | Herefs |
| 51 M7 | **Lett's Green** | Kent |
| 69 H5 | **Letty Green** | Herts |
| 133 L2 | **Letwell** | Rothm |
| 223 H3 | **Leuchars** | Fife |
| 282 g5 | **Leumrabhagh** | W Isls |
| 282 g4 | **Leurbost** | W Isls |
| 5 G5 | **Levalsa Meor** | Cnwll |
| 114 D8 | **Levedale** | Staffs |
| 70 C2 | **Level's Green** | Essex |
| 153 H6 | **Leven** | E R Yk |
| 222 F7 | **Leven** | Fife |
| 157 G5 | **Levens** | Cumb |
| 69 K3 | **Levens Green** | Herts |
| 131 G1 | **Levenshulme** | Manch |
| 281 d8 | **Levenwick** | Shet |
| 282 d6 | **Leverburgh** | W Isls |
| 103 J1 | **Leverington** | Cambs |
| 68 D5 | **Leverstock Green** | Herts |
| 119 L2 | **Leverton** | Lincs |
| 9 j2 | **Le Villocq** | Guern |
| 90 F7 | **Levington** | Suffk |
| 162 E4 | **Levisham** | N York |
| 65 L6 | **Lew** | Oxon |
| 11 K6 | **Lewannick** | Cnwll |
| 12 B5 | **Lewdown** | Devon |

22 F5 **Lewes** E Susx
31 K8 **Leweston** Dorset
54 F2 **Leweston** Pembks
51 K4 **Lewisham** Gt Lon
51 L4 **Lewisham Crematorium** Gt Lon
250 F6 **Lewiston** Highld
42 E4 **Lewistown** Brdgnd
79 L4 **Lewis Wych** Herefs
67 H7 **Lewknor** Oxon
11 L2 **Leworthy** Devon
28 B3 **Leworthy** Devon
40 C3 **Lewson Street** Kent
147 J8 **Lewth** Lancs
12 B5 **Lewtrenchard** Devon
72 D2 **Lexden** Essex
30 C4 **Lexworthy** Somset
5 K2 **Ley** Cnwll
52 E7 **Leybourne** Kent
159 K4 **Leyburn** N York
114 B2 **Leycett** Staffs
68 F2 **Leygreen** Herts
68 C6 **Ley Hill** Bucks
139 H3 **Leyland** Lancs
139 H7 **Leyland Green** St Hel
245 G1 **Leylodge** Abers
269 J5 **Leys** Abers
233 K7 **Leys** P & K
53 M5 **Leysdown-on-Sea** Kent
234 F6 **Leysmill** Angus
234 B5 **Leys of Cossans** Angus
80 D2 **Leysters** Herefs
51 K2 **Leyton** Gt Lon
51 K2 **Leytonstone** Gt Lon
11 L6 **Lezant** Cnwll
3 H4 **Lezerea** Cnwll
266 F4 **Lhanbryde** Moray
60 F2 **Libanus** Powys
199 G4 **Libberton** S Lans
211 J5 **Liberton** C Edin
98 E2 **Lichfield** Staffs
98 C8 **Lickey** Worcs
81 M1 **Lickey End** Worcs
98 B8 **Lickey Rock** Worcs
36 D5 **Lickfold** W Susx
12 B6 **Liddaton Green** Devon
228 B3 **Liddesdale** Highld
47 J3 **Liddington** Swindn
132 F4 **Lidgate** Derbys
88 E4 **Lidgate** Suffk
143 G7 **Lidget** Donc
134 C6 **Lidgett** Notts
24 F4 **Lidham Hill** E Susx
85 K7 **Lidlington** C Beds
53 G6 **Lidsing** Kent
222 E1 **Liff** Angus
98 D7 **Lifford** Birm
11 M5 **Lifton** Devon
11 M5 **Liftondown** Devon
83 H4 **Lighthorne** Warwks
83 H4 **Lighthorne Heath** Warwks
50 B6 **Lightwater** Surrey
114 E3 **Lightwood** C Stke
113 L3 **Lightwood Green** Ches E
112 F3 **Lightwood Green** Wrexhm
100 C8 **Lilbourne** Nhants
190 E1 **Lilburn Tower** Nthumb
114 A8 **Lilleshall** Wrekin
68 E2 **Lilley** Herts
48 C3 **Lilley** W Berk
201 H8 **Lilliesleaf** Border
84 D7 **Lillingstone Dayrell** Bucks
84 D7 **Lillingstone Lovell** Bucks
31 K8 **Lillington** Dorset
17 K4 **Lilliput** Poole
29 L2 **Lilstock** Somset
97 G1 **Lilyhurst** Shrops
139 J4 **Limbrick** Lancs
68 D2 **Limbury** Luton
79 L2 **Limebrook** Herefs
140 B5 **Limefield** Bury
197 K1 **Limekilnburn** S Lans
210 E2 **Limekilns** Fife
209 M5 **Limerigg** Falk
19 G7 **Limerstone** IoW
167 J1 **Limestone Brae** Nthumb
64 A1 **Lime Street** Worcs
31 J6 **Limington** Somset
197 J5 **Limmerhaugh** E Ayrs
107 H3 **Limpenhoe** Norfk
45 M6 **Limpley Stoke** Wilts
51 L8 **Limpsfield** Surrey
51 L8 **Limpsfield Chart** Surrey
16 F1 **Linby** Notts
36 C5 **Linchmere** W Susx
176 C3 **Lincluden** D & G
135 K5 **Lincoln** Lincs
135 K5 **Lincoln Crematorium** Lincs
81 J2 **Lincomb** Worcs
7 L6 **Lincombe** Devon
27 J2 **Lincombe** Devon

156 F6 **Lindale** Cumb
156 C7 **Lindal in Furness** Cumb
22 E2 **Lindfield** W Susx
36 B4 **Lindford** Hants
141 H4 **Lindley** Kirk
150 B6 **Lindley Green** N York
130 F4 **Lindow End** Ches E
80 F2 **Lindridge** Worcs
70 F2 **Lindsell** Essex
89 K6 **Lindsey** Suffk
89 K6 **Lindsey Tye** Suffk
30 E4 **Liney** Somset
18 B2 **Linford** Hants
52 E3 **Linford** Thurr
149 K8 **Lingbob** C Brad
170 F7 **Lingdale** R & Cl
79 L2 **Lingen** Herefs
38 B4 **Lingfield** Surrey
130 A2 **Lingley Green** Warrtn
107 G2 **Lingwood** Norfk
258 F3 **Linicro** Highld
64 B1 **Linkend** Worcs
48 A7 **Linkenholt** Hants
24 E2 **Linkhill** Kent
11 L7 **Linkinhorne** Cnwll
211 J1 **Linktown** Fife
266 E4 **Linkwood** Moray
95 J5 **Linley** Shrops
80 F4 **Linley Green** Herefs
96 F4 **Linleygreen** Shrops
210 C4 **Linlithgow** W Loth
190 C5 **Linshiels** Nthumb
272 D8 **Linsidemore** Highld
67 M2 **Linslade** C Beds
107 G7 **Linstead Parva** Suffk
178 A7 **Linstock** Cumb
82 B1 **Linthurst** Worcs
141 H5 **Linthwaite** Kirk
213 H7 **Lintlaw** Border
267 K3 **Lintmill** Moray
202 B7 **Linton** Border
88 B6 **Linton** Cambs
115 M8 **Linton** Derbys
63 K2 **Linton** Herefs
39 J3 **Linton** Kent
150 E6 **Linton** Leeds
149 H3 **Linton** N York
191 K7 **Linton** Nthumb
115 M8 **Linton Heath** Derbys
63 K2 **Linton Hill** Herefs
151 G4 **Linton-on-Ouse** N York
18 B2 **Linwood** Hants
136 B2 **Linwood** Lincs
208 D6 **Linwood** Rens
283 C9 **Lionacleit** W Isls
282 h1 **Lional** W Isls
23 J4 **Lions Green** E Susx
36 C4 **Liphook** Hants
114 A5 **Lipley** Shrops
129 G1 **Liscard** Wirral
28 F4 **Liscombe** Somset
6 B2 **Liskeard** Cnwll
36 A5 **Liss** Hants
153 J4 **Lissett** E R Yk
36 A5 **Liss Forest** Hants
136 B3 **Lissington** Lincs
89 G6 **Liston** Essex
43 J5 **Lisvane** Cardif
44 D2 **Liswerry** Newpt
121 J8 **Litcham** Norfk
42 D5 **Litchard** Brdgnd
84 C4 **Litchborough** Nhants
48 C8 **Litchfield** Hants
138 D8 **Litherland** Sefton
87 G6 **Litlington** Cambs
23 J7 **Litlington** E Susx
87 L5 **Little Abington** Cambs
101 L8 **Little Addington** Nhants
173 K5 **Little Airies** D & G
69 G2 **Little Almshoe** Herts
82 D3 **Little Alne** Warwks
138 C6 **Little Altcar** Sefton
69 K5 **Little Amwell** Herts
158 B1 **Little Asby** Cumb
98 E3 **Little Aston** Staffs
19 G7 **Little Atherfield** IoW
170 D8 **Little Ayton** N York
71 J5 **Little Baddow** Essex
46 A2 **Little Badminton** S Glos
177 J2 **Little Bampton** Cumb
71 G1 **Little Bardfield** Essex
86 D4 **Little Barford** Bed
122 C5 **Little Barningham** Norfk
65 J4 **Little Barrington** Gloucs
129 L5 **Little Barrow** Ches W
162 D6 **Little Barugh** N York
180 B3 **Little Bavington** Nthumb
90 F5 **Little Bealings** Suffk
162 F2 **Littlebeck** N York
47 L5 **Little Bedwyn** Wilts

73 G2 **Little Bentley** Essex
69 H5 **Little Berkhamsted** Herts
84 F3 **Little Billing** Nhants
68 B3 **Little Billington** C Beds
63 G1 **Little Birch** Herefs
146 F7 **Little Bispham** Bpool
90 C5 **Little Blakenham** Suffk
166 B4 **Little Blencow** Cumb
98 C3 **Little Bloxwich** Wsall
21 G3 **Little Bognor** W Susx
116 A1 **Little Bolehill** Derbys
130 E2 **Little Bollington** Ches E
50 E8 **Little Bookham** Surrey
28 E8 **Littleborough** Devon
135 G3 **Littleborough** Notts
140 E4 **Littleborough** Rochdl
41 G4 **Littlebourne** Kent
83 K6 **Little Bourton** Oxon
101 G6 **Little Bowden** Leics
88 D5 **Little Bradley** Suffk
79 K3 **Little Brampton** Herefs
95 J7 **Little Brampton** Shrops
71 K4 **Little Braxted** Essex
234 F3 **Little Brechin** Angus
16 B4 **Littlebredy** Dorset
85 H8 **Little Brickhill** M Keyn
114 D6 **Little Bridgeford** Staffs
84 C3 **Little Brington** Nhants
73 G2 **Little Bromley** Essex
164 E4 **Little Broughton** Cumb
130 B6 **Little Budworth** Ches W
251 H1 **Littleburn** Highld
71 G8 **Little Burstead** Essex
87 L7 **Littlebury** Essex
87 K7 **Littlebury Green** Essex
118 D7 **Little Bytham** Lincs
70 F3 **Little Canfield** Essex
137 G3 **Little Carlton** Lincs
134 F8 **Little Carlton** Notts
101 M2 **Little Casterton** Rutlnd
153 H6 **Little Catwick** E R Yk
86 B1 **Little Catworth** Cambs
137 G3 **Little Cawthorpe** Lincs
46 B6 **Little Chalfield** Wilts
68 C7 **Little Chalfont** Bucks
40 B6 **Little Chart** Kent
87 L7 **Little Chesterford** Essex
39 H4 **Little Cheveney** Kent
46 E8 **Little Cheverell** Wilts
87 J7 **Little Chishill** Cambs
73 H3 **Little Clacton** Essex
65 K6 **Little Clanfield** Oxon
164 E5 **Little Clifton** Cumb
145 H6 **Little Coates** NE Lin
81 M6 **Little Comberton** Worcs
24 C5 **Little Common** E Susx
39 G2 **Little Comp** Kent
65 K1 **Little Compton** Warwks
178 B7 **Little Corby** Cumb
89 H7 **Little Cornard** Suffk
47 H8 **Littlecott** Wilts
80 E5 **Little Cowarne** Herefs
65 L8 **Little Coxwell** Oxon
160 C4 **Little Crakehall** N York
101 H8 **Little Cransley** Nhants
105 H3 **Little Cressingham** Norfk
138 C7 **Little Crosby** Sefton
165 H5 **Little Crosthwaite** Cumb
115 J4 **Little Cubley** Derbys
117 K8 **Little Dalby** Leics
63 K4 **Littledean** Gloucs
63 G1 **Little Dewchurch** Herefs
88 D3 **Little Ditton** Cambs
63 G4 **Little Doward** Herefs
47 M7 **Littledown** Hants
103 L6 **Little Downham** Cambs
152 F4 **Little Driffield** E R Yk
105 H1 **Little Dunham** Norfk
232 F7 **Little Dunkeld** P & K
71 G3 **Little Dunmow** Essex
33 K4 **Little Durnford** Wilts
70 F2 **Little Easton** Essex
116 B3 **Little Eaton** Derbys
105 K3 **Little Ellingham** Norfk
32 B2 **Little Elm** Somset
84 B4 **Little Everdon** Nhants
87 H4 **Little Eversden** Cambs
65 J6 **Little Faringdon** Oxon
160 D4 **Little Fencote** N York
142 E1 **Little Fenton** N York
105 H1 **Little Fransham** Norfk
68 C4 **Little Gaddesden** Herts
62 F2 **Little Garway** Herefs
102 C7 **Little Gidding** Cambs
91 H4 **Little Glemham** Suffk
63 K2 **Little Gorsley** Herefs
86 F4 **Little Gransden** Cambs
117 J3 **Little Green** Notts
32 B1 **Little Green** Somset
136 F2 **Little Grimsby** Lincs

134 E3 **Little Gringley** Notts
162 C7 **Little Habton** N York
70 B3 **Little Hadham** Herts
118 F3 **Little Hale** Lincs
116 D3 **Little Hallam** Derbys
70 D4 **Little Hallingbury** Essex
14 B6 **Littleham** Devon
27 H6 **Littleham** Devon
67 L6 **Little Hampden** Bucks
21 H6 **Littlehampton** W Susx
32 D8 **Little Hanford** Dorset
85 G1 **Little Harrowden** Nhants
66 F7 **Little Haseley** Oxon
153 J7 **Little Hatfield** E R Yk
122 E7 **Little Hautbois** Norfk
54 D4 **Little Haven** Pembks
37 J4 **Littlehaven** W Susx
98 E3 **Little Hay** Staffs
131 K2 **Little Hayfield** Derbys
115 G7 **Little Haywood** Staffs
114 D8 **Little Heath** Staffs
49 G4 **Little Heath** W Berk
8 B2 **Littlehempston** Devon
80 D2 **Little Hereford** Herefs
72 D1 **Little Horkesley** Essex
69 L2 **Little Hormead** Herts
23 G4 **Little Horsted** E Susx
141 J2 **Little Horton** C Brad
46 F6 **Little Horton** Wilts
67 J1 **Little Horwood** Bucks
142 C6 **Little Houghton** Barns
84 F3 **Little Houghton** Nhants
191 J3 **Littlehoughton** Nthumb
132 C4 **Little Hucklow** Derbys
139 L7 **Little Hulton** Salfd
48 D4 **Little Hungerford** W Berk
161 G7 **Little Hutton** N York
114 F6 **Little Ingestre** Staffs
85 H2 **Little Irchester** Nhants
153 H4 **Little Kelk** E R Yk
32 C2 **Little Keyford** Somset
67 K5 **Little Kimble** Bucks
83 H5 **Little Kineton** Warwks
67 L7 **Little Kingshill** Bucks
175 K3 **Little Knox** D & G
156 D2 **Little Langdale** Cumb
33 H4 **Little Langford** Wilts
70 E5 **Little Laver** Essex
130 B4 **Little Leigh** Ches W
71 H4 **Little Leighs** Essex
139 M6 **Little Lever** Bolton
85 G6 **Little Linford** M Keyn
31 G6 **Little Load** Somset
66 F4 **Little London** Bucks
103 J4 **Little London** Cambs
23 J3 **Little London** E Susx
70 C1 **Little London** Essex
88 D8 **Little London** Essex
63 L3 **Little London** Gloucs
34 E1 **Little London** Hants
48 F7 **Little London** Hants
150 B7 **Little London** Leeds
119 H7 **Little London** Lincs
119 M6 **Little London** Lincs
136 F5 **Little London** Lincs
120 C7 **Little London** Norfk
94 C5 **Little London** Powys
132 D5 **Little Longstone** Derbys
114 B3 **Little Madeley** Staffs
81 H7 **Little Malvern** Worcs
129 H6 **Little Mancot** Flints
89 G8 **Little Maplestead** Essex
80 F7 **Little Marcle** Herefs
27 J8 **Little Marland** Devon
49 L2 **Little Marlow** Bucks
121 H6 **Little Massingham** Norfk
106 D2 **Little Melton** Norfk
243 K4 **Littlemill** Abers
253 H2 **Littlemill** Highld
62 C6 **Little Mill** Mons
66 F7 **Little Milton** Oxon
68 A7 **Little Missenden** Bucks
41 K5 **Little Mongeham** Kent
133 G7 **Littlemoor** Derbys
30 D4 **Little Moor** Somset
66 D6 **Littlemore** Oxon
167 H8 **Little Musgrave** Cumb
112 F7 **Little Ness** Shrops
129 G4 **Little Neston** Ches W
75 G6 **Little Newcastle** Pembks
168 E7 **Little Newsham** Dur
31 G7 **Little Norton** Somset
73 J1 **Little Oakley** Essex
101 K6 **Little Oakley** Nhants
85 J4 **Little Odell** Bed
68 E2 **Little Offley** Herts
114 C8 **Little Onn** Staffs
167 G7 **Little Ormside** Cumb
177 K7 **Little Orton** Cumb
104 C5 **Little Ouse** Cambs

150 F4 **Little Ouseburn** N York
116 B5 **Littleover** C Derb
100 F6 **Little Oxendon** Nhants
99 G6 **Little Packington** Warwks
39 J4 **Little Pattenden** Kent
86 D3 **Little Paxton** Cambs
10 C8 **Little Petherick** Cnwll
138 D1 **Little Plumpton** Lancs
107 G1 **Little Plumstead** Norfk
118 B5 **Little Ponton** Lincs
104 B6 **Littleport** Cambs
104 B6 **Littleport Bridge** Cambs
19 J3 **Little Posbrook** Hants
27 J8 **Little Potheridge** Devon
142 B2 **Little Preston** Leeds
84 B4 **Little Preston** Nhants
130 C6 **Littler** Ches W
102 E7 **Little Raveley** Cambs
143 K3 **Little Reedness** E R Yk
150 E5 **Little Ribston** N York
65 J3 **Little Rissington** Gloucs
65 L1 **Little Rollright** Oxon
132 E6 **Little Rowsley** Derbys
121 L6 **Little Ryburgh** Norfk
190 E4 **Little Ryle** Nthumb
96 B3 **Little Ryton** Shrops
166 D3 **Little Salkeld** Cumb
88 C8 **Little Sampford** Essex
49 K6 **Little Sandhurst** Br For
97 L2 **Little Saredon** Staffs
129 J6 **Little Saughall** Ches W
88 F3 **Little Saxham** Suffk
262 C8 **Little Scatwell** Highld
87 J5 **Little Shelford** Cambs
82 F2 **Little Shrewley** Warwks
13 L1 **Little Silver** Devon
147 G7 **Little Singleton** Lancs
151 K8 **Little Skipwith** N York
142 E4 **Little Smeaton** N York
121 L5 **Little Snoring** Norfk
45 M2 **Little Sodbury** S Glos
45 L2 **Little Sodbury End** S Glos
34 E4 **Little Somborne** Hants
46 D2 **Little Somerford** Wilts
114 A6 **Little Soudley** Shrops
148 E2 **Little Stainforth** N York
169 K6 **Little Stainton** Darltn
129 J5 **Little Stanney** Ches W
86 B3 **Little Staughton** Bed
137 H7 **Little Steeping** Lincs
114 E5 **Little Stoke** Staffs
25 K2 **Littlestone-on-Sea** Kent
90 D3 **Little Stonham** Suffk
100 E3 **Little Stretton** Leics
95 K5 **Little Stretton** Shrops
166 D6 **Little Strickland** Cumb
102 E8 **Little Stukeley** Cambs
114 C5 **Little Sugnall** Staffs
129 J4 **Little Sutton** Ches W
96 C6 **Little Sutton** Shrops
179 M3 **Little Swinburne** Nthumb
175 H4 **Little Sypland** D & G
66 A2 **Little Tew** Oxon
72 C2 **Little Tey** Essex
103 L8 **Little Thetford** Cambs
161 G7 **Little Thirkleby** N York
122 B4 **Little Thornage** Norfk
147 G7 **Little Thornton** Lancs
169 L2 **Little Thorpe** Dur
100 C4 **Littlethorpe** Leics
150 D2 **Littlethorpe** N York
88 D5 **Little Thurlow** Suffk
88 D5 **Little Thurlow Green** Suffk
52 D3 **Little Thurrock** Thurr
233 M5 **Littleton** Angus
45 H6 **Littleton** BaNES
129 K6 **Littleton** Ches W
175 G4 **Littleton** D & G
17 H2 **Littleton** Dorset
34 F4 **Littleton** Hants
31 H5 **Littleton** Somset
36 E2 **Littleton** Surrey
50 D5 **Littleton** Surrey
46 B3 **Littleton Drew** Wilts
45 H1 **Littleton-on-Severn** S Glos
46 E8 **Littleton Pannell** Wilts
27 J7 **Little Torrington** Devon
72 C5 **Little Totham** Essex
165 H6 **Little Town** Cumb
169 J2 **Littletown** Dur
148 B8 **Little Town** Lancs
130 C1 **Little Town** Warrtn
99 J2 **Little Twycross** Leics
156 C7 **Little Urswick** Cumb
53 K1 **Little Wakering** Essex
87 L7 **Little Walden** Essex
89 J6 **Little Waldingfield** Suffk
121 K4 **Little Walsingham** Norfk
71 H4 **Little Waltham** Essex
52 D1 **Little Warley** Essex

82 A8 **Little Washbourne** Gloucs
144 B1 **Little Weighton** E R Yk
101 K5 **Little Weldon** Nhants
89 H3 **Little Welnetham** Suffk
136 F2 **Little Welton** Lincs
90 C7 **Little Wenham** Suffk
96 E2 **Little Wenlock** Wrekin
31 K5 **Little Weston** Somset
19 K5 **Little Whitefield** IoW
106 F8 **Little Whittingham Green** Suffk
180 B5 **Little Whittington** Nthumb
49 K3 **Littlewick Green** W & M
87 L3 **Little Wilbraham** Cambs
15 K2 **Littlewindsor** Dorset
64 C4 **Little Witcombe** Gloucs
81 H3 **Little Witley** Worcs
66 E8 **Little Wittenham** Oxon
83 G8 **Little Wolford** Warwks
98 C2 **Littlewood** Staffs
51 H6 **Little Woodcote** Gt Lon
67 L3 **Littleworth** Bucks
65 L7 **Littleworth** Oxon
98 C1 **Littleworth** Staffs
114 E7 **Littleworth** Staffs
21 L3 **Littleworth** W Susx
81 K5 **Littleworth** Worcs
82 B3 **Littleworth** Worcs
50 B2 **Littleworth Common** Bucks
88 D6 **Little Wratting** Suffk
85 J2 **Little Wymington** Bed
69 G2 **Little Wymondley** Herts
98 C2 **Little Wyrley** Staffs
113 J7 **Little Wytheford** Shrops
88 F7 **Little Yeldham** Essex
71 G4 **Littley Green** Essex
132 C4 **Litton** Derbys
158 F7 **Litton** N York
45 H8 **Litton** Somset
15 M4 **Litton Cheney** Dorset
282 g4 **Liurbost** W Isls
129 H2 **Liverpool** Lpool
141 J3 **Liversedge** Kirk
13 J7 **Liverton** Devon
171 G7 **Liverton** R & Cl
171 G7 **Liverton Mines** R & Cl
39 L3 **Liverton Street** Kent
210 E5 **Livingston** W Loth
210 D5 **Livingston Village** W Loth
128 E5 **Lixwm** Flints
3 H8 **Lizard** Cnwll
124 D3 **Llaingoch** IoA
94 C7 **Llaithddu** Powys
93 J3 **Llan** Powys
109 L7 **Llanaber** Gwynd
109 G3 **Llanaelhaearn** Gwynd
77 J1 **Llanafan** Cerdgn
78 D4 **Llanafan-Fawr** Powys
78 D5 **Llanafan-fechan** Powys
125 J3 **Llanallgo** IoA
109 G4 **Llanarmon** Gwynd
112 A5 **Llanarmon Dyffryn Ceiriog** Wrexhm
128 E8 **Llanarmon-yn-Ial** Denbgs
76 D4 **Llanarth** Cerdgn
62 D5 **Llanarth** Mons
58 F5 **Llanarthne** Carmth
128 D3 **Llanasa** Flints
124 F2 **Llanbabo** IoA
92 D7 **Llanbadarn Fawr** Cerdgn
94 D7 **Llanbadarn Fynydd** Powys
78 F5 **Llanbadarn-y-garreg** Powys
62 D7 **Llanbadoc** Mons
124 F1 **Llanbadrig** IoA
44 D1 **Llanbeder** Newpt
109 K6 **Llanbedr** Gwynd
61 K3 **Llanbedr** Powys
79 G6 **Llanbedr** Powys
128 D7 **Llanbedr-Dyffryn-Clwyd** Denbgs
125 J4 **Llanbedrgoch** IoA
108 F5 **Llanbedrog** Gwynd
126 E6 **Llanbedr-y-Cennin** Conwy
125 K7 **Llanberis** Gwynd
43 G7 **Llanbethery** V Glam
94 D8 **Llanbister** Powys
42 F7 **Llanblethian** V Glam
55 L2 **Llanboidy** Carmth
43 J4 **Llanbradach** Caerph
93 K3 **Llanbrynmair** Powys
42 F8 **Llancadle** V Glam
43 G7 **Llancarfan** V Glam
62 D6 **Llancayo** Mons
62 D2 **Llancillo** Herefs
63 G3 **Llancloudy** Herefs
92 E5 **Llancynfelyn** Cerdgn
43 J6 **Llandaff** Cardif
109 K6 **Llandanwg** Gwynd
57 K6 **Llandarcy** Neath
58 A6 **Llandawke** Carmth
125 J5 **Llanddaniel Fab** IoA

58 F5 **Llanddarog** Carmth
77 G1 **Llanddeiniol** Cerdgn
125 K6 **Llanddeiniolen** Gwynd
111 J4 **Llandderfel** Gwynd
59 L4 **Llanddeusant** Carmth
124 F3 **Llanddeusant** IoA
61 G1 **Llanddew** Powys
56 E7 **Llanddewi** Swans
77 J4 **Llanddewi Brefi** Cerdgn
78 E5 **Llanddewi'r Cwm** Powys
62 D4 **Llanddewi Rhydderch** Mons
55 K4 **Llanddewi Velfrey** Pembks
78 F2 **Llanddewi Ystradenni** Powys
126 F7 **Llanddoget** Conwy
125 K4 **Llanddona** IoA
55 M4 **Llanddowror** Carmth
127 H4 **Llanddulas** Conwy
109 K7 **Llanddwywe** Gwynd
125 J4 **Llanddyfnan** IoA
110 B4 **Llandecwyn** Gwynd
60 F1 **Llandefaelog** Powys
61 H1 **Llandefaelog-Tre'r-Graig** Powys
78 F8 **Llandefalle** Powys
125 K5 **Llandegfan** IoA
112 B1 **Llandegla** Denbgs
79 G3 **Llandegley** Powys
62 C8 **Llandegveth** Mons
108 D5 **Llandegwning** Gwynd
59 H4 **Llandeilo** Carmth
78 F6 **Llandeilo Graban** Powys
78 B8 **Llandeilo'r Fan** Powys
74 D6 **Llandeloy** Pembks
62 E6 **Llandenny** Mons
44 E1 **Llandevaud** Newpt
44 E2 **Llandevenny** Mons
63 G2 **Llandinabo** Herefs
94 B5 **Llandinam** Powys
55 J3 **Llandissilio** Pembks
63 G6 **Llandogo** Mons
42 F7 **Llandough** V Glam
43 J7 **Llandough** V Glam
59 L2 **Llandovery** Carmth
42 E7 **Llandow** V Glam
77 J6 **Llandre** Carmth
92 D6 **Llandre** Cerdgn
75 K6 **Llandre Isaf** Pembks
111 K4 **Llandrillo** Denbgs
127 G4 **Llandrillo-yn-Rhos** Conwy
78 E3 **Llandrindod Wells** Powys
112 D8 **Llandrinio** Powys
126 F3 **Llandudno** Conwy
126 F4 **Llandudno Junction** Conwy
78 B7 **Llandulas** Powys
125 H8 **Llandwrog** Gwynd
59 H6 **Llandybie** Carmth
58 D6 **Llandyfaelog** Carmth
59 H5 **Llandyfan** Carmth
76 B7 **Llandyfriog** Cerdgn
125 H3 **Llandyfrydog** IoA
126 B5 **Llandygai** Gwynd
75 M3 **Llandygwydd** Cerdgn
112 B3 **Llandynan** Denbgs
128 D6 **Llandyrnog** Denbgs
94 F4 **Llandyssil** Powys
76 D7 **Llandysul** Cerdgn
43 K5 **Llanedeyrn** Cardif
57 G3 **Llanedi** Carmth
78 E7 **Llaneglwys** Powys
92 D2 **Llanegryn** Gwynd
58 F4 **Llanegwad** Carmth
125 H1 **Llaneilian** IoA
127 G4 **Llanelian-yn-Rhôs** Conwy
111 L2 **Llanelidan** Denbgs
79 H8 **Llanelieu** Powys
62 C5 **Llanellen** Mons
56 F5 **Llanelli** Carmth
56 F4 **Llanelli Crematorium** Carmth
110 D7 **Llanelltyd** Gwynd
61 K4 **Llanelly** Mons
78 E5 **Llanelwedd** Powys
109 L6 **Llanenddwyn** Gwynd
108 E6 **Llanengan** Gwynd
111 G8 **Llanerch** Powys
95 H4 **Llanerch** Powys
125 G3 **Llanerchymedd** IoA
94 B2 **Llanerfyl** Powys
124 E3 **Llanfachraeth** IoA
110 E7 **Llanfachreth** Gwynd
124 F5 **Llanfaelog** IoA
108 C6 **Llanfaelrhys** Gwynd
62 E4 **Llanfaenor** Mons
126 B4 **Llanfaes** IoA
61 G2 **Llanfaes** Powys
124 E2 **Llanfaethlu** IoA
109 L5 **Llanfair** Gwynd
94 D2 **Llanfair Caereinion** Powys
77 H5 **Llanfair Clydogau** Cerdgn
128 D8 **Llanfair Dyffryn Clwyd** Denbgs
126 D5 **Llanfairfechan** Conwy
125 J6 **Llanfair-is-gaer** Gwynd

62 D5 **Llanfair Kilgeddin** Mons
75 K5 **Llanfair-Nant-Gwyn** Pembks
125 J5 **Llanfair P G** IoA
127 J5 **Llanfair Talhaiarn** Conwy
94 F8 **Llanfair Waterdine** Shrops
125 H6 **Llanfair-y-Cwmwd** IoA
124 E2 **Llanfairynghornwy** IoA
124 E4 **Llanfair-yn-Neubwll** IoA
55 K3 **Llanfallteg** Carmth
55 K3 **Llanfallteg West** Carmth
92 D7 **Llanfarian** Cerdgn
112 B7 **Llanfechain** Powys
124 F2 **Llanfechell** IoA
128 E7 **Llanferres** Denbgs
124 F2 **Llanfflewyn** IoA
124 F3 **Llanfigael** IoA
76 E7 **Llanfihangel-ar-arth** Carmth
111 J2 **Llanfihangel Glyn Myfyr** Conwy
78 C8 **Llanfihangel Nant Bran** Powys
79 H4 **Llanfihangel-nant-Melan** Powys
79 G2 **Llanfihangel Rhydithon** Powys
44 F2 **Llanfihangel Rogiet** Mons
61 H2 **Llanfihangel Tal-y-llyn** Powys
58 E4 **Llanfihangel-uwch-Gwili** Carmth
92 E8 **Llanfihangel-y-Creuddyn** Cerdgn
111 L8 **Llanfihangel-yng-Ngwynfa** Powys
124 E4 **Llanfihangel yn Nhowyn** IoA
92 E2 **Llanfihangel-y-pennant** Gwynd
109 J3 **Llanfihangel-y-pennant** Gwynd
109 L4 **Llanfihangel-y-traethau** Gwynd
78 F8 **Llanfilo** Powys
62 B4 **Llanfoist** Mons
111 H4 **Llanfor** Gwynd
62 C8 **Llanfrechfa** Torfn
110 B3 **Llanfrothen** Gwynd
61 G2 **Llanfrynach** Powys
128 D8 **Llanfwrog** Denbgs
124 E3 **Llanfwrog** IoA
112 A7 **Llanfyllin** Powys
59 G3 **Llanfynydd** Carmth
129 G8 **Llanfynydd** Flints
75 L6 **Llanfyrnach** Pembks
94 B1 **Llangadfan** Powys
56 D3 **Llangadog** Carmth
59 K3 **Llangadog** Carmth
125 G6 **Llangadwaladr** IoA
112 B5 **Llangadwaladr** Powys
125 H6 **Llangaffo** IoA
58 C5 **Llangain** Carmth
78 C6 **Llangammarch Wells** Powys
42 E6 **Llangan** V Glam
63 G3 **Llangarron** Herefs
61 H2 **Llangasty-Talyllyn** Powys
59 G4 **Llangathen** Carmth
61 K3 **Llangattock** Powys
62 D3 **Llangattock Lingoed** Mons
62 F4 **Llangattock-Vibon-Avel** Mons
112 B6 **Llangedwyn** Powys
125 H4 **Llangefni** IoA
42 D4 **Llangeinor** Brdgnd
125 H6 **Llangeinwen** IoA
77 H3 **Llangeitho** Cerdgn
76 C7 **Llangeler** Carmth
92 C2 **Llangelynin** Gwynd
58 E6 **Llangendeirne** Carmth
57 G4 **Llangennech** Carmth
56 D6 **Llangennith** Swans
61 K3 **Llangenny** Powys
127 H6 **Llangernyw** Conwy
108 E5 **Llangian** Gwynd
57 K4 **Llangiwg** Neath
74 E5 **Llangloffan** Pembks
75 L6 **Llanglydwen** Carmth
126 C4 **Llangoed** IoA
75 L3 **Llangoedmor** Cerdgn
112 B3 **Llangollen** Denbgs
75 J6 **Llangolman** Pembks
61 H2 **Llangors** Powys
62 F6 **Llangovan** Mons
111 G5 **Llangower** Gwynd
76 B4 **Llangranog** Cerdgn
125 H5 **Llangristiolus** IoA
63 G3 **Llangrove** Herefs
62 E2 **Llangua** Mons
79 H1 **Llangunllo** Powys
58 D5 **Llangunnor** Carmth
93 K7 **Llangurig** Powys
111 J3 **Llangwm** Conwy
62 E7 **Llangwm** Mons
55 G5 **Llangwm** Pembks
108 C5 **Llangwnnadl** Gwynd
128 D6 **Llangwyfan** Denbgs
125 H4 **Llangwyllog** IoA
77 H1 **Llangwyryfon** Cerdgn
77 H4 **Llangybi** Cerdgn
109 G3 **Llangybi** Gwynd

62 D7 **Llangybi** Mons
57 H5 **Llangyfelach** Swans
128 D7 **Llangynhafal** Denbgs
61 J3 **Llangynidr** Powys
55 M3 **Llangynin** Carmth
76 C6 **Llangynllo** Cerdgn
58 C6 **Llangynog** Carmth
78 E6 **Llangynog** Powys
111 K6 **Llangynog** Powys
42 C4 **Llangynwyd** Brdgnd
61 H2 **Llanhamlach** Powys
42 F5 **Llanharan** Rhondd
42 F5 **Llanharry** Rhondd
62 D8 **Llanhennock** Mons
61 K7 **Llanhilleth** Blae G
125 J6 **Llanidan** IoA
93 L6 **Llanidloes** Powys
108 D5 **Llaniestyn** Gwynd
79 H7 **Llanigon** Powys
92 D8 **Llanilar** Cerdgn
42 E5 **Llanilid** Rhondd
76 D3 **Llanina** Cerdgn
77 H4 **Llanio** Cerdgn
43 J5 **Llanishen** Cardif
62 F6 **Llanishen** Mons
126 C6 **Llanllechid** Gwynd
78 C5 **Llanlleonfel** Powys
62 D7 **Llanllowell** Mons
94 C3 **Llanllugan** Powys
58 C5 **Llanllwch** Carmth
94 D5 **Llanllwchaiarn** Powys
76 E7 **Llanllwni** Carmth
109 H1 **Llanllyfni** Gwynd
56 D6 **Llanmadoc** Swans
42 E7 **Llanmaes** V Glam
44 E1 **Llanmartin** Newpt
94 E5 **Llanmerewig** Powys
42 E7 **Llanmihangel** V Glam
55 M5 **Llanmiloe** Carmth
56 F6 **Llanmorlais** Swans
127 K5 **Llannefydd** Conwy
56 F3 **Llannon** Carmth
108 F4 **Llannor** Gwynd
76 F2 **Llanon** Cerdgn
62 C5 **Llanover** Mons
58 D3 **Llanpumsaint** Carmth
111 M6 **Llanrhaeadr-ym-Mochnant** Powys
74 D6 **Llanrhian** Pembks
56 F6 **Llanrhidian** Swans
126 F4 **Llanrhos** Conwy
126 F7 **Llanrhychwyn** Conwy
124 F2 **Llanrhyddlad** IoA
76 F1 **Llanrhystud** Cerdgn
62 F3 **Llanrothal** Herefs
125 J7 **Llanrug** Gwynd
43 K5 **Llanrumney** Cardif
126 F7 **Llanrwst** Conwy
56 A3 **Llansadurnen** Carmth
59 J3 **Llansadwrn** Carmth
125 K4 **Llansadwrn** IoA
56 C3 **Llansaint** Carmth
57 J5 **Llansamlet** Swans
126 F4 **Llansanffraid Glan Conwy** Conwy
127 J6 **Llansannan** Conwy
42 F6 **Llansannor** V Glam
61 H2 **Llansantffraed** Powys
78 D2 **Llansantffraed-Cwmdeuddwr** Powys
78 F4 **Llansantffraed-in-Elvel** Powys
76 F2 **Llansantffraid** Cerdgn
112 C7 **Llansantffraid-ym-Mechain** Powys
59 H2 **Llansawel** Carmth
112 B6 **Llansilin** Powys
62 E6 **Llansoy** Mons
60 F2 **Llanspyddid** Powys
54 F6 **Llanstadwell** Pembks
56 C3 **Llansteffan** Carmth
78 F6 **Llanstephan** Powys
62 C8 **Llantarnam** Torfn
55 L5 **Llanteg** Pembks
62 D4 **Llanthewy Skirrid** Mons
62 B2 **Llanthony** Mons
62 E4 **Llantilio-Crossenny** Mons
62 C4 **Llantilio Pertholey** Mons
24 F3 **Llantrisant** IoA
62 D7 **Llantrisant** Mons
43 G5 **Llantrisant** Rhondd
43 G5 **Llantrithyd** V Glam
43 G4 **Llantwit Fardre** Rhondd
42 E7 **Llantwit Major** V Glam
112 B3 **Llantysilio** Denbgs
11 G5 **Llanuwchllyn** Gwynd
44 E1 **Llanvaches** Newpt
62 F8 **Llanvair Discoed** Mons
62 D4 **Llanvapley** Mons
62 D4 **Llanvetherine** Mons
62 C1 **Llanveynoe** Herefs

62 C3 **Llanvihangel Crucorney** Mons
62 D5 **Llanvihangel Gobion** Mons
62 E4 **Llanvihangel-Ystern-Llewern** Mons
63 G2 **Llanwarne** Herefs
111 K7 **Llanwddyn** Powys
62 B4 **Llanwenarth** Mons
76 F6 **Llanwenog** Cerdgn
44 D2 **Llanwern** Newpt
58 A4 **Llanwinio** Carmth
125 H8 **Llanwnda** Gwynd
74 F4 **Llanwnda** Pembks
76 F6 **Llanwnnen** Cerdgn
94 B4 **Llanwnog** Powys
42 F3 **Llanwonno** Rhondd
59 K3 **Llanwrda** Carmth
93 G3 **Llanwrin** Powys
78 D3 **Llanwrthwl** Powys
78 B5 **Llanwrtyd** Powys
78 B6 **Llanwrtyd Wells** Powys
94 C3 **Llanwyddelan** Powys
112 C7 **Llanyblodwel** Shrops
58 B6 **Llanybri** Carmth
76 F6 **Llanybydder** Carmth
55 J2 **Llanycefn** Pembks
75 G5 **Llanychaer Bridge** Pembks
77 H6 **Llanycrwys** Carmth
111 G7 **Llanymawddwy** Gwynd
112 C7 **Llanymynech** Powys
124 E3 **Llanynghenedl** IoA
128 C7 **Llanynys** Denbgs
112 F1 **Llan-y-pwll** Wrexhm
78 E3 **Llanyre** Powys
109 H4 **Llanystumdwy** Gwynd
61 H2 **Llanywern** Powys
55 H3 **Llawhaden** Pembks
112 C5 **Llawnt** Shrops
93 K5 **Llawryglyn** Powys
129 H8 **Llay** Wrexhm
125 G3 **Llechcynfarwy** IoA
61 G2 **Llechfaen** Powys
61 H5 **Llechrhyd** Caerph
75 L3 **Llechryd** Cerdgn
124 F4 **Llechylched** IoA
77 H1 **Lledrod** Cerdgn
111 G4 **Llidiardau** Gwynd
77 G7 **Llidiartnenog** Carmth
111 M3 **Llidiart-y-parc** Denbgs
108 F3 **Llithfaen** Gwynd
128 D4 **Lloc** Flints
79 H7 **Llowes** Powys
60 F6 **Llwydcoed** Rhondd
60 F6 **Llwydcoed Crematorium** Rhondd
111 K8 **Llwydiarth** Powys
128 C6 **Llwyn** Denbgs
76 E3 **Llwyncelyn** Cerdgn
76 C4 **Llwyndafydd** Cerdgn
94 F3 **Llwynderw** Powys
58 A2 **Llwyn-drain** Pembks
62 C4 **Llwyn-du** Mons
108 F3 **Llwyndyrys** Gwynd
92 D2 **Llwyngwril** Gwynd
56 F5 **Llwynhendy** Carmth
112 C4 **Llwynmawr** Wrexhm
60 F5 **Llwyn-on** Myr Td
55 L4 **Llwyn-y-brain** Carmth
77 G4 **Llwyn-y-groes** Cerdgn
42 F3 **Llwynypia** Rhondd
112 D6 **Llynclys** Shrops
125 G4 **Llynfaes** IoA
128 E6 **Llyn-y-pandy** Flints
127 H4 **Llysfaen** Conwy
76 E3 **Llyswen** Cerdgn
79 G7 **Llyswen** Powys
42 E6 **Llysworney** V Glam
55 H2 **Llys-y-frân** Pembks
60 C1 **Llywel** Powys
132 E2 **Load Brook** Sheff
210 C4 **Loan** Falk
202 E3 **Loanend** Nthumb
211 J6 **Loanhead** Mdloth
176 C7 **Loaningfoot** D & G
196 C4 **Loans** S Ayrs
27 H3 **Lobb** Devon
12 B5 **Lobhillcross** Devon
238 B7 **Lochailort** Highld
227 K3 **Lochaline** Highld
172 D3 **Lochans** D & G
176 C3 **Locharbriggs** D & G
216 E4 **Lochavich** Ag & B
217 J2 **Lochawe** Ag & B
283 c11 **Loch Baghasdail** W Isls
283 c11 **Lochboisdale** W Isls
227 H7 **Lochbuie** Ag & B
248 E4 **Lochcarron** Highld
227 L6 **Lochdon** Ag & B
227 L5 **Lochdonhead** Ag & B
206 B3 **Lochead** Ag & B
219 K2 **Lochearnhead** Stirlg

222 F1 **Lochee** C Dund
239 G7 **Locheilside Station** Highld
251 G4 **Lochend** Highld
283 c8 **Locheport** W Isls
283 c8 **Loch Euphoirt** W Isls
176 B4 **Lochfoot** D & G
206 E1 **Lochgair** Ag & B
222 C8 **Lochgelly** Fife
206 D2 **Lochgilphead** Ag & B
217 K7 **Lochgoilhead** Ag & B
222 D4 **Lochieheads** Fife
266 F3 **Lochill** Moray
253 J4 **Lochindorb Lodge** Highld
270 E4 **Lochinver** Highld
262 B7 **Lochluichart** Highld
176 E2 **Lochmaben** D & G
283 d8 **Lochmaddy** W Isls
260 E6 **Loch Maree Hotel** Highld
283 d8 **Loch nam Madadh** W Isls
222 B7 **Lochore** Fife
194 E1 **Lochranza** N Ayrs
235 J3 **Lochside** Abers
176 C3 **Lochside** D & G
252 F1 **Lochside** Highld
264 C4 **Lochslin** Highld
183 G7 **Lochton** S Ayrs
234 E3 **Lochty** Angus
223 J5 **Lochty** Fife
228 B4 **Lochuisge** Highld
208 B7 **Lochwinnoch** Rens
187 G6 **Lochwood** D & G
5 H3 **Lockengate** Cnwll
176 F3 **Lockerbie** D & G
47 H5 **Lockeridge** Wilts
34 C5 **Lockerley** Hants
44 D7 **Locking** N Som
130 C1 **Locking Stumps** Warrtn
152 F6 **Lockington** E R Yk
116 D6 **Lockington** Leics
113 M6 **Lockleywood** Shrops
51 L6 **Locksbottom** Gt Lon
19 G5 **Locksgreen** IoW
19 H2 **Locks Heath** Hants
162 E5 **Lockton** N York
101 H3 **Loddington** Leics
101 H7 **Loddington** Nhants
7 L5 **Loddiswell** Devon
107 G4 **Loddon** Norfk
87 L3 **Lode** Cambs
98 F7 **Lode Heath** Solhll
15 L4 **Loders** Dorset
98 C7 **Lodge Hill Crematorium** Birm
36 D6 **Lodsworth** W Susx
142 A3 **Lofthouse** Leeds
159 K8 **Lofthouse** N York
142 A3 **Lofthouse Gate** Wakefd
171 G7 **Loftus** R & Cl
197 H6 **Logan** E Ayrs
156 A4 **Loganbeck** Cumb
210 C6 **Loganlea** W Loth
114 A4 **Loggerheads** Staffs
235 H3 **Logie** Angus
223 G3 **Logie** Fife
253 K2 **Logie** Moray
243 M3 **Logie Coldstone** Abers
256 B4 **Logie Newton** Abers
235 G3 **Logie Pert** Angus
232 E5 **Logierait** P & K
257 G6 **Logierieve** Abers
55 K2 **Login** Carmth
87 H2 **Lolworth** Cambs
259 M6 **Lonbain** Highld
152 C6 **Londesborough** E R Yk
51 H3 **London** Gt Lon
5 G5 **London Apprentice** Cnwll
39 M6 **London Beach** Kent
68 F6 **London Colney** Herts
160 D5 **Londonderry** N York
85 H2 **London End** Nhants
118 D4 **Londonthorpe** Lincs
260 D4 **Londubh** Highld
260 C4 **Lonemore** Highld
45 H5 **Long Ashton** N Som
97 H8 **Long Bank** Worcs
117 L3 **Long Bennington** Lincs
181 G5 **Longbenton** N Tyne
65 J1 **Longborough** Gloucs
16 A4 **Long Bredy** Dorset
98 C7 **Longbridge** Birm
83 G3 **Longbridge** Warwks
32 E3 **Longbridge Deverill** Wilts
84 C2 **Long Buckby** Nhants
177 J7 **Longburgh** Cumb
31 L8 **Longburton** Dorset
8 B3 **Long Cause** Devon
117 J6 **Long Clawson** Leics
132 D8 **Longcliffe** Derbys
8 C3 **Longcombe** Devon
35 G7 **Long Common** Hants
114 D7 **Long Compton** Staffs

83 G8 **Long Compton** Warwks
47 K1 **Longcot** Oxon
67 G5 **Long Crendon** Bucks
17 J1 **Long Crichel** Dorset
177 H7 **Longcroft** Cumb
50 C6 **Longcross** Surrey
95 K2 **Longden** Shrops
95 K2 **Longden Common** Shrops
50 F5 **Long Ditton** Surrey
115 H8 **Longdon** Staffs
81 J7 **Longdon** Worcs
98 D1 **Longdon Green** Staffs
81 J7 **Longdon Heath** Worcs
113 K8 **Longdon upon Tern** Wrekin
13 K4 **Longdown** Devon
3 J4 **Longdowns** Cnwll
143 H2 **Long Drax** N York
133 J5 **Long Duckmanton** Derbys
116 E5 **Long Eaton** Derbys
52 D5 **Longfield** Kent
99 K6 **Longford** Covtry
115 L4 **Longford** Derbys
64 B3 **Longford** Gloucs
50 D4 **Longford** Gt Lon
38 D2 **Longford** Kent
113 L5 **Longford** Shrops
114 A7 **Longford** Wrekin
222 E1 **Longforgan** P & K
212 F7 **Longformacus** Border
191 G6 **Longframlington** Nthumb
129 L5 **Long Green** Ches W
81 J8 **Long Green** Worcs
17 L3 **Longham** Dorset
121 L8 **Longham** Norfk
66 B4 **Long Hanborough** Oxon
257 L4 **Longhaven** Abers
119 K2 **Long Hedges** Lincs
191 J8 **Longhirst** Nthumb
63 K3 **Longhope** Gloucs
275 b6 **Longhope** Ork
191 H7 **Longhorsley** Nthumb
191 J3 **Longhoughton** Nthumb
83 K2 **Long Itchington** Warwks
165 J3 **Longlands** Cumb
115 L4 **Longlane** Derbys
100 A8 **Long Lawford** Warwks
64 B3 **Longlevens** Gloucs
141 G3 **Longley** Calder
141 J6 **Longley Kirk**
81 G5 **Longley Green** Worcs
233 L6 **Longleys** P & K
31 G6 **Long Load** Somset
268 D4 **Longmanhill** Abers
67 L4 **Long Marston** Herts
151 H5 **Long Marston** N York
82 E5 **Long Marston** Warwks
166 F5 **Long Marton** Cumb
95 K7 **Long Meadowend** Shrops
89 H6 **Long Melford** Suffk
36 B4 **Longmoor Camp** Hants
266 E4 **Longmorn** Moray
131 H5 **Longmoss** Ches E
64 C8 **Long Newton** Gloucs
201 J7 **Longnewton** Border
212 B6 **Long Newton** E Loth
169 K7 **Longnewton** S on T
63 M4 **Longney** Gloucs
212 A4 **Longniddry** E Loth
96 B3 **Longnor** Shrops
132 B6 **Longnor** Staffs
34 F2 **Longparish** Hants
178 A6 **Longpark** Cumb
148 E4 **Long Preston** N York
147 M8 **Longridge** Lancs
114 E8 **Longridge** Staffs
210 C6 **Longridge** W Loth
209 L5 **Longriggend** N Lans
153 H7 **Long Riston** E R Yk
2 D5 **Longrock** Cnwll
114 F1 **Longsdon** Staffs
139 G7 **Longshaw** Wigan
269 J6 **Longside** Abers
140 D6 **Long Sight** Oldham
113 L4 **Longslow** Shrops
87 H2 **Longstanton** Cambs
34 D3 **Longstock** Hants
55 K5 **Longstone** Pembks
86 F4 **Longstowe** Cambs
106 D5 **Long Stratton** Norfk
84 F5 **Long Street** M Keyn
47 H8 **Longstreet** Wilts
35 M2 **Long Sutton** Hants
119 M7 **Long Sutton** Lincs
31 G6 **Long Sutton** Somset
102 D4 **Longthorpe** C Pete
89 K2 **Long Thurlow** Suffk
166 B6 **Longthwaite** Cumb
114 E3 **Longton** C Stke
138 F3 **Longton** Lancs
177 L5 **Longtown** Cumb

62 C1 **Longtown** Herefs
9 e3 **Longueville** Jersey
96 C4 **Longville in the Dale** Shrops
113 K8 **Long Waste** Wrekin
116 D6 **Long Whatton** Leics
67 J6 **Longwick** Bucks
66 E8 **Long Wittenham** Oxon
180 C1 **Longwitton** Nthumb
175 H3 **Longwood** D & G
96 D2 **Longwood** Shrops
66 A7 **Longworth** Oxon
212 C6 **Longyester** E Loth
57 K5 **Lon-las** Swans
269 J4 **Lonmay** Abers
258 D7 **Lonmore** Highld
6 B4 **Looe** Cnwll
39 J3 **Loose** Kent
13 G2 **Loosebeare** Devon
119 K6 **Loosegate** Lincs
67 K7 **Loosley Row** Bucks
268 A5 **Lootcherbrae** Abers
34 B4 **Lopcombe Corner** Wilts
30 F8 **Lopen** Somset
113 G5 **Loppington** Shrops
190 E5 **Lorbottle** Nthumb
20 C5 **Lordington** W Susx
104 B1 **Lordsbridge** Norfk
53 G6 **Lords Wood** Medway
233 J6 **Lornty** P & K
116 C2 **Loscoe** Derbys
15 L3 **Loscombe** Dorset
266 E2 **Lossiemouth** Moray
113 K5 **Lostford** Shrops
130 D5 **Lostock Gralam** Ches W
130 D5 **Lostock Green** Ches W
139 H3 **Lostock Hall** Lancs
139 K6 **Lostock Hall Fold** Bolton
139 K6 **Lostock Junction** Bolton
5 J3 **Lostwithiel** Cnwll
274 C6 **Lothbeg** Highld
149 G6 **Lothersdale** N York
274 C6 **Lothmore** Highld
49 L1 **Loudwater** Bucks
116 F7 **Loughborough** Leics
116 F7 **Loughborough Crematorium** Leics
57 G5 **Loughor** Swans
70 B7 **Loughton** Essex
85 G7 **Loughton** M Keyn
96 E6 **Loughton** Shrops
118 E7 **Lound** Lincs
134 D2 **Lound** Notts
107 K4 **Lound** Suffk
13 J7 **Lounston** Devon
116 C7 **Lount** Leics
136 F2 **Louth** Lincs
140 B2 **Love Clough** Lancs
19 M1 **Lovedean** Hants
34 B6 **Lover** Wilts
142 F8 **Loversall** Donc
70 F6 **Loves Green** Essex
160 E3 **Lovesome Hill** N York
55 J5 **Loveston** Pembks
31 K5 **Lovington** Somset
142 C4 **Low Ackworth** Wakefd
180 D2 **Low Angerton** Nthumb
63 M1 **Lowbands** Gloucs
172 C2 **Low Barbeth** D & G
136 A5 **Low Barlings** Lincs
162 C3 **Low Bell End** N York
148 A2 **Low Bentham** N York
157 K7 **Low Biggins** Cumb
157 K2 **Low Borrowbridge** Cumb
132 E2 **Low Bradfield** Sheff
149 H6 **Low Bradley** N York
166 A2 **Low Braithwaite** Cumb
143 K7 **Low Burnham** N Linc
191 J5 **Low Buston** Nthumb
164 C6 **Lowca** Cumb
151 L5 **Low Catton** E R Yk
169 H7 **Low Coniscliffe** Darltn
178 B7 **Low Crosby** Cumb
117 H2 **Lowdham** Notts
169 K8 **Low Dinsdale** Darltn
113 H5 **Lowe** Shrops
142 E3 **Low Eggborough** N York
131 K8 **Low Hill** Staffs
160 B6 **Low Ellington** N York
30 B4 **Lower Aisholt** Somset
16 E2 **Lower Ansty** Dorset
64 B2 **Lower Apperley** Gloucs
66 F3 **Lower Arncott** Oxon
13 K5 **Lower Ashton** Devon
49 H2 **Lower Assendon** Oxon
138 D2 **Lower Ballam** Lancs
139 G1 **Lower Bartle** Lancs
48 F3 **Lower Basildon** W Berk
79 M4 **Lower Bearwood** Herefs
37 K5 **Lower Beeding** W Susx
101 L5 **Lower Benefield** Nhants

82 A2 **Lower Bentley** Worcs
97 H5 **Lower Beobridge** Shrops
116 D1 **Lower Birchwood** Derbys
83 L5 **Lower Boddington** Nhants
2 B4 **Lower Boscaswell** Cnwll
36 C2 **Lower Bourne** Surrey
83 H7 **Lower Brailes** Warwks
247 L4 **Lower Breakish** Highld
131 H2 **Lower Bredbury** Stockp
81 J4 **Lower Broadheath** Worcs
79 L4 **Lower Broxwood** Herefs
80 E8 **Lower Buckenhill** Herefs
80 C7 **Lower Bullingham** Herefs
33 K7 **Lower Burgate** Hants
14 B3 **Lower Burrowton** Devon
80 A4 **Lower Burton** Herefs
86 D6 **Lower Caldecote** C Beds
63 L7 **Lower Cam** Gloucs
44 D7 **Lower Canada** N Som
83 M3 **Lower Catesby** Nhants
78 E8 **Lower Chapel** Powys
33 G5 **Lower Chicksgrove** Wilts
47 L8 **Lower Chute** Wilts
51 K2 **Lower Clapton** Gt Lon
97 L7 **Lower Clent** Worcs
13 K2 **Lower Creedy** Devon
131 L4 **Lower Crossings** Derbys
141 K6 **Lower Cumberworth** Kirk
57 L3 **Lower Cwmtwrch** Powys
139 K3 **Lower Darwen** Bl w D
85 L2 **Lower Dean** Bed
141 K6 **Lower Denby** Kirk
260 C7 **Lower Diabaig** Highld
23 J5 **Lower Dicker** E Susx
95 L6 **Lower Dinchope** Shrops
95 H6 **Lower Down** Shrops
150 F3 **Lower Dunsforth** N York
80 E6 **Lower Egleton** Herefs
131 L8 **Lower Elkstone** Staffs
115 J3 **Lower Ellastone** Staffs
67 G5 **Lower End** Bucks
85 H7 **Lower End** M Keyn
84 F3 **Lower End** Nhants
85 H3 **Lower End** Nhants
47 J8 **Lower Everleigh** Wilts
19 G4 **Lower Exbury** Hants
41 J5 **Lower Eythorne** Kent
45 G4 **Lower Failand** N Som
35 L4 **Lower Farringdon** Hants
50 E4 **Lower Feltham** Gt Lon
21 G3 **Lower Fittleworth** W Susx
154 c6 **Lower Foxdale** IoM
112 E5 **Lower Frankton** Shrops
54 F4 **Lower Freystrop** Pembks
36 A2 **Lower Froyle** Hants
8 D1 **Lower Gabwell** Devon
263 G2 **Lower Gledfield** Highld
31 G2 **Lower Godney** Somset
97 L5 **Lower Gornal** Dudley
86 C8 **Lower Gravenhurst** C Beds
86 D8 **Lower Green** Herts
87 J8 **Lower Green** Herts
38 E5 **Lower Green** Kent
39 G5 **Lower Green** Kent
121 L4 **Lower Green** Norfk
97 K2 **Lower Green** Staffs
88 E2 **Lower Green** Suffk
91 H4 **Lower Hacheston** Suffk
50 E5 **Lower Halliford** Surrey
15 M1 **Lower Halstock Leigh** Dorset
53 J5 **Lower Halstow** Kent
17 K4 **Lower Hamworthy** Poole
40 F5 **Lower Hardres** Kent
79 K3 **Lower Harpton** Herefs
53 H6 **Lower Hartlip** Kent
116 C1 **Lower Hartshay** Derbys
67 J4 **Lower Hartwell** Bucks
114 C4 **Lower Hatton** Staffs
156 B5 **Lower Hawthwaite** Cumb
79 K4 **Lower Hergest** Herefs
66 C2 **Lower Heyford** Oxon
147 H4 **Lower Heysham** Lancs
52 F4 **Lower Higham** Kent
90 E8 **Lower Holbrook** Suffk
112 F5 **Lower Hordley** Shrops
21 G3 **Lower Horncroft** W Susx
140 B1 **Lowerhouse** Lancs
141 J5 **Lower Houses** Kirk
81 H5 **Lower Howsell** Worcs
130 D1 **Lower Irlam** Salfd
116 C3 **Lower Kilburn** Derbys
46 A1 **Lower Kilcott** Gloucs
204 D7 **Lower Killeyan** Ag & B
16 A3 **Lower Kingcombe** Dorset
51 H8 **Lower Kingswood** Surrey
129 H7 **Lower Kinnerton** Ches W
44 F6 **Lower Langford** N Som
223 G6 **Lower Largo** Fife
115 G4 **Lower Leigh** Staffs
82 F8 **Lower Lemington** Gloucs

78 C2 **Lower Llanfadog** Powys
27 J5 **Lower Lovacott** Devon
27 L3 **Lower Loxhore** Devon
63 H4 **Lower Lydbrook** Gloucs
79 M2 **Lower Lye** Herefs
43 K4 **Lower Machen** Newpt
62 D1 **Lower Maes-coed** Herefs
17 L2 **Lower Mannington** Dorset
32 C2 **Lower Marston** Somset
63 H6 **Lower Meend** Gloucs
30 B4 **Lower Merridge** Somset
83 L7 **Lower Middleton Cheney** Nhants
31 J2 **Lower Milton** Somset
82 A6 **Lower Moor** Worcs
63 J8 **Lower Morton** S Glos
69 K6 **Lower Nazeing** Essex
82 F3 **Lower Norton** Warwks
32 C6 **Lower Nyland** Dorset
43 J7 **Lower Penarth** V Glam
97 K4 **Lower Penn** Staffs
18 E5 **Lower Pennington** Hants
139 G2 **Lower Penwortham** Lancs
130 E5 **Lower Peover** Ches E
140 D5 **Lower Place** Rochdl
67 H4 **Lower Pollicott** Bucks
82 E6 **Lower Quinton** Warwks
53 H5 **Lower Rainham** Medway
90 B7 **Lower Raydon** Suffk
29 J3 **Lower Roadwater** Somset
147 M3 **Lower Salter** Lancs
46 D3 **Lower Seagry** Wilts
70 C4 **Lower Sheering** Essex
85 K6 **Lower Shelton** C Beds
49 J3 **Lower Shiplake** Oxon
83 L3 **Lower Shuckburgh** Warwks
65 H3 **Lower Slaughter** Gloucs
141 L3 **Lower Soothill** Kirk
63 K5 **Lower Soudley** Gloucs
41 H7 **Lower Standen** Kent
46 D3 **Lower Stanton St Quintin** Wilts
53 H4 **Lower Stoke** Medway
63 K8 **Lower Stone** Gloucs
98 D3 **Lower Stonnall** Staffs
105 K4 **Lower Stow Bedon** Norfk
17 G3 **Lower Street** Dorset
24 C5 **Lower Street** E Susx
122 F4 **Lower Street** Norfk
88 F5 **Lower Street** Suffk
90 D5 **Lower Street** Suffk
130 C3 **Lower Stretton** Warrtn
15 K3 **Lower Stroud** Dorset
68 D2 **Lower Sundon** C Beds
19 H2 **Lower Swanwick** Hants
65 H2 **Lower Swell** Gloucs
83 J7 **Lower Tadmarton** Oxon
14 C2 **Lower Tale** Devon
115 G4 **Lower Tean** Staffs
107 J3 **Lower Thurlton** Norfk
3 G5 **Lower Town** Cnwll
13 G7 **Lower Town** Devon
80 E6 **Lower Town** Herefs
74 F5 **Lower Town** Pembks
11 L7 **Lower Trebullett** Cnwll
3 K4 **Lower Treluswell** Cnwll
83 H6 **Lower Tysoe** Warwks
91 G5 **Lower Ufford** Suffk
13 K6 **Lower Upcott** Devon
35 H7 **Lower Upham** Hants
53 G5 **Lower Upnor** Medway
29 L4 **Lower Vexford** Somset
130 B3 **Lower Walton** Warrtn
16 E3 **Lower Waterston** Dorset
44 E8 **Lower Weare** Somset
84 C3 **Lower Weedon** Nhants
79 K5 **Lower Welson** Herefs
81 L7 **Lower Westmancote** Worcs
17 G2 **Lower Whatcombe** Dorset
32 B2 **Lower Whatley** Somset
130 B4 **Lower Whitley** Ches W
63 L7 **Lower Wick** Gloucs
81 J5 **Lower Wick** Worcs
35 K3 **Lower Wield** Hants
23 K6 **Lower Willingdon** E Susx
130 F5 **Lower Withington** Ches E
49 K2 **Lower Woodend** Bucks
33 K4 **Lower Woodford** Wilts
16 A2 **Lower Wraxall** Dorset
81 H6 **Lower Wyche** Worcs
141 J3 **Lower Wyke** C Brad
100 F2 **Lowesby** Leics
107 L5 **Lowestoft** Suffk
164 F6 **Loweswater** Cumb
181 G7 **Low Fell** Gatesd
37 L3 **Lowfield Heath** W Susx
208 D2 **Low Gartachorrans** Stirlg
179 L6 **Low Gate** Nthumb
178 C7 **Low Gettbridge** Cumb
157 K3 **Lowgill** Cumb
148 A3 **Lowgill** Lancs

150 B2 **Low Grantley** N York
150 B4 **Low Green** N York
97 H7 **Low Habberley** Worcs
30 F5 **Low Ham** Somset
150 C5 **Low Harrogate** N York
163 G1 **Low Hawsker** N York
166 B2 **Low Hesket** Cumb
152 A2 **Low Hutton** N York
156 D5 **Lowick** Cumb
101 L7 **Lowick** Nhants
203 G5 **Lowick** Nthumb
156 D5 **Lowick Bridge** Cumb
156 D5 **Lowick Green** Cumb
166 C6 **Low Knipe** Cumb
150 B3 **Low Laithe** N York
168 E5 **Lowlands** Dur
62 C7 **Lowlands** Torfn
136 C4 **Low Langton** Lincs
131 K3 **Low Leighton** Derbys
164 F5 **Low Lorton** Cumb
162 E7 **Low Marishes** N York
134 F6 **Low Marnham** Notts
203 H6 **Low Middleton** Nthumb
161 L4 **Low Mill** N York
141 J2 **Low Moor** C Brad
169 J2 **Low Moorsley** Sundld
164 C6 **Low Moresby** Cumb
156 F6 **Low Newton** Cumb
164 F5 **Low Rogerscales** Cumb
165 G2 **Low Row** Cumb
165 K3 **Low Row** Cumb
178 D6 **Low Row** Cumb
159 H3 **Low Row** N York
172 C2 **Low Salchrie** D & G
144 B5 **Low Santon** N Linc
82 E2 **Lowsonford** Warwks
123 G6 **Low Street** Norfk
52 E3 **Low Street** Thurr
106 D4 **Low Tharston** Norfk
166 D6 **Lowther** Cumb
166 C6 **Lowther Castle** Cumb
153 H4 **Lowthorpe** E R Yk
12 F2 **Lowton** Devon
30 B7 **Lowton** Somset
139 J8 **Lowton** Wigan
139 J8 **Lowton Common** Wigan
139 J8 **Lowton St Mary's** Wigan
210 D2 **Low Torry** Fife
136 E5 **Low Toynton** Lincs
142 B7 **Low Valley** Barns
156 E6 **Low Wood** Cumb
160 F1 **Low Worsall** N York
156 E2 **Low Wray** Cumb
29 G7 **Loxbeare** Devon
36 F3 **Loxhill** Surrey
27 L3 **Loxhore** Devon
27 L3 **Loxhore Cott** Devon
83 G4 **Loxley** Warwks
115 H5 **Loxley Green** Staffs
81 G7 **Loxter** Herefs
44 D7 **Loxton** N Som
36 F4 **Loxwood** W Susx
277 L7 **Loyal Lodge** Highld
100 F6 **Lubenham** Leics
119 M2 **Lucasgate** Lincs
50 B7 **Lucas Green** Surrey
29 G2 **Luccombe** Somset
19 K7 **Luccombe Village** IoW
203 J7 **Lucker** Nthumb
11 M7 **Luckett** Cnwll
89 G6 **Lucking Street** Essex
46 B2 **Luckington** Wilts
46 B4 **Lucknam** Wilts
28 F3 **Luckwell Bridge** Somset
80 B2 **Lucton** Herefs
169 G8 **Lucy Cross** N York
283 c12 **Ludag** W Isls
145 H8 **Ludborough** Lincs
7 J4 **Ludbrook** Devon
55 K4 **Ludchurch** Pembks
141 G3 **Luddenden** Calder
140 F3 **Luddenden Foot** Calder
40 C3 **Luddenham Court** Kent
52 E5 **Luddesdown** Kent
143 L4 **Luddington** N Linc
82 E5 **Luddington** Warwks
102 C6 **Luddington in the Brook** Nhants
136 D2 **Ludford** Lincs
96 C8 **Ludford** Shrops
67 G4 **Ludgershall** Bucks
34 B1 **Ludgershall** Wilts
2 D4 **Ludgvan** Cnwll
123 H7 **Ludham** Norfk
96 C8 **Ludlow** Shrops
30 F8 **Ludney** Somset
32 F6 **Ludwell** Wilts
169 K2 **Ludworth** Dur
69 J1 **Luffenhall** Herts
11 L3 **Luffincott** Devon

212 B3 **Luffness** E Loth
197 H6 **Lugar** E Ayrs
212 D4 **Luggate Burn** E Loth
80 B3 **Lugg Green** Herefs
209 K4 **Luggiebank** N Lans
129 M3 **Lugsdale** Halton
208 C8 **Lugton** E Ayrs
80 D7 **Lugwardine** Herefs
247 J3 **Luib** Highld
80 A7 **Lulham** Herefs
99 H1 **Lullington** Derbys
23 J6 **Lullington** E Susx
45 M8 **Lullington** Somset
45 G6 **Lulsgate Bottom** N Som
81 G4 **Lulsley** Worcs
16 F6 **Lulworth Camp** Dorset
140 F3 **Lumb** Calder
140 C3 **Lumb** Lancs
140 E3 **Lumbutts** Calder
142 D2 **Lumby** N York
209 H5 **Lumloch** E Duns
244 D3 **Lumphanan** Abers
222 B8 **Lumphinnans** Fife
255 K7 **Lumsden** Abers
235 H5 **Lunan** Angus
234 D5 **Lunanhead** Angus
221 K1 **Luncarty** P & K
152 E6 **Lund** E R Yk
143 G1 **Lund** N York
233 L8 **Lundie** Angus
223 G6 **Lundin Links** Fife
223 G6 **Lundin Mill** Fife
106 E5 **Lundy Green** Norfk
281 e4 **Lunna** Shet
52 F7 **Lunsford** Kent
24 C5 **Lunsford's Cross** E Susx
138 D7 **Lunt** Sefton
79 M4 **Luntley** Herefs
14 E1 **Luppitt** Devon
7 L4 **Lupridge** Devon
141 M4 **Lupset** Wakefd
157 J6 **Lupton** Cumb
36 D5 **Lurgashall** W Susx
29 G7 **Lurley** Devon
136 F6 **Lusby** Lincs
8 B3 **Luscombe** Devon
7 H5 **Luson** Devon
218 E8 **Luss** Ag & B
215 J7 **Lussagiven** Ag & B
258 D5 **Lusta** Highld
13 H6 **Lustleigh** Devon
80 B3 **Luston** Herefs
235 G2 **Luthermuir** Abers
222 E3 **Luthrie** Fife
97 L6 **Lutley** Dudley
13 L7 **Luton** Devon
14 C2 **Luton** Devon
68 E3 **Luton** Luton
53 G5 **Luton** Medway
100 C6 **Lutterworth** Leics
7 H3 **Lutton** Devon
7 K3 **Lutton** Devon
119 M6 **Lutton** Lincs
102 C6 **Lutton** Nhants
29 H3 **Luxborough** Somset
5 H3 **Luxulyan** Cnwll
140 E7 **Luzley** Tamesd
275 H1 **Lybster** Highld
95 J6 **Lydbury North** Shrops
28 B4 **Lydcott** Devon
25 K3 **Lydd** Kent
41 H6 **Lydden** Kent
41 K2 **Lydden** Kent
101 J4 **Lyddington** Rutlnd
29 L4 **Lydeard St Lawrence** Somset
49 H7 **Lyde Green** Hants
12 C5 **Lydford** Devon
31 J5 **Lydford on Fosse** Somset
140 D3 **Lydgate** Calder
140 E4 **Lydgate** Rochdl
95 H5 **Lydham** Shrops
47 G2 **Lydiard Green** Wilts
47 G2 **Lydiard Millicent** Wilts
47 G2 **Lydiard Tregoze** Swindn
138 D7 **Lydiate** Sefton
98 B8 **Lydiate Ash** Worcs
32 B8 **Lydlinch** Dorset
63 J6 **Lydney** Gloucs
55 J7 **Lydstep** Pembks
97 L6 **Lye** Dudley
44 F6 **Lye Cross** N Som
68 B6 **Lye Green** Bucks
38 D6 **Lye Green** E Susx
82 E2 **Lye Green** Warwks
97 G8 **Lye Head** Worcs
32 D2 **Lye's Green** Wilts
66 B8 **Lyford** Oxon
40 F6 **Lymbridge Green** Kent
15 H4 **Lyme Regis** Dorset
40 F7 **Lyminge** Kent

18 E4 **Lymington** Hants
21 H6 **Lyminster** W Susx
130 D2 **Lymm** Warrtn
40 F8 **Lympne** Kent
44 C8 **Lympsham** Somset
14 A5 **Lympstone** Devon
28 C1 **Lynbridge** Devon
28 F2 **Lynch** Somset
241 L3 **Lynchat** Highld
106 C2 **Lynch Green** Norfk
18 D2 **Lyndhurst** Hants
101 K3 **Lyndon** Rutlnd
98 F6 **Lyndon Green** Birm
199 L5 **Lyne** Border
50 C5 **Lyne** Surrey
113 G5 **Lyneal** Shrops
63 J1 **Lyne Down** Herefs
13 K6 **Lyneham** Devon
65 K3 **Lyneham** Oxon
46 F3 **Lyneham** Wilts
178 C4 **Lyneholmford** Cumb
191 K7 **Lynemouth** Nthumb
245 G2 **Lyne of Skene** Abers
275 b6 **Lyness** Ork
122 B7 **Lyng** Norfk
30 E5 **Lyng** Somset
79 K4 **Lynhales** Herefs
28 C1 **Lynmouth** Devon
98 D3 **Lynn** Staffs
114 B8 **Lynn** Wrekin
254 E6 **Lynn of Shenval** Moray
40 B3 **Lynsted** Kent
11 H2 **Lynstone** Cnwll
28 C1 **Lynton** Devon
16 C1 **Lyon's Gate** Dorset
79 L4 **Lyonshall** Herefs
17 J3 **Lytchett Matravers** Dorset
17 J4 **Lytchett Minster** Dorset
280 C4 **Lyth** Highld
138 D2 **Lytham** Lancs
138 D2 **Lytham St Anne's** Lancs
95 L2 **Lythbank** Shrops
171 K8 **Lythe** N York
279 J3 **Lythmore** Highld

## M

3 J4 **Mabe Burnthouse** Cnwll
137 J3 **Mablethorpe** Lincs
131 H5 **Macclesfield** Ches E
131 H5 **Macclesfield Crematorium** Ches E
268 C3 **Macduff** Abers
192 E6 **Macharioch** Ag & B
43 K4 **Machen** Caerph
194 D4 **Machrie** N Ayrs
192 D4 **Machrihanish** Ag & B
214 D5 **Machrins** Ag & B
93 G3 **Machynlleth** Powys
56 F5 **Machynys** Carmth
116 A4 **Mackworth** Derbys
211 M4 **Macmerry** E Loth
12 D3 **Maddaford** Devon
221 G3 **Madderty** P & K
33 J2 **Maddington** Wilts
210 B4 **Maddiston** Falk
21 G5 **Madehurst** W Susx
114 B3 **Madeley** Staffs
96 F3 **Madeley** Wrekin
114 B2 **Madeley Heath** Staffs
29 L8 **Madford** Devon
87 H3 **Madingley** Cambs
80 A7 **Madley** Herefs
81 J5 **Madresfield** Worcs
2 C5 **Madron** Cnwll
125 H3 **Maenaddwyn** IoA
126 F6 **Maenan** Conwy
75 J6 **Maenclochog** Pembks
42 F6 **Maendy** V Glam
3 K5 **Maenporth** Cnwll
110 C3 **Maentwrog** Gwynd
76 C3 **Maen-y-groes** Cerdgn
11 H1 **Maer** Cnwll
114 B4 **Maer** Staffs
59 J3 **Maerdy** Carmth
42 E2 **Maerdy** Rhondd
112 D7 **Maesbrook** Shrops
112 D6 **Maesbury** Shrops
112 D6 **Maesbury Marsh** Shrops
44 C2 **Maes-glas** Newpt
55 L2 **Maesgwynne** Carmth
128 E7 **Maeshafn** Denbgs
76 C6 **Maesllyn** Cerdgn
78 D6 **Maesmynis** Powys
78 E5 **Maesmynis** Powys
42 C3 **Maesteg** Brdgnd
59 G5 **Maesybont** Carmth
43 J3 **Maesycwmmer** Caerph
70 D5 **Magdalen Laver** Essex

254 F3 **Maggieknockater** Moray
70 C2 **Maggots End** Essex
23 K5 **Magham Down** E Susx
138 D7 **Maghull** Sefton
100 B6 **Magna Park** Leics
44 E2 **Magor** Mons
37 L4 **Maidenbower** W Susx
32 D3 **Maiden Bradley** Wilts
8 D1 **Maidencombe** Torbay
15 G3 **Maidenhayne** Devon
45 H5 **Maiden Head** N Som
49 L3 **Maidenhead** W & M
168 F1 **Maiden Law** Dur
16 B3 **Maiden Newton** Dorset
182 F1 **Maidens** S Ayrs
49 L4 **Maiden's Green** Br For
136 F4 **Maidenwell** Lincs
55 G7 **Maiden Wells** Pembks
84 B5 **Maidford** Nhants
84 D8 **Maids Moreton** Bucks
39 J2 **Maidstone** Kent
101 G8 **Maidwell** Nhants
281 e6 **Mail** Shet
44 C1 **Maindee** Newpt
169 J4 **Mainsforth** Dur
234 D3 **Mains of Balhall** Angus
244 E8 **Mains of Balnakettle** Abers
254 B5 **Mains of Dalvey** Highld
235 H1 **Mains of Haulkerton** Abers
255 J6 **Mains of Lesmoir** Abers
176 B7 **Mainsriddle** D & G
95 G6 **Mainstone** Shrops
64 A3 **Maisemore** Gloucs
98 E7 **Major's Green** Worcs
116 B3 **Makeney** Derbys
7 K7 **Malborough** Devon
131 L3 **Malcoff** Derbys
50 F6 **Malden Rushett** Gt Lon
71 K5 **Maldon** Essex
148 F3 **Malham** N York
259 H4 **Maligar** Highld
237 H1 **Mallaig** Highld
237 K1 **Mallaigvaig** Highld
211 G6 **Malleny Mills** C Edin
70 C2 **Mallows Green** Essex
125 G6 **Malltraeth** IoA
93 J1 **Mallwyd** Gwynd
46 D2 **Malmesbury** Wilts
28 D1 **Malmsmead** Devon
113 H2 **Malpas** Ches W
4 D6 **Malpas** Cnwll
44 C1 **Malpas** Newpt
63 L2 **Malswick** Gloucs
136 F3 **Maltby** Lincs
133 K1 **Maltby** Rothm
170 B8 **Maltby** S on T
137 J3 **Maltby le Marsh** Lincs
72 E3 **Malting Green** Essex
40 B6 **Maltman's Hill** Kent
152 B2 **Malton** N York
81 H5 **Malvern Link** Worcs
81 H6 **Malvern Wells** Worcs
80 F1 **Mamble** Worcs
62 C6 **Mamhilad** Mons
3 J6 **Manaccan** Cnwll
94 D3 **Manafon** Powys
282 e6 **Manais** W Isls
13 H6 **Manaton** Devon
137 G2 **Manby** Lincs
99 J4 **Mancetter** Warwks
140 C8 **Manchester** Manch
129 H6 **Mancot** Flints
240 A3 **Mandally** Highld
103 K5 **Manea** Cambs
98 E4 **Maney** Birm
169 G8 **Manfield** N York
15 L3 **Mangerton** Dorset
45 K4 **Mangotsfield** S Glos
68 E2 **Mangrove Green** Herts
3 H5 **Manhay** Cnwll
282 e6 **Manish** W Isls
140 E3 **Mankinholes** Calder
129 L5 **Manley** Ches W
61 J6 **Manmoel** Caerph
224 C7 **Mannel** Ag & B
47 H7 **Manningford Bohune** Wilts
47 H7 **Manningford Bruce** Wilts
141 J1 **Manningham** C Brad
37 K5 **Manning's Heath** W Susx
17 L1 **Mannington** Dorset
73 G1 **Manningtree** Essex
245 K3 **Mannofield** C Aber
55 H7 **Manorbier** Pembks
55 H6 **Manorbier Newton** Pembks
59 J4 **Manordeilo** Carmth
201 K6 **Manorhill** Border
74 F5 **Manorowen** Pembks
51 L2 **Manor Park** Gt Lon
51 L2 **Manor Park Crematorium** Gt Lon

79 M6 **Mansell Gamage** Herefs
80 A6 **Mansell Lacy** Herefs
157 K6 **Mansergh** Cumb
197 J8 **Mansfield** E Ayrs
133 K7 **Mansfield** Notts
133 K7 **Mansfield & District Crematorium** Notts
133 K7 **Mansfield Woodhouse** Notts
156 D6 **Mansriggs** Cumb
32 D7 **Manston** Dorset
41 K2 **Manston** Kent
142 B1 **Manston** Leeds
17 J1 **Manswood** Dorset
118 B4 **Manthorpe** Lincs
118 E8 **Manthorpe** Lincs
144 A7 **Manton** N Linc
134 C4 **Manton** Notts
101 J3 **Manton** Rutlnd
47 H5 **Manton** Wilts
70 C2 **Manuden** Essex
70 E4 **Manwood Green** Essex
31 L5 **Maperton** Somset
134 E7 **Maplebeck** Notts
68 C8 **Maple Cross** Herts
49 G4 **Mapledurham** Oxon
49 G8 **Mapledurwell** Hants
37 J6 **Maplehurst** W Susx
52 C6 **Maplescombe** Kent
115 K2 **Mapleton** Derbys
38 C3 **Mapleton** Kent
116 D3 **Mapperley** Derbys
117 G3 **Mapperley Park** C Nott
15 L3 **Mapperton** Dorset
82 C2 **Mappleborough Green** Warwks
153 K7 **Mappleton** E R Yk
141 M5 **Mapplewell** Barns
16 E1 **Mappowder** Dorset
4 C5 **Marazanvose** Cnwll
2 E5 **Marazion** Cnwll
113 J2 **Marbury** Ches E
103 J4 **March** Cambs
186 E3 **March** S Lans
66 C7 **Marcham** Oxon
113 K5 **Marchamley** Shrops
113 K5 **Marchamley Wood** Shrops
115 J5 **Marchington** Staffs
115 J6 **Marchington Woodlands** Staffs
108 E6 **Marchros** Gwynd
112 E2 **Marchwiel** Wrexhm
18 F2 **Marchwood** Hants
42 D7 **Marcross** V Glam
80 C6 **Marden** Herefs
39 J4 **Marden** Kent
47 G7 **Marden** Wilts
70 E6 **Marden Ash** Essex
39 J5 **Marden Beech** Kent
38 D7 **Mardens Hill** E Susx
39 J5 **Marden Thorn** Kent
69 H3 **Mardlebury** Herts
62 C4 **Mardy** Mons
101 G2 **Marefield** Leics
136 E7 **Mareham le Fen** Lincs
136 E6 **Mareham on the Hill** Lincs
116 C2 **Marehay** Derbys
21 H3 **Marehill** W Susx
23 G2 **Maresfield** E Susx
144 E2 **Marfleet** C KuH
129 H8 **Marford** Wrexhm
57 L7 **Margam** Neath
42 B4 **Margam Crematorium** Neath
32 D7 **Margaret Marsh** Dorset
70 F5 **Margaret Roding** Essex
71 G6 **Margaretting** Essex
71 G7 **Margaretting Tye** Essex
41 K1 **Margate** Kent
195 G4 **Margnaheglish** N Ayrs
174 F5 **Margrie** D & G
170 F7 **Margrove Park** R & Cl
104 E2 **Marham** Norfk
11 J2 **Marhamchurch** Cnwll
102 C3 **Marholm** C Pete
125 J3 **Marian-glas** IoA
28 C6 **Mariansleigh** Devon
53 K4 **Marine Town** Kent
244 F2 **Marionburgh** Abers
259 H4 **Marishader** Highld
6 F2 **Maristow** Devon
176 E2 **Marjoriebanks** D & G
30 F1 **Mark** Somset
38 D5 **Markbeech** Kent
137 H4 **Markby** Lincs
30 E2 **Mark Causeway** Somset
38 F7 **Mark Cross** E Susx
116 B4 **Markeaton** C Derb
116 B4 **Markeaton Crematorium** C Derb
99 L3 **Market Bosworth** Leics
102 C2 **Market Deeping** Lincs
113 L5 **Market Drayton** Shrops
100 F6 **Market Harborough** Leics

334 Market Lavington - Merton

46 E8 **Market Lavington** Wilts
118 A8 **Market Overton** Rutlnd
136 B2 **Market Rasen** Lincs
136 D4 **Market Stainton** Lincs
133 L6 **Market Warsop** Notts
152 D7 **Market Weighton** E R Yk
105 K7 **Market Weston** Suffk
100 B2 **Markfield** Leics
61 J6 **Markham** Caerph
134 E5 **Markham Moor** Notts
222 E6 **Markinch** Fife
150 C3 **Markington** N York
212 C3 **Markle** E Loth
45 K6 **Marksbury** BaNES
19 H5 **Mark's Corner** IoW
72 C2 **Marks Tey** Essex
6 D3 **Markwell** Cnwll
68 D4 **Markyate** Herts
81 H7 **Marl Bank** Worcs
47 J5 **Marlborough** Wilts
80 C4 **Marlbrook** Herefs
98 B8 **Marlbrook** Worcs
82 C5 **Marlcliff** Warwks
8 C2 **Marldon** Devon
23 K4 **Marle Green** E Susx
91 H3 **Marlesford** Suffk
41 G5 **Marley** Kent
41 K4 **Marley** Kent
113 J2 **Marley Green** Ches E
180 F7 **Marley Hill** Gatesd
106 C2 **Marlingford** Norfk
54 C5 **Marloes** Pembks
49 K2 **Marlow** Bucks
95 K8 **Marlow** Herefs
49 K1 **Marlow Bottom** Bucks
38 C4 **Marlpit Hill** Kent
24 C4 **Marlpits** E Susx
38 C7 **Marlpits** E Susx
116 D3 **Marlpool** Derbys
32 C7 **Marnhull** Dorset
131 J2 **Marple** Stockp
131 J2 **Marple Bridge** Stockp
142 E6 **Marr** Donc
159 K3 **Marrick** N York
55 L5 **Marros** Carmth
141 G5 **Marsden** Kirk
181 K6 **Marsden** S Tyne
148 F8 **Marsden Height** Lancs
158 F5 **Marsett** N York
67 K5 **Marsh** Bucks
149 J8 **Marsh** C Brad
30 C8 **Marsh** Devon
68 F4 **Marshall's Heath** Herts
68 F5 **Marshalswick** Herts
122 D6 **Marsham** Norfk
66 E7 **Marsh Baldon** Oxon
48 B5 **Marsh Benham** W Berk
41 J4 **Marshborough** Kent
95 K5 **Marshbrook** Shrops
145 K7 **Marshchapel** Lincs
68 D2 **Marsh Farm** Luton
43 L5 **Marshfield** Newpt
45 M4 **Marshfield** S Glos
11 G4 **Marshgate** Cnwll
66 F3 **Marsh Gibbon** Bucks
14 B4 **Marsh Green** Devon
38 C4 **Marsh Green** Kent
113 K8 **Marsh Green** Wrekin
103 L2 **Marshland St James** Norfk
133 H4 **Marsh Lane** Derbys
63 H5 **Marsh Lane** Gloucs
138 D4 **Marshside** Sefton
29 H2 **Marsh Street** Somset
15 J3 **Marshwood** Dorset
159 K3 **Marske** N York
170 E6 **Marske-by-the-Sea** R & Cl
139 K7 **Marsland Green** Wigan
130 D5 **Marston** Ches W
79 L4 **Marston** Herefs
118 A3 **Marston** Lincs
66 D5 **Marston** Oxon
97 J1 **Marston** Staffs
114 E6 **Marston** Staffs
99 G4 **Marston** Warwks
46 D7 **Marston** Wilts
98 F6 **Marston Green** Solhll
99 K5 **Marston Jabbet** Warwks
31 K6 **Marston Magna** Somset
65 H7 **Marston Meysey** Wilts
115 J4 **Marston Montgomery** Derbys
85 K7 **Marston Moretaine** C Beds
115 L5 **Marston on Dove** Derbys
83 M6 **Marston St Lawrence** Nhants
80 D4 **Marston Stannett** Herefs
100 F6 **Marston Trussell** Nhants
63 H3 **Marstow** Herefs
68 A4 **Marsworth** Bucks
47 L7 **Marten** Wilts
130 F4 **Marthall** Ches E
123 J7 **Martham** Norfk
33 J7 **Martin** Hants
41 K6 **Martin** Kent
136 B7 **Martin** Lincs
136 D6 **Martin** Lincs
166 B6 **Martindale** Cumb
136 C7 **Martin Dales** Lincs
33 H6 **Martin Drove End** Hants
28 B1 **Martinhoe** Devon
81 K3 **Martin Hussingtree** Worcs
130 C2 **Martinscroft** Warrtn
16 C4 **Martinstown** Dorset
90 F6 **Martlesham** Suffk
90 F6 **Martlesham Heath** Suffk
55 H5 **Martletwy** Pembks
81 H3 **Martley** Worcs
31 G7 **Martock** Somset
131 G6 **Marton** Ches E
130 C6 **Marton** Ches W
156 C7 **Marton** Cumb
153 J7 **Marton** E R Yk
153 K2 **Marton** E R Yk
135 G3 **Marton** Lincs
170 C7 **Marton** Middsb
150 F3 **Marton** N York
162 C6 **Marton** N York
95 G3 **Marton** Shrops
83 J2 **Marton** Warwks
150 E2 **Marton-le-Moor** N York
50 E7 **Martyr's Green** Surrey
35 G4 **Martyr Worthy** Hants
275 b3 **Marwick** Ork
27 K3 **Marwood** Devon
250 E1 **Marybank** Highld
262 F8 **Maryburgh** Highld
245 J4 **Maryculter** Abers
213 H7 **Marygold** Border
208 F5 **Maryhill** C Glas
235 H2 **Marykirk** Abers
63 G6 **Maryland** Mons
51 H3 **Marylebone** Gt Lon
139 H6 **Marylebone** Wigan
254 D4 **Marypark** Moray
164 D3 **Maryport** Cumb
172 E7 **Maryport** D & G
12 B6 **Marystow** Devon
12 C6 **Mary Tavy** Devon
235 H4 **Maryton** Angus
244 D4 **Marywell** Abers
245 L4 **Marywell** Abers
235 G6 **Marywell** Angus
160 B6 **Masham** N York
71 G5 **Mashbury** Essex
180 F4 **Mason** N u Ty
157 L7 **Masongill** N York
196 D7 **Masonhill Crematorium** S Ayrs
133 J4 **Mastin Moor** Derbys
70 D5 **Matching** Essex
70 D5 **Matching Green** Essex
70 D5 **Matching Tye** Essex
180 C4 **Matfen** Nthumb
39 G5 **Matfield** Kent
45 G1 **Mathern** Mons
81 G6 **Mathon** Herefs
74 E6 **Mathry** Pembks
122 C4 **Matlask** Norfk
132 F7 **Matlock** Derbys
132 F7 **Matlock Bank** Derbys
132 F8 **Matlock Bath** Derbys
132 F7 **Matlock Dale** Derbys
64 B4 **Matson** Gloucs
165 L6 **Matterdale End** Cumb
134 D2 **Mattersey** Notts
134 D2 **Mattersey Thorpe** Notts
49 H7 **Mattingley** Hants
105 L1 **Mattishall** Norfk
105 L1 **Mattishall Burgh** Norfk
196 F5 **Mauchline** E Ayrs
269 G6 **Maud** Abers
9 e2 **Maufant** Jersey
65 J2 **Maugersbury** Gloucs
154 g4 **Maughold** IoM
250 C4 **Mauld** Highld
85 L7 **Maulden** C Beds
166 E7 **Maulds Meaburn** Cumb
160 E5 **Maunby** N York
80 D5 **Maund Bryan** Herefs
29 J5 **Maundown** Somset
107 K1 **Mautby** Norfk
115 H8 **Mavesyn Ridware** Staffs
137 G6 **Mavis Enderby** Lincs
164 E1 **Mawbray** Cumb
139 G5 **Mawdesley** Lancs
42 B5 **Mawdlam** Brdgnd
3 H6 **Mawgan** Cnwll
4 D2 **Mawgan Porth** Cnwll
130 D8 **Maw Green** Ches E
4 A5 **Mawla** Cnwll
3 K5 **Mawnan** Cnwll
3 K5 **Mawnan Smith** Cnwll
101 H8 **Mawsley** Nhants
137 J5 **Mawthorpe** Lincs
102 C2 **Maxey** C Pete
99 G6 **Maxstoke** Warwks
40 F6 **Maxted Street** Kent
201 J7 **Maxton** Border
41 J7 **Maxton** Kent
176 C4 **Maxwell Town** D & G
11 J4 **Maxworthy** Cnwll
57 H6 **Mayals** Swans
114 D2 **May Bank** Staffs
183 H1 **Maybole** S Ayrs
50 C7 **Maybury** Surrey
37 H3 **Mayes Green** Surrey
23 K2 **Mayfield** E Susx
211 K6 **Mayfield** Mdloth
115 J2 **Mayfield** Staffs
50 C7 **Mayford** Surrey
63 L3 **May Hill** Gloucs
72 D6 **Mayland** Essex
72 C6 **Maylandsea** Essex
23 K3 **Maynard's Green** E Susx
98 D7 **Maypole** Birm
41 G2 **Maypole** Kent
62 F4 **Maypole** Mons
107 J4 **Maypole Green** Norfk
89 J3 **Maypole Green** Suffk
91 G2 **Maypole Green** Suffk
49 H3 **May's Green** Oxon
50 E7 **May's Green** Surrey
26 C7 **Mead** Devon
45 K7 **Meadgate** BaNES
67 K6 **Meadle** Bucks
169 H3 **Meadowfield** Dur
95 H3 **Meadowtown** Shrops
12 A6 **Meadwell** Devon
157 H4 **Meal Bank** Cumb
164 F2 **Mealrigg** Cumb
165 H2 **Mealsgate** Cumb
150 C8 **Meanwood** Leeds
148 E4 **Mearbeck** N York
31 G3 **Meare** Somset
30 D6 **Meare Green** Somset
30 E5 **Meare Green** Somset
208 F7 **Mearns** E Rens
85 G2 **Mears Ashby** Nhants
99 J1 **Measham** Leics
156 F6 **Meathop** Cumb
153 H7 **Meaux** E R Yk
7 G2 **Meavy** Devon
101 H5 **Medbourne** Leics
26 D7 **Meddon** Devon
134 B5 **Meden Vale** Notts
136 F8 **Medlam** Lincs
147 H8 **Medlar** Lancs
49 K2 **Medmenham** Bucks
180 D7 **Medomsley** Dur
35 K3 **Medstead** Hants
53 G6 **Medway Crematorium** Kent
131 K7 **Meerbrook** Staffs
79 L5 **Meer Common** Herefs
70 B1 **Meesden** Herts
113 L7 **Meeson** Wrekin
12 D1 **Meeth** Devon
88 E4 **Meeting Green** Suffk
122 F6 **Meeting House Hill** Norfk
58 B5 **Meidrim** Carmth
94 E1 **Meifod** Powys
233 L6 **Meigle** P & K
186 A3 **Meikle Carco** D & G
209 J8 **Meikle Earnock** S Lans
207 G6 **Meikle Kilmory** Ag & B
232 F7 **Meikle Obney** P & K
233 J7 **Meikleour** P & K
256 C5 **Meikle Wartle** Abers
56 E3 **Meinciau** Carmth
114 E3 **Meir** C Stke
114 E3 **Meir Heath** Staffs
87 H6 **Melbourn** Cambs
116 C6 **Melbourne** Derbys
152 A7 **Melbourne** E R Yk
4 F4 **Melbur** Cnwll
26 F7 **Melbury** Devon
32 E6 **Melbury Abbas** Dorset
16 B1 **Melbury Bubb** Dorset
16 A1 **Melbury Osmond** Dorset
16 A1 **Melbury Sampford** Dorset
85 K2 **Melchbourne** Bed
16 E2 **Melcombe Bingham** Dorset
12 D4 **Meldon** Devon
180 D2 **Meldon** Nthumb
180 D2 **Meldon Park** Nthumb
87 H6 **Meldreth** Cambs
220 C7 **Meldrum** Stirlg
216 C4 **Melfort** Ag & B
234 E4 **Melgund Castle** Angus
128 C3 **Meliden** Denbgs
55 K4 **Melinau** Pembks
93 H4 **Melin-byrhedyn** Powys
60 B6 **Melincourt** Neath
127 G7 **Melin-y-coed** Conwy
94 D2 **Melin-y-ddol** Powys
111 K2 **Melin-y-wig** Denbgs
166 D5 **Melkinthorpe** Cumb
179 G6 **Melkridge** Nthumb
46 C6 **Melksham** Wilts
3 H5 **Mellangoose** Cnwll
48 C3 **Mell Green** W Berk
166 B2 **Mellguards** Cumb
147 M2 **Melling** Lancs
138 E7 **Melling** Sefton
138 E7 **Melling Mount** Sefton
106 B8 **Mellis** Suffk
260 D2 **Mellon Charles** Highld
260 E1 **Mellon Udrigle** Highld
139 K2 **Mellor** Lancs
131 K2 **Mellor** Stockp
139 J2 **Mellor Brook** Lancs
32 B1 **Mells** Somset
107 H8 **Mells** Suffk
166 E3 **Melmerby** Cumb
159 K5 **Melmerby** N York
160 E7 **Melmerby** N York
277 K4 **Melness** Highld
89 G4 **Melon Green** Suffk
15 L3 **Melplash** Dorset
201 H6 **Melrose** Border
275 b6 **Melsetter** Ork
160 B1 **Melsonby** N York
141 H5 **Meltham** Kirk
141 H5 **Meltham Mills** Kirk
144 B2 **Melton** E R Yk
91 G5 **Melton** Suffk
152 B5 **Meltonby** E R Yk
122 A5 **Melton Constable** Norfk
117 K7 **Melton Mowbray** Leics
144 D5 **Melton Ross** N Linc
260 B3 **Melvaig** Highld
112 E8 **Melverley** Shrops
112 E7 **Melverley Green** Shrops
278 E3 **Melvich** Highld
15 G2 **Membury** Devon
269 H4 **Memsie** Abers
234 C4 **Memus** Angus
5 J4 **Menabilly** Cnwll
4 B5 **Menagissey** Cnwll
125 K5 **Menai Bridge** IoA
106 F6 **Mendham** Suffk
90 D2 **Mendlesham** Suffk
90 C3 **Mendlesham Green** Suffk
6 B2 **Menheniot** Cnwll
81 G2 **Menithwood** Worcs
185 K2 **Mennock** D & G
149 L7 **Menston** C Brad
220 E7 **Menstrie** Clacks
143 H1 **Menthorpe** N York
67 M3 **Mentmore** Bucks
238 C6 **Meoble** Highld
96 B1 **Meole Brace** Shrops
35 J7 **Meonstoke** Hants
52 D5 **Meopham** Kent
52 D6 **Meopham Green** Kent
52 D5 **Meopham Station** Kent
103 J7 **Mepal** Cambs
86 C8 **Meppershall** C Beds
79 K6 **Merbach** Herefs
130 E3 **Mere** Ches E
32 D4 **Mere** Wilts
138 E4 **Mere Brow** Lancs
140 C2 **Mereclough** Lancs
98 E4 **Mere Green** Birm
81 L3 **Mere Green** Worcs
130 C5 **Mere Heath** Ches W
53 H6 **Meresborough** Medway
39 G3 **Mereworth** Kent
99 G7 **Meriden** Solhll
246 E2 **Merkadale** Highld
17 K3 **Merley** Poole
54 F4 **Merlin's Bridge** Pembks
113 G7 **Merrington** Shrops
54 F7 **Merrion** Pembks
31 G8 **Merriott** Somset
12 D7 **Merrivale** Devon
36 F1 **Merrow** Surrey
17 K2 **Merry Field Hill** Dorset
68 E8 **Merry Hill** Herts
97 K4 **Merryhill** Wolves
100 A2 **Merry Lees** Leics
6 B2 **Merrymeet** Cnwll
40 D7 **Mersham** Kent
51 H8 **Merstham** Surrey
20 E6 **Merston** W Susx
19 J6 **Merstone** IoW
4 D6 **Merther** Cnwll
58 C5 **Merthyr** Carmth
78 D7 **Merthyr Cynog** Powys
43 H7 **Merthyr Dyfan** V Glam
42 D6 **Merthyr Mawr** Brdgnd
61 G6 **Merthyr Tydfil** Myr Td
61 G7 **Merthyr Vale** Myr Td
27 J8 **Merton** Devon

Merton - Minto 335


51 H5 Merton Gt Lon
105 H4 Merton Norfk
66 E3 Merton Oxon
28 D7 Meshaw Devon
72 C3 Messing Essex
143 M6 Messingham N Linc
106 F7 Metfield Suffk
6 E1 Metherell Cnwll
135 L7 Metheringham Lincs
222 F7 Methil Fife
222 F7 Methilhill Fife
142 B2 Methley Leeds
142 B3 Methley Junction Leeds
256 F4 Methlick Abers
221 J2 Methven P & K
104 E4 Methwold Norfk
104 E4 Methwold Hythe Norfk
107 H5 Mettingham Suffk
122 D4 Metton Norfk
5 G6 Mevagissey Cnwll
142 D7 Mexborough Donc
280 C2 Mey Highld
108 D5 Meyllteyrn Gwynd
65 G7 Meysey Hampton Gloucs
282 e3 Miabhig W Isls
282 e3 Miavaig W Isls
63 G2 Michaelchurch Herefs
79 K8 Michaelchurch Escley Herefs
79 J5 Michaelchurch-on-Arrow Powys
43 K5 Michaelstone-y-Fedw Newpt
43 J7 Michaelston-le-Pit V Glam
10 F6 Michaelstow Cnwll
7 K1 Michelcombe Devon
35 G3 Micheldever Hants
35 G2 Micheldever Station Hants
34 D5 Michelmersh Hants
90 D3 Mickfield Suffk
133 K1 Micklebring Donc
171 J8 Mickleby N York
142 C1 Micklefield Leeds
68 D7 Micklefield Green Herts
50 F8 Mickleham Surrey
116 A5 Mickleover C Derb
149 K7 Micklethwaite C Brad
165 J1 Micklethwaite Cumb
168 B6 Mickleton Dur
82 E6 Mickleton Gloucs
142 B2 Mickletown Leeds
129 K5 Mickle Trafford Ches W
132 F4 Mickley Derbys
160 C7 Mickley N York
89 G4 Mickley Green Suffk
180 C6 Mickley Square Nthumb
269 H3 Mid Ardlaw Abers
275 c2 Midbea Ork
244 E3 Mid Beltie Abers
18 B4 Mid Bockhampton Dorset
210 E5 Mid Calder W Loth
280 C8 Mid Clyth Highld
268 B4 Mid Culbeuchly Abers
49 H2 Middle Assendon Oxon
66 C2 Middle Aston Oxon
66 B2 Middle Barton Oxon
177 H4 Middlebie D & G
232 C2 Middlebridge P & K
31 G8 Middle Chinnock Somset
67 H2 Middle Claydon Bucks
142 C6 Middlecliffe Barns
13 G5 Middlecott Devon
64 E6 Middle Duntisbourne Gloucs
159 L5 Middleham N York
133 H4 Middle Handley Derbys
105 K6 Middle Harling Norfk
6 B1 Middlehill Cnwll
46 B5 Middlehill Wilts
96 B5 Middlehope Shrops
206 E1 Middle Kames Ag & B
82 C6 Middle Littleton Worcs
114 B3 Middle Madeley Staffs
79 L8 Middle Maes-coed Herefs
16 C1 Middlemarsh Dorset
115 J3 Middle Mayfield Staffs
74 C7 Middle Mill Pembks
12 C7 Middlemore Devon
40 A7 Middle Quarter Kent
136 A2 Middle Rasen Lincs
8 D1 Middle Rocombe Devon
147 M3 Middle Salter Lancs
170 C6 Middlesbrough Middsb
165 L2 Middlesceugh Cumb
157 J5 Middleshaw Cumb
159 K7 Middlesmoor N York
30 B6 Middle Stoford Somset
53 H4 Middle Stoke Medway
169 H4 Middlestone Dur
169 H4 Middlestone Moor Dur
30 F1 Middle Stoughton Somset
141 L4 Middlestown Wakefd
63 M6 Middle Street Gloucs
5 K2 Middle Taphouse Cnwll
201 L4 Middlethird Border
224 B6 Middleton Ag & B
157 K5 Middleton Cumb
132 D7 Middleton Derbys
132 E8 Middleton Derbys
89 H7 Middleton Essex
34 F2 Middleton Hants
80 D1 Middleton Herefs
147 H4 Middleton Lancs
141 M2 Middleton Leeds
149 L6 Middleton N York
162 D5 Middleton N York
101 J5 Middleton Nhants
120 E8 Middleton Norfk
180 C2 Middleton Nthumb
203 H6 Middleton Nthumb
221 L6 Middleton P & K
140 C6 Middleton Rochdl
96 C7 Middleton Shrops
112 D5 Middleton Shrops
91 K2 Middleton Suffk
56 D7 Middleton Swans
98 F4 Middleton Warwks
83 L7 Middleton Cheney Nhants
140 C6 Middleton Crematorium Rochdl
114 F4 Middleton Green Staffs
202 F8 Middleton Hall Nthumb
168 B5 Middleton-in-Teesdale Dur
91 J2 Middleton Moor Suffk
169 K8 Middleton One Row Darltn
161 G1 Middleton-on-Leven N York
20 F6 Middleton-on-Sea W Susx
80 C2 Middleton on the Hill Herefs
152 E6 Middleton on the Wolds E R Yk
96 E5 Middleton Priors Shrops
160 E7 Middleton Quernhow N York
169 K8 Middleton St George Darltn
96 F6 Middleton Scriven Shrops
66 D2 Middleton Stoney Oxon
160 B2 Middleton Tyas N York
155 H1 Middletown Cumb
10 b3 Middle Town IoS
44 F4 Middletown N Som
95 H1 Middletown Powys
83 H6 Middle Tysoe Warwks
34 C3 Middle Wallop Hants
130 D6 Middlewich Ches E
34 B4 Middle Winterslow Wilts
11 K7 Middlewood Cnwll
79 K6 Middlewood Herefs
33 K4 Middle Woodford Wilts
90 C3 Middlewood Green Suffk
197 G4 Middleyard E Ayrs
64 B6 Middle Yard Gloucs
30 E4 Middlezoy Somset
169 H5 Middridge Dur
45 M6 Midford BaNES
139 G3 Midge Hall Lancs
178 E7 Midgeholme Cumb
48 E5 Midgham W Berk
140 F3 Midgley Calder
141 L5 Midgley Wakefd
37 J2 Mid Holmwood Surrey
141 K7 Midhopestones Sheff
36 C6 Midhurst W Susx
20 D5 Mid Lavant W Susx
201 H7 Midlem Border
250 D4 Mid Mains Highld
31 H5 Midney Somset
207 G7 Midpark Ag & B
45 K8 Midsomer Norton BaNES
136 E5 Mid Thorpe Lincs
277 K4 Midtown Highld
137 G8 Midville Lincs
83 G3 Mid Warwickshire Crematorium Warwks
131 H3 Midway Ches E
281 e3 Mid Yell Shet
244 A2 Migvie Abers
31 L7 Milborne Port Somset
16 F3 Milborne St Andrew Dorset
31 L6 Milborne Wick Somset
180 D4 Milbourne Nthumb
46 D2 Milbourne Wilts
166 F5 Milburn Cumb
45 K1 Milbury Heath S Glos
150 F2 Milby N York
83 K8 Milcombe Oxon
89 J6 Milden Suffk
104 E8 Mildenhall Suffk
47 J5 Mildenhall Wilts
79 K1 Milebrook Powys
39 J4 Milebush Kent
46 E5 Mile Elm Wilts
72 E2 Mile End Essex
63 H5 Mile End Gloucs
107 G5 Mile End Suffk
121 K7 Mileham Norfk
22 C5 Mile Oak Br & H
39 H4 Mile Oak Kent
98 F3 Mile Oak Staffs
80 D2 Miles Hope Herefs
210 E1 Milesmark Fife
140 C7 Miles Platting Manch
53 K4 Mile Town Kent
202 E6 Milfield Nthumb
116 B3 Milford Derbys
26 D6 Milford Devon
94 D5 Milford Powys
114 F7 Milford Staffs
36 E2 Milford Surrey
54 E5 Milford Haven Pembks
18 D5 Milford on Sea Hants
63 H5 Milkwall Gloucs
9 a1 Millais Jersey
36 B5 Milland W Susx
36 C5 Milland Marsh W Susx
140 F3 Mill Bank Calder
165 H5 Millbeck Cumb
257 J3 Millbreck Abers
36 C2 Millbridge Surrey
85 K7 Millbrook C Beds
34 E8 Millbrook C Sotn
6 E4 Millbrook Cnwll
9 c3 Millbrook Jersey
140 E7 Millbrook Tamesd
131 J2 Mill Brow Stockp
245 H2 Millbuie Abers
250 F1 Millbuie Highld
196 E5 Millburn S Ayrs
8 B5 Millcombe Devon
107 G3 Mill Common Norfk
107 H7 Mill Common Suffk
24 E3 Millcorner E Susx
263 H5 Millcraig Highld
7 L3 Mill Cross Devon
115 J1 Milldale Staffs
49 J2 Mill End Bucks
103 G7 Mill End Cambs
63 L7 Millend Gloucs
87 G8 Mill End Herts
211 K5 Millerhill Mdloth
132 C5 Miller's Dale Derbys
115 M1 Millers Green Derbys
70 E5 Miller's Green Essex
209 H5 Millerston C Glas
140 D4 Millgate Lancs
88 C6 Mill Green Cambs
70 F6 Mill Green Essex
69 G5 Mill Green Herts
119 H6 Mill Green Lincs
106 C6 Mill Green Norfk
113 L6 Millgreen Shrops
98 D3 Mill Green Staffs
115 H7 Mill Green Staffs
89 J6 Mill Green Suffk
89 K4 Mill Green Suffk
90 D3 Mill Green Suffk
91 H3 Mill Green Suffk
79 K5 Millhalf Herefs
14 F2 Millhayes Devon
147 K2 Millhead Lancs
198 B3 Millheugh S Lans
23 L6 Mill Hill E Susx
69 G8 Mill Hill Gt Lon
206 F5 Millhouse Ag & B
165 K3 Millhouse Cumb
176 F2 Millhousebridge D & G
141 K7 Millhouse Green Barns
142 C6 Millhouses Barns
133 G3 Millhouses Sheff
208 C6 Milliken Park Rens
55 G4 Millin Cross Pembks
152 C5 Millington E R Yk
114 C5 Millmeece Staffs
157 H6 Millness Cumb
220 E4 Mill of Drummond P & K
208 C3 Mill of Haldane W Duns
155 M6 Millom Cumb
11 H3 Millook Cnwll
2 F5 Millpool Cnwll
11 G8 Millpool Cnwll
207 K8 Millport N Ayrs
157 G6 Mill Side Cumb
39 H2 Mill Street Kent
122 B7 Mill Street Norfk
90 C1 Mill Street Suffk
132 F4 Millthorpe Derbys
157 L4 Millthrop Cumb
245 J3 Milltimber C Aber
243 J2 Milltown Abers
255 J8 Milltown Abers
5 J3 Milltown Cnwll
177 K4 Milltown D & G
133 G7 Milltown Derbys
27 K3 Milltown Devon
244 E3 Milltown of Campfield Abers
254 F4 Milltown of Edinvillie Moray
244 E3 Milltown of Learney Abers
221 L6 Milnathort P & K
208 F4 Milngavie E Duns
140 D5 Milnrow Rochdl
157 H6 Milnthorpe Cumb
142 A4 Milnthorpe Wakefd
258 B6 Milovaig Highld
80 E1 Milson Shrops
40 A3 Milstead Kent
33 L2 Milston Wilts
118 F5 Milthorpe Lincs
84 B6 Milthorpe Nhants
114 E2 Milton C Stke
87 K3 Milton Cambs
178 D6 Milton Cumb
172 F4 Milton D & G
175 L1 Milton D & G
116 A6 Milton Derbys
248 A3 Milton Highld
250 E5 Milton Highld
251 G2 Milton Highld
263 K5 Milton Highld
280 D6 Milton Highld
208 B5 Milton Inver
52 E4 Milton Kent
254 D7 Milton Moray
267 K4 Milton Moray
44 D6 Milton N Som
44 D1 Milton Newpt
134 E5 Milton Notts
66 C8 Milton Oxon
83 K8 Milton Oxon
233 G3 Milton P & K
233 H4 Milton P & K
55 H6 Milton Pembks
31 G6 Milton Somset
219 H7 Milton Stirlg
208 D4 Milton W Duns
16 F2 Milton Abbas Dorset
12 A6 Milton Abbot Devon
211 H6 Milton Bridge Mdloth
68 B1 Milton Bryan C Beds
31 L3 Milton Clevedon Somset
6 F2 Milton Combe Devon
67 G6 Milton Common Oxon
27 G8 Milton Damerel Devon
63 L5 Milton End Gloucs
65 H7 Milton End Gloucs
85 K4 Milton Ernest Bed
129 K7 Milton Green Ches W
48 C1 Milton Hill Oxon
85 G7 Milton Keynes M Keyn
47 J7 Milton Lilbourne Wilts
84 E4 Milton Malsor Nhants
231 H8 Milton Morenish P & K
244 C3 Milton of Auchinhove Abers
222 E7 Milton of Balgonie Fife
208 D1 Milton of Buchanan Stirlg
209 H4 Milton of Campsie E Duns
251 J3 Milton of Leys Highld
243 L4 Milton of Tullich Abers
32 D5 Milton on Stour Dorset
40 A2 Milton Regis Kent
23 J6 Milton Street E Susx
65 K3 Milton-under-Wychwood Oxon
29 L5 Milverton Somset
83 H2 Milverton Warwks
114 F5 Milwich Staffs
128 E5 Milwr Flints
216 F7 Minard Ag & B
33 G7 Minchington Dorset
64 C7 Minchinhampton Gloucs
202 C6 Mindrum Nthumb
29 H2 Minehead Somset
112 C1 Minera Wrexhm
46 F1 Minety Wilts
109 L4 Minffordd Gwynd
237 K6 Mingarrypark Highld
136 F6 Miningsby Lincs
11 J8 Minions Cnwll
196 C8 Minishant S Ayrs
111 G8 Minllyn Gwynd
173 K2 Minnigaff D & G
41 J2 Minnis Bay Kent
268 D4 Minnonie Abers
130 D7 Minshull Vernon Ches E
150 E3 Minskip N York
18 D2 Minstead Hants
20 D3 Minsted W Susx
41 J2 Minster Kent
53 L4 Minster Kent
180 B7 Minsteracres Nthumb
95 J2 Minsterley Shrops
65 L5 Minster Lovell Oxon
63 M4 Minsterworth Gloucs
16 C2 Minterne Magna Dorset
16 C2 Minterne Parva Dorset
136 C5 Minting Lincs
269 J6 Mintlaw Abers
120 E7 Mintlyn Crematorium Norfk
188 F2 Minto Border

| | | |
|---|---|---|
| 95 K5 | **Minton** Shrops | |
| 55 H4 | **Minwear** Pembks | |
| 98 F5 | **Minworth** Birm | |
| 164 C7 | **Mirehouse** Cumb | |
| 280 D4 | **Mireland** Highld | |
| 141 K4 | **Mirfield** Kirk | |
| 64 D5 | **Miserden** Gloucs | |
| 43 G2 | **Miskin** Rhondd | |
| 43 G5 | **Miskin** Rhondd | |
| 134 D1 | **Misson** Notts | |
| 100 C6 | **Misterton** Leics | |
| 134 F1 | **Misterton** Notts | |
| 15 K1 | **Misterton** Somset | |
| 73 G1 | **Mistley** Essex | |
| 73 H1 | **Mistley Heath** Essex | |
| 51 H5 | **Mitcham** Gt Lon | |
| 63 K3 | **Mitcheldean** Gloucs | |
| 4 D4 | **Mitchell** Cnwll | |
| 186 E7 | **Mitchellslacks** D & G | |
| 62 F5 | **Mitchel Troy** Mons | |
| 180 E2 | **Mitford** Nthumb | |
| 4 B5 | **Mithian** Cnwll | |
| 114 D8 | **Mitton** Staffs | |
| 84 B8 | **Mixbury** Oxon | |
| 141 G2 | **Mixenden** Calder | |
| 131 L8 | **Mixon** Staffs | |
| 90 B4 | **Moats Tye** Suffk | |
| 130 F4 | **Mobberley** Ches E | |
| 115 G3 | **Mobberley** Staffs | |
| 79 L6 | **Moccas** Herefs | |
| 127 G4 | **Mochdre** Conwy | |
| 94 C5 | **Mochdre** Powys | |
| 173 J5 | **Mochrum** D & G | |
| 18 B2 | **Mockbeggar** Hants | |
| 39 H4 | **Mockbeggar** Kent | |
| 164 E6 | **Mockerkin** Cumb | |
| 7 J4 | **Modbury** Devon | |
| 114 E4 | **Moddershall** Staffs | |
| 125 J2 | **Moelfre** IoA | |
| 112 B6 | **Moelfre** Powys | |
| 125 J8 | **Moel Tryfan** Gwynd | |
| 187 G5 | **Moffat** D & G | |
| 86 C5 | **Moggerhanger** C Beds | |
| 116 A8 | **Moira** Leics | |
| 40 D5 | **Molash** Kent | |
| 246 F6 | **Mol-chlach** Highld | |
| 128 F7 | **Mold** Flints | |
| 141 J4 | **Moldgreen** Kirk | |
| 70 E2 | **Molehill Green** Essex | |
| 71 H3 | **Molehill Green** Essex | |
| 152 F7 | **Molescroft** E R Yk | |
| 180 E2 | **Molesden** Nthumb | |
| 102 B8 | **Molesworth** Cambs | |
| 28 E5 | **Molland** Devon | |
| 129 J5 | **Mollington** Ches W | |
| 83 K5 | **Mollington** Oxon | |
| 209 J4 | **Mollinsburn** N Lans | |
| 76 F3 | **Monachty** Cerdgn | |
| 245 G2 | **Mondynes** Abers | |
| 90 F3 | **Monewden** Suffk | |
| 221 J1 | **Moneydie** P & K | |
| 49 L3 | **Moneyrow Green** W & M | |
| 185 J5 | **Moniaive** D & G | |
| 223 J1 | **Monifieth** Angus | |
| 234 D7 | **Monikie** Angus | |
| 222 E4 | **Monimail** Fife | |
| 75 K3 | **Monington** Pembks | |
| 142 B6 | **Monk Bretton** Barns | |
| 69 H7 | **Monken Hadley** Gt Lon | |
| 142 D2 | **Monk Fryston** N York | |
| 80 E6 | **Monkhide** Herefs | |
| 177 K7 | **Monkhill** Cumb | |
| 96 E5 | **Monkhopton** Shrops | |
| 80 B4 | **Monkland** Herefs | |
| 27 H6 | **Monkleigh** Devon | |
| 42 D7 | **Monknash** V Glam | |
| 12 E2 | **Monkokehampton** Devon | |
| 181 J4 | **Monkseaton** N Tyne | |
| 89 K5 | **Monks Eleigh** Suffk | |
| 37 K5 | **Monk's Gate** W Susx | |
| 131 G5 | **Monks Heath** Ches E | |
| 48 F7 | **Monk Sherborne** Hants | |
| 40 F7 | **Monks Horton** Kent | |
| 29 K3 | **Monksilver** Somset | |
| 100 A6 | **Monks Kirby** Warwks | |
| 90 F2 | **Monk Soham** Suffk | |
| 98 E8 | **Monkspath** Solhll | |
| 67 K6 | **Monks Risborough** Bucks | |
| 137 H6 | **Monksthorpe** Lincs | |
| 70 F2 | **Monk Street** Essex | |
| 62 D6 | **Monkswood** Mons | |
| 14 E2 | **Monkton** Devon | |
| 41 J2 | **Monkton** Kent | |
| 196 D5 | **Monkton** S Ayrs | |
| 181 H6 | **Monkton** S Tyne | |
| 42 D7 | **Monkton** V Glam | |
| 45 M6 | **Monkton Combe** BaNES | |
| 32 E3 | **Monkton Deverill** Wilts | |
| 46 A6 | **Monkton Farleigh** Wilts | |
| 30 C5 | **Monkton Heathfield** Somset | |
| 33 H8 | **Monkton Up Wimborne** Dorset | |
| 15 H3 | **Monkton Wyld** Dorset | |
| 181 K7 | **Monkwearmouth** Sundld | |
| 35 K5 | **Monkwood** Hants | |
| 97 L4 | **Monmore Green** Wolves | |
| 63 G4 | **Monmouth** Mons | |
| 79 L6 | **Monnington on Wye** Herefs | |
| 173 J6 | **Monreith** D & G | |
| 31 H7 | **Montacute** Somset | |
| 139 K5 | **Montcliffe** Bolton | |
| 112 F8 | **Montford** Shrops | |
| 113 G8 | **Montford Bridge** Shrops | |
| 255 L8 | **Montgarrie** Abers | |
| 94 F4 | **Montgomery** Powys | |
| 140 A7 | **Monton** Salfd | |
| 235 H4 | **Montrose** Angus | |
| 9 i3 | **Mont Saint** Guern | |
| 34 C2 | **Monxton** Hants | |
| 132 C6 | **Monyash** Derbys | |
| 256 C8 | **Monymusk** Abers | |
| 220 F2 | **Monzie** P & K | |
| 209 J5 | **Moodiesburn** N Lans | |
| 222 F4 | **Moonzie** Fife | |
| 150 D8 | **Moor Allerton** Leeds | |
| 15 K3 | **Moorbath** Dorset | |
| 136 E6 | **Moorby** Lincs | |
| 79 L4 | **Moorcot** Herefs | |
| 17 K1 | **Moor Crichel** Dorset | |
| 17 L3 | **Moordown** Bmouth | |
| 130 B3 | **Moore** Halton | |
| 68 B3 | **Moor End** C Beds | |
| 141 G2 | **Moor End** Calder | |
| 12 F1 | **Moor End** Devon | |
| 63 L6 | **Moorend** Gloucs | |
| 147 G6 | **Moor End** Lancs | |
| 151 J8 | **Moor End** N York | |
| 143 H4 | **Moorends** Donc | |
| 35 G7 | **Moorgreen** Hants | |
| 69 J2 | **Moor Green** Herts | |
| 116 E2 | **Moorgreen** Notts | |
| 132 F5 | **Moorhall** Derbys | |
| 79 M6 | **Moorhampton** Herefs | |
| 149 L8 | **Moorhead** C Brad | |
| 141 K2 | **Moor Head** Leeds | |
| 177 H8 | **Moorhouse** Cumb | |
| 177 K7 | **Moorhouse** Cumb | |
| 142 D5 | **Moorhouse** Donc | |
| 134 E6 | **Moorhouse** Notts | |
| 51 L8 | **Moorhouse Bank** Surrey | |
| 30 E4 | **Moorland** Somset | |
| 30 F3 | **Moorlinch** Somset | |
| 151 H4 | **Moor Monkton** N York | |
| 164 D7 | **Moor Row** Cumb | |
| 165 H1 | **Moor Row** Cumb | |
| 170 F7 | **Moorsholm** R & Cl | |
| 32 D7 | **Moorside** Dorset | |
| 138 E1 | **Moor Side** Lancs | |
| 147 K8 | **Moor Side** Lancs | |
| 150 C8 | **Moorside** Leeds | |
| 136 E8 | **Moor Side** Lincs | |
| 140 E6 | **Moorside** Oldham | |
| 40 E7 | **Moorstock** Kent | |
| 98 C6 | **Moor Street** Birm | |
| 53 H6 | **Moor Street** Medway | |
| 5 M2 | **Moorswater** Cnwll | |
| 142 C5 | **Moorthorpe** Wakefd | |
| 12 C7 | **Moortown** Devon | |
| 18 A3 | **Moortown** Hants | |
| 19 G7 | **Moortown** IoW | |
| 150 D7 | **Moortown** Leeds | |
| 144 D7 | **Moortown** Lincs | |
| 113 K7 | **Moortown** Wrekin | |
| 263 K3 | **Morangie** Highld | |
| 237 K2 | **Morar** Highld | |
| 267 H4 | **Moray Crematorium** Moray | |
| 102 C5 | **Morborne** Cambs | |
| 13 H1 | **Morchard Bishop** Devon | |
| 15 J4 | **Morcombelake** Dorset | |
| 101 K3 | **Morcott** Rutlnd | |
| 112 D6 | **Morda** Shrops | |
| 17 H3 | **Morden** Dorset | |
| 51 H5 | **Morden** Gt Lon | |
| 80 D7 | **Mordiford** Herefs | |
| 169 J5 | **Mordon** Dur | |
| 95 H5 | **More** Shrops | |
| 29 G6 | **Morebath** Devon | |
| 189 K1 | **Morebattle** Border | |
| 147 H3 | **Morecambe** Lancs | |
| 47 H2 | **Moredon** Swindn | |
| 261 J1 | **Morefield** Highld | |
| 41 G7 | **Morehall** Kent | |
| 7 L4 | **Moreleigh** Devon | |
| 231 H8 | **Morenish** P & K | |
| 164 C6 | **Moresby Parks** Cumb | |
| 35 G6 | **Morestead** Hants | |
| 16 F4 | **Moreton** Dorset | |
| 70 D5 | **Moreton** Essex | |
| 80 C2 | **Moreton** Herefs | |
| 67 G6 | **Moreton** Oxon | |
| 114 B8 | **Moreton** Staffs | |
| 115 J5 | **Moreton** Staffs | |
| 129 G2 | **Moreton** Wirral | |
| 113 J6 | **Moreton Corbet** Shrops | |
| 13 H5 | **Moretonhampstead** Devon | |
| 65 J1 | **Moreton-in-Marsh** Gloucs | |
| 80 E5 | **Moreton Jeffries** Herefs | |
| 113 J7 | **Moretonmill** Shrops | |
| 83 H4 | **Moreton Morrell** Warwks | |
| 80 C6 | **Moreton on Lugg** Herefs | |
| 83 H4 | **Moreton Paddox** Warwks | |
| 84 B5 | **Moreton Pinkney** Nhants | |
| 113 K4 | **Moreton Say** Shrops | |
| 63 M5 | **Moreton Valence** Gloucs | |
| 76 B4 | **Morfa** Cerdgn | |
| 109 K4 | **Morfa Bychan** Gwynd | |
| 125 H8 | **Morfa Dinlle** Gwynd | |
| 60 C6 | **Morfa Glas** Neath | |
| 108 E3 | **Morfa Nefyn** Gwynd | |
| 43 H5 | **Morganstown** Cardif | |
| 33 L6 | **Morgan's Vale** Wilts | |
| 212 C5 | **Morham** E Loth | |
| 92 D7 | **Moriah** Cerdgn | |
| 166 E6 | **Morland** Cumb | |
| 130 F3 | **Morley** Ches E | |
| 116 C3 | **Morley** Derbys | |
| 168 E5 | **Morley** Dur | |
| 141 L2 | **Morley** Leeds | |
| 130 F3 | **Morley Green** Ches E | |
| 106 B3 | **Morley St Botolph** Norfk | |
| 11 L7 | **Mornick** Cnwll | |
| 211 H5 | **Morningside** C Edin | |
| 209 L7 | **Morningside** N Lans | |
| 106 E5 | **Morningthorpe** Norfk | |
| 180 E2 | **Morpeth** Nthumb | |
| 235 H3 | **Morphie** Abers | |
| 115 J7 | **Morrey** Staffs | |
| 115 G1 | **Morridge Side** Staffs | |
| 57 J5 | **Morriston** Swans | |
| 121 M3 | **Morston** Norfk | |
| 27 H2 | **Mortehoe** Devon | |
| 133 J2 | **Morthen** Rothm | |
| 49 G6 | **Mortimer** W Berk | |
| 49 G6 | **Mortimer Common** W Berk | |
| 80 A3 | **Mortimer's Cross** Herefs | |
| 48 F6 | **Mortimer West End** Hants | |
| 51 G4 | **Mortlake** Gt Lon | |
| 51 G4 | **Mortlake Crematorium** Gt Lon | |
| 166 B3 | **Morton** Cumb | |
| 177 L7 | **Morton** Cumb | |
| 133 H7 | **Morton** Derbys | |
| 19 K6 | **Morton** IoW | |
| 118 E6 | **Morton** Lincs | |
| 134 F1 | **Morton** Lincs | |
| 117 J1 | **Morton** Notts | |
| 112 D6 | **Morton** Shrops | |
| 135 H7 | **Morton Hall** Lincs | |
| 211 J5 | **Mortonhall Crematorium** C Edin | |
| 160 D4 | **Morton-on-Swale** N York | |
| 122 C8 | **Morton on the Hill** Norfk | |
| 168 F6 | **Morton Tinmouth** Dur | |
| 2 B4 | **Morvah** Cnwll | |
| 6 B3 | **Morval** Cnwll | |
| 248 F7 | **Morvich** Highld | |
| 96 F4 | **Morville** Shrops | |
| 96 F4 | **Morville Heath** Shrops | |
| 26 C7 | **Morwenstow** Cnwll | |
| 133 H3 | **Mosborough** Sheff | |
| 196 F3 | **Moscow** E Ayrs | |
| 97 G5 | **Mose** Shrops | |
| 165 K4 | **Mosedale** Cumb | |
| 98 D6 | **Moseley** Birm | |
| 97 L4 | **Moseley** Wolves | |
| 81 J3 | **Moseley** Worcs | |
| 139 L6 | **Moses Gate** Bolton | |
| 224 B6 | **Moss** Ag & B | |
| 142 F5 | **Moss** Donc | |
| 112 D1 | **Moss** Wrexhm | |
| 255 K7 | **Mossat** Abers | |
| 281 e4 | **Mossbank** Shet | |
| 139 G8 | **Moss Bank** St Hel | |
| 164 C5 | **Mossbay** Cumb | |
| 196 D6 | **Mossblown** S Ayrs | |
| 130 D2 | **Mossbrow** Traffd | |
| 189 H3 | **Mossburnford** Border | |
| 175 G1 | **Mossdale** D & G | |
| 184 D2 | **Mossdale** E Ayrs | |
| 147 H7 | **Moss Edge** Lancs | |
| 130 D4 | **Moss End** Ches E | |
| 209 K7 | **Mossend** N Lans | |
| 164 F5 | **Mosser Mains** Cumb | |
| 131 H7 | **Mossley** Ches E | |
| 140 E7 | **Mossley** Tamesd | |
| 188 C6 | **Mosspaul Hotel** Border | |
| 177 G8 | **Moss Side** Cumb | |
| 253 G1 | **Moss-side** Highld | |
| 138 D2 | **Moss Side** Lancs | |
| 138 D7 | **Moss Side** Sefton | |
| 267 G4 | **Mosstodloch** Moray | |
| 174 E4 | **Mossyard** D & G | |
| 139 G5 | **Mossy Lea** Lancs | |
| 15 K2 | **Mosterton** Dorset | |
| 140 C7 | **Moston** Manch | |
| 113 J6 | **Moston** Shrops | |
| 130 E7 | **Moston Green** Ches E | |
| 128 E4 | **Mostyn** Flints | |
| 32 E6 | **Motcombe** Dorset | |
| 7 H5 | **Mothecombe** Devon | |
| 166 A5 | **Motherby** Cumb | |
| 209 K7 | **Motherwell** N Lans | |
| 51 G5 | **Motspur Park** Gt Lon | |
| 51 L4 | **Mottingham** Gt Lon | |
| 34 D5 | **Mottisfont** Hants | |
| 18 F7 | **Mottistone** IoW | |
| 140 F8 | **Mottram in Longdendale** Tamesd | |
| 131 H8 | **Mottram St Andrew** Ches E | |
| 9 j3 | **Mouilpied** Guern | |
| 129 L5 | **Mouldsworth** Ches W | |
| 232 D3 | **Moulin** P & K | |
| 22 E6 | **Moulsecoomb** Br & H | |
| 48 E2 | **Moulsford** Oxon | |
| 85 H7 | **Moulsoe** M Keyn | |
| 263 H5 | **Moultavie** Highld | |
| 130 C5 | **Moulton** Ches W | |
| 119 J6 | **Moulton** Lincs | |
| 160 C2 | **Moulton** N York | |
| 84 F2 | **Moulton** Nhants | |
| 88 D2 | **Moulton** Suffk | |
| 43 G7 | **Moulton** V Glam | |
| 119 J7 | **Moulton Chapel** Lincs | |
| 107 H2 | **Moulton St Mary** Norfk | |
| 119 K6 | **Moulton Seas End** Lincs | |
| 4 C4 | **Mount** Cnwll | |
| 5 K1 | **Mount** Cnwll | |
| 141 H4 | **Mount** Kirk | |
| 141 G2 | **Mountain** C Brad | |
| 61 G7 | **Mountain Ash** Rhondd | |
| 199 K4 | **Mountain Cross** Border | |
| 40 E5 | **Mountain Street** Kent | |
| 4 B6 | **Mount Ambrose** Cnwll | |
| 89 H8 | **Mount Bures** Essex | |
| 24 D3 | **Mountfield** E Susx | |
| 263 G7 | **Mountgerald House** Highld | |
| 4 B5 | **Mount Hawke** Cnwll | |
| 3 H7 | **Mount Hermon** Cnwll | |
| 4 E3 | **Mountjoy** Cnwll | |
| 200 C2 | **Mount Lothian** Mdloth | |
| 70 F7 | **Mountnessing** Essex | |
| 63 G8 | **Mounton** Mons | |
| 131 G8 | **Mount Pleasant** Ches E | |
| 115 M8 | **Mount Pleasant** Derbys | |
| 116 B2 | **Mount Pleasant** Derbys | |
| 169 H4 | **Mount Pleasant** Dur | |
| 153 L7 | **Mount Pleasant** E R Yk | |
| 23 G4 | **Mount Pleasant** E Susx | |
| 105 K4 | **Mount Pleasant** Norfk | |
| 88 E5 | **Mount Pleasant** Suffk | |
| 82 B2 | **Mount Pleasant** Worcs | |
| 180 E7 | **Mountsett Crematorium** Dur | |
| 116 F8 | **Mountsorrel** Leics | |
| 33 H6 | **Mount Sorrel** Wilts | |
| 141 G2 | **Mount Tabor** Calder | |
| 36 E3 | **Mousehill** Surrey | |
| 2 D5 | **Mousehole** Cnwll | |
| 176 E4 | **Mouswald** D & G | |
| 131 G8 | **Mow Cop** Ches E | |
| 189 L2 | **Mowhaugh** Border | |
| 100 D2 | **Mowmacre Hill** C Leic | |
| 100 E5 | **Mowsley** Leics | |
| 240 D7 | **Moy** Highld | |
| 252 E5 | **Moy** Highld | |
| 248 D7 | **Moyle** Highld | |
| 75 J3 | **Moylegrove** Pembks | |
| 205 L8 | **Muasdale** Ag & B | |
| 245 K5 | **Muchalls** Abers | |
| 63 G1 | **Much Birch** Herefs | |
| 80 E6 | **Much Cowarne** Herefs | |
| 62 F1 | **Much Dewchurch** Herefs | |
| 30 F6 | **Muchelney** Somset | |
| 31 G6 | **Muchelney Ham** Somset | |
| 70 B3 | **Much Hadham** Herts | |
| 138 F3 | **Much Hoole** Lancs | |
| 138 F3 | **Much Hoole Town** Lancs | |
| 5 L3 | **Muchlarnick** Cnwll | |
| 80 F8 | **Much Marcle** Herefs | |
| 96 E3 | **Much Wenlock** Shrops | |
| 52 E3 | **Mucking** Thurr | |
| 52 E3 | **Muckingford** Thurr | |
| 16 C4 | **Muckleford** Dorset | |
| 114 A4 | **Mucklestone** Staffs | |
| 96 E4 | **Muckley** Shrops | |
| 137 G3 | **Muckton** Lincs | |
| 27 K3 | **Muddiford** Devon | |
| 23 J4 | **Muddles Green** E Susx | |
| 18 B5 | **Mudeford** Dorset | |
| 31 J7 | **Mudford** Somset | |

| | | |
|---|---|---|
| 31 J7 | **Mudford Sock** Somset |
| 31 G2 | **Mudgley** Somset |
| 53 M4 | **Mud Row** Kent |
| 208 F4 | **Mugdock** Stirlg |
| 246 F1 | **Mugeary** Highld |
| 115 M3 | **Mugginton** Derbys |
| 115 M3 | **Muggintonlane End** Derbys |
| 168 D1 | **Muggleswick** Dur |
| 268 C5 | **Muirden** Abers |
| 234 E7 | **Muirdrum** Angus |
| 268 C6 | **Muiresk** Abers |
| 233 M8 | **Muirhead** Angus |
| 222 D6 | **Muirhead** Fife |
| 209 J5 | **Muirhead** N Lans |
| 197 K5 | **Muirkirk** E Ayrs |
| 209 J2 | **Muirmill** Stirlg |
| 244 C1 | **Muir of Fowlis** Abers |
| 266 D4 | **Muir of Miltonduff** Moray |
| 250 F2 | **Muir of Ord** Highld |
| 233 G7 | **Muir of Thorn** P & K |
| 239 J7 | **Muirshearlich** Highld |
| 257 J4 | **Muirtack** Abers |
| 221 G5 | **Muirton** P & K |
| 250 E1 | **Muirton Mains** Highld |
| 233 J6 | **Muirton of Ardblair** P & K |
| 158 F3 | **Muker** N York |
| 106 D3 | **Mulbarton** Norfk |
| 267 G6 | **Mulben** Moray |
| 2 C4 | **Mulfra** Cnwll |
| 27 J2 | **Mullacott Cross** Devon |
| 3 H7 | **Mullion** Cnwll |
| 3 H7 | **Mullion Cove** Cnwll |
| 137 K5 | **Mumby** Lincs |
| 80 F5 | **Munderfield Row** Herefs |
| 80 F5 | **Munderfield Stocks** Herefs |
| 123 G4 | **Mundesley** Norfk |
| 104 F4 | **Mundford** Norfk |
| 107 G4 | **Mundham** Norfk |
| 72 C6 | **Mundon Hill** Essex |
| 40 B6 | **Mundy Bois** Kent |
| 165 L4 | **Mungrisdale** Cumb |
| 251 H1 | **Munlochy** Highld |
| 195 L1 | **Munnoch** N Ayrs |
| 80 F7 | **Munsley** Herefs |
| 96 C6 | **Munslow** Shrops |
| 13 G5 | **Murchington** Devon |
| 82 C7 | **Murcot** Worcs |
| 66 E4 | **Murcott** Oxon |
| 46 D1 | **Murcott** Wilts |
| 279 L3 | **Murkle** Highld |
| 239 G5 | **Murlaggan** Highld |
| 49 H7 | **Murrell Green** Hants |
| 234 C8 | **Murroes** Angus |
| 103 H2 | **Murrow** Cambs |
| 67 K2 | **Mursley** Bucks |
| 40 B2 | **Murston** Kent |
| 234 C4 | **Murthill** Angus |
| 233 G7 | **Murthly** P & K |
| 151 K5 | **Murton** C York |
| 167 G6 | **Murton** Cumb |
| 169 K1 | **Murton** Dur |
| 181 H5 | **Murton** N Tyne |
| 202 F3 | **Murton** Nthumb |
| 15 G3 | **Musbury** Devon |
| 162 B6 | **Muscoates** N York |
| 211 K4 | **Musselburgh** E Loth |
| 117 L4 | **Muston** Leics |
| 163 K6 | **Muston** N York |
| 97 K8 | **Mustow Green** Worcs |
| 51 H1 | **Muswell Hill** Gt Lon |
| 175 H5 | **Mutehill** D & G |
| 107 K5 | **Mutford** Suffk |
| 220 F4 | **Muthill** P & K |
| 14 B2 | **Mutterton** Devon |
| 114 A8 | **Muxton** Wrekin |
| 279 L5 | **Mybster** Highld |
| 59 L3 | **Myddfai** Carmth |
| 113 G6 | **Myddle** Shrops |
| 76 E4 | **Mydroilyn** Cerdgn |
| 147 K7 | **Myerscough** Lancs |
| 3 L4 | **Mylor** Cnwll |
| 3 K4 | **Mylor Bridge** Cnwll |
| 75 K6 | **Mynachlog ddu** Pembks |
| 128 D5 | **Mynydd-llan** Flints |
| 95 J5 | **Myndtown** Shrops |
| 62 F8 | **Mynydd-bach** Mons |
| 57 J5 | **Mynydd-Bach** Swans |
| 92 F8 | **Mynydd Buch** Cerdgn |
| 56 D3 | **Mynyddgarreg** Carmth |
| 128 F7 | **Mynydd Isa** Flints |
| 126 B6 | **Mynydd Llandygai** Gwynd |
| 108 E5 | **Mynytho** Gwynd |
| 245 G4 | **Myrebird** Abers |
| 189 G6 | **Myredykes** Border |
| 49 L7 | **Mytchett** Surrey |
| 140 E2 | **Mytholm** Calder |
| 140 F3 | **Mytholmroyd** Calder |
| 138 D1 | **Mythop** Lancs |
| 150 F3 | **Myton-on-Swale** N York |

| | | |
|---|---|---|
| | **N** | |
| 260 C3 | **Naast** Highld |
| 139 J2 | **Nab's Head** Lancs |
| 282 d6 | **Na Buirgh** W Isls |
| 151 J6 | **Naburn** C York |
| 149 L8 | **Nab Wood Crematorium** C Brad |
| 40 D6 | **Naccolt** Kent |
| 40 F4 | **Nackington** Kent |
| 90 F7 | **Nacton** Suffk |
| 153 G4 | **Nafferton** E R Yk |
| 64 C7 | **Nag's Head** Gloucs |
| 63 J4 | **Nailbridge** Gloucs |
| 30 B5 | **Nailsbourne** Somset |
| 44 F5 | **Nailsea** N Som |
| 99 L2 | **Nailstone** Leics |
| 64 B7 | **Nailsworth** Gloucs |
| 264 D8 | **Nairn** Highld |
| 37 K2 | **Nalderswood** Surrey |
| 3 G4 | **Nancegollan** Cnwll |
| 2 D4 | **Nancledra** Cnwll |
| 108 E5 | **Nanhoron** Gwynd |
| 128 E5 | **Nannerch** Flints |
| 116 E8 | **Nanpantan** Leics |
| 4 F4 | **Nanpean** Cnwll |
| 2 B5 | **Nanquidno** Cnwll |
| 5 H2 | **Nanstallon** Cnwll |
| 60 F4 | **Nant-ddu** Powys |
| 76 C4 | **Nanternis** Cerdgn |
| 58 F4 | **Nantgaredig** Carmth |
| 43 H4 | **Nantgarw** Rhondd |
| 78 D2 | **Nant-glas** Powys |
| 127 K7 | **Nantglyn** Denbgs |
| 93 L8 | **Nantgwyn** Powys |
| 110 B2 | **Nant Gwynant** Gwynd |
| 109 J1 | **Nantlle** Gwynd |
| 112 C6 | **Nantmawr** Shrops |
| 78 E2 | **Nantmel** Powys |
| 109 L2 | **Nantmor** Gwynd |
| 126 B7 | **Nant Peris** Gwynd |
| 113 L1 | **Nantwich** Ches E |
| 61 H5 | **Nant-y-Bwch** Blae G |
| 58 E5 | **Nant-y-caws** Carmth |
| 62 C6 | **Nant-y-derry** Mons |
| 42 C3 | **Nantyffyllon** Brdgnd |
| 61 K5 | **Nantyglo** Blae G |
| 112 C5 | **Nant-y-gollen** Shrops |
| 42 D3 | **Nant-y-moel** Brdgnd |
| 126 D5 | **Nant-y-pandy** Conwy |
| 67 K7 | **Naphill** Bucks |
| 81 K5 | **Napleton** Worcs |
| 148 E5 | **Nappa** N York |
| 83 L3 | **Napton on the Hill** Warwks |
| 55 J4 | **Narberth** Pembks |
| 100 C4 | **Narborough** Leics |
| 104 E1 | **Narborough** Norfk |
| 6 C4 | **Narkurs** Cnwll |
| 109 H2 | **Nasareth** Gwynd |
| 100 F7 | **Naseby** Nhants |
| 84 F8 | **Nash** Bucks |
| 51 L6 | **Nash** Gt Lon |
| 79 K3 | **Nash** Herefs |
| 44 D2 | **Nash** Newpt |
| 80 E1 | **Nash** Shrops |
| 97 H7 | **Nash End** Worcs |
| 67 K5 | **Nash Lee** Bucks |
| 35 K2 | **Nash's Green** Hants |
| 52 D5 | **Nash Street** Kent |
| 102 B4 | **Nassington** Nhants |
| 64 A6 | **Nastend** Gloucs |
| 69 K2 | **Nasty** Herts |
| 158 D1 | **Nateby** Cumb |
| 147 J2 | **Nateby** Lancs |
| 157 H5 | **Natland** Cumb |
| 89 L5 | **Naughton** Suffk |
| 65 G2 | **Naunton** Gloucs |
| 81 K7 | **Naunton** Worcs |
| 81 M5 | **Naunton Beauchamp** Worcs |
| 135 K0 | **Navenby** Lincs |
| 70 D7 | **Navestock** Essex |
| 70 E7 | **Navestock Side** Essex |
| 274 D5 | **Navidale House Hotel** Highld |
| 264 B7 | **Navity** Highld |
| 161 L5 | **Nawton** N York |
| 89 K8 | **Nayland** Suffk |
| 69 L6 | **Nazeing** Essex |
| 69 L6 | **Nazeing Gate** Essex |
| 18 B4 | **Neacroft** Hants |
| 99 J6 | **Neal's Green** Warwks |
| 281 e5 | **Neap** Shet |
| 115 H2 | **Near Cotton** Staffs |
| 156 E3 | **Near Sawrey** Cumb |
| 51 G2 | **Neasden** Gt Lon |
| 169 J8 | **Neasham** Darltn |
| 57 L5 | **Neath** Neath |
| 35 M3 | **Neatham** Hants |
| 123 G7 | **Neatishead** Norfk |
| 77 G2 | **Nebo** Cerdgn |
| 127 G8 | **Nebo** Conwy |

| | | |
|---|---|---|
| 109 H2 | **Nebo** Gwynd |
| 125 H2 | **Nebo** IoA |
| 105 H2 | **Necton** Norfk |
| 270 F2 | **Nedd** Highld |
| 180 F2 | **Nedderton** Nthumb |
| 89 K5 | **Nedging** Suffk |
| 89 L5 | **Nedging Tye** Suffk |
| 106 E7 | **Needham** Norfk |
| 90 C4 | **Needham Market** Suffk |
| 88 E2 | **Needham Street** Suffk |
| 87 G1 | **Needingworth** Cambs |
| 96 F7 | **Neen Savage** Shrops |
| 80 F1 | **Neen Sollars** Shrops |
| 96 E6 | **Neenton** Shrops |
| 108 E3 | **Nefyn** Gwynd |
| 208 E7 | **Neilston** E Rens |
| 43 H3 | **Nelson** Caerph |
| 148 F8 | **Nelson** Lancs |
| 198 E4 | **Nemphlar** S Lans |
| 45 G7 | **Nempnett Thrubwell** BaNES |
| 167 H2 | **Nenthall** Cumb |
| 167 H2 | **Nenthead** Cumb |
| 201 L5 | **Nenthorn** Border |
| 13 J3 | **Neopardy** Devon |
| 22 B4 | **Nep Town** W Susx |
| 128 F7 | **Nercwys** Flints |
| 204 C5 | **Nereabolls** Ag & B |
| 209 H7 | **Nerston** S Lans |
| 202 F6 | **Nesbit** Nthumb |
| 149 K6 | **Nesfield** N York |
| 129 G4 | **Ness** Ches W |
| 112 F7 | **Nesscliffe** Shrops |
| 129 G4 | **Neston** Ches W |
| 46 B5 | **Neston** Wilts |
| 96 E5 | **Netchwood** Shrops |
| 131 G4 | **Nether Alderley** Ches E |
| 33 K1 | **Netheravon** Wilts |
| 201 H4 | **Nether Blainslie** Border |
| 268 E4 | **Netherbrae** Abers |
| 117 J6 | **Nether Broughton** Leics |
| 198 C4 | **Netherburn** S Lans |
| 15 L3 | **Netherbury** Dorset |
| 177 L4 | **Netherby** Cumb |
| 150 D6 | **Netherby** N York |
| 16 C3 | **Nether Cerne** Dorset |
| 176 F2 | **Nethercleuch** D & G |
| 31 K7 | **Nether Compton** Dorset |
| 83 M2 | **Nethercote** Warwks |
| 11 L3 | **Nethercott** Devon |
| 27 H3 | **Nethercott** Devon |
| 256 E7 | **Nether Crimond** Abers |
| 267 G3 | **Nether Dallachy** Moray |
| 63 H7 | **Netherend** Gloucs |
| 15 L2 | **Nether Exe** Devon |
| 24 C3 | **Netherfield** E Susx |
| 117 G8 | **Netherfield** Leics |
| 117 G3 | **Netherfield** Notts |
| 24 D4 | **Netherfield Road** E Susx |
| 186 D4 | **Nether Fingland** S Lans |
| 143 J7 | **Nethergate** N Linc |
| 122 B5 | **Nethergate** Norfk |
| 33 K5 | **Netherhampton** Wilts |
| 133 H4 | **Nether Handley** Derbys |
| 234 B7 | **Nether Handwick** Angus |
| 142 C8 | **Nether Haugh** Rothm |
| 15 J2 | **Netherhay** Dorset |
| 134 E4 | **Nether Headon** Notts |
| 116 B2 | **Nether Heage** Derbys |
| 84 C3 | **Nether Heyford** Nhants |
| 186 F4 | **Nether Howcleugh** S Lans |
| 147 K2 | **Nether Kellet** Lancs |
| 257 K3 | **Nether Kinmundy** Abers |
| 115 H5 | **Netherland Green** Staffs |
| 133 K5 | **Nether Langwith** Notts |
| 175 J6 | **Netherlaw** D & G |
| 245 J5 | **Netherley** Abers |
| 176 D1 | **Nethermill** D & G |
| 257 G3 | **Nethermuir** Abers |
| 51 J7 | **Netherne-on-the-Hill** Surrey |
| 141 H4 | **Netheroyd Hill** Kirk |
| 132 E4 | **Nether Padley** Derbys |
| 208 E7 | **Netherplace** E Rens |
| 151 J5 | **Nether Poppleton** C York |
| 165 K3 | **Nether Row** Cumb |
| 99 H1 | **Netherseal** Derbys |
| 161 G4 | **Nether Silton** N York |
| 95 G8 | **Nether Skyborry** Shrops |
| 30 B3 | **Nether Stowey** Somset |
| 70 E5 | **Nether Street** Essex |
| 46 E6 | **Netherstreet** Wilts |
| 141 H6 | **Netherthong** Kirk |
| 133 J5 | **Netherthorpe** Derbys |
| 234 E4 | **Netherton** Angus |
| 13 L8 | **Netherton** Devon |
| 97 L5 | **Netherton** Dudley |
| 48 A7 | **Netherton** Hants |
| 63 G2 | **Netherton** Herefs |
| 141 H5 | **Netherton** Kirk |
| 209 K8 | **Netherton** N Lans |
| 190 E4 | **Netherton** Nthumb |

| | | |
|---|---|---|
| 66 B7 | **Netherton** Oxon |
| 233 H5 | **Netherton** P & K |
| 97 G6 | **Netherton** Shrops |
| 208 F3 | **Netherton** Stirlg |
| 141 L4 | **Netherton** Wakefd |
| 82 A7 | **Netherton** Worcs |
| 155 H1 | **Netherton** Cumb |
| 280 E1 | **Nethertown** Highld |
| 148 C8 | **Nethertown** Lancs |
| 115 J8 | **Nethertown** Staffs |
| 199 J4 | **Netherurd** Border |
| 34 C4 | **Nether Wallop** Hants |
| 155 L2 | **Nether Wasdale** Cumb |
| 165 K2 | **Nether Welton** Cumb |
| 65 J3 | **Nether Westcote** Gloucs |
| 99 G5 | **Nether Whitacre** Warwks |
| 186 B2 | **Nether Whitecleuch** S Lans |
| 67 H4 | **Nether Winchendon** Bucks |
| 191 G8 | **Netherwitton** Nthumb |
| 253 J7 | **Nethy Bridge** Highld |
| 19 G2 | **Netley** Hants |
| 34 D8 | **Netley Marsh** Hants |
| 13 L3 | **Nettacott** Devon |
| 49 G2 | **Nettlebed** Oxon |
| 31 L1 | **Nettlebridge** Somset |
| 15 L3 | **Nettlecombe** Dorset |
| 19 J8 | **Nettlecombe** IoW |
| 68 C5 | **Nettleden** Herts |
| 135 K4 | **Nettleham** Lincs |
| 39 H3 | **Nettlestead** Kent |
| 39 H3 | **Nettlestead Green** Kent |
| 19 L5 | **Nettlestone** IoW |
| 169 H1 | **Nettlesworth** Dur |
| 144 E7 | **Nettleton** Lincs |
| 46 B3 | **Nettleton** Wilts |
| 46 B3 | **Nettleton Shrub** Wilts |
| 7 G5 | **Netton** Devon |
| 33 K3 | **Netton** Wilts |
| 59 K4 | **Neuadd** Carmth |
| 93 K8 | **Neuadd-ddu** Powys |
| 77 K7 | **Neuadd Fawr** Carmth |
| 53 G1 | **Nevendon** Essex |
| 75 J4 | **Nevern** Pembks |
| 101 H4 | **Nevill Holt** Leics |
| 176 C5 | **New Abbey** D & G |
| 268 F3 | **New Aberdour** Abers |
| 51 K6 | **New Addington** Gt Lon |
| 150 B6 | **Newall** Leeds |
| 35 J4 | **New Alresford** Hants |
| 233 K6 | **New Alyth** P & K |
| 102 E3 | **Newark** C Pete |
| 275 f2 | **Newark** Ork |
| 117 L1 | **Newark-on-Trent** Notts |
| 153 G7 | **New Arram** E R Yk |
| 209 L7 | **Newarthill** N Lans |
| 52 D6 | **New Ash Green** Kent |
| 117 L1 | **New Balderton** Notts |
| 40 F7 | **Newbarn** Kent |
| 52 D5 | **New Barn** Kent |
| 69 H7 | **New Barnet** Gt Lon |
| 85 G2 | **New Barton** Nhants |
| 211 K6 | **Newbattle** Mdloth |
| 190 F2 | **New Bewick** Nthumb |
| 177 G6 | **Newbie** D & G |
| 146 E2 | **Newbiggin** Cumb |
| 155 K4 | **Newbiggin** Cumb |
| 166 B5 | **Newbiggin** Cumb |
| 166 D1 | **Newbiggin** Cumb |
| 166 E5 | **Newbiggin** Cumb |
| 167 L5 | **Newbiggin** Dur |
| 168 F1 | **Newbiggin** Dur |
| 159 G4 | **Newbiggin** N York |
| 159 H5 | **Newbiggin** N York |
| 181 H1 | **Newbiggin-by-the-Sea** Nthumb |
| 233 L7 | **Newbigging** Angus |
| 234 C7 | **Newbigging** Angus |
| 234 D8 | **Newbigging** Angus |
| 199 H4 | **Newbigging** S Lans |
| 158 C2 | **Newbiggin-on-Lune** Cumb |
| 100 B8 | **New Bilton** Warwks |
| 133 G5 | **Newbold** Derbys |
| 116 C7 | **Newbold** Leics |
| 100 B7 | **Newbold on Avon** Warwks |
| 82 F6 | **Newbold on Stour** Warwks |
| 83 G4 | **Newbold Pacey** Warwks |
| 99 M7 | **Newbold Revel** Warwks |
| 99 L3 | **Newbold Verdon** Leics |
| 136 F8 | **New Bolingbroke** Lincs |
| 102 D2 | **Newborough** C Pete |
| 125 G6 | **Newborough** IoA |
| 115 J6 | **Newborough** Staffs |
| 83 M7 | **Newbottle** Nhants |
| 181 H8 | **Newbottle** Sundld |
| 135 K5 | **New Boultham** Lincs |
| 91 G6 | **Newbourne** Suffk |
| 84 F7 | **New Bradwell** M Keyn |
| 133 G5 | **New Brampton** Derbys |
| 169 G2 | **New Brancepeth** Dur |
| 210 F4 | **Newbridge** C Edin |
| 43 K2 | **Newbridge** Caerph |

338 **Newbridge - Newtown**


76 F3 **Newbridge** Cerdgn
2 C5 **Newbridge** Cnwll
4 C6 **Newbridge** Cnwll
176 C3 **Newbridge** D & G
34 C7 **Newbridge** Hants
18 F6 **Newbridge** IoW
162 D5 **New Bridge** N York
66 B6 **Newbridge** Oxon
112 D3 **Newbridge** Wrexhm
81 J7 **Newbridge Green** Worcs
62 D8 **Newbridge-on-Usk** Mons
78 E4 **Newbridge on Wye** Powys
128 F6 **New Brighton** Flints
129 G1 **New Brighton** Wirral
116 D2 **New Brinsley** Notts
171 G6 **New Brotton** R & Cl
179 K5 **Newbrough** Nthumb
112 D1 **New Broughton** Wrexhm
106 B5 **New Buckenham** Norfk
13 J2 **Newbuildings** Devon
257 J6 **Newburgh** Abers
269 H4 **Newburgh** Abers
222 C3 **Newburgh** Fife
138 F5 **Newburgh** Lancs
161 J7 **Newburgh Priory** N York
180 E6 **Newburn** N u Ty
139 L6 **New Bury** Bolton
32 B1 **Newbury** Somset
48 C5 **Newbury** W Berk
32 D3 **Newbury** Wilts
51 L1 **Newbury Park** Gt Lon
166 E6 **Newby** Cumb
148 E6 **Newby** Lancs
148 C2 **Newby** N York
163 J4 **Newby** N York
170 C8 **Newby** N York
156 E5 **Newby Bridge** Cumb
177 L8 **Newby Cross** Cumb
178 B7 **Newby East** Cumb
166 E6 **Newby Head** Cumb
268 E5 **New Byth** Abers
177 L8 **Newby West** Cumb
160 E5 **Newby Wiske** N York
62 F4 **Newcastle** Mons
95 G7 **Newcastle** Shrops
76 B7 **Newcastle Emlyn** Carmth
178 C2 **Newcastleton** Border
114 D2 **Newcastle-under-Lyme** Staffs
181 G6 **Newcastle upon Tyne** N u Ty
75 L4 **Newchapel** Pembks
131 G8 **Newchapel** Staffs
38 A5 **Newchapel** Surrey
61 J5 **Newchurch** Blae G
79 L5 **Newchurch** Herefs
19 J6 **Newchurch** IoW
25 K1 **Newchurch** Kent
62 F7 **Newchurch** Mons
79 H5 **Newchurch** Powys
115 J7 **Newchurch** Staffs
148 E7 **Newchurch in Pendle** Lancs
106 D2 **New Costessey** Norfk
164 F2 **New Cowper** Cumb
211 K4 **Newcraighall** C Edin
142 B4 **New Crofton** Wakefd
92 D8 **New Cross** Cerdgn
51 K4 **New Cross** Gt Lon
30 F7 **New Cross** Somset
197 J8 **New Cumnock** E Ayrs
24 E4 **New Cut** E Susx
268 F6 **New Deer** Abers
181 H3 **New Delaval** Nthumb
140 F6 **New Delph** Oldham
50 D2 **New Denham** Bucks
37 J3 **Newdigate** Surrey
84 D3 **New Duston** Nhants
151 K5 **New Earswick** C York
116 D2 **New Eastwood** Notts
142 E7 **New Edlington** Donc
266 E4 **New Elgin** Moray
153 J7 **New Ellerby** E R Yk
49 L5 **Newell Green** Br For
51 L4 **New Eltham** Gt Lon
82 C3 **New End** Worcs
24 F2 **Newenden** Kent
102 D3 **New England** C Pete
88 E6 **New England** Essex
63 L2 **Newent** Gloucs
141 L2 **New Farnley** Leeds
129 H3 **New Ferry** Wirral
169 G4 **Newfield** Dur
181 G8 **Newfield** Dur
264 B4 **Newfield** Highld
102 D4 **New Fletton** C Pete
48 E8 **Newfound** Hants
142 C2 **New Fryston** Wakefd
54 D2 **Newgale** Pembks
185 G7 **New Galloway** D & G
122 A3 **Newgate** Norfk
69 J6 **Newgate Street** Herts
223 G5 **New Gilston** Fife
10 b2 **New Grimsby** IoS
113 K2 **Newhall** Ches E
115 M7 **Newhall** Derbys
203 K7 **Newham** Nthumb
181 H3 **New Hartley** Nthumb
211 H4 **Newhaven** C Edin
132 C7 **Newhaven** Derbys
23 G7 **Newhaven** E Susx
50 D6 **New Haw** Surrey
55 K6 **New Hedges** Pembks
181 H8 **New Herrington** Sundld
140 E5 **Newhey** Rochdl
121 J4 **New Holkham** Norfk
144 D3 **New Holland** N Linc
171 K8 **Newholm** N York
133 K6 **New Houghton** Derbys
121 H6 **New Houghton** Norfk
209 L6 **Newhouse** N Lans
158 D7 **New Houses** N York
139 H7 **New Houses** Wigan
157 J4 **New Hutton** Cumb
52 F7 **New Hythe** Kent
22 F3 **Newick** E Susx
40 F8 **Newingreen** Kent
41 G7 **Newington** Kent
53 J6 **Newington** Kent
66 F7 **Newington** Oxon
95 K6 **Newington** Shrops
64 B8 **Newington Bagpath** Gloucs
58 E2 **New Inn** Carmth
62 C7 **New Inn** Torfn
95 H8 **New Invention** Shrops
106 E2 **New Lakenham** Norfk
198 E4 **New Lanark** S Lans
144 D2 **Newland** C KuH
156 D6 **Newland** Cumb
143 K2 **Newland** E R Yk
63 H5 **Newland** Gloucs
143 H3 **Newland** N York
66 A5 **Newland** Oxon
28 E3 **Newland** Somset
81 H5 **Newland** Worcs
211 L6 **Newlandrig** Mdloth
188 E7 **Newlands** Border
165 K3 **Newlands** Cumb
180 D7 **Newlands** Nthumb
266 F6 **Newlands of Dundurcas** Moray
138 E5 **New Lane** Lancs
130 C1 **New Lane End** Warrtn
177 K2 **New Langholm** D & G
137 G8 **New Leake** Lincs
269 H5 **New Leeds** Abers
142 A6 **New Lodge** Barns
139 G3 **New Longton** Lancs
172 F2 **New Luce** D & G
2 D5 **Newlyn** Cnwll
4 D3 **Newlyn East** Cnwll
256 F7 **Newmachar** Abers
209 L7 **Newmains** N Lans
51 G5 **New Malden** Gt Lon
70 D4 **Newman's End** Essex
89 H6 **Newman's Green** Suffk
88 C3 **Newmarket** Suffk
282 g3 **Newmarket** W Isls
170 E6 **New Marske** R & Cl
66 D5 **New Marston** Oxon
112 E4 **New Marton** Shrops
245 H7 **New Mill** Abers
188 D4 **Newmill** Border
2 D4 **New Mill** Cnwll
68 A4 **New Mill** Herts
141 J6 **New Mill** Kirk
267 J5 **Newmill** Moray
141 M4 **Newmillerdam** Wakefd
234 C3 **Newmill of Inshewan** Angus
211 G5 **Newmills** C Edin
4 E4 **New Mills** Cnwll
131 K3 **New Mills** Derbys
210 D2 **Newmills** Fife
63 G5 **Newmills** Mons
94 D3 **New Mills** Powys
221 L1 **Newmiln** P & K
197 G3 **Newmilns** E Ayrs
18 C4 **New Milton** Hants
73 H1 **New Mistley** Essex
75 H7 **New Moat** Pembks
112 F5 **Newnes** Shrops
71 G5 **Newney Green** Essex
63 K5 **Newnham** Gloucs
49 H8 **Newnham** Hants
86 E7 **Newnham** Herts
40 B4 **Newnham** Kent
84 B3 **Newnham** Nhants
80 E2 **Newnham** Worcs
134 D6 **New Ollerton** Notts
98 E4 **New Oscott** Birm
268 F5 **New Pitsligo** Abers
10 C6 **New Polzeath** Cnwll
11 L5 **Newport** Cnwll
17 G3 **Newport** Dorset
143 L2 **Newport** E R Yk
87 L8 **Newport** Essex
63 K7 **Newport** Gloucs
274 F3 **Newport** Highld
19 H6 **Newport** IoW
44 C1 **Newport** Newpt
123 K8 **Newport** Norfk
75 H4 **Newport** Pembks
114 A7 **Newport** Wrekin
223 G2 **Newport-on-Tay** Fife
85 G6 **Newport Pagnell** M Keyn
37 G5 **Newpound Common** W Susx
196 C6 **New Prestwick** S Ayrs
76 D3 **New Quay** Cerdgn
4 D3 **Newquay** Cnwll
72 F2 **New Quay** Essex
106 F1 **New Rackheath** Norfk
79 H3 **New Radnor** Powys
166 B3 **New Rent** Cumb
180 C7 **New Ridley** Nthumb
149 H7 **New Road Side** N York
25 K2 **New Romney** Kent
143 G8 **New Rossington** Donc
92 F8 **New Row** Cerdgn
148 A8 **New Row** Lancs
142 B2 **Newsam Green** Leeds
220 F8 **New Sauchie** Clacks
131 G6 **Newsbank** Ches E
256 C5 **Newseat** Abers
147 K8 **Newsham** Lancs
160 E5 **Newsham** N York
168 E8 **Newsham** N York
181 H3 **Newsham** Nthumb
142 B4 **New Sharlston** Wakefd
143 H2 **Newsholme** E R Yk
148 E5 **Newsholme** Lancs
203 K6 **New Shoreston** Nthumb
181 J8 **New Silksworth** Sundld
170 F7 **New Skelton** R & Cl
141 J5 **Newsome** Kirk
118 B4 **New Somerby** Lincs
69 H8 **New Southgate Crematorium** Gt Lon
137 H6 **New Spilsby** Lincs
139 J6 **New Springs** Wigan
201 H6 **Newstead** Border
116 E1 **Newstead** Notts
203 J7 **Newstead** Nthumb
209 K7 **New Stevenston** N Lans
79 L4 **New Street** Herefs
116 D8 **New Swannington** Leics
142 D1 **Newthorpe** N York
116 E2 **Newthorpe** Notts
53 G1 **New Thundersley** Essex
22 D4 **Newtimber** W Susx
135 L2 **Newtoft** Lincs
217 G7 **Newton** Ag & B
189 G2 **Newton** Border
42 C6 **Newton** Brdgnd
86 E6 **Newton** C Beds
87 J5 **Newton** Cambs
119 M8 **Newton** Cambs
43 K6 **Newton** Cardif
129 J6 **Newton** Ches W
129 L7 **Newton** Ches W
129 M4 **Newton** Ches W
146 D2 **Newton** Cumb
133 J7 **Newton** Derbys
79 L1 **Newton** Herefs
79 L8 **Newton** Herefs
80 C4 **Newton** Herefs
251 G2 **Newton** Highld
252 D2 **Newton** Highld
263 L6 **Newton** Highld
280 D6 **Newton** Highld
147 G8 **Newton** Lancs
148 B5 **Newton** Lancs
157 J7 **Newton** Lancs
142 C2 **Newton** Leeds
118 D4 **Newton** Lincs
211 K5 **Newton** Mdloth
266 C3 **Newton** Moray
267 G4 **Newton** Moray
152 D1 **Newton** N York
101 J6 **Newton** Nhants
121 H8 **Newton** Norfk
117 J3 **Newton** Notts
180 C6 **Newton** Nthumb
190 D5 **Newton** Nthumb
198 F6 **Newton** S Lans
209 H6 **Newton** S Lans
98 C4 **Newton** Sandw
112 F4 **Newton** Shrops
29 K3 **Newton** Somset
115 G6 **Newton** Staffs
89 J7 **Newton** Suffk
210 E3 **Newton** W Loth
100 C7 **Newton** Warwks
34 B6 **Newton** Wilts
13 K8 **Newton Abbot** Devon
177 G7 **Newton Arlosh** Cumb
169 H5 **Newton Aycliffe** Dur
170 B5 **Newton Bewley** Hartpl
85 H5 **Newton Blossomville** M Keyn
85 K2 **Newton Bromswold** Nhants
99 K2 **Newton Burgoland** Leics
203 L8 **Newton-by-the-Sea** Nthumb
135 L2 **Newton by Toft** Lincs
6 C2 **Newton Ferrers** Cnwll
7 G5 **Newton Ferrers** Devon
282 c7 **Newton Ferry** W Isls
106 E4 **Newton Flotman** Norfk
211 K6 **Newtongrange** Mdloth
45 G1 **Newton Green** Mons
100 E4 **Newton Harcourt** Leics
140 C7 **Newton Heath** Manch
245 K5 **Newtonhill** Abers
141 M3 **Newton Hill** Wakefd
151 G6 **Newton Kyme** N York
160 B5 **Newton-le-Willows** N York
139 H8 **Newton-le-Willows** St Hel
211 K6 **Newtonloan** Mdloth
67 K1 **Newton Longville** Bucks
208 F7 **Newton Mearns** E Rens
234 F3 **Newtonmill** Angus
241 J4 **Newtonmore** Highld
160 C1 **Newton Morrell** N York
55 G5 **Newton Mountain** Pembks
171 H7 **Newton Mulgrave** N York
222 B5 **Newton of Balcanquhal** P & K
223 J6 **Newton of Balcormo** Fife
151 H4 **Newton on Ouse** N York
162 E4 **Newton-on-Rawcliffe** N York
113 H7 **Newton on the Hill** Shrops
191 H5 **Newton-on-the-Moor** Nthumb
135 G5 **Newton on Trent** Lincs
14 C4 **Newton Poppleford** Devon
66 F1 **Newton Purcell** Oxon
99 H2 **Newton Regis** Warwks
166 B4 **Newton Reigny** Cumb
13 K3 **Newton St Cyres** Devon
122 E8 **Newton St Faith** Norfk
45 L6 **Newton St Loe** BaNES
27 G8 **Newton St Petrock** Devon
115 M6 **Newton Solney** Derbys
34 E3 **Newton Stacey** Hants
173 K2 **Newton Stewart** D & G
34 B3 **Newton Tony** Wilts
27 J5 **Newton Tracey** Devon
170 D8 **Newton under Roseberry** R & Cl
180 E2 **Newton Underwood** Nthumb
151 M6 **Newton upon Derwent** E R Yk
35 L4 **Newton Valence** Hants
187 H7 **Newton Wamphray** D & G
138 F2 **Newton with Scales** Lancs
61 J5 **Newtown** Blae G
129 M4 **Newtown** Ches W
2 F5 **Newtown** Cnwll
11 K6 **Newtown** Cnwll
164 E1 **Newtown** Cumb
166 C6 **Newtown** Cumb
177 L6 **Newtown** Cumb
178 C6 **Newtown** Cumb
185 J1 **Newtown** D & G
131 K3 **Newtown** Derbys
14 C3 **Newtown** Devon
28 D6 **Newtown** Devon
15 L2 **Newtown** Dorset
17 K1 **New Town** Dorset
32 F7 **New Town** Dorset
33 G7 **New Town** Dorset
23 H3 **New Town** E Susx
63 K6 **Newtown** Gloucs
18 D2 **Newtown** Hants
35 J8 **Newtown** Hants
48 C6 **Newtown** Hants
80 B4 **Newtown** Herefs
80 C8 **Newtown** Herefs
80 E6 **Newtown** Herefs
81 G7 **Newtown** Herefs
240 B3 **Newtown** Highld
19 G5 **Newtown** IoW
139 G4 **Newtown** Lancs
101 L7 **New Town** Nhants
190 E6 **Newtown** Nthumb
202 F6 **Newtown** Nthumb
203 G8 **Newtown** Nthumb
17 K4 **Newtown** Poole
94 D5 **Newtown** Powys
61 G7 **Newtown** Rhondd
112 F7 **Newtown** Shrops
113 H5 **Newtown** Shrops
30 C8 **Newtown** Somset
98 C3 **Newtown** Staffs
131 H7 **Newtown** Staffs
139 H6 **Newtown** Wigan
32 F5 **Newtown** Wilts
47 L4 **New Town** Wilts
47 L6 **Newtown** Wilts
81 K4 **Newtown** Worcs

Newtown - Norton 339

98 B7 Newtown Worcs
3 J6 Newtown-in-St Martin Cnwll
100 B2 Newtown Linford Leics
208 C7 Newtown of Beltrees Rens
201 J6 Newtown St Boswells Border
100 B3 Newtown Unthank Leics
61 J6 New Tredegar Caerph
198 D5 New Trows S Lans
133 H6 New Tupton Derbys
233 L7 Newtyle Angus
103 K2 New Walsoken Cambs
145 H6 New Waltham NE Lin
133 H4 New Whittington Derbys
211 M5 New Winton E Loth
66 A4 New Yatt Oxon
50 D1 Newyears Green Gt Lon
216 F5 Newyork Ag & B
136 D8 New York Lincs
181 H5 New York N Tyne
150 B3 New York N York
79 L4 Nextend Herefs
54 F6 Neyland Pembks
154 b6 Niarbyl IoM
63 K5 Nibley Gloucs
45 K3 Nibley S Glos
63 L7 Nibley Green Gloucs
29 K7 Nicholashayne Devon
56 F7 Nicholaston Swans
178 D5 Nickies Hill Cumb
150 D4 Nidd N York
245 L3 Nigg C Aber
264 C5 Nigg Highld
45 L5 Nimlet BaNES
179 H8 Ninebanks Nthumb
47 G2 Nine Elms Swindn
80 E2 Nineveh Worcs
74 C7 Nine Wells Pembks
24 C5 Ninfield E Susx
18 F6 Ningwood IoW
201 L8 Nisbet Border
202 B3 Nisbet Hill Border
19 H8 Niton IoW
208 E7 Nitshill C Glas
52 C7 Noah's Ark Kent
52 E1 Noak Bridge Essex
70 D8 Noak Hill Gt Lon
141 L6 Noblethorpe Barns
95 L2 Nobold Shrops
84 C3 Nobottle Nhants
135 L6 Nocton Lincs
107 H3 Nogdam End Norfk
66 E4 Noke Oxon
54 E3 Nolton Pembks
54 D3 Nolton Haven Pembks
113 H2 No Man's Heath Ches W
99 H2 No Man's Heath Warwks
6 B3 No Man's Land Cnwll
28 E8 Nomansland Devon
34 B7 Nomansland Wilts
113 H6 Noneley Shrops
41 H5 Nonington Kent
157 H6 Nook Cumb
178 B3 Nook Cumb
51 G5 Norbiton Gt Lon
146 F7 Norbreck Bpool
81 G6 Norbridge Herefs
113 J2 Norbury Ches E
115 J3 Norbury Derbys
51 J5 Norbury Gt Lon
95 J5 Norbury Shrops
114 B6 Norbury Staffs
113 J2 Norbury Common Ches E
114 B7 Norbury Junction Staffs
81 J2 Norchard Worcs
130 B4 Norcott Brook Ches W
146 F7 Norcross Lancs
103 L3 Nordelph Norfk
140 C5 Norden Rochdl
96 F4 Nordley Shrops
202 D4 Norham Nthumb
141 G3 Norland Town Calder
130 B5 Norley Ches W
10 C4 Norleywood Hants
23 G4 Norlington E Susx
135 K2 Normanby Lincs
143 M4 Normanby N Linc
162 C6 Normanby N York
170 D7 Normanby R & Cl
136 B1 Normanby le Wold Lincs
102 D5 Norman Cross Cambs
50 B8 Normandy Surrey
24 C6 Norman's Bay E Susx
14 C2 Norman's Green Devon
116 B5 Normanton C Derb
117 L3 Normanton Leics
118 B2 Normanton Lincs
134 E8 Normanton Notts
101 K2 Normanton Rutlnd
142 B3 Normanton Wakefd
33 K3 Normanton Wilts
99 K1 Normanton le Heath Leics
116 E7 Normanton on Soar Notts
117 G5 Normanton on the Wolds Notts
134 F6 Normanton on Trent Notts
147 G8 Normoss Lancs
36 D2 Norney Surrey
46 C6 Norrington Common Wilts
6 E1 Norris Green Cnwll
116 B8 Norris Hill Leics
141 K3 Norristhorpe Kirk
105 J4 Northacre Norfk
68 B3 Northall Bucks
160 E4 Northallerton N York
121 M8 Northall Green Norfk
19 G1 Northam C Sotn
27 H5 Northam Devon
84 E3 Northampton Nhants
81 J2 Northampton Worcs
133 K3 North Anston Rothm
49 M5 North Ascot Br For
66 C1 North Aston Oxon
69 H6 Northaw Herts
30 D8 Northay Somset
34 E6 North Baddesley Hants
229 G3 North Ballachulish Highld
31 K5 North Barrow Somset
121 K4 North Barsham Norfk
53 G1 North Benfleet Essex
20 F6 North Bersted W Susx
212 C2 North Berwick E Loth
168 F4 North Bitchburn Dur
181 H2 North Blyth Nthumb
19 K2 North Boarhunt Hants
18 B4 North Bockhampton Dorset
102 C2 Northborough C Pete
41 K5 Northbourne Kent
13 H5 North Bovey Devon
46 B7 North Bradley Wilts
12 C6 North Brentor Devon
32 B3 North Brewham Somset
36 E3 North Bridge Surrey
24 D2 Northbridge Street E Susx
35 G3 Northbrook Hants
66 D3 Northbrook Oxon
86 F6 North Brook End Cambs
27 H3 North Buckland Devon
107 H2 North Burlingham Norfk
31 K5 North Cadbury Somset
135 J4 North Carlton Lincs
134 B3 North Carlton Notts
143 M1 North Cave E R Yk
64 E5 North Cerney Gloucs
22 F3 North Chailey E Susx
36 E5 Northchapel W Susx
33 L7 North Charford Hants
191 H2 North Charlton Nthumb
51 G6 North Cheam Gt Lon
31 M5 North Cheriton Somset
15 K4 North Chideock Dorset
68 B5 Northchurch Herts
152 D8 North Cliffe E R Yk
135 G5 North Clifton Notts
169 H4 North Close Dur
137 G2 North Cockerington Lincs
228 E8 North Connel Ag & B
42 B5 North Cornelly Brdgnd
3 K7 North Corner Cnwll
145 J7 North Cotes Lincs
11 L4 Northcott Devon
14 D1 Northcott Devon
29 K8 Northcott Devon
4 A6 North Country Cnwll
66 D7 Northcourt Oxon
107 K5 North Cove Suffk
160 D2 North Cowton N York
85 H6 North Crawley M Keyn
52 A4 North Cray Gt Lon
121 J4 North Creake Norfk
30 D6 North Curry Somset
152 E5 North Dalton E R Yk
150 E5 North Deighton N York
27 K4 North Devon Crematorium Devon
41 L1 Northdown Kent
151 L8 North Duffield N York
259 G2 North Duntulm Highld
51 G5 North East Surrey Crematorium Gt Lon
133 G6 Northedge Derbys
41 G6 North Elham Kent
136 E2 North Elkington Lincs
121 L7 North Elmham Norfk
142 D5 North Elmsall Wakefd
67 H8 Northend Bucks
19 L3 North End C Port
177 K7 North End Cumb
32 D5 North End Dorset
145 H2 North End E R Yk
153 K7 North End E R Yk
71 G3 North End Essex
33 J7 North End Hants
35 J5 North End Hants
116 F8 North End Leics
119 H3 North End Lincs
137 H2 North End Lincs
144 D7 North End Lincs
145 J7 North End Lincs
144 E3 North End N Linc
44 E5 North End N Som
85 J2 North End Nhants
105 K5 North End Norfk
191 G6 North End Nthumb
138 C6 North End Sefton
21 G6 North End W Susx
21 J5 North End W Susx
83 J5 Northend Warwks
131 G2 Northenden Manch
49 L1 Northend Woods Bucks
260 B4 North Erradale Highld
100 D3 North Evington C Leic
71 K7 North Fambridge Essex
144 B3 North Ferriby E R Yk
98 C7 Northfield Birm
245 K2 Northfield C Aber
144 C2 Northfield E R Yk
102 A2 Northfields Lincs
52 D4 Northfleet Kent
153 H5 North Frodingham E R Yk
33 L8 North Gorley Hants
106 E5 North Green Norfk
91 G3 North Green Suffk
91 J2 North Green Suffk
135 K5 North Greetwell Lincs
152 C2 North Grimston N York
52 F6 North Halling Medway
20 B6 North Hayling Hants
203 G6 North Hazelrigg Nthumb
28 C4 North Heasley Devon
37 G6 North Heath W Susx
29 J6 North Hele Devon
11 K7 North Hill Cnwll
50 D2 North Hillingdon Gt Lon
66 D6 North Hinksey Village Oxon
37 J2 North Holmwood Surrey
7 K3 North Huish Devon
135 J6 North Hykeham Lincs
24 E2 Northiam E Susx
86 C6 Northill C Beds
63 L5 Northington Gloucs
35 H3 Northington Hants
144 D7 North Kelsey Lincs
251 H2 North Kessock Highld
144 F4 North Killingholme N Linc
160 F5 North Kilvington N York
100 D6 North Kilworth Leics
18 B3 North Kingston Hants
118 F1 North Kyme Lincs
153 L2 North Landing E R Yk
119 K1 Northlands Lincs
65 G4 Northleach Gloucs
67 K5 North Lee Bucks
160 D7 North Lees N York
14 E3 Northleigh Devon
27 L4 Northleigh Devon
40 F6 North Leigh Kent
66 A4 North Leigh Oxon
134 F3 North Leverton with Habblesthorpe Notts
12 C3 Northlew Devon
82 C5 North Littleton Worcs
31 H3 Northload Bridge Somset
105 L6 North Lopham Norfk
101 K3 North Luffenham Rutlnd
20 C4 North Marden W Susx
67 J3 North Marston Bucks
211 K7 North Middleton Mdloth
190 E1 North Middleton Nthumb
256 E3 North Millbrex Abers
172 D4 North Milmain D & G
28 C5 North Molton Devon
66 B6 Northmoor Oxon
48 E1 North Moreton Oxon
234 B4 Northmuir Angus
20 E6 North Mundham W Susx
134 F7 North Muskham Notts
152 D8 North Newbald E R Yk
83 K7 North Newington Oxon
47 H7 North Newnton Wilts
30 D4 North Newton Somset
20 B6 Northney Hants
63 L7 North Nibley Gloucs
48 D8 North Oakley Hants
52 C2 North Ockendon Gt Lon
50 E2 Northolt Gt Lon
128 F6 Northop Flints
129 G6 Northop Hall Flints
170 C6 North Ormesby Middsb
136 E1 North Ormsby Lincs
141 K3 Northorpe Kirk
118 E8 Northorpe Lincs
119 G4 Northorpe Lincs
143 M8 Northorpe Lincs
160 E5 North Otterington N York
31 H3 Northover Somset
31 H6 Northover Somset
135 L1 North Owersby Lincs
141 H2 Northowram Calder
15 L1 North Perrott Somset
30 D4 North Petherton Somset
11 K4 North Petherwin Cnwll
105 H2 North Pickenham Norfk
81 M4 North Piddle Worcs
15 M3 North Poorton Dorset
17 H5 Northport Dorset
18 B2 North Poulner Hants
210 F3 North Queensferry Fife
28 C4 North Radworthy Devon
118 D2 North Rauceby Lincs
122 E4 Northrepps Norfk
137 G3 North Reston Lincs
150 C6 North Rigton N York
18 B4 North Ripley Hants
131 H6 North Rode Ches E
165 H4 North Row Cumb
120 E8 North Runcton Norfk
146 C2 North Scale Cumb
135 G6 North Scarle Lincs
181 H2 North Seaton Nthumb
181 H2 North Seaton Colliery Nthumb
228 E6 North Shian Ag & B
181 J5 North Shields N Tyne
53 K2 North Shoebury Sthend
146 F8 North Shore Bpool
102 F3 North Side C Pete
164 C5 North Side Cumb
170 F7 North Skelton R & Cl
145 L8 North Somercotes Lincs
160 D7 North Stainley N York
167 J7 North Stainmore Cumb
52 D3 North Stifford Thurr
45 L5 North Stoke BaNES
48 F2 North Stoke Oxon
21 H5 North Stoke W Susx
88 B2 North Street Cambs
33 K7 North Street Hants
35 K4 North Street Hants
40 D4 North Street Kent
53 H4 North Street Medway
48 F4 North Street W Berk
203 K6 North Sunderland Nthumb
11 K3 North Tamerton Cnwll
12 F2 North Tawton Devon
209 K1 North Third Stirlg
145 H8 North Thoresby Lincs
282 d6 Northton W Isls
12 C1 North Town Devon
31 J2 North Town Somset
49 L3 North Town W & M
122 A8 North Tuddenham Norfk
180 E5 North Walbottle N u Ty
122 F5 North Walsham Norfk
35 H2 North Waltham Hants
35 M1 North Warnborough Hants
29 L5 Northway Somset
57 G7 Northway Swans
70 D6 North Weald Bassett Essex
134 F3 North Wheatley Notts
8 C2 North Whilborough Devon
130 C5 Northwich Ches W
45 H6 North Wick BaNES
45 H2 Northwick S Glos
30 E1 Northwick Somset
81 J4 Northwick Worcs
45 H7 North Widcombe BaNES
136 C2 North Willingham Lincs
133 H6 North Wingfield Derbys
118 B7 North Witham Lincs
104 E4 Northwold Norfk
114 D2 Northwood C Stke
132 E6 Northwood Derbys
50 E1 Northwood Gt Lon
19 H5 Northwood IoW
113 G5 Northwood Shrops
63 L4 Northwood Green Gloucs
31 L7 North Wootton Dorset
120 E6 North Wootton Norfk
31 J3 North Wootton Somset
46 B4 North Wraxall Wilts
47 H3 North Wroughton Swindn
142 E5 Norton Donc
23 G7 Norton E Susx
64 B2 Norton Gloucs
130 A3 Norton Halton
86 E8 Norton Herts
18 E6 Norton IoW
62 F3 Norton Mons
44 D6 Norton N Som
152 B2 Norton N York
84 B3 Norton Nhants

340 Norton - Ormesby

133 L5 Norton Notts
79 K2 Norton Powys
170 B6 Norton S on T
133 G3 Norton Sheff
95 L7 Norton Shrops
96 D2 Norton Shrops
96 E6 Norton Shrops
97 G3 Norton Shrops
89 J2 Norton Suffk
57 H7 Norton Swans
20 F5 Norton W Susx
46 C2 Norton Wilts
81 K5 Norton Worcs
82 B5 Norton Worcs
32 F2 Norton Bavant Wilts
114 D5 Norton Bridge Staffs
98 C2 Norton Canes Staffs
79 M6 Norton Canon Herefs
122 B6 Norton Corner Norfk
135 H7 Norton Disney Lincs
32 C4 Norton Ferris Wilts
30 B5 Norton Fitzwarren Somset
18 E6 Norton Green IoW
45 H6 Norton Hawkfield BaNES
70 F6 Norton Heath Essex
113 M4 Norton in Hales Shrops
114 D1 Norton in the Moors C Stke
99 J2 Norton-Juxta-Twycross Leics
150 F2 Norton-le-Clay N York
82 F3 Norton Lindsey Warwks
89 K2 Norton Little Green Suffk
45 J6 Norton Malreward BaNES
70 E6 Norton Mandeville Essex
45 M7 Norton St Philip Somset
107 H4 Norton Subcourse Norfk
31 G7 Norton sub Hamdon Somset
79 L5 Norton Wood Herefs
134 F7 Norwell Notts
134 E7 Norwell Woodhouse Notts
106 E2 Norwich Norfk
122 E8 Norwich (St Faith) Crematorium Norfk
281 f1 Norwick Shet
220 F8 Norwood Clacks
133 J3 Norwood Derbys
25 K1 Norwood Kent
70 E5 Norwood End Essex
141 H2 Norwood Green Calder
50 E3 Norwood Green Gt Lon
37 K2 Norwood Hill Surrey
103 H4 Norwoodside Cambs
101 G4 Noseley Leics
7 G5 Noss Mayo Devon
160 C6 Nosterfield N York
88 C6 Nosterfield End Cambs
248 D6 Nostie Highld
65 G3 Notgrove Gloucs
42 B6 Nottage Brdgnd
6 D3 Notter Cnwll
116 F4 Nottingham C Nott
16 C6 Nottington Dorset
142 A5 Notton Wakefd
46 C5 Notton Wilts
71 J5 Nounsley Essex
81 J2 Noutard's Green Worcs
89 H3 Nowton Suffk
95 K1 Nox Shrops
49 G2 Nuffield Oxon
152 C6 Nunburnholme E R Yk
116 E1 Nuncargate Notts
166 C2 Nunclose Cumb
99 K5 Nuneaton Warwks
66 E7 Nuneham Courtenay Oxon
51 K4 Nunhead Gt Lon
153 J6 Nunkeeling E R Yk
151 H4 Nun Monkton N York
32 B2 Nunney Somset
32 B2 Nunney Catch Somset
80 D6 Nunnington Herefs
161 L6 Nunnington N York
190 F7 Nunnykirk Nthumb
145 H6 Nunsthorpe NE Lin
151 J6 Nunthorpe C York
170 C7 Nunthorpe Middsb
170 D8 Nunthorpe Village Middsb
33 K5 Nunton Wilts
160 D7 Nunwick N York
179 K4 Nunwick Nthumb
63 J7 Nupdown S Glos
67 L3 Nup End Bucks
64 A5 Nupend Gloucs
49 L4 Nuptown Br For
34 E7 Nursling Hants
36 A6 Nursted Hants
46 F6 Nursteed Wilts
97 J3 Nurton Staffs
20 C6 Nutbourne W Susx
21 J3 Nutbourne W Susx
37 M1 Nutfield Surrey
116 E3 Nuthall Notts
87 H8 Nuthampstead Herts
37 J5 Nuthurst W Susx
23 G2 Nutley E Susx
35 J2 Nutley Hants
140 B4 Nuttal Lane Bury
143 G7 Nutwell Donc
280 E3 Nybster Highld
20 E7 Nyetimber W Susx
36 B6 Nyewood W Susx
13 G1 Nymet Rowland Devon
13 G2 Nymet Tracey Devon
64 A7 Nympsfield Gloucs
29 L6 Nynehead Somset
30 F4 Nythe Somset
20 F5 Nyton W Susx

## O

100 D3 Oadby Leics
53 J6 Oad Street Kent
81 J3 Oakall Green Worcs
115 G3 Oakamoor Staffs
210 E5 Oakbank W Loth
12 D3 Oak Cross Devon
43 J2 Oakdale Caerph
29 L6 Oake Somset
97 J3 Oaken Staffs
147 K6 Oakenclough Lancs
96 F1 Oakengates Wrekin
129 G5 Oakenholt Flints
169 G3 Oakenshaw Dur
141 J2 Oakenshaw Kirk
133 H8 Oakerthorpe Derbys
76 E4 Oakford Cerdgn
29 G6 Oakford Devon
29 G6 Oakfordbridge Devon
131 H6 Oakgrove Ches E
101 J2 Oakham Rutlnd
114 B1 Oakhanger Ches E
36 A4 Oakhanger Hants
31 K2 Oakhill Somset
38 E3 Oakhurst Kent
87 H2 Oakington Cambs
78 E5 Oaklands Powys
63 M4 Oakle Street Gloucs
85 K4 Oakley Bed
66 F4 Oakley Bucks
210 D1 Oakley Fife
35 H1 Oakley Hants
67 H7 Oakley Oxon
17 K3 Oakley Poole
106 D7 Oakley Suffk
50 A4 Oakley Green W & M
93 L6 Oakley Park Powys
64 C6 Oakridge Gloucs
168 F5 Oaks Dur
139 K1 Oaks Lancs
95 K2 Oaks Shrops
64 E8 Oaksey Wilts
115 J5 Oaks Green Derbys
178 C4 Oakshaw Ford Cumb
35 M5 Oakshott Hants
99 J1 Oakthorpe Leics
169 K8 Oak Tree Darltn
116 C4 Oakwood C Derb
179 L5 Oakwood Nthumb
149 J8 Oakworth C Brad
40 C3 Oare Kent
28 D2 Oare Somset
47 H6 Oare Wilts
118 D4 Oasby Lincs
30 F5 Oath Somset
234 D4 Oathlaw Angus
50 E6 Oatlands Park Surrey
216 D1 Oban Ag & B
95 H7 Obley Shrops
232 F7 Obney P & K
31 L7 Oborne Dorset
118 E8 Obthorpe Lincs
90 D1 Occold Suffk
275 J1 Occumster Highld
196 F6 Ochiltree E Ayrs
116 C4 Ockbrook Derbys
98 B4 Ocker Hill Sandw
81 H3 Ockeridge Worcs
50 D7 Ockham Surrey
237 G6 Ockle Highld
37 H3 Ockley Surrey
80 E6 Ocle Pychard Herefs
153 G2 Octon E R Yk
31 H7 Odcombe Somset
45 L6 Odd Down BaNES
81 L3 Oddingley Worcs
65 J2 Oddington Gloucs
66 E4 Oddington Oxon
85 J4 Odell Bed
12 C2 Odham Devon
49 H8 Odiham Hants
141 J2 Odsal C Brad
86 F7 Odsey Cambs
33 K5 Odstock Wilts
99 K2 Odstone Leics
83 J2 Offchurch Warwks
82 C6 Offenham Worcs
131 H2 Offerton Stockp
181 J7 Offerton Sundld
22 F5 Offham E Susx
39 G2 Offham Kent
21 H5 Offham W Susx
114 B5 Offleymarsh Staffs
86 E2 Offord Cluny Cambs
86 E2 Offord D'Arcy Cambs
90 C5 Offton Suffk
14 E3 Offwell Devon
47 J4 Ogbourne Maizey Wilts
47 J4 Ogbourne St Andrew Wilts
47 J4 Ogbourne St George Wilts
141 G2 Ogden Calder
180 E3 Ogle Nthumb
129 K3 Oglet Lpool
42 D6 Ogmore V Glam
42 C6 Ogmore-by-Sea V Glam
42 E4 Ogmore Vale Brdgnd
126 C6 Ogwen Bank Gwynd
32 D8 Okeford Fitzpaine Dorset
12 E3 Okehampton Devon
132 E7 Oker Side Derbys
37 H3 Okewood Hill Surrey
13 K7 Olchard Devon
84 F1 Old Nhants
245 L2 Old Aberdeen C Aber
35 J4 Old Alresford Hants
270 E2 Oldany Highld
185 J3 Old Auchenbrack D & G
116 F3 Old Basford C Nott
49 G8 Old Basing Hants
121 L7 Old Beetley Norfk
82 D2 Oldberrow Warwks
190 F2 Old Bewick Nthumb
136 F6 Old Bolingbroke Lincs
150 B7 Old Bramhope Leeds
133 G5 Old Brampton Derbys
175 J1 Old Bridge of Urr D & G
106 B5 Old Buckenham Norfk
48 C7 Old Burghclere Hants
38 F2 Oldbury Kent
98 C5 Oldbury Sandw
97 G5 Oldbury Shrops
99 J4 Oldbury Warwks
63 J8 Oldbury Naite S Glos
63 J8 Oldbury-on-Severn S Glos
46 B1 Oldbury on the Hill Gloucs
161 J5 Old Byland N York
143 G7 Old Cantley Donc
169 J3 Old Cassop Dur
42 D6 Old Castle Brdgnd
62 C2 Oldcastle Mons
113 G2 Oldcastle Heath Ches W
95 G4 Old Churchstoke Powys
145 H6 Old Clee NE Lin
29 J3 Old Cleeve Somset
134 C6 Old Clipstone Notts
127 H4 Old Colwyn Conwy
134 B2 Oldcotes Notts
183 G3 Old Dailly S Ayrs
117 H6 Old Dalby Leics
132 B4 Old Dam Derbys
269 H6 Old Deer Abers
31 H1 Old Ditch Somset
142 E8 Old Edlington Donc
169 H5 Old Eldon Dur
153 J8 Old Ellerby E R Yk
91 H8 Old Felixstowe Suffk
149 H8 Oldfield C Brad
81 J2 Oldfield Worcs
102 D4 Old Fletton C Pete
32 C1 Oldford Somset
63 H3 Old Forge Herefs
62 F2 Old Furnace Herefs
131 L1 Old Glossop Derbys
143 J3 Old Goole E R Yk
10 b2 Old Grimsby IoS
69 K3 Old Hall Green Herts
89 H4 Oldhall Green Suffk
122 F5 Old Hall Street Norfk
140 D6 Oldham Oldham
213 G5 Oldhamstocks E Loth
70 C5 Old Harlow Essex
72 E3 Old Heath Essex
120 F3 Old Hunstanton Norfk
102 F7 Old Hurst Cambs
157 J5 Old Hutton Cumb
4 D6 Old Kea Cnwll
208 D4 Old Kilpatrick W Duns
69 G3 Old Knebworth Herts
106 E2 Old Lakenham Norfk
45 K4 Oldland S Glos
148 B8 Old Langho Lancs
154 f5 Old Laxey IoM
119 L2 Old Leake Lincs
152 B1 Old Malton N York
256 E6 Oldmeldrum Abers
142 C1 Old Micklefield Leeds
11 M7 Oldmill Cnwll
83 G2 Old Milverton Warwks
44 C7 Oldmixon N Som
90 B3 Old Newton Suffk
169 J3 Old Quarrington Dur
116 F3 Old Radford C Nott
79 J3 Old Radnor Powys
256 B6 Old Rayne Abers
25 J2 Old Romney Kent
22 B6 Old Shoreham W Susx
276 C4 Oldshoremore Highld
38 F3 Old Soar Kent
45 L3 Old Sodbury S Glos
118 C5 Old Somerby Lincs
161 H6 Oldstead N York
84 E7 Old Stratford Nhants
232 B2 Old Struan P & K
97 K6 Old Swinford Dudley
157 K2 Old Tebay Cumb
160 F6 Old Thirsk N York
140 F2 Old Town Calder
157 J6 Old Town Cumb
166 B2 Old Town Cumb
23 K7 Old Town E Susx
10 c3 Old Town IoS
190 B7 Old Town Nthumb
140 B8 Old Trafford Traffd
133 H6 Old Tupton Derbys
178 B6 Oldwall Cumb
56 E6 Oldwalls Swans
86 C6 Old Warden C Beds
28 F6 Oldways End Somset
102 B7 Old Weston Cambs
280 E6 Old Wick Highld
50 C4 Old Windsor W & M
40 E4 Old Wives Lees Kent
50 C7 Old Woking Surrey
84 F7 Old Wolverton M Keyn
113 G7 Old Woods Shrops
279 K5 Olgrinmore Highld
115 J7 Olive Green Staffs
187 G1 Oliver Border
34 F5 Oliver's Battery Hants
281 d4 Ollaberry Shet
247 H1 Ollach Highld
130 F4 Ollerton Ches E
134 D6 Ollerton Notts
113 L6 Ollerton Shrops
77 H4 Olmarch Cerdgn
88 C7 Olmstead Green Cambs
85 H5 Olney M Keyn
279 L3 Olrig House Highld
98 E7 Olton Solhll
45 J2 Olveston S Glos
81 J3 Ombersley Worcs
134 D6 Ompton Notts
179 H5 Once Brewed Nthumb
154 e6 Onchan IoM
131 L8 Onecote Staffs
89 K3 Onehouse Suffk
62 E4 Onen Mons
79 M2 Ongar Street Herefs
95 L7 Onibury Shrops
229 G3 Onich Highld
60 C5 Onllwyn Neath
114 B3 Onneley Staffs
36 E1 Onslow Village Surrey
130 B5 Onston Ches W
116 B2 Openwoodgate Derbys
260 B5 Opinan Highld
266 F5 Orbliston Moray
258 D7 Orbost Highld
137 J6 Orby Lincs
30 C6 Orchard Portman Somset
33 J2 Orcheston Wilts
62 F2 Orcop Herefs
62 F2 Orcop Hill Herefs
268 A4 Ord Abers
244 E2 Ordhead Abers
244 A3 Ordie Abers
267 G5 Ordiequish Moray
179 L7 Ordley Nthumb
134 D4 Ordsall Notts
24 F5 Ore E Susx
80 B2 Oreleton Common Herefs
96 E7 Oreton Shrops
91 K5 Orford Suffk
130 B2 Orford Warrtn
17 H4 Organford Dorset
115 J8 Orgreave Staffs
40 C8 Orlestone Kent
80 C2 Orleton Herefs
81 G2 Orleton Worcs
85 G1 Orlingbury Nhants
165 J5 Ormathwaite Cumb
170 C7 Ormesby R & Cl

Ormesby St Margaret - Park Street 341

123 K8 Ormesby St Margaret Norfk
123 K8 Ormesby St Michael Norfk
260 D2 Ormiscaig Highld
211 M5 Ormiston E Loth
236 F7 Ormsaigmore Highld
206 A4 Ormsary Ag & B
138 E6 Ormskirk Lancs
168 F1 Ornsby Hill Dur
214 C6 Oronsay Ag & B
275 b5 Orphir Ork
51 M5 Orpington Gt Lon
138 D8 Orrell Sefton
139 G7 Orrell Wigan
139 G6 Orrell Post Wigan
154 d4 Orrisdale IoM
175 J5 Orroland D & G
52 D3 Orsett Thurr
114 C8 Orslow Staffs
117 K3 Orston Notts
165 H4 Orthwaite Cumb
147 K5 Ortner Lancs
157 K1 Orton Cumb
101 H7 Orton Nhants
97 K4 Orton Staffs
102 D4 Orton Longueville C Pete
99 J3 Orton-on-the-Hill Leics
177 K8 Orton Rigg Cumb
102 C4 Orton Waterville C Pete
87 H5 Orwell Cambs
139 K2 Osbaldeston Lancs
139 K1 Osbaldeston Green Lancs
151 K5 Osbaldwick C York
99 L3 Osbaston Leics
112 D7 Osbaston Shrops
19 H5 Osborne IoW
118 E4 Osbournby Lincs
129 L6 Oscroft Ches W
258 E8 Ose Highld
116 D7 Osgathorpe Leics
135 M1 Osgodby Lincs
143 G1 Osgodby N York
163 J5 Osgodby N York
247 H1 Oskaig Highld
226 E4 Oskamull Ag & B
71 G3 Onslow Green Essex
115 K3 Osmaston Derbys
16 D6 Osmington Dorset
16 D6 Osmington Mills Dorset
142 A1 Osmondthorpe Leeds
161 G3 Osmotherley N York
66 D6 Osney Oxon
40 C3 Ospringe Kent
141 L4 Ossett Wakefd
134 E6 Ossington Notts
72 D7 Ostend Essex
50 F3 Osterley Gt Lon
161 K6 Oswaldkirk N York
139 L2 Oswaldtwistle Lancs
112 D5 Oswestry Shrops
52 B7 Otford Kent
39 K3 Otham Kent
39 K3 Otham Hole Kent
30 F4 Othery Somset
150 B6 Otley Leeds
90 E4 Otley Suffk
90 F4 Otley Green Suffk
34 F6 Otterbourne Hants
148 F4 Otterburn N York
190 C7 Otterburn Nthumb
206 E2 Otter Ferry Ag & B
11 H4 Otterham Cnwll
30 C2 Otterhampton Somset
53 H5 Otterham Quay Kent
11 G4 Otterham Station Cnwll
282 c7 Otternish W Isls
50 C6 Ottershaw Surrey
281 e3 Otterswick Shet
14 C5 Otterton Devon
18 F3 Otterwood Hants
14 C3 Ottery St Mary Devon
41 G6 Ottinge Kent
145 H3 Ottringham E R Yk
177 J7 Oughterby Cumb
158 F6 Oughtershaw N York
164 F3 Oughterside Cumb
132 F1 Oughtibridge Sheff
130 D2 Oughtrington Warrtn
161 J7 Oulston N York
177 H8 Oulton Cumb
142 B2 Oulton Leeds
122 C6 Oulton Norfk
114 B7 Oulton Staffs
114 E4 Oulton Staffs
107 L4 Oulton Suffk
107 L5 Oulton Broad Suffk
122 C6 Oulton Street Norfk
102 A5 Oundle Nhants
97 K5 Ounsdale Staffs
166 E4 Ousby Cumb
88 E3 Ousden Suffk
143 L3 Ousefleet E R Yk
181 G8 Ouston Dur
203 J6 Outchester Nthumb
41 G5 Out Elmstead Kent
156 E3 Outgate Cumb
158 D2 Outhgill Cumb
82 D2 Outhill Warwks
114 B5 Outlands Staffs
141 G4 Outlane Kirk
145 K3 Out Newton E R Yk
147 H7 Out Rawcliffe Lancs
103 K3 Outwell Norfk
33 K7 Outwick Hants
37 M2 Outwood Surrey
142 A3 Outwood Wakefd
140 B6 Outwood Gate Bury
116 C7 Outwoods Leics
114 B7 Outwoods Staffs
142 A3 Ouzlewell Green Leeds
141 G2 Ovenden Calder
87 H1 Over Cambs
130 C6 Over Ches W
64 A3 Over Gloucs
45 H2 Over S Glos
115 L4 Over Burrows Derbys
81 M7 Overbury Worcs
16 D6 Overcombe Dorset
31 K7 Over Compton Dorset
139 K6 Overdale Crematorium Bolton
102 B5 Over End Cambs
132 F5 Overgreen Derbys
98 F4 Over Green Warwks
132 D6 Over Haddon Derbys
147 K2 Over Kellet Lancs
66 B3 Over Kiddington Oxon
31 G4 Overleigh Somset
115 J8 Overley Staffs
63 G4 Over Monnow Mons
65 L2 Over Norton Oxon
130 F5 Over Peover Ches E
129 J4 Overpool Ches W
272 B3 Overscaig Hotel Highld
116 A8 Overseal Derbys
161 G4 Over Silton N York
40 D4 Oversland Kent
82 C4 Oversley Green Warwks
84 F2 Overstone Nhants
30 B3 Over Stowey Somset
122 E3 Overstrand Norfk
31 G7 Over Stratton Somset
33 J3 Overstreet Wilts
130 E4 Over Tabley Ches E
83 L7 Overthorpe Nhants
245 J1 Overton C Aber
129 M4 Overton Ches W
35 G1 Overton Hants
147 H4 Overton Lancs
151 J5 Overton N York
80 C1 Overton Shrops
56 E7 Overton Swans
141 L4 Overton Wakefd
112 E3 Overton Wrexhm
112 E3 Overton Bridge Wrexhm
130 F7 Overton Green Ches E
157 K7 Overtown Lancs
209 L8 Overtown N Lans
47 H3 Overtown Swindn
142 A4 Overtown Wakefd
34 C3 Over Wallop Hants
99 H5 Over Whitacre Warwks
133 J5 Over Woodhouse Derbys
66 B1 Over Worton Oxon
66 E8 Overy Oxon
67 J3 Oving Bucks
20 E6 Oving W Susx
22 E6 Ovingdean Br & H
180 D6 Ovingham Nthumb
168 E7 Ovington Dur
88 F6 Ovington Essex
35 H4 Ovington Hants
105 J3 Ovington Norfk
180 C6 Ovington Nthumb
19 H3 Ower Hants
34 D7 Ower Hants
16 E5 Owermoigne Dorset
95 H5 Owlbury Shrops
133 G2 Owlerton Sheff
64 A7 Owlpen Gloucs
91 G1 Owl's Green Suffk
49 K6 Owlsmoor Br For
67 J6 Owlswick Bucks
135 K2 Owmby Lincs
144 D6 Owmby Lincs
35 G6 Owslebury Hants
142 E5 Owston Donc
101 G2 Owston Leics
143 K7 Owston Ferry N Linc
145 H1 Owstwick E R Yk
145 J2 Owthorne E R Yk
117 H5 Owthorpe Notts
170 C5 Owton Manor Hartpl
104 E3 Oxborough Norfk
15 L3 Oxbridge Dorset
136 F4 Oxcombe Lincs
133 J5 Oxcroft Derbys
71 G1 Oxen End Essex
157 H5 Oxenholme Cumb
140 F1 Oxenhope C Brad
156 D5 Oxen Park Cumb
31 G3 Oxenpill Somset
64 D1 Oxenton Gloucs
47 L7 Oxenwood Wilts
66 D6 Oxford Oxon
66 E5 Oxford Crematorium Oxon
68 E8 Oxhey Herts
180 F8 Oxhill Dur
83 H6 Oxhill Warwks
97 K3 Oxley Wolves
72 C4 Oxley Green Essex
24 C3 Oxley's Green E Susx
103 K6 Oxlode Cambs
189 J3 Oxnam Border
122 E6 Oxnead Norfk
50 F6 Oxshott Surrey
50 E6 Oxshott Heath Surrey
141 L7 Oxspring Barns
51 K8 Oxted Surrey
201 G2 Oxton Border
151 H7 Oxton N York
117 G1 Oxton Notts
56 F7 Oxwich Swans
56 F7 Oxwich Green Swans
121 K6 Oxwick Norfk
271 L7 Oykel Bridge Hotel Highld
256 B6 Oyne Abers
57 H7 Oystermouth Swans
64 A8 Ozleworth Gloucs

## P

282 h3 Pabail W Isls
16 D1 Packers Hill Dorset
116 B8 Packington Leics
114 D1 Packmoor C Stke
83 G2 Packmores Warwks
234 C5 Padanaram Angus
67 H1 Padbury Bucks
51 H3 Paddington Gt Lon
130 C2 Paddington Warrtn
41 G7 Paddlesworth Kent
52 E6 Paddlesworth Kent
39 G4 Paddock Wood Kent
113 H5 Paddolgreen Shrops
140 F8 Padfield Derbys
130 C2 Padgate Warrtn
70 F7 Padhams Green Essex
140 B1 Padiham Lancs
149 L4 Padside N York
10 C7 Padstow Cnwll
48 F5 Padworth W Berk
169 G4 Page Bank Dur
20 E7 Pagham W Susx
72 D8 Paglesham Essex
8 C3 Paignton Torbay
100 A7 Pailton Warwks
23 K3 Paine's Cross E Susx
115 G5 Painleyhill Staffs
79 G6 Painscastle Powys
180 C6 Painshawfield Nthumb
152 B4 Painsthorpe E R Yk
64 C5 Painswick Gloucs
40 C3 Painter's Forstal Kent
208 E6 Paisley Rens
107 L5 Pakefield Suffk
89 J2 Pakenham Suffk
111 J4 Pale Gwynd
88 D6 Pale Green Essex
34 B3 Palestine Hants
49 L4 Paley Street W & M
98 C4 Palfrey Wsall
106 C7 Palgrave Suffk
16 F4 Pallington Dorset
11 H7 Palmersbridge Cnwll
69 J8 Palmers Green Gt Lon
196 F7 Palmerston E Ayrs
43 H7 Palmerstown V Glam
175 K3 Palnackie D & G
174 C2 Palnure D & G
133 J6 Palterton Derbys
48 F7 Pamber End Hants
48 F7 Pamber Green Hants
48 F6 Pamber Heath Hants
81 L8 Pamington Gloucs
17 K2 Pamphill Dorset
87 K5 Pampisford Cambs
31 G2 Panborough Somset
234 E8 Panbride Angus
11 K1 Pancrasweek Devon
43 G7 Pancross V Glam
43 J4 Pandy Caerph
92 D3 Pandy Gwynd
111 G5 Pandy Gwynd
62 C3 Pandy Mons
93 K3 Pandy Powys
112 B4 Pandy Wrexhm
111 L2 Pandy'r Capel Denbgs
127 G6 Pandy Tudur Conwy
71 H2 Panfield Essex
48 F4 Pangbourne W Berk
22 D5 Pangdean W Susx
80 E5 Panks Bridge Herefs
150 D5 Pannal N York
150 C5 Pannal Ash N York
243 L4 Pannanich Wells Hotel Abers
112 D7 Pant Shrops
128 E4 Pantasaph Flints
74 F5 Panteg Pembks
5 K1 Pantersbridge Cnwll
42 E5 Pant-ffrwyth Brdgnd
109 H2 Pant Glas Gwynd
93 G4 Pantglas Powys
59 G4 Pant-Gwyn Carmth
57 J5 Pant-lasau Swans
93 J7 Pant Mawr Powys
136 C4 Panton Lincs
128 B7 Pant-pastynog Denbgs
93 G3 Pantperthog Gwynd
93 L8 Pant-y-dwr Powys
94 E3 Pant-y-ffridd Powys
57 H3 Pantyffynnon Carmth
61 L7 Pantygaseg Torfn
42 D3 Pant-y-gog Brdgnd
75 K7 Pantymenyn Carmth
128 E6 Pant-y-mwyn Flints
107 G1 Panxworth Norfk
164 F4 Papcastle Cumb
280 E6 Papigoe Highld
212 D4 Papple E Loth
116 F1 Papplewick Notts
86 F3 Papworth Everard Cambs
86 F2 Papworth St Agnes Cambs
5 H4 Par Cnwll
41 J3 Paramour Street Kent
139 G5 Parbold Lancs
31 J4 Parbrook Somset
37 G6 Parbrook W Susx
111 G5 Parc Gwynd
55 K4 Parc Gwyn Crematorium Pembks
75 M2 Parcllyn Cerdgn
44 E1 Parc Seymour Newpt
164 E5 Pardshaw Cumb
91 G3 Parham Suffk
186 D7 Park D & G
178 F6 Park Nthumb
3 H3 Park Bottom Cnwll
140 E7 Park Bridge Tamesd
38 E6 Park Corner E Susx
49 G1 Park Corner Oxon
49 K2 Park Corner W & M
138 D2 Park Crematorium Lancs
85 K4 Park End Bed
63 J5 Parkend Gloucs
179 K4 Park End Nthumb
38 F4 Parkers Green Kent
73 K1 Parkeston Essex
90 F8 Parkeston Quay Essex
40 D7 Park Farm Kent
129 G4 Parkgate Ches W
165 H1 Parkgate Cumb
176 D1 Parkgate D & G
24 C4 Parkgate E Susx
71 G1 Parkgate Essex
19 J2 Park Gate Hants
39 L6 Parkgate Kent
52 B6 Parkgate Kent
150 A7 Park Gate Leeds
37 K2 Parkgate Surrey
81 L1 Park Gate Worcs
70 C2 Park Green Essex
90 D2 Park Green Suffk
234 F5 Parkgrove Crematorium Angus
208 E4 Parkhall W Duns
27 G6 Parkham Devon
26 F6 Parkham Ash Devon
116 B1 Park Head Derbys
63 H7 Park Hill Gloucs
117 J1 Parkhill Notts
245 K1 Parkhill House Abers
63 G6 Parkhouse Mons
57 G7 Parkmill Swans
51 G3 Park Royal Gt Lon
169 L1 Parkside Dur
209 L7 Parkside N Lans
129 J8 Parkside Wrexhm
17 K4 Parkstone Poole
68 F6 Park Street Herts

37 H4 **Park Street** W Susx
141 H3 **Park Wood Crematorium** Calder
17 M3 **Parley Green** Dorset
150 F8 **Parlington** Leeds
49 J1 **Parmoor** Bucks
70 B5 **Parndon** Essex
70 C5 **Parndon Wood Crematorium** Essex
28 B2 **Parracombe** Devon
75 H4 **Parrog** Pembks
164 F3 **Parsonby** Cumb
133 G1 **Parson Cross** Sheff
103 H2 **Parson Drove** Cambs
72 E4 **Parson's Heath** Essex
116 A6 **Parson's Hill** Derbys
208 F5 **Partick** C Glas
130 D2 **Partington** Traffd
137 H6 **Partney** Lincs
164 C6 **Parton** Cumb
22 B3 **Partridge Green** W Susx
62 B3 **Partrishow** Powys
115 K1 **Parwich** Derbys
70 E6 **Paslow Wood Common** Essex
84 F7 **Passenham** Nhants
36 B4 **Passfield** Hants
70 D7 **Passingford Bridge** Essex
102 D3 **Paston** C Pete
123 G4 **Paston** Norfk
114 F6 **Pasturefields** Staffs
12 B3 **Patchacott** Devon
22 D5 **Patcham** Br & H
68 F7 **Patchetts Green** Herts
21 J5 **Patching** W Susx
27 L2 **Patchole** Devon
45 J3 **Patchway** S Glos
149 L3 **Pateley Bridge** N York
72 D4 **Paternoster Heath** Essex
30 F5 **Pathe** Somset
222 E8 **Pathhead** Fife
211 L6 **Pathhead** Mdloth
82 E3 **Pathlow** Warwks
221 K5 **Path of Condie** P & K
70 B2 **Patmore Heath** Herts
183 K1 **Patna** E Ayrs
47 G7 **Patney** Wilts
154 C5 **Patrick** IoM
160 B4 **Patrick Brompton** N York
139 M8 **Patricroft** Salfd
145 J3 **Patrington** E R Yk
145 J3 **Patrington Haven** E R Yk
41 G4 **Patrixbourne** Kent
165 L7 **Patterdale** Cumb
97 J4 **Pattingham** Staffs
84 C4 **Pattishall** Nhants
71 K2 **Pattiswick Green** Essex
96 D4 **Patton** Shrops
2 D5 **Paul** Cnwll
84 D6 **Paulerspury** Nhants
144 F3 **Paull** E R Yk
33 K4 **Paul's Dene** Wilts
45 K7 **Paulton** BaNES
80 F5 **Paunton** Herefs
191 G6 **Pauperhaugh** Nthumb
114 B8 **Pave Lane** Wrekin
85 K4 **Pavenham** Bed
30 D2 **Pawlett** Somset
202 C6 **Pawston** Nthumb
82 E7 **Paxford** Gloucs
202 E3 **Paxton** Border
40 B4 **Payden Street** Kent
14 C2 **Payhembury** Devon
3 H2 **Paynter's Lane End** Cnwll
148 E5 **Paythorne** Lancs
80 A1 **Paytoe** Herefs
22 F7 **Peacehaven** E Susx
132 B4 **Peak Dale** Derbys
132 B4 **Peak Forest** Derbys
119 J8 **Peak Hill** Lincs
102 D2 **Peakirk** C Pete
39 H4 **Pearson's Green** Kent
80 E8 **Peartree Green** Herefs
45 K7 **Peasedown St John** BaNES
116 C2 **Peasehill** Derbys
122 B8 **Peaseland Green** Norfk
48 C3 **Peasemore** W Berk
91 H2 **Peasenhall** Suffk
37 L4 **Pease Pottage** W Susx
37 G2 **Peaslake** Surrey
129 M1 **Peasley Cross** St Hel
25 G3 **Peasmarsh** E Susx
30 E8 **Peasmarsh** Somset
36 E2 **Peasmarsh** Surrey
269 G3 **Peathill** Abers
223 H5 **Peat Inn** Fife
100 D5 **Peatling Magna** Leics
100 D6 **Peatling Parva** Leics
96 C6 **Peaton** Shrops
89 G8 **Pebmarsh** Essex
82 D6 **Pebworth** Worcs

140 F2 **Pecket Well** Calder
129 M8 **Peckforton** Ches E
51 J4 **Peckham** Gt Lon
100 A3 **Peckleton** Leics
111 M6 **Pedairffordd** Powys
40 F8 **Pedlinge** Kent
97 K7 **Pedmore** Dudley
30 F4 **Pedwell** Somset
200 B5 **Peebles** Border
154 C5 **Peel** IoM
138 D2 **Peel** Lancs
19 K3 **Peel Common** Hants
41 G7 **Peene** Kent
39 M7 **Peening Quarter** Kent
116 C7 **Peggs Green** Leics
68 E1 **Pegsdon** C Beds
180 F2 **Pegswood** Nthumb
41 K3 **Pegwell** Kent
247 H2 **Peinchorran** Highld
259 G5 **Peinlich** Highld
54 F3 **Pelcomb** Pembks
54 F3 **Pelcomb Bridge** Pembks
54 F3 **Pelcomb Cross** Pembks
72 E4 **Peldon** Essex
39 G6 **Pell Green** E Susx
98 C3 **Pelsall** Wsall
98 C3 **Pelsall Wood** Wsall
181 G8 **Pelton** Dur
181 G8 **Pelton Fell** Dur
164 F1 **Pelutho** Cumb
5 L4 **Pelynt** Cnwll
56 F5 **Pemberton** Carmth
139 H7 **Pemberton** Wigan
39 M4 **Pembles Cross** Kent
56 D4 **Pembrey** Carmth
79 M4 **Pembridge** Herefs
55 G6 **Pembroke** Pembks
54 F6 **Pembroke Dock** Pembks
39 G5 **Pembury** Kent
4 D5 **Penair** Cnwll
63 H1 **Pen-allt** Herefs
63 G5 **Penallt** Mons
55 J7 **Penally** Pembks
5 G6 **Penare** Cnwll
43 J7 **Penarth** V Glam
55 J4 **Penblewin** Pembks
92 E6 **Pen-bont Rhydybeddau** Cerdgn
76 B5 **Penbryn** Cerdgn
58 E2 **Pencader** Carmth
109 G3 **Pencaenewydd** Gwynd
212 A5 **Pencaitland** E Loth
124 F5 **Pencarnisiog** IoA
76 B7 **Pencarreg** Carmth
10 F6 **Pencarrow** Cnwll
61 H2 **Pencelli** Powys
57 G5 **Penclawdd** Swans
42 E5 **Pencoed** Brdgnd
80 E5 **Pencombe** Herefs
63 G2 **Pencoyd** Herefs
63 H3 **Pencraig** Herefs
111 K6 **Pencraig** Powys
2 B4 **Pendeen** Cnwll
60 E5 **Penderyn** Rhondd
55 L5 **Pendine** Carmth
140 B7 **Pendlebury** Salfd
148 D7 **Pendleton** Lancs
81 H8 **Pendock** Worcs
10 E6 **Pendoggett** Cnwll
31 H8 **Pendomer** Somset
43 G6 **Pendoylan** V Glam
42 D5 **Pendre** Brdgnd
93 G3 **Penegoes** Powys
3 K3 **Penelewey** Cnwll
55 J2 **Pen-ffordd** Pembks
43 J2 **Pengam** Caerph
43 K6 **Pengam** Cardif
51 K5 **Penge** Gt Lon
10 F5 **Pengelly** Cnwll
125 H1 **Pengorffwysfa** IoA
6 B2 **Pengover Green** Cnwll
62 C5 **Pen-groes-oped** Mons
127 K4 **Pengwern** Denbgs
3 H7 **Penhale** Cnwll
4 E3 **Penhale** Cnwll
3 J3 **Penhale** Cnwll
6 E4 **Penhale** Cnwll
4 C4 **Penhallow** Cnwll
3 H3 **Penhalurick** Cnwll
3 H3 **Penhalvean** Cnwll
47 H1 **Penhill** Swindn
44 E1 **Penhow** Newpt
24 C4 **Penhurst** E Susx
92 D2 **Peniarth** Gwynd
211 H7 **Penicuik** Mdloth
58 D4 **Peniel** Carmth
127 L7 **Peniel** Denbgs
259 H8 **Penifiler** Highld
192 F3 **Peninver** Ag & B
125 K7 **Penisarwaun** Gwynd
141 K7 **Penistone** Barns

3 K5 **Penjerrick** Cnwll
130 A2 **Penketh** Warrtn
183 G3 **Penkill** S Ayrs
97 L1 **Penkridge** Staffs
11 H3 **Penlean** Cnwll
32 E1 **Penleigh** Wilts
112 F3 **Penley** Wrexhm
57 H5 **Penllergaer** Swans
124 F3 **Pen-llyn** IoA
42 E6 **Penllyn** V Glam
125 G6 **Pen-lon** IoA
110 E2 **Penmachno** Conwy
43 J2 **Penmaen** Caerph
56 F7 **Penmaen** Swans
126 E4 **Penmaenan** Conwy
126 E4 **Penmaenmawr** Conwy
110 C7 **Penmaenpool** Gwynd
43 G7 **Penmark** V Glam
126 C3 **Penmon** IoA
109 K3 **Penmorfa** Gwynd
4 D5 **Penmount Crematorium** Cnwll
125 J5 **Penmynydd** IoA
67 M8 **Penn** Bucks
97 K4 **Penn** Wolves
92 F3 **Pennal** Gwynd
268 F3 **Pennan** Abers
76 F3 **Pennant** Cerdgn
111 K5 **Pennant** Denbgs
93 J4 **Pennant** Powys
111 K6 **Pennant-Melangell** Powys
57 G7 **Pennard** Swans
95 J3 **Pennerley** Shrops
13 K2 **Pennicott** Devon
156 C7 **Pennington** Cumb
18 D4 **Pennington** Hants
139 J6 **Pennington Green** Wigan
61 H2 **Pennorth** Powys
68 A7 **Penn Street** Bucks
45 L4 **Pennsylvania** S Glos
156 D6 **Penny Bridge** Cumb
226 F7 **Pennycross** Ag & B
123 G7 **Pennygate** Norfk
227 G7 **Pennyghael** Ag & B
183 H1 **Pennyglen** S Ayrs
133 L4 **Penny Green** Derbys
119 K6 **Penny Hill** Lincs
28 F8 **Pennymoor** Devon
75 L3 **Penparc** Cerdgn
92 D7 **Penparcau** Cerdgn
43 J2 **Penpedairheol** Caerph
62 C6 **Penpedairheol** Mons
62 C6 **Penperlleni** Mons
10 F5 **Penpethy** Cnwll
5 J4 **Penpillick** Cnwll
3 K3 **Penpol** Cnwll
5 K4 **Penpoll** Cnwll
3 G3 **Penponds** Cnwll
10 F7 **Penpont** Cnwll
186 C7 **Penpont** D & G
60 E2 **Penpont** Powys
7 J4 **Penquit** Devon
11 L7 **Penrest** Cnwll
76 B7 **Penrherber** Carmth
75 M4 **Pen-rhiw** Pembks
43 G2 **Penrhiwceiber** Rhondd
57 K3 **Pen Rhiwfawr** Neath
76 C6 **Penrhiw-llan** Cerdgn
76 C6 **Penrhiw-pal** Cerdgn
108 F5 **Penrhos** Gwynd
124 D3 **Penrhos** IoA
62 E5 **Penrhos** Mons
59 L6 **Penrhos** Powys
125 K5 **Penrhos garnedd** Gwynd
127 G3 **Penrhyn Bay** Conwy
92 D6 **Penrhyncoch** Cerdgn
109 L4 **Penrhyndeudraeth** Gwynd
126 F3 **Penrhyn-side** Conwy
56 F7 **Penrice** Swans
194 D2 **Penrioch** N Ayrs
166 C4 **Penrith** Cumb
10 B8 **Penrose** Cnwll
166 A5 **Penruddock** Cumb
3 K4 **Penryn** Cnwll
127 J4 **Pensarn** Conwy
81 G2 **Pensax** Worcs
129 G3 **Pensby** Wirral
32 C4 **Penselwood** Somset
45 J6 **Pensford** BaNES
81 L6 **Pensham** Worcs
181 H8 **Penshaw** Sundld
38 E4 **Penshurst** Kent
38 E4 **Penshurst Station** Kent
11 K8 **Pensilva** Cnwll
97 K5 **Pensnett** Dudley
13 H2 **Penstone** Devon
94 C5 **Penstrowed** Powys
5 G5 **Pentewan** Cnwll
125 K6 **Pentir** Gwynd
4 C3 **Pentire** Cnwll
55 J5 **Pentlepoir** Pembks

89 G6 **Pentlow** Essex
89 G6 **Pentlow Street** Essex
120 F8 **Pentney** Norfk
178 B3 **Pentonbridge** Cumb
34 D2 **Penton Grafton** Hants
34 D2 **Penton Mewsey** Hants
125 J4 **Pentraeth** IoA
128 C7 **Pentre** Denbgs
129 H6 **Pentre** Flints
62 C6 **Pentre** Mons
62 E7 **Pentre** Mons
94 C6 **Pentre** Powys
94 E5 **Pentre** Powys
95 G5 **Pentre** Powys
42 E2 **Pentre** Rhondd
112 E7 **Pentre** Shrops
112 D3 **Pentre** Wrexhm
77 G6 **Pentre bach** Cerdgn
128 F4 **Pentre Bach** Flints
61 G6 **Pentrebach** Myr Td
78 B8 **Pentre-bach** Powys
94 E1 **Pentrebeirdd** Powys
125 H5 **Pentre Berw** IoA
110 D1 **Pentre-bont** Conwy
112 D2 **Pentrebychan Crematorium** Wrexhm
76 C7 **Pentre-cagel** Carmth
112 A1 **Pentre-celyn** Denbgs
93 J2 **Pentre-celyn** Powys
57 J6 **Pentre-chwyth** Swans
112 D5 **Pentre-clawdd** Shrops
76 D7 **Pentre-cwrt** Carmth
112 B2 **Pentredwr** Denbgs
109 J4 **Pentrefelin** Gwynd
125 H1 **Pentrefelin** IoA
128 F5 **Pentre Ffwrndan** Flints
111 G1 **Pentrefoelas** Conwy
75 L6 **Pentregalar** Pembks
76 C5 **Pentregat** Cerdgn
59 H5 **Pentre-Gwenlais** Carmth
109 L6 **Pentre Gwynfryn** Gwynd
128 E5 **Pentre Halkyn** Flints
95 H7 **Pentre Hodrey** Shrops
127 K5 **Pentre Isaf** Conwy
128 C7 **Pentre Llanrhaeadr** Denbgs
94 E4 **Pentre Llifior** Powys
78 C4 **Pentre-llwyn-llwyd** Powys
92 D8 **Pentre-llyn** Cerdgn
111 J1 **Pentre-llyn-cymmer** Conwy
93 J3 **Pentre-Maw** Powys
42 E6 **Pentre Meyrick** V Glam
62 B6 **Pentre-piod** Torfn
44 B2 **Pentre-poeth** Newpt
76 D4 **Pentre'rbryn** Cerdgn
77 H5 **Pentre'r-felin** Cerdgn
126 F6 **Pentre'r Felin** Conwy
60 D1 **Pentre'r-felin** Powys
127 L7 **Pentre Saron** Denbgs
126 F7 **Pentre-tafarn-y-fedw** Conwy
59 M2 **Pentre ty gwyn** Carmth
116 C1 **Pentrich** Derbys
33 H7 **Pentridge** Dorset
61 K7 **Pen-twyn** Caerph
63 G5 **Pen-twyn** Mons
61 L6 **Pen-twyn** Torfn
43 K2 **Pentwynmaur** Caerph
43 H5 **Pentyrch** Cardif
5 H4 **Penwithick** Cnwll
48 C6 **Penwood** Hants
60 C4 **Penwyllt** Powys
59 H4 **Penybanc** Carmth
78 F2 **Penybont** Powys
112 B6 **Pen-y-bont** Powys
111 L6 **Pen-y-bont-fawr** Powys
75 L4 **Pen-y-bryn** Pembks
60 C4 **Pen-y-cae** Powys
112 D3 **Penycae** Wrexhm
62 E8 **Pen-y-cae-mawr** Mons
108 C6 **Penycaerau** Gwynd
128 D4 **Pen-y-cefn** Flints
62 F5 **Pen-y-clawdd** Mons
43 G4 **Pen-y-coedcae** Rhondd
54 D2 **Pen-y-cwn** Pembks
42 D5 **Pen-y-fai** Brdgnd
128 D5 **Pen-y-felin** Flints
129 G7 **Penyffordd** Flints
125 J8 **Penyffridd** Gwynd
92 D6 **Pen-y-garn** Cerdgn
111 L6 **Pen-y-Garnedd** Powys
61 J1 **Pen-y-genffordd** Powys
108 C5 **Pen-y-graig** Gwynd
42 F3 **Penygraig** Rhondd
59 G6 **Penygroes** Carmth
109 H1 **Penygroes** Gwynd
126 D8 **Pen-y-Gwryd** Gwynd
42 F6 **Pen-y-lan** V Glam
56 E4 **Pen-y-Mynydd** Carmth
129 G7 **Penymynydd** Flints
126 C8 **Pen-y-pass** Gwynd
62 E5 **Pen-yr-Heol** Mons

60 F6 **Pen-yr-Heolgerrig** Myr Td
125 H2 **Penysarn** IoA
112 B1 **Pen-y-stryt** Denbgs
60 E6 **Penywaun** Rhondd
57 L3 **Penywern** Neath
2 D5 **Penzance** Cnwll
81 L5 **Peopleton** Worcs
130 F5 **Peover Heath** Ches E
36 D2 **Peper Harow** Surrey
113 K6 **Peplow** Shrops
70 F5 **Pepper's Green** Essex
68 D3 **Pepperstock** C Beds
196 C3 **Perceton** N Ayrs
269 H3 **Percyhorner** Abers
9 i3 **Perelle** Guern
34 B1 **Perham Down** Wilts
29 G2 **Periton** Somset
50 F2 **Perivale** Gt Lon
14 B4 **Perkins Village** Devon
181 G8 **Perkinsville** Dur
134 C5 **Perlethorpe** Notts
3 K3 **Perranarworthal** Cnwll
4 B4 **Perranporth** Cnwll
2 E5 **Perranuthnoe** Cnwll
3 K3 **Perranwell** Cnwll
4 C4 **Perranwell** Cnwll
3 K3 **Perran Wharf** Cnwll
4 C4 **Perranzabuloe** Cnwll
64 E6 **Perrott's Brook** Gloucs
98 D5 **Perry** Birm
98 D5 **Perry Barr** Birm
98 D5 **Perry Barr Crematorium** Birm
71 K3 **Perry Green** Essex
70 B4 **Perry Green** Herts
46 E1 **Perry Green** Wilts
63 J1 **Perrystone Hill** Herefs
15 H2 **Perry Street** Somset
114 C5 **Pershall** Staffs
81 L6 **Pershore** Worcs
86 B2 **Pertenhall** Bed
221 K3 **Perth** P & K
221 K2 **Perth Crematorium** P & K
112 E5 **Perthy** Shrops
80 E7 **Perton** Herefs
97 J3 **Perton** Staffs
32 E4 **Pertwood** Wilts
102 D4 **Peterborough** C Pete
102 D3 **Peterborough Crematorium** C Pete
79 L7 **Peterchurch** Herefs
245 J3 **Peterculter** C Aber
257 L2 **Peterhead** Abers
169 L2 **Peterlee** Dur
35 M6 **Petersfield** Hants
68 F3 **Peter's Green** Herts
50 F4 **Petersham** Gt Lon
27 H8 **Peters Marland** Devon
43 L5 **Peterstone Wentlooge** Newpt
43 G6 **Peterston-super-Ely** V Glam
63 H2 **Peterstow** Herefs
12 C7 **Peter Tavy** Devon
40 F5 **Petham** Kent
11 K4 **Petherwin Gate** Cnwll
12 C1 **Petrockstow** Devon
85 H5 **Petsoe End** M Keyn
40 E6 **Pet Street** Kent
24 F4 **Pett** E Susx
90 E3 **Pettaugh** Suffk
40 F5 **Pett Bottom** Kent
234 C7 **Petterden** Angus
198 F4 **Pettinain** S Lans
91 G4 **Pettistree** Suffk
29 H6 **Petton** Devon
113 G6 **Petton** Shrops
51 M5 **Petts Wood** Gt Lon
211 J2 **Pettycur** Fife
46 A2 **Petty France** S Glos
257 G7 **Pettymuk** Abers
36 E6 **Petworth** W Susx
23 L6 **Pevensey** E Susx
24 B6 **Pevensey Bay** E Susx
47 H7 **Pewsey** Wilts
49 J2 **Pheasant's Hill** Bucks
81 L3 **Phepson** Worcs
181 H8 **Philadelphia** Sundld
26 D6 **Philham** Devon
200 F7 **Philiphaugh** Border
2 F3 **Phillack** Cnwll
3 L3 **Philleigh** Cnwll
70 F3 **Philpot End** Essex
210 E4 **Philpstoun** W Loth
63 J2 **Phocle Green** Herefs
49 J7 **Phoenix Green** Hants
241 J5 **Phoines** Highld
31 G5 **Pibsbury** Somset
164 D6 **Pica** Cumb
99 G4 **Piccadilly** Warwks
68 D5 **Piccotts End** Herts
142 E6 **Pickburn** Donc
162 D6 **Pickering** N York

34 E2 **Picket Piece** Hants
18 B2 **Picket Post** Hants
99 H7 **Pickford** Covtry
99 H7 **Pickford Green** Covtry
160 E6 **Pickhill** N York
95 K3 **Picklescott** Shrops
130 D4 **Pickmere** Ches E
30 B5 **Pickney** Somset
114 A6 **Pickstock** Wrekin
139 L3 **Pickup Bank** Bl w D
27 H3 **Pickwell** Devon
101 G1 **Pickwell** Leics
46 B5 **Pickwick** Wilts
118 D5 **Pickworth** Lincs
101 L1 **Pickworth** Rutlnd
129 K5 **Picton** Ches W
128 D3 **Picton** Flints
160 F1 **Picton** N York
23 G6 **Piddinghoe** E Susx
67 K8 **Piddington** Bucks
84 F4 **Piddington** Nhants
66 F4 **Piddington** Oxon
16 D3 **Piddlehinton** Dorset
16 D3 **Piddletrenthide** Dorset
103 G7 **Pidley** Cambs
169 G7 **Piercebridge** Darltn
275 c1 **Pierowall** Ork
64 C2 **Piff's Elm** Gloucs
180 E1 **Pigdon** Nthumb
82 F3 **Pigeon Green** Warwks
17 K2 **Pig Oak** Dorset
79 L5 **Pig Street** Herefs
132 D7 **Pikehall** Derbys
17 K2 **Pilford** Dorset
70 E7 **Pilgrims Hatch** Essex
135 H1 **Pilham** Lincs
45 G4 **Pill** N Som
6 D2 **Pillaton** Cnwll
6 D2 **Pillatonmill** Cnwll
83 G5 **Pillerton Hersey** Warwks
83 G5 **Pillerton Priors** Warwks
79 J2 **Pilleth** Powys
142 A7 **Pilley** Barns
18 E4 **Pilley** Hants
18 E4 **Pilley Bailey** Hants
44 C2 **Pillgwenlly** Newpt
27 H5 **Pillhead** Devon
147 IIG **Pilling** Lancs
147 G6 **Pilling Lane** Lancs
45 H2 **Pilning** S Glos
25 K4 **Pilot Inn** Kent
132 B7 **Pilsbury** Derbys
15 J3 **Pilsdon** Dorset
102 B2 **Pilsgate** C Pete
132 E5 **Pilsley** Derbys
133 H7 **Pilsley** Derbys
107 H1 **Pilson Green** Norfk
23 G3 **Piltdown** E Susx
27 K4 **Pilton** Devon
101 M6 **Pilton** Nhants
101 K3 **Pilton** Rutlnd
31 K3 **Pilton** Somset
56 E7 **Pilton Green** Swans
148 C7 **Pimlico** Lancs
84 B7 **Pimlico** Nhants
17 H1 **Pimperne** Dorset
119 H6 **Pinchbeck** Lincs
119 G6 **Pinchbeck Bars** Lincs
119 G6 **Pinchbeck West** Lincs
143 G4 **Pincheon Green** Donc
170 D7 **Pinchinthorpe** R & Cl
139 H4 **Pincock** Lancs
138 E5 **Pinfold** Lancs
89 G3 **Pinford End** Suffk
56 D4 **Pinged** Carmth
49 G5 **Pingewood** W Berk
69 H2 **Pin Green** Herts
13 M3 **Pinhoe** Devon
99 H7 **Pinkett's Booth** Covtry
46 B2 **Pinkney** Wilts
99 K7 **Pinley** Covtry
82 F2 **Pinley Green** Warwks
90 E7 **Pin Mill** Suffk
182 F4 **Pinminnoch** S Ayrs
182 F4 **Pinmore** S Ayrs
14 C5 **Pinn** Devon
50 E1 **Pinner** Gt Lon
50 E1 **Pinner Green** Gt Lon
113 K2 **Pinsley Green** Ches E
81 M5 **Pinvin** Worcs
182 F5 **Pinwherry** S Ayrs
133 J8 **Pinxton** Derbys
80 C6 **Pipe and Lyde** Herefs
80 B1 **Pipe Aston** Herefs
114 A3 **Pipe Gate** Shrops
98 E2 **Pipehill** Staffs
253 G2 **Piperhill** Highld
11 J5 **Pipers Pool** Cnwll
101 J6 **Pipewell** Nhants
27 J3 **Pippacott** Devon

139 H3 **Pippin Street** Lancs
79 G7 **Pipton** Powys
50 B7 **Pirbright** Surrey
50 B7 **Pirbright Camp** Surrey
201 K7 **Pirnie** Border
194 D2 **Pirnmill** N Ayrs
68 F1 **Pirton** Herts
81 K5 **Pirton** Worcs
92 E7 **Pisgah** Cerdgn
49 H1 **Pishill** Oxon
108 E3 **Pistyll** Gwynd
232 B2 **Pitagowan** P & K
269 H3 **Pitblae** Abers
221 J2 **Pitcairngreen** P & K
264 C5 **Pitcalnie** Highld
256 C6 **Pitcaple** Abers
233 M2 **Pitcarity** Angus
64 B5 **Pitchcombe** Gloucs
67 J3 **Pitchcott** Bucks
119 J5 **Pitcher Row** Lincs
96 C5 **Pitchford** Shrops
67 J6 **Pitch Green** Bucks
36 C3 **Pitch Place** Surrey
50 B8 **Pitch Place** Surrey
254 D4 **Pitchroy** Moray
31 L4 **Pitcombe** Somset
42 D6 **Pitcot** V Glam
212 E4 **Pitcox** E Loth
256 B8 **Pitfichie** Abers
256 C3 **Pitglassie** Abers
264 B2 **Pitgrudy** Highld
234 E4 **Pitkennedy** Angus
222 E5 **Pitlessie** Fife
232 D4 **Pitlochry** P & K
256 B6 **Pitmachie** Abers
241 K3 **Pitmain** Highld
256 F6 **Pitmedden** Abers
30 B7 **Pitminster** Somset
234 E5 **Pitmuies** Angus
256 B8 **Pitmunie** Abers
31 G5 **Pitney** Somset
222 C2 **Pitroddie** P & K
223 G4 **Pitscottie** Fife
52 F1 **Pitsea** Essex
140 E7 **Pitses** Oldham
84 E2 **Pitsford** Nhants
68 B4 **Pitstone** Bucks
29 J7 **Pitt** Devon
34 F5 **Pitt** Hants
245 G8 **Pittarrow** Abers
63 L7 **Pitt Court** Gloucs
223 K6 **Pittenweem** Fife
222 D7 **Pitteuchar** Fife
169 J2 **Pittington** Dur
256 C6 **Pittodrie House Hotel** Abers
34 B4 **Pitton** Wilts
38 F3 **Pitt's Wood** Kent
269 H3 **Pittulie** Abers
10 C7 **Pityme** Cnwll
169 H2 **Pity Me** Dur
40 B6 **Pivington** Kent
106 E8 **Pixey Green** Suffk
37 J1 **Pixham** Surrey
209 L5 **Plains** N Lans
10 D6 **Plain Street** Cnwll
96 C4 **Plaish** Shrops
51 L2 **Plaistow** Gt Lon
36 F5 **Plaistow** W Susx
34 C7 **Plaitford** Hants
139 J7 **Plank Lane** Wigan
124 E4 **Plas Cymyran** IoA
48 D6 **Plastow Green** Hants
39 G2 **Platt** Kent
139 J7 **Platt Bridge** Wigan
113 H4 **Platt Lane** Shrops
39 L3 **Platts Heath** Kent
169 H1 **Plawsworth** Dur
38 F3 **Plaxtol** Kent
25 O3 **Playden** E Susx
90 F5 **Playford** Suffk
49 H4 **Play Hatch** Oxon
4 C6 **Playing Place** Cnwll
63 M1 **Playley Green** Gloucs
95 K2 **Plealey** Shrops
209 M2 **Plean** Stirlg
222 C4 **Pleasance** Fife
139 J2 **Pleasington** Bl w D
139 K2 **Pleasington Crematorium** Bl w D
133 K6 **Pleasley** Derbys
133 K6 **Pleasleyhill** Notts
32 B8 **Pleck** Dorset
70 E2 **Pledgdon Green** Essex
142 A4 **Pledwick** Wakefd
9 J2 **Pleinheaume** Guern
9 a1 **Plemont** Jersey
129 K5 **Plemstall** Ches W
179 G6 **Plenmeller** Nthumb
71 G4 **Pleshey** Essex
248 C5 **Plockton** Highld

95 J6 **Plowden** Shrops
95 J3 **Plox Green** Shrops
40 B6 **Pluckley** Kent
40 B6 **Pluckley Station** Kent
40 B6 **Pluckley Thorne** Kent
41 J3 **Plucks Gutter** Kent
164 F3 **Plumbland** Cumb
157 G4 **Plumgarths** Cumb
130 E5 **Plumley** Ches E
156 D7 **Plumpton** Cumb
166 C3 **Plumpton** Cumb
22 E4 **Plumpton** E Susx
84 B5 **Plumpton** Nhants
84 D6 **Plumpton End** Nhants
22 E4 **Plumpton Green** E Susx
166 C4 **Plumpton Head** Cumb
51 L3 **Plumstead** Gt Lon
122 E4 **Plumstead** Norfk
122 C4 **Plumstead Green** Norfk
117 G5 **Plumtree** Notts
39 K4 **Plumtree Green** Kent
117 K5 **Plungar** Leics
40 B7 **Plurenden** Kent
16 D2 **Plush** Dorset
11 J6 **Plusha** Cnwll
11 K7 **Plushabridge** Cnwll
76 C5 **Plwmp** Cerdgn
6 F4 **Plymouth** C Plym
7 G4 **Plympton** C Plym
7 G4 **Plymstock** C Plym
14 B2 **Plymtree** Devon
161 K5 **Pockley** N York
152 B6 **Pocklington** E R Yk
119 H7 **Pode Hole** Lincs
31 J6 **Podimore** Somset
85 J3 **Podington** Bed
114 B4 **Podmore** Staffs
73 G4 **Point Clear** Essex
118 F5 **Pointon** Lincs
18 A5 **Pokesdown** Bmouth
11 L4 **Polapit Tamar** Cnwll
270 C6 **Polbain** Highld
6 C3 **Polbathic** Cnwll
210 D6 **Polbeth** W Loth
5 G1 **Polbrock** Cnwll
102 E6 **Polebrook** Nhants
81 J5 **Pole Elm** Worcs
23 K6 **Polegate** E Susx
130 C4 **Polelane Ends** Ches W
141 G4 **Pole Moor** Kirk
99 H3 **Polesworth** Warwks
2 B6 **Polgigga** Cnwll
270 D6 **Polglass** Highld
5 G5 **Polgooth** Cnwll
185 H2 **Polgown** D & G
21 H6 **Poling** W Susx
21 H5 **Poling Corner** W Susx
5 J4 **Polkerris** Cnwll
123 G5 **Pollard Street** Norfk
142 F4 **Pollington** E R Yk
228 B2 **Polloch** Highld
208 F6 **Pollokshaws** C Glas
208 F6 **Pollokshields** C Glas
5 G5 **Polmassick** Cnwll
5 J4 **Polmear** Cnwll
210 B3 **Polmont** Falk
237 L4 **Polnish** Highld
5 L4 **Polperro** Cnwll
5 K5 **Polruan** Cnwll
31 H2 **Polsham** Somset
89 K7 **Polstead** Suffk
89 K7 **Polstead Heath** Suffk
216 C7 **Poltalloch** Ag & B
3 J7 **Poltescoe** Cnwll
13 M3 **Poltimore** Devon
211 J6 **Polton** Mdloth
202 A3 **Polwarth** Border
11 J6 **Polyphant** Cnwll
10 C6 **Polzeath** Cnwll
211 H7 **Pomathorn** Mdloth
132 B6 **Pomeroy** Derbys
78 F7 **Ponde** Powys
102 F5 **Pondersbridge** Cambs
69 K7 **Ponders End** Gt Lon
3 J3 **Ponsanooth** Cnwll
155 J2 **Ponsonby** Cumb
3 J7 **Ponsongath** Cnwll
13 G7 **Ponsworthy** Devon
9 e4 **Pontac** Jersey
59 H6 **Pontamman** Carmth
58 E6 **Pontantwn** Carmth
57 K4 **Pontardawe** Neath
57 G4 **Pontarddulais** Swans
58 F4 **Pont-ar-gothi** Carmth
60 C2 **Pont-ar-Hydfer** Powys
59 K4 **Pont-ar-llechau** Carmth
58 E3 **Pontarsais** Carmth
129 G7 **Pontblyddyn** Flints
126 E8 **Pont Cyfyng** Conwy
126 F6 **Pont Dolgarrog** Conwy

| | | |
|---|---|---|
| 94 B5 | **Pontdolgoch** Powys | |
| 44 C2 | **Pont-Ebbw** Newpt | |
| 142 C3 | **Pontefract** Wakefd | |
| 142 C4 | **Pontefract Crematorium** Wakefd | |
| 180 E4 | **Ponteland** Nthumb | |
| 93 G7 | **Ponterwyd** Cerdgn | |
| 95 K2 | **Pontesbury** Shrops | |
| 95 K2 | **Pontesbury Hill** Shrops | |
| 95 K2 | **Pontesford** Shrops | |
| 112 C4 | **Pontfadog** Wrexhm | |
| 75 H5 | **Pontfaen** Pembks | |
| 78 D8 | **Pont-faen** Powys | |
| 76 B4 | **Pontgarreg** Cerdgn | |
| 75 K4 | **Pontgarreg** Pembks | |
| 56 E3 | **Ponthenry** Carmth | |
| 62 C8 | **Ponthir** Torfn | |
| 76 A6 | **Ponthirwaun** Cerdgn | |
| 43 J3 | **Pontllanfraith** Caerph | |
| 57 H5 | **Pontlliw** Swans | |
| 61 H6 | **Pontlottyn** Caerph | |
| 109 H1 | **Pontlyfni** Gwynd | |
| 56 F3 | **Pont Morlais** Carmth | |
| 60 D5 | **Pontneddfechan** Neath | |
| 62 B7 | **Pontnewydd** Torfn | |
| 62 B6 | **Pontnewynydd** Torfn | |
| 180 E8 | **Pontop** Dur | |
| 126 C7 | **Pont Pen-y-benglog** Gwynd | |
| 77 K2 | **Pontrhydfendigaid** Cerdgn | |
| 111 G6 | **Pont Rhyd-sarn** Gwynd | |
| 42 C4 | **Pont Rhyd-y-cyff** Brdgnd | |
| 42 B3 | **Pont-rhyd-y-fen** Neath | |
| 77 K1 | **Pontrhydygroes** Cerdgn | |
| 62 C7 | **Pontrhydyrun** Torfn | |
| 62 E2 | **Pontrilas** Herefs | |
| 94 D1 | **Pont Robert** Powys | |
| 125 J7 | **Pont-rug** Gwynd | |
| 24 B4 | **Ponts Green** E Susx | |
| 76 D6 | **Pontshaen** Cerdgn | |
| 63 J3 | **Pontshill** Herefs | |
| 61 G5 | **Pontsticill** Myr Td | |
| 60 D6 | **Pont Walby** Neath | |
| 76 B7 | **Pontwelly** Carmth | |
| 56 E3 | **Pontyates** Carmth | |
| 58 F6 | **Pontyberem** Carmth | |
| 112 D4 | **Pont-y-blew** Wrexhm | |
| 129 K7 | **Pontybodkin** Flints | |
| 42 F5 | **Pontyclun** Rhondd | |
| 42 D3 | **Pontycymer** Brdgnd | |
| 75 K5 | **Pontyglasier** Pembks | |
| 42 F3 | **Pontygwaith** Rhondd | |
| 75 K5 | **Pontygynon** Pembks | |
| 110 E1 | **Pont-y-pant** Conwy | |
| 62 B7 | **Pontypool** Torfn | |
| 62 C7 | **Pontypool Road** Torfn | |
| 43 G4 | **Pontypridd** Rhondd | |
| 74 E7 | **Pont-yr-hafod** Pembks | |
| 42 D4 | **Pont-yr-Rhyl** Brdgnd | |
| 43 K3 | **Pontywaun** Caerph | |
| 3 H3 | **Pool** Cnwll | |
| 10 b2 | **Pool** IoS | |
| 150 C6 | **Pool** Leeds | |
| 17 K4 | **Poole** Poole | |
| 17 K3 | **Poole Crematorium** Poole | |
| 64 E8 | **Poole Keynes** Gloucs | |
| 260 D4 | **Poolewe** Highld | |
| 166 B6 | **Pooley Bridge** Cumb | |
| 105 L7 | **Pooley Street** Norfk | |
| 131 H7 | **Poolfold** Staffs | |
| 80 D5 | **Pool Head** Herefs | |
| 63 L1 | **Poolhill** Gloucs | |
| 221 H7 | **Pool of Muckhart** Clacks | |
| 95 G1 | **Pool Quay** Powys | |
| 88 F7 | **Pool Street** Essex | |
| 38 C3 | **Pooting's** Kent | |
| 35 H2 | **Popham** Hants | |
| 51 K3 | **Poplar** Gt Lon | |
| 91 K2 | **Poplar Street** Suffk | |
| 19 G5 | **Porchfield** IoW | |
| 106 F3 | **Poringland** Norfk | |
| 3 H4 | **Porkellis** Cnwll | |
| 28 F2 | **Porlock** Somset | |
| 28 F1 | **Porlock Weir** Somset | |
| 206 B7 | **Portachoillan** Ag & B | |
| 248 B5 | **Port-an-Eorna** Highld | |
| 228 D6 | **Port Appin** Ag & B | |
| 205 G3 | **Port Askaig** Ag & B | |
| 206 E5 | **Portavadie** Ag & B | |
| 207 H5 | **Port Bannatyne** Ag & B | |
| 45 G4 | **Portbury** N Som | |
| 177 H6 | **Port Carlisle** Cumb | |
| 204 C4 | **Port Charlotte** Ag & B | |
| 19 K3 | **Portchester** Hants | |
| 19 K2 | **Portchester Crematorium** Hants | |
| 170 C6 | **Port Clarence** S on T | |
| 206 F4 | **Port Driseach** Ag & B | |
| 56 E7 | **Port Einon** Swans | |
| 204 E7 | **Port Ellen** Ag & B | |
| 256 D7 | **Port Elphinstone** Abers | |
| 182 C8 | **Portencalzie** D & G | |
| 195 K1 | **Portencross** N Ayrs | |
| 154 b8 | **Port Erin** IoM | |
| 16 B5 | **Portesham** Dorset | |
| 267 J3 | **Portessie** Moray | |
| 154 g4 | **Port e Vullen** IoM | |
| 54 F4 | **Portfield Gate** Pembks | |
| 12 A5 | **Portgate** Devon | |
| 10 D6 | **Port Gaverne** Cnwll | |
| 208 B4 | **Port Glasgow** Inver | |
| 267 H3 | **Portgordon** Moray | |
| 274 D5 | **Portgower** Highld | |
| 4 D2 | **Porth** Cnwll | |
| 42 F3 | **Porth** Rhondd | |
| 3 K6 | **Porthallow** Cnwll | |
| 5 L4 | **Porthallow** Cnwll | |
| 42 B6 | **Porthcawl** Brdgnd | |
| 10 B8 | **Porthcothan** Cnwll | |
| 2 B6 | **Porthcurno** Cnwll | |
| 108 D3 | **Porth Dinllaen** Gwynd | |
| 260 B5 | **Port Henderson** Highld | |
| 74 D5 | **Porthgain** Pembks | |
| 2 B6 | **Porthgwarra** Cnwll | |
| 114 D2 | **Porthill** Staffs | |
| 4 D6 | **Porthkea** Cnwll | |
| 43 G8 | **Porthkerry** V Glam | |
| 3 G8 | **Porthleven** Cnwll | |
| 109 K4 | **Porthmadog** Gwynd | |
| 2 C4 | **Porthmeor** Cnwll | |
| 3 J5 | **Porth Navas** Cnwll | |
| 4 F4 | **Portholland** Cnwll | |
| 3 K6 | **Porthoustock** Cnwll | |
| 5 H5 | **Porthpean** Cnwll | |
| 4 A5 | **Porthtowan** Cnwll | |
| 112 F2 | **Porthwgan** Wrexhm | |
| 58 F5 | **Porthyrhyd** Carmth | |
| 112 C6 | **Porth-y-Waen** Shrops | |
| 218 C8 | **Portincaple** Ag & B | |
| 9 a1 | **Portinfer** Jersey | |
| 143 K2 | **Portington** E R Yk | |
| 216 F5 | **Portinnisherrich** Ag & B | |
| 165 H6 | **Portinscale** Cumb | |
| 10 D6 | **Port Isaac** Cnwll | |
| 44 F4 | **Portishead** N Som | |
| 267 K3 | **Portknockie** Moray | |
| 245 K4 | **Portlethen** Abers | |
| 175 L4 | **Portling** D & G | |
| 4 F7 | **Portloe** Cnwll | |
| 172 D6 | **Port Logan** D & G | |
| 6 A4 | **Portlooe** Cnwll | |
| 264 E3 | **Portmahomack** Highld | |
| 5 G6 | **Portmellon** Cnwll | |
| 236 E4 | **Port Mor** Highld | |
| 18 E4 | **Portmore** Hants | |
| 171 J7 | **Port Mulgrave** N York | |
| 228 E6 | **Portnacroish** Ag & B | |
| 282 h3 | **Portnaguran** W Isls | |
| 204 B6 | **Portnahaven** Ag & B | |
| 246 D2 | **Portnalong** Highld | |
| 282 h3 | **Port nan Giuran** W Isls | |
| 282 c7 | **Port nan Long** W Isls | |
| 282 h1 | **Port Nis** W Isls | |
| 211 J4 | **Portobello** C Edin | |
| 181 G7 | **Portobello** Gatesd | |
| 98 B4 | **Portobello** Wolves | |
| 219 J7 | **Port of Menteith** Stirlg | |
| 282 h1 | **Port of Ness** W Isls | |
| 33 L4 | **Porton** Wilts | |
| 12 A7 | **Portontown** Devon | |
| 172 B4 | **Portpatrick** D & G | |
| 10 D6 | **Port Quin** Cnwll | |
| 228 D6 | **Port Ramsay** Ag & B | |
| 3 G2 | **Portreath** Cnwll | |
| 259 H7 | **Portree** Highld | |
| 154 b8 | **Port St Mary** IoM | |
| 3 M4 | **Portscatho** Cnwll | |
| 19 L4 | **Portsea** C Port | |
| 278 E3 | **Portskerra** Highld | |
| 45 G1 | **Portskewett** Mons | |
| 22 C6 | **Portslade** Br & H | |
| 22 C6 | **Portslade-by-Sea** Br & H | |
| 172 B3 | **Portslogan** D & G | |
| 19 L4 | **Portsmouth** C Port | |
| 140 D3 | **Portsmouth** Calder | |
| 154 d7 | **Port Soderick** IoM | |
| 19 L3 | **Port Solent** C Port | |
| 217 G3 | **Portsonachan Hotel** Ag & B | |
| 267 M3 | **Portsoy** Abers | |
| 129 H3 | **Port Sunlight** Wirral | |
| 34 F8 | **Portswood** C Sotn | |
| 57 L7 | **Port Talbot** Neath | |
| 57 J6 | **Port Tennant** Swans | |
| 236 E7 | **Portuairk** Highld | |
| 80 B6 | **Portway** Herefs | |
| 80 C8 | **Portway** Herefs | |
| 98 B6 | **Portway** Sandw | |
| 82 C1 | **Portway** Worcs | |
| 204 B6 | **Port Wemyss** Ag & B | |
| 173 J6 | **Port William** D & G | |
| 6 D4 | **Portwrinkle** Cnwll | |
| 174 D7 | **Portyerrock** D & G | |
| 13 J3 | **Posbury** Devon | |
| 96 E3 | **Posenhall** Shrops | |
| 88 F5 | **Poslingford** Suffk | |
| 199 L6 | **Posso** Border | |
| 12 F6 | **Postbridge** Devon | |
| 67 H7 | **Postcombe** Oxon | |
| 17 J4 | **Post Green** Dorset | |
| 40 F7 | **Postling** Kent | |
| 106 F2 | **Postwick** Norfk | |
| 244 D4 | **Potarch** Abers | |
| 68 B1 | **Potsgrove** C Beds | |
| 68 C5 | **Potten End** Herts | |
| 41 H2 | **Potten Street** Kent | |
| 163 H7 | **Potter Brompton** N York | |
| 106 D5 | **Pottergate Street** Norfk | |
| 135 L6 | **Potterhanworth** Lincs | |
| 135 M6 | **Potterhanworth Booths** Lincs | |
| 123 J7 | **Potter Heigham** Norfk | |
| 46 E7 | **Potterne** Wilts | |
| 46 E7 | **Potterne Wick** Wilts | |
| 67 L6 | **Potter Row** Bucks | |
| 69 H6 | **Potters Bar** Herts | |
| 147 J5 | **Potters Brook** Lancs | |
| 97 J6 | **Potter's Cross** Staffs | |
| 68 E6 | **Potters Crouch** Herts | |
| 39 M4 | **Potter's Forstal** Kent | |
| 99 K7 | **Potters Green** Covtry | |
| 23 H3 | **Potter's Green** E Susx | |
| 69 K3 | **Potters Green** Herts | |
| 69 G3 | **Pottersheath** Herts | |
| 100 B4 | **Potters Marston** Leics | |
| 115 J4 | **Potter Somersal** Derbys | |
| 84 E6 | **Potterspury** Nhants | |
| 257 H8 | **Potterton** Abers | |
| 150 F8 | **Potterton** Leeds | |
| 121 L7 | **Potthorpe** Norfk | |
| 32 D3 | **Pottle Street** Wilts | |
| 161 G2 | **Potto** N York | |
| 86 E5 | **Potton** C Beds | |
| 120 F7 | **Pott Row** Norfk | |
| 72 C3 | **Pott's Green** Essex | |
| 131 J4 | **Pott Shrigley** Ches E | |
| 11 J1 | **Poughill** Cnwll | |
| 13 K1 | **Poughill** Devon | |
| 18 B2 | **Poulner** Hants | |
| 46 E7 | **Poulshot** Wilts | |
| 65 G7 | **Poulton** Gloucs | |
| 129 G2 | **Poulton** Wirral | |
| 147 G2 | **Poulton-le-Fylde** Lancs | |
| 65 G7 | **Poulton Priory** Gloucs | |
| 97 G8 | **Pound Bank** Worcs | |
| 16 C4 | **Poundbury** Dorset | |
| 57 G6 | **Poundffald** Swans | |
| 38 D7 | **Poundgate** E Susx | |
| 23 H3 | **Pound Green** E Susx | |
| 88 E4 | **Pound Green** Suffk | |
| 97 G7 | **Pound Green** Worcs | |
| 37 L3 | **Pound Hill** W Susx | |
| 66 F2 | **Poundon** Bucks | |
| 38 E5 | **Poundsbridge** Kent | |
| 13 G7 | **Poundsgate** Devon | |
| 11 H3 | **Poundstock** Cnwll | |
| 48 C6 | **Pound Street** Hants | |
| 23 J3 | **Pounsley** E Susx | |
| 174 C5 | **Pouton** D & G | |
| 91 H1 | **Pouy Street** Suffk | |
| 37 L3 | **Povey Cross** Surrey | |
| 190 F3 | **Powburn** Nthumb | |
| 13 M5 | **Powderham** Devon | |
| 15 L3 | **Powerstock** Dorset | |
| 176 F5 | **Powfoot** D & G | |
| 81 G6 | **Pow Green** Herefs | |
| 177 H7 | **Powhill** Cumb | |
| 81 J5 | **Powick** Worcs | |
| 221 J7 | **Powmill** P & K | |
| 16 E5 | **Poxwell** Dorset | |
| 50 C4 | **Poyle** Slough | |
| 22 C5 | **Poynings** W Susx | |
| 31 L6 | **Poyntington** Dorset | |
| 131 H3 | **Poynton** Ches E | |
| 113 J8 | **Poynton** Wrekin | |
| 113 J7 | **Poynton Green** Wrekin | |
| 55 G3 | **Poyston Cross** Pembks | |
| 89 K4 | **Poystreet Green** Suffk | |
| 2 F5 | **Praa Sands** Cnwll | |
| 52 A6 | **Pratt's Bottom** Gt Lon | |
| 3 G4 | **Praze-an-Beeble** Cnwll | |
| 3 H7 | **Predannack Wollas** Cnwll | |
| 113 J5 | **Prees** Shrops | |
| 147 G6 | **Preesall** Lancs | |
| 113 J5 | **Prees Green** Shrops | |
| 112 D4 | **Preesgweene** Shrops | |
| 113 J4 | **Prees Heath** Shrops | |
| 113 J4 | **Prees Higher Heath** Shrops | |
| 113 J5 | **Prees Lower Heath** Shrops | |
| 190 E4 | **Prendwick** Nthumb | |
| 76 D6 | **Pren-gwyn** Cerdgn | |
| 109 K3 | **Prenteg** Gwynd | |
| 129 G2 | **Prenton** Wirral | |
| 129 L1 | **Prescot** Knows | |
| 29 K8 | **Prescott** Devon | |
| 96 F7 | **Prescott** Shrops | |
| 112 F7 | **Prescott** Shrops | |
| 233 J2 | **Presnerb** Angus | |
| 202 C6 | **Pressen** Nthumb | |
| 128 C3 | **Prestatyn** Denbgs | |
| 131 H4 | **Prestbury** Ches E | |
| 64 E2 | **Prestbury** Gloucs | |
| 79 K2 | **Presteigne** Powys | |
| 31 K3 | **Prestleigh** Somset | |
| 139 M6 | **Prestolee** Bolton | |
| 213 H7 | **Preston** Border | |
| 22 D6 | **Preston** Br & H | |
| 13 K7 | **Preston** Devon | |
| 16 D6 | **Preston** Dorset | |
| 144 F2 | **Preston** E R Yk | |
| 64 F7 | **Preston** Gloucs | |
| 68 F2 | **Preston** Herts | |
| 40 D3 | **Preston** Kent | |
| 41 H3 | **Preston** Kent | |
| 139 G2 | **Preston** Lancs | |
| 203 K8 | **Preston** Nthumb | |
| 101 J3 | **Preston** Rutlnd | |
| 96 C1 | **Preston** Shrops | |
| 29 K4 | **Preston** Somset | |
| 89 J5 | **Preston** Suffk | |
| 8 D3 | **Preston** Torbay | |
| 46 F3 | **Preston** Wilts | |
| 47 K4 | **Preston** Wilts | |
| 82 E2 | **Preston Bagot** Warwks | |
| 67 G1 | **Preston Bissett** Bucks | |
| 29 L5 | **Preston Bowyer** Somset | |
| 113 J6 | **Preston Brockhurst** Shrops | |
| 130 B4 | **Preston Brook** Halton | |
| 35 J3 | **Preston Candover** Hants | |
| 84 B4 | **Preston Capes** Nhants | |
| 139 H1 | **Preston Crematorium** Lancs | |
| 48 F1 | **Preston Crowmarsh** Oxon | |
| 84 F4 | **Preston Deanery** Nhants | |
| 82 E2 | **Preston Green** Warwks | |
| 113 H7 | **Preston Gubbals** Shrops | |
| 113 G8 | **Preston Montford** Shrops | |
| 82 F5 | **Preston on Stour** Warwks | |
| 169 L7 | **Preston on Tees** S on T | |
| 130 B3 | **Preston on the Hill** Halton | |
| 79 M7 | **Preston on Wye** Herefs | |
| 211 L4 | **Prestonpans** E Loth | |
| 157 H6 | **Preston Patrick** Cumb | |
| 31 H7 | **Preston Plucknett** Somset | |
| 41 H3 | **Preston Street** Kent | |
| 159 K4 | **Preston-under-Scar** N York | |
| 113 L8 | **Preston upon the Weald Moors** Wrekin | |
| 80 D6 | **Preston Wynne** Herefs | |
| 140 B6 | **Prestwich** Bury | |
| 180 E4 | **Prestwick** Nthumb | |
| 196 C6 | **Prestwick** S Ayrs | |
| 67 L7 | **Prestwood** Bucks | |
| 97 K6 | **Prestwood** Staffs | |
| 42 E3 | **Price Town** Brdgnd | |
| 104 B7 | **Prickwillow** Cambs | |
| 31 H1 | **Priddy** Somset | |
| 12 B1 | **Priestacott** Devon | |
| 132 C5 | **Priestcliffe** Derbys | |
| 132 C5 | **Priestcliffe Ditch** Derbys | |
| 157 H7 | **Priest Hutton** Lancs | |
| 197 H3 | **Priestland** E Ayrs | |
| 141 H3 | **Priestley Green** Calder | |
| 95 H4 | **Priest Weston** Shrops | |
| 52 E6 | **Priestwood Green** Kent | |
| 100 B5 | **Primethorpe** Leics | |
| 122 B8 | **Primrose Green** Norfk | |
| 213 H7 | **Primrosehill** Border | |
| 103 H5 | **Primrose Hill** Cambs | |
| 133 J8 | **Primrose Hill** Derbys | |
| 97 L6 | **Primrose Hill** Dudley | |
| 138 E6 | **Primrose Hill** Lancs | |
| 202 C7 | **Primsidemill** Border | |
| 55 K4 | **Princes Gate** Pembks | |
| 67 K6 | **Princes Risborough** Bucks | |
| 83 J1 | **Princethorpe** Warwks | |
| 12 E7 | **Princetown** Devon | |
| 20 C5 | **Prinsted** W Susx | |
| 128 C7 | **Prion** Denbgs | |
| 178 B5 | **Prior Rigg** Cumb | |
| 96 B8 | **Priors Halton** Shrops | |
| 83 L4 | **Priors Hardwick** Warwks | |
| 97 G1 | **Priorslee** Wrekin | |
| 83 L4 | **Priors Marston** Warwks | |
| 64 C2 | **Priors Norton** Gloucs | |
| 47 H1 | **Priory Vale** Swindn | |
| 79 J6 | **Priory Wood** Herefs | |
| 42 F4 | **Prisk** V Glam | |
| 45 K7 | **Priston** BaNES | |
| 106 C5 | **Pristow Green** Norfk | |
| 53 J2 | **Prittlewell** Sthend | |
| 35 L5 | **Privett** Hants | |
| 27 K3 | **Prixford** Devon | |
| 4 E5 | **Probus** Cnwll | |

212 B3 **Prora** E Loth
164 F3 **Prospect** Cumb
3 G5 **Prospidnick** Cnwll
268 E3 **Protstonhill** Abers
180 D6 **Prudhoe** Nthumb
2 E5 **Prussia Cove** Cnwll
45 J6 **Publow** BaNES
69 K2 **Puckeridge** Herts
30 E7 **Puckington** Somset
45 K4 **Pucklechurch** S Glos
81 K7 **Puckrup** Gloucs
130 E5 **Puddinglake** Ches W
129 H5 **Puddington** Ches W
28 E8 **Puddington** Devon
105 L5 **Puddledock** Norfk
16 E3 **Puddletown** Dorset
80 D3 **Pudleston** Herefs
141 K1 **Pudsey** Leeds
21 H3 **Pulborough** W Susx
114 A7 **Puleston** Wrekin
129 J7 **Pulford** Ches W
16 D1 **Pulham** Dorset
106 D6 **Pulham Market** Norfk
106 E6 **Pulham St Mary** Norfk
63 J8 **Pullens Green** S Glos
96 B2 **Pulley** Shrops
85 L8 **Pulloxhill** C Beds
210 E5 **Pumpherston** W Loth
77 J7 **Pumsaint** Carmth
75 G6 **Puncheston** Pembks
15 M5 **Puncknowle** Dorset
23 K3 **Punnett's Town** E Susx
19 M2 **Purbrook** Hants
52 C3 **Purfleet** Thurr
30 D3 **Puriton** Somset
71 K6 **Purleigh** Essex
51 J6 **Purley** Gt Lon
49 G4 **Purley** W Berk
95 G7 **Purlogue** Shrops
46 C5 **Purlpit** Wilts
103 K6 **Purls Bridge** Cambs
32 B7 **Purse Caundle** Dorset
81 K1 **Purshull Green** Worcs
95 J7 **Purslow** Shrops
142 C4 **Purston Jaglin** Wakefd
15 J1 **Purtington** Somset
63 K6 **Purton** Gloucs
63 K6 **Purton** Gloucs
47 G2 **Purton** Wilts
47 G1 **Purton Stoke** Wilts
84 D6 **Pury End** Nhants
65 M7 **Pusey** Oxon
80 E7 **Putley** Herefs
80 F7 **Putley Green** Herefs
64 A5 **Putloe** Gloucs
51 G4 **Putney** Gt Lon
51 G4 **Putney Vale Crematorium** Gt Lon
27 H3 **Putsborough** Devon
67 L4 **Puttenham** Herts
36 D2 **Puttenham** Surrey
89 G7 **Puttock End** Essex
16 C6 **Putton** Dorset
84 E6 **Puxley** Nhants
44 E6 **Puxton** N Som
56 E4 **Pwll** Carmth
54 F6 **Pwllcrochan** Pembks
61 L5 **Pwll-du** Mons
111 M1 **Pwll-glas** Denbgs
78 E8 **Pwllgloyw** Powys
108 F4 **Pwllheli** Gwynd
63 G8 **Pwllmeyric** Mons
58 A5 **Pwll Trap** Carmth
42 B3 **Pwll-y-glaw** Neath
126 F4 **Pydew** Conwy
116 D1 **Pye Bridge** Derbys
22 D4 **Pyecombe** W Susx
44 D2 **Pye Corner** Newpt
114 F8 **Pye Green** Staffs
42 B5 **Pyle** Brdgnd
29 L5 **Pyleigh** Somset
31 K3 **Pylle** Somset
103 K6 **Pymoor** Cambs
15 L3 **Pymore** Dorset
50 D7 **Pyrford** Surrey
67 G7 **Pyrton** Oxon
101 J8 **Pytchley** Nhants
11 K2 **Pyworthy** Devon

## Q

94 F7 **Quabbs** Shrops
19 H5 **Quadring** Lincs
19 H5 **Quadring Eaudike** Lincs
67 H3 **Quainton** Bucks
43 H3 **Quaker's Yard** Myr Td
80 F8 **Quaking Houses** Dur
81 e7 **Quarff** Shet
34 C2 **Quarley** Hants

116 B3 **Quarndon** Derbys
19 K5 **Quarr Hill** IoW
208 B5 **Quarrier's Village** Inver
118 E3 **Quarrington** Lincs
169 J3 **Quarrington Hill** Dur
130 A6 **Quarrybank** Ches W
97 L6 **Quarry Bank** Dudley
266 D3 **Quarrywood** Moray
207 K6 **Quarter** N Ayrs
197 L1 **Quarter** S Lans
97 G5 **Quatford** Shrops
97 G5 **Quatt** Shrops
168 F2 **Quebec** Dur
64 A4 **Quedgeley** Gloucs
104 B7 **Queen Adelaide** Cambs
53 K4 **Queenborough** Kent
31 K6 **Queen Camel** Somset
45 J5 **Queen Charlton** BaNES
28 E7 **Queen Dart** Devon
81 K7 **Queenhill** Worcs
32 C4 **Queen Oak** Dorset
19 J6 **Queen's Bower** IoW
141 H2 **Queensbury** C Brad
129 H6 **Queensferry** Flints
112 E6 **Queen's Head** Shrops
209 H6 **Queenslie** C Glas
85 L5 **Queen's Park** Bed
84 E3 **Queen's Park** Nhants
39 H4 **Queen Street** Kent
46 F2 **Queen Street** Wilts
209 J3 **Queenzieburn** N Lans
70 D1 **Quendon** Essex
100 E1 **Queniborough** Leics
65 H6 **Quenington** Gloucs
147 K4 **Quernmore** Lancs
98 D4 **Queslett** Birm
6 C2 **Quethiock** Cnwll
48 E4 **Quick's Green** W Berk
105 L6 **Quidenham** Norfk
35 G1 **Quidhampton** Hants
33 K5 **Quidhampton** Wilts
113 H5 **Quina Brook** Shrops
84 B5 **Quinbury End** Nhants
98 C6 **Quinton** Dudley
84 E4 **Quinton** Nhants
84 F4 **Quinton Green** Nhants
4 D3 **Quintrell Downs** Cnwll
115 H3 **Quixhall** Staffs
213 H6 **Quixwood** Border
12 A3 **Quoditch** Devon
220 E3 **Quoig** P & K
116 F8 **Quorn** Leics
199 G5 **Quothquan** S Lans
275 d5 **Quoyburray** Ork
275 b4 **Quoyloo** Ork

## R

39 K4 **Rabbit's Cross** Kent
69 G3 **Rableyheath** Herts
177 G8 **Raby** Cumb
129 H4 **Raby** Wirral
199 K6 **Rachan Mill** Border
126 C6 **Rachub** Gwynd
28 E7 **Rackenford** Devon
21 H4 **Rackham** W Susx
122 F8 **Rackheath** Norfk
176 D4 **Racks** D & G
275 a5 **Rackwick** Ork
115 M4 **Radbourne** Derbys
140 B6 **Radcliffe** Bury
191 K5 **Radcliffe** Nthumb
117 H4 **Radcliffe on Trent** Notts
84 D8 **Radclive** Bucks
65 L7 **Radcot** Oxon
263 J7 **Raddery** Highld
29 J5 **Raddington** Somset
223 H5 **Radernie** Fife
99 J7 **Radford** Covtry
83 H2 **Radford Semele** Warwks
30 B3 **Radlet** Somset
68 F7 **Radlett** Herts
28 C6 **Radley** Devon
66 D7 **Radley** Oxon
70 F6 **Radley Green** Essex
130 B8 **Radmore Green** Ches E
67 J7 **Radnage** Bucks
45 K8 **Radstock** BaNES
84 B7 **Radstone** Nhants
83 J5 **Radway** Warwks
114 B1 **Radway Green** Ches E
85 K4 **Radwell** Bed
86 E8 **Radwell** Herts
88 C7 **Radwinter** Essex
88 C7 **Radwinter End** Essex
43 H5 **Radyr** Cardif
118 D2 **RAF College (Cranwell)** Lincs
265 H8 **Rafford** Moray
117 H7 **Ragdale** Leics

95 L5 **Ragdon** Shrops
2 D6 **Raginnis** Cnwll
62 E5 **Raglan** Mons
134 F5 **Ragnall** Notts
252 F6 **Raigbeg** Highld
81 K4 **Rainbow Hill** Worcs
138 F7 **Rainford** St Hel
52 B3 **Rainham** Gt Lon
53 H6 **Rainham** Medway
129 L2 **Rainhill** St Hel
129 L2 **Rainhill Stoops** St Hel
131 J4 **Rainow** Ches E
140 B7 **Rainsough** Bury
160 E7 **Rainton** N York
134 B8 **Rainworth** Notts
157 K1 **Raisbeck** Cumb
167 G2 **Raise** Cumb
152 C3 **Raisthorpe** N York
222 C2 **Rait** P & K
136 F3 **Raithby** Lincs
137 G6 **Raithby** Lincs
171 K8 **Raithwaite** N York
36 B5 **Rake** Hants
140 B5 **Rakewood** Rochdl
241 J4 **Ralia** Highld
77 G6 **Ram** Carmth
258 B7 **Ramasaig** Highld
3 J4 **Rame** Cnwll
6 E5 **Rame** Cnwll
45 K3 **Ram Hill** S Glos
40 C6 **Ram Lane** Kent
16 A2 **Rampisham** Dorset
146 E3 **Rampside** Cumb
87 J2 **Rampton** Cambs
134 F4 **Rampton** Notts
140 B4 **Ramsbottom** Bury
47 K4 **Ramsbury** Wilts
35 L6 **Ramsdean** Hants
48 E7 **Ramsdell** Hants
65 M4 **Ramsden** Oxon
81 L6 **Ramsden** Worcs
71 H8 **Ramsden Bellhouse** Essex
71 H7 **Ramsden Heath** Essex
102 F6 **Ramsey** Cambs
73 J1 **Ramsey** Essex
154 f3 **Ramsey** IoM
102 F6 **Ramsey Forty Foot** Cambs
102 E6 **Ramsey Heights** Cambs
72 D6 **Ramsey Island** Essex
102 F5 **Ramsey Mereside** Cambs
102 E6 **Ramsey St Mary's** Cambs
41 L2 **Ramsgate** Kent
149 K2 **Ramsgill** N York
168 B1 **Ramshaw** Dur
91 H7 **Ramsholt** Suffk
189 K5 **Ramshope** Nthumb
115 H3 **Ramshorn** Staffs
12 F4 **Ramsley** Devon
36 E4 **Ramsnest Common** Surrey
136 D4 **Ranby** Lincs
134 C3 **Ranby** Notts
136 B4 **Rand** Lincs
50 F7 **Randalls Park Crematorium** Surrey
64 B5 **Randwick** Gloucs
208 C6 **Ranfurly** Rens
115 K7 **Rangemore** Staffs
45 K2 **Rangeworthy** S Glos
196 E8 **Rankinston** E Ayrs
101 H1 **Ranksborough** Rutlnd
71 H3 **Rank's Green** Essex
139 L3 **Rann** Bl w D
230 D4 **Rannoch Station** P & K
29 G2 **Ranscombe** Somset
134 C2 **Ranskill** Notts
114 D6 **Ranton** Staffs
114 D7 **Ranton Green** Staffs
123 G8 **Ranworth** Norfk
220 D8 **Raploch** Stirlg
275 d2 **Rapness** Ork
30 E7 **Rapps** Somset
175 K5 **Rascarrel** D & G
207 J2 **Rashfield** Ag & B
81 L2 **Rashwood** Worcs
151 G2 **Raskelf** N York
61 J5 **Rassau** Blae G
141 H3 **Rastrick** Calder
248 E7 **Ratagan** Highld
100 B2 **Ratby** Leics
99 J3 **Ratcliffe Culey** Leics
116 E6 **Ratcliffe on Soar** Notts
117 G8 **Ratcliffe on the Wreake** Leics
33 L2 **Ratfyn** Wilts
269 J4 **Rathen** Abers
222 F3 **Rathillet** Fife
148 D4 **Rathmell** N York
210 F5 **Ratho** C Edin
210 F4 **Ratho Station** C Edin
267 J3 **Rathven** Moray

34 E6 **Ratlake** Hants
83 J5 **Ratley** Warwks
41 H4 **Ratling** Kent
95 K4 **Ratlinghope** Shrops
120 B8 **Rattan Row** Norfk
280 C2 **Rattar** Highld
165 K3 **Ratten Row** Cumb
165 L1 **Ratten Row** Cumb
147 H7 **Ratten Row** Lancs
7 L3 **Rattery** Devon
89 K3 **Rattlesden** Suffk
23 K7 **Ratton Village** E Susx
233 J6 **Rattray** P & K
165 L1 **Raughton** Cumb
165 L2 **Raughton Head** Cumb
85 K1 **Raunds** Nhants
133 J1 **Ravenfield** Rothm
155 K3 **Ravenglass** Cumb
81 G4 **Ravenhills Green** Worcs
107 H4 **Raveningham** Norfk
138 C6 **Raven Meols** Sefton
163 H2 **Ravenscar** N York
154 e4 **Ravensdale** IoM
86 B4 **Ravensden** Bed
158 E2 **Ravenseat** N York
133 L8 **Ravenshead** Notts
113 K2 **Ravensmoor** Ches E
141 K4 **Ravensthorpe** Kirk
84 C1 **Ravensthorpe** Nhants
99 L1 **Ravenstone** Leics
85 G5 **Ravenstone** M Keyn
158 C2 **Ravenstonedale** Cumb
198 F4 **Ravenstruther** S Lans
159 L1 **Ravensworth** N York
163 G2 **Raw** N York
151 J5 **Rawcliffe** C York
143 H3 **Rawcliffe** E R Yk
143 H3 **Rawcliffe Bridge** E R Yk
150 B7 **Rawdon** Leeds
150 B8 **Rawdon Crematorium** Leeds
40 B3 **Rawling Street** Kent
142 C8 **Rawmarsh** Rothm
98 C1 **Rawnsley** Staffs
71 J8 **Rawreth** Essex
14 E1 **Rawridge** Devon
140 B3 **Rawtenstall** Lancs
90 B7 **Raydon** Suffk
190 C7 **Raylees** Nthumb
53 H1 **Rayleigh** Essex
15 H3 **Raymond's Hill** Devon
71 H3 **Rayne** Essex
51 G5 **Raynes Park** Gt Lon
88 B2 **Reach** Cambs
140 A1 **Read** Lancs
49 H4 **Reading** Readg
49 H4 **Reading Crematorium** Readg
25 G1 **Reading Street** Kent
41 L2 **Reading Street** Kent
166 E7 **Reagill** Cumb
2 F4 **Realwa** Cnwll
263 K1 **Rearquhar** Highld
117 H8 **Rearsby** Leics
113 L1 **Rease Heath** Ches E
279 G3 **Reay** Highld
41 H2 **Reculver** Kent
29 K7 **Red Ball** Devon
55 J6 **Redberth** Pembks
68 E4 **Redbourn** Herts
144 B7 **Redbourne** N Linc
63 G5 **Redbrook** Gloucs
113 H3 **Redbrook** Wrexhm
40 B8 **Redbrook Street** Kent
253 H2 **Redburn** Highld
179 H6 **Redburn** Nthumb
170 E6 **Redcar** R & Cl
175 K2 **Redcastle** D & G
251 G2 **Redcastle** Highld
87 K4 **Red Cross** Cambs
165 H2 **Red Dial** Cumb
210 B3 **Redding** Falk
210 B3 **Reddingmuirhead** Falk
131 H1 **Reddish** Stockp
82 B2 **Redditch** Worcs
82 B2 **Redditch Crematorium** Worcs
88 F4 **Rede** Suffk
106 F6 **Redenhall** Norfk
34 C1 **Redenham** Hants
179 K3 **Redesmouth** Nthumb
235 J2 **Redford** Abers
234 E6 **Redford** Angus
36 C5 **Redford** W Susx
188 C3 **Redfordgreen** Border
42 F4 **Redgate** Rhondd
221 K2 **Redgorton** P & K
105 L7 **Redgrave** Suffk
245 H3 **Redhill** Abers
17 L3 **Red Hill** Bmouth
86 F8 **Redhill** Herts
45 G6 **Redhill** N Som
37 L1 **Redhill** Surrey

82 D4 **Red Hill** Warwks
107 H6 **Redisham** Suffk
45 H4 **Redland** Bristl
275 C3 **Redland** Ork
90 E1 **Redlingfield** Suffk
90 E1 **Redlingfield Green** Suffk
88 D1 **Red Lodge** Suffk
140 C4 **Red Lumb** Rochdl
32 B4 **Redlynch** Somset
33 L6 **Redlynch** Wilts
164 F4 **Redmain** Cumb
81 H2 **Redmarley** Worcs
63 L1 **Redmarley D'Abitot** Gloucs
169 K6 **Redmarshall** S on T
117 L4 **Redmile** Leics
159 J4 **Redmire** N York
245 G8 **Redmyre** Abers
98 C8 **Rednal** Birm
112 E6 **Rednal** Shrops
201 J6 **Redpath** Border
260 B6 **Redpoint** Highld
11 K2 **Red Post** Cnwll
139 H6 **Red Rock** Wigan
55 L4 **Red Roses** Carmth
191 K6 **Red Row** Nthumb
4 A6 **Redruth** Cnwll
46 D6 **Redstocks** Wilts
233 J8 **Redstone** P & K
55 J4 **Redstone Cross** Pembks
114 C1 **Red Street** Staffs
140 B6 **Redvales** Bury
125 J3 **Red Wharf Bay** IoA
44 E2 **Redwick** Newpt
45 H2 **Redwick** S Glos
169 G6 **Redworth** Darltn
87 H8 **Reed** Herts
107 J3 **Reedham** Norfk
143 K3 **Reedness** E R Yk
136 D6 **Reeds Beck** Lincs
140 B3 **Reeds Holme** Lancs
135 L5 **Reepham** Lincs
122 B7 **Reepham** Norfk
159 J3 **Reeth** N York
99 H7 **Reeves Green** Solhll
154 f3 **Regaby** IoM
270 C5 **Reiff** Highld
37 L1 **Reigate** Surrey
163 L7 **Reighton** N York
256 F7 **Reisque** Abers
280 D5 **Reiss** Highld
4 C4 **Rejerrah** Cnwll
3 G4 **Releath** Cnwll
2 F4 **Relubbus** Cnwll
253 J2 **Relugas** Moray
49 J2 **Remenham** Wokham
49 J2 **Remenham Hill** Wokham
116 F6 **Rempstone** Notts
64 E5 **Rendcomb** Gloucs
91 H2 **Rendham** Suffk
91 H4 **Rendlesham** Suffk
208 E5 **Renfrew** Rens
86 B5 **Renhold** Bed
133 J4 **Renishaw** Derbys
191 J3 **Rennington** Nthumb
208 C3 **Renton** W Duns
166 E2 **Renwick** Cumb
123 J8 **Repps** Norfk
116 A6 **Repton** Derbys
251 J3 **Resaurie** Highld
5 G6 **Rescassa** Cnwll
5 G5 **Rescorla** Cnwll
237 L7 **Resipole** Highld
3 G3 **Reskadinnick** Cnwll
263 J6 **Resolis** Highld
60 C6 **Resolven** Neath
218 C5 **Rest and be thankful** Ag & B
213 J6 **Reston** Border
3 K4 **Restronguet** Cnwll
234 D5 **Reswallie** Angus
4 F2 **Reterth** Cnwll
134 D3 **Retford** Notts
5 G2 **Retire** Cnwll
71 J7 **Rettendon** Essex
4 E3 **Retyn** Cnwll
136 E7 **Revesby** Lincs
7 K7 **Rew** Devon
13 H8 **Rew** Devon
13 M3 **Rewe** Devon
19 H5 **Rew Street** IoW
12 A5 **Rexon** Devon
107 K7 **Reydon** Suffk
105 L2 **Reymerston** Norfk
55 J5 **Reynalton** Pembks
56 E6 **Reynoldston** Swans
11 L7 **Rezare** Cnwll
62 D6 **Rhadyr** Mons
77 L6 **Rhandirmwyn** Carmth
78 D2 **Rhayader** Powys
250 F2 **Rheindown** Highld
128 E5 **Rhes-y-cae** Flints

112 B3 **Rhewl** Denbgs
128 D7 **Rhewl** Denbgs
128 D3 **Rhewl-fawr** Flints
128 D4 **Rhewl Mostyn** Flints
270 E3 **Rhicarn** Highld
276 D5 **Rhiconich** Highld
263 J5 **Rhicullen** Highld
60 D6 **Rhigos** Rhondd
261 G1 **Rhireavach** Highld
273 K7 **Rhives** Highld
43 J5 **Rhiwbina** Cardif
110 D2 **Rhiwbryfdir** Gwynd
43 L4 **Rhiwderyn** Newpt
125 K7 **Rhiwen** Gwynd
42 F4 **Rhiwinder** Rhondd
111 H4 **Rhiwlas** Gwynd
125 K6 **Rhiwlas** Gwynd
112 B5 **Rhiwlas** Powys
43 G5 **Rhiwsaeson** Rhondd
30 C4 **Rhode** Somset
39 H4 **Rhoden Green** Kent
140 C6 **Rhodes** Rochdl
133 L4 **Rhodesia** Notts
40 F6 **Rhodes Minnis** Kent
74 C6 **Rhodiad-y-brenin** Pembks
175 J3 **Rhonehouse** D & G
43 G8 **Rhoose** V Glam
58 C2 **Rhos** Carmth
128 D7 **Rhos** Denbgs
57 K4 **Rhos** Neath
125 G2 **Rhosbeirio** IoA
125 J4 **Rhoscefnhir** IoA
124 D4 **Rhoscolyn** IoA
54 E6 **Rhoscrowther** Pembks
128 F6 **Rhosesmor** Flints
109 G4 **Rhos-fawr** Gwynd
125 J8 **Rhosgadfan** Gwynd
125 G2 **Rhosgoch** IoA
79 H5 **Rhosgoch** Powys
76 F2 **Rhos Haminiog** Cerdgn
75 L4 **Rhoshill** Pembks
108 C5 **Rhoshirwaun** Gwynd
109 H3 **Rhoslan** Gwynd
92 C2 **Rhoslefain** Gwynd
112 D2 **Rhosllanerchrugog** Wrexhm
125 J2 **Rhôs Lligwy** IoA
59 H4 **Rhosmaen** Carmth
125 H4 **Rhosmeirch** IoA
124 E5 **Rhosneigr** IoA
112 E2 **Rhosnesni** Wrexhm
127 G4 **Rhôs-on-Sea** Conwy
112 E1 **Rhosrobin** Wrexhm
56 D7 **Rhossili** Swans
125 J8 **Rhostryfan** Gwynd
112 D2 **Rhostyllen** Wrexhm
125 G2 **Rhosybol** IoA
111 M7 **Rhos y-brithdir** Powys
112 D4 **Rhosygadfa** Shrops
77 H1 **Rhos-y-garth** Cerdgn
111 H4 **Rhos-y-gwaliau** Gwynd
108 D4 **Rhos-y-llan** Gwynd
112 D3 **Rhosymedre** Wrexhm
79 K1 **Rhos-y-meirch** Powys
207 M2 **Rhu** Ag & B
128 C5 **Rhuallt** Denbgs
207 G4 **Rhubodach** Ag & B
130 A7 **Rhuddall Heath** Ches W
76 F6 **Rhuddlan** Cerdgn
127 L4 **Rhuddlan** Denbgs
79 G5 **Rhulen** Powys
205 M6 **Rhunahaorine** Ag & B
110 B3 **Rhyd** Gwynd
58 D4 **Rhydargaeau** Carmth
77 G7 **Rhydcymerau** Carmth
81 J6 **Rhydd** Worcs
109 K1 **Rhyd-Ddu** Gwynd
57 K5 **Rhydding** Neath
127 K6 **Rhydgaled** Conwy
110 F1 **Rhydlanfair** Conwy
76 C5 **Rhydlewis** Cerdgn
108 C5 **Rhydlios** Gwynd
111 G2 **Rhyd-lydan** Conwy
76 E6 **Rhydowen** Cerdgn
77 G2 **Rhydrosser** Cerdgn
79 J5 **Rhydspence** Herefs
128 F8 **Rhydtalog** Flints
111 G4 **Rhyd-uchaf** Gwynd
108 E4 **Rhyd-y-clafdy** Gwynd
112 C5 **Rhydycroesau** Shrops
92 D7 **Rhydyfelin** Cerdgn
43 H4 **Rhydyfelin** Rhondd
127 H4 **Rhyd-y-foel** Conwy
57 K4 **Rhydyfro** Neath
125 K6 **Rhyd-y-groes** Gwynd
110 F7 **Rhydymain** Gwynd
62 C5 **Rhyd-y-meirch** Mons
128 E6 **Rhydymwyn** Flints
92 D6 **Rhyd-y pennau** Cerdgn
92 D3 **Rhyd-yr-onnen** Gwynd
110 C3 **Rhyd-y-sarn** Gwynd

127 K3 **Rhyl** Denbgs
61 H5 **Rhymney** Caerph
222 B3 **Rhynd** P & K
255 K6 **Rhynie** Abers
264 C4 **Rhynie** Highld
97 H8 **Ribbesford** Worcs
139 H2 **Ribbleton** Lancs
138 E2 **Ribby** Lancs
139 K1 **Ribchester** Lancs
132 F7 **Riber** Derbys
144 F6 **Riby** Lincs
151 K8 **Riccall** N York
188 F7 **Riccarton** Border
196 E4 **Riccarton** E Ayrs
80 C1 **Richards Castle** Herefs
50 C3 **Richings Park** Bucks
50 F4 **Richmond** Gt Lon
159 M2 **Richmond** N York
133 H3 **Richmond** Sheff
9 i2 **Richmond Fort** Guern
29 L4 **Rich's Holford** Somset
114 E7 **Rickerscote** Staffs
44 F7 **Rickford** N Som
7 L7 **Rickham** Devon
105 L8 **Rickinghall** Suffk
70 D1 **Rickling** Essex
70 D1 **Rickling Green** Essex
68 D8 **Rickmansworth** Herts
188 E1 **Riddell** Border
116 C1 **Riddings** Derbys
27 L8 **Riddlecombe** Devon
149 K7 **Riddlesden** C Brad
45 H7 **Ridge** BaNES
17 H5 **Ridge** Dorset
69 G7 **Ridge** Herts
33 G4 **Ridge** Wilts
78 E3 **Ridgebourne** Powys
37 L1 **Ridge Green** Surrey
45 G6 **Ridgehill** N Som
99 J4 **Ridge Lane** Warwks
41 G6 **Ridge Row** Kent
133 H3 **Ridgeway** Derbys
82 B3 **Ridgeway** Worcs
81 G5 **Ridgeway Cross** Herefs
88 E7 **Ridgewell** Essex
23 H3 **Ridgewood** E Susx
85 J8 **Ridgmont** C Beds
180 B6 **Riding Mill** Nthumb
52 D6 **Ridley** Kent
179 H6 **Ridley** Nthumb
113 J1 **Ridley Green** Ches E
123 G5 **Ridlington** Norfk
101 J3 **Ridlington** Rutlnd
123 G5 **Ridlington Street** Norfk
179 L2 **Ridsdale** Nthumb
161 J5 **Rievaulx** N York
177 J5 **Rigg** D & G
209 K5 **Riggend** N Lans
253 G2 **Righoul** Highld
157 K5 **Rigmadon Park** Cumb
137 H4 **Rigsby** Lincs
198 E6 **Rigside** S Lans
139 J3 **Riley Green** Lancs
115 J8 **Rileyhill** Staffs
11 K7 **Rilla Mill** Cnwll
11 K7 **Rillaton** Cnwll
162 E7 **Rillington** N York
148 D6 **Rimington** Lancs
31 K6 **Rimpton** Somset
145 J2 **Rimswell** E R Yk
75 G7 **Rinaston** Pembks
97 G4 **Rindleford** Shrops
175 H3 **Ringford** D & G
132 F3 **Ringinglow** Sheff
106 C1 **Ringland** Norfk
23 H3 **Ringles Cross** E Susx
39 L2 **Ringlestone** Kent
139 M6 **Ringley** Bolton
23 G5 **Ringmer** E Susx
7 J5 **Ringmore** Devon
13 L8 **Ringmore** Devon
138 F5 **Ring o'Bells** Lancs
254 E3 **Ringorm** Moray
103 H3 **Ring's End** Cambs
107 H5 **Ringsfield** Suffk
107 H6 **Ringsfield Corner** Suffk
68 C4 **Ringshall** Herts
90 B4 **Ringshall** Suffk
90 B5 **Ringshall Stocks** Suffk
101 L8 **Ringstead** Nhants
120 F3 **Ringstead** Norfk
18 A3 **Ringwood** Hants
41 K5 **Ringwould** Kent
2 F5 **Rinsey** Cnwll
2 F5 **Rinsey Croft** Cnwll
23 H5 **Ripe** E Susx
116 C2 **Ripley** Derbys
18 B4 **Ripley** Hants
150 C4 **Ripley** N York
50 D7 **Ripley** Surrey

144 B2 **Riplingham** E R Yk
35 K6 **Riplington** Hants
150 D2 **Ripon** N York
118 E6 **Rippingale** Lincs
41 K5 **Ripple** Kent
81 K7 **Ripple** Worcs
140 F4 **Ripponden** Calder
204 D7 **Risabus** Ag & B
80 D4 **Risbury** Herefs
144 A5 **Risby** N Linc
88 F2 **Risby** Suffk
43 K3 **Risca** Caerph
153 J7 **Rise** E R Yk
38 F7 **Riseden** E Susx
39 H6 **Riseden** Kent
119 H5 **Risegate** Lincs
135 K5 **Riseholme** Lincs
164 D4 **Risehow** Cumb
85 L3 **Riseley** Bed
49 H6 **Riseley** Wokham
90 E2 **Rishangles** Suffk
139 L2 **Rishton** Lancs
140 F4 **Rishworth** Calder
140 A3 **Rising Bridge** Lancs
116 D4 **Risley** Derbys
130 C1 **Risley** Warrtn
150 B2 **Risplith** N York
47 L6 **Rivar** Wilts
71 K4 **Rivenhall End** Essex
41 J6 **River** Kent
36 D6 **River** W Susx
87 L2 **River Bank** Cambs
250 F1 **Riverford** Highld
38 D2 **Riverhead** Kent
32 C8 **Rivers Corner** Dorset
139 J5 **Rivington** Lancs
28 E6 **Roachill** Devon
84 E5 **Roade** Nhants
106 F4 **Road Green** Norfk
178 C4 **Roadhead** Cumb
198 E3 **Roadmeetings** S Lans
197 H7 **Roadside** E Ayrs
279 L4 **Roadside** Highld
29 J3 **Roadwater** Somset
258 D7 **Roag** Highld
146 D3 **Roa Island** Cumb
183 H2 **Roan of Craigoch** S Ayrs
87 J8 **Roast Green** Essex
43 K6 **Roath** Cardif
188 D3 **Roberton** Border
198 F7 **Roberton** S Lans
24 D3 **Robertsbridge** E Susx
141 J3 **Roberttown** Kirk
55 J4 **Robeston Wathen** Pembks
177 H4 **Robgill Tower** D & G
131 H8 **Robin Hill** Staffs
139 G5 **Robin Hood** Lancs
141 M2 **Robin Hood** Leeds
98 E7 **Robin Hood Crematorium** Solhll
88 E7 **Robinhood End** Essex
163 G2 **Robin Hood's Bay** N York
6 F2 **Roborough** Devon
27 K7 **Roborough** Devon
129 K2 **Roby** Knows
139 G6 **Roby Mill** Lancs
115 J4 **Rocester** Staffs
54 E3 **Roch** Pembks
140 D5 **Rochdale** Rochdl
140 C5 **Rochdale Crematorium** Rochdl
5 G3 **Roche** Cnwll
52 F5 **Rochester** Medway
189 M6 **Rochester** Nthumb
53 J1 **Rochford** Essex
80 E2 **Rochford** Worcs
54 E3 **Roch Gate** Pembks
10 C7 **Rock** Cnwll
57 L6 **Rock** Neath
191 J2 **Rock** Nthumb
21 K4 **Rock** W Susx
81 G1 **Rock** Worcs
14 B3 **Rockbeare** Devon
33 K7 **Rockbourne** Hants
177 K6 **Rockcliffe** Cumb
175 L4 **Rockcliffe** D & G
177 K6 **Rockcliffe Cross** Cumb
131 H8 **Rock End** Staffs
8 D2 **Rockend** Torbay
129 H2 **Rock Ferry** Wirral
264 E3 **Rockfield** Highld
62 F4 **Rockfield** Mons
28 D1 **Rockford** Devon
18 B2 **Rockford** Hants
96 C3 **Rockgreen** Shrops
63 K8 **Rockhampton** S Glos
10 F5 **Rockhead** Cnwll
95 G7 **Rockhill** Shrops
81 L1 **Rock Hill** Worcs
101 J5 **Rockingham** Nhants
105 K4 **Rockland All Saints** Norfk
107 G3 **Rockland St Mary** Norfk

105 K4 **Rockland St Peter** Norfk
134 E5 **Rockley** Notts
47 H4 **Rockley** Wilts
140 C3 **Rockliffe** Lancs
207 L1 **Rockville** Ag & B
49 J1 **Rockwell End** Bucks
29 L6 **Rockwell Green** Somset
64 B6 **Rodborough** Gloucs
47 H2 **Rodbourne** Swindn
46 D2 **Rodbourne** Wilts
79 K3 **Rodd** Herefs
190 E2 **Roddam** Nthumb
16 B5 **Rodden** Dorset
168 F3 **Roddymoor** Dur
46 A8 **Rode** Somset
130 F8 **Rode Heath** Ches E
131 G6 **Rode Heath** Ches E
282 d7 **Rodel** W Isls
113 J8 **Roden** Wrekin
29 J3 **Rodhuish** Somset
113 K8 **Rodington** Wrekin
113 K8 **Rodington Heath** Wrekin
63 L5 **Rodley** Gloucs
150 B8 **Rodley** Leeds
64 D7 **Rodmarton** Gloucs
22 F6 **Rodmell** E Susx
40 B3 **Rodmersham** Kent
40 B3 **Rodmersham Green** Kent
31 H1 **Rodney Stoke** Somset
115 K3 **Rodsley** Derbys
30 C3 **Rodway** Somset
150 E3 **Roecliffe** N York
140 E8 **Roe Cross** Tamesd
69 G5 **Roe Green** Herts
87 G8 **Roe Green** Herts
139 M7 **Roe Green** Salfd
51 G4 **Roehampton** Gt Lon
37 J4 **Roffey** W Susx
273 H7 **Rogart** Highld
36 B6 **Rogate** W Susx
156 E3 **Roger Ground** Cumb
44 B2 **Rogerstone** Newpt
282 d7 **Roghadal** W Isls
44 F2 **Rogiet** Mons
66 F8 **Roke** Oxon
181 K7 **Roker** Sundld
123 J8 **Rollesby** Norfk
100 F3 **Rolleston** Leics
117 K1 **Rolleston** Notts
115 L6 **Rolleston on Dove** Staffs
153 K6 **Rolston** E R Yk
44 D6 **Rolstone** N Som
39 L7 **Rolvenden** Kent
39 L7 **Rolvenden Layne** Kent
168 C6 **Romaldkirk** Dur
160 E4 **Romanby** N York
199 K3 **Romanno Bridge** Border
28 C6 **Romansleigh** Devon
40 A7 **Romden Castle** Kent
258 F6 **Romesdal** Highld
17 L1 **Romford** Dorset
52 B1 **Romford** Gt Lon
131 J2 **Romiley** Stockp
52 C6 **Romney Street** Kent
34 D6 **Romsey** Hants
97 H6 **Romsley** Shrops
98 B7 **Romsley** Worcs
206 B8 **Ronachan** Ag & B
46 C7 **Rood Ashton** Wilts
167 L2 **Rookhope** Dur
19 H6 **Rookley** IoW
19 H7 **Rookley Green** IoW
44 D8 **Rooks Bridge** Somset
29 K4 **Rooks Nest** Somset
160 B5 **Rookwith** N York
145 H2 **Roos** E R Yk
146 D2 **Roose** Cumb
146 E2 **Roosebeck** Cumb
86 B4 **Roothams Green** Bed
35 K4 **Ropley** Hants
35 K4 **Ropley Dean** Hants
35 K4 **Ropley Soke** Hants
118 C5 **Ropsley** Lincs
269 K6 **Rora** Abers
95 H3 **Rorrington** Shrops
267 H6 **Rosarie** Moray
4 C4 **Rose** Cnwll
147 H8 **Roseacre** Lancs
28 D6 **Rose Ash** Devon
198 D3 **Rosebank** S Lans
75 J6 **Rosebush** Pembks
11 H3 **Rosecare** Cnwll
4 D3 **Rosecliston** Cnwll
162 C3 **Rosedale Abbey** N York
72 C2 **Rose Green** Essex
89 J7 **Rose Green** Suffk
89 K6 **Rose Green** Suffk
20 E7 **Rose Green** W Susx
272 C7 **Rosehall** Highld
269 G3 **Rosehearty** Abers

23 G4 **Rose Hill** E Susx
140 B2 **Rose Hill** Lancs
113 G8 **Rosehill** Shrops
266 C3 **Roseisle** Moray
23 K7 **Roselands** E Susx
54 F5 **Rosemarket** Pembks
263 K8 **Rosemarkie** Highld
29 L7 **Rosemary Lane** Devon
233 J6 **Rosemount** P & K
4 F2 **Rosenannon** Cnwll
3 K6 **Rosenithon** Cnwll
23 J3 **Roser's Cross** E Susx
5 H3 **Rosevean** Cnwll
3 M4 **Rosevine** Cnwll
2 F4 **Rosewarne** Cnwll
211 J6 **Rosewell** Mdloth
169 L6 **Roseworth** S on T
3 G3 **Roseworthy** Cnwll
166 D7 **Rosgill** Cumb
2 B6 **Roskestal** Cnwll
258 D7 **Roskhill** Highld
3 K6 **Roskorwell** Cnwll
165 K2 **Rosley** Cumb
211 J6 **Roslin** Mdloth
115 L8 **Rosliston** Derbys
207 L2 **Rosneath** Ag & B
175 G6 **Ross** D & G
203 J5 **Ross** Nthumb
129 J8 **Rossett** Wrexhm
150 D5 **Rossett Green** N York
143 G8 **Rossington** Donc
208 D5 **Rossland** Rens
63 J2 **Ross-on-Wye** Herefs
280 C8 **Roster** Highld
130 E3 **Rostherne** Ches E
165 H7 **Rosthwaite** Cumb
115 J3 **Roston** Derbys
2 E5 **Rosudgeon** Cnwll
210 F2 **Rosyth** Fife
190 F6 **Rothbury** Nthumb
117 H8 **Rotherby** Leics
38 E7 **Rotherfield** E Susx
49 H3 **Rotherfield Greys** Oxon
49 H3 **Rotherfield Peppard** Oxon
133 H1 **Rotherham** Rothm
133 J1 **Rotherham Crematorium** Rothm
84 D4 **Rothersthorpe** Nhants
49 H7 **Rotherwick** Hants
266 F6 **Rothes** Moray
207 H6 **Rothesay** Ag & B
256 D4 **Rothiebrisbane** Abers
267 L6 **Rothiemay** Moray
242 C2 **Rothiemurchus Lodge** Highld
256 C4 **Rothienorman** Abers
100 D1 **Rothley** Leics
180 C1 **Rothley** Nthumb
256 B5 **Rothmaise** Abers
142 A2 **Rothwell** Leeds
144 F7 **Rothwell** Lincs
101 H7 **Rothwell** Nhants
142 A2 **Rothwell Haigh** Leeds
153 G5 **Rotsea** E R Yk
234 B2 **Rottal Lodge** Angus
22 F6 **Rottingdean** Br & H
164 C8 **Rottington** Cumb
176 D3 **Roucan** D & G
176 D3 **Roucan Loch Crematorium** D & G
19 H7 **Roud** IoW
121 H7 **Rougham** Norfk
89 H3 **Rougham Green** Suffk
114 E4 **Rough Close** Staffs
40 F3 **Rough Common** Kent
148 E7 **Roughlee** Lancs
243 K1 **Roughpark** Abers
136 D6 **Roughton** Lincs
122 E4 **Roughton** Norfk
97 G4 **Roughton** Shrops
30 F3 **Roughway** Kent
72 B6 **Roundbush** Essex
68 F7 **Round Bush** Herts
70 E4 **Roundbush Green** Essex
68 E3 **Round Green** Luton
15 K1 **Roundham** Somset
150 D8 **Roundhay** Leeds
98 C5 **Rounds Green** Sandw
52 E5 **Round Street** Kent
37 G5 **Roundstreet Common** W Susx
46 E6 **Roundway** Wilts
234 B5 **Roundhill** Angus
15 G4 **Rousdon** Devon
66 C2 **Rousham** Oxon
82 B4 **Rous Lench** Worcs
207 K6 **Routenburn** N Ayrs
153 H7 **Routh** E R Yk
67 J7 **Rout's Green** Bucks
10 F7 **Row** Cnwll
157 G5 **Row** Cumb
166 E4 **Row** Cumb

177 L3 **Rowanburn** D & G
218 E7 **Rowardennan** Stirlg
131 K2 **Rowarth** Derbys
35 H8 **Row Ash** Hants
44 F7 **Rowberrow** Somset
19 G6 **Rowborough** IoW
46 E6 **Rowde** Wilts
12 F3 **Rowden** Devon
126 E5 **Rowen** Conwy
115 K2 **Rowfield** Derbys
178 F6 **Rowfoot** Nthumb
30 C5 **Rowford** Somset
71 H3 **Row Green** Essex
72 F3 **Rowhedge** Essex
37 H4 **Rowhook** W Susx
82 F2 **Rowington** Warwks
132 D5 **Rowland** Derbys
20 B5 **Rowland's Castle** Hants
180 E7 **Rowland's Gill** Gatesd
36 B2 **Rowledge** Surrey
168 E1 **Rowley** Dur
144 B1 **Rowley** E R Yk
95 H2 **Rowley** Shrops
141 J5 **Rowley Hill** Kirk
98 B6 **Rowley Regis** Sandw
98 B6 **Rowley Regis Crematorium** Sandw
62 D2 **Rowlstone** Herefs
37 G3 **Rowly** Surrey
19 K3 **Rowner** Hants
82 B1 **Rowney Green** Worcs
34 E7 **Rownhams** Hants
164 E7 **Rowrah** Cumb
67 K3 **Rowsham** Bucks
132 E6 **Rowsley** Derbys
131 G4 **Rows of Trees** Ches E
48 C1 **Rowstock** Oxon
136 A8 **Rowston** Lincs
133 J6 **Rowthorne** Derbys
129 K6 **Rowton** Ches W
95 J1 **Rowton** Shrops
95 K7 **Rowton** Shrops
113 K7 **Rowton** Wrekin
50 D6 **Row Town** Surrey
201 L7 **Roxburgh** Border
144 A4 **Roxby** N Linc
171 H7 **Roxby** N York
86 C4 **Roxton** Bed
70 F5 **Roxwell** Essex
169 G6 **Royal Oak** Darltn
138 C2 **Royal Oak** Lancs
113 K3 **Royal's Green** Ches E
239 M7 **Roy Bridge** Highld
141 K5 **Roydhouse** Kirk
69 L5 **Roydon** Essex
106 C7 **Roydon** Norfk
120 F7 **Roydon** Norfk
69 L5 **Roydon Hamlet** Essex
142 B1 **Royston** Barns
87 G7 **Royston** Herts
140 D6 **Royton** Oldham
9 e2 **Rozel** Jersey
112 D3 **Ruabon** Wrexhm
224 D5 **Ruaig** Ag & B
4 E6 **Ruan High Lanes** Cnwll
4 E6 **Ruan Lanihorne** Cnwll
3 H7 **Ruan Major** Cnwll
3 J8 **Ruan Minor** Cnwll
63 J3 **Ruardean** Gloucs
63 J4 **Ruardean Hill** Gloucs
63 J4 **Ruardean Woodside** Gloucs
98 C7 **Rubery** Birm
283 c12 **Rubha Ban** W Isls
166 C2 **Ruckcroft** Cumb
80 B7 **Ruckhall** Herefs
40 D8 **Ruckinge** Kent
136 F4 **Ruckland** Lincs
96 C3 **Ruckley** Shrops
161 G1 **Rudby** N York
180 D5 **Rudchester** Nthumb
116 F5 **Ruddington** Notts
63 K5 **Ruddle** Gloucs
5 G4 **Ruddlemoor** Cnwll
63 M3 **Rudford** Gloucs
46 B8 **Rudge** Somset
45 J2 **Rudgeway** S Glos
37 G4 **Rudgwick** W Susx
63 J2 **Rudhall** Herefs
130 D5 **Rudheath** Ches W
130 E5 **Rudheath Woods** Ches E
71 K6 **Rudley Green** Essex
46 B5 **Rudloe** Wilts
43 K4 **Rudry** Caerph
153 H2 **Rudston** E R Yk
131 J8 **Rudyard** Staffs
189 G2 **Ruecastle** Border
138 F4 **Rufford** Lancs
151 H5 **Rufforth** C York
111 K3 **Rug** Denbgs
100 B8 **Rugby** Warwks

115 G7 **Rugeley** Staffs
27 K2 **Ruggaton** Devon
30 C6 **Ruishton** Somset
50 E2 **Ruislip** Gt Lon
267 H5 **Rumbach** Moray
221 J7 **Rumbling Bridge** P & K
107 G7 **Rumburgh** Suffk
168 F4 **Rumby Hill** Dur
10 B8 **Rumford** Cnwll
210 B4 **Rumford** Falk
43 K6 **Rumney** Cardif
30 B6 **Rumwell** Somset
129 L3 **Runcorn** Halton
20 E6 **Runcton** W Susx
104 C2 **Runcton Holme** Norfk
36 C2 **Runfold** Surrey
105 L2 **Runhall** Norfk
107 J1 **Runham** Norfk
107 L2 **Runham** Norfk
29 L6 **Runnington** Somset
71 J6 **Runsell Green** Essex
139 G4 **Runshaw Moor** Lancs
171 J7 **Runswick** N York
233 L2 **Runtaleave** Angus
71 J8 **Runwell** Essex
49 J4 **Ruscombe** Wokham
80 E8 **Rushall** Herefs
106 D6 **Rushall** Norfk
47 H7 **Rushall** Wilts
98 C3 **Rushall** Wsall
89 H3 **Rushbrooke** Suffk
96 C5 **Rushbury** Shrops
69 J1 **Rushden** Herts
85 J2 **Rushden** Nhants
53 K5 **Rushenden** Kent
38 F7 **Rusher's Cross** E Susx
12 B7 **Rushford** Devon
105 J7 **Rushford** Norfk
73 H4 **Rush Green** Essex
52 B2 **Rush Green** Gt Lon
69 G2 **Rush Green** Herts
130 D2 **Rush Green** Warrtn
23 L3 **Rushlake Green** E Susx
107 K6 **Rushmere** Suffk
90 E6 **Rushmere St Andrew** Suffk
36 C3 **Rushmoor** Surrey
79 K3 **Rushock** Herefs
81 K1 **Rushock** Worcs
131 G1 **Rusholme** Manch
130 B7 **Rushton** Ches W
101 J6 **Rushton** Nhants
96 D2 **Rushton** Shrops
131 J7 **Rushton Spencer** Staffs
81 J4 **Rushwick** Worcs
169 H5 **Rushyford** Dur
219 K7 **Ruskie** Stirlg
118 E1 **Ruskington** Lincs
156 E5 **Rusland** Cumb
37 K3 **Rusper** W Susx
63 K5 **Ruspidge** Gloucs
71 H4 **Russell Green** Essex
49 H1 **Russell's Water** Oxon
90 F1 **Russel's Green** Suffk
37 K3 **Russ Hill** Surrey
38 E5 **Rusthall** Kent
21 H6 **Rustington** W Susx
163 G6 **Ruston** N York
153 G3 **Ruston Parva** E R Yk
162 F1 **Ruswarp** N York
96 D5 **Ruthall** Shrops
201 K7 **Rutherford** Border
209 G6 **Rutherglen** S Lans
5 G2 **Ruthernbridge** Cnwll
128 D8 **Ruthin** Denbgs
245 K3 **Ruthrieston** C Aber
267 K6 **Ruthven** Abers
233 L5 **Ruthven** Angus
241 K4 **Ruthven** Highld
4 F3 **Ruthvoes** Cnwll
165 H3 **Ruthwaite** Cumb
176 E5 **Ruthwell** D & G
52 A5 **Ruxley Corner** Gt Lon
63 G3 **Ruxton Green** Herefs
112 F7 **Ruyton-XI-Towns** Shrops
180 B4 **Ryal** Nthumb
15 J3 **Ryall** Dorset
81 K7 **Ryall** Worcs
52 E7 **Ryarsh** Kent
67 G6 **Rycote** Oxon
156 E2 **Rydal** Cumb
19 K5 **Ryde** IoW
25 G3 **Rye** E Susx
113 H5 **Ryebank** Shrops
81 H8 **Rye Cross** Worcs
63 J3 **Ryeford** Herefs
25 G3 **Rye Foreign** E Susx
25 H3 **Rye Harbour** E Susx
145 G3 **Ryehill** E R Yk
49 H5 **Ryeish Green** Wokham
81 H8 **Rye Street** Worcs

102 A1 **Ryhall** Rutlnd
142 B5 **Ryhill** Wakefd
181 K8 **Ryhope** Sundld
133 J6 **Rylah** Derbys
135 K4 **Ryland** Lincs
116 F4 **Rylands** Notts
149 H4 **Rylstone** N York
31 J8 **Ryme Intrinseca** Dorset
151 J7 **Ryther** N York
180 E6 **Ryton** Gatesd
162 D7 **Ryton** N York
97 G3 **Ryton** Shrops
99 L6 **Ryton** Warwks
99 K8 **Ryton-on-Dunsmore** Warwks
180 E6 **Ryton Woodside** Gatesd

**S**

148 D8 **Sabden** Lancs
70 E7 **Sabine's Green** Essex
69 J3 **Sacombe** Herts
69 J3 **Sacombe Green** Herts
169 G1 **Sacriston** Dur
169 J7 **Sadberge** Darltn
194 B4 **Saddell** A & B
100 E5 **Saddington** Leics
120 D8 **Saddle Bow** Norfk
22 D5 **Saddlescombe** W Susx
157 G2 **Sadgill** Cumb
87 L7 **Saffron Walden** Essex
55 H6 **Sageston** Pembks
105 H3 **Saham Hills** Norfk
105 H3 **Saham Toney** Norfk
129 K7 **Saighton** Ches W
213 K5 **St Abbs** Border
212 F6 **St Agnes** Border
4 B5 **St Agnes** Cnwll
68 F5 **St Albans** Herts
4 D5 **St Allen** Cnwll
9 j3 **St Andrew** Guern
223 J4 **St Andrews** Fife
43 H7 **St Andrew's Major** V Glam
15 L4 **St Andrews Well** Dorset
138 C2 **St Anne's** Lancs
187 G7 **St Ann's** D & G
12 A8 **St Ann's Chapel** Cnwll
7 J5 **St Ann's Chapel** Devon
3 K6 **St Anthony** Cnwll
23 L7 **St Anthony's Hill** E Susx
63 G7 **St Arvans** Mons
128 B5 **St Asaph** Denbgs
42 F8 **St Athan** V Glam
9 c3 **St Aubin** Jersey
5 G4 **St Austell** Cnwll
164 C8 **St Bees** Cumb
5 H4 **St Blazey** Cnwll
5 H4 **St Blazey Gate** Cnwll
201 J7 **St Boswells** Border
9 b3 **St Brelade** Jersey
9 b3 **St Brelade's Bay** Jersey
10 D8 **St Breock** Cnwll
10 F7 **St Breward** Cnwll
63 H6 **St Briavels** Gloucs
54 C5 **St Brides** Pembks
42 D6 **St Bride's Major** V Glam
44 E1 **St Brides Netherwent** Mons
43 H6 **St Brides super-Ely** V Glam
44 C3 **St Brides Wentlooge** Newpt
6 E3 **St Budeaux** C Plym
82 D7 **Saintbury** Gloucs
2 C6 **St Buryan** Cnwll
45 M5 **St Catherine** BaNES
217 J5 **St Catherines** A & B
64 B6 **St Chloe** Gloucs
58 A5 **St Clears** Carmth
6 A1 **St Cleer** Cnwll
4 D6 **St Clement** Cnwll
9 e4 **St Clement** Jersey
11 H5 **St Clether** Cnwll
207 G5 **St Colmac** A & B
4 E2 **St Columb Major** Cnwll
4 D2 **St Columb Minor** Cnwll
4 E3 **St Columb Road** Cnwll
269 K4 **St Combs** Abers
106 F6 **St Cross South Elmham** Suffk
235 J2 **St Cyrus** Abers
221 G3 **St David's** P & K
74 B7 **St David's** Pembks
4 B6 **St Day** Cnwll
29 K2 **St Decumans** Somset
4 F3 **St Dennis** Cnwll
62 E1 **St Devereux** Herefs
75 K3 **St Dogmaels** Pembks
75 G6 **St Dogwells** Pembks
6 D1 **St Dominick** Cnwll
42 E8 **St Donats** V Glam
46 E6 **St Edith's Marsh** Wilts
10 D6 **St Endellion** Cnwll
4 E3 **St Enoder** Cnwll

4 D5 **St Erme** Cnwll
6 D3 **St Erney** Cnwll
2 E4 **St Erth** Cnwll
2 F4 **St Erth Praze** Cnwll
10 B8 **St Ervan** Cnwll
4 E1 **St Eval** Cnwll
5 G5 **St Ewe** Cnwll
43 H6 **St Fagans** Cardif
269 K6 **St Fergus** Abers
220 B2 **St Fillans** P & K
55 J6 **St Florence** Pembks
11 G3 **St Gennys** Cnwll
127 K4 **St George** Conwy
44 D6 **St George** N Som
43 H6 **St George's** V Glam
50 D6 **St George's Hill** Surrey
6 D3 **St Germans** Cnwll
27 J7 **St Giles in the Wood** Devon
11 L4 **St Giles-on-the-Heath** Devon
3 K4 **St Gluvia's** Cnwll
78 D1 **St Harmon** Powys
168 F5 **St Helen Auckland** Dur
164 D4 **St Helens** Cumb
24 E5 **St Helens** E Susx
19 L6 **St Helens** IoW
139 G8 **St Helens** St Hel
139 G8 **St Helens Crematorium** St Hel
51 H5 **St Helier** Gt Lon
9 d3 **St Helier** Jersey
2 E5 **St Hilary** Cnwll
42 F7 **St Hilary** V Glam
14 C1 **Saint Hill** Devon
38 B6 **Saint Hill** W Susx
61 K6 **St Illtyd** Blae G
69 G2 **St Ippollitts** Herts
54 D5 **St Ishmael's** Pembks
10 C8 **St Issey** Cnwll
6 C2 **St Ive** Cnwll
87 G1 **St Ives** Cambs
2 E3 **St Ives** Cnwll
17 M2 **St Ives** Dorset
122 F7 **St James** Norfk
84 E3 **St James's End** Nhants
107 G7 **St James South Elmham** Suffk
4 F1 **St Jidgey** Cnwll
6 E4 **St John** Cnwll
9 c1 **St John** Jersey
168 D4 **St Johns** Dur
154 c5 **St John's** IoM
38 E2 **St Johns** Kent
50 C7 **St Johns** Surrey
81 J4 **St Johns** Worcs
27 J5 **St John's Chapel** Devon
167 K3 **St John's Chapel** Dur
103 L1 **St John's Fen End** Norfk
120 C8 **St John's Highway** Norfk
199 G6 **St John's Kirk** S Lans
184 F6 **St John's Town of Dalry** D & G
51 H2 **St John's Wood** Gt Lon
154 e3 **St Jude's** IoM
2 B5 **St Just** Cnwll
3 L4 **St Just-in-Roseland** Cnwll
256 D5 **St Katherines** Abers
3 K6 **St Keverne** Cnwll
10 E7 **St Kew** Cnwll
10 E7 **St Kew Highway** Cnwll
6 A3 **St Keyne** Cnwll
5 H2 **St Lawrence** Cnwll
72 D6 **St Lawrence** Essex
19 J8 **St Lawrence** IoW
9 c2 **St Lawrence** Jersey
41 K2 **St Lawrence** Kent
67 M5 **St Leonards** Bucks
17 M2 **St Leonards** Dorset
24 E5 **St Leonards** E Susx
39 H2 **St Leonard's Street** Kent
2 B6 **St Levan** Cnwll
43 H7 **St Lythans** V Glam
10 E7 **St Mabyn** Cnwll
222 C3 **St Madoes** P & K
79 L8 **St Margarets** Herefs
69 K5 **St Margarets** Herts
41 K6 **St Margaret's at Cliffe** Kent
275 c6 **St Margaret's Hope** Ork
107 G6 **St Margaret South Elmham** Suffk
154 d7 **St Marks** IoM
3 J6 **St Martin** Cnwll
6 B4 **St Martin** Cnwll
9 j3 **St Martin** Guern
9 e2 **St Martin** Jersey
221 L1 **St Martin's** P & K
112 D4 **St Martins** Shrops
112 D4 **St Martin's Moor** Shrops
9 c2 **St Mary** Jersey
34 F1 **St Mary Bourne** Hants
8 D2 **St Marychurch** Torbay
42 F7 **St Mary Church** V Glam
52 A5 **St Mary Cray** Gt Lon
42 E6 **St Mary Hill** V Glam

25 K2 **St Mary in the Marsh** Kent
51 H1 **St Marylebone Crematorium** Gt Lon
275 d5 **St Mary's** Ork
25 K2 **St Mary's Bay** Kent
44 F5 **St Mary's Grove** N Som
53 H4 **St Mary's Hoo** Medway
62 F4 **St Maughans** Mons
62 F4 **St Maughans Green** Mons
3 L4 **St Mawes** Cnwll
4 E2 **St Mawgan** Cnwll
6 D2 **St Mellion** Cnwll
43 K5 **St Mellons** Cardif
10 B7 **St Merryn** Cnwll
5 G4 **St Mewan** Cnwll
4 F6 **St Michael Caerhays** Cnwll
30 D5 **St Michael Church** Somset
4 D6 **St Michael Penkevil** Cnwll
39 M6 **St Michaels** Kent
80 D2 **St Michaels** Worcs
147 J1 **St Michael's on Wyre** Lancs
107 G6 **St Michael South Elmham** Suffk
10 D7 **St Minver** Cnwll
223 J6 **St Monans** Fife
5 L1 **St Neot** Cnwll
86 D3 **St Neots** Cambs
74 E5 **St Nicholas** Pembks
43 H6 **St Nicholas** V Glam
41 J2 **St Nicholas at Wade** Kent
209 L1 **St Ninians** Stirlg
107 J3 **St Olaves** Norfk
73 H4 **St Osyth** Essex
9 b2 **St Ouen** Jersey
63 G2 **St Owens Cross** Herefs
52 A5 **St Pauls Cray** Gt Lon
69 G3 **St Paul's Walden** Herts
9 b2 **St Peter** Jersey
9 k3 **St Peter Port** Guern
9 i3 **St Peter's** Guern
41 L2 **St Peter's** Kent
86 E1 **St Peter's Hill** Cambs
55 G7 **St Petrox** Pembks
5 L2 **St Pinnock** Cnwll
196 D6 **St Quivox** S Ayrs
3 J8 **St Ruan** Cnwll
9 k2 **St Sampson** Guern
9 i3 **St Saviour** Guern
9 d3 **St Saviour** Jersey
4 F4 **St Stephen** Cnwll
6 E3 **St Stephens** Cnwll
11 L5 **St Stephens** Cnwll
10 F6 **St Teath** Cnwll
10 F7 **St Tudy** Cnwll
54 F7 **St Twynnells** Pembks
5 K4 **St Veep** Cnwll
235 G6 **St Vigeans** Angus
5 G2 **St Wenn** Cnwll
63 G2 **St Weonards** Herefs
43 H6 **St y-Nyll** V Glam
7 L7 **Salcombe** Devon
14 D5 **Salcombe Regis** Devon
72 D4 **Salcott-cum-Virley** Essex
130 F2 **Sale** Traffd
137 J4 **Saleby** Lincs
81 L4 **Sale Green** Worcs
24 D2 **Salehurst** E Susx
59 H4 **Salem** Carmth
92 E6 **Salem** Cerdgn
227 H4 **Salen** A & B
237 K7 **Salen** Highld
139 K1 **Salesbury** Lancs
85 H7 **Salford** C Beds
65 L2 **Salford** Oxon
140 B8 **Salford** Salfd
82 C5 **Salford Priors** Warwks
37 L2 **Salfords** Surrey
123 G8 **Salhouse** Norfk
221 J8 **Saline** Fife
33 K5 **Salisbury** Wilts
33 K4 **Salisbury Crematorium** Wilts
166 D3 **Salkeld Dykes** Cumb
122 C6 **Salle** Norfk
136 F5 **Salmonby** Lincs
65 G3 **Salperton** Gloucs
86 B5 **Salph End** Bed
209 L6 **Salsburgh** N Lans
114 F6 **Salt** Staffs
164 E2 **Salta** Cumb
149 L8 **Saltaire** C Brad
6 E3 **Saltash** Cnwll
263 K6 **Saltburn** Highld
170 F6 **Saltburn-by-the-Sea** R & Cl
117 M6 **Saltby** Leics
155 K3 **Saltcoats** Cumb
195 L3 **Saltcoats** N Ayrs
177 G8 **Salt Cotes** Cumb
138 D2 **Saltcotes** Lancs
22 F6 **Saltdean** Br & H
164 C5 **Salterbeck** Cumb
148 F6 **Salterforth** Lancs

130 C6 **Salterswall** Ches W
33 K4 **Salterton** Wilts
137 H1 **Saltfleet** Lincs
137 H2 **Saltfleetby All Saints** Lincs
137 J1 **Saltfleetby St Clement** Lincs
137 H2 **Saltfleetby St Peter** Lincs
45 K5 **Saltford** BaNES
122 B3 **Salthouse** Norfk
98 E5 **Saltley** Birm
44 D2 **Saltmarsh** Newpt
143 K3 **Saltmarshe** E R Yk
129 J6 **Saltney** Flints
162 C6 **Salton** N York
27 H6 **Saltrens** Devon
181 G6 **Saltwell Crematorium** Gatesd
180 E3 **Saltwick** Nthumb
40 F8 **Saltwood** Kent
21 K6 **Salvington** W Susx
81 K3 **Salwarpe** Worcs
15 K3 **Salway Ash** Dorset
82 C3 **Sambourne** Warwks
113 M6 **Sambrook** Wrekin
139 H2 **Samlesbury** Lancs
139 J2 **Samlesbury Bottoms** Lancs
29 K7 **Sampford Arundel** Somset
29 K3 **Sampford Brett** Somset
12 F2 **Sampford Courtenay** Devon
29 K7 **Sampford Moor** Somset
29 J8 **Sampford Peverell** Devon
12 D7 **Sampford Spiney** Devon
275 e3 **Samsonlane** Ork
73 G3 **Samson's Corner** Essex
212 B5 **Samuelston** E Loth
204 C2 **Sanaigmore** A & B
2 C5 **Sancreed** Cnwll
152 D7 **Sancton** E R Yk
31 G2 **Sand** Somset
247 M8 **Sandaig** Highld
165 H3 **Sandale** Cumb
142 A4 **Sandal Magna** Wakefd
236 F4 **Sandavore** Highld
130 E7 **Sandbach** Ches E
207 K3 **Sandbank** A & B
17 K5 **Sandbanks** Poole
267 L3 **Sandend** Abers
51 J6 **Sanderstead** Gt Lon
167 G7 **Sandford** Cumb
13 J2 **Sandford** Devon
17 H4 **Sandford** Dorset
18 B3 **Sandford** Hants
19 J7 **Sandford** IoW
44 E7 **Sandford** N Som
197 L2 **Sandford** S Lans
112 E6 **Sandford** Shrops
113 J5 **Sandford** Shrops
66 D6 **Sandford-on-Thames** Oxon
31 K6 **Sandford Orcas** Dorset
66 B2 **Sandford St Martin** Oxon
41 G8 **Sandgate** Kent
269 H3 **Sandhaven** Abers
172 D5 **Sandhead** D & G
142 C8 **Sandhill** Rothm
16 B2 **Sandhills** Dorset
31 L8 **Sandhills** Dorset
150 E7 **Sand Hills** Leeds
66 E5 **Sandhills** Oxon
36 D3 **Sandhills** Surrey
180 A5 **Sandhoe** Nthumb
216 F7 **Sandhole** A & B
152 B8 **Sand Hole** E R Yk
143 L2 **Sandholme** E R Yk
119 K4 **Sandholme** Lincs
49 K6 **Sandhurst** Br For
64 B2 **Sandhurst** Gloucs
39 K7 **Sandhurst** Kent
24 E2 **Sandhurst Cross** Kent
151 L4 **Sand Hutton** N York
160 E6 **Sandhutton** N York
116 E4 **Sandiacre** Derbys
137 K3 **Sandilands** Lincs
130 B5 **Sandiway** Ches W
33 K7 **Sandleheath** Hants
66 C6 **Sandleigh** Oxon
32 C6 **Sandley** Dorset
53 G7 **Sandling** Kent
130 F6 **Sandlow Green** Ches E
281 c5 **Sandness** Shet
71 H6 **Sandon** Essex
87 G8 **Sandon** Herts
114 E5 **Sandon** Staffs
114 E6 **Sandon Bank** Staffs
19 K6 **Sandown** IoW
6 A3 **Sandplace** Cnwll
68 F5 **Sandridge** Herts
46 D6 **Sandridge** Wilts
120 F5 **Sandringham** Norfk
67 K8 **Sands** Bucks
171 K8 **Sandsend** N York
156 B6 **Sand Side** Cumb
157 G6 **Sandside** Cumb

| | | |
|---|---|---|
| 143 J6 | **Sandtoft** N Linc | |
| 39 M3 | **Sandway** Kent | |
| 41 K4 | **Sandwich** Kent | |
| 166 A6 | **Sandwick** Cumb | |
| 281 e8 | **Sandwick** Shet | |
| 282 g3 | **Sandwick** W Isls | |
| 164 C7 | **Sandwith** Cumb | |
| 164 C7 | **Sandwith Newtown** Cumb | |
| 86 D5 | **Sandy** C Beds | |
| 136 E8 | **Sandy Bank** Lincs | |
| 129 H6 | **Sandycroft** Flints | |
| 23 K3 | **Sandy Cross** E Susx | |
| 80 F4 | **Sandy Cross** Herefs | |
| 187 J7 | **Sandyford** D & G | |
| 13 K7 | **Sandygate** Devon | |
| 154 e3 | **Sandygate** IoM | |
| 54 D5 | **Sandy Haven** Pembks | |
| 147 H3 | **Sandylands** Lancs | |
| 149 K8 | **Sandy Lane** C Brad | |
| 113 M4 | **Sandylane** Staffs | |
| 57 G7 | **Sandylane** Swans | |
| 46 D5 | **Sandy Lane** Wilts | |
| 112 F3 | **Sandy Lane** Wrexhm | |
| 13 G4 | **Sandy Park** Devon | |
| 177 L5 | **Sandysike** Cumb | |
| 63 G2 | **Sandyway** Herefs | |
| 277 G3 | **Sangobeg** Highld | |
| 276 F3 | **Sangomore** Highld | |
| 130 B2 | **Sankey Bridges** Warrtn | |
| 81 H2 | **Sankyn's Green** Worcs | |
| 236 E6 | **Sanna Bay** Highld | |
| 282 g3 | **Sanndabhaig** W Isls | |
| 195 G2 | **Sannox** N Ayrs | |
| 185 K1 | **Sanquhar** D & G | |
| 155 K2 | **Santon** Cumb | |
| 154 d7 | **Santon** IoM | |
| 155 K2 | **Santon Bridge** Cumb | |
| 105 G6 | **Santon Downham** Suffk | |
| 100 B5 | **Sapcote** Leics | |
| 81 G2 | **Sapey Common** Herefs | |
| 105 J8 | **Sapiston** Suffk | |
| 102 E8 | **Sapley** Cambs | |
| 115 K4 | **Sapperton** Derbys | |
| 64 D6 | **Sapperton** Gloucs | |
| 118 D5 | **Sapperton** Lincs | |
| 119 K6 | **Saracen's Head** Lincs | |
| 280 D7 | **Sarclet** Highld | |
| 19 H2 | **Sarisbury** Hants | |
| 42 D5 | **Sarn** Brdgnd | |
| 108 D5 | **Sarn** Gwynd | |
| 93 L4 | **Sarn** Powys | |
| 94 F5 | **Sarn** Powys | |
| 58 B5 | **Sarnau** Carmth | |
| 76 B5 | **Sarnau** Cerdgn | |
| 111 J4 | **Sarnau** Gwynd | |
| 78 E8 | **Sarnau** Powys | |
| 112 C8 | **Sarnau** Powys | |
| 108 E6 | **Sarn Bach** Gwynd | |
| 79 L5 | **Sarnesfield** Herefs | |
| 112 D7 | **Sarn-wen** Powys | |
| 59 H6 | **Saron** Carmth | |
| 76 C7 | **Saron** Carmth | |
| 125 H7 | **Saron** Gwynd | |
| 125 J6 | **Saron** Gwynd | |
| 68 D7 | **Sarratt** Herts | |
| 41 H2 | **Sarre** Kent | |
| 65 L3 | **Sarsden** Oxon | |
| 34 C2 | **Sarson** Hants | |
| 168 E2 | **Satley** Dur | |
| 41 H7 | **Satmar** Kent | |
| 159 G3 | **Satron** N York | |
| 28 B6 | **Satterleigh** Devon | |
| 156 D4 | **Satterthwaite** Cumb | |
| 49 H2 | **Satwell** Oxon | |
| 244 F1 | **Sauchen** Abers | |
| 233 J8 | **Saucher** P & K | |
| 235 G2 | **Sauchieburn** Abers | |
| 63 L5 | **Saul** Gloucs | |
| 134 F2 | **Saundby** Notts | |
| 55 K6 | **Saundersfoot** Pembks | |
| 67 J6 | **Saunderton** Bucks | |
| 27 H3 | **Saunton** Devon | |
| 37 G6 | **Sausthorpe** Lincs | |
| 4 C6 | **Saveock** Cnwll | |
| 14 F4 | **Saverley Green** Staffs | |
| 41 K4 | **Savile Town** Kirk | |
| 83 L2 | **Sawbridge** Warwks | |
| 70 C4 | **Sawbridgeworth** Herts | |
| 63 G5 | **Sawdon** N York | |
| 16 D5 | **Sawley** Derbys | |
| 48 D6 | **Sawley** Lancs | |
| 50 C2 | **Sawley** N York | |
| 87 K5 | **Sawston** Cambs | |
| 102 D6 | **Sawtry** Cambs | |
| 17 L7 | **Saxby** Leics | |
| 35 K3 | **Saxby** Lincs | |
| 44 C4 | **Saxby All Saints** N Linc | |
| 17 J7 | **Saxelbye** Leics | |
| 90 C3 | **Saxham Street** Suffk | |
| 135 H4 | **Saxilby** Lincs | |
| 122 A4 | **Saxlingham** Norfk | |
| 106 E4 | **Saxlingham Green** Norfk | |
| 106 E4 | **Saxlingham Nethergate** Norfk | |
| 106 E4 | **Saxlingham Thorpe** Norfk | |
| 91 J3 | **Saxmundham** Suffk | |
| 117 H3 | **Saxondale** Notts | |
| 88 D3 | **Saxon Street** Cambs | |
| 91 G2 | **Saxtead** Suffk | |
| 90 F2 | **Saxtead Green** Suffk | |
| 90 F2 | **Saxtead Little Green** Suffk | |
| 122 C5 | **Saxthorpe** Norfk | |
| 151 G8 | **Saxton** N York | |
| 22 D4 | **Sayers Common** W Susx | |
| 161 L8 | **Scackleton** N York | |
| 134 D2 | **Scaftworth** Notts | |
| 152 C1 | **Scagglethorpe** N York | |
| 214 D5 | **Scalasaig** Ag & B | |
| 143 L2 | **Scalby** E R Yk | |
| 163 H4 | **Scalby** N York | |
| 85 L4 | **Scald End** Bed | |
| 84 E1 | **Scaldwell** Nhants | |
| 178 B6 | **Scaleby** Cumb | |
| 178 B6 | **Scalebyhill** Cumb | |
| 166 E2 | **Scale Houses** Cumb | |
| 146 E2 | **Scales** Cumb | |
| 165 K5 | **Scales** Cumb | |
| 166 B1 | **Scalesceugh** Cumb | |
| 117 H6 | **Scalford** Leics | |
| 171 H7 | **Scaling** N York | |
| 171 H8 | **Scaling Dam** R & Cl | |
| 281 d7 | **Scalloway** Shet | |
| 136 E4 | **Scamblesby** Lincs | |
| 141 G4 | **Scammonden** Kirk | |
| 228 C1 | **Scamodale** Highld | |
| 162 F7 | **Scampston** N York | |
| 135 J4 | **Scampton** Lincs | |
| 251 H4 | **Scaniport** Highld | |
| 141 G4 | **Scapegoat Hill** Kirk | |
| 163 J5 | **Scarborough** N York | |
| 4 F4 | **Scarcewater** Cnwll | |
| 133 K6 | **Scarcliffe** Derbys | |
| 150 E7 | **Scarcroft** Leeds | |
| 280 C2 | **Scarfskerry** Highld | |
| 168 D8 | **Scargill** Dur | |
| 224 D6 | **Scarinish** Ag & B | |
| 130 D5 | **Scarisbrick** Lancs | |
| 165 H4 | **Scarness** Cumb | |
| 105 J1 | **Scarning** Norfk | |
| 117 J3 | **Scarrington** Notts | |
| 138 E6 | **Scarth Hill** Lancs | |
| 151 G8 | **Scarthingwell** N York | |
| 145 H6 | **Scartho** NE Lin | |
| 144 B6 | **Scawby** N Linc | |
| 142 E6 | **Scawsby** Donc | |
| 142 E6 | **Scawthorpe** Donc | |
| 161 J6 | **Scawton** N York | |
| 22 F3 | **Scayne's Hill** W Susx | |
| 61 H2 | **Scethrog** Powys | |
| 131 G8 | **Scholar Green** Ches E | |
| 141 H1 | **Scholemoor Crematorium** C Brad | |
| 141 J3 | **Scholes** Kirk | |
| 141 J6 | **Scholes** Kirk | |
| 150 E8 | **Scholes** Leeds | |
| 142 B8 | **Scholes** Rothm | |
| 139 J6 | **Scholes** Wigan | |
| 142 B3 | **Scholey Hill** Leeds | |
| 169 H6 | **School Aycliffe** Dur | |
| 141 H1 | **School Green** C Brad | |
| 130 C6 | **School Green** Ches W | |
| 49 H5 | **Schoolgreen** Wokham | |
| 15 J2 | **School House** Dorset | |
| 141 L5 | **Scissett** Kirk | |
| 74 F5 | **Scleddau** Pembks | |
| 134 C4 | **Scofton** Notts | |
| 106 C7 | **Scole** Norfk | |
| 221 L2 | **Scone** P & K | |
| 247 H2 | **Sconser** Highld | |
| 222 F8 | **Scoonie** Fife | |
| 135 M8 | **Scopwick** Lincs | |
| 261 G1 | **Scoraig** Highld | |
| 152 F6 | **Scorborough** E R Yk | |
| 4 B6 | **Scorrier** Cnwll | |
| 7 K1 | **Scorriton** Devon | |
| 147 K6 | **Scorton** Lancs | |
| 160 C3 | **Scorton** N York | |
| 122 F7 | **Sco Ruston** Norfk | |
| 178 B7 | **Scotby** Cumb | |
| 160 B2 | **Scotch Corner** N York | |
| 147 J4 | **Scotforth** Lancs | |
| 114 C2 | **Scot Hay** Staffs | |
| 135 L4 | **Scothern** Lincs | |
| 118 C5 | **Scotland** Lincs | |
| 181 G2 | **Scotland Gate** Nthumb | |
| 222 C7 | **Scotlandwell** P & K | |
| 139 J6 | **Scot Lane End** Bolton | |
| 279 K5 | **Scotscalder Station** Highld | |
| 177 L4 | **Scotsdike** Cumb | |
| 180 C2 | **Scot's Gap** Nthumb | |
| 255 L7 | **Scotsmill** Abers | |
| 208 F5 | **Scotstoun** C Glas | |
| 180 F6 | **Scotswood** N u Ty | |
| 143 M7 | **Scotter** Lincs | |
| 143 L7 | **Scotterthorpe** Lincs | |
| 118 D7 | **Scottlethorpe** Lincs | |
| 143 M7 | **Scotton** Lincs | |
| 150 D4 | **Scotton** N York | |
| 160 B3 | **Scotton** N York | |
| 122 F6 | **Scottow** Norfk | |
| 118 D4 | **Scott Willoughby** Lincs | |
| 105 K3 | **Scoulton** Norfk | |
| 115 H5 | **Scounslow Green** Staffs | |
| 276 B7 | **Scourie** Highld | |
| 276 A7 | **Scourie More** Highld | |
| 281 d8 | **Scousburgh** Shet | |
| 140 E6 | **Scouthead** Oldham | |
| 279 K2 | **Scrabster** Highld | |
| 189 J3 | **Scraesburgh** Border | |
| 136 F6 | **Scrafield** Lincs | |
| 190 D4 | **Scrainwood** Nthumb | |
| 119 L3 | **Scrane End** Lincs | |
| 100 E2 | **Scraptoft** Leics | |
| 123 K8 | **Scratby** Norfk | |
| 151 M4 | **Scrayingham** N York | |
| 24 D3 | **Scrays** E Susx | |
| 118 E3 | **Scredington** Lincs | |
| 137 H6 | **Scremby** Lincs | |
| 202 F3 | **Scremerston** Nthumb | |
| 117 J3 | **Screveton** Notts | |
| 136 E6 | **Scrivelsby** Lincs | |
| 150 E4 | **Scriven** N York | |
| 134 C2 | **Scrooby** Notts | |
| 115 K5 | **Scropton** Derbys | |
| 136 D8 | **Scrub Hill** Lincs | |
| 233 K4 | **Scruschloch** Angus | |
| 160 D4 | **Scruton** N York | |
| 178 B4 | **Scuggate** Cumb | |
| 277 L4 | **Scullomie** Highld | |
| 121 K5 | **Sculthorpe** Norfk | |
| 143 M5 | **Scunthorpe** N Linc | |
| 56 E7 | **Scurlage** Swans | |
| 30 E8 | **Sea** Somset | |
| 15 K1 | **Seaborough** Dorset | |
| 114 C3 | **Seabridge** Staffs | |
| 41 G8 | **Seabrook** Kent | |
| 181 K6 | **Seaburn** Sundld | |
| 129 H2 | **Seacombe** Wirral | |
| 150 E8 | **Seacroft** Leeds | |
| 137 L7 | **Seacroft** Lincs | |
| 119 K4 | **Seadyke** Lincs | |
| 259 H8 | **Seafield** Highld | |
| 210 D6 | **Seafield** W Loth | |
| 211 J4 | **Seafield Crematorium** C Edin | |
| 23 H7 | **Seaford** E Susx | |
| 138 C8 | **Seaforth** Sefton | |
| 117 G8 | **Seagrave** Leics | |
| 46 D3 | **Seagry Heath** Wilts | |
| 169 L1 | **Seaham** Dur | |
| 203 L6 | **Seahouses** Nthumb | |
| 38 E2 | **Seal** Kent | |
| 36 D1 | **Seale** Surrey | |
| 163 J6 | **Seamer** N York | |
| 170 C8 | **Seamer** N York | |
| 195 K2 | **Seamill** N Ayrs | |
| 123 J6 | **Sea Palling** Norfk | |
| 144 D6 | **Searby** Lincs | |
| 40 E2 | **Seasalter** Kent | |
| 155 J2 | **Seascale** Cumb | |
| 156 B3 | **Seathwaite** Cumb | |
| 165 H8 | **Seathwaite** Cumb | |
| 156 E6 | **Seatle** Cumb | |
| 165 H7 | **Seatoller** Cumb | |
| 6 C4 | **Seaton** Cnwll | |
| 164 D4 | **Seaton** Cumb | |
| 14 F4 | **Seaton** Devon | |
| 169 L1 | **Seaton** Dur | |
| 153 J6 | **Seaton** E R Yk | |
| 41 H4 | **Seaton** Kent | |
| 181 H3 | **Seaton** Nthumb | |
| 101 K4 | **Seaton** Rutlnd | |
| 181 G4 | **Seaton Burn** N Tyne | |
| 170 C5 | **Seaton Carew** Hartpl | |
| 181 H4 | **Seaton Delaval** Nthumb | |
| 152 B7 | **Seaton Ross** E R Yk | |
| 181 H3 | **Seaton Sluice** Nthumb | |
| 15 K4 | **Seatown** Dorset | |
| 161 J3 | **Seave Green** N York | |
| 19 L5 | **Seaview** IoW | |
| 177 G8 | **Seaville** Cumb | |
| 30 F7 | **Seavington St Mary** Somset | |
| 30 F7 | **Seavington St Michael** Somset | |
| 62 C7 | **Sebastopol** Torfn | |
| 165 K2 | **Sebergham** Cumb | |
| 99 H2 | **Seckington** Warwks | |
| 157 L4 | **Sedbergh** Cumb | |
| 63 H8 | **Sedbury** Gloucs | |
| 158 F4 | **Sedbusk** N York | |
| 82 B7 | **Sedgeberrow** Worcs | |
| 117 M4 | **Sedgebrook** Lincs | |
| 104 D6 | **Sedge Fen** Suffk | |
| 169 K5 | **Sedgefield** Dur | |
| 120 F4 | **Sedgeford** Norfk | |
| 32 E5 | **Sedgehill** Wilts | |
| 97 L4 | **Sedgley** Dudley | |
| 140 B7 | **Sedgley Park** Bury | |
| 157 H5 | **Sedgwick** Cumb | |
| 24 E4 | **Sedlescombe** E Susx | |
| 67 J5 | **Sedrup** Bucks | |
| 40 B4 | **Seed** Kent | |
| 46 D6 | **Seend** Wilts | |
| 46 D6 | **Seend Cleeve** Wilts | |
| 68 B8 | **Seer Green** Bucks | |
| 107 G4 | **Seething** Norfk | |
| 138 D7 | **Sefton** Sefton | |
| 138 D7 | **Sefton Town** Sefton | |
| 181 G4 | **Seghill** Nthumb | |
| 114 D6 | **Seighford** Staffs | |
| 125 K6 | **Seion** Gwynd | |
| 97 J4 | **Seisdon** Staffs | |
| 112 C5 | **Selattyn** Shrops | |
| 35 M4 | **Selborne** Hants | |
| 142 F1 | **Selby** N York | |
| 20 F3 | **Selham** W Susx | |
| 51 J5 | **Selhurst** Gt Lon | |
| 201 G7 | **Selkirk** Border | |
| 63 H2 | **Sellack** Herefs | |
| 281 e2 | **Sellafirth** Shet | |
| 2 C5 | **Sellan** Cnwll | |
| 30 B7 | **Sellick's Green** Somset | |
| 40 E7 | **Sellindge** Kent | |
| 40 D4 | **Selling** Kent | |
| 46 D6 | **Sells Green** Wilts | |
| 98 D7 | **Selly Oak** Birm | |
| 23 H6 | **Selmeston** E Susx | |
| 51 K6 | **Selsdon** Gt Lon | |
| 64 B6 | **Selsey** Gloucs | |
| 20 D8 | **Selsey** W Susx | |
| 38 A6 | **Selsfield Common** W Susx | |
| 157 H3 | **Selside** Cumb | |
| 158 D7 | **Selside** N York | |
| 41 H6 | **Selsted** Kent | |
| 116 D1 | **Selston** Notts | |
| 29 G2 | **Selworthy** Somset | |
| 89 K6 | **Semer** Suffk | |
| 46 C6 | **Semington** Wilts | |
| 32 E5 | **Semley** Wilts | |
| 118 F5 | **Sempringham** Lincs | |
| 50 C7 | **Send** Surrey | |
| 50 D7 | **Send Marsh** Surrey | |
| 43 H3 | **Senghenydd** Caerph | |
| 2 B6 | **Sennen** Cnwll | |
| 2 B6 | **Sennen Cove** Cnwll | |
| 60 D2 | **Sennybridge** Powys | |
| 134 C2 | **Serlby** Notts | |
| 161 G7 | **Sessay** N York | |
| 104 C1 | **Setchey** Norfk | |
| 18 D3 | **Setley** Hants | |
| 211 M4 | **Seton Mains** E Loth | |
| 148 E3 | **Settle** N York | |
| 152 C2 | **Settrington** N York | |
| 29 L4 | **Seven Ash** Somset | |
| 64 F3 | **Sevenhampton** Gloucs | |
| 47 J1 | **Sevenhampton** Swindn | |
| 51 M2 | **Seven Kings** Gt Lon | |
| 38 E2 | **Sevenoaks** Kent | |
| 38 E3 | **Sevenoaks Weald** Kent | |
| 60 B5 | **Seven Sisters** Neath | |
| 64 D4 | **Seven Springs** Gloucs | |
| 72 D2 | **Seven Star Green** Essex | |
| 45 G2 | **Severn Beach** S Glos | |
| 81 K6 | **Severn Stoke** Worcs | |
| 86 B4 | **Sevick End** Bed | |
| 40 D7 | **Sevington** Kent | |
| 88 B7 | **Sewards End** Essex | |
| 69 K7 | **Sewardstonebury** Essex | |
| 68 C3 | **Sewell** C Beds | |
| 153 K2 | **Sewerby** E R Yk | |
| 3 H5 | **Seworgan** Cnwll | |
| 118 A7 | **Sewstern** Leics | |
| 161 G2 | **Sexhow** N York | |
| 65 H1 | **Sezincote** Gloucs | |
| 282 h1 | **Sgiogarstaigh** W Isls | |
| 67 G5 | **Shabbington** Bucks | |
| 97 J2 | **Shackerley** Shrops | |
| 99 K2 | **Shackerstone** Leics | |
| 116 C5 | **Shacklecross** Derbys | |
| 36 D2 | **Shackleford** Surrey | |
| 140 D3 | **Shade** Calder | |
| 282 g1 | **Shader** W Isls | |
| 169 J3 | **Shadforth** Dur | |
| 107 J6 | **Shadingfield** Suffk | |
| 40 C7 | **Shadoxhurst** Kent | |
| 150 D7 | **Shadwell** Leeds | |
| 105 J6 | **Shadwell** Norfk | |
| 87 H7 | **Shaftenhoe End** Herts | |
| 32 E6 | **Shaftesbury** Dorset | |
| 142 F6 | **Shaftholme** Donc | |
| 142 B5 | **Shafton** Barns | |
| 142 B5 | **Shafton Two Gates** Barns | |

139 K7 **Shakerley** Wigan
47 L6 **Shalbourne** Wilts
18 F6 **Shalcombe** IoW
35 L3 **Shalden** Hants
35 L2 **Shalden Green** Hants
13 L8 **Shaldon** Devon
18 F6 **Shalfleet** IoW
71 H1 **Shalford** Essex
36 F2 **Shalford** Surrey
71 H2 **Shalford Green** Essex
114 D5 **Shallowford** Staffs
40 E4 **Shalmsford Street** Kent
84 C7 **Shalstone** Bucks
36 F2 **Shamley Green** Surrey
234 D3 **Shandford** Angus
207 L2 **Shandon** Ag & B
264 D5 **Shandwick** Highld
100 F4 **Shangton** Leics
181 G3 **Shankhouse** Nthumb
19 K7 **Shanklin** IoW
166 D7 **Shap** Cumb
17 H2 **Shapwick** Dorset
30 F3 **Shapwick** Somset
98 F5 **Shard End** Birm
116 D5 **Shardlow** Derbys
97 L2 **Shareshill** Staffs
142 B4 **Sharlston** Wakefd
142 B4 **Sharlston Common** Wakefd
98 E7 **Sharman's Cross** Solhll
53 G4 **Sharnal Street** Medway
85 K3 **Sharnbrook** Bed
140 C3 **Sharneyford** Lancs
100 B5 **Sharnford** Leics
16 D1 **Sharnhill Green** Dorset
139 G1 **Sharoe Green** Lancs
150 D2 **Sharow** N York
68 D1 **Sharpenhoe** C Beds
190 D5 **Sharperton** Nthumb
123 H7 **Sharp Green** Norfk
63 K6 **Sharpness** Gloucs
38 B6 **Sharpthorne** W Susx
11 J7 **Sharptor** Cnwll
81 L2 **Sharpway Gate** Worcs
122 A4 **Sharrington** Norfk
97 H7 **Shatterford** Worcs
41 J4 **Shatterling** Kent
132 D3 **Shatton** Derbys
7 G2 **Shaugh Prior** Devon
15 J3 **Shave Cross** Dorset
113 M1 **Shavington** Ches E
140 F1 **Shaw** C Brad
140 D6 **Shaw** Oldham
47 G2 **Shaw** Swindn
48 C5 **Shaw** W Berk
46 C6 **Shaw** Wilts
113 L8 **Shawbirch** Wrekin
282 f2 **Shawbost** W Isls
113 J7 **Shawbury** Shrops
140 D5 **Shawclough** Rochdl
63 K2 **Shaw Common** Gloucs
190 F3 **Shawdon Hill** Nthumb
100 C7 **Shawell** Leics
34 F6 **Shawford** Hants
140 D4 **Shawforth** Lancs
69 J1 **Shaw Green** Herts
139 G4 **Shaw Green** Lancs
150 C3 **Shaw Green** N York
185 L7 **Shawhead** D & G
150 C3 **Shaw Mills** N York
198 C3 **Shawsburn** S Lans
32 E3 **Shear Cross** Wilts
176 D5 **Shearington** D & G
100 D5 **Shearsby** Leics
30 D5 **Shearston** Somset
12 B1 **Shebbear** Devon
114 B6 **Shebdon** Staffs
279 H3 **Shebster** Highld
208 F7 **Sheddens** E Rens
35 H8 **Shedfield** Hants
132 B7 **Sheen** Staffs
133 G5 **Sheepbridge** Derbys
180 E7 **Sheep Hill** Dur
141 J4 **Sheepridge** Kirk
141 M1 **Sheepscar** Leeds
64 C5 **Sheepscombe** Gloucs
7 G1 **Sheepstor** Devon
12 C1 **Sheepwash** Devon
181 G2 **Sheepwash** Nthumb
45 G4 **Sheepway** N Som
99 J3 **Sheepy Magna** Leics
99 J3 **Sheepy Parva** Leics
70 D4 **Sheering** Essex
53 K4 **Sheerness** Kent
50 D6 **Sheerwater** Surrey
36 A6 **Sheet** Hants
2 D5 **Sheffield** Cnwll
133 G2 **Sheffield** Sheff
49 G5 **Sheffield Bottom** W Berk
133 G3 **Sheffield City Road Crematorium** Sheff

22 F2 **Sheffield Green** E Susx
86 C7 **Shefford** C Beds
276 B4 **Sheigra** Highld
96 E3 **Sheinton** Shrops
95 K7 **Shelderton** Shrops
98 F6 **Sheldon** Birm
132 C6 **Sheldon** Derbys
14 D1 **Sheldon** Devon
40 D4 **Sheldwich** Kent
40 D4 **Sheldwich Lees** Kent
141 H2 **Shelf** Calder
106 C6 **Shelfanger** Norfk
82 D3 **Shelfield** Warwks
98 C3 **Shelfield** Wsall
82 D3 **Shelfield Green** Warwks
117 H3 **Shelford** Notts
99 L5 **Shelford** Warwks
202 D4 **Shellacres** Nthumb
70 E6 **Shelley** Essex
141 K5 **Shelley** Kirk
89 L7 **Shelley** Suffk
141 K5 **Shelley Far Bank** Kirk
65 L8 **Shellingford** Oxon
70 F5 **Shellow Bowells** Essex
81 G3 **Shelsley Beauchamp** Worcs
81 G3 **Shelsley Walsh** Worcs
85 K2 **Shelton** Bed
106 E5 **Shelton** Norfk
117 K3 **Shelton** Notts
95 L1 **Shelton** Shrops
106 E5 **Shelton Green** Norfk
116 C5 **Shelton Lock** C Derb
114 C4 **Shelton Under Harley** Staffs
95 H4 **Shelve** Shrops
80 C6 **Shelwick** Herefs
70 F8 **Shenfield** Essex
83 J6 **Shenington** Oxon
67 F7 **Shenley** Herts
85 G8 **Shenley Brook End** M Keyn
68 F6 **Shenleybury** Herts
85 G7 **Shenley Church End** M Keyn
79 M7 **Shenmore** Herefs
173 J2 **Shennanton** D & G
98 E3 **Shenstone** Staffs
97 J8 **Shenstone** Worcs
98 E3 **Shenstone Woodend** Staffs
99 K3 **Shenton** Leics
102 F1 **Shepeau Stow** Lincs
69 H2 **Shephall** Herts
51 G3 **Shepherd's Bush** Gt Lon
49 H2 **Shepherd's Green** Oxon
63 L6 **Shepherds Patch** Gloucs
41 H5 **Shepherdswell** Kent
141 J6 **Shepley** Kirk
63 J8 **Shepperdine** S Glos
50 D5 **Shepperton** Surrey
50 D5 **Shepperton Green** Surrey
87 H5 **Shepreth** Cambs
116 E7 **Shepshed** Leics
30 F7 **Shepton Beauchamp** Somset
31 K2 **Shepton Mallet** Somset
31 L4 **Shepton Montague** Somset
39 J3 **Shepway** Kent
170 B4 **Sheraton** Dur
31 L7 **Sherborne** Dorset
65 H4 **Sherborne** Gloucs
45 H7 **Sherborne** Somset
48 F7 **Sherborne St John** Hants
83 G3 **Sherbourne** Warwks
169 J2 **Sherburn** Dur
163 G7 **Sherburn** N York
169 J2 **Sherburn Hill** Dur
142 D1 **Sherburn in Elmet** N York
37 G1 **Shere** Surrey
121 K5 **Shereford** Norfk
34 C6 **Sherfield English** Hants
49 G7 **Sherfield on Loddon** Hants
140 B3 **Sherfin** Lancs
8 A6 **Sherford** Devon
17 H4 **Sherford** Dorset
97 G1 **Sheriffhales** Shrops
151 K3 **Sheriff Hutton** N York
122 D3 **Sheringham** Norfk
85 H6 **Sherington** M Keyn
22 B3 **Shermanbury** W Susx
120 F5 **Shernborne** Norfk
33 G3 **Sherrington** Wilts
46 B2 **Sherston** Wilts
116 F3 **Sherwood** C Nott
134 D6 **Sherwood Forest Crematorium** Notts
209 H6 **Shettleston** C Glas
139 H6 **Shevington** Wigan
139 H5 **Shevington Moor** Wigan
139 G6 **Shevington Vale** Wigan
6 D4 **Sheviock** Cnwll
141 H2 **Shibden Head** C Brad
19 H6 **Shide** IoW
202 C5 **Shidlaw** Nthumb
248 F7 **Shiel Bridge** Highld

248 C1 **Shieldaig** Highld
176 D2 **Shieldhill** D & G
210 B4 **Shieldhill** Falk
199 G5 **Shieldhill House Hotel** S Lans
209 K7 **Shields** N Lans
237 J6 **Shielfoot** Highld
234 C4 **Shielhill** Angus
207 L4 **Shielhill** Inver
66 A6 **Shifford** Oxon
97 G2 **Shifnal** Shrops
191 J4 **Shilbottle** Nthumb
169 G5 **Shildon** Dur
208 D7 **Shillford** E Rens
29 H6 **Shillingford** Devon
66 E8 **Shillingford** Oxon
13 L4 **Shillingford Abbot** Devon
13 L5 **Shillingford St George** Devon
32 D8 **Shillingstone** Dorset
86 C8 **Shillington** C Beds
190 B4 **Shillmoor** Nthumb
65 K5 **Shilton** Oxon
99 L6 **Shilton** Warwks
106 D6 **Shimpling** Norfk
89 H5 **Shimpling** Suffk
89 H4 **Shimpling Street** Suffk
169 H3 **Shincliffe** Dur
181 H8 **Shiney Row** Sundld
49 H5 **Shinfield** Wokham
86 F6 **Shingay** Cambs
91 J6 **Shingle Street** Suffk
8 B2 **Shinnersbridge** Devon
272 D5 **Shinness** Highld
38 F3 **Shipbourne** Kent
105 J2 **Shipdham** Norfk
44 E7 **Shipham** Somset
8 D2 **Shiphay** Torbay
49 J3 **Shiplake** Oxon
49 H3 **Shiplake Row** Oxon
44 D7 **Shiplate** N Som
149 L8 **Shipley** C Brad
116 D3 **Shipley** Derbys
97 H4 **Shipley** Shrops
37 H6 **Shipley** W Susx
37 M3 **Shipley Bridge** Surrey
40 C7 **Shipmeadow** Suffk
107 H5 **Shipmeadow** Suffk
104 C6 **Shippea Hill Station** Cambs
66 C7 **Shippon** Oxon
83 G7 **Shipston on Stour** Warwks
67 J2 **Shipton** Bucks
64 F3 **Shipton** Gloucs
151 H4 **Shipton** N York
96 D5 **Shipton** Shrops
34 B2 **Shipton Bellinger** Hants
15 L4 **Shipton Gorge** Dorset
20 C7 **Shipton Green** W Susx
46 C1 **Shipton Moyne** Gloucs
66 C4 **Shipton-on-Cherwell** Oxon
152 C7 **Shiptonthorpe** E R Yk
65 L3 **Shipton-under-Wychwood** Oxon
67 J7 **Shirburn** Oxon
138 D5 **Shirdley Hill** Lancs
166 E4 **Shire** Cumb
133 K6 **Shirebrook** Derbys
133 G1 **Shiregreen** Sheff
45 G4 **Shirehampton** Bristl
181 H4 **Shiremoor** N Tyne
62 F8 **Shirenewton** Mons
98 D3 **Shire Oak** Wsall
133 L3 **Shireoaks** Notts
40 B8 **Shirkoak** Kent
133 H8 **Shirland** Derbys
96 E4 **Shirlett** Shrops
34 E8 **Shirley** C Sotn
115 L3 **Shirley** Derbys
51 K6 **Shirley** Gt Lon
98 E7 **Shirley** Solhll
80 A3 **Shirl Heath** Herefs
35 H8 **Shirrell Heath** Hants
206 D2 **Shirvan** Ag & B
27 L3 **Shirwell** Devon
194 E5 **Shiskine** N Ayrs
168 C3 **Shittlehope** Dur
79 M3 **Shobdon** Herefs
18 B2 **Shobley** Hants
13 K2 **Shobrooke** Devon
117 H7 **Shoby** Leics
113 G2 **Shocklach** Ches W
113 G2 **Shocklach Green** Ches W
53 K2 **Shoeburyness** Sthend
41 K5 **Sholden** Kent
19 G2 **Sholing** C Sotn
164 D5 **Shoose** Cumb
95 K1 **Shoot Hill** Shrops
10 B7 **Shop** Cnwll
26 D7 **Shop** Cnwll
20 E6 **Shopwyke** W Susx
140 D4 **Shore** Rochdl
51 J2 **Shoreditch** Gt Lon

30 C6 **Shoreditch** Somset
52 B6 **Shoreham** Kent
22 C6 **Shoreham-by-Sea** W Susx
202 E4 **Shoreswood** Nthumb
35 J5 **Shorley** Hants
64 F7 **Shorncote** Gloucs
52 E5 **Shorne** Kent
52 E5 **Shorne Ridgeway** Kent
6 B3 **Shorta Cross** Cnwll
23 G3 **Shortbridge** E Susx
36 C2 **Shortfield Common** Surrey
23 H4 **Shortgate** E Susx
98 E5 **Short Heath** Birm
36 A4 **Shortheath** Hants
98 B3 **Short Heath** Wsall
4 C5 **Shortlanesend** Cnwll
196 E4 **Shortlees** E Ayrs
86 B6 **Shortstown** Bed
19 G7 **Shorwell** IoW
45 L7 **Shoscombe** BaNES
106 E4 **Shotesham** Norfk
71 J8 **Shotgate** Essex
90 F8 **Shotley** Suffk
180 D8 **Shotley Bridge** Dur
180 C8 **Shotleyfield** Nthumb
90 F8 **Shotley Gate** Suffk
90 F8 **Shotley Street** Suffk
40 D4 **Shottenden** Kent
36 C4 **Shottermill** Surrey
82 E4 **Shottery** Warwks
83 K6 **Shotteswell** Warwks
91 H6 **Shottisham** Suffk
116 A2 **Shottle** Derbys
116 A2 **Shottlegate** Derbys
169 K5 **Shotton** Dur
169 L3 **Shotton** Dur
129 H6 **Shotton** Flints
180 F3 **Shotton** Nthumb
202 C7 **Shotton** Nthumb
169 K3 **Shotton Colliery** Dur
210 A1 **Shotts** N Lans
129 H5 **Shotwick** Ches W
266 D5 **Shougle** Moray
104 D2 **Shouldham** Norfk
104 D2 **Shouldham Thorpe** Norfk
81 J3 **Shoulton** Worcs
39 G7 **Shover's Green** E Susx
114 B2 **Shraleybrook** Staffs
112 F8 **Shrawardine** Shrops
81 J2 **Shrawley** Worcs
50 C3 **Shreding Green** Bucks
82 F2 **Shrewley** Warwks
96 B1 **Shrewsbury** Shrops
33 J2 **Shrewton** Wilts
20 F6 **Shripney** W Susx
47 K1 **Shrivenham** Oxon
105 K5 **Shropham** Norfk
72 E2 **Shrub End** Essex
80 D6 **Shucknall** Herefs
88 C6 **Shudy Camps** Cambs
64 D3 **Shurdington** Gloucs
49 K4 **Shurlock Row** W & M
82 B3 **Shurnock** Worcs
279 J4 **Shurrery** Highld
279 J5 **Shurrery Lodge** Highld
30 B2 **Shurton** Somset
99 G5 **Shustoke** Warwks
13 L2 **Shute** Devon
14 F3 **Shute** Devon
83 J7 **Shutford** Oxon
114 D7 **Shut Heath** Staffs
81 K8 **Shuthonger** Gloucs
84 E5 **Shutlanger** Nhants
13 M6 **Shutterton** Devon
97 K2 **Shutt Green** Staffs
99 H2 **Shuttington** Warwks
133 J5 **Shuttlewood** Derbys
140 B4 **Shuttleworth** Bury
282 f2 **Siabost** W Isls
282 g1 **Siadar** W Isls
100 E6 **Sibbertoft** Nhants
95 K6 **Sibdon Carwood** Shrops
83 H7 **Sibford Ferris** Oxon
83 H7 **Sibford Gower** Oxon
88 F8 **Sible Hedingham** Essex
70 F2 **Sibley's Green** Essex
11 J7 **Siblyback** Cnwll
119 K2 **Sibsey** Lincs
119 K1 **Sibsey Fenside** Lincs
102 B4 **Sibson** Cambs
99 K3 **Sibson** Leics
280 D5 **Sibster** Highld
117 K2 **Sibthorpe** Notts
134 E5 **Sibthorpe** Notts
91 J2 **Sibton** Suffk
89 H3 **Sicklesmere** Suffk
150 E6 **Sicklinghall** N York
30 C3 **Sidbrook** Somset
14 D4 **Sidbury** Devon
96 F6 **Sidbury** Shrops

| | |
|---|---|
| 142 B6 **Sid Cop** Barns | |

142 B6 **Sid Cop** Barns
44 E7 **Sidcot** N Som
51 M4 **Sidcup** Gt Lon
164 D4 **Siddick** Cumb
131 G5 **Siddington** Ches E
64 F7 **Siddington** Gloucs
81 L1 **Sidemoor** Worcs
122 F3 **Sidestrand** Norfk
14 D4 **Sidford** Devon
20 D7 **Sidlesham** W Susx
20 D6 **Sidlesham Common** W Susx
24 D5 **Sidley** E Susx
14 D5 **Sidmouth** Devon
96 B6 **Siefton** Shrops
13 H7 **Sigford** Devon
153 J6 **Sigglesthorne** E R Yk
42 E7 **Sigingstone** V Glam
65 K5 **Signet** Oxon
48 F6 **Silchester** Hants
117 G8 **Sileby** Leics
155 L6 **Silecroft** Cumb
106 C3 **Silfield** Norfk
77 G5 **Silian** Cerdgn
34 F6 **Silkstead** Hants
141 L6 **Silkstone** Barns
141 L6 **Silkstone Common** Barns
181 J8 **Silksworth** Sundld
118 E3 **Silk Willoughby** Lincs
176 F8 **Silloth** Cumb
163 H4 **Silpho** N York
149 J6 **Silsden** C Brad
86 B8 **Silsoe** C Beds
32 C5 **Silton** Dorset
211 G7 **Silverburn** Mdloth
157 G7 **Silverdale** Lancs
114 C2 **Silverdale** Staffs
157 G7 **Silverdale Green** Lancs
71 K3 **Silver End** Essex
268 D3 **Silverford** Abers
122 D6 **Silvergate** Norfk
91 H3 **Silverlace Green** Suffk
105 F8 **Silverley's Green** Suffk
84 C6 **Silverstone** Nhants
53 J7 **Silver Street** Kent
31 J4 **Silver Street** Somset
13 M2 **Silverton** Devon
4 B5 **Silverwell** Cnwll
96 E7 **Silvington** Shrops
131 K1 **Simmondley** Derbys
179 K4 **Simonburn** Nthumb
28 D3 **Simonsbath** Somset
29 L7 **Simonsburrow** Devon
140 A1 **Simonstone** Lancs
158 F4 **Simonstone** N York
202 C4 **Simprim** Border
85 H8 **Simpson** M Keyn
54 E3 **Simpson Cross** Pembks
202 C3 **Sinclair's Hill** Border
196 F7 **Sinclairston** E Ayrs
160 E6 **Sinderby** N York
179 K8 **Sinderhope** Nthumb
130 E2 **Sinderland Green** Traffd
49 J5 **Sindlesham** Wokham
116 B5 **Sinfin** C Derb
67 J1 **Singleborough** Bucks
51 L7 **Single Street** Gt Lon
40 C7 **Singleton** Kent
147 G8 **Singleton** Lancs
20 E4 **Singleton** W Susx
52 E5 **Singlewell** Kent
39 K5 **Sinkhurst Green** Kent
244 B1 **Sinnarhard** Abers
162 C5 **Sinnington** N York
81 J3 **Sinton** Worcs
81 J3 **Sinton Green** Worcs
50 D3 **Sipson** Gt Lon
61 J5 **Sirhowy** Blae G
39 K6 **Sissinghurst** Kent
45 K4 **Siston** S Glos
11 L4 **Sitcott** Devon
3 G5 **Sithney** Cnwll
3 G5 **Sithney Common** Cnwll
3 G5 **Sithney Green** Cnwll
40 B3 **Sittingbourne** Kent
97 H5 **Six Ashes** Shrops
61 K6 **Six Bells** Blae G
136 C2 **Sixhills** Lincs
88 B4 **Six Mile Bottom** Cambs
40 F6 **Sixmile Cottages** Kent
33 G7 **Sixpenny Handley** Dorset
9 C2 **Six Rues** Jersey
91 L3 **Sizewell** Suffk
275 d5 **Skaill** Ork
197 G7 **Skares** E Ayrs
245 K5 **Skateraw** Abers
213 G4 **Skateraw** E Loth
259 G7 **Skeabost** Highld
160 B2 **Skeeby** N York
101 G3 **Skeffington** Leics
145 K4 **Skeffling** E R Yk

133 K7 **Skegby** Notts
134 F5 **Skegby** Notts
137 L7 **Skegness** Lincs
264 B1 **Skelbo** Highld
264 B1 **Skelbo Street** Highld
142 D5 **Skelbrooke** Donc
119 K4 **Skeldyke** Lincs
135 J5 **Skellingthorpe** Lincs
131 H3 **Skellorn Green** Ches E
142 E5 **Skellow** Donc
141 K5 **Skelmanthorpe** Kirk
138 F6 **Skelmersdale** Lancs
207 K5 **Skelmorlie** N Ayrs
278 B5 **Skelpick** Highld
185 K6 **Skelston** D & G
151 J4 **Skelton** C York
166 B4 **Skelton** Cumb
143 J3 **Skelton** E R Yk
150 E2 **Skelton** N York
159 K3 **Skelton** N York
170 F7 **Skelton** R & Cl
156 E2 **Skelwith Bridge** Cumb
137 H5 **Skendleby** Lincs
245 G2 **Skene House** Abers
62 F3 **Skenfrith** Mons
153 G5 **Skerne** E R Yk
277 L4 **Skerray** Highld
276 C6 **Skerricha** Highld
147 J3 **Skerton** Lancs
99 L5 **Sketchley** Leics
57 H6 **Sketty** Swans
57 K5 **Skewen** Neath
151 K2 **Skewsby** N York
122 E6 **Skeyton** Norfk
122 E6 **Skeyton Corner** Norfk
279 H3 **Skiall** Highld
137 H1 **Skidbrooke** Lincs
137 H1 **Skidbrooke North End** Lincs
144 C1 **Skidby** E R Yk
282 h1 **Skigersta** W Isls
29 H5 **Skilgate** Somset
118 A6 **Skillington** Lincs
176 F7 **Skinburness** Cumb
210 B2 **Skinflats** Falk
48 C6 **Skinners Green** W Berk
171 G6 **Skinningrove** R & Cl
206 E7 **Skipness** Ag & B
177 L2 **Skipper's Bridge** D & G
165 L2 **Skiprigg** Cumb
153 J5 **Skipsea** E R Yk
153 J5 **Skipsea Brough** E R Yk
149 H5 **Skipton** N York
160 E6 **Skipton-on-Swale** N York
151 L8 **Skipwith** N York
153 J7 **Skirlaugh** E R Yk
199 J5 **Skirling** Border
49 J1 **Skirmett** Bucks
152 A4 **Skirpenbeck** E R Yk
166 E4 **Skirwith** Cumb
158 C7 **Skirwith** N York
280 E3 **Skirza** Highld
178 B5 **Skitby** Cumb
67 J6 **Skittle Green** Bucks
247 L4 **Skulamus** Highld
95 G8 **Skyborry Green** Shrops
72 C3 **Skye Green** Essex
253 J6 **Skye of Curr** Highld
149 J4 **Skyreholme** N York
140 E2 **Slack** Calder
140 E6 **Slackcote** Oldham
157 G6 **Slack Head** Cumb
137 K5 **Slackholme End** Lincs
256 F3 **Slacks of Cairnbanno** Abers
64 C5 **Slad** Gloucs
14 D1 **Slade** Devon
27 J2 **Slade** Devon
28 E5 **Slade** Devon
48 E1 **Slade End** Oxon
52 B4 **Slade Green** Gt Lon
97 L2 **Slade Heath** Staffs
133 K2 **Slade Hooton** Rothm
10 E8 **Sladesbridge** Cnwll
81 J8 **Slades Green** Worcs
178 F8 **Slaggyford** Nthumb
148 C5 **Slaidburn** Lancs
141 G5 **Slaithwaite** Kirk
132 E8 **Slaley** Derbys
180 A7 **Slaley** Nthumb
209 M4 **Slamannan** Falk
68 B3 **Slapton** Bucks
8 B6 **Slapton** Devon
84 C6 **Slapton** Nhants
140 D6 **Slattocks** Rochdl
37 L5 **Slaugham** W Susx
46 B4 **Slaughterford** Wilts
101 G4 **Slawston** Leics
36 B3 **Sleaford** Hants
118 E2 **Sleaford** Lincs
166 E6 **Sleagill** Cumb

113 H6 **Sleap** Shrops
113 L8 **Sleapford** Wrekin
69 G5 **Sleapshyde** Herts
272 B6 **Sleasdairidh** Highld
81 J8 **Sledge Green** Worcs
152 E3 **Sledmere** E R Yk
178 C3 **Sleetbeck** Cumb
17 J3 **Sleight** Dorset
168 B8 **Sleightholme** Dur
162 F1 **Sleights** N York
17 H4 **Slepe** Dorset
280 E2 **Slickly** Highld
193 J4 **Sliddery** N Ayrs
247 G3 **Sligachan** Highld
207 K1 **Sligrachan** Ag & B
63 L6 **Slimbridge** Gloucs
114 C5 **Slindon** Staffs
20 F5 **Slindon** W Susx
37 H4 **Slinfold** W Susx
126 B6 **Sling** Gwynd
162 B7 **Slingsby** N York
68 D3 **Slip End** C Beds
86 F7 **Slip End** Herts
101 L7 **Slipton** Nhants
115 G8 **Slitting Mill** Staffs
216 C7 **Slockavullin** Ag & B
175 G2 **Slogarie** D & G
122 F6 **Sloley** Norfk
13 H5 **Sloncombe** Devon
137 J5 **Sloothby** Lincs
50 C3 **Slough** Slough
50 B3 **Slough Crematorium** Bucks
30 C7 **Slough Green** Somset
37 L5 **Slough Green** W Susx
248 E4 **Slumbay** Highld
50 C8 **Slyfield Green** Surrey
147 J3 **Slyne** Lancs
201 K6 **Smailholm** Border
140 F5 **Smallbridge** Rochdl
13 K3 **Smallbrook** Devon
63 H7 **Smallbrook** Gloucs
123 G6 **Smallburgh** Norfk
132 B4 **Smalldale** Derbys
132 C3 **Smalldale** Derbys
22 C5 **Small Dole** W Susx
116 C3 **Smalley** Derbys
116 C3 **Smalley Common** Derbys
116 C3 **Smalley Green** Derbys
37 M2 **Smallfield** Surrey
98 E6 **Small Heath** Birm
25 G1 **Small Hythe** Kent
15 G2 **Smallridge** Devon
114 D2 **Smallthorne** C Stke
168 E8 **Smallways** N York
130 F7 **Smallwood** Ches E
147 H6 **Small Wood Hey** Lancs
105 K7 **Smallworth** Norfk
34 E1 **Smannell** Hants
158 C1 **Smardale** Cumb
39 L5 **Smarden** Kent
39 L5 **Smarden Bell** Kent
38 E5 **Smart's Hill** Kent
203 H5 **Smeafield** Nthumb
237 J5 **Smearisary** Highld
30 B8 **Smeatharpe** Devon
40 E7 **Smeeth** Kent
100 E5 **Smeeton Westerby** Leics
150 B3 **Smelthouses** N York
275 G2 **Smerral** Highld
97 J5 **Smestow** Staffs
98 C6 **Smethwick** Sandw
130 F7 **Smethwick Green** Ches E
116 B7 **Smisby** Derbys
19 J5 **Smitheclose** IoW
81 H5 **Smith End Green** Worcs
178 B6 **Smithfield** Cumb
147 J5 **Smith Green** Lancs
142 A6 **Smithies** Barns
29 J8 **Smithincott** Devon
87 H7 **Smith's End** Herts
70 E3 **Smith's Green** Essex
88 D7 **Smith's Green** Essex
260 C4 **Smithston** Highld
252 D3 **Smithton** Highld
140 D5 **Smithy Bridge** Rochdl
130 E5 **Smithy Green** Ches E
131 G3 **Smithy Green** Stockp
116 C2 **Smithy Houses** Derbys
99 M5 **Smockington** Leics
277 G3 **Smoo** Highld
72 D3 **Smythe's Green** Essex
185 L5 **Snade** D & G
95 J3 **Snailbeach** Shrops
88 C2 **Snailwell** Cambs
163 G6 **Snainton** N York
143 G3 **Snaith** E R Yk
132 B2 **Snake Pass Inn** Derbys
160 C6 **Snape** N York
91 J3 **Snape** Suffk
138 D5 **Snape Green** Lancs

91 J4 **Snape Street** Suffk
51 L1 **Snaresbrook** Gt Lon
99 K2 **Snarestone** Leics
135 L3 **Snarford** Lincs
25 J2 **Snargate** Kent
25 J1 **Snave** Kent
81 L4 **Sneachill** Worcs
95 H5 **Snead** Powys
106 D5 **Sneath Common** Norfk
162 F1 **Sneaton** N York
162 F2 **Sneatonthorpe** N York
135 M4 **Snelland** Lincs
130 F5 **Snelson** Ches E
115 J3 **Snelston** Derbys
105 K5 **Snetterton** Norfk
120 F4 **Snettisham** Norfk
116 C8 **Snibston** Leics
64 A1 **Snig's End** Gloucs
190 E5 **Snitter** Nthumb
135 K1 **Snitterby** Lincs
82 F3 **Snitterfield** Warwks
132 E7 **Snitterton** Derbys
96 D8 **Snitton** Shrops
40 B6 **Snoadhill** Kent
79 K7 **Snodhill** Herefs
52 F6 **Snodland** Kent
39 G4 **Snoll Hatch** Kent
141 L7 **Snowden Hill** Barns
69 L1 **Snow End** Herts
82 C8 **Snowshill** Gloucs
106 B7 **Snow Street** Norfk
19 L2 **Soake** Hants
43 H5 **Soar** Cardif
7 K7 **Soar** Devon
60 E1 **Soar** Powys
35 J7 **Soberton** Hants
35 J8 **Soberton Heath** Hants
166 C5 **Sockbridge** Cumb
160 E1 **Sockburn** Darltn
128 C5 **Sodom** Denbgs
112 E3 **Sodylt Bank** Shrops
104 B8 **Soham** Cambs
104 B8 **Soham Cotes** Cambs
282 c7 **Solas** W Isls
54 E4 **Solbury** Pembks
26 E8 **Soldon** Devon
26 E8 **Soldon Cross** Devon
35 K4 **Soldridge** Hants
40 E5 **Sole Street** Kent
52 E5 **Sole Street** Kent
98 F7 **Solihull** Solhll
80 L4 **Sollers Dilwyn** Herefs
80 E8 **Sollers Hope** Herefs
138 F4 **Sollom** Lancs
74 C7 **Solva** Pembks
177 J3 **Solwaybank** D & G
101 G1 **Somerby** Leics
144 D6 **Somerby** Lincs
116 C1 **Somercotes** Derbys
18 B5 **Somerford** Dorset
64 E8 **Somerford Keynes** Gloucs
20 D7 **Somerley** W Susx
107 K4 **Somerleyton** Suffk
115 J4 **Somersal Herbert** Derbys
136 F5 **Somersby** Lincs
103 G7 **Somersham** Cambs
90 C5 **Somersham** Suffk
66 D2 **Somerton** Oxon
31 H5 **Somerton** Somset
89 G4 **Somerton** Suffk
113 J8 **Somerwood** Shrops
21 K6 **Sompting** W Susx
49 J4 **Sonning** Wokham
49 H3 **Sonning Common** Oxon
49 H4 **Sonning Eye** Oxon
112 E2 **Sontley** Wrexhm
18 B4 **Sopley** Hants
46 B2 **Sopworth** Wilts
174 C5 **Sorbie** D & G
279 L4 **Sordale** Highld
225 H3 **Sorisdale** Ag & B
197 G5 **Sorn** E Ayrs
280 C4 **Sortat** Highld
136 D4 **Sotby** Lincs
136 B6 **Sots Hole** Lincs
107 J6 **Sotterley** Suffk
128 F6 **Soughton** Flints
67 L2 **Soulbury** Bucks
166 B5 **Soulby** Cumb
167 H8 **Soulby** Cumb
66 D1 **Souldern** Oxon
85 J3 **Souldrop** Bed
113 K2 **Sound** Ches E
267 G5 **Sound Muir** Moray
45 J4 **Soundwell** S Glos
12 D4 **Sourton** Devon
156 B6 **Soutergate** Cumb
121 H8 **South Acre** Norfk
41 H7 **South Alkham** Kent
50 E3 **Southall** Gt Lon

8 B7 **South Allington** Devon
210 A1 **South Alloa** Falk
64 E2 **Southam** Gloucs
83 K3 **Southam** Warwks
20 F3 **South Ambersham** W Susx
19 G1 **Southampton** C Sotn
34 F7 **Southampton Crematorium** Hants
133 K3 **South Anston** Rothm
50 A5 **South Ascot** W & M
40 C7 **South Ashford** Kent
18 E4 **South Baddesley** Hants
229 H4 **South Ballachulish** Highld
151 J5 **South Bank** C York
170 C6 **South Bank** R & Cl
31 K5 **South Barrow** Somset
51 H6 **South Beddington** Gt Lon
11 K4 **South Beer** Cnwll
53 G2 **South Benfleet** Essex
20 F6 **South Bersted** W Susx
18 B4 **South Bockhampton** Dorset
51 L5 **Southborough** Gt Lon
38 F5 **Southborough** Kent
18 A5 **Southbourne** Bmouth
20 C5 **Southbourne** W Susx
15 K3 **South Bowood** Dorset
143 G5 **South Bramwith** Donc
7 K3 **South Brent** Devon
32 B4 **South Brewham** Somset
45 H5 **South Bristol Crematorium** Bristl
191 K6 **South Broomhill** Nthumb
105 K2 **Southburgh** Norfk
107 H2 **South Burlingham** Norfk
152 F5 **Southburn** E R Yk
31 K5 **South Cadbury** Somset
135 J4 **South Carlton** Lincs
134 B3 **South Carlton** Notts
144 A2 **South Cave** E R Yk
64 F7 **South Cerney** Gloucs
22 F4 **South Chailey** E Susx
15 H2 **South Chard** Somset
191 H2 **South Charlton** Nthumb
32 B6 **South Cheriton** Somset
169 G5 **South Church** Dur
53 J2 **Southchurch** Sthend
168 E7 **South Cleatlam** Dur
152 D8 **South Cliffe** E R Yk
135 G5 **South Clifton** Notts
137 G2 **South Cockerington** Lincs
42 B5 **South Cornelly** Brdgnd
11 H3 **Southcott** Cnwll
12 D3 **Southcott** Devon
13 H6 **Southcott** Devon
27 H7 **Southcott** Devon
47 H7 **Southcott** Wilts
67 K5 **Southcourt** Bucks
107 K7 **South Cove** Suffk
121 J4 **South Creake** Norfk
141 H5 **South Crosland** Kirk
100 F2 **South Croxton** Leics
152 E6 **South Dalton** E R Yk
52 C5 **South Darenth** Kent
143 H1 **South Duffield** N York
23 G6 **Southease** E Susx
136 E2 **South Elkington** Lincs
142 D5 **South Elmsall** Wakefd
192 E6 **Southend** Ag & B
145 K4 **South End** E R Yk
33 J7 **South End** Hants
81 G6 **South End** Herefs
144 E4 **South End** N Linc
105 K5 **South End** Norfk
47 J4 **Southend** Wilts
53 J2 **Southend Crematorium** Sthend
53 J2 **Southend-on-Sea** Sthend
165 L3 **Southernby** Cumb
39 L4 **Southernden** Kent
42 D7 **Southerndown** V Glam
176 C7 **Southerness** D & G
260 B5 **South Erradale** Highld
14 C4 **Southerton** Devon
104 C4 **Southery** Norfk
52 C2 **South Essex Crematorium** Gt Lon
72 B8 **South Fambridge** Essex
48 A3 **South Fawley** W Berk
144 B4 **South Ferriby** N Linc
144 C3 **South Field** E R Yk
209 M4 **Southfield** Falk
52 D5 **Southfleet** Kent
19 J7 **Southford** IoW
69 J8 **Southgate** Gt Lon
120 E5 **Southgate** Norfk
121 J4 **Southgate** Norfk
122 C6 **Southgate** Norfk
57 G7 **Southgate** Swans
38 A4 **South Godstone** Surrey
18 B2 **South Gorley** Hants
181 G5 **South Gosforth** N u Ty

71 G8 **South Green** Essex
72 F3 **South Green** Essex
53 J7 **South Green** Kent
105 L1 **South Green** Norfk
106 D8 **South Green** Suffk
211 G4 **South Gyle** C Edin
71 H7 **South Hanningfield** Essex
20 C3 **South Harting** W Susx
20 B6 **South Hayling** Hants
203 G6 **South Hazelrigg** Nthumb
67 M6 **South Heath** Bucks
23 G6 **South Heighton** E Susx
169 K2 **South Hetton** Dur
142 B5 **South Hiendley** Wakefd
11 L7 **South Hill** Cnwll
31 G5 **South Hill** Somset
66 D6 **South Hinksey** Oxon
26 C6 **South Hole** Devon
37 J2 **South Holmwood** Surrey
52 B2 **South Hornchurch** Gt Lon
31 J2 **South Horrington** Somset
7 K6 **South Huish** Devon
135 J6 **South Hykeham** Lincs
181 J7 **South Hylton** Sundld
86 C6 **Southill** C Beds
35 G1 **Southington** Hants
144 D8 **South Kelsey** Lincs
251 H2 **South Kessock** Highld
144 F4 **South Killingholme** N Linc
160 F6 **South Kilvington** N York
100 D7 **South Kilworth** Leics
142 C5 **South Kirkby** Wakefd
13 J7 **South Knighton** Devon
119 G2 **South Kyme** Lincs
209 H7 **South Lanarkshire Crematorium** S Lans
14 E4 **Southleigh** Devon
66 B5 **South Leigh** Oxon
134 F3 **South Leverton** Notts
82 C6 **South Littleton** Worcs
51 H5 **South London Crematorium** Gt Lon
105 L7 **South Lopham** Norfk
101 K3 **South Luffenham** Rutlnd
23 G5 **South Malling** E Susx
47 J2 **South Marston** Swindn
51 H8 **South Merstham** Surrey
190 E2 **South Middleton** Nthumb
142 D2 **South Milford** N York
7 K6 **South Milton** Devon
69 G6 **South Mimms** Herts
72 D7 **Southminster** Essex
28 C5 **South Molton** Devon
180 F8 **South Moor** Dur
66 B7 **Southmoor** Oxon
48 E1 **South Moreton** Oxon
234 B5 **Southmuir** Angus
20 E6 **South Mundham** W Susx
134 F8 **South Muskham** Notts
152 D8 **South Newbald** E R Yk
83 J8 **South Newington** Oxon
33 J4 **South Newton** Wilts
133 J8 **South Normanton** Derbys
51 J5 **South Norwood** Gt Lon
37 M1 **South Nutfield** Surrey
52 D2 **South Ockendon** Thurr
86 D2 **Southoe** Cambs
90 E2 **Southolt** Suffk
137 G4 **South Ormsby** Lincs
102 B3 **Southorpe** C Pete
141 L4 **South Ossett** Wakefd
160 E5 **South Otterington** N York
16 B3 **Southover** Dorset
24 B2 **Southover** E Susx
135 L1 **South Owersby** Lincs
141 H3 **Southowram** Calder
37 K1 **South Park** Surrey
15 L1 **South Perrott** Dorset
31 G7 **South Petherton** Somset
11 K6 **South Petherwin** Cnwll
105 G3 **South Pickenham** Norfk
6 E3 **South Pill** Cnwll
7 M6 **South Pool** Devon
15 M3 **South Poorton** Dorset
138 D4 **Southport** Sefton
138 D5 **Southport Crematorium** Lancs
210 F3 **South Queensferry** C Edin
28 C4 **South Radworthy** Devon
118 D2 **South Rauceby** Lincs
121 J6 **South Raynham** Norfk
131 H1 **South Reddish** Stockp
122 E4 **Southrepps** Norfk
137 G3 **South Reston** Lincs
136 B6 **Southrey** Lincs
65 J6 **Southrop** Gloucs
35 K2 **Southrope** Hants
104 C2 **South Runcton** Norfk
135 G7 **South Scarle** Notts
19 L4 **Southsea** C Port
112 D1 **Southsea** Wrexhm

228 E7 **South Shian** Ag & B
181 J5 **South Shields** S Tyne
181 J6 **South Shields Crematorium** S Tyne
138 C1 **South Shore** Bpool
168 E5 **Southside** Dur
137 H1 **South Somercotes** Lincs
150 D3 **South Stainley** N York
52 D3 **South Stifford** Thurr
45 L6 **South Stoke** BaNES
48 F2 **South Stoke** Oxon
21 H5 **South Stoke** W Susx
40 D7 **South Stour** Kent
40 D4 **South Street** Kent
40 D4 **South Street** Kent
52 D6 **South Street** Kent
199 H3 **South Tarbrax** S Lans
12 F3 **South Tawton** Devon
3 G3 **South Tehidy** Cnwll
137 G4 **South Thoresby** Lincs
168 E7 **South Thorpe** Dur
35 K4 **South Town** Hants
107 L2 **Southtown** Norfk
30 D7 **Southtown** Somset
166 B2 **Southwaite** Cumb
107 H1 **South Walsham** Norfk
51 J3 **Southwark** Gt Lon
35 L2 **South Warnborough** Hants
37 J5 **Southwater** W Susx
37 H5 **Southwater Street** W Susx
31 H2 **Southway** Somset
70 E8 **South Weald** Essex
16 D8 **Southwell** Dorset
117 J1 **Southwell** Notts
50 E4 **South West Middlesex Crematorium** Gt Lon
67 H7 **South Weston** Oxon
11 J4 **South Wheatley** Cnwll
19 L2 **Southwick** Hants
101 M5 **Southwick** Nhants
30 E2 **Southwick** Somset
181 J7 **Southwick** Sundld
22 C6 **Southwick** W Susx
46 B7 **Southwick** Wilts
45 H7 **South Widcombe** BaNES
100 D4 **South Wigston** Leics
40 D7 **South Willesborough** Kent
136 C3 **South Willingham** Lincs
169 L4 **South Wingate** Dur
133 G8 **South Wingfield** Derbys
118 B7 **South Witham** Lincs
107 K8 **Southwold** Suffk
34 F4 **South Wonston** Hants
107 H2 **Southwood** Norfk
31 J4 **Southwood** Somset
71 K7 **South Woodham Ferrers** Essex
120 E7 **South Wootton** Norfk
46 B6 **South Wraxall** Wilts
12 F4 **South Zeal** Devon
141 G3 **Sowerby** Calder
160 F6 **Sowerby** N York
141 G3 **Sowerby Bridge** Calder
165 L3 **Sowerby Row** Cumb
147 G7 **Sower Carr** Lancs
28 F6 **Sowerhill** Somset
62 B7 **Sowhill** Torfn
88 D5 **Sowley Green** Suffk
141 G4 **Sowood** Calder
6 F2 **Sowton** Devon
14 A4 **Sowton** Devon
140 F4 **Soyland Town** Calder
122 F5 **Spa Common** Norfk
88 D7 **Spain's End** Essex
119 H7 **Spalding** Lincs
143 J1 **Spaldington** E R Yk
86 C1 **Spaldwick** Cambs
135 G6 **Spalford** Notts
118 E4 **Spanby** Lincs
49 G7 **Spanish Green** Hants
122 B7 **Sparham** Norfk
122 B7 **Sparhamill** Norfk
156 D5 **Spark Bridge** Cumb
166 B5 **Sparket** Cumb
31 K5 **Sparkford** Somset
98 E6 **Sparkhill** Birm
7 H3 **Sparkwell** Devon
121 L8 **Sparrow Green** Norfk
132 B4 **Sparrowpit** Derbys
39 G6 **Sparrows Green** E Susx
34 F4 **Sparsholt** Hants
47 M2 **Sparsholt** Oxon
167 K1 **Spartylea** Nthumb
115 H4 **Spath** Staffs
162 C5 **Spaunton** N York
30 C3 **Spaxton** Somset
239 L7 **Spean Bridge** Highld
21 K3 **Spear Hill** W Susx
34 D5 **Spearywell** Hants
67 K7 **Speen** Bucks
48 C5 **Speen** W Berk

163 L7 **Speeton** N York
129 K3 **Speke** Lpool
38 E5 **Speldhurst** Kent
70 C4 **Spellbrook** Herts
39 H6 **Spelmonden** Kent
65 M3 **Spelsbury** Oxon
141 K3 **Spen** Kirk
49 H5 **Spencers Wood** Wokham
130 F7 **Spen Green** Ches E
159 L5 **Spennithorne** N York
169 H4 **Spennymoor** Dur
82 C3 **Spernall** Warwks
13 G5 **Spestos** Devon
81 K4 **Spetchley** Worcs
17 H2 **Spetisbury** Dorset
107 H7 **Spexhall** Suffk
267 G3 **Spey Bay** Moray
253 K6 **Speybridge** Highld
254 E3 **Speyview** Moray
137 G6 **Spilsby** Lincs
203 J6 **Spindlestone** Nthumb
133 J4 **Spinkhill** Derbys
263 J2 **Spinningdale** Highld
133 L6 **Spion Kop** Notts
46 E4 **Spirthill** Wilts
129 H3 **Spital** Wirral
134 C1 **Spital Hill** Donc
135 K2 **Spital in the Street** Lincs
23 G4 **Spithurst** E Susx
212 A4 **Spittal** E Loth
152 B5 **Spittal** E R Yk
279 L5 **Spittal** Highld
202 F3 **Spittal** Nthumb
55 G2 **Spittal** Pembks
233 H7 **Spittalfield** P & K
243 K6 **Spittal of Glenmuick** Abers
233 H2 **Spittal of Glenshee** P & K
189 G2 **Spittal-on-Rule** Border
122 E8 **Spixworth** Norfk
10 C7 **Splatt** Cnwll
11 J5 **Splatt** Cnwll
12 E2 **Splatt** Devon
23 G2 **Splayne's Green** E Susx
43 K6 **Splottlands** Cardif
130 E3 **Spodegreen** Ches E
150 E5 **Spofforth** N York
116 C4 **Spondon** C Derb
129 G7 **Spon Green** Flints
106 B4 **Spooner Row** Norfk
105 G1 **Sporle** Norfk
212 E4 **Spott** E Loth
201 J3 **Spottiswoode** Border
84 D1 **Spratton** Nhants
36 B3 **Spreakley** Surrey
13 G3 **Spreyton** Devon
7 G4 **Spriddlestone** Devon
135 K3 **Spridlington** Lincs
209 G5 **Springburn** C Glas
177 K5 **Springfield** D & G
71 H5 **Springfield** Essex
222 F5 **Springfield** Fife
168 F5 **Spring Gardens** Dur
98 B3 **Springhill** Staffs
98 D2 **Springhill** Staffs
175 K1 **Springholm** D & G
196 D3 **Springside** N Ayrs
135 H2 **Springthorpe** Lincs
141 L7 **Spring Vale** Barns
181 G7 **Springwell** Sundld
129 K3 **Springwood Crematorium** Lpool
145 F1 **Sproatley** E R Yk
130 E6 **Sproston Green** Ches W
142 E7 **Sprotbrough** Donc
90 D6 **Sproughton** Suffk
202 B6 **Sprouston** Border
106 E1 **Sprowston** Norfk
117 M6 **Sproxton** Leics
161 K6 **Sproxton** N York
112 F5 **Spunhill** Shrops
130 A8 **Spurstow** Ches E
15 M4 **Spyway** Dorset
74 D6 **Square & Compass** Pembks
97 G4 **Stableford** Shrops
114 C4 **Stableford** Staffs
132 F2 **Stacey Bank** Sheff
148 E3 **Stackhouse** N York
55 G7 **Stackpole** Pembks
105 L5 **Stacksford** Norfk
140 C3 **Stacksteads** Lancs
7 G4 **Staddiscombe** C Plym
143 L2 **Staddlethorpe** E R Yk
131 L5 **Staden** Derbys
66 F7 **Stadhampton** Oxon
283 b10 **Stadhlaigearraidh** W Isls
166 D2 **Staffield** Cumb
259 H3 **Staffin** Highld
114 E7 **Stafford** Staffs
114 E6 **Stafford Crematorium** Staffs
85 J5 **Stagsden** Bed

141 M7 **Stainborough** Barns
164 D5 **Stainburn** Cumb
150 C6 **Stainburn** N York
118 B7 **Stainby** Lincs
141 M5 **Staincross** Barns
168 E6 **Staindrop** Dur
50 D5 **Staines** Surrey
118 E6 **Stainfield** Lincs
136 B5 **Stainfield** Lincs
143 G5 **Stainforth** Donc
148 E2 **Stainforth** N York
147 G8 **Staining** Lancs
141 G4 **Stainland** Calder
163 G1 **Stainsacre** N York
133 J6 **Stainsby** Derbys
157 H5 **Stainton** Cumb
166 C5 **Stainton** Cumb
177 L7 **Stainton** Dur
133 L1 **Stainton** Donc
168 D7 **Stainton** Dur
170 B7 **Stainton** Middsb
159 K3 **Stainton** N York
135 L4 **Stainton by Langworth** Lincs
163 H3 **Staintondale** N York
136 C1 **Stainton le Vale** Lincs
146 E1 **Stainton with Adgarley** Cumb
165 H6 **Stair** Cumb
196 E6 **Stair** E Ayrs
142 B6 **Stairfoot** Barns
172 F4 **Stairhaven** D & G
171 H7 **Staithes** N York
181 G2 **Stakeford** Nthumb
147 H6 **Stake Pool** Lancs
19 M2 **Stakes** Hants
32 B7 **Stalbridge** Dorset
32 B7 **Stalbridge Weston** Dorset
123 H6 **Stalham** Norfk
123 H6 **Stalham Green** Norfk
40 B5 **Stalisfield Green** Kent
105 L4 **Stalland Common** Norfk
31 K7 **Stallen** Dorset
145 G5 **Stallingborough** NE Lin
159 G5 **Stalling Busk** N York
114 E4 **Stallington** Staffs
147 G6 **Stalmine** Lancs
147 G6 **Stalmine Moss Side** Lancs
140 E8 **Stalybridge** Tamesd
00 E7 **Stambourne** Essex
88 D7 **Stambourne Green** Essex
102 A2 **Stamford** Lincs
191 J2 **Stamford** Nthumb
129 L6 **Stamford Bridge** Ches W
151 M5 **Stamford Bridge** E R Yk
180 C4 **Stamfordham** Nthumb
51 J2 **Stamford Hill** Gt Lon
147 G7 **Stanah** Lancs
69 G5 **Stanborough** Herts
68 B2 **Stanbridge** C Beds
17 K2 **Stanbridge** Dorset
149 H8 **Stanbury** C Brad
140 B6 **Stand** Bury
209 K5 **Stand** N Lans
210 B4 **Standburn** Falk
97 K2 **Standeford** Staffs
39 L5 **Standen** Kent
39 K7 **Standen Street** Kent
32 D1 **Standerwick** Somset
36 B4 **Standford** Hants
164 D4 **Standingstone** Cumb
64 A5 **Standish** Gloucs
139 H5 **Standish** Wigan
139 H6 **Standish Lower Ground** Wigan
66 B6 **Standlake** Oxon
34 F5 **Standon** Hants
69 K3 **Standon** Herts
114 C4 **Standon** Staffs
69 K3 **Standon Green End** Herts
90 D1 **Standwell Green** Suffk
210 A7 **Stane** N Lans
121 K7 **Stanfield** Norfk
86 D7 **Stanford** C Beds
40 F7 **Stanford** Kent
95 H1 **Stanford** Shrops
80 F5 **Stanford Bishop** Herefs
81 G2 **Stanford Bridge** Worcs
113 M6 **Stanford Bridge** Wrekin
48 E4 **Stanford Dingley** W Berk
65 M8 **Stanford in the Vale** Oxon
52 E3 **Stanford le Hope** Thurr
100 D7 **Stanford on Avon** Nhants
116 F7 **Stanford on Soar** Notts
81 G2 **Stanford on Teme** Worcs
70 D7 **Stanford Rivers** Essex
133 J5 **Stanfree** Derbys
170 F7 **Stanghow** R & Cl
102 D4 **Stanground** C Pete
139 L2 **Stanhill** Lancs
121 H4 **Stanhoe** Norfk
199 K7 **Stanhope** Border
168 C3 **Stanhope** Dur

40 C7 **Stanhope** Kent
115 M7 **Stanhope Bretby** Derbys
101 K6 **Stanion** Nhants
97 J8 **Stanklin** Worcs
116 C3 **Stanley** Derbys
180 F8 **Stanley** Dur
133 J7 **Stanley** Notts
221 K1 **Stanley** P & K
97 G6 **Stanley** Shrops
114 E1 **Stanley** Staffs
142 A3 **Stanley** Wakefd
116 C3 **Stanley Common** Derbys
168 F3 **Stanley Crook** Dur
142 A3 **Stanley Ferry** Wakefd
138 F6 **Stanley Gate** Lancs
114 E1 **Stanley Moor** Staffs
64 E1 **Stanley Pontlarge** Gloucs
22 E5 **Stanmer** Br & H
68 F8 **Stanmore** Gt Lon
34 F5 **Stanmore** Hants
48 C3 **Stanmore** W Berk
179 G2 **Stannersburn** Nthumb
89 H4 **Stanningfield** Suffk
141 K1 **Stanningley** Leeds
180 F3 **Stannington** Nthumb
132 F2 **Stannington** Sheff
180 F3 **Stannington Station** Nthumb
79 L3 **Stansbatch** Herefs
88 F5 **Stansfield** Suffk
115 J1 **Stanshope** Staffs
89 G5 **Stanstead** Suffk
69 K5 **Stanstead Abbotts** Herts
89 G5 **Stanstead Street** Suffk
52 D6 **Stansted** Kent
70 D2 **Stansted Mountfitchet** Essex
115 M7 **Stanton** Derbys
82 C8 **Stanton** Gloucs
62 C3 **Stanton** Mons
191 G8 **Stanton** Nthumb
115 J2 **Stanton** Staffs
105 K8 **Stanton** Suffk
116 B6 **Stanton by Bridge** Derbys
116 D4 **Stanton by Dale** Derbys
45 H6 **Stanton Drew** BaNES
47 J1 **Stanton Fitzwarren** Swindn
66 D6 **Stanton Harcourt** Oxon
133 J7 **Stanton Hill** Notts
132 E6 **Stanton in Peak** Derbys
96 B7 **Stanton Lacy** Shrops
132 E7 **Stanton Lees** Derbys
96 D5 **Stanton Long** Shrops
117 G5 **Stanton on the Wolds** Notts
45 K6 **Stanton Prior** BaNES
47 G6 **Stanton St Bernard** Wilts
66 E5 **Stanton St John** Oxon
46 C3 **Stanton St Quintin** Wilts
89 J2 **Stanton Street** Suffk
100 A1 **Stanton under Bardon** Leics
113 J6 **Stanton upon Hine Heath** Shrops
45 J6 **Stanton Wick** BaNES
63 L4 **Stantway** Gloucs
112 F6 **Stanwardine in the Field** Shrops
113 G6 **Stanwardine in the Wood** Shrops
72 D2 **Stanway** Essex
64 F1 **Stanway** Gloucs
72 D2 **Stanway Green** Essex
90 F1 **Stanway Green** Suffk
50 D4 **Stanwell** Surrey
50 D4 **Stanwell Moor** Surrey
85 J1 **Stanwick** Nhants
177 L7 **Stanwix** Cumb
283 b10 **Staoinebrig** W Isls
162 D4 **Stape** N York
17 L2 **Stapehill** Dorset
113 L2 **Stapeley** Ches E
115 L7 **Stapenhill** Staffs
41 J4 **Staple** Kent
29 J6 **Staple Cross** Devon
24 E3 **Staple Cross** E Susx
37 L5 **Staplefield** W Susx
30 C7 **Staple Fitzpaine** Somset
87 K5 **Stapleford** Cambs
69 J4 **Stapleford** Herts
117 L7 **Stapleford** Leics
135 H8 **Stapleford** Lincs
116 E4 **Stapleford** Notts
33 J3 **Stapleford** Wilts
70 D8 **Stapleford Abbotts** Essex
70 D7 **Stapleford Tawney** Essex
30 B5 **Staplegrove** Somset
30 B6 **Staplehay** Somset
98 B8 **Staple Hill** Worcs
39 K5 **Staplehurst** Kent
19 H6 **Staplers** IoW
40 D3 **Staplestreet** Kent
178 C4 **Stapleton** Cumb
79 L2 **Stapleton** Herefs

99 L4 **Stapleton** Leics
169 H8 **Stapleton** N York
95 L3 **Stapleton** Shrops
31 G6 **Stapleton** Somset
30 B8 **Stapley** Somset
86 C3 **Staploe** Bed
80 F7 **Staplow** Herefs
222 E6 **Star** Fife
75 M5 **Star** Pembks
44 E7 **Star** Somset
150 D4 **Starbeck** N York
159 G7 **Starbotton** N York
14 A6 **Starcross** Devon
83 H1 **Stareton** Warwks
132 F7 **Starkholmes** Derbys
140 A5 **Starling** Bury
70 C1 **Starlings Green** Essex
24 D4 **Starr's Green** E Susx
106 E6 **Starston** Norfk
8 B6 **Start** Devon
168 D7 **Startforth** Dur
46 D3 **Startley** Wilts
41 J4 **Statenborough** Kent
130 D2 **Statham** Warrtn
30 E5 **Stathe** Somset
117 K5 **Stathern** Leics
169 L3 **Station Town** Dur
86 C2 **Staughton Green** Cambs
86 C2 **Staughton Highway** Cambs
63 H4 **Staunton** Gloucs
64 A1 **Staunton** Gloucs
117 L3 **Staunton in the Vale** Notts
79 L3 **Staunton on Arrow** Herefs
79 L6 **Staunton on Wye** Herefs
156 E5 **Staveley** Cumb
157 G3 **Staveley** Cumb
133 H5 **Staveley** Derbys
150 E3 **Staveley** N York
8 B2 **Staverton** Devon
64 C2 **Staverton** Gloucs
83 M3 **Staverton** Nhants
46 B6 **Staverton** Wilts
64 C3 **Staverton Bridge** Gloucs
30 E3 **Stawell** Somset
29 J6 **Stawley** Somset
280 E5 **Staxigoe** Highld
163 J6 **Staxton** N York
92 E5 **Staylittle** Cerdgn
93 J5 **Staylittle** Powys
147 G7 **Staynall** Lancs
117 K1 **Staythorpe** Notts
149 L6 **Stead** C Brad
159 K8 **Stean** N York
151 K2 **Stearsby** N York
30 C2 **Steart** Somset
71 G2 **Stebbing** Essex
71 G2 **Stebbing Green** Essex
98 E6 **Stechford** Birm
39 L5 **Stede Quarter** Kent
36 C6 **Stedham** W Susx
179 L7 **Steel** Nthumb
38 E7 **Steel Cross** E Susx
210 D1 **Steelend** Fife
188 F7 **Steele Road** Border
155 L6 **Steel Green** Cumb
113 J4 **Steel Heath** Shrops
80 C4 **Steen's Bridge** Herefs
35 M6 **Steep** Hants
19 J8 **Steephill** IoW
140 F3 **Steep Lane** Calder
17 H6 **Steeple** Dorset
72 D6 **Steeple** Essex
46 C7 **Steeple Ashton** Wilts
66 C2 **Steeple Aston** Oxon
66 C2 **Steeple Barton** Oxon
88 D7 **Steeple Bumpstead** Essex
67 H2 **Steeple Claydon** Bucks
102 C7 **Steeple Gidding** Cambs
33 H3 **Steeple Langford** Wilts
86 F6 **Steeple Morden** Cambs
149 J7 **Steeton** C Brad
258 D5 **Stein** Highld
180 E6 **Stella** Gatesd
40 F6 **Stelling Minnis** Kent
30 F6 **Stembridge** Somset
5 G3 **Stenalees** Cnwll
185 K4 **Stenhouse** D & G
210 A2 **Stenhousemuir** Falk
136 D3 **Stenigot** Lincs
259 H3 **Stenscholl** Highld
116 B5 **Stenson Fields** Derbys
212 D4 **Stenton** E Loth
282 g3 **Steornabhagh** W Isls
55 K5 **Stepaside** Pembks
51 K3 **Stepney** Gt Lon
131 H2 **Stepping Hill** Stockp
85 K8 **Steppingley** C Beds
209 H5 **Stepps** N Lans
91 J3 **Sternfield** Suffk
27 K2 **Sterridge** Devon

46 F7 **Stert** Wilts
88 C3 **Stetchworth** Cambs
69 G2 **Stevenage** Herts
24 C4 **Steven's Crouch** E Susx
196 B3 **Stevenston** N Ayrs
35 H1 **Steventon** Hants
48 C1 **Steventon** Oxon
88 B6 **Steventon End** Essex
85 K4 **Stevington** Bed
85 K6 **Stewartby** Bed
209 G7 **Stewartfield** S Lans
196 E2 **Stewarton** E Ayrs
67 K2 **Stewkley** Bucks
30 D7 **Stewley** Somset
137 G2 **Stewton** Lincs
19 L6 **Steyne Cross** IoW
21 L4 **Steyning** W Susx
54 E5 **Steynton** Pembks
26 C8 **Stibb** Cnwll
121 L6 **Stibbard** Norfk
27 G7 **Stibb Cross** Devon
47 J6 **Stibb Green** Wilts
102 B4 **Stibbington** Cambs
201 L5 **Stichill** Border
5 G5 **Sticker** Cnwll
136 F7 **Stickford** Lincs
12 F4 **Sticklepath** Devon
29 J4 **Sticklepath** Somset
87 K8 **Stickling Green** Essex
136 F8 **Stickney** Lincs
121 L3 **Stiffkey** Norfk
81 G5 **Stifford's Bridge** Herefs
53 J6 **Stiff Street** Kent
39 J4 **Stile Bridge** Kent
31 G3 **Stileway** Somset
283 b10 **Stilligarry** W Isls
151 J7 **Stillingfleet** N York
151 J2 **Stillington** N York
169 K6 **Stillington** S on T
102 D5 **Stilton** Cambs
63 L7 **Stinchcombe** Gloucs
16 D4 **Stinsford** Dorset
95 J3 **Stiperstones** Shrops
98 D7 **Stirchley** Birm
96 F2 **Stirchley** Wrekin
257 L3 **Stirling** Abers
220 D8 **Stirling** Stirlg
86 D2 **Stirtloe** Cambs
149 H5 **Stirton** N York
71 J2 **Stisted** Essex
47 K5 **Stitchcombe** Wilts
3 J4 **Stithians** Cnwll
6 C2 **St Ive Cross** Cnwll
99 J8 **Stivichall** Covtry
130 C6 **Stixwould** Lincs
129 K5 **Stoak** Ches W
199 L5 **Stobo** Border
17 H5 **Stoborough** Dorset
17 H5 **Stoborough Green** Dorset
188 E4 **Stobs Castle** Border
191 J7 **Stobswood** Nthumb
71 G7 **Stock** Essex
44 F6 **Stock** N Som
34 D4 **Stockbridge** Hants
198 C6 **Stockbriggs** S Lans
53 H6 **Stockbury** Kent
48 B5 **Stockcross** W Berk
3 K4 **Stockdale** Cnwll
165 L2 **Stockdalewath** Cumb
40 C5 **Stocker's Hill** Kent
101 H4 **Stockerston** Leics
82 A3 **Stock Green** Worcs
63 J1 **Stocking** Herefs
99 J5 **Stockingford** Warwks
84 F5 **Stocking Green** M Keyn
70 C1 **Stocking Pelham** Herts
14 F2 **Stockland** Devon
30 C2 **Stockland Bristol** Somset
38 E5 **Stockland Green** Kent
13 K1 **Stockleigh English** Devon
13 K2 **Stockleigh Pomeroy** Devon
46 E5 **Stockley** Wilts
79 L7 **Stockley Hill** Herefs
30 F7 **Stocklinch** Somset
79 M4 **Stockmoor** Herefs
131 H2 **Stockport** Stockp
131 H2 **Stockport Crematorium** Stockp
141 L8 **Stocksbridge** Sheff
180 C6 **Stocksfield** Nthumb
80 C3 **Stockton** Herefs
107 H4 **Stockton** Norfk
95 G3 **Stockton** Shrops
97 G3 **Stockton** Shrops
83 K3 **Stockton** Warwks
33 G3 **Stockton** Wilts
114 B8 **Stockton** Wrekin
114 E1 **Stockton Brook** Staffs
130 B3 **Stockton Heath** Warrtn
170 B6 **Stockton-on-Tees** S on T
81 G2 **Stockton on Teme** Worcs

151 L4 **Stockton on the Forest** C York
64 D4 **Stockwell** Gloucs
97 K3 **Stockwell End** Wolves
115 G7 **Stockwell Heath** Staffs
45 J5 **Stockwood** Bristl
16 B1 **Stockwood** Dorset
82 B3 **Stock Wood** Worcs
147 J4 **Stodday** Lancs
41 H3 **Stodmarsh** Kent
122 B4 **Stody** Norfk
270 D2 **Stoer** Highld
31 J8 **Stoford** Somset
33 J4 **Stoford** Wilts
29 K3 **Stogumber** Somset
30 B2 **Stogursey** Somset
99 K7 **Stoke** Covtry
26 D6 **Stoke** Devon
20 B6 **Stoke** Hants
48 B8 **Stoke** Hants
53 H4 **Stoke** Medway
15 K2 **Stoke Abbott** Dorset
101 H5 **Stoke Albany** Nhants
90 D1 **Stoke Ash** Suffk
117 H3 **Stoke Bardolph** Notts
80 F3 **Stoke Bliss** Worcs
84 E5 **Stoke Bruerne** Nhants
88 E6 **Stoke by Clare** Suffk
89 K7 **Stoke-by-Nayland** Suffk
13 L3 **Stoke Canon** Devon
35 G3 **Stoke Charity** Hants
11 L7 **Stoke Climsland** Cnwll
80 E5 **Stoke Cross** Herefs
50 E7 **Stoke D'Abernon** Surrey
102 A6 **Stoke Doyle** Nhants
101 J4 **Stoke Dry** Rutlnd
80 E7 **Stoke Edith** Herefs
98 F4 **Stoke End** Warwks
33 H5 **Stoke Farthing** Wilts
104 D3 **Stoke Ferry** Norfk
8 C5 **Stoke Fleming** Devon
17 G5 **Stokeford** Dorset
8 C3 **Stoke Gabriel** Devon
45 J3 **Stoke Gifford** S Glos
99 L4 **Stoke Golding** Leics
85 G5 **Stoke Goldington** M Keyn
50 B3 **Stoke Green** Bucks
134 F4 **Stokeham** Notts
67 L1 **Stoke Hammond** Bucks
113 L5 **Stoke Heath** Shrops
81 L2 **Stoke Heath** Worcs
106 E3 **Stoke Holy Cross** Norfk
13 L8 **Stokeinteignhead** Devon
80 E5 **Stoke Lacy** Herefs
66 E2 **Stoke Lyne** Oxon
67 K5 **Stoke Mandeville** Bucks
67 J7 **Stokenchurch** Bucks
51 J2 **Stoke Newington** Gt Lon
8 B6 **Stokenham** Devon
114 D2 **Stoke-on-Trent** C Stke
64 D2 **Stoke Orchard** Gloucs
50 B2 **Stoke Poges** Bucks
81 M2 **Stoke Pound** Worcs
80 C4 **Stoke Prior** Herefs
81 L2 **Stoke Prior** Worcs
27 L4 **Stoke Rivers** Devon
118 B6 **Stoke Rochford** Lincs
49 G2 **Stoke Row** Oxon
30 E5 **Stoke St Gregory** Somset
30 C6 **Stoke St Mary** Somset
31 L2 **Stoke St Michael** Somset
96 D7 **Stoke St Milborough** Shrops
95 K7 **Stokesay** Shrops
107 J1 **Stokesby** Norfk
161 H1 **Stokesley** N York
31 G7 **Stoke sub Hamdon** Somset
67 G7 **Stoke Talmage** Oxon
32 B5 **Stoke Trister** Somset
113 L6 **Stoke upon Tern** Shrops
114 D3 **Stoke-upon-Trent** C Stke
16 E1 **Stoke Wake** Dorset
81 L2 **Stoke Wharf** Worcs
30 C2 **Stolford** Somset
70 E7 **Stondon Massey** Essex
67 J4 **Stone** Bucks
63 K8 **Stone** Gloucs
25 H2 **Stone** Kent
52 C4 **Stone** Kent
133 L2 **Stone** Rothm
31 J4 **Stone** Somset
114 E5 **Stone** Staffs
97 J8 **Stone** Worcs
103 J5 **Stonea** Cambs
30 F1 **Stone Allerton** Somset
45 J8 **Ston Easton** Somset
44 D7 **Stonebridge** N Som
105 J5 **Stonebridge** Norfk
99 G6 **Stonebridge** Warwks
102 F3 **Stone Bridge Corner** C Pete
133 H7 **Stonebroom** Derbys
141 H2 **Stone Chair** Calder

23 K6 **Stone Cross** E Susx
38 D7 **Stone Cross** E Susx
39 G7 **Stone Cross** E Susx
38 E5 **Stone Cross** Kent
40 D7 **Stone Cross** Kent
41 K4 **Stone Cross** Kent
89 G4 **Stonecross Green** Suffk
39 H6 **Stonecrouch** Kent
44 F4 **Stone-edge-Batch** N Som
144 E2 **Stoneferry** C KuH
206 D5 **Stonefield Castle Hotel** Ag & B
39 G7 **Stonegate** E Susx
162 D1 **Stonegate** N York
161 L7 **Stonegrave** N York
81 K5 **Stonehall** Worcs
179 J4 **Stonehaugh** Nthumb
245 J6 **Stonehaven** Abers
143 H6 **Stone Hill** Donc
6 F4 **Stonehouse** C Plym
158 D5 **Stone House** Cumb
64 A6 **Stonehouse** Gloucs
179 G7 **Stonehouse** Nthumb
198 C4 **Stonehouse** S Lans
83 H1 **Stoneleigh** Warwks
113 K1 **Stoneley Green** Ches E
86 C2 **Stonely** Cambs
35 M5 **Stoner Hill** Hants
117 L6 **Stonesby** Leics
66 B4 **Stonesfield** Oxon
73 H2 **Stones Green** Essex
38 F2 **Stone Street** Kent
89 K6 **Stone Street** Suffk
89 K7 **Stone Street** Suffk
107 H7 **Stone Street** Suffk
40 E7 **Stonestreet Green** Kent
165 J7 **Stonethwaite** Cumb
266 F3 **Stonewells** Moray
52 D4 **Stonewood** Kent
283 b10 **Stoneybridge** W Isls
97 L8 **Stoneybridge** Worcs
210 C6 **Stoneyburn** W Loth
18 D1 **Stoney Cross** Hants
100 D3 **Stoneygate** C Leic
72 D7 **Stoneyhills** Essex
172 D4 **Stoneykirk** D & G
132 E4 **Stoney Middleton** Derbys
100 B4 **Stoney Stanton** Leics
32 B4 **Stoney Stoke** Somset
31 L3 **Stoney Stratton** Somset
95 J2 **Stoney Stretton** Shrops
245 K1 **Stoneywood** C Aber
209 L2 **Stoneywood** Falk
90 D3 **Stonham Aspal** Suffk
98 D3 **Stonnall** Staffs
49 H1 **Stonor** Oxon
101 G4 **Stonton Wyville** Leics
80 D2 **Stony Cross** Herefs
81 G5 **Stony Cross** Herefs
34 D7 **Stonyford** Hants
133 K6 **Stony Houghton** Derbys
84 F7 **Stony Stratford** M Keyn
98 D1 **Stonywell** Staffs
28 B4 **Stoodleigh** Devon
29 G7 **Stoodleigh** Devon
21 H3 **Stopham** W Susx
68 E2 **Stopsley** Luton
10 C7 **Stoptide** Cnwll
129 G3 **Storeton** Wirral
81 G6 **Storeyard Green** Herefs
138 F6 **Stormy Corner** Lancs
282 g3 **Stornoway** W Isls
81 H5 **Storridge** Herefs
21 J4 **Storrington** W Susx
157 G6 **Storth** Cumb
151 M7 **Storwood** E R Yk
266 E2 **Stotfield** Moray
86 E7 **Stotfold** C Beds
96 F6 **Stottesdon** Shrops
100 E3 **Stoughton** Leics
50 C8 **Stoughton** Surrey
20 C4 **Stoughton** W Susx
81 L5 **Stoulton** Worcs
97 K6 **Stourbridge** Dudley
97 K6 **Stourbridge Crematorium**
Dudley
17 G1 **Stourpaine** Dorset
81 J1 **Stourport-on-Severn** Worcs
32 C6 **Stour Provost** Dorset
32 D6 **Stour Row** Dorset
141 M2 **Stourton** Leeds
97 K6 **Stourton** Staffs
83 G7 **Stourton** Warwks
32 C4 **Stourton** Wilts
32 B7 **Stourton Caundle** Dorset
31 G4 **Stout** Somset
281 e8 **Stove** Shet
107 J7 **Stoven** Suffk
200 F4 **Stow** Border
135 H3 **Stow** Lincs
104 C2 **Stow Bardolph** Norfk

105 J4 **Stow Bedon** Norfk
104 B2 **Stowbridge** Norfk
87 L3 **Stow-cum-Quy** Cambs
63 H5 **Stowe** Gloucs
95 H8 **Stowe** Shrops
114 F6 **Stowe by Chartley** Staffs
84 C3 **Stowehill** Nhants
31 L6 **Stowell** Somset
45 H7 **Stowey** BaNES
12 B3 **Stowford** Devon
12 B5 **Stowford** Devon
14 D4 **Stowford** Devon
28 B3 **Stowford** Devon
89 J2 **Stowlangtoft** Suffk
86 C1 **Stow Longa** Cambs
71 K7 **Stow Maries** Essex
90 B3 **Stowmarket** Suffk
65 J2 **Stow-on-the-Wold** Gloucs
40 F7 **Stowting** Kent
40 F6 **Stowting Common** Kent
90 C3 **Stowupland** Suffk
253 J8 **Straanruie** Highld
234 F2 **Stracathro Hospital** Angus
244 F5 **Strachan** Abers
217 H6 **Strachur** Ag & B
106 E8 **Stradbroke** Suffk
46 D8 **Stradbrook** Wilts
88 E5 **Stradishall** Suffk
104 D2 **Stradsett** Norfk
118 B1 **Stragglethorpe** Lincs
117 H4 **Stragglethorpe** Notts
47 L4 **Straight Soley** Wilts
211 J5 **Straiton** Mdloth
183 K2 **Straiton** S Ayrs
256 F7 **Straloch** Abers
232 F3 **Straloch** P & K
115 H4 **Stramshall** Staffs
154 e6 **Strang** IoM
140 B7 **Strangeways** Salfd
63 H2 **Strangford** Herefs
172 C3 **Stranraer** D & G
77 K2 **Strata Florida** Cerdgn
49 G6 **Stratfield Mortimer** W Berk
49 G6 **Stratfield Saye** Hants
49 G7 **Stratfield Turgis** Hants
86 D5 **Stratford** C Beds
51 K2 **Stratford** Gt Lon
91 H3 **Stratford St Andrew** Suffk
90 B8 **Stratford St Mary** Suffk
33 K4 **Stratford sub Castle** Wilts
33 J5 **Stratford Tony** Wilts
82 F4 **Stratford-upon-Avon** Warwks
260 C4 **Strath** Highld
270 E4 **Strathan** Highld
277 K3 **Strathan** Highld
197 K2 **Strathaven** S Lans
208 F3 **Strathblane** Stirlg
270 F7 **Strathcanaird** Highld
248 E5 **Strathcarron** Highld
227 K6 **Strathcoil** Ag & B
243 K1 **Strathdon** Abers
223 H4 **Strathkinness** Fife
210 B4 **Strathloanhead** W Loth
241 G5 **Strathmashie House** Highld
222 C5 **Strathmiglo** Fife
262 E8 **Strathpeffer** Highld
232 D4 **Strathtay** P & K
195 G4 **Strathwhillan** N Ayrs
278 E3 **Strathy** Highld
278 E3 **Strathy Inn** Highld
219 J4 **Strathyre** Stirlg
11 J1 **Stratton** Cnwll
16 C4 **Stratton** Dorset
64 E6 **Stratton** Gloucs
66 F2 **Stratton Audley** Oxon
31 L1 **Stratton-on-the-Fosse** Somset
47 H2 **Stratton St Margaret** Swindn
106 D4 **Stratton St Michael** Norfk
122 E7 **Stratton Strawless** Norfk
223 J4 **Stravithie** Fife
29 K3 **Stream** Somset
22 E4 **Streat** E Susx
51 J4 **Streatham** Gt Lon
68 D2 **Streatley** C Beds
48 E3 **Streatley** W Berk
14 E5 **Street** Devon
147 K5 **Street** Lancs
162 C2 **Street** N York
31 H3 **Street** Somset
99 M7 **Street Ashton** Warwks
112 E4 **Street Dinas** Shrops
23 K3 **Street End** E Susx
40 F4 **Street End** Kent
20 D7 **Street End** W Susx
180 F7 **Street Gate** Gatesd
98 F1 **Streethay** Staffs
151 H6 **Street Houses** N York
160 D3 **Streetlam** N York
116 C2 **Street Lane** Derbys
98 D4 **Streetly** Wsall

98 D4 **Streetly Crematorium** Wsall
88 C5 **Streetly End** Cambs
31 K3 **Street on the Fosse** Somset
95 K6 **Strefford** Shrops
233 J8 **Strelitz** P & K
116 E3 **Strelley** Notts
151 K4 **Strensall** C York
81 L7 **Strensham** Worcs
30 D2 **Stretcholt** Somset
8 C5 **Strete** Devon
80 B4 **Stretford** Herefs
80 C4 **Stretford** Herefs
130 F1 **Stretford** Traffd
87 K7 **Strethall** Essex
103 K8 **Stretham** Cambs
20 E5 **Strettington** W Susx
113 G1 **Stretton** Ches W
133 H7 **Stretton** Derbys
118 B8 **Stretton** Rutlnd
97 K1 **Stretton** Staffs
115 L6 **Stretton** Staffs
130 C3 **Stretton** Warrtn
99 J1 **Stretton en le Field** Leics
80 E6 **Stretton Grandison** Herefs
83 J1 **Stretton-on-Dunsmore** Warwks
82 F7 **Stretton on Fosse** Warwks
80 B6 **Stretton Sugwas** Herefs
99 M7 **Stretton under Fosse** Warwks
96 D4 **Stretton Westwood** Shrops
269 H5 **Strichen** Abers
131 J2 **Strines** Stockp
30 B2 **Stringston** Somset
85 H3 **Strixton** Nhants
63 H7 **Stroat** Gloucs
248 D5 **Stromeferry** Highld
275 b4 **Stromness** Ork
218 F5 **Stronachlachar** Stirlg
207 G3 **Stronafian** Ag & B
271 H4 **Stronchrubie** Highld
207 K3 **Strone** Ag & B
239 J7 **Strone** Highld
239 L6 **Stronenaba** Highld
217 J2 **Stronmilchan** Ag & B
228 C3 **Strontian** Highld
39 L7 **Strood** Kent
52 F5 **Strood** Medway
37 J1 **Strood Green** Surrey
36 F6 **Strood Green** W Susx
64 B6 **Stroud** Gloucs
35 L6 **Stroud** Hants
50 C5 **Stroude** Surrey
53 J1 **Stroud Green** Essex
64 A5 **Stroud Green** Gloucs
118 B5 **Stroxton** Lincs
246 D1 **Struan** Highld
232 B2 **Struan** P & K
137 H3 **Strubby** Lincs
107 G2 **Strumpshaw** Norfk
198 C3 **Strutherhill** S Lans
222 F5 **Struthers** Fife
250 C4 **Struy** Highld
124 F3 **Stryd-y-Facsen** IoA
112 D2 **Stryt-issa** Wrexhm
257 H3 **Stuartfield** Abers
98 D3 **Stubbers Green** Wsall
19 J3 **Stubbington** Hants
140 B4 **Stubbins** Lancs
106 E4 **Stubbs Green** Norfk
32 F8 **Stubhampton** Dorset
133 G4 **Stubley** Derbys
139 H7 **Stubshaw Cross** Wigan
118 A2 **Stubton** Lincs
33 L8 **Stuckton** Hants
148 E2 **Studfold** N York
49 L3 **Stud Green** W & M
68 C4 **Studham** C Beds
177 H7 **Studholme** Cumb
17 K6 **Studland** Dorset
82 C2 **Studley** Warwks
46 D4 **Studley** Wilts
82 C2 **Studley Common** Warwks
150 C2 **Studley Roger** N York
150 C2 **Studley Royal** N York
103 L7 **Stuntney** Cambs
23 K4 **Stunts Green** E Susx
114 C5 **Sturbridge** Staffs
135 H2 **Sturgate** Lincs
88 D6 **Sturmer** Essex
32 C8 **Sturminster Common** Dorset
17 J2 **Sturminster Marshall** Dorset
32 C8 **Sturminster Newton** Dorset
41 G3 **Sturry** Kent
144 B7 **Sturton** N Linc
135 H4 **Sturton by Stow** Lincs
134 F3 **Sturton le Steeple** Notts
106 C7 **Stuston** Suffk
151 G7 **Stutton** N York
90 D8 **Stutton** Suffk
131 G3 **Styal** Ches E
148 A8 **Stydd** Lancs

Stynie - Tannington 355


267 G4 Stynie Moray
134 C2 Styrrup Notts
218 D6 Succoth Ag & B
81 G5 Suckley Worcs
81 G4 Suckley Green Worcs
101 L7 Sudborough Nhants
91 J4 Sudbourne Suffk
118 C3 Sudbrook Lincs
45 G2 Sudbrook Mons
135 L4 Sudbrooke Lincs
115 K5 Sudbury Derbys
50 F2 Sudbury Gt Lon
89 H7 Sudbury Suffk
140 C5 Sudden Rochdl
81 J3 Suddington Worcs
64 D5 Sudgrove Gloucs
163 H4 Suffield N York
122 E5 Suffield Norfk
113 K8 Sugdon Wrekin
114 B5 Sugnall Staffs
80 B6 Sugwas Pool Herefs
247 J5 Suisnish Highld
154 e3 Sulby IoM
84 A6 Sulgrave Nhants
48 F4 Sulham W Berk
48 F5 Sulhamstead W Berk
48 F5 Sulhamstead Abbots W Berk
48 F5 Sulhamstead Bannister W Berk
21 J4 Sullington W Susx
281 d4 Sullom Shet
281 d4 Sullom Voe Shet
43 J8 Sully V Glam
150 B3 Summerbridge N York
4 E4 Summercourt Cnwll
121 G4 Summerfield Norfk
97 J8 Summerfield Worcs
49 H1 Summer Heath Bucks
55 K5 Summerhill Pembks
98 D2 Summerhill Staffs
112 D1 Summer Hill Wrexhm
169 G6 Summerhouse Darltn
157 H5 Summerlands Cumb
133 G4 Summerley Derbys
20 D5 Summersdale W Susx
140 B5 Summerseat Bury
66 D5 Summertown Oxon
140 D6 Summit Oldham
140 E4 Summit Rochdl
157 L1 Sunbiggin Cumb
50 E5 Sunbury Surrey
185 K6 Sundaywell D & G
204 C3 Sunderland Ag & B
165 G4 Sunderland Cumb
147 H4 Sunderland Lancs
181 K7 Sunderland Sundld
169 H3 Sunderland Bridge Dur
181 J7 Sunderland Crematorium Sundld
200 D8 Sundhope Border
68 D2 Sundon Park Luton
38 D2 Sundridge Kent
145 H4 Sunk Island E R Yk
50 B5 Sunningdale W & M
50 B5 Sunninghill W & M
66 D7 Sunningwell Oxon
168 F3 Sunniside Dur
180 F7 Sunniside Gatesd
140 A4 Sunny Bank Lancs
169 G4 Sunny Brow Dur
116 B5 Sunnyhill C Derb
139 K3 Sunnyhurst Bl w D
220 D7 Sunnylaw Stirlg
66 D5 Sunnymead Oxon
47 K8 Sunton Wilts
50 F5 Surbiton Gt Lon
119 H6 Surfleet Lincs
119 J6 Surfleet Seas End Lincs
107 G2 Surlingham Norfk
72 C3 Surrex Essex
37 L3 Surrey & Sussex Crematorium W Susx
122 D4 Sustead Norfk
143 L7 Susworth Lincs
26 F8 Sutcombe Devon
26 F8 Sutcombemill Devon
106 B4 Suton Norfk
137 G5 Sutterby Lincs
119 J4 Sutterton Lincs
86 E5 Sutton C Beds
102 B4 Sutton C Pete
103 J7 Sutton Cambs
7 K6 Sutton Devon
13 G2 Sutton Devon
142 E5 Sutton Donc
23 H7 Sutton E Susx
51 H6 Sutton Gt Lon
41 K5 Sutton Kent
142 D3 Sutton N York
123 H6 Sutton Norfk
117 K4 Sutton Notts
66 B6 Sutton Oxon
54 E4 Sutton Pembks
96 C1 Sutton Shrops
97 G6 Sutton Shrops
112 E6 Sutton Shrops
113 L5 Sutton Shrops
129 M1 Sutton St Hel
114 B7 Sutton Staffs
91 G6 Sutton Suffk
21 G4 Sutton W Susx
37 H2 Sutton Abinger Surrey
52 C5 Sutton at Hone Kent
101 G5 Sutton Bassett Nhants
46 D3 Sutton Benger Wilts
31 J8 Sutton Bingham Somset
116 E6 Sutton Bonington Notts
120 B7 Sutton Bridge Lincs
99 L3 Sutton Cheney Leics
98 E4 Sutton Coldfield Birm
98 F4 Sutton Coldfield Crematorium Birm
66 D8 Sutton Courtenay Oxon
119 M7 Sutton Crosses Lincs
134 D3 Sutton cum Lound Notts
116 E6 Sutton Fields Notts
66 B5 Sutton Green Oxon
50 C8 Sutton Green Surrey
112 F2 Sutton Green Wrexhm
160 D6 Sutton Howgrave N York
133 K7 Sutton in Ashfield Notts
149 H7 Sutton-in-Craven N York
100 B4 Sutton in the Elms Leics
131 H5 Sutton Lane Ends Ches E
97 G3 Sutton Maddock Shrops
30 E3 Sutton Mallet Somset
33 G5 Sutton Mandeville Wilts
129 L2 Sutton Manor St Hel
80 D6 Sutton Marsh Herefs
31 K6 Sutton Montis Somset
144 E1 Sutton-on-Hull C KuH
137 K3 Sutton on Sea Lincs
151 J3 Sutton-on-the-Forest N York
115 L5 Sutton on the Hill Derbys
134 F6 Sutton on Trent Notts
16 D5 Sutton Poyntz Dorset
103 H1 Sutton St Edmund Lincs
119 L7 Sutton St James Lincs
80 C6 Sutton St Nicholas Herefs
34 F3 Sutton Scotney Hants
39 K2 Sutton Street Kent
83 G7 Sutton-under-Brailes Warwks
161 G6 Sutton-under-Whitestonecliffe N York
151 L6 Sutton upon Derwent E R Yk
39 K3 Sutton Valence Kent
32 E3 Sutton Veny Wilts
32 E7 Sutton Waldron Dorset
130 A4 Sutton Weaver Ches W
45 H7 Sutton Wick BaNES
66 C8 Sutton Wick Oxon
137 G4 Swaby Lincs
116 A7 Swadlincote Derbys
105 G2 Swaffham Norfk
87 L3 Swaffham Bulbeck Cambs
88 B2 Swaffham Prior Cambs
122 F5 Swafield Norfk
161 G2 Swainby N York
80 B7 Swainshill Herefs
106 E3 Swainsthorpe Norfk
45 M5 Swainswick BaNES
83 J7 Swalcliffe Oxon
40 F2 Swalecliffe Kent
144 F7 Swallow Lincs
135 J6 Swallow Beck Lincs
33 G5 Swallowcliffe Wilts
49 H6 Swallowfield Wokham
133 J3 Swallow Nest Rothm
70 F7 Swallows Cross Essex
34 E1 Swampton Hants
17 K6 Swanage Dorset
67 K2 Swanbourne Bucks
43 J8 Swanbridge V Glam
97 G4 Swancote Shrops
130 E5 Swan Green Ches W
144 C2 Swanland E R Yk
52 B5 Swanley Kent
52 B5 Swanley Village Kent
35 J7 Swanmore Hants
116 C8 Swannington Leics
122 C7 Swannington Norfk
135 J6 Swanpool Garden Suburb Lincs
52 D4 Swanscombe Kent
57 J6 Swansea Swans
57 J5 Swansea Crematorium Swans
72 C2 Swan Street Essex
122 F6 Swanton Abbot Norfk
121 M8 Swanton Morley Norfk
121 M5 Swanton Novers Norfk
53 J7 Swanton Street Kent
98 C5 Swan Village Sandw
116 C1 Swanwick Derbys
19 H2 Swanwick Hants
118 D3 Swarby Lincs
106 D3 Swardeston Norfk
116 B6 Swarkestone Derbys
191 H6 Swarland Nthumb
191 H5 Swarland Estate Nthumb
35 H3 Swarraton Hants
149 J6 Swartha C Brad
156 C7 Swarthmoor Cumb
118 F4 Swaton Lincs
87 G2 Swavesey Cambs
18 D4 Sway Hants
118 C7 Swayfield Lincs
34 F7 Swaythling C Sotn
80 F3 Sweet Green Worcs
13 K3 Sweetham Devon
38 D7 Sweethaws E Susx
39 K4 Sweetlands Corner Kent
11 G3 Sweets Cnwll
5 J3 Sweetshouse Cnwll
91 H3 Swefling Suffk
99 K1 Swepstone Leics
66 A1 Swerford Oxon
130 F6 Swettenham Ches E
61 K7 Swffryd Blae G
39 L4 Swift's Green Kent
90 E4 Swilland Suffk
138 F1 Swillbrook Lancs
142 B2 Swillington Leeds
27 L5 Swimbridge Devon
27 L5 Swimbridge Newland Devon
65 L4 Swinbrook Oxon
141 K2 Swincliffe Kirk
150 C4 Swincliffe N York
28 B3 Swincombe Devon
148 E5 Swinden N York
135 H7 Swinderby Lincs
64 D2 Swindon Gloucs
190 D6 Swindon Nthumb
97 J5 Swindon Staffs
47 H2 Swindon Swindn
153 J8 Swine E R Yk
143 J3 Swinefleet E R Yk
45 K5 Swineford S Glos
85 L2 Swineshead Bed
119 H3 Swineshead Lincs
119 H3 Swineshead Bridge Lincs
275 H1 Swiney Highld
100 C7 Swinford Leics
66 C5 Swinford Oxon
41 G6 Swingfield Minnis Kent
41 H6 Swingfield Street Kent
89 K6 Swingleton Green Suffk
203 K7 Swinhoe Nthumb
145 G8 Swinhope Lincs
159 J5 Swinithwaite N York
80 F7 Swinmore Common Herefs
115 J2 Swinscoe Staffs
165 H6 Swinside Cumb
118 D7 Swinstead Lincs
135 L4 Swinthorpe Lincs
202 C4 Swinton Border
160 B6 Swinton N York
162 D8 Swinton N York
142 C7 Swinton Rothm
140 A7 Swinton Salfd
100 C1 Swithland Leics
263 G6 Swordale Highld
238 B5 Swordland Highld
278 C4 Swordly Highld
130 D3 Sworton Heath Ches E
77 J2 Swyddffynnon Cerdgn
49 G1 Swyncombe Oxon
114 D4 Swynnerton Staffs
15 M5 Swyre Dorset
112 B6 Sycharth Powys
93 L7 Sychnant Powys
94 B2 Sychtyn Powys
129 G8 Sydallt Wrexhm
64 D5 Syde Gloucs
51 K4 Sydenham Gt Lon
67 H6 Sydenham Oxon
12 A7 Sydenham Damerel Devon
36 E4 Sydenhurst Surrey
121 H5 Syderstone Norfk
16 C3 Sydling St Nicholas Dorset
48 C7 Sydmonton Hants
97 H2 Sydnal Lane Shrops
117 K2 Syerston Notts
140 D4 Syke Rochdl
143 G4 Sykehouse Donc
106 E7 Syleham Suffk
56 F3 Sylen Carmth
281 e5 Symbister Shet
196 D5 Symington S Ayrs
199 G6 Symington S Lans
15 K4 Symondsbury Dorset
63 H4 Symonds Yat Herefs
150 A8 Sympson Green C Brad
15 J2 Synderford Dorset
76 D4 Synod Inn Cerdgn
278 B7 Syre Highld
64 F3 Syreford Gloucs
84 C7 Syresham Nhants
100 D1 Syston Leics
118 B3 Syston Lincs
81 J2 Sytchampton Worcs
84 F2 Sywell Nhants


## T


130 E4 Tabley Hill Ches E
66 C3 Tackley Oxon
106 C4 Tacolneston Norfk
151 G7 Tadcaster N York
132 C5 Taddington Derbys
65 G1 Taddington Gloucs
27 H7 Taddiport Devon
48 F6 Tadley Hants
86 F5 Tadlow Cambs
83 J7 Tadmarton Oxon
45 L5 Tadwick BaNES
51 G7 Tadworth Surrey
61 H5 Tafarnaubach Blae G
75 J5 Tafarn-y-bwlch Pembks
128 E7 Tafarn-y-Gelyn Denbgs
43 H5 Taff's Well Rhondd
93 J3 Tafolwern Powys
57 L7 Taibach Neath
263 L3 Tain Highld
280 B3 Tain Highld
282 e5 Tairbeart W Isls
60 F2 Tai'r Bull Powys
70 E3 Takeley Essex
70 E3 Takeley Street Essex
78 F8 Talachddu Powys
128 D3 Talacre Flints
14 C3 Talaton Devon
54 D4 Talbenny Pembks
43 G5 Talbot Green Rhondd
17 L4 Talbot Village Bmouth
14 C3 Taleford Devon
93 K3 Talerddig Powys
76 D5 Talgarreg Cerdgn
79 G8 Talgarth Powys
246 D3 Talisker Highld
114 C1 Talke Staffs
114 C1 Talke Pits Staffs
178 D7 Talkin Cumb
260 E6 Talladale Highld
187 H2 Talla Linnfoots Border
183 K3 Tallaminnock S Ayrs
113 G3 Tallarn Green Wrexhm
164 F4 Tallentire Cumb
59 H2 Talley Carmth
102 B2 Tallington Lincs
112 D2 Tallwrn Wrexhm
277 K4 Talmine Highld
58 B4 Talog Carmth
77 G4 Talsarn Cerdgn
109 L4 Talsarnau Gwynd
4 E2 Talskiddy Cnwll
125 J4 Talwrn IoA
112 F2 Talwrn Wrexhm
92 E5 Tal-y-bont Cerdgn
126 F6 Tal-y-Bont Conwy
109 L7 Tal-y-bont Gwynd
126 C5 Tal-y-bont Gwynd
61 H3 Talybont-on-Usk Powys
126 F5 Tal-y-Cafn Conwy
62 E4 Tal-y-coed Mons
42 F5 Tal-y-garn Rhondd
92 F2 Tal-y-llyn Gwynd
109 J1 Talysarn Gwynd
61 L6 Tal-y-Waun Torfn
93 H3 Talywern Powys
139 J7 Tamer Lane End Wigan
6 F3 Tamerton Foliot C Plym
99 G3 Tamworth Staffs
119 L3 Tamworth Green Lincs
151 G4 Tancred N York
74 E7 Tancredston Pembks
38 B3 Tandridge Surrey
180 F7 Tanfield Dur
180 F8 Tanfield Lea Dur
54 F3 Tangiers Pembks
47 L8 Tangley Hants
20 E5 Tangmere W Susx
283 b13 Tangusdale W Isls
158 F1 Tan Hill N York
275 d4 Tankerness Ork
142 A7 Tankersley Barns
40 F2 Tankerton Kent
280 D6 Tannach Highld
245 H6 Tannachie Abers
234 D4 Tannadice Angus
98 D8 Tanner's Green Worcs
90 F2 Tannington Suffk

209 J6 **Tannochside** N Lans
132 F7 **Tansley** Derbys
102 B5 **Tansor** Nhants
180 E7 **Tantobie** Dur
170 C8 **Tanton** N York
97 K8 **Tanwood** Worcs
82 D1 **Tanworth in Arden** Warwks
110 C3 **Tan-y-Bwlch** Gwynd
127 J6 **Tan-y-fron** Conwy
112 D1 **Tan-y-fron** Wrexhm
110 C3 **Tan-y-grisiau** Gwynd
76 B5 **Tan-y-groes** Cerdgn
282 d6 **Taobh Tuath** W Isls
49 M3 **Taplow** Bucks
205 L6 **Tarbert** Ag & B
206 D5 **Tarbert** Ag & B
282 e5 **Tarbert** W Isls
218 D6 **Tarbet** Ag & B
238 C5 **Tarbet** Highld
276 B6 **Tarbet** Highld
129 K2 **Tarbock Green** Knows
196 E5 **Tarbolton** S Ayrs
199 H2 **Tarbrax** S Lans
82 B2 **Tardebigge** Worcs
244 B7 **Tarfside** Angus
244 B3 **Tarland** Abers
138 F4 **Tarleton** Lancs
138 E5 **Tarlscough** Lancs
64 D7 **Tarlton** Gloucs
44 D8 **Tarnock** Somset
164 F1 **Tarns** Cumb
156 F4 **Tarnside** Cumb
130 A7 **Tarporley** Ches W
28 F4 **Tarr** Somset
17 H2 **Tarrant Crawford** Dorset
32 F8 **Tarrant Gunville** Dorset
32 F8 **Tarrant Hinton** Dorset
17 H2 **Tarrant Keyneston** Dorset
17 J1 **Tarrant Launceston** Dorset
17 J1 **Tarrant Monkton** Dorset
17 H1 **Tarrant Rawston** Dorset
17 H1 **Tarrant Rushton** Dorset
23 G6 **Tarring Neville** E Susx
80 E7 **Tarrington** Herefs
247 J6 **Tarskavaig** Highld
256 F5 **Tarves** Abers
129 L6 **Tarvin** Ches W
129 L6 **Tarvin Sands** Ches W
106 D4 **Tasburgh** Norfk
96 F4 **Tasley** Shrops
65 M3 **Taston** Oxon
115 K7 **Tatenhill** Staffs
84 F6 **Tathall End** M Keyn
147 M2 **Tatham** Lancs
136 F3 **Tathwell** Lincs
51 L7 **Tatsfield** Surrey
129 L7 **Tattenhall** Ches W
121 J6 **Tatterford** Norfk
121 J5 **Tattersett** Norfk
136 D8 **Tattershall** Lincs
136 C8 **Tattershall Bridge** Lincs
136 D7 **Tattershall Thorpe** Lincs
90 D7 **Tattingstone** Suffk
90 D7 **Tattingstone White Horse** Suffk
15 H1 **Tatworth** Somset
267 H6 **Tauchers** Moray
30 C6 **Taunton** Somset
30 B6 **Taunton Deane Crematorium** Somset
122 D8 **Taverham** Norfk
70 E3 **Taverners Green** Essex
55 L4 **Tavernspite** Pembks
12 C7 **Tavistock** Devon
12 F3 **Taw Green** Devon
27 K5 **Tawstock** Devon
131 K4 **Taxal** Derbys
217 G3 **Taychreggan Hotel** Ag & B
205 M7 **Tayinloan** Ag & B
63 L3 **Taynton** Gloucs
65 K4 **Taynton** Oxon
216 F1 **Taynuilt** Ag & B
223 H2 **Tayport** Fife
215 L7 **Tayvallich** Ag & B
136 C2 **Tealby** Lincs
181 G7 **Team Valley** Gatesd
247 K6 **Teangue** Highld
263 G7 **Teanord** Highld
157 K2 **Tebay** Cumb
68 C2 **Tebworth** C Beds
13 J4 **Tedburn St Mary** Devon
81 M8 **Teddington** Gloucs
50 F5 **Teddington** Gt Lon
80 F3 **Tedstone Delamere** Herefs
80 F3 **Tedstone Wafer** Herefs
170 D6 **Teesport** R & Cl
170 C7 **Teesside Crematorium** Middsb
170 B7 **Teesside Park** S on T
84 D1 **Teeton** Nhants
33 G4 **Teffont Evias** Wilts

33 G4 **Teffont Magna** Wilts
75 L5 **Tegryn** Pembks
117 M8 **Teigh** Rutlnd
12 F5 **Teigncombe** Devon
13 K7 **Teigngrace** Devon
13 L7 **Teignmouth** Devon
188 D4 **Teindside** Border
96 F2 **Telford** Wrekin
97 G1 **Telford Crematorium** Wrekin
46 A7 **Tellisford** Somset
22 F6 **Telscombe** E Susx
22 F7 **Telscombe Cliffs** E Susx
231 J4 **Tempar** P & K
176 E2 **Templand** D & G
11 G7 **Temple** Cnwll
211 K7 **Temple** Mdloth
99 G8 **Temple Balsall** Solhll
76 F4 **Temple Bar** Cerdgn
45 J7 **Temple Cloud** BaNES
32 B6 **Templecombe** Somset
88 D5 **Temple End** Suffk
41 J6 **Temple Ewell** Kent
82 D4 **Temple Grafton** Warwks
65 G2 **Temple Guiting** Gloucs
142 F3 **Temple Hirst** N York
133 H6 **Temple Normanton** Derbys
245 H7 **Temple of Fiddes** Abers
250 F5 **Temple Pier** Highld
166 E5 **Temple Sowerby** Cumb
28 F8 **Templeton** Devon
55 J4 **Templeton** Pembks
168 E1 **Templetown** Dur
86 D4 **Tempsford** C Beds
80 E2 **Tenbury Wells** Worcs
55 K6 **Tenby** Pembks
73 H2 **Tendring** Essex
73 H2 **Tendring Green** Essex
73 H2 **Tendring Heath** Essex
104 B4 **Ten Mile Bank** Norfk
73 G3 **Tenpenny Heath** Essex
39 M6 **Tenterden** Kent
71 J4 **Terling** Essex
113 K8 **Tern** Wrekin
113 L5 **Ternhill** Shrops
176 B3 **Terregles** D & G
151 L2 **Terrington** N York
120 C7 **Terrington St Clement** Norfk
120 C8 **Terrington St John** Norfk
98 E8 **Terry's Green** Warwks
39 H3 **Teston** Kent
34 D7 **Testwood** Hants
64 C8 **Tetbury** Gloucs
64 C8 **Tetbury Upton** Gloucs
112 F5 **Tetchill** Shrops
11 L3 **Tetcott** Devon
136 F5 **Tetford** Lincs
145 J7 **Tetney** Lincs
145 J7 **Tetney Lock** Lincs
67 G6 **Tetsworth** Oxon
97 K3 **Tettenhall** Wolves
97 K3 **Tettenhall Wood** Wolves
86 E4 **Tetworth** Cambs
133 J7 **Teversal** Notts
87 K3 **Teversham** Cambs
188 C5 **Teviothead** Border
69 H4 **Tewin** Herts
69 H4 **Tewin Wood** Herts
81 K8 **Tewkesbury** Gloucs
40 B3 **Teynham** Kent
149 M8 **Thackley** C Brad
164 F6 **Thackthwaite** Cumb
166 A5 **Thackthwaite** Cumb
21 J3 **Thakeham** W Susx
67 H6 **Thame** Oxon
50 F5 **Thames Ditton** Surrey
52 A3 **Thamesmead** Gt Lon
41 K2 **Thanet Crematorium** Kent
40 F4 **Thanington** Kent
199 G5 **Thankerton** S Lans
106 D4 **Tharston** Norfk
48 D5 **Thatcham** W Berk
129 L1 **Thatto Heath** St Hel
70 F1 **Thaxted** Essex
160 D5 **Theakston** N York
143 M4 **Thealby** N Linc
31 G2 **Theale** Somset
48 F5 **Theale** W Berk
153 G8 **Thearne** E R Yk
131 G8 **The Bank** Ches E
96 E3 **The Bank** Shrops
64 F6 **The Beeches** Gloucs
91 K2 **Theberton** Suffk
115 G6 **The Blythe** Staffs
95 J4 **The Bog** Shrops
82 A4 **The Bourne** Worcs
247 H2 **The Braes** Highld
97 K4 **The Bratch** Staffs
80 C3 **The Broad** Herefs
212 F4 **The Brunt** E Loth
154 e5 **The Bungalow** IoM

81 J2 **The Burf** Worcs
64 C4 **The Butts** Gloucs
64 C5 **The Camp** Gloucs
113 H3 **The Chequer** Wrexhm
86 C3 **The City** Bed
67 J7 **The City** Bucks
65 L2 **The Common** Oxon
34 B4 **The Common** Wilts
46 F2 **The Common** Wilts
39 H5 **The Corner** Kent
95 K6 **The Corner** Shrops
84 E4 **The Counties Crematorium** Nhants
154 d3 **The Cronk** IoM
100 E6 **Theddingworth** Leics
137 J2 **Theddlethorpe All Saints** Lincs
137 J2 **Theddlethorpe St Helen** Lincs
196 C1 **The Den** N Ayrs
63 J4 **The Forest of Dean Crematorium** Gloucs
79 L3 **The Forge** Herefs
40 A6 **The Forstal** Kent
40 D7 **The Forstal** Kent
113 L5 **The Fouralls** Shrops
53 J5 **The Garden of England Crematorium** Kent
156 A5 **The Green** Cumb
71 J3 **The Green** Essex
162 D2 **The Green** N York
32 E4 **The Green** Wilts
81 K7 **The Grove** Worcs
37 G5 **The Haven** W Susx
64 B2 **The Haw** Gloucs
170 C4 **The Headland** Hartpl
156 A6 **The Hill** Cumb
49 K3 **The Holt** Wokham
80 C2 **The Hundred** Herefs
28 D8 **Thelbridge Cross** Devon
40 C8 **The Leacon** Kent
67 L6 **The Lee** Bucks
154 e2 **The Lhen** IoM
209 G7 **The Linn Crematorium** E Rens
105 L7 **Thelnetham** Suffk
266 F4 **The Lochs** Moray
106 D7 **Thelveton** Norfk
130 C2 **Thelwall** Warrtn
130 F1 **The Manchester Crematorium** Manch
95 H4 **The Marsh** Powys
122 B6 **Themelthorpe** Norfk
180 F8 **The Middles** Dur
39 J7 **The Moor** Kent
57 H7 **The Mumbles** Swans
209 H8 **The Murray** S Lans
81 K8 **The Mythe** Gloucs
63 G6 **The Narth** Mons
245 G4 **The Neuk** Abers
83 M7 **Thenford** Nhants
46 F5 **Theobald's Green** Wilts
36 C1 **The Park Crematorium** Hants
63 L7 **The Quarry** Gloucs
39 M4 **The Quarter** Kent
64 C3 **The Reddings** Gloucs
87 G7 **Therfield** Herts
61 J1 **The Rhôs** Powys
142 F7 **The Rose Hill Crematorium** Donc
220 D3 **The Ross** P & K
36 C2 **The Sands** Surrey
46 A4 **The Shoe** Wilts
96 F4 **The Smithies** Shrops
87 K5 **The Spike** Cambs
83 G1 **The Spring** Warwks
62 B7 **The Square** Torfn
38 F4 **The Stair** Kent
25 G2 **The Stocks** Kent
36 A3 **The Straits** Hants
46 D7 **The Strand** Wilts
105 H6 **Thetford** Norfk
165 L2 **Thethwaite** Cumb
2 E3 **The Towans** Cnwll
68 E2 **The Vale Crematorium** Luton
80 C5 **The Vauld** Herefs
97 G2 **The Wyke** Shrops
70 C7 **Theydon Bois** Essex
151 L7 **Thicket Priory** N York
46 B4 **Thickwood** Wilts
136 D5 **Thimbleby** Lincs
161 G3 **Thimbleby** N York
129 G3 **Thingwall** Wirral
161 G6 **Thirkleby** N York
161 G6 **Thirlby** N York
201 H4 **Thirlestane** Border
160 B5 **Thirn** N York
160 F6 **Thirsk** N York
144 F1 **Thirtleby** E R Yk
147 H8 **Thistleton** Lancs
118 B7 **Thistleton** Rutlnd
104 D8 **Thistley Green** Suffk
152 C4 **Thixendale** N York

179 M3 **Thockrington** Nthumb
103 H2 **Tholomas Drove** Cambs
151 G2 **Tholthorpe** N York
55 J5 **Thomas Chapel** Pembks
166 B3 **Thomas Close** Cumb
255 L4 **Thomastown** Abers
82 C3 **Thomas Town** Warwks
105 J4 **Thompson** Norfk
52 E5 **Thong** Kent
159 H5 **Thoralby** N York
134 C5 **Thoresby** Notts
137 J4 **Thoresthorpe** Lincs
144 F8 **Thoresway** Lincs
145 G8 **Thorganby** Lincs
151 L7 **Thorganby** N York
162 C3 **Thorgill** N York
107 J8 **Thorington** Suffk
89 K8 **Thorington Street** Suffk
149 H5 **Thorlby** N York
70 C3 **Thorley** Herts
18 F6 **Thorley** IoW
70 C3 **Thorley Houses** Herts
18 F6 **Thorley Street** IoW
161 H7 **Thormanby** N York
170 B7 **Thornaby-on-Tees** S on T
122 B4 **Thornage** Norfk
84 E8 **Thornborough** Bucks
160 D6 **Thornborough** N York
141 J1 **Thornbury** C Brad
12 A1 **Thornbury** Devon
80 E3 **Thornbury** Herefs
45 J1 **Thornbury** S Glos
177 J8 **Thornby** Cumb
100 E8 **Thornby** Nhants
131 K7 **Thorncliff** Staffs
146 D2 **Thorncliffe Crematorium** Cumb
15 J2 **Thorncombe** Dorset
36 F3 **Thorncombe Street** Surrey
86 C5 **Thorncott Green** C Beds
19 G7 **Thorncross** IoW
90 D1 **Thorndon** Suffk
12 D4 **Thorndon Cross** Devon
143 H5 **Thorne** Donc
31 H7 **Thorne** Somset
7 M2 **Thornecroft** Devon
27 G7 **Thornehillhead** Devon
150 E7 **Thorner** Leeds
98 D3 **Thornes** Staffs
141 M4 **Thornes** Wakefd
29 K6 **Thorne St Margaret** Somset
50 D3 **Thorney** Bucks
102 F3 **Thorney** C Pete
135 G5 **Thorney** Notts
30 F6 **Thorney** Somset
18 B4 **Thorney Hill** Hants
103 G3 **Thorney Toll** Cambs
30 D6 **Thornfalcon** Somset
31 K8 **Thornford** Dorset
179 H6 **Thorngrafton** Nthumb
30 E4 **Thorngrove** Somset
145 G3 **Thorngumbald** E R Yk
121 G3 **Thornham** Norfk
90 C1 **Thornham Magna** Suffk
90 D1 **Thornham Parva** Suffk
102 B3 **Thornhaugh** C Pete
19 G1 **Thornhill** C Sotn
43 J5 **Thornhill** Caerph
186 C7 **Thornhill** D & G
132 D3 **Thornhill** Derbys
141 L4 **Thornhill** Kirk
219 L7 **Thornhill** Stirlg
43 J5 **Thornhill Crematorium** Cardif
141 K4 **Thornhill Lees** Kirk
141 J3 **Thornhills** Calder
153 H3 **Thornholme** E R Yk
17 G2 **Thornicombe** Dorset
202 D6 **Thornington** Nthumb
168 E3 **Thornley** Dur
169 K3 **Thornley** Dur
179 J7 **Thornley Gate** Nthumb
208 F7 **Thornliebank** E Rens
88 E4 **Thorns** Suffk
131 K2 **Thornsett** Derbys
130 F3 **Thorns Green** Ches E
165 H5 **Thornthwaite** Cumb
149 L4 **Thornthwaite** N York
234 B6 **Thornton** Angus
84 E8 **Thornton** Bucks
141 H1 **Thornton** C Brad
152 A6 **Thornton** E R Yk
222 E7 **Thornton** Fife
146 F7 **Thornton** Lancs
100 A2 **Thornton** Leics
136 D6 **Thornton** Lincs
170 B7 **Thornton** Middsb
202 E4 **Thornton** Nthumb
54 E5 **Thornton** Pembks
138 D7 **Thornton** Sefton

144 D4 **Thornton Curtis** N Linc
138 D7 **Thornton Garden of Rest Crematorium** Sefton
129 K5 **Thornton Green** Ches W
209 G8 **Thorntonhall** S Lans
51 J5 **Thornton Heath** Gt Lon
129 G3 **Thornton Hough** Wirral
148 F6 **Thornton-in-Craven** N York
158 B8 **Thornton in Lonsdale** N York
160 F4 **Thornton-le-Beans** N York
151 L3 **Thornton-le-Clay** N York
162 E6 **Thornton le Dale** N York
144 D8 **Thornton le Moor** Lincs
160 F5 **Thornton-le-Moor** N York
129 K5 **Thornton-le-Moors** Ches W
160 F5 **Thornton-le-Street** N York
213 G4 **Thorntonloch** E Loth
159 G5 **Thornton Rust** N York
160 A5 **Thornton Steward** N York
160 C5 **Thornton Watlass** N York
70 C6 **Thornwood Common** Essex
201 J3 **Thornydykes** Border
165 L6 **Thornythwaite** Cumb
117 K3 **Thoroton** Notts
150 F6 **Thorp Arch** Leeds
115 J2 **Thorpe** Derbys
152 F6 **Thorpe** E R Yk
137 J3 **Thorpe** Lincs
149 H3 **Thorpe** N York
107 J4 **Thorpe** Norfk
117 K2 **Thorpe** Notts
50 C5 **Thorpe** Surrey
106 D7 **Thorpe Abbotts** Norfk
116 E7 **Thorpe Acre** Leics
117 K7 **Thorpe Arnold** Leics
142 D4 **Thorpe Audlin** Wakefd
162 F8 **Thorpe Bassett** N York
53 K2 **Thorpe Bay** Sthend
101 K4 **Thorpe by Water** Rutlnd
133 G1 **Thorpe Common** Rothm
99 H2 **Thorpe Constantine** Staffs
106 F1 **Thorpe End** Norfk
73 H3 **Thorpe Green** Essex
139 H3 **Thorpe Green** Lancs
89 J4 **Thorpe Green** Suffk
142 B8 **Thorpe Hesley** Rothm
142 F5 **Thorpe in Balne** Donc
101 G5 **Thorpe Langton** Leics
169 K5 **Thorpe Larches** Dur
50 C5 **Thorpe Lea** Surrey
135 H4 **Thorpe le Fallows** Lincs
73 J3 **Thorpe-le-Soken** Essex
152 C7 **Thorpe le Street** E R Yk
101 H7 **Thorpe Malsor** Nhants
83 M6 **Thorpe Mandeville** Nhants
122 E4 **Thorpe Market** Norfk
122 D8 **Thorpe Marriot** Norfk
89 J4 **Thorpe Morieux** Suffk
91 L3 **Thorpeness** Suffk
141 M2 **Thorpe on the Hill** Leeds
135 H6 **Thorpe on the Hill** Lincs
106 F2 **Thorpe St Andrew** Norfk
137 J7 **Thorpe St Peter** Lincs
133 K3 **Thorpe Salvin** Rothm
100 F1 **Thorpe Satchville** Leics
169 L6 **Thorpe Thewles** S on T
136 B8 **Thorpe Tilney** Lincs
151 G4 **Thorpe Underwood** N York
101 H7 **Thorpe Underwood** Nhants
102 A7 **Thorpe Waterville** Nhants
142 F2 **Thorpe Willoughby** N York
104 C2 **Thorpland** Norfk
73 G3 **Thorrington** Essex
13 L2 **Thorverton** Devon
68 E4 **Thrales End** C Beds
106 C8 **Thrandeston** Suffk
101 M7 **Thrapston** Nhants
165 G3 **Threapland** Cumb
149 H4 **Threapland** N York
113 G3 **Threapwood** Ches W
115 G3 **Threapwood** Staffs
115 G3 **Threapwood Head** Staffs
183 J2 **Threave** S Ayrs
63 G3 **Three Ashes** Herefs
37 L3 **Three Bridges** W Susx
4 B5 **Three Burrows** Cnwll
39 K5 **Three Chimneys** Kent
79 G7 **Three Cocks** Powys
57 G6 **Three Crosses** Swans
23 L3 **Three Cups Corner** E Susx
80 F3 **Three Gates** Worcs
123 G7 **Threehammer Common** Norfk
11 J5 **Three Hammers** Cnwll
103 K3 **Three Holes** Norfk
118 E4 **Threekingham** Lincs
39 H7 **Three Leg Cross** E Susx
17 L1 **Three Legged Cross** Dorset
49 H5 **Three Mile Cross** Wokham
4 C6 **Threemilestone** Cnwll
210 E4 **Three Miletown** W Loth
24 F4 **Three Oaks** E Susx
201 G4 **Threepwood** Border
165 K5 **Threlkeld** Cumb
70 D5 **Threshers Bush** Essex
149 H3 **Threshfield** N York
107 J1 **Thrigby** Norfk
167 L6 **Thringarth** Dur
116 D8 **Thringstone** Leics
160 D4 **Thrintoft** N York
87 J6 **Thriplow** Cambs
133 K2 **Throapham** Rothm
103 G2 **Throckenhalt** Lincs
69 J1 **Throcking** Herts
180 E5 **Throckley** N u Ty
82 A5 **Throckmorton** Worcs
17 M3 **Throop** Bmouth
16 F4 **Throop** Dorset
180 D2 **Throphill** Nthumb
190 E5 **Thropton** Nthumb
209 M1 **Throsk** Stirlg
64 D5 **Througham** Gloucs
185 L6 **Throughgate** D & G
12 F4 **Throwleigh** Devon
40 C4 **Throwley** Kent
40 C4 **Throwley Forstal** Kent
116 E5 **Thrumpton** Notts
134 D4 **Thrumpton** Notts
280 D7 **Thrumster** Highld
145 J6 **Thrunscoe** NE Lin
190 F4 **Thrunton** Nthumb
65 L7 **Thrup** Oxon
64 B6 **Thrupp** Gloucs
66 C4 **Thrupp** Oxon
12 B5 **Thrushelton** Devon
117 H8 **Thrussington** Leics
34 C2 **Thruxton** Hants
80 B8 **Thruxton** Herefs
142 D8 **Thrybergh** Rothm
116 C5 **Thulston** Derbys
53 G1 **Thundersley** Essex
100 C1 **Thurcaston** Leics
133 K2 **Thurcroft** Rothm
26 E8 **Thurdon** Cnwll
122 D4 **Thurgarton** Norfk
117 J2 **Thurgarton** Notts
141 L7 **Thurgoland** Barns
100 B4 **Thurlaston** Leics
83 L1 **Thurlaston** Warwks
30 C6 **Thurlbear** Somset
118 E8 **Thurlby** Lincs
135 H7 **Thurlby** Lincs
137 J4 **Thurlby** Lincs
85 L3 **Thurleigh** Bed
7 K6 **Thurlestone** Devon
88 D5 **Thurlow** Suffk
30 C5 **Thurloxton** Somset
141 K7 **Thurlstone** Barns
107 J4 **Thurlton** Norfk
130 F8 **Thurlwood** Ches E
100 D2 **Thurmaston** Leics
100 E3 **Thurnby** Leics
123 H8 **Thurne** Norfk
53 H7 **Thurnham** Kent
102 B6 **Thurning** Nhants
122 B5 **Thurning** Norfk
142 C6 **Thurnscoe** Barns
165 K1 **Thursby** Cumb
140 D1 **Thursden** Lancs
121 L5 **Thursford** Norfk
36 D3 **Thursley** Surrey
279 K3 **Thurso** Highld
128 F3 **Thurstaston** Wirral
89 J2 **Thurston** Suffk
140 E6 **Thurston Clough** Oldham
177 K7 **Thurstonfield** Cumb
141 J5 **Thurstonland** Kirk
89 J2 **Thurston Planch** Suffk
107 G3 **Thurton** Norfk
115 L4 **Thurvaston** Derbys
105 L2 **Thuxton** Norfk
158 F3 **Thwaite** N York
90 D2 **Thwaite** Suffk
156 E4 **Thwaite Head** Cumb
149 K7 **Thwaites** C Brad
107 G4 **Thwaite St Mary** Norfk
149 K7 **Thwaites Brow** C Brad
153 G2 **Thwing** E R Yk
221 J3 **Tibbermore** P & K
186 C6 **Tibbers** D & G
63 M3 **Tibberton** Gloucs
81 L4 **Tibberton** Worcs
113 L7 **Tibberton** Wrekin
187 K2 **Tibbie Shiels Inn** Border
106 C5 **Tibenham** Norfk
133 J7 **Tibshelf** Derbys
152 E5 **Tibthorpe** E R Yk
39 H7 **Ticehurst** E Susx
35 H5 **Tichborne** Hants
101 L2 **Tickencote** Rutlnd
44 F4 **Tickenham** N Som
85 H6 **Tickford End** M Keyn
134 B1 **Tickhill** Donc
96 B5 **Ticklerton** Shrops
116 B6 **Ticknall** Derbys
153 G7 **Tickton** E R Yk
98 E8 **Tidbury Green** Solhll
47 L7 **Tidcombe** Wilts
67 G6 **Tiddington** Oxon
82 F4 **Tiddington** Warwks
46 C4 **Tiddleywink** Wilts
38 F7 **Tidebrook** E Susx
6 C3 **Tideford** Cnwll
6 C3 **Tideford Cross** Cnwll
63 H7 **Tidenham** Gloucs
132 C4 **Tideswell** Derbys
48 F4 **Tidmarsh** W Berk
83 G7 **Tidmington** Warwks
33 J7 **Tidpit** Hants
34 B1 **Tidworth** Wilts
54 E5 **Tiers Cross** Pembks
84 D5 **Tiffield** Nhants
234 E3 **Tigerton** Angus
282 b7 **Tigh a Ghearraidh** W Isls
282 b7 **Tigharry** W Isls
206 F4 **Tighnabruaich** Ag & B
7 L3 **Tigley** Devon
86 B2 **Tilbrook** Cambs
52 D4 **Tilbury** Thurr
88 E7 **Tilbury Green** Essex
88 F7 **Tilbury Juxta Clare** Essex
98 F6 **Tile Cross** Birm
99 H7 **Tile Hill** Covtry
98 F8 **Tilehouse Green** Solhll
49 G4 **Tilehurst** Readg
36 C2 **Tilford** Surrey
37 L4 **Tilgate** W Susx
37 L4 **Tilgate Forest Row** W Susx
31 J4 **Tilham Street** Somset
80 F8 **Tillers Green** Gloucs
221 G7 **Tillicoultry** Clacks
198 D4 **Tillietudlem** S Lans
72 E6 **Tillingham** Essex
80 B6 **Tillington** Herefs
36 E6 **Tillington** W Susx
80 B6 **Tillington Common** Herefs
244 F2 **Tillybirloch** Abers
244 E1 **Tillyfourie** Abers
256 F7 **Tillygreig** Abers
221 K6 **Tillyrie** P & K
41 J5 **Tilmanstone** Kent
120 C7 **Tilney All Saints** Norfk
120 C8 **Tilney High End** Norfk
120 C8 **Tilney St Lawrence** Norfk
33 H1 **Tilshead** Wilts
113 J4 **Tilstock** Shrops
113 G1 **Tilston** Ches W
130 A7 **Tilstone Bank** Ches W
130 A7 **Tilstone Fearnall** Ches W
68 B2 **Tilsworth** C Beds
101 G2 **Tilton on the Hill** Leics
64 B7 **Tiltups End** Gloucs
70 E2 **Tilty** Essex
136 B7 **Timberland** Lincs
131 H7 **Timbersbrook** Ches E
29 G2 **Timberscombe** Somset
149 M5 **Timble** N York
29 H5 **Timewell** Devon
177 K4 **Timpanheck** D & G
130 F2 **Timperley** Traffd
45 K7 **Timsbury** BaNES
34 D6 **Timsbury** Hants
282 d3 **Timsgarry** W Isls
282 d3 **Timsgearraidh** W Isls
89 H2 **Timworth** Suffk
89 H2 **Timworth Green** Suffk
16 E4 **Tincleton** Dorset
178 E7 **Tindale** Cumb
169 G5 **Tindale Crescent** Dur
84 C6 **Tingewick** Bucks
141 L3 **Tingley** Leeds
68 C1 **Tingrith** C Beds
12 A5 **Tinhay** Devon
34 E2 **Tinker's Hill** Hants
132 E6 **Tinkersley** Derbys
133 H2 **Tinsley** Sheff
37 L3 **Tinsley Green** W Susx
10 F5 **Tintagel** Cnwll
63 G7 **Tintern Parva** Mons
31 H7 **Tintinhull** Somset
140 F8 **Tintwistle** Derbys
176 D3 **Tinwald** D & G
101 M2 **Tinwell** Rutlnd
28 D2 **Tippacott** Devon
103 K4 **Tipp's End** Norfk
18 C4 **Tiptoe** Hants
97 L5 **Tipton** Sandw
98 B5 **Tipton Green** Sandw
14 C4 **Tipton St John** Devon
72 C4 **Tiptree** Essex
72 C4 **Tiptree Heath** Essex
78 B7 **Tirabad** Powys
206 A6 **Tiretigan** Ag & B
64 B2 **Tirley** Gloucs
61 H6 **Tirphil** Caerph
166 C5 **Tirril** Cumb
129 G7 **Tir-y-fron** Flints
32 F5 **Tisbury** Wilts
37 G4 **Tisman's Common** W Susx
115 K1 **Tissington** Derbys
26 D5 **Titchberry** Devon
19 J3 **Titchfield** Hants
19 J2 **Titchfield Common** Hants
102 A7 **Titchmarsh** Nhants
121 G3 **Titchwell** Norfk
117 J4 **Tithby** Notts
79 L3 **Titley** Herefs
69 G2 **Titmore Green** Herts
51 L7 **Titsey** Surrey
11 J2 **Titson** Cnwll
114 D4 **Tittensor** Staffs
121 K7 **Tittleshall** Norfk
81 J1 **Titton** Worcs
130 A7 **Tiverton** Ches W
29 G8 **Tiverton** Devon
106 D6 **Tivetshall St Margaret** Norfk
106 D6 **Tivetshall St Mary** Norfk
29 G2 **Tivington** Somset
141 L6 **Tivy Dale** Barns
114 F7 **Tixall** Staffs
101 L3 **Tixover** Rutlnd
281 d9 **Toab** Shet
133 H8 **Toadhole** Derbys
116 B1 **Toadmoor** Derbys
226 F1 **Tobermory** Ag & B
215 L3 **Toberonochy** Ag & B
283 b10 **Tobha Mor** W Isls
256 C5 **Tocher** Abers
267 K3 **Tochieneal** Moray
46 F3 **Tockenham** Wilts
46 F3 **Tockenham Wick** Wilts
170 E7 **Tocketts** R & Cl
139 K3 **Tockholes** Bl w D
45 J2 **Tockington** S Glos
151 G5 **Tockwith** N York
32 D7 **Todber** Dorset
191 G7 **Todburn** Nthumb
68 C2 **Toddington** C Beds
82 B8 **Toddington** Gloucs
69 G2 **Todds Green** Herts
82 F8 **Todenham** Gloucs
234 C7 **Todhills** Angus
177 L6 **Todhills** Cumb
169 G4 **Todhills** Dur
140 E3 **Todmorden** Calder
133 K3 **Todwick** Rothm
87 G4 **Toft** Cambs
130 E4 **Toft** Ches E
118 E8 **Toft** Lincs
281 e4 **Toft** Shet
83 L1 **Toft** Warwks
168 F5 **Toft Hill** Dur
136 D7 **Toft Hill** Lincs
107 J4 **Toft Monks** Norfk
135 L2 **Toft next Newton** Lincs
121 K6 **Toftrees** Norfk
105 K1 **Toftwood** Norfk
191 K5 **Togston** Nthumb
247 J6 **Tokavaig** Highld
49 H3 **Tokers Green** Oxon
282 h2 **Tolastadh** W Isls
4 F3 **Toldish** Cnwll
29 K4 **Tolland** Somset
32 F7 **Tollard Farnham** Dorset
32 F7 **Tollard Royal** Wilts
142 E6 **Toll Bar** Donc
99 K8 **Tollbar End** Covtry
16 B3 **Toller Fratrum** Dorset
16 A3 **Toller Porcorum** Dorset
151 H3 **Tollerton** N York
117 G4 **Tollerton** Notts
15 L2 **Toller Whelme** Dorset
72 D5 **Tollesbury** Essex
72 D5 **Tolleshunt D'Arcy** Essex
72 D4 **Tolleshunt Knights** Essex
72 C5 **Tolleshunt Major** Essex
16 F3 **Tolpuddle** Dorset
282 h2 **Tolsta** W Isls
51 G5 **Tolworth** Gt Lon
252 E6 **Tomatin** Highld
239 M1 **Tomchrasky** Highld
239 K3 **Tomdoun** Highld
250 B6 **Tomich** Highld
250 F2 **Tomich** Highld
263 J5 **Tomich** Highld
272 F7 **Tomich** Highld
254 D7 **Tomintoul** Moray
83 K3 **Tomlow** Warwks
250 F3 **Tomnacross** Highld
254 D6 **Tomnavoulin** Moray
114 E1 **Tompkin** Staffs

| | | | |
|---|---|---|---|
| 62 C6 **Ton** Mons | 18 E6 **Totland** IoW | 29 H4 **Treborough** Somset | 3 J7 **Trelan** Cnwll |
| 62 D7 **Ton** Mons | 132 F4 **Totley** Sheff | 4 E3 **Trebudannon** Cnwll | 11 H4 **Trelash** Cnwll |
| 38 F4 **Tonbridge** Kent | 132 F4 **Totley Brook** Sheff | 11 L6 **Trebullett** Cnwll | 4 E4 **Trelassick** Cnwll |
| 42 D5 **Tondu** Brdgnd | 8 B3 **Totnes** Devon | 10 E6 **Treburgett** Cnwll | 5 L4 **Trelawne** Cnwll |
| 29 L6 **Tonedale** Somset | 116 E4 **Toton** Notts | 11 L7 **Treburley** Cnwll | 128 C4 **Trelawnyd** Flints |
| 92 C3 **Ton fanau** Gwynd | 224 F4 **Totronald** Ag & B | 10 B8 **Treburrick** Cnwll | 3 K6 **Treleague** Cnwll |
| 141 K2 **Tong** C Brad | 258 F3 **Totscore** Highld | 5 J2 **Trebyan** Cnwll | 3 K7 **Treleaver** Cnwll |
| 40 C4 **Tong** Kent | 51 J1 **Tottenham** Gt Lon | 60 C1 **Trecastle** Powys | 58 A3 **Trelech** Carmth |
| 97 H2 **Tong** Shrops | 104 C1 **Tottenhill** Norfk | 11 K6 **Trecogo** Cnwll | 58 B3 **Trelech a'r Betws** Carmth |
| 116 C7 **Tonge** Leics | 69 H8 **Totteridge** Gt Lon | 12 F2 **Trecott** Devon | 74 B6 **Treleddyd-fawr** Pembks |
| 40 C4 **Tong Green** Kent | 68 C3 **Totternhoe** C Beds | 74 F5 **Trecwn** Pembks | 3 K4 **Trelew** Cnwll |
| 36 C1 **Tongham** Surrey | 140 A5 **Tottington** Bury | 60 F6 **Trecynon** Rhondd | 43 H2 **Trelewis** Myr Td |
| 175 H4 **Tongland** D & G | 139 L2 **Tottleworth** Lancs | 11 J6 **Tredaule** Cnwll | 10 E5 **Treligga** Cnwll |
| 97 H2 **Tong Norton** Shrops | 34 D8 **Totton** Hants | 2 C5 **Tredavoe** Cnwll | 10 D6 **Trelights** Cnwll |
| 141 J2 **Tong Street** C Brad | 49 L4 **Touchen End** W & M | 61 J5 **Tredegar** Blae G | 10 E6 **Trelill** Cnwll |
| 277 K5 **Tongue** Highld | 151 G7 **Toulston** N York | 10 F8 **Tredethy** Cnwll | 11 K6 **Trelinnoe** Cnwll |
| 118 F7 **Tongue End** Lincs | 30 B4 **Toulton** Somset | 64 C1 **Tredington** Gloucs | 4 F4 **Trelion** Cnwll |
| 43 H5 **Tongwynlais** Cardif | 264 D4 **Toulvaddie** Highld | 83 G6 **Tredington** Warwks | 3 L3 **Trelissick** Cnwll |
| 42 B2 **Tonmawr** Neath | 39 J3 **Tovil** Kent | 5 H3 **Tredinnick** Cnwll | 63 G6 **Trellech** Mons |
| 57 L5 **Tonna** Neath | 5 G5 **Towan** Cnwll | 5 K2 **Tredinnick** Cnwll | 62 F6 **Trelleck Grange** Mons |
| 43 H4 **Ton-teg** Rhondd | 10 B7 **Towan** Cnwll | 5 M3 **Tredinnick** Cnwll | 128 D4 **Trelogan** Flints |
| 69 J4 **Tonwell** Herts | 207 J5 **Toward** Ag & B | 6 B3 **Tredinnick** Cnwll | 4 F1 **Trelow** Cnwll |
| 42 F3 **Tonypandy** Rhondd | 207 J5 **Toward Quay** Ag & B | 10 C8 **Tredinnick** Cnwll | 3 J6 **Trelowarren** Cnwll |
| 42 F4 **Tonyrefail** Rhondd | 84 D5 **Towcester** Nhants | 61 H1 **Tredomen** Powys | 6 B3 **Trelowia** Cnwll |
| 66 E7 **Toot Baldon** Oxon | 2 D3 **Towednack** Cnwll | 75 J4 **Tredrissi** Pembks | 3 M3 **Treluggan** Cnwll |
| 70 D6 **Toot Hill** Essex | 67 H6 **Towersey** Oxon | 10 D7 **Tredrizzick** Cnwll | 95 G3 **Trelystan** Powys |
| 34 E7 **Toothill** Hants | 244 A1 **Towie** Abers | 62 D8 **Tredunnock** Mons | 109 K3 **Tremadog** Gwynd |
| 47 G2 **Toothill** Swindn | 168 E3 **Tow Law** Dur | 61 H1 **Tredustan** Powys | 11 H5 **Tremail** Cnwll |
| 51 H5 **Tooting** Gt Lon | 103 J4 **Town End** Cambs | 2 B6 **Treen** Cnwll | 75 M3 **Tremain** Cerdgn |
| 51 H4 **Tooting Bec** Gt Lon | 156 C4 **Town End** Cumb | 2 C3 **Treen** Cnwll | 11 J4 **Tremaine** Cnwll |
| 160 F7 **Topcliffe** N York | 156 E1 **Town End** Cumb | 5 J4 **Treesmill** Cnwll | 6 B1 **Tremar** Cnwll |
| 106 F5 **Topcroft** Norfk | 156 F6 **Town End** Cumb | 133 J2 **Treeton** Rothm | 6 D3 **Trematon** Cnwll |
| 106 F5 **Topcroft Street** Norfk | 166 E5 **Town End** Cumb | 74 E4 **Trefasser** Pembks | 6 B2 **Trembraze** Cnwll |
| 85 L3 **Top End** Bed | 208 C4 **Townend** W Duns | 125 G5 **Trefdraeth** IoA | 128 C5 **Tremeirchion** Denbgs |
| 143 G4 **Topham** Donc | 166 C1 **Towngate** Cumb | 61 J1 **Trefecca** Powys | 2 C5 **Tremethick Cross** Cnwll |
| 140 C6 **Top of Hebers** Rochdl | 102 C1 **Towngate** Lincs | 93 L5 **Trefeglwys** Powys | 5 G2 **Tremore** Cnwll |
| 88 E7 **Toppesfield** Essex | 138 E6 **Town Green** Lancs | 77 H2 **Trefenter** Cerdgn | 128 D4 **Tre-Mostyn** Flints |
| 139 L5 **Toppings** Bolton | 107 G1 **Town Green** Norfk | 54 F2 **Treffgarne** Pembks | 3 K6 **Trenance** Cnwll |
| 106 D4 **Toprow** Norfk | 141 J7 **Townhead** Barns | 74 E7 **Treffgarne Owen** Pembks | 4 D1 **Trenance** Cnwll |
| 13 M5 **Topsham** Devon | 156 F2 **Town Head** Cumb | 43 G4 **Trefforest** Rhondd | 10 C8 **Trenance** Cnwll |
| 128 F7 **Top-y-rhos** Flints | 164 E3 **Townhead** Cumb | 74 D6 **Treffynnon** Pembks | 5 H5 **Trenarren** Cnwll |
| 194 D5 **Torbeg** N Ayrs | 166 E4 **Townhead** Cumb | 61 H4 **Trefil** Blae G | 96 F1 **Trench** Wrekin |
| 273 H8 **Torboll** Highld | 176 D1 **Townhead** D & G | 77 G4 **Trefilan** Cerdgn | 49 G3 **Trench Green** Oxon |
| 251 H3 **Torbreck** Highld | 148 K1 **Town Head** N York | 74 D5 **Trefin** Pembks | 4 E4 **Trendeal** Cnwll |
| 8 B2 **Torbryan** Devon | 175 J2 **Townhead of Greenlaw** D & G | 112 C6 **Treflach Wood** Shrops | 2 D3 **Trendrine** Cnwll |
| 239 J7 **Torcastle** Highld | 210 F1 **Townhill** Fife | 112 C8 **Trefnannau** Powys | 10 D8 **Treneague** Cnwll |
| 8 B6 **Torcross** Devon | 169 K3 **Town Kelloe** Dur | 128 C5 **Trefnant** Denbgs | 3 H5 **Trenear** Cnwll |
| 251 G1 **Tore** Highld | 12 A7 **Townlake** Devon | 112 C6 **Trefonen** Shrops | 11 H5 **Treneglos** Cnwll |
| 5 J4 **Torfrey** Cnwll | 139 K7 **Town Lane** Wigan | 108 F2 **Trefor** Gwynd | 2 F4 **Trenerth** Cnwll |
| 206 C6 **Torinturk** Ag & B | 22 F4 **Town Littleworth** E Susx | 124 F4 **Trefor** IoA | 5 K4 **Trenewan** Cnwll |
| 135 G4 **Torksey** Lincs | 139 J8 **Town of Lowton** Wigan | 10 F5 **Trefrew** Cnwll | 10 F6 **Trenewth** Cnwll |
| 45 M3 **Tormarton** S Glos | 38 E7 **Town Row** E Susx | 126 F7 **Trefriw** Conwy | 11 H4 **Trengune** Cnwll |
| 194 D4 **Tormore** N Ayrs | 48 E7 **Towns End** Hants | 11 K5 **Tregadillett** Cnwll | 4 D3 **Treninnick** Cnwll |
| 252 E2 **Tornagrain** Highld | 30 E7 **Townsend** Somset | 63 G5 **Tre-gagle** Mons | 4 C3 **Trenowah** Cnwll |
| 244 D2 **Tornaveen** Abers | 2 F4 **Townshend** Cnwll | 125 H4 **Tregaian** IoA | 3 J4 **Trenoweth** Cnwll |
| 251 G6 **Torness** Highld | 104 F6 **Town Street** Suffk | 62 E5 **Tregare** Mons | 31 K7 **Trent** Dorset |
| 169 G4 **Toronto** Dur | 45 K1 **Townwell** S Glos | 3 K6 **Tregarne** Cnwll | 114 D3 **Trentham** C Stke |
| 227 L5 **Torosay Castle** Ag & B | 202 C7 **Town Yetholm** Border | 77 J3 **Tregaron** Cerdgn | 116 E5 **Trentlock** Derbys |
| 165 G3 **Torpenhow** Cumb | 151 K4 **Towthorpe** C York | 126 B6 **Tregarth** Gwynd | 135 G3 **Trent Port** Lincs |
| 210 C4 **Torphichen** W Loth | 152 D3 **Towthorpe** E R Yk | 4 E2 **Tregaswith** Cnwll | 114 D3 **Trent Vale** C Stke |
| 244 E3 **Torphins** Abers | 151 G7 **Towton** N York | 10 F5 **Tregatta** Cnwll | 3 G4 **Trenwheal** Cnwll |
| 6 E4 **Torpoint** Cnwll | 127 K4 **Towyn** Conwy | 5 G2 **Tregawne** Cnwll | 42 E6 **Treoes** V Glam |
| 8 D2 **Torquay** Torbay | 129 H2 **Toxteth** Lpool | 11 J5 **Tregeare** Cnwll | 42 E2 **Treorchy** Rhondd |
| 8 D2 **Torquay Crematorium** Torbay | 137 G7 **Toynton All Saints** Lincs | 112 B5 **Tregeiriog** Wrexhm | 10 E7 **Trequite** Cnwll |
| 200 F3 **Torquhan** Border | 137 G7 **Toynton Fen Side** Lincs | 124 F1 **Tregele** IoA | 92 E5 **Tre'r-ddol** Cerdgn |
| 7 H4 **Torr** Devon | 137 G7 **Toynton St Peter** Lincs | 10 E7 **Tregellist** Cnwll | 42 F6 **Trerhyngyll** V Glam |
| 259 K6 **Torran** Highld | 38 D3 **Toy's Hill** Kent | 4 E6 **Tregenna** Cnwll | 6 C3 **Trerulefoot** Cnwll |
| 209 G4 **Torrance** E Duns | 196 E6 **Trabboch** E Ayrs | 2 B5 **Tregeseal** Cnwll | 76 A5 **Tresaith** Cerdgn |
| 196 D2 **Torranyard** N Ayrs | 196 F6 **Trabbochburn** E Ayrs | 3 K4 **Tregew** Cnwll | 4 E5 **Tresawle** Cnwll |
| 29 J3 **Torre** Somset | 3 J6 **Traboe** Cnwll | 60 F6 **Tre-Gibbon** Rhondd | 97 J4 **Trescott** Staffs |
| 260 E8 **Torridon** Highld | 29 K6 **Tracebridge** Somset | 3 J6 **Tregidden** Cnwll | 2 F5 **Trescowe** Cnwll |
| 260 D8 **Torridon House** Highld | 264 D8 **Tradespark** Highld | 4 F5 **Tregidgeo** Cnwll | 4 C3 **Tresean** Cnwll |
| 247 J4 **Torrin** Highld | 60 E1 **Trallong** Powys | 5 G5 **Tregiskey** Cnwll | 46 A1 **Tresham** Gloucs |
| 194 B4 **Torrisdale** Ag & B | 211 L4 **Tranent** E Loth | 74 D6 **Treglemais** Pembks | 4 E5 **Tresillian** Cnwll |
| 278 B4 **Torrisdale** Highld | 129 H2 **Tranmere** Wirral | 11 H3 **Tregole** Cnwll | 10 F6 **Tresinney** Cnwll |
| 274 C4 **Torrish** Highld | 278 F5 **Trantelbeg** Highld | 3 J4 **Tregolls** Cnwll | 11 H3 **Treskinnick Cross** Cnwll |
| 147 J3 **Torrisholme** Lancs | 278 F5 **Trantlemore** Highld | 10 C7 **Tregonce** Cnwll | 11 J5 **Tresmeer** Cnwll |
| 272 E7 **Torrobull** Highld | 180 F2 **Tranwell** Nthumb | 4 F2 **Tregonetha** Cnwll | 11 G4 **Tresparrett** Cnwll |
| 245 L3 **Torry** C Aber | 59 J5 **Trapp** Carmth | 4 F6 **Tregony** Cnwll | 232 B3 **Tressait** P & K |
| 210 D2 **Torryburn** Fife | 212 D4 **Traprain** E Loth | 11 G5 **Tregoodwell** Cnwll | 281 d6 **Tresta** Shet |
| 9 h4 **Torteval** Guern | 82 D1 **Trap's Green** Warwks | 4 F3 **Tregoss** Cnwll | 281 f3 **Tresta** Shet |
| 176 D3 **Torthorwald** D & G | 48 A6 **Trapshill** W Berk | 79 H7 **Tregoyd** Powys | 134 F4 **Treswell** Notts |
| 21 G6 **Tortington** W Susx | 200 D6 **Traquair** Border | 5 H4 **Tregrehan Mills** Cnwll | 3 G3 **Treswithian** Cnwll |
| 81 J1 **Torton** Worcs | 49 G5 **Trash Green** W Berk | 76 D6 **Tre-groes** Cerdgn | 92 E5 **Tre Taliesin** Cerdgn |
| 63 L8 **Tortworth** S Glos | 148 F8 **Trawden** Lancs | 5 H2 **Tregullon** Cnwll | 6 B2 **Trethawle** Cnwll |
| 259 H7 **Torvaig** Highld | 77 J1 **Trawscoed** Cerdgn | 10 D7 **Tregunna** Cnwll | 10 F4 **Trethevey** Cnwll |
| 156 C4 **Torver** Cumb | 110 D4 **Trawsfynydd** Gwynd | 11 J6 **Tregunnon** Cnwll | 2 B6 **Trethewey** Cnwll |
| 209 M2 **Torwood** Falk | 42 F3 **Trealaw** Rhondd | 4 D2 **Tregurrian** Cnwll | 43 J4 **Trethomas** Caerph |
| 201 G5 **Torwoodlee** Border | 138 F1 **Treales** Lancs | 94 D4 **Tregynon** Powys | 4 F4 **Trethosa** Cnwll |
| 134 D2 **Torworth** Notts | 4 C4 **Treamble** Cnwll | 58 D5 **Tre-gynwr** Carmth | 5 H4 **Trethurgy** Cnwll |
| 247 L1 **Toscaig** Highld | 124 D4 **Trearddur Bay** IoA | 43 G3 **Trehafod** Rhondd | 74 C6 **Tretio** Pembks |
| 86 E3 **Toseland** Cambs | 258 F6 **Treaslane** Highld | 6 D3 **Trehan** Cnwll | 63 G2 **Tretire** Herefs |
| 148 D4 **Tosside** Lancs | 10 C7 **Treator** Cnwll | 43 H2 **Treharris** Myr Td | 61 J3 **Tretower** Powys |
| 89 J3 **Tostock** Suffk | 43 G7 **Tre Aubrey** V Glam | 10 E6 **Treharrock** Cnwll | 128 F8 **Treuddyn** Flints |
| 258 B6 **Totaig** Highld | 42 F4 **Trebanog** Rhondd | 10 B7 **Trehemborne** Cnwll | 11 K6 **Trevadlock** Cnwll |
| 259 G6 **Tote** Highld | 57 K4 **Trebanos** Neath | 77 G6 **Treherbert** Carmth | 10 F4 **Trevalga** Cnwll |
| 259 J4 **Tote** Highld | 11 K7 **Trebartha** Cnwll | 42 E2 **Treherbert** Rhondd | 129 J8 **Trevalyn** Wrexhm |
| 36 C6 **Tote Hill** W Susx | 10 E5 **Trebarwith** Cnwll | 6 C2 **Trehunist** Cnwll | 10 D7 **Trevanger** Cnwll |
| 35 H3 **Totford** Hants | 11 J5 **Trebeath** Cnwll | 11 L6 **Trekenner** Cnwll | 10 D7 **Trevanson** Cnwll |
| 137 H3 **Tothill** Lincs | 10 C6 **Trebetherick** Cnwll | 10 E5 **Treknow** Cnwll | 2 D5 **Trevarrack** Cnwll |

| | | |
|---|---|---|
| 4 E3 | Trevarren Cnwll | |
| 4 D2 | Trevarrian Cnwll | |
| 5 G6 | Trevarrick Cnwll | |
| 3 J3 | Trevarth Cnwll | |
| 55 L4 | Trevaughan Carmth | |
| 58 D4 | Tre-Vaughan Carmth | |
| 2 D3 | Treveal Cnwll | |
| 4 C3 | Treveal Cnwll | |
| 10 F6 | Treveighan Cnwll | |
| 4 B4 | Trevellas Downs Cnwll | |
| 5 L2 | Trevelmond Cnwll | |
| 4 D3 | Trevemper Cnwll | |
| 5 G6 | Treveor Cnwll | |
| 4 E5 | Treverbyn Cnwll | |
| 5 G3 | Treverbyn Cnwll | |
| 3 J5 | Treverva Cnwll | |
| 2 B6 | Trevescan Cnwll | |
| 62 B6 | Trevethin Torfn | |
| 10 F5 | Trevia Cnwll | |
| 6 C1 | Trevigro Cnwll | |
| 3 L3 | Trevilla Cnwll | |
| 4 D4 | Trevilson Cnwll | |
| 4 F4 | Treviscoe Cnwll | |
| 4 F6 | Treviskey Cnwll | |
| 4 E2 | Trevithick Cnwll | |
| 4 F6 | Trevithick Cnwll | |
| 4 D3 | Trevoll Cnwll | |
| 10 B7 | Trevone Cnwll | |
| 112 C3 | Trevor Wrexhm | |
| 2 B6 | Trevorgans Cnwll | |
| 10 C7 | Trevorrick Cnwll | |
| 10 B7 | Trevose Cnwll | |
| 3 G5 | Trew Cnwll | |
| 10 F6 | Trewalder Cnwll | |
| 61 J1 | Trewalkin Powys | |
| 10 F5 | Trewarmett Cnwll | |
| 4 E6 | Trewarthenick Cnwll | |
| 11 G5 | Trewassa Cnwll | |
| 2 F5 | Trewavas Cnwll | |
| 11 J6 | Treween Cnwll | |
| 2 B4 | Trewellard Cnwll | |
| 11 J5 | Trewen Cnwll | |
| 3 H5 | Trewennack Cnwll | |
| 55 G7 | Trewent Pembks | |
| 95 G1 | Trewern Powys | |
| 10 E6 | Trewetha Cnwll | |
| 10 E7 | Trewethern Cnwll | |
| 6 D3 | Trewidland Cnwll | |
| 3 K7 | Trewillis Cnwll | |
| 6 B2 | Trewint Cnwll | |
| 11 J6 | Trewint Cnwll | |
| 3 M4 | Trewithian Cnwll | |
| 11 L8 | Trewoodloe Cnwll | |
| 3 H7 | Trewoon Cnwll | |
| 5 G4 | Trewoon Cnwll | |
| 4 E6 | Treworga Cnwll | |
| 4 D5 | Treworgan Cnwll | |
| 4 E7 | Treworlas Cnwll | |
| 11 G4 | Treworld Cnwll | |
| 3 M3 | Treworthal Cnwll | |
| 62 C3 | Tre-wyn Mons | |
| 10 B7 | Treyarnon Cnwll | |
| 20 D3 | Treyford W Susx | |
| 17 L2 | Trickett's Cross Dorset | |
| 178 E5 | Triermain Cumb | |
| 75 G7 | Triffleton Pembks | |
| 11 K4 | Trillacott Cnwll | |
| 169 K4 | Trimdon Dur | |
| 169 K4 | Trimdon Colliery Dur | |
| 169 K3 | Trimdon Grange Dur | |
| 122 F4 | Trimingham Norfk | |
| 91 G7 | Trimley Lower Street Suffk | |
| 91 G7 | Trimley St Martin Suffk | |
| 91 G7 | Trimley St Mary Suffk | |
| 97 H7 | Trimpley Worcs | |
| 56 E4 | Trimsaran Carmth | |
| 70 C4 | Trims Green Herts | |
| 27 J2 | Trimstone Devon | |
| 231 K3 | Trinafour P & K | |
| 61 K7 | Trinant Caerph | |
| 68 A5 | Tring Herts | |
| 67 M4 | Tringford Herts | |
| 68 A4 | Tring Wharf Herts | |
| 234 F3 | Trinity Angus | |
| 9 d2 | Trinity Jersey | |
| 221 G3 | Trinity Gask P & K | |
| 29 L4 | Triscombe Somset | |
| 239 H8 | Trislaig Highld | |
| 4 D5 | Trispen Cnwll | |
| 191 J7 | Tritlington Nthumb | |
| 4 E3 | Troan Cnwll | |
| 232 E7 | Trochry P & K | |
| 61 H6 | Troedrhiwfuwch Caerph | |
| 76 B6 | Troedyraur Cerdgn | |
| 61 G6 | Troedyrhiw Myr Td | |
| 127 G5 | Trofarth Conwy | |
| 9 C2 | Trois Bois Jersey | |
| 3 G3 | Troon Cnwll | |
| 196 C5 | Troon S Ayrs | |
| 219 H5 | Trossachs Pier Stirlg | |

| | | |
|---|---|---|
| 89 H1 | Troston Suffk | |
| 11 J4 | Troswell Cnwll | |
| 81 K4 | Trotshill Worcs | |
| 52 D7 | Trottiscliffe Kent | |
| 36 B6 | Trotton W Susx | |
| 190 B7 | Troughend Nthumb | |
| 140 D3 | Trough Gate Lancs | |
| 156 F2 | Troutbeck Cumb | |
| 165 L5 | Troutbeck Cumb | |
| 156 F3 | Troutbeck Bridge Cumb | |
| 133 H4 | Troway Derbys | |
| 46 B7 | Trowbridge Wilts | |
| 116 E3 | Trowell Notts | |
| 46 B7 | Trowle Common Wilts | |
| 68 D4 | Trowley Bottom Herts | |
| 106 E2 | Trowse Newton Norfk | |
| 150 C8 | Troy Leeds | |
| 32 C2 | Trudoxhill Somset | |
| 30 B6 | Trull Somset | |
| 142 F5 | Trumfleet Donc | |
| 258 C4 | Trumpan Highld | |
| 80 F7 | Trumpet Herefs | |
| 87 J4 | Trumpington Cambs | |
| 50 C5 | Trumpsgreen Surrey | |
| 122 F4 | Trunch Norfk | |
| 147 G7 | Trunnah Lancs | |
| 4 D6 | Truro Cnwll | |
| 11 K5 | Truscott Cnwll | |
| 13 K6 | Trusham Devon | |
| 115 L4 | Trusley Derbys | |
| 137 K3 | Trusthorpe Lincs | |
| 97 J4 | Trysull Staffs | |
| 66 B7 | Tubney Oxon | |
| 8 B4 | Tuckenhay Devon | |
| 97 H5 | Tuckhill Shrops | |
| 3 G3 | Tuckingmill Cnwll | |
| 32 F5 | Tuckingmill Wilts | |
| 18 A5 | Tuckton Bmouth | |
| 4 F5 | Tucoyse Cnwll | |
| 88 E1 | Tuddenham Suffk | |
| 90 E5 | Tuddenham Suffk | |
| 38 F4 | Tudeley Kent | |
| 169 H3 | Tudhoe Dur | |
| 63 H3 | Tudorville Herefs | |
| 108 D4 | Tudweiliog Gwynd | |
| 36 E3 | Tuesley Surrey | |
| 64 B4 | Tuffley Gloucs | |
| 34 F2 | Tufton Hants | |
| 75 H6 | Tufton Pembks | |
| 101 G3 | Tugby Leics | |
| 96 D6 | Tugford Shrops | |
| 203 K7 | Tughall Nthumb | |
| 220 E8 | Tullibody Clacks | |
| 251 H6 | Tullich Highld | |
| 264 D4 | Tullich Highld | |
| 232 F5 | Tulliemet P & K | |
| 256 E5 | Tulloch Abers | |
| 216 F8 | Tullochgorm Ag & B | |
| 240 B7 | Tulloch Station Highld | |
| 232 F8 | Tullybeagles Lodge P & K | |
| 233 J5 | Tullymurdoch P & K | |
| 255 L7 | Tullynessle Abers | |
| 51 J4 | Tulse Hill Gt Lon | |
| 58 F6 | Tumble Carmth | |
| 71 K2 | Tumbler's Green Essex | |
| 136 D7 | Tumby Lincs | |
| 136 E8 | Tumby Woodside Lincs | |
| 231 L4 | Tummel Bridge P & K | |
| 38 F5 | Tunbridge Wells Kent | |
| 177 G3 | Tundergarth D & G | |
| 122 F5 | Tungate Norfk | |
| 45 K7 | Tunley BaNES | |
| 114 D1 | Tunstall C Stke | |
| 145 J2 | Tunstall E R Yk | |
| 40 A3 | Tunstall Kent | |
| 157 K8 | Tunstall Lancs | |
| 160 B3 | Tunstall N York | |
| 107 J2 | Tunstall Norfk | |
| 114 B6 | Tunstall Staffs | |
| 91 H4 | Tunstall Suffk | |
| 181 J8 | Tunstall Sundld | |
| 132 B5 | Tunstead Derbys | |
| 122 F7 | Tunstead Norfk | |
| 131 K4 | Tunstead Milton Derbys | |
| 35 K1 | Tunworth Hants | |
| 80 C7 | Tupsley Herefs | |
| 49 G7 | Turgis Green Hants | |
| 65 G4 | Turkdean Gloucs | |
| 100 F4 | Tur Langton Leics | |
| 46 A6 | Turleigh Wilts | |
| 97 H6 | Turleygreen Shrops | |
| 140 B4 | Turn Lancs | |
| 79 L7 | Turnastone Herefs | |
| 182 F2 | Turnberry S Ayrs | |
| 6 F4 | Turnchapel C Plym | |
| 116 A2 | Turnditch Derbys | |
| 139 J2 | Turner Green Lancs | |
| 23 L3 | Turner's Green E Susx | |
| 82 E2 | Turner's Green Warwks | |
| 38 A6 | Turner's Hill W Susx | |

| | | |
|---|---|---|
| 16 F4 | Turners Puddle Dorset | |
| 69 K6 | Turnford Herts | |
| 211 G4 | Turnhouse C Edin | |
| 16 F1 | Turnworth Dorset | |
| 268 C6 | Turriff Abers | |
| 139 L4 | Turton Bottoms Bl w D | |
| 103 G4 | Turves Cambs | |
| 85 J5 | Turvey Bed | |
| 49 J1 | Turville Bucks | |
| 49 H1 | Turville Heath Bucks | |
| 84 B7 | Turweston Bucks | |
| 187 L3 | Tushielaw Inn Border | |
| 115 L6 | Tutbury Staffs | |
| 82 A1 | Tutnall Worcs | |
| 63 G3 | Tutshill Gloucs | |
| 122 E6 | Tuttington Norfk | |
| 11 M7 | Tutwell Cnwll | |
| 134 E5 | Tuxford Notts | |
| 275 b3 | Twatt Ork | |
| 281 d6 | Twatt Shet | |
| 209 J4 | Twechar E Duns | |
| 201 H6 | Tweedbank Border | |
| 202 F3 | Tweedmouth Nthumb | |
| 187 G1 | Tweedsmuir Border | |
| 4 B6 | Twelveheads Cnwll | |
| 24 C3 | Twelve Oaks E Susx | |
| 130 F6 | Twemlow Green Ches E | |
| 118 F7 | Twenty Lincs | |
| 45 L6 | Twerton BaNES | |
| 50 F4 | Twickenham Gt Lon | |
| 64 B3 | Twigworth Gloucs | |
| 22 C3 | Twineham W Susx | |
| 22 C3 | Twineham Green W Susx | |
| 45 L7 | Twinhoe BaNES | |
| 89 H7 | Twinstead Essex | |
| 28 D5 | Twitchen Devon | |
| 95 J7 | Twitchen Shrops | |
| 41 H4 | Twitham Kent | |
| 12 E7 | Two Bridges Devon | |
| 132 E7 | Two Dales Derbys | |
| 99 G3 | Two Gates Staffs | |
| 8 C1 | Two Mile Oak Cross Devon | |
| 27 J2 | Two Pots Devon | |
| 68 D6 | Two Waters Herts | |
| 99 J2 | Twycross Leics | |
| 67 G2 | Twyford Bucks | |
| 35 G6 | Twyford Hants | |
| 100 F2 | Twyford Leics | |
| 118 B6 | Twyford Lincs | |
| 121 M6 | Twyford Norfk | |
| 49 J4 | Twyford Wokham | |
| 80 C8 | Twyford Common Herefs | |
| 61 H5 | Twyn-carno Caerph | |
| 175 G4 | Twynholm D & G | |
| 81 K8 | Twyning Gloucs | |
| 81 L7 | Twyning Green Gloucs | |
| 59 L4 | Twynllanan Carmth | |
| 43 H7 | Twyn-yr-Odyn V Glam | |
| 62 E6 | Twyn-y-Sheriff Mons | |
| 101 L7 | Twywell Nhants | |
| 79 M7 | Tyberton Herefs | |
| 98 E5 | Tyburn Birm | |
| 57 H3 | Tycroes Carmth | |
| 111 L7 | Tycrwyn Powys | |
| 120 A7 | Tydd Gote Lincs | |
| 119 M8 | Tydd St Giles Cambs | |
| 119 M7 | Tydd St Mary Lincs | |
| 20 B6 | Tye Hants | |
| 70 D2 | Tye Green Essex | |
| 71 J3 | Tye Green Essex | |
| 88 B8 | Tye Green Essex | |
| 141 J1 | Tyersal C Brad | |
| 139 K7 | Tyldesley Wigan | |
| 40 F3 | Tyler Hill Kent | |
| 67 L8 | Tylers Green Bucks | |
| 70 D6 | Tyler's Green Essex | |
| 51 K8 | Tylers Green Surrey | |
| 42 F3 | Tylorstown Rhondd | |
| 93 L7 | Tylwch Powys | |
| 111 J3 | Ty-nant Conwy | |
| 111 H6 | Ty-nant Gwynd | |
| 218 E1 | Tyndrum Stirlg | |
| 112 C3 | Ty'n-dwr Denbgs | |
| 181 J5 | Tynemouth N Tyne | |
| 181 J5 | Tynemouth Crematorium N Tyne | |
| 60 E7 | Tynewydd Rhondd | |
| 212 D3 | Tyninghame E Loth | |
| 185 K4 | Tynron D & G | |
| 42 F4 | Ty'n-y-bryn Rhondd | |
| 43 K4 | Ty'n-y-coedcae Caerph | |
| 125 J3 | Tynygongl IoA | |
| 77 J1 | Tynygraig Cerdgn | |
| 126 F5 | Ty'n-y-Groes Conwy | |
| 43 G4 | Tyn-y-nant Rhondd | |
| 85 G6 | Tyringham M Keyn | |
| 98 E6 | Tyseley Birm | |
| 42 C6 | Tythegston Brdgnd | |
| 131 H4 | Tytherington Ches E | |
| 45 K1 | Tytherington S Glos | |

| | | |
|---|---|---|
| 32 C2 | Tytherington Somset | |
| 32 F3 | Tytherington Wilts | |
| 15 H2 | Tytherleigh Devon | |
| 46 D4 | Tytherton Lucas Wilts | |
| 68 F6 | Tyttenhanger Herts | |
| 5 J4 | Tywardreath Cnwll | |
| 5 J4 | Tywardreath Highway Cnwll | |
| 126 F4 | Tywyn Conwy | |
| 92 C3 | Tywyn Gwynd | |

## U

| | | |
|---|---|---|
| 91 H1 | Ubbeston Green Suffk | |
| 45 G7 | Ubley BaNES | |
| 160 C2 | Uckerby N York | |
| 23 H3 | Uckfield E Susx | |
| 81 K7 | Uckinghall Worcs | |
| 64 C2 | Uckington Gloucs | |
| 96 D2 | Uckington Shrops | |
| 209 J6 | Uddingston S Lans | |
| 198 E6 | Uddington S Lans | |
| 24 F3 | Udimore E Susx | |
| 256 F6 | Udny Green Abers | |
| 257 G6 | Udny Station Abers | |
| 47 H3 | Uffcott Wilts | |
| 29 K8 | Uffculme Devon | |
| 102 B2 | Uffington Lincs | |
| 47 L1 | Uffington Oxon | |
| 96 C1 | Uffington Shrops | |
| 102 B3 | Ufford C Pete | |
| 91 G5 | Ufford Suffk | |
| 83 J3 | Ufton Warwks | |
| 48 F5 | Ufton Nervet W Berk | |
| 194 B5 | Ugadale Ag & B | |
| 7 K4 | Ugborough Devon | |
| 107 J7 | Uggeshall Suffk | |
| 162 F1 | Ugglebarnby N York | |
| 132 E2 | Ughill Sheff | |
| 70 D2 | Ugley Essex | |
| 70 D2 | Ugley Green Essex | |
| 171 J8 | Ugthorpe N York | |
| 224 F4 | Uig Ag & B | |
| 258 B6 | Uig Highld | |
| 258 F4 | Uig Highld | |
| 282 d3 | Uig W Isls | |
| 259 G7 | Uigshader Highld | |
| 226 D8 | Uisken Ag & B | |
| 280 D7 | Ulbster Highld | |
| 165 L6 | Ulcat Row Cumb | |
| 137 H5 | Ulceby Lincs | |
| 144 E5 | Ulceby N Linc | |
| 144 E5 | Ulceby Skitter N Linc | |
| 39 L4 | Ulcombe Kent | |
| 165 H3 | Uldale Cumb | |
| 63 M7 | Uley Gloucs | |
| 191 J7 | Ulgham Nthumb | |
| 261 J1 | Ullapool Highld | |
| 82 D2 | Ullenhall Warwks | |
| 64 D4 | Ullenwood Gloucs | |
| 151 H7 | Ulleskelf N York | |
| 100 B6 | Ullesthorpe Leics | |
| 133 J2 | Ulley Rothm | |
| 80 E5 | Ullingswick Herefs | |
| 246 D1 | Ullinish Lodge Hotel Highld | |
| 164 E6 | Ullock Cumb | |
| 156 B4 | Ulpha Cumb | |
| 157 G6 | Ulpha Cumb | |
| 153 J4 | Ulrome E R Yk | |
| 281 e4 | Ulsta Shet | |
| 71 K5 | Ulting Wick Essex | |
| 98 E7 | Ulverley Green Solhll | |
| 156 C7 | Ulverston Cumb | |
| 17 K6 | Ulwell Dorset | |
| 185 J1 | Ulzieside D & G | |
| 27 L6 | Umberleigh Devon | |
| 271 H2 | Unapool Highld | |
| 157 C4 | Underbarrow Cumb | |
| 178 B2 | Under Burnmouth Border | |
| 141 J1 | Undercliffe C Brad | |
| 96 B1 | Underdale Shrops | |
| 157 K6 | Underley Hall Cumb | |
| 39 J4 | Underling Green Kent | |
| 38 E3 | Under River Kent | |
| 116 D2 | Underwood Notts | |
| 104 D7 | Undley Suffk | |
| 44 E2 | Undy Mons | |
| 154 e6 | Union Mills IoM | |
| 39 H7 | Union Street E Susx | |
| 133 G4 | Unstone Derbys | |
| 133 G4 | Unstone Green Derbys | |
| 140 B6 | Unsworth Bury | |
| 165 L1 | Unthank Cumb | |
| 166 B3 | Unthank Cumb | |
| 166 E3 | Unthank Cumb | |
| 132 F4 | Unthank Derbys | |
| 202 F3 | Unthank Nthumb | |
| 47 H7 | Upavon Wilts | |
| 16 C2 | Up Cerne Dorset | |
| 53 H5 | Upchurch Kent | |

360 Upcott - Wainfleet All Saints


28 D5 Upcott Devon
79 K5 Upcott Herefs
50 B6 Updown Hill Surrey
88 D3 Upend Cambs
13 L2 Up Exe Devon
122 C7 Upgate Norfk
106 B5 Upgate Street Norfk
106 F5 Upgate Street Norfk
16 A2 Uphall Dorset
210 E5 Uphall W Loth
13 K1 Upham Devon
35 H6 Upham Hants
79 M3 Uphampton Herefs
81 J2 Uphampton Worcs
44 C7 Uphill N Som
139 G6 Up Holland Lancs
208 D8 Uplawmoor E Rens
63 L2 Upleadon Gloucs
170 E6 Upleatham R & Cl
40 C2 Uplees Kent
15 L4 Uploders Dorset
29 J7 Uplowman Devon
15 H4 Uplyme Devon
20 C4 Up Marden W Susx
52 C2 Upminster Gt Lon
31 J7 Up Mudford Somset
49 G8 Up Nately Hants
14 E1 Upottery Devon
95 K6 Upper Affcot Shrops
263 G2 Upper Ardchronie Highld
97 H7 Upper Arley Worcs
66 F4 Upper Arncott Oxon
83 L7 Upper Astrop Nhants
48 F4 Upper Basildon W Berk
141 K3 Upper Batley Kirk
22 B5 Upper Beeding W Susx
101 L5 Upper Benefield Nhants
82 B2 Upper Bentley Worcs
278 F5 Upper Bighouse Highld
133 J8 Upper Birchwood Derbys
43 H4 Upper Boat Rhondd
83 L5 Upper Boddington Nhants
92 D5 Upper Borth Cerdgn
83 G7 Upper Brailes Warwks
247 L4 Upper Breakish Highld
80 B7 Upper Breinton Herefs
81 J4 Upper Broadheath Worcs
117 J6 Upper Broughton Notts
48 D5 Upper Bucklebury W Berk
33 K7 Upper Burgate Hants
52 E5 Upper Bush Medway
177 L8 Upperby Cumb
86 D6 Upper Caldecote C Beds
44 D7 Upper Canada N Som
18 D1 Upper Canterton Hants
83 M3 Upper Catesby Nhants
98 B8 Upper Catshill Worcs
78 D7 Upper Chapel Powys
30 C5 Upper Cheddon Somset
33 G5 Upper Chicksgrove Wilts
47 L8 Upper Chute Wilts
51 K2 Upper Clapton Gt Lon
34 D2 Upper Clatford Hants
64 E4 Upper Coberley Gloucs
21 K6 Upper Cokeham W Susx
115 G2 Upper Cotton Staffs
96 C2 Upper Cound Shrops
142 B5 Upper Cudworth Barns
141 K6 Upper Cumberworth Kirk
59 L6 Upper Cwmtwrch Powys
267 G4 Upper Dallachy Moray
41 K5 Upper Deal Kent
85 L2 Upper Dean Bed
141 K6 Upper Denby Kirk
178 E5 Upper Denton Cumb
23 J5 Upper Dicker E Susx
95 L6 Upper Dinchope Shrops
279 H3 Upper Dounreay Highld
73 K1 Upper Dovercourt Essex
219 L6 Upper Drumbane Stirlg
150 F3 Upper Dunsforth N York
36 E2 Upper Eashing Surrey
263 K7 Upper Eathie Highld
80 E6 Upper Egleton Herefs
131 L7 Upper Elkstone Staffs
115 J3 Upper Ellastone Staffs
132 B4 Upper End Derbys
34 E1 Upper Enham Hants
97 H5 Upper Farmcote Shrops
35 L4 Upper Farringdon Hants
63 L5 Upper Framilode Gloucs
35 M2 Upper Froyle Hants
258 E6 Upperglen Highld
31 H2 Upper Godney Somset
86 C8 Upper Gravenhurst C Beds
88 B8 Upper Green Essex
62 D3 Upper Green Mons
88 E2 Upper Green Suffk
48 A6 Upper Green W Berk
63 H2 Upper Grove Common Herefs
132 F7 Upper Hackney Derbys
36 B1 Upper Hale Surrey
50 E5 Upper Halliford Surrey
52 E6 Upper Halling Medway
101 K2 Upper Hambleton Rutlnd
40 F4 Upper Harbledown Kent
40 F5 Upper Hardres Court Kent
79 M4 Upper Hardwick Herefs
38 C6 Upper Hartfield E Susx
116 C2 Upper Hartshay Derbys
64 D3 Upper Hatherley Gloucs
114 C4 Upper Hatton Staffs
142 C8 Upper Haugh Rothm
96 C7 Upper Hayton Shrops
141 J4 Upper Heaton Kirk
151 L4 Upper Helmsley N York
79 J4 Upper Hergest Herefs
84 C3 Upper Heyford Nhants
66 D2 Upper Heyford Oxon
80 B4 Upper Hill Herefs
52 B5 Upper Hockenden Kent
141 K4 Upper Hopton Kirk
81 H5 Upper Howsell Worcs
131 K7 Upper Hulme Staffs
36 F4 Upper Ifold Surrey
65 J7 Upper Inglesham Swindn
46 A1 Upper Kilcott Gloucs
57 G6 Upper Killay Swans
217 J2 Upper Kinchrackine Ag & B
47 L3 Upper Lambourn W Berk
98 C2 Upper Landywood Staffs
44 F7 Upper Langford N Som
133 K5 Upper Langwith Derbys
223 G6 Upper Largo Fife
115 G4 Upper Leigh Staffs
45 H6 Upper Littleton N Som
244 F4 Upper Lochton Abers
115 H8 Upper Longdon Staffs
86 D8 Upper & Lower Stondon C Beds
97 H4 Upper Ludstone Shrops
275 H1 Upper Lybster Highld
63 J4 Upper Lydbrook Gloucs
80 C6 Upper Lyde Herefs
79 M2 Upper Lye Herefs
79 L8 Upper Maes-coed Herefs
141 K7 Upper Midhope Sheff
140 F6 Uppermill Oldham
81 J1 Upper Milton Worcs
46 E1 Upper Minety Wilts
82 A5 Upper Moor Worcs
141 K2 Upper Moor Side Leeds
267 G6 Upper Mulben Moray
96 E5 Upper Netchwood Shrops
115 G4 Upper Nobut Staffs
20 F3 Upper Norwood W Susx
132 E4 Upper Padley Derbys
18 D4 Upper Pennington Hants
67 H4 Upper Pollicott Bucks
151 J5 Upper Poppleton C York
82 E6 Upper Quinton Warwks
34 D6 Upper Ratley Hants
65 J3 Upper Rissington Gloucs
80 E2 Upper Rochford Worcs
174 E3 Upper Ruscoe D & G
80 F3 Upper Sapey Herefs
46 D3 Upper Seagry Wilts
85 K6 Upper Shelton C Beds
122 C3 Upper Sheringham Norfk
207 K5 Upper Skelmorlie N Ayrs
65 H3 Upper Slaughter Gloucs
63 K5 Upper Soudley Gloucs
79 K4 Upper Spond Herefs
41 H7 Upper Standen Kent
86 C3 Upper Staploe Bed
185 L6 Upper Stepford D & G
106 E3 Upper Stoke Norfk
84 C4 Upper Stowe Nhants
33 K7 Upper Street Hants
106 D7 Upper Street Norfk
123 G7 Upper Street Norfk
123 G8 Upper Street Norfk
88 F5 Upper Street Suffk
90 C5 Upper Street Suffk
90 D8 Upper Street Suffk
81 K7 Upper Strensham Worcs
68 D2 Upper Sundon C Beds
65 H2 Upper Swell Gloucs
142 A7 Upper Tankersley Barns
106 E4 Upper Tasburgh Norfk
115 G4 Upper Tean Staffs
141 H6 Upperthong Kirk
133 J4 Upperthorpe Derbys
143 J7 Upperthorpe N Linc
113 G3 Upper Threapwood Ches W
36 E6 Upperton W Susx
115 L1 Upper Town Derbys
132 F6 Uppertown Derbys
168 D3 Upper Town Dur
80 D5 Upper Town Herefs
280 D1 Uppertown Highld
45 G6 Upper Town N Som
89 J2 Upper Town Suffk
59 G6 Upper Tumble Carmth
83 H6 Upper Tysoe Warwks
91 G4 Upper Ufford Suffk
64 F7 Upperup Gloucs
47 J3 Upper Upham Wilts
53 G5 Upper Upnor Medway
234 E8 Upper Victoria Angus
32 B1 Upper Vobster Somset
83 L6 Upper Wardington Oxon
84 F7 Upper Weald M Keyn
84 B3 Upper Weedon Nhants
23 G4 Upper Wellingham E Susx
45 L5 Upper Weston BaNES
106 E7 Upper Weybread Suffk
81 J5 Upper Wick Worcs
35 K3 Upper Wield Hants
67 H4 Upper Winchendon Bucks
132 F8 Upperwood Derbys
33 K3 Upper Woodford Wilts
48 E7 Upper Wootton Hants
46 A4 Upper Wraxall Wilts
81 H6 Upper Wyche Worcs
13 L1 Uppincott Devon
101 J3 Uppingham Rutlnd
17 K1 Uppington Dorset
96 D2 Uppington Shrops
161 G5 Upsall N York
202 D4 Upsettlington Border
69 L7 Upshire Essex
34 E4 Up Somborne Hants
41 H3 Upstreet Kent
16 B2 Up Sydling Dorset
89 K1 Upthorpe Suffk
67 J5 Upton Bucks
102 C3 Upton C Pete
102 D7 Upton Cambs
129 J6 Upton Ches W
11 H2 Upton Cnwll
11 K7 Upton Cnwll
165 K3 Upton Cumb
7 K6 Upton Devon
14 C2 Upton Devon
16 E6 Upton Dorset
17 J4 Upton Dorset
153 J5 Upton E R Yk
129 L2 Upton Halton
34 E7 Upton Hants
47 M7 Upton Hants
99 K3 Upton Leics
135 H2 Upton Lincs
84 D3 Upton Nhants
107 H1 Upton Norfk
117 J1 Upton Notts
134 E4 Upton Notts
48 D2 Upton Oxon
65 K4 Upton Oxon
55 G6 Upton Pembks
171 G6 Upton R & Cl
50 B3 Upton Slough
29 H5 Upton Somset
31 G5 Upton Somset
142 D5 Upton Wakefd
82 D4 Upton Warwks
32 E4 Upton Wilts
129 G2 Upton Wirral
63 K2 Upton Bishop Herefs
45 K5 Upton Cheyney S Glos
96 E5 Upton Cressett Shrops
63 J2 Upton Crews Herefs
11 K8 Upton Cross Cnwll
86 C8 Upton End C Beds
35 L1 Upton Grey Hants
129 J5 Upton Heath Ches W
13 K2 Upton Hellions Devon
32 F3 Upton Lovell Wilts
96 C1 Upton Magna Shrops
32 B3 Upton Noble Somset
13 L3 Upton Pyne Devon
64 B4 Upton St Leonards Gloucs
32 E1 Upton Scudamore Wilts
81 L4 Upton Snodsbury Worcs
2 F3 Upton Towans Cnwll
81 K7 Upton upon Severn Worcs
81 L2 Upton Warren Worcs
20 F4 Upwaltham W Susx
87 L1 Upware Cambs
103 K3 Upwell Norfk
16 C5 Upwey Dorset
70 C2 Upwick Green Herts
102 E6 Upwood Cambs
46 F7 Urchfont Wilts
80 C5 Urdimarsh Herefs
150 D1 Ure Bank N York
169 L7 Urlay Nook S on T
130 E1 Urmston Traffd
266 F4 Urquhart Moray
161 J2 Urra N York
250 E1 Urray Highld
235 H4 Usan Angus
169 G2 Ushaw Moor Dur
62 D7 Usk Mons
136 A1 Usselby Lincs
181 H7 Usworth Sundld
130 A6 Utkinton Ches W
149 J7 Utley C Brad
13 J3 Uton Devon
136 F1 Utterby Lincs
115 H5 Uttoxeter Staffs
108 B6 Uwchmynydd Gwynd
50 D2 Uxbridge Gt Lon
281 f2 Uyeasound Shet
54 F4 Uzmaston Pembks


## V


9 k2 Vale Guern
124 E4 Valley IoA
50 B6 Valley End Surrey
10 F6 Valley Truckle Cnwll
259 J4 Valtos Highld
282 e3 Valtos W Isls
52 F2 Vange Essex
61 L6 Varteg Torfn
281 e3 Vatsetter Shet
258 D7 Vatten Highld
61 G5 Vaynor Myr Td
9 i2 Vazon Bay Guern
281 e6 Veensgarth Shet
79 H7 Velindre Powys
29 K3 Vellow Somset
26 E6 Velly Devon
26 F8 Venngreen Devon
95 H2 Vennington Shrops
14 C4 Venn Ottery Devon
13 J3 Venny Tedburn Devon
11 L7 Venterdon Cnwll
19 J8 Ventnor IoW
7 H3 Venton Devon
47 M7 Vernham Dean Hants
47 M7 Vernham Street Hants
95 L7 Vernolds Common Shrops
17 L1 Verwood Dorset
4 E7 Veryan Cnwll
4 F6 Veryan Green Cnwll
14 E4 Vicarage Devon
146 C2 Vickerstown Cumb
141 J6 Victoria Barns
61 J5 Victoria Blae G
5 G3 Victoria Cnwll
281 e5 Vidlin Shet
266 F3 Viewfield Moray
209 J6 Viewpark N Lans
52 D6 Vigo Kent
9 k3 Village de Putron Guern
9 a1 Ville la Bas Jersey
9 i3 Villiaze Guern
24 D3 Vinehall Street E Susx
23 K4 Vines Cross E Susx
39 K2 Vinters Park Crematorium Kent
50 C5 Virginia Water Surrey
11 M4 Virginstow Devon
32 B1 Vobster Somset
281 d5 Voe Shet
79 L7 Vowchurch Herefs
130 B1 Vulcan Village St Hel


## W


168 F6 Wackerfield Dur
106 D5 Wacton Norfk
81 K5 Wadborough Worcs
67 H4 Waddesdon Bucks
8 C3 Waddeton Devon
138 E7 Waddicar Sefton
144 B8 Waddingham Lincs
148 C7 Waddington Lancs
135 K6 Waddington Lincs
13 K6 Waddon Devon
16 B5 Waddon Dorset
10 D7 Wadebridge Cnwll
30 D8 Wadeford Somset
101 M6 Wadenhoe Nhants
69 K4 Wadesmill Herts
39 G7 Wadhurst E Susx
132 F5 Wadshelf Derbys
46 B5 Wadswick Wilts
142 F8 Wadworth Donc
127 K7 Waen Denbgs
128 D6 Waen Denbgs
112 C7 Waen Powys
112 B8 Waen Fach Powys
125 K6 Waen-pentir Gwynd
125 K6 Waen-wen Gwynd
95 J3 Wagbeach Shrops
62 B6 Wainfelin Torfn
137 J7 Wainfleet All Saints Lincs

137 J7 **Wainfleet Bank** Lincs
137 J8 **Wainfleet St Mary** Lincs
107 G5 **Wainford** Norfk
11 H3 **Wainhouse Corner** Cnwll
52 F5 **Wainscott** Medway
44 E5 **Wain's Hill** N Som
141 G2 **Wainstalls** Calder
158 C1 **Waitby** Cumb
145 H7 **Waithe** Lincs
142 A4 **Wakefield** Wakefd
141 M4 **Wakefield Crematorium** Wakefd
98 E6 **Wake Green** Birm
101 L3 **Wakerley** Nhants
72 C2 **Wakes Colne** Essex
107 K8 **Walberswick** Suffk
21 G5 **Walberton** W Susx
180 E5 **Walbottle** N u Ty
175 J1 **Walbutt** D & G
178 B6 **Walby** Cumb
31 J2 **Walcombe** Somset
118 E4 **Walcot** Lincs
143 M3 **Walcot** N Linc
95 J6 **Walcot** Shrops
96 D1 **Walcot** Shrops
47 H2 **Walcot** Swindn
82 D4 **Walcot** Warwks
100 C6 **Walcote** Leics
106 C7 **Walcot Green** Norfk
136 B8 **Walcott** Lincs
123 G5 **Walcott** Norfk
159 H6 **Walden** N York
159 H6 **Walden Head** N York
142 E4 **Walden Stubbs** N York
53 G6 **Walderslade** Medway
20 C5 **Walderton** W Susx
15 L4 **Walditch** Dorset
115 J4 **Waldley** Derbys
169 H1 **Waldridge** Dur
91 G6 **Waldringfield** Suffk
23 J3 **Waldron** E Susx
133 J3 **Wales** Rothm
31 K6 **Wales** Somset
136 B1 **Walesby** Lincs
134 D5 **Walesby** Notts
63 H3 **Walford** Herefs
79 M1 **Walford** Herefs
113 G7 **Walford** Shrops
114 C5 **Walford** Statfs
113 G7 **Walford Heath** Shrops
113 M2 **Walgherton** Ches E
84 F1 **Walgrave** Nhants
18 E4 **Walhampton** Hants
139 L7 **Walkden** Salfd
181 H6 **Walker** N u Ty
200 D5 **Walkerburn** Border
148 B7 **Walker Fold** Lancs
134 F1 **Walkeringham** Notts
134 F1 **Walkerith** Lincs
69 H2 **Walkern** Herts
80 C5 **Walker's Green** Herefs
98 D7 **Walker's Heath** Birm
222 C7 **Walkerton** Fife
18 C5 **Walkford** Dorset
7 G1 **Walkhampton** Devon
152 F8 **Walkington** E R Yk
133 G2 **Walkley** Sheff
140 C2 **Walk Mill** Lancs
82 B2 **Walkwood** Worcs
179 L5 **Wall** Nthumb
98 E2 **Wall** Staffs
183 H2 **Wallacetown** S Ayrs
196 C6 **Wallacetown** S Ayrs
22 F5 **Wallands Park** E Susx
129 G1 **Wallasey** Wirral
156 B6 **Wall End** Cumb
80 B4 **Wall End** Herefs
53 J4 **Wallend** Medway
80 F7 **Waller's Green** Herefs
178 B6 **Wallhead** Cumb
97 K5 **Wall Heath** Dudley
180 C5 **Wall Houses** Nthumb
48 F1 **Wallingford** Oxon
51 H6 **Wallington** Gt Lon
19 K2 **Wallington** Hants
86 F8 **Wallington** Herts
98 C3 **Wallington Heath** Wsall
75 G7 **Wallis** Pembks
17 L4 **Wallisdown** Poole
37 H3 **Walliswood** Surrey
281 C6 **Walls** Shet
181 H5 **Wallsend** N Tyne
165 K5 **Wallthwaite** Cumb
96 C5 **Wall under Haywood** Shrops
211 L4 **Wallyford** E Loth
41 L5 **Walmer** Kent
138 F3 **Walmer Bridge** Lancs
140 B5 **Walmersley** Bury
41 H3 **Walmestone** Kent
98 F5 **Walmley** Birm
98 F5 **Walmley Ash** Birm

137 G4 **Walmsgate** Lincs
30 D3 **Walpole** Somset
107 H8 **Walpole** Suffk
120 B7 **Walpole Cross Keys** Norfk
120 B8 **Walpole Highway** Norfk
120 B8 **Walpole St Andrew** Norfk
120 B8 **Walpole St Peter** Norfk
30 E2 **Walrow** Somset
98 C4 **Walsall** Wsall
98 D3 **Walsall Wood** Wsall
140 D3 **Walsden** Calder
99 K7 **Walsgrave on Sowe** Covtry
89 K1 **Walsham le Willows** Suffk
140 A5 **Walshaw** Bury
150 F5 **Walshford** N York
103 K1 **Walsoken** Norfk
199 H4 **Walston** S Lans
69 G1 **Walsworth** Herts
67 K7 **Walter's Ash** Bucks
38 D5 **Walters Green** Kent
43 G7 **Walterston** V Glam
62 D2 **Walterstone** Herefs
40 E5 **Waltham** Kent
145 H7 **Waltham** NE Lin
69 K7 **Waltham Abbey** Essex
35 H7 **Waltham Chase** Hants
69 K7 **Waltham Cross** Herts
117 L6 **Waltham on the Wolds** Leics
49 K4 **Waltham St Lawrence** W & M
71 G1 **Waltham's Cross** Essex
51 K1 **Walthamstow** Gt Lon
102 D3 **Walton** C Pete
178 C6 **Walton** Cumb
133 G6 **Walton** Derbys
150 F6 **Walton** Leeds
100 D6 **Walton** Leics
85 H7 **Walton** M Keyn
79 J3 **Walton** Powys
95 L7 **Walton** Shrops
31 G4 **Walton** Somset
114 D5 **Walton** Staffs
114 D6 **Walton** Staffs
91 G8 **Walton** Suffk
20 D6 **Walton** W Susx
142 A4 **Walton** Wakefd
83 G4 **Walton** Warwks
113 K7 **Walton** Wrekin
64 C1 **Walton Cardiff** Gloucs
55 H2 **Walton East** Pembks
32 C7 **Walton Elm** Dorset
83 L8 **Walton Grounds** Nhants
44 E4 **Walton-in-Gordano** N Som
130 B3 **Walton Lea Crematorium** Warrtn
139 H2 **Walton-le-Dale** Lancs
50 E5 **Walton-on-Thames** Surrey
114 F7 **Walton-on-the-Hill** Staffs
51 G7 **Walton on the Hill** Surrey
73 K3 **Walton on the Naze** Essex
117 G7 **Walton on the Wolds** Leics
115 L7 **Walton-on-Trent** Derbys
44 E4 **Walton Park** N Som
54 D4 **Walton West** Pembks
149 H5 **Waltonwrays Crematorium** N York
128 D4 **Walwen** Flints
128 E4 **Walwen** Flints
128 E5 **Walwen** Flints
179 L5 **Walwick** Nthumb
169 G7 **Walworth** Darltn
51 J3 **Walworth** Gt Lon
169 G6 **Walworth Gate** Darltn
54 E4 **Walwyn's Castle** Pembks
15 G1 **Wambrook** Somset
177 H7 **Wampool** Cumb
36 D1 **Wanborough** Surrey
47 J2 **Wanborough** Swindn
68 E3 **Wandon End** Herts
51 H4 **Wandsworth** Gt Lon
107 J7 **Wangford** Suffk
100 D1 **Wanlip** Leics
186 C4 **Wanlockhead** D & G
23 K6 **Wannock** E Susx
102 B3 **Wansford** C Pete
153 G4 **Wansford** E R Yk
39 J4 **Wanshurst Green** Kent
51 L1 **Wanstead** Gt Lon
32 B3 **Wanstrow** Somset
63 K6 **Wanswell** Gloucs
48 B1 **Wantage** Oxon
81 H4 **Wants Green** Worcs
45 L3 **Wapley** S Glos
83 J2 **Wappenbury** Warwks
84 C6 **Wappenham** Nhants
23 K4 **Warbleton** E Susx
66 F8 **Warborough** Oxon
102 F7 **Warboys** Cambs
146 F8 **Warbreck** Bpool
11 H4 **Warbstow** Cnwll
130 D2 **Warburton** Traffd

167 H7 **Warcop** Cumb
53 M5 **Warden** Kent
179 L5 **Warden** Nthumb
98 E5 **Ward End** Birm
86 C6 **Warden Street** C Beds
90 B2 **Ward Green** Suffk
85 L8 **Wardhedges** C Beds
83 L6 **Wardington** Oxon
130 B8 **Wardle** Ches E
140 D4 **Wardle** Rochdl
181 H6 **Wardley** Gatesd
101 H3 **Wardley** Rutlnd
140 A7 **Wardley** Salfd
132 D5 **Wardlow** Derbys
131 J3 **Wardsend** Ches E
103 K7 **Wardy Hill** Cambs
69 K4 **Ware** Herts
17 H5 **Wareham** Dorset
25 J1 **Warehorne** Kent
203 J7 **Warenford** Nthumb
203 J6 **Waren Mill** Nthumb
203 H7 **Warenton** Nthumb
69 K4 **Wareside** Herts
86 E4 **Waresley** Cambs
81 J1 **Waresley** Worcs
39 K2 **Ware Street** Kent
49 L4 **Warfield** Br For
8 C5 **Warfleet** Devon
119 H5 **Wargate** Lincs
49 J3 **Wargrave** Wokham
80 B7 **Warham** Herefs
121 L3 **Warham All Saints** Norfk
121 L3 **Warham St Mary** Norfk
179 K3 **Wark** Nthumb
202 C5 **Wark** Nthumb
27 M6 **Warkleigh** Devon
101 K7 **Warkton** Nhants
83 L7 **Warkworth** Nhants
191 K5 **Warkworth** Nthumb
160 E4 **Warlaby** N York
140 E4 **Warland** Calder
5 K1 **Warleggan** Cnwll
46 A6 **Warleigh** BaNES
141 G3 **Warley Town** Calder
51 K7 **Warlingham** Surrey
177 G5 **Warmanbie** D & G
115 M1 **Warmbrook** Derbys
142 B4 **Warmfield** Wakefd
130 D7 **Warmingham** Ches E
102 B5 **Warmington** Nhants
83 K5 **Warmington** Warwks
32 E2 **Warminster** Wilts
45 K4 **Warmley** S Glos
142 E7 **Warmsworth** Donc
16 E5 **Warmwell** Dorset
81 K4 **Warndon** Worcs
35 J6 **Warnford** Hants
37 J4 **Warnham** W Susx
37 J4 **Warnham Court** W Susx
21 H5 **Warningcamp** W Susx
37 K5 **Warninglid** W Susx
131 H5 **Warren** Ches E
54 F7 **Warren** Pembks
170 D5 **Warrenby** R & Cl
198 F5 **Warrenhill** S Lans
49 K3 **Warren Row** W & M
69 H7 **Warren's Green** Herts
40 B5 **Warren Street** Kent
85 H4 **Warrington** M Keyn
130 B2 **Warrington** Warrtn
211 H4 **Warriston** C Edin
211 H4 **Warriston Crematorium** C Edin
19 H2 **Warsash** Hants
132 B7 **Warslow** Staffs
133 L6 **Warsop Vale** Notts
152 D5 **Warter** E R Yk
152 C6 **Warter Priory** E R Yk
160 B6 **Warthermaske** N York
151 L5 **Warthill** N York
24 D5 **Wartling** E Susx
117 J7 **Wartnaby** Leics
138 E2 **Warton** Lancs
147 K2 **Warton** Lancs
190 E5 **Warton** Nthumb
99 H3 **Warton** Warwks
83 G2 **Warwick** Warwks
178 B7 **Warwick Bridge** Cumb
178 B7 **Warwick-on-Eden** Cumb
178 B3 **Warwicksland** Cumb
275 C3 **Wasbister** Ork
156 B1 **Wasdale Head** Cumb
131 L3 **Wash** Derbys
70 C1 **Washall Green** Herts
5 H1 **Washaway** Cnwll
8 B4 **Washbourne** Devon
30 F1 **Washbrook** Somset
90 D6 **Washbrook** Suffk
29 G7 **Washfield** Devon
159 J2 **Washfold** N York
29 J3 **Washford** Somset

28 E8 **Washford Pyne** Devon
135 L5 **Washingborough** Lincs
181 H7 **Washington** Sundld
21 J4 **Washington** W Susx
98 E5 **Washwood Heath** Birm
48 E6 **Wasing** W Berk
168 D2 **Waskerley** Dur
83 G3 **Wasperton** Warwks
135 M6 **Wasps Nest** Lincs
161 J6 **Wass** N York
29 K2 **Watchet** Somset
47 K1 **Watchfield** Oxon
30 E2 **Watchfield** Somset
157 H3 **Watchgate** Cumb
165 G2 **Watchill** Cumb
8 D2 **Watcombe** Torbay
165 J7 **Watendlath** Cumb
13 H6 **Water** Devon
140 C3 **Water** Lancs
87 K2 **Waterbeach** Cambs
20 E5 **Waterbeach** W Susx
177 H3 **Waterbeck** D & G
121 J4 **Waterden** Norfk
66 D5 **Water Eaton** Oxon
97 K1 **Water Eaton** Staffs
86 C5 **Water End** Bed
86 C5 **Water End** Bed
85 L7 **Water End** C Beds
164 F6 **Waterend** Cumb
152 B8 **Water End** E R Yk
88 B7 **Water End** Essex
68 D5 **Water End** Herts
69 G6 **Water End** Herts
115 H1 **Waterfall** Staffs
208 F7 **Waterfoot** E Rens
140 C3 **Waterfoot** Lancs
69 J4 **Waterford** Herts
142 D2 **Water Fryston** Wakefd
11 G6 **Watergate** Cnwll
156 E2 **Waterhead** Cumb
200 B3 **Waterheads** Border
168 F3 **Waterhouses** Dur
115 H2 **Waterhouses** Staffs
39 H3 **Wateringbury** Kent
64 D6 **Waterlane** Gloucs
10 F7 **Waterloo** Cnwll
133 H7 **Waterloo** Derbys
79 L5 **Waterloo** Herefs
247 K4 **Waterloo** Highld
209 L8 **Waterloo** N Lans
122 E7 **Waterloo** Norfk
233 G7 **Waterloo** P & K
55 G6 **Waterloo** Pembks
17 K4 **Waterloo** Poole
138 C8 **Waterloo** Sefton
29 J8 **Waterloo Cross** Devon
125 J6 **Waterloo Port** Gwynd
19 M2 **Waterlooville** Hants
166 B6 **Watermillock** Cumb
102 C4 **Water Newton** Cambs
98 F5 **Water Orton** Warwks
66 F6 **Waterperry** Oxon
29 J6 **Waterrow** Somset
21 G4 **Watersfield** W Susx
139 L3 **Waterside** Bl w D
68 B7 **Waterside** Bucks
165 H2 **Waterside** Cumb
143 H5 **Waterside** Donc
184 C1 **Waterside** E Ayrs
196 F2 **Waterside** E Ayrs
209 H4 **Waterside** E Duns
139 K6 **Water's Nook** Bolton
258 A7 **Waterstein** Highld
66 F6 **Waterstock** Oxon
54 F5 **Waterston** Pembks
84 C8 **Water Stratford** Bucks
42 B5 **Water Street** Neath
113 K7 **Waters Upton** Wrekin
156 D5 **Water Yeat** Cumb
68 E7 **Watford** Herts
84 B2 **Watford** Nhants
149 L2 **Wath** N York
160 D7 **Wath** N York
142 C7 **Wath upon Dearne** Rothm
104 C1 **Watlington** Norfk
67 G8 **Watlington** Oxon
116 E2 **Watnall** Notts
280 B5 **Watten** Highld
105 K8 **Wattisfield** Suffk
89 K5 **Wattisham** Suffk
15 K4 **Watton** Dorset
152 F6 **Watton** E R Yk
105 J3 **Watton** Norfk
69 J3 **Watton-at-Stone** Herts
105 J3 **Watton Green** Norfk
70 D8 **Wattons Green** Essex
209 K5 **Wattston** N Lans
42 F3 **Wattstown** Rhondd
43 K3 **Wattsville** Caerph
144 B2 **Wauldby** E R Yk

244 E5 **Waulkmill** Abers
57 H6 **Waunarlwydd** Swans
92 D7 **Waunfawr** Cerdgn
125 J7 **Waunfawr** Gwynd
57 G4 **Waungron** Swans
61 J5 **Waunlwyd** Blae G
85 H7 **Wavendon** M Keyn
165 H1 **Waverbridge** Cumb
129 K7 **Waverton** Ches W
165 H1 **Waverton** Cumb
153 H8 **Wawne** E R Yk
123 J6 **Waxham** Norfk
145 J2 **Waxholme** E R Yk
41 K2 **Way** Kent
13 H8 **Waye** Devon
15 J1 **Wayford** Somset
15 L3 **Waytown** Dorset
28 F8 **Way Village** Devon
44 D6 **Way Wick** N Som
29 K3 **Weacombe** Somset
65 L6 **Weald** Gt Lon
50 F1 **Wealdstone** Gt Lon
150 D7 **Weardley** Leeds
44 E8 **Weare** Somset
27 H6 **Weare Giffard** Devon
167 K3 **Wearhead** Dur
30 F5 **Wearne** Somset
158 B2 **Weasdale** Cumb
121 J7 **Weasenham All Saints** Norfk
121 J7 **Weasenham St Peter** Norfk
140 B8 **Weaste** Salfd
98 D8 **Weatheroak Hill** Worcs
130 B5 **Weaverham** Ches W
115 J7 **Weaverslake** Staffs
152 E2 **Weaverthorpe** N York
44 D7 **Webbington** Somset
45 K4 **Webb's Heath** S Glos
82 B2 **Webheath** Worcs
80 A7 **Webton** Herefs
256 F5 **Wedderlairs** Abers
149 G6 **Wedding Hall Fold** N York
41 J3 **Weddington** Kent
99 K5 **Weddington** Warwks
46 F7 **Wedhampton** Wilts
31 G1 **Wedmore** Somset
98 C4 **Wednesbury** Sandw
97 L3 **Wednesfield** Wolves
135 G6 **Weecar** Notts
67 K3 **Weedon** Bucks
84 C3 **Weedon** Nhants
84 B6 **Weedon Lois** Nhants
98 F3 **Weeford** Staffs
8 A2 **Week** Devon
27 K5 **Week** Devon
28 C7 **Week** Devon
13 H1 **Weeke** Devon
34 F5 **Weeke** Hants
101 J7 **Weekley** Nhants
11 J3 **Week St Mary** Cnwll
153 G7 **Weel** E R Yk
73 H3 **Weeley** Essex
73 H3 **Weeley Crematorium** Essex
73 H3 **Weeley Heath** Essex
232 B5 **Weem** P & K
114 E7 **Weeping Cross** Staffs
82 C4 **Weethley** Warwks
104 F5 **Weeting** Norfk
145 K4 **Weeton** E R Yk
138 D1 **Weeton** Lancs
150 C6 **Weeton** N York
150 C8 **Weetwood** Leeds
140 C3 **Weir** Lancs
112 E6 **Weirbrook** Shrops
6 E2 **Weir Quay** Devon
281 d5 **Weisdale** Shet
133 L5 **Welbeck Abbey** Notts
106 B2 **Welborne** Norfk
118 C1 **Welbourn** Lincs
151 M2 **Welburn** N York
160 F2 **Welbury** N York
118 C4 **Welby** Lincs
103 K6 **Welches Dam** Cambs
26 D7 **Welcombe** Devon
191 G6 **Weldon Bridge** Nthumb
100 E7 **Welford** Nhants
48 B4 **Welford** W Berk
82 D5 **Welford-on-Avon** Warwks
101 G5 **Welham** Leics
134 E3 **Welham** Notts
69 G6 **Welham Green** Herts
36 A2 **Well** Hants
137 H5 **Well** Lincs
160 C6 **Well** N York
81 H7 **Welland** Worcs
81 J7 **Welland Stone** Worcs
234 D7 **Wellbank** Angus
49 L1 **Well End** Bucks
69 G7 **Well End** Herts
83 G4 **Wellesbourne** Warwks

83 G4 **Wellesbourne Mountford** Warwks
68 F2 **Well Head** Herts
52 B6 **Well Hill** Kent
48 D4 **Wellhouse** W Berk
51 M4 **Welling** Gt Lon
85 H2 **Wellingborough** Nhants
121 J7 **Wellingham** Norfk
135 K8 **Wellingore** Lincs
155 K2 **Wellington** Cumb
80 C5 **Wellington** Herefs
29 L6 **Wellington** Somset
96 E1 **Wellington** Wrekin
81 G7 **Wellington Heath** Herefs
80 C6 **Wellington Marsh** Herefs
45 L7 **Wellow** BaNES
18 F6 **Wellow** IoW
134 D6 **Wellow** Notts
69 L3 **Wellpond Green** Herts
31 J2 **Wells** Somset
99 K3 **Wellsborough** Leics
113 M1 **Wells Green** Ches E
141 G1 **Wells Head** C Brad
121 K3 **Wells-next-the-sea** Norfk
70 F3 **Wellstye Green** Essex
13 L1 **Well Town** Devon
221 G3 **Welltree** P & K
210 E1 **Wellwood** Fife
103 L4 **Welney** Norfk
113 G4 **Welshampton** Shrops
63 H4 **Welsh Bicknor** Herefs
113 H4 **Welsh End** Shrops
112 E5 **Welsh Frankton** Shrops
74 F6 **Welsh Hook** Pembks
63 G3 **Welsh Newton** Herefs
94 F2 **Welshpool** Powys
42 F6 **Welsh St Donats** V Glam
165 K2 **Welton** Cumb
144 B2 **Welton** E R Yk
135 K4 **Welton** Lincs
84 B2 **Welton** Nhants
137 J6 **Welton le Marsh** Lincs
136 E2 **Welton le Wold** Lincs
145 J3 **Welwick** E R Yk
69 G4 **Welwyn** Herts
69 G4 **Welwyn Garden City** Herts
113 H5 **Wem** Shrops
30 D3 **Wembdon** Somset
50 F2 **Wembley** Gt Lon
7 G5 **Wembury** Devon
12 F1 **Wembworthy** Devon
207 K5 **Wemyss Bay** Inver
77 J1 **Wenallt** Cerdgn
87 K8 **Wendens Ambo** Essex
66 E3 **Wendlebury** Oxon
105 J1 **Wendling** Norfk
67 L5 **Wendover** Bucks
3 H5 **Wendron** Cnwll
87 G5 **Wendy** Cambs
10 F7 **Wenfordbridge** Cnwll
107 J8 **Wenhaston** Suffk
102 E7 **Wennington** Cambs
52 B3 **Wennington** Gt Lon
147 M2 **Wennington** Lancs
132 E7 **Wensley** Derbys
159 K5 **Wensley** N York
142 D4 **Wentbridge** Wakefd
95 J5 **Wentnor** Shrops
103 K7 **Wentworth** Cambs
142 B8 **Wentworth** Rothm
141 M7 **Wentworth Castle** Barns
43 H7 **Wenvoe** V Glam
79 M5 **Weobley** Herefs
80 A5 **Weobley Marsh** Herefs
21 H5 **Wepham** W Susx
104 D3 **Wereham** Norfk
97 K3 **Wergs** Wolves
109 K4 **Wern** Gwynd
61 H3 **Wern** Powys
95 G1 **Wern** Powys
112 D4 **Wern** Shrops
131 J1 **Werneth Low** Tamesd
56 F6 **Wernffrwd** Swans
128 F6 **Wern-y-gaer** Flints
102 D3 **Werrington** C Pete
11 L5 **Werrington** Cnwll
114 E2 **Werrington** Staffs
129 K5 **Wervin** Ches W
138 E1 **Wesham** Lancs
133 G8 **Wessington** Derbys
42 F8 **West Aberthaw** V Glam
121 G8 **West Acre** Norfk
202 F4 **West Allerdean** Nthumb
7 L6 **West Alvington** Devon
33 K3 **West Amesbury** Wilts
28 E5 **West Anstey** Devon
160 B4 **West Appleton** N York
136 E5 **West Ashby** Lincs
20 D5 **West Ashling** W Susx
46 C7 **West Ashton** Wilts

168 F5 **West Auckland** Dur
163 H5 **West Ayton** N York
30 A4 **West Bagborough** Somset
61 K6 **West Bank** Blae G
129 L3 **West Bank** Halton
136 C4 **West Barkwith** Lincs
171 J8 **West Barnby** N York
212 E3 **West Barns** E Loth
121 K5 **West Barsham** Norfk
15 K4 **West Bay** Dorset
122 C4 **West Beckham** Norfk
50 D4 **West Bedfont** Surrey
41 G3 **Westbere** Kent
72 D2 **West Bergholt** Essex
48 D5 **West Berkshire Crematorium** W Berk
15 M5 **West Bexington** Dorset
120 F8 **West Bilney** Norfk
22 D6 **West Blatchington** Br & H
181 J6 **West Boldon** S Tyne
117 M3 **Westborough** Lincs
17 L4 **Westbourne** Bmouth
20 B5 **Westbourne** W Susx
32 C5 **West Bourton** Dorset
141 J2 **West Bowling** C Brad
40 E6 **West Brabourne** Kent
105 J2 **West Bradenham** Norfk
148 C7 **West Bradford** Lancs
31 J3 **West Bradley** Somset
141 L5 **West Bretton** Wakefd
117 G4 **West Bridgford** Notts
168 B6 **West Briscoe** Dur
98 C5 **West Bromwich** Sandw
98 C5 **West Bromwich Crematorium** Sandw
41 K1 **Westbrook** Kent
48 B4 **Westbrook** W Berk
46 D5 **Westbrook** Wilts
28 B4 **West Buckland** Devon
30 B6 **West Buckland** Somset
159 H5 **West Burton** N York
21 G4 **West Burton** W Susx
84 B8 **Westbury** Bucks
95 J2 **Westbury** Shrops
46 C8 **Westbury** Wilts
32 E1 **Westbury Leigh** Wilts
63 L4 **Westbury on Severn** Gloucs
45 H3 **Westbury-on-Trym** Bristl
31 H1 **Westbury-sub-Mendip** Somset
168 E2 **West Butsfield** Dur
143 L6 **West Butterwick** N Linc
138 D2 **Westby** Lancs
50 D6 **West Byfleet** Surrey
172 E8 **West Cairngaan** D & G
107 K1 **West Caister** Norfk
210 D6 **West Calder** W Loth
31 J6 **West Camel** Somset
16 E6 **West Chaldon** Dorset
48 A1 **West Challow** Oxon
7 L6 **West Charleton** Devon
15 M2 **West Chelborough** Dorset
191 J6 **West Chevington** Nthumb
21 J3 **West Chiltington** W Susx
31 G8 **West Chinnock** Somset
47 H8 **West Chisenbury** Wilts
50 D8 **West Clandon** Surrey
41 K6 **West Cliffe** Kent
53 J2 **Westcliff-on-Sea** Sthend
31 H8 **West Coker** Somset
7 L2 **West Combe** Devon
31 L3 **Westcombe** Somset
31 K2 **West Compton** Somset
16 A4 **West Compton Abbas** Dorset
65 J3 **Westcote** Gloucs
66 B2 **Westcote Barton** Oxon
67 H4 **Westcott** Bucks
14 B2 **Westcott** Devon
37 H1 **Westcott** Surrey
151 L7 **West Cottingwith** N York
47 J6 **Westcourt** Wilts
143 G3 **West Cowick** E R Yk
57 H7 **West Cross** Swans
11 K4 **West Curry** Cnwll
165 K1 **West Curthwaite** Cumb
23 J7 **Westdean** E Susx
20 E4 **West Dean** W Susx
34 B5 **West Dean** Wilts
102 C2 **West Deeping** Lincs
129 J1 **West Derby** Lpool
104 D3 **West Dereham** Norfk
27 J3 **West Down** Devon
33 H2 **Westdown Camp** Wilts
10 F6 **Westdowns** Cnwll
50 D3 **West Drayton** Gt Lon
134 D5 **West Drayton** Notts
280 B2 **West Dunnet** Highld
52 B5 **Wested** Kent
144 C2 **West Ella** E R Yk
85 J4 **West End** Bed
49 L5 **West End** Br For

43 K3 **West End** Caerph
87 G2 **West End** Cambs
177 K7 **West End** Cumb
144 A2 **West End** E R Yk
144 F2 **West End** E R Yk
145 H2 **West End** E R Yk
64 A5 **Westend** Gloucs
34 F7 **West End** Hants
35 K4 **West End** Hants
69 H5 **West End** Herts
69 J6 **West End** Herts
139 L2 **West End** Lancs
150 B8 **West End** Leeds
145 K8 **West End** Lincs
44 F5 **West End** N Som
149 L4 **West End** N York
151 H7 **West End** N York
105 H2 **West End** Norfk
107 K1 **West End** Norfk
48 E2 **West End** Oxon
45 L1 **West End** S Glos
31 L4 **West End** Somset
50 B6 **West End** Surrey
50 E6 **West End** Surrey
49 K4 **West End** W & M
22 B4 **West End** W Susx
32 F6 **West End** Wilts
33 G6 **West End** Wilts
46 E3 **West End** Wilts
49 G6 **West End Green** Hants
179 H6 **Westend Town** Nthumb
40 F7 **Westenhanger** Kent
279 K6 **Westerdale** Highld
161 L2 **Westerdale** N York
251 G5 **Wester Drumashie** Highld
90 E5 **Westerfield** Suffk
20 F6 **Westergate** W Susx
51 L8 **Westerham** Kent
180 F5 **Westerhope** N u Ty
8 C2 **Westerland** Devon
45 K3 **Westerleigh** S Glos
45 L3 **Westerleigh Crematorium** S Glos
210 D4 **Wester Ochiltree** W Loth
223 K6 **Wester Pitkierie** Fife
235 G4 **Westerton** Angus
20 E5 **Westerton** W Susx
281 C6 **Westerwick** Shet
51 G6 **West Ewell** Surrey
39 H3 **West Farleigh** Kent
83 M5 **West Farndon** Nhants
112 E6 **West Felton** Shrops
45 K8 **Westfield** BaNES
164 C5 **Westfield** Cumb
24 E4 **Westfield** E Susx
279 J3 **Westfield** Highld
209 J4 **Westfield** N Lans
105 K2 **Westfield** Norfk
210 B4 **Westfield** W Loth
16 D1 **Westfields** Dorset
80 C7 **Westfields** Herefs
233 J6 **Westfields of Rattray** P & K
53 G6 **Westfield Sole** Kent
135 K3 **West Firsby** Lincs
163 K6 **West Flotmanby** N York
29 L6 **Westford** Somset
142 B1 **West Garforth** Leeds
167 L3 **Westgate** Dur
143 K6 **Westgate** N Linc
121 L3 **Westgate** Norfk
141 K2 **Westgate Hill** C Brad
41 K1 **Westgate on Sea** Kent
122 D7 **Westgate Street** Norfk
48 C2 **West Ginge** Oxon
47 K7 **West Grafton** Wilts
49 H7 **West Green** Hants
33 L5 **West Grimstead** Wilts
37 J6 **West Grinstead** W Susx
142 E2 **West Haddlesey** N York
84 C1 **West Haddon** Nhants
48 D2 **West Hagbourne** Oxon
97 K7 **West Hagley** Worcs
107 J7 **Westhall** Suffk
116 D3 **West Hallam** Derbys
116 C3 **West Hallam Common** Derbys
144 A4 **West Halton** N Linc
16 C6 **Westham** Dorset
23 L6 **Westham** E Susx
51 K2 **West Ham** Gt Lon
30 F2 **Westham** Somset
20 E5 **Westhampnett** W Susx
133 H4 **West Handley** Derbys
66 B8 **West Hanney** Oxon
71 H7 **West Hanningfield** Essex
33 K5 **West Harnham** Wilts
45 H7 **West Harptree** BaNES
20 C3 **West Harting** W Susx
30 D6 **West Hatch** Somset
32 F5 **West Hatch** Wilts
234 E8 **West Haven** Angus

31 G2 **Westhay** Somset
138 F6 **Westhead** Lancs
104 B2 **West Head** Norfk
98 C7 **West Heath** Birm
48 E7 **West Heath** Hants
274 D5 **West Helmsdale** Highld
48 C1 **West Hendred** Oxon
68 E6 **West Hertfordshire Crematorium** Herts
163 G7 **West Hesterton** N York
44 D6 **West Hewish** N Som
80 D6 **Westhide** Herefs
245 J2 **Westhill** Abers
14 C4 **West Hill** Devon
38 A6 **West Hoathly** W Susx
17 G5 **West Holme** Dorset
31 J3 **Westholme** Somset
80 B5 **Westhope** Herefs
95 L6 **Westhope** Shrops
52 D1 **West Horndon** Essex
83 L5 **Westhorp** Nhants
119 H5 **Westhorpe** Lincs
90 B2 **Westhorpe** Suffk
31 J2 **West Horrington** Somset
50 D8 **West Horsley** Surrey
203 G7 **West Horton** Nthumb
41 H7 **West Hougham** Kent
139 K6 **Westhoughton** Bolton
157 L7 **Westhouse** N York
133 H8 **Westhouses** Derbys
17 L3 **West Howe** Bmouth
29 G4 **West Howetown** Somset
50 F8 **Westhumble** Surrey
221 K2 **West Huntingtower** P & K
30 D2 **West Huntspill** Somset
68 E4 **West Hyde** C Beds
50 C1 **West Hyde** Herts
40 F8 **West Hythe** Kent
28 C2 **West Ilkerton** Devon
48 C3 **West Ilsley** W Berk
20 C6 **West Itchenor** W Susx
137 G7 **West Keal** Lincs
47 G5 **West Kennett** Wilts
195 K1 **West Kilbride** N Ayrs
52 C6 **West Kingsdown** Kent
46 A3 **West Kington** Wilts
128 F2 **West Kirby** Wirral
162 F7 **West Knapton** N York
16 D5 **West Knighton** Dorset
32 E4 **West Knoyle** Wilts
203 G5 **West Kyloe** Nthumb
7 J4 **Westlake** Devon
30 F7 **West Lambrook** Somset
70 B3 **Westland Green** Herts
41 K6 **West Langdon** Kent
229 H4 **West Laroch** Highld
20 E3 **West Lavington** W Susx
46 E8 **West Lavington** Wilts
168 F8 **West Layton** N York
116 E6 **West Leake** Notts
202 C5 **West Learmouth** Nthumb
161 G2 **West Lees** N York
13 G1 **West Leigh** Devon
27 H5 **Westleigh** Devon
29 J7 **Westleigh** Devon
29 L5 **West Leigh** Somset
91 K2 **Westleton** Suffk
121 J8 **West Lexham** Norfk
95 J2 **Westley** Shrops
89 G2 **Westley** Suffk
88 C4 **Westley Waterless** Cambs
151 K3 **West Lilling** N York
67 J5 **Westlington** Bucks
199 K3 **West Linton** Border
177 L6 **Westlinton** Cumb
45 M4 **West Littleton** S Glos
48 B2 **West Lockinge** Oxon
51 G3 **West London Crematorium** Gt Lon
16 F6 **West Lulworth** Dorset
152 E2 **West Lutton** N York
31 J4 **West Lydford** Somset
28 C1 **West Lyn** Devon
30 D5 **West Lyng** Somset
120 D7 **West Lynn** Norfk
52 E7 **West Malling** Kent
81 H6 **West Malvern** Worcs
20 C4 **West Marden** W Susx
134 E5 **West Markham** Notts
41 J3 **Westmarsh** Kent
145 H5 **West Marsh** NE Lin
148 F5 **West Marton** N York
32 E6 **West Melbury** Dorset
142 C7 **West Melton** Rothm
35 K6 **West Meon** Hants
35 K5 **West Meon Hut** Hants
35 K5 **West Meon Woodlands** Hants
72 E4 **West Mersea** Essex
22 E4 **Westmeston** E Susx
180 C6 **West Mickley** Nthumb

69 J4 **Westmill** Herts
69 K2 **Westmill** Herts
15 L3 **West Milton** Dorset
51 J3 **Westminster** Gt Lon
53 K4 **West Minster** Kent
50 E5 **West Molesey** Surrey
30 C5 **West Monkton** Somset
17 L2 **West Moors** Dorset
17 H3 **West Morden** Dorset
201 J5 **West Morriston** Border
149 K7 **West Morton** C Brad
31 J6 **West Mudford** Somset
234 A5 **Westmuir** Angus
162 B6 **West Ness** N York
169 K7 **West Newbiggin** Darltn
164 F2 **Westnewton** Cumb
153 K8 **West Newton** E R Yk
120 F6 **West Newton** Norfk
30 D5 **West Newton** Somset
51 J4 **West Norwood** Gt Lon
51 J4 **West Norwood Crematorium** Gt Lon
181 J5 **Westoe** S Tyne
13 J8 **West Ogwell** Devon
45 L5 **Weston** BaNES
114 A1 **Weston** Ches E
14 D2 **Weston** Devon
14 E5 **Weston** Devon
16 D8 **Weston** Dorset
129 L3 **Weston** Halton
35 M6 **Weston** Hants
79 L4 **Weston** Herefs
69 H1 **Weston** Herts
119 J6 **Weston** Lincs
149 M6 **Weston** N York
84 B6 **Weston** Nhants
134 F6 **Weston** Notts
95 H8 **Weston** Shrops
96 D5 **Weston** Shrops
112 D6 **Weston** Shrops
114 F6 **Weston** Staffs
48 B4 **Weston** W Berk
80 D7 **Weston Beggard** Herefs
46 B1 **Westonbirt** Gloucs
101 G5 **Weston by Welland** Nhants
35 G3 **Weston Colley** Hants
88 C4 **Weston Colville** Cambs
35 L2 **Weston Corbett** Hants
114 E3 **Weston Coyney** C Stke
84 F3 **Weston Favell** Nhants
88 C5 **Weston Green** Cambs
97 H1 **Weston Heath** Shrops
119 J7 **Weston Hills** Lincs
99 K6 **Weston in Arden** Warwks
85 K8 **Westoning** C Beds
44 F4 **Weston-in-Gordano** N Som
68 C1 **Westoning Woodend** C Beds
114 B6 **Weston Jones** Staffs
122 C8 **Weston Longville** Norfk
112 F6 **Weston Lullingfields** Shrops
6 F3 **Weston Mill Crematorium** C Plym
66 D3 **Weston-on-the-Green** Oxon
35 L2 **Weston Patrick** Hants
112 D4 **Weston Rhyn** Shrops
82 D7 **Weston Subedge** Gloucs
44 C6 **Weston-Super-Mare** N Som
44 D6 **Weston-super-Mare Crematorium** N Som
67 K5 **Weston Turville** Bucks
97 H1 **Weston-under-Lizard** Staffs
63 J3 **Weston under Penyard** Herefs
113 J5 **Weston-under-Redcastle** Shrops
83 J1 **Weston under Wetherley** Warwks
115 M3 **Weston Underwood** Derbys
85 G5 **Weston Underwood** M Keyn
116 C6 **Weston-upon-Trent** Derbys
30 E4 **Westonzoyland** Somset
32 D7 **West Orchard** Dorset
47 H5 **West Overton** Wilts
152 A3 **Westow** N York
11 L4 **West Panson** Devon
245 H4 **West Park** Abers
17 L3 **West Parley** Dorset
39 G3 **West Peckham** Kent
11 L4 **West Peeke** Devon
180 F8 **West Pelton** Dur
31 J3 **West Pennard** Somset
4 C3 **West Pentire** Cnwll
86 C2 **West Perry** Cambs
28 F2 **West Porlock** Somset
30 F6 **Westport** Somset
16 D1 **West Pulham** Dorset
26 F7 **West Putford** Devon
29 K3 **West Quantoxhead** Somset
210 B3 **Westquarter** Falk
43 J7 **Westra** V Glam
13 L2 **West Raddon** Devon

169 J1 **West Rainton** Dur
135 L2 **West Rasen** Lincs
145 G7 **West Ravendale** NE Lin
121 J6 **West Raynham** Norfk
134 D3 **West Retford** Notts
48 E3 **Westridge Green** W Berk
210 B5 **Westrigg** W Loth
180 F6 **West Road Crematorium** N u Ty
65 J8 **Westrop** Swindn
160 F2 **West Rounton** N York
104 D8 **West Row** Suffk
121 H6 **West Rudham** Norfk
122 D3 **West Runton** Norfk
201 K3 **Westruther** Border
103 H4 **Westry** Cambs
212 A5 **West Saltoun** E Loth
13 J2 **West Sandford** Devon
281 e3 **West Sandwick** Shet
159 K6 **West Scrafton** N York
181 G2 **West Sleekburn** Nthumb
123 K7 **West Somerton** Norfk
16 D4 **West Stafford** Dorset
134 F1 **West Stockwith** Notts
20 D5 **West Stoke** W Susx
158 F2 **West Stonesdale** N York
30 F1 **West Stoughton** Somset
32 C6 **West Stour** Dorset
41 H3 **West Stourmouth** Kent
89 G1 **West Stow** Suffk
47 H6 **West Stowell** Wilts
35 H3 **West Stratton** Hants
40 A4 **West Street** Kent
41 K4 **West Street** Kent
52 F4 **West Street** Medway
89 K1 **West Street** Suffk
89 G2 **West Suffolk Crematorium** Suffk
160 C7 **West Tanfield** N York
5 K2 **West Taphouse** Cnwll
206 D5 **West Tarbert** Ag & B
21 J6 **West Tarring** W Susx
191 H6 **West Thirston** Nthumb
20 C6 **West Thorney** W Susx
133 J4 **Westthorpe** Derbys
117 G6 **West Thorpe** Notts
52 C3 **West Thurrock** Thurr
52 E3 **West Tilbury** Thurr
35 K5 **West Tisted** Hants
136 B3 **West Torrington** Lincs
45 G6 **West Town** BaNES
20 B7 **West Town** Hants
80 B3 **West Town** Herefs
44 F5 **West Town** N Som
31 J4 **West Town** Somset
32 B3 **West Town** Somset
34 C5 **West Tytherley** Hants
103 K1 **West Walton** Norfk
103 K1 **West Walton Highway** Norfk
165 J2 **Westward** Cumb
27 G5 **Westward Ho!** Devon
40 C6 **Westwell** Kent
65 J5 **Westwell** Oxon
40 C5 **Westwell Leacon** Kent
34 C7 **West Wellow** Hants
7 G5 **West Wembury** Devon
222 E8 **West Wemyss** Fife
87 J2 **Westwick** Cambs
168 D7 **Westwick** Dur
44 D6 **West Wick** N Som
122 F6 **Westwick** Norfk
88 C5 **West Wickham** Cambs
51 K5 **West Wickham** Gt Lon
55 H5 **West Williamston** Pembks
46 C7 **West Wiltshire Crematorium** Wilts
120 E8 **West Winch** Norfk
34 B4 **West Winterslow** Wilts
20 C7 **West Wittering** W Susx
159 J5 **West Witton** N York
14 B3 **Westwood** Devon
41 K2 **Westwood** Kent
52 D5 **Westwood** Kent
116 D1 **Westwood** Notts
179 H6 **Westwood** Nthumb
46 A7 **Westwood** Wilts
179 K2 **West Woodburn** Nthumb
48 B6 **West Woodhay** W Berk
99 H8 **Westwood Heath** Covtry
32 C2 **West Woodlands** Somset
143 J7 **Westwoodside** N Linc
35 M3 **West Worldham** Hants
21 K6 **West Worthing** W Susx
88 C5 **West Wratting** Cambs
67 K8 **West Wycombe** Bucks
180 D6 **West Wylam** Nthumb
46 B4 **West Yatton** Wilts
52 D5 **West Yoke** Kent
26 D7 **West Youlstone** Cnwll
53 H5 **Wetham Green** Kent
178 B7 **Wetheral** Cumb

150 F6 **Wetherby** Leeds
89 K3 **Wetherden** Suffk
90 D2 **Wetheringsett** Suffk
71 H1 **Wethersfield** Essex
90 D2 **Wetherup Street** Suffk
114 F2 **Wetley Rocks** Staffs
130 C7 **Wettenhall** Ches E
132 B8 **Wetton** Staffs
152 E4 **Wetwang** E R Yk
114 B5 **Wetwood** Staffs
47 K7 **Wexcombe** Wilts
50 C3 **Wexham** Slough
50 C2 **Wexham Street** Bucks
122 C3 **Weybourne** Norfk
36 C1 **Weybourne** Surrey
106 E7 **Weybread** Suffk
106 E7 **Weybread Street** Suffk
50 D6 **Weybridge** Surrey
15 G3 **Weycroft** Devon
279 L3 **Weydale** Highld
34 D2 **Weyhill** Hants
16 C6 **Weymouth** Dorset
16 C6 **Weymouth Crematorium** Dorset
84 F8 **Whaddon** Bucks
87 G6 **Whaddon** Cambs
64 B4 **Whaddon** Gloucs
33 L5 **Whaddon** Wilts
46 C6 **Whaddon** Wilts
166 C6 **Whale** Cumb
133 K5 **Whaley** Derbys
131 K3 **Whaley Bridge** Derbys
133 K5 **Whaley Thorns** Derbys
280 D8 **Whaligoe** Highld
148 C8 **Whalley** Lancs
139 L1 **Whalley Banks** Lancs
180 D3 **Whalton** Nthumb
119 K6 **Whaplode** Lincs
103 G1 **Whaplode Drove** Lincs
83 K5 **Wharf** Warwks
148 D2 **Wharfe** N York
147 J8 **Wharles** Lancs
85 J6 **Wharley End** C Beds
179 K5 **Wharmley** Nthumb
132 F1 **Wharncliffe Side** Sheff
152 C3 **Wharram-le-Street** N York
130 C6 **Wharton** Ches W
80 C4 **Wharton** Herefs
159 L2 **Whashton** N York
157 H6 **Whasset** Cumb
83 G6 **Whatcote** Warwks
99 G3 **Whateley** Warwks
89 L6 **Whatfield** Suffk
15 H1 **Whatley** Somset
32 B2 **Whatley** Somset
45 K3 **Whatley's End** S Glos
24 D4 **Whatlington** E Susx
40 F6 **Whatsole Street** Kent
116 B1 **Whatstandwell** Derbys
117 K4 **Whatton** Notts
173 K5 **Whauphill** D & G
159 H2 **Whaw** N York
4 B6 **Wheal Rose** Cnwll
107 J4 **Wheatacre** Norfk
67 G7 **Wheatfield** Oxon
68 F4 **Wheathampstead** Herts
96 E7 **Wheathill** Shrops
31 J5 **Wheathill** Somset
141 G3 **Wheatley** Calder
36 A3 **Wheatley** Hants
66 E6 **Wheatley** Oxon
169 K3 **Wheatley Hill** Dur
142 F6 **Wheatley Hills** Donc
148 E8 **Wheatley Lane** Lancs
97 J1 **Wheaton Aston** Staffs
112 D1 **Wheatsheaf** Wrexhm
29 G3 **Wheddon Cross** Somset
40 F6 **Wheelbarrow Town** Kent
67 K8 **Wheelerend Common** Bucks
49 J4 **Wheeler's Green** Wokham
39 L4 **Wheeler's Street** Kent
36 E3 **Wheelerstreet** Surrey
130 E7 **Wheelock** Ches E
130 E8 **Wheelock Heath** Ches E
139 J3 **Wheelton** Lancs
142 C3 **Wheldale** Wakefd
151 L6 **Wheldrake** C York
65 H7 **Whelford** Gloucs
68 C6 **Whelpley Hill** Bucks
165 J3 **Whelpo** Cumb
128 F4 **Whelston** Flints
69 J3 **Whempstead** Herts
151 K2 **Whenby** N York
89 G4 **Whepstead** Suffk
90 E7 **Wherstead** Suffk
34 E3 **Wherwell** Hants
132 C4 **Wheston** Derbys
39 G4 **Whetsted** Kent
69 H8 **Whetstone** Gt Lon
100 C4 **Whetstone** Leics

165 G1 **Wheyrigg** Cumb
155 L6 **Whicham** Cumb
83 H8 **Whichford** Warwks
180 F6 **Wickham** Gatesd
12 B3 **Whiddon** Devon
13 G4 **Whiddon Down** Devon
90 D6 **Whight's Corner** Suffk
234 D6 **Whigstreet** Angus
84 C2 **Whilton** Nhants
11 L2 **Whimble** Devon
14 B3 **Whimple** Devon
123 H5 **Whimpwell Green** Norfk
105 K2 **Whinburgh** Norfk
147 H7 **Whin Lane End** Lancs
175 H4 **Whinnie Liggate** D & G
177 J8 **Whinnow** Cumb
257 K5 **Whinnyfold** Abers
169 K7 **Whinny Hill** S on T
19 H5 **Whippingham** IoW
68 C3 **Whipsnade** C Beds
13 M4 **Whipton** Devon
132 F3 **Whirlow** Sheff
135 H6 **Whisby** Lincs
117 L8 **Whissendine** Rutlnd
121 K7 **Whissonsett** Norfk
218 C8 **Whistlefield** Ag & B
217 J8 **Whistlefield Inn** Ag & B
49 J4 **Whistley Green** Wokham
129 L2 **Whiston** Knows
85 G3 **Whiston** Nhants
133 J2 **Whiston** Rothm
114 D8 **Whiston** Staffs
115 G2 **Whiston** Staffs
97 H3 **Whiston Cross** Shrops
115 G2 **Whiston Eaves** Staffs
129 L2 **Whiston Lane End** Knows
99 H5 **Whitacre Fields** Warwks
155 K5 **Whitbeck** Cumb
81 G4 **Whitbourne** Herefs
181 K6 **Whitburn** S Tyne
210 C6 **Whitburn** W Loth
129 J4 **Whitby** Ches W
171 K8 **Whitby** N York
129 J5 **Whitbyheath** Ches W
212 F7 **Whitchester** Border
45 J5 **Whitchurch** BaNES
67 J3 **Whitchurch** Bucks
43 J5 **Whitchurch** Cardif
12 C7 **Whitchurch** Devon
34 F1 **Whitchurch** Hants
63 H4 **Whitchurch** Herefs
48 F3 **Whitchurch** Oxon
74 C7 **Whitchurch** Pembks
113 J3 **Whitchurch** Shrops
15 J3 **Whitchurch Canonicorum** Dorset
48 F3 **Whitchurch Hill** Oxon
16 D5 **Whitcombe** Dorset
95 J5 **Whitcot** Shrops
95 G6 **Whitcott Keysett** Shrops
40 E5 **Whiteacre** Kent
99 G5 **Whiteacre Heath** Warwks
71 J1 **Whiteash Green** Essex
29 K7 **White Ball** Somset
139 L2 **Whitebirk** Bl w D
250 E8 **Whitebridge** Highld
63 G6 **Whitebrook** Mons
257 G8 **Whitecairns** Abers
51 J3 **Whitechapel** Gt Lon
147 L7 **White Chapel** Lancs
82 C7 **White Chapel** Worcs
75 K5 **Whitechurch** Pembks
63 H5 **Whitecliffe** Gloucs
72 C1 **White Colne** Essex
139 J4 **White Coppice** Lancs
211 K5 **Whitecraig** E Loth
63 J6 **Whitecroft** Gloucs
172 F3 **Whitecrook** D & G
2 E4 **Whitecross** Cnwll
3 H6 **White Cross** Cnwll
10 D8 **Whitecross** Cnwll
210 C4 **Whitecross** Falk
81 H8 **White End** Worcs
263 J2 **Whiteface** Highld
194 D3 **Whitefarland** N Ayrs
183 H1 **Whitefaulds** S Ayrs
140 B6 **Whitefield** Bury
28 C4 **Whitefield** Devon
29 K5 **Whitefield** Somset
129 K2 **Whitefield Lane End** Knows
256 C6 **Whiteford** Abers
130 C6 **Whitegate** Ches W
49 H8 **Whitehall** Hants
275 e3 **Whitehall** Ork
37 H6 **Whitehall** W Susx
164 C7 **Whitehaven** Cumb
40 C3 **Whitehill** Kent
99 L1 **Whitehill** Leics
36 A4 **Whitehill and Bordon** Hants
268 B3 **Whitehills** Abers

256 A8 **Whitehouse** Abers
206 C6 **Whitehouse** Ag & B
98 E4 **Whitehouse Common** Birm
212 D3 **Whitekirk** E Loth
168 C3 **White Kirkley** Dur
16 D3 **White Lackington** Dorset
30 F7 **Whitelackington** Somset
81 L4 **White Ladies Aston** Worcs
67 K6 **Whiteleaf** Bucks
180 E7 **White-le-Head** Dur
19 J2 **Whiteley** Hants
19 J7 **Whiteley Bank** IoW
131 H4 **Whiteley Green** Ches E
50 E6 **Whiteley Village** Surrey
22 D2 **Whitemans Green** W Susx
58 E4 **White Mill** Carmth
253 J1 **Whitemire** Moray
116 F3 **Whitemoor** C Nott
5 G3 **Whitemoor** Cnwll
116 B2 **Whitemoor** Derbys
131 H7 **Whitemoor** Staffs
281 d6 **Whiteness** Shet
71 J3 **White Notley** Essex
65 M4 **Whiteoak Green** Oxon
45 L7 **White Ox Mead** BaNES
34 B6 **Whiteparish** Wilts
137 G4 **White Pit** Lincs
256 F7 **Whiterashes** Abers
70 E4 **White Roding** Essex
280 E6 **Whiterow** Highld
265 G8 **Whiterow** Moray
64 B5 **Whiteshill** Gloucs
23 J4 **Whitesmith** E Susx
139 G3 **White Stake** Lancs
30 D8 **Whitestaunton** Somset
13 K3 **Whitestone** Devon
80 D6 **White Stone** Herefs
13 L4 **Whitestone Cross** Devon
89 K7 **Whitestreet Green** Suffk
152 B2 **Whitewall Corner** N York
49 K3 **White Waltham** W & M
45 L6 **Whiteway** BaNES
64 C5 **Whiteway** Gloucs
148 B6 **Whitewell** Lancs
12 E8 **Whiteworks** Devon
41 J6 **Whitfield** Kent
84 B7 **Whitfield** Nhants
179 H7 **Whitfield** Nthumb
63 K8 **Whitfield** S Glos
179 H7 **Whitfield Hall** Nthumb
14 F3 **Whitford** Devon
128 D4 **Whitford** Flints
143 K3 **Whitgift** E R Yk
114 D6 **Whitgreave** Staffs
174 C6 **Whithorn** D & G
195 G6 **Whiting Bay** N Ayrs
142 B1 **Whitkirk** Leeds
55 L3 **Whitland** Carmth
188 E4 **Whitlaw** Border
196 D6 **Whitletts** S Ayrs
142 E4 **Whitley** N York
49 H5 **Whitley** Readg
133 G1 **Whitley** Sheff
46 C5 **Whitley** Wilts
181 J4 **Whitley Bay** N Tyne
181 J4 **Whitley Bay Crematorium** N Tyne
179 L7 **Whitley Chapel** Nthumb
114 C6 **Whitley Heath** Staffs
141 K4 **Whitley Lower** Kirk
38 D3 **Whitley Row** Kent
98 E8 **Whitlock's End** Solhll
63 M5 **Whitminster** Gloucs
17 L1 **Whitmore** Dorset
114 C3 **Whitmore** Staffs
29 J7 **Whitnage** Devon
83 H3 **Whitnash** Warwks
79 J5 **Whitney-on-Wye** Herefs
165 G3 **Whitrigg** Cumb
177 H7 **Whitrigg** Cumb
177 H7 **Whitrigglees** Cumb
33 K7 **Whitsbury** Hants
202 D3 **Whitsome** Border
44 D2 **Whitson** Newpt
40 E2 **Whitstable** Kent
11 K3 **Whitstone** Cnwll
190 F4 **Whittingham** Nthumb
95 K5 **Whittingslow** Shrops
133 H4 **Whittington** Derbys
64 E3 **Whittington** Gloucs
157 K7 **Whittington** Lancs
104 E3 **Whittington** Norfk
112 E5 **Whittington** Shrops
97 J6 **Whittington** Staffs
98 F2 **Whittington** Staffs
99 J4 **Whittington** Warwks
81 K4 **Whittington** Worcs
133 G5 **Whittington Moor** Derbys
84 D6 **Whittlebury** Nhants
139 H3 **Whittle-le-Woods** Lancs

102 F4 **Whittlesey** Cambs
87 K5 **Whittlesford** Cambs
139 L4 **Whittlestone Head** Bl w D
143 M3 **Whitton** N Linc
190 F6 **Whitton** Nthumb
79 J2 **Whitton** Powys
169 K6 **Whitton** S on T
80 D1 **Whitton** Shrops
90 D5 **Whitton** Suffk
47 L4 **Whittonditch** Wilts
180 C7 **Whittonstall** Nthumb
48 C7 **Whitway** Hants
133 K4 **Whitwell** Derbys
68 F3 **Whitwell** Herts
19 J8 **Whitwell** IoW
160 D3 **Whitwell** N York
101 K2 **Whitwell** Rutlnd
151 M3 **Whitwell-on-the-Hill** N York
122 B7 **Whitwell Street** Norfk
116 D8 **Whitwick** Leics
142 B3 **Whitwood** Wakefd
140 D4 **Whitworth** Lancs
113 H4 **Whixall** Shrops
150 F4 **Whixley** N York
168 E7 **Whorlton** Dur
161 G2 **Whorlton** N York
80 D3 **Whyle** Herefs
51 J7 **Whyteleafe** Surrey
63 H7 **Wibdon** Gloucs
141 J2 **Wibsey** C Brad
100 B6 **Wibtoft** Warwks
81 H3 **Wichenford** Worcs
40 B4 **Wichling** Kent
18 B5 **Wick** Bmouth
14 E2 **Wick** Devon
280 E6 **Wick** Highld
45 K4 **Wick** S Glos
30 B2 **Wick** Somset
30 F5 **Wick** Somset
42 D7 **Wick** V Glam
21 H6 **Wick** W Susx
33 L6 **Wick** Wilts
81 M6 **Wick** Worcs
88 B1 **Wicken** Cambs
84 E7 **Wicken** Nhants
87 K8 **Wicken Bonhunt** Essex
136 A3 **Wickenby** Lincs
85 K5 **Wick End** Bed
133 J2 **Wickersley** Rothm
89 K6 **Wicker Street Green** Suffk
71 H8 **Wickford** Essex
19 K2 **Wickham** Hants
48 B5 **Wickham** W Berk
71 K5 **Wickham Bishops** Essex
41 H3 **Wickhambreaux** Kent
88 E4 **Wickhambrook** Suffk
82 C7 **Wickhamford** Worcs
90 C2 **Wickham Green** Suffk
48 B4 **Wickham Green** W Berk
48 B5 **Wickham Heath** W Berk
91 G4 **Wickham Market** Suffk
107 J2 **Wickhampton** Norfk
89 G7 **Wickham St Paul** Essex
90 C2 **Wickham Skeith** Suffk
88 F4 **Wickham Street** Suffk
90 C1 **Wickham Street** Suffk
106 B3 **Wicklewood** Norfk
122 D5 **Wickmere** Norfk
44 D6 **Wick St Lawrence** N Som
23 J5 **Wickstreet** E Susx
45 L1 **Wickwar** S Glos
70 D1 **Widdington** Essex
140 D1 **Widdop** Calder
191 K7 **Widdrington** Nthumb
191 J7 **Widdrington Station** Nthumb
13 G7 **Widecombe in the Moor** Devon
6 B3 **Widegates** Cnwll
11 H2 **Widemouth Bay** Cnwll
181 G4 **Wide Open** N Tyne
71 G6 **Widford** Essex
70 B4 **Widford** Herts
47 G1 **Widham** Wilts
19 M2 **Widley** Hants
67 L7 **Widmer End** Bucks
117 G6 **Widmerpool** Notts
51 L5 **Widmore** Gt Lon
129 L2 **Widnes** Halton
129 L2 **Widnes Crematorium** Halton
14 F3 **Widworthy** Devon
139 H6 **Wigan** Wigan
139 H7 **Wigan Crematorium** Wigan
31 G7 **Wigborough** Somset
14 C4 **Wiggaton** Devon
120 D8 **Wiggenhall St Germans** Norfk
104 B1 **Wiggenhall St Mary Magdalen** Norfk
104 B1 **Wiggenhall St Mary the Virgin** Norfk
88 D6 **Wiggens Green** Essex
132 B7 **Wiggenstall** Staffs

112 E4 **Wiggington** Shrops
151 J4 **Wigginton** C York
68 B5 **Wigginton** Herts
83 J8 **Wigginton** Oxon
99 G2 **Wigginton** Staffs
68 B5 **Wigginton Bottom** Herts
148 E4 **Wigglesworth** N York
177 J8 **Wiggonby** Cumb
21 H3 **Wiggonholt** W Susx
151 G6 **Wighill** N York
121 L3 **Wighton** Norfk
97 K4 **Wightwick** Wolves
132 F5 **Wigley** Derbys
34 B7 **Wigley** Hants
80 A2 **Wigmore** Herefs
53 G6 **Wigmore** Medway
135 G5 **Wigsley** Notts
102 A6 **Wigsthorpe** Nhants
100 D4 **Wigston** Leics
100 D3 **Wigston Fields** Leics
100 A5 **Wigston Parva** Leics
134 B3 **Wigthorpe** Notts
119 J4 **Wigtoft** Lincs
165 H1 **Wigton** Cumb
174 C4 **Wigtown** D & G
141 L8 **Wigtwizzle** Sheff
150 D7 **Wike** Leeds
101 H5 **Wilbarston** Nhants
151 M5 **Wilberfoss** E R Yk
103 K8 **Wilburton** Cambs
85 G2 **Wilby** Nhants
105 L5 **Wilby** Norfk
90 F1 **Wilby** Suffk
47 H6 **Wilcot** Wilts
112 F7 **Wilcott** Shrops
44 E2 **Wilcrick** Newpt
132 F5 **Wilday Green** Derbys
131 K6 **Wildboarclough** Ches E
86 B4 **Wilden** Bed
81 J1 **Wilden** Worcs
104 D7 **Wilde Street** Suffk
34 D1 **Wildhern** Hants
69 H5 **Wildhill** Herts
209 L8 **Wildmanbridge** S Lans
98 B8 **Wildmoor** Worcs
143 K8 **Wildsworth** Lincs
116 F4 **Wilford** C Nott
116 F4 **Wilford Hill Crematorium** Notts
113 K3 **Wilkesley** Ches E
264 E3 **Wilkhaven** Highld
210 F5 **Wilkieston** W Loth
69 G5 **Wilkin's Green** Herts
136 E7 **Wilksby** Lincs
29 J8 **Willand** Devon
24 C2 **Willards Hill** E Susx
113 L1 **Willaston** Ches E
129 H4 **Willaston** Ches W
85 G7 **Willen** M Keyn
99 K8 **Willenhall** Covtry
98 B4 **Willenhall** Wsall
144 C2 **Willerby** E R Yk
163 H6 **Willerby** N York
82 D7 **Willersey** Gloucs
79 K6 **Willersley** Herefs
40 D7 **Willesborough** Kent
40 D7 **Willesborough Lees** Kent
51 G2 **Willesden** Gt Lon
27 L4 **Willesleigh** Devon
46 B1 **Willesley** Wilts
29 K4 **Willett** Somset
96 F3 **Willey** Shrops
100 B6 **Willey** Warwks
50 B8 **Willey Green** Surrey
83 L6 **Williamscot** Oxon
42 F4 **Williamstown** Rhondd
69 G1 **Willian** Herts
82 E5 **Willicote** Warwks
70 E5 **Willingale** Essex
23 K6 **Willingdon** E Susx
87 H1 **Willingham** Cambs
135 H3 **Willingham by Stow** Lincs
88 C4 **Willingham Green** Cambs
86 C5 **Willington** Bed
116 A6 **Willington** Derbys
169 G4 **Willington** Dur
39 K3 **Willington** Kent
83 G7 **Willington** Warwks
129 M6 **Willington Corner** Ches W
181 H5 **Willington Quay** N Tyne
143 J1 **Willitoft** E R Yk
29 K3 **Williton** Somset
137 J5 **Willoughby** Lincs
83 M2 **Willoughby** Warwks
119 K2 **Willoughby Hills** Lincs
117 H6 **Willoughby-on-the-Wolds** Notts
100 C5 **Willoughby Waterleys** Leics
135 J1 **Willoughton** Lincs
130 B4 **Willow Green** Ches W
71 H3 **Willows Green** Essex

45 K5 **Willsbridge** S Glos
12 D6 **Willsworthy** Devon
30 F6 **Willtown** Somset
82 E4 **Wilmcote** Warwks
45 K6 **Wilmington** BaNES
14 F3 **Wilmington** Devon
23 J6 **Wilmington** E Susx
52 B4 **Wilmington** Kent
131 G3 **Wilmslow** Ches E
99 G3 **Wilnecote** Staffs
139 K1 **Wilpshire** Lancs
149 K8 **Wilsden** C Brad
118 D3 **Wilsford** Lincs
33 K3 **Wilsford** Wilts
47 G7 **Wilsford** Wilts
28 D1 **Wilsham** Devon
141 H6 **Wilshaw** Kirk
150 A3 **Wilsill** N York
39 K6 **Wilsley Green** Kent
39 K6 **Wilsley Pound** Kent
63 H2 **Wilson** Herefs
116 C6 **Wilson** Leics
198 F2 **Wilsontown** S Lans
85 L6 **Wilstead** Bed
102 B1 **Wilsthorpe** Lincs
67 L4 **Wilstone** Herts
67 M4 **Wilstone Green** Herts
164 D8 **Wilton** Cumb
63 H2 **Wilton** Herefs
162 F6 **Wilton** N York
170 D6 **Wilton** R & Cl
33 J4 **Wilton** Wilts
47 K6 **Wilton** Wilts
188 E3 **Wilton Dean** Border
88 B7 **Wimbish** Essex
88 C8 **Wimbish Green** Essex
51 G5 **Wimbledon** Gt Lon
103 J5 **Wimblington** Cambs
130 D7 **Wimboldsley** Ches W
17 K3 **Wimborne Minster** Dorset
33 H8 **Wimborne St Giles** Dorset
104 C2 **Wimbotsham** Norfk
87 G5 **Wimpole** Cambs
82 F5 **Wimpstone** Warwks
32 B5 **Wincanton** Somset
136 F6 **Winceby** Lincs
130 C4 **Wincham** Ches W
210 E4 **Winchburgh** W Loth
64 F2 **Winchcombe** Gloucs
25 G4 **Winchelsea** E Susx
25 G4 **Winchelsea Beach** E Susx
35 G5 **Winchester** Hants
39 J5 **Winchet Hill** Kent
49 J8 **Winchfield** Hants
68 B8 **Winchmore Hill** Bucks
69 J8 **Winchmore Hill** Gt Lon
131 J6 **Wincle** Ches E
133 G1 **Wincobank** Sheff
164 D7 **Winder** Cumb
156 F3 **Windermere** Cumb
83 H7 **Winderton** Warwks
250 F2 **Windhill** Highld
131 J3 **Windlehurst** Stockp
50 A6 **Windlesham** Surrey
10 B7 **Windmill** Cnwll
132 C4 **Windmill** Derbys
23 L5 **Windmill Hill** E Susx
30 D7 **Windmill Hill** Somset
65 J4 **Windrush** Gloucs
267 L4 **Windsole** Abers
50 B4 **Windsor** W & M
64 B7 **Windsoredge** Gloucs
89 H4 **Windsor Green** Suffk
83 G1 **Windy Arbour** Warwks
222 F7 **Windygates** Fife
131 G5 **Windyharbour** Ches E
129 G8 **Windy Hill** Wrexhm
22 C3 **Wineham** W Susx
145 J5 **Winestead** E R Yk
148 F7 **Winewall** Lancs
106 C6 **Winfarthing** Norfk
19 J6 **Winford** IoW
45 G6 **Winford** N Som
79 K6 **Winforton** Herefs
16 F5 **Winfrith Newburgh** Dorset
67 L3 **Wing** Bucks
101 K3 **Wing** Rutlnd
169 L3 **Wingate** Dur
139 K6 **Wingates** Bolton
191 G7 **Wingates** Nthumb
133 G6 **Wingerworth** Derbys
68 C2 **Wingfield** C Beds
106 E7 **Wingfield** Suffk
46 B7 **Wingfield** Wilts
106 E7 **Wingfield Green** Suffk
41 H4 **Wingham** Kent
41 G6 **Wingmore** Kent
67 L3 **Wingrave** Bucks
134 E7 **Winkburn** Notts
49 L4 **Winkfield** Br For

49 L5 **Winkfield Row** Br For
115 H1 **Winkhill** Staffs
38 D3 **Winkhurst Green** Kent
12 F1 **Winkleigh** Devon
150 C2 **Winksley** N York
18 B4 **Winkton** Dorset
180 E6 **Winlaton** Gatesd
180 E6 **Winlaton Mill** Gatesd
280 D5 **Winless** Highld
112 C7 **Winllan** Powys
147 J6 **Winmarleigh** Lancs
35 G5 **Winnall** Hants
49 J5 **Winnersh** Wokham
130 C5 **Winnington** Ches W
164 D5 **Winscales** Cumb
44 E7 **Winscombe** N Som
130 C6 **Winsford** Ches W
28 F4 **Winsford** Somset
27 J3 **Winsham** Devon
15 J1 **Winsham** Somset
115 M7 **Winshill** Staffs
57 J5 **Winshwen** Swans
166 D4 **Winskill** Cumb
35 K1 **Winslade** Hants
46 A6 **Winsley** Wilts
67 J2 **Winslow** Bucks
65 G5 **Winson** Gloucs
34 D8 **Winsor** Hants
156 F4 **Winster** Cumb
132 E7 **Winster** Derbys
168 F7 **Winston** Dur
90 E3 **Winston** Suffk
64 D5 **Winstone** Gloucs
27 J8 **Winswell** Devon
16 D5 **Winterborne Came** Dorset
17 G2 **Winterborne Clenston** Dorset
16 D5 **Winterborne Herringston** Dorset
16 F2 **Winterborne Houghton** Dorset
17 G3 **Winterborne Kingston** Dorset
16 C5 **Winterborne Monkton** Dorset
16 F2 **Winterborne Stickland** Dorset
17 G3 **Winterborne Tomson** Dorset
17 G2 **Winterborne Whitechurch** Dorset
17 H3 **Winterborne Zelston** Dorset
45 J3 **Winterbourne** S Glos
48 C4 **Winterbourne** W Berk
16 B4 **Winterbourne Abbas** Dorset
47 G4 **Winterbourne Bassett** Wilts
33 L4 **Winterbourne Dauntsey** Wilts
33 L4 **Winterbourne Earls** Wilts
33 L4 **Winterbourne Gunner** Wilts
47 G4 **Winterbourne Monkton** Wilts
16 B4 **Winterbourne Steepleton** Dorset
33 J3 **Winterbourne Stoke** Wilts
48 F1 **Winterbrook** Oxon
149 G4 **Winterburn** N York
144 A3 **Winteringham** N Linc
130 E8 **Winterley** Ches E
142 B4 **Wintersett** Wakefd
34 B4 **Winterslow** Wilts
144 A4 **Winterton** N Linc
123 K7 **Winterton-on-Sea** Norfk
137 K6 **Winthorpe** Lincs
135 G8 **Winthorpe** Notts
17 L4 **Winton** Bmouth
167 H8 **Winton** Cumb
23 H6 **Winton** E Susx
160 F3 **Winton** N York
162 F8 **Wintringham** N York
102 B7 **Winwick** Cambs
100 D8 **Winwick** Nhants
130 B1 **Winwick** Warrtn
115 M1 **Wirksworth** Derbys
113 J3 **Wirswall** Ches E
103 J2 **Wisbech** Cambs
103 J2 **Wisbech St Mary** Cambs
37 G5 **Wisborough Green** W Susx
55 K5 **Wiseman's Bridge** Pembks
134 E2 **Wiseton** Notts
64 D5 **Wishanger** Gloucs
209 L7 **Wishaw** N Lans
98 F4 **Wishaw** Warwks
50 D7 **Wisley** Surrey
136 D5 **Wispington** Lincs
40 B7 **Wissenden** Kent
107 H7 **Wissett** Suffk
104 D4 **Wissington** Norfk
89 J8 **Wissington** Suffk
95 K6 **Wistanstow** Shrops
113 L5 **Wistanswick** Shrops
113 L1 **Wistaston** Ches E
130 D8 **Wistaston Green** Ches E
131 G5 **Wisterfield** Ches E
55 H3 **Wiston** Pembks
198 F6 **Wiston** S Lans
21 K4 **Wiston** W Susx
102 F7 **Wistow** Cambs

100 E4 **Wistow** Leics
142 F1 **Wistow** N York
148 C8 **Wiswell** Lancs
103 J7 **Witcham** Cambs
17 J1 **Witchampton** Dorset
103 K7 **Witchford** Cambs
31 G6 **Witcombe** Somset
71 K4 **Witham** Essex
32 B3 **Witham Friary** Somset
118 D8 **Witham on the Hill** Lincs
135 H7 **Witham St Hughs** Lincs
136 E3 **Withcall** Lincs
22 D5 **Withdean** Br & H
23 D5 **Witherenden Hill** E Susx
28 D8 **Witheridge** Devon
99 J4 **Witherley** Leics
137 H3 **Withern** Lincs
145 J2 **Withernsea** E R Yk
153 K7 **Withernwick** E R Yk
106 F7 **Withersdale Street** Suffk
88 D5 **Withersfield** Suffk
156 F5 **Witherslack** Cumb
5 G2 **Withiel** Cnwll
29 H4 **Withiel Florey** Somset
5 G2 **Withielgoose** Cnwll
64 F4 **Withington** Gloucs
80 D6 **Withington** Herefs
131 G1 **Withington** Manch
96 D1 **Withington** Shrops
115 G4 **Withington** Staffs
130 F5 **Withington Green** Ches E
80 D6 **Withington Marsh** Herefs
28 F8 **Withleigh** Devon
139 J3 **Withnell** Lancs
82 B1 **Withybed Green** Worcs
99 L6 **Withybrook** Warwks
29 J3 **Withycombe** Somset
38 D6 **Withyham** E Susx
45 K7 **Withy Mills** BaNES
28 E4 **Withypool** Somset
45 H5 **Withywood** Bristl
36 E3 **Witley** Surrey
90 E5 **Witnesham** Suffk
65 M5 **Witney** Oxon
102 B3 **Wittering** C Pete
25 G2 **Wittersham** Kent
98 D5 **Witton** Blrm
107 G2 **Witton** Norfk
123 G5 **Witton** Norfk
169 G2 **Witton Gilbert** Dur
107 J3 **Witton Green** Norfk
168 F4 **Witton le Wear** Dur
168 F4 **Witton Park** Dur
29 K5 **Wiveliscombe** Somset
35 K3 **Wivelrod** Hants
22 E3 **Wivelsfield** E Susx
22 E3 **Wivelsfield Green** E Susx
22 E3 **Wivelsfield Station** W Susx
72 F3 **Wivenhoe** Essex
72 F2 **Wivenhoe Cross** Essex
122 A3 **Wiveton** Norfk
73 H2 **Wix** Essex
82 C4 **Wixford** Warwks
73 H2 **Wix Green** Essex
113 J6 **Wixhill** Shrops
88 E6 **Wixoe** Suffk
85 J8 **Woburn** C Beds
85 H8 **Woburn Sands** M Keyn
49 G6 **Wokefield Park** W Berk
50 C7 **Woking** Surrey
50 B7 **Woking Crematorium** Surrey
49 K5 **Wokingham** Wokham
13 K8 **Wolborough** Devon
51 K7 **Woldingham** Surrey
163 J8 **Wold Newton** E R Yk
145 G8 **Wold Newton** NE Lin
199 H6 **Wolfclyde** S Lans
80 F3 **Wolferlow** Herefs
120 E6 **Wolferton** Norfk
83 M2 **Wolfhampcote** Warwks
233 H8 **Wolfhill** P & K
179 G7 **Wolf Hills** Nthumb
74 F6 **Wolf's Castle** Pembks
54 F3 **Wolfsdale** Pembks
97 K6 **Wollaston** Dudley
85 H3 **Wollaston** Nhants
95 H1 **Wollaston** Shrops
116 E4 **Wollaton** C Nott
13 J6 **Wolleigh** Devon
113 K5 **Wollerton** Shrops
97 L6 **Wollescote** Dudley
115 G7 **Wolseley Bridge** Staffs
168 D3 **Wolsingham** Dur
114 D2 **Wolstanton** Staffs
140 C5 **Wolstenholme** Rochdl
99 L8 **Wolston** Warwks
176 E8 **Wolsty** Cumb
66 D5 **Wolvercote** Oxon
97 K4 **Wolverhampton** Wolves
113 G5 **Wolverley** Shrops

97 J7 **Wolverley** Worcs
48 E7 **Wolverton** Hants
41 H6 **Wolverton** Kent
84 F7 **Wolverton** M Keyn
82 F3 **Wolverton** Warwks
32 C4 **Wolverton** Wilts
48 E7 **Wolverton Common** Hants
62 F7 **Wolvesnewton** Mons
99 L6 **Wolvey** Warwks
99 L5 **Wolvey Heath** Warwks
170 B5 **Wolviston** S on T
161 L6 **Wombleton** N York
97 K5 **Wombourne** Staffs
142 B7 **Wombwell** Barns
41 H5 **Womenswold** Kent
142 E4 **Womersley** N York
62 F5 **Wonastow** Mons
36 F2 **Wonersh** Surrey
13 L4 **Wonford** Devon
12 F4 **Wonson** Devon
35 G3 **Wonston** Hants
49 M2 **Wooburn** Bucks
49 M1 **Wooburn Green** Bucks
49 M1 **Wooburn Moor** Bucks
11 M1 **Woodacott** Devon
159 J6 **Woodale** N York
133 J3 **Woodall** Rothm
123 G8 **Woodbastwick** Norfk
134 F4 **Woodbeck** Notts
82 C4 **Wood Bevington** Warwks
117 G2 **Woodborough** Notts
47 G7 **Woodborough** Wilts
14 E3 **Woodbridge** Devon
32 E7 **Woodbridge** Dorset
91 G5 **Woodbridge** Suffk
84 D6 **Wood Burcote** Nhants
14 B5 **Woodbury** Devon
14 B4 **Woodbury Salterton** Devon
64 B6 **Woodchester** Gloucs
40 B8 **Woodchurch** Kent
129 G2 **Woodchurch** Wirral
29 G2 **Woodcombe** Somset
51 J6 **Woodcote** Gt Lon
48 F3 **Woodcote** Oxon
114 B8 **Woodcote** Wrekin
81 L1 **Woodcote Green** Worcs
48 B7 **Woodcott** Hants
63 G7 **Woodcroft** Gloucs
33 G7 **Woodcutts** Dorset
122 B6 **Wood Dalling** Norfk
88 D3 **Woodditton** Cambs
66 D5 **Woodeaton** Oxon
55 J6 **Wooden** Pembks
85 K6 **Wood End** Bed
86 B2 **Wood End** Bed
103 H8 **Wood End** Cambs
50 E3 **Wood End** Gt Lon
69 J2 **Wood End** Herts
228 B3 **Woodend** Highld
84 B5 **Woodend** Nhants
115 K6 **Woodend** Staffs
210 B5 **Woodend** W Loth
20 D5 **Woodend** W Susx
82 D1 **Wood End** Warwks
99 H4 **Wood End** Warwks
99 J6 **Wood End** Warwks
97 L3 **Wood End** Wolves
136 E6 **Wood Enderby** Lincs
70 E2 **Woodend Green** Essex
33 L6 **Woodfalls** Wilts
26 C8 **Woodford** Cnwll
8 B5 **Woodford** Devon
63 K7 **Woodford** Gloucs
69 L8 **Woodford** Gt Lon
101 L8 **Woodford** Nhants
131 H3 **Woodford** Stockp
51 L1 **Woodford Bridge** Gt Lon
84 A5 **Woodford Halse** Nhants
69 L8 **Woodford Wells** Gt Lon
98 C6 **Woodgate** Birm
29 K7 **Woodgate** Devon
121 K8 **Woodgate** Norfk
121 M8 **Woodgate** Norfk
20 F6 **Woodgate** W Susx
81 M2 **Woodgate** Worcs
51 J1 **Wood Green** Gt Lon
33 L7 **Woodgreen** Hants
66 A5 **Woodgreen** Oxon
136 D6 **Woodhall** Lincs
159 H4 **Woodhall** N York
141 K1 **Woodhall Hill** Leeds
136 C7 **Woodhall Spa** Lincs
67 H3 **Woodham** Bucks
169 H5 **Woodham** Dur
50 D6 **Woodham** Surrey
71 J7 **Woodham Ferrers** Essex
71 K6 **Woodham Mortimer** Essex
71 K5 **Woodham Walter** Essex
97 L3 **Wood Hayes** Wolves

256 E4 **Woodhead** Abers
30 E5 **Woodhill** Somset
181 H1 **Woodhorn** Nthumb
181 H1 **Woodhorn Demesne** Nthumb
141 L1 **Woodhouse** Leeds
116 F8 **Woodhouse** Leics
133 H3 **Woodhouse** Sheff
142 B3 **Woodhouse** Wakefd
116 F8 **Woodhouse Eaves** Leics
131 H7 **Woodhouse Green** Staffs
211 H6 **Woodhouselee** Mdloth
177 L4 **Woodhouselees** D & G
133 H3 **Woodhouse Mill** Sheff
177 K8 **Woodhouses** Cumb
140 D7 **Woodhouses** Oldham
98 D2 **Woodhouses** Staffs
115 J7 **Woodhouses** Staffs
8 D4 **Woodhuish** Devon
103 G8 **Woodhurst** Cambs
22 E6 **Woodingdean** Br & H
141 L3 **Woodkirk** Leeds
256 F7 **Woodland** Abers
7 J4 **Woodland** Devon
8 B1 **Woodland** Devon
168 D5 **Woodland** Dur
40 F7 **Woodland** Kent
182 F4 **Woodland** S Ayrs
13 H3 **Woodland Head** Devon
245 H4 **Woodlands** Abers
142 E6 **Woodlands** Donc
17 L1 **Woodlands** Dorset
18 E1 **Woodlands** Hants
52 C6 **Woodlands** Kent
150 D5 **Woodlands** N York
29 L3 **Woodlands** Somset
98 F5 **Woodlands (Coleshill) Crematorium** Warwks
49 L3 **Woodlands Park** W & M
47 M4 **Woodlands St Mary** W Berk
163 J5 **Woodlands (Scarborough) Crematorium** N York
143 M5 **Woodlands (Scunthorpe) Crematorium** N Linc
31 J3 **Woodland Street** Somset
132 F2 **Woodland View** Sheff
112 F5 **Wood Lane** Shrops
114 C2 **Wood Lane** Staffs
7 L5 **Woodleigh** Devon
142 B2 **Woodlesford** Leeds
131 J1 **Woodley** Stockp
49 J4 **Woodley** Wokham
63 M7 **Woodmancote** Gloucs
64 E2 **Woodmancote** Gloucs
64 E5 **Woodmancote** Gloucs
20 C5 **Woodmancote** W Susx
22 C4 **Woodmancote** W Susx
81 L6 **Woodmancote** Worcs
35 H2 **Woodmancott** Hants
153 G8 **Woodmansey** E R Yk
36 C5 **Woodmansgreen** W Susx
51 H7 **Woodmansterne** Surrey
14 B5 **Woodmanton** Devon
46 B7 **Woodmarsh** Wilts
115 J7 **Woodmill** Staffs
33 H6 **Woodminton** Wilts
41 J4 **Woodnesborough** Kent
102 A4 **Woodnewton** Nhants
116 D1 **Woodnook** Notts
121 M6 **Wood Norton** Norfk
139 G1 **Woodplumpton** Lancs
105 K3 **Woodrising** Norfk
142 B2 **Wood Row** Leeds
97 K6 **Woodrow** Worcs
24 B3 **Wood's Corner** E Susx
79 K5 **Woods Eaves** Herefs
113 M5 **Woodseaves** Shrops
114 B6 **Woodseaves** Staffs
47 J4 **Woodsend** Wilts
133 L3 **Woodsetts** Rothm
16 E4 **Woodsford** Dorset
39 G6 **Wood's Green** E Susx
50 B5 **Woodside** Br For
164 D4 **Woodside** Cumb
70 C6 **Woodside** Essex
223 G6 **Woodside** Fife
51 J5 **Woodside** Gt Lon
18 E5 **Woodside** Hants
69 H5 **Woodside** Herts
233 J7 **Woodside** P & K
40 B4 **Woodside Green** Kent
66 C4 **Woodstock** Oxon
75 H7 **Woodstock** Pembks
102 D4 **Woodston** C Pete
123 H7 **Wood Street** Norfk
36 E1 **Wood Street Village** Surrey
133 J5 **Woodthorpe** Derbys
116 F8 **Woodthorpe** Leics
137 H4 **Woodthorpe** Lincs
106 F4 **Woodton** Norfk
147 L7 **Wood Top** Lancs

27 G6 **Woodtown** Devon
138 C5 **Woodvale** Sefton
22 E6 **Woodvale Crematorium** Br & H
116 A7 **Woodville** Derbys
114 B5 **Woodwall Green** Staffs
102 E7 **Wood Walton** Cambs
33 H7 **Woodyates** Dorset
28 B1 **Woody Bay** Devon
80 C2 **Woofferton** Shrops
31 H2 **Wookey** Somset
31 H2 **Wookey Hole** Somset
17 G5 **Wool** Dorset
27 H2 **Woolacombe** Devon
41 H5 **Woolage Green** Kent
41 H5 **Woolage Village** Kent
63 H7 **Woolaston** Gloucs
63 H6 **Woolaston Common** Gloucs
30 E3 **Woolavington** Somset
36 C6 **Woolbeding** W Susx
14 D4 **Woolbrook** Devon
29 H4 **Woolcotts** Somset
141 J6 **Wooldale** Kirk
202 F7 **Wooler** Nthumb
13 J1 **Woolfardisworthy** Devon
26 F6 **Woolfardisworthy** Devon
140 B5 **Woolfold** Bury
199 G2 **Woolfords** S Lans
48 E5 **Woolhampton** W Berk
80 E8 **Woolhope** Herefs
16 E1 **Woolland** Dorset
45 J6 **Woollard** BaNES
69 K5 **Woollensbrook** Herts
45 L5 **Woolley** BaNES
102 C8 **Woolley** Cambs
26 D7 **Woolley** Cnwll
133 G7 **Woolley** Derbys
141 M5 **Woolley** Wakefd
131 K1 **Woolley Bridge** Derbys
49 K3 **Woolley Green** W & M
81 M3 **Woolmere Green** Worcs
69 H3 **Woolmer Green** Herts
30 D4 **Woolmerston** Somset
15 J1 **Woolminstone** Somset
39 L6 **Woolpack** Kent
89 K3 **Woolpit** Suffk
89 K3 **Woolpit Green** Suffk
83 L2 **Woolscott** Warwks
13 J2 **Woolsgrove** Devon
180 F5 **Woolsington** N u Ty
95 L4 **Woolstaston** Shrops
117 L5 **Woolsthorpe** Lincs
118 B6 **Woolsthorpe-by-Colsterworth** Lincs
19 G2 **Woolston** C Sotn
7 L5 **Woolston** Devon
7 L6 **Woolston** Devon
95 K6 **Woolston** Shrops
112 D6 **Woolston** Shrops
29 K3 **Woolston** Somset
31 L5 **Woolston** Somset
130 C2 **Woolston** Warrtn
64 D1 **Woolstone** Gloucs
85 G7 **Woolstone** M Keyn
47 L2 **Woolstone** Oxon
8 A2 **Woolston Green** Devon
129 K2 **Woolton** Lpool
48 B6 **Woolton Hill** Hants
90 E7 **Woolverstone** Suffk
46 A8 **Woolverton** Somset
51 L3 **Woolwich** Gt Lon
79 L5 **Woonton** Herefs
80 D3 **Woonton** Herefs
190 F2 **Wooperton** Nthumb
114 A3 **Woore** Shrops
90 F1 **Wootten Green** Suffk
85 K6 **Wootten** Bed
18 C4 **Wootton** Hants
79 L5 **Wootton** Herefs
19 J5 **Wootton** IoW
41 H6 **Wootton** Kent
144 D4 **Wootton** N Linc
84 E4 **Wootton** Nhants
66 B3 **Wootton** Oxon
66 C6 **Wootton** Oxon
112 E6 **Wootton** Shrops
114 C6 **Wootton** Staffs
115 H3 **Wootton** Staffs
46 F3 **Wootton Bassett** Wilts
19 J5 **Wootton Bridge** IoW
85 K6 **Wootton Broadmead** Bed
19 J5 **Wootton Common** IoW
29 G2 **Wootton Courtenay** Somset
15 J3 **Wootton Fitzpaine** Dorset
47 J6 **Wootton Rivers** Wilts
48 E8 **Wootton St Lawrence** Hants
82 E3 **Wootton Wawen** Warwks
81 K4 **Worcester** Worcs
51 G6 **Worcester Park** Gt Lon
97 K6 **Wordsley** Dudley
97 G4 **Worfield** Shrops

17 H5 **Worgret** Dorset
86 B5 **Workhouse End** Bed
164 D5 **Workington** Cumb
134 B4 **Worksop** Notts
136 F4 **Worlaby** Lincs
144 C5 **Worlaby** N Linc
67 L5 **Worlds End** Bucks
19 L1 **Worlds End** Hants
48 C3 **World's End** W Berk
22 E3 **Worlds End** W Susx
44 D6 **Worle** N Som
130 C8 **Worleston** Ches E
107 J5 **Worlingham** Suffk
28 D8 **Worlington** Devon
104 D8 **Worlington** Suffk
90 F2 **Worlingworth** Suffk
150 D3 **Wormald Green** N York
62 E1 **Wormbridge** Herefs
104 D1 **Wormegay** Norfk
62 F1 **Wormelow Tump** Herefs
132 C5 **Wormhill** Derbys
80 A7 **Wormhill** Herefs
72 D1 **Wormingford** Essex
66 F5 **Worminghall** Bucks
82 B7 **Wormington** Gloucs
31 J2 **Worminster** Somset
223 G2 **Wormit** Fife
83 K4 **Wormleighton** Warwks
69 K6 **Wormley** Herts
36 E3 **Wormley** Surrey
69 K6 **Wormleybury** Herts
143 G4 **Wormley Hill** Donc
39 M2 **Wormshill** Kent
80 A5 **Wormsley** Herefs
50 B8 **Worplesdon** Surrey
132 F1 **Worrall** Sheff
63 J4 **Worrall Hill** Gloucs
142 A7 **Worsbrough** Barns
142 A7 **Worsbrough Bridge** Barns
142 B7 **Worsbrough Dale** Barns
139 M7 **Worsley** Salfd
139 H7 **Worsley Mesnes** Wigan
122 F6 **Worstead** Norfk
140 C1 **Worsthorne** Lancs
7 H4 **Worston** Devon
148 D7 **Worston** Lancs
41 K4 **Worth** Kent
31 H2 **Worth** Somset
37 L4 **Worth** W Susx
37 M4 **Worth Abbey** W Susx
106 B7 **Wortham** Suffk
95 H2 **Worthen** Shrops
112 F2 **Worthenbury** Wrexhm
121 M7 **Worthing** Norfk
21 K6 **Worthing** W Susx
21 J5 **Worthing Crematorium** W Susx
116 C7 **Worthington** Leics
17 J7 **Worth Matravers** Dorset
62 F5 **Worthybrook** Mons
48 F8 **Worting** Hants
141 M7 **Wortley** Barns
141 L1 **Wortley** Leeds
159 G5 **Worton** N York
46 E7 **Worton** Wilts
106 F6 **Wortwell** Norfk
95 G3 **Wotherton** Shrops
101 M2 **Wothorpe** C Pete
7 H3 **Wotter** Devon
37 H2 **Wotton** Surrey
63 M8 **Wotton-under-Edge** Gloucs
67 G4 **Wotton Underwood** Bucks
85 G7 **Woughton on the Green** M Keyn
52 F6 **Wouldham** Kent
97 H5 **Woundale** Shrops
73 J1 **Wrabness** Essex
27 J4 **Wrafton** Devon
136 B4 **Wragby** Lincs
142 C4 **Wragby** Wakefd
106 C2 **Wramplingham** Norfk
7 K3 **Wrangaton** Devon
142 D5 **Wrangbrook** Wakefd
119 M2 **Wrangle** Lincs
119 M1 **Wrangle Common** Lincs
119 M1 **Wrangle Lowgate** Lincs
29 L7 **Wrangway** Somset
30 D6 **Wrantage** Somset
144 C6 **Wrawby** N Linc
44 F4 **Wraxall** N Som
31 K4 **Wraxall** Somset
147 M2 **Wray** Lancs
156 E3 **Wray Castle** Cumb
50 C4 **Wraysbury** W & M
147 M2 **Wrayton** Lancs
138 E2 **Wrea Green** Lancs
156 B5 **Wreaks End** Cumb
166 B1 **Wreay** Cumb
166 B6 **Wreay** Cumb
36 B2 **Wrecclesham** Surrey

181 G7 **Wrekenton** Gatesd
162 D5 **Wrelton** N York
113 K2 **Wrenbury** Ches E
163 H5 **Wrench Green** N York
106 D4 **Wreningham** Norfk
107 K6 **Wrentham** Suffk
141 M3 **Wrenthorpe** Wakefd
95 K3 **Wrentnall** Shrops
143 H2 **Wressle** E R Yk
144 B6 **Wressle** N Linc
86 E5 **Wrestlingworth** C Beds
104 D3 **Wretton** Norfk
112 E2 **Wrexham** Wrexhm
97 H8 **Wribbenhall** Worcs
96 E6 **Wrickton** Shrops
139 G5 **Wrightington Bar** Lancs
70 D4 **Wright's Green** Essex
114 B2 **Wrinehill** Staffs
44 F6 **Wrington** N Som
45 K8 **Writhlington** BaNES
71 G6 **Writtle** Essex
96 E1 **Wrockwardine** Wrekin
143 H7 **Wroot** N Linc
149 L8 **Wrose** C Brad
52 D7 **Wrotham** Kent
52 D7 **Wrotham Heath** Kent
97 J3 **Wrottesley** Staffs
47 H3 **Wroughton** Swindn
19 J7 **Wroxall** IoW
82 F1 **Wroxall** Warwks
96 D2 **Wroxeter** Shrops
122 F8 **Wroxham** Norfk
83 K7 **Wroxton** Oxon
115 K3 **Wyaston** Derbys
70 F7 **Wyatt's Green** Essex
119 K3 **Wyberton East** Lincs
119 J3 **Wyberton West** Lincs
86 D4 **Wyboston** Bed
113 M2 **Wybunbury** Ches E
81 L2 **Wychbold** Worcs
38 C7 **Wych Cross** E Susx
115 K8 **Wychnor** Staffs
35 M3 **Wyck** Hants
65 J3 **Wyck Rissington** Gloucs
168 E7 **Wycliffe** Dur
149 G8 **Wycoller** Lancs
117 K6 **Wycomb** Leics
67 L8 **Wycombe Marsh** Bucks
69 K1 **Wyddial** Herts
40 D6 **Wye** Kent
63 G5 **Wyesham** Mons
117 L7 **Wyfordby** Leics
141 J2 **Wyke** C Brad
13 K3 **Wyke** Devon
15 G3 **Wyke** Devon
32 D5 **Wyke** Dorset
96 E3 **Wyke** Shrops
50 A8 **Wyke** Surrey
31 L4 **Wyke Champflower** Somset
163 H6 **Wykeham** N York
99 K7 **Wyken** Covtry
97 H4 **Wyken** Shrops
16 C7 **Wyke Regis** Dorset
112 F6 **Wykey** Shrops
99 L4 **Wykin** Leics
180 D6 **Wylam** Nthumb
98 E4 **Wylde Green** Birm
33 H3 **Wylye** Wilts
117 G6 **Wymeswold** Leics
85 J2 **Wymington** Bed
117 M7 **Wymondham** Leics
106 C3 **Wymondham** Norfk
42 E3 **Wyndham** Brdgnd
16 B3 **Wynford Eagle** Dorset
169 L5 **Wynyard Park** S on T
169 L5 **Wynyard Village** S on T
81 M5 **Wyre Piddle** Worcs
117 G6 **Wysall** Notts
80 C2 **Wyson** Herefs
98 D8 **Wythall** Worcs
66 C5 **Wytham** Oxon
165 K7 **Wythburn** Cumb
131 G2 **Wythenshawe** Manch
165 G5 **Wythop Mill** Cumb
86 F1 **Wyton** Cambs
144 F1 **Wyton** E R Yk
90 B2 **Wyverstone** Suffk
89 L2 **Wyverstone Street** Suffk
118 A5 **Wyville** Lincs

**Y**

143 M6 **Yaddlethorpe** N Linc
19 G7 **Yafford** IoW
160 E4 **Yafforth** N York
8 C3 **Yalberton** Torbay
39 H3 **Yalding** Kent
166 C5 **Yanwath** Cumb
65 G4 **Yanworth** Gloucs

152 B5 **Yapham** E R Yk
21 G6 **Yapton** W Susx
44 D7 **Yarborough** N Som
19 K6 **Yarbridge** IoW
136 F1 **Yarburgh** Lincs
14 F1 **Yarcombe** Devon
28 D6 **Yard** Devon
98 E6 **Yardley** Birm
98 E6 **Yardley Crematorium** Birm
84 E6 **Yardley Gobion** Nhants
85 G4 **Yardley Hastings** Nhants
98 E7 **Yardley Wood** Birm
79 J3 **Yardro** Powys
30 B5 **Yarford** Somset
80 E6 **Yarkhill** Herefs
31 H2 **Yarley** Somset
31 L5 **Yarlington** Somset
169 L8 **Yarm** S on T
18 E5 **Yarmouth** IoW
27 L5 **Yarnacott** Devon
46 C7 **Yarnbrook** Wilts
13 H6 **Yarner** Devon
114 D5 **Yarnfield** Staffs
27 K6 **Yarnscombe** Devon
66 C5 **Yarnton** Oxon
80 B2 **Yarpole** Herefs
200 D7 **Yarrow** Border
30 E2 **Yarrow** Somset
200 D7 **Yarrow Feus** Border
200 E7 **Yarrowford** Border
80 A6 **Yarsop** Herefs
102 B4 **Yarwell** Nhants
45 L3 **Yate** S Glos
49 K6 **Yateley** Hants
46 F4 **Yatesbury** Wilts
48 E4 **Yattendon** W Berk
80 A2 **Yatton** Herefs
44 E6 **Yatton** N Som
46 C4 **Yatton Keynell** Wilts
19 K6 **Yaverland** IoW
15 H4 **Yawl** Devon
135 H1 **Yawthorpe** Lincs
105 K1 **Yaxham** Norfk
102 D5 **Yaxley** Cambs
106 C8 **Yaxley** Suffk
79 M6 **Yazor** Herefs
50 E3 **Yeading** Gt Lon
150 B7 **Yeadon** Leeds
157 H7 **Yealand Conyers** Lancs
157 H7 **Yealand Redmayne** Lancs
157 H7 **Yealand Storrs** Lancs
7 H4 **Yealmbridge** Devon
7 H4 **Yealmpton** Devon
170 E6 **Yearby** R & Cl
164 F2 **Yearngill** Cumb
161 J7 **Yearsley** N York
113 G7 **Yeaton** Shrops
115 K3 **Yeaveley** Derbys
202 E7 **Yeavering** Nthumb
162 F6 **Yedingham** N York
66 A6 **Yelford** Oxon
27 J4 **Yelland** Devon
86 F3 **Yelling** Cambs
100 D8 **Yelvertoft** Nhants
7 G1 **Yelverton** Devon
106 F3 **Yelverton** Norfk
32 B6 **Yenston** Somset
13 H3 **Yeoford** Devon
11 L5 **Yeolmbridge** Cnwll
28 E5 **Yeo Mill** Devon
27 G6 **Yeo Vale** Devon
31 J7 **Yeovil** Somset
31 H7 **Yeovil Crematorium** Somset
31 J7 **Yeovil Marsh** Somset
31 J6 **Yeovilton** Somset
55 H5 **Yerbeston** Pembks
275 b4 **Yesnaby** Ork
190 E4 **Yetlington** Nthumb
31 K8 **Yotminster** Dorset
8 B4 **Yetson** Devon
14 B5 **Yettington** Devon
221 H6 **Yetts o'Muckhart** Clacks
141 H2 **Yews Green** C Brad
98 C4 **Yew Tree** Sandw
125 J6 **Y Felinheli** Gwynd
75 L2 **Y Ferwig** Cerdgn
109 G4 **Y Ffor** Gwynd
128 C8 **Y Gyffylliog** Denbgs
85 K2 **Yielden** Bed
97 K7 **Yieldingtree** Worcs
198 E3 **Yieldshields** S Lans
50 D3 **Yiewsley** Gt Lon
111 K3 **Y Maerdy** Conwy
112 D2 **Y Nant** Wrexhm
43 G3 **Ynysboeth** Rhondd
43 J3 **Ynysddu** Caerph
57 J5 **Ynysforgan** Swans
42 F3 **Ynyshir** Rhondd
92 D5 **Ynyslas** Cerdgn
42 F5 **Ynysmaerdy** Rhondd

57 K4 **Ynysmeudwy** Neath
57 J5 **Ynystawe** Swans
60 C4 **Ynyswen** Powys
42 E2 **Ynyswen** Rhondd
43 G3 **Ynysybwl** Rhondd
92 D3 **Ynysymaengwyn** Gwynd
158 F6 **Yockenthwaite** N York
95 K2 **Yockleton** Shrops
143 K3 **Yokefleet** E R Yk
208 E5 **Yoker** C Glas
151 J5 **York** C York
139 L1 **York** Lancs
151 J6 **York City Crematorium** C York
40 E3 **Yorkletts** Kent
63 J5 **Yorkley** Gloucs
49 L7 **York Town** Surrey
113 H7 **Yorton Heath** Shrops
132 D6 **Youlgreave** Derbys
152 B5 **Youlthorpe** E R Yk
151 G3 **Youlton** N York
69 K3 **Youngsbury** Herts
71 H3 **Young's End** Essex
115 J7 **Yoxall** Staffs
91 J2 **Yoxford** Suffk
108 D6 **Y Rhiw** Gwynd
93 G7 **Ysbyty Cynfyn** Cerdgn
110 F2 **Ysbyty Ifan** Conwy
77 K1 **Ysbyty Ystwyth** Cerdgn
128 D5 **Ysceifiog** Flints
92 E4 **Ysgubor-y-Coed** Cerdgn
57 L3 **Ystalyfera** Neath
42 F3 **Ystrad** Rhondd
76 F4 **Ystrad Aeron** Cerdgn
60 D4 **Ystradfellte** Powys
77 L6 **Ystrad Ffin** Carmth
60 B5 **Ystradgynlais** Powys
77 K2 **Ystrad Meurig** Cerdgn
43 J3 **Ystrad Mynach** Caerph
42 F6 **Ystradowen** V Glam
92 F7 **Ystumtuen** Cerdgn
257 G5 **Ythanbank** Abers
256 B4 **Ythanwells** Abers
256 F5 **Ythsie** Abers

## Z

13 G2 **Zeal Monachorum** Devon
32 C4 **Zeals** Wilts
4 C4 **Zelah** Cnwll
2 C3 **Zennor** Cnwll
3 J7 **Zoar** Cnwll
116 F6 **Zouch** Notts

# Ten money-saving offers on AA products and services

Call the telephone number shown below for each product, quoting the reference number, or visit the web site as requested

## AA Driving School

Learning to drive?

**Buy 2 AA driving lessons, get 1 FREE***

Call: **0800 975 3683**

*Offer closes 1.07.2010. Only 1 free hour of tuition will be given per pupil. Offer not available to existing AA Driving School pupils and cannot be used in conjunction with any other offer. Offer subject to instructor availability. AA driving instructors are self-employed franchisees and all contracts for the provision of driving tuition are between the pupil and the instructor. Only one voucher redeemable per pupil. This vouchers has no monetary value. Full terms and conditions are available at AAdrivingschool.co.uk (Given on calling 0800 107 2045).

## AA Travel Shop

**10% discount at AAtravelshop.com***

For AA car accessories and much more, plus free p&p on all orders over £15**

Enter promo code: **'ATLAS 10'** at the basket

Terms & conditions apply. *On marked prices only. Valid until 1/07/2010. Subject to availability.
**Applies to UK mainland and standard delivery only.

## AA Breakdown Cover

**Join the UK's No.1 choice in breakdown assistance from £39***

Call: **0800 316 9386**

*£39 is for annual Vehicle Membership (Roadside). £39 only available to new Members joining by phone and when paying by recurring annual payment only. Applies to first 12 months of cover only and is not available for existing Members or at renewal and cannot be applied respectively. Offer cannot be used in conjunction with any other offer, nor can it be used in a breakdown situation. Offer may be withdrawn or varied at any time.

## AA Van Insurance

**5% discount for AA Members***

Up to £250 for replacement locks if your van keys are lost or stolen

Call: **0800 294 2740**

*Discount only available to existing AA Personal Members when they become new AA Van Insurance customers and is only applicable for the first year of the policy. Discount not available retrospectively or for specialist schemes. Discount not available online or in conjunction with any other discount, promotion or offer. Offer can be withdrawn or varied at any time.

## AA Home Insurance

**10% discount for AA Members***

Accidental damage cover on buildings insurance as standard

Call: **0800 032 2175** quoting ref: 351

*Discount only available to existing AA Personal Members when they become new AA Home Insurance customers and is only applicable for the first year of the policy. Discount not available retrospectively or for specialist schemes. Discount not available online or in conjunction with any other discount, promotion or offer. Offer can be withdrawn or varied at any time.

## AA Travel Insurance

**10% OFF AA Travel Insurance**

If you have a holiday planned this year, trust the AA to take care of you

Call: **0800 072 3407** and quote 'AAAV09'

Terms and Conditions apply. AA Travel Insurance is arranged by Drakefield Insurance Services Limited, an AA group company, authorised and regulated by the Financial Services Authority.

## AA European Breakdown Cover

Driving in Europe?

**Save £10 now on our European Breakdown cover on trips of 6 days or more***

Call: **0800 294 0298** and quote 'UK Atlas 2010'

Different rates apply to different lengths of cover/parties of more than eight and supplements may apply (e.g. for older vehicles and trailers). Information correct at time of going to print (13/3/09) but subject to change. Offer available by phone and quoting 'UK Atlas 2010' and is not available in a breakdown situation. Discount not available online or in conjunction with any other discount, promotion or offer. Offer can be withdrawn or varied at any time. Offer ends 1/07/2010.

## AA Car Insurance

**10% discount for AA Members***

A panel of over 20 leading insurers

Call: **0800 197 4675** quoting ref: 350

*Discount only available to existing AA Personal Members when they become new AA Motor Insurance customers and is only applicable for the first year of the policy. Discount not available retrospectively or for specialist schemes. Discount not available online or in conjunction with any other discount, promotion or offer. Offer can be withdrawn or varied at any time.

## AA Caravan Insurance

**10% discount for AA Members***

Choose from three levels of cover

Call: **0800 107 1477**

*Discount only available to existing AA Personal Members when they become new AA Caravan Insurance customers and is only applicable for the first year of the policy. Discount not available retrospectively or for specialist schemes. Discount not available in conjunction with any other discount, promotion or offer. Offer can be withdrawn or varied at any time.

## AA Motorcycle Insurance

**5% discount for AA Members***

Protected No Claims Discount available

Call: **0800 107 9771**

*Discount only available to existing AA Personal Members when they become new AA Motorcycle Insurance customers and is only applicable for the first year of the policy. Discount not available retrospectively or for specialist schemes. Discount not available online or in conjunction with any other discount, promotion or offer. Offer can be withdrawn or varied at any time.

# Map pages north

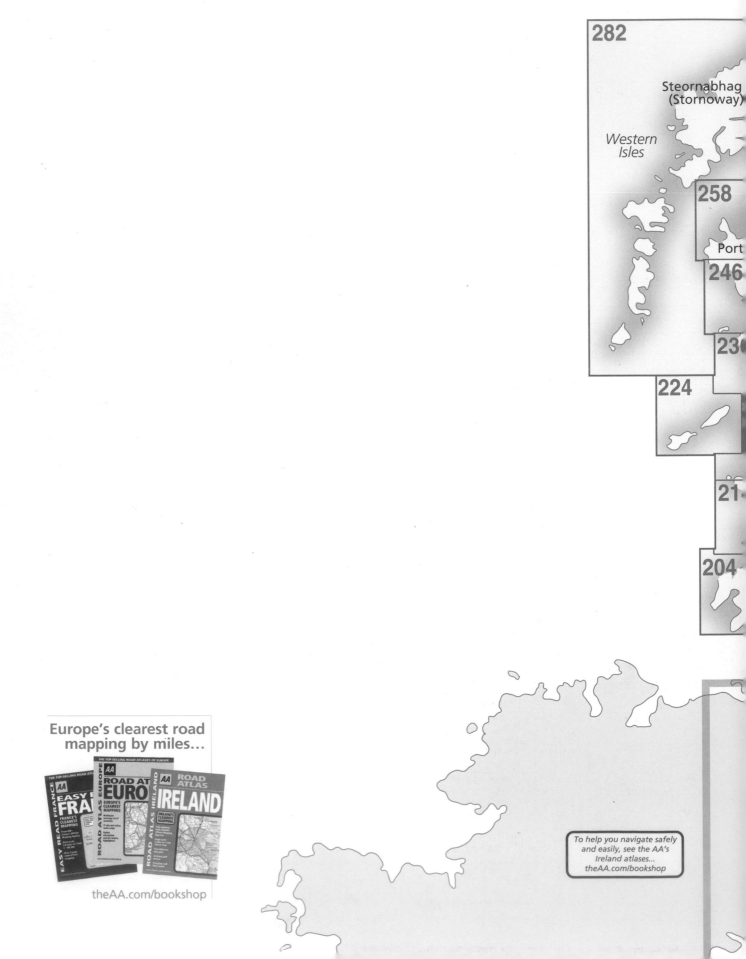

282

Steornabhag
(Stornoway)

Western
Isles

258

Port

246

23

224

21

204